TRANSACTIONS

OF THE

AMERICAN PHILOSOPHICAL SOCIETY

HELD AT PHILADELPHIA
FOR PROMOTING USEFUL KNOWLEDGE

———

NEW SERIES—VOLUME 43, PART 2
1953

———

ENCYCLOPEDIC DICTIONARY
OF ROMAN LAW

ADOLF BERGER

City College, New York
and
French University (Ecole Libre des Hautes Etudes), New York

———

THE AMERICAN PHILOSOPHICAL SOCIETY
INDEPENDENCE SQUARE
PHILADELPHIA 6

SEPTEMBER, 1953

Copyright 1953 by The American Philosophical Society

Library of Congress Catalogue
Card Number: 53–7641

PREFACE

The idea of preparing a Dictionary of Roman Law in encyclopedic form came to my mind soon after my arrival in the United States, as I became more familiar with the status of Roman Law in American schools and legal writing. The idea grew further while I was working with my friend, Professor A. Arthur Schiller of Columbia University School of Law, on a complete bibliography of the Romanistic literature published in English since 1939. It became increasingly clear to me that many a reader must encounter great difficulties in understanding the technical language of papers concerned with Roman Law. The severely restricted place occupied by Roman Law in college and university curricula has produced a situation in which it is entirely true that *Romanistica non leguntur*.

That I finally undertook the work, despite a variety of difficulties, may be attributed in large measure to the warm encouragement I received from scholars in various fields of Roman antiquities. They approved my plan enthusiastically and stressed the usefulness of a dictionary as I conceived it, designed for teachers and students of Roman Law in the classroom, for students of legal history who have no or only little Latin, and for readers of juristic or literary Latin works in translations which not always are reliable when legal terms or problems are involved. In particular, the idea of an encyclopedic dictionary with extensive bibliographies met with the approbation of everyone consulted.

Now, after several years of intensive work, after several decades of study and research in my chosen field, I may be permitted to offer this Dictionary to all who are interested in ancient Rome's legal institutions, sources, history, and language, to scholars and students, both beginners and those more advanced, with the wish and hope that the *cupida legum iuventus* may include in its desire for knowledge of the law that legal system which, even in our own day, is the foundation and the intellectual background of the law of a large part of the world.

No one is more aware of the deficiencies of a work of this kind than the author himself. The selection of the entries from all the domains of Roman Law, the maintenance of a proper proportion in presenting the various topics without concessions to those more familiar or more interesting to the author personally, and the necessity of remaining within the limits of a single volume, all created embarrassing difficulties. For the principles of selection and organization finally adopted, the reader is referred to the Introduction.

Preparation of the Dictionary would not have been possible if the American Philosophical Society had not been generous with renewed grants-in-aid from the very beginning of the project. I wish to express my deepest gratitude to the Society for this assistance and encouragement and for accepting the Dictionary for publication in its *Transactions*.

I am further gratefully indebted to the Mid-European Studies Center of the National Committee for a Free Europe for the helpful interest it took in my work in its later stages. Thankful mention must also be made of the Social Science Research Council for grants in the years 1946 and 1949.

Invaluable assistance was rendered by several colleagues who assumed the tedious task of polishing the manuscript linguistically and stylistically. My most sincere thanks are due Professors M. I. Finley of the Newark College of Rutgers University, Jacob Hammer of Hunter College, Lionel Casson of New York University, and Naphtali Lewis of Brooklyn College for the service they have rendered to me in true friendship.

A. B.

New York, June 15, 1952

MALVAE

UXORI OPTIMAE PIISSIMAE
CONSOCIAE LABORUM MEORUM

S.

ENCYCLOPEDIC DICTIONARY OF ROMAN LAW

ADOLF BERGER

CONTENTS

INTRODUCTION

This Dictionary has several purposes: to explain technical Roman legal terms, to translate and elucidate those Latin words which have a specific connotation when used in a juristic context or in connection with a legal institution or question, and to provide a brief picture of Roman legal institutions and sources as a sort of a first introduction to them.

The objectives of the work, not the juristic character of available Latin writings, therefore, determined the inclusion or exclusion of any single word or phrase. Since the Dictionary is not intended to be a complete Latin-English dictionary for all words which occur in the writings of the Roman jurists or in the various codifications of Roman law, the reader must consult a general Latin-English lexicon for ordinary words that have no specific meaning in law or juristic language. In this respect, as in others, the present work differs fundamentally from Heumann's *Handlexikon zu den Quellen des römischen Rechts* (in the excellent edition by Emil Seckel, 1907). On the other hand, numerous entries concern words and phrases which occur only in non-juristic sources, literary writings or inscriptions, but which must, nevertheless, receive attention if the Dictionary is truly to survey all fields of the vast province of Roman law; private, criminal, public, administrative, sacral, and military law, taxation, etc. Many entries, furthermore, deal with Latin terms of medieval or modern coinage, unknown to the ancient Romans, but now widely accepted in the Romanistic literature.

All the more important entries are encyclopedic as well as lexicographical. That is to say, an attempt has been made in each case to depict as succinctly as possible, the historical development of the legal institution or term it defines, the use of certain words in the language of the jurists or the imperial chancery, and particular attention has been given to important substantial changes from early law to classical law and again in the reforms of Justinian. Additional matter is indicated by cross-references, printed in small capitals. Analogous terms and institutions are also noted by small capitals, sometimes in the body of the text, sometimes at the end of an entry. (As a matter of course, with a few exceptions, every Latin word used to explain or illustrate a term has its own entry even when that fact is not specifically indicated by the use of small capitals.) Synonyms and antonyms are indicated in many entries.

Considerable attention has been given to the sources themselves. A large number of entries are devoted to them, ranging in time from the archaic regal ordinances (the *leges regiae*) to Justinian's codification, and, in more limited measure, to post-Justinian Byzantine and medieval writings and collections of laws. Basic definitions, legal rules of fundamental importance, and characteristic utterances of the jurists are given in literal translations within quotation marks, followed by a citation of the pertinent source. Titles of the Institutes, Digest and Justinian's Code or Novels that deal *ex professo* with a specific topic are noted at the end of the entry. Substantial interpolations by which classical institutions and terms were eliminated as well as the more reliable linguistic criteria have been taken into consideration.

BIBLIOGRAPHY

The extensive bibliographical apparatus is intended for a wide circle of readers. For that reason, space has been given to publications in English, many of which may be unknown to the international guild of Romanists, at the same time that works in other languages are fully represented in the interest of readers in other countries and of students and research workers who have a mastery of other languages. Stress has been primarily placed on the international Romanistic literature of the twentieth century. Earlier works are cited only when they have remained standard treatments or did not lose their importance despite later publications. All recent publications have been taken into account in so far as they were available. A few books that were not accessible to the author have been included after their usefulness was ascertained by correspondence with scholars abroad.

To insure completeness and at the same time to avoid wasteful duplication, the bibliography was divided into two distinct parts. A General Bibliography in twenty chapters appears as a block at the end of the Dictionary. It comprises textbooks and comprehensive general presentations, which as a matter of rule are not repeated in the bibliographies appended to the single entries, and literature concerning general problems of the development of Roman law, the sources and their editions, and the influence of Roman law on modern legal systems. The Anglo-American reader will find Chapter X, "Roman Law and the Anglo-American World" of special interest. It is a first attempt to provide an extensive bibliography of works and articles on the part played by Roman law in the development of the common law and on the value of the study of Roman law in countries in the sphere of Anglo-American law. Chapter XIV on Roman law in non-juristic sources, Chapter VI on the legal policies of the emperors, and Chapter XI concerned with the literature on the place of Roman law in legal education, are also first attempts at systematic bibliographic treatment.

The second part of the bibliographical apparatus is the specialized section, scattered throughout the Dictionary among the individual entries. Here, too, the aim was to satisfy both the beginner and the expert. First place has been assigned to the renowned encyclopedias: the *Realenzyklopaedie der klassischen Altertumswissenschaft* (*RE*) of Pauly, Wissowa, Kroll *et al.*, the *Dictionnaire des antiquités grecques et romaines* of Daremberg and Saglio (*DS*), the *Nuovo Digesto Italiano* (*NDI*), De Ruggiero's *Dizionario epigrafico* (*DE*) and the very recent *Oxford Classical Dictionary* (*OCD*). Then come the special monographs, periodical articles, essays in volumes published in honor of, or in memory of distinguished scholars, congress publications, anniversary papers, and the like. Frequent reference has been made to doctoral dissertations in various languages, since at the very least they provide good bibliographies. On rare occasions special attention is drawn to reliable bibliographical references collected in other papers. In general, an effort has been made in the individual bibliographies to indicate appropriate sections within a larger work or publications whose titles do not suggest a discussion of the entry concerned. When the index word is mentioned in the bibliography it is frequently abbreviated to the initial letter.

Bibliographical omissions are unavoidable even when remarkable papers are involved. I am confident, however, that the selections scrupulously compiled will enable the reader to find without any difficulty the literature left out in this book.

GLOSSARY

A selected English-Latin Glossary is appended for the benefit of readers who have little or no familiarity with Latin legal terminology. It includes the more important terms in English whose Latin counterparts are not virtually the same. Thus, "sale" or "lease" are included, but not "senate" or "consul," "formula" or "exceptio." Terms connected with administration are generally omitted. The Latin words of the Glossary are covered by pertinent entries in the Dictionary proper together with the cross-references. Thus the reader will have the opportunity to become acquainted not only with the term itself but also its legal significance and applications.

LIST OF ABBREVIATIONS

ABayAW. Abhandlungen der Bayerischen Akademie der Wissenschaften (Munich).

ACDR. Atti del Congresso Internazionale di diritto romano, 1933; Bologna 1–2, Roma 1–2 (1934, 1935).

ACIVer. Atti del Congresso Internazionale di diritto romano e di storia del diritto, Verona, 1948; vol. 1 ff. (in press).

ACSR. Atti dei Congressi Nazionali di Studi Romani.

ADO–RIDA; see *RIDA.*

Aeg. Aegyptus. Rivista italiana di egittologia e di papirologia.

AG. Archivio giuridico.

AHDE. Anuario de Historia del Derecho Español (Madrid).

AmJPhilol. American Journal of Philology.

ANap. Atti dell' Accademia di Scienze morali e politiche della Società Reale di Napoli.

AnBari. Annali della Facoltà di giurisprudenza dell' Università di Bari.

AnCam. Annali dell' Università di Camerino. Sezione giuridica.

AnCat. Annali del Seminario giuridico dell' Università di Catania.

AnGren. Annales de l'Université de Grenoble. Section Lettres, Droit.

AnMac. Annali dell' Università di Macerata.

AnMes. Annali dell' Instituto delle Scienze giuridiche dell' Università di Messina.

AnPal. Annali del Seminario giuridico dell' Università di Palermo.

AnPer. Annali dell' Istituto giuridico dell' Università di Perugia.

AnTr.　Annali Triestini di diritto, economia e politica (a cura dell' Università di Trieste).

Ant.　Antonym.

AntCl.　Antiquité Classique (Brussels).

APad.　Atti dell' Accademia scientifica di Padova.

APrAW.　Abhandlungen der Preussischen Akademie der Wissenschaften in Berlin, philosophisch-historische Klasse.

ArCP.　Archiv für civilistische Praxis.

ArPap.　Archiv für Papyrusforschung.

ASächGW.　Abhandlungen der Sächsischen Gesellschaft der Wissenschaften in Leipzig, philosophisch-historische Klasse.

Ath.　Athenaeum. Studi periodici di lettere, e storia dell' antichità (Pavia).

ATor.　Atti dell' Accademia delle Scienze di Torino.

AVen.　Atti dell' Istituto Veneto di Scienze, Lettere ed Arti.

BerSächGW.　Berichte der Sächsischen Gesellschaft der Wissenschaften, Leipzig, philosophisch-historische Klasse.

Bibl.　Bibliography.

BIDR.　Bullettino dell' Istituto del diritto romano.

C.　*Codex Justinianus.*

CambLJ.　Cambridge Law Journal.

CentCodPav.　Per il XIV Centenario della codificazione giustinianea. Studi pubblicati dalla Facoltà di giurisprudenza di Pavia, 1934.

ClJ.　Classical Journal.

ClMed.　Classica et Medievalia (Kopenhagen).

ClPhilol.　Classical Philology.

ConfCast.　Conferenze romanistiche tenute nell' Univ. di Pavia nell' anno 1939 a ricordo di G. Castelli, Milano 1940.

ConfInst.　Conférences faites à l'Institut de droit rom. en 1947, Paris 1950.

ConfMil.　Conferenze pel XIV Centenario della Pandette, Milan, 1931.

CRAI.　ComptesRendus de l'Académie des Inscriptions et des Belles Lettres.

CristDirPriv.　Cristianesimo e diritto privato. Pubblicazione dell' Università del Sacro Cuore, Milan, 1935.

D.　*Digesta Iustiniani.*

DE.　Dizionario epigrafico di antichità romane, ed. E. De Ruggiero.

DS.　Dictionnaire des antiquités grecques et romaines, ed. Ch. Daremberg and E. Saglio.

Ét.　Études.

Fg.　Festgabe.

Fil.　Il Filangieri.

FIR.　Fontes Iuris Romani Anteiustiniani, ed. Riccobono, Baviera, Ferrini, Furlani, Arangio-Ruiz, 1-3 (Florence, 1940–1943).

Fr. Vat.　Fragmenta Vaticana.

Fschr.　Festschrift.

GGA.　Göttingische Gelehrte Anzeigen.

GrZ.　Grünhut's Zeitschrift für das öffentliche und Privatrecht der Gegenwart.

Her.　Hermes.

Hist.　Historia. Studi storici per l' antichità classica (Milan).

IhJb.　Ihering's Jahrbücher für die Dogmatik des heutigen römischen und deutschen Privatrechts.

Inst.　*Institutiones Iustiniani.*

JRS.　Journal of Roman Studies.

JurR.　Juridical Review.

Kl.　Klio. Beiträge zur alten Geschichte.

KrVj.　Kritische Vierteljahresschrift für Gesetzgebung und Rechtswissenschaft.

LQR.　Law Quarterly Review.

Mél.　Mélanges.

MemBol.　Memorie dell' Accademia della Scienze e Lettere dell' Istituto di Bologna.

MemLinc.　Memorie dell' Accademia dei Lincei.

MemLomb.　Memorie dell' Istituto Lombardo di Scienze e Lettere.

MemTor.　Memorie dell' Istituto giuridico dell' Università di Torino.

Mn.　Mnemosyne. Bibliotheca philologica Batava.

Mous.　Mouseion. Rivista di scienze classiche (Naples).

NDI.　Nuovo Digesto Italiano.

Nov.　*Novellae Instiniani.*

NRHD.　Nouvelle Revue historique de droit français et étranger (since 1922 *Revue historique* etc. = *RHD*).

OCD.　The Oxford Classical Dictionary.

PBritSR.　Papers of the British School at Rome.

PubMod.　Pubblicazioni della Facolà di giurisprudenza di Modena.

RAC.　Reallexikon für Antike und Christentum.

RBSG.　Rassegna bibliografica delle scienze giuridiche, sociali e politiche.

RDCiv.　Rivista di diritto civile.

RDCom.　Rivista di diritto commerciale.

RDNav.　Rivista di diritto di navigazione.

RE.　Realenzyklopädie der klassischen Altertumswissenschaft, ed. Paully, Wissowa, Kroll, Mittelhaus, and Ziegler.

Rec.　Recueil.

RendBol.　Rendiconti dell' Accademia delle Scienze e Lettere dell' Istituto di Bologna, Classe di scienze morali.

RendLinc.　Rendiconti dell' Accademia dei Lincei.

RendLomb.　Rendiconti dell' Istituto Lombardo di Scienze e Lettere.

RHD.　Revue historique de droit français et étranger (since 1922 continuation of *NRHD*).

RIDA.　Revue internationale des droits de l'antiquité. Since 1952 published under the title: *Archives d'histoire du droit oriental et Revue internationale des droits de l'antiquité* (= *ADO–RIDA*).

RISG.　Rivista italiana per le scienze giuridiche.

RStDIt.　Rivista di storia del dirittto italiano.

SbBerl.　Sitzungsberichte der Preussischen Akademie der Wissenschaften Berlin, philosophisch-historische Klasse.

SbHeid.　Sitzungsberichte der Heidelberger Akademie der Wissenschaften, phil.-hist. Klasse.

SbLeipz.　Sitzungsberichte der Sächsischen Gesellschaft der Wissenschaften in Leipzig.

SbMünch.　Sitzungsberichte der Bayrischen Akademie der Wissenschaften, München, phil.-hist. Klasse.

SbWien.　Sitzungsberichte der Akademie der Wissenschaften Wien, phil.-hist. Klasse.

Scr.—Scritti.

SDHI.　Studia et documenta historiae et iuris.

Sem.　Seminar. An annual extraordinary number of *The Jurist* (Washington, D. C.).

St.　Studi (in onore, in memoria, and the like with the name of the scholar honored).

StDocSD.　Studi e documenti di storia e diritto.

StCagl.　Studi economico- giuridici dell' Università di Cagliari.

StPav.　Studi nelle scienze giuridiche e sociali dell' Istituto di esercitazioni presso la Facoltà di giurisprudenza dell' Università di Pavia.

StSas.　Studi Sassaresi.

StSen.　Studi Senesi.

StUrb.　Studi Urbinati.　.

Symb.　Symbolae.

TAmPhilolAs.　Transactions of the American Philological Association.

Syn.　Synonym.

TR.　Tijdschrift voor Rechtsgeschiedenis (= *Revue d'Histoire de droit* (Haarlem—La Haye).

Trad.　Traditio. Studies in Ancient and Medieval History, Thought and Religion (Washington, D. C.).

TulLR.　Tulane Law Review.

Varia.　Varia. Études de droit romain. Publications de l' Institut de droit romain de l'Université de Paris, 1952.

ZSS.　Zeitschrift der Savigny-Stiftung für Rechtsgeschichte, Romanistische Abteilung.

ZVR.　Zeitschrift für vergleichende Rechtswissenschaft.

A

A. Abbreviation for *absolvo* written by judges of criminal courts (see QUAESTIONES) on wooden tablets (see TABELLAE) to indicate a vote for acquittal. See ABSOLUTIO. A condemnatory vote was expressed by the letter $C = condemno$ (= I condemn). In criminal matters submitted to the popular assemblies (see COMITIA) the abbreviations used were: $L = libero$ for acquittal, and $D = damno$ for condemnation. The abbreviation NL (= *non liquet*) meant that the case was not clear to the voter.—See LIQUERE.

A. Abbreviation for *antiquo*, written by the participants in a popular assembly (see COMITIA) on wooden tablets, indicated a vote against the proposed bill. *Antiquo* = I leave it in the ancient state, I reject. On the contrary, the abbreviation $UR = uti\ rogas$ (as you propose) was used for an affirmative vote. —See LEX, ROGATIO.

A, ab. These prepositions appear in the official titles of the heads of certain divisions in the imperial chancery; see the following items. Some of these officials were later called *magistri*.

A censibus. An official of the imperial chancery charged with the examination of the financial situation of persons who aspired to admission to the senatorial or equestrian rank. Such admission depended upon the possession of a considerable property.—See CENSUS, ORDO SENATORIUS, EQUITES.

Kalopothakes, *DE* 2, 114.

A cognitionibus. The chief of the division of the imperial chancery concerned with judicial matters.— See COGNITIO.

De Ruggiero, *DE* 2, 320; v. Premerstein, *RE* 4, 220.

A commentariis. See COMMENTARII, COMMENTARIENSIS.

A consiliis. See A STUDIIS.

A diplomatibus. See DIPLOMA.

A libellis. The head of the division of the imperial chancery which dealt with all kinds of petitions addressed to the emperor. His later title was *magister libellorum*.—See LIBELLUS.

Thédénat, *DS* 3, 1174; v. Premerstein, *RE* 13, 15.

A memoria. A high official of the imperial chancery who prepared the drafts for the emperor's public allocutions.

Bloch, *DS* 2, 723; Fluss, *RE* 15, 655.

A rationibus. The head of the division of the imperial chancery which was concerned with the emperor's financial matters and the control of the fiscal administration throughout the whole empire. From the time of Claudius he was an official of the state and not an imperial functionary.—See PROCURATOR A RATIONIBUS, RATIONES.

Rostowzew, *DE* 3, 133.

A studiis. An imperial official (from the middle of the first century) somewhat connected with the emperor's judicial activity, probably his special counsel in more complicated legal and governmental matters. Later his title was *magister a studiis*. A similar office may have been that of the *a consiliis*.

Kübler, *RE* 4A, 397; Chapot, *DS* 4, 1546; O. Hirschfeld, *Kaiserl. Verwaltungsbeamte*[2] (1905) 332; Bersanetti, *Epigraphica* 9 (1947) 56.

Ab actis. See ACTA.

Ab epistulis. The director of the imperial secretariat which was subdivided into two departments, one for Latin (*ab epistulis Latinis*) and one for Greek letters (*ab epistulis Graecis*). The office was concerned with the private and official correspondence of the emperor, in both civil and military matters, and also with the appointment of military officers.—See EPISTULA, SCRINIUM EPISTULARUM.

Rostowzew, *RE* 6, 210; Bloch, *DS* 2, 712; De Ruggiero, *DE* 2, 2133.

Ab intestato. See INTESTATUS.

Abactor. See ABIGEUS.

Abactus. A magistrate forced to resign his office by the decision of a popular assembly.—See LEX SEMPRONIA DE ABACTIS.

Abactus partus. See PARTUS ABACTUS.

Abalienare. See ALIENATIO. The term is used primarily of alienations through MANCIPATIO.

Berger, *Kritische Vierteljahresschr. für Gesetzgebung und Rechtswiss.* 14 (1912) 414; De Visscher, *Rev. Études Latines* 1936, 130 (= *Nouvelles Études,* 1949, 257).

Abdicatio. Renunciation, abandonment. In private law, the term is used of the renunciation of an inheritance or a guardianship (*abdicatio tutelae*). The abandonment of a child (*abdicatio liberorum*) by the head of a family (*pater familias*) was forbidden by the law, as expressly stated by Diocletian (C. 8.46.6), but was nevertheless practiced. In public law *abdicatio* indicates the resignation of a magistrate or an imperial official from his post.—See EXPONERE LIBERUM.

Leonhard, *RE* 1; Neumann, *RE* 1; Humbert, *DS* 1; for *abdicatio tutelae:* Perozzi, *RendBol* 1918/9 (= *Scritti* 3, 215); Solazzi, *RendLomb* 51 (1918) 873; *idem, St. Pavia* 6 (1921) 116; Sachers, *RE* 7A, 1532; for *abdicatio liberorum:* Düll, *ZSS* 63 (1943) 71.

Abigeatus. Cattle stealing (rustling) from a stable or pasture. Unlike an ordinary theft (see FURTUM) it was prosecuted as a public crime (see CRIMINA PUBLICA) and punished more severely.—D. 47.14; C. 9.37.

Hartmann, *RE* 1; Humbert, *DS* 1; Berger, *Sem* 2 (1944) 23.

Abigeus. A cattle thief, a rustler. Syn. *abactor.*—See ABIGEATUS.

Abiurare. To deny a debt on oath; to hold back fraudulently.—See IUSIURANDUM.

Wlassak, *RE* 1; D. Daube, *Studies in biblical law,* 1947, 229.

Aboleri. See ABOLITIO.

Abolitio. (From *abolere.*) In penal law, the annulment of an accusation and consequently of the whole trial through deletion of the name of the individual charged with a crime from the list of accused persons. See ACCUSATIO. *Abolitio publica* (= general abolition) was ordered by the emperor on the occasion of some happy event or of thanksgiving festivities (*gratulatio*). Withdrawal of the accusation by the accuser (*desistere*) or his death produced *abolitio*. *Aboleri* = extinction of the right of suing or prosecuting a person in civil or criminal matters.—D. 48.16; C. 9.42; 43.45.

Saglio, *DS* 1; A. Leschtsch, *A. paschalis*, Diss. Freiburg, 1904; P. Duparc, *Origines de la grâce dans le droit pénal rom.*, 1942, 24.

Abortio (abortus). Abortion. For *abortio* caused by a poisonous drink (*poculum abortionis*), see VENENUM.

Waszink, *RAC* 1 (1950).

Abrogare legem. To annul a statute in its entirety by an abrogating legislative act. A law may also lose its binding force by disuse (DESUETUDO) which is the expression of a "tacit consent of the whole people" (D. 1.3.32.1).—See DEROGARE.

Absens, absentia. (In judicial trials.) The Twelve Tables already provided that the absent party automatically lost the case to the party present. Under the formulary procedure a plaintiff who did not appear in court was deemed to have renounced his claim. The absence of the defendant in the first stage of the trial before the magistrate (IN IURE) might under certain circumstances lead to the seizure of his property; see MISSIO IN BONA; his non-appearance before the judge (*apud iudicem*) might lead to his condemnation; see CONDEMNATIO, CONTUMACIA, EREMODICIUM. The normal consequences of the absence could be annulled by an extraordinary praetorian measure (RESTITUTIO IN INTEGRUM) if it was justified by important reasons such as sickness, acting in the interest of the state, and the like.

Wlassak, *RE* 1; Kipp, *RE* 6, 417; Fliniaux, *Ét Girard* 1, 1912; Solazzi, *St. Simoncelli*, 1917; *idem, Concorso dei creditori* 1 (1917) 66, 70 (Bibl.).

Absentes, absentia. Persons absent enjoy a particular protection in cases in which the defense of their rights required their presence. The remedies were various. In the case of justified absence the praetor could annul by means of RESTITUTIO IN INTEGRUM any rights acquired to the prejudice of the absent person; see the foregoing item. Property of persons absent in service of the state (such as governors of provinces, officials, soldiers) could not be acquired by USUCAPIO. Such persons were also excused from civil charges, as TUTELA, CURA. A particular defense was granted to Roman citizens who became prisoners of war. See CAPTIVI, POSTLIMINIUM. In contractual relations the absence of the creditor does not interrupt the prescription of his actions. The distinction *absentes—praesentes* is of importance in the conclusion of verbal and consensual contracts: whereas the former require the presence of the contracting parties, the latter can be concluded *inter absentes* by means of a letter (*epistula*) or a messenger (*nuntius*).—In Justinian's rules on LONGI TEMPORIS PRAESCRIPTIO, *inter praesentes* means that the owner of the immovable and the factual possessor live in the same province. Ant. *inter absentes.*—See COMMEATUS, STIPULATIO INTER ABSENTES.

Wlassak, *RE* 1; Guarneri-Citati *NDI* 1 (*s.v. assenza*).

Absolutio. (From *absolvere*.) Refers to a judgment by which the defendant in a civil trial or the accused in a criminal one was absolved. In the formulary procedure the term was expressly used in the formula to authorize the judge to render an absolutory judgment (*absolvito*).—See SENTENTIA.

Wlassak, *RE* 1; Leonhard, *ibid.*

Absolutorius. There was a maxim in classical Roman law (Gai Inst. 4, 114): *omnia judicia absolutoria sunt* = all civil trials may lead to an absolution (of the defendant). If the defendant satisfied the plaintiff after LITIS CONTESTATIO but before the judgment (SENTENTIA), the judge had to render an absolutory judgment. The rule was accepted by some jurists only with regard to IUDICIA BONAE FIDEI, but by the second century it was generally recognized.

Abstinere(se)hereditate. The praetorian law granted the so-called SUI ET NECESSARII HEREDES the right to refuse the paternal inheritance (*ius abstinendi*) in order to avoid the acceptance of an insolvent inheritance which otherwise would fall to them automatically.—C. 2.38.—See PRO HEREDE GERERE.

Absumptio. See RES QUAE USU CONSUMUNTUR.

Aburnius Valens. A Roman jurist under Hadrian and Antoninus Pius, author of an extensive treatise on *fideicommissa*.

Jörs, *RE* 1 (no. 2); Orestano *NDI* 1.

Abusus. See RES QUAE USU CONSUMUNTUR.

Abuti. To abuse, to make bad use of a thing or a right, particularly with the intention to harm another.—See AEMULATIO.

Riccobono, *BIDR* 46 (1939) 1; Appleton, *Rev. générale du droit* 55 (1931) 115.

Accensi. Non-armed soldiers without any property qualification. They were mustered into a special CENTURIA and formed a reserve troop which in battle took the place of fallen legionaries. Syn. *velati* (= clothed with a military cloak).—*Accensi* were also the orderlies of higher magistrates (with *imperium*).

Cichorius—Kubitschek, *RE* 1; Humbert—De la Berge—Saglio, *DS* 1; De Ruggiero, *DE* 1; Vogel, *ZSS* 67 (1950) 86.

Acceptilatio. An oral form of dissolving oral obligations, according to the rule that obligations contracted *verbis* had to be dissolved in the same way (orally). The stipulatory debtor asked his creditor: "What I promised to you, have you received it (*habesne acceptum*)?" The latter answered "I have (*habeo*)." Later, Greek words were admitted. In order to dissolve an obligation other than an oral one by *accepti-*

latio, which was the safest form of receipt, the parties transferred the obligation into a *stipulatio* to which an *acceptilatio* was afterwards applied. This extension of *acceptilatio* was introduced by the jurist AQUILIUS GALLUS who composed the formula of the novating *stipulatio,* called *stipulatio Aquiliana.*—D. 46.4; C. 8.43.

Leonhard, *RE* 1; Natalucci, *NDI* 1; De Ruggiero, *Scritti A. Marghieri* (1921) 415; Wlassak, *ZSS* 42 (1921) 394; Bohacek, *AnPal* 11 (1923) 379; Cugia, *A. solutioni comparatur,* 1924; *idem, St. Mancaleoni,* 1938, 111; *idem, St. Bonolis* I (1942) 247; Michon, *Rec. Gény* I (1934) 42; Solazzi, *Estinzione dell'obbligazione* I² (1935) 246; P. Meylan, *A. et paiement,* 1934; G. Lombardi, *Ricerche in tema di ius gentium* 1946, 185; Daube, *ZSS* 66 (1948) 119.

Acceptum habere. See ACCEPTILATIO; syn. *acceptum facere, accepto ferre.*

Acceptum rogare. The debtor's question in ACCEPTILATIO.

Accessio. (From *accedere.*) The union of one thing (land or movable) with another either by natural forces or artificially (mechanically, *iungere*) so that they form an organic unity (a whole, *accessio materiae*). The cases of *accessio* were very manifold. If the things mixed, melted, woven, etc., belonged to different owners, the question of ownership over the new whole might involve difficulties. A general rule was that when one of the things was only an accessory of the other, the ownership of the latter was decisive. Outward appearance, usage or custom determine which was principal and which accessory.—D. 22.1. —See FERRUMINATIO, INTEXERE, LITTERAE, PICTURA, PLANTARE, SUPERFICIES, EXHIBERE.

Leonhard, *RE* 1; Baudry, *DS* 1; Sanfilippo, *NDI* 1; Riccobono, *AnPal* 5 (1917); Guarneri-Citati, *AnMac* 1926, 1929; *idem, AnMes* 1927; *AnPal* 14 (1930).

Accessio possessionis. Addition of possession. In some particular cases (LONGI TEMPORIS PRAESCRIPTIO, USUCAPIO, INTERDICTUM UTRUBI), the periods of possession of two or more successive holders were added together to the benefit of the last one. Syn. *accessio temporis.*

Zanzucchi, *AG* 72 (1904) 177, 353; 76 (1906) 3; P. Krüger, *ZSS* 26 (1905) 144; Suman, *RISG* 59 (1917) 225; Ratti, *St. Bonfante* 1 (1930) 263.

Accessio temporis. See ACCESSIO POSSESSIONIS.

Accipere iudicium. See IUDICIUM ACCIPERE.

Acclamatio. A demonstration of esteem and friendly feeling in the form of fixed cheers, tendered to high magistrates and later to the emperors when they appeared in public on certain occasions. A victorious general was acclaimed by a loud salutation when he entered the city of Rome in triumph. In the senate, acclamation was a sign of approval of the emperor's *oratio* (see ORATIO PRINCIPIS). It was considered a vote and noted in records of the senate (*acta senatus*). —See TRIUMPHUS.

De Ruggiero, *DE* 1, 72; Saglio, *DS* 1; Klauser, *RAC* 1 (1950) 221; Dessau, *Ephemeris epigraphica* 7 (1892) 429; Seeck, *Rheinisches Museum* 48 (1893) 199; O. Hirschfeld, *Kleine Schriften,* 1913, 691; Charlesworth, *JRS* 33 (1943).

Accursius. A famous glossator (1182–1260), professor at the law school in Bologna. He compiled the glosses of other glossators (see GLOSSATORES) in a general collection called *glossa ordinaria.*

Monti, *NDI* 1; E. Landsberg, *Die Glosse des A.,* 1883; Genzmer, *Fschr Wenger* 2 (1945) 223; Torrelli, *RStDIt* 7 (1934) 429.

Accusatio. (From *accusare.*) Except for a few instances of a civil nature this means accusation in criminal affairs in the Roman criminal procedure of the last century of the Republic. Prosecution began at the initiative of a citizen (not a magistrate) who assumed the role of the accuser by denouncing the wrongdoer and filing a charge against him with the chairman of the competent criminal court (*quaestio*). This first step of the accuser was called *nomen deferre* (*nominis delatio*), he being the *delator* (denouncer). If the magistrate accepted the accusation (*nomen recipere*), normally presented by writing (*libellus accusatorius*), he ordered its registration (*inscriptio*) in the official record of persons to face a criminal trial. The *accusatio* could be supported by the signatures (*subscriptio*) of additional accusers. In order to prevent malicious accusations, an oath (IURAMENTUM CALUMNIAE) was imposed on the accuser.—In civil matters, *accusatio* is used in connection with a guardian alleged to be dishonest or negligent (see TUTOR SUSPECTUS), with a freedman, ungrateful to his patron (see INGRATUS), and with an undutiful testament (see QUERELA INOFFICIOSI TESTAMENTI).—D. 48.2; C. 9.1; 2.—See CALUMNIA, CAPITIS ACCUSATIO, EDICTUM CONSTANTINI, PRAEVARICATIO, TERGIVERSATIO, REPETERE ACCUSATIONEM.

Leonhard, *RE* 1; Vinet, *DS* 1; Lauria, *NDI* 1; *idem, A.-inquisitio, ANap* 56 (1934); Wlassak, *SbWien* 184, 1 (1917), 194 (1920); Hitzig, *RE* 4 (*s.v. delatio nominis*).

Accusator. An accuser in a criminal trial.

Accusatorius libellus. See ACCUSATIO.

Acilius (Atilius ?), Lucius. A jurist of the early second century B.C., author of a commentary on the Twelve Tables.

Klebs, *RE* 1, 252 (no. 7).

Acqu-. See ADQU-.

Acta. Records drawn up by officials, concerning their activity and proceedings developed before them as well as certain binding declarations of private individuals (donations, testimony, etc.) made before them (*apud acta*). Syn. *gesta,* sometimes *commentarii.* The term for the performance of binding deeds, entered into the *acta,* is in later times *insinuare.*—*Ab actis* = a general designation for officials concerned with *acta* (secretaries = *scribae,* the subordinate personnel in the pertinent offices).

Kubitschek, *RE* 1; Weiss, *RE* Suppl. 7 (*s.v. gesta*); Humbert, *DS* 1; De Ruggiero, *DE* 1.

Acta Caesaris. Acts performed or ordered by an emperor before his death. They had to be respected by his successor who was obliged to take an oath to that effect upon accepting the throne. A similar oath with regard to *acta Caesaris* was also compulsory for senators. Syn. *acta principis,* which may also mean the records of imperial orations, decisions, etc.

Acta diurna. An official law bulletin, introduced by Caesar for the publication of statutes and decrees of the senate (SENATUSCONSULTA) as well as of important news concerning the state, and the imperial family.

Acta militaria. Records pertaining to the administration of larger military units, as, e.g., legions, in which there was a file for each soldier summarizing his service and his financial affairs (proceeds, savings, and the like).

Kubitschek, *RE* 1, 286; Humbert, *DS* 1; O. Hirschfeld, *Kleine Schriften,* 1913, 682.

Acta populi. Another designation for ACTA DIURNA. They were also called *acta urbis, urbana, publica,* since they contained news about important local events.

Acta senatus. Records of the discussions in the senate, another of Caesar's innovations (see ACTA DIURNA). Orations of the emperor delivered in the senate were also published there.

Humbert, *DS* 1; De Ruggiero, *DE* 1, 45; O'Brien Moore, *RE* Suppl. 6, 770; O. Hirschfeld, *Kleine Schriften,* 1913, 689.

Actio. In the definition of the jurist Celsus, "nothing else than the right of an individual to sue in a trial for what is due to him" (D. 45.1.51; Inst. 4.6 pr.). In the formal sense *actio* is referred to the action of a plaintiff by which he initiates a suit (*actione experiri, actionem exercere*) as well to the whole proceedings, or to the formula granted for a specific claim. In this last meaning *actio* is synonymous with *iudicium,* both being applied to particular formulae. —See IUDICIUM, PETITIO, DARE ACTIONEM, DENEGARE, REPETERE ACTIONEM, PERIRE.—Inst. 4.6; D. 44.7; C. 4.10.—In the following presentation the different types of actions appear under ACTIONES; the specific actions are dealt with either under the name of the legal institution with which they are connected or under their own denomination.

Wlassak, *RE* 1; Anon., *DS* 1; Landucci, *NDI* 1; Brugi, *NDI* 1 (*s.v. azione*); Albertario, *In tema di classificazione delle azioni,* 1928 (= *Studi* 4 [1946] 219); Arangio-Ruiz, *Cours de droit romain. Les actions,* Naples, 1935; G. Pugliese, *Actio e diritto subbiettivo,* 1939; Biondi, *ACDR,* Roma II (1935) 185.

Actio ad exhibendum. See EXHIBERE.

Actio ad supplendam legitimam. See PARS LEGITIMA; QUERELA INOFFICIOSI TESTAMENTI.

Balis, *ZSS* 55 (1935) 272.

Actio aestimatoria. See ACTIO QUANTI MINORIS, AESTIMATUM, EMPTIO.—D. 19.3.

Actio aquae pluviae arcendae. Action against the owner of a neighboring plot of land for having constructed a work which might change the natural flow of rain-water to the detriment of the plaintiff's property. The *actio* had to be brought before damage was done; the defendant when defeated had to re- move the construction. Originating in the Twelve Tables, the *actio* acquired a different aspect in Justinian's law since its availability was considerably reformed.—D. 39.3.

G. Baviera, *Scritti* 1 (1909); Berger, *ZSS* 31 (1910) 405; Schönbauer, *ZSS* 54 (1934); M. Sargenti, *L'a.a.p.a.,* 1940.

Actio arbitraria. See ACTIO DE EO QUOD CERTO LOCO, ACTIONES ARBITRARIAE.

Actio arborum furtim caesarum. The Twelve Tables introduced this *actio* against anyone who secretly cut down trees belonging to another's property. The fixed penalty of 25 asses for each tree was later changed to double value by the praetorian action *de arboribus succisis,* modeled after the decemviral action. Moreover, the wrongdoer could be sued for the damage done through the ACTIO LEGIS AQUILIAE. —D. 47.7.

P. Huvelin, *Le furtum,* 1915, 67; Fliniaux, *St. Bonfante* 1 (1929) 523; Berger, *St. Riccobono* 1 (1936) 614; E. Carrelli, *SDHI* 5 (1939) 327; idem, *AnBari* 2 (1939); Kiessling, *Jour. of jur. papyrology* 4 (1950) 317.

Actio auctoritatis (de auctoritate). The transferor of quiritary ownership over a RES MANCIPI through MANCIPATIO was obliged to defend the transferee against a claim of ownership (REI VINDICATIO) by a third person (see EVICTIO). In this context AUCTORITAS means a kind of guaranty in case of eviction. If the transferor failed to do so or the transferee lost the case, the latter had *actio auctoritatis* for double the price paid. This liability on the part of the *mancipio dans* (the transferor) lasted according to the Twelve Tables two years for immovables, one year for all other things, because after these periods the transferee acquired full ownership through USUCAPIO. Where *usucapio* by the transferee was excluded, as, for instance, in the case of stolen things, or of a transferee who was a foreigner (*hostis*) the liability for *auctoritas* of the transferor was unlimited in time, "eternal" (*aeterna auctoritas*).

Leist, *RE* 2, 2276; Ferrini, *NDI* 1 (*s.v. auctoritatis a.*); E. Levy, *Die Konkurrenz der Aktionen,* 2, 1 (1922) 238; P. F. Girard, *Mélanges* 2 (1923) 5, 153, 290; Leifer, *ZSS* 56 (1936) 136; v. Lübtow, *Fschr Koschaker* 2 (1939) 117; De Visscher, *RHD* 16 (1937) 574; (= *Nouvelles Études,* 1949, 179); Giffard, *RHD* 17 (1938) 339; P. Noailles, *Fas et ius,* 1948, 339; M. Kaser, *Eigentum und Besitz,* 1943, passim; idem, *ZSS* 68 (1951) 168, 174; Magdelain, *RID.A* 5 (= *Mél De Visscher* 4, 1950) 145.

Actio calumniae. See IUDICIUM CALUMNIAE.

Actio calumniosa. An action brought by a plaintiff only with the purpose of chicanery.—See CALUMNIA.

Actio Calvisiana. The patron's right to inherit from his freedman was protected by this action against fraudulent alienation by the latter in the case of intestacy. If the freedman's testament contained dispositions to defraud the patron the analogous action for annulment of such dispositions was the *actio Fabiana.*—See FRAGMENTUM DE FORMULA FABIANA.

E. Levy, *Privatstrafe und Schadensersatz* (1915) 69.

Actio certae creditae pecuniae. See MUTUUM.

Actio civilis in factum. See ACTIO PRAESCRIPTIS VERBIS.

Actio civilis incerti. See ACTIO PRAESCRIPTIS VERBIS.

Actio commodati. See COMMODATUM.

Actio communi dividundo. Action among co-owners for division of common property. Along with this primary function, the *actio* served for the settlement of all other controversial questions that might arise from common ownership, e.g., from unequal distribution of profits from, or expenses on, the common thing. The *actio* belongs to the category of IUDICIA BONAE FIDEI; thus the judge had the possibility of taking into account and adjusting the various reciprocal liabilities among the co-owners (*praestationes personales*).—D. 10.3; C. 3.37; 38.—See COMMUNIO, COMMUNIS, SOCIETAS, DIVISIO, ACTIONES DUPLICES, ADIUDICATIO.

> A. Berger, *Zur Entwicklungsgeschichte der Teilungsklagen im klassischen röm. Recht,* 1912; Albertario, *Studi* 4 (1946, ex 1913) 167; Arangio-Ruiz, *RISG* 52 (1912) 223; Biondi, *AnPer.* 1913; Ein, *BIDR* 39 (1931) 73; Frezza, *RISG* 7 (1932) 3.

Actio conducti. See LOCATIO CONDUCTIO.

Actio confessoria. See VINDICATIO SERVITUTIS, CONFESSIO IN IURE.

Actio constitutoria. See CONSTITUTUM.

Actio curationis causa utilis (iudicium curationis utile). The name given by Justinian to the action granted the *curator* of a *minor* for recovery of expenses or losses he had incurred in connection with the management of the ward's affairs.—See MINORES, CURATOR MINORIS.

Actio damni infecti. See DAMNUM INFECTUM.

Actio de aestimato. See AESTIMATUM.

Actio de albo corrupto. Action for spoiling, damaging or falsifying the praetorian edict promulgated on the ALBUM. The *actio* is penal, *in factum,* and popular. See ACTIONES IN FACTUM, ACTIONES POPULARES, ALBUM, EDICTUM.

Actio de arboribus succisis. See ACTIO ARBORUM FURTIM CAESARUM.

Actio de deiectis vel effusis. A praetorian action against a householder for throwing things or pouring liquids from his dwelling, so as to harm people on the street. The householder is responsible also if his slave, guest, or child did so. Justinian listed such cases among obligations which arise "as if from a delict" (*obligationes quae quasi ex delicto nascuntur*). Similar responsibility arose when things were located or suspended on the outside of a house or in a window in such a way as to endanger passers-by. The pertinent action was *actio de positis ac suspensis.* —See HOSPES.

> Fioretti, *NDI* 5 (*s.v. effusa*); G. A. Palazzo, *Obbligazioni quasi ex delicto,* 1919.

Actio de dolo. See ACTIO DOLI.

Actio de dote (dotis). In some interpolated passages the name for the action for recovery of a dowry (*actio rei uxoriae*), thoroughly reformed by Justinian. —See DOS.

Actio de eo quod certo loco. If someone promised by STIPULATIO a performance at a certain place, the creditor could sue him only there since the fulfillment of the obligation at another place might be more expensive to the debtor. By this praetorian action the judge was given the possibility of taking into account the difference. The action is also termed *arbitraria* for a reason which is not quite clear; its classical formula had not the *arbitrium*-clause which was the characteristic feature of the so-called ACTIONES ARBITRARIAE.—D. 13.4; C. 3.18.—See PLURIS PETITIO LOCO.

> G. v. Beseler, *Edictum de eo quod certo loco,* 1907; Dumas, *NRHD* 34 (1910) 610; Arangio-Ruiz, *BIDR* 25 (1912) 130, 26 (1913) 147; Biondi, *AnPal* 1 (1916) 19; idem, *BIDR* 26 (1913) 5, 153; Lenel, *ZSS* 37 (1916) 121; Beseler, *TR* 8 (1928) 326; S. G. Huwardas, *Beiträge zur Lehre von den actiones arbitrariae,* 1932; Astuti, *AnCam* 11, 2 (1937) 157; L. Wenger, *Institutes of the R. law of civil procedure,* 1940, 151; Biscardi, *StSen* 60 (1948) 656 (Bibl.); D'Ors, *RIDA* 4 (1950) 435.

Actio de in rem verso. See PECULIUM.

Actio de modo agri. If land is transferred by MANCIPATIO the transferee has this *actio* against the transferor if the area of the transferred land proves to be less than asserted by the former owner. The latter must pay double the proportionate part of the price.

> Cuq, *DS* 3, 1958.

Actio (iudicium) de moribus. The action of a husband against his wife in case of divorce for misconduct. The *actio,* which in ancient times may have been merely a criminal accusation, is penal in character and, under certain circumstances, may cause the divorced wife to lose her whole dowry. The action was abolished by Justinian.—C. 5.17.

> Klingmüller, *RE* 9 (*s.v. iudicium, de m.*); Cuq, *DS* 3, 2001; Wolff, *ZSS* 54 (1934) 315 (Bibl.); Volterra, *RISG* 85 (1948) 115.

Actio de pastu pecoris. Action for damage caused by another man's cattle grazing on the plaintiff's property. Belongs to the category of ACTIONES NOXALES.—See NOXA.

> Fliniaux, *Mél Cornil* 1 (1926) 245; Carrelli, *AnBari* 2 (1939) 3.

Actio de pauperie. Action for damage done by a domestic four-footed animal (*quadrupes*). Its owner had either to compensate for the damage (*pauperies*) or surrender the animal (*noxae dedere*). See NOXA. Justinian extended the *actio* to another case of liability of animal owners. Keeping a dog or a savage animal near the road was prohibited by the edict of the *aediles* and the injured victim was entitled to redress. Justinian granted an *actio de pauperie* in such a case in addition to the aedilician action.

> Robbe, *NDI* 9 (*s.v. pauperies*); Haymann, *ZSS* 42 (1921); E. Levy, *Konkurrenz der Aktionen,* 2, 1 (1922) 225; Biondi, *AnPal* 10 (1925) 3; Kerr Wylie, *St. Riccobono* 4 (1936) 459; Robbe, *RISG* N.S. 7 (1932) 327; Lenel, *ZSS* 47 (1937) 2; Visconti, *St. Solmi* 1 (1941) 157; Düll, *ZSS* 61 (1941) 1; Condanari-Michler, *Fschr Wenger* 1 (1944) 236.

Actio de peculio. See PECULIUM.

Actio de pecunia constituta. See CONSTITUTUM.

Actio de positis ac suspensis. See ACTIO DE DEIECTIS VEL EFFUSIS.

Actio de rationibus distrahendis. Action for double damages against a guardian guilty of embezzlement; it was available only after the termination of the guardianship.—D. 27.3.

> Sachers, *RE* 7A, 1563; Solazzi, *Rend Lomb* 50 (1917) 178; 53 (1920) 121; Levy, *Konkurrenz der Aktionen 2,* 1 (1922) 247.

Actio de servo corrupto. See ACTIO SERVI CORRUPTI.

Actio de termino moto. Action against the person who intentionally removed and set at another place a boundary stone in order to change the boundary of a landed property to the prejudice of the owner. Such an action could be brought by any citizen.—See TERMINUM MOVERE, ACTIONES POPULARES.

Actio de tigno iuncto. See TIGNUM IUNCTUM.

Actio de universitate. A postclassical name for HEREDITATIS PETITIO.

> E. Albertario, *Studi* 4 (1946) 65.

Actio depensi. A surety by SPONSIO who paid the principal debtor's debt because the latter failed to do so, had an *actio depensi* according to the Lex Publilia (about 200 B.C.) if within six months after the payment he was not reimbursed by the principal debtor. —See SPONSIO.

> Eisele F., *Beitrage zur rom. Rechtsgesch.,* 1896, 25.

Actio depositi. See DEPOSITUM.

Actio doli (de dolo). Action for fraud (*dolus, dolus malus*), introduced by the praetor Aquilius Gallus in 66 B.C. In the praetorian edict, it was generally promised for restitution of damages by the following announcement: "When acts are alleged to have been done *dolo malo* (by fraud), if there is no other action available in such a case and there appears to be just cause, I shall grant an action" (D. 4.3.1.1). Its applicability was gradually extended, even in Justinian's law. *Actio doli* belongs to the category of ACTIONES IN FACTUM; it is of penal character, infaming, limited to one year (after Constantine to three years) from the time the fraud was committed, and available only when no other remedy, particularly a contractual one, could be applied. Because of its general applicability the *actio* is called by Cicero "a drag-net of all ill-will" (*De nat. deorum* 3.30.74).

> F. Litten, *Festg. K. Güterbock,* 1910, 255; G. Maier, *Prätorische Bereicherungsklagen,* 1932, 35; F. Palumbo, *L'azione di dolo,* 1935; Buckland, *LQR* 55 (1939); G. Longo, *Contributi alla dottrina del dolo,* 1937.

Actio dotis. See ACTIO DE DOTE.

Actio empti (ex empto). See EMPTIO.

Actio ex stipulatu. See STIPULATIO.

Actio ex testamento. Action of a legatee against the heir to enforce a legacy bequeathed *per damnationem* or *sinendi modo.* See LEGATUM.

Actio exercitoria. See EXERCITOR.

Actio Fabiana. See ACTIO CALVISIANA.

Actio familiae (h)erciscundae. Action among coheirs (COHEREDES) in order to bring about division of the common property inherited.—D. 10.2; C. 3.36; 38.—See DIVISIO, FAMILIA.

> Frezza, *NDI* 1; Sciascia, *AG* 132 (1945) 75; see ACTIO COMMUNI DIVIDUNDO.

Actio fiduciae. See FIDUCIA.

Actio finium regundorum. Action between neighbors to settle a dispute over the boundaries (*fines*) of their lands. The judge (an arbitrator, often an expert land-surveyor = *agrimensor*) could transfer a piece of land from one party to another into full ownership (ADIUDICATIO). D. 10.1; C. 3.39.

> Humbert, *DS* 2 (*s.v. finium reg. a.*); Arangio-Ruiz, *BIDR* 32 (1922) 5; Buckland, *RHD* 15 (1936) 741.

Actio funeraria. The praetor granted an action to a person who arranged a funeral at his own expenses without being obliged to do so. The heir who did not fulfil his duty of piety towards the deceased because of negligence or absence, was liable.—D. 11.7; C. 3.44.—See FUNUS, SUMPTUS FUNERUM.

> Cuq, *DS* 2, 1405; De Francisci, *Fil* 40 (1915); *idem, AnPer* 32 (1920); E. Levy, *Privatstrafe und Schadensersatz,* 1915, 33; Donatuti, *SDHI* 8 (1942) 18.

Actio furti. See FURTUM.

Actio furti concepti. See FURTUM CONCEPTUM.

Actio furti non exhibiti. See FURTUM NON EXHIBITUM.

Actio furti oblati. See FURTUM CONCEPTUM.

Actio furti prohibiti. See FURTUM PROHIBITUM.

Actio hypothecaria. See HYPOTHECA.

Actio incerti. ACTIO EX STIPULATU and ACTIO EX TESTAMENTO have sometimes the addition *incerti*. *Actio civilis incerti* is a Justinian creation.—See ACTIO PRAESCRIPTIS VERBIS, LEGATUM, STIPULATIO.

> De Villa, *A.i.* 1932; Giffard, *SDHI* 3 (1938) 152; *idem, RHD* 16 (1937) 670.

Actio in iudicem qui litem suam facit. See IUDEX QUI, etc.

Actio iniuriarum. See INIURIA.

Actio institoria. See INSTITOR.

Actio institutoria. See ACTIO QUAE INSTITUIT OBLIGATIONEM.

Actio interrogatoria. See INTERROGATIO.

Actio iudicati. See IUDICATUM.

Actio iurisiurandi. See IURAMENTUM VOLUNTARIUM.

Actio legis Aquiliae. See LEX AQUILIA.

Actio legis Plaetoriae. See LEX PLAETORIA.

Actio locati. See LOCATIO CONDUCTIO.

Actio mandati. See MANDATUM.

Actio negatoria (negativa). Action brought by the owner of a landed property against anyone who, without denying the plaintiff's ownership, claimed a servitude or usufruct over his property. The aim of the *actio* was judicial recognition that the plaintiff has full ownership not encumbered by any right of the

defendant. See ACTIO PROHIBITORIA, VINDICATIO SER-
VITUTIS, CAUTIO DE NON AMPLIUS TURBANDO.

Arangio-Ruiz, *Azioni confessorie e negatorie*, 1908; Biondi,
AnMes 3 (1929) ; Bohacek, *BIDR* 44 (1937), 46 (1939).

Actio negotiorum gestorum. See NEGOTIORUM GESTIO.

Actio oneris aversi. Action against the master of a
ship for fraud committed in the delivery of cargo.

P. Huvelin, *Le Furtum* (1915) 511; Solazzi, *RDNav* 2
(1936) ; De Santis, *SDHI* 12 (1946) 89.

Actio operarum. See OPERAE LIBERTI.

Actio Pauliana. See FRAUS, INTERDICTUM FRAUDA-
TORIUM.

Actio pigneraticia. See PIGNUS, HYPOTHECA.

Actio praescriptis verbis. Not a classical term; the
classical jurists speak of *agere praescriptis verbis* when
"common and usual names of actions are lacking,"
that is to say, when the foundation of an action is a
bilateral transaction for reciprocal performances which
do not conform to the typical and recognized species
of contracts. The name *praescriptis verbis* originates
from the fact that in the respective *formula* the factual background of the action had to be described,
praescriptis verbis rem gestam demonstrare. Justinian's collaborators created the term *actio praescriptis verbis* and extended the applicability of the
action although the formulary procedure had been
out of use for centuries. It was qualified by Justinian as an *actio bonae fidei* and had a general function, being adaptable to very different legal situations
in which the plaintiff after performing his duty claimed
the performance of the reciprocal duty by the defendant. The terminology is not stable, the *actio* is
also called *actio civilis incerti, civilis in factum,* and
by other names.—D. 19.5; C. 4.64.

Audibert, *Mél. Gérardin*, 1907; P. Meylan, *Origine et
nature de l'a.p.v.* 1919; P. De Francisci, *Synallagma*, 1–2
(1913/16) ; Kretschmer, *ZSS* 59 (1939) 190; Thayer,
Tulane LR 19 (1949) 62; P. Voci, *Contratto* (1946) 234.

Actio principalis. See ACTIONES DIRECTAE.

Actio pro socio. See SOCIETAS.—Syn. IUDICIUM SO-
CIETATIS.

Actio prohibitoria. An action similar to ACTIO NEGA-
TORIA. Its existence in classical law is controversial.
It is assumed that its INTENTIO aims at recognition
of the plaintiff's right to forbid the defendant to exercise a certain right (servitude, usufruct) over the
plaintiff's property. See VINDICATIO SERVITUTIS.

Bortolucci, *BIDR* 21 (1909) ; R. Henle, *Unus casus*, 1915,
138; Biondi, *AnMes* 3 (1929).

Actio protutelae. Action against a person who acts
as a guardian (*pro tutore*) without having been
legally appointed.

Peters, *ZSS* 32 (1911) 243; Solazzi, *AS* 91 (1924) 150.

Actio Publiciana in rem. An honorary action (*actio
honoraria*) created by a praetor named Publicius and
granted to the bonitary (IN BONIS) owner of a thing
for reclaiming property of which he has lost possession. The plaintiff has to prove only that he
acquired the thing under conditions which put him
in the position to usucapt it. It is an *actio ficticia,*
the fiction being that the plaintiff had already acquired full property by a completed *usucapio*. The
function of the *actio Publiciana* was the same as that
of REI VINDICATIO, which, however, the plaintiff could
not use because he had no quiritary ownership.—
D. 6.2.—See ACTIONES FICTICIAE, EXCEPTIO IUSTI
DOMINII.

Lécrivain, *DS* 4 (*s.v. Publ. a.*) ; Montel, *NDI* 10; Perozzi,
BIDR 7 (1894) ; V. Seeler, *ZSS* 21 (1900) ; Pflüger, *ibid.*
42 (1921) 469; Carrelli, *SDHI* 3 (1937) 20; De Sarlo,
St Solazzi (1948) 203.

Actio quae instituit obligationem. Improperly called
institutoria, a term unknown to the sources. If a
woman intervened for another person by assuming
a contractual obligation for him, her intercession
being void, the praetor granted the creditor an action
directly against the real debtor who personally was
not obliged.—See INTERCESSIO, SENATUSCONSULTUM
VELLAEANUM.

Bortolucci, *A.q.i.o.,* 1915; Carelli, *RISG* 12 (1937) 63;
Beretta, *RISG* N.S. 2 (1948) 367.

Actio quae restituit obligationem (restitutoria).
When a creditor lost his *actio* against his debtor because of a novatory intercession by a woman, the
praetor granted him the primary action since the
woman's intercession was void. See INTERCESSIO,
SENATUSCONSULTUM VELLAEANUM.

Carrelli, *SDHI* 3 (1937) 305; Beretta, *RISG* 2 (1948) 368.

Actio quanti minoris. See EMPTIO.—D. 21.1.

Pringsheim, *ZSS* 69 (1952) 234.

Actio quasi institoria. See INSTITOR.

Actio quasi Serviana. See PIGNUS, HYPOTHECA.

Actio quod iussu. See IUSSUM.

Actio quod metus causa. See METUS.

Actio rationibus distrahendis. See ACTIO DE RATIO-
NIBUS DISTRAHENDIS.

Actio recepticia. See RECEPTUM ARGENTARII.

Actio redhibitoria. See EMPTIO.

Actio rei uxoriae. See DOS.

Actio rerum amotarum. Action for recovery of
things stolen by the wife from her husband in view
of an imminent divorce. The milder qualification "for
having taken things away" instead of "having stolen"
(*furtum*) was chosen to avoid the infaming *actio
furti* between husband and wife.—D. 25.2; C. 5.21.—
See RETENTIONES DOTALES.

Zanzucchi, *RISG* 42 (1906) ; 47 (1910) ; Kretschmar, *ZSS*
59 (1939) 199.

Actio rescissoria. In a few cases an action is granted
for the annulment of a legal situation created by special circumstances, as in the case of the return of a
soldier from captivity or of a person who had been
absent in public service. By bringing this *actio*
within a year after their return, they could rescind
the usucapion (*rescindere usucapionem*) achieved during their absence. See ABSENTES.

Carrelli, *SDHI* 3 (1937) 20; P. Collinet, *La nature des
actions*, 1948, 457.

Actio restitutoria. See ACTIO QUAE RESTITUIT OBLI-GATIONEM.

Actio Rutiliana. An action devised by the praetor Rutilius to the benefit of the purchaser of the property of a bankrupt debtor (*bonorum emptor*). For debts due to the latter, whose universal successor the *bonorum emptor* was, he sued in the name of the other (see INTENTIO), but asks for condemnation in his own name. Another *actio* granted to the *bonorum emptor* was the so-called *actio Serviana* by which he sued under the fiction "as if he were the heir" (*ficto se herede*) if the bankrupt died. See ACTIONES FIC-TICIAE, CONVERTERE, BONORUM VENDITIO.

Actio sepulcri violati. A praetorian, penal action in case of violation of a grave.—D. 47.12; C. 9.19.—See SEPULCRUM, VIOLATIO SEPULCRI.

Actio sequestraria. See SEQUESTER.

Actio servi corrupti (de servo corrupto). Action by a slave's master in case of his slave's corruption. Those liable were persons who persuaded the slave to commit robbery or some other crime, moral misconduct or luxury, to flee from his master, and the like, so that the slave became worse (*deterior factus*). The corruptor (*instigator, sollicitator*) is responsible only when he did it purposely (*dolo malo*). He had to pay not only the lessening in value of the slave but also double damages done by the slave.—D. 11.3; C. 6.2.

> Kleinfeller, *RE* 4; Schiller, *Columbia Law Rev.* 30 (1930) 839; *idem, St. Riccobono* 4 (1936) 79.

Actio Serviana. See PIGNUS, HYPOTHECA.

Actio Serviana. Of the *bonorum emptor,* see ACTIO RUTILIANA, VENDITIO BONORUM.

Actio subsidiaria. An action granted to a ward against a municipal magistrate for having appointed an incapable guardian or having failed to demand adequate guarantee from the appointed guardian (see CAUTIO REM PUPILLI SALVAM FORE). Roman and provincial magistrates were not answerable under this action.—D. 27.8; C. 5.75.

> Sachers, *RE* 7A, 1581; E. Levy, *Privatstrafe und Schaden-sersatz,* 1915, 41; Brugi, *Mél Girard* 1 (1912) 143; Berger, *KrVj* 16 (1914) 84.

Actio tributoria. A praetorian action lying against a father or master whose son (or slave) doing commercial business with his *peculium,* contracted debts with the knowledge of the father (master), and the *peculium* subsequently became insolvent. The remainder of the *peculium* was to be shared proportionally among the creditors and the father (master) if anything was due to him. Claims on the part of the creditors that an unfair distribution has been made by the father (master) could be sued by *actio tributoria.*—D. 14.4. —See PECULIUM.

> L. Lemarié, *De l'a.t.,* Thèse, Paris, 1910.

Actio tutelae. See TUTELA.—D. 27.3.

Actio vectigalis (actio quae de fundo vectigali proposita est). See AGER VECTIGALIS.

Actio venditi. See EMPTIO.

Actio vi bonorum raptorum. See VIS, RAPINA.

Actiones adiectiliae qualitatis. See EXERCITOR NAVIS.

Actiones aediliciae. Actions introduced by the aedilician edict. They were concerned with the sale of slaves and animals (see EMPTIO) and damages caused by animals, see ACTIO DE PAUPERIE.—C. 4.58.—See EDICTUM AEDILIUM CURULIUM.

Actiones annales. See ACTIO TEMPORALES.

> Beretta, *RISG* 2 (1948) 353.

Actiones arbitrariae. Actions the formula of which contained the so-called arbitrary clause authorizing the judge to bid the defendant by an *arbitrium* (*arbitratus*), an interlocutory order, to satisfy the defendant's claim by restoring or producing (*exhibere*) the object claimed ("*nisi arbitrio tuo* [of the judge] *res restituatur, exhibeatur*"). If the defendant did so, he was absolved; if not, the final judgment condemned him to pay a sum of money, which was more disadvantageous to him than the immediate fulfillment of the judge's order (he might be condemned to a higher amount, he had to pay a fourfold amount in the *actio quod metus causa* [see METUS], he incurred infamy in *actio doli,* etc.). It is controversial whether the words *"arbitrio tuo"* were in the formula and whether the term *arbitrariae actiones* was used by the classical jurists.

> Biondi, *BIDR* 26 (1913) 1, 153; *idem, St sulle actiones arbitrariae e l'arbitrium iudicis,* 1913; May, *Mél Girard* 2 (1912) 151; Lenel, *Fschr Sohm,* 1914, 201; Berger, *KrVj* 16 (1914) 122; Levy, *ZSS* 36 (1915) 1; R. Düll, *Der Gütegedanke,* 1931; M. Kaser, *Restituere als Prozessgegenstand,* 1932; G. Huwardas, *Beiträge zur Lehre von den a.a.,* 1932; Herdlitczka, *Zur Lehre vom Zwischenurteil bei den a.a.,* 1930; *idem, Skizzen zum röm. Zivilprozess,* 1934; Schönbauer, *St. Riccobono* 2 (1936) 371; F. Schulz, *Class. R. Law,* 1951, 37.

Actiones bonae fidei. See IUDICIA BONAE FIDEI.

Actiones (formulae) certae. Actions with a precisely specified object, sum of money or a thing, claimed by the plaintiff. Ant. *actiones incertae.* In the formulary procedure the object in dispute was defined in the INTENTIO of the formula. Hence the distinction: *intentio certa* and *incerta.* In the latter the plaintiff's claim is directed to *"quidquid"* (= whatever it will appear that the defendant has to pay or do).

Actiones civiles. Actions which protected rights recognized by the IUS CIVILE. Their origin lay in the Twelve Tables, in certain statutes or in the creative activity of the jurists. Ant. *actiones honorariae,* see ACTIONES PRAETORIAE, ACTIONES AEDILICIAE.

Actiones contrariae. See ACTIONES DIRECTAE.

Actiones directae. (1) Actions the formula of which could be extended through an appropriate modification to analogous factual circumstances, not covered by the original formula. The modified formula was an *actio utilis,* as opposed to the original *actio directa.* (2) Actions arising from certain contracts which normally created liability in one party, as, e.g., in the case of a deposit or mandate the action of the depositor or mandator, were *actiones directae*. Under exceptional circumstances, however, the party primarily bound, the depositee or the mandatary, had a claim against the other party. Such actions are called by Justinian *contrariae* as opposed to the *actiones directae* of the parties who as a matter of rule are creditors in such contracts. The same holds true for non-contractual situations, such as guardianship, since the guardian had an *actio contraria* (*iudicium contrarium*) against the ward. Other terms for *actio directa* are *actio principalis,* and rarely, *iudicium rectum.* The concept of *actio contraria* is controversial.—D. 27.4; C. 5.58.

Manigk, *RE* 9 (*s.v. iudicium contrarium*); J. Partsch, *Studien zur negotiorum gestio,* 1913, 47; Biondi, *AnPal* 7 (1920) 59; Kübler, *ZSS* 38 (1917) 73; Lenel, *Edictum perpetuum* 3 (1927) 318; G. Provera, *SDHI* 8 (1942) 113; *idem, St. Solazzi,* 1948, 345; V. Arangio-Ruiz, *Il mandato,* 1949, 45.

Actiones duplices. See IUDICIA DUPLICIA.

Actiones famosae. Actions in which the condemnation of the defendant involved INFAMIA: he became *infamis* (*ignominiosus*). Such *actiones* were: *actiones furti, vi bonorum raptorum, iniuriarum, de dolo, mandati, depositi,* and others. Syn. *actiones turpes.*

Sachers, *RE* 7A, 1434; Zanzucchi, *RISG* 42 (1906) 1; 47 (1910) 3, 237.

Actiones ficticiae. Praetorian actions adapted by the use of a fiction in the formula to legal situations not protected by the original formula. For instance, some actions became available to foreigners under the fiction "as if they were Roman citizens." In the ACTIO PUBLICIANA the claim for recovery of a thing was based on the fiction that *usucapio* has been completed. Actions granted to, or against, a successor by praetorian law (*bonorum possessor*) contained the fiction "as if he were *heres.*"

Riccobono, *TR* 9 (1929) 1.

Actiones hereditariae. Actions in favor of, or against, the heir, connected with an inheritance.—Inst. 4.12; C. 4.16.

Actiones honorariae. Actions originating in praetorian or aedilician law.—See ACTIONES AEDILICIAE, ACTIONES PRAETORIAE. Ant. *actiones civiles.*

M. Kaser, *Das altröm. ius,* 1949, 94.

Actiones in bonum et aequum conceptae. This term, mentioned only once (D. 4.5.8), refers to certain *actiones in factum,* primarily in cases of torts in which the CONDEMNATIO contained the clause *quantum bonum et aequum* (or simply *aequum*) *videbitur.* It authorized the judge to fix the sum of condemnation at his discretion "as it would seem to him just and fair." The foundation of the *actiones* was not a contractual relation between the parties but a behavior of the defendant which caused some harm to the plaintiff. Such actions were, e.g., *actiones rei uxoriae, funeraria, iniuriarium, sepulcri violati,* and

the action against the judge *qui litem suam facit.* In origin, there certainly were formal and substantial differences between these *actiones* and IUDICIA BONAE FIDEI. The disappearance of the formulary procedure furthered their equalization fully completed in Justinian law.

Thomas, *NRHD* 25 (1901) 541; Pringsheim, *ZSS* 52 (1932) 85; Kaser, *RIDA* 2 (1949) 512.

Actiones in duplum. See ACTIONES IN SIMPLUM.

Actiones in factum. See FORMULAE IN IUS CONCEPTAE.

Actiones in id quod pervenit. Actions by which the plaintiff claimed only what the defendant obtained to his detriment.—See ACTIONES POENALES, PERVENIRE AD ALIQUEM.

F. Schulz, *Die actiones in id etc.,* Diss. Breslau, 1905; G. H. Maier, *Praetorische Bereicherungsklagen,* 1932; E. Albertario, *Studi* 4 (1946) 289 (seven articles).

Actiones in ius conceptae. See FORMULAE IN IUS CONCEPTAE.

Actiones in personam. Actions in which the plaintiff based his claim on a contractural or delictual obligation of the defendant. Ant. *actiones in rem* = actions in which the plaintiff asserts a right to a certain thing (ownership, servitude) possessed by the defendant. This basic distinction is expressed by a different wording of the INTENTIO in the formula: in the *actiones in personam* the defendant is sued for *dare, facere, praestare oportere* (= to give, to do or to perform something), in the *actiones in rem* the plaintiff affirms that the corporeal object he claims is his or that he has a certain right over the adversary's property. The former actions lie against the person obligated by a contract or a wrongdoing, the latter may be brought against any person who withholds the thing involved from the plaintiff. *Actiones in rem* are also called *vindicationes* (REI VINDICATIO, VINDICATIO SERVITUTIS); to *actiones in personam* the term *condictiones* is applied, in post-classical and Justinian law the term *actiones personales.*

G. Segre, *BIDR* 41 (1933); S. Grosso, *Problemi di diritti reali,* 1944, 74; Albertario, *Studi* 4 (1946) 221; B. Biondi, *Le servità prediali nel dir. rom.,* 1946, 14.

Actiones in rem. See ACTIONES IN PERSONAM.

De Villa, *NDI* 6 (*in rem a.*); Kaser, *Besitz und Verschulden bei dinglichen Klagen, ZSS* 51 (1931) 92.

Actiones in simplum. It is a general rule that the aim of each action is the simple value of what the plaintiff claims (*simplum*). There are, however, *actiones* in which the defendant is condemned to pay twofold (*duplum*), threefold (*triplum*), even fourfold (*quadruplum*) the value. The liability of the defendant is doubled, for instance, in certain actions when he deliberately denies. See INFITIATIO. Higher rates of condemnation occur in cases of theft.—See FURTUM, DUPLUM.

Actiones incertae. See ACTIONES CERTAE.

Actiones interrogatoriae. See INTERROGATIO IN IURE.

Actiones mixtae. The term, doubtless of non-classical

origin, is used in various meanings. IUDICIA DUPLICIA are so called likewise actions which simultaneously serve different purposes (recovery of a thing and penalty), finally actions which are both in rem and in personam (*actiones quod metus causa*, see ACTIONES IN PERSONAM).

> Berger, *St Simoncelli*, 1915, 184 (Bibl.); *idem*, *ZSS* 36 (1915) 218; U. v. Lübtow, *Ediktstitel quod metus causa*, 1932, 292; P. Voci, *Risarcimento e pena privata*, 1939, 91.

Actiones mutuae. See MUTUAE PETITIONES.

Actiones noxales. See NOXA.

Actiones perpetuae. Generally actions could be brought without limit of time. Such were all *actiones civiles*. A constitution of Theodosius II (A.D. 424) introduced a thirty-year period of prescription for all actions with a few exceptions. Since then all actions which extinguished after thirty years, we called *perpetuae*.—Inst. 4.12; C. 7.39.—See PRAE-SCRIPTIO TRIGINTA ANNORUM.

Actiones personales. Postclassical and Justinian term for ACTIONES IN PERSONAM.

Actiones poenales. Also called *actiones quibus poenam persequimur*. Actions by which the plaintiff sued for payment of a penalty because of a private offence committed by the defendant. Penal actions are transmissible only to the heir of the plaintiff, but not to the heir of the defendant, except in certain cases for his enrichment (*in id quod ad eum pervenit*, or *quantum locupletior factus est*).—See DELICTA.

> P. De Francisci, *St sopra le azioni penali*, 1912; E. Levy, *Privatstrafe und Schadensersatz*, 1915; Riccobono, *ZSS* 47 (1927); G. Maier, *Praetorische Bereicherungsklagen*, 1932; P. Voci, *Risarcimento e pena privata* (1939) 6, 150; E. Albertario, *St* 4 (1946) 303, 371; Beretta, *RISG* 2 (1948) 353.

Actiones populares. Actions which can be brought by "any one among the people" (*quivis [quilibet] ex populo*). They are of praetorian origin and serve to protect public interest (*ius populi*). They are penal, and in case of condemnation of the offender the plaintiff receives the penalty paid. Such actions are: *actiones de albo corrupto, sepulchri violati, de termino moto, de positis ac suspensis*, etc. There are instances, however, established in statutes or local ordinances, in which the penalty was paid to the state or municipal treasury, or divided between the *aerarium* and the accuser, as, e.g., provided in a decree of the Senate in the case of damage to aqueducts.—D. 47.23.

> Cuq, *DS* 4 (*s.v. popularis actio*); Kübler, *RE* 4A, 157; C. Fadda, *Azione popolare*, 1894; T. Mommsen, *Gesammelte Schriften* 3 (1905) 375.

Actiones praeiudiciales. Actions in which decision in a preliminary question is passed (*praeiudicium*) being decisive on a second suit. E.g., when a patron wants to sue his freedman for failure in accomplishing his duties, the preliminary question is *an libertus sit*, i.e., whether the defendant is really his freedman. In such actions absolution or condemnation is not implied, the judge's statement (*pronuntiatio*) being only an answer to the question involved.—See FORMULAE PRAEIUDICIALES, PRAEIUDICIA, INTENTIO.

> Siber, *Fschr Wenger* 1 (1944) 69.

Actiones praetoriae. Actions originating in pretorian law. They either contained an extension of civil actions (*actiones civiles*) to analogous new cases or granted protection to legal transactions or situations not recognized by IUS CIVILE. The most creative innovations among the *actiones praetoriae* were the *actiones (formulae) in factum, actiones ficticiae*, and *actiones utiles*. See ACTIONES TEMPORALES.

> Beretta, *RISG* 2 (1948) 353.

Actiones praescriptis verbis. See ACTIO PRAESCRIPTIS VERBIS.

Actiones privatae. Actions protecting the private interests of an individual. Ant. ACTIONES POPULARES. Similar in meaning is the term *iudicia privata* covering civil trials in private affairs subject in classical law to the judgment of a private judge, but in later times, after the nationalization of the civil proceedings, without this feature.

Actiones quibus poenam persequimur. See ACTIONES POENALES.

Actiones quibus rem persequimur (actiones rei persequendae gratia comparatae). Also called in the literature *rei persecutoriae* = actions in which the object of the trial is a thing, a sum of money, restitution or indemnity. Such are all *actiones in rem* and *actiones in personam* of contractual origin. Ant. ACTIONES POENALES. There are *actiones* arising from offences of a delictual character in which the plaintiff's claims embrace both objectives, redress and penalty, as for instance in case of theft, or of *actiones in duplum*. The distinction is important as far as the liability of the heirs is concerned.—See ACTIONES MIXTAE, IN SIMPLUM, POENALES.

> A. Giffard, *Études sur les obligations et les actions*, II *Les actions personnelles reipersecutoires*, 1941.

Actiones speciales. See IUDICIA GENERALIA.

Actiones temporales (temporariae). Actions which could be brought only within a limited period of time. Such were ACTIONES PRAETORIAE, mostly limited to one year (*actiones annales*). ACTIONES AEDILICIAE were limited to six months only.—Inst. 4.12. —See ACTIONES PERPETUAE.

Actiones stricti iuris. See IUDICIA BONAE FIDEI.

Actiones turpes. See ACTIONES FAMOSAE.

Actiones utiles. Actions introduced through the activity of praetors and jurists by a modification of an already existing formula to cover legal situations and transactions for which the original formula did not suffice. The mechanism of the *actiones utiles* contributed considerably to the development of the law. The original action is called *directa*.—See ACTIONES DIRECTAE.

> I. Alibrandi, *Opere* 1 (1896) 149; Seckel, in *Heumann's Handlexikon*⁹ (1907) 608; G. Bortolucci, *A. utilis*, 1909;

Riccobono, *TR* 9 (1929) 33; Dekkers, *Rev. Univ. Bruxelles* 41 (1935/6) 232; P. Collinet, *La nature des actions,* 1947, 403.

Actiones vulgares. Common, usual actions, opposed to *actiones utiles,* or *actiones in factum.*

Actor. The plaintiff in a civil trial, particularly after the LITIS CONTESTATIO. Syn. *is qui agit, agens, petitor.* Before the *litis contestatio* he is designated as *is qui agere vult. Actrix* = a female plaintiff. Ant. *reus, is cum quo agitur.*—See REUS, AGERE.
Wlassak, *RE* 1.

Actor. In private law, a manager of another's business or affairs, an agent. Frequently a slave is appointed for this purpose.—C. 5.61.
Daube, *LQR* 62 (1946) 269; A. Burdese, *Autorizzazione ad alienare,* 1950, 25.

Actor domus augustae. See ACTOR REI PRIVATAE.

Actor praediorum fiscalium. The administrator of landed property belonging to the fisc.—C. 11.72.

Actor publicus. See ACTOR UNIVERSITATIS.

Actor rei privatae (actor domus augustae). The administrator of the Emperor's private property. See RES PRIVATA, DOMUS AUGUSTA.
De Ruggiero, *DE* 1.

Actor rei publicae. See ACTOR UNIVERSITATIS.

Actor universitatis (collegii, municipii). The agent, representative of a corporate body by whom "is being acted and done (*agatur et fiat*) all that has to be acted and done on the common behalf" (D. 3.4.1.1). Corporate bodies of public law had also their *actores* (*actor municipum, actor civitatis*), who in case of litigation represent them in court both as plaintiffs and as defendants. In this character they are also called *defensores.* Sporadically the term *actor rei publicae* or *actor publicus* also appears.—D. 3.4.
Habel, *RE* 1, 330; Humbert, *DS* 1 (*a. publ.*); De Ruggiero, *DE* 1, 66; Ramadier, *Ét. Girard* 1 (1913) 259.

Actrix. See ACTOR in a civil trial.

Actum. Added at the end of a written document and followed by the name of the locality refers to the place where the deed was performed ("done at . . .").

Actus. The right to drive a draft animal or vehicles over another's property. It is a rustic servitude and also implies the right of passage (*ius eundi*). See SERVITUTES PRAEDIORUM RUSTICORUM, INTERDICTUM DE ITINERE ACTUQUE PRIVATO.—D. 43.19.
Leonhard, *RE* 1, 331; De Ruggiero, *DE* 1, 70; Scialoja, *St giur.* 1 (1932) 389; Arangio-Ruiz, *St Brugi,* 1910; Landucci, *AVen* 65 (1906) 1307; Meylan, *St Albertoni,* 1 (1935) 134.

Actus legitimi. Certain formal legal transactions governed by the strict formalism of the ancient law, which could not be subject to a suspensive condition or a term (*dies*), such as formal conveyance of property (through MANCIPATIO or IN IURE CESSIO), ACCEPTILATIO, and a few others. In these transactions no interval was admitted between their conclusion and their effectiveness.—See DIES.
E. F. Bruck, *Bedingungsfeindliche Rechtsgeschäfte,* 1904.

Actus rerum. Court days on which the judicial activity of the private judges (jurors = *iudices*) was exercised (*cum res aguntur*).—See IUDEX.
Wlassak, *RE* 1.

Ad exemplum. See EXEMPLUM.

Adaeratio. Calculation in money for payment in cash instead of supplies in kind to the state (ANNONA) or in matter of wages.
Seeck, *RE* 1; Heichelheim, *OCD*; Persson, *Staat und Manufaktur* (Lund, 1923) 104.

Adcrescendi ius. See IUS ADCRESCENDI.

Addicere (addictio). To assign, adjudge, adjudicate a thing being the object of a controversy. When property is conveyed by IN IURE CESSIO the praetor *addicit rem. Addicere iudicem* (or *arbitrum*) = to appoint a judge (or an arbitrator). *Addicere* is also referred to persons: a free man caught in the commission of a theft was assigned to the person from whom he has stolen. For *addicere* in auctions, see AUCTIO. —See also ADDICTUS.
Wlassak *RE* 1; Cogliolo, *NDI* 1; Carrelli, *AnBari* 1939, 122; Lévy-Bruhl, *Nouvelles études sur le très ancien dr. rom.,* 1947, 141; Kaser, *Fschr Wenger* 1 (1944) 117.

Addictio bonorum libertatum servandarum causa. In order to prevent testamentary manumissions from becoming void when the appointed heir refused to accept an insolvent inheritance, an enactment of Marc Aurel made it possible to assign the inheritance to another person, primarily to the slaves freed in the last will, who had to carry out all the dispositions concerned with manumissions.—Inst. 3.11.
Humbert, *DS* 1.

Addictio in diem. An agreement between buyer and seller giving the latter the right to declare the sale annulled if, within a certain time, he received an offer of a higher price (*adiectio*) for the object sold. In such a case the first buyer had the possibility to increase his bid and to keep the thing.—D. 18.2.
Cogliolo, *NDI;* Senn, *NRHD* 37 (1913); Longo, *BIDR* 31 (1921); H. Sieg, *Quellenkritische Studien zur Bessergebotsklausel im röm. Kaufrecht,* 1933; Archi, *St Ratti,* 1934, 325; Levy, *Zu den Rücktrittsverboten des röm. Kaufs, Symbolae Frib. Lenel,* 1932; Romano, *StPav* 22 (1937); Henle, *Fschr Koschaker* 2 (1939) 169; Alvaro D'Ors, *In diem addictio,* Madrid, 1945.

Addictus. A debtor who had failed to pay his debt and against whom a personal execution (MANUS INIECTIO) was initiated could be adjudged to the creditor in the earliest times and held prisoner by the latter (under the Twelve Tables). He remained free, but after sixty days he could be sold beyond the boundaries of Rome (beyond the Tiber river = *trans Tiberim*) which effected loss of citizenship and of freedom.—See DIES IUSTI, TIBERIS.
Leist, *RE* 1; Humbert, *DS* 1.

Ademptio. From *adimere.* Cancellation, revocation of a prior disposition, as, for instance, withdrawal of a *peculium* which had been granted to a son or slave (*ademptio peculii*).—See ADEMPTIO LEGATI, ADEMPTIO LIBERTATIS.

Ademptio bonorum. Confiscation of property by a public authority as an act of punishment.—See CON-FISCATIO, PUBLICATIO BONORUM.

U. Brasiello, *Repressione penale*, 1937, 324.

Ademptio legati. A legacy could be annulled by the testator either expressly by a statement in a later will or codicil, or through a subsequent, intentional (*animus adimendi legatum*) alienation of the thing bequeathed or through its transfer to another legatee (*translatio legati*). In a similar manner a testamentary manumission could be revoked either expressly or tacitly when the testator alienated the slave or bequeathed him to another person (*ademptio libertatis*).—Inst. 2.21; D. 34.4; 40.6.

Leonhard, *RE* 1; Messina-Vitrano, *AnPal* 3 (1917) 3; Solazzi, *Scritti Mancaleoni, StSas* 16, (1938) 186; Sanfilippo, *AnPal* 17 (1937) 105, 120; Koschaker, *ConfCast* 1940, 87; Albertario, *St* 4 (1946) 42; Arnò, *L'alienazione della cosa legata, MemTor* 44 (1939).

Ademptio libertatis. See ADEMPTIO LEGATI.—D. 40.6.

Adesse. In a judicial trial, to be present in court as a party to the proceedings; to assist a party as his advocate.—See ADVOCATUS.

Adfatus. An imperial enactment (in the language of the imperial chancery).

Adfines. See ADFINITAS.

Adfinitas. Relationship between one consort and near relatives (parents, brothers and sisters, children) of the other consort. Marriage between persons so related was forbidden: it was void and punished as incestuous.—See INCESTUS.

Leonhard, *RE* 1; Baudry, *DS* 2; A. Guarino, *Affinitas*, 1939; Castello, *Osservazioni sui divieti di matrimonio fra parenti ed affini, RendLomb* 72 (1939); *idem, Diritto familiare*, 1942, 142.

Adfirmator. A person who affirms the trustworthiness or solvency of another before an official. He was answerable for fraudulent false information.

Leonhard, *RE* 1.

Adgnatio, adgnatus. See AGNATIO, AGNATUS.

Adiectio. See ADDICTIO IN DIEM. *Adiectio* = a higher bid at an auction.—C. 10.3.—See AUCTIO, SUBHASTATIO.

Adiectus solutionis causa. A person to whom a debt due to another, the primary creditor, was to be paid.

S. Cugia, *A.s.c.,* Naples, 1919; Riccobono, *AnPal* 14 (1930) 401; G. Wesenberg, *Verträge zu Gunsten Dritter,* 1949, 21.

Adire hereditatem. See ADITIO HEREDITATIS.

Aditio hereditatis. The acceptance of an inheritance by an heir (HERES) appointed in a last will or inheriting under the law. Only a certain category of heirs (see HERES VOLUNTARIUS) was obliged to declare expressly their willingness to accept the estate, whereas the nearest relatives belonging to the family of the testator (HERES NECESSARIUS, HERES SUUS ET NECESSARIUS) acquired the inheritance automatically under the law (*ipso iure*) without any particular formality. The ancient form of *aditio hereditatis* was CRETIO, later forms were: acting as an heir (PRO HEREDE GERERE) and an informal declaration of intent (*aditio nuda voluntate*). An acceptance once made was irrevocable.—D. 29.2; C. 6.30.

Solazzi, *I modi di accettazione dell'eredità, StPav* 1919; Dulckeit, *Erblasserwille und Erwerbswille bei Antretung der Erbschaft,* 1934; H. Krüger, *ZSS* 64 (1944) 394.

Aditus. Syn. *ius adeundi.* With some rustic servitudes there is connected the right of walking to the place burdened with the servitude if the exercise of the servitude by the person so entitled would otherwise be impossible.—See SERVITUTES PRAEDIORUM RUSTICORUM.

Adiudicatio. The part of the procedural formula by which the judge was permitted to adjudge (*adiudicare*) the object to the parties to the trial in so-called divisory actions (*actio communi dividundo, actio familiae erciscundae*). Beyond the controversies, concerned with the division of common property, *adiudicatio* by the judge also occurs when he adjudicates someone's property to another or to the fisc.

Wlassak, *RE* 1; Baudry, *DS* 1; Arangio-Ruiz, *BIDR* 32 (1922) 5.

Adiutores. Assistant officers in the various branches of administration of the Empire, as well as in the imperial chancery and household.

De Ruggiero, *DE* 1; Habel, *RE* 2; Saglio, *DS* 1; Berger, *ClPhilol* 43 (1948) 233; Jones, *JRS* 39 (1949) 54.

Adl-. See ALL-.

Adlecti. Subordinate officers in the emperor's secretariat and in other imperial offices.—See the following item.

Adlectio. The emperors used to confer the title and rank of ex-magistrates (*adlectio inter consulares, praetorios, quaestorios, tribunicios*) on persons who never before had been in service or had held an office of a rank lower than that which was conferred on them. The person thus distinguished (*adlectus*) became qualified for the next higher magistracy. An *adlectus inter praetorios,* for instance, could be elected to the consulship. Moreover, the *adlecti* became members of the senate in the group of retired magistrates of the rank given them. An *adlectio in senatum* was frequently practiced with regard to imperial PROCURATORES of equestrian rank. See LECTIO SENATUS.—Another kind of *adlectio* was the admission of persons of plebeian origin to the patriciate. —*Adlectio* is also the admission of a new member into a corporation, as well as that of a new citizen into the *municipales* (*adlectio inter cives,* see LEX CASSIA) or of a new councillor into the ORDO DE-CURIONUM.—See DECRETUM DECURIONUM.

Schmidt, *RE* 1; Humbert, *DS* 1; De Ruggiero, *DE* 1; O'Brien-Moore, *RE* Suppl. 6, 760 (*a. in senatum*); Borzsak, *RE* 18, 1110 (*s.v. ornamenta*).

Adminiculum. A legal support or remedy which strengthens a person in his legal situation or gives him the possibility to improve it (e.g., an appeal, see APPELLATIO).

Administrare (administratio). Refers both to the management of private affairs (property, *peculium*, tutorship) and to the exercise of a public office (magistracy, governorship, *administratio rerum publicarum*). Hence *administrator* is used of the highest officials of the state.—D. 26.7; 50.8; C. 5.37; 11.31; 38; 1.49.—See EXCUTERE RATIONES.

Orestano, *St Bonolis* 1 (1942) 11.

Admissionalis. See the following item.

Seeck, *RE* 1.

Admissiones. Admission to an audience with the emperor was granted by a special office, *officium admissionum,* under the supervision of a *magister admissionum.* The intervening officer was the *admissionalis.*

Schmidt, *RE* 1; De Ruggiero, *DE* 1, 92.

Admissum. A general and not sharply defined term for criminal offenses. It is used particularly in later sources. *In admisso deprehendere* = to catch in the very act.

Berger, *KrVj* 16 (1912) 414; De Dominicis, *AVen* 92 (1932/3) 1215.

Admittere. To commit an illicit act (a wrongdoing).

Adnotatio. A decision of the emperor written in the margin of a petition addressed to him. In some texts it is distinguished from an imperial rescript (RESCRIPTUM) from which it differed in form, not in content. The differences between *adnotatio* and *rescriptum* which might have arisen from the fact that the *adnotatio* was originally a written instruction for drafting a rescript by the imperial chancery, gradually vanished. In criminal proceeding *adnotatio* (from *adnotare*) means noting a person on the list of those who are to be summoned or deported.

Seeck, *RE* 1.

Adoptio. Through *adoptio* a person who is under the paternal power of the head of his family comes under the *patria potestas* of another (*adoptator, pater adoptivus*). The change of family (*mutatio familiae*) is the characteristic feature of the *adoptio*, while in an *adrogatio*, i.e., the adoption of a person *sui iuris* who is himself the head of a family, there is a fusion of two families since the *adrogatus* enters into another family together with all persons subject to his paternal power. The legal effects are equal in both cases; the adopted persons have the same rights (succession) and duties (*sacra*) as natural sons.—D. 1.7; Inst. 1.11; 3–10; C. 8.47.—See the following items, DATIO IN ADOPTIONEM, ADROGATIO (Bibl.).

Leonhard, *RE* 1; Baudry, *DS* 1; Bellelli, *NDI* 1 (*s.v. adozione*); Wenger, *RAC* 1 (1942); De Ruggiero, *DE* 1; C. G. Bergmann, *Beiträge zum röm. Adoptionsrecht,* 1912; Albertario, *St. Ratti* 1934, 667; Monier, *St Albertoni* 1 (1935) 235; M. H. Prevost, *Les adoptions politiques à Rome,* 1949.

Adoptio in fratrem. See FRATER.

Adoptio minus plena. A weaker form of *adoptio* in Justinian law by which the ties with the former family of the adopted person were not completely destroyed, particularly in the field of the rights of succession. Ant. *adoptio plena* which produced the effects of the ancient *adoptio.*

Lavaggi, *SDHI* 12 (1946) 45, 115.

Adoptio per populum. Refers to *adrogatio* since in earlier times the approval by the people (*auctoritas populi*) was required for the validity of a change of family (MUTATIO FAMILIAE).

Castelli, *Scritti giuridici,* 1923, 189.

Adoptio plena. See ADOPTIO MINUS PLENA.

Adoptivus. Connected with adoption. *Filius adoptivus,* or simply *adoptivus* = the adopted person. *Pater adoptivus* = the adopting father.

Adoratio purpurae. Worshipping the emperor by kneeling before him and kissing his purple garment.

Seeck, *RE* 1; Avery, *Mem. Amer. Acad. Rome* 17 (1940).

Adp-. See APP-.

Adplumbatio. See FERRUMINATIO, PLUMBATURA.

Leonhard, *RE* 1; Pampaloni, *Scritti* 1 (1941) 7.

Adprehendere rem. To take hold of a thing. It is a symbolic gesture to affirm the right of ownership in a trial (REI VINDICATIO) or in the act of transfer of ownership through MANCIPATIO. In a larger sense, to take physical possession of a thing.

Adprobare. To approve, as another jurist's opinion. According to a statute, LEX AELIA SENTIA, exceptional manumissions of slaves contrary to the rules therein set forth had to be approved by a special court.— *Adprobare opus* = to approve of a work (*opus*) done by a hired craftsman. *Adprobare* was an important act in the hire contract (LOCATIO CONDUCTIO OPERIS FACIENDI) since after approval the risk of destruction or deterioration of the work passed upon the person who ordered it.—Syn. *probare.*

Samter, *ZSS* 26 (1905) 125.

Adpromissio (adpromissor). The obligation of a surety who guaranteed for the debt of the principal debtor through *stipulatio.* The different forms of suretyship were *sponsio, fideiussio, fidepromissio,* according to the expression used by the surety (*sponsor, fideiussor, fidepromissor*) when he assumed liability in a stipulation additional to that of the principal (*spondeo, fide mea esse iubeo* = I bid you trust my faith, *fide promitto* = I pledge my faith). The obligation of the surety was for the same thing and could not be assumed for a larger sum or under heavier conditions than that of the principal. As a matter of rule, the accessory character of the suretyship depended upon the validity and the existence of the principal obligation, but in the case of *sponsio* and *fidepromissio* this rule was weakened. Besides, the liability arising from these two forms lasted only two years and did not bind the heirs. In Justinian's law all three forms were fused into one, the *fideiussio,* whereas in earlier times *sponsio* was accessible only to Roman citizens, and *sponsio* and *fidepromissio* could be applied to guarantee only obligations from verbal contracts. In Justinian's law all these and other minor differences vanished.—Inst. 3.20; D.46.1; C. 2.23; 8.40.—See LEX APULEIA DE SPONSU, LEX CICEREIA, LEX CORNELIA DE ADPROMISSORIBUS.

Leonhard, *RE* 1; 6 (*s.vv. fideiussio, fidepromissio*); Cuq, *DS* 3, 557; Anon. *NDI* 5 (*s.v. fideiussio*); E. Levy, *Sponsio, fidepromissio, fideiussio,* 1907; Donatuti, *AnPer* 38 (1927) 1; Solazzi, *BIDR* 38 (1930) 19; Buckland, *RHD* 7 (1928), 460; 12 (1933) 116; W. Flume, *Studien zur Akzessorietät der röm. Bürgschaftsstipulationen,* 1932; G. Bo, *Contributi alla dottrina dell'obbligazione fideiussoria,* 1934; Archi, *ConfCast,* 1940, 259; F. De Martino, *Garenzie personali dell'obbligazione,* 1 (1940); G. Nocera, *Insolvenza e responsabilità sussidiaria,* 1942, 59; Levy, *Sem* 2 (1944) 6 (= *BIDR* 55–56, *Post-Bellum* [1951] 207); Beretta, *Scr Ferrini* 1 (Univ. Sacro Cuore, Milan, 1947) 80.

Adpulsus pecoris ad aquam. The right to drive one's cattle through another's (the neighbor's) property to water. The right is connected with certain rustic servitudes to secure the access of the cattle to the watering-place.

Adquirere (adquisitio). To acquire (ownership, possession, an inheritance, an obligation). The ability to acquire for other persons is dealt with by Inst. 2.9; 3.28; C. 4.27; the acquisition of an inheritance D. 29.2; C. 6.30; of ownership D. 41.1; of possession D. 29.2; C. 7.32; through *adrogatio* Inst. 3.10.

Leonhard, *RE* 1, 284.

Adquirere per universitatem. See UNIVERSITAS.

Adrogatio. See ADOPTIO, ADOPTIO PER POPULUM.—Inst. 3.10.

Leonhard, *RE* 1; Humbert, *DS* 1; Bellelli, *NDI* 1; G. Beseler, *Subsiciva,* 1929, 1; Bellelli, *AG* 116 (1936) 65; idem, *SDHI* 3 (1937) 140; Lavaggi, *SDHI* 12 (1946) 115; Cosentini, *AnCat* 2 (1948) 235.

Adrogatio per rescriptum principis. Adoption of a person *sui iuris* granted by a rescript of the emperor. No further formalities were necessary.

Adscribere. When referring to last wills, to make a legacy or to add a specific clause (e.g., a condition, a term) to a testamentary disposition.

Adscripticii. A class of COLONI in the later Empire who were bound to their landlord's soil which they cultivated. Although their legal status was that of free men and citizens, they were subject to certain personal restrictions and burdens which made their position similar to serfdom.—See COLONATUS.

Saumagne, *Byzantion* 12 (1937).

Adsertio. (From *adserere.*) Any assertion made before court. An *adsertio* acquired particular importance when the personal status of a person was contested. Hence, *adsertor libertatis* was he who, in a trial about the status of an alleged slave, asserted and defended his liberty. In the form of enfranchisement called MANUMISSIO VINDICTA (= manumission in the form of a fictitious trial) the intervention of an *adsertor libertatis* was necessary. He claimed the liberty of the slave involved, and the manumittor then failed to deny this assertion.—C. 7.17.—See INGENUITAS, VINDICATIO IN LIBERTATEM.

Leonhard, *RE* 1; *DS* 1 (*s.v. assertor*); M. Nicolau, *Causa liberalis,* 1933, 122; Noailles, *Rev. des Études Latines* 20 (1942) 121; Van Oven, *TR* 18 (1950) 159, 177; P. Noailles, *Du droit sacré au droit civil,* 1950, 177.

Adsertor libertatis. See the foregoing item.

Adsessores. Legal advisers who assisted magistrates and judges in judicial activity. They belonged to the *consilium* (council), hence their name *consiliarii.* In the later classical period their activity was very extensive. The jurist Paul who wrote a monograph on the duties of *adsessores* enumerates as lying in the sphere of their activity: *cognitiones, postulationes, libelli, edicta, decreta, epistulae.* The terms cover the whole magisterial and judicial activity in court and beyond procedural questions. Under the later Empire each official had at least one *adsessor.* The *adsessores* were appointed by the government with a salary. An *adsessor* who helped a magistrate or judge in drafting a decision was responsible for advice given in ignorance or inconsiderateness (*imprudentia*). The opinion of *adsessores* was not binding on the magistrate or judge.—D. 1.22; C. 1.51, 52.

Seeck, *RE* 1 (*assessores*); Humbert, *DS* 1; De Ruggiero, *DE* 1; Kübler, *RAC* 1 (1943) 803; Hitzig, *Die Assessoren der röm. Magistrate,* 1893.

Adsessorium. Appears in the title of works by the jurists, Sabinus and Puteloanus, each work cited only once in the Digest. Thus the character of those writings cannot be specified. They probably dealt with cases which the authors drew from their assessorial practice.—See ADSESSORES.

Adsidui. The term appears in the Twelve Tables in connection with processual guarantees (see VINDEX). "For an *adsiduus* only an *adsiduus* may be a guarantee, while for a *proletarius* any one may guaranty" (Gell. n. Att. 16.10.5). *Adsidui* are those who belong to the five classes of the so-called Servian constitution (CENTURIAE) with a patrimony from 100,000 down to 12,500 asses. Syn. *locupletes, classici.* Ant. *proletarii.*

Kubitschek, *RE* 1; Pascal, *Rivista di filol. e istruzione classica* 30 (1902); M. F. Peterlongo-Lepri, *Saggi sul patrimonio* 1 (1942) 25.

Adsignatio. The assignment of public land (AGER PUBLICUS) to private individuals, municipalities or colonies in ownership or usufruct. The distribution was regulated by statutes (agrarian legislation = LEGES AGRARIAE) which fixed the size and conditions of the grant.

Kubitschek, *RE* 1; Vancura, *RE* 12, 1155; De Ruggiero, *DE* 1; Fraccaro, *Scr Ferrini* 1 (Univ. Sacro Cuore, Milan, 1947) 262.

Adsignatio liberti. According to a decree of the senate of the early Empire, the patron of a freedman was permitted to assign (*assignare*) his right of patronage, those of inheritance included, to one of his children or grandchildren under his paternal power. The patron who thus disposed, either in a last will or orally, is called *adsignator.*—Inst. 3.8; D. 38.4.

Leonhard, *RE* 1; De Ruggiero, *DE* 1; G. La Pira, *La successione intestata,* 1930, 203; Harada, *ZSS* 59 (1939) 498; E. Cosentini, *St sui liberti* 2 (1950).

Adstipulatio (adstipulator). A promise by an additional *stipulatio,* in which the debtor of the original stipulation promised the same thing (*idem*) to another person (*adstipulator*). The latter is entitled to sue the debtor in the case of non-payment. The internal relation between the first and the subsidiary creditor is normally a mandate (agency), therefore the first creditor or his heirs might recover the sum paid to his agent (*procurator*) through *actio mandati.* *Adstipulatio* was primarily applied when a person wanted to make sure that the payment would be made after his death, since a direct stipulation *post mortem* was invalid.—See MANDATUM, LEX AQUILIA, STIPULATIO POST MORTEM.

Pernice, *ZSS* 19 (1898) 178; Pringsheim, *ZSS* 42 (1921) 305; Desserteaux, *Capitis deminutio* 2 (1919) 229; R. Orestano, *Ius singulare,* *AnMac* 11 (1937), 79; F. de Martino, *Le garenzie personali dell'obbligazione,* 1940.

Adtributio. The assignment of debts owed to, or by, an inheritance, by a judge or an arbitrator on the occasion of its division. With reference to AGER PULICUS *adtributio* is syn. with ASSIGNATIO.—See ACTIO FAMILIAE HERCISCUNDAE.

De Ruggiero, *DE* 1, 111.

Adulescens. A person under twenty-five years of age, but over fourteen.—Syn. *minor, adultus.*—See IUVENIS, MINORES.

Berger, *RE* 15, 1861 (Bibl.); Axelson, *Mélanges Marouzeau,* 1948, 7.

Adulter, adultera. See ADULTERIUM.

Adulterator. A counterfeiter of coins.—See FALSUM.

Adulterinus. Counterfeit, e.g., a coin, a last will.—Syn. *falsus, reprobus.*

Adulterium. A statutory punishment of adultery, which was considered a criminal offence only when committed by a married woman (*adultera*) was introduced by the Augustean law, *Lex Julia de adulteriis coërcendis* (before 18 B.C.). Earlier customary law admitted only immediate revenge of the husband on the adulteress or punishment by him after consultation with the family council (*consilium propinquorum*) in a procedure similar to a judicial trial (see IUDICIUM DOMESTICUM). Under the Julian statute, the father of the adulterous woman was permitted to kill her and her partner (*adulter*) if he surprised them in his or her husband's house. The husband's rights were rather limited; he was forced to divorce her, for otherwise he made himself guilty of matchmaking (LENOCINIUM). Besides, he or his father had to accuse the adulteress of *adulterium* which now

became a public crime prosecuted before a criminal court. Any Roman citizen could bring in the accusation if the husband or his father did not do so within two months after the divorce. The statutory term for other accusers was four additional months. The penalty was banishment of the adulteress and confiscation of one-third of her property, together with the loss of a part of her dowry. The legislation of Constantine, later confirmed by Justinian, introduced the death penalty for *adulterium.*—D. 48.5; C. 9.9.—See LEX IULIA DE ADULTERIIS, LENA, ACTIO DE MORIBUS, BINAE NUPTIAE.

Hartmann, *RE* 1; Humbert, *DS* 1; Chiazzese, *NDI* 1; C. W. Westrup, *Observations sur la notion de la fidelité,* 1927; Volterra, *StCagl* 1928; idem, *RendLomb* 63 (1930) 182; *St Bonfante* 2 (1930) 109; Bandini, *St Ratti,* 1934; C. Corsanego, *La repressione romana dell'adulterio,* 1936; Biondi, *StSas* 16 (1938); De Dominicis, *SDHI* 16 (1950) 1.

Adultus. See ADULESCENS.

Adventicium (adventicius). Acquisitions made by a slave or *filius familias* with means not taken from the master's or father's property.—See DOS, PECULIUM ADVENTICIUM.

Leonhard, *RE* 1; Albertario, *Studi* 1 (1933) 283.

Adversarius. The adversary in a lawsuit.

Advocatio. Both the profession of an advocate and his assistance to a party in a legal controversy.—See ADVOCATUS.

Advocatus. The term is applied to persons who exercise the profession of an advocate (*advocatio*), i.e., a legal adviser, while *iurisperitus* is a legal scholar, expert in law, a man learned in law. The *advocatus* assisted his clients (*clientes*) with juristic advice before and during the trial, in both civil and criminal matters, and pleaded for them in court. The latter activity was originally reserved to persons specially trained in rhetoric (*oratores*). Under the Republic the *advocatus* was not paid for his services; under the Principate compensation was gradually permitted. See HONORARIUM, PALMARIUM, LEX CINCIA. Syn. *patronus, causidicus.*—C. 2.7; 9; 12.10; 61.—See SENATUSCONSULTUM DE ADVOCATIONE, SENATUS CONSULTUM CLAUDIANUM, ERROR ADVOCATORUM.

Kubitschek, *RE* 1; Humbert, *DS* 1; De Ruggiero, *DE* 1; Seidl, *RE* 4A (*s.v. synegoros*); M. Travers, *Les corporations d'avocats sous l'Empire rom.,* Thèse, Paris, 1894; Pierantoni, *Gli avvocati di Roma antica,* 1900; Weiss, *ZSS* 32 (1911) 363; Tamassia, *APad* 33 (1917) 51; White, *Amer. Law Rev.* 53 (1919) 481; Wenger, *Die Anwaltschaft im röm. Recht,* in J. Magnus, *Die Rechtsanwaltschaft,* 1929, 452; E. P. Parks, *The R. rhetorical schools as a preparation for the courts,* Baltimore, 1945; F. M. De Robertis, *I rapporti di lavoro,* 1946, 189; U. E. Paoli, *La vita romana,* 5th ed. 1948, 252.

Advocatus fisci. First appointed by Hadrian for the defense of the interests of the fisc both extrajudicially and in courts. He is not directly concerned with the fiscal administration.—Syn. *patronus fisci.*—C. 2.8.

Kubitschek, *RE* 1; Humbert, *DS* 1; De Ruggiero, *DE* 1, 125.

Aedes. (In sing.) A building of sacred character (often *aedes sacra*) of a lower degree sacrally than a temple (*templum*). See DEPOSITIO IN AEDE. (Pl.) In juristic texts, syn. for *aedificium* and is applied primarily to urban buildings while the rustic ones are called *villae*. Juristically the terms *aedes* and *aedificium* include the soil (*solum*) and what is built upon it (*superficies*). Moreover, everything that is within the building and serves for perpetual use (e.g., tubes for water supply) is a part of the building as its accessory and shares the legal situation of the whole.—See VITIUM AEDIUM.

De Ruggiero, *DE* 1; Weinstock, *RE* 5A (*templum*).

Aedificatio. Building a house. The construction of houses is governed by building regulations (statutes, *senatusconsulta*, imperial enactments) and is subject to the supervision of magistrates (*aediles, censores* for public buildings, under the Empire the *praefectus urbi* and his staff). Among the imperial enactments the building regulation by the Emperor Zeno (C. 8.10.12, 474–491) is the most important. The interests of the neighbors are protected by OPERIS NOVI NUNTIATIO, a kind of protestation against a new construction which may be detrimental to the owners of adjacent buildings or lands. On the other hand, the house builder who gives sufficient guaranty is protected by a special interdict *ne vis fiat aedificanti* (= that force should not be used against the builder of a house) against any disturbance. Unless special permission is granted, building on public places is prohibited. Demolition of constructions already erected may be enforced by an interdict INTERDICTUM DE LOCIS PUBLICIS.—See LEX IULIA DE MODO AEDIFICIORUM, ZENONIANAE CONSTITUTIONES, OPERIS NOVI NUNTIATIO.—C. 8.10.

Leonhard, *RE* 1; Berger, *RE* 9, 1656, 1670; Voigt, *Die röm. Baugesetze, BerSächGW* 1903; Biondi, *BIDR* 44 (1936/7) 363; Capocci, *SDHI* 7 (1941) 155.

Aedificia. There is a distinction between private buildings (*aedificia privata*) which are in private ownership and public buildings (*aedificia publica*) which are *res publicae* and under the management and supervision of public officials.—See AEDES, AEDIFICATIO, OPERA PUBLICA.—C. 8.10.

De Ruggiero, *DE* 1.

Aediles cereales. These officials were created by Caesar in 44 B.C. and given specific functions in the administration of grain for the city of Rome.

De Ruggiero, *DE* 1, 222.

Aediles curules. Created in 367 B.C. as a patrician magistracy ranking in the hierarchy between the praetors and the quaestors. Their charges which in certain measure coincided with those of the *aediles plebis,* were rather extensive: public order and security in Rome, the traffic in the city, management of public buildings, *cura annonae* (food supply) as well as water supply, the supervision over markets, market transactions (such as the sale of slaves and animals), and weights and measures used in the market, and the like. A particularly heavy burden of theirs was the *cura ludorum,* arrangement of the public games, on which they often spent considerable sums of their own in order to obtain the support of the people in the furtherance of their careers. The creation of this magistracy is linked with the organization of the games inasmuch as the AEDILES PLEBIS were not rich enough to afford such expenses. The *aediles curules* had criminal jurisdiction in minor offenses. They were magistrates without *imperium*. —See ACTIONES AEDILICIAE, EDICTUM AEDILIUM CURULIUM, CURA ANNONAE, DIES FASTI.

Kubitschek, *RE* 1; Humbert, *DS* 1; Stella-Maranca, *NDI* 1 (*aedilitas*); Anon., *NDI* 5 (*edili*); H. Vincent, *Le droit des édiles,* 1922; De Ruggiero, *DE* 1; Sherwin-White, *OCD*; E. Manni, *Per la storia dei municipii,* 1947, 245.

Aediles plebis. Plebeian officers elected by the plebeians, to serve as assistants of the plebeian tribunes whose orders they had to carry out (*collegae minores*). Until the creation of the AEDILES CURULES (patrician magistrates), their responsibility was rather large and embraced the same fields which were later assigned to the new magistracy, the AEDILES CURULES. They enjoyed inviolability like the tribunes of the *plebs*. After the creation of the patrician *aediles,* they were somewhat in the shadow in spite of a certain similarity in function. The plebeian *aediles* had no outward sign of their official rank. For their activity in the archives see LEX VALERIA HORATIA ON SENATUSCONSULTA.

Siber, *RE* 21, 168; De Ruggiero, *DE* 1, 220; Humbert, *DS* 1; Momigliano, *Bull. della commissione archeologica comunale di Roma* 60 (1932/3) 218; E. Manni, *Per la storia dei municipii,* 1947, 221.

Aedilicius. Connected with the activity of the *aediles.* See ACTIONES AEDILICIAE, EDICTUM AEDILIUM CURULIUM.

Aelius Gallus (Caius). A little known jurist of the end of the Republic, author of a juristic glossary: "On the meaning of juristic terms."

Klebs, *RE* 1, 492, no. 58.

Aelius Paetus Catus (Sextus). Consul in 198 B.C.; he published a manual under the title *"Tripertita,"* divided into three parts: the Twelve Tables, a commentary on them, and the forms of *legis actiones* (procedure). The work was later called *Ius Aelianum*.

Klebs, *RE* 1, 527, no. 105; Danneberg, *RE* 10 (*ius Aelianum*); Zocco Rosa, *NDI* 7 (*ius Aelianum*); F. Schulz, *History of Roman legal science,* 1946, 35.

Aelius Tubero. See TUBERO.

Aemulatio. Making use of a right not for one's own profit, but only with the intention of doing damage to another. The term is not of Roman juristic coinage, it was created in the Middle Ages and means abuse or misuse of a right. The classical rule, stressed several times in the sources, that "there is no fraud, no wrong, no violence when one does something he has the right to do," or "when one avails himself of his own right" (D. 50.17; 55; 155.1) was somehow modified in Justinian's law under the influence of Christian ethics.—See NEMO (NULLUS) VIDETUR, etc., NEMO DAMNUM, etc., UTI SUO IURE.

Riccobono, *NDI* 1; De Villiers, *Nuisances in Roman Law, LQR* 17 (1901) 387; M. Rotondi, *CentCodPav,* 1934; Riccobono, *La teoria dell'abuso di diritto nella dottrina romana, BIDR* 46 (1939) 1; Stella-Maranca, *St Albertoni* 2 (1933) 449; Kreller, *Missbrauch der Rechte, Ztschr für ausländisches und internationales Privatrecht* 2 (1937) 1; Bartošek, *ACIVer* 3 (1952) 191 (Bibl. 235).

Aequitas (aequum). Related to justice (*iustitia, iustum*) but distinguished from the positive law, *ius.* One of the fundamental principles which direct or should direct the development of law; it is the corrective and creative element in such development. A law which is guided by *aequitas* is *ius aequum,* its antonym is *ius iniquum.* In the legal sphere *aequitas* may be realized either by interpreting the existing law or by supplementing it where an exact legal provision is missing. *Aequitas,* as the word itself indicates, implies the element of equality. Transferred into the province of law it postulates equal treatment of all according to the conceptions nurtured in the social (common) conscience of the people which change, of course, when social and economic conditions undergo a change. The Roman *aequitas* fulfilled its functions in the development of the Roman law. When the legal norms established in earlier law, written or not written, became inadequate to the social and economic necessities of the later age, the *aequitas* went into operation both in private law and in civil procedure as well as in judicial practice. The *ius honorarium* was a large field in which the postulates of equity were realized. On the other hand, the jurists also contributed a great deal in the same direction. Since the end of the Republic many juristic decisions were inspired by the principle of *aequitas;* among the classical jurists the most prolific contributor was Papinian. This is the meaning of the famous definition of the jurist Celsus—put at the very beginning of the Digest (D.1.1.1 pr.)—*"ius est ars boni er aequi"* (= law is the art of finding the good and the just) which has recently been depreciated—unjustly—as an empty rhetorical phrase. The Roman jurists as well as the officials who administered the law were perfectly aware of the nature of *aequitas* although they have not left an exact definition of the word. It was precisely through their exercise of that "art" and by their perfect understanding what was *bonum et aequum* that the Roman jurists brought *ius* to the peak it reached in the classical period. *Aequitas* sometimes appears to be opposed to the *ius* then in force, particularly when it enters into its corrective function (when, for instance, the *aequitas* of the praetor is placed ahead of the rigidity of the ancient law, *ius civile*), and, at times, it is strongly connected with *ius,* even being presented as its substance, as in the Ciceronian saying, "the law is the established *aequitas*" (*aequitas constituta, Top.* 9) where *ius* and *aequitas* appear inseparable. *Aequitas* has its natural foundation in any human society, in its customs, and in its ethical and social conceptions as well, and becomes law either through customary practice or by legislative enactments (this is the Ciceronian *aequitas constituta*); the connection between *aequitas* and *ius naturale* is evident. Hence the frequent references to *aequitas naturalis,* reminiscent of the references to *naturalis ratio.* It is often adduced by the jurists as the reason for criticism of, or doubts about, the fairness of an existing legal rule. The classical *aequitas* was a fertile soil for the influence of Christian ethical doctrines. The evolution found its expression in Justinian's codification in which not only the conception of *aequitas* acquired a broader aspect but the terminology was also enriched by the addition of references to terms like *pietas, caritas, humanitas, benignitas, clementia.* Many interpolations referring to these ideas testify to that tendency of the emperor, but not all of them added new doctrines and rules to the classical Roman law, since the *aequum* was too deeply rooted in the conscience of the jurists. The place the classical *aequitas* acquired in Justinian's legal system is neatly characterized by the following detail. A principle of fundamental importance formulated in a rescript of the emperor Antoninus Pius (doubtless at the suggestion of a jurist of his council) to the effect that "though changes in solemn forms are not easily to be admitted, yet where *aequitas* demands it help should be granted" (D. 4.1.7 pr.) is repeated, as a general rule, in the final title of Justinian's Digest *On Rules of Ancient Law,* under the name of the jurist Marcellus (D. 50.17.183) from whose *Digesta* the quotation of the rescript was excerpted in one of the initial books of the Digest. Attempts to eliminate all references to *aequitas, aequum, aequissimum est, aequitas naturalis,* etc., wherever they appear in excerpts of classical juristic works, must be rejected as one of those uncritical exaggerations which have been so frequent in the modern search for interpolations, although nobody will deny that some of those references belong to the compilers.—See IUS, IUS EST ARS BONI ET AEQUI, BENIGNUS.

Kipp, *RE* 1; Humbert, *DS* 1; Riccobono, *NDI* 1; Jonkers, *RAC* 1 (1941); Fadda, *L'equità ed il metodo dei giureconsulti rom.,* 1880; W. W. Buckland, *Equity in Rom. law,* 1911; Brice, *Rom. aequitas and English equity, Georgetown Law Journal* 2 (1913); Beseler, *ZSS* 45 (1925) 453; Guarneri-Citati, *Indice*² (1927) 7; idem, *St Riccobono,* 1 (1936) 704; idem, *Fschr Koschaker* 1 (1939) 120; Sokolowski, *St Bonfante* 1 (1929) 190; Ragusa, *Diritto e equità da Cicerone ai giureconsulti classici, AG* 103 (1930) 87, 224; Giannini, *AG* 105 (1931) 194; Pringsheim, *ZSS* 52 (1932) 86; C. A. Maschi, *La concezione naturalistica,*

1937, 311; M. P. Guibal, *De l'influence de la philosophie sur le dr. rom.*, 1937, 162; Albertario, *Studi* 5 (1937) 107; Devilla, *Ae. naturalis*, *StSas* 16 (1938) 125; Bastnagel, *BIDR* 45 (1948) 356; Condanari-Michler, *St Besta* 3 (1939) 505; Biondi, *Scr Ferrini* (Pavia, 1947, reprints, 1943) 210; Riccobono, *BIDR* 53/4 (1948) 32 (= *AnPal* 20 [1949] 39); idem, *Lineamenti della storia delle fonti*, 1949, 108; Ridder, *Aequitas non equity*, *Archiv für Rechts- und Sozialphilosophie* 39 (1951) 181.

Aequum et bonum. See BONUM ET AEQUUM, AEQUI-TAS, IUS EST ARS BONI ET AEQUI.

Aër. The air. Belongs to the category of RES COM-MUNES OMNIUM.—See CAELUM.

Lardone, *Air Law Rev. 2* (1931); Riccobono, *Riv di diritto aeronautico* 1 (1938).

Aerarii. Citizens excluded from the centuriate and tribal organization (TRIBUS) by the censors and subject to the payment of a special poll-tax. They were not permitted to vote in *comitia centuriata* and *comitia tributa*. Assignment to the *aerarii* was a form of administrative punishment.—See NOTA CENSORIA.

Kubitschek, *RE* 1; Humbert, *DS* 1; De Ruggiero, *DE* 1, 311.

Aerarium militare. A special military treasury instituted by Augustus. It provided pensions for veterans and was supported by donations of the emperor and by the income from sales—and inheritance taxes. The funds of the *aerarium militare* were administered by *praefecti aerarii militaris*.—See CENTESIMA RERUM VENALIUM, VICESIMA HEREDITATIUM.

Aerarium populi Romani. State treasury, also called *aerarium Saturni* because it was located in the temple of Saturn. It was also a central archive for documents connected with the financial and general administration, for statutes passed by the popular assemblies (LEX LICINIA IUNIA), *senatusconsulta,* and generally for all documents in which the state was interested, such as contracts with private individuals (see TABULAE PUBLICAE, TABULAE CENSORIAE). Originally under the directorship of the quaestors, then of the praetors, it was submitted by Augustus to the control of the senate. In the Principate the chiefs of the *aerarium* were the *praefecti aerarii Saturni.* The *aerarium populi Romani* is to be distinguished from the treasury of the emperor (see FISCUS). The distinction gradually lost importance since the imperial treasury absorbed the revenues of the *aerarium* more and more.—See TABULARIUM.

Kubitschek, *RE* 1; Sachers, *RE* 4A, 1964; Humbert and Guillaume, *DS* 1; De Ruggiero, *DE* 1, 309; Stella-Maranca, *NDI* 1; Foligno, *NDI* 5 (*s.v. erario*); Frank, *JRS* 23 (1933) 143; S. v. Bolla, *Die Entwicklung des Fiscus,* 1938; Sutherland, *Amer. Jour. of Philology* 67 (1945) 151; Mattingly, *OCD;* O'Brien-Moore, *RE* Suppl. 6, 790; Jones, *JRS* 40 (1950) 23.

Aerarium Saturni. See AERARIUM POPULI ROMANI.

Aes. A copper coin, often syn. with AS. In a broader sense = money.—See the following items.

Kubitschek, *RE* 1; Mattingly, *OCD; idem, Numismatic Chronicle*, 1943, 21.

Aes alienum. "What we owe to another," a debt. Ant. *aes suum* = "what another owes to us" (D. 50.16.213.1).

Humbert, *DS* 1; De Ruggiero, *DE* 1, 312.

Aes confessum. See CONFESSIO IN IURE.

Aes equestre. The sum of money allotted to a cavalry-man for the purchase of a horse.—See EQUITES, LEGIS ACTIO PER PIGNORIS CAPIONEM.·

Kubitschek, *RE* 1; Humbert, *DS* 1.

Aes et libra. See PER AES ET LIBRAM.

Lévy-Bruhl, *LQR* 60 (1944) 51.

Aes hordearium (hordiarium). The allowance for the purchase of fodder for a cavalryman's horse.— See EQUITES, LEGIS ACTIO PER PIGNORIS CAPIONEM.

Schwahn, *RE* 7A, 57; Humbert, *DS* 1.

Aes militare. The soldier's pay.—See TRIBUS, LEGIS ACTIO PER PIGNORIS CAPIONEM.

Aes publicum. See COLLATIO.

Aes rude. Uncoined bronze which served to estimate the value of things before coinage was introduced.

Aestimatio. The valuation in money of things, or of damages and all kinds of losses one suffered through another's wrongful doing or by his non-fulfillment of a contractual obligation. Particularly important in the recovery of damages was the estimation of the interest (INTERESSE) of the person who endured them.—See VERITAS.

Orestano, *AnCam* 10 (1936) 227.

Aestimatio dotis. The valuation in money of the things which are constituted as a dowry. When the restitution of the latter (*dos aestimata*) became an issue, only its fixed value entered into consideration, if a choice between restoration in kind and the return of a sum of money has not been agreed upon.

Volterra, *RendLomb* 66 (1933), 1014; Wolff, *ZSS* 53 (1933) 331.

Aestimatio litis. See LITIS AESTIMATIO.

Aestimatorius. See AESTIMATUM, ACTIO QUANTI MINORIS, INIURIA.

Aestimatum. A transaction by which one receives goods, estimated at a fixed amount, from another on the condition that within a certain time the recipient will either return the goods or pay the sum agreed upon. Such agreements were generally made with second-hand dealers who kept the profit when they sold the goods at a higher price. In the meantime the ownership normally remained with the real owner, who did not care whether the recipient finally decided to buy the things for himself or sold them to another. In the case of non-fulfillment of the transaction the owner had an action called *de aestimato* or *aestimatoria.*—D. 19.3.

De Medio, *Il contractus aestimatorius,* 1900; De Francisci, *Synallagma* 1 (1913) 85; Buckland, *Mél. Cornil* 1 (1926) 139; idem, *RHD* 12 (1933) 217; P. Voci, *Contratto* (1946) 256; Pezzana, *AG* 140 (1951) 53.

Aetas. When used without any specific attribute (as, for instance, *aetas minor, maior, perfecta, adulta*), the word may indicate any human age. In particular, in locutions connected with the protection of minors (such as *remedium* or *beneficium aetatis*, VENIA AETA-TIS), *aetas* refers to minors, whereas when it is applied to the age of persons liberated from public charges (*munera*) or tutorship (*tutela*), elderly people are meant. For the influence of the various stages of human life on legal capacity, see INFANS PUBERES, IMPUBERES, MAIORES, IMPRUDENTIA, SUAE AETATIS FIERI, MINORES.—See also the following entries.

Leonhard, *RE* 1; Berger, *RE* 15, 1862.

Aetas legitima. Not a technically exact term. Usually refers to persons who have attained their majority, as in phrases like *post legitimam aetatem, legitimam aetatem complere*. A favorite word in the language of Justinian's compilers and appears frequently in interpolated texts. Sometimes there is doubt about its actual significance because of the lack of precision in the term *legitimus* in Justinian's language.—See LEGITIMUS.

Berger, *RE* 15, 1683.

Aetas perfecta. Not a technical term. Generally refers to the age of majority.

Berger, *RE* 15, 1682.

Aetas pupillaris. See PUPILLUS.

Aetatis suae fieri. See SUAE AETATIS FIERI.

Aeterna auctoritas. See ACTIO AUCTORITATIS.

Aeterna urbs. Rome (in later imperial constitutions). —See URBS, ROMA.

Aeternitas. Eternity, immortality. The term was one of the titles of the emperor in the later Empire (*aeternitas imperialis, aeternitas nostra*).

Cumont, *Rev. d'hist. et littérature réligieuse* 1 (1896) 435; L. Berlinger, *Titulatur der röm. Kaiser*, 1935, 25; Charlesworth, *Harvard Theolog. Rev.* 29 (1936) 122; Ensslin, *Gott-Kaiser, SbMünch* 1943, 6. Heft, 77.

Adf-. See AFF-.

Affectio (affectus). A favorable disposition of one's mind towards a person or a thing. See AFFECTIO MARITALIS. With reference to juristic transactions the term is used in the same sense as *animus* (= will, intention) and is charged with the same suspicion of Byzantine origin (see ANIMUS). The value which a person attaches to an object (the so-called *pretium affectionis*) is generally irrelevant when restitution of damages done to it is demanded.

Guarneri-Citati, *Indice* (1927) 8.

Affectio maritalis. Conjugal affection conceived as a continuous (not momentary) state of mind is a basic element of intent in the Roman marriage. It presumes the intention of living as husband and wife for life and of procreating legitimate children. The attempt to eliminate the *affectio maritalis* from the conception of marriage by the assumption that the pertinent texts are interpolated must be considered a failure.—See CONCUBINATUS.

Ehrhardt, *RE* 17, 1479; E. Albertario, *Studi* 1 (1933)

197; G. Longo, *BIDR* 46 (1939) 119; E. Volterra, *La conception du mariage* (Padova, 1940) 37; Wolff, *ZSS* 67 (1950) 296 (Bibl.); P. Rasi, *Consensus facit nuptias*, 1946.

Affectio societatis. Used with reference to the intention of the parties to a contract of partnership.—See SOCIETAS.

Salvadore, *Rivista di dir. civile* 3 (1911) 681; Arangio-Ruiz, *La società*, 1950, 63; van Oven, *TR* 19 (1951) 452.

Africanus, Sextus Caecilius. A Roman jurist of the middle of the second century after Christ, a younger contemporary of Julian and probably his pupil. He is the author of a collection of *responsa*, published under the title of *Quaestiones* (in nine books); many of them represent the opinion of Julian. From his twenty-book-collection of *Epistulae* one text only is preserved.

Jors, *RE* 3 (*s.v. Caecilius*, no. 29); Orestano, *NDI* 1; Buhl, *ZSS* 2 (1881) 180; Lenel, *ZSS* 51 (1931) 1; Degrassi, *Epigraphica* 3 (1941) 23.

Agens vice (vicem, vices). See VICE.

Agentes in rebus. Since the fourth century after Christ, a body of more than a thousand persons whose official duties varied widely in character. They acted chiefly as police officers. Their competence also embraced the provinces where during their frequent travels, they had to inspect the state post and to report about misdemeanors and corruption of officials in other fields of administration. They developed a system of spying and denunciation and they exercised a great influence at the imperial court as informers and secret police, not seldom misusing their position. A group of them charged with the control of the *cursus publicus* (= state post) were called *curiosi* in allusion to their inquisitive activity.—C. 12.20; 21. —See SCHOLAE.

Seeck, *RE* 1; Humbert, *DS* 1; De Ruggiero, *DE* 1, 355; O. Hirschfeld, *Kleine Schriften*, 1913, 624; E. Stein, *ZSS* 41 (1920) 194; A. E. R. Boak, *Univ. of Michigan Studies, Human. Series*, 14 (1924) 68.

Ager. Any kind of rural land, both arable and pasture, not including buildings and *villae* (country-houses, farm-houses). The principal division is: *ager privatus*, in private ownership, and *ager publicus*, state land considered to belong to the Roman people. The various types of public land assigned to private individuals are explained in the following items. The nature of some of them varied in the course of time owing to the manifold agrarian legislation (see LEGES AGRARIAE). In the last analysis, through the gradual assignment of the *ager publicus* to private individuals by various forms, all the land which in the earliest times was *ager publicus* became *ager privatus*.

Kubitschek, *RE* 1; De Ruggiero, *DE* 1; Kaser, *Typen der röm. Bodenrechte in der späteren Republik*, *ZSS* 62 (1942); M. Weber, *Röm. Agrargeschichte in ihrer Bedeutung für das Staats- und Privatrecht*, 1891 (Italian translation in *Biblioteca di Storia economica*, 2, 1891, 1894).

Ager adsignatus. See ADSIGNATIO.

Ager colonicus. Land destined as the territory of a

new colony. It was assigned to the colonists in ownership.

Ager compascuus. Pasture land assigned to the inhabitants of the adjacent plots, for their collective use at a small fee (*scriptura*).

Ager desertus. Land abandoned by its owner and not cultivated. Imperial legislation took care of bringing such land into agricultural economy.—C. 11.59.

> Leonhard, *RE* 5, 249; Humbert, *DS* 2 (*s.v. deserti agri*); Kaser, *RE* Suppl. 7, 690; Charvin, *Les constitutions du Code Théod. sur les a.d., La Belgique judiciaire* 58 (1900); Meyer-Collins, *Derelictio* (Diss. Erlangen, 1930) 89; E. Levy, *West Roman Vulgar Law*, 1951, 194.

Ager emphyteuticarius (emphyteuticus). Land which is the object of a contract of *emphyteusis*. Syn. *ager vectigalis*.—See EMPHYTEUSIS.—D. 6.3.

Ager limitaneus. See LIMEN.

Ager limitatus. Land, the boundaries of which were settled by a land-surveyor.

Ager occupatorius. (1) Enemy land occupied by the Romans and annexed to the territory of the state; (2) part of the AGER PUBLICUS which was open to free occupation and use by anybody, the ownership, however, being reserved to the state which had the right to claim it back at any time. Holders of such land (*possessores*) could dispose of it by various transactions and by testament. The agrarian legislation (see LEGES AGRARIAE) imposed some limits on the extension of an *ager occupatorius*.

> Kaser, *RE* Suppl. 7, 689; *idem*, *ZSS* 62 (1942) 27; F. Bozza, *Possessio dell'ager publicus*, 1939.

Ager privatus. See AGER.

Ager privatus vectigalisque. Land which originally was *ager publicus* became quiritary property of the buyer when sold by public sale. The acquirer had to pay an annual rent to the state. The *ager privatus vectigalisque* passed to the heirs of the owner as part of his succession, but it could not be sold by him. Later agrarian legislation introduced some modifications.

> Kaser, *ZSS* 62 (1942) 6.

Ager provincialis. See FUNDUS PROVINCIALIS.

Ager publicus. The land which belongs to the state (the Roman people). The principal source of its increase was military conquest. Portions of the *ager publicus* could become private property by assignment (*adsignatio, ager adsignatus*) or by sale (*ager quaestorius*, since such sales of state property are made by the quaestors). Lease of the *ager publicus* to individuals was also practiced, either in perpetuity, for long terms or for short periods. The lessee paid a rent (*vectigal*).—See AGER, LEGES AGRARIAE, AGER SCRIPTURARIUS.

> Kubitschek, *RE* 1; Schwahn, *RE* 7A, 10; Humbert, *DS* 1; Albertario, *NDI* 1; Jones, *OCD*; De Ruggiero *DE* 1; Guiraud, *Rev. des questions historiques* 44 (1909) 397; T. Frank, *JRSt* 17 (1917) 141; Zancan, *ATor* 67 (1932); *idem*, *A.p.*, *Pubbl. Facoltà Lettere Univ. Padova*, 8 (1935); F. Bozza, *Possessio dell'a.p.*, 1939; Carcaterra,

AnBari 4 (1941) 101; Kaser, *Eigentum und Besitz*, 1943, 239 and *passim;* Tibiletti, *Ath* 26 (1948) 173, 27 (1949) 3.

Ager quaestorius. See AGER PUBLICUS.

> Kaser, *ZSS* 62 (1942) 43.

Ager Romanus. The Roman soil comprising the territory of the city of Rome, later, the territory divided into thirty-five tribes (*tribus*), and, finally, the whole of Italy.

Ager scripturarius. A plot of public land granted to private individuals for pasture on payment of a special tax (*scriptura*).

> C. Trapenard, *L'a.s.*, 1908.

Ager stipendiarius, tributarius. See PRAEDIA STIPENDIARIA, PRAEDIA TRIBUTARIA.

Ager vectigalis. Land belonging to the state or municipality and leased in perpetuity. Originally the lease of state land was performed by the censors and the term was limited to five years (*leges censoriae, leges locationis*). In postclassical law, the *ager vectigalis* is identified with *ager emphyteuticarius*. It was hereditary and the lease could not be annulled if the lessee or his heir paid the rent regularly. The pretorian action for the recovery of such land from a third person holding it unlawfully was modeled after the *rei vindicatio* although the lessee was not a full owner (*actio vectigalis* or *quae de fundo vectigali proposita est*). In the largest sense, any public land given in lease to an individual for a rent (*vectigal*) is called *ager vectigalis*.—See AGER PRIVATUS VECTIGALISQUE.

> Humbert, *DS* 1; Bolla, *NDI* 1; Bassanelli, *La colonia perpetua*, 1933; Beseler, *SDHI* 3 (1937) 360; Lanfranchi, *Studi sull'ager vectigalis* 1 (1938) 2 (*AnCam* 13, 1939, 163) 3 (*AnTriest* 11, 1940); Kaser, *ZSS* 62 (1942) 34.

Ager viritanus. Public land assigned individually (*viritim*) to a private person, mostly under the form of AGER PRIVATUS VECTIGALISQUE. This assignment is not connected with the foundation of a colony.

> Kübler, *Geschichte des röm. Rechts*, 1925, 120.

Agere. In a civil trial, the procedural activity of the plaintiff (*is qui agit*). Ant. *is cum quo agitur* = the defendant.—See ACTOR, IS QUI AGIT.

> Wlassak, *RE* 1 (*s.v. actor*); Fadda, *NDI* 1.

Agere. When referring to the activity of the jurists, indicates their activity as legal advisers in a specific controversy. In particular, they assisted the party to a trial in drafting the formula to be used by him, in advising him about the use of prescribed oral forms, in acting personally in the first stage of the trial before the magistrate, or in instructing the party's advocate. This activity gave the jurists the opportunity to develop new, unprecedented formulas.

> Berger, *RE* 10, 1162.

Agere causas. See CAUSAS DICERE.

Agere cum plebe, populo, senatu. See IUS AGENDI CUM PLEBE, POPULO, SENATU.

Agere iumentum. See IUS AGENDI IUMENTUM.

Agere per sponsionem. (1) In interdictal proceedings, a special form of trial when the defendant did not immediately obey the praetor's order. At the plaintiff's demand a normal trial was initiated in order to establish whether or not the defendant had fulfilled the interdictal order. The *sponsio* trial involved a penal element since the defendant bound himself by a stipulation (*sponsio*) to pay the plaintiff a penalty (*poena*) if his failure to obey the interdict was proved. In the case of an *interdictum duplex* each party had to promise to pay a penalty if defeated, the defendant by *sponsio*, his adversary by *restipulatio*. Thus a counterpart to *agere per sponsionem* is *agere ex restipulatione*. The *sponsio* was only a measure to compel the party involved to fulfil the command of the magistrate. If, however, the restitution or exhibition ordered by the magistrate was still not accomplished, or if the defendant continued to interfere with the plaintiff, contrary to a prohibitory interdict issued, a specific action followed, called *iudicium secutorium*, the aim of which was to procure for the plaintiff full satisfaction for all damages and losses he had suffered from the obstinate behavior of the defendant. (2) Another form of *agere per sponsionem* is applied when the question of ownership of a thing is involved. The party in possession of the thing promised the adversary a certain sum by *sponsio* (*stipulatio*) in the event that the latter proved his ownership over the controversial thing. The action which followed was based on the *sponsio* and the decision thereon was actually a decision on the ownership. Here the *sponsio* had no penal character and therefore the defeated possessor did not pay the sum stipulated in the *sponsio*, the function of which is described as follows: "through it, it is judged over the thing itself" (*per eam de re ipsa iudicatur*, Gaius, *Inst.* 4.94). Hence it is called *sponsio praeiudicialis* because the legal situation established in the decision in the *sponsio* suit was prejudicial for all claims connected with the ownership (the delivery of the thing, or of its fruits, and the like).—See SPONSIO, PROVOCARE SPONSIONE.

Berger, *RE* 9, 1693; Jobbé-Duval, *Ét. sur la procédure civile I. Agere p.s.*, 1896; Bozza, *St Bonfante* 2 (1930) 589; Carcaterra, *AnBari* 2 (1940) 52; Kaser, *Eigentum u. Besitz*, 1943, 282; Siber, *Fschr Wenger* 1 (1944) 69; Arangio-Ruiz, *La parola del passato* 8 (1948) 142; v. Lübtow, *ZSS* 68 (1951) 337.

Agere praescriptis verbis. See ACTIO PRAESCRIPTIS VERBIS.

Agerius. See AULUS.

Agnasci. To enter by birth (or by adoption) into the agnatic group. The term is primarily used with reference to a person (son or grandson) born after the death of a testator. He becomes the testator's heir (*heres suus*) by reason of the fact that he would have fallen in directly under the testator's paternal power if the latter were still alive. See POSTUMI. The term is also applied to children born during the testator's lifetime after a will has been made.—See the following items.

Agnatio. The relationship among persons (*agnati*) who are under the paternal power (*patria potestas*) of the same head of a family (*pater familias*) or who would have been if he were still alive. The agnatic tie is created by descendance in the male line from a common ancestor. From earliest times *agnatio* was the basis for rights of succession by intestacy according to the *ius civile*. Guardianship also falls on the nearest *agnatus*.—Ant. *cognatio*.—Inst. 1.15; 3.2.— See HERES SUUS.

Leonhard, *RE* 1; Baudry, *DS* 1; Paoli, *NDI* 1; Lenel, *ZSS* 37 (1914); Perozzi, *BIDR* 31 (1921) 88; Michon, *Mél Cornil* 2 (1926) 113; G. Goutelle, *La lutte entre l'agnation et cognation à propos du Sencons. Tertullianum*, 1934; Carcaterra, *AnBari* 2 (1940); C. Castello, *Diritto familiare*, 1942, 123; Guarino, *SDHI* 10 (1944) 290; idem, *AnCat* 1 (1947) 330, 3 (1949) 204; Lepri, *St Solazzi*, 1948, 299; Solazzi, *ANap* 63 (1950).

Agnati (agnatus). See AGNATIO, AGNASCI.—Ant. COGNATI.

Agnatio postumi. See AGNASCI, POSTUMI.

Agnatus proximus. The nearest relative among the *agnati*. In matters of intestate succession and guardianship an *agnatus proximus* excludes the *agnatus* of a remoter degree.—Ant. *agnatus inferioris gradus*.

Lenel, *ZSS* 37 (1917) 129.

Agnitio bonorum possessionis. The request of a person addressed to the praetor that he be granted the possession of an inheritance (*bonorum possessio*) as successor according to the praetorian law (*bonorum possessor*).—See BONORUM POSSESSIO.

Leonhard, *RE* 1; Arangio-Ruiz, *FIR* 3 (1943) no. 61; H. Krüger, *ZSS* 64 (1944) 397, 405.

Agnoscere. A general term for the assumption of legal duties or the acknowledgment of a specific legal situation or transaction.—D. 25.3.

Agnoscere bonorum possessionem. See AGNITIO BONORUM POSSESSIONIS. Syn. *petere bonorum possessionem*.

Agnoscere liberum (partum). To acknowledge the paternity of a child. A *senatusconsultum de agnoscendis liberis* established certain rules in the case of pregnancy of a divorced wife, designed to protect her rights against the former husband as well as the latter's if the child was not his. The wife had to declare formally to the husband *se ex eo praegnatem esse*.—D. 25.3.—See SENATUS CONSULTUM PLANCIANUM.

Agnoscere signum. See SIGNUM.

Agrimensores. Land(field) surveyors. Syn. *mensores agrorum, agrarii*, or simply *mensores*. The earliest were priests (*augures*) since the Romans attached a religious significance to the boundaries of a city or of a settlement and the act of tracing the boundaries was celebrated with sacred rites. Later, they were private individuals, experts in surveying. An *agrimensor* engaged for the delimitation of a plot of land was not considered to be hired by *locatio conductio;* his services were treated as liberal, not salaried, services. See HONORARIUM. He was responsible, however, for fraud committed in the fulfillment of his professional duties. A special action was granted against an *agrimensor* who made a false report on boundaries (*qui falsum modum dixerit*). Under the Principate the *agrimensores* were trained in special schools. Some were appointed as state officials, chiefly for military purposes (division and assignment of conquered land, limitation of military camps). In their private activity they functioned as arbitrators in controversies about boundaries of private property or as experts in judicial trials on such matters.—See CONTROVERSIA DE FINE, DE LOCO.—D. 11.6; C. 12.27.

Fordyce and Balsdon, *OCD* (v. *gromatici*); Kubitschek, *RE* 1; Schulten, *RE* 7 (*gromatici*); Fabricius, *RE* 15 (*mensor*); Humbert, *DS* 1; Bolla, *NDI* 1; De Ruggiero, *DE* 1; E. Levy, *Privatstrafe und Schadensersatz*, 1915, 52; idem, *Konkurrenz der Klagen* 2, 1 (1922) 241; Beeson, *Cl Philol* 23 (1928) 1; Albertario, *SDHI* 9 (1943) 27.

Aio. "I affirm." The word is used by a party to a trial to stress his rights to the object in dispute, or to assert the status of liberty of a man (*hunc hominem liberum esse aio*).

Ait (aiunt). In juristic writings, opinions of other jurists are thus introduced in this way, e.g., *Labeo ait*. In the commentaries on the praetorian edict, the words *praetor ait* (*inquit*) precede a literal quotation. Excerpts from statutes, senatusconsults and imperial enactments are also often attached to *ait*.

Ala. A cavalry unit of about five hundred men within the auxiliary armies (AUXILIA) under the command of a *praefectus alae* (since Augustus). The auxiliary cavalry has to be distinguished from the cavalry units within the legions (*equites legionis*).

Cichorius, *RE* 1; Kübler, *RE* 6, 279; De Ruggiero, *DE* 1.

Album. A board painted white, exposed in public and accessible to the people, on which announcements (*edicta*) of the magistrates were written. Forgery of the text or damage intentionally done to the *album* (*corrumpere, corruptio*) can be prosecuted by any citizen through the *actio de albo corrupto*.—See ALBUM PRAETORIS, ACTIO DE ALBO CORRUPTO.

Schmidt, *RE* 1; Guillaume-Saglio-Humbert, *DS* 1; Anon. *NDI* 1; Schulz, *JRS* 32 (1942) 88.

Album collegii. A list of the members of a *collegium* as well as the bulletin board for internal announcements in an association.

De Ruggiero, *DE* 1, 393.

Album curiae (decurionum, ordinis decurionum). The list of the members of municipal councils. It was published on a white board.—See CURIA, DECURIONES, PROSCRIPTIO ALBI.—D. 50.3.

De Ruggiero, *DE* 1, 392; Kornemann, *RE* 4, 587; V. Hoesen and Johnson, *Jour. Egyptian Arch.*, 12 (1926) 116.

Album iudicum. The list of citizens qualified to assume the function of juror in judicial trials, both civil and criminal. Under the Republic the *album iudicum* was prepared every year by the praetorian office. Political points of view often influenced the composition of the list. The jurors for a specific trial were selected by agreement of the parties or by lot (*sortitio*). The parties had the right to reject persons inacceptable to them (*reicere, reiectio*).—See FERRE IUDICEM.

Steinwenter, *RE* 9, 2466; Guillemin-Saglio-Humbert, *DS* 1; Fraccaro, *RendLomb* 52 (1919) 335; Kreller, *ZSS* 45 (1925).

Album praetoris. A white board on which the praetorian edict was publicly announced together with its legal rules, procedural formulae (actions, exceptions, interdicts) and praetorian measures. A plaintiff who wanted to sue his adversary might lead him before the *album* and indicate there the formula of action he wished to apply against the defendant.

Album senatorium. The list of the members of the senate.

De Ruggiero, *DE* 1, 390.

Alea. In juristic language the term indicates any game of chance (not only dice). Claims arising from such games, which were generally forbidden, were not actionable. The Justinian law admitted certain exceptions.—See LEX ALEARIA, LEX CORNELIA DE ALEATORIBUS, LEX TITIA DE ALEATORIBUS.—C. 3.43.

Leonhard-Hartmann, *RE* 1; Humbert, *DS* 1.

Aleator. A gambler.—D. 11.5; C.3.43.—See ALEA.

Alfenus Varus. A Roman jurist of the end of the Republic, pupil of Servius Sulpicius Rufus, author of an extensive work, *Digesta,* in forty books.

Klebs-Jörs, *RE* 1; Orestano, *NDI* 1; H. Krüger, *St Bonfante* 2 (1930) 326; L. De Sarlo, *Alfeno Varo e i suoi Digesta*, 1940.

Alienatio. Alienation, the transfer of property through a transaction (sale, donation). Certain things are not alienable (RES LITIGIOSAE, land constituted as a dowry, *fundus dotalis*) and, on the other hand, certain persons are not permitted to alienate their property because of the lack of legal ability to act by themselves (persons under guardianship or curatorship). Insolvent debtors were prohibited from alienating their property fraudulently to the detriment of the creditors (*in fraudem creditorum*). See INTERDICTUM FRAUDATORIUM. For fraudulent alienation by a freedman to the detriment of his patron, see ACTIO CALVISIANA. For the alienation of a thing bequeathed in a last will to a legatee, see ADEMPTIO LEGATI.—Inst. 2.8; C. 4.51; 52.

De Ruggiero, *DE* 1; Del Prete, *NDI* 1; De Robertis, *AnBari* 2 (1939) 71; Brasiello, *SDHI* 15 (1949) 114; A. Burdese, *Autorizzazione ad alienare*, 1950.

Alienatio hereditatis. The transfer of an inheritance before or after its acceptance by the heir is achieved by IN IURE CESSIO HEREDITATIS. The alienation of an anticipated inheritance of a person still alive by a presumptive successor was not only void, but the seller also became unworthy (*indignus*) losing thereby his right to receive anything from that particular inheritance.

Alienatio in fraudem creditorum. See ALIENATIO, INTERDICTUM FRAUDATORIUM.

Alienatio iudicii mutandi causa facta. The transfer of a thing which is expected to be the object of litigation in the near future, in order to change the conditions of the trial to the disadvantage of the adversary. The transaction could be rescinded by the praetor through *in integrum restitutio*. In particular an alienation to a person of greater power (POTENTIORES) was forbidden.—D. 4.7; C. 2.54.

Partsch, *De l'édit sur l'a.i.m.*, 1900; Mitteis, *ZSS* 30 (1909) 451; Lenel, *ZSS* 37 (1916) 104; Kretschmar, *ZSS* 40 (1919) 136, 48 (1928) 566; L. Charvet, *La restitutio in integrum des majeurs*, 1920, 93.

Alieni iuris esse. To be legally dependent upon the power of another. Syn. *alieno iuri subiectus, in potestate alicuius esse*. The power (*ius, potestas*) of another fell into different types and consequently there was a distinction among persons *alieni iuris*. The most important group was that of persons subject to the paternal power (PATRIA POTESTAS) of the head of the family (PATER FAMILIAS). Other persons *alieno iuri subiecti* were wives under the power of the husbands (*manus*), persons *in mancipio* (see MANCIPIUM), and slaves (*servi*) under the *dominica potestas* of their masters. Ant. *sui iuris esse*. Persons *alieni iuris* might become *sui iuris* either through legal acts, which differed according to the form of *potestas*, or in consequence of certain events. Persons subject to paternal power become *sui iuris* through the death of the *pater familias*, unless they then come under the power of another person, as, e.g., a grandson became subject to the *patria potestas* of his father if they both had been under the *potestas* of the grandfather. The release of a person *alieni iuris* from paternal power in the lifetime of the father was achieved by EMANCIPATIO, that of a slave by MANUMISSIO.—See PATER FAMILIAS, PATRIA POTESTAS, SUI IURIS ESSE.—Inst. 1.8; 4.7; D. 1.6; 14.5; C. 4.26.

Alienigenus. A foreigner (born in a foreign country).

Alieno iuri subiectus. See ALIENI IURIS ESSE.

Alieno nomine. In the name (in behalf) of another (e.g., *agere, possidere*, etc.). See NEMO ALIENO NOMINE.—Ant. *suo* (*proprio*) *nomine*. Acting *alieno nomine* was subject to various restrictions which in the course of time were gradually repealed.

G. Beseler, *Juristische Miniaturen*, 1929, 92.

Alienum. (Noun.) All that belongs to another.

Alienum aes. See AES ALIENUM.

Alienum negotium. Another man's affair. See NEGOTIORUM GESTIO. The law intervened in cases in which a person managed another's affairs without being authorized by him.

Alienus. See ALIENUM. Ant. PROPRIUS.

Alimenta. Nourishment, the necessities of life, means of support. Under the Principate a reciprocal right to, and duty of, sustenance between parents and children was established. Imperial constitutions and the jurisdiction of the *cognitio extra ordinem* enlarged the circle of persons obliged to reciprocal support (grandparents and grandchildren, wards, even illegitimate children), which reached its apogee in Justinian's law. This introduced a general obligation to provide *alimenta* for impoverished relatives as a duty of piety (*officium pietatis*). For *alimenta* as a public institution, see ALIMENTARIUS, FACULTATES, ORATIO MARCI.—D. 25.3; C. 5.26; 50.

De Ruggiero, *DE* 1, 408; Roberti, *Il diritto agli alimenti, Miscellanea Vermeersch* 2 (1935); E. Albertario, *Studi* 1 (1933) 249; Lanfranchi, *SDHI* 6 (1940) 5; G. Longo, *AnMac* 17 (1948) 215; Sachers, *Fschr Schulz* 1 (1951) 310.

Alimenta legata. Legacy of sustenance. It comprised food (*cibaria*), clothing (*vestiaria*) and lodging (*habitatio*). The extent of such a legacy is broadly discussed by the jurists in D. 34.1. It was normally combined with landed property as security.—See LEGATUM PENORIS.

B. Biondi, *Successione testamentaria*, 1943, 463.

Alimentarius. Connected with the distribution of *alimenta* (provisions) among the poor. *Pueri alimentarii* (*puellae alimentariae*) are indigent children who received *alimenta* from either imperial or private foundations (*arca alimentaria, pecuniae alimentariae*). The supervision of all such organizations in Italy and in the provinces was assigned to special *procuratores* (*quaestores, praefecti*) *alimentorum*.

Kubitschek, *RE* 1; Orestano, *NDI* 1; De Ruggiero, *DE* 1, 402, 408.

Alluvio. What a river has gradually added to the land along its bank. The landowner acquires ownership of the added soil (*accessio*). If, however, a river swept away a piece of land and attached it to another's property, the former owner did not lose his rights to the land carried away unless the accession had became inseparable from the neighbor's land, as when, for instance, the trees stroke roots into the latter.—C. 7.41.

Leonhard, *RE* 1 (*adluvio*); Baudry, *DE* 1; Pampaloni, *StSen* 43 (1929) 214; Naber, *Ath* 10 (1932) 37; Guarneri-Citati, *BIDR* 43 (1935) 25; Branca, *AnTr* 12 (1941) 50.

Alma urbs. In later imperial constitutions refers to Constantinople.

Alter alteri obligatur (tenetur). Each party is obligated to the other contractual partner. The phrase applies to reciprocal obligations in consensual contracts in which each party is bound to "what each has to perform for another *ex aequo et bono* (according to what is just and fair)," Gai Inst. 3.137, Iust. Inst. 3.22.3.

Altercatio. A legal controversy. *Altercationes* = alternating speeches of the advocates in a trial. Also a cross-examination of a witness.

Steinwenter, *ZSS* 65 (1947) 92.

Alterum tantum. As much again. Syn. *duplum*. The expression is applied to actions in which the plaintiff is condemned to pay twofold the value of the object in dispute. See ACTIONES IN SIMPLUM, DUPLUM.

Altiores. Persons of the highest social rank.—See HONESTIORES.

Alumnus. A child nourished and brought up by a person not related to him by blood.—See EXPOSITIO.

De Ruggiero, *DE* 1; Volterra, *St Besta* 1 (1939) 455.

Alveus derelictus. A river bed abandoned by the flowing water. It belonged to the landowners on the banks in proportion to the extent of their holdings, while the new river bed was in the same legal situation in which the former was: it became a *flumen publicum* (a public river) if it had been such before.—See FLUMINA.

De Ruggiero, *DE* 1; Scialoja, *St* 1 (1933, ex 1889) 391; Andrich, *AG* 56 (1896) 101, 57 (1896) 59; Riccobono, *St Schupfer* 1 (1898) 217; Guarneri-Citati, *AnMac* 1 (1926) 107; Branca, *AnTr* 12 (1941) 54.

Amatorius. See VENENUM.

Ambigere. To doubt, dispute, call into question. Legal decisions or rules are often introduced apodictically by *non est ambigendum, non ambigitur* (= there is no doubt).

Berger, *KrV* 14 (1912) 415; Guarneri-Citati, *Indice²* (1927) 10.

Ambigua vox. An obscure, ambiguous term. When it is used in a statute, "that meaning of it ought rather to be accepted which is blameless (*vitio caret* = free from fault), particularly when the intention of the law can also be thereby concluded" (D. 1.3.19).— See INTERPRETATIO.

Ambiguitas (ambiguus). Ambiguity, vagueness. The terms are used with predilection by Justinian and his compilers. But the phrase *non est ambigui iuris* (= it is a certain law) is frequent in Diocletian's constitutions. The monograph *"De ambiguitatibus"* ascribed to the jurist Julian may be a collection of doubtful questions collected in a later period from the jurist's works.—See AMBIGERE, AMBIGUA VOX.

Himmelschein, *Symbolae Friburgenses Lenel* (1932) 409.

Ambire. To canvass in elections for magisterial posts.

Ambitio. Bias, partiality (e.g., of a judge).

Ambitus. Unlawful maneuvers in elections. A series of statutes (see LEX AURELIA, CALPURNIA, CORNELIA, CORNELIA BAEBIA, CORNELIA FULVIA, IULIA, POETELIA, POMPEIA) dealt with dishonest and corrupt electoral practices by the candidates for magistracies (bribery, banquets, circus plays, canvassing by unworthy means). The legislation against *ambitus* may not have been very effective since the various prohibitions had to be repeated under the Republic time and again and the penalties became more and more severe (pecuniary fines, loss of *ius honorum*, exclusion from the senate [*lex Calpurnia* of 67 B.C.], infamy, exile) until the *lex Iulia* of Augustus of 18 B.C. introduced some moderations.

Hartmann, *RE* 1; Humbert, *DS* 1; G. Chaigne, *L'ambitus et les mœurs électorales des Romains,* 1911.

Ambitus. An open space two and a half Roman feet in width (*duo pedes et semis = sestertius pes*) between neighboring houses. Originally required by the Twelve Tables, it fell later into disuse. See PARIES COMMUNIS, SERVITUS ONERIS FERENDI. New building regulations were introduced by the Emperor Zeno (474–491). See AEDIFICATIO, ZENONIANAE CONSTITUTIONES.

Brugi, *RISG* 4 (1887); Berger, *ACDR* Roma, 1 (1934) 57.

Ambulare. The passing of a thing, a right or possession, from one person to another or successively to several persons by a change in the legal situation.

Amica. See PAELEX.

Castello, *Matrimonio e concubinato* (1940), 31, 41.

Amici Augusti. Outstanding persons, senators or knights (*equites*), admitted to solemn receptions by the emperor. They have no official position. From Diocletian's time the title *amici Augusti* was automatically granted to higher court officials.

Oehler, *RE* 1, 1831; Ciccotti, *DE* 1.

Amicitia (foedus amicitiae). A treaty of friendship between Rome and another state establishing peaceful and friendly relations.—See AMICUS POPULI ROMANI.

Gallet, *RHD* 16 (1937) 235; Heuss, *Klio, Beiheft* 31 (1933) 12, 78; Paradisi, *Scr Ferrini* 2 (Univ. Sacro Cuore, Milan, 1947) 178; Manni, *Rivista di filol. clas.* 1949, 79.

Amicus populi Romani. A title granted by the senate to individuals who rendered special services to the Republic. A state with which Rome has a friendship treaty. See AMICITIA. A stronger degree of international relations with Rome was that of *societas,* by which a foreign state became an ally (*socius*) of the Roman state (*populi Romani*) and was bound to give military aid in the event of war.

V. Ferrenbach, *Die amici p. R. republikanischer Zeit,* 1895.

Amovere. To purloin, put aside. The term has a milder color than *furari* (*furtum committere* = to steal) and is applied when there is no real theft, as, for instance, when important documents or things belonging to an inheritance are hidden by the heir. For *amovere* between spouses, see ACTIO RERUM AMOTARUM.

Ampliatio. In Roman criminal procedure the reiteration of all the evidence when the jury declared that the case has not been sufficiently elucidated and required further (*amplius*) investigation.

Humbert, *DS* 1; Berger, *OCD;* Balsdon, *Papers of the Brit. School at Rome,* 1938, 109.

Amplissimus ordo. The senate.—See SENATUS.

Amplitudo. A distinctive title of the highest functionaries in the later Empire ("your Excellency").

Anastasianae leges. See LEGES ANASTASIANAE.

Anatocismus. The transformation of interest due and not paid into a new interest bearing principal. The term is unknown in juristic sources. Syn. *usurae usurarum*. Although forbidden, it was practiced in

Cicero's time as *anatocismus anniversarius* (= annually compounded interest). Justinian forbade it definitely.

Leonhard, *RE* 1; Caillemer, *DS* 1.

Anatolius. A law professor in Beirut, one of the compilers of the Digest. Anatolius (the same?) is known as a commentator on Justinian's Code.

Hartmann, *RE* 1, 2073; Berger, *Byz.* 17 (1945) 1 (Bibl.).

Ancilla. A female slave.—See PARTUS ANCILLAE, PROSTITUERE.

De Ruggiero, *DE* 1; F. M. De Robertis, *La organizzazione e la tecnica produttiva*, 1946, 156.

Aneglogistus. Exempt from the duty of giving account. The term is used on a guardian appointed in a testament and relieved by the testator from giving account of his administration of the ward's property. The guardian was, however, liable for fraud in spite of the testator's order.

Arangio-Ruiz and Colombo, *Jour. of Juristic Papyrology* 4 (1950) 121.

Angaria (angariae). Compulsory service in the imperial post or in the transportation of persons or things in official business (*cursus publicus*). The same term indicates the animals (oxen, horses = *veredi*) as well as the carriages to be provided for that purpose. Later imperial legislation dealt with the organization of official transportation and postal service, which had become a great burden to landowners.—C. 12.50.

Seeck, *RE* 1; Humbert, *DS* 1, 1659; Rostowzew, *Klio* 6 (1906) 249.

Angustus clavus. A narrow purple stripe on the tunic, a distinctive mark of the equestrian rank.—Ant. *latus clavus* (for senators).—See CLAVUS LATUS.

Hula, *RE* 4, 6; De Ruggiero, *DE* 2, 306.

Animadversio (animadvertere). Any kind of punishment, but most often capital punishment. *Animadversio gladio* (*animadversio capitis*) = decapitation. *Animadversus* = a man who was executed in conformity to a death sentence.

Animalia. A distinction was made between wild animals living in a natural state of liberty (*ferae bestiae*) and those who go away and come back to their former place (pigeons, bees, stags). The latter belonged to the occupant and as long as they retain the habit of returning to his property (*consuetudo, animus revertendi*).—See FERAE, ANIMUS REVERTENDI, ACTIO DE PAUPERIE.

Animalia quae collo dorsove domantur. Domestic animals of draft and burden (horses, oxen, asses, mules, but not elephants and camels). They are RES MANCIPI.—See PECUS.

Animus. The intention (will) of a person concluding a transaction with another or acting unilaterally in order to accomplish an act with legal effects. *Animus* is also connected with certain wrongdoing in order to stress that the person acted intentionally (*animus furandi, iniuriae faciendae, occidendi,* etc.). With reference to last wills and testaments, the syn. term *voluntas* (*testantis, testatoris*) prevails. Intention is distinguished from what a person declared orally whether by solemn, prescribed words or informally or in writing. A contradiction between intention (*animus, voluntas*) and the words expressed (*verba*) might influence the validity of the act accomplished. After the archaic and preclassical periods of rigid formalism in legal transactions, the importance of the *animus* (*voluntas*) with regard to the validity of the act was gradually recognized already in classical time, although there is in the modern Romanistic literature a tendency to ascribe all occurrences of *animus* in Justinian's codification, chiefly in the contractual domain, to the emperor's innovation or at least to postclassical origin. The tendency mentioned is doubtless an exaggeration though the interpolation of many texts in which the *animus* is emphatically stressed is beyond the question. The connection between *animus* and various legal institutions differs in intensity; its significance in the Roman doctrine of possession (*animo possidere*) is particularly well elaborated. Syn. with *animus* is sometimes AFFECTIO (*affectus*), sometimes *mens*, as in the phrase *eo animo ut* (*ea mente ut*) = with the intention that.—See VOLUNTAS and the following items.

Guarneri-Citati, *Indice*[2] (1927) 10; *idem, Fschr Koschaker* 1 (1939) 122; Donatuti, *BIDR* 34 (1925); Sokolowski, *Mél Cornil* 2 (1926); Riccobono, *ibid.* 378; *idem, ACDR Roma* 1 (1934); Pringsheim, *LQR* 49 (1933) 45; Albertario, *Studi* 5 (1937) 125; Maschi, *Studi sull'interpretazione dei legati. Verba e voluntas*, 1938.

Animus adimendi legatum. See ADEMPTIO LEGATI.

Animus contrahendi. (Or *animus contrahendae obligationis.*) Occurs in a few texts. Sometimes the type of the contract is specified: *animus emendi, vendendi, transigendi, promittentis, stipulantium, compensandi,* etc.

Animus damni dandi. The intention to damage a thing. It is used in connection with damages done to testaments.

Animus decipiendi. The intention to deceive (defraud) another.

Animus derelinquendi (derelinquentis). See DERELICTIO.

Animus donandi. The intention to make a gift.—See DONATIO.

Pringsheim, *ZSS* 42 (1921) 273; Biondi, *Scr Ferrini* 1 (Univ. Sacro Cuore, Milan, 1947) 133.

Animus furandi (furis, furti faciendi). See FURTUM.

Berger, *BIDR* 32 (1922, printed 1915) 182; Albertario, *A.f.* (1923, = *Studi* 3 [1936] 209).

Animus iniuriae (faciendae). See INIURIA.

Animus intercedendi. See INTERCESSIO.

Animus legandi. See LEGATUM.

Animus liberorum procreandorum. Procreation of children is considered to be an element of intent in concluding a marriage.

Animus lucrandi (lucri faciendi). See FURTUM.

Animus negotia aliena gerendi. See NEGOTIORUM GESTIO.

> Riccobono, *AnPal* 3/4 (1917), 170; Rabel, *St Bonfante* 4 (1930); Erhardt, in *Freiburger Rechtsgesch. Abhandlungen* 5 (*Romanist. Studien* 1935).

Animus novandi. See NOVATIO.

> Guarneri-Citati, *Indice* 2 (1927) 11; Scialaja, *St Perozzi*, 1925; Cornil, *Mél Fournier*, 1907, 87; Hägerström, *Der röm. Obligationsbegriff* 2 (1941) Beil. p. 199.

Animus occidendi. The intention to kill a man.

Animus possidendi. The term, common in literature, is rare in juristic sources, which also speak of *animus possidentis,* but mostly of *animo adquirere possessionem* or *retinere possessionem.*—See POSSESSIO.

> Rotondi, *BIDR* 30 (1920) 1 (= *Scr giur.* 3, 1922, 94).

Animus recipiendi. Refers to the intention of a person acting on behalf of another without authorization (*negotiorum gestor*) to be reimbursed subsequently for his services.

Animus revertendi. Used of animals which have the habit of returning to 'their quarters. Thus, their owner does not lose ownership. See ANIMALIA. Similarly the master of a slave retained his power as long as the slave had the intention to return to the master.

Animus societatis. See SOCIETAS.

Annalis actio (or **exceptio**). An action (or exception) available for only one year to anyone who wished to make use of it. See ACTIONES TEMPORALES. Both these remedies are of praetorian origin.

Anniculus. A one-year-old child.—See CAUSAE PROBATIO.

Anniversarius. See ANATOCISMUS, CANON.

Annona. Has different meanings which all, however, are somehow connected with the supply of provisions: the general supply of grain for the city of Rome, the free distribution of grain and bread to needy people, food for the army, food sold by the government to the people for cash, taxes in natural products, and, finally, the central administration of the food supply. Originally the responsibility for the provisioning of Rome was vested with the *aediles,* under the later Republic and in the Empire the *cura annonae* was enlarged under the supervision of the *praefectus annonae* assisted by a staff of auxiliary officials.—D. 48.12; C. 40.16.—See ANNONA CIVICA, ANNONA MILITARIS, CURA ANNONAE, PRAEFECTUS ANNONAE, PROSECUTOR, LEX IULIA DE ANNONA.

> Schwahn, *RE* 7A, 76; Stevenson, *OCD*; Kalsbach, *RAC* 1 (1950); Oehler, *RE* 1; Humbert, *DS* 1; Rostowzew, *RE* 7 (*frumentum*); De Ruggiero, *DE* 1; A. Segrè, *Byz.* 16 (1943) 392.

Annona civica (civilis). The supply of food from Egypt and Africa for the provisioning of Rome, and later of Constantinople. The term is also used to indicate the gratuitous distribution of food to the poor, also known as *annona publica.*—C. 11.25.—See FRUMENTATIONES, LEGES FRUMENTARIAE.

> Van Berchem, *Les distributions de blé etc. sous l'Empire,* 1939.

Annona militaris. Provisions supplied by the population in the provinces for the maintenance of troops and government officials. In the later Empire this, originally an emergency measure, became a permanent institution as a form of taxation in kind.—C. 12.38.

> De Ruggiero, *DE* 1; A. Segrè, *loc. cit.;* Van Berchem, *Mém. de la Société des Antiquaires en France* 80 (1937) 117.

Annona publica. See ANNONA CIVICA.

Annonarius. (Adj.) Connected with food administration.—See ANNONA.

Annua bima trima die. A frequent clause in legacies of annual payments (pensions): the bequeathed sum was to be paid over a period of three years in equal installments. The phrase also appears in sales when the price was to be paid in the same way.

Annus continuus. A full calendar year of 365 consecutive days. Ant. *annus utilis.*

Annus utilis. A one-year period (365 days) not counting the days during which the party involved was unable to act in court for personal reasons (disease, captivity, absence in official business) or because of the absence of his adversary or the inactivity of the judicial authorities.—See DIES UTILES, TEMPUS UTILE.

> Kübler, *RE* 5A, 485.

Annuum. A payment or an allowance which recurs every year. *Annua legata* = legacies consisting of annual payments.—See LEGATUM ANNUUM.

Anonymus. An anonymous juristic writer of the late sixth century after Christ, author of a concise summary (*index*) of the Digest which served as a basis for the compilation of the Digest portion of the BASILICA. He can be identified as the author of a collection of ecclesiastical and lay legal sources, the so-called *Nomocanon 14 titulorum,* and of a compilation of allegedly controversial rules in Justinian's Digest. From the title of the latter work (*Peri enantiophaneion*), later Byzantine authors invented the name Enantiophanes of a jurist. The identity of the author of the Digest index and the compilations mentioned is controversial but without good reasons.

> Peters, *Die oström. Digestenkommentare, BerSächGW* 1913, 11; Spulber, *Archives d'hist. du dr. oriental* 1 (1937) 307; Pringsheim, *Seminar* 4 (1946) 21 (= *BIDR* 55-56, Post-Bellum, 1951, 302); Scheltema, *R. D* 30 (1952) 14.

Anquisitio. The earliest form of judicial trial in criminal matters conducted by a magistrate in the presence of an informal assembly of citizens (*contio*) who attended the whole proceedings, the examination of the accused and the hearing of witnesses, in order to be able to pass final judgment in case the accused appealed from the condemnation by the magistrate. An acquittal by the latter is final, however.

> Hartmann, *RE* 1; Brecht, *ZSS* 59 (1939) 271.

Antecessores. Prominent teachers in the law schools of the late Empire.

> Humbert, *DS* 1.

Antestatus. One of the solemn witnesses at a *mancipatio* in the earliest law. His role in the act is not quite clear and he disappeared soon (there is no mention of him in Gaius).

> Leist, *RE* 1; Kaser, *RE* 5A, 1025; Kunkel, *RE* 14, 999; De Ruggiero, *DE* 1, 491; Schupfer, *RISG* 47 (1910) 333; Bonfante, *Corso di dir. rom. 2, 2* (1928) 138.

Anthianus. See FURIUS ANTHIANUS.

Antichresis. An agreement between creditor and debtor by which the former was granted the right to use the thing pledged (land or house) and to obtain income therefrom in lieu of interest. The creditor might lease the property, live on it, or use it otherwise. He kept possession until the debt was paid.

> Leonhard, *RE* 1; Manigk, *Gläubigerbefriedigung durch Nutzung.* 1910; *idem, RE* 20, 1276.

Antinomia. Justinian uses this Greek term, for which he did not find a Latin synonym, to indicate a contradiction between legal norms. He proudly, though mistakenly, stresses that his codification is free from contradictory statements (*Deo auctore* 8 = C. 1.17.1.8).

Antipherna. Gifts given by the husband to the wife as a counterpart to the dowry (in Greek *pherné*).— See DONATIO ANTE NUPTIAS.

Antiqui. As a noun, or as an adjective in connection with *legum auctores, conditores, prudentes,* etc., refers to former jurists, particularly those of more remote times. In Justinian's language by *antiqui* the classical jurists are meant.—See VETERES, IUS ANTIQUUM.

Antiquo. See A (abbreviation for *antiquo*).

Antiquum ius. See IUS ANTIQUUM, VETUS IUS.

Anulus. A ring. It was an old Roman custom that freeborn men wore rings *signandi causa,* i.e., for sealing written instruments they made or witnessed (e.g., last wills). Syn. *anulus signatorius.*—See IUS ANULI AUREI, EQUITES.

Apertissimus. Most evident, conclusive. It is one of Justinian's favorite superlatives, often applied to means of evidence (*apertissimae probationes*).—See PROBATIONES.

> Guarneri-Citati, *Indice*² (1927) 11.

Apertura testamenti (tabularum, codicillorum). In connection with the introduction of an inheritance tax (VICESIMA HEREDITATIUM), certain formalities were fixed for the opening of a last will in the presence of a special official. From Hadrian's time the competent office was the *statio vicesimae.* After the acknowledgment of the signatures and seals by· the witnesses, the testament was opened (*aperire*) and read aloud in public (*recitatio testamenti*). Later it was deposited in the archives together with a record of the whole act of *apertura.* Persons interested in the document were permitted to see it (*inspicere*) and to make a copy (*describere*).—D. 29.3; 6.32; 52.

> Wenger, *RE* 2A, 2407; B. Biondi, *Successione testamentaria,* 1943, 601; Arangio-Ruiz, *FIR* 1943, nos. 57, 58.

Apices. When used with a pertinent adjective, such as *divini, sacri, augusti,* indicates an imperial letter.

Apices iuris. Juristic subtlety, sophistry.

Apocha. A written receipt in which the creditor declares that he has received (*"scripsi accepisse"*) the sum due him. In Justinian's law an *apocha* was fully valid only if it was not gainsaid within thirty days. *Apocha publica* = an official receipt issued for the payment of taxes. Syn. *securitates.*—C. 10.22.

> Leonhard, *RE* 1; Paoli, *NDI* 1; Frese, *ZSS* 18 (1897); Appleton, *St Scialoja* 2 (1905) 503.

Apochae Pompeianae. Receipts on wax tablets found in 1875 in the house of a banker in Pompei.

> Arangio-Ruiz, *FIR* (1943) 400.

Apostata. A person who abandoned the Christian faith. Penalties imposed on apostates by the Christian emperors included infamy, loss of the right to make a last will or to take under one, and loss of the right to receive a donation. Constantine added confiscation of property for those who turned to Judaism.—C. 1.7.

> Humbert, *DS* 1 (*apostasie*).

Apostoli. See APPELLO. Syn. *libelli dimissorii.*— D. 49.6.—See LITTERAE DIMISSORIAE.

Apparitores. Subordinate officials performing auxiliary services in the offices of magistrates and imperial officials, such as secretaries (*scribae*), messengers (*viatores*), heralds (*praecones*). The *apparitores* normally served for longer periods of time and thus became valuable aides to their superiors who were appointed for one year only. Their influence increased considerably during the Empire. They were organized in associations (*collegia, decuriae apparitorum*). In the absolute monarchy they constituted an important element in the bureaucratic organization of the government. A series of imperial constitutions of the fourth and fifth centuries dealt with·the privileges and duties of the *apparitores* of the higher officials, as we learn from Justinian's Code 12.52(53)–59(60); 61(62).—See IMMUNES, DECURIAE APPARITORUM.

> Habel, *RE* 2; Humbert, *DS* 1; De Ruggiero, *DE* 1; Waltzing, *DE* 2, 351, 369; Eliachévitch, *La personnalité juridique,* 1942, 241; Düll, *ZSS* 53 (1943) 393.

Appellatio (appello). An appeal by a litigant to a higher judicial court when the judgment of the lower one was not in his favor. Introduced in the extraordinary proceedings (*cognitio extra ordinem*) as a new procedural remedy, then gradually reformed, finally by Justinian, the *appellatio* developed into a general institution applicable to all judgments, in both civil and criminal matters, except those of the praetorian prefect and decisions of a merely administrative character. Frivolous appeals were punished by pecuniary fines. Later, *appellatio* became syn. with *provocatio,* which in earlier times applied only to criminal cases.—D. 49.1–13; C. 7.62–70.—See

CONSULTATIO, EDICTUM DE APPELLATIONIBUS, INIUS-
TUS, ORATIO MARCI, and the following items.

> Kipp, *RE* 2; Hartmann, *ibid.;* Humbert, *DS* 1; Orestano,
> *NDI* 1; E. Perrot, *L'appel dans la procédure de l'ordo
> iudiciorum,* 1907; Lauria, *AG* 97 (1927); Sanfilippo,
> *AnCam* 8 (1934); Düll, *ZSS* 56 (1936); Wenger, *RAC*
> 1 (1942).

Appellator. The party to a trial who appeals from an
unfavorable judgment.—See APPELLATIO, APELLO.

Appellatorii libelli. See APPELLO.

Appello. "I appeal." This word was pronounced by
a litigant in order to announce that he was appealing
from the judgment or decree of a magistrate to a
higher court. When made in writing in so-called
libelli appellatorii the appeal had to be filed with the
judge of the lower court whose decision was being
opposed. The latter then wrote a report (*litterae
dimissoriae, libelli dimissorii, apostoli*) by which he
"dismissed" the case and transmitted the appeal to
the higher court through the intermediary of the
appellator himself. Until the decision of the higher
tribunal was rendered, the first judgment remained
without effect.

Appius Claudius Caecus. A renowned jurist of about
300 B.C.

> Münzer, *RE* 3, 2681; Schulz, *History of Roman legal
> science* (1946) 9.

Applicatio. See CLIENTES, IUS APPLICATIONIS.

Apud. Connected with the name of a jurist (e.g.,
apud Iulianum), used to introduce a specific opinion
of the jurist, or of a critical or explanatory remark
(*nota*) made by a later jurist to the opinion of an
earlier one (e.g., *apud Labeonem Proculus notat*).—
—See NOTAE.

> Sciascia, *BIDR* 49–50 (1947) 430.

Apud acta. See ACTA.

Apud iudicem. See IN IURE, IN IUDICIO.

Aqua. Often employed for the servitudes of using
water from or through another's property. In this
meaning it is syn. with *ius (servitus) aquae.* Distinctions are made as to the time during which the
right may be exercised. Thus *aqua aestiva* can be
used only in the summer time, *aqua cottidiana* every
day, *aqua diurna* only in the daytime, and *aqua nocturna* at night.—D. 43.20; C. 3.34.—See SERVITUS
AQUAEDUCTUS, SERVITUS AQUAE HAUSTUS.

Aqua et igni interdictio. See INTERDICERE AQUA ET
IGNI.

Aqua pluvia. Rain water. See ACTIO AQUAE PLUVIAE
ARCENDAE, SERVITUS STILLICIDII.

Aqua profluens. Flowing water. It ranks among the
RES COMMUNES OMNIUM.—See FLUMINA.

Aqua publica. (Syn. *aqua in usu publico.*) Flowing
or stagnant water destined for the common use of
the population of a community. The category embraces waters in FLUMINA PUBLICA, LACUS, STAGNUM,
FOSSA.

> De Ruggiero, *DE* 1; E. Costa, *Le acque nel diritto rom.,*
> 1919; Bonfante, *Scritti giur.* 4 (1926) 242; M. Lauria,

AnMac 8 (1932) 243; G. Longo, *RISG* 1928, 244; *idem,
St Ratti,* 1934, 57; Grosso, *Scritti Santi Romano* 4 (1940)
175.

Aquaeductus. Aqueducts for public use were under
particular protection of the law. A decree of the
Senate of 11 B.C., statutes (such as the LEX QUINCTIA)
and frequent imperial enactments, especially in the
later Empire, contained detailed provisions, backed
by penal sanctions, designed to prevent damage to
aqueducts.—Water conduits for private purposes
were protected by interdicts.—C. 11.43.—See SERVI-
TUS AQUAEDUCTUS, INTERDICTUM DE AQUA, ACTIONES
POPULARES.

> Leonhard, *RE* 2; Labatut, *DS* 1; De Ruggiero, *DE* 1,
> 537; Gianzana, *NDI* 1 (*s.v. acque private*); Herschel,
> *The two books on the water supply of Frontinus,* New
> York, 1913; Kornemann, *RE* 4, 1784; Weiss, *ZSS* 45
> (1925) 87; De Robertis, *La espropriazione per pubblica
> utilità,* 1936, 95; Riccobono, *FIR* 1² (1941) 276.

Aquaeductus Venafranus. See EDICTUM DE AQUAE-
DUCTU VENAFRANO.

Aquae haustus. See SERVITUS AQUAE HAUSTUS.

Aquarius. A subordinate officer in the water administration. In a private household, *aquarius* is usually
a slave who takes care of the water supply.

> De Ruggiero, *DE* 1, 587.

Aquila, Iulius. A little known Roman jurist, contemporary with Ulpian, author of a collection of
responsa.

> Berger, *RE* 10, 167.

Aquilia(Aquilia lex). See LEX AQUILIA.

Aquiliana stipulatio. See ACCEPTILATIO, AQUILIUS
GALLUS.

Aquilius Gallus, Gaius. One of the most creative
jurists under the Republic, praetor in 66 B.C. His
name is linked with the introduction of the STIPU-
LATIO AQUILIANA and the ACTIO DOLI.—See also
POSTUMI AQUILIANI.

> Klebs-Jörs, *RE* 2, 327; Orestano, *NDI* 1; Beseler, *BIDR*
> 50 (1931) 314.

Ara. An altar for sacrifices located either in a temple,
in any *locus sacer,* as a sanctuary, or in any other
place. Along with the consecration of an *ara,* rules
(*lex arae*) were issued concerning its use.

> De Ruggiero, *DE* 1, 578.

Ara legis Hadrianae. The stone on which the inscription concerning the so-called *Lex Hadriana* was
found (in Tunisia).—See LEX MANCIANA.

> Riccobono, *FIR* 1² (1941) 493.

Arbiter. In a judicial trial, in controversies which
required specific professional or technical knowledge
the magistrate could appoint an expert (*arbiter*) instead of a judge (*iudex*) so that the judgment should
be rendered by someone better qualified than the
average Roman citizen listed in the panel of judges
(*album iudicum*). The discretionary powers of an
arbiter in making his decision were not so severely
restricted by the praetor's instructions as in ordinary
trials. The division of common property (*communio*)

or a common inheritance was assigned to an *arbiter* as was the establishment of boundaries between adjoining lands.—See ADDICERE, ADIUDICATIO, LEGIS ACTIO PER IUDICIS ARBITRIVE POSTULATIONEM, IUDEX.

Wlassak, *RE* 2; De Ruggiero, *DE* 1; R. Düll, *Der Güte-gedanke im röm. Civilprozessrecht,* 1931; Kaser, *Fschr Wenger* 1 (1944) 115.

Arbiter datus (delegatus, pedaneus). A person appointed by a judicial magistrate to examine a particular point in dispute in a civil trial, e.g., to check accounts, to establish the solvency of a guarantor, or to calculate the *quarta Falcidia* (see LEX FALCIDIA).

Wlassak, *RE* 2, 410.

Arbiter ex compromisso. An arbitrator chosen by voluntary agreement of the parties (COMPROMISSUM) to decide their dispute. His decision (*sententia, pro-nuntiatio arbitri*) could be enforced only when the parties had, through reciprocal stipulations strengthened by penalties, assumed the obligation of fulfilling the arbitrator's judgment. Generally the duties of the *arbiter* were fixed in the parties' agreement, the *arbiter* had more liberty, however, than a *iudex* bound by the formula in the formulary proceedings. The appointment of an *arbiter* is an extrajudicial arrangement; later it received protection of the praetor, who, by coercive measures, might compel the *arbiter* to carry out the duties conferred on him by the parties involved and assumed by him without the intervention of a magistrate.—See RECEPTUM ARBITRI, COMPROMISSUM (Bibl.).

Arbitrari. The activity of an *arbiter.*

Arbitrarius. Depending upon the decision of the judge (*iudex*).—See ACTIONES ARBITRARIAE.

Arbitratus. See ARBITRIUM.

Arbitratus (arbitrium) iudicis. See ACTIONES ARBITRARIAE.

Arbitrium. A judgment, decision of an arbitrator. Syn. *arbitratus.* See ARBITER. The entire proceedings ending with a decision by an *arbiter* is also called *arbitrium,* as is the interlocutory decision which could be handed down by the judge (*iudex*) in a civil trial (in literature *arbitrium de restituendo*) under authority of the clause in the formula (*clausula arbitraria*): *neque et res arbitrio tuo* (*sc. iudicis*) *restituatur,* see ACTIONES ARBITRARIAE.—See the foregoing entries, IURGIUM, RECEPTUM ARBITRI.

Wlassak, *RE* 2.

Arbitrium (arbitratus) boni viri. The judgment, opinion of an honest, upright man to whom a controversial point has been submitted.

Scaduto, *AnPal* 11 (1923) 24; Riccobono, *Mél Cornil 2* (1926) 310; Albertario, *Studi* 3 (1936) 283, 329; Grosso, *SDHI* 1 (1935) 83; *idem, Riv. di dir. commerciale* 402 (1942) 227; Frezza, *Nuova Riv. di dir. com.* 2 (1949) 41.

Arbitrium iudicis (iudicantis). See ACTIONES ARBITRARIAE, ARBITRIUM.

Arbitrium liti(s) aestimandae. Proceedings for the estimation of the value of an object in dispute in money.—See LITIS AESTIMATIO.

Kipp, *RE* 1, 687; Huvelin, *Mél Gérardin,* 1907, 319.

Arbitrium tutelae. ACTIO (IUDICIUM) TUTELAE. See TUTOR.—C. 5.57.

Arbores caedere. For conflicts arising in connection with the cutting of trees by a neighbor or by an unauthorized person, see INTERDICTUM DE ARBORIBUS CAEDENDIS, ACTIO ARBORUM FURTIM CAESARUM.—D. 43.27; 47.7.

Arca. A cash-box, in a larger sense the treasury of a community (*arca municipalis*) or of a public or private corporation (*arca collegii*). *Arca publica* is the treasury of Rome; its divisions connected with specific purposes are *arca frumentaria, arca olearia,* etc., for revenues and expenses resulting from the sale and purchase of grain, oil and the like. *Arca fisci* (*fiscalis, Caesaris*) is the state treasury under the Empire. *Arca praefecturae* is a particular treasury under the administration of the *praefectus praetorio.*

Habel, *RE* 2; Humbert, *DS* 1; Fuchs, *DE* 1, 627; Beseler, *ZSS* 46 (1926) 86.

Arca alimentaria. See ALIMENTARIUS.

Arca collegii. The treasury of an association.—See COLLEGIUM.

De Ruggiero, *DE* 1, 629.

Arca fisci, praefecturae, publica. See ARCA.

Arca provincialis. The treasury of a province, supported by contributions of the provincial municipalities primarily for religious expenditures and for the public games.

Arcadius Charisius. See CHARISIUS.

Arcarius. The treasurer (cashier) in an *arca.* In public *arcae,* he is the chief officer in charge of the treasury.—C. 10.72.—See ARCA.

Habel, *RE* 2; Humbert, *DS* 1; Fuchs, *DE* 1, 633.

Arcarius. (Adj.) See NOMINA ARCARIA.

Archiater sacri palatii. A physician-in-ordinary to the emperor and the imperial family.—C. 12.13.

Archiepiscopus. An archbishop.

Architectus. The profession of an *architectus* was considered one of the noblest liberal professions. An *architectus* who deceived his client in the accomplishment of the work ordered was prosecuted by an action similar to that against a dishonest land-surveyor.—See AGRIMENSORES.

Area. See LOCUS.

Arenarii. Men who hired themselves out for fights with wild beasts in the circus (*arena*). They were free men but were treated as slaves by their employers, and belonged to the most despised social class.

Pollack, *RE* 2.

Argentaria. A banker's business. Syn. *mensa argentaria.*

Argentarii. Bankers, owners of a banking firm. They performed various financial operations such as money changing, purchase and sale of coins, loans on interest, and on mortgage, and the like. Exact and honest bookkeeping was obligatory of them since their books (*rationes*) enjoyed public confidence (*fides publica*), and had to be produced (*edere ra-*

tiones, editio rationum) in trials in which their clients were involved, as evidence even when the banker himself was not a party. The duty to produce their books in court was precisely formulated in the praetorian edict, and a special action was granted against an *argentarius* who refused to do so. When suing his customer for a money debt (*actio qua argentarius experitur*) the *argentarius* had to deduct from his claim whatever he owed to the customer (*agere cum compensatione*) since, when he demanded "one penny more" (*plus nummo uno*), he lost the case because of PLUSPETITIO.—Women were excluded from the banking business.—D. 2.13.—See MENSA, RELEGARE PECUNIAM.

Oehler, *RE* 2; Saglio-Humbert, *DS* 1; De Ruggiero, *DE* 1; La Fortuna, *NDI* 1; Voigt, *ASächGW* 10 (1888) 516; A. Rossello, *Argentarii* 1, 1891; Mitteis, *ZSS* 19 (1898) 203; R. Beigel, *Rechnungswesen und Buchführung der Römer*, 1904, 206; E. Levy, *Privatstrafe und Schadensersatz*, 1915, 61; Platon, *NHRD* 33 (1909) 10; L. De Sarlo, *Il documento come oggetto dei rapporti*, 1935, 257; Solazzi, *Compensazione* 2 (1950) 31.

Argentum. (1) Silver money; (2) the silver objects in a household. They might be altogether the object of one legacy (*argentum legatum*).—D. 34.2; C. 10.78.

De Ruggiero, *DE* 1.

Arguere. To accuse (and generally, to convict) a person of a crime.

Argumentum. A general term for all means of evidence.—See PROBATIO, ARRA.

Aristo, Titius. A Roman jurist, member of the council of the emperor Trajan, author of annotations (*notae*) to the works of some jurists of the Augustan period.—See DECRETA FRONTIANA.

Orestano, *NDI* 1, 206; Mommsen, *Jurist. Schriften* 2 (1905) 22; Sciascia, *BIDR* 49–50 (1948) 415.

Arma. See VIS ARMATA, TELUM.

Arra (arrha). A sum of money or a thing (a ring, for instance) given as an earnest at the conclusion of a sale. In the classical law it was considered a means of evidence only (*argumentum emptionis contractae*). The origin of the institution lies in Greek sale practices. In Justinian's law the buyer might withdraw from the purchase by forfeiting the *arra*, whereas the seller had to double the amount he received from the buyer if he wanted to cancel the sale. This function of the *arra*—the parties' right to cancel the sale (hence the name *arra poenitentialis* in literature)—evidently was excluded when the formalities set by Justinian (written deed, intervention of a notary) had been completed.

Foligno, *NDI* 1; G. Calogirou, *Die a. im Vermögensrecht*, 1911; Senn, *NRHD* 37 (1913) 571; F. Bergold, *Gesch. und Wesen des arrhabo und der a.*, Diss. Erlangen, 1923; Cornil, *ZSS* 48 (1928) 55; E. Popesco, *La fonction pénitentielle des arrhes dans la vente*, 1925; Carusi, *St Bonfante* 4 (1930) 503; J. Partsch, *Aus nachgelassenen Schriften*, 1931, 262; Levy, *Symb Frib Lenel*, 1931, 133; Simonetos, *Fschr Koschaker* 3 (1939); Massei, *BIDR* 48 (1941) 215; Steinwenter, *RAC* 1 (1943); F. De Zulueta, *The Rom.*

Law of sale, 1945, 22; F. Pringsheim, *The Greek law of sale* (Weimar, 1950) 333.

Arra sponsalicia. See SPONSALIA.—C. 5.1.

Koschaker, *ZSS* 33 (1912); Cornil, *ZSS* 48 (1928); Volterra, *RISG* 2, 4, 5 (1927–1930); Grattier, *Dictionnaire de droit canon.* 1 (1935) 1050.

Arrianus. A Roman jurist of the classical period, known only as the author of a monograph on interdicts.

Jörs, *RE* 2, 1229.

Arrius Menander. A Roman jurist who lived under Septimius Severus and Caracalla (early third century) and was a member of their councils (*consilia*). He is the author of a treatise on military law (*De re militari*).

Jörs, *RE* 2, 1257.

Ars magica. See MAGIA.

Artes liberales. See OPERAE LIBERALES, STUDIA LIBERALIA.

Articulus. A legal rule or a special provision in a written legal enactment.

Artifices. Artists versed in fine arts or skilled in the practice of a manual art. They were exempt from compulsory public services (*munera*) in order to be given the opportunity of developing their knowledge and skillfulness and of instructing others. A constitution of the Emperor Constantine of A.D. 337 (C. 10.66.1) contains a list of some forty professions entitled to such exemptions. Along with physicians and veterinarians there are mentioned painters, sculptors, architects, goldsmiths, silversmiths, potters, armorers, glaziers, fullers, carpenters, etc.

Arvales fratres. Arval brethren, a group of twelve priests of senatorial origin whose duty it was to observe certain rituals and to perform sacrifices in honor of the goddess Dea Dia and the deities worshipped as protectors of agriculture. Protocols of their priestly functions are preserved epigraphically. After the reorganization of the college of Arvals by Augustus their activity was more and more devoted to the glorification of the Emperor (who was automatically a member of the group) and his family.

As. A Roman coin, originally of one pound of bronze (*as libralis*). As a monetary unit the *as* was divided into twelve *unciae*. In juristic language, the term served as a conception of a whole; hence an heir who inherited the entire estate was named *heres ex asse*. Similarly, parts of an inheritance were indicated by the corresponding terms used for an *uncia* and its multiples. *Heres ex semisse* was an heir whose share was a half of the estate. In general, the term involves the whole of an object referred to, as, for instance, a legacy *ex asse* or *ex asse possidere*. In later times the *as* was reduced to four, and then to two ounces (*unciae*).—See ASSIS DISTRIBUTIO, UNCIA.

Kubitschek, *RE* 2; Hultsch, *RE* Suppl. 1; Lenormant, *RS* 1; Pampaloni, *RISG* 52 (1912) 131.

Ascendentes (adscendentes). Relatives in the ascending line (parents, grandparents, great-grandparents) on both the father's (*per virilem sexum*) and mother's side (*per matrem*). Ant. *descendentes.* Syn. *superiores.*

Ass-. See ADS-.

Assis distributio. A pamphlet of the jurist Maecianus on the division of the *as.*—See AS.

Pampaloni, *RISG* 52 (1912) 131.

Astrologi. Although frequently prosecuted together with others who *illicitam divinationem pollicentur* (illegally predict the future) as exercising a prohibited profession, they did not disappear from Rome, especially since several emperors believed in astrology (as Vespasian, Hadrian, Septimius Severus, Caracalla) and the high society was not adverse to them. A course of strong action against the astrologers (often identified with *Chaldaei* and *mathematici*) began with Diocletian who condemned the *ars mathematica.* Generally only the practice of astrology as a profession (*exercitio, professio*) for the prediction of future events was punished. The knowledge (*notitia*) as such was not interdicted. Diocletian's successors followed his severe regime against the astrologers, especially with regard to foreigners.

Riess, *RE* 2; Bouché-Leclercq, *DS* 2, 316; Rogers, *Classical Philology* 26 (1931) 203; Cramer, *Sem* 9 (1951) 1.

Ateius Capito. See CAPITO.

Athanasius. A Byzantine jurist of the second half of the sixth century, author of an epitome of Justinian's Novels (about A.D. 572) systematically arranged in 22 titles.

Edition: C. G. E. Heimbach, *Anecdota* 1, 1838; Berger, *BIDR* Suppl. Post-Bellum, 55/56 (1951) 135.

Athleta. Athletes who exercised their profession for the sake of glory and bravery (*gloriae et virtutis causa*) were granted certain privileges, such as exemption from public charges (MUNERA) and taxes. The *Lex Aquilia* does not apply when an *athleta* killed his adversary in the fight by accident because the element of *iniuria* was lacking. See LEX AQUILIA. Unlike actors and gladiators, athletes enjoyed high esteem.—C. 10.54.

Atilianus tutor. See LEX ATILIA.

Atilicinus. A jurist of about the middle of the first century after Christ.

Joers, *RE* 2; Ferrini, *Opere* 2 (1929) 87.

Atilius. An unknown jurist of the second century B.C. —See SEMPRONIUS.

Atrox. Atrocious, dreadful. The attribute is applied to certain crimes accomplished with particular violence and cruelty, hence involving greater culpability and more severe punishment.

Atrox iniuria. See INIURIA ATROX.

Atrox vis. See VIS.

Attestatio. Unknown in the classical juristic language, the term is used in later imperial constitutions in the sense of testimony. Syn. *testatio, testimonium.*

Auctio. A public sale by auction. It was applied in certain cases. See SECTIO BONORUM, BONORUM VEN-

DITIO. When the auction was in the interest of the state, the *auctio* was performed by a *quaestor,* whereas when the sale of the property of an insolvent debtor was ordered at the request of his private creditors, a representative of the latter managed the sale. The owner himself might initiate a public sale of his property on his own behalf. The conditions of the *auctio* were publicly announced (*praedicere*); the assignment to the highest bidder *addicere.*—See HASTA, SUBHASTATIO, LICITARI.

Leist, *RE* 2, 2270; Humbert, *DS* 1; Platon, *NHRD* 33 (1909) 137.

Auctor. A person who by giving his approval, i.e., exercising his *auctoritas,* made valid the transaction of another person who was not able to conclude a transaction by himself. Such a person acting as an *auctor* was primarily the guardian (*tutor*) who *auctoritatem suam interponit* to the transaction concluded by his ward by declaring: *auctor fio* ("I approve"). Of the legally incapable ward it is said that he acts *tutore auctore. Auctor* is also used for the predecessor in title who transfers his right on another (a seller, for instance) and through the transaction assumes the guaranty that the acquirer will not be evicted from the thing transferred.—See LAUDARE AUCTOREM.

Auctor. In penal law, the person by whose influence, instigation or order, a crime was committed.

Humbert, *DS* 1.

Auctor legis. The proposer of a statute. Syn. *rogator.* Similarly, an emperor is named as *auctor senatusconsulti,* i.e., of the senatusconsult decreed on his proposal. Of the senators who by their *auctoritas* (approval) promote the passage of a law in the popular assemblies, it is said *patres auctores fiunt.*— See AUCTORITAS SENATUS.

Auctorati. Persons who hired themselves out for fighting as gladiators. Their condition was not far from that of slaves.—See ARENARII, GLADIATORES.

Kübler, *DE* 1, 769.

Auctores. With or without the qualifiers *iuris,* or *iuris scientiae,* or *scholae* = jurisprudents.

Humbert, *DS* 1.

Auctoritas. Authority, prestige; it is rather a moral power than a legal one. The term is used with regard to groups or persons who command obedience and respect. In this sense, legal and literary texts speak of *auctoritas* of the people (*populi*), of the emperor (*principis*), of the magistrates, judges, and jurisconsults, of a father or parents, as well as of that of a statute, of the law in general or of judicial judgments. A legally technical meaning *auctoritas* acquired in some fields of the private and public law. The significance of *auctoritas* varies according to the context in which it is used. Thus, in private law *auctoritas* occurs when a tutor acts as an *auctor* giving his assent (*auctoritatem interponere*) to a transaction concluded by his ward (*pupillus*) or by a woman under his guardianship. By his *auctoritas* he gives legal weight to the transaction. *Auctoritas* is also the guaranty assumed by the vendor when transferring his property.—See AUCTOR, ACTIO AUCTORITATIS, DENUNTIATIO EX AUCTORITATE, and the following items.

Leist, *RE* 2; Bozzi, *NDI* 1; Heinze, *Hermes* 60 (1925) 348; De Visscher, *RHD* 1933, 603 (= *Nouvelles Études,* 1949, 141); *idem, La jurisprudence romaine et la notion de l'auctoritas, Recueil Gény* 1 (1934) 32; *idem, RHD* 1937, 573; F. Fürst, *A. im Privat- und öffentlichen Leben der röm. Republik,* Diss. Marburg, 1934; F. Schulz, *Principles* 1936, 164; Kahrstedt, *Das Problem der a., Göttingische Gelehrte Anzeigen* 200 (1938) 17; R. Heinze, *Vom Geist des Römertums* (1938) 1; Wagenvoort-Tellenbach, *RAC* 1 (1943); Staedler, *ZSS* 61 (1941) 77, 100; 63 (1943) 384; H. Lévy-Bruhl, *Ann. Univ. Lyon* 1942 (= *Nouvelles Études,* 1947, 14); De Francisci, *Arcana imperii,* 3, 1 (1948) 245 (Bibl.); Amirante, *St Solazzi* (1948) 375; Brasiello, *ibid.* 689; Schönbauer, *St Wien,* 224, 2 (1946) 68; P. Noailles, *Fas et ius* (1948) 223; *idem, Du droit sacré au droit civil,* 1950, 236; Magdelain, *RIDA* 5 (= *Mél De Visscher* 4, 1950) 127; Roussier, *RHD* 29 (1951) 231.

Auctoritas patris. The approval by, the authority of, the head of a family (*pater familias*).

Solazzi, *Iura* 2 (1951) 133.

Auctoritas patrum. The ratification of statutes (and elections) voted in the popular assemblies by the senate (*patres auctores fiunt*). The word *"patrum"* is reminiscent of the original senate composed of patricians. Originally given subsequent to the vote of the *comitia,* the *auctoritas patrum* became later rather a mere formality when the procedure was changed and the senate gave its authorization before the matter passed to the *comitia* or *concilia plebis.*— See AUCTORITAS SENATUS, SENATUS, LEX MAENIA, LEX VALERIA HORATIA.

Lengle, *RE* 6A, 2467; O'Brien-Moore, *RE* Suppl. 6, 668, 677; Humbert, *DS* 1; Biscardi, *BIDR* 48 (1941) 403; Guarino, *Studi Solazzi* (1948); Biscardi, *RHD* 29 (1951) 151.

Auctoritas populi. Mentioned in connection with ADROGATIO for the validity of which the approval by the people assembled was necessary.

Auctoritas praefecti (praesidis). The personal authority and influence of the prefects (particularly of the *praefectus praetorio*) or of the provincial governors.

Auctoritas principis (principalis). The use of *auctoritas* with reference to the emperor first appears in the autobiography of Augustus (see RES GESTAE) in which he affirms, after having transferred the *res publica* to the senate and the people and after having received the title *Augustus* (January, 27 B.C.): "I was superior to all others in authority (*auctoritate praestiti*), but I had no more power (*potestas*) than my colleagues in the magistracy." *Auctoritas* means here personal authority, moral and social influence, while *potestas* embraces legal power. *Auctoritas* has no specific legal content, although after Augustus it

entered the official terminology. Generally speaking, it is the personal prestige, the authority, the high esteem which the emperor enjoyed as the first citizen in the state (*princeps*). It gave all his acts and orders a particular importance and significance in legislative, judicial, and administrative fields. Senatusconsults were issued *ex auctoritate principis* and the authorization of the jurists to give answers to legal questions addressed to them (*ius respondendi*) was referred to the *auctoritas principis.* In a few texts the *auctoritas* of certain emperors is stressed (Hadrian, Septimius Severus). Some emperors define their *auctoritas* as the source of their commands and decisions (*ex auctoritate nostra*) or underline the *auctoritas* of their rescripts and enactments. Thus their *auctoritas* is transferred to their ordinances themselves. Through the increasingly binding force of the imperial constitutions, the frequency of administrative orders of the emperors, and the privileges and distinctions granted to individuals by them, the content of *auctoritas principis* went beyond the mere personal authority and assumed sometimes the aspect of sovereignty. The term was never legally defined, not even under the absolute monarchy, although it is very frequent in imperial constitutions of the fourth and fifth centuries.—See CONSTITUTIONES PRINCIPUM, PRINCEPS.

A. v. Premerstein, *Vom Wesen und Werden des Prinzipats,* 1937; Kübler, *KrVj* 30 (1938) 29; A. Magdelain, *A.p.,* 1947; P. De Francisci, *Arcana imperii* 3, 1 (1948) 303; Kunkel, *ZSS* 66 (1948) 437; M. Grant, *From imperium to auctoritas,* 1946, 424; Pugliese and Carratelli, *La parola del passato* 10 (1949) 29; Last, *JRS* 40 (1950) 119.

Auctoritas prudentium. See AUCTORITAS.

Auctoritas rei iudicatae, auctoritas rerum similiter iudicatarum. See RES IUDICATA.

Auctoritas senatus. The previous or subsequent approval by the senate of statutes or elections voted in the popular assemblies. It is syn. with *auctoritas patrum* in the earlier centuries of the Roman history. In the later Republic the term is applied to those decrees of the senate which did not become *senatusconsulta* because of a formal defect or the intercession of a magistrate. In phrases like *auctoritas senatusconsulti, auctoritas* means the same thing as in references to statutes or other enactments.—See SENATUSCONSULTUM, AUCTORITAS, LEX PUBLILIA PHILONIS, AUCTORITAS PATRUM, INTERCESSIO.

Leist, *RE* 2, 2275; O'Brien-Moore, *RE* Suppl. 6, 718; Humbert, *DS* 1, 545; Volterra, *NDI* 12, 44; Kunkel, *ZSS* 66 (1948) 437.

Auctoritas tutoris. The cooperation (consent) of the guardian in transactions concluded by the ward (an *impubes,* a woman).—Inst. 1.21; D. 26.8; C. 5.59.— See AUCTORITAS, TUTELA.

Sachers, *RE* 7A, 1554; Solazzi, *ANap* 57 (1935) 212; *idem, SDHI* 12 (1946) 7; De Visscher, *ibid.* 9 (1943) 116; Solazzi, *Iura* 2 (1951) 133.

Audientia. Unknown in the language of the classical jurists the term is used in later imperial constitutions for legal proceedings, the judgment included.

Albertario, *SDHI* 2 (1936) 161.

Audientia episcopalis. See EPISCOPALIS AUDIENTIA.

Auditores. Law students attending the lectures of jurists. A group of pupils of the jurist Servius Sulpicius Rufus appears in the Digest as *auditores Servii.*

Auditorium. The audience hall in the imperial palace, used also as a court room. Later *auditorium* often means the court itself, sometimes even not an imperial one.

Kubitschek, *RE* 2; Humbert, *DS* 1.

Aufidius Chius. An unknown Roman jurist, of the first post-Christian century, mentioned only once in the Digest.

Jörs, *RE* 2, 2291 (no. 17).

Aufidius Namusa. One of the last Roman jurists under the Republic, a pupil of Servius Sulpicius Rufus and the editor of an extensive work composed of excerpts from the writings of Servius' disciples (*auditores Servii*).—See AUDITORES.

Jörs, *RE* 2, 2294 (no. 31); Kübler, *RE* 4A, 858.

Aufidius Tucca. Another of the pupils of Servius Sulpicius Rufus, like Aufidius Namusa.—See AUDITORES.

Jörs, *RE* 2, 2296 (no. 39).

Augures. A college of high priests among the *sacerdotes populi Romani*. Originally they were only three, but later their number gradually increased until 15 (16?). Certain priestly rituals were in their exclusive competence, in particular the interpretation of all kinds of auspices (*auspicia, auguria*) on any occasion when consultation of the will of the gods was obligatory (the appointment of high priests, of the *flamen Dialis* or of high magistrates [= *inauguratio*], the opening of *comitia* meetings, the performance of an important public action). Besides these official *augures* (*augures publici*), there were numerous *augures privati*, both in Rome and in Italy, who assisted citizens in their private *auspicia.* —See AGRIMENSORES, LEX DOMITIA, AUSPICIA, LEX OGULNIA, TEMPLUM, IUS AUGURIUM, COMMENTARII SACERDOTUM, DIVINATIO.

Wissowa, *RE* 2; *idem, Religion und Kultus der Römer,* 1902, 450, 523; Muller and Waszink, *RAC* 1, 975; Spinazzola, *DE* 1; F. David, *Le droit augural et la divination officielle chez les Rom.,* 1905; H. Baranger, *La théorie des auspices,* Thèse, Paris, 1941, 102; Coli, *SDHI* 17 (1951) 73.

Augusta. An honorary title of the emperor's wife conferred by the senate. The first *Augusta* was Livia, Augustus' wife; the title was conferred on her after her death. Exceptionally, the title was given also to a daughter of the emperor.

Neumann, *RE* 2, 2371; De Ruggiero, *DE* 1, 925.

Augustales. Persons associated in colleges devoted to the cult of Augustus. They were either priests (*sodales Augustales,* in Italian municipalities *seviri* [*sexviri*] *Augustales*) or private individuals corporate in a *collegium* (*corpus*) *Augustalium.*

Neumann, *RE* 2; Humbert, *DS* 1; v. Premerstein, *DE* 1, 828, 834; L. R. Taylor, *TAmPhilolA* 45 (1914) 238; Nock, *Mél Bidez* 2 (1934) 627; Hammond, *OCD* (1949) 783.

Augustalis. See PRAEFECTUS AUGUSTALIS.—D. 1.17; C. 1.37.

Augusti. Two emperors, each being simultaneously head of the state.—See CONSORS IMPERII.

Augustus. An honorary title conferred on the first Roman emperor, the founder of the Roman Principate, C. Iulius Caesar Octavianus (27 B.C.–A.D. 14), and then given by the Senate to his successors. It became later the usual title of the emperors. Justinian called himself *Semper Augustus.*—See CONSORTES IMPERII.

Neumann, *RE* 2; Schönbauer, *SbWien,* 224, 2 (1946) 67; M. Grant, *From imperium to auctoritas,* 1946, 444 (Bibl.).

Augustus. (Adj.) Connected with, or originating from, the emperor. The word occurs frequently in imperial constitutions.—See DOMUS AUGUSTA.

A(ulus) Agèrius. In Gaius' Institutes this fictitious name is used in the formulae of several actions for the plaintiff (*is qui agit,* hence Agerius). The defendant appears there as N(umerius) Negidius, an imaginary name originating in the words *numerare* and *negare,* since the defendant is the man who has to pay and normally denies the plaintiff's claim.

Wlassak, *RE* 1, 794.

Aurea. Golden words (sentences). It is the second title of Gaius' *Res Cottidianae,* probably added to the work in a later time.—See GAIUS, RES COTIDIANAE.

Aureus. A Roman gold coin of high value. As a monetary unit it was introduced by Caesar, equal to one hundred sesterces. Its gold content gradually diminished with the various monetary reforms. In Justinian's legislation it was substituted for one thousand sesterces (*sestertium*) in classical texts. Syn. SOLIDUS.

Lenormant, *DS* 1; Cesano, *Bull. della Commissione archeol. comunale di Roma,* 5, 6 (1929, 1930); Mattingly, *OCD* 210 (*s.v.* coinage); M. Bahrfeldt, *Die röm. Goldmünzenprägung,* 1923.

Aurum argentumque. A special tax imposed on merchants once in five years. Syn. *collatio lustralis.*

Ferrari, *AVen* 99, 2 (1939/40) 193.

Aurum coronarium. A conquered country had to provide the victorious Roman general an amount in gold as a contribution to be used for the manufacturing of a crown for the triumphant commander when he returned to Rome.—See TRIUMPHUS.—C. 10.76.

Kubitschek, *RE* 2; Humbert, *DS* 1; Moschella, *NDI* 4 (*s.v. coronarium aurum*); Schubart, *Arch. für Papyrusforschung* 14 (1941) 44; T. Klausen, *Mitt. Deutsch. Archäol. Inst. Rom, Röm. Abt.* 59 (1944, published 1948) 129; *idem, RAC* 1, 1014; Lacombrade, *Rev. études anciennes* 51 (1949) 54.

Aurum tironicum. See TEMO.

Kubitschek, *RE* 1; Humbert, *DS* 1.

Aurum vicesimarium. See VICESIMA MANUMISSIONUM.

Auspicato. After having obtained approval of the gods through favorable *auspicia*.

Auspicia. The observation of certain natural phenomena by competent priests (AUGURES) in order to explore whether or not the gods approve an important public action about to be launched. When the signs observed (*ex coelo* = from the sky, such as thunder, *ex avibus* = from the flight of birds, *ex tripudio* = feeding chickens from a tripedal vessel, etc.) were interpreted by the priests in an unfavorable sense, the action was dropped. The right to order *auspicia* (*ius auspiciorum*) was a prerogative of the higher magistrates and was sometimes misused in order to thwart an action proposed by another magistrate. The non-observance of *auspicia* or action in defiance of an unfavorable prediction (*contra auspicia facta*) might lead to the annulment of the whole action by the competent magistrate.—See OBNUNTIATIO.

Wissowa, *RE* 2; *idem, Religion u. Kultus der Römer*, 1902, 454; Bouché-Leclercq, *DS* 1; Stella-Maranca, *NDI* 1; Ericsson, *Arch. für Religionswiss.* 33 (1936) 294; H. Baranger, *La théorie des auspices,* Thèse, Paris, 1941; Coli, *SDHI* 17 (1951) 96.

Authenticum. The original of a written document. *Authenticae tabulae testamenti* = the original written will of a testator.—Ant. *tabulae descriptae* (= a copy).—See EXEMPLUM.

Authenticum (or **Authenticae** *sc. Novellae*). A collection of 134 Novels promulgated by Justinian between A.D. 535 and 556, after the publication of the second edition of his Code. The Greek Novels are translated into Latin therein, not always quite correctly. The date (eleventh century?) and place of the origin of the *Authenticum* are unknown. It was first considered a forgery, but the Law School in Bologna established its authenticity (hence the name *Authenticum*).—See NOVELLAE IUSTINIANI.

Tamassia, *AVen* 1908; Scherillo, *ACSR* 1935; *Index titulorum Authentici in novem collationes digesti, Sem* 2 (1944) 82.

Auxilia. Military units recruited in the provinces from men lacking Roman citizenship (*peregrini*) and therefore excluded from service in the legions. The *auxiliarii* (= the soldiers of the *auxilia*) were discharged after twenty-five years of service (*missio honesta*). On that occasion they were granted Roman citizenship in a document called a *diploma*.

De Ruggiero, *DE* 1, 952; *Corpus Inscr. Latinarum* 16; Riccobono, *FIR* 1² (1941) 223; Porteous, *OCD;* G. L. Cheesman, *The a. of the imperial army,* 1914; R. Marichal, *L'occupation rom. de la Basse Égypte. Le statut des auxilia,* 1945.

Auxiliarii. See AUXILIA.

Auxilium. The assistance, protection given by the plebeian tribunes, first to plebeians only and later to all citizens, against wrongful acts of the magistrates.—See TRIBUNI PLEBIS, INTERCESSIO.

Aversio. *Emere per aversionem* (*in aversione* or *aversione*) to buy with a lump sum.

Avulsio. The term does not appear in Roman juristic language, but is familiar in literature. It indicates a piece of land carried away from its owner's property by flowing water and attached to another's land.—See ALLUVIO.

Leonhard, *RE* 2; Pampaloni, *Scritti* 1 (1941) 431 (ex 1884), 507 (ex 1885); *idem, StSen* 43 (1929) 214.

Azo (Azzo). A famous glossator (see GLOSSATORES), professor in the Law School in Bologna (1190–1229), renowned for his commentary to Justinian's Code (*Summa Codicis*).

Orestano, *NDI* 2, 172 (*s.v. Azzone*); Maitland, *Select passages from the works of Bracton and Azo,* 1895.

B

Bacchanalia. Orgiastic rites in the worship of Bacchus, forbidden by the SENATUSCONSULTUM DE BACCHANALIBUS.

De Ruggiero, *DE* 1, 957.

Baldus (de Ubaldis). A famous post-glossator, pupil of Bartolus, professor of law in various Italian universities. He died about 1400.—See GLOSSATORES.

L'opera di Baldo (per cura dell'Univ. di Perugia) 1901; Monti, *NDI* 2 (Bibl.).

Balineum (balnearia, balneum). A bath-house. Theft committed here, *furtum balnearium,* is considered as a theft to be punished more severely.—D. 47.17.—See BALNEATOR.

De Ruggiero, *DE* 1, 964.

Balneator. The owner of a bath-house or the lessee of a public bathing establishment. The supervision of baths and of their management was in the competence of the *aediles*. A *balneator* who exploited his enterprise for immoral purposes ("as happens in certain provinces," D. 3.2.4.2) was published as a procurer (see LENO).—C. 4.59.—See BALINEUM.

Barbari. Originally the Romans used this name for any foreign people with a strange language and savage customs. Later the term was extended to enemies of the Roman state and to countries not bound to Rome by a treaty.

Ruge, *RE* 2; Humbert, *DS* 1; Vismara, *Scr Ferrini* 1 (Univ. Sacro Cuore, Milan, 1947) 445.

Bartolus De Saxoferrato (1313–1357). Professor of law in Perugia. He was one of the so-called postglossators, commentators on Justinian's codification in the fourteenth century, and exercised great influence on the development of late medieval law.—See GLOSSATORES.

Monti, *NDI* 2; Buonamici, *B. de S. in Pisa,* 1914; J. L. van de Kamp, *B. de S. Leven, werken,* etc., Amsterdam, 1936; A. T. Scheedy, *B. on social conditions in the fourteenth century,* 1942 (New York).

Basilica. A Byzantine codification (termed by Byzantine writers *Basilikos* [*sc. nomos*], i.e., imperial

[law]) in sixty books. It was initiated by the Emperor of Byzance, Basil the Macedonian, and completed in the reign of his son, Leo the Wise, early in the tenth century. Starting from a sharp criticism of Justinian's codification for having dealt with the same topics in its various parts, Leo ordered the collection into single titles of provisions, taken from Justinian's Institutes, Digest, and Code, and also from the Novels, which dealt with each particular topic. He followed, however, Justinian's example by further ordering that superfluous, controversial, and obsolete matters be omitted. Apart from some legal provisions of the legislation of post-Justinian emperors the *Basilica* are thus an abridged Greek summary of Justinian's codification, at times even a more or less literal translation of single texts thereof. Works of writers of Justinian's time were exploited in a large measure for the codification, in particular, for the Digest texts a summary (*index*) by an unknown author (see ANONYMUS), for excerpts from Justinian's Code a commentary thereon by THALELAEUS. Only about two-thirds of the *Basilica* are preserved in the known manuscripts. The contents of the missing portions are revealed by a repertory ("table of contents"), called TIPOUKEITOS (= "where is what"). Some of the *Basilica* manuscripts are also provided with scholia, i.e., excerpts from juristic literature written on Justinian's legislation during his lifetime and afterwards (the so-called "older" scholia); a considerable number of scholia belong to juristic works of post-Basilican times. The scholia preserved are even more incomplete than the *Basilica* themselves, some manuscripts of the *Basilica* being preserved without scholia at all. The *Basilica* constitute a legal monument of the highest importance for our knowledge of Justinian and post-Justinian law in the Byzantine Empire, and for the criticism of some texts of Justinian's Digest and Code in instances in which the Greek text of the *Basilica* and their scholia is better preserved than in the Latin manuscripts of Justinian's legislation.

Edition (with Latin translation): G. E. Heimbach, *Basilicorum libri 60*, 1–6 (1833–1870), Suppl. 1, ed. Zachariae v. Lingenthal (1846), Suppl. 2, ed. Mercati and Ferrini (1897); ed. without translation by J. Zepos, *Basilica* (2nd ed., Athens, 1910–1912).—Lawson, *LQR* 46, 47. (1930, 1931); *idem, ZSS* 49 (1929); Arangio-Ruiz, *St Albertoni* 1 (1925); Scheltema, *Probleme der Basiliken, TR* 16 (1939) 320; Guarino, *Scr Ferrini* (Univ. Pavia), 1946, 307; Berger, *Scritti Ferrini* 3 (Univ. Sacro Cuore, Milan, 1948) 194; *idem, To kata podas, BIDR* 55–56 (1952) 65.

Beatissimus. An attribute of the emperors in the fourth century.

De Ruggiero, *DE* 1, 984.

Beatitudo. A title of the highest church dignitaries.

Bellum. According to a tradition, it was the legendary founder of Rome, Romulus, who granted the Roman people the right to decide about war, and—according to Cicero (*De rep.* 2.17.31)—it was the third king of Rome, Tullus Hostilius who introduced the formal declaration of war (*bellum indicere*) by the *fetiales* since a war waged without prior declaration to the enemy was considered unjust (*iniustum*) and impious (*impium*). Later it was in the competence of the *comitia centuriata* to decide about the declaration of war (*lex de bello indicendo*).—See SENATUS, DENUNTIARE, FETIALES, INDICERE BELLUM, LEGES DE BELLO INDICENDO, IUS FETIALE, OCCUPATIO, DEDITIO, INDUTIAE, REPETITIO RERUM.

Liebenam, *RE* 4, 696; Berger, *RE* Suppl. 7, 383; Larsen, *OCD* 958; C. Phillipson, *Intern. law of Greece and Rome* 2 (1911) 166; E. Seckel, *Krieg und Recht in Rom.*, 1915; Heuss, *Klio, Beiheft* 31 (1933) 18.

Beneficiarii. Soldiers of a lower rank to whom their superiors granted the liberation from certain duties (*munera*). In the Empire the term indicates not only persons who had obtained a benefit (*beneficium*) from the emperor or from a military commander but also the assistants (staff) of high military and civil officials.

Domaszewski, *RE* 3; Masquelez, *DS* 1; De Ruggiero, *DE* 1, 994; O. Hirschfeld, *Kleine Schriften*, 1913, 581; Lopuszanski, *AntCl* 20 (1951) 7.

Beneficium. A legal benefit or remedy of an exceptional character, granted in certain legal situations or to a specific category of persons by a statute, the praetorian edict, a senatusconsult or by the emperor (imperial constitutions). With regard to this last source the term is applied to privileges granted by the emperor to individuals, groups of persons, municipalities or whole provinces.—See COMMENTARII BENEFICIORUM.

Leonhard, *RE* 3; Baudry, *DS* 1; De Ruggiero, *DE* 1; Orestano, *St Riccobono* 3 (1936) 473.

Beneficium abstinendi. Syn. *ius abstinendi.*—See ABSTINERE (SE) HEREDITATE.

Beneficium aetatis. See VENIA AETATIS, RESTITUTIO IN INTEGRUM.

Beneficium cedendarum actionum. Before paying the principal's debt the surety could demand cession of the actions the creditor had against the principal and other sureties.—See CESSIO.

G. Nocera, *Insolvenza e responsabilità sussidiaria*, 1942, 89.

Beneficium competentiae. The term coined in literature and generally accepted although unknown in Roman juristic language indicates the right of a debtor in certain cases to be condemned only "to what he can do (pay)" (*in id quod* [*quantum*] *facere potest* was the pertinent clause, inserted into the *condemnatio* part of the formula). *Facere* means here "as far as his means permit" (*quatenus facultates eius permittunt*). The exceptional measure is granted in actions in which there was a specific relationship between plaintiff and defendant (for instance, when the debtor was an ascendant, a patron or a former partner of the creditor, actions between husband and wife) or in which the claim had a specific character (claim by the donee for fulfillment of a donation promised, payment of a dowry promised but not given, restitution of a dowry). Soldiers may oppose the *beneficium competentiae* in any claim directed against them. The financial capacity of the defendant was differently estimated (*taxatio*) in the various cases. The *beneficium competentiae* was strictly personal and not available to sureties. Its purpose was to protect the debtor from being deprived of the necessary means of subsistence.—See FACULTATES, FACERE POSSE, CONDEMNATIO.

> Weiss, *RE* 17 (*s.v. Notbedarf*); Pampaloni, *RISG* 52 (1912) 198; Zanzucchi, *BIDR* 29 (1916) 61; A. Levet, *Le bénéfice de compétence*, 1927; Guarino, *RendLomb* 72, 2 (1938/9) 355, 401; *idem, Fschr Koschaker* 2 (1939) 49; *idem, SDHI* 7 (1941) 5; *idem, RISG* 14 (1939) 153; *idem, Scr Ferrini* 1 (Univ. Sacro Cuore, Milan, 1947) 299.

Beneficium divisionis. Hadrian limited the liability of *fideiussores* (sureties by FIDEIUSSIO) to the share resulting from the division of the principal debt by the number of solvent sureties.

> Collinet, *St Albertoni* 1 (1935) 271; G. Nocera, *Insolvenza* (1942) 101, 198.

Beneficium excussionis (or ordinis). Both terms coined in literature. Justinian gave a surety the right to compel the creditor who had sued him before the principal, to sue the principal first.

Beneficium inventarii. According to an enactment of Justinian, an heir had the right to call for an inventory of the inheritance. This gave him the benefit that he was liable for the debts of the testator and the legacies only to the amount of three quarters of the estate, the remaining fourth being reserved to him as the so-called *quarta Falcidia* (see LEX FALCIDIA). The inventory was made in the presence of a notary and representatives of the creditors of the estate. Failure to request the *beneficium inventarii* within the prescribed term (thirty days after notice of his institution as an heir) made the *heres* fully liable and deprived him of the Falcidian quarter.—See INVENTARIUM, SEPARATIO BONORUM.

Beneficium ordinis. See BENEFICIUM EXCUSSIONIS.

Beneficium separationis. See SEPARATIO BONORUM.

Benigna interpretatio. A liberal, beneficial interpretation of a legal provision or of an individual expression of will in legal transactions or testaments. "Laws are to be interpreted in a more liberal manner provided that their intention be respected" (D. 1.3.18). "In criminal matters a more benign interpretation (sc. in favor of the accused) should be applied" (D. 50.17.155.2)—See INTERPRETATIO, RES DUBIAE, HUMANITAS, and the following item.

Benigne (benignius), benignitas. All these expressions are used in legal texts to introduce decisions which, dictated by considerations of a moral rather than a legal nature, are contrary to the strict rules of law. Good will, charity, benevolence, and humanity are frequently invoked in order to save a transaction or legal situation in favor of a person, without any further argumentation. Sometimes the decision is given abruptly (*sed benignius est*), just contrary to the one which may be expected. The classicality of such texts has long been suspected and the terms mentioned above have been considered criteria of interpolations. There is no doubt that many of the decisions based exclusively on *benignitas* and similar conceptions, such as *pietas, caritas, benevolentia, clementia,* are not of classical origin. The influence of Christian doctrines and philosophical ideas is undeniable. But a general stigmatization of all the pertinent texts invoking *benignitas* may be one of the usual exaggerations in the interpolationistic research. *Benignitas* and analogous terms are familiar in Cicero and other literary sources. There is no reason to exclude a saying like this one: "In doubtful matters preference should always be given to the more benign (benevolent, liberal) solution" (*semper in dubiis benigniora praeferenda sunt*), inserted in the Digest title "On various rules of the ancient law" (50.17.56), from the classical law. The rule appears in other texts in similar words. The road from *benignitas* to *aequitas* is not a long one and one text (D. 1.3.25, by Modestinus) speaks directly of *aequitatis benignitas.*—See BENIGNA INTERPRETATIO, AEQUITAS.

> Guarneri-Citati, *Indice delle parole,* etc. 2 (1927) 14 and *Fschr Koschaker* 1 (1939) 123; Albertario, *BIDR* 33 (1923) 65, 73; Laborderie-Boulou, *RHD* 26 (1948) 137; Berger, *In dubiis benigniora, ACIVer* 1 (1951) 187 (= *Sem* 9 [1951] 36).

Berytus. Beirut. There was a famous law school here which flourished particularly in the fifth and sixth centuries after Christ. It had a fixed curriculum and its professors (*antecessores*) were appointed by the state. Two of them (Dorotheus and Anatolius) were selected by Justinian, who speaks of the Phoenician city with high praise ("the city of the laws," *legum nutrix* = the nurse of the laws), for collaboration in his codification. Fifth-century teachers at *Berytus:* Patricius, Cyrillus, Domninus, Demosthenes, and Eudoxius, were held in great esteem.—C. 11.22.

> Kübler, *RE* 1A, 398; P. De Francisci, *Vita e studi a Berito,* 1912; Peters, *Die oströmischen Digestenkommentare,* 1913, 60; Pringsheim, *Beryt und Bologna, Fschr Lenel* 1921, 204; P. Collinet, *Histoire de l'école de droit à Beyrouth,* 1925.

Bes. Two-thirds of an *as* (= eight *unciae*). *Bes* indicates two-thirds of any whole (an estate, for instance).—See AS.

Bestiae ferae. See FERAE BESTIAE, ANIMUS REVERTENDI, OBICERE BESTIIS.

Bimus. See ANNUA, BIMA DIE.

Bina sponsalia. See BINAE NUPTIAE.

Binae nuptiae. The Latin language has no word for bigamy. Speaking of bigamy, later juristic language used the locution *binas uxores habere.* According to the Roman conception of marriage the existence of two simultaneous marriages was legally impossible since the first marriage was considered automatically dissolved through the absence of the essential elements (AFFECTIO MARITALIS, uninterrupted living in common). The praetorian edict punished, however, with infamy a person who attempted to constitute two marital unions at the same time. Two betrothals (*bina sponsalia*) were punished as well. Under certain conditions, a bigamist might be accused of STUPRUM, a bigamous woman of adultery. In post-classical law bigamy was punished as a specific crime.—See INFAMIA.

Volterra, *St Ratti* (1933) 299; P. Rasi, *Consensus facit nuptias* (1946) 194.

Binas uxores habere. See BINAE NUPTIAE.

Bis idem exigere. To claim (to sue for) the same thing twice from the same debtor. "Good faith does not allow (*bona fides non patitur*) the same thing to be twice exacted" (D. 50.17.57). The same is expressed in the rule: *bis de eadem re ne sit actio*.—See EADEM RES, RES IUDICATA, LITIS CONTESTATIO, REPETERE ACTIONEM.

Biondi, *AnPal* 7 (1920) 38.

Bona. The whole of a person's property. The term has a specific application in the praetorian law (*in bonis esse, missio in bona*), and in the law of succession, both civil and praetorian. See BONORUM POSSESSIO. *Bona* as a whole embraces not only corporeal things but also rights and debts. In certain loculations, however, it is employed in the sense of corporeal things only. Syn. (often) *patrimonium*.—See the following items, IN BONIS ESSE, MISSIO IN BONA, CONSECRATIO, UNIVERSITAS BONORUM.

Leonhard, *RE* 3; Humbert, *DS* 1; Donatuti, *NDI* 2; Pfaff, *Fschr Hanausek*, 1925; P. Collinet, *B. et patrimonium*, *Études Andréades* (Athens, 1940) 377; Lemarignier, *L'apparition du mot bona*, *RHD* 21 (1942) 224.

Bona adventicia. See PECULIUM ADVENTICIUM.

Bona caduca. See CADUCA.

Bona damnatorum. Property confiscated from persons condemned to capital punishment (loss of life, liberty or citizenship) in a criminal trial.—D. 48.20; C. 9.49.—See PUBLICATIO.

Humbert, *DS* 1; De Ruggiero, *DE* 1; L. Clerici, *Economia e finanze dei Romani*, 1943, 497.

Bona fides. Honesty, uprightness, good faith. The term has various applications. Generally it is opposed to *mala fides, fraus, dolus, dolus malus*. Certain common rules are derived from *bona fides*, such as: "*bona fides* requires that what has been agreed upon be done" (D. 19.2.21) which is expressed in other words by the saying: "*bona fides* demands highest equity (honesty, *aequitas*) in contracts" (D. 16.3.31 pr.). What is dishonest, immoral is considered *contra bonam fidem*. In contractual law, the *bona fides* is particularly important not only because of the rules mentioned above, but also because certain types of contract are based on *bona fides*, as the reciprocal confidence, honesty, good faith of the parties,

at both the conclusion and the execution of the assumed duties. Trials arising from such contracts are judged from the point of view of honesty and fairness (*iudicia bonae fidei*). Acting *bona fide* (e.g., *emere, vendere, solvere, facere*) or exercising certain rights connected with a factual situation (*bona fide possidere*) presumes the belief of a person that what he is doing is lawful and does not violate another's right. Such an erroneous belief may even be to the detriment of the person involved, as when a free man *bona fide* considers himself a slave and acts as such (*liber homo bona fide serviens*).—See FIDES (Bibl.), IUDICIA BONAE FIDEI, CONTRACTUS BONAE FIDEI, LIBER HOMO, etc., USUCAPIO, BIS IDEM EXIGERE, POSSESSOR BONAE FIDEI.

Leonhard, *RE* 3; Humbert, *DS* 1; Montel, *NDI* 2; Bonfante, *Scritti giur.* 2 (1926) 708; Pringsheim, *ConfMil* 1931, 201; Collinet, *Mél Fournier*, 1929, 71; J. Faure, *Iusta causa et bonne foi*, Lausanne, 1936.

Bona liberti. A freedman's property.—See ADSIGNATIO LIBERTI.

Bona materna. Everything that a *filius familias* acquires from his mother through a testament or by intestacy. *Bona materni generis* are his acquisitions from maternal ascendants. Though the ownership of these *bona* goes to his father (*pater familias*), the latter according to a law of Constantine, has not the right to alienate them, but he has the usufruct during his lifetime.—C. 6.60.

Bona materni generis. See BONA MATERNA.

Bona proscriptorum. See PROSCRIPTIO.—C. 9.49.

Bona vacantia. An estate without any heir under a will or by intestacy. In earlier law, it could be acquired by USUCAPIO PRO HEREDE. Under the Empire it was taken by the fisc, which also assumed the debts of the deceased. Syn. *bona vacua*.—C. 10.10.—See PROCURATOR HEREDITATIUM.

Leonhard, *RE* 3; Humbert, *DS* 1; Erdmann, *RE* 7A, 2026.

Bona vi rapta. See RAPINA.

Bonae fidei possessor. See POSSESSOR BONAE FIDEI.

Bonam copiam iurare. See IURARE BONAM COPIAM.

Boni mores. (Ant. *mali mores*.) Customary principles of good, honest and moral behavior, recognized and traditionally observed by the people (*mores populi, mores antiqui*). The locution acquires legal importance when something is done in violation of what, according to common feelings, is required by the *boni mores* (*adversus* or *contra bonos mores*).—See MORES, CONTRA BONOS MORES, ILLICITUS.

Senn, *Recueil d'études en l'honneur de F. Gény* 1 (1935) 53; Kaser, *ZSS* 60 (1940) 100.

Bonis interdicere. See INTERDICTIO BONORUM.

Bonorum addictio. See ADDICTIO BONORUM.

Bonorum cessio. See CESSIO BONORUM.

Bonorum collatio. See COLLATIO BONORUM.

Bonorum curator. See CURATOR BONORUM.

Bonorum distractio. See DISTRACTIO BONORUM.

Bonorum emptio. The counterpart to *bonorum venditio*.—See BONORUM VENDITIO.

Bonorum emptor. The buyer of the property of a bankrupt.—See BONORUM VENDITIO, ACTIO RUTILIANA, DEDUCTIO.

Bonorum interdictio. See INTERDICERE BONIS.

Bonorum possessio. The law of succession introduced by the praetors as a system of inheritance parallel to that of the *ius civile,* in order to correct certain iniquities (*iniquitates*) in the latter. Literally *bonorum possessio* means the possession of an estate given by the praetor to a person (*bonorum possessor*) without regard to whether or not he had the right of succession in the specific case under the civil law (*ius civile*). Practically the *bonorum possessor* had a legal position similar to that of a universal successor without being called *heres,* since that term is reserved to those who succeeded into the entire property of the deceased under the *ius civile.* An old rule says: *praetor heredes facere non potest* (= the praetor cannot make *heredes,* Gai *Inst.* 3.32; Iust. *Inst.* 3.9.2), but he might give a person factual possession of the inheritance and thus create a legal situation similar to that of the civil *heres.* In granting *bonorum possessio,* the praetor originally followed the rules of succession of the *ius civile,* but in the later development, new rules of succession were introduced by him which differed essentially from the civil law. Thus conflicts might arise between persons claiming their rights to an inheritance on the ground of the civil law and those who obtained possession of the estate from the praetor. The praetorian law was ultimately triumphant. The most important advantage of the praetorian *bonorum possessor* was the INTERDICTUM QUORUM BONORUM, available to him against anyone who held things belonging to the estate. In comparison with *hereditatis petitio* the procedural benefits of this remedy were so important (especially in the matter of evidence) that even civil law successors (*heredes*) asked for *bonorum possessio* in order to profit by the praetorian protection. The *bonorum possessor* has the actions of the civil *heres,* but he might use them only as *actiones utiles* with the fiction "as if he were *heres.*" For the recovery of single objects he had the *actio Publiciana* instead of the *rei vindicatio,* which makes his situation as a plaintiff much easier. With the disappearance of the formulary procedure, the differences between the two systems gradually lost their significance. The imperial legislation promoted the fusion of the two systems which in the past had created a dualism, with its unavoidable conflicting situations in specific cases. Under Justinian, the fusion is completed. Terms used before for the civil law of succession were now used with reference to the *bonorum possessio;* the *bonorum possessores* are mentioned alongside the *heredes* in interpolated texts either expressly or by the general expression *"ceteri successores."* A *bonorum possessio* was given by the praetor (*dare bonorum possessionem*) only on request. There was no *bonorum possessio ipso iure.* No one acquired the *bonorum possessio* against his will. For the different kinds of *bonorum possessio,* see the following items.—Inst. 3.9.; D. 37.1; 38.13; C. 6.9.—See AGNITIO BONORUM POSSESSIONIS, INTERDICTUM QUORUM BONORUM, USUCAPIO PRO HEREDE, HEREDITATIS PETITIO POSSESSORIA.

　Leonhard, *RE* 3; Humbert, *DS* 1; Donatuti, *NDI* 2; Crescenzio, *NDI* 12, 940; Biondi, *Concetti fondamentali del dir. ereditario* 1 (1946) 83; Timbal, *RHD* 19–20, (1940–41) 368.

Bonorum possessio ab intestato. See BONORUM POSSESSIO INTESTATI.

Bonorum possessio contra tabulas. In certain cases, the praetor granted the possession of the estate contrary to the will of the testator, in particular when an emancipated son was passed over in silence in the will, without being either instituted as heir or expressly disinherited. Other dispositions of the will, such as manumissions, legacies, appointments of guardians, disinheritances remained valid. Special rules on behalf of a patron and his children provided for a *bonorum possessio* contrary to the will of his freedman; see BONORUM POSSESSIO DIMIDIAE PARTIS.—D. 37.4; 5; C. 6.12; 13.

　Düll, *RE* 17 (*s.v. Noterbrecht*); L. Maissonnier, *B.p.c.t.,* These Bordeaux, 1905; G. La Pira, *La successione ereditaria intestata e contro il testamento,* 1930.

Bonorum possessio cum re. Cases of *bonorum possessio* in which the *bonorum possessor* retained the inheritance against the claim of the *heres* under *ius civile.* *Cum re* (= *cum effectu*) = effectively. Ant. *bonorum possessio sine re* (= without effect), when in a conflict between the *heres* and the *bonorum possessor,* the latter was defeated. When the praetors began to grant *bonorum possessio* against the rules of the *ius civile,* the *bonorum possessio* was mostly *sine re;* in the later development the *bonorum possessio cum re* prevailed.

Bonorum possessio decretalis. Ant. *bonorum possessio edictalis.* The latter occurred when the *bonorum possessio* was given by the praetor in cases fixed in the praetorian edict. *Bonorum possessio decretalis* instead was when the praetor after investigation of the specific circumstances granted the *bonorum possessio* in a case not foreseen in the edict. The praetor's decree was issued in such cases in court (*pro tribunali*) whereas the *bonorum possessio edictalis* was given more informally (*de plano*). Examples of *bonorum possessio decretalis* are the *bonorum possessio* granted to the mother of an unborn child (BONORUM POSSESSIO VENTRIS NOMINE) and the BONORUM POSSESSIO EX CARBONIANO EDICTO.

　Solazzi, *AG* 100 (1928) 17.

Bonorum possessio dimidiae partis. This took place when a freedman died without leaving a testament and his heirs in intestacy were only adopted children or a wife *in manu*. In this case the praetor granted the patron a *bonorum possessio* of half the freedman's property. The same happened when a freedman who had no children or disinherited them, did not leave his patron (or the latter's children) a half of his estate. In the latter case the *bonorum possessio* was *contra tabulas*.

G. La Pira, *Successione hereditaria intestata*, 1930, 395; C. Cosentini, *St sui liberti* 1 (1948) 189, 2 (1950) 24, 155.

Bonorum possessio edictalis. See BONORUM POSSESSIO DECRETALIS.

Bonorum possessio ex Carboniano edicto (Carboniana). The praetorian edict provided that an *impubes* whose legitimacy was contested might be granted a temporary *bonorum possessio intestati* until he reached puberty and his status of a legitimate child was decided in his favor.—D. 37.10; C. 6.17.

Niedermeyer, *ZSS* 50 (1930) 78.

Bonorum possessio ex testamento militis. See TESTAMENTUM MILITIS.—D. 37.13.

Bonorum possessio furiosi nomine. A *bonorum possessio decretalis* granted to the curator of an insane. It was provisory and became definite when the insane regained capacity.—D. 37.3.

H. Krüger, *ZSS* 64 (1944) 408.

Bonorum possessio intestati (ab intestato). Succession according to praetorian law in case of intestacy. Taking into consideration the cognatic tie alongside the agnatic one (an emancipated son, for instance) and favoring in a larger measure the relatives and the surviving spouse of the deceased the praetor admitted to an intestate succession a number of persons excluded by the *ius civile*. The praetorian successors on intestacy were classified in four groups (classes), which the jurists identified by adding the word *"unde"* (*ex ea parte edicti unde . . . vocantur* = from that part of the edict under which the pertinent group was entitled to the *bonorum possessio*). Persons of a lower-ranking group were eligible only when there were no successors in the foregoing class or if the existing successors repudiated the inheritance (*successio ordinum*). The first group, *unde liberi,* embraced all children of the deceased, including those emancipated, but excluding children adopted into another family. An emancipated son did not exclude his children who had remained in the family of his father (i.e., their grandfather). Later, according to an innovation ascribed to the jurist Julian (*nova clausula Iuliani*), the emancipated son received half of the appropriate portion of the estate, the other half being reserved for his children. The second group, *unde legitimi,* embraced the *agnates* who were *heredes* under the civil law (*heredes legitimi*). The third group, *unde cognati,* comprized cognates until the sixth and (partly) seventh degrees, primarily persons excluded from inheritance under the *ius civile*. An innovation here was also the *successio graduum;* if the nearest cognate failed to claim the *bonorum possessio* or refused the succession, the right to claim passed to the cognates of the next degree. In the fourth class, reciprocal rights to succession were given to husband and wife in the absence of persons entitled in the foregoing classes, regardless of whether or not the wife was *in manu* of her husband. In an analogous manner, the praetorian law reformed the intestate succession of a freedman's estate establishing in a somewhat complicated manner seven classes of eligible persons, from the children of the freedman to the cognates of his patron.—D. 38.6–8; 11: C. 6.14; 15; 18.

G. La Pira, *La successione ereditaria intestata e contro il testamento*, 1930.

Bonorum possessio iuris civilis adiuvandi (confirmandi) gratia. A *bonorum possessio* given to a person who is entitled to the inheritance under the civil law (*ius civile*).

Bonorum possessio iuris civilis corrigendi (emendandi) gratia. A *bonorum possessio* given to persons not entitled under the *ius civile* to the exclusion of those so entitled.

Bonorum possessio iuris civilis supplendi gratia. A *bonorum possessio* given to a person who is not entitled to inherit under the *ius civile,* but without the exclusion of persons so entitled; when, for instance, an emancipated son inherits under praetorian law together with those not emancipated.

Bonorum possessio liberti intestati. See BONORUM POSSESSIO INTESTATI.

Lavaggi, *StCagl* 30 (1946).

Bonorum possessio litis ordinandae gratia. A *bonorum possessio* granted exceptionally to persons who would be entitled to a *bonorum possessio intestati,* in order to enable them to impugn the will of the deceased as *testamentum inofficiosum*.—See QUERELA INOFFICIOSI TESTAMENTI

Bonorum possessio secundum tabulas. A *bonorum possessio* given to the heirs instituted in a will, which although void under the *ius civile* was, however, valid according to the praetorian law, the requirements of which were less formal than those of the *ius civile*. —D. 37.11; C. 6.11.—See TESTAMENTUM, TESTAMENTUM PRAETORIUM.

Bonorum possessio sine re. See BONORUM POSSESSIO CUM RE.

Arnò, *Mem. Accad. di Modena* 12 (1914).

Bonorum possessio unde cognati. See BONORUM POSSESSIO INTESTATI.

Bonorum possessio unde legitimi. See BONORUM POSSESSIO INTESTATI.

Bonorum possessio unde liberi. See BONORUM POSSESSIO INTESTATI.

Bonorum possessio unde vir et uxor. See BONORUM POSSESSIO INTESTATI.

Bonorum possessio ventris nomine. A *bonorum possessio* granted to a pregnant woman whose child is presumed to be the successor of the deceased father.

This is provisory until the legitimacy of the child born and his rights of succession are established.—D. 37.9.

Bonorum possessionem petere. See AGNITIO BONORUM POSSESSIONES.

Bonorum possessor. A person to whom the praetor granted a *bonorum possessio.* "He succeeds in the place of the deceased under praetorian law" (Gai *Inst.* 4.34).—See BONORUM POSSESSIO and the following items, AGNITIO BONORUM POSSESSIONIS, ACTIONES FICTICIAE.

Bonorum proscriptio. See PROSCRIBERE BONA.

Bonorum sectio. See SECTIO BONORUM.

Bonorum separatio. See SEPARATIO BONORUM.

Bonorum venditio. The sale of the whole property (*bona*) of an insolvent debtor who even after it had been given into possession (*missio in possessionem*) of a creditor or creditors, failed to come to terms with them. The sale, an auction, was managed by a *magister* under the supervision of the praetor. The property is assigned to the highest bidder (*bonorum emptor, bonorum emptio*). The buyer had an interdict (*interdictum possessorium*) to obtain the possession of things belonging to the debtor's *bona* that were held by another.—Inst. 3.12; C. 7.72.—See LEX VENDITIONIS, DEDUCTIO.

Leonhard, *RE* 3 (*s.v. b. emptio*); Beaudry-Beauchet-Collinet, *DS* 5 (*s.v. venditio b.*); Armuzzi, *AG* 72 (1904) 496; Triandafil, *Du rôle du curator et magister dans la b. v., Rev. de droit et sociologie* 1 (1916); Rotondi, *Cent CodPav,* 1933; Carrelli, *SDHI* 4 (1937) 429, 10 (1944) 302; Solazzi, *Il concorso dei creditori* 2 (1938) 61, 130; *idem, La compensazione* 2 (1950) 65.

Bonum et aequum (aequum et bonum). (Also without "*et.*") Right and equitable, fair (ness) and just (ice). The words appear in the definition of *ius* by the jurist Celsus (*ius est ars boni et aequi*), in the formula of *actiones in aequum et bonum conceptae,* and in the phrase *ex bono et aequo.* The locution *bonum aequum* appears also in the comparative degree *melius aequius.*—See AEQUITAS.

Pringsheim, *ZSS* 52 (1932) 78; A. Leyval, *Notion d'enrichissement injuste. Une application de b. et ae.,* Thèse, Alger, 1935, 68; Maschi, *La concezione naturalistica,* 1937, 182; Riccobono, *BIDR* 53–54 (1948) 31 (= *AnPal* 20 [1949] 39); v. Lübtow, *ZSS* 66 (1948) 533; Beretta, *St Solazzi,* 1948, 264.

Bonus pater familias. The average type of an honest, prudent (*prudens*) and industrious (*diligens, studiosus*) man (father of a family), whose behavior in relations with other citizens is given as a pattern of an upright man and may be required from any one. Acting contrary to what a *bonus pater familias* would do in a given situation may serve as a basis for measuring his culpability and liability in a specific case.—See DILIGENS PATER FAMILIAS.

Sachers, *RE* 18, p. 4, 2154; Predella, *NDI* 2; Fadda, *Atti Accad. Napoli* 32 (1901); D'Ameglio, *Monitore dei Tribunali,* 1930, 441.

Bonus vir. See ARBITIUM BONI VIRI, VIR BONUS, BONUS PATER FAMILIAS.

Brevi manu traditio. See TRADITIO BREVI MANU.

Breviarium Alaricianum (Alarici). See LEX ROMANA VISIGOTHORUM.

Brevis (breve). Any kind of lists and registers used in fiscal administration of the later Empire; in particular financial reports of public officials about payments (taxes) received and administrative expenditures. Such reports had to be made in four-month-periods (*breves quadrimenstrui*). *Brevis* was also used for lists of tax-debtors. In military administration, *brevis* = a list concerning the supply of provisions for the army (see ANNONA MILITARIS).—C. 1.42.

Seeck, *RE* 3; Karlowa, *Röm. Rechtsgeschichte* 1 (1885) 907.

Brutus, M. Iunius. A republican jurist of the second century B.C., author of a work on the *ius civile* (partly *responsa*).

Bulgarus. A glossator of the twelfth century.—See IRNERIUS, GLOSSATORES.

Monti, *NDI* 2; H. Kantorowicz, *Studies in the Glossators of the R. Law* (1938) 62, 241.

Bustum. The place where the body of a dead person was burned or buried. The Twelve Tables excluded the *usucapio* of such places.—See ROGUS, USTRINA.

Mau, *RE* 3; Cuq, *DS* 2, 1394.

C

C. Abbreviation for *condemno.*—See A.

Cadaver. A dead body. Burning or burying a corpse within the boundaries of the city of Rome was prohibited by the Twelve Tables. An insult to the body, before or during the funeral, was considered an insult to the heir, who had the *actio iniuriarum* directly against the offender since "a contumely done to the deceased concerns the heirs' reputation" (D. 47.10. 1.4). Theft committed on a dead body was punished by compulsory labor in mines (*metalla*), in certain circumstances (use of arms) by death. Justinian prohibited the seizure of the body of a dead debtor, a custom which seems to have been practiced to compel the heirs to pay his debts.

Cadavera punitorum. The bodies of persons condemned to death and executed; these must be delivered to their relatives for burial.—D. 48.24.

Cadere causa. To lose a case in court, primarily for an excessive claim (*plus petere*).—See PLUSPETITIO.

Caduca. Testamentary dispositions made in favor of persons who, according to certain statutes (*leges caducariae*), were incapable of acquiring under a will. The term indicates also the inheritance itself or the legacy which became vacant because of the incapacity of the heir or legatee or because of other reasons (death of the beneficiary before the opening of the testament or his refusal to accept the gift). Dispositions which became void during the testator's life are styled *in causa caduci*. The treatment of *caduca* and the things *in causa caduci* was identical: they were assigned to persons who benefited by the testament if they had children. If such heirs or legatees were lacking the *caduca* went to the "treasury of the Roman people" (*aerarium*, later *fiscus*). Already in the later Empire some cases of *caduca* were abolished. In an extensive constitution Justinian abrogated the whole institution of *caduca* ("*De caducis tollendis*," C. 6.51.1) and fixed new general rules concerning testamentary dispositions which became vacant for any reason. A fundamental rule in the law of *caduca* was that the person who benefited by them received them with all charges (*cum onere*) imposed by the testator, such as legacies, or manumissions. —See CADUCORUM VINDICATIO.

  Leonhard, *RE* 3 (*s.v. bona c.*); Humbert, *DS* 2 (*s.v. bona c.*); Barbieri, *St Bonfante* 1 (1929) 565; Levet, *RHD* 14 (1935); v. Bolla, *ZSS* 59 (1939) 546; Vaccaro Delogu, *L'accrescimento nel dir. ereditario*, 1941, 145; Solazzi, *SDHI* 6 (1940) 165; idem, *ANap* 61 (1942) 71; B. Biondi, *Successione testamentaria*, 1943, 143; Besnier, *RIDA* 2 (1949) 93.

Caducorum vindicatio. The claim of a beneficiary to whom vacant parts of an inheritance or vacant legacies were awarded.—See CADUCA, COELIBES, ORBI.

Caecilius Africanus. See AFRICANUS.

Caecus. Blind (*caecitas* = blindness). A blind man could not witness a written testament. He was also unable to assume a guardianship.—See TESTAMENTUM CAECI.

Caelebs, caelibatus. See COELEBS, COELIBATUS.

Caelestis. Celestial, divine. Referred in the later Empire to the emperor's enactments or letters.

Caelius Sabinus. A Roman jurist (consul in A.D. 69), who was the head of the Sabinian group. He wrote a commentary on the aedilician edict.—See SABINIANI, EDICTUM AEDILIUM CURULIUM.

  Jörs, *RE* 3, 1272 (no. 32).

Caelum (coelum). The aerial space over a private or public property (*supra locum, caelum agri*). Although air is not in private ownership, the immediate space over any property must remain free (*liberum*) from another's interference in so far as its use, necessary to the owner, is impaired by a neighbor or anybody else.—See FUMUS, PROIECTIO, SERVITUTES LUMINUM, AËR.

  Pampaloni, *Sulla condizione dello spazio aereo, AG* 48 (1892) 32; Bonfante, *Corso di dir. rom.* 2, 1 (1926) 219.

Caesar. The name was originally a *cognomen* (= surname) of the emperor Augustus as adoptive son of C. Iulius Caesar and was used as such by the members of his adoptive family. Later it was assumed by the emperors as a part of their imperial title ("*Imperator Caesar . . .*"). Until Hadrian's time the descendants of an emperor also bore this title but thereafter only the destined successor and co-regents used it. Under Diocletian's reform of the government (tetrarchy) two emperors were *Augusti*

and the other two *Caesares* (lower in rank and designate successors to the *Augusti*).—See PRINCEPS.

  Neumann, *RE* 3, 1287.

Caesariani. Originally all servants in the imperial household were so termed. Later the term was applied to subordinate fiscal officials, concerned primarily with the seizure (confiscation) of property.

Calata comitia. See COMITIA CALATA.

Calator. A slave assigned to the personal service of his master and at his disposal on call. *Calatores* (*kalatores*) were also servants of the members of pontifical guilds.

  Samter, *RE* 3; De Ruggiero, *DE* 2.

Calculus. In Justinian constitutions, the judgment of a judge or an arbitrator. In the meaning of calculation (reckoning) *calculus* is syn. with *computatio*.— C. 2.5.—See ERROR CALCULI.

  Solazzi, *RendLomb* 58 (1925) 307.

Calendarium. See KALENDARIUM.

Calliditas. Shrewdness.—See STELLIONATUS.

Callistratus. A Roman jurist, presumably of Greek origin. He lived under Septimius Severus and Caracalla, and wrote *Institutiones, Quaestiones,* and works on criminal and fiscal law. The term *edictum monitorium* which appears in the title of one of his writings, is not clear.

  Kotz-Dobrz, *RE* Suppl. 3; Orestano, *NDI* 2; H. Krüger, *St Bonfante* 2 (1930) 327; J. B. Nordeblad, *Index verborum quae Callistrati libris continentur* 1 (A–Is), Lund, 1934; Schulz, *History of Rom. legal science*, 1946, 193.

Calumnia. Trickery, deception in legal transactions or in the interpretation of legal norms or of manifestations of will. In a technical sense *calumnia* refers to both civil and criminal matters. In the first case it is a malicious vexation (*vexare*) of a person with suits (*litibus*) "brought merely in order to trouble the adversary and with the hope for success through a mistake or injustice of the judge" (Gai Inst. 4.178). In civil proceedings the defendant too may commit *calumnia* if he denies the plaintiff's claim merely for chicanery. The principal remedies to prevent *calumnia* in civil trials is IUSIURANDUM (*iuramentum*) CALUMNIAE applicable to either party, and (in classical law) IUDICIUM CALUMNIAE only in favor of a defendant maliciously sued. In the field of the private law there is still another form of *calumnia* if a person receives money in order to annoy another with vexatious trials (civil, criminal or fiscal). The person to whose detriment such an illicit arrangement was made, was granted against the man who received the money a praetorian action, proposed in the Edict, for four times the sum which had been given him as the price of his complicity.—In criminal law *calumnia* (*crimen calumniae*) was committed when a person accused another in full knowledge that the latter is innocent. Such a *falsa accusatio* made in bad faith was punished by branding the *calumniator* with the letter *K* (abbreviation for *kalumniator*) on the forehead, and by the imposition of various disabilities: infamy, inability to be in the future a prosecutor in a criminal trial, other procedural disadvantages, and exclusion from competition for a public office. The *crimen calumniae* of the *falsus accusator* had to be proved in a special proceeding; the mere acquittal of the person he had accused was not sufficient to stigmatize him as a *calumniator*. A *lex Remmia* (about 80 B.C.) set the rule that a *calumniator* was to be tried before the same tribunal (*quaestio*) before which he had prosecuted the innocent accused.—D. 3.6; C. 9.46.

Hitzig, *RE* 3; Humbert, *DS* 2; Lauria, *NDI* 2; G. Maier, *Prätorische Bereicherungsklagen*, 1932, 55; E. Levy, *Vom römischen Anklagevergehen, ZSS* 53 (1933) 151; Lauria, *St Ratti*, 1934, 97.

Calumnia notatus. A person convicted of *crimen calumniae* (malicious accusation).—See CALUMNIA, CALUMNIATOR.

Calumniari. To commit *calumnia*.—See CALUMNIA, CALUMNIATOR.

Calumniator. A person "who harasses others with suits brought through fraud and deception," D. 50.16.233 pr. (*calumniari*). A *calumniator* proved and pronounced guilty of *crimen calumniae* was exposed to various penalties.—D. 3.6; C. 9.46.—See CALUMNIA.

Calumniosus. Involving *calumnia*.—See CALUMNIA, ACTIO CALUMNIOSA.

Cancellare. To mark crosses over a written document (a testament, a promissory note) in order to annul it.
Sanfilippo, *AnPal* 17 (1937) 133.

Cancellarii. Auxiliary officials in the chancery of a high functionary, charged with secretarial services. They seem to have been of importance in the offices of the provincial governors.—C. 1.51.

Candidati. Members of the body-guard of the emperor (in the later Empire). They are first mentioned in A.D. 350.
Seeck, *RE* 3, 1468.

Candidatus. An aspirant to a magistracy. The competitors for a magisterial post appeared in public during the electoral period in glittering white togas (*toga candida*, hence the name *candidatus*), surrounded by friends and slaves, to appeal for the support of the voters. Unfair practices were forbidden and punished if they constituted the crime of AMBITUS.—See moreover LEX POMPEIA, NOMENCLATOR, PROFESSIO (in elections).
Kübler, *DE* 2.

Candidatus Caesaris (or **principis**). A candidate recommended by the emperor to the senate for an official post. The following appointment by the senate was a mere formality. The emperor's recommendation was considered a distinction; it is found as such in numerous inscriptions.—See QUAESTORES CANDIDATI PRINCIPIS.
Kubitschek, *RE* 3, 1469; Kübler, *DE* 2, 65.

Canon. The term (of Greek origin and unknown in Justinian's Institutes and Digest) appears in two different meanings in later imperial constitutions and Justinian's Novels: (1) a regular annual payment of a fixed (*fixus*) amount as a rent in a lease for a long term or in perpetuity (*emphyteusis*) or as a land-tax paid to the state. As a tax it was only exceptionally increased or lessened (see PERAEQUATIO) by the tax assessors. It is distinguished from extraordinary payments of duties which were neither regular nor fixed; (2) syn. with *regula* (*iuris*) or *norma* (= legal rule). In the language of the Novels *canon* occurs mostly in the sense of Church legal rules in contradistinction to legal rules of secular origin.—See the following items.
Humbert, *DS* 1; L. Wenger, *SbWien* 220, 2 (1942); Berger, *Fschr Schulz* 2 (1951) 9.

Canon anniversarius. A tax or duty paid *per annum*. The term appears with reference to an impost paid by Jewish synagogues.

Canon aurarius. A tax or duty paid in gold. Ant. *canon frumentarius* = a tax or duty paid in kind.—C. 11.23.

Canon emphyteuticarius (emphyteuticus). The annual rent paid by an *emphyteuta* to the landlord (the emperor or a private individual) in a lease in perpetuity or for a long term.—See EMPHYTEUSIS.

Canon frumentarius. See CANON AURARIUS.

Canones ecclesiastici. The rules of the Church (ecclesiastical laws).
B. Biondi, *Giustiniano Primo, principe e legislatore cattolico*, 1936, 92.

Canones largitionalium titulorum. See LARGITIONALIA.—C. 10.23.

Canonica. Regular taxes (duties) paid by the possessors of *fundi emphyteuticarii* or of land belonging to the private patrimony of the emperor.

Canonicarius. A collector of taxes (*canones*).
Seeck, *RE* 3; Wenger, *Canon* (see above), 46.

Canticum. A defamatory poem. Syn. CARMEN FAMOSUM.

Capacitas. (Adj. CAPAX.) A general conception of legal capacity is unknown to the Romans. The term is used only with reference to certain acts or legal transactions. Elsewhere *capacitas* is expressed by *ius* (= the right to do something) or by a specific term, as, for instance, the capacity to make a will = *testamenti factio*. More frequent is the use of the adjective *capax* (= capable, able) to denote physical or mental capacity and legal capacity as well (e.g., to contract an obligation or to accept the payment of a debt). Restrictions of legal capacity are manifold and they vary pursuant to certain personal qualities of the individual involved (age, sex, citizenship, dependency upon paternal power, etc.) or to the legal domain to which they apply (obligations, acquisition of property, procedure, etc.). Persons capable (*capaces*) in one regard may be incapable in another.

For *capacitas* in the law of successions, see the following item, COELIBES, ORBI, LEX FURIA, LEX VOCONIA, LEX IULIA ET PAPIA, CADUCA, TESTAMENTI FACTIO.

Leonhard, *RE* 3; B. Biondi, *Successione testamentaria,* 1943, 133.

Capax. In the law of succession, a person able to take under a will (= *qui capere potest*). See CAPACITAS. A person might be fully *capax* (*capax solidi*) when he could take the whole gift (inheritance or legacy) left to him in a last will and testament, or partially *capax* (*capax portionis*) when only a portion thereof was accessible to him.

Capax doli. A person capable of perceiving the fraudulent character of his action. Those who are below the age of puberty generally are not considered *capaces doli,* nor are persons with mental defects, who are not responsible for their actions.—See IMPUBES.

Capere. To acquire either by USUCAPIO or (more frequently) on the occasion of a person's death (*mortis causa*).—D. 39.6.

Capio. Sometimes syn. with USUCAPIO. *Mortis causa capiones* = all kinds of benefits a person receives through, or on the occasion of, another's death (conditional gifts) "except those forms of acquisition which have specific names" (D. 39.6.31 pr.), such as *hereditas, legatum, fideicommissum.*—D. 39.6; C. 8.56.—See PIGNORIS CAPIO.

Ferrini, *NDI* 2 (*s.v. capioni*).

Capitalis. A criminal matter in which the penalty may be death, loss of liberty or loss of Roman citizenship.—See CAPUT, CAUSA CAPITALIS, CRIMEN, QUAESTIO, POENA CAPITALIS, SENTENTIA, TRESVIRI CAPITALES.

Levy, *Die röm. Capitalstrafe, SbHeid* 1931; Brasiello, *RBSG* 9 (1934) 220.

Capitatio. A general expression for taxes paid per head (*caput*), either as a poll-tax (*capitatio humana*) or an animal tax (*capitatio animalium*). The *capitatio humana*—to be distinguished from land tax, *iugatio terrena*—was paid only by persons of lower classes (hence it was called also *capitatio plebeia*), not wealthy enough to pay taxes *ex censu,* i.e., on their whole property as evaluated on the occasion of a *census.* The *capitatio humana* became a general institution under Diocletian. In earlier times the poll-tax (*tributum capitis*) was paid only in certain provinces. Exemptions were admissible; they were granted to minors, widows, etc. Only healthy persons able to work (men from 14 to 65) were assessed, but not in equal measure.—C. 11.49.

Seeck, *RE* 3; Humbert, *DS* 1; F. Leo, *Die c. plebeia und die c. humana,* 1903; A. Piganiol, *L'impôt de la c.,* 1916; F. Lot, *RHD* 4 (1925) 177; idem, *L'impôt foncier et la capitation personnelle* (*Bibliothèque des Hautes Études,* 253), 1928; C. Bellieni, *C. plebeia e c. humana,* 1931; Piganiol, *Rev. historique* 166 (1935); A. Deleage, *La c. du Bas-Empire,* 1945; A. Segrè, *Trad* 3 (1945) 114.

Capitatio animalium. A tax levied per head of cattle (from the times of Diocletian.)—See CAPITATIO.

Thibault, *Rev. générale de droit et de la législation* 23 (1899) 320.

Capitatio humana (or **plebeia**). See CAPITATIO.

Schwahn, *RE* 7A, 68; Lécrivain, *DS* 5, 435; Thibault, *Rev. gén. du droit et de la législation* 23 (1899) 290.

Capite censi. Persons registered not as to their property which was below the lowest census for military service, but simply as to their existence as living individuals, primarily as heads (*caput*) of a family.—See PROLETARII.

Gabba, *Ath* 27 (1949) 198.

Capite minuti. Persons who have undergone a CAPITIS DEMINUTIO.—Inst. 1.16; D. 4.5.—See CAPITIS DEMINUTIO.

Capite puniri (or **plecti**). To suffer the death penalty.—See CAPITALIS, POENA.

Capitis accusatio. An accusation of a crime which carried the death penalty for the culprit.

Capitis amputatio. Decapitation. Syn. *decollatio.*

Capitis deminutio. The loss of *caput* (the civil status of a person which implies the legal ability to conclude legally valid transactions and to be the subject of rights recognized by the law) through the loss of one of the three elements thereof, freedom, Roman citizenship or membership in a Roman family. Syn. *minutio capitis.* For the various degrees of *capitis deminutio,* see CAPUT.—Inst. 1.16; 4.5.—See RESTITUTIO IN INTEGRUM PROPTER CAPITIS DEMINUTIONEM.

Leonhard, *RE* 3; Baudry, *DS* 1; Anon., *NDI* 2 (*s.v. deminutio*); Berger, *OCD* (*s.v. deminutio c.*); F. Dessertaux, *Études sur la formation hist. de la c. d.,* 1–3 (1909–1928); idem, *TR* 8 (1928) 129; U. Coli, *Saggi critici sulle fonti del dir. rom. I. C. d.,* 1922; Ambrosino, *SDHI* 6 (1940) 369; Kaser, *Iura* 3 (1952) 48.

Capito, Gaius Ateius. A jurist of the Augustan epoch. He adhered to older doctrines and was highly estimated by his contemporaries. He wrote a treatise on pontifical law and an extensive collection of Miscellanies (*Coniectanea*).

Jörs, *RE* 2, 1904 (no. 8); Berger, *OCD* 164; Grosso, *Quaderni di Roma* 1 (1947) 335; L. Strzelecki, *De A. Capitone, nuptiarum caerimoniarum interprete,* Wroclaw, 1947.

Capitulum. Some statutes were divided into chapters, *capitula.*—*Capitulum* is also a single provision of an agreement.

Captatorius. A disposition in a will by which the testator instituted an heir or bequeathed a legacy on the condition that the beneficiary shall grant a gift to another person in his will was called *captatoria institutio* (*scriptura*) or *captio.* Such a disposition was not valid.

Captio. See the foregoing item.—See also PIGNORIS CAPIO.

Captivitas. Captivity. When a Roman citizen was captured as a prisoner by an enemy (*hostis*) with whom the Romans were at war, he became a slave of the enemy. The same rule was observed by the Romans with regard to foreigners whom they made prisoners in a war. After his return the Roman war prisoner (*captivus*) regained his legal status by virtue of a specific Roman legal institution (see POST-LIMINIUM). A Roman captured (kidnapped) by a bandit (*latro*) did not become his slave; his legal status remained unchanged.—D. 49.16; C. 1.3.—See POSTLIMINIUM, REDEMPTUS AB HOSTIBUS, LEX COR-NELIA.

Leonhard, *RE* 3; L. Sertorio, *La prigionia di guerra*, 1915; Ratti, *RISG* N.S. 1, 2 (1926–27); *idem, BIDR* 35 (1927) 105; *idem, AnMac* 1 (1927); H. Krüger, *ZSS* 51 (1931) 203; Levy, *ClPhilol* 38 (1943) 159; Di Marzo, *St Solazzi*, 1948, 1; Leicht, *RStDIt* 22 (1949) 181; L. Amirante, *Captivitas e postliminium*, 1950.

Captivus. A prisoner of war.—D. 49.15; C. 1.3.—See the foregoing item.

Caput. In Roman sources the term has different meanings. Generally it signifies an individual, hence the distinction between *caput liberum* (= a free person) and *caput servile* (= a slave). In connection with *deminutio* (*deminutio capitis* = the loss of *caput*) *caput* = the civil status of a Roman citizen, for which three elements were necessary: to be a free man (*status libertatis*), to have Roman citizenship (*status civitatis*) and to belong to a Roman family (*status familiae*) either as its head (*pater familias*) or as a member. The loss of one of these elements involved the *capitis deminutio*, with all its legal consequences. The gravest effects were connected with the loss of freedom (*capitis deminutio maxima*) in the case of enslavement of a citizen or reducing a freedman to slavery, because the loss of liberty entailed the loss of citizenship and family ties. A lesser degree (*capitis deminutio media*) in which a person lost citizenship without losing liberty also resulted in loss of membership in family. See INTERDICERE AQUA ET IGNI. Loss of family (*capitis deminutio minima*) occurred when a person's agnatic family ties were dissolved either by his entry into another family (*adoptio, adrogatio,* marriage of a woman with *in manum conventio*) or by his becoming the head of a new family (*emancipatio*). The consequences of this lowest degree of *capitis deminutio* were originally perceptible only in economic and social fields (loss of the rights of inheritance in the former family, dissolution of partnership, extinction of personal servitudes, and the like). Some of these consequences were later mitigated by the praetorian law which recognized cognatic family ties. Thus the *capitis deminutio minima* gradually lost its original significance; under Justinian it is almost without any importance at all. See CAPITIS DEMINUTIO.—Other meanings of *caput* are: a section of a statute, edict or imperial constitution (syn. CAPITULUM); the principal of a debt as distinguished from the interest; in tax administration, *caput* denotes a tax unit or an individual person as a tax-payer. For *caput* in connection with the death penalty, see ANIMADVERSIO,

CAPITE PUNIRI, CAPITIS ACCUSATIO, CAPITALIS, POENA CAPITIS, CONSECRATIO.—Inst. 1.16; D. 4.5.

Radin, *Mél Fournier*, 1929; Gioffredi, *SDHI* 11 (1945) 301; Lot, *L'étendue de caput fiscal, RHD* 4 (1925) 5, 177; A. Déléage, *La capitation du Bas-Empire*, 1945.

Caput aquae. The place where the water originates (*aqua nascitur*). It is either the source or the river or lake from which the water is initially drawn. The servitude of *aquaeductus* could be constituted on any *caput aquae*.—See FONS.

Carbonianum edictum. See BONORUM POSSESSIO EX CARBONIANO EDICTO.

Carcer. A jail. Imprisonment was not a repressive measure, it served only for the detention of persons during investigation or trial, or after sentence pending execution.

Berger, *OCD* (*s.v. prison*); Grand, *La prison et la notion d'emprisonnement, RHD* 19 (1940) 58.

Carcer privatus. A private prison. It was used for the incarceration of recalcitrant slaves, and—in earlier times—of debtors who failed to pay their debt. Private prisons were prohibited by the emperors Zeno and Justinian.—C. 9.5.—See NEXUM.

Humbert, *DS* 1; Hitzig, *RE* 3.

Caritas. Love, affection. Appears in a few juristic texts as a psychological and humane element which had to be taken into consideration in certain legal situations which required mild and benevolent treatment. *Caritas* belongs to the group of terms, such as *benignitas, clementia, humanitas,* which are put forward to recommend an exceptionally benignant dealing with a specific case. Reminiscences of Christian *caritas* may occur in some interpolated texts, but the term cannot be excluded from the language of the classical jurists since it is used in contemporary literary texts.—See BENIGNE.

Albertario, *Studi* 5 (1937) 21; Maschi, *AnTr* 18 (1948) 51; *idem, Ius* 1 (1950) 266.

Carmen famosum. A defamatory poem (libel), lampoon, pasquinade. Syn. *canticum, libellus famosus.* It is one of the graver cases of personal offense (*iniuria*) and is punished by deportation.—See the following item.—See LIBELLUS FAMOSUS, INTESTABILIS.

Leonhard, *RE* 3; Brasiello, *NDI* 2.

Carmen malum. Sometimes identified with *carmen famosum.* Originally it was a specific wrongdoing, a kind of sorcery (mentioned already in the Twelve Tables) committed by pronouncing magic formulae to bring harm to a person or his property.—See OCCENTARE, INCANTARE.

Carnifex. An executioner. He was not permitted to live in Rome.

Cartilius. An unknown jurist of the late Republic.

H. Krüger, *St Bonfante* 2 (1930) 328.

Cascellius. A jurist of the late Republic, author of the formula called IUDICIUM CASCELLIANUM.

Jörs, *RE* 3, 1634; Ferrini, *Opere* 2 (1929) 53.

Cassare. To annul (a law, an agreement).

Cassiani. See CASSIUS, SABINIANI.

Cassius, Gaius Cassius Longinus. A prominent jurist of the first century after Christ. He followed Sabinus in the leadership of the so-called Sabinian school (SABINIANI), hence also called CASSIANI. His principal work was an extensive treatise on *ius civile.*— See GAIUS.

Jörs, *RE* 3 (no. 63); C. Arnò, *Pubbl. Fac. Giuridica Modena* 4 (1925); *idem, Mél Cornil* 1 (1926) 97.

Castellum. A small fortified place (diminutive of *castrum*). People living in a *castellum* sometimes had an organization similar to that of small communities (*vici, pagi*).—C. 11.60.

Kubitschek, *RE* 3; De Ruggiero, *DE* 2.

Castellum (aquae). A water reservoir, public or private (syn. *receptaculum*). A servitude of drawing water from another's *castellum* (*ius aquae ducendae ex castello*) was protected by a special interdict *de aqua ex castello ducenda.*—D. 43.20.

Berger, *RE* 9, 1631; De Ruggiero, *DE* 2, 132; Thierry, *DS* 1, 937; Orestano, *BIDR* 43 (1935) 297.

Castigare (castigatio). To chastise, castigate. Corporal punishment was applied to both slaves (with a whip, *flagellum*) and free persons (with a club, *fustis*) either as an additional punishment, or in lieu of a pecuniary fine when the culprit could not pay, or as a coërcive measure for minor offenses. Soldiers were punished by *castigatio* for disobedience or violation of military discipline. Outside the penal law fathers, masters, and instructors were permitted to castigate their sons, slaves and apprentices, respectively. Syn. *verberare (verberatio)*.

Hitzig, *RE* 3; Humbert, *DS* 1; Fougères, *DS* 2 (*s.v. flagellum*); Lécrivain, *DS* 5 (*verber*); U. Brasiello, *Repressione penale,* 1937, 386.

Castra. A military camp serving either as a permanent quarter for troops or a temporary center of attack or defense, or for a short night stay of a military unit in march. *In castris* = during the military service, in war time.

Domaszewski, *RE* 3; De Ruggiero, *DE* 2; Saglio, *DS* 1, 941.

Castratio. Emasculation, castration. *Castratus* = eunuch. The imperial legislation of the early Empire (Domitian, Hadrian) tried to suppress this custom practiced primarily on slaves, but without success, since the prohibition of *castratio* was repeated several times and the penalties were constantly aggravated, until Constantine and later Justinian, imposed the death penalty.—C. 4.42.—See EUNUCHUS.

Hitzig, *RE* 3; Humbert, *DS* 1.

Castrense peculium. See PECULIUM CASTRENSE.

Castrensiani. Servants and subordinate employees in the imperial household. Syn. *familia castrensis.*— See MINISTERIALES.—C. 12.25.

Ensslin, *RE* Suppl. 6, 493; Dunlap, *Univ. of Michigan Studies, Humanistic Ser.* 14 (1924) 215; Giffard, *RHD* 14 (1935) 239.

Castrensis (procurator castrensis). The superintendent of the imperial household. His title was also *castrensis sacri palatii.*

Seeck, *RE* 3; Heron de Villefosse, *DS* 1; Dunlap, *loc. cit.* 207.

Casus. An accident, an event which happened without any human intervention or fault. Terminology is varied: *casus, casus fortuitus, casus maior, vis maior.* According to a general principle "no one is responsible for a *casus*" (*casus a nullo praestatur,* D. 50.17.23), the owner of a thing suffered the damage caused by a *casus* unless another has assumed responsibility for such losses. In the contractual field *casus* might make it impossible for the debtor to fulfill his obligation (e.g., destruction of the thing to be delivered to the creditor). Normally, the debtor was not liable for such accidents unless there was a special agreement extending his risk to such cases.— See CUSTODIA, DILIGENTIA, FORTUITUS.

De Medio, *BIDR* 20 (1908) 157; F. Schulz, *Rechtsvergleichende Forschungen über die Zufallshaftung, ZVR* 25, 27 (1910, 1912) Buckland, *Harvard LR* 46 (1933); G. I. Luzzatto, *Caso fortuito e forza maggiore* 1 (1938); Condanari-Michler, *Scr Ferrini* 3 (Univ. Sacro Cuore, Milan, 1948) 102.

Catholicus. (Adj.) Connected with the Christian faith (*fides, religio*) or Church (*ecclesia*).

For bibl. see B. Biondi, *Guide bibliografiche, Dir. rom.* (1944) *s.v. Chiesa Cattolica,* p. 139.

Cato, M. Porcius Cato. Surnamed also *Censorius* (or *Maior*), consul 195 B.C., censor 184 B.C. He is named by Cicero "an expert in *ius civile,* the best of all" (*De orat.* 1.171). His work "On agriculture" (*De agricultura,* written about 160 B.C.) contains forms of agrarian contracts. He was the initiator of the *Senatusconsultum de Bacchanalibus.* His son, M. Porcius Cato Licinianus, is known as the author of an extensive work *De iuris disciplina,* probably a treatise on the *ius civile.* One of the two (more likely the son) was the author of the so-called REGULA CATONIANA.

Jörs, *Röm. Rechtswissenschaft* (1888) 267, 283; McDonald, *OCD* 173 (no. 1).

Catoniana regula. See REGULA CATONIANA, CATO.

Caupo. An inn-keeper. He assumed liability for things left in his custody by an agreement, *receptum cauponum.* The praetorian Edict fixed the pertinent rules equally to the responsibility of ship-owners and keepers of public stables.—D. 4.9; 47.5.—See RECEPTUM NAUTARUM.

Causa. One of the vaguest terms of the Roman juristic language. Starting from the basic meaning of cause, reason, inducement, the jurists use it in very different senses. Thus, *causa* indicates a legal situation in such phrases as *in eadem causa est,* or *alia causa est. Causa* is the reason for which some judicial measures (actions, exceptions, interdicts) were introduced by the praetor. *Causa* is also the purpose for which an action is brought in a specific controversy, or a legal disposition is made (*causa dotis, causa legati*). Not infrequently *causa* refers to the trial itself or the matter from which it originated; see CAUSAE COGNITIO. Sometimes *causa* is roughly identical with ANIMUS when it alludes to the subjective motive, intention, or purpose of a person. In this sense its use is simply unlimited because it may be applied to elements recognized by the law as well as to inducements which are immoral and condemned by law (*causa turpis, iniusta, illicita,* and similar). *Causa* receives a specific juridical content when it implies the legal title or foundation on which a person bases its claim against another or a legal situation is created, as, e.g., in phrases like *causa venditionis, donationis, hereditaria, legati, fideicommissi, iudicati,* etc. In certain legal institutions *causa,* particularly when qualified as *iusta causa,* acquires a specific coloration, as in TRADITIO, USUCAPIO, MANUMISSIO, etc. In the domain of the law of contracts, i.e., in bilateral transactions, the Romans did not elaborate a special doctrine of *causa.* There are mentions of *causa* with regard to some specific contracts, but a general theory can hardly be drawn out. Finally, with reference to certain things (land, slaves) when their restitution *cum sua causa* is involved, *causa* means the accessories, proceeds, fruits, or the child born of a slave. See the following items.—See CADERE CAUSA, FALSA CAUSA, IUSTA CAUSA, and the following items.

> Leonhard, *RE* 3; Brunelli, *NDI* 3; Bonfante, *Scr. giur.* 3, 125; V. A. Georgescu, *Le mot causa dans le latin juridique,* Jasi, 1936 (reprinted in *Ét. de philologie juridique,* Bucharest, 1939); De Bois-Juzan, *De la c. en dr. français,* 1939, 155; Bibl. in Betti, *Istituzioni* 1 (1942) 122; Miniconi, *Rev. Ét. Latines* 21 (1943/4) 82; De Sarlo, *BIDR* 51/2 (1948) 99; P. J. Miniconi, *Causa et ses dérivés,* Thèse, Paris, 1951; F. Schwarz, *Die Grundlage der Condictio* (1952) 120.

Causa cadere. See CADERE CAUSA.

Causa capitalis. A criminal matter or trial in which the loss of the defendant's CAPUT (life, freedom or Roman citizenship) was at stake. Syn. *res capitalis, crimen capitale;* ant. *causa pecuniaria.*

> E. Levy, *Die röm. Kapitalstrafe, SbHeid* 1931.

Causa cognita. See CAUSAE COGNITIO, PASSIM.

Causa criminalis. A judicial matter connected with a crime.

Causa Curiana. See CURIANA CAUSA.

Causa iudicati. See IUDICATUM.

> Pflueger, *ZSS* 43 (1923) 153.

Causa liberalis. A trial in which the question whether an individual was a slave or a free man, was involved. Syn. *iudicium liberale.*—D. 40.12; C. 7.16.—See PRAETOR DE LIBERALIBUS CAUSIS, ORDINARE LITEM, VERGINIA.

> Nicolau, C. 1., Paris, 1933; H. Krüger, *St Riccobono 2* (1936) 227; P. Noailles, *Le procès de Virginie, Rev. Ét. Latines,* 20 (1942) 106 (= *Fas et ius,* 1948, 187); Di Paola, *AnCat* 2 (1948) 266; Van Oven, *TR* 18 (1950) 159.

Causa lucrativa. A matter in which one acquires a thing without any reciprocal, equivalent expenditure.

DONATIO, LEGATUM, USUCAPIO PRO HEREDE are so named.—See RES LUCRATIVAE.

> Di Marzo, *BIDR* 15, 17 (1903, 1905).

Causa manumissionis. See CAUSAE PROBATIO, MANUMISSIO.

Causa pecuniaria. A judicial matter in which the issue is the payment of a sum of money (debts, damages, fines). Ant. CAUSA CAPITALIS, CRIMINALIS.

Causa poenalis. See IUDICIA POENALIA, POENALIS.

Causa possessionis, traditionis, usucapionis. See POSSESSIO, TRADITIO, USUCAPIO.

Causa turpis. See CONDICTIO OB TURPEM CAUSAM.

Causae coactio. See CAUSAE CONIECTIO.

Causae cognitio (causam cognoscere). The judicial examination of the case, particularly of its factual background in the course of the proceedings, both in the first stage of the trial before the magistrate (*in iure*) and in the second (*apud iudicem*) before the private judge. Several ordinary and extraordinary measures to be ordered by the judicial magistrate, as, e.g., IN INTEGRUM RESTITUTIO, MISSIONES IN POSSESSIONEM, CAUTIONES, could be applied only *causa cognita,* i.e., after a thorough *causa cognitio.* Ant. CITRA CAUSAE COGNITIONEM.

> Wlassak, *RE* 4, 206; Lévy-Bruhl, *TR* 5 (1924) 383; M. Lemosse, *Cognitio,* 1944, 185.

Causae collectio. See the following item.

Causae coniectio. A summary presentation of the case before the juror (IUDEX) by the parties or their advocates. Syn. *causae collectio.*

> Wlassak, *RE* 4 (*s.v. coniectio*).

Causae probatio. A special procedure designed to examine certain factual elements in matters involving Roman citizenship or personal status. *Erroris causae probatio:* when a marriage was concluded in error by persons of differing legal status. *Anniculi causae probatio:* a LATINUS IUNIANUS, who had been freed before the age of thirty and had married a Roman woman, acquired Roman citizenship if there was a one-year-old child born in this marriage. The wife and child became Roman citizens too. Also in some exceptional cases of MANUMISSIO (of a slave under thirty years or as a token of particular gratitude) the fairness of the motives was examined by the competent official through a *causae probatio.*—See SENATUS-CONSULTUM PEGASIANUM.

> Leonhard, *RE* 3; De Dominicis, *AnPer* 58 (1947–48) 109.

Causam perorare (orare). To argue the case before the judge (see IUDEX).

Causa perpetua. See PERPETUA CAUSA.

Causaria. See MISSIO.

Causas agere. See the following item.

Causas dicere. To plead the causes of others before the courts as an advocate. Hence *causidicus* = the advocate. Syn. *causas agere, orare.*

Causidicus. See CAUSAS DICERE, ADVOCATUS.

> Kubitschek, *RE* 3; Conrat, *Mél. Fitting I* (1907) 303.

Cautela. Used by Justinian's compilers in lieu of *cautio*.—See CAUTIO.

Guarneri-Citati, *Indice*[2] (1927) 16.

Cautio. Denotes the obligation assumed as a guaranty for the execution of an already existing obligation or of a duty which is not protected by the law. The simplest form (*nuda cautio*) is a promise by a mere *stipulatio* (*nuda stipulatio, repromissio*) which gives the creditor the advantages of a stipulatory obligation. Other forms were a pledge (*pignus* or *hypotheca*) or guaranty assumed by a person other than the principal debtor (a surety). "A thing gives more security than a person" (D. 50, 17, 25). Also an oath (*cautio iuratoria*) was used to strengthen an obligation. For the different application of *cautiones,* which frequently are called simply *stipulationes,* see the following items. *Cautio* is also used to indicate a written declaration of the debtor confirming his obligation and issued for the purpose of evidence. For the application of *cautio* with reference to a preceding *stipulatio,* see CAUTIO STIPULATORIA.—See STIPULATIO, SATISDATIO, IDONEUS, REPROMISSIO.

Leonhard, *RE* 3; Humbert, *DS* 1; *Laborderie, Revue générale de droit* 33 (1909) 439; A. Palermo, *Il procedimento cauzionale nel dir. rom.,* 1942.

Cautio amplius non agi (peti). A *cautio* given by the plaintiff who acts on behalf of another person as his procurator (*procuratorio nomine*) to guarantee the defendant that he would not be sued for the same claim again by the principal.—See PROCURATOR.

Debray, *NHRD* 36 (1912) 3; A. Palermo, *Procedimento cauzionale cit.,* 23.

Cautio damni infecti. A security given against apprehended damage. The pertinent *stipulatio* created a legal tie between the owner of the immovable threatened and the owner of the adjacent building the rundown conditions of which endangered the former's property. If the *cautio damni infecti* was refused and later damage was really done, the praetor granted the owner of the damaged property an action with a fictitious formula based on the fiction that *cautio damni infecti* had been given.—D. 39.2.—See DAMNUM INFECTUM, MISSIO IN POSSESSIONEM DAMNI INFECTI CAUSA.

G. Branca, *Danno temuto,* 1937; Palermo, *op. cit.* 35.

Cautio de bonis (dotibus) conferendis. A *cautio* by which an emancipated son or draughter promised to accomplish their duties of *collatio*.—See COLLATIO BONORUM, COLLATIO DOTIS.

A. Guarino, *Collatio bonorum,* 1937.

Cautio de dolo. See DOLUS, STIPULATIO DE DOLO.

Cautio de evictione. See EVICTIO.

Cautio de non amplius turbando. A *cautio* given by the defendant in an ACTIO NEGATORIA to the effect that he will not disturb the owner of a plot of land by claiming a servitude thereon. A similar *cautio* is given in an *actio confessoria* to the beneficiary of a servitude by the defendant binding himself not to put any obstacle in the exercise of the servitude.—See VINDICATIO SERVITUTIS.

Cautio de rato (cautio ratam rem dominum habiturum). A *cautio* given in a trial by a representative (*procurator*) of the creditor to the effect that the latter (the principal, *dominus negotii*) will approve of what his *procurator* had done and will not sue the debtor a second time in the same matter. Tutors and curators as well had to give such a security in the name of their wards. In later law the *cautio de rato* was required only when there were reasonable doubts about the powers of the representative (for instance, in the case of absence of the principal.—See PROCURATOR, TUTOR, CAUTIO AMPLIUS NON AGI.

Palermo, *op. cit.* 23.

Cautio de servo persequendo. A security given by a person holding another's slave for the pursuit of the latter in case he would run away.—See SERVUS FUGITIVUS.

Cautio ex lege Falcidia. A security given the heir by the legatee to return what he might receive beyond the limits established by the *lex Falcidia*.—See LEX FALCIDIA.

Cautio ex operis novi nuntiatione. See OPERIS NOVI NUNTIATIO.

Cautio fructuaria. See CAUTIO USUFRUCTUARIA (syn.).

Cautio indemnitatis. A security given a person that he would not suffer any loss or damage from a transaction or an event which may happen.

Cautio iudicatum solvi. See IUDICATUM.

Brunelli, *NDI* 3; Duquesne, *Mél Gerardin,* 1907; *idem, Mél Fitting* 1 (1907); Palermo, *op. cit.* 22; P. Gay-Lugny, *C.i.s.,* Thèse, Paris, 1906.

Cautio iudicio sisti. A security given by the defendant to appear in court.—See VADIMONIUM, EXSECUTOR.

Cautio iuratoria. The strengthening of an obligation by oath.—See IUSIURANDUM, CAUTIO.

Cautio legatorum nomine. A security given by the heir that all that the testator ordered in connection with a legacy would be fulfilled. In the case of refusal by the heir to assume this obligation by *stipulatio* the legatee might ask the praetor to be put in possession of the heir's property (*missio in possessionem legatorum servandorum causa*).—See LEGATUM, MISSIO IN POSSESSIONEM.

Palermo, *op. cit.* 41, 93; Solazzi, *RISG* 86 (1949) 38.

Cautio Muciana. A security given by a legatee (extended later to heirs) to whom a legacy was bequeathed under a negative condition that he would not do a certain thing. The fulfillment of such a condition could be established only at the death of the legatee. In order to give the legatee the opportunity of receiving the legacy during his lifetime this *cautio* was introduced (by the Republican jurist Q. Mucius Scaevola) by which he obligated himself not to act against the condition imposed. If, despite this promise he did the act forbidden, he was compelled to return all that he benefited by the legacy including the profits (*fructus*).

> Kübler, *RE* 16, 445; Bozzi, *NDI* 3; Levy, *ZSS* 24 (1904) 122; H. Krüger, *Mél Girard* 2 (1912); Beseler, *ZSS* 47 (1927) 60; Solazzi, *SDHI* 10 (1944); B. Biondi, *Successione testamentaria*, 1943, 545; idem, *BIDR* 49–50 (1947) 241.

Cautio pro praede litis et vindiciarum. A security connected with the proceedings with *sponsio* (AGERE PER SPONSIONEM) and given by the party who received the temporary possession of the object in dispute, in order to guarantee its restitution together with the fruits in the case he lost the suit.—See PRAEDES LITIS ET VINDICIARUM.

> Palermo, *op. cit.* 21.

Cautio ratam rem dominum habiturum. See CAUTIO DE RATO.

Cautio rei uxoriae. A stipulation concerning the restitution of the dowry in case of divorce.—See DOS.

Cautio rem adulescentis salvam fore. See the following item.

> Berger, *RE* 15, 1878.

Cautio rem pupilli salvam fore. A guaranty given by the guardian to the effect that his administration of the ward's patrimony will not prove detrimental to it. Testamentary guardians were free from giving such a security. A similar *cautio* (*rem adulescentis salvam fore*) was imposed on the curator of a minor. —Inst. 1.24; D. 46.6; C. 5.42.—See TUTELA, CURATOR MINORIS.

> Sachers, *RE* 7A, 1569; H. Weymuller, *Contribution à l'histoire de l'actio tutelae*, 1901; Rotondi, *Scritti* 2 (1922, ex 1912) 268; Palermo, *op. cit., passim*.

Cautio stipulatoria. (A non-Roman term.) A written declaration by a debtor confirming that he assumed an obligation through *stipulatio*. The frequent usage of such documents in postclassical development influenced the transformation of the *stipulatio* into a written form of promise since the legislation of the later emperors considered a written declaration of promise a sufficient proof that an oral *stipulatio* had taken place regardless of whether this has happened or not.—See STIPULATIO.

> Platon, *NHRD* 33 (1909) 438; Riccobono, *ZSS* 35 (1914) 217; 43 (1922) 262; H. Steinacker, *Die antiken Grundlagen der frühmittelalterlichen*, Urkunde, 1927, 83; P. Collinet, *Études historiques sur le droit de Justinien* 1 (1912) 59; V. De Gautard, *Les rapports entre la stipulation et l'écrit stipulatoire*, Thèse, Lausanne, 1931; A. Segrè, *Aeg* 25 (1945) 65.

Cautio suspecti heredis. See SATISDATIO SUSPECTI HEREDIS.

Cautio usufructuaria. A security given by the usufructuary to the owner of the *res in usufructu* to guarantee that he would fulfill his duties and would not abuse his rights as an usufructuary.—D. 7.9.

> R. de Ruggiero, *St Scialoja* 1 (1905); Grosso, *ATor* 72 (1936); Palermo, *op. cit.* 39, 102.

Cautio vadimonium sisti. See VADIMONIUM.

Cautum (caveri) iubere. The order of the praetor to give security (CAUTIO). Ant. *cautum denegare*.

> Woess, *ZSS* 53 (1933) 378; Palermo, *Procedimento cauzionale*, 1942, 62.

Cavere. To give security through a ÇAUTIO (*stipulatio, pignus*, surety).—See IDONEUS.

Cavere. (When referring to the jurists' activity.) Drafting agreements (*sponsiones, mancipationes*) and last wills which the jurists composed upon request of private individuals.

> Leonhard, *RE* 3, 1085; Berger, *RE* 10, 1162.

Caveri. (When referring to provisions of statutes ["*lege cavetur*"], senatusconsults, etc.) The statute (senatusconsult) provides that. . . . With reference to last wills and testaments *caveri* denotes the dispositions of the testator.

Cedere. (Transitive.) To cede, transfer to another a right or an action or to constitute a servitude (*cedere usumfructum, aquaeductum*, etc.) in favor of another.—See CESSIO.

Cedere. (Intransitive.) With regard to terms fixed for the fulfillment of an obligation: *dies cedit* means the day "on which the sum is beginning to be owed"; *dies venit* = the day "on which the sum due can be demanded (sued for)" (D. 50.16.213 pr.). For legacies, see DIES CEDENS.

Cedere actione (lite). To recede from, to withdraw, an action. Syn. *desistere*.

> Leonhard, *RE* 3.

Cedere actionem. See CESSIO.

Cedere bonis. See CESSIO BONORUM.

Cedere foro. To leave the *forum*, i.e., when a money-banker (*nummularius*) gave up his place of business on the *forum* because of bankruptcy.

Cedere in iure. See IN IURE CESSIO.

Celeres. Cavalrymen in the earlier times. They were organized in three centuriae, each recruited from one of the original three Roman *tribus*, and were commanded by *tribuni celerum*.—See TRIBUS, RAMNES.

> Kübler, *RE* 6, 272; Saglio, *DS* 1; Berger, *RE* Suppl. 7, 397 (s.v. *Lex Iunia*).

Celsitudo. An honorific title of the emperor (*celsitudo imperatoria*). The emperors addressed the *praefecti praetorio* in rescripts with *celsitudo* ("your highness").—Syn. AMPLITUDO.

> P. Koch, *Byzantinische Beamtentitel*, 1905, 108.

Celsus, P. Iuventius. A prominent Roman jurist of the first decades of the second century after Christ. He succeeded his father, P. Iuventius Celsus the Older, a less known jurist, in the leadership of the Proculian School. *Celsus* was praetor, consul and member of the Emperor Hadrian's council. Among his works *Digesta, Epistulae* and *Quaestiones* are of a high value.

> Diehl, *RE* 10, 1363; Orestano, *NDI* 3; Gianturco, *St Fadda* 5 (1906); F. Stella-Maranca, *Intorno ai frammenti di Celso*, 1915.

Censere. Used for the resolutions of the senate (*senatus censuit* or *censuerunt* [*sc. senatores*]). *Censere,* with reference to censors and their subordinates, indicates the activity connected with the evaluation of the citizens' property for tax purposes.

Censitores. (Syn. *censores.*) Appraisers, special officials in the later Empire sent to provinces for the purpose of estimation of landed property in connection with the assessment of taxes.—C. 11.58.

Censitus. (From *censeri.*) A taxpayer whose property has been estimated and charged with a land-tax. Later, the payer of a poll-tax was also called *censitus.* Ant. *incensitus.*—C. 11.48; 50.

Censores. Censorship was created in 443 B.C. as a non-permanent magistracy. *Censores* were elected once in five years (LUSTRUM) and were in office for eighteen months. Thus through three years and a half there were no censors at all, and during that time their functions passed to other magistrates, chiefly the consuls. The *censores* had no imperium, and yet their authority was exceptionally great so that even ex-consuls competed for censorship. Their ordinances were valid for the whole quinquennial period until the appointment of new censors. Their most important tasks were the preparation of the CENSUS and making the list of the senators (LECTIO SENATUS). For further functions of the *censores* and various problems connected with censorship see CURA MORUM, NOTA, LEGES CENSORIAE, TABULAE CENSORIAE, LEX DE CENSORIA POTESTATE, LEX AEMILIA, LEX OVINIA, LEX PUBLILIA PHILONIS, TRIBUS, CENSUS EQUITUM. The censorship lost its importance in the late first century after Christ.

Kubitschek, *RE* 3; Humbert, *DS* 1; Manca, *NDI* 3; De Ruggiero, *DE* 2; Treves, *OCD*; M. Nowak, *Die Strafverhängungen der c.,* Diss. Breslau, 1909; O. Leuze, *Zur Gesch. der röm. Zensur* 1 (1909); E. Schmähling, *Die Sittenaufsicht der Zensoren,* 1938; Klotz, *Rheinisches Museum für Philologie,* 1939; Plachy, *BIDR* 47 (1940) 104; R. V. Cram, *Harvard St of Class. Philology* 51 (1940) 71; A. Calderini, *La censura in Roma antica,* 1944; Siber, *Fschr Schulz* 1 (1951) 466.

Censorius. (Adj.) Connected with the office and functions of the censors.—See NOTA, LEGES CENSORIAE, LEX DE CENSORIA POTESTATE.

Censorius. (Noun.) An ex-censor.

Censu manumissio. See MANUMISSIO CENSU.

Censuales. Officials of the later Empire, in Rome and Constantinople, subordinate to the *praefectus urbi* and concerned with the taxation of senators and various other matters, similar to those which in the Republic belonged to the tasks of *aediles* (games, administration of public buildings, survey of students studying in the capital, police functions, and the like). In other cities *censuales* were primarily active in making taxation lists.—See MAGISTER CENSUS.—C. 10.71.

Seeck, *RE* 3.

Censualis. (Adj.) See CENSUS, FORMA CENSUALIS.

Census. The registration of citizens combined with the estimation of their property and their assignment to CENTURIAE. Upon summons by the censors the head of a family had to appear before them and make a declaration under oath (*professio censualis*) concerning his family and property. Taxation (as long as direct taxation in Italy existed, i.e., until 167 B.C.) followed the evaluation of the property. By an edict preceding the *census* (*lex censui censendo*), the censors announced publicly the principles to be observed in making the returns required, and the rules they would follow in the evaluation of the moral conduct of the citizens.—See NOTA CENSORIA, FORMA CENSUALIS, A CENSIBUS. *Census* is also the term for the list of the taxpayers.—D. 50.15; C. 11.58; 49.

Kubitschek, *RE* 3; Seeck, *RE* 5, 1184; Schwahn, *RE* 7A, 63; Kalopothakes, *DE* 2; Stevenson, *OCD*; Garofalo, *BIDR* 13 (1900) 273; Cavaignac, *Revue de philologie* 1934, 72; Bourne, *Classical Weekly* 45 (1951/2) 152.

Census equitum. The inspection of cavalrymen and their horses by the censors.

Centenarius. An official with a salary of 100,000 sesterces (since the time of Hadrian). Also a private individual with a property valued at the sum mentioned above.

Centesima. (*Sc. usura.*) One per cent interest per month, i.e., 12 per cent per annum.—See USURAE CENTESIMAE.

Kubitschek, *RE* 3; Humbert, *DS* 1.

Centesima rerum venalium. A tax on sales at auction (one per cent) introduced by Augustus, reduced by Tiberius to *ducentesima* (one-half per cent), then again restored as *centesima.*

Kubitschek, *RE* 3; Moschella, *NDI*; Rostowzew, *DE* 2, 582; R. Cagnat, *Ét. historiques sur les impôts indirects à Rome,* 1882, 227.

Centonarii. Voluntary firemen.—See FABRI.

H. J. Loane, *Industry and commerce in R.,* 1938, 73.

Centumviri. A special court for trials concerning inheritances and property affairs (*vindicationes*) of a higher value. The centumviral panel was composed originally of 105 jurors (3 from each of the 35 TRIBUS) divided into groups (*tribunalia*). Later their number increased to 180. After the normal procedure *in iure* (before the magistrate) the matter went to a court selected from the centumviral list. The form of proceeding before the *centumviri* was always the *legis actio,* even when this form was generally substituted by the formulary procedure. The *centumviri* disappeared in the third century after Christ.—See LEX CREPEREIA, HASTA, PROVOCATIO.

Wlassak, *RE* 3; Gayet, *DS* 1; Moschella, *NDI* 3; De Ruggiero, *DE* 2; Berger, *OCD*; Olivier-Martin, *Le tribunal des c.,* 1904; Jobbé-Duval, *NRHD* 28–29 (1904–1905); F. Bozza, *Sulla competenza dei c.,* 1928; Koschaker, *ZSS* 50 (1930) 679; M. Nicolau, *Causa liberalis,* 1933, 35.

Centuria. Tradition ascribes to the king Servius Tullius the organization of the Roman people (well-to-do men, capable to military service) in *centuriae* (units of about a hundred persons) which assembled in so-called COMITIA CENTURIATA. The connection of this political reform with the military formations is obvious. This tradition is rejected by many scholars as unreliable. As a military unit the *centuria* is a group of one hundred (later less) soldiers, under the command of a *centurio*. In later development sixty *centuriae* formed a legion.—See COMITIA CENTURIATA (Bibl.), PROLETARII.

Kubitschek, *RE* 3; Humbert, *DS* 1; Moschella, *NDI* 3; De Ruggiero, *DE* 2; Mattingly, *OCD*; A. Rosenberg, *Zenturienverfassung*, 1911; Giorgi, *Le origini dell'ordinamento centuriato, St storici per l'antichità classica* 5 (1912); Arangio-Ruiz, *La riforma dell'ordinamento centuriato, Scr Arnò*, 1928; H. M. D. Parker, *The Rom. legions*, 1928; Fraccaro, *St Bonfante* 1 (1929) 103; *idem, Ath* 12 (1934); De Sanctis, *Riv. di filol. e d'istruzione class.* 1933; Zancan, *AVen* 1933-34, 869; G. Giannelli, *Atene e Roma* 37 (1935); Cavaignac, *RIDA* 2 (= *Mél De Visscher* 1 (1949) 173.

Centuria praerogativa. The *centuria* which, selected by lot, voted first in the *comitia centuriata*.

Centuria vigilum. See VIGILES.

Centurio. The military commander of a *centuria*. The *centuriones* of the first line (*hastati*) were of a lower rank than those of the second line (*principes*); the latter were of a lower rank than those of the third line (*triarii*). The first *centurio* in the legion was the *centurio primi pili* or *primipilus*.—See CENTURIA (Bibl.).

Domaszewski, *RE* 3; Parker, *OCD*; Th. Wegeleben, *Die Rangordnung der röm. Centurionen*, Diss. Berlin, 1913; Parker, *JRS* 26 (1936) 45; De Laet, *AntCl* 9 (1940) 13.

Cerae. Wax-tablets. They were used for short letters, receipts, brief written agreements, testaments and codicils (*codicilli cerati*). Syn. *tabellae ceratae*.—See APOCHAE POMPEIANAE.

Lafaye, *DS* 5, p. 3 (*s.v. tabellae*).

Cernere hereditatem. See CRETIO.

Certa et sollemnia verba. See VERBA CERTA ET SOLLEMNIA, SOLLEMNIA VERBA.

Certamen. (From *certare* = to fight.) Applied to lawsuits.

Certum. (Noun.) A fixed sum or quantity of things being the object of an obligation or of a claim in a trial (*obligatio certi, condictio certi, certum petere*). *Certum* is "where the object (*quid*), the quality (*quale*), and the quantity (*quantum*) is expressly evident" (D. 45.1.74). Ant. *incertum*. The distinction *certum*—*incertum* is important in the law of obligations and in the civil procedure.—C. 4.2.—See CERTUS, CONDICTIO CERTI, CONDICTIO INCERTI, LEGIS ACTIO PER CONDICTIONEM, LEGIS ACTIO PER IUDICIS POSTULATIONEM.

Certus. Exactly determined, such as a sum of money, a specific object, the price in a sale (*pretium*), a slave indicated by name, a limited plot of land (*fundus Cornelianus*), a date fixed by calendar, a determined

place (see ACTIO DE EO QUOD CERTO LOCO), etc.—See CONDICTIO CERTAE PECUNIAE, CONDICTIO CERTAE REI.

Cessare (cessatio). When referring to actions, procedural measures, or statutory provisions, to become inapplicable, unsuitable, to lose validity. When used of a person bound to do something (a guardian, *procurator, debtor*) = to neglect, to fail to fulfil his duties.

Cessicius tutor. See TUTOR CESSICIUS, IN IURE CESSIO TUTELAE.

Cessio. The transfer of a creditor's rights to another person. It was not directly feasible in Roman classical law. The obligatory relationship (*obligatio*) was strictly personal. The transfer could, however, be managed in another way, either by a novatory promise of the debtor to pay to a new creditor (the transferee) the thing he owed the former creditor, or by the transfer of the action against the debtor by appointment of the transferee as the creditor's representative through a mandate (*cedere, mandare, transferre actionem*) to sue the debtor. The cessionary was *procurator in rem suam* (a representative on behalf of his own) inasmuch as the condemnation of the debtor was in his favor. This form of *cessio* was more popular because the first way (*novatio*) was impossible if the debtor refused to cooperate. But certain inconveniences were involved in a *cessio actionis*, too, because the debtor might pay the former creditor until the action of the cessionary was brought against him, and, besides, the appointment of the transferee by *mandatum* became invalid through the death of the primary creditor (the mandator). In the later law a notification of the cession performed, made to the debtor by the creditor, improved the situation of the cessionary. In further development the cessionary was granted, in certain specific cases, an *actio utilis* against the debtor. This became a general rule in Justinian's law.—See BENEFICIUM CEDENDARUM ACTIONUM, LEX ANASTASIANA.

Biondi, *NDI* 3; Schulz, *ZSS* 27 (1906) 82; Eisele, *ibid.* 46; Beseler, *Beiträge* 3 (1913) 172; Drechsler, *Actio utilis des Cessionars*, Diss. Freiburg, 1914.

Cessio bonorum. A debtor who became insolvent without his fault might voluntarily surrender his property to the creditors in order to avoid an execution by a compulsory sale thereof which involved infamy. The measure was introduced in favor of the debtors by the *Lex Iulia de cessione bonorum*.—D. 42.3; C. 7.71.

Wlassak, *RE* 3; Weiss, *RE* Suppl. 6, 61; Humbert, *DS* 1 (*s.v. bonorum c.*); Donatuti, *NDI* 3; Zanzucchi, *BIDR* 29 (1918) 71; Guénoun, *La c. b.*, Paris, 1920; Woess, *ZSS* 43 (1923) 485; S. Solazzi, *Concorso dei creditori* 4 (1943) 130; *Acta Divi Augusti* 1 (1945) 152 (Bibl.).

Cessio in iure. See IN IURE CESSIO.

Ceteri (ceterae). Used by the compilers in order to introduce a generalization of what originally referred only to a certain category of persons or things (as, for instance, *heredes et ceteri successores, ceteri con-*

tractus).—See BONORUM POSSESSIO, SUCCESSORES CETERI.

Guarneri-Citati, *Indice delle parole,* etc.² (1927) 17.

Charisius, Aurelius Arcadius. A little known jurist of the late third or the first half of the fourth century after Christ. He wrote monographs on the office of the *praefectus praetorio,* on witnesses and on public charges (*munera*).

Jors, *RE* 3, 2146.

Charta. The material on which a document is written. In the later Empire the term (or *chartula*) indicates the document itself.

L. De Sarlo, *Il documento oggetto di rapporti,* 1935, 33.

Chartularius. An official in the late Empire dealing primarily with the registers of taxpayers.—C. 12.49.

Chirographum. A promissory note written by the debtor and delivered to the creditor. Gaius mentions it as a *litterarum obligatio* used by peregrines (the name [= handwriting] reveals the Greek origin of the institution). Used by Romans the *chirographum* had the value of any written document, and was considered only an evidence of a previous *stipulatio.* It was later applied even without a preceding stipulatory promise. An *exceptio non numeratae pecuniae* (i.e., an objection to the effect that the creditor did not give any money to the debtor) could be opposed to a claim from a *chirographum,* but only within five years after the issuance of the *chirographum* (two years in Justinian's law). Later it could not be oppugned at all.—C. 8.26.

Lécrivain, *DS* 5, 156; M. Kroell, *Le rôle de l'écrit dans la preuve de contrat,* 1906, 137; Messina-Vitrano, *AG* 80 (1908) 94; Riccobono, *ZSS* 43 (1922) 320; Arangio-Ruiz, *FIR* 3 (1943) no. 130; L. de Sarlo, *Il documento come oggetto dei rapporti* (1935) 7, 35.

Christiani. In pagan Rome Christians were considered enemies of the state (*hostes publici*) and as such they were exposed to persecution and punishment for *crimen maiestatis.* Besides, the secret meetings of the Christians were punishable under the *lex Iulia de collegiis* as illicit associations (*collegia illicita*). Still in the early third century mentions of *illicita Christianorum coitio* (gathering) appear; it is likely that a special enactment was later issued against Christian associations. A milder practice was exercised with regard to the so-called COLLEGIA FUNERATICIA (TENUIORUM), but administrative coercive measures ordered in police proceedings (*coercitio*) by the discretionary power of the magistrates were always applicable. Refusal to take part in religious ceremonies dedicated to the celebration of gods or the emperor as a god was considered as a confession to profess Christianity in the same measure as an open declaration, "I am a Christian," sufficed for an accusation of *crimen maiestatis.* A particular practice was introduced in connection with the persecution by the emperor Decius; the production of a certificate that an individual participated in pagan sacrifices issued by a competent commission was an evidence that he was not a Christian; see LIBELLUS LIBELLATICI.—C. 1.10.—See CRIMEN MAIESTATIS, ECCLESIA.

M. Conrat (Cohn), *Die Christenverfolgungen,* 1897; Mattingly, *OCD* (*s.v. persecutio*); Mommsen, *Juristische Schriften* 3 (1907, ex 1890) 389; R. Rota, *Il delitto politico nell'età antica,* 1907, 138; Costa, *Crimini e pene,* 1921, 105 (Bibl.); Saleilles, *Mél Girard* 2 (1912); Vitale, *Rev. de philologie* 49 (1925); Schnorr v. Carolsfeld, *Gesch. der juristischen Person* 1 (1933) 243; P. W. Duff, *Personality in Rom. private law,* 1938, 169; Levy, *BIDR* 45 (1938) 122; G. Bovini, *La proprietà ecclesiastica e la condizione giuridica della Chiesa,* 1949, 145.

Cibaria. Food, provisions. Interpretative rules for *cibaria* in legacies are abundant in juristic writings. *Cibaria* is also the daily remuneration granted to imperial officials during their service travels through the empire.—D. 34.1.—See SALARIUM.

Fiebiger, *RE* 3; Fournier, *DS* 2.

Cingulum. A girdle. In later imperial constitutions it denotes symbolically the rank of a high civil or military state official.

Kübler, *RE* 7A, 2024.

Cinna. An unknown jurist of the first half of the first century after Christ.

Berger, *RE* Suppl. 3, 250.

Cino da Pistoia. A renowned postglossator (died 1314).—See GLOSSATORES.

Monti, *NDI* 3 (Bibl.).

Cippus. A boundary stone. Syn. *terminus.*—See TERMINARE.

Circumcisio. Circumcision was first generally prohibited by Hadrian. Later Antoninus Pius permitted it as a special concession to Jews. The interdiction of *circumcisio* of slaves was always in force, but evidently it was practiced since several imperial constitutions repeated the prohibition. A circumcised slave became free.—C. 1.10.

Hitzig, *RE* 3; Zmigryder-Konopka, *Les Romains et la circoncision des Juifs, Eos* 33 (1931) 334.

Circumscribere (circumscriptio). To defraud the partner in a transaction. It is a statutory term in the LEX PLAETORIA which forbade the *circumscriptio adulescentium* (defrauding young men).

Humbert, *DS* 1.

Circumvenire legem. To evade a law by trickery.

Citra causae cognitionem. Without investigation of the truth. Certain declarations of individuals made before an official (*professiones*) were accepted for registration only on the ground of the person's allegations. Similarly some orders of the praetor were issued on the assumption that what has been proffered by the party was true, without any further examination of the factual or legal situation. A typical case of such procedure is the issuance of an interdict.— See CAUSAE COGNITIO, INTERDICTUM.

Montevecchi, *Aeg* 28 (1948) 145.

Citare. To call a person to court as a witness. The term is not syn. with *in ius vocare* (see IN IUS VOCATIO).

Civilis. Connected with the *cives* (citizens) or a *civitas* (state, city, community). When opposed to *criminalis, civilis* means a private matter as contrasted with a criminal one. Another juxtaposition is *civilis—naturalis* (*possessio, obligatio*) in which *civilis* alludes to a connection with the *ius civile,* whereas *naturalis* lacks such a connection and means only a natural, real state of things.—See IUS CIVILE, NATURALIS.

Civiliter. Opposed to *criminaliter* = through a civil trial; opposed to *naturaliter* = according to *ius civile.*

Civis. A Roman citizen (also *civis Romanus*), unless a citizen of another city or state is meant.—See CIVITAS ROMANA.

Civis Romanus. A Roman citizen, i.e., any person who either by birth or otherwise became an integral part of the Roman people (*populus Romanus*) and as such enjoyed public and private rights connected with Roman citizenship. Only a small group of citizens (not born as Roman citizens) was deprived of public rights, e.g., *cives sine suffragio,* former slaves (freedmen) and in certain cases former peregrines.—See CIVITAS, ROMANA, CIVITATES SINE SUFFRAGIO.

De Ruggiero, *DE* 2; Lévy-Bruhl, *ACDR* Roma 2, 471.

Civitas Romana. Roman citizenship. Beside freedom (*status libertatis*) Roman citizenship was an essential condition for being subject of rights, both private and public. Citizenship was acquired principally by birth of parents, Roman citizens. A child born in a legitimate marriage, was Roman citizen, even if the father alone was citizen, for children took status of their fathers. Therefore, a child born *ex iustis nuptiis* of a peregrine father and a Roman mother, was a peregrine. Decisive was the status at the time of conception. See LEX MINICIA. Through manumission a slave became not only free but also a Roman citizen. Admission of peregrines to Roman citizenship was effected by a special concession either in favor of individuals or larger groups, inhabitants of a city or country. Under the Republic, Roman citizenship was granted by the Roman people and later by the emperor. Particular services rendered to the state (military service or special merits, see also LEX VISELLIA) were the occasion for granting citizenship to individuals (*viritim, singillatim*). Political tendencies dictated the acceptance of foreign elements in larger groups into the orbit of Roman citizenship. Between 90 and 87 B.C. the whole of Italy obtained Roman citizenship; later it was extended gradually to cities and provinces abroad until the Emperor Caracalla (A.D. 212, Dig. 1.5.17) granted Roman citizenship to all inhabitants "of the Roman world" (*in orbe Romano*), with the exception of *dediticii.*

See CONSTITUTIO ANTONINIANA. The rights of the Roman citizens comprized the right to compete for a magistracy (*ius honorum*), to vote in public assemblies (*ius suffragii*), to appeal to the people in the case of condemnation in a criminal trial, to conclude a Roman marriage, full legal capacity and admission to solemn legal Roman forms. Among the duties of a Roman citizen the principal was military service in a legion and payment of taxes which in the course of times were subject to various reforms. The loss of liberty (*capitis deminutio maxima*) involved the loss of citizenship, but there was also a loss of citizenship without loss of liberty (*capitis deminutio media*), as in the case of *interdictio aqua et igni* or *deportatio.* —See CAPUT, REIECTIO CIVITATIS.

Kornemann, *RE* Suppl. 1, 304; Humbert, *DS* 1; De Ruggiero, *DE* 2; Colagrosso, *NDI* 3, 201; Sherwin-White, *OCD* (*s.v.* citizenship); C. E. Goodfellow, *Roman citizenship,* 1935; Zancan, *AVen* 95 (1935/6); Bernardi, *Ath* 16 (1938) 239; A. N. Sherwin-White, *The Roman citizenship* 1939; Lombardi, *AG* 126 (1941) 192; De Visscher, *La dualité de droits de cité dans le monde romain, Bull. Cl. de Lettres Acad. Royale de Belgique* 33 (1947) 50; *idem, AnCat* 3 (1949) 1; Arangio-Ruiz, *Scr Carnelutti* 4 (1950) 53; Schönbauer, *Anzeiger Akad. d. Wissensch. Wien, hist.-philos. Klasse,* 1949, 343; *idem, Jour. Juristic Papyrology* 6 (1952) 17; Niccolini, *Atti Accad. Lincei,* 1946; C. Castello, *L'acquisto della cittadinanza e i suoi riflessi nel dir. rom.,* 1951; De Visscher, *ADO–RIDA* 1 (1952) 401.

Civitas optimo iure. Roman citizenship granted to foreigners (or municipalities) with all the rights enjoyed by a native Roman citizen.

Civitates (civitas). All *cives* (citizens) of a larger or smaller territorial, political unit (state, city, colony, municipality) form a *civitas.* Hence the term is also applied to an autonomous unit itself and the Romans speak of their own state as a *civitas* ("*nostra*") as well as of other states (*civitas Atheniensium*) or a group of states (*civitates Graecorum*). The term is, however, especially used with regard to foreign *civitates* (*civitates peregrinae*) in the sense of a large group of free individuals living together and organized as a legal social unit (*societas;* Cicero: *coetus hominum iure sociati, De republ.* 6.13.13).—See the following items.

Kornemann, *RE* Suppl. 1, 300; Sherwin-White, *OCD* 195; De Ruggiero *DE* 2; Lombardi, *AG* 126 (1941) 193.

Civitates foederatae. Allied cities and communities in Italy and the provinces with which Rome concluded a treaty (*foedus*). They enjoyed certain privileges and exemption from taxation and lived according to their own laws (*suis legibus uti*), but they were seldom granted exemption from military service.—See FOEDUS.

Kornemann, *RE* Suppl. 1, 302; De Ruggiero, *DE* 2, 255; Sherwin-White, *The Roman citizenship,* 1939, 157.

Civitates liberae et immunes. Free cities enjoying a high degree of self-government and exemption from taxes. The status of a *civitas libera* was granted either by a *lex data* (a charter decreed by the Roman people, the senate, or later, by the emperor) or by a treaty of alliance (*foedus*) with Rome (*civitates liberae et foederatae*), by which the autonomous position of the *civitates liberae* was guaranteed in a stronger way since the treaty could not be unilaterally revoked, except in the case of war. According to a Roman conception "a people is free when it is not subject to the power of another people" (D. 49.15. 7.1).

> De Ruggiero, *DE* 2, 258; Sherwin-White, *op. cit.* 150; Heuss, *Die völkerrechtlichen Grundlagen,* Klio, Beiheft 31 (1933) 99; Vittinghoff, *ZSS* 68 (1951) 472.

Civitates sine suffragio. Cities with limited Roman citizenship, being deprived of the right to vote in the popular assemblies. They were not enrolled into a Roman *tribus,* and thus their accession to *comitia tributa* was excluded.

> Kübler, *RE* 4A, 1897; Kornemann, *RE* Suppl. 1, 309; Zmigryder-Konopka, *Eos* 32 (1929) 587; Bernardi, *Ath* 1938, 239; Sherwin-White, *op. cit.* 38; E. Manni, *Per la storia dei municipii,* 1947, 56.

Civitates stipendiariae. *Civitates* subject to the payment of tributes and imposts to Rome. Ant. *civitates immunes.*—See STIPENDIUM.

Clam. Secretly. An act is committed *clam* when it is done with the intention to conceal it (*animo celandi*) before another person since otherwise a controversy with the latter would be unavoidable. The term is of particular importance in the doctrine of *possessio* (see CLANDESTINA POSSESSIO) and in the INTERDICTUM QUOD VI AUT CLAM.

> M. David, *L'interdit quod vi aut clam,* 1947, 18.

Clamor. A friendly call, applause. It is the most usual element of ACCLAMATIO. As a cry in danger it had a certain importance in connection with the theft (*furtum*) when a person surprised and attacked by a burglar called for help. Already the Twelve Tables mention the *clamor* applied in a similar situation (*endoplorato*).

> Berger, *St Albertoni* 1 (1933) 381; Wieacker, *Fschr Wenger* 1 (1944) 129.

Clandestina possessio. Possession acquired secretly (see CLAM) against or without the will of the owner or the actual possessor. Such possession was stigmatized as *possessio vitiosa* (= defective) and was exposed to an *exceptio vitiosae possessionis* by the person from whom the thing had been taken away. —See POSSESSIO, INIUSTA.

Clara persona. A senator or his wife. Execution on their property in the case of insolvency was made in a milder form (*honestius*); there was no *missio in possessionem* and the sale of the property was performed according to a *senatusconsult* (of an unknown date) by a special curator (*curator distrahendorum bonorum gratia*).

Clarigatio. A solemn oral declaration addressed by the FETIALES in the name of the Roman people to a foreign state. It concerned territories or things claimed by the Romans. If the claims were not satisfied by the foreign state, a formal declaration of war followed.—See INDICTIO BELLI.

> Volterra, *Scr Carnelutti* 4 (1950) 245.

Clarissimatus. The dignity of a person who belongs to the class of *clarissimi.* Syn. *dignitas clarissima.*— See CLARISSIMUS.

Clarissimus. (*Clarissimus vir, clarissima persona.*) An honorary title of senators and high officials of senatorial rank. A senator's wife had the right to the title *clarissima.*—C. 3.24; 5.33.—See CLARA PERSONA, SPECTABILIS.

> Seeck, *RE* 3, 2628; P. Koch, *Byzantinische Beamtentitel,* 1903; De Ruggiero, 2, 267; O. Hirschfeld, *Kleine Schriften,* 1913, 647.

Classiarii. (*Sc. milites*). Marines in the Roman navy (*classis*). Syn. *classici.*—C. 11.13.

Classici. See CLASSIARII.

Classicus. A person enlisted in the first class of wealthy persons on occasion of the CENSUS. The property required was 100,000 asses. Persons listed in the lower classes were *infra classem.*—See LEX VOCONIA.

> Kübler, *RE* 3, 2628; Gabba, *Ath* 27 (1949) 173.

Classis. The Roman navy. Also the name of the five groups of citizens distinguished according to their wealth in the politico-military reform ascribed to Servius Tullius (see CENTURIA). The classes comprized only the foot-soldiers of the army.—See NAUARCHUS.

> Kübler, *RE* 3, 2630; De Ruggiero, *DE* 2, 271; C. G. Starr, Jr., *The Rom. Imperial Navy,* 31 B.C.–A.D. 324 (Ithaca, 1941); Wickert, *Würzburger Jahrbücher für die Altertumswissenschaft* 4 (1949) 100.

Claudius. This name, particularly in notes to the *Digesta* of the jurist, Q. Cervidius SCAEVOLA, refers to the jurist, Claudius TRYPHONINUS.

Clausula. A specific legal provision of a statute, a senatusconsult or of the praetorian edict. Also a particular clause of an agreement between private individuals (e.g., of a *stipulatio*).—See DOLUS MALUS, NOVA CLAUSULA.

> Leonhard, *RE* 4.

Clausula doli. (*De dolo malo.*) See DOLUS MALUS.

Clausus (clusus). A slave put into jail by his master. —See CARCER PRIVATUS.

> Wenger, *ZSS* 61 (1941) 357.

Claves. Keys. The delivery of *claves* (*traditio clavium*) of a storage-room (a granary or a wine-cellar) was considered in later law the delivery of the merchandise itself by the seller to the buyer. Such kind of delivery is called in literature a "symbolic tradition."

> Riccobono, *ZSS* 34 (1913) 197; F. Schulz, *Einführung in das Studium der Digesten,* 1916, 68.

Clavus latus. A broad purple stripe on the toga or tunic. The *clavus latus* (*laticlavus*) on the tunic was a mark of distinction of senators and their sons, hence the senatorial rank itself is indicated as *latus clavus* (the bestowal by the emperor = *conferre latum clavum;* to obtain the senatorial rank upon request = *impetrare latum clavum*). The privilege of a *latus clavus* was later extended to higher dignitaries of the empire (*laticlavii*). Ant. *clavus angustus* = a narrow stripe on the border of the toga, a distinction mark for persons of equestrian rank.—See TOGA PRAETEXTA, ADLECTIO.

   Hula, *RE* 4, 6; De Ruggiero, *DE* 2, 306; Balsdon, *OCD*.

Clementia. Referred to gracious acts of the emperor. Later emperors, Justinian included, like to speak of their clemency (*placet nostrae clementiae*).

   Dahlmann, *C. Caesaris, Neue Jahrb. für Wissensch. und Jugendbildung* 70 (1934) 17.

Clementissimus. A title of the emperors since the third century.

   De Ruggiero, *DE* 2.

Clerici. The title of the Code of Justinian, 1.3 (*De episcopis et clericis*) contains a series of imperial constitutions of the Christian emperors (A.D. 313–534) concerning the particular legal situation of ecclesiastical persons and various privileges granted to clergymen (in judicial matters, with regard to testamentary dispositions, exemption from guardianship and public charges, etc.).

   Génestal, *NRHD* 32 (1908) 161; F. Ferrari dalle Spade, *Immunità ecclesiastiche, AVen* 99 (1939–1940) 115, 162, 171, 196.

Clientela. See CLIENTES.

Clientes. In the earliest period *clientes* were strangers who had migrated to Rome where they submitted themselves to patrician families (*gentes*) in order to obtain their protection. Men from vanquished countries also looked for a similar relation. (See DEDITIO.) Clientship created reciprocal duties. The *clientes* worked for their patrons, who in turn gave them protection in case of need, especially in judicial matters. The *clientes* were free men, but in fact their situation was half servile. Later their situation improved considerably although their social authority and dignity remained always low. They were permitted to acquire property and many of them became gradually well-to-do people. The *clientes* had to assist the patron and his family in the case of need, and to ransom him when he had fallen into captivity. They appeared in public as his retainers and were subject to his jurisdiction. The whole relationship being based on reciprocal confidence (*fides*) the patron could not sue his client before court nor testify against him. A reciprocal duty bound the client. Fraud committed by the patron on his client stood under religious sanctions; the pertinent provision derives from the Twelve Tables (*sacer esto*). Clientship (*clientela*) was hereditary but lost its original force and meaning in the course of time. The *clientes* were gradually absorbed by other strata of the population, primarily by the plebeians. In quite a different sense *clientes* is used with reference to the clients of an advocate.—See IUS APPLICATIONIS, DOTARE, GENS.

   Premerstein, *RE* 4; Humbert, *DS* 2; Anon., *NDI* 3; Momigliano, *OCD*; G. Curis, *Clientela e schiavitù,* 1902; S. L. Mohler, *Class. Studies in honor of J. C. Rolfe,* Philadelphia, 1931, 239; Lemosse, *RIDA* 3 (= *Mél De Visscher* 2, 1949) 46.

Cloaca. A sewer. Protection of public health (*salubritas civitatum*) and of private interests required at times the intervention of judicial or administrative authorities in the case of defective sewers.—See INTERDICTA DE CLOACIS, INTERDICTA DE REFICIENDO, SERVITUS CLOACAE IMMITTENDAE.—D. 43.23.

Coactio causae (in breve). See CAUSAE CONIECTIO.

Coactor. A collector of taxes or of money paid by sellers at a public auction.

   Leist, *RE* 2, 227; v. Premerstein, *RE* 4; De Ruggiero, *DE* 2, 314; Platon, *NRHD* 33 (1909) 149.

Coactus volui. An expression used in the doctrine of *metus* (duress), indicating that an individual although acting under duress is nevertheless acting willingly, something he would not have done if he were free (e.g., accepting an inheritance under duress). This opinion was shared only by a few jurists.—See METUS.

   U. v. Lübtow, *Quod metus causa gestum erit,* 1932, 61.

Codex. Wooden tablets covered with wax or sheets of papyrus or parchment, bound together in book form. A booklet of few pages = *codicilli.* In the late Empire, collections of imperial constitutions were designated as *codices* (see below).

   Wünsch, *RE* 4.

Codex accepti et expensi (depensi). A cash-book into which a Roman used to note the sums received (*acceptum*) and paid out (*expensum*). A *codex* (*liber*) *rationum domesticarum* was used for similar purposes. The entries might be used as evidence in a trial, but they did not have the force of full proof. Only bookkeeping of bankers enjoyed particular confidence.—See ARGENTARII, NOMINA ARCARIA, NOMINA TRANSSCRIPTICIA.

   Humbert, *DS* 1; Leonhard, *RE* 4; Aru, *NDI* 3; R. Beigel, *Rechnungswesen und Buchführung der Römer* (Karlsruhe, 1904) 181; Voigt, *ASächGW* 10 (1888) 544, 552.

Codex Gregorianus. The earliest private, systematic collection of imperial constitutions, published not before A.D. 291 by an unknown author (Gregorius?). The oldest constitution is by Hadrian. The *Codex Gregorianus* is not preserved and is known in excerpts only from the FRAGMENTA VATICANA, COLLATIO, CONSULTATIO, LEX ROMANA BURGUNDIONUM, LEX ROMANA VISIGOTHORUM, and an appendix thereto. A continuation of this collection is the *Codex Hermogenianus.* Both compilations acquired seemingly a considerable authority although composed as private enterprises, since Justinian refers to them as the sources for his Code.

Editions: G. Haenel, *Corpus iuris anteiustiniani* 2 (1837); P. Krüger, *Collectio* 3, 224; Baviera, *FIR* 2² (1940) 655. Bibl.: Baudry, *DS* 1; Jörs, *RE* 4; Scherillo, *NDI* 4; Rotondi, *Scritti* 1 (1922, ex 1914) 111; Scherillo, *St Ratti,* 1934, 247; F. Schulz, *History of R. legal science,* 1946, 287, 309.

Codex Hermogenianus. A collection supplementary to the *Codex Gregorianus* containing constitutions of Diocletian from 291 until 294. The composer of the compilation was one Hermogenianus (not identical with the jurist Hermogenianus?). Excerpts of the *Codex Hermogenianus* are preserved in the same sources as those of the CODEX GREGORIANUS. Several constitutions of the years 295–305, 314, and 364–365 were added later to the original Code.

Editions: G. Haenel, *Corpus iuris anteiustiniani* 2 (1837); P. Krüger, *Collectio* 3, 249; Baviera, *FIR* 2² (1940) 665. Bibl.: Baudry, *DS* 1; Jörs, *RE* 4; Scherillo, *NDI* 4; *idem, St Ratti,* 1934, 247; Rotondi, *Scritti* 1 (1922, ex 1914) 118.

Codex Iustinianus. In 528 Justinian charged a commission composed of high officials and lawyers with the task of compiling a collection of imperial constitutions. For earlier imperial enactments the three *Codices, Gregorianus, Hermogenianus,* and *Theodosianus,* had to be used. The Code published April 7, 529, soon proved obsolete because of the copious later legislative activity of the emperor. Therefore a new edition (*Codex repetitae praelectionis*) was ordered in 533, and published in the middle of December, 534. The latest constitution therein is of November 4, 534, the earliest by Hadrian who is represented in the Code by one enactment only (6.23.1). The Code is divided into twelve books, the books into titles. Within each title the constitutions are chronologically arranged and provided with information concerning the emperor, the destinatary to whom they were issued and the date of issue. As in the Digest, the compilers were authorized to make appropriate changes in the texts of the constitutions of former emperors for which a comparison with the pertinent texts in the *Codex Theodosianus* is very instructive, showing both the technique and the extent of the interpolations accomplished.—See QUINQUAGINTA DECISIONES.

Editions: P. Krueger, *Codex Iustinianus* 1877; *idem, Corpus Iuris Civilis* 2¹⁰ (1929). Vocabularies: Longo, *Vocabolario delle costituzioni di Giustiniano, BIDR* 10 1898); Marchi, *Le interpolazioni risultanti dal confronto etc. BIDR* 18 (1906); Chiazzese, *Confronti testuali, AnPal* 17 (1933); R. Mayr-M. San Nicolò, *Vocabularium Codicis Iustiniani,* 1–2 (1920, 1923); Bibl.: Baudry, *DS* 1; Jörs, *RE* 4; Anon., *NDI* 3 (s.v. Codice di Giustiniano); Berger, *OCD* 207; Rotondi, *Tecnica dei compilatori del Cod. Giust., Studi sulle fonti del Cod. Giust., Scritti giur.* 1 (1922) 71, 110; Schulz, *ZSS* 50 (1930); *idem, St Bonfante* 1 (1929); *idem, ACII* 1 (1935); Collinet, *L'originalité du Code de Just., ACII* 1 (1935); for the remnants of the first edition of the Code Schulz, *History of R. legal science,* 1946, 318; Berger, *BIDR* 55–56 (1952) 110; for Justinian's legisla-

tion during the compilation of the Digest: Longo, *BIDR* 19 (1907) 132; De Francisci, *BIDR* 22, 23, 27, 31 (1910, 1911, 1915, 1921).

Codex (liber) rationum domesticarum. A housebook in which proceeds and expenses were entered.—See CODEX ACCEPTI ET EXPENSI.

Codex repetitae praelectionis. See CODEX IUSTINIANUS.

Codex Theodosianus. An official collection of imperial constitutions from A.D. 312 (Constantine) until 438 when the Code was published by Theodosius II. The Code is divided into sixteen books, the books into titles. The compiling commission was authorized by the emperor to omit obsolete provisions and superfluous phrases, to make additions, emendations and alterations. A large portion of the Theodosian Code found acceptance in the *Lex Romana Visigothorum,* and later in Justinian's Code, not without abridgements and alterations. The Theodosian Code was in force in the East until its abrogation by the Code of Justinian (first edition 529) and in Italy until the conquest by Justinian in 554. The *Codex Theodosianus* is not preserved as a whole; a great portion thereof is known through the *Lex Romana Visigothorum,* the existing manuscripts contain only parts of the codification.—See CODEX IUSTINIANUS, INTERPRETATIONES.

Editions: Mommsen, *Theodosiani libri XVI,* 1905; P. Krueger, *C.Th.* 1923–1926 (only books I–VIII); Engl. translation: C. Pharr, *The Theodosian Code and Novels, and the Sirmondian Constitutions,* Princeton, 1952. Vocabulary: Gradenwitz, *Heidelberger Index zum Theodosianus,* 1925, Suppl. 1929. Bibl.: Mommsen, *Juristische Schriften* 2 (1905), several articles; Baudry, *DS* 1; Jörs, *RE* 4; Scherillo, *NDI* 3; Gradenwitz, *ZSS* 34 (1913), 38 (1917); G. Ferrari, *Osservazioni sulla trasmissione diplomatica del C. T.,* 1915; Wieacker, *Lateinische Kommentare zum C. Th., Symb. Frib. Lenel,* 1931; Scherillo, *St Ratti,* 1934, 247; *idem, St Albertoni* 1 (1935) 515; Archi, *SDHI* 2 (1936); Scherillo, *SDHI* 6 (1940) 408, 8 (1942) 5; Higgins, *Reliability of titles and dates in C. Th., Byz* 10 (1935) 621; Solazzi, *Glossemi e interpolazioni, SDHI* 10 (1944); 13–14 (1948).

Codicilli. A written document containing dispositions of a testator to be valid after his death (*mortis causa*), but not the institution of an heir which was permissible only in a testament. The recognition of *codicilli* is somehow connected with the institution of *fideicommissa* (under Augustus). Distinction is made between *codicilli testamento confirmati* (a codicil confirmed in a later or earlier testament) and *non confirmati* (not mentioned in a testament). While the former codicil might contain various dispositions (legacies, manumissions, appointment of a guardian) and was considered as a part of a testament (*pars testamenti*), the latter was reserved for *fideicommissa* only. There were also *codicilli ab intestato,* i.e., *codicilli* in which the testator charged his heirs on intestacy with *fideicommissa.* In classical law no specific form was required for *codicilli.* Later imperial legislation required the presence of witnesses. Justinian introduced even oral *codicilli*. A testator might dispose in his testament that in case of its invalidation because of formal deficiencies, it should be treated as a codicil.—Inst. 2.25; D. 29.7; C. 6.36.

Seeck, *RE* 4; Saglio, *DS* 1; Accardi-Pasqualino, *NDI* 3; De Ruggiero, *DE* 2; B. Biondi, *La convalidazione del codicillo*, 1911; Kortenbeutel, *Ein Kodizill eines röm. Kaisers*, *APrAW* 1939, no. 13; Scarlata-Fazio, *La successione codicillare*, 1939; Guarino, *ZSS* 62 (1942) 209; idem, *SDHI* 10 (1944) 317; Biondi, *Successione testamentaria*, 1946, 612.

Codicillus. A diploma of appointment of an official by the emperor or granting a special privilege.—See ILLUSTRIS, EPISTULA.

Piganiol, *CRAI* 1947, 376.

Coelibes (caelibes). Unmarried persons. The Augustan legislation excluded *coelibes* of a certain age wholly or partially from inheritance.—See LEX IULIA DE MARITANDIS ORDINIBUS.—C. 8.57.

Leonhard, *RE* (*s.v. caelibatus*); Manca, *NDI* 3 (*s.v. caelibes*).

Coëmptio. A contractual form of acquisition of *manus* over the wife by the husband (*conventio in manum*) through a fictitious sale (*mancipatio*) by which the woman, and consequently the power over her, were transferred to him by her father. When the woman was not under paternal power (*sui iuris*), she herself accomplished a self-mancipation. *Coëmptio* is closely connected with the conclusion of a marriage (*coëmptio matrimonii causa facta*) except in the case of *coëmptio fiduciae causa*.—See MANUS, and the following item.

Leonhard, *RE* 4; Kunkel, *RE* 14, 2269; Anon., *NDI* 4; Pezozzi, *Scritti* 3 (1948, ex 1904) 528; Carrelli, *AnMac* 9 (1933) 189; E. Volterra, *La conception du mariage* (Padova, 1940) 23; Dull, *Fschr Wenger* 1 (1944) 211; H. Lévy-Bruhl, *Nouvelles Études* 1947, 74; Köstler, *ZSS* 65 (1947) 47; Kaser, *Das altrom. ius*, 1949, 315.

Coëmptio fiduciae causa (fiduciaria). A *coëmptio* concluded not for the purpose of matrimony but in order to get rid of a disagreeable guardian. After the *coëmptio* has been made the woman "is remancipated by her partner (*coemptionator*) to another man of her choice and having been manumitted by him, she has him as a guardian (*tutor fiduciarius*)." This form of *coëmptio* was applied also (until Hadrian) to give the woman the possibility to make a testament (Gaius, Inst. 1.114–115a).

W. Erbe, *Fiducia*, 1940, 165.

Coëmptionator. See COËMPTIO FIDUCIAE CAUSA.

Coërcitio. (From *coërcere*.) The magistrates had the power of enforcing obedience to their commands and of punishing minor disorderly offenses by certain coercive or repressive measures (prison, fines, pledge). Generally there was no appeal against acts of magisterial coercion which were made without any ordinary proceeding at the discretion of the individual magistrate.—See MULTA.

Neumann, *RE* 4; Kübler, *RE* 14, 421; Lécrivain, *DE* 3, 1528; De Dominicis, *NDI* 3; Brasiello, *Repressione penale*, 1937, 32; Lengle, *RE* 6A, 2475.

Coetus amplissimus. In later imperial constitutions, the senate.

Cogere. See COACTUS VOLUI, NECESSITAS.

Cogere senatum. See SENATUM COGERE.

Cogitatio. A thought, an intention, a design. "Nobody is punished for his thoughts (intentions)" (*cogitationis poenam nemo patitur*, D. 48.19.18). "The intention to commit a theft does not make a person a thief" (D. 47.2.1.1).

Cognati. Relatives united by the cognatic tie.—See COGNATIO, AGNATI.

Solazzi, *La successione dei cognati*, *ANap* 58 (1937) 63.

Cognatio. Blood relationship. Normally the AGNATI are also *cognati* even when the natural tie does not occur. Thus, adopted family members are not only *agnati* (under the same paternal power) but also *cognati*. *Cognatio* includes persons related through females, as well as former *agnati* who given in adoption, emancipated or otherwise, lost the agnatic kinship. The praetorian law protected the rights of succession of *cognati* which finally superseded those of *agnati*. The distinction *agnatio*—*cognatio* gradually lost its practical significance.—Inst. 3.5.—See AGNATI (Bibl.), UNDE COGNATI.

Baudry, *DS* 1; Leonhard, *RE* 4; Anon., *NDI* 3; Perozzi, *St Brugi*, 1910 (= *Scritti* 3, 61); Maschi, *La concezione naturalistica*, 1937, 143; C. Castello, *Diritto familiare*, 1942, 123; Guarino, *SDHI* 10 (1944) 290.

Cognatio civilis (legitima). See AGNATIO.

Cognatio ex transverso gradu. Collateral relationship (in the side line).

Cognatio legitima. COGNATIO CIVILIS; see AGNATIO.

Cognatio naturalis. *Cognatio*. Ant. *cognatio civilis*. Also applied to the relationship between a mother and her illegitimate child, and to the relationship between slaves (syn. *cognatio servilis*).

Cognatio servilis. See COGNATIO NATURALIS, SERVUS.

Cognitio. (From *cognoscere*). The examination of a judicial case (and eventually a decision) by a magistrate or a juror (*iudex*). The *cognitio* comprehends all that is done by the judicial authority during the proceedings, civil or criminal, in order to establish the facts which led to the controversy (hearing of the parties and their counselors, of witnesses and experts, examination of documents and other means of evidence). The extension of the activity, termed as *causae cognitio*, depended upon the competence of the inquiring person (*qui cognoscit*) as well upon the matter involved in the *causae cognitio*. Thus, for instance, the *causae cognitio* by the praetor took one form when he was requested to grant an *in integrum restitutio* and another when he ordered a *missio in possessionem* or a *cautio*, or appointed a guardian. The *cognitio* also differed in the various strata of the Roman civil procedure. In criminal matters *cognitio* covers the whole proceeding, judgment included.—See CAUSAE COGNITIO.

> Wlassak, *RE* 4; Kleinfeller, *RE* 4, 218; Thédénat, *DS* 1; De Ruggiero, *DE* 2; Lauria, *ANap* 56 (1934) 305; M. Lemosse, *Cognitio, étude sur le rôle du juge,* 1944.

Cognitio caesariana. See COGNITIO SACRA.

Cognitio extra ordinem (extraordinaria). The latest form of civil proceedings which, originally concurrent with the formulary procedure as "extraordinary" (*extra ordinem, sc. iudiciorum privatorum*), later became exclusive. The *cognitio extra ordinem* was based on the idea that the administration of justice is a function of the state, while in the previous forms of proceedings the trial was dominated by the parties under the moderation and supervision of the magistrate. The characteristic feature of the *cognitio extra ordinem* which appeared at the beginning of the Empire, is that the private juror disappears and his place is taken by a public official acting as a delegate of the emperor or of a high functionary. When the new procedure became general, there was no more bipartition of the trial nor a formula, the whole proceeding being under control of the same functionary or his delegate. In criminal matters the new procedure under the Principate, *cognitio extra ordinem,* was opposite to the procedure before perpetual courts (see QUAESTIONES). Here, too, the imperial jurisdictional official held the trial in his hands from beginning to end and rendered the final sentence.—The jurisdiction of the *cognitio extra ordinem* in which the jurists efficiently collaborated assisting the jurisdictional officers with their advice, contributed considerably to the development of the law.—D. 50.13. —See APPELLATIO.

> Wlassak, *RE* 4; Sachers, *RE* Suppl. 7, 793; R. Samter, *Nichtförmliches Gerichtsverfahren,* 1911; Riccobono, *La c.e.o. e il suo influsso sul ius civile, Mél Cornil* 2 (1926); Balogh, *ACDR Roma* 2 (1935) 269; Drestano, *StCagl* 26 (1938) 153; De Robertis, *AnBari, N.S.* 4 (1941) 3; Santi Di Paola, *AnCat* 2 (1948) 252; Riccobono, *RIDA* 3 (= *Mél De Visscher* 2 (1949) 277.

Cognitio sacra (or caesariana). The examination and decision of a judicial matter by the emperor or his delegate.—See A COGNITIONIBUS.

> De Laet, *AntCl* 1945, 145.

Cognitionalis. Connected with judicial *cognitio.* The term is widely used in later imperial constitutions.

Cognitor. A representative of a party in a civil trial. He was appointed in a prescribed, solemn form in the presence of the adversary, contrary to another type of a representative in litigation, the PROCURATOR, who was informally appointed. The intervention of a representative found its expression in the procedural formula since the principal was mentioned in the INTENTIO, while the CONDEMNATIO was formulated in favor of the representative. In practice the *cognitor* had the *actio iudicati* for the execution of the judgment (see CESSIO), but a praetorian remedy (*translatio iudicii*) was foreseen to make the formula work

for the real creditor. In Justinian's law the only representative in litigation is the *procurator.*—See EXCEPTIO COGNITORIA, IUDICATUM, and the following item. *Cognitor* in later imperial constitutions = a judge (*qui litem cognoscit*).—See the following entry.

> Leist, *RE* 4; C. Wirbel, *Le c.,* 1911; Debray, *NRHD* 36 (1912); Berger, *GrZ* 40 (1913) 663.

Cognitor in rem suam. A plaintiff in a trial, formally appointed as a *cognitor* and being in fact the real creditor as the cessionary of the original creditor who transferred his right against the debtor to him. See CESSIO. Similar is the situation of a *procurator in rem suam.*

Cognitores praediorum. Vouchers (examiners) who on their responsibility certified the correctness of the data concerning landed property, given as a pledge (*subsignatio*) by persons who assumed certain obligations towards a municipality.

> E. G. Hardy, *Three Spanish charters* (1912) 80, 110.

Cognomen. A surname following the first name (*praenomen*) and the name of the gens of a person (*nomen gentilicium*).—See NOMEN.

Cognoscere. See COGNITIO.

Cohaerere. See CORPUS EX COHAERENTIBUS.

Coheredes. Co-heirs. When an estate was left to more than one person, instituted as *heredes,* or when several persons inherited it in intestacy, in equal or unequal shares, they were *coheredes* and had the same legal position as co-owners. Division could be obtained either by arrangement or through judicial proceeding by an *actio familiae erciscundae.*—See FAMILIA, DIVISIO, ACTIO FAMILIAE ERCISCUNDAE.

Cohors. A contingent of five hundred (in the legions) or thousand soldiers (in certain auxiliary troops).

> De Ruggiero, *DE* 2.

Cohors. In administration, the subordinate personnel in the office of a high magistrate, an imperial official or a provincial governor. Of particular importance were the *cohortes* attached to the office of the *praefecti praetorio* (*cohortes praetoriae*), organized as military units under their command. They became in the course of time a highly influential military and political factor in the empire until their abolition by Constantine.—See PRAETORIANUS, PRAETORIUM.

> Cagnat, *DS* 5, 603; M. Durry, *Les cohortes prétoriennes,* 1938; A. Passerini, *Le coorti pretorie,* 1939.

Cohortes vigilum. See VIGILES.

Cohortales (cohortalini). Subordinate officials in the office of the *praefecti praetorio* and provincial governors in the later Empire.—C. 3.25; 12.57.—See COHORS.

Coire. See IUS COËUNDI.

Collatio (conlatio). The contribution of money (*pecunia, aes*) for the erection of a monument, a gravestone or a public building. When the contributor was a municipality or another public body, the construction was designated as erected *aere publico.*

> De Ruggiero, *DE* 2, 602.

Collatio bonorum. A contribution to the estate to be made by emancipated children (*collatio emancipati*) and including all their gains made after the emancipation, if they wanted to participate together with the non-emancipated children in the intestate inheritance of their father according to praetorian law (*bonorum possessio unde cognati*). The reason was that if the emancipated children had remained under the paternal power of the deceased, all their acquisitions would have increased his property. On similar principles was based the *collatio dotis* with regard to the dowry which a daughter had received from her father. This *collatio* applied also to testamentary successions. The rules concerning the *collatio dotis* which were somewhat different from those of the *collatio emancipati,* influenced the development of the latter towards an extension to cases which were not foreseen at its origin. *Collationes* were made originally through an effective import of the goods acquired, later an appropriate *cautio* sufficed; see CAUTIO DE BONIS CONFERENDIS.—D. 37.6; C. 6.20.

Leonhard, *RE* 3, 704 (*s.v. bonorum c.*); Baudry, *DS* 1 (*s.v. bonorum c.*); A. Guarino, *Collatio bonorum*, 1937; idem, *RendLomb* 73 (1939), *ZSS* 59 (1939) 509, and *Le collazioni ereditarie* (Corso, Napoli, 1944), *BIDR* 49–50 (1947) 259.

Collatio donationis. Based on the same principles as COLLATIO BONORUM. It was introduced by Justinian for all kinds of donations made by ascendants to their descendants and for all kinds of succession.

Collatio donationis ante nuptias. A *collatio* introduced in the late fifth century after Christ and applied to gifts made by a man to his betrothed. See DONATIO ANTE NUPTIAS. The rules were similar to those of the *collatio dotis.*—See COLLATIO BONORUM.

Collatio dotis. See COLLATIO BONORUM.—D. 37.7; C. 6.20.

Pringsheim, *SDHI* 4 (1938); Leonhard, *RE* 3, 705 (*s.v. bonorum c.*).

Collatio emancipati. See COLLATIO BONORUM.

Collatio legum Mosaicarum et Romanarum. An anonymous compilation composed between A.D. 390 and 428 with the purpose to compare some selected Roman legal norms, chiefly of penal character, with the Mosaic law. The collection is known also under the name *Lex Dei* because some manuscripts have the title *Lex Dei quam Dominus praecepit ad Moysen.*

Editions: P. Krüger, *Collectio* 3; Kübler in Huschke's *Jurisprudentia Antejustiniana* 2, 2 (1927).—Jörs, *RE* 4; Moschella, *NDI* 3; F. Triebs, *Studien zur Lex Dei*, 1–2 (1905–1907); M. Hyamson, *Mos. et Rom. L. Coll.* 1913; N. Smits, *Mos. etc. Coll.,* Haarlem, 1934; E. Volterra, *MemLinc* 1930; Ostersetzer, *Revue Études Juives*, 99 (1934); Kübler, *ZSS* 56 (1936) 356; K. v. Hohenlohe, *Ursprung und Zweck der C.,* 1935; idem, *Archiv für kath. Kirchenrecht*, 1939; Schulz, *SDHI* 2 (1936) 20; idem, *The manuscripts of the C.,* Symbolae van Oven, 1946, 313 (= *BIDR* 55/56 Post-Bellum, 1951, 50), and *History of Rom. legal science*, 1946, 311, 344; Wolff, *Scr Ferrini* 4 (1949) 77. For glosses: Volterra, *RStDIt* 9 (1936) 366.

Collatio lustralis. See AURUM ARGENTUMQUE.

Collationes. In the later Empire, the term covers various contributions, ordinary and extraordinary, in kind, money or labor, imposed on possessors (lessees) of emphyteuticary land belonging to the emperor (*fundi patrimoniales*), to the fisc or to public corporate bodies (*civitates*). The term occurs in the rubrics of several titles in Justinian's Code (10.28; 11.65; 74; 75) although it does not appear in the single imperial constitutions therein. Possessions of the DOMUS AUGUSTA and the RES PRIVATA of the emperor were exempt from such *collationes.*—C. 11.75.

Collator. A tax payer (in later imperial constitutions).

Collectarii. Money-changers. They were united in associations.—See ARGENTARII.

Platon, *NRHD* 33 (1909) 23.

Collectio causae. See CAUSAE CONIECTIO.

Collegae. Members of the same association (*collegium*). Also co-guardians and co-heirs are *collegae.* In public law *collegae* are officials who simultaneously hold the same office and "have the same power" (D. 50.16.173 pr.), as e.g., consuls, praetors in the same year of service).—See COMPARATIO.

Neumann, *RE* 4; Kübler, *RE* 14, 407; Frezza, *St Solazzi*, 1948, 508.

Collegatarii. Legatees to whom the testator bequeathed the same object. The IUS ADCRESCENDI applies to a common legacy.—See CONCURSU PARTES FIUNT.

Collegia. Associations of both private and public character, unions of different kinds and for different purposes (professional, cultural, charitable, religious). There were *collegia* of priests (*collegia sacerdotum, pontificum*) of tradesmen, craftsmen and workmen, of public officials, clubs for social gatherings, etc. Originally they had (probably since the Twelve Tables) the right to assembly (*coire, ius coëundi*), they were permitted to issue statutes concerning their organization, activity, and the rights and duties of their members (LEGES COLLEGIORUM). Gradually, particularly under the imperial legislation, they have been granted certain rights as associations, such as both to have and to free slaves and to acquire legacies under a testament. The rule "if anything is owed to a *universitas,* is not due to its members," and vice versa "what the *universitas* owes, the members do not owe" (D. 3.4.7.1) shows that the conception of a *universitas* (*collegium*) as a corporate body (corporation), separated from the individual members, came through. Generally they had a common fund (ARCA) and a representative (ACTOR UNIVERSITATIS) who acted on their behalf. From the beginning, restrictions were imposed on *collegia* to prevent them from acting against the laws and engaging in subversive activities. When doing so, they were considered illegal (*illicita*), were dissolved and a criminal prosecution of the members followed. Analogous terms are: *corpus, universitas, societas, sodalicium.*—D. 47.22.—See the following items, LEX CLODIA,

LEX IULIA DE COLLEGIIS, LEGES COLLEGIORUM, CON-
VENTUS COLLEGII, FABRI, ORDO COLLEGII, PACTIO
COLLEGII.

> Kornemann, *RE* 4; Baudry-Gayet-Humbert, *DS* 1; Berra,
> *NDI* 3; De Martino, *NDI* 9, 931; Waltzing, *DE* 2; *idem,
> Études historiques sur les corporations professionelles,* 1–3
> (1895–1899); Groag, *Vierteljahreschr. für Sozial- und
> Wirtschaftsgesch.* 2 (1904) 481; U. Coli, *Collegia e sodali-
> tates,* 1913; La Piana, *L'immigrazione a Roma, Ricerche
> religiose* 2 (1926) 508; De Robertis, *AnBari* 1933 II, 3;
> *idem, Il diritto associativo romano,* 1938; Lo Bianco,
> *Storia dei collegi artigiani dell'Impero,* 1934; Schnorr v.
> Carolsfeld *Zur Geschichte der juristischen Person* 1
> (1933); A. Calderini, *Le associazioni professionali in R.
> antica,* 1933; P. W. Duff, *Personality in Rom. private law,*
> 1938; A. P. Torri, *Le corporazioni romane,* 1940; B.
> Eliachevitch, *La personnalité juridique en dr. privé rom.,*
> 1942; Accame, *Bull. Comm. Archeol. del Governorato di
> Roma,* 10 (1942) App. 12; Arangio-Ruiz, *FIR* 3 (1943),
> nos. 32 ff; Berger, *Epigraphica* 9 (1947) 44; F. Schulz,
> *Rom. classical law,* 1951, 95.

Collegia apparitorum. Associations of APPARITORES.

> Waltzing, *DE* 2, 351; 369.

Collegia familiarum. Associations of the members of
a family for the construction and maintenance of a
common grave.

> De Ruggiero, *DE* 3, 30.

Collegia funeraticia. Associations of poor men for
the purpose of assuring each member of a decent
funeral. The expenses were from a common fund
collected through monthly fees (*stips menstrua*) paid
by the members. Named also *collegia tenuiorum.*
Early Christian communities were organized as *collegia tenuiorum.*

> Cuq, *DS* 2, 1402; De Vincenti, *DE* 3; Saleilles, *Mél
> Girard* 2 (1912) 470; M. Roberti, *St Zanzucchi* (*Pubbl.
> Univ. Sacro Cuore, vol. 14,* Milan, 1927); Besnier, *Mél
> Albert Dufourcq,* 1932; De Robertis, *AnBari* 1933, I, 101;
> Monti, *St Riccobono* 3 (1936); G. Bovini, *La proprietà
> ecclesiastica,* 96 (1947) 114.

Collegia illicita. Associations that were considered illegal, not because they lacked formal requirements
(authorization), but because their aims and purposes
were ostensibly directed against the state or the
public order. They are frequently mentioned in the
last period of the Republic.—See COLLEGIA, LEX IULIA
DE COLLEGIIS.

> F. De Robertis, *AnBari* 1933, I, 134; *idem, St di dir penale
> rom.,* 1943, 94.

Collegia magistratuum. Not *collegia* in the strict
sense of the word; they are groups of magistrates
who were COLLEGAE in office.

> Fadda, *St Brugi,* 1910, 139.

Collegia sacerdotum. Colleges of priests performing
the same priestly duties (*collegia pontificum, augurum, flaminum, fetialium,* etc.)—See NOMINATIO.

Collegia tenuiorum. See COLLEGIA FUNERATICIA.

Collegia veteranorum. Associations of veterans.

> Waltzing, *DE* 2, 350; 368.

Collegiati. Members of corporate bodies, particularly
in the provinces. In Rome and Constantinople the
term *corporati* prevailed. The membership in associations of artisans and workmen was compulsory.
—C. 11.18.

> Kornemann, *RE* 4, 460; G. Kühn, *De opificum Romanorum
> condicione,* Diss. Halle 1910, 27.

Colliberti. Slaves simultaneously manumitted by their
master. Usually manumissions of a larger number
of slaves were ordered in testaments.—See LEX FUFIA
CANINIA.

> Thibault, *Mél Fournier,* 1929, 725.

Collocare domicilium. See DOMICILIUM.

Collocare filiam in matrimonium. To give away a
daughter in marriage.

Collocare pecuniam. To invest money (*in nomina =*
in loans).

> Kübler, *Mél Girard* 2 (1912) 49.

Collusio. (From COLLUDERE.) A secret understanding between two or more persons for the purpose of
obtaining fraudulently an illegal profit or injure a
third person, primarily through a fictitious (*perlusorium iudicium*) trial. Collusion frequently occurred
between a patron and his freedman in order to make
the latter be declared free-born.—D. 40.16; C. 7.20.
—See SENATUSCONSULTUM NINNIANUM.

> Leist, *RE* 4; H. Krüger, *St Riccobono* 2 (1936) 247.

Colonatus. In the late Empire from the fourth century on, the legal, economic, and social situation of
coloni, i.e., rural laborers bound to the soil which
they cultivated for the landowner. Their connection
with the soil was so close that its alienation involved
their transfer to the acquirer. The original condition
of *coloni* was that of perpetual tenants. It became
hereditary in the course of time and assumed the
aspect of serfdom from which they could be freed
under certain circumstances. Legally they were free
and Roman citizens. Desertion from the land did
not change their status since they could be reclaimed
by the landowner. People in distress voluntarily
accepted the condition of *coloni.*—C. 11.48; 51–53;
64; 69.—See ADSCRIPTICII.

> Seeck, *RE* 4; Humbert, *DS* 1; Schulten, *DE* 2; Bolke-
> stein, *De colonatu romano,* Amsterdam, 1909; H. F. Pel-
> ham, *The imperial domains and the colonate,* Oxford, 1911;
> Rostowzew, *Studien zur Geschichte des Kolonats,* 1910;
> *idem, The problem of the origin of serfdom, Jour. of land
> and public utility economics,* 1926, 148; R. Clausing, *The
> Rom. colonate,* New York, 1925; Saumagne, *Byzantion*
> 12 (1937) 487; Collinet, *Recueil de la Société J. Bodin,*
> 2 (Bruxelles, 1937) 85 and *Studi Bizantini e Neoellenici*
> 5 (1938) 600; Ganshof, *AntCl* 14 (1945) 262.

Coloni. Citizens of a colony (*colonia*); farmers on
land taken on lease. For *coloni* in the later Empire,
see COLONATUS.

Coloni adscripticii. See ADSCRIPTICII.

Coloni dominici. *Coloni* on land belonging to the
private property of the Emperor.—C. 11.69.

Coloni partiarii. Tenant-farmers who gave the landowners a portion of the products as a rent (instead
of a rent in money). They shared profits and losses
with the owner as if there existed partnership (*societas*) between them and the owners.

v. Bolla, *RE* 18, 4, 2480; Ferrini, *Opere* 3 (1929, ex 1893) 1; P. Brunn, *Die colonia partiaria,* Diss. Berlin, 1907.

Coloni patrimoniales. Coloni on land belonging to the PATRIMONIUM PRINCIPIS.

Coloniae. The first Roman colonies composed of Roman citizens were founded on the Roman coast line. Later colonization expanded through Italy for military, naval, political, and commercial purposes. Some colonies were founded on the basis of IUS LATII granted to their citizens (*colonia Latina, Latini coloniarii*). Under Augustus colonization comprized the provinces on the Mediterranean. Colonies were named after their founders. Their organization, settled in a charter (*lex coloniae, leges colonicae*), varied with the times. They were administered by *duoviri iuri dicundo* whose competence was similar to that of consuls and praetors in Rome.

Kornemann, *RE* 4, 567; Lenormant, *DS* 1; Scherillo, *NDI* 3; Schulten, *DE* 2, 415; Sherwin-White, *OCD* (*s.v.* colonization); J. S. Reid, *Municipalities of the R. empire,* 1913, 60; Abbott, *ClPhilol* 10 (1915) 123; E. Pais, *Storia della colonizzazione della Roma antica,* 1 (1923); Salmon, *JRS* 26 (1936) 47; A. N. Sherwin-White, *The Roman citizenship,* 1939; Degrassi, *Atti Accad. Lincei,* Ser. 8, vol. 2 (1950) 281; Vittinghoff, *ZSS* 68 (1951) 440.

Colonia Latina. A colony the citizens of which were granted only the IUS LATII, and not Roman citizenship. They were *Latini coloniarii.* A Roman citizen who took domicile in a *colonia Latina* at its foundation, lost Roman citizenship and became a Latin.

Vittinghoff, *ZSS* 68 (1951) 475.

Colonia partiaria. See COLONI PARTIARII.

Comes domesticorum. The commander of the court garrison.

Seeck, *RE* 4, 648.

Comes domorum. The superintendent of imperial buildings.

Seeck, *RE* 4, 651.

Comes formarum. See COMITES.

Comes Orientis. The ruler of the *Dioecesis Orientis* (Syria, Palestine, etc.).—C. 1.36; 12.56.

Seeck, *RE* 4, 662; G. Downey, *A study of the C.O. and the consulares Syriae,* Diss. Princeton, 1939.

Comes portus. See COMITES.

Comes rei militaris. Military commanders who received this distinctive title after important achievements in the provinces.—C.12.12; 1.47.

Seeck, *RE* 4, 662; Grossi-Gondi, *DE* 2, 516.

Comes rei privatae (rerum privatarum). These directed the administration of the imperial domains. Property confiscations of persons condemned in criminal trials, vacant inheritances and seizures of all kind belonged to his competence.—C. 1.33; 12.6. —See PROCURATOR REI PRIVATAE, COMES SACRI PATRIMONII.

Seeck, *RE* 4, 664; Grossi-Gondi, *DE* 2, 497.

Comes sacrae vestis. The supervisor of the imperial wardrobe.

Seeck, *RE* 4, 671.

Comes sacrarum largitionum. The highest officer in the financial administration of the state and head of the state treasury. He is also the highest judicial authority in tax matters. There was no appeal to the emperor against his decisions.—C. 12.6; 1.32.— See LARGITIONES.

Samonati, *DE* 4, 409; Grossi-Gondi, *DE* 2, 495; Seeck, *RE* 4, 671.

Comes sacri cubiculi. The chamberlain of the imperial palace.

Comes sacri palatii. The marshal of the imperial residence. His fuller title was *comes et castrensis sacri palatii.*—C. 12.13.

Comes sacri patrimonii. The chief of the administration of the emperor's patrimony. The office, created at the end of the fifth century, assumed a part of the duties of the *comes rerum privatarum.*— C. 1.34.

Seeck, *RE* 2, 675.

Comes sacri stabuli. The imperial equerry.

Seeck, *RE* 4, 677.

Comitatenses largitionum. The staff of the office of the COMES SACRARUM LARGITIONUM.—See LARGITIONES.

Comitatus. All the *comites* forming the retinue of the emperor.

Comites. In the Republic and the early Empire, subordinate officials in the office of a magistrate (see COHORS) or provincial governor.

Comites. In the later Empire, *comes* was the title of high military and civil officials. In almost each branch of the administration it was conferred on more important functionaries who under the Principate were simply *curatores.* Thus a *comes formarum* headed the administration of water supply, a *comes portus* had the supervision of the ports, a *comes riparum et alvei Tiberis et cloacarum* supervised the rivers, the Tiber and the sewers. Some of those officials of particular significance in the government of the later Empire are mentioned in the following items. The dignity of a *comes* = *comitiva.* There were three degrees of *comitivae: primi, secundi, tertii ordinis.* Besides, the title of a *comes* was granted to meritorious persons, even such who never had served in official capacity. The *comites* in general, but particularly those of the highest class residing in the imperial palace and in daily contact with the emperor, became the most influential persons in the later Empire.—C. 12.6; 10–14.—See the foregoing and the following items.

Seeck, *RE* 4; Humbert, *DS* 1; Grossi-Gondi, *DE* 2.

Comites Augusti. These appear about the middle of the second century as advisers of the emperor during his travels.

Seeck, *RE* 4, 626.

Comites commerciorum. Supervisors of the trade with the adjacent states and custom officers.

Seeck, *RE* 4, 643; Grossi-Gondi, *DE* 2, 507.

Comites consistoriani. Members of the imperial council (*consistorium*).—C. 12.10.

Seeck, *RE* 4, 644; Grossi-Gondi, *DE* 2, 482.

Comites dispositionum. Directors of the department of the imperial chancery for private (not governmental) matters of the emperor (*scrinium dispositionum*).

Seeck, *RE* 4, 647.

Comitia. Assemblies of the Roman people (*populus Romanus*) for legislative and judicial purposes as well as for elections. They are to be distinguished from the assemblies of the plebs alone, *concilia plebis.* For the various *comitia,* see the following entries. The *comitia* were convoked by a high magistrate who had the IUS AGENDI CUM POPULO. Only matters presented by the convoking magistrate could be submitted to vote and amendments to the proposals were not admitted. An informal gathering of the people, CONTIO, might take place before the *comitia* assembled in order to discuss the subjects on which the citizens had to vote in the *comitia.*

Liebenam, *RE* 4; Humbert, *DS* 1; Ferrini, *NDI* 3; De Ruggiero, *DE* 2, 804; Mattingly, *OCD*; G. W. Botsford, *The Rom. assemblies,* 1909; Marchi, *L'infrequentia nei c., RendLomb* 45 (1912) 72; E. Pais, *Ricerche sulla storia* 4 (1921) 49; Siber, *ZSS* 57 (1937) 233; Brecht, *ZSS* 59 (1939); G. Nocera, *Il potere dei comizi,* 1940; Cosentini, *AG* 131 (1944) 130.

Comitia calata. One of the ancient forms of *comitia* convoked (*calata*) by the *pontifex maximus* for special religious purposes. There the opportunity to make a will was given the citizens (*testamentum calatis comitiis*).

Kübler, *RE* 4; B. Biondi, *Successione testamentaria,* 1943, 47.

Comitia centuriata. A popular assembly based upon the division of the people into CENTURIAE, classified according to the value of the property of the individual citizens. Primarily a military unit, the *centuria* was also a voting unit with one vote only, determined by the majority of its members. Originally the *comitia centuriata* had large legislative functions, but they lost them gradually to the benefit of *comitia tributa.* They retained, however, other prerogatives, such as the election of magistrates, the decision about war and peace, and jurisdiction as a court of appeal in capital matters.—See LEX DE BELLO INDICENDO, POMERIUM, PROVOCATIO.

G. Rotondi, *Leges publicae populi Romani,* 1912, 31 (Bibl.); Tibiletti, *Ath* 27 (1929) 172, 210; Siber, *ZSS* 57 (1937) 263; Momigliano, *SDHI* 4 (1938) 509; Guarino, *St Solazzi,* 1948, 27; Dell'Oro, *La parola del passato* 14 (1950) 132; De Visscher, *RHD* 29 (1951) 34; Gallo, *SDHI* 18 (1952) 128.

Comitia curiata. The earliest legislative assembly based upon the division of the people into CURIAE. At the beginning of the Republic they were deprived of their legislative functions and their competence was limited to voting the LEX CURIATA DE IMPERIO by which the magistrates were vested with *imperium,* and to approving certain legal acts connected with the family system, as *adrogatio* and testaments.—See POMERIUM.

Siber, *RE* 21, 128.

Comitia tributa. The basis of this popular assembly of patricians and plebeians was the division of the Roman territory into local, district organizations, TRIBUS. Originally limited to less important matters (the election of minor magistrates, restricted jurisdiction as a court of appeal) their competence increased in the second half·of the fourth century B.C. when they superseded the *comitia centuriata* in legislative matters.—See LEX CORNELIA POMPEIA, TRIBUNI PLEBIS, PROVOCATIO.

G. Rotondi, *Leges publicae populi Rom.,* 1912, 36 (Bibl.).

Comitialis morbus. See MORBUS COMITIALIS.

Comitiatus maximus. See COMITIA CENTURIATA.

E. Pais, *Ricerche sulla storia* 1 (1915) 408.

Comitium. The place at the forum of Rome where the curial assemblies (*comitia curiata*) took place.

De Ruggiero, *DE* 2.

Comitiva. See COMITES.

Commeatus. In military service, a furlough. A soldier on leave of absence is not considered absent in the interest of the state. He becomes an *emansor* when he does not return in time, or a *desertor,* when his absence lasts a longer time.—C. 12.42.

Commendare (commendatio). Recommendation of a candidate for an office in Roman or provincial administration by the emperor when the appointment depended upon a popular assembly or the senate (from the time of Tiberius).—See CANDIDATUS PRINCIPIS.

Brassloff, *RE* 4; De Ruggiero, *DE* 2; Balsdon, *OCD*; O'Brien-Moore, *RE* Suppl. 6, 780.

Commendare. See DEPONERE.

Commentariensis. An officer in a record-office. In the military administration he had similar functions as the A COMMENTARIIS.—*Commentarienses* were also officials in public prisons. One of their tasks was to superintend the execution of corporal punishments.—See COMMENTARII.

V. Premerstein, *RE* 4, 759; De Ruggiero, *DE* 2, 540.

Commentarii. Records (a journal) kept in the offices of higher magistrates about their official activities (*commentarii consulares, censorii, commentarii* of provincial governors). The recording officers = *a commentariis* (as, e.g., *a commentariis praefecti praetorio, praefecti vigilum*). This also was the title of the director of the pertinent division of the imperial chancery.—As a type of juristic writings *commentarii* has no technical meaning. Apparently they were notes for lecturing purposes. The Institutes of Gaius are divided into four *commentarii*; he denoted his other works also as *commentarii.*

V. Premerstein, *RE* 4, 726, 759; Thédenat, *DS* 1 (*s.v. commentarium*); De Ruggiero, *DE* 2; Kübler, *RE* 6, 499; F. Schulz, *History of Roman legal science* (1946) 340.

Commentarii beneficiorum. A special register in the imperial chancery for enactments granting personal privileges.—See BENEFICIUM.

V. Premerstein, *RE* 4, 741 ; De Robertis, *AnBari* 1941, 185.

Commentarii principum. Records kept in the imperial chancery for imperial enactments. There were apparently separate divisions in the imperial record office in which various types of imperial constitutions (*commentarii epistularum, edictorum,* etc.) were kept under the supervision of one or more *a commentariis.* The *Semestria* (*Semenstria*) of the emperor Marcus Aurelius had perhaps some connection with his legislative activity as excerpts from the *commentarii* made public every six months. Of particular importance were the *commentarii* of civil and criminal trials which had taken place before the emperor.

V. Premerstein, *RE* 4, 739 ; Bresslau, *ZSS* 6 (1886).

Commentarii sacerdotum (pontificum, augurum). Records (diaries) kept in the archives of the various colleges of priests. The *commentarii pontificum* contained reports on their activities, statutes of their temples, rules of sacral law, and the like.

V. Premerstein, *RE* 4, 729 ; Rose, *OCD* ; G. Rohde, *Kultsatzungen der röm. Pontifices,* 1936 ; F. Norden, *Aus röm. Priesterbüchern,* Lund, 1939 ; C. W. Westrup, *Introduction to early R. law,* 4, 1 (1950) 35.

Commercium. The right to buy and to sell reciprocally (*Epit.* Ulp. 19.5). In other words the legal ability to conclude valid transactions in order to acquire or to sell goods. *Commercio interdicere* = to deprive a person (for instance, a spendthrift) of this right. Similarly certain things are exempt from being the object of *commercium*; see RES CUIUS COMMERCIUM NON EST. For *commercium* in international trade relations, see IUS COMMERCII.—C. 4.63.

Leonhard, *RE* 4; Humbert, *DS* 1; M. P. Charlesworth, *Trade routes and commerce in the R. Empire,* Cambridge, 1926; O. E. Powers, *Studies in the commercial vocabulary of early Latin,* Chicago, 1944; Sautel, in *Varia. Ét. de droit rom.,* Paris, 1952; Kaser, *St Arangio-Ruiz* 2 (1952) 131.

Comminatio. A threat applied by a magistrate to a party in a trial to the effect that certain consequences will result if his order is not followed, as, e.g., payment of interest if the debt is not paid at the date fixed.—C. 7.57.

Commiscere (commixtio). To mingle things together. The product resulting from the mixing together of materials belonging to different owners was owned by them in common, when the materials were of the same kind, or when they were of different but inseparable sorts.

Pampaloni, *BIDR* 37 (1929) 38.

Commissoria lex. (In sales.) An additional clause in a sale (*emptio venditio*) under which the seller had the right to rescind the contract if the buyer failed to pay the price or its remainder within a certain time.—D. 18.3.

Leonhard, *RE* 4; Humbert, *DS* 1; F. Wieacker, *Er-*

füllungszwang und Widerruf im röm. Kaufrecht, 1932; Levy, *Symb Frib Lenel* 1932; Archi, *St Ratti,* 1934, 325; Biscardi, *StSen* 60 (1948) 611.

Commissoria lex. (In a pledge.) An agreement between creditor and debtor by which the former becomes owner of the pledge if the debtor fails to pay the debt at the date fixed. Constantine forbade such agreement.—C. 8.34.—See IUS DISTRAHENDI, PIGNUS.

Naber, *Mn* 32 (1904) ; Raape, *Verfallsklausel beim Pfand,* 1 (1913) ; A. Burdese, *L. c. e ius vendendi* (*Mem. Ist. Giur. Torino,* 63) 1949; Kaser, *ZSS* 67 (1950) 557.

Commissum. In fiscal law, a confiscation of goods, primarily for the violation of custom provisions.—D. 39.4; C. 4.61.

Commissum. In penal law, a criminal offence. Syn. *admissum.*

Humbert, *DS* 1; De Dominicis, *AVen* 92 (1932–33) 1215.

Committere. To commit an unlawful act (*committere crimen, delictum, scelus, furtum, adulterium*). In contractual law: to forfeit a right or an advantage or to incur a penalty by committing an act to which according to the agreement of the parties involved such consequences were attached (*committere stipulationem*). In passive form (*committi*), as in phrases like *stipulatio* (*cautio*) *committitur,* the term indicates that a certain obligation becomes binding because the suspensive condition under which the promise was given was realized.

Committi fisco (or similar). To incur a confiscation.—See COMMISSUM (in fiscal law).

Commixtio. See COMMISCERE.

Commodator. See COMMODATUM.

Commodatum. A gratuitous loan of a thing (originally movables, later also immovables) to be returned by the borrower to the lender (*commodator*) on the terms fixed in the agreement or reasonably corresponding to the purpose of the loan. *Commodatum* belongs to the so-called real contracts concluded by the delivery (*re*) of the thing and is governed by *bona fides.* Normally *commodatum* was to the exclusive benefit of the borrower; therefore his liability for the use of the thing is extensive (*diligentia, custodia*). He is not responsible for damages caused to the thing by accidents beyond his control (*casus*). The lender had an action (*actio commodati*) against the borrower for the misuse or the return of the thing, whereas the borrower might sue with *actio commodati contraria* for the recovery of extraordinary expenses and for damages caused by the fault of the lender.—D. 13.6; C. 4.23.—See FIDUCIA CUM AMICO.

Leonhard, *RE* 4; Humbert, *DS* 1; C. Ferrini, *Opere* 3, 81; G. Segrè, *St Fadda* 6 (1906) 313; R. De Ruggiero, *BIDR* 19 (1907) 5; Cicogna, *ibid.* 235; Schulz, *GrZ* 38 (1911) 12; J. Stock, *Zum Begriff der donatio,* 1932; Pflüger, *ZSS* 65 (1947) 121.

Commodum. Advantage, profit. Legal benefits, resulting from statutes or *senatusconsulta* are designated as *commoda,* similarly the rights connected with a certain legal situation (possession, ownership) as well as proceeds, such as interest, wages, and the like. Ant. *incommodum, onus*. "It is natural that he who suffers the disadvantage of a thing should have also the profits thereof" (Inst. 3.23.3; D. 50.17.10). A similar saying is: "he who bears the risk should have also the profit." The rule applies to the contract of sale (*emptio venditio*) to the effect that the buyer who bears the risk (*periculum*) of deterioration, destruction or disappearance of the thing purchased but not yet delivered has the right to its products and increase after the conclusion of the sale.—See EMPTIO VENDITIO.

Commodum repraesentationis. See REPRAESENTARE.

Commonitorium. A letter of reminding, an order. *Commonitorium sacrum* = an order of the emperor to an official.

Seeck, *RE* 4.

Commorientes. Persons who died in the same accident (e.g., a shipwreck). There were certain rules concerning the simultaneous death of parents who died together with their children: children below the age of puberty (*impuberes*) were presumed to have died before their parents, whereas children over that age (*puberes*) had to be considered dead after their parents. The rules, which probably originate in Justinian's law, had to be observed in the case of succession. Syn. *simul (pariter) perire (decedere)*. Ant. *supervivere* (= to survive).

Beseler, *ZSS* 44 (1924) 373; G. Donatuti, *Le praesumptiones nel diritto rom.*, 1930, 22; *idem, Rivista di dir. privato* 3 (1933) 198.

Communicare. To share a thing with another by making him co-owner thereof or by dividing it or its proceeds with him.

Communicare lucrum cum damno. To share profits and losses with another. This is a fundamental principle of the contract of partnership (*societas*) except for losses caused by fraud or negligence of one of the partners. In relations among successors, especially when an heir was obliged to deliver the inheritance wholly or partially to a *fideicommissarius*, reciprocal stipulations were made in order to guarantee the common participation in profits and losses (*de lucro et damno communicando*).

Communio. Common ownership. It arises when two or more persons buy or acquire through inheritance or legacy the same thing in common. They have either equal or unequal shares thereof, the thing remaining physically undivided (*pro indiviso*). The co-owners have the same legal situation with reference to the whole and participate according to their shares in the produces (*fructus*) and expenses. Each of them may freely dispose of his share but not beyond it. Division of the common property becomes necessary when the co-owners disagree (*communio est mater rixarum* = common ownership is the mother of disputes). It is achieved by the *actio communi dividundo*, or in the case of common inheritance by

the *actio familiae (h)erciscundae*. These divisory actions offer an opportunity for settling other controversies among co-owners, such as restitution of expenses made on the common thing by one co-owner, equalization of profits and damages and the like (so-called *praestationes personales*).—D. 10.2; 3; C. 3.36; 37; 38; 4.52.—See ADIUDICATIO, IUS PROHIBENDI, ACTIO COMMUNI DIVIDUNDO, IUS ADCRESCENDI, NEMO INVITUS.

Leonhard, *RE* 4; Biondi, *NDI* 4; A. Berger, *Zur Entwicklungsgeschichte der Teilungsklagen*, 1912; Bonfante, *BIDR* 25 (1912); Riccobono, *Dalla communio del diritto quiritario, Oxford Essays in legal history*, 1913; *idem, Dal diritto rom. classico al dir. moderno, AnPal* 3-4 (1917) 165; Ein, *BIDR* 39 (1931); Branca, *RISG* 6 (1931) 215, 7 (1932) 247; Borettini, *RISG* 7 (1932) 459; J. Gaudemet, *Le régime juridique de l'indivision en dr. rom.*, 1934; Solazzi, *ANap* 57 (1935) 127; Arangio-Ruiz, *La società* (Corso), 1950, 32; Ambrosino, *SDHI* 16 (1950) 188.

Communio incidens. The term is used in literature to indicate common ownership which arose without interference of the co-owners, as in the case of an inheritance or legacy awarded to two or several persons who thus "fell in together into common property" ("*incidimus in communionem*").

Arangio-Ruiz, *St Riccobono* 4 (1936) 355; Donatuti, *St Albertario* 1 (1952).

Communio sacrorum. See SACRA.

Communis. (Adj.) A thing may be *communis* (common property) to all (see RES COMMUNES OMNIUM), or belong to a corporate body (*corpus, collegium*) or to two or more persons, *res communis* (see COMMUNIO). *Commune* (a noun) embraces all that several persons have in common. It may be ownership, or another right, as *superficies, ius in agro vectigali*. In the denomination of the *actio communi dividundo*, *commune* is used in this large sense. *Communis* is also what is in the interest of more persons or the whole society (*communis utilitas*) or concerns more persons (*communis culpa, periculum*). *Communia* (pl. noun) = rules which equally apply to similar legal institutions; several titles in the Code contain such common rules, as, e.g., *communia de legatis et fideicommissis* (C. 6.43).—See IUS COMMUNE, UTILITAS.

Communiter agere. To act on behalf of more persons or a corporation.—See STIPULATIO COMMUNIS.

Comparare. See PARARE, COMPARATIO LITTERARUM.

Comparatio. An agreement between colleagues in office concerning the division of competence or the assignment of the performance of a specific official act to one of them.—See COLLEGAE.

Comparatio litterarum. The comparison of handwritings. Experts on handwriting (*comparatores*) were heard in a trial when doubts about the authenticity of a written document arose.

Compascere. To exercise the right of common pasturage (*ius compascendi, ius compascui*).

Compatroni. Co-patrons who manumitted a common slave.

Compendium. A profit. Syn. *lucrum,* ant. *dispendium.*

Compensatio. Occurred in classical law when the judge on grounds of good faith (only in a *bonae fidei iudicium*) took into consideration what the plaintiff owed to the defendant from another transaction and condemned the defendant to pay the balance only if his debt was larger. Later a set off of reciprocal debts was available under certain circumstances through *exceptio doli.* The practice of the *cognitio extra ordinem* favored the development of the institution and thus it became a general form of extinction of obligations which operated even beyond the judicial courts. In this final stage *compensatio* worked *ipso iure* (= by the force of law) and not *ope exceptionis* (through an exception) when reciprocal debts between two persons met together.—D. 16.2; C. 4.31.
—See ARGENTARII, DEDUCTIO.

> Leonhard, *RE* 4; Humbert, *DS* 1; Biondi, *NDI* 3; Brass-loff, *ZSS* 22 (1901); P. Kretschmar, *Entwicklung der Compensation,* 1907; Leonhard, *Mél Girard* 2 (1912); B. Biondi, *La compensazione, AnPal* 12 (1929); Solazzi, *La compensazione*[2] (1950); Kreller, *Iura* 2 (1951) 82.

Comperendinatio. (In a criminal trial, particularly on extortion, *repetundae.*) Compulsory division of the case into two proceedings (*actio, prima, actio secunda*). Voting took place at the end of the second hearing.—See LEX SERVILIA DE REPETUNDIS and the following item.

> Kipp, *RE* 4, 790; Balsdon, *Papers of the British School of Rome,* 1928, 98.

Comperendinus dies. The third following day. On that day after the appointment of the *iudex* the parties had to appear before him (in the *legis actio* proceedings).—Syn. *perendinus dies.*

> Kipp, *RE* 4 (*s.v. comperendinatio*); Humbert, *DS* 2, 177 (*s.v. dies*); Ferrini, *NDI* 3.

Competens. When applied to procedural elements as *actio, iudex, poena, tribunal,* etc., indicates the action, the judge, etc., pertinent (competent) to the specific case. Justinian's compilers often substituted the term *competens* in place of the classical expression which in Justinian's time was obsolete because of the reformed organization of the procedure and administration of justice.

> Guarneri-Citati, *Indice*[2] (1927) 19; Berger, *KrVj* 1914, 142.

Competere. *Actio competit* is used of actions which were granted by the *ius civile,* while praetorian actions are "given" (*a praetore dantur*). When used with reference to other actions than those of *ius civile* the term may be frequently of compilatory origin.

> P. Krüger, *ZSS* 16 (1895) 1; Guarneri-Citati, *Indice*[2] (1927) 19; Vinci, *AnCat* 2 (1948) 365.

Competitor. (In later imperial constitutions.) An imperial official of the treasury charged with the seizure of goods submitted to confiscation. Syn. (sometimes) *petitor.*

Componere (compositio). To draft the text of a legal instrument (a testament, a codicil, a *stipulatio,* a compromise, or a procedural formula).

Componere controversiam. To settle a dispute by a compromise.

Compos mentis. Fresh of mind, mentally healthy. Ant. *demens.*

Comprobare. See ADPROBARE. Syn. PROBARE.

Compromissum (compromittere). An agreement of the parties to submit their controversy to an *arbitrator* (*compromittere in aliquem de aliqua re*). It normally provided for the payment of a penalty by the defeated party defaulted in the fulfilment of the arbitrator's decision (*pecunia compromissa*).—See ARBITER EX COMPROMISSO.

> Leist, *RE* 4; De Ruggiero, *DE* 1, 615; La Pira, *St Riccobono* 2 (1936) 187; Roussier, *RHD* 18 (1939) 167.

Computare. To reckon, to include in an account (e.g., *in quartam Falcidiam*). Syn. *calculus. Error computationis* = ERROR CALCULI.

Conatus. (In penal law.) An attempt to commit a crime. The Roman jurists did not elaborate a general theory of the criminal attempt, nor did they establish any rule as to when an attempt should be punished. With regard to some crimes preparations made with criminal intent were declared to be liable to punishment (as, for instance, some cases under the *Lex Cornelia de sicariis*), with regard to others they were not. Nor is a clear distinction made between intent to commit a crime (*consilium, voluntas sceleris*) and an actual but unsuccessful attempt. However, juristic and literary texts distinguish between intended and not committed crimes (*cogitata, non perfecta scelera*) and those actually carried out (*exitus, factum, eventus*). In a rescript of Hadrian we read: "With regard to crimes intention is taken into consideration, and not the result (*exitus*)" (D. 48.8.14). Similarly a late imperial constitution of A.D. 397 (preserved in the Theodosian Code 9.26.1, but not accepted into Justinian's Code) contains, in connection with the *Lex Iulia de ambitu,* the rule: "Statutes (the laws) punish equally a crime and the intention to commit it (*sceleris voluntas*)." These dicta not only did not become a general rule but are even contradicted by other texts in legal sources.—See COGITATIO.

> Costa, *Il conato criminoso, BIDR* 31 (1921) 20.

Concedere. To concede, to grant another a right (e.g., a servitude). Sometimes syn. with *cedere.* When referring to a debt = to remit, to release from an obligation.

Concepta verba. Appears in a text by Gaius (4.30) as synonymous with the *formula* in the formulary procedure.—See CONCEPTIO VERBORUM.

> Solazzi, *Fschr Wenger* 2 (1945) 54.

Conceptio. A conception. The time of conception is decisive for the personal status of the child. In classical law the child was free if at any time between the conception and the birth the mother was a free person. Similarly the time of conception is of importance in the doctrine of posthumous children (*postumi*), inasmuch as there was a difference according as the conception took place before or after the testament was made.

Conceptio verborum. The drafting of a legally important oral declaration (an oath, a stipulation) or a written procedural instrument (*formula, interdictum, libellus*).

Conceptus. Conceived and not yet born. See CONCEPTIO. Syn. *in utero esse*. The law protects the interests of a child not yet born, in particular his rights of succession and for this purpose the child whose birth is expected (*nasciturus*) is treated as if it were already born (*pro nato habetur*).—See POSTUMI, NASCITURUS.

Albertario, *St* 1 (1933) 3; Castello, *St Solazzi*, 1948, 232; idem, *RIDA* 4 (1950) 267; Bastošek, *RIDA* 2 (1949) 28.

Concilia plebis. Assemblies of the *plebs* alone. They met originally by *curiae* and later (LEX PUBLILIA VOLERONIS) by *tribus* (*concilia plebis tributa*). Resolutions passed by the *concilia plebis = plebiscita*. Three statutes are cited in connection with the legislative power of the plebeian assemblies (LEX PUBLILIA PHILONIS, VALERIA HORATIA, HORTENSIA) but the extant evidence is not precise enough to admit of an exact understanding of their significance. The last statute (287 B.C.) is the most concrete in this obscure history. The plebiscites were passed upon the motion of the plebeian tribunes.—See PLEBISCITA, TRIBUNI PLEBIS.

Kornemann, *RE* 4; Humbert, *DS* 1; Vaglieri, *DE* 2; G. W. Botsford, *The Roman assemblies*, 1909, 119.

Concilia provinciarum. Provincial assemblies composed of leading personages as representatives (*legati*) of the various political entities in the province. The original purpose of these gatherings was of a religious character: to celebrate the cult of the divinity of the emperor (Augustus) in the capital of the province. Their activity developed considerably. They maintained a direct contact with the governor of the province through envoys and exercised a kind of control over his activity which might result in a criminal prosecution of the governor at Rome. In the second half of the third century they began to disappear.

Kornemann, *RE* Suppl. 4 (*s.v. koinon* = the Greek term for *c.*); E. G. Hardy, *St in R. history*, 2nd ed., 1910, 235.

Conciliabulum. A settlement, a community of lesser extent than a municipality (*municipium*). The organs of local administration were similar to those of a municipality, including an administrative council (*ordo decurionum*). Some *conciliabula* may have been important market places since *conciliabulum* often appears in connection with a FORUM.—See MUNICIPIUM.

Schulten, *RE* 4; Grenier, *DS* 5, 856.

Concilium manumissionum. An advisory board of five senators and five *equites* constituted to examine the reasonableness of exceptional manumissions (of slaves under thirty or when the master was under twenty). Such councils existed also in the provinces under the chairmanship of the governor.

Concilium propinquorum. See CONSILIUM PROPINQUORUM.

Concipere. See CONCEPTA VERBA, CONCEPTIO VERBORUM, CONCEPTIO, CONCEPTUS.

Concordans matrimonium. (Syn. *concordantes vir et uxor*.) A marriage in which husband and wife live in perfect accord. The terms occur in connection with the problem of whether the father of the wife may exercise his *patria potestas* in order to dissolve such a marriage.

Volterra, *RIDA* 1 (1948) 232.

Concubina. See CONCUBINATUS.

Concubinatus. A concubinage. The sources do not contain any definition of *concubinatus*. It is a permanent, monogamous union of men and women not legally married. It differs from marriage through the lack of AFFECTIO MARITALIS and of the *honor matrimonii* (the social dignity of a woman living with a man in a legitimate marriage). *Concubinatus* was not prohibited by law and the LEX IULIA DE ADULTERIIS did not apply to persons living in *concubinatus*. Restrictions which barred the conclusion of a valid marriage were also binding with regard to *concubinatus*. The relation did not produce any legal consequences. Justinian favored the transformation of the *concubinatus* into marriage by establishing the presumption that a union with a free woman of honest life (*honestae vitae*) is considered a valid marriage unless the parties declared in a written document before witnesses that they were living in *concubinatus*. —D. 25.7; C. 5.26.—See PAELEX.

Leonhard, *RE* 4; Baudry, *DS* 1; De Ruggiero, *DE* 2; P. M. Meyer, *Der röm. Konkubinat*, 1895; Costa, *BIDR* 11 (1900) 233; J. Plassard, *Le concubinat rom. sous le Haut-Empire*, 1921; G. Castelli, *Il concubinato e la legislazione Augustea, Scritti* 1 (1923) 143; Bonfante, *St Perozzi*, 1925, 283 (=*Studi* 4, 563); E. J. Jonkers, *Invloed van het Christendom op de romeinsche wetgewing betreffend het concubinaat*, 1938; C. Castello, *In tema di matrimonio e concubinato nel mondo rom.*, 1940; Janeau, *De l'adrogation des liberi naturales*, 1947, 29.

Concubitus. Coition. The term occurs in the classical rule concerning the conclusion of a marriage. *Nuptias non concubitus, sed consensus facit* (= consent, not intercourse, constitutes marriage, D. 35.1.15; 50.17.30).—See MATRIMONIUM, NUPTIAE.

Concurrentia delicta. See DELICTA CONCURRENTIA.

Concurrere. Said of actions which lie in favor of one person for the same thing (*de eadem re*). *Actiones concurrentes* are to be distinguished from actions which arise from the same fact but have different aims, as for instance in the case of a theft, see FURTUM. The claimant could sue only with one of the concurrent actions *de eadem re* according to the rule "if one was chosen the other is consumed" (D. 47.7.34 pr.; D. 50.17.43 pr.).

> Leonhard, *RE* 4; Humbert, *DS* 1; Peters, *ZSS* 32 (1911) 179; I. Alibrandi, *Del concorso delle azioni, Opere* 1 (1896); E. Levy, *Die Konkurrenz der Aktionen*, 1–2, 1 (1918, 1922); Liebman, *Azioni concorrenti, St Ratti*, 1934; Naber, *Mn* 52–53 (1924–25); Betti, *Istituzioni* I² (1942) 335 (Bibl.).

Concursu partes fiunt. When the same thing (inheritance, legacy) or the same right is assigned to several persons all share equally therein, unless the testator disposed otherwise.

Concursus causarum. Occurs when a person to whom a determined thing is due becomes owner thereof under a different title. The obligation to deliver the thing automatically becomes void, "because what is ours cannot be given to us" (Gaius Inst. 4.4). Thus the performance of the duty becomes impossible. In later development another more equitable solution was found. The obligation of the debtor was extinguished only when the creditor got the thing gratuitously (*ex causa lucrativa*), for instance, by legacy or donation.

> C. Ferrini, *Opere* 3 (1929, ex 1891) 385; Schulz, *ZSS* 38 (1917) 114.

Concussio. (From *concutere*.) Extortion of money or gifts through intimidation, misuse of authority by an official or by a person who falsely assumes an official character.—D. 47.13; C. 12.61.

> Hitzig, *RE* 4.

Condemnare. To condemn the defendant in a civil trial to the payment of a sum of money (see CONDEMNATIO) or the accused in a criminal trial. Ant. *absolvere*.

> Hitzig, *RE* 4 (for criminal procedure).

Condemnatio. (In formulary proceedings.) "That part of the formula by which the judge (*iudex*) is empowered to condemn or to absolve the defendant" (G. 4.43). In the *condemnatio* either a fixed amount was indicated (*condemnatio certa*) or a maximum sum was fixed which the judge could not exceed (*dumtaxat* = not exceeding). In certain formulas no sum at all was indicated, the judge being authorized to fix the sum of the condemnation at his discretion by expressions such as the following: *quanti ea res est* (or *erit* = what the value of the matter in dispute is, *sc.* at the time when the formula was set or when judgment will be pronounced respectively), or simply by *quidquid* ("whatever" may appear appropriate to the judge, as in cases when the obligation concerned an *incertum*), or, in exceptional cases, by the phrase *quantum aequum videbitur* (= as much as will appear equitable to the judge). In the so-called IUDICIA BONAE FIDEI the *condemnatio* contained the clause *ex fide bona* (according to [in] good faith).—See SENTENTIA, TAXATIO, EGREDI, and the following items.

> Leist, *RE* 4; Beretta, *St Solazzi* 1948, 264.

Condemnatio certa (certae pecuniae). A *condemnatio* in which the judge is instructed to condemn the defendant to pay a fixed sum. Ant. *condemnatio incerta.*—See CONDEMNATIO.

Condemnatio cum deductione. See DEDUCTIO.

Condemnatio incerta (incertae pecuniae). A *condemnatio* in which the sum is indefinite. Ant. *condemnatio certa*. The *condemnatio incerta* is either unlimited or limited by a maximum (*cum taxatione*).—See CONDEMNATIO.

Condemnatio in quantum facere potest. (*Sc.* the defendant.) A condemnation to what the defendant is able to pay.—See BENEFICIUM COMPETENTIAE.

Condemnatio pecuniaria. A *condemnatio* to pay a sum of money. The classical law did not admit of any other condemnation in a civil trial than a pecuniary one. In suits in which the plaintiff claimed the delivery of a specific thing an evaluation in money (see LITIS AESTIMATIO) was necessary to make the conversion into money in the *condemnatio* possible, unless the defendant preferred to satisfy the plaintiff by the delivery of the thing in dispute before the judgment was passed.—See ABSOLUTORIUS.

> Pfaff, *Juristische Vierteljahresschr.*, 18 (1902) '49; Schlossmann, *IhJb* 46 (1904); Levy, *ZSS* 42 (1921) 476; M. Nicolau and P. Collinet, *RHD* 15 (1936) 751; S. Riccobono, Jr., *AnPal* 17 (1937) 43; Wenger, *ZSS* 59 (1939) 316; Gioffredi, *SDHI* 12 (1946) 136; *idem, Contributi allo studio del processo civ. rom.*, 1947, 46; v. Lübtow, *ZSS* 68 (1951) 321.

Condere iura. To establish, to create law. In referring to jurists, the term *conditores iuris* is used to mean those of them who, through their *responsa* given on the ground of their *ius respondendi*, contributed to the development of the law.—See IUS RESPONDENDI, RESPONSA, INTERPRETATIO.

> Magdelain, *RHD* 28 (1950) 6.

Condicere. In the earliest civil procedure syn. with *denuntiare* (= to announce, to give notice, to declare). It applies to the act of the claimant in the LEGIS ACTIO PER CONDICTIONEM, by which he summoned the defendant *in iure* to appear before the magistrate again after thirty days to continue the proceedings with the appointment of the *iudex*. Since this *legis actio* served only for claims *in personam* and for a specific object, the terms *condicere* and *condictio* were used for *actiones in personam* by which a *dare facere oportere* (obligations to give or to do) was claimed. For further development, see CONDICTIONES and the entries referring to the various *condictiones*.—See ACTIONES IN PERSONAM.

Condicio. The legal or social status of a person. In the imperial criminal law the social condition of a person was of importance for the kind of penalty to be applied to him.—See HONESTIORES, HUMILIORES, POTENTIORES.

Condicio. A condition, i.e., a clause added to a transaction or a testamentary disposition which makes the validity thereof dependent upon the occurrence or non-occurrence of a future event; the clause is introduced by *si* or *nisi* (*si non*). The event may be either a natural one when it is independent of human activity, or it is a fact to be done or not done by the party involved or by a third person (*condicio potestativa*). Until the fulfillment of the condition (*pendente condicione*) there is a state of uncertainty about the effects attached to its realization, to wit, as to whether the transaction will enter into force (suspensive condition) or be dissolved (resolutive condition). The technical terms for the period between the conclusion of the transaction and the fulfillment of the condition are *in suspenso esse, suspensus sub condicione,* and the like. Conditions may be added to almost all legal transactions and acts (stipulations, sales, leases, institutions of heirs, legacies, manumissions, etc.) except the so-called ACTUS LEGITIMI.—D. 28.7; 35.1; C. 6.25; 6.46.—For the various kinds of *condicio* see the following items; see DISIUNCTIVO MODO, DIES CEDENS, DIES CERTUS, NUBERE.

Leonhard, *RE* 4; Orestano, *NDI* 3; De Ruggiero, *DE* 2; E. F. Bruck, *Bedingungsfeindliche Rechtsgeschäfte,* 1904; Vassalli, *BIDR* 1915 (= *Scritti* 1, 1939, 245); R. Popovic, *Condicionis implendae causa datum, Zürcher Beiträge zur Rechtswissenschaft* 73, 1919; Bohacek, *AnPal* 11 (1924) 329; Riccobono, *St Perozzi,* 1925; G. Grosso, *Contributo allo studio dell'adempimento della condizione, MemTor* 1930; idem, *ATor* 65 (1929) 455; V. Scialoja, *Negozi giuridici,* 1933, 96; D. Ochsenbein, *Transmissibilité héréditaire de l'oblig. conditionnelle,* Génève, 1935; Flume, *TR* 14 (1936) 19; Donatuti, *SDHI* 3 (1937); idem, *Lo statulibero,* 1940, 16; Betti, *Retroattività della condizione, Scr Ferrini* (Univ. Pavia, 1946); Grosso, *SDHI* 8 (1942) 290.

Condicio deficit. The *condicio* is not fulfilled.

Condicio facti. See CONDICIO IURIS.

Condicio illicita. See CONDICIO TURPIS.

Condicio impletur (impleta est). The *condicio* is fulfilled. Syn. *condicio existit (extitit).* Sometimes a condition which has not been fulfilled is considered as if it were fulfilled. This is the case primarily, "when the person who is interested in the non-fulfillment of the condition acts so as to prevent its fulfillment" (D. 50.17.161 = 35.1.24). Such a fiction is applied to manumissions imposed upon an heir under a condition the realization of which depends upon himself. The rule was later extended to stipulations.

G. Grosso, *La finzione dell'adempimento della condizione,* 1930; Donatuti, *SDHI* 3 (1937) 63; B. Biondi, *Successione testamentaria,* 1946, 537.

Condicio impossibilis. A condition which in the nature of things cannot be fulfilled. A typical example is "if you will touch the sky with your finger." For testamentary dispositions the doctrine of the Sabinians, who considered such a condition non-existent (*pro non scripta*) was accepted by later jurists and Justinian.

I. Alibrandi, *Opere* 1 (1896) 192; R. De Ruggiero, *BIDR* 16 (1904); Manenti, *St Scialoja* 1 (1905); Cugusi, *St Fadda* 5 (1906); Beseler, *SDHI* 7 (1941) 186; Cooper, *Tulane LR* 16 (1942) 433.

Condicio institutionis. A condition attached to the institution of an heir by the testator.—D. 28.7.—See CONDICIO TESTAMENTI.

Condicio iuris. A requirement imposed by law for the validity of a legal transaction. *Condiciones iuris* are not real conditions, since they are neither uncertain nor do they make the validity of the transaction depend upon a future event. They are indispensable requisites fixed by the law. Where they are not observed, the transaction is void. Ant. *condicio facti* = real conditions imposed by the will of the party (*testator, donator*) or parties involved.

Condicio iurisiurandi. A testamentary condition imposed on an heir or legatee to take an oath that he would fulfill the testator's wish. Such conditions were usual in testamentary manumissions. When added to other dispositions such a condition might be dispensed with by the praetor or replaced by a *cautio.*

Cuq, *DS* 3, 772; Messina-Vitrano, *AnPer* 33 (1921) 600.

Condicio mixta. A condition which partly depends upon, and partly is independent of, the will of the party involved, as, for instance, when its fulfillment depends partly upon a natural event or the will of a third party.—Syn. *condicio promiscua.*

Condicio pendet. See CONDICIO.

Condicio potestativa. A condition the realization of which depends upon the will of a specific person. It may consist in doing (*condicio faciendi*) or not doing (*condicio non faciendi*) something. In the latter case only after the death of the person upon whom the *condicio* was imposed could it be established that he had not acted against the condition. See CAUTIO MUCIANA. The term *condicio potestativa* is not of classical origin; the classical jurists speak of *condicio in potestate (arbitrio) alicuius* (= a condition depending upon one's capacity or will).

Condicio tacita. A condition which is understood in a transaction, as, for instance, the conclusion of a marriage with regard to a dowry constituted in advance.

Condicio testamenti. A testamentary condition connected with the institution of heirs, legacies, *fideicommissa,* manumissions. Specific rules apply to such conditions. The underlying one is that in the first place the testator's intention is decisive.—See CONDICIO IMPOSSIBILIS, TURPIS.—D. 28.7; 35.1; C. 6.46.

I. Alibrandi, *Opere,* 1895.

Condicio turpis (illicita). A condition the fulfillment of which involves the perpetration of an act violating a legal or moral norm (*contra bonos mores*). Such conditions made the contract void; when added to a testamentary disposition, originally they had to be vacated by the praetor, later they were considered as *condiciones impossibiles* and were treated as if they were not written (*pro non scriptis*).—See CONDICIO IMPOSSIBILIS, ILLICITUS.

R. De Ruggiero, *BIDR* 16 (1904) 167; Suman, *Fil* 1917; Messina-Vitrano, *I negozi iuris civilis sotto condizione illecita, AnPer* 33 (1921) 583; Cicogna, *StSen* 54 (1940) 48.

Condicionalis. A legal transaction (*obligatio, stipulatio, emptio,* etc.) or testamentary disposition (institution of an heir, legacy, manumission) attended with a condition. Ant. *purus* = unconditional.

Condicionaliter. See SUB CONDICIONE. Ant. *pure.*— See PURUS.

Condiciones disiunctivae. See DISIUNCTIVO MODO.

Condictio (condictiones). As *actio in personam* it arose from the ancient LEGIS ACTIO PER CONDICTIONEM (see CONDICERE). The *condictiones* acquired increasing application. Gaius (Inst. 4.5; 17) defines *condictio* as "any *actio in personam* by which we claim (*intendimus*) an obligation to give or to do (*dare facere oportere*)," without giving any specific cause of action. Originally limited to a fixed sum (*certa pecunia*) and a specific thing (*certa res*), the *condictio* was extended to uncertain claims (*incertum*) and Justinian admitted them for all kinds of things, movables and immovables, fungibles and not fungibles. A particular domain of the application of *condictio* is an unjust enrichment when a person acquires something from another's property at the latter's expenses, without any legal ground (*sine causa*) or dishonestly (*ex iniusta causa*). "It is a matter of natural equity that no one should be enriched to the detriment of another" (D. 12.6.14; see LOCUPLETIOR FIERI). This doctrine of Justinian infiltrated the classical texts through numerous interpolations and made the *condictio* a general action for the most varied claims when a specifically termed action was not available.—See ACTIONES IN PERSONAM, CONDICERE, and the following items.

Kipp, *RE* 4; Humbert and Lécrivain, *DS* 4 (*s.v. per condictionem actio*); Landucci, *NDI* 3; I. Koschembahr-Lyskowski, *C. als Bereicherungsklage,* 1–2 (1903, 1907); R. v. Mayr, *Die c. des röm. Privatrechts,* 1905; M. Freudenthal, *Zur Entwicklungsgesch. der. c.,* 1910; F. de Visscher, *La c. et le système de la procédure formulaire,* 1923; E. Beaudonnat, *L'évolution générale des condictions,* Paris, 1926; Haymann, *IhJb* 77 (1927) 188; G. H. Maier, *Die prätorischen Bereicherungsklagen,* 1932; A. P. Leyval, *De la notion d'enrichissement en dr. rom.,* Thèse, Alger, 1935; Oliver, *D. 12.1, etc. De condictionibus,* Cambridge, 1937; Robbe, *SDHI* 7 (1941); Frezza, *Nuova RDCom* 2 (1949) 42; Solazzi, *ANap* 62 (1941); Donatuti, *Studi Parmensi* 1 (1951) 35; U. von Lübtow, *Beiträge zur Lehre von der condictio,* 1952; F. Schwarz, *Die Grundlage der c. im klassischen röm. Recht,* 1952.

Condictio causa data causa non secuta (ob causam dati or datorum). An action granted a person who has given something to another in anticipation of a specific event (e.g., a dowry given for a future marriage) or the performance of a specific act by the receiver, upon the failure of the expected event or act to materialize. Through this *condictio* the giver recovered the thing given.—D. 12.4; C. 4.6.

Kretschmar, *ZSS* 61 (1941).

Condictio cautionis. An action of the debtor for the return of a written acknowledgment of his debt which he had repaid.

Condictio certae pecuniae. An action for the payment of a fixed sum promised by a *stipulatio.*

Condictio certae rei. An action based on a *stipulatio* for the delivery of a specific thing (*certa res*). This *condictio* is also called *condictio triticaria,* a term which was originally applied when a fixed amount of wheat (*triticum*) was due, and was generalized by Justinian to apply to all kinds of fungible goods.— D. 13.3.

Beretta, *SDHI* 9 (1943) 223.

Condictio certi. An action for a *certum.* A Justinian creation, "it lies when a *certum* is claimed from any cause, from any obligation" (D. 12.1.9 pr.).—See CERTUM.

Giffard, *ConfInst* 1947 (1950) 55.

Condictio ex causa furtiva. See FURTUM.

Condictio ex iniusta causa. See CONDICTIO OB INIUSTAM CAUSAM.

Condictio ex lege. This name was given by Justinian to the post-classical *condictio,* which became a general action employed for the prosecution of any claim which an imperial enactment acknowledged as actionable without giving the action a specific name.— D. 13.2; C. 4.9.—See CONDICTIO.

Condictio ex paenitentia. See PAENITENTIA.

Condictio furtiva. (Syn. *condictio ex causa furtiva.*) —See FURTUM.

Condictio incerti. A *condictio* by which an *incertum* is claimed. The term appears mostly in interpolated texts.—See CERTUM.

Trampedach, *ZSS* 17 (1896) 97, 365; Pflüger, *ZSS* 18 (1897) 75; idem, *Condictio und kein Ende, Fg P. Krüger,* 1911; v. Mayr, *ZSS* 24–25 (1903–1904); Benigni, *Fil* 31 (1906); Naber, *RStDIt* 8 (1935) 284; Kretschmar, *ZSS* 59 (1939) 128; Giffard, *RIDA* 4 (1950) 499.

Condictio indebiti. An action for the recovery of a payment made in error for a not existing debt (*indebitum*). Both the parties, the giver and the receiver, must have acted in error. If the latter took the payment in bad faith, he was treated as a thief. *Indebitum* was also a debt which existed at *ius civile,* but could be annulled by an peremptory exception. —D. 12.6; C. 4.5.

Solazzi, *ANap* 59 (1939); idem, *SDHI* 9 (1943) 55; C. Sanfilippo, *C.i.,* 1943; F. Schwarz, *ZSS* 68 (1951) 266.

Condictio liberationis. A post-classical form of a *condictio incerti,* granted to a debtor against his creditor in order to obtain from him a formal release from a debt which became invalid.

Archi, *St Solazzi,* 1948, 740.

Condictio ob causam datorum. See CONDICTIO CAUSA DATA CAUSA NON SECUTA.

Condictio ob iniustam causam. An action for the recovery of money paid for an illegal cause, as, e.g., for a debt contracted under duress.—D. 12.5; C. 4.9. —See USURAE.

Pflüger, *ZSS* 32 (1911) 168.

Condictio ob turpem causam. An action for the recovery of money the acceptance of which by the receiver was immoral, as, e.g., for not committing a crime.—D. 12.5; C. 4.7.

Condictio possessionis. An action for the recovery of possession of a thing which the adversary had obtained from the plaintiff without legal cause. In comparison with the interdictal protection (see IN-TERDICTA), the *condictio* had the advantage of being an *actio perpetua*.

De Villa, *StSas* 10 (1932).

Condictio sine causa. An action for the recovery of a thing given for a specific purpose (*causa*) which failed afterwards, as, e.g., a dowry given in view of a future marriage which, however, was not concluded, or a gift made by a donor in contemplation of his imminent death (*mortis causa*), which then did not occur.—D. 12.7; C. 4.9.

Condictio triticaria. An action for the return of a quantity of grain (*triticum*) or other fungibles which had been given as a loan.—See CONDICTIO CERTAE REI, MUTUUM.—D. 13.3.

Collinet, *St Perozzi*, 1925; Kretschmar, *ZSS* 59 (1939) 128.

Conditores iuris. See IURISCONSULTUS, CONDERE IURA.

Conductio. See LOCATIO.

Conductor agri vectigalis. See AGER VECTIGALIS.

Conductor operarum. See LOCATIO CONDUCTIO OPE-RARUM.

Conductor operis. See LOCATIO CONDUCTIO OPERIS FACIENDI.

Conductor rei. See LOCATIO CONDUCTIO REI.

Conductores. Lessees. Holders of large private and public estates used to sublease small portions thereof to minor lessees (*coloni*) for a rent (a third or higher part of the produce) and personal services.—C. 11.72.

Rostowzew, *DE* 2, 586; Lécrivain, *DS* 3, 967.

Conductores vectigalium. Persons who leased from the state the right to collect *vectigalia* (revenues from state property, such as land, mines, salt-works).—C. 10.57.—See VECTIGAL, PUBLICANI.

Rostowzew, *DE* 2.

Confarreatio. The earliest form of CONVENTIO IN MANUM in order to conclude a marriage between patricians. It was a solemn ceremony in the presence of ten witnesses and a high priest. The term comes from the use of a cake of spelt (*far, panis farreus*) in the ceremony. When the *confarreatio* fell into disuse, it remained obligatory only for the marriage of flamines.

Leonhard, *RE* 4; Kunkel, *RE* 14, 2270; De Ruggiero, *DE* 2; S. Perozzi, *Scritti* 3 (1948, ex 1904) 528; Fowler, *JRS* 6 (1916) 185; Brassloff, *St Bonfante* 2 (1929) 363; Carrelli, *AnMac* 9 (1933) 207; Noailles, *RHD* 15 (1936); E. Volterra, *La conception du mariage* (Padova, 1940), 14; Koestler, *ZSS* 65 (1947) 44; M. Kaser, *Das altröm. Ius*, 1949, 342.

Conferre. To contribute money or goods; see CON-FERRE IN SOCIETATEM, COLLATIO, COLLATIO BONORUM, COLLATIO DOTIS, COLLATIO DONATIONIS.

Conferre imperium (magistratum, potestatem). To confer power upon a high magistrate or the emperor.—See IMPERIUM, LEX CURIATA DE IMPERIO, LEX DE IMPERIO.

Conferre in societatem. To contribute a share as a partner of a company (*societas*).—See SOCIETAS.

Guarneri-Citati, *BIDR* 42 (1934) 183.

Confessio. (From *confiteri*.) Admission of liability by the defendant in full or partial conformity with the plaintiff's claim. *Confessio* may occur in either stage of the civil trial, *in iure* or *apud iudicem*.—D. 42.2; C. 7.59.—See the following items.

Kipp, *RE* 4; Cuq, *DS* 3, 744.

Confessio apud iudicem. An acknowledgment of the plaintiff's claim by the defendant before the judge. It was treated only as a means of evidence. The judge could evaluate it at his discretion.

Confessio in iure. An acknowledgment of the plaintiff's claim made by the defendant (*confessus*) before the magistrate in the stage of the proceedings *in iure*. A *confessus* "is like a *iudicatus* (condemned by the judge's judgment) since he is condemned to a certain degree by his own judgment" (D. 42.2.1). The rule goes back to the Twelve Tables with regard to claims of a fixed sum. They ordered that an amount of money admitted by the defendant (*aes confessum*) was subject to execution in the same way as a thing adjudged by a judgment. When the defendant admitted his liability but did not express it in a fixed sum, immediate execution was impossible and the whole matter went as a suit based on confession (*actio confessoria*) to the judge whose task was to assess the liability of the defendant. By his *confessio* the latter avoided condemnation to a double amount (*duplum*) in those actions in which his denial (see INFITIATIO) would have produced such effect.

Kipp, *RE* 4; Cuq, *DS* 3; A. Giffard, *La c.*, 1900; Betti, *AVen* 74 (1915) 1453; idem, *ATor* 50 (1914–15) 700; Collinet, *NRHD* 29 (1925); W. Püschel, *Confessus pro iudicato est*, 1924; Wlassak, *Konfessio in iure*, *SbMünch* 1934; Wenger, *ZSS* 59 (1939); Pflüger, *ZSS* 64 (1944) 360; S. di Paola, *Confessio in iure* 1 (Milan, 1952).

Confideiussores. Two or more sureties, *fideiussores*, for the same debt.—See BENEFICIUM DIVISIONIS.

Confinium. A strip of land constituting a border between two adjoining plots. It was to be left unploughed and was excluded from *usucapio*. Syn. *fines*.—See ACTIO FINIUM REGUNDORUM, CONTRO-VERSIA DE FINE.

Confirmare tutorem. To confirm a guardian. In certain cases, when the testamentary appointment of a guardian was not quite certain, when the testament was defective, or when the appointment was made by a person who had no *patria potestas* over the ward (the mother, or the father of an emancipated son) the praetor could take the will of the testator into consideration and confirm the guardian appointed.—D. 26.3; C. 5.29.

Sachers, *RE* 7A, 1511; Solazzi, *RendLomb* 53 (1920) 359.

Confirmatio codicillorum. See CODICILLI.

Confirmatio donationis. A donation which might be invalidated by an exception opposed by the donor (*exceptio legis Cinciae*) became valid if the donor died without having revoked the donation. According to an *oratio* of the emperors Severus and Caracalla a donation between husband and wife (*donatio inter virum et uxorem*) became valid, if the donor confirmed the donation in his testament.

Siber, *ZSS* 43 (1933); De Robertis, *AnBari* 1935; Biondi, *Successione testamentaria* (1943) 666, 714.

Confiscari (confiscatio). Seizure by, and for, the fisc. —See PUBLICATIO.—C. 9.48.

Humbert, *DS* 1.

Confiteri, confessus. See CONFESSIO. Syn. *fateri*.

Confuga. (From *confugere*.) A person persecuted by an enemy, by creditors or for a crime, who takes refuge in a place which is inviolable, e.g., in a temple (*in aede sacra*) or under a statue of a reigning or dead emperor (*ad statuam Caesaris*).—C. 1.25.

P. Timbal Duclaux de Martin, *Droit d'asile*, 1939, 27; Gioffredi, *SDHI* 12 (1946) 187.

Confugere ad ecclesiam. To take refuge in a church. —C. 1.12.

Confusio. (From *confundere*.) Mingling of liquids. When they belong to different owners, the mixture is owned by them in common as in the case of COMMISCERE.

Pampaloni, *BIDR* 37 (1929) 38; Baudry, *DS* 1; Leonhard, *RE* 4.

Confusio. In the law of obligations this occurs when the right of the creditor and the obligation of the debtor meet in the same person, as when the debtor becomes heir of the creditor or *vice versa*. *Confusio* effects the extinction of the obligation.

Baudry, *DS* 1; Leonhard, *RE* 4; S. Cugia, *Confusione extinguitur obligatio*, 1927; item, *La confusione dell'obligazione*, Corso, 1943; S. Solazzi, *L'estinzione dell'obligazione*, I² (1935) 277; A. Hollfelder, *Die c. im röm. R.*, 1930; G. Wesenberg, *Der Zusammenfall in einer Person von Hauptschuld und Bürgschaftsschuld*, 1935; Biondi, *Istituti fondamentali del dir. ereditario* 2 (1948) 126.

Confusio. (In the law of servitudes.) If ownership of an immovable, encumbered by a servitude, and the right of servitude meet in the same person, the servitude, praedial or personal, is extinguished through *confusio*, which in such cases is also termed CONSOLIDATIO.

Congiarium. Money or valuable commodities distributed among the people on specific occasions. This custom, introduced by Caesar, was followed by the emperors as a gesture of liberality (*liberalitas*) on such occasions as accession to the throne, a victory in war, or another solemn event. The example of the emperors was imitated by triumphant generals and wealthy individuals. Tokens (TESSERAE NUMMARIAE) redeemable in money, were also thrown to the people on such occasions.—See MISSILIA.

Rostowzew, *RE* 4; Bervé, *RE* 13 (*s.v. liberalitas*); Espérandieu, *DE* 2; Thédenat, *DS*; D. Van Berchem, *Distribution de blé et d'argent*, Genève, 1939.

Coniectanea. A collection of miscellanea. The word appears as the title of juristic works of Capito and Alfenus Varus.

Coniectio. See CAUSAE CONIECTIO.

Coniunctim. Jointly. Heirs instituted *coniunctim* became co-heirs with equal shares. A condition imposed *coniunctim* upon several persons is binding on all. Ant. DISIUNCTIM, SEPARATIM.

Coniunctio. An institution of several heirs for the same estate or of several legatees for the same thing in common. The estate (or legacy) became common property of the *coheredes* (or *collegatarii*). The heirs or legatees thus awarded are termed *coniuncti*. —See CONIUNCTIM.

Coniunctio maris et feminae. A basic element of the Roman marriage when connected with AFFECTIO MARITALIS and intended as a community for ever (CONSORTIUM *omnis vitae*).—See NUPTIAE.

Conl-. See COLL-.

Connubium. See CONUBIUM.

Conrei. See CORREI.

Consanguinei. See CONSANGUINITAS. Ant. UTERINI. The distinction has significance in the law of succession.

Leonhard, *RE* 4.

Consanguinitas. The relationship between brothers and sisters begotten by the same father. In a larger sense, blood relationship.—See IUS CONSANGUINITATIS, NECESSITUDO.

Conscientia (conscius). Knowledge of a crime committed by another. Such knowledge did not entail punishment except in cases in which denunciation to the authorities was obligatory, as, e.g., in case of high treason (see MAIESTAS, PERDUELLIO).

Consciscere sibi mortem. To commit suicide. Suicide committed by a person accused of a crime in order to avoid condemnation was considered a confession of guilt and his property was confiscated. Trials for high treason were continued in spite of the suicide of the accused.—Syn. *manus sibi inferre*.— D. 48.21; C. 9.50.—See SUICIDIUM, LIBERA FACULTAS MORTIS.

Rogers, *TAmPhilolAs* 64 (1933) 18; Volterra, *RStDIt* 6 (1933) 393; F. Vittinghoff, *Der Staatsfeind in der rom. Kaiserzeit*, 1936, 52.

Conscius. See CONSCIENTIA.

Conscius fraudis. One who participates in a debtor's fraudulent activities in order to deceive the latter's creditors. Syn. *particeps fraudis*. A praetorian action for damages lies against him.—See FRAUS.

Humbert, *DS* 1.

Conscribere. To write down a legal document, in particular a testament or codicil.

Conscripti. See PATRES CONSCRIPTI.

Consecrare (consecratio). See RES SACRAE.

Consecratio. As a sanction for a crime committed against the state or community this was the assignment of the offender and his property to the gods; this made him an outlaw (*sacer*), deprived him of protection by men and excluded him from human society. The *consecratio,* both *capitis* and *bonorum,* is the lot of a person whom the laws declared SACER. —See LEGES SACRATAE.

> Wissowa, *RE* 4; De Ruggiero, *DE* 1, 144.

Consecratio. (With regard to deceased emperors.) The enrollment of the dead emperor among gods, deification.—See DIVUS.

> G. Hertling, *Konsecration im rom. Sakralrecht,* 1911; S. Brassloff, *Studien zur röm. Rechtsgeschichte,* 1925; Bickerman, *Arch. für Religionswissenschaft* 27 (1929); F. Vittinghoff, *Der Staatsfeind in der röm. Kaiserzeit,* 1936, 77; Bruck, *Sem* 7 (1949) 12 (Bibl.).

Consensus. (From *consentire.*) In private law = consent. It is either unilateral when a person gives his assent (approval) to an act performed by another (*consensus curatoris,* of a father or parents, of a magistrate), or bilateral when two persons agree upon a transaction. The *consensus* must be complete (*in unum* = on the same matter) and free from any external influence (duress = *vis, metus,* error). Although *consensus* is the basic element of all agreements between two or more persons, there are some contracts (*emptio venditio, locatio conductio, mandatum, societas*) which are concluded (*obligatio consensu contracta*) when merely a *consensus* of the parties exists and is expressed (*nudus consensus*), as opposed to other contracts for the conclusion of which further elements are required, such as the delivery of a thing (*res*), the use of words (*verba*) or a written form (*litterae*). *Consensus* may be given expressly in spoken or written words, or tacitly, simply by·gesture or other behavior leaving no doubt as to the consent of the party (*tacite, tacitus consensus*). —Inst. 3.22.—See CONTRACTUS, NUTUS.

> Leonhard, *RE* 4; Perozzi, *St Schupfer,* 1 (Turin, 1898); Hägerström, *ZSS* 63 (1943) 268.

Consensus. In public law this refers to the manifestation of the collective approval of the people (*consensus populi*), the senate (*consensus senatus*), a municipal council, and the like.

> De Ruggiero, *DE* 2.

Consensus contrarius. A consensual contract (see CONSENSUS) could be rescinded by a contrary agreement of the parties if neither of them had yet fulfilled his obligation (*re integra, re nondum soluta*). Syn. *dissensus.*

> Siber, *ZSS* 42 (1922); Stoll, *ZSS* 44 (1924).

Consentire. See CONSENSUS.

Conservi. Fellow slaves belonging to the same master.

Consignare (consignatio). To seal a written document (e.g., a testament). Syn. *signare.*

Consiliarii (consiliarii Augusti). Members of the emperor's *consilium;* generally members of any council.

> De Ruggiero, *DE* 2, 616; Checchini, *AVen* 58 (1909).

Consilium. Advice. It is to be distinguished from a mandate (*mandatum*) and does not create any responsibility for the person who gave it if it pro-duced bad results. "Everybody may decide for himself whether the advice is to his advantage" (17.1.2.6). —*Consilium* of the person who performs a deed means his decision, intention, particularly when referring to prohibited acts.—See OPE CONSILIO.

> Last, *AnPal* 15 (1936) 253.

Consilium decurionum. A municipal senate.—See DECURIONES.

> De Ruggiero, *RE* 2, 611.

Consilium magistratuum. Higher magistrates (consuls, praetors, censors, aediles, governors of the provinces, prefects, etc.) used to have advisory boards composed of jurists and experts in various fields. They asked the *consilium* for advice in important matters, but were not obliged to follow it.—See ADSESSORES.

> Liebenam, *RE* 4; De Ruggiero, *DE* 2, 610; G. Cicogna, *I consigli dei magistrati romani e il c. principis,* 1910.

Consilium principis. The imperial council. Following a Republican institution, the council of the magistrates (CONSILIUM MAGISTRATUUM), the emperors beginning with Augustus used to consult a body of advisors convoked in cases of particular importance. Hadrian organized it as a permanent council composed of members (jurists, high imperial functionaries of equestrian rank, and senators) appointed for life (*consiliarii,* from the time of Diocletian *a consiliis sacris*). In the later Empire the council, called CONSISTORIUM (*sacrum*), functioned rather as a privy council of the emperor in legislative, judicial and administrative matters. Many famous jurists of the classical period were members of the *consilium.* They exercised a great influence on the development of the law as crystallized in imperial enactments. The participation of the praetorian prefects gave the *consilium principis* also a political character.

> Orestano, *NDI* 3; Balsdon, *OCD*; Seeck, *RE* 4, 926; De Ruggiero, *DE* 2, 614; Cuq, *Mémoires de l'Académie des Inscr. et Belles-Lettres,* 1 S. 9 (1884); Cicogna, *Il consilium principis, consistorium,* 1902; *idem, I consigli dei magistrati romani e il cons. princ.,* 1910; Orestano, *Il potere normativo degli imperatori,* 1937, 51.

Consilium propinquorum (necessariorum). A family council composed of older members. Sometimes friends participated therein (*consilium propinquorum et amicorum*). According to an ancient custom the head of a family used to consult this council before punishing a member of the family for criminal offenses, for instance his wife or daughter for adultery (see ADULTERIUM). But he was not bound by the opinion of the *consilium,* which was only an advisory board to assist the head of the family in internal family matters, and had no judicial competence.

> De Ruggiero, *DE* 2, 609; Volterra, *RISG* 85 (1948) 112.

Consilium publicum. The senate.

> De Ruggiero, *DE* 2, 610.

Consilium quaestionis. The jury in a criminal trial. —See QUAESTIONES.

Consistentes. Persons who sojourn temporarily at a place which is neither their birth-place nor their domicile. The term is applied primarily to merchants (*negotiatores*).

Kornemann, *RE* 4, 922; De Ruggiero, *DE* 2.

Consistere (*cum aliquo, adversus aliquem*). To sue a person for a civil claim or to denounce another for an unfair action (e.g., a slave denounces his master for concealing a testament).

Consistorium. See COMITES CONSISTORIANI, CONSILIUM PRINCIPIS.

Seeck, *RE* 4, 930; Humbert, *DS* 1; De Ruggiero, *DE* 2, 618; Mattingly, *OCD*; Cicogna, *Il consilium principis, consistorium,* 1902.

Consobrini. Children of brothers or sisters, cousins. Children of two brothers = *patrueles* (*fratres* or *sorores*).

Consolidatio. The extinction of a personal servitude by merger when the ownership of an immovable, burdened with a servitude and the right thereto meet in the same person. It happens, for instance, when the owner becomes heir of the usufructuary (*fructuarius*) or *vice versa.*—See CONFUSIO.

Consortes imperii. Colleagues in power. Colleagues in the tribunate = *consortes tribuniciae potestatis.* Syn. *participes.* With reference to emperors, the *consors* of the reigning emperor was his colleague only formally being appointed solely to secure the succession after the death of the emperor, who alone had the title *Augustus.* Normally he was the emperor's son appointed in the same manner as the emperor. In this way the imperial power was perpetuated in the family.—See COLLEGAE.

De Ruggiero, *DE* 2; Lécrivain, *DS* 4, 651.

Consortes litis. Two or more plaintiffs or defendants in the same trial.—C. 3.40.

Redenti, *AG* 99 (1907).

Consortium. (In ancient law.) The community of goods among co-heirs after the death of their *pater familias* when the property remained undivided. This common enjoyment of family property served as a model for a contractual *consortium* among individuals, members of different families, not connected by a tie of common succession. The *consortes* had broader powers to act for the whole group, with regard both to acquisitions and alienations (manumission of slaves) since each was considered the owner of the whole. According to Gaius (3.154a), this ancient *consortium* was "a legal and simultaneously a natural *societas,* called *ercto non cito*" (with ownership not divided).

Sachers, *RE* 18, 4, 2149; Frezza, *NDI* 3; *idem, Riv. di filol e istr. class.* 1934, 33; Cicogna, *St in mem. P. Rossi; StSen* 1932; Rabel, *Mnemosyna Pappoulia,* 1934; Arangio-Ruiz, *BIDR* 42 (1934) 601; P. Noailles, *Études de dr. rom.* 51; Lévy-Bruhl, *Atti IV Congr. Intern. Papir. giur.* (Firenze, 1935) 293 (= *Nouvelles Ét.,* 1947, 51); C. A. Maschi, *Disertiones, Ricerche intorno alla divisibilità del c. nel diritto rom. clas.,* 1935; *idem, Concezione naturalistica,* 1937, 306; Albertario, *Studi* 5 (1937) 467; Wie-

acker, *Hausgenossenschaft und Erbeinsetzung,* 1940; Solazzi, *SDHI* 12 (1946) 7; E. Schlechter, *Contrat de société,* 1947, 182; De Visscher, *Nouvelles Études,* 1949, 267; Albanese, *Successione ereditaria, AnPal* 20 (1949) 9; Daube, *Juridical Review* 62 (1950) 71; Arangio-Ruiz, *La società (Corso),* 1950, 3; Weiss, *Fschr Schulz* 2 (1951) 84.

Consortium omnis vitae. A community for the whole life. It is a basic element of the Roman marriage, mentioned in the definition of marriage by Modestinus (D. 23.2.1); see NUPTIAE. It is not affected by the possibility of divorce.

Solazzi, *AnMac* 5 (1930) 27; Erhardt, *ZSS* 57 (1937) 357.

Conspiratio. A plot by several persons for criminal purposes (e.g., to bribe witnesses, to break out of prison).

Constante matrimonio. During the existence of a valid marriage.

Constantinopolitana urbs (Constantinopolis). The former Byzantium, refounded by Constantine in A.D. 330 as *Nova Roma.* It replaced Rome as the capital of the Empire and "enjoyed the prerogatives of ancient Rome (*Roma vetus*)," C. 1.2.6.

Oberhummer, *RE* 4; Mattingly, *OCD*.

Constare. See RES QUAE PONDERE . . . CONSTANT.

Constat inter omnes. It is the common opinion of the jurists. Syn. *generaliter constat, omnes consentiunt.*

Schwarz, *Fschr Schulz* 2 (1951) 208.

Constituere. To constitute, create a legal situation, relation or an obligatory binding (*servitutem, obligationem, dotem,* etc.)—See the following items.

Leonhard, *RE* 4; Baudry, *DS* 1.

Constituere debitum. See CONSTITUTUM DEBITI.

Constituere iura (ius). To create laws. The expression is applied to all kinds of legislative activity (of the people, the praetor, the senate, the emperors, and the jurists) and even to legal customs (*ius moribus constitutum*).—See CONDERE IURA.

Constituere procuratorem (tutorem). To appoint a representative (a guardian).

Constitutio. (In the meaning of a legal rule) outside the domain of imperial legislative activity (see CONSTITUTIONES PRINCIPUM). Very rarely used in texts that are not free from the suspicion of postclassical origin. In one postclassical source appears a *constitutio Rutiliana* which established a specific rule regarding a defective purchase of a *res mancipi* from a woman without the approval of her guardian (Fr. Vat. 1). Its author was probably the Republican jurist Publius Rutilius Rufus.

Constitutio Antoniniana de civitate. A constitution of the emperor Caracalla (A.D. 212) by which all inhabitants of the empire, organized in *civitates* with local autonomy, were granted the Roman citizenship, except the so-called PEREGRINI DEDITICII. The constitution is preserved on a Greek papyrus (of Giessen, I no. 40, ed. P. M. Meyer). There is, however, a lacuna on a decisive point which has led to an abundant literature. The problems involved are still controversial.—See PRAENOMEN.

Kübler, *RE* 19, 641; Anon., *NDI* 5 (*Editto di Caracalla*); Bry, *Ét. Girard* (1912); G. Segrè, *BIDR* 32 (1922); *idem, St Perozzi*, 1925, 137; E. Bickerman, *Das Edikt des Kaisers Caracalla*, 1925; Capocci, *Mem Linc*, Ser. 6, 1, 1925; P. M. Meyer, *ZSS* 46, 1926; Schönbauer, *ZSS* 51 (1931) 303; Stroux, *Philologus* 88 (1933) 272; Wilhelm, *Amer. Jour. of Archaeology* 38 (1934); Jones, *JRS* 26 (1936) 223; Sherwin-White, *The R. citizenship* (1939) 218; Schubart, *Aeg* 20 (1940) 31; Heichelheim, *Jour. of Eg. Arch.* 26 (1940); A. Segrè, *Rend. Pontif. Accad. di Archeol.,* 16 (1940) 181; Riccobono, *FIR* 2² (1941) no. 88; Wenger, *ArPap* 14 (1941) 195; D'Ors, *Emerita* 11 (1943) 297; *idem, AHDE* 15 (1944) 162, 17 (1947) 586; Arangio-Ruiz, *L'application du droit rom. en Égypte après la c. A., Bull. de l'Institut d'Égypte* 29 (1947) 89; Bell, *JRS* 37 (1947) 17; Wenger, *RIDA* 3 (1949) 527; Keil, *Anzeiger Akad. Wiss. Wien*, 1948, 143; D. Magie, *Rom. rule in Asia Minor* 2 (1950) 1555; Henne, *ConfInst* 1947 (1950) 92; De Visscher, *AnCat* 3 (1949) 15; Schönbauer, *Jour. juristic papyrology* 6 (1952) 36; Taubenschlag, *ibid.* 130 (Bibl.).—For imperial constitutions preserved in papyri, Taubenschlag, *ibid.* 121.

Constitutio Rutiliana. See CONSTITUTIO.

Constitutionarius. An official entrusted with copying the imperial constitutions and keeping them under control.

Constitutiones generales. See CONSTITUTIONES PRINCIPUM, CONSTITUTIONES SPECIALES.

Constitutiones imperiales. See CONSTITUTIONES PRINCIPUM.

Constitutiones personales. Imperial enactments by which private individuals were granted personal privileges as a reward for meritorious service rendered to the emperor or the state.

De Robertis, *AnBari* 4 (1941) 360.

Constitutiones principum (principales, imperiales, sacrae). *Constitutiones* is a general term which embraces all types of imperial enactment; see EDICTA, DECRETA, MANDATA, RESCRIPTA. "What the emperor ordained (*principi placuit*) has the force (*vigor*) of a statute (*lex*)" or ". . . is applied as if it were a statute (*legis vicem obtinet*)" (D. 1.4.1 pr.; Gaius 1.5). Such principles were established in the early second century after Christ. We are told by Gaius (*loc. cit.*) that there never had been any doubt about it, and yet in the early Principate the emperor used to present his legislative proposals personally in an *oratio* before the senate for its approval by which they acquired full legal force. This approval afterwards became a simple formality, so that the *oratio* itself was considered a law. A legislative character was attributed in the first place to the *edicta* and to those enactments indicated as *constitutiones generales* (*decreta, rescripta*) in which the emperor expressly declared that his decision issued in a specific case should henceforth be applied in analogous cases. Rescripts and decrees issued without such a clause also acquired the force of legal norms in the last analysis, since on the one hand the judges normally followed the principles settled therein (although legally they were not bound to do so) and on the other hand by appeal

to the imperial court a contrary decision of a lower court might be changed in accordance with the rules issued by the emperor in previous cases.—D. 1.4; C. 1.14.

Jörs, *RE* 4; Costa, *NDI* 3; Berger, *OCD*; Riccobono, *FIR* 2² (1941) 295; Fass, *Arch. für Urkundenforschung* 1 (1908) 221; E. Vernay, *Ét. Girard* 2 (1913); Kreller, *ZSS* 41 (1920) 262; Lardone, *St Riccobono* 1 (1936); Orestano, *Il potere normativo degli imperatori e le costituzioni imperiali*, 1937; Volterra, *St Besta* 1 (1939) 449; F. v. Schwind, *Publikation der Gesetze*, 1940, 129; De Robertis, *Sull'efficacia normativa delle cost. imperiali, AnBari* 4 (1941, 1, 281); *idem, ZSS* 62 (1942) 255; Luzzatto, *Scr. Ferrini* (Univ. Pavia, 1946) 263.

Constitutiones Sirmondianae. A private collection of sixteen imperial constitutions issued between 333 and 425 concerning ecclesiastical matters (first edited by J. Sirmondi, 1631). The collection was compiled by an unknown author in the Western Empire. Ten of the constitutions are preserved in the Codex Theodosianus, but their text in the *Constitutiones Sirmondianae* is more complete.

Edition: in Mommsen's edition of the *Codex Theodosianus.*—Jörs, *RE* 4; Scherillo, *NDI* 3.—Translation, in C. Pharr, *Codex Theodosianus* (Princeton, N. J., 1952) 477.

Constitutiones speciales. Imperial constitutions general in character but limited to particular categories of persons or legal relations. Ant. *constitutiones generales* binding on the whole people, and CONSTITUTIONES PERSONALES.

De Robertis, *AnBari* 4 (1941) 340.

Constitutum. A formless promise to pay an already existing debt, either of one's own (*constitutum debiti proprii*) or of another (*constitutum debiti alieni*) on a fixed date and at a fixed place. The sum so promised is called *pecunia constituta*. This is not a novation, the creditor being able to sue the debtor according to the previous terms. The fulfillment of a *constitutum* may be claimed by a special action, *actio de pecunia constituta* (*constitutoria*). It is an *actio in factum*, strengthened by the promise of a penalty of one half of the original debt (*sponsio dimidiae partis*). A *constitutum* could also cover debts originating from wrongdoings. The institution was reformed by Justinian in many respects.—D. 13.5; C. 4.18.—See the following items.

Humbert, *DS* 1; Anon., *NDI* 3; J. Déjardin, *L'action de pec. const.* 1914; A. Philippin, *Le pacte de constitut*, 1929; Willems, *Mél Cornil* 2 (1926) 615; G. Astuti, *La promessa di pagamento* 1, *AnCam* 11 (1937), 2 (Pubbl. Catania 7, 1941).

Constitutum debiti alieni. A promise to pay (CONSTITUTUM) another's debt. This is a formless kind of surety. Its validity depends upon that of the principal debt.—See RECEPTUM ARGENTARII.

Constitutum debiti proprii. A *constitutum* between parties already involved in an obligatory relationship. See CONSTITUTUM. The purpose of this *constitutum*, also called *pactum de constituto*, is to modify some elements of the previous obligation, such as the date or the place of the payment.

Koschaker, *ZSS* 63 (1943) 470.

Constitutum est. When referring to a legal norm, this indicates that it originates from an imperial constitution.—See CONSTITUTIONES PRINCIPUM.

Constitutum possessorium. Not a classical term. In literature it denotes the legal situation of a person who transferred possession (*possessio*) of a thing to another but continued to hold it (*detinere*) under another title. Possessory protection is consequently given to the new possessor. A *constitutum possessorium* took place when the seller of an immovable remained therein as a tenant. A contrary change of a possessory situation, when the actual holder of a thing (*detentor*) acquired possession thereof was *traditio brevi manu*, since the thing was not delivered over by *traditio* but remained in the detention of the same person.—See DETENTIO.

Aru, *NDI* 3; F. Schulz, *Einführung in das Studium der Digesten*, 1916, 73; Buckland, *RHD* 4 (1925) 355; Luzzatto, *AG* 108 (1932) 244; H. H. Pflüger, *Zur Lehre vom Erwerb des Eigentums*, 1937, 65.

Constitutus. Said of a person or a thing that is in a certain legal situation; it also means settled by law (imperial constitutions), legally established. The term appears frequently in interpolated texts, particularly when *constitutus* is substituted for a specific period of time (*tempus constitutum*) which had been fixed in the ancient law and was then changed in postclassical or Justinian's law.

Guarneri-Citati, *Indice*, 2nd ed. (1927) *s.v. constituere*.

Consuetudo. (Also *consuetudo longa, inveterata, vetus*.) A custom, usage. Syn. *mores, mores diuturni, mores* (or *mos*) *maiorum* (= custom observed by the ancestors). *Consuetudo* constantly observed through a long period is the source of the so-called customary law, generally observed by the people. Cicero (*De invent.* 2.22.67) defines it as the law which has been approved by the will of all being observed for a long time, and classical jurists speak of a silent consent of the people (*tacitus consensus populi, tacita civium conventio*, D. 1.3.32.1; 35). Yet it is not an autonomous source of law. Without legislative action by a law-making organ, through a statute, the praetorian edict, a senatusconsult, or imperial enactment, it was not binding upon the judge, though its influence on jurisdiction or on the interpretation of the will of the parties to a transaction may have been considerable. "Custom is the best interpreter of statutes" (D. 1.3.37). In ancient times, before the first Roman codification in the Twelve Tables, the whole law was customary. Legal customs observed constantly and generally in relations with foreigners, could easily acquire statutory force when confirmed by the praetor. To change legal customs regularly and immutably observed was not easy and the emperors had frequently opposed customs, par-

ticularly those imported from the provinces in their enactments. A custom could not abrogate an existing law (DESUETUDO).—D. 1.3; C. 8.52.—See IUS SCRIPTUM, LONGAEVUS USUS, USUS, INTERPRES.

S. Brie, *Zur Lehre vom Gewohnheitsrecht*, 1899; E. Lambert, *Études de droit commun* 1 (1903) 111, 389; O. Kniebe, *Zur Lehre vom Gewohnheitsrecht im vorjust. Recht*, Heidelberg, 1908; Solazzi, *AG* 102 (1929) 3; *idem*, *St Albertoni* 1 (1935) 35; Steinwenter, *St Bonfante* 2 (1930) 419; A. Lebrun, *La coutume*, Thèse, Caen, 1932, 198; Schiller, *Virginia Law Rev.* 24 (1938) 268; Gaudemet, *RHD* 17 (1938) 141; Riccobono, *BIDR* 46 (1939) 333; Kaser, *ZSS* 59 (1939) 59; Rech, *Mos maiorum*, Diss. Marburg, 1936; Senn, *Introduction à l'étude du droit comparé*, 1 (1938) 218; B. Paradisi, *Storia del diritto italiano* (Lezioni) 1951, 228; Lombardi, *SDHI* 17 (1951) 281.

Consuetudo civitatis (provinciae, regionis). Legal customs of a local character observed in autonomous cities, provinces or particular regions.

Niedermeyer, *Byzant.-Neugriech. Jahrb.* 2 (1921) 87.

Consuetudo fori. A constant court practice. The term is mentioned only once in juristic sources (D. 50.13.1.10) with reference to the honorarium of an advocate; a judge, when settling a lawyer's fee, should have taken into consideration the practice of the court among other circumstances. In Justinian's language analogous expressions are *usus iudiciorum* and *observatio iudicialis*. In all instances the court practice refers to procedural matters and not to substantive law. The term *usus fori* which occurs in the literature is not Roman.

Consuetudo revertendi. See ANIMALIA, ANIMUS REVERTENDI.

Consulares. Ex-consuls. They became members of the senate after their year of service. Governors of provinces, dictators, and censors were often chosen from among the *consulares*. See ADLECTIO. Hadrian created the institution of four circuit-judges to administer law in Italy and they, too, were called *consulares*. In the later Empire some governors of provinces had the title *consulares*.

Kübler, *RE* 4; Humbert, *DS* 1; Paribeni, *DE* 2.

Consulere (iurisperitum). To ask a jurisconsult for an opinion in a legal matter.—See IURISCONSULTI.

Consules. The supreme Roman magistrates in the Republic, as successors to the royal power (*potestas regia*). Two *consules* elected by the people in centuriate assemblies governed the state for one year. Originally both *consules* were patricians, since 367 B.C. one had to be a plebeian (see LEX LICINIA SEXTIA). The creation of other magistracies and the activity of the senate and the popular assemblies produced a gradual weakening of their originally unlimited power, which further was hampered by the plebeian tribunes (*intercessio*). Their functions as military commanders remained undiminished, however. Their jurisdictional attributions were checked by the right of appeal to the *comitia* in criminal matters; in civil affairs they lost them to the praetors. Under the Principate the consulship remained in existence but gradually became a merely honorary function. The *consules* were appointed for short periods (four, or even two months) but they kept some political rights (convocation of, and presidency in, the senate) and exercised some minor administrative functions. Their social position remained high, however, since they were granted all honors and insignia of the highest magistrates, as in the earliest Principate. They continued to give their name to the year until this system of dating was abolished by Justinian in 537. They retained some competence in manumissions when they were in active service, but as a whole their official functions were insignificant.—D. 1.10; C. 12.3.—See DICTATOR, CONSULARES, MAGISTRATUS, PROCONSUL, IMPERIUM, SENATUSCONSULTUM ULTIMUM, DIES ET CONSUL, and the following items.

Kübler, *RE* 4; Humbert, *DS* 1; Anon., *NDI* 3; De Ruggiero, *RE* 2, 679 (a list of consuls by Vaglieri, *ibid.*); Treves, *OCD*; De Sanctis, *Rivista di filologia*, 1929, 1; Groag, *Wiener Studien*, 1929, 143.

Consules honorarii. Persons to whom the emperor granted the title of consul as an honorary distinction in the late Empire. They had no effective functions.

Consules ordinarii. Consuls who entered office on January 1 and whose names were given to the whole year in the official dating system.

Consules suffecti. Consuls elected by extraordinary vote when the post of a *consul* became vacant during the year of service because of death or some other reason.

Consultatio. (From *consultare*.) A request addressed by a lower judge in a proceeding of *cognitio extra ordinem* to his superior, the future appellate judge in the case, for an opinion in a legal matter to be decided upon. This practice led to the development of a specific procedure whereby a *consultatio* was addressed to the emperor by a judge whose decision was subject to an appeal to the imperial court. The *consultatio* was made in a detailed report (*relatio*) containing a statement of the subject of the controversy and the written objections (*preces refutatoriae, libelli refutatorii*) of the parties, who had been informed in advance of the contents of the judge's report. The emperor decided on the basis of the written materials submitted to him. In particular, judicial matters of the provinces were transmitted in this way to the emperor who expressed his point of view in a rescript sent to the first judge. The latter in turn notified the parties of the imperial decision. The parties themselves were forbidden to address the imperial chancery directly unless a year elapsed without an answer. This was the procedure of a *consultatio* before judgment (*ante sententiam*). The same procedure was used in the case of an appeal to the imperial court (*appellatio more consultationis*) from the time of Constantine. Justinian's predecessor, Justin, admitted a hearing of the parties

before the imperial court in the course of this proceeding.—D. 49.1; C. 7.61; 62.—See RESCRIPTUM.

Lécrivain, *DS* 4 (*s.v. relatio*); Kipp, *RE* 2, 206; 4, 1142; Partsch, *Nachr. Ges. der Wissenschaften Göttingen*, 1911; E. Andt, *Procédure par rescrit*, 1920.

Consultatio veteris cuiusdam iurisconsulti. An anonymous booklet written in the Western Empire in the late fifth or early sixth century containing a collection of juristic opinions on real and imaginary cases. The author used the Sentences of Paul and a number of constitutions from the three *Codices*, Gregorianus, Hermogenianus and Theodosianus.

Editions: P. Krüger, *Collectio* 3 (1890) 201; Kübler in Huschke's *Iurisprudentia anteiustiniana*⁶, 2, 2 (1927) 490; Baviera, *FIR* 1² (1940) 593.—Jörs, *RE* 4; Moschella, *NDI* 3; Conrat and Kantorowicz, *ZSS* 34 (1913) 46; Volterra, *ACII* 2 (1935) 399; *idem, RStDIt* 8 (1935) 144 (for glosses and interpolations).

Consultator (consultor, consulens). One who asks a jurist for his opinion in a legal matter.—See CONSULERE, IURISCONSULTI.

Berger, *RE* 10, 1165.

Consultissima lex. A well-considered law.

Consultissimus vir. A man learned in the law.

Consulto. See DOLUS.

Consumere. See ABUSUS, RES QUAE USU CONSUMUNTUR.

Leonhard, *RE* 4.

Consumere, consumi. (With regard to actions.) When a plaintiff has two different actions against the same adversary for the same claim, "through the use of one action the other is extinguished" ("consumed," *per alteram actionem altera consumitur*). This principle does not apply to *actiones poenales*. A "consumptive" effect is also connected with the LITIS CONTESTATIO, to wit, that the plaintiff loses the right to repeat an action once *litis contestatio* has been achieved.—See CONCURRERE, BIS DE EADEM RE.

Leist, *RE* 4, 1147 (*consumptio actionis*); Gradenwitz, *Festg. Bekker, Aus röm. und bürgerl. Recht*, 1907, 383.

Consumere fructus. See FRUCTUS CONSUMPTI.

Contendere. To litigate, hence *contentio* = a dispute brought to trial.

Contentio. See the foregoing item.

Contentiosus. See IURISDICTIO CONTENTIOSA.

Contestatio. (From *contestari*.) A declaration made before witnesses. The term is connected with the invitation extended to persons to be witnesses to a fact or an oral statement, by the words *"testes estote"* (= be witnesses). Later *contestatio* is also used with regard to declarations made before a public official.—See TESTATIO, TESTIS, TRANSFERRE DOMICILIUM.

Contestatio litis. See LITIS CONTESTATIO.

Contextus. The content of a written document, e.g., of a testament. With regard to testaments, it is required that they be made *uno contextu*, i.e., in one act, without interruption.

B. Biondi, *Successione testamentaria*, 1943, 57.

Continens. *In* (*ex*) *continenti* = immediately, without delay. Ant. *ex intervallo*. The locution *in continenti* is used in connection with the right of a father to kill an adulterous daughter caught *in flagranti;* see ADULTERIUM, LEX IULIA DE ADULTERIIS.

Continentia (aedificia). Buildings outside of Rome, but adjacent to the walls of the city. They were considered part of Rome and consequently a child born therein was held to have been born in Rome.—See URBS.

Continuus. See ANNUS, TEMPUS CONTINUUM.

Contio. A popular informal meeting convoked by a magistrate in order to communicate to the people (*verba facere ad populum*) news of an important military event or an edict issued by him, or to inform them about subject matters to be dealt with in the next formal *comitia*, which might even be held on the same day. Thus, laws, elections and judicial matters were discussed in a *contio* before they were subject to vote or decision in the assembly proper where discussion was not permitted. A *contio* was less solemn and was not preceded by *auspicia*. No voting took place. Plebeian tribunes were wont to use *contiones* for political purposes.

> Liebenam, *RE* 4; Humbert, *DS* 1; De Ruggiero, *DE* 2; Treves, *OCD*.

Contra. Against (e.g., to decide, to render judgment). Ant. SECUNDUM.

Contra bonos mores. See BONI MORES. "It is to be held that we may not do things (*facta*) which violate good customs" (D. 28.7.15). A condition imposed on a person not to marry or not to procreate children in a legal marriage, suing parents or patrons in court, a mandate to commit a theft or to hurt another, and the like, were considered to be *contra bonos mores.*— See CONDICTIO TURPIS, CONDICTIO OB TURPEM CAUSAM, ILLICITUS.

> Koschembahr-Lyskowski, *Mél Cornil* 2 (1926); J. Macqueron, *L'histoire de la cause immorale dans les obligations*, 1924; H. R. Mezger, *Stipulationen und letztwillige Verfügungen c. b. m.* 1929 (Diss. Gottingen); Siber, *St Bonfante* 4 (1930) 103; Kaser, *ZSS* 60 (1940) 100; Riccobono, *Scr. Ferrini* (Univ. Pavia) 1947, 75.

Contra legem facere. See FRAUS LEGI FACTA.

Contra tubulas. Contrary to the testamentary dispositions of the testator.—See BONORUM POSSESSIO CONTRA TABULAS.

Contra vindicare. See IN IURE CESSIO.

Contractus. (From *contrahere.*) A contract. There is no exact definition of *contractus* in the sources, nor did the Roman jurists develop a general theory of contracts. The characteristic element of a *contractus* is the agreement, the concurrence of the wills of the parties, to create an actionable, obligatory bond between them. (Much larger is the use of the verb *contrahere* which at times appears in a sense other than the creation of a contract; locutions such as *contrahere delictum* or *contrahere crimen* have nothing to do with a contractual obligation.) Originally limited to obligations recognized by the *ius civile,* the term *contractus* even in the classical period acquired a wider sense, embracing obligatory relations recognized by the praetorian law and covering the whole domain of contractual obligations, so that the jurist Paul could say: "Every obligation should be considered a contract, so that wherever a person assumes an obligation he is considered to have concluded a contract" (D. 5.1.20). The term *contractus*, although not rare in classical sources, is therefore far less frequent than *obligatio*. The real picture of the Roman concept of *contractus* was overshadowed by the fact that for some typical contracts specific names were created, such as *emptio venditio, locatio conductio, depositum, commodatum*, etc. (see below); on the other hand, for the fundamental element of a contract, the consent of the contracting parties (see CONSENSUS), other expressions were available which covered both the consent itself and the whole transaction (*conventio, pactio, pactum conventum*, also *negotium*). In the Roman system of obligations, the *contractus* appears as the source of four principal classes of obligations according to the fundamental division established in Gaius' Institutes (4.88): "every obligation arises either from a *contractus* (*ex contractu*) or from a wrongdoing (*ex delicto*)." The subdivision of the contracts into four groups, formulated also by Gaius (4.89 ff.) and accepted by Justinian (Inst. 3.13 ff.), is based on specific elements which create unilateral or bilateral obligations. The four groups are: (1) Contracts which are validly concluded by the mere consent (*nudo consensu*) of the parties. As a matter of fact, all contracts require consent of the contracting parties, but this particular category requires nothing more than the consent. It includes sale (*emptio venditio*), lease and hire (*locatio conductio*), mandate (*mandatum*), and partnership (*societas*). (2) Contracts concluded by *res* (*obligationes re contractae*), i.e., the handing over of a thing by one party (the future creditor) to the other (the future debtor). Such contracts are loan (*mutuum*), deposit (*depositum*), a gratuitous loan of a thing (*commodatum*) and pledge (*pignus*). (3) Contracts concluded by the pronunciation of solemn, prescribed words (*certa verba, obligatio verbis contracta*); such are *stipulatio, dotis dictio* and *iurata promissio liberti.* (4) Contracts concluded through the instrument of *litterae* (*obligatio litteris contracta*), i.e., of written entries in the account books of a professional banker or any private individual; see NOMINA TRANSSCRIPTICIA, EXPENSILATIO. For the specific contracts, see the pertinent entries; for the subjective elements of importance in the conclusion of a contract see CONSENSUS, VOLUNTAS, ERROR, METUS, DOLUS; see also CONVENTIO, NEGOTIUM, PACTIO, PACTUM, TRANSACTIO and the following items.

> Leonhard, *RE* 4; Riccobono, *NDI* 4, 30; Brasiello, *NDI* 8, 1203; Berger, *OCD*; De Francisci, *Synallagma*, 1–2

(1913, 1916); Bonfante, *Scritti* 3 (1926) 107 (several articles); Riccobono, *AnPal* 3-4 (1917) 689; *idem, La formazione della teoria generale del contratto, St Bonfante* 1 (1930) 123; Bortolucci, *ACII* 1 (1935); Nocera, *La definizione bizantina di contratto, RISG* 11 (1936) 278; Collinet, *LQR* 98 (1932) 488; Lauria, *SDHI* 4 (1938) 135; Brasiello, *SDHI* 10 (1944); Grosso, *Il sistema romano dei contratti*, 2nd ed. 1950; P. Voci, *Scr. Ferrini* (Univ. Pavia, 1946) 383; *idem, La dottrina del contratto,* 1946; Archi, *Scritti Ferrini* (Univ. Pavia, 1946) 659; Van Oven, *Iura* 1 (1950) 21; Dulckeit, *Fschr Schulz* 1 (1951) 153.

Contractus bonae fidei. A term created by Justinian for contracts which in the classical period gave rise to *actiones (formulae, iudicia) bonae fidei*. They involved the good faith of the parties and required fairness in the performance of the duties assumed. All consensual contracts as well as the real contracts (*re,* the latter with the exception of the loan, *mutuum*) belong to this category of contracts.—See CONTRACTUS, USURAE EX PACTIO, IUDICIA BONAE FIDEI.

S. Di Marzo, *B. f. c.,* 1904; Bibl. in Guarneri-Citati, *Indice, St Riccobono* 1 (1936) 713.

Contractus (pactum) in favorem tertii. The term is unknown in the sources. The Romanistic literature considers as such a contract a transaction in which a person who is not a representative of a third person, accepts a promise in favor of the latter, who does not himself participate in the transaction. As a matter of principle, such a transaction was void and the third person did not acquire any action therefrom. See NEMO ALTERI STIPULARI POTEST. Only a son could conclude such a transaction in favor of his father, a slave for his master, a guardian for his ward. In Justinian's law some exceptions were admitted.

Riccobono, *AnPal* 14 (1930) 399; G. Pacchioni, *Contratti in f. t.,* 3rd ed. 1933; Bonfante, *Studi* 3 (1926) 243; *idem, CentCodPav* (1934) 211; Vazny, *BIDR* 40 (1932); *idem, St Riccobono* 4 (1936) 261; Cornil, *St Riccobono* 4 (1936) 241; Albertario, *Fschr Koschaker* 2 (1939) 16 (Bibl.); G. Wesenberg, *Verträge zugunsten Dritter,* 1949; Frezza, *NuovaRDCom* 3 (1950) 12.

Contractus innominati. Unnamed contracts. The term, unknown in the sources, is used for transactions which, although of a certain typical structure, were not termed by a specific name. Once only the expression "anonymous *synallagma*" appears in a Byzantine text. From *contractus innominati* arise bilateral duties: each party assumes the obligation to give (*dare*) or to do (*facere*) something. Four types of such contracts are distinguished: (1) *do ut des* (one party transfers the ownership of a thing to another who has to do the same in return); (2) *do ut facias* (one party gives the other a thing whereas the other has to perform a service); (3) *facio ut des* (an inverse transaction to that under 2); and (4) *facio ut facias* (a reciprocal exchange of performances of the most different kinds). If one of the parties fulfilled his duty and the other did not, the former has an action for the recovery of the thing given or for indemnification for the service performed (CONDICTIO CAUSA DATA CAUSA NON SECUTA, ACTIO DOLI). Some of the *contractus innominati* became so typical that already in classical times they received a specific denomination (PERMUTATIO, AESTIMATUM); others were discussed by the jurists and solved in various manners, particularly with regard to the question whether the party who first performed his obligation had an action to compel the other to perform his. Some jurists were not disinclined to such an action (*in factum,* with a description of the agreement in the formula, *praescriptis verbis agere*). The history and theory of such contracts appear in the sources in a somewhat confused picture because the pertinent texts are thoroughly interpolated, leaving the classical ideas hardly recognizable, and because of the multiform terminology concerning the remedies granted to the one party who had performed his duty to enforce the reciprocal performance on the part of the other.—See ACTIO PRAESCRIPTIS VERBIS.

P. De Francisci, *Synallagma, Storia e dottrina dei cosidetti contratti innominati,* 1-2 (1913, 1916); Partsch, *Aus nachgelassenen Schriften,* 1933, 3; Collinet, *Mnem Pappoulia,* 1934, 93; Kretschmar, *ZSS* 61 (1941); Grosso, *Il sistema romano dei contratti,* 2nd ed. 1950, 176; Giffard, *ConfInst* 1947 (1950) 68.

Contractus iudicum. In Justinian's language, contracts concluded by high administrative officials in Constantinople and the provinces as private individuals. The emperor greatly limited their liberty to conclude certain transactions. Forbidden were purchases of immovables and movables (except for personal use), contracts for the construction of a building for their private use, and the acceptance of gifts, unless with a special permission of the emperor. Such transactions made by *iudices* (a general Justinian term for high governmental officials) were void.—C. 1.53.

Contractus suffragii. See SUFFRAGIUM.

Contradicere (contradictio). To oppose, object, make a contrary statement, deny, particularly with regard to a claim in a judicial proceeding.—See NARRATIO.

P. Collinet, *La procédure par libelle* (1932) 209, 295; Lemosse, *St Solazzi,* 1948, 470.

Contradictor. The opponent in a trial who contests the plaintiff's claim, particularly in trials concerning paternity or the personal status of a person (as a free man or a free-born).

Contradictorii libelli. See LIBELLI CONTRADICTORII.

Contrahere. Used in different applications: concluding a marriage or betrothal, committing a crime, assuming an obligation through a bilateral agreement (see CONTRACTUS), accepting an inheritance, performing procedural activities, and in a general sense, performing any act of legal significance.

Betti, *BIDR* 25 (1912) 65 and 28 (1915) 3, 329; P. Voci, *Dottrina del contratto* (1946) 12; Grosso, *Il sistema romano dei contratti,* 2nd ed. 1950, 32.

Contrarius. See CONSENSUS CONTRARIUS, ACTIONES DIRECTAE.

Contrectatio (contrectare). Laying hands on another's thing with a view to taking, misappropriating, meddling with, misusing another's thing. The term appears in the Roman definition of theft (FURTUM) and its application goes far beyond the simple taking away of another's property without his consent.

Buckland, *LQR* 57 (1941) 467; Cohen, *RIDA* 2 (1949) 134; *Niederländer, ZSS* 67 (1950) 240.

Contrectator. A thief.—See CONTRECTATIO.

Controversia. A general term for a legal controversy between private individuals, a dispute before a court. With regard to jurists and their works, *controversia* means a difference of opinion among persons learned in the law, particularly between representatives of the two juristic schools, the Sabinians and Proculians.—See PROCULIANI, SABINIANI.

Albertario, *Studi* 4 (1940) 263.

Controversia de fine (finibus). A dispute between neighbors about the boundaries of rural property when only the five-foot-border strip was involved. The controversy was called *iurgium* (not *lis*) and was settled in a friendly manner by arbitrators, usually with the assistance of experts (AGRIMENSORES). See LEX MAMILIA ROSCIA. When the controversial strip of land was wider than five feet, the quarrel became a CONTROVERSIA DE LOCO.

Kübler, *RE* 9, 959; Brugi, *NDI* 4 (*controversiae agrorum*); Schulten, *DE* 3, 93.

Controversia de loco. See the foregoing item.

Contubernales. A man and woman living together but not united in a legal marriage (*iustae nuptiae*). See CONTUBERNIUM. Inscriptions show that not only slaves but also free persons and freedmen were thus designated.—See CONTUBERNIUM.

De Ruggiero, *DE* 2, 1188; Castello, *Matrimonio* (1940) 32.

Contubernales (milites). See CONTUBERNIUM (military).

Contubernium. A permanent, marriage-like union between slaves. Masters favored the maintenance of slave families. Children of such unions were *liberi naturales*. *Contubernium* is also a lasting union of a master and his female slave.—See CONTUBERNALES, SENATUSCONSULTUM CLAUDIANUM.

Fiebiger, *RE* 4; Masquelez, *DS* 1; Brugi, *NDI* 4; A. de Manaricua, *El matrimonio de los esclavos, Analecta Gregoriana*, 23 (1940); C. Castello, *Matrimonio* (1940) 32.

Contubernium. (Military.) A group of ten soldiers living under the same tent. Hence *contubernales* = tent-companions.

De Ruggiero, *DE* 2.

Contumacia. (Adj. *contumax*.) Non-obedience to an order of a magistrate in general, to a judicial magistrate or a judge in particular, the refusal to answer or another form of contempt of court. A specific form of *contumacia* is non-appearance in court in spite of a summons or hiding to avoid a summons.
—See ABSENS, EREMODICIUM, EDICTA PEREMPTORIA.

Kipp, *RE* 4; Humbert, *DS* 1; P. Petot, *Le défaut in iudicio,* 1912; A. Steinwenter, *Versäumnisverfahren,* 1914;

Solazzi, *St Simoncelli,* 1917; Volterra, *BIDR* 38 (1930); Brasiello, *StUrb* 7 (1933); L. Aru, *Il processo civile contumaciale,* 1934.

Contumacia. (In military service.) Insubordination, disobedience to a superior's order. *Contumacia* towards a high commander or the governor of a province in his military capacity was punished by death. *Petulantia* is more serious insubordination (impudence, audacity), as when a soldier raised hand against his superior. It was punished by death when the superior was of a higher military rank.—See DELICTA MILITUM.

Contumaciter. (In imperial constitutions.) To behave as a *contumax,* to be guilty of *contumacia* in a civil trial. Syn. *per contumaciam.*—See CONTUMACIA.

Contumax. See CONTUMACIA.

Contumelia. An insult. It is considered a kind of INIURIA, but it is not precisely defined. It is characterized as synonymous with the Greek *hybris.*—See CONVICIUM.

Contutores. Two or more guardians of the same ward (*plures tutores*). Such plurality could be established by testament, by appointment of the magistrate, or by law, when two *tutores legitimi* were entitled to the same guardianship being relatives of the ward in equal degree. Co-owners manumitting a common slave might become co-tutors, too.—D. 26.7; C. 5.40; 42; 52.—See TUTOR GERENS, TUTOR CESSANS.

Sachers, *RE* 7A, 1526, 1551, 1575; Peters, *ZSS* 32 (1911) 226; Levy, *ZSS* 37 (1916) 14; A. Lecompte, *La pluralité des tuteurs,* 1927; Solazzi, *ANap* 57 (1935) 221; Arangio-Ruiz, *ibid.* 61 (1942) 271; G. Nocera, *Insolvenza,* 1942, 227; Solazzi, *SDHI* 12 (1946) 7; Frezza, *St Solazzi,* 1948, 514.

Conubium. The legal capacity of a man to conclude a valid marriage. *Conubium* is "the faculty to marry (*uxorem ducere*) legally" (Epit. Ulp. 5.3).—See IUS CONUBII, MATRIMONIUM, MATRIMONIUM IUSTUM.

Leonhard, *RE* 4; Kunkel, *RE* 14, 2262; Humbert, *DS* 1; De Ruggiero, *DE* 2, 265; C. Cosentini, *St sui liberti* 1 (1948) 50; E. Nardi, *La reciproca posizione successoria dei coniugi privi di c.,* 1938; Costanzi, *Sul divieto di c. fra patrizi e plebei, ACSR* 2 (1929); Volterra, *St Albertario,* 2 (1950) 347; De Visscher, *ADO–RIDA* 1 (1952) 401.

Convalescere. To become legally valid after an original invalidity or uncertainty about the validity. As a matter of rule, "what is defective (*vitiosum*) in the beginning cannot become valid by lapse of time" (D. 50.17.29).

Conveniens est (convenit). It is proper, suitable (e.g., to equity, to good faith, or to what has been said before). The phrase *conveniens est dicere* (= it is proper to say) frequently precedes juristic decisions.

Convenienter. Used similarly to CONVENIENS EST.

Convenire. (1) To come together, "to assemble from different places in one place" (D. 2.14.1.3). It refers to gatherings of members of an association (*collegium*) and the like. (2) When said of two persons = "to agree upon a thing from different impulses of the mind" (D. *ibid.*). Hence "*conventio* is a general term and applies to all matters upon which persons dealing one with another agree in order to conclude a contract or to settle a dispute." The term is so comprehensive that "there is no contract, no obligation, which does not involve an agreement" (D. *ibid.*). *Convenire* may denote the agreement as a whole or single clauses thereof (*nominatim convenire*).—Syn. *consentire*.

Convenire aliquem. To sue a person in court.

Convenit. (Generally said.) It is held, assumed, generally accepted.—See CONVENIENS EST.

Conventio. See CONVENIRE under (2). Later classical jurists distinguished three kinds (*species*) of *conventiones: publicae* (*ex publica causa*), such as peace treaties concluded by the commanding generals; *privatae* (*ex privata causa*), agreements in private matters such as contracts at civil law (*conventiones legitimae*) and at *ius gentium* (*conventiones iuris gentium*).

Condanari Michler, *RE* 18, 2135; Riccobono, *St Bonfante* 1 (1930) 146; G. Lombardi, *Ricerche in tema di ius gentium* (1946) 193, 215.

Conventio. In later procedural terminology, see LIBELLUS CONVENTIONIS.—See CONVENIRE (ALIQUEM).

Conventio in manum. An agreement accompanying the conclusion of a marriage, by which the wife entered into the family of her husband and acquired the legal position of a daughter (*filiae familias loco*) dependent upon his power (*manus*).—See MANUS (Bibl.), COËMPTIO, CONFARREATIO, USUS.

Conventionalis. Based on a *conventio*, i.e., an agreement between the parties. The term is applied to stipulations (*stipulationes*) to be distinguished from *stipulationes praetoriae*, imposed by the praetor in certain proceedings, and *stipulationes iudiciales*, imposed by the judge.—See STIPULATIONES PRAETORIAE.

Conventiones legitimae, publicae, privatae. See CONVENTIO.

Conventum. Occurs only in combination with *pactum*.—See PACTUM CONVENTUM.

Conventus. A gathering of the people in the provinces for judicial purposes (hence the name *conventus juridicus*) on days fixed by the governor, who, during his travels through the province, made a halt in larger cities in order to administer justice. The institution was created at the beginning of the Principate.

Kornemann, *RE* 4, 1173; Schulten, *DE* 2, 1189; Humbert, *DS* 1; Accardi-Pasqualino, *NDI* 4.

Conventus civium Romanorum. A permanent organization of Roman citizens in the provinces, under the chairmanship of a *curator* (*civium Romanorum*).

Kornemann, *RE* 4, 1179; Schulten, *DE* 2, 1196.

Conventus collegii. A meeting of the members of an association.

Conventus iuridicus. See CONVENTUS.

J. Coroi, *Le c. i. en Égypte aux trois premiers siècles de l'Empire rom.*, 1935.

Convertere. (With regard to the formula in the formulary proceedings.) To transfer the *condemnatio* clause of the formula to a person other than the one mentioned in the *intentio*, for instance, when the plaintiff's representative in the trial is the cessionary (*procurator in rem suam*) of the primary creditor, or when the *bonorum emptor* acquired the creditor's property.—See CONDEMNATIO, INTENTIO, TRANSLATIO IUDICII, ACTIO RUTILIANA, BONORUM EMPTIO.

Convicium. A verbal offense against a person's honor. It is considered an INIURIA when committed by loud shouting in public (*vociferatio*).—See INGRATUS.

Convincere. To convict a person of a crime as his accuser (see ACCUSATIO) or to prove one's rights in a civil trial against the assertions of the adversary.

Convocare. (In public law.) To convoke the senate, a popular assembly, a CONTIO. In criminal law: to assemble a number of accomplices (TURBA) to commit a criminal assault together.

Cooptatio. The election of new members of a *collegium* by its existing members. It was also practiced in priestly colleges (COLLEGIA SACERDOTUM). *Cooptatio* took place in the college of the tribunes if the full number of tribunes was not 'elected by the plebeian assembly or if the post of a tribune became vacant. The LEX TREBONIA abolished the tribunician *cooptatio*.

Wissowa, *RE* 4; Paribeni, *DE* 2.

Copulare matrimonium (nuptias). To conclude a marriage.

Cordi. An enactment by Justinian, beginning with the word *"Cordi"* by which the second edition of his Code was promulgated (November 16, 534).—See CODEX IUSTINIANUS.

Cornicularii. Soldiers who received the distinctive military sign, *corniculum*. They were used as adjutants of their military commanders and for secretarial work. Under the Empire higher civil officials also had their *cornicularii*.—C. 12.57.

Fiebiger, *RE* 4; Pottier, *DS* 1; Breccia, *DE* 2.

Corona. See VENDITIO SUB CORONA.

Corporalis. Corporeal, connected with a CORPUS.—See RES CORPORALES.

Corporaliter. (Adv., syn. *corpore*). See POSSESSIO.

Corporati. Members of a compulsory association (guild) of professional artisans.—See COLLEGIATI.

Leonhard, *RE* 4, 1645.

Corpore possidere. See POSSESSIO, POSSESSIO NATURALIS.

Corpus. A human body (alive or dead). *Corpus liberum* = a free person.—See VITIUM CORPORIS.

Corpus. A corporeal thing; it is syn. with *res corporalis* and opposed to non-corporeal things, to rights (*ius, iura*). *Corpora nummorum* = pieces of money, coins, distinguished from a sum of money (*summa*). *Corpus* is also used to denote a whole, embracing a number of things, as, for instance, *corpus patrimonii* = the whole estate, *corpus gregis* = the whole herd, *corpus servorum* = all the slaves belonging to one master. With regard to a union of persons, a corporate body, *corpus* is syn. with COLLEGIUM.—D. 47.22.

Schnorr v. Carolsfeld, *Zur Gesch. der juristischen Person,* 1 (1933) 147; De Robertis, *Il diritto associativo rom.* 1938; De Visscher, *Scr Ferrini* 4 (Univ. Sacro Cuore, Milan, 1949) 43; K. Olivecrona, *Three essays in R. law,* 1949, 18.

Corpus. (With reference to the literary activity of a jurist.) Refers to the whole of his writings (e.g., *corpus Ulpiani*). Syn. *universa scripta.*

F. Schulz, *Epitome Ulpiani,* 1926, 20; *idem, History of R. legal science,* 1946, 181; Albertario, *Studi* 5 (1937) 497.

Corpus ex cohaerentibus. (*Corpus quod ex pluribus inter se cohaerentibus constat.*) A thing composed of several, physically united things of the same or different material, which serves a given economic or social use (e.g., a building, a ship). Through the junction the component parts lose their legal individuality and share the legal situation of the whole. They become property of the owner of the whole. The term *universitas rerum,* when used for such kind of things, is probably of postclassical origin. Ant. *res singularis* on the one hand, *corpus ex distantibus* on the other.—See ACCESSIO, FERRUMINATIO, and the following item.

Corpus ex distantibus. An agglomeration of things, physically not united but considered one thing, a unit from the economic and social point of view. The typical example is a herd (*grex*). Legally such a *corpus* is treated as a whole and may be, as such, the object of legal transactions (sale, lease) or claims (*vindicatio gregis*). But the individual things belonging to such a *corpus* may also be made the object of transactions and claims, without, however, changing the collective character of the whole. Ant. *corpus ex cohaerentibus.*

Bianco, *NDI* 4, 371 (*s.v. cose semplici*).

Corpus Hermogeniani. See CODEX HERMOGENIANUS.

Corpus iuris civilis. A collective designation of the Emperor Justinian's codification, used first in the edition by Dionysius Gothofredus (Godefroy) in 1583. The denomination embraces the INSTITUTIONES, the DIGESTA (or PANDECTAE), the CODEX (CODEX IUSTINIANUS) and the NOVELLAE. No collective title was given to his codification by Justinian himself. He mentions only once (C. 5.13.1 pr.) *omne corpus iuris* (= the entire domain of law).

Riccobono, *NDI* 4; Ebrard, *Die Entstehung des C. I. nach den acht Einführungsgesetzen Justinians, Schweizer Beiträge zur allgem. Gesch.* 5 (1947) 28; E. H. Kaden, *Justinien législateur, Mémoires de la Faculté de droit de Genève* 6 (1941) 41; F. Wieacker, *Vom röm. Recht,* 1944, 146; De Clercq, *Dictionnaire de droit canonique* 4 (1947) 644.

Correctores civitatium. Imperial officials supervising the financial administration of certain *municipia.* In the later Empire, *corrector* appears as the title of high governmental dignitaries, in particular of provincial governors.

V. Premerstein, *RE* 4; Cagnat, *DS* 1; Orestano, *NDI* 4; Mancini, *DE* 2.

Correi (conrei). Two or more debtors owing the same debt.—See DUO REI.

Leonhard, *RE* 4 (*conreus*); Willems, *Mél Cornil* 2 (1926).

Corrumpere. To bribe (a judge, an arbitrator, a magistrate); to forge a document (a testament = *corrumpere tabulas testamenti,* accounts = *rationes,* a promissory bill = *corrumpere chirographum*).

Corrumpere album. See ALBUM, ACTIO DE ALBO CORRUPTO.

Corrumpere servum. See ACTIO SERVI CORRUPTI.

Corruptio (corruptor) servi. See ACTIO SERVI CORRUPTI.

Kleinfeller, *RE* 4.

Coruncanius, Tiberius. Consul in 280 B.C. and the first plebeian to be chief pontiff. He is also mentioned as the first jurist who explained the law in public by discussing private cases and giving opinions in legal questions (RESPONSA).

Jörs, *RE* 4 (no. 3).

Cratinus. A law professor in Constantinople and member of the commission which compiled the Digest.

Creatio. The election of a magistrate in a popular assembly or the appointment of a magistrate or a pontiff. See MAGISTRATUS. In the later Empire, *creatio* is appointment to any public service.—C. 10.68; 70.

Brassloff, *RE* 4.

Credere. To trust, to have confidence in a person as an honest debtor (*fidem sequi*). Hence *pecuniam* (*rem*) *credere* = to lend money (a thing). *Pecunia* (*res*) *credita* is the sum of money (the thing) given in loan. In a larger sense, *credere* is syn. with *mutuum dare* (i.e., to lend money) and *creditum* with *mutuum.* In a narrower sense, *creditum* is a loan when the same object is to be returned to the loangiver, creditor. "A creditor is not only he who lent money but anyone to whom anything is due for any reason whatsoever" (D. 50.16.11), in other words "anybody who has any action, a civil one, an honorary one or an *actio in factum*" (D. 44.7.42.1).—D. 12.1; C.4.1.—See FRAUDARE.

Leonhard, *RE* 4.

Creditor. See CREDERE.

Creditor pigneraticius. A creditor who received security from the debtor in the form of a pledge (*pignus*).—See PIGNUS, FRUCTUS REI PIGNERATAE, FURTUM POSSESSIONIS.

Ratti, *StUrb* 1 (1927) 3.

Creditum. See CREDERE, IUS CREDITI.

Creditur. It is presumed.—See PRAESUMPTIO.

Crematio (vivi). Death by being burned. It was already known in the Twelve Tables as a penalty for arson. Syn. *exurere, exurendum damnari, igni necari.*—See INCENDIARIUS.

Cretio. (From *cernere.*) The earliest form of acceptance of an inheritance (see ADITIO HEREDITATIS) by the heir appointed in a testament. The prescribed formula of the oral declaration of acceptance was "Whereas A appointed me as his *heres* in his testament, I deliberately accept (*adeo cernoque*) (Gaius 2.166). The testator might impose this solemn form as obligatory and disinherit the heir in the case of omission. Normally *cretio* had to be declared within one hundred days from the time when the heir had notice of his appointment (*cretio vulgaris*) if the testator did not dispose otherwise. *Cretio* was formally abolished in A.D. 407.

Leonhard, *RE* 4; Lévy-Bruhl, *NRHD* 38 (1914) 153; Buckland, *TR* 3 (1922) 239; Solazzi, *StPav* 5 (1919); Besnier, *RHD* 10 (1931) 324; G. Dulckeit, *Erblasserwille und Erwerbswille*, 1934, 115; Archi, *SDHI* 2 (1936) 44; Arangio-Ruiz, *FIR* 3 (1946) nos. 59, 60; B. Biondi, *Istituti fondamentali del dir. ered.* 2 (1948) 49; *idem, St Solazzi*, 1948, 67; F. La Rosa, *AnCat* 4 (1950) 372.

Crimen. May denote the accusation of a crime and the following trial as well as the crime itself, if it is punishable by a public penalty after condemnation of the culprit in a trial conducted under a formal accusation in the forms prescribed for criminal matters. Ant. is *delictum* which, in classical terminology, applied to private offenses to be prosecuted by the aggrieved person himself and punished by a penalty to be paid to the latter. In postclassical language the two terms are used interchangeably since public prosecution absorbed the wrongdoings previously classified as *delicta*. The Roman criminal legislation did not produce a comprehensive penal code. Under the Republic, a series of statutes dealt with crimes and their punishment; a further development was brought by some decrees of the senate and in a large measure by imperial constitutions. Through an extensive interpretation the jurists contributed to the application of older statutes to crimes not comprised by the original statute. This happened, for instance, with the *Lex Cornelia de falsis* and the *Lex Cornelia de sicariis et veneficis* and many others. But, generally speaking, only a few juristic writings dealt with merely criminal matters.—D. 47.11; C. 3.15.—See DELICTUM, MALEFICIUM, ADMISSUM, POENA, and the following items. For the individual criminal offenses, see the pertinent entries.

Hitzig, *RE* 4; Humbert, *DS* 1; Brasiello, *NDI* 4; Berger, *OCD* 489; Albertario, *Delictum e crimen*, 1924 (= *Studi* 3 [1936] 143); Lauria, *SDHI* 4 (1938) 188.

Crimen annonae. Unfair machinations, connected with the food supply and perpetrated in order to increase prices.—See ANNONA, LEX IULIA DE ANNONA.

Crimen calumniae. See CALUMNIA.

Crimen capitale. See CAPITALIS.

Crimen expilatae hereditatis. Plundering an inheritance before the instituted or legitimate heir entered it. It did not become a criminal offense until an enactment of Marcus Aurelius. Until then not only was it not punished but it might even lead to the acquisition of ownership over the things lawlessly appropriated through USUCAPIO PRO HEREDE.—D. 47.19; C. 9.32.

Leonhard, *RE* 4; Baudry, *DS* 2 (*s.v. expilatio*); Solazzi, *RendLomb* 69 (1936) 978.

Crimen fraudati vectigalis. The crime of tax evasion. —See FRAUDARE VECTIGAL, VECTIGAL.

Crimen legis Fabiae. See LEX FABIA, PLAGIUM.

Crimen maiestatis. (*Sc. imminutae, laesae, violatae.*) A crime "committed against the Roman people and its security" according to the LEX IULIA MAIESTATIS (D. 48.4.1.1). A *crimen maiestatis* could be committed not only by Roman citizens and not only on Roman territory. Several kinds of wrongs were termed *crimen maiestatis*: high treason, sedition, criminal attack against a magistrate, desertion, and the like. Under the Principate the term was extended to any offense where the safety of the emperor or his family is involved. In the later period, the term *maiestas* covered the sphere of PERDUELLIO, hence a distinction between these two crimes can hardly be made. The profession of Christianity was treated as *crimen maiestatis.*—D. 48.4; C. 9.8.—See LEX CORNELIA DE MAIESTATE, LEX VARIA, LEX APULEIA, OBSES.

Kübler, *RE* 14; Humbert and Lécrivain, *DS* 3; Charlesworth, *OCD* (all *s.v. maiestas*); Berger, *ibid.* 663; Anon., *NDI* 7 (*s.v. lesa maestà*); E. Pollack, *Der Majestätsgedanke im röm. Recht*, 1908; Ciaceri, *St storici per l'antichità classica* 2–3 (1909–1910); Robinson, *Georgetown LJ* 8 (1919) 14; F. Vittinghoff, *Der Staatsfeind in der röm. Kaiserzeit*, 1926; P. M. Schisas, *Offences against the state*, London, 1926; A. Mellor, *Les conceptions de crime politique sous la Rep. rom.*, 1934; C. A. Brecht, *Perduellio*, 1938; *idem, ZSS* 64 (1944) 354; Cramer, *Sem* 9 (1951) 9.

Crimen repetundarum. See REPETUNDAE.

Crimen suspecti tutoris. See TUTOR SUSPECTUS.

Crimina extraordinaria. See CRIMINA PUBLICA.

Crimina levia (leviora). Minor wrongdoings which are tried and punished by a magistrate in a simplified procedure (*de plano*).—See COERCITIO, DE PLANO.

Crimina publica. Crimes against the public and social order which were defined by special statutes (*leges iudiciorum publicorum*) and tried in *iudicia publica*. The pertinent statutes (listed under LEX) settled also the penalties. The prosecution of *crimina publica* started with ACCUSATIO. The procedure was regulated either by the specific statute or by a general one, as the LEX IULIA IUDICIORUM PUBLICORUM. Ant. *crimina extraordinaria* (*quae extra ordinem coërcentur*) are opposed to the *crimina publica* which *legibus coërcentur*. Their repression was introduced by imperial legislation, in a large measure in instructions given to the provincial governors. New kinds of crimes, unknown in the past, were thus submitted to criminal prosecution, and some wrongs previously defined as private offenses (as some kinds of theft, ABIGEATUS, STELLIONATUS) were treated as public crimes and prosecuted through public accusation.— D. 47.11.—See IUDICIA PUBLICA, QUAESTIO.

Criminalis. Connected with a criminal matter (*criminalis accusatio, causa*). Ant. *civilis*.

Criminaliter. See CIVILITER.

Crux. A cross. It was used as an instrument for the execution of persons condemned to death (*in* [*ad*] *crucem damnare*). *Crucifixion* was considered the most cruel form of the death penalty. Therefore it was applied to slaves; hence the term *servile supplicium*. Under the Empire crucifixion was also used for Roman citizens, but only in the case of individuals of the lower class (*humiliores*) convicted of particularly heavy crimes. It was abolished by Constantine. A wooden pillar to which slaves were bound to be flogged, was also called *crux*.

Cubicularius. A groom in the imperial chamber (*cubiculum*).—C. 12.5.

Rostowzew, *RE* 4; Saglio, *DS* 1; Besta, *NDI* 4; J. E. Dunlap, *Univ. Michigan Studies, Human. Ser.* 14 (1924) 182.

Cubiculum. The bed-chamber of the emperor and the empress.—See CUBICULARIUS, PRAEPOSITUS SACRI CUBICULI.

Cesano, *DE* 2, 1280.

Culleus. A leather sack used for the execution of the death penalty by drowning the culprit (*poena cullei*). The penalty was applied in the case of murder of a near relative (*parricidium*).—See LEX POMPEIA.

Hitzig, *RE* 4; Humbert, *DS* 1; Radin, *JRS* 10 (1920) 119; Düll, *ACDR* Roma 2 (1935).

Culpa. (In contractual relations.) A negligence on the part of a debtor who failed to foresee the consequences of his behavior with regard to the performance of the duties assumed in a contract. "There is no *culpa* if everything was done that a very careful man should have done" (D. 19.2.25.7). The responsibility of the debtor for his *culpa* is not settled in a uniform way for all kinds of contracts. There is no general rule in this respect, although some underlying ideas are not lacking, such as the liability for *culpa* of a contracting party who has received profit from a transaction (*utilitas contrahentis*) or in contractual relations governed by good faith (*bona fides*). Among those responsible for *culpa* were artisans and experts who took on a piece of work and afterwards proved lacking in the necessary professional knowledge (*imperitia*). On the other hand, in actions in which condemnation would have rendered the defendant infamous, his *culpa* is not taken into consideration. "In contracts we are liable sometimes only for *dolus* (*fraud*), sometimes also for *culpa*" (D. 13.6.5.2). The whole question of liability for *culpa* in the Roman contractual law is among the most crucial points in the literature, primarily because of the manifold changes introduced into classical texts by Justinian's compilers, guided by the tendency to increase the debtor's responsibility, and because of the absence of precise classical definition of various more or less technical terms in this domain, such as *custodia, diligentia, neglegentia*. In spite of a copious literature on the problem, the opinions of scholars are still divergent in fundamental points.—*Culpa* in criminal offenses or wrongdoings harmful to others is not so problematical. In some instances it means simply a fault of the guilty wrongdoer for which he is held responsible. As to private wrongs (*crimina privata, delicta*), *culpa* as negligence ("when a man failed to foresee what a careful [*diligens*] man would have foreseen," D. 9.2.31) it is scarcely conceivable in many cases (theft, robbery). In damage to property (*damnum*) a negligent behavior (carelessness) was taken into consideration and the jurists frequently dealt with cases of this kind. With regard to damage to property (see LEX AQUILIA) Justinian extended the liability of the wrongdoer to the "slightest negligence" (*culpa levissima*, D. 9.2.44 pr.). *Crimina publica* were punished only when the offender acted intentionally (*sciens dolo malo*); negligence remained without penalty. Where, in a later development, *culpa* was held to deserve a penalty, the latter was a minor one. Among such instances of punishable negligence were acts committed under a sudden impulse (*impetus*) or in a state of intoxication (*ebrietas, per vinum*).—Although in delictual matters *culpa* appears in a somewhat different light from that in the contractual sphere, the conception that *culpa* is something intermediate between *dolus* (*dolus malus* = evil intention, fraud) and *casus* (accident) is common to both domains.—See DOLUS, CASUS, IMPERITIA, NEGLEGENTIA, CUSTODIA, DILIGENTIA, and the following items.

Leonhard, *RE* 4; Baudry, *DS* 1; De Medio, *St Fadda* 2 (1906); *idem, BIDR* 17, 18 (1905–1906); Kübler, *Das Utilitätsprinzip, Fg Gierke,* 2 (1911) 256; Gradenwitz, *ZSS* 34 (1914); Binding, *ZSS* 39 (1919); K. Heldrich, *Verschulden beim Vertragsabschluss,* 1924; Kübler, *Rechtsidee und Staatsgedanke (Fschr Binder,* 1930), 63; Arangio-Ruiz, *Responsabilità contrattuale,* 2nd ed. 1933; Vazny, *ACII* 1 (1935) 345; Kübler, *Les degrès de faute, Études Lambert* 1 (1938); Pflüger, *ZSS* 65 (1947) 120; Brasiello, *SDHI* 12 (1946) 148; Condanari-Michler, *Scr Ferrini* 3 (Univ. Sacro Cuore, Milan, 1948) 28; Marton, *RIDA* 3 (= *Mél De Visscher* 2, 1949) 182; Visky, *ibid.* 437; F. H. Lawson, *Negligence in the civil law,* 1950, 36.

Culpa in concreto. (A term unknown in Roman juristic language.) Occurs when a person does not apply the same care (*diligentia*) in the interest of his creditor which he observes in his own matters (*diligentia quam suis*). Such degree of attention is required of a partner in a *societas,* of a guardian in the administration of the ward's affairs, and of a husband in the administration of the dowry.

L. Sertorio, *La c. i. c.,* 1914.

Culpa in eligendo. Negligence involved in choosing an inappropriate person for a work which someone assumed to do. Under certain circumstances the person who made the negligent choice was responsible for the damages caused by the unskilled workman (particularly in *locatio conductio operis faciendi*).

Culpa in faciendo. A negligent doing which caused damage to another's property or body. Ant. *culpa in non faciendo* = negligent omission.

Culpa lata and **culpa levis.** These constitute a distinction according to the gravity of the negligence. There are no specific criteria, the estimation of the degree is left to the judge. "*Culpa lata* is an immoderate negligence, i.e., not understanding what all understand" (50.16.213.2). *Culpa lata* (also called *culpa latior* or *culpa magna*) is considered equal to *dolus* (D. 50.16.226). Ant. *culpa levis,* a lower degree of *culpa,* is called once, in connection with the *lex Aquilia, culpa levissima* (D. 9.2.44 pr.).

De Medio, Binding, *ll. cc.* under CULPA; Lenel, *ZSS* 38 (1918) 263.

Cum re. See BONORUM POSSESSIO CUM RE.

Cunabula (iuris, legum). Basic principles, elements of the law.

Cura (curatio). Appears as a technical term both in public (administrative) and private law. In the first domain *cura* embraces the duties of public officials connected with various branches of administration, in the second field it comprises duties of private individuals to protect the interests of private individuals who because of physical or mental defects, youth or absence, cannot take care personally of their affairs. The *cura* in private law, known already in the Twelve Tables, is similar to guardianship (TUTELA). The differences which had existed originally between the two institutions as far as the rights and duties of the tutors and curators were concerned, were gradually abolished; in postclassical and Justinian law the equalization is completed, in a large measure through the insertion of *cura* into texts which originally dealt with *tutela.* Persons entrusted with *cura* are called *curatores,* both in public and private law. In the following entries the *curae* of the private law are listed under *curator,* those (more important) of the public law under *curatores.*—Inst. 1.23; D. 26.7; 27.5; 7; 9; 10; C. 5.31–34; 36–49; 57; 60–69.—See EXCEPTIO CURATORIA.

Kornemann, *RE* 4; Leonhard, *ibid.* 4; Thédenat, *DS* 1; Anon., *NDI* 4; Solazzi, *NDI* (*s.v. tutela*) 12; De Ruggiero, *DE* 2.

Cura annonae. The care for corn supply. Under the Republic the aediles were responsible for the *cura annonae* and all matters pertaining to it (regulation of prices, prevention of monopolies, supply of corn to the troops in Italy, and the like). Their administration was often a failure and created catastrophic situations. Augustus reorganized the whole matter of provisioning of Rome by the creation of a new office under the direction of the PRAEFECTUS ANNONAE.—See ANNONA.

Humbert, *DS* 1.

Cura minorum. See CURATOR MINORIS, MINORES.

Cura morum. The supervision of public morals. The term corresponds to the REGIMEN MORUM of the censors under the Republic. It is particularly connected with Augustus and his "care for law and morals" (*cura legum et morum*).

A. v. Premerstein, *Vom Werden und Wesen des Prinzipats, ABayAW* 15 (1937) 149; Schmähling, *Die Sittenaufsicht der Zensoren,* 1938.

Cura prodigi. See CURATOR PRODIGI, PRODIGUS.

Curatio. Syn. with CURA, in both private and public law.

Curator adiunctus tutori. See CURATOR IMPUBERIS.

Curator bonorum. The administrator of the estate of an insolvent debtor. He was appointed in certain cases only when the creditors, who were granted possession thereof (MISSIO IN POSSESSIONEM), had no right to sell it (e.g., the heir being a *pupillus,* absent in the interest of the state, or a prisoner of war). A *curator bonorum* was also appointed when it was uncertain whether there would be an heir or not. His duty was to protect the estate from losses.—D. 42.7.

G. Solazzi, *Concorso dei creditori* 2 (1938).

Curator collegii. A leading functionary in professional, religious and other kinds of associations. If there was a *magister collegii* (a chairman), the *curator* was his deputy. His functions depended upon the character and aims of the association.

Kornemann, *RE* 4, 122.

Curator distrahendorum bonorum gratia. See DISTRACTIO BONORUM.—See CLARA PERSONA.

Curator furiosi. A *curator* of an insane person of whom it is said: "he cannot make any transaction because he does not understand what he is doing" (D. 50.17.5). The *curator* took care of the person and administered the property of his ward. He could be appointed by the father of the lunatic in a testament; if there was no testamentary disposition, the nearest agnate was, according to the Twelve Tables, entitled to assume the *cura furiosi.* When the curatorship was ended the *curator* could be sued in an *actio negotiorum gestorum* for bad management of the ward's patrimonial affairs.—D. 27.10; C. 5.70.—See FURIOSUS, IUDICIUM CURATIONIS.

De Francisci, *BIDR* 30 (1921) 154; Guarino, *SDHI* 10 (1944) 374.

Curator impuberis (pupilli). Wards who had a guardian (*pupilli*), in exceptional cases could have (besides the tutor) a curator, appointed by a magistrate at the request of the guardian and at the latter's responsibility (*curator adiunctus, actor, adiutor*). This occurred when the tutor was old or permanently ill—which was not a ground for his removal—or when the property of the *pupillus* was large and located at distant places. In Justinian's law the *curator adiunctus* became an autonomous institution; he was appointed by an official and the tutor was not responsible for his assistant's activity.—D. 27.10.—See IMPUBES, PUPILLUS.

Sachers, *RE* 7A, 1526; R. Taubenschlag, *Vormundschaftsrechtliche Studien,* 1913, 47; Solazzi, *C. i.,* 1917.

Curator minoris. A *curator* of a *minor* (a person under twenty-five) *sui iuris*. Originally appointed for specific matters in order to protect the inexperienced minor against transactions in which his youth might have been exploited, the *curator minoris* became under Marcus Aurelius a legal institution, since the remedy of the LEX PLAETORIA and the praetorian RESTITUTIO IN INTEGRUM proved insufficient. Appointed at the request of the minor the *curator* assisted him in concluding transactions by giving his consent (*consensus*). The remedy of the *restitutio in integrum* remained in force for minors acting without a curator. It was a general rule that a minor could not make his position worse when he acted without the approval of his curator. In postclassical and Justinian's law the *curator minoris* became a matter of rule and was assimilated to *tutela* in many respects.—See CURA MINORES (Bibl.), LEX PLAETORIA, IUDICIUM CURATIONIS, TUTOR SUSPECTUS.

Berger, *RE* 15, 1870; Albertario, *ZSS* 33 (1912) 245 (= *Studi* 1 (1935) 407; G. Solazzi, *La minore età*, 1913; idem, *RISG* 54 (1914); Y. Arangio-Riuz, *Il mandato*, 1949, 23; A. Burdese, *Autorizzazione ad alienare*, 1950, 14.

Curator muti, surdi. A *curator* of a dumb or deaf person. His attributions were analogous to those of other curators. Similarly a person who suffered from a chronic disease which did not permit him to manage his affairs, might have a curator.

Curator prodigi. A *curator* of a spendthrift. He is known as early as in the Twelve Tables; he was appointed on behalf of the nearest relatives of the spendthrift in order to save his property for his presumptive heirs. The rights and duties of a *curator prodigi* are similar to those of a *curator furiosi* (except the care for the person of the *prodigus*). The appointment of a *curator prodigi* was preceded by a decree of the praetor, *interdictio bonorum,* which excluded the spendthrift from the administration of his property. See INTERDICERE BONIS. For transactions by which the *prodigus* assumed duties or alienated something from his property, he needed the consent of his *curator*. He was not permitted to make a testament.—See PRODIGUS.—D. 27.10; C. 5.70.

De Francisci, *BIDR* 30 (1921) 154; Solazzi, *St Bonfante* 1 (1930) 47.

Curator pupilli. See CURATOR IMPUBERIS.

Curator surdi. See CURATOR MUTI.

Curator ventri datus. A *curator* appointed for the defense of the interests of a child not yet born.—See VENTER, NASCITURUS, CONCEPTUS.—D. 37.9.

Anon., *NDI* 4; Solazzi, *RISG* 54 (1914) 277.

Curatores. (In public law.) Commissioners entrusted with certain branches of the administration. Augustus appointed several *curatores* and charged them with the administration or supervision (*cura, curatio*) of public institutions and works which under the Republic attributed to *quaestors* and *aediles,* such as public roads (*curatores viarum*), aqueducts (*curatores aquarum*), public buildings (*curatores operum publicorum*) and the conservacy of the bed and banks of the Tiber (*curatores alvei et riparum Tiberis*). *Curatores* were active also in municipalities.—See MAGISTRI, PROCURATORES and the following items.

Kornemann, *RE* 4; Sacchi, *NDI* 4; De Ruggiero, *DE* 2; Thédenat, *DS* 1, 1621.

Curatores aedium sacrarum. *Curatores* of imperial buildings.—See SUBCURATOR.

Kornemann, *RE* 4, 1787.

Curatores alvei Tiberis. See CURATORES.

Thédenat, *DS* 1, 1623.

Curatores annonae. See CURA ANNONAE.

Curatores aquarum. *Curatores* of aqueducts and administrators of the water supply.—See SUBCURATOR.

Kornemann, *RE* 4, 1784; De Ruggiero, *DE* 1, 548; T. Ashby, *Aqueducts of ancient Rome*, 1935, 17.

Curatores civitatis. See CURATORES REI PUBLICAE.

Curatores civium Romanorum. See CONVENTUS CIVIUM ROMANORUM.

Curatores frumenti. See PRAEFECTI FRUMENTI DANDI.

Curatores kalendarii. See KALENDARIUM.

Kornemann, *RE* 4, 1805.

Curatores ludorum. *Curatores* for extraordinary games (*ludi*) given by the emperor to the people.

Kornemann, *RE* 4, 1798.

Curatores operum publicorum. Officials for the management of public buildings (administration, lease, construction, contracts with contractors, etc.). Their competence was sometimes extended to other public institutions which found expression in their official title, appropriately enlarged.—See SUBCURATOR, OPERA PUBLICA.

Kornemann, *RE* 4, 1787, 1802; Thédenat, *DS* 1, 1622.

Curatores praesidii. Administrative officers in military garrisons.

Youtie, *TAmPhilolAs* 81 (1950) 110.

Curatores regionum. See CURATORES URBIS ROMAE.

Curatores rei publicae (civitatis). Officials in Italian cities appointed by the emperor for the supervision and administration of municipal finances. They had jurisdiction in matters connected with the financial administration and intervened in transactions concerning municipal property. In the later Empire their competence appears somewhat diminished as a result of a general centralizing tendency in the administration of the state.

Kornemann, *RE* 4, 1806; Lacour-Gayet, *DS* 1, 1619; Mancini, *DE* 2; Liebenam, *Philologus* 56 (1897) 290; Lucas, *JRS* 1940, 56; Cassarino, *AnCat* 2 (1948); A. Lécrivain, *Le c. r. p.* 1920; D. Magie, *Rom. rule in Asia Minor* 2 (1950) 1454.

Curatores urbis Romae. Officials who took care of the districts (*regiones*) of the city of Rome.—See REGIONES URBIS ROMAE.

Curatores viarum. Officials charged with the maintenance and supervision of public roads (*cura viarum*). Primarily the adjacent communities had to contribute funds and labor for constructing and repairing the roads. But the state treasury and the imperial fisc made also considerable contributions. There were also special *curatores* for larger roads, as *curatores viae Appiae, Flaminiae*, etc.

Kornemann, *RE* 4, 1781; Chapot, *DS* 5, 788.

Curiae. The earliest units, probably based on a territorial principle, into which the Roman people was divided. There were originally thirty *curiae*, ten in each TRIBUS. It seems that in the original stage only patricians belonged to the curial organization; later the plebeians were admitted. The political character of the *curiae* manifested itself in the COMITIA CURIATA in which each *curia* had one vote. Their purpose was also military, since each of them had to contribute one hundred men for the infantry and ten for the cavalry. A land plot was assigned to the *curia* for common use. The leader of a *curia* was the *curio*, the head of all *curiae* was the *curio maximus*, originally perhaps identical with the king. A *flamen curialis* took care of the common worship and religious matters of the members of the *curiae*. For *curiae* in the later Empire, see ORDO DECURIONUM.

Kübler, *RE* 4; Momigliano, *OCD*; Lacour-Gayet, *DS* 1; Gervasio, *DE* 2; Besta, *NDI* 4.

Curiae municipiorum. The citizens of the municipalities (*municipes*) were organized in groups called *curiae* or *tribus*. *Curia* is also the council of administration, the senate, of a *municipium* (syn. *ordo decurionum*), and the building in which the council held its sessions.—See ORDO DECURIONUM.

Gaudemet, *Iura* 2 (1951) 44.

Curiales. Members of a municipal council (*curia, ordo decurionum*) in the later Empire. Syn. *decuriones*. —C. 3.25; 10.22.

Gaudemet, *Iura* 2 (1951) 44.

Curiana causa. A famous trial (*clarissima causa*) before the centumviral court dealing with a case of a *substitutio pupillaris* for a son whose birth was expected but did not materialize. The case in which the jurist Q. Mucius Scaevola appeared for the heirs on intestacy, is mentioned in several writings of Cicero.—See CENTUMVIRI.

Perrin, *RHD* 27 (1949) 354; J. Stroux, *Röm. Rechtswissenschaft und Rhetorik* (Potsdam, 1949) 42.

Curio. See CURIA.

De Ruggiero, *DE* 2.

Curiosi. See AGENTES IN REBUS.—C. 12.22.

Humbert, *DS* 1, 1667; Hirschfeld, *SbBerl* 39, 1 (1891).

Cursor. A courier, messenger in imperial postal service.

Cicolini, *DE* 2.

Cursus honorum. The order in which the Republican magistracies had to be held by a Roman citizen to make him a capable candidate for a higher magistracy. The lowest degree in the magisterial career was the quaestorship which was followed by the aedilship and praetorship. The consulship was the top magistracy. Censorship did not belong to the

cursus honorum. Syn. *ordo magistratuum*. In the Empire there was not a fixed *cursus honorum*, either in the senatorial or equestrian career, since the emperor had full liberty to confer official titles on persons who never before had been in service (see ADLECTIO).—See LEX CORNELIA DE MAGISTRATIBUS, LEX VILLIA.

Kübler, *RE* 14, 405.

Cursus publicus. The official postal service organized in the early Principate for the transportation of official personages or of things in the interest of, or belonging to, the State or the emperor, or connected somehow with the administration. It served also for the official correspondence with the rest of Italy and the provinces. Reorganized by Hadrian, who charged the fisc with its supervision, the postal service was again reformed by Diocletian and his successors and became a compulsory service (*munus*) shouldered by landowners and wealthy people who had to contribute in various ways to a proper functioning of the institution.—C. 12.50.—See CURSUS VELOX, AGENTES IN REBUS, ANGARIA, DIPLOMA, EVECTIO, MANSIO, PARANGARIA, VEREDI, PRAEFECTUS VEHICULORUM.

Seeck, *RE* 4; Humbert, *DS* 1; Bellino, *DE* 2; A. E. R. Boak, *Univ. of Michigan Studies, Human. Series* 14 (1924) 74; E. J. Holmberg, *Zur Gesch. des c. p.*, Uppsala, 1933; H. G. Pflaum, *Essai sur le c. p. dans le Haut-Empire, Mém. Acad. Insc. et Belles-Lettres*, 14, 1 (1940) 189; Labrousse, *Mél d'archéologie et d'hist. de l'École franç. de Rome*, 1940, 150.

Cursus velox. Fast post-service (see CURSUS PUBLICUS) to be distinguished from *cursus clabularis* (from *clabula* = a heavy carriage) for the transportation of food and luggage for soldiers.

Curulis. Refers to magistrates who had the right to seat on a SELLA CURULIS during their official activity. —See MAGISTRATUS, AEDILES CURULES.

Custodela. An ancient Latin term, syn. with *custodia*. It appears in the form prescribed for the *testamentum per aes et libram*. The FAMILIAE EMPTOR assumed the custody of the hereditary things. The *custodela* is a counterpart to a likewise ancient term *mandatela*, used in the same formula and indicating the wish (order) of the testator concerning the distribution of the inheritance.

Weiss, *ZSS* 42 (1921) 104.

Custodes corporis. Bodyguards of the emperor and of high military commanders in peace as well as in war.—See EQUITES SINGULARES.

Paribeni, *DE* 2, 1237; idem, *Mitteilungen deutsch. kais. Archäol. Instituts, Röm. Abt.* 20 (1905) 321.

Custodia. Custody, safe keeping, watching. The term appears in connection with the responsibility of the debtor in some specific contracts. It belongs to those not precisely defined and oscillating expressions concerning contractual responsibility (see CULPA), which through manipulations of the compilers of the Digest became nebulous. Moreover, the *custodia* itself is sometimes accompanied by adjectives, such as *dili-*

gens, plena, which seem to presuppose a gradation thereof. Expressions like *exactissima diligentia custodiendae rei* exclude a precise separation of the terms combined. Responsibility for *custodia* arose when it was expressly agreed upon or from contracts concluded primarily in the interest of the party who held another's thing to be returned later to the owner, as in the case of a gratuitous loan (*commodatum*) or when persons were involved whose business it was to assume the custody of other people's things, as storehouse keepers, shipmasters, innkeepers, etc. (see RECEPTUM NAUTARUM) or in certain cases of LOCATIO CONDUCTIO OPERIS FACIENDI (see FULLO). Since on the one hand *custodia* is linked with *culpa, neglegentia,* or *diligentia,* on the other hand it is opposed to VIS MAIOR (see CASUS), it has been assumed that *custodia* entailed a higher degree of responsibility than for *culpa* only; in particular, it involved the duty of a more careful custody, and consequently, liability for a simple, lesser accident (not for *vis maior*), such as theft which through a more attentive guarding by the debtor could be prevented. Another theory does not consider *custodia* a specific degree of responsibility between *culpa* and *vis maior,* but a diligent care for things belonging to another. One who expressly promised *custodia* (*custodiam praestare,* see PACTUM CUSTODIAE) or concluded a transaction which involved *custodia,* was obliged to apply particular diligence and to perform the pertinent duties with every possible means being also responsible for persons employed therefor. In cases of *custodia* even a slight omission created the liability of the debtor. *Custodia* is not to be separated from *diligentia,* for there is no *custodia* without *diligentia.* —*Custodia* is also used in the normal meaning of the word, outside the domain of contracts, as, e.g., with regard to the custody of things belonging to an inheritance by the *familiae emptor* (see TESTAMENTUM PER AES ET LIBRAM, FAMILIAE EMPTOR), or that of the *missus in possessionem* (see MISSIONES IN POSSESSIONEM). *Custodia* is identified there with *observatio rerum* (= watching, guarding things).—See CULPA, SARCINATOR.

Rabel, *NDI* 4; Humbert, *DS* 1; Lusignani, *Responsabilità per c.,* 1–3 (1902, 1903, 1905); Schulz, *Ztschr. für vergleichende Rechtswiss.* 25 (1911) 459, 27 (1912) 145; idem, *KrVj* 50 (1912) 22; Seckel, in Heumann's *Handlexikon⁹* (1914) 117; Haymann, *ZSS* 40 (1919) 167, 48 (1928) 318; Kunkel, *ZSS* 45 (1925) 268; Vazny, *AnPal* 12 (1926) 101; J. Paris, *La responsabilité de la c.,* 1926; Carrelli, *RBSG* 6 (1931) 604; V. Arangio-Ruiz, *Responsabilità contrattuale²,* 1933, 62; G. I. Luzzatto, *Caso fortuito e forza maggiore* I. *Responsabilità per c.* 1938; Krückmann, *ZSS* 63 (1943) 48, 64 (1944) 1; Pflüger, *ZSS* 65 (1947) 121; De Robertis, *AnBari* 10 (1949) 58; Rosenthal, *ZSS* 68 (1951) 222.

Custodia reorum. Detention of persons involved in a criminal matter in a jail, to have them at the disposal of the inquiring officials. After condemnation the culprits were held in prison for the execution of the sentence.—D. 48.3; C. 9.4.—See CARCER.

Berger, *OCD* (s.v. prison).

Custodire partum. See INSPICERE VENTREM.

Custos. A jailer. See CUSTODIA REORUM. Prisoners who escaped from jail profiting by the negligence of the *custodes* received a milder punishment than those who broke out by their own efforts (*effractores*) or in conspiracy with other prisoners.

Custos. (In a *traditio.*) The buyer of a larger amount of merchandise could appoint a *custos* (= a guard, an attendant) before taking it away. The delivery of the things (*traditio*) was considered fulfilled by such appointment, and the seller was free from any risk.

Riccobono, *ZSS* 34 (1913) 200.

Custos iuris civilis. Title given the praetor by Cicero.

Custos urbis. Refers to the PRAEFECTUS URBI.

Keune, *RE* 4, 1903; Humbert, *DS* 1.

Custos ventris. See SENATUSCONSULTUM PLANCIANUM.

Cyrillos. See KYRILLOS.

D

D. Abbreviation for *damno* (= I condemn), see A.

Damnare. To condemn a defendant in a civil trial (see CONDEMNATIO) or an accused in a criminal proceeding. In the latter meaning the term is mostly used of a condemnatory judgment for crimes punished by death (*in crimine capitali*). With reference to testamentary dispositions *damnare* = to impose upon an heir or legatee the duty to perform a service or a payment to the benefit of a third person.

Betti, *RISG* 56 (1915) 31; A. Hägerström, *Der Obligationsbegriff* 1 (1927) 443; M. Kaser, *Das Altröm. Ius,* 1949, 127.

Damnare ad bestias. See BESTIIS OBICERE.

Damnare in metallum (metalla). See METALLUM.

Damnas. Occurred in the form of a legacy called *legatum per damnationem: heres meus damnas esto dare* (= my heir shall be obliged to give).—See LEGATUM PER DAMNATIONEM.

Thomas, *RHD* 10 (1931) 211.

Damnatio. See DAMNARE, CONDEMNATIO.

Damnatio in ludum. See LUDI GLADIATORII, GLADIATORES.

Damnatio memoriae. A disgrace inflicted on the memory of a person (*memoria damnata*) condemned to death and executed, or dead before the criminal prosecution was finished. Only crimes against the state, such as treason (*maiestas, perduellio*) brought about this *ignominia post mortem,* the extinction of the memory of the individual thus stigmatized. His name was canceled on documents and destroyed on monuments; his last will and donations *mortis causa* lost validity. The *damnatio memoriae* was also applied to emperors, whose conduct was unworthy, during their lifetime or posthumously. The pertinent decree was issued by the senate.

Brassloff, *RE* 4; Balsdon, *OCD*; Orestano, *BIDR* 44 (1937) 327; Vittinghoff, *Der Staatsfeind in der röm. Kaiserzeit. Untersuchungen zur damnatio memoriae,* 1936.

Damnatus. Condemned in a criminal trial for a crime calling for capital punishment.—D. 48.20; C. 4.49.— See BONA DAMNATORUM.

Damnosus. Threatening (involving) loss. In relations between neighbors the term indicates a defective building which may damage the neighboring property.—See DAMNUM INFECTUM.

Daube, *St Solazzi* (1948) 117.

Damnum. A loss, expenditure, suffered by the victim of an offense, particularly a loss ensuing for the owner of a thing from a damage done thereto. "He who suffered damage through his own fault is not considered to have sustained damage" (D. 50.17.203). Responsibility for damages inflicted on another's property is either contractual (resulting from duties assumed in a contract) or delictual resulting from a tort, a wrongful act (*delictum*) committed by an offender.—See COMMUNICARE, NEMO DAMNUM FACIT, SARCIRE.

Leonhard, *RE* 4; Baudry, *DS* 1; E. Levy, *Privatstrafe und Schadensersatz,* 1915; Thomas, *RHD* 10 (1931) 211; Ratti, *BIDR* 40 (1932) 169; P. Voci, *Risarcimento del danno e processo formulare,* 1938, 19; idem, *St Ferrini* 2 (Univ. Sacro Cuore, Milan, 1947) 361; Daube, *On the use of the term d., St Solazzi,* 1948, 93.

Damnum decidere. To come to terms concerning the damages to be paid by the offender to the person who sustained a loss.

Daube, *St Solazzi,* 1948, 99.

Damnus emergens. A real factual loss which one suffers in his property, a loss which can be evaluated in money (pecuniary loss). Ant. *lucrum cessans* = a loss of a reasonable profit. Both terms do not belong to the Roman juristic language, but the distinction between two kinds of losses is classical.

P. Voci, *Risarcimento del danno,* 1938, 63.

Damnum fatale. A damage done by an unavoidable accident (VIS MAIOR).

Damnum infectum (or **nondum factum**). A damage not yet done but threatening one's property by the defective state of a neighbor's property. Originally the owner of the threatened property had against his neighbor an *actio damni infecti* (which even after the introduction of the formulary procedure was conducted in the form of *legis actio*). Later praetorian law introduced specific remedies, see CAUTIO DAMNI INFECTI, MISSIO IN POSSESSIONEM DAMNI INFECTI NOMINE.—See VITIUM AEDIUM, DENUNTIATIO DOMUM.

Baudry, *DS* 1; Cuq, *DS* 5, 933; Branca, *St Ratti,* 1934, 161; idem, *Danno temuto,* 1937; M. F. Lepri, *Missiones in possessionem,* 1939, 90.

Damnum iniuria datum. See LEX AQUILIA.

Damnum praestare. To make good the loss incurred by a person whose property was damaged.—See SARCIRE, RESARCIRE.

Dardanarius. A merchant in corn and other kind of food who through illicit machinations raised the prices or used forged weights.

Rostowzew, *RE* 7, 142.

Dare. To give, hand over a thing for the purpose of making the receiver the owner thereof. This is the general meaning when a contractual obligation concerned a *dare*. The contents of the term might be limited by the indication of a minor purpose, as, e.g., *pignori dare* (= to give as a pledge), *utendum dare* (= to give for use), *precario dare* (= to give as a PRECARIUM).—See CONTRACTUS INNOMINATI.—*Dare,* in criminal trials, connected with a sentence, in phrases as *dare in metalla, ad bestias, in exsilium,* etc. = to condemn.—*Dare* in the meaning of "to appoint" refers to the appointment of a *tutor* or *curator* by a magistrate or a private person or of a representative or agent for one's private affairs. *Dare bonorum possessionem* refers to the praetorian act of granting a BONORUM POSSESSIO.—See the following items.

Grosso, *In materia di obbligazioni di dare, SDHI* 6 (1940); F. Pastori, *Profilo dogmatico dell'obbligazione rom.,* 1951, 118.

Dare actionem. To grant an action. The praetor "gives an action" in cases where the *ius civile* refused it. In a larger sense *dare actionem* (or *iudicium*) is the praetor's approval of the formula agreed upon by the parties. Ant. DENEGARE ACTIONEM (= *non dare actionem*). Syn. REDDERE ACTIONEM.— D. 44.5.

P. Krüger, *ZSS* 16 (1895) 1.

Dare iudicem. To appoint a judge in a civil trial.— See IUDEX.

Datio. An act of giving (*dare*). It applies to all meanings of DARE (*datio tutoris, bonorum possessionis, iudicis, pignoris,* etc.).

Datio dotis. Constitution of a dowry by immediately handing it over. *Datio dotis* is also the term employed for the delivery of things promised as a dowry by *dictio, promissio* or *pollicitatio dotis.*

Datio in solutum. The payment of a thing other than that which originally was due to the creditor who accepts it as a discharge of the former obligation. The creditor was not obliged to do so. Only in Justinian's law a debtor who had no cash at his disposal could offer payment in immovables at a fair price.

H. Steiner, *D. i. s.,* 1914; De Francisci, *L'evizione della res data i. s.,* 1915; Solazzi, *RendLomb* 61 (1928) 341; M. Ricca-Barberis, *L'evizione nella d. i. s., RISG* 6 (1931) 3; S. Solazzi, *L'estinzione dell'obbligazione,* 2nd ed. 1935, 161.

Datio tutoris. See TUTOR DATIVUS.

De actionibus. A dissertation written in Greek (*peri agogon*), of pre-Justinian origin and dealing generally with various more important actions. It is rather the work of a practitioner than of a scholar.

Editions: G. E. Heimbach (Jr.), *Observationes iuris Graeco-Romani* 1 (1830); Zachariae, *ZSS* 14 (1893) 88; J. and P. Zepos, *Jus Graeco-Romanum* 3 (Athens, 1931) 301.—Ferrini, *Opere* 1 (1929) 365; G. Segrè, *Mél Girard* 2 (1913) 543; Brugi, *Annuario dell'Istituto di storia del dir. rom. Catania* 13–14 (1914–15); P. Collinet, *La procédure par libelle*, 1932, 501; Scheltema, *TR* 17 (1940) 420.

De gradibus (cognationum). A dissertation on the degrees of cognatic relationship, written by an unknown jurist, presumably of the classical period.

Editions: in all collections of *Fontes,* see General Bibliography, Ch. XII.—Berger, *RE* 10, 1192; Scherillo, *StCagl* 18 (1931) 65.

De peculiis. A Byzantine dissertation, called not quite appropriately *Tractatus de peculiis* in the literature. Written about the middle of the eleventh century it deals with various topics connected with the reciprocal acquisitions and rights of succession of father and son, of some kinds of *peculia* and the like. The unknown author who is quite familiar with Justinian's legislation, the post-Justinian legal literature as well as with the BASILICA, is particularly interested in the son's acquisitions on which the father has only a usufruct.

Editions: G. E. Heimbach (Jr.), *Anecdota* 2 (1840) 247; J. and P. Zepos, *Jus Graeco-romanum* 3 (Athens, 1931) 345.—Berger, *Scr Ferrini* 3 (Univ. Sacro Cuore, Milan, 1948) 174.

De plano. In matters of minor importance the magistrate acted more informally, "from the level" "out of court," without any preceding *causae cognitio,* either personally or through officials of his bureau acting under his supervision. The proceedings were public and there was no platform (*tribunal*) for the acting officers. Ant. *pro tribunali.*—See CRIMINA LEVIA.

Düll, *ZSS* 52 (1932) 170; Wenger, *ibid.* 59 (1932) 62; 62 (1942) 366.

Debere. To owe, to be under an obligation to pay a sum or to perform something, an obligation of contractual or delictual origin which was suable at *ius civile* or *ius praetorium.*—See DEBITUM, DEBITOR.

G. Segrè, *St Bonfante* 3 (1930) 524.

Debitor. A debtor, "he from whom money may be exacted against his will" (D. 50.16.108). Therefore a *debitor* is not he who "has a just exception against the creditor's claim" (D. 50.17.66). Syn. *reus debendi.* Ant. *creditor.*—See DEBERE.

Debitor civitatis (reipublicae). A debtor of a *civitas* or municipality. He could not obtain any honorary position (*honor*) until he paid his debt. Such debtors were subject to special executory measures.—C. 11.33; 40.

Debitor debitoris. A debtor's debtor.—C. 4.15.

Debitor fisci. A debtor of the fisc. Imperial legislation established special rules for the execution of fiscal claims.—C. 10.2.

Debitor reipublicae. See DEBITOR CIVITATIS.

Debitum. Both the object of the obligation (*id quod debetur* = what is due) and the obligatory tie between debtor and creditor. Ant. *indebitum.*

Humbert, *DS* 2.

Decanus. A low ranking officer in a legion, commander of a unit of ten soldiers (*contubernium*). A *decanus* at the imperial court was an official of a lower rank in the service of the empress.—C. 12.26.

Fiebiger, *RE* 4; Seeck, *ibid.* 2246 (no. 2).

Decedere de possessione. To give up, to abandon possession.—See MISSIONES IN POSSESSIONEM.

Decemprimi. (Also *decemprimi curiales.*) A group of ten persons selected from the members of a larger body (the senate under the Republic where the *decemprimi* were the heads of the senatorial *decuriae,* municipal senates, sacerdotal colleges). They enjoyed special privileges. In the military hierarchy of the later Empire *decemprimi* occupied a privileged position in the military unit attached to the imperial palace (*domestici*).

Brandis, *RE* 4; Humbert, *DS* 2.

Decemvirales leges. See LEX DUODECIM TABULARUM, DECEMVIRI LEGIBUS SCRIBUNDIS.

Decemviri agris dandis assignandis. See TRIUMVIRI COLONIAE DEDUCENDAE.

De Ruggiero, *DE* 2, 430.

Decemviri legibus scribundis. A commission composed of ten persons appointed in 451 B.C. for the codification of laws. They continued their work in the following year. During the two years of their work, the activity of all magistracies was suspended and the *decemviri* assumed the governmental functions vested in the consular *imperium.*—See LEX DUODECIM TABULARUM, VERGINIA.

Kübler, *RE* 4, 2257; Berger, *RE* 4A, 1905; Momigliano, *OCD*; Humbert, *DS* 2; Moschella, *NDI* 4.

Decemviri sacris faciundis. See DUOVIRI SACRIS FACIUNDIS.

Decemviri stlitibus iudicandis. Originally minor judicial magistrates (see VIGINTISEXVIRI), they became later chairmen of the judicial courts formed within the tribunal of the CENTUMVIRI.

Humbert, *DS* 2; Kübler, *RE* 4, 2260; Vaglieri, *DE* 2; M. Nicolau, *Causa liberalis,* 1933, 16.

Decernere. To issue a decree (*decretum*) when applied to the senate; to decide a judicial matter when applied to a decision of a magistrate or the emperor —See DECRETA.

Decessor. A predecessor in office. A provincial official whose successor in office had already been appointed, was required to remain in service until the new incumbent arrived in the province. Ant. *successor.*—C. 1.49.

Decidere. To decide about a judicial matter by judgment (see DECISIO); to settle a controversy by a transaction between the adversaries or by an oath.— See TRANSACTIO, IUSIURANDUM VOLUNTARIUM.

Decidere damnum. See DAMNUM DECIDERE.

Decima. One-tenth. One-tenth of the estate was the part which according to the Augustan LEX IULIA ET PAPIA POPPAEA one spouse could take when the other died intestate. An increase of this tenth part by further tenths was permitted in proportion to the number of children. The pertinent provisions (*decimariae sc. leges*) were abolished in A.D. 410.—C. 8.57.

Decisio. See DECIDERE, QUINQUAGINTA DECISIONES.

Declarare. To declare (e.g., *voluntatem* = one's will). With reference to judicial judgments = to establish a specific legal situation (ownership, a servitude).

Decoctor. (From *decoquere*.) An embezzler or a bankrupt, whose property was sold through BONORUM VENDITIO. In a later trial he was obliged to give a *cautio iudicatum solvi* (a security for the payment of the judgment debt).

Decollatio. Decapitation. Syn. *capitis amputatio*.

Decreta. See DECERNERE, BONORUM POSSESSIO DECRETALIS, and the following items.

Decreta decurionum. Decrees issued by the municipal senate (*ordo decurionum*) on various matters. They could not be rescinded unless public utility required such a measure.—D. 50.9; C. 10.47.—See DECRETA MAGISTRATUUM.

Decreta Frontiana (Frontiniana). A juristic work (collection of decisions of the imperial court?), attributed to the jurist Titius Aristo.—See ARISTO.

T. Mommsen, *Jur. Schriften* 2 (1905) 22.

Decreta magistratuum. Orders of the magistrates of a judicial (*interdicta, missiones in possessionem*, or concerning *bonorum possessiones*) or administrative character (imposition of fines, *multae*, or ordaining a *pignoris capio*) to enforce compliance with their ordinances. In matters concerning guardianship or curatorship *decreta* are very frequent. *Decreta* are issued after *causae cognitio* and *pro tribunali*. The *decreta* of provincial governors had a similar character.—C. 5.72.—See IN INTEGRUM RESTITUTIO.

Hesky, *RE* 4; De Ruggiero, *DE* 2; Jobbé-Duval, *St Bonfante* 3 (1930) 165.

Decreta principum. Imperial enactments (decrees) issued by the emperor in the exercise of jurisdiction in civil and criminal matters, both as final judgments and as interlocutory decisions during the proceedings. They rank among the imperial constitutions and had some importance, although no binding force, in similar future cases inasmuch as they could be considered and applied as precedents. When published by order of the emperor they acquired general validity as the edicts of the emperor.—See CONSTITUTIONES PRINCIPUM (Bibl.).

Decretum divi Marci. A decree of the emperor Marcus Aurelius forbidding creditors to take arbitrarily away things or money due from their debtors, without resorting for help to the competent authorities. "Creditors should claim what they believe to be due to them through the intermediary of a judge" (D. 4.2.13). A creditor who contrary to that decree proceeded on his own with force against the debtor lost his claim.

Decuma. The tenth part (*pars decima*) of natural produce paid in kind (corn, wine, oil) as a rent or property-tax in Italy and provinces.

Liebenam, *RE* 4; Humbert, *DS* 2; Kaser, *ZSS* 62 (1942) 61; De Ruggiero, *DE* 2; L. Clerici, *Economia e finanze dei Romani*, 1 (1943) 477.

Decuria. A group (unit) of ten men. In ancient times, the *decuria* had a military and political character, since the CURIAE, into which the oldest TRIBUS were divided (altogether 30 *curiae*), were composed of ten *decuriae*, each of them with ten men. *Decuriae* were also the smallest units in the cavalry. The Roman senate had also its *decuriae* (of ten men) and preserved this name afterwards when its *decuriae* were groups of one tenth of the whole number of the senators. Finally, professional corporations and those of·subaltern officials as well, were divided in *decuriae*, often with more than ten members. Imperial constitutions of the fourth century deal with various *decuriae* of officials in the city of Rome (*decuria urbis Romae*), such as fiscal clerks (*fiscales*), *scribae* (*librarii* = copyists), *censuales* (= tax assessment clerks).—C. 11.14.—See the following items.

Kübler, *RE* 4; Humbert, *DS* 2; Bellino, *DE* 2; Moschella, *NDI* 4.

Decuria lictoria. See LICTORES.

Decuriae apparitorum. Associations of *apparitores*, organized in *decuriae*. They were granted some rights as corporate bodies (inheriting, holding and manumitting slaves).—See DECURIALES.

Kornemann, *RE* 4, 401; P. W. Duff, *Personality in R. private law*, 1938, 32, 101; B. Eliachévitch, *Personnalité juridique* 1942, 241; Jones, *JRS* 39 (1949) 40.

Decuriae iudicum. Groups of jurors (of 300 each?) in the list of persons qualified for this service. Originally there were three *decuriae*, of senators, *equites* and *tribuni aerarii*, respectively. The first to be eliminated were the *tribuni aerarii*; then Augustus removed the senators after which the equestrian class alone functioned as judges. The number of *decuriae iudicum* increased to five.

Kübler, *RE* 6, 299.

Decuriae senatus. See DECURIA.

Decuriales. Members of *decuriae* in private corporations or of associations of subaltern officers (*decuriae apparitorum*).

De Ruggiero, *DE* 2.

Decurio. The commander of a small cavalry unit, *decuria*.—See TURMA.

Mancini, *DE* 2.

Decurionatus. The office of a *decurio*.—See DECURIONES, ORDO DECURIONUM.

Decuriones. Members of a municipal senate (*ordo decurionum*) elected for life. Vacant posts were filled at five-year intervals. Eligible were former municipal magistrates with a census of at least one hundred thousand sesterces. Persons of particular worth to the *municipium* and its protectors (*patroni municipii*) residing in Rome were honored by membership in the municipal senate. The *decuriones* decided about all matters involving the interests of the community, appointed local magistrates, and functioned as a court of appeal on fines imposed by municipal officers.—D. 50.2; C. 10.32; 33; 35; 12.16.—See ORDO DECURIONUM, DECRETA DECURIONUM, ALBUM CURIAE, DUAE PARTES.

Kübler, *RE* 4; Kornemann, *RE* 16, 621; Humbert, *DS* 2; Mancini, *DE* 2, 1515; Gaudemet, *Iura* 2 (1951) 44.

Decuriones pedanei. Members of the municipal senate who had not been municipal magistrates before. They were appointed by *duoviri* (or *quattuorviri*) *iuri dicundo* to seats which became vacant because of the death of a *decurio* or his removal, as the result of a condemnation in a criminal trial.

Mommsen, *Jur. Schriften*, 3 (1907) 38.

Dedere noxae. See NOXA.

De Visscher, *Noxalité*, 1947, 400 and *passim*.

Dedere se hosti. To surrender to the enemy in the course of a war.—See DEDITIO, DEDITICII.

Dedicatio. A religious ceremony by which an object (a temple or an altar) was consecrated to gods. Solemn words were pronounced on such an occasion by a pontiff and sometimes by a magistrate, in conformity with the statute or decree of the senate by which the *consecratio* was ordained (*lex dedicationis*).—See RES SACRAE, LOCUS SACER, DUOVIRI AEDI DEDICANDAE.

Wissowa, *RE* 4; Pottier, *DS* 2; De Ruggiero, *DE* 1, 144; 2, 1553; S. Brassloff, *Studien zur röm. Rechtsgeschichte*, 1925; Paoli, *RHD* 24–25 (1947) 185.

Dediticii. The citizens of a foreign state or community who, vanquished in a war with Rome, surrendered to the power and protection of Rome (*deditio*). They constituted a specific group of the Roman population; they were free but lacked all public rights and citizenship (*nullius civitatis*). Their legal status as *peregrini dediticii* could be improved by unilateral concessions granted by Rome to individuals or groups. But even the general grant of Roman citizenship to peregrines by the constitution of the emperor Caracalla excluded the *dediticii*. The status of *dediticii*, termed by Justinian *dediticia libertas*, was abolished by him (C. 7.5.1).—See CONSTITUTIO ANTONINIANA (Bibl.), DEDITIO, DEDITICII EX LEGE AELIA SENTIA.

Sherwin-White, *OCD*; Schulten, *RE* 4; Gayet and Humbert, *DS* 2; Moore, *Arch. f. lat. Lexikographie*, 11 (1900) 81; G. Moinier, *Les peregrines déditices*, 1930; G. Bozzoni, *La const. Antoniniana e i d.*, 1933; Stroux, *Philologus* 88 (1933) 287; Momigliano, *Ann. Scuola Norm. Superiore di Pisa* Ser. 2, v. 3 (1934) 361; Luzzatto, *SDHI* 2 (1936) 211; A. d'Ors, *AHDE* 15 (1944) 162; Bell, *JRS* 37 (1947) 17; Tsherikover, *Jour. juristic Papyrology* 4 (1950) 203; Schönbauer, *ibid.* 6 (1952) 17.

Dediticii ex lege Aelia Sentia. Slaves who had been found guilty of a crime, had been put in bonds by their masters by way of punishment, or had been handed over to fight with men or beasts, could become free through manumission, but they obtained freedom of the lowest degree and could never be admitted to Roman citizenship. They were unable to make a will or to inherit under one.

Deditio. The surrender of an enemy community defeated in war with Rome. Its territory was annexed, and its citizens became *peregrini dediticii*.—See DEDITICII.

E. Täubler, *Imperium Romanum*, 1913, 14; Heuss, *Völkerrechtliche Grundlagen der röm. Aussenpolitik*, 1933, 60; Frezza, *SDHI* 4 (1938) 412.; Paradisi, *St Solmi* 1 (1941) 287; A. Magdelain, *Les origines de la sponsio*, 1943, 87; De Visscher, *St Riccobono* 2 (1936); *idem*, *CRAI* 1946, 82; *idem*, *Noxalité*, 1947, 72; Lévy-Bruhl, *Nouvelles études*, 1947, 116; La Rosa, *Iura* 1 (1950) 283; Piganiol, *RIDA* 5 (1950) 339.

Dedoken. The Greek text of Justinian's constitution by which the Digest was promulgated (Dec. 16, 533). It apparently was an earlier draft than the Latin edition, *Tanta*, and is frequently more exact than the latter.—See TANTA, DIGESTA IUSTINIANI.

Ebrard, *ZSS* 40 (1919) 113; Berger, *Byzantion* 17 (1944/5) 14 (= *BIDR* 55–56, *Suppl. Post-Bellum*, 1952, 275)

Deducere in coloniam. To take colonists from Rome or some other place to a colony to be founded.

Deducere in domum. See DEDUCTIO IN DOMUM.

Deducere in iudicium. To bring a suit in court to the joinder of issue (see LITIS CONTESTATIO). Thus the *in iure* stage was finished and the trial could enter the second stage before the judge (*apud iudicem*).—See RES IN IUDICIUM DEDUCTA, EXCEPTIO REI IUDICATAE.

Deductio. (In suits of a *bonorum emptor*.) If the buyer of the property of an insolvent debtor (see BONORUM EMPTOR, BONORUM VENDITIO) sued somebody, he had to do so *cum deductione*, i.e., to deduct from his claim whatever he himself owed to the defendant as the bankrupt's successor. This was a kind of compensation but it went farther than the normal COMPENSATIO since debts of a different nature (e.g., money with debts in kind) might be set off and even debts falling due in the future were taken into account.

Solazzi, *St Fadda* 1 (1906) 347; *idem, Concorso dei creditori* 2 (1938) 146; *idem, Compensazione*[2] (1950) 65.

Deductio in domum mariti. The solemn introduction of the bride into the husband's house, accompanied by religious ceremonies. It was considered the beginning of the marriage.

E. Levy, *Hergang der röm. Ehescheidung*, 1925, 68; M. Rage-Brocard, *Rites de mariage. La d.*, 1934; Orestano, *BIDR* 47 (1940) 306.

Deductio quae moribus fit. See VIS EX CONVENTU.

Deductio servitutis. The constitution of a servitude by the seller of an immovable in favor of either the alienated land or of another plot owned by himself. Thus the seller either conceded the buyer a servitude on his own land or reserved such a right for his property (*deducta servitute*).—See DEDUCTIO USUSFRUCTUS.

S. Solazzi, *Requisiti e modi di costituzione delle servitù prediali*, 1947, 87; 135.

Deductio ususfructus. A mode of constituting a usufruct on behalf of the owner who transfers his property to another (*deducto usufructu*) or of a legatee in a testament. Syn. with *deducere* are *detrahere, excipere.*

> Humbert, *DS* 2; U. v. Lübtow, *Schenkungen der Eltern,* 1949, 24; D'Ors, *Fschr Schulz* 1 (1951) 270; Sanfilippo, *AnCat* 4 (1950) 152.

Defectus conditionis. See CONDITIO DEFICIT.

Defendere. To defend one's own (*defendere propriam causam*) or another's matter (*defendere alienam causam,* for instance of an absent person) in court. *Defendere* another means "to do what the principal would do in the trial and to give appropriate security (*cavere*)" (D. 3.3.35.3). A party to a trial who does not fulfil his procedural duties or is not duly represented, is considered *indefensus* (not defended) and must submit to disagreeable executory measures. *Defendere* may also refer to the defended object or right (*defendere fundum, servitutem, hereditatem, possessionem,* etc.).—See INDEFENSUS.

Defendi potest. Introduces a legal opinion (= "it may be affirmed").

Defensio. The activity of DEFENDERE oneself or another in a civil or a criminal trial. *Defensio* is also the procedural means by which one combats his adversary's claim, an *exceptio,* for instance. "No one of those who deny their debt is prohibited from using another kind of defense" (D. 50.17.43).—*Defensio* is also the payment of another's debt.

> Wlassak, *ZSS* 25 (1904) 124; Frese, *St Bonfante* 4 (1930) 420.

Defensor. A person who defends another's interests in a trial with or without authorization (*defensor absentis*) or on account of his legal relation to the plaintiff or defendant (as his tutor or curator). Public corporate bodies may have a *defensor* too, such as an *actor municipii, syndicus, defensor coloniae, defensor rei publicae.*—D. 3.3.—See DEFENDERE, DEFENSIO.

Defensor civitatis. An official appointed by the emperor (for the first time in A.D. 364) for the defense of the poor classes of the population (hence he is also called *defensor plebis*) against exactions by the great landowners and powerful citizens (*potentiores*). High ex-officials, even senators, were appointed to this office, in later times by the *praefectus praetorio,* or elected by a group of distinguished citizens of the community. The *defensores civitatis* gradually became supervisors of all officials in the provinces and they transmitted to the governor complaints received concerning his subordinates. They also obtained jurisdiction in smaller civil affairs and even developed police functions in certain cases, not to speak of their extensive interference in administrative matters.—C. 1.55.—See ACTOR UNIVERSITATIS.

> Seeck, *RE* 4; Desjardins, *DS* 2; Mancini, *DE* 2; Romano, *NDI* 4; Chenon, *NRHD* 13 (1889) 321, 515; Baale, *D. C.,* Diss. Amsterdam, 1904; Rees, *Jour. juristic papyrology* 6 (1952) 73.

Defensor plebis. See DEFENSOR CIVITATIS.

> Hoepffner, *RHD* 17 (1938) 225.

Defensores senatus. These were introduced about the middle of the fourth century for the defense of the members of the senate in Constantinople against vexations by provincial governors and tax-collectors to which senatorial landowners were exposed in the provinces. The *defensores senatus* (who were elected by the senate) disappeared in the fifth century.

> Seeck, *RE* 4.

Deferre. To denounce a crime committed by another person to the authorities. In the later Empire, slaves who denounced certain crimes (such as counterfeit of money, desertion, abduction of woman) received liberty (*libertate donari*) as a reward' (*praemium*). See DENUNTIARE. *Deferre se* = to denounce oneself in a fiscal matter (e.g., to be unable to take under a will; see CAPAX) which might result in a seizure of property by the fisc.—C. 7.13.—See DELATIO, DELATORES, DEFERRE FISCO.

Deferre fisco. To denounce to the fisc a case in which it would be entitled to seize private property. The imperial legislation sought repeatedly' to curb the abuse of denunciations and inflicted severe penalties not only on false informers. Apparently, denunciations concerning unpaid custom duties were frequent. The jurist Marcian wrote a monograph *De delatoribus* ("On denouncers") in which numerous imperial constitutions dealing with denunciations are listed along with a schedule of articles dutiable on import (D. 39.4.16.7, see PORTORIUM). Smuggling of those goods was severely punished.

> Berger, *RE* 17, 1476; Solazzi, *BIDR* 49–50 (1947) 405.

Deferre hereditatem. An inheritance, both testamentary and intestate was considered *delata* (conferred), "when somebody may obtain it by acceptance" (D. 50.16.151). See ADITIO HEREDITATIS. The heir had only to declare that he accepts it. The term *deferre* is also applied to *bonorum possessiones,* legacies and testamentary substitutions. *Deferre* occurs normally at the time of the death of the person whose succession is inherited. It might occur later, when the heir was instituted under condition or when the heir instituted refused to accept the inheritance. *Deferre* on intestacy took place when there was no valid testament; it could not concur with a testamentary *delatio* because according to an ancient rule, "no one can decease partly *testatus,* partly *intestatus*" (see NEMO PRO PARTE TESTATUS).—See TRANSMITTERE, TRANSMISSIO.

Deferre iusiurandum. See IUSIURANDUM NECESSARIUM.

Deferre tutelam. To designate a guardian by testament (*ex testamento*) or to confer guardianship according to the law. See TUTELA. The term is also applied to curatorship (see CURA).

Deficere. With regard to judicial measures (e.g., *actio deficit*) indicates that in the case in question an action (exception, interdict) had to be denied. In the passive voice, *defici* (e.g., *iure, actione*) refers to a person deficient in a right or action.

Deficere. (Intrans.) See CONDICIO DEFICIT.

Definitio. Appears both in the sense of an explanation of a term and in that of a legal rule. The Roman jurists do not give definitions very often, and those given by them are not always exact or exhaustive. They rather avoided definitions which might have become a hindrance to later adaptations required by the necessities of life. "Every definition in civil law is perilous since there is little that could not be subverted (overthrown)," the jurist Javolenus said (D. 50.17.202). Justinian's compilers did not share this prejudice. In later imperial constitutions *definitio* = a judgment in a trial.

Pringsheim, *Fg Lenel,* 1921, 251; Himmelschein, *Symbolae Friburgenses Lenel,* 1931, 420; Masi, *AG* 121 (1939) 138; M. Villey, *Recherches sur la littérature didactique du dr. rom.,* 1945, 44; Biondi, *Scr Ferrini* (Univ. Pavia, 1946) 240; Schulz, *History of R. legal science,* 1946, 66; 336.

Definitiones. The title of a work of the jurist Papinian. The excerpts from the work preserved in the Digest show that *definitiones* cannot be unrestrictedly identified with *regulae.* A work of the jurist Q. Mucius Scaevola, with the Greek title *Horoi* (= *definitiones*) may have had a similar character.

Definitiva sententia. A postclassical term for the final judgment in a civil trial, to be distinguished from interlocutory, preliminary decisions (*interlocutiones*).—Syn. DEFINITIO.

Biondi, *St Bonfante* 4 (1930) 50.

Defixiones. See EXECRATIONES.

Kuhnert, *RE* 4; Lafaye, *DS* 5, 4; Cesano, *DE* 2.

Defraudator. See FRAUDATOR.

Defunctus. A deceased person. The term is primarily used when questions connected with his inheritance or specific hereditary objects are involved. —See MORS, MORTALITAS, STATUS DEFUNCTI.

S. Solazzi, *Contro la rappresentanza del defunto,* 1916; Jobbé-Duval, *Les morts malfaisants,* 1924; Volterra, *Processi penali contro i defunti, RIDA* 3 (1949) 485.

Deicere. To throw down; see ACTIO DE DEIECTIS ET EFFUSIS.—D. 9.3.

Deicere de possessione. To dispossess a person from an immovable, chiefly when the action is connected with the use of physical force.—See INTERDICTUM DE VI.

Leonhard, *RE* 4; Humbert, *DS* 2; Levy, *Scr Ferrini* 3 (Univ. Sacro Cuore, Milan, 1948) 136.

Deicere e saxo Tarpeio. To throw down from the Tarpeian rock. It was a way of executing the death penalty on slaves who committed a theft and were caught in the very act (*furtum manifestum*), as well as in cases of high treason and false testimony. Introduced by the Twelve Tables, it was abolished in the third century after Christ.—See TESTIMONIUM FALSUM.

Taubenschlag, *RE* 4A, 2330; E. Pais, *Ricerche sulla storia e sul dir. pubbl. di Roma,* 4 (1921) 17.

Deiectio gradus. Degradation from rank as a military punishment.

Deierare (deiurare). Syn. *iurare.* The term belongs to ancient Latin and is used once in the praetorian Edict with reference to an oath imposed on the defendant by the praetor.

Delatio. See DELATORES.

Delatio fisco. See DEFERRE FISCO.

Delatio hereditatis. See DEFERRE HEREDITATEM.

Delatio iurisiurandi. See IUSIURANDUM NECESSARIUM.

Delatio nominis. See ACCUSATIO.

Delatores. Accusers in a criminal trial; see ACCUSATIO. Some individuals professionally assumed the role of accusers for political reasons. Malicious prosecution was punished.—C. 10.11.—See QUADRUPLATORES, NUNTIARE FISCO, DEFERRE FISCO.

Kleinfeller, *RE* 4; Humbert, *DS* 2; De Ruggiero, *DE* 2; Flint, *ClJ* 8 (1912); G. Bossière, *L'accusation publique et les délateurs,* 1911.

Delegare ab argentario. See RELEGARE PECUNIAM.

Delegare iurisdictionem. See IURISDICTIO DELEGATA.

Delegatio. An order given by one person (*is qui delegat*) to another (*is qui delegatur*) to pay a debt to, or to assume an obligation towards, a third person (*is cui delegatur*). The term covers various transactions serving different purposes. The most practical form occurs when a creditor orders his debtor to pay the debt to a third party of whom he himself is a debtor. "He who orders a payment is considered as if he paid himself" (D. 46.3.56). A *delegatio* may serve also novatory purposes (*novatio*) when the creditor orders his debtor to promise (not to pay) a third person something. In this case a new obligation arises towards the third person in the place of that of the *delegans.* Such changes in the person of the debtor or creditor may occur only with the consent of the persons involved. A *delegatio* may also serve for the performance of a donation (when the donor orders his debtor to pay his debt to another) or for the constitution of a dowry (when the father of the bride orders his debtor to pay the debt to his son-in-law).—D. 46.2; C. 8.41.—See EXPROMITTERE.

Leonhard, *RE* 4; F. Kempner, *Untersuchung über die Kausalbeziehung der Delegation,* Greifswald, 1919; P. Rutsaert, *Étude sur la délégation,* Gand, 1929; G. Hubrecht, *Observations sur la nature de la délégation,* Bordeaux, 1931; Andreoli, *RISG* 7 (1932) 385; Aru, *BIDR* 44 (1937) 332; S. Cugia, *Indagine sulla delegazione,* 1947.

Delegatio. (In taxation matters.) An imperial order by which the annual amount to be levied in taxes, both in money and in kind, was established. The *praefectus praetorio* assessed the amount for the provinces and notified the governors who were responsible for the collection in their provinces.

Seeck, *RE* 4, 2431.

Delere. To cancel a written document (a testament, for instance) totally or partially. The pertinent dispositions became void.—D. 28.4.

Deliberare (deliberatio) de adeunda hereditate. An heir who was not obliged to accept an inheritance (*heres voluntarius*) was granted a certain time in which to decide whether to accept it or not.—See TEMPUS AD DELIBERANDUM, ADITIO HEREDITATIS.— D. 28.8; C. 6.30.

S. Solazzi, *Spatium deliberandi,* 1912; *idem, SDHI* 3 (1937) 450, 6 (1940) 337.

Delicta concurrentia. Several crimes committed by the same person either in different acts or in one. "Never do several concurrent crimes cause impunity to be granted for any of them" (D. 47.1.2 pr.). This rule concerned private crimes, as when, for instance, one kidnapped another's slave and killed him. The culprit could be sued for private penalty by *actio furti* and by *actio legis Aquiliae* for damages. As to crimes prosecuted by the state (*crimina publica*) imperial legislation provided that they be tried before the same court.

Humbert, *DS* 1 (*concursus delictorum*).

Delicta militum. Military crimes or offences are either purely military or common to civilians as well. A special military crime (*delictum militare*) is one "which somebody commits as a soldier" (D. 49.16.2 pr.). Minor military penalties included: pecuniary fines, castigation, additional service, transfer to another branch of service; more severe penalties were degradation and dishonorable discharge. Several military crimes were punished by death, particularly in wartime. A soldier could neither be condemned to compulsory labor in the mines nor tortured. Specific offences against military discipline included insubordination, disobedience (*contumacia*), idleness (*segnitia*), negligence (*desidia*). Milder treatment, and sometimes full forgiveness, were granted to recruits (*tirones*) unfamiliar with military discipline. A rule which defined generally the behavior of a soldier was: "A soldier who is a disturber of the peace (*turbator pacis*) shall be punished by death" (D. 49.16.16.1). —D. 49.16.—See DISCIPLINA.

Taubenschlag, *RE* 15 (*s.v. Militärstrafrecht*); Cagnat, *DS* 3 (*s.v. militum poenae*); J. Bouquié, *Les juges militaires* (Bruxelles, 1884) 142; J. Bray, *Essai sur le droit pénal militaire des Rom.,* 1894; A. Müller, *Die Strafjustiz im röm. Heere, Neue Jahrbücher für das klass. Altertum* 9 (1906); C. Andrieux, *La repression des fautes militaires,* Lyon, 1927.

Delicta privata—publica. See DELICTUM.

Delictum. A wrongdoing prosecuted through a private action of the injured individual and punished by a pecuniary penalty paid to the plaintiff. For the distinction, *crimen—delictum,* see CRIMEN. The actions by which the injured person sued for a penalty were ACTIONES POENALES, and the procedure was that of a civil action. The typical private offenses are *furtum* (theft), *rapina* (robbery), *iniuria* (personal offence), and *damnum iniuria datum* (damage done to property). *Delictum* is the source of one group of obligations (*obligationes ex delicto*) which

in the fundamental division of obligations is opposed to the contractual ones (*obligationes ex contractu*). The group of private wrongdoings was enlarged by the praetorian law through the creation of *obligationes,* called *quasi ex delicto,* arising from some minor offences. "No one should improve his condition by a *delictum*" (D. 50.17.134.1). The distinction *delicta privata—publica* which corresponds to the classical distinction of *delicta* and *crimina,* is of postclassical origin.—D. 47.1.—See CRIMEN, CRIMINA PUBLICA.

Hitzig, *RE* 4; Baudry, *DS* 2; Brasiello, *NDI* 4; 8, 1206; Lauria, *SDHI* 4 (1938) 182; Roberti, *St Calisse* 1 (1940) 161.

Delictum militare. See DELICTA MILITUM.

Delinquere. To commit a wrongdoing, an unlawful act, a crime (*crimen*), or a private offence (*delictum*).

Demens (noun dementia). Insane, lunatic. Legally he is treated as a *furiosus* and subject to a curatorship.—See CURATOR FURIOSI (called also *curator dementis*), FURIOSUS.

Audibert, *Études I. La folie et la prodigalité,* 1892, 11; Solazzi, *Dementia, Mouseion* 2 (1924); *idem, AG* 143 (1952) 16; Lenel, *ZSS* 45 (1925) 514.

Deminutio (deminuere). Refers to all acts of transferring or alienating property. Some persons, such as those who are under curatorship, are forbidden to make transactions by which their property is lessened.

Deminutio capitis. See CAPITIS DEMINUTIO.

Demolire (demolitio). To destroy. The owner of a building could destroy it when he pleased provided that such action did not violate the rights of, or cause damages to, his neighbor. Where it might, the demolition was regarded as a new structure (*opus novum*) and was liable to an objection by the neighbor, see OPERIS NOVI NUNTIATIO. Also in the case of a party wall (see PARIES COMMUNIS) the demolition by one of the owners could give rise to a controversy. Syn. *destruere.*

Berger, *RE* 18, 561; Daube, *Class. Quarterly* 44 (1950) 119.

Demonstrare (demonstratio). To denote, explain, describe, define (a thing, a term, a plot of land, etc.). It refers primarily to testamentary clauses by which the testator defined the persons or things mentioned in his testament.—See DEMONSTRATIO FALSA.

Demonstratio. As a part of the written formula in the formulary procedure this defined the subject matter of the claim with a phrase initiated with *quod* (= whereas, inasmuch as, e.g., the plaintiff sold a slave to the defendant). A *demonstratio* was required where the claim (*intentio*) was uncertain (*incerta*), since it defined more precisely the object of the controversy (*res de qua agitur*), which was of importance for a future trial on the same subject and for an eventual objection that the matter had already been dealt with in court (*exceptio rei iudicatae*).

Arangio-Ruiz, *St Cagliari* 4 (1912).

Demonstratio falsa. The use of inappropriate words in the description of a person or a thing in a last will, or of words which in common speech mean something other than what the testator intended to express. *"Falsa demonstratio non nocet"* (= "the erroneous denotation is not prejudicial," D. 35.1.33 pr.). In numerous cases the jurists interpret a *falsa demonstratio* in favor of the validity of the testamentary disposition.—With regard to the *demonstratio* in the formula (see the foregoing item) the plaintiff's claim is not impaired if the object of the trial is not correctly described in the formula; an overstatement or an understatement (*plus aut minus positum*) is without any effect on the plaintiff's claim.—D. 35.1.

> Eisele, *JhJb* 65 (1915) 18; Bang, *JhJb* 66 (1916) 336; Donatuti, *St Perozzi*, 1925, 311; Grosso, *St Bonfante 2* (1930) 187; B. Biondi, *Successione testamentaria*, 1943, 521; Flume, *Fschr Schulz* 1 (1951) 224.

Demosthenes. A Byzantine jurist of the fifth century, probably a professor in the law school of Beirut.

> Kübler, *RE* 5, 190.

Denarius. A Roman silver coin (after 269 B.C.), originally equal to ten copper asses and four *sestertii nummi.*—See EDICTUM DIOCLETIANI DE PRETIIS.

> Lenormant, *DS* 2; Cesano, *DE* 2; De Ruggiero, *RendLinc* 17 (1908) 250; Mattingly and Robinson, *Numismatic Chronicle* 1938, 1; Mattingly, *OCD* 210 (*s.v. coinage*).

Denegare actionem (denegatio actionis). The refusal by the praetor to grant the plaintiff the action (*legis actio, formula*) he requested. "He who has the power to give an action may refuse it" (D. 50.17.102.1). The competent magistrate (the praetor primarily) did so at his own discretion, but the plaintiff could repeatedly sue the defendant before another praetor. *Denegare actionem* was decreed by the magistrate in various instances when already *in iure* it appeared beyond a doubt that the plaintiff had no cause of action, that he had no capacity to act personally in court, or when his claim was immoral or not suable under either *ius civile* or praetorian law and the praetor was not willing to grant a new action. Syn. *non dare actionem.*—D. 44.5.—See DARE ACTIONEM.

> Leist, *RE* 5; Lenel, *ZSS* 30 (1909) 333; R. Düll, *Denegationsrecht und praetorische Jurisdiction*, 1915; R. Mewaldt, *Denegare actionem*, 1912; H. Lévy-Bruhl, *La d. a. dans la procédure formulaire*, 1924; Wenger, *Practor und Formel, SberMünch* 1926, 33; De Martino, *Giurisdizione*, 1937, 70; Polacek, *ZSS* 63 (1943) 406; Lauria, *Scr Ferrini* (Univ. Pavia, 1946) 644.

Denegare bonorum possessionem. To reject a request for BONORUM POSSESSIO.—See AGNITIO BONORUM POSSESSIONIS.

Denegare cautionem. See CAUTUM IUBERE.

Denegare exceptionem. A counterpart to *denegare actionem:* when the praetor rejected the demand of the defendant for the insertion of an *exceptio* into the formula.

Denegare interdictum. The refusal of an interdict by the praetor.—See INTERDICTUM.

Denegare iurisdictionem. To exclude a person from judicial protection in court (before the magistrate)

and from assuming the role of a petitioner. It differs from *denegare actionem* where the magistrate in his capacity as a jurisdictional organ issued a decree of *denegatio* after the party had appeared before him and presented his case.

> R. Düll, *Denegationsrecht*, 1915, 59; idem, *ZSS* 57 (1937) 77.

Denuntiare. (Syn. *nuntiare.*) To give notice, to intimate, to announce. The term applies both to official declarations addressed to private individuals and to announcements made by the latter to the competent authorities. Similarly, there was a *denuntiare* when a private person gave notice to another of a legally important fact or of his intention where such an act was necessary for proceeding with a legal remedy. *Denuntiare* was prescribed, for instance, in the case of *evictio:* when sued by a third person for recovery of the thing bought the buyer had to notify the seller thereof. A creditor who was going to sell the pledge had to give the debtor notice. Similarly a creditor who ceded his rights against the debtor to another (see CESSIO) had to act in order to compel the debtor to pay the new creditor. An heir who had a right on intestacy, when disinherited by the testator, had to *denuntiare* his intention to sue for the nullification of the testament.—See CONDICERE, SENATUSCONSULTUM PLANCIANUM, COMMISSORIA LEX.

> Kipp, *RE* 5; Humbert, *DS* 2; A. Burdese, *Lex commissoria*, 1949, 15.

Denuntiare bellum (denuntiatio belli). A declaration of war by which a state of war between two countries was initiated. *Indicere bellum* has similar significance. The two verbs sometimes appear side by side.—See BELLUM.

> Walbank, *ClPhil* 1949, 15.

Denuntiare testibus testimonium. To summon a witness in a criminal trial. It could be done either by a magistrate or by the accuser.

> Kaser, *RE* 5A, 1049.

Denuntiatio domum. A specific form of *denuntiatio* in the case of DAMNUM INFECTUM, which must precede the proceedings connected with *cautio damni infecti* or *missio in possessionem.* By this private act, the plaintiff informs the adversary of his intention to proceed against him for *damnum infectum.* If the adversary is absent, the *denuntiatio* is made to his representative or to a tenant in the house.

Denuntiatio ex auctoritate. Summons of the adversary (in the late Empire) authorized by a public official.—See DENUNTIATIO LITIS.

> A. J. Boyé, *La denuntiatio*, 1922, 206.

Denuntiatio litis. A summons of the defendant by the magistrate in the procedure *cognitio extra ordinem* of the classical period. In the later Empire the summons was a private act with the assistance of an official person and under official authorization (*denuntiatio ex auctoritate*).—See REPARATIO TEMPORUM.

Kipp, *RE* 5; Leonhard, *RE* 13 (*s.v. litis den.*); Steinwenter, *Studien zum röm. Versäumnisverfahren*, 1914; A. J. Boyé, *La d. introductive d'instance sous le Principat*, 1922.

Denuntiator. The prosecutor in a criminal trial; police officers in the late Empire who had to denounce criminal offences to be prosecuted by the State. Syn. *nuntiator.*

Kübler, *RE* 5; Humbert, *DS* 2; De Ruggiero, *DE* 2.

Denuntiatores (lictores denuntiatores). Assistants of the *curatores urbis Romae*. *Denuntiatores* were also subordinate officials who announced the public games (*ludi*).

Kübler, *RE* 5; *idem, RE* 13, 515.

Deo auctore. The initial words of Justinian's constitution of December 15, 530, addressed to Tribonianus, his principal collaborator in the composition of the Digest (DIGESTA), by which the emperor's plan concerning this part of his codification was announced. The enactment reveals the emperor's ideas about the whole work and contains instructions to be followed in its compilation.

Depellere manum. To remove, throw off the claimant's hand who had touched the shoulder of the defendant in exercising the so-called MANUS INIECTIO. —See VINDEX.

M. Kaser, *Das altröm. Ius,* 1949, 195.

Depensum. (From *dependere.*) What the surety paid to the creditor on behalf of the principal debtor.— See ACTIO DEPENSI.

Deponere (depositio). To resign one's office (*officium*) or guardianship (*tutelam*).—For *deponere* = to deposit, see DEPOSITIO, DEPOSITUM.

Deportatio. Perpetual banishment of a person condemned for a crime. It was the severest form of banishment since it included additional penalties, such as seizure of the whole property, loss of Roman citizenship, confinement to a definite place. Under the Principate it replaced the former *interdictio aqua et igni*. The emperor could grant the deportee full amnesty, which restored him to his former rights (*postliminium*). Places of *deportatio* were islands (*in insulam*) near the Italian shore or an oasis in the Libyan desert.—D. 48.22.—See RELEGATIO, EXILIUM.

Kleinfeller, *RE* 4; Berger, *OCD* (*s.v. relegatio*); J. Strachan-Davidson, *Problems of Roman criminal law,* 2 (1912) 57; Brasiello, *La repressione penale,* 1937, 294 and *passim*; Devilla, *StSas* 23 (1950) 1.

Depositio in aede. A debtor who wants to pay his debt and was unable to do so because the creditor refused to accept the payment, was absent or unable to accept it, or was uncertain (as, for instance, when the heirs of the original creditor were yet unknown), might deposit the sum due in a temple (*in aede sacra*) or in a public office (*in loco publico*) designated by an official. In a similar situation was a slave, manumitted in a testament under the condition that he render accounts and pay the balance, when the heir was absent or unknown. It is controversial whether such a *depositio* effectuated an immediate liberation of the debtor. It seems that the various cases were treated differently in this regard.

R. De Ruggiero, *StCagl* 1 (1909) 121; G. Solazzi, *Estinzione dell'obbligazione* 1² (1935) 140, 160; Catalano, *AnCat* 3 (1949).

Depositum. A deposit. *Depositum* is both the object given a person for custody, and the contract itself by which somebody assumed the duty to watch over the depositor's thing without any remuneration. The contract, which was exclusively in the interest of the depositor, was concluded by handing over the deposit to the depositary (*obligatio re contracta*). The latter was not allowed to use the thing and had to return it to the owner at his demand, with all proceeds and accessories. He was liable for *dolus*, but not for negligence (*culpa*). An *actio depositi* lay against him when he refused to return the deposit or otherwise violated his duties. The condemnation in *actio depositi* rendered the depositary infamous (see INFAMIA). On the other hand, he had an *actio depositi contraria* against the depositor for the recovery of expenses and losses incurred in connection with the deposit.—D. 16.3; C. 4.34.—See FIDUCIA CUM AMICO, PACTUM NE DOLUS PRAESTETUR, and the following items.

Leonhard, *RE* 5; Humbert, *DS* 2; Anon., *NDI* 4; Taubenschlag, *GrZ* 34 (1907); Schulz, *Ztschr. für vergl. Rechtswiss.* 25 (1911) 464, 27 (1912) 144; R. De Ruggiero, *BIDR* 19 (1907) 5; G. Rotondi, *Scritti* 2 (1922) 1; J. Paoli, *Lis infitiando crescit in duplum,* 1933, 170; C. Longo, *Corso di dir. rom. Il deposito,* 1933; Albertario, *Studi* 4 (1936) 247; Sachers, *Fschr Koschaker* 2 (1939) 80.

Depositum irregolare. A deposit of money or other fungibles wherein the depositary had to return not the same things, but the same quantity (*tantundem*) of money or things. The transaction, called in literature *depositum irregolare,* became a loan (*mutuum*) when the depositary had the right to use the things. A deposit of an amount of money (coins) in a sealed bag was a normal *depositum*. Such deposits were made with bankers who assumed the custody of the money.

G. Segrè, *BIDR* 18 (1906) 132; C. Longo, *BIDR* 19 (1907) 187; Bonifacio, *BIDR* 49–50 (1948) 80; Schulz, *Ferrini* 4 (Univ. Sacro Cuore, Milan, 1949) 254; Seidl, *Fschr Schulz* 1 (1951) 373.

Depositum miserabile. A deposit made in a time of emergency (a shipwreck, fire, riot; see TUMULTUS). The depositary's liability was greater than in an ordinary deposit. He had to pay double damages in the case of fraud or denial. The term is not of Roman juristic language.

Deprehendere (deprehensio). To catch a criminal in the very act. A thief surprised when committing the theft = *fur manifestus*.—See ADMISSUM, FURTUM MANIFESTUM.

Derectarius (directarius). A burglar who sneaks into a dwelling furtively. He was punished more severely than an ordinary thief.

> Hitzig, *RE* 5, 1166.

Derelictio. (From *derelinquere.*) The abandonment of a thing by its owner with the intention of getting rid thereof. A *res derelicta* is subject to *occupatio,* by which the occupant immediately acquires property. *Derelinquere* is also coupled with certain procedural terms (*accusationem, litem*) when a person withdraws an accusation or an action.

> Berger, *BIDR* 32 (1922, reprints published 1915); J. J. Meyer-Collins, *D.* (Diss. Erlangen, 1932); H. Krüger, *Mnemosyna Pappulia,* 1934; Arnò, *ATor* 76/II (1941) 261; A. Cuenod, *Usucapio pro derelicto,* 1943 (Thèse, Lausanne).

Derelictus. See ALVEUS DERELICTUS, PRO DERELICTO HABERE.

Derelinquere. See DERELICTIO. Syn. *pro derelicto habere;* see USUCAPIO.

Derivatio. See FLUMINA PUBLICA.

Derogare legi. Refers primarily to a partial annulment of a statute; see ABROGARE. *Derogatorius* = a derogating enactment.

Descendentes. Relatives in a descending line (children, grandchildren, great-grandchildren) through males (*ex virili sexu, per mares, ex masculis,* etc.) or females (*ex femino sexu*).—See VENIRE EX ALIQUO.

Descendere ex. (E.g., *lege duodecim tabularum.*) Indicates the origin of a legal norm or institution.

Describere. To make a copy of a document, a private one (a testament) or one which was deposited in a public archive.—See LIBER LIBELLORUM.

Descriptio (describere). (In the tax administration of the later Empire.) The assessment of taxes.—C. 10.22; 36.—See RES LUCRATIVAE.

Deserere. To renounce a right (a servitude, an usufruct); to withdraw an accusation (*accusationem*) or to discontinue a suit after the *litis contestatio* (*litem*). Syn. *desistere actione, destituere.*—See EREMODICIUM, TESTAMENTUM DESERTUM, VADIMONIUM DESERTUM, TERGIVERSATIO.

Deserere (desertio, desertor). To abandon the military service without leave. More severe cases of desertion were punished with death, as, for instance, leaving the field of combat before the enemy.—C. 12.45.—See EMANSOR, TRANSFUGA, PERFUGA, FUSTUARIUM SUPPLICIUM.

> Fiebiger, *RE* 5; Jullian, *DS* 2; R. Latrille, *La repression de la désertion,* Toulouse, 1919; V. Arangio-Ruiz, *Sul reato di diserzione,* in *Rariora,* 1946, 271.

Desiderare. To apply to a judicial magistrate for granting an action, an *interdictum,* or a *restitutio in integrum.*

Desiderium. A written or oral request addressed to a judicial magistrate.—See PRECES.

Designatio. The emperor's proposal concerning candidates for a magistracy to be elected by the senate.—See COMMENDATIO, CANDIDATUS PRINCIPIS, DESTINATIO.

Designatus. A magistrate (consul, praetor, etc.) elected for the following year.—See RENUNTIATIO.

> De Ruggiero, *DE* 2.

Desinere possidere. See DOLO DESINERE POSSIDERE.

Desistere. To withdraw an accusation in a criminal trial; to drop a civil suit. Syn. *cedere actione, deserere, destituere.*—See TERGIVERSATIO.

Despondere. To betroth.—See SPONSALIA.

Destinare. To assign, appoint a person for certain functions or tasks; to designate a thing for a specific use.

Destinatio (of magistrates). The official nomination of candidates for consulship and praetorship to be elected by the popular assemblies (*designatio*) in the early Principate. The assemblies had to confirm the candidacies proposed by a gathering composed of senators and *equites* (not by senators alone, as has been assumed hitherto). The procedure in voting and selecting the candidates is now known from a statute preserved on a bronze tablet (*tabula Hebana*) and recently discovered in the R. colony of Heba (Etruria).

> Coli, *BIDR* 53–54 (1948) 369; De Visscher, *Bull. Acad. de Belgique, Cl. Lettres,* 5 sér., 35 (1949) 191; *idem, RHD* 29 (1951) 1; Nesselhauf, *Historia* 1 (1950) 110; Schönbauer, *RIDA* 6 (1951) 201; Levi, *Parola del passato* 14 (1950) 158; De Visscher, *ibid.* 118.

Destituere. See DESERERE.

Destruere. See DEMOLIRE.

Desuetudo. A long continued non-application of a legal norm. Although *desuetudo* does not formally abrogate a law, the latter easily falls into oblivion and loses its force in practice. "Laws are repealed not only by the will of the legislator but also by disuse through the tacit consent of all men" (D. 1.3.32.1). In connection with the compilation of the Digest Justinian ordered that laws which had vanished by *desuetudo* should not be taken into consideration.—*In desuetudinem abire* = to pass out of use.—See ABROGARE LEGEM.

> Steinwenter, *RE* 16, 295; Solazzi, *AG* 102 (1929) 3.

Detentio. (From *detinere.*) A simple holding of a thing without having possession (in legal sense) or ownership thereof. *Detentio* is not a technical term and is used in a rather looser sense. He who has *detentio* (*detentor*) cannot use possessory remedies. He holds another's thing on the ground of an agreement with him (lease, deposit, *commodatum*), who remains legal possessor; the *detentor* "renders service to another's possession." The Roman term for *detentio* is *possessio naturalis.* Syn. *tenere, detentare.* In Justinian's language the use of the respective words is confusing.—See CONSTITUTUM POSSESSORIUM, POSSESSIO.

> J. Duquesne, *Distinction de la possession et de la détention,* 1898; S. Brassloff, *Possessio,* 1928; Radin, *St Bonfante* 3 (1930) 151; Albertario, *Studi* 2 (1941) 161; Kaser, *Deutsche Landesreferate zum III Intern. Kongress für Rechtsvergleichung in London,* 1950.

Detentor (detentator). See DETENTIO. The term occurs only in later imperial constitutions.

Determinare. To set limits, to settle (terms for a judicial action), to define the extent of a servitude.

Detestari (detestatio). To give notice to another (*denuntiatio*) in the presence of witnesses (*testes*).

Detestatio sacrorum. A solemn declaration made by a person in *comitia* to the effect that he is leaving his *gens* or family in order to pass into another. He renounced the participation in the sacred rites of his former social group. The interpretation of the term is controversial.

Kübler, *RE* 3, 1331; 1A, 1682; Anon., *NDI* 11, 964.

Detestatus. A culprit convicted of a crime through the testimony of witnesses.

Detinere. See DETENTIO, CONSTITUTUM POSSESSORIUM.

Detrahere usumfructum. See DEDUCTIO USUSFRUCTUS.

Detrimentum. A loss, damage. Syn. *damnum*.

Devocare. (In imperial constitutions.) To summon a person to render public services or assume a public charge.

Deus. Frequently interpolated in classical texts for the plural *dii* (= gods).—See DII.

R. De Ruggiero, *StCagl* 1 (1909) 140.

Devolutus. (From *devolvere*.) Used with regard to a succession, guardianship or ownership conferred on a person.

Devotio. An honorific title used in the later Empire in writings addressed to high officials (*"devotio tua"*). In another sense, the term is connected with the tax administration in the later Empire.

Devotio. A malediction addressed through a magic formula to the infernal gods requesting them to destroy a certain person.—See EXSECRATIO.

Wissowa, *RE* 5; Bouché-Leclercq, *DS* 2; Cesano, *DE* 2.

Devotissimus vir. The title of a subaltern official. It appears first in the second half of the fourth century after Christ. It alludes to the loyalty towards the emperor.

O. Hirschfeld, *Kleine Schriften*, 1913, 678.

Diarium. Daily records, an official diary, in particular in a fiscal office (*statio*).

Dicere. Appears frequently in such interpolated phrases as *dicere ut, dici potest* (= it may be said), *dicet aliquis, dicendum est* (= it is to say), and the like. Such phrases do not, however, indicate that what follows is not of classical origin.

Guarneri-Citati, *Indice*² (1927) 29; idem, *Fschr Koschaker*, 1 (1939) 131.

Dicere. Denotes the assertions of the parties and their advocates in a trial.—See IUS DICERE, DICERE SENTENTIAM, CAUSAS DICERE.

Dicere causas. See CAUSAS DICERE.

Dicere diem. (In a criminal trial.) To summon the accused to appear before the magistrate on a fixed day.

Dicere dotem. See DICTIO DOTIS.

Dicere ius. See IUS DICERE, IURISDICTIO.

Dicere legem. To insert a specific clause in a testament or contract.—See DICTUM, LEGES CONTRACTUS.

Dicere multam. See MULTA.

Dicere sententiam. (When referring to a judge.) To pronounce a judgment.

Dicere sententiam in senatu. To give a vote in the senate.

Dicio Romana (or Romani nominis). The supreme political power, sovereignty of the Roman state.

Dicis causa (gratia). For the sake of form, *pro forma*. The phrase refers to transactions made in a certain form in order to conceal the true purposes of the parties and to obtain legal results other than those which normally are connected with that form of transaction.—See IMAGINARIUS, SIMULATIO, NUMMUS UNUS.

Rabel, *ZSS* 27 (1906) 307; Betti, *BIDR* 42 (1934) 306.

Dicta. An informal statement made by the seller concerning the existence of specific distinctive traits or the absence of certain defects in the object sold (particularly in a slave). The seller is liable if his assertion proves to be untrue. Similar significance is attached to *promissa*, when the assertion is more formal and made as an explicit promise of the qualities specified. The two terms appear together as *dicta et promissa*.—See EMPTIO.

R. Monier, *La garantie contre les vices cachés*, 1930, 50; Haymann, *ZSS* 51 (1931) 476; Krückmann, *ZSS* 59 (1939) 1.

Dictare (dictatio). To dictate the contents of a written document; it primarily refers to testaments. For *dictare* with reference to the formula in the formulary procedure, see EDITIO ACTIONIS.

Dictator. An extraordinary magistrate under the Republic, appointed in times of internal troubles (sedition) or external difficulties of particular gravity. The appointment was made by one of the consuls for a maximal period of six months. If the danger passed earlier, the *dictator* was obliged to resign. A *dictator* had unlimited legislative, administrative, and judicial power, and was not hampered by the intercession of the tribunes. The dictatorship of Sulla (82 B.C.) and Caesar (49 B.C.), established by special statutes, were of a different character. The last constitutional dictatorship was at the end of the third century B.C.—See MAGISTER EQUITUM, MAGISTER POPULI, PROVOCATIO.

Liebenam, *RE* 5; Humbert, *DS* 2; De Robertis, *NDI* 4; Bruno, *DE* 2; Sherwin-White, *OCD*; F. Bandel, *Die röm. Diktaturen*, 1910; Soltau, *Hermes* 49 (1914) 352; Kornemann, *Kl* 14 (1914) 190; Birt, *Rheinisches Museum* 76 (1927) 198; Momigliano, *Bull. Comm. Arch. Communale di Roma*, 58 (1930); Wilcken, *APrAW* 1940, no. 1; Gintowt, *Mél De Visscher* 1 (*RIDA* 2, 1949) 25; A. Dell'Oro, *La formazione dello stato patrizio-plebeo* 1950, 49.

Dictator comitiorum habendorum causa. An extraordinary magistrate appointed for the special purpose of convoking a popular assembly for elections when the higher magistrates were absent from Rome (e.g., commanding the army).

Liebenam, *RE* 5, 383.

Dictator municipii. The head of the administration in the earliest *municipia,* assisted by one or two *aediles,* and later also by two quaestors.—See MUNICIPIUM, MAGISTRATUS MUNICIPALES.

Kornemann, *RE* 14, 615; Liebenam, *RE* 5, 389; H. Rudolph, *Stadt und Staat im röm. Italien,* 1935, 14; E. Manni, *Per la storia dei municipii,* 1947, 93.

Dictio dotis. A form of constituting a dowry through a unilateral promise expressed in prescribed words (*certa et sollemnia verba*) ". . . *doti tibi erit*" by the woman, her paternal ancestor or her debtor. The *dictio dotio* was abolished by an imperial constitution of Theodosius II (428 A.D., C. 5.11.6) which introduced formless promises of a dowry.—See POLLICITATIO DOTIS.

Leonhard, *RE* 5; Lauria, *ANap* 58 (1937) 221; Daube, *JurR* 51 (1939) 11; Solazzi, *SDHI* (1940); Hägerström, *Der. röm. Obligationsbegriff* 2 (1941) 182; Berger, *Bull. Acad. Sciences Cracovie,* 1909, 75; *idem, Jour. of Juristic Papyrology* 1 (1945) 13 (= *BIDR* 55–56, Suppl. Post-Bellum 1951, 99); Riccobono, *BIDR* 49–50 (1948) 39; F. Bonifacio, *Novazione,* 1950, 58; Kaser, *SDHI* 17 (1951) 169.

Dictum. See DICTA.

Diei dictio, diem dicere. See DICERE DIEM.

Dies. A day, a date specified in a clause of a transaction or testamentary disposition and connecting the beginning (*ex die*) or the end (*in diem, ad diem*) of the validity thereof with a fixed date. The so-called ACTUS LEGITIMI could not be limited by *dies.*—See CEDERE, SINE DIE, and the following items.

Humbert, *DS* 2; De Ruggiero, *DE* 2; Pagge, *NDI* 12 (*s.v. termine*); R. De Ruggiero, *BIDR* 15 (1903) 5; Vassalli, *BIDR* 27 (1915); *idem, St giuridici* 1 (1939) 245; Solazzi, *Iura* 1 (1950) 34.

Dies cedens (legati). The day on which the legatee becomes entitled to the legacy. If he dies after that day, his heir acquires his right. The *dies cedens* generally is the day of the testator's death; if the legacy depends upon a condition, *dies cedens* is the day on which the condition is fulfilled. A counterpart to the *dies cedens* is the *dies veniens (legati)* = the day on which the legatee or his heir may claim payment of the legacy. It is normally the day on which the heir accepts the inheritance. Under certain circumstances both days fall together as, for instance, when the condition attached to the legacy is fulfilled after the acceptance of the inheritance by the heir.—D. 36.2; C. 6.53.—See CEDERE.

Sommer, *ZSS* 34 (1913) 394.

Dies certus. A day of which one is certain that it will come (*certus an*) and when it will come (*certus quando*). Such days are calendar-days. Ant. *dies incertus,* an uncertain day, either uncertain as to when it will come (*incertus quando,* as, e.g., the day of a person's death) or whether it will come at all (*in-*

certus an, as, e.g., the day of a person's marriage). A *dies incertus 'an* and *incertus quando* is equal to a condition (*condicio*).

C. Appleton, *Revue générale de droit* 50 (1926) 154.

Dies coeptus pro impleto habetur. A day begun is held to be completed. The rule is applied to USUCAPIO (D. 44.3.15 pr.).

Dies comitiales. Days on which the popular assemblies (*comitia*) could be convoked.—See LEX PUPIA.

Bouché-Leclercq, *DS* 2, 992.

Dies comperendinus. See COMPEREDINUS DIES.

Dies diffisus. See DIFFINDERE.

Dies et consul. Official dating was by indication of the calendar-day and the consuls of the year (*cum die et consule, die et consule adiecto*). It was used for statutes, senatusconsults, imperial enactments, and private documents. Ant. *sine die et consule.*—See CONSUL.

Dies fasti. Days on which court sessions could be held and magistrates and jurors could exercise their judicial activity. Ant. *dies nefasti.* See DO DICO ADDICO. The origin of this distinction goes back to the earliest times of Roman history. First the pontiffs established the official calendar in which the single days were indicated as *fasti* or *nefasti* by the abbreviations *F* and *N.* Afterwards the *aediles* took care of the calendar. The annual schedule of *dies fasti* and *nefasti* was termed *fasti.*—See DIES NEFASTI.

Schön, *RE* 6 (*s.v. fasti*); Bouché-Leclercq, *DS* 2 (*s.v. fasti*); De Ruggiero, *DE* 2, 1780; Stella-Maranca, *NDI* 5 (*s.v. fasti dies*); Paoli, *RHD* 30 (1952) 293.

Dies fatalis. The last day of a term within which a certain performance had to be done in order to prevent the loss of a right or some other detrimental consequence.

Dies festi. See FERIAE.

Dies incertus. See DIES CERTUS.

Brunetti, *D. i.,* 1893; Segrè, *RISG* 18 (1895).

Dies iuridici. A later term for court-days.

Dies iusti. A thirty-day period granted by the Twelve Tables to debtors who had acknowledged their debt in court (*aes confessum*) or were condemned by judgment, to gather the sum to be paid. If the thirty days elapsed and the debt was not paid, the debtor was brought to the praetor who adjudged him to the creditor. The latter was allowed to fetter the debtor and keep him in prison for 60 days.—See ADDICTUS, TEMPUS IUDICATI.

Dies mortis. The day of death. In classical law, stipulations to pay a sum after the debtor's or creditor's death (*post mortem*) were void because an obligation could not arise for the heir, neither as creditor nor as debtor. Similar treatment was extended to promises connected with the day preceding the death of the creditor or debtor (*pridie quam moriar,* or *pridie quam morieris* in the stipulatory question). Justinian declared such stipulations valid.

—See MANDATUM POST MORTEM, OBLIGATIO POST MORTEM, STIPULATIO POST MORTEM.

F. Vassalli, *Di clausole relative al dies mortis nel legato e nella stipulatio*, 1910; Solazzi, *Iura* 1 (1950) 49.

Dies nefasti. Days on which the praetor was not allowed to pronounce one of the three solemn words *do, dico, addico*. Ant. DIES FASTI. Therefore, *legis actiones* and jurisdiction were forbidden on those days. Likewise, popular assemblies did not meet on those holidays which were devoted to religious ceremonies and public festivals.—See DIES FASTI (Bibl.), DO DICO ADDICO.

Wissowa, *RE* 6, 2015.

Dies legitimus. See LEGITIMUS.

Dies praesens. See PRAESENTI DIE.

Dies utiles. Days on which certain acts could be performed in court (before the magistrates). When a certain number of days was fixed for declarations or requests to be made before a magistrate, as, for instance, one hundred days for the demand of *bonorum possessio,* only *dies utiles* were reckoned.—See ANNUS UTILIS.

Dies veniens (legati). See DIES CEDENS.

Diffarreatio. The formal dissolution of a marriage concluded by CONFARREATIO to free the woman from the *manus* tie.—See DIVORTIUM.

De Ruggiero, *DE* 2, 397; Leonhard, *RE* 5.

Differentiae. Distinctions. The title of a work by the jurist Modestinus. Some of the texts preserved reveal a tendency to stress the differences existing among similar legal institutions or terms.

Diffindere. To defer a trial to another day because of the sickness of the judge or of one of the parties (*dies diffisus*). The measure was already known in the Twelve Tables.

Digerere. See DIGESTA.

Digesta. (From *digerere*.) In juristic literature. Some jurists (Alfenus Varus, Celsus, Julian, Scaevola, Marcellus) wrote comprehensive works under this title. Neither the system nor the kind of presentation is uniform, but the general feature is that both *ius civile* and praetorian law are taken into consideration. Often excerpts from earlier works of the same author (*Responsa, Quaestiones*) are collected and put into a somewhat systematic order (*digerere*).

Mommsen, *Jurist. Schriften* 2, 90; Jörs, *RE* 5, 485.

Digesta Iustiniani. The main part of Justinian's legislative work. Announced on December 15, 530 by the constitution *"Deo Auctore,"* it was published on December 16, 533 by the constitutions *"Tanta"* (in Latin) and *"Dedoken"* (in Greek) and it entered into force two weeks later. The grandiose work is a compilation of excerpts from the juristic literature of the classical epoch. More than 9,000 texts are distributed into fifty books, each of which—except for books 30–32 on legacies and *fideicommissa*—are divided into titles of various extent containing the texts pertinent to the topic indicated in the super-scription (*rubrica*) of the title. Each text is preceded by an *inscriptio* denoting the classical author and title of the work from which it was taken. By a special instruction of the emperor, the compilers were authorized to omit all superfluous, imperfect, and obsolete material and to make alterations in the excerpted fragments taking into consideration the changes introduced by later imperial legislative activity and Justinian's own enactments. The commission composed of law professors in Constantinople and Beirut, high officials, and prominent practitioners, under the chairmanship of TRIBONIANUS, made use of that authorization in a very large measure, not only in order to introduce into the collected texts later legislative changes but also to insert some reforms of the older law where the classical doctrines or ideas seemed to them less appropriate for their time. Justinian's statement that "many things and of highest importance (*multa et maxima*) have been changed" (*Tanta*, 10) corresponds exactly to the truth. Innumerable alterations (suppressions, additions, substitutions), sometimes wholly opposite to what had been said by a classical jurist, were accomplished with the purpose of modernizing the law as it stood in texts written three to five centuries earlier. Those alterations are called interpolations (*emblemata Triboniani*). The copies of the classical works, which the compilers had at their disposal, were provided with marginal or interlinear remarks (glosses), inserted by the readers in postclassical times; thus the glosses entered into the Digest, willingly accepted by the compilers for whom they facilitated the compilatory task in a large measure. The research into interpolations and postclassical alterations in the Digest is one of the most important features of modern Romanistic literature, the efforts of which are devoted to the segregation in each text of what was said therein originally by the jurist from what had been added or changed afterwards. In order to avoid controversial discussions and confusing commentaries to this part of his codification, Justinian allowed only explanatory writings, summaries, and additional notes to the single title to be made in the future and forbade commentaries of a polemical, critical and controversial character. The other official title of the Digest was *Pandectae*.—See INDEX FLORENTINUS, TANTA, DEDOKEN.

Editions see General Bibliography, Ch. XII.—Jörs, *RE* 5; Riccobono, *NDI* 4; Baudry, *DS* 4 (*s.v. Pandectae*); Berger, *OCD*; F. Hoffmann, *Die Compilation der Digesten Justinians*, 1900; Longo, *BIDR* 19 (1907) 132; De Francisci, *BIDR* 22, 23, 27 (1910, 1911, 1914); H. Peters, *Die oström. Digestenkommentare und die Entstehung der Digesten, BerSächGW* 65 (1913); H. Krüger, *Die Herstellung der Digesten Justinians und der Gang der Excerption,* 1932; De Francisci, *Premesse storiche alla critica del Digesto, ConfMil* 1931, 1; Collinet, *L'originalité du Digeste, ibid.* 39; De Visscher, *Le Digeste, ibid.* 53 (= *Nouvelles Études,* 1949, 331); Arangio-Ruiz, *Precedenti scolastici del Digesto, ibid.* 285; Rotondi, *Scr giuridici* 1 (1922)

87; Berger, *Justinian's ban upon the commentaries to the Digest, Bull. Polish Institute of Arts and Sciences in America* 3 (1945) 656 (= *BIDR* 55–56, Suppl. Post-Bellum, 1951, offpr. 1948, 124).

Digestum novum, vetus. Some manuscripts of the Digest contain only one-third of the work. The first third, from Book 1 through Book 24, is called *Digestum vetus,* the last third (Books 39–50) *Digestum novum,* and the middle portion *Infortiatum.* This division of the Digest into three parts is only accidental.

Kantorowicz, *ZSS* 31 (1919) 40; De Francisci, *BIDR* 33 (1923) 162.

Dignitas. The respect and esteem which the magistrates and senators enjoyed among the people. *Dignitas populi Romani* = the greatness and power of the Roman people. In the later Empire, *dignitas* refers to the highest administrative offices. The hierarchy of the dignitates = *ordo dignitatum.*—C. 12.1; 8; 1.52.—See ORDINARIUS.

H. Wegehaupt, *Die Bedeutung von d. in den Schriften der republikanischen Zeit,* Diss. Breslau, 1932.

Dignitas patricia. See PATRICIATUS.

Dii. Gods. They could not be instituted as heirs in a testament. Exceptions, however, were admitted by senatusconsults and imperial constitutions in favor of some deities (in Rome of *Jovis Tarpeius,* and in the provinces of only one provincial deity). Legacies were permitted and subject to a deduction according to the *Lex Falcidia,* as all other legacies. The temple dedicated to the cult of the deity honored by the gift, was the beneficiary. For the pertinent legislation of the Christian emperors, see ECCLESIA.

Scialoja, *St giuridici* 2 (1934) 241; B. Biondi, *Successione testamentaria,* 1943, 128.

Diiudicare (diiudicatio). To decide a judicial controversy by judgment.

Dilatio. The adjournment of a trial. At the request of either party, only one *dilatio* might be granted in pecuniary matters. In criminal trials the accuser could request for an adjournment twice, the accused three times.—D. 2.12; C. 3.11.—See DIFFINDERE, and the following item.

Dilatio instrumentorum (personarum) gratia. An adjournment granted for the presentation of documentary evidence (only to the defendant since the plaintiff had to prepare the necessary documents before suing) or in order to give absent persons involved in the trial the opportunity to appear in court. The extension of the term granted depended upon the remoteness of the place from which the persons had to arrive or the documents to be brought.

Bortolucci, *St Riccobono* 2 (1936) 441.

Dilatorius. See EXCEPTIONES DILATORIAE.

Dilectum edicere. To order a mobilization of the army.

Liebenam, *RE* 5; Cagnat, *DS* 2; De Ruggiero, *DE* 2.

Diligens pater familias. A careful head of a family. The way he manages his affairs is presented as a model of caution and prudence.—See BONUS PATER FAMILIAS.

Sachers, *RE* 18, 4, 2154; Buckland, *St Bonfante* 2 (1930) 87.

Diligentia. Cautious conduct, carefulness. Lack of *diligentia* might cause liability of the person who was contractually obligated to a careful, cautious conduct, where another's interests were involved. The term is linked with others concerning contractual liability, and appears at times in texts which are not free of suspicion as to their classical origin. Complete elimination of the term from the classical juristic thinking is out of the question. Ant. *neglegentia.*—See CULPA, CUSTODIA.

Kunkel, *ZSS* 45 (1925) 266; Krückmann, *ZSS* 64 (1944) 5; Pflüger, *ZSS* 65 (1947) 121.

Diligentia quam suis. Carefulness (diligence) which a man applies in his own affairs. It is referred to when the duties of a guardian in the management of the ward's property or those of a partner in a *societas* are defined.—See CULPA IN CONCRETO.

Ehrhardt, *Mnem Pappulia,* 1934, 101.

Dilucida intervalla. See INTERVALLA.

Dimissorius. See LITTERAE DIMISSORIAE.

Dimittere. In obligatory relations *dimittere creditorem* = to satisfy the creditor; *dimittere debitorem* = to release the debtor.

Dimittere uxorem. To dismiss, to send away one's wife (e.g., in the case of adultery). Such an act is sufficient for a divorce if the husband gives up his *affectio maritalis* and repudiates the wife with the intention of dissolving the marriage.

Dioecesis. (As an administrative unit.) The union of several provinces. Through Diocletian's reform the whole Roman Empire was divided into twelve *dioeceses.* Later the number was increased to fifteen. The governor of a *dioecesis,* to whom the governors of the pertinent provinces were subordinated, was the *vicarius.* Three or four *dioeceses* were united into a *praefectura* under a *praefectus praetorio.* There were two *praefecturae* in the Western Empire (Italia, Gallia) and two in the Eastern Empire (Oriens, Illyricum). This administrative division of the Empire was reflected in the appeal proceedings in judicial matters. The provincial governors were judges in the first instance (*iudices ordinarii,* in Justinian's language called simply *iudices*). The second instance was the *vicarius,* from whose decisions an appeal to the emperor was admissible. The judgments of the *praefectus praetorio* as the head of a *praefectura,* rarely were submitted to the emperor since his judicial functions were held to be exercised in the place of the emperor (*vice sacra*).—See VICARIUS, VICARIUS IN URBE, VICARIUS PRAEFECTI PRAETORIO.

Kornemann, *RE* 5, 727; Jullian, *DS* 2.

Dioecesis urbica. The territory of Rome as a judicial district in which justice was administered by officials residing in Rome. Italy was divided into dictricts (*regiones*) submitted to the judicial competence of *iuridici.*—See REGIONES ITALIAE.

Diploma. Written permission to use the imperial post, delivered by a special official of the imperial chancery (*a diplomatibus*).

Humbert, *DS* 1, 1648.

Diploma honestae missionis. See AUXILIA, MISSIO, and the following item.

Diploma militare. A certificate in the form of a diptych issued to veteran soldiers after the completion of their military service (normally twenty, in the AUXILIA twenty-five years). The *diploma* conferred Roman citizenship on a peregrine soldier, his wife and children or granted him the *ius conubii* (= the right to conclude a legal Roman marriage). If the veteran had lived in a marital union with a woman, the *diploma* convalidated it into a legal marriage. Some tax immunities might also be included in a *diploma.* —See DIPTYCHUM.

Wünsch, *RE* 5; Lammert, *RE* 15, 1666; Wenger, *RE* 2A, 2416; Thédenat, *DS* 2; Vaglieri, *DE* 2, 198; H. M. D. Parker, *The R. legions,* 1928, 102, 239; Nesselhauf, *Corpus Inscr. Latinarum* 16 (1936); Riccobono, *FIR* 1² (1941) 223 (Bibl.).

Diptychum. A written document composed of two rectangular tablets of bronze or wood, joined together by a string passed through holes in the edges. Often three tablets were used bound in the same way together like a booklet (*triptychum*). The text of the document was written twice, once on the inner pages (*scriptura interior*), tied around with the string and sealed by the witnesses, and a second time on the outside pages (*scriptura exterior*) which could be read without opening the inner part.—See TABULA, TABULAE CERATAE.

Wenger, *RE* 2A, 2417; Wünsch, *RE* 5, 1163.

Directarius. See DERECTARIUS.

Directus. Straight, immediate. Used in various connections to denote that an act produces directly the results normally attached thereto, contrary to analogous legal institutions which are only indirectly effective. Thus, for instance, *libertas directa* is liberty given in a testament through a direct manumissory disposition of the testator and is opposed to *libertas fideicommissaria* where the slave becomes free through a manumission by the heir; the direct institution of an heir (*institutio directa*) is opposed to a SUBSTITUTIO. For the meaning of *directus* in connection with certain types of actions, see ACTIONES DIRECTAE.

Diribitio. The scrutiny of votes in popular assemblies by special scrutinizers (*diribitores*) appointed for each *centuria* or *tribus.*

G. Rotondi, *Leges publicae populi Romani,* 1912, 142.

Diribitores. See DIRIBITIO.

Liebenam, *RE* 5; Humbert, *DS* 1, 1386.

Dirimere. To settle a controversy (*dirimere controversiam*) by the decision of a judge or an arbitrator; to dissolve (a marriage, a partnership).

Discedere. To recede, to withdraw as a party from an agreement, or from a trial; to give up possession (*a possessione*); to dissolve a marriage by divorce.

Disceptatio. (From *disceptare.*) A legal dispute, a trial. It may denote both the debate on the controversial matter before court and the decision itself. *Disceptatio domestica* = a friendly dispute within the domestic community.

Düll, *ZSS* 63 (1943) 67.

Disceptator. He who examines and settles a controversy, an arbitrator or judge.

Discessio. (From *discedere.*) Voting (in the senate) by division. The senator who voted for the motion took one place, those who opposed it, another (*sententiam pedibus ferre,* Gellius, *Noct. Att.* 3.18.2).— See SENATORES PEDARII, SENATUSCONSULTA.

O'Brien-Moore, *RE* Suppl. 6, 711; 716.

Discidium. A divorce.

Discindere. (In later imperial constitutions). To dismiss from public service.

Disciplina. Rules affecting orderly conduct, primarily in military service (*disciplina militaris*). Disorderly conduct of soldiers, disobedience, insubordination, and the like, were treated as lesser military delicts. See DELICTA MILITUM, CASTIGATIO, REGENS EXERCITUM. —*Disciplina publica* = public order.—See SEDITIOSI.

J. Sulzer, *Beiträge zur inneren Geschichte des röm. Heeres,* Basel, 1923; O. Mauch, *Der lateinische Begriff d.,* Diss. Basel, 1941; S. v. Bolla, *Aus röm. und bürgerlichem Erbrecht,* 1950, 6; Solazzi, *SDHI* 17 (1951) 249.

Discussor. An official in the later Empire who verified the accounts of expenditures for public buildings and the records connected with tax administration.—C. 10.30.—*Discussor census,* see INSPECTOR.

Seeck, *RE* 5.

Discutere matrimonium. To dissolve a marriage (or a betrothal = *discutere sponsalia*).

Disiunctim. See CONIUNCTIM. Different interpretative rules were applied to legacies left joint *disiunctim.* See the following item.

Disiunctivo modo. Alternatively (*aut . . . aut, sive . . . sive* = either . . . or). Conditions imposed *disiunctivo modo* = *conditiones disiunctivae.* Generally the person on whom they were imposed had the choice between them.

Dispendium. Expense, loss. Syn. *impensae, impendium*; ant. *compendium, lucrum.*

Dispensatio aerarii. Supervision over the administration of the treasury (AERARIUM POPULI ROMANI). It belonged to the competence of the senate.

Dispensator. A financial manager of a wealthy landowner. The emperor also had *dispensatores* = paymasters, cashiers of the imperial purse.

Dispensator pauperum. See OECONOMUS ECCLESIAE.

Displicere. See PACTUM DISPLICENTIAE.

Dispositio. (In later imperial constitutions.) An arrangement made by a testator in his last will or the testament as a whole (*ultima dispositio*).

Dispositiones. Private (not governmental) affairs and correspondence of the emperor (in the late Empire).—See COMES DISPOSITIONUM.

Disputatio fori. Mentioned only once by Pomponius with reference to the times following the promulgation of the Twelve Tables (D. 1.2.2.5). The term seems to indicate discussions of legal problems by the jurists in a public place (in court?).

V. Lübtow, *ZSS* 66 (1948) 467.

Disputationes. Juristic writings containing cases discussed by the jurists in their activity as teachers. The discussions might have started from real cases in which the jurists were asked for opinion (*responsum*).—See TRYPHONINUS.

Dissensus. (From *dissentire*.) See CONSENSUS CONTRARIUS.

Hupka, *ZSS* 52 (1932) 1.

Dissimulatio. In the case of *iniuria* (insult), disregarding (neglecting) an offense by the person insulted who leaves the matter without giving any sign of outraged feeling. "The insult is abolished by *dissimulatio*" (*dissimulatione aboletur*, D. 47.10.17.1). —See INIURIA.

Dissolvere (dissolutio). To dissolve (a marriage by divorce, a partnership), to cancel (a contract, an obligatory tie).

Distractio bonorum. An institution similar to BONORUM VENDITIO (sale of the property of an insolvent debtor). The sale was by individual items (not in a lump), probably without any foregoing *missio in bona*. *Distractio bonorum* did not involve infamy. Originally applied as an exception in the case of the insolvency of a senator (see CLARA PERSONA), a ward or a lunatic, the *distractio bonorum* became a general institution under Justinian.

Solazzi, *Concorso dei creditori* 2 (1938) 199; 3 (1940) 1; Cosentini, *SDHI* 11 (1945) 1; Lepri, *Scr Ferrini* 2 (Univ. Sacro Cuore, Milan, 1947) 99.

Distractio pignoris. See IUS DISTRAHENDI.—D. 20.5; C. 8.27; 28.

Distrahere. To sell (a pledge, see IUS DISTRAHENDI, DISTRACTIO BONORUM), to dissolve (a contract, a marriage). Syn. *dissolvere*, ant. *contrahere*.

Diurnus. See AQUA DIURNA, FUR DIURNUS, OPERAE DIURNAE.

Divalis. Refers to enactments and utterances made by the emperor.

Ensslin, *SbMünch* 1943, 6, 72.

Divertere. To divorce ("to go in different ways").— See DIVORTIUM.

Dividere. See DIVISIO.

Divina domus. See DOMUS AUGUSTA.

Divinatio. As the art of predicting and interpreting certain natural phenomena (*auspicia, auguria*) this is a part of the activity of *augures* and their occult science.—AUGURES, HARUSPICES.

Hopfner, *RE* 14, 1258 (*s.v. mantike*); Bouché-Leclercq, *DS* 2; Pease, *OCD*; Cramer, *Sem* 10 (1952) 44.

Divinatio. (In a criminal trial.) A preliminary stage in which an accuser is chosen among several persons who brought the same accusation against a person. Plurality of accusers in the same trial was not admissible.

Hitzig, *RE* 5; Humbert, *DS* 2; Berger, *OCD*.

Divinitas. Divinity; a title applied to the emperor.— See DIVALIS, DIVUS, DIVINUS.

Herzog-Hauser, *RE* Suppl. 4, 806 (*s.v. Kaiserkult*); L. R. Taylor, *The divinity of the R. emperor*, Middletown, 1931; Ensslin, *Gottkaiser, SbMünch* 1943, Heft 6, *passim*.

Divinus. Pertaining to gods; in the later Empire, connected with the person of the emperor or issued by him (enactments, privileges, gracious acts). Syn. *divalis*.—See IUS DIVINUM, RES DIVINI IURIS, DOMUS DIVINA.

Divisio. Division of common property. It can be achieved either by mutual agreement or by an action: among co-heirs by the ACTIO FAMILIAE HERCISCUNDAE, among co-owners by the ACTIO COMMUNI DIVIDUNDO. An analogous action, although not for dividing common property, but for the regulation of controversial land boundaries, was the ACTIO FINIUM REGUNDORUM. All these actions have some procedural peculiarities, among them a special clause in the formula, ADIUDICATIO.—See COMMUNIO.

Divisio inter liberos. (Made by the father.) See TESTAMENTUM PARENTIS INTER LIBEROS.

Divortium. A divorce. It was achieved without formalities, simply by a definitive cessation of the common life of the consorts, initiated by common agreement or by one of them, thereby proving that there was no longer any *affectio maritalis* between the spouses. Therefore, a temporary abandonment of the common dwelling by the wife in a state of excitement (*per calorem*) was not considered a *divortium*. If the conclusion of a marriage was accompanied by a *conventio in manum*, the dissolution of such agreement had to be accomplished by a contrary act (*diffarreatio* in the case of *confarreatio*, *remancipatio* or *emancipatio* in the case of *coëmptio*). Usually, however, a unilateral declaration by the divorcing spouse (*repudium*) followed the separation, either by writing, *per epistulam*—the letter had to be signed by seven witnesses—or orally, directly or indirectly by a messenger (*per nuntium*). Legislation of the Christian emperors often dealt with *divortium*; they introduced some restrictions and imposed pecuniary sanctions on the party who repudiated his consort without any just ground. The principle of the dissolubility of marriages, however, always remained in force. In Justinian's law written notification of a divorce (*libellus divortii, repudii*) became obligatory.—D. 24.2; C. 5.24.—See FILIA FAMILIAS.

Leonhard, *RE* 5; Kunkel, *RE* 14, 2275; Baudry, *DS* 2; Anon., *NDI* 5; E. Levy, *Hergang der röm. Ehescheidung*, 1925; Solazzi, *BIDR* 34 (1925) 1, 295; Corbett, *LQR* 45 (1929); Volterra, *St Ratti*, 1934, 394; *idem, St Riccobono* 3 (1936) 201; Basanoff, *ibid.* 177; L. Caes, *La dissolution volontaire du mariage sine manu*, Louvain, 1935; G. Longo, *BIDR* 40 (1932) 202; Jonkers, *SDHI* 5 (1939) 123; Rasi, *Consensus facit nuptias*, 1946, 125; Volterra, *RIDA* 1 (1948) 224; Solazzi, *Il divorzio della liberta*, *BIDR* 51–52 (1948) 327; P. Noailles, *Les tabous du mariage*, in *Fas et ius*, 1948, 1; Wolff, *ZSS* 67 (1950) 261.

Divortium bona gratia. (In Justinian law.) A divorce caused by reasons which cannot be charged to either of the consorts, as when the marriage remained childless for three years because of a physical deficiency of one of the consorts, or the absence of the husband as a prisoner of war for five years, mental disease, etc.

Tabera, *ACII* 1 (1935) 195; Solazzi, *RendLomb* 71 (1938) 511; Wolff, *ZSS* 67 (1950) 270.

Divortium ex iusta causa. A divorce caused by the bad behavior of one of the consorts (adultery or immoral conduct of the wife, the husband's living with a concubine or his false accusation of the wife for adultery) in Justinian's law. The culpable consort was subject to pecuniary sanctions (loss of the dowry or nuptial donations, and, under certain circumstances, even loss of a quarter of property). Ant. *divortium sine causa,* when there was no reasonable ground for the divorce. It was valid, but the party who divorced was liable to money penalties.

Divus (diva). A title granted an emperor or empress after the death if a *consecratio* had taken place by which the deceased entered among the deities of the state.—See DIVINITAS, NOSTER.

Herzog-Hauser, *RE* Suppl. 4, 806 (*s.v. Kaiserkult*); De Ruggiero, *DE* 4, 44; Martroye, *Bull. de la Société des Antiquaires de France*, 1928, 297; L. R. Taylor, *The divinity of the R. emperor*, 1931; A. d'Ors, *AHDE* 14 (1942/3) 33; Ensslin, *Gottkaiser, SbMünch* 1943, Heft 6.

Do, dico, addico. The three solemn words (*tria solemnia verba*) pronounced by the praetor in the exercise of his jurisdictional activity in the *in-iure*-stage of the process. *Dare* referred to his granting an action (*formula, iudicium*), an exception, an interdict, possession, or to his appointment of a guardian, a judge, and the like. *Dicere* was applied to some of his commands, such as *dicere diem, dicere multam; addicere* is linked with the approval of what happened *in iure* (e.g., *in iure cessio*), see also ADDICERE.—See DIES FASTI.

Wlassak, *ZSS* 25 (1903) 85; Düll, *ZSS* 57 (1937) 76; F. De Martino, *Giurisdizione*, 1937, 59; Pugliese, *Lezioni sul processo civile r.*, 1947, 45; P. Noailles, *Du droit sacré au dr. civil*, 1950, 284.

Documentum. A document. The term is unknown in classical juristic language, but is used in post-classical imperial constitutions.—See INSTRUMENTUM.

Dodrans. Three quarters of an *as* (nine *unciae*), hence three quarters of an inheritance.—See AS.

Dolo desinere possidere. To give up fraudulently possession of a thing with the purpose to be unable to restore it to the true owner or legal possessor. He who does so "is treated as if he still possessed the thing" (D. 50.17.137; 157.1).—See REI VINDICATIO, EXHIBERE, POSSESSOR FICTUS.

Lenel, *GrZ* 37 (1910) 534; Pissard, *NRH* 35 (1910); Levy, *ZSS* 42 (1921) 505; Kaser, *ZSS* 51 (1931) 109.

Dolo malo. (Syn. *dolose.*) Intentionally, with evil intention (malice). The term receives often greater emphasis by the addition of *sciens* (knowingly) to indicate that the wrongdoer committed the offence with full knowledge of the unlawfulness of his act. "No one is considered to act fraudulently (*dolo*) who avails himself of his right" (D. 50.17.55), or "who fulfills the order of a judge" (*iussum iudicis,* D. *ibid.* 167.1).—See DOLUS.

Dolose. See DOLO MALO, DOLUS.

Dolus. Defined by Labeo (D. 4.3.1.2) as follows: "any cunning, deceit, or contrivance used to defraud, deceive or cheat another." Syn. *dolus malus.* Ant. on the one hand *dolus bonus* (simple shrewdness), on the other hand BONA FIDES. In transactions governed by *bona fides* (*negotia bonae fidei*) and protected by actions (*iudicia*) *bonae fidei* the judge's duty was to take into consideration fraudulent conduct of the parties and to reject claims or defenses based on *dolus.* In actions governed by *ius strictum* (such as arising from *stipulatio*) the defendant must oppose *exceptio doli* if he wanted to object that the plaintiff's claim was founded on *dolus.* A person deceived *dolo* (*malo*) by another, had the ACTIO DOLI against him, introduced by praetorian law, when another special action was not available. In transactions under strict law liability for *dolus* could be assumed by a special *clausula doli*, included in, or attached to the principal *stipulatio.* Through this clause the promisor guaranteed that there was not nor will be any fraud (*dolum malum abesse afuturumque esse*). An agreement excluding liability for *dolus* (*pactum ne dolus praestetur*) was void.—In criminal offenses *dolus* means the intention of the wrongdoer to commit the crime, which presupposes his knowledge of the unlawfulness of the act. Republican statutes dealing with criminal offences generally expressly stress the *scientia* of the culprit (*sciens dolo malo*). Similar expressions are: *consulto, consilio, voluntate, sciens prudensque.*—D. 4.3; C. 2.20.—See ACTIO DOLI, CULPA, CAPAX DOLI, EXCEPTIO DOLI, CONSILIUM, DOLO MALO, IN INTEGRUM RESTITUTIO, STIPULATIO DE DOLO.

Humbert, *DS* 2; Litten, *Fg Güterbock*, 1910; Schulz, *ZSS* 33 (1912); Charvet, *La restitutio in integrum des majeurs*, 1920, 41; G. Rotondi, *Scr giur.* 2 (1922) 371; K. Heldrich, *Das Verschulden beim Vertragsabschluss*, 1924; J. Duquesne *In integrum restitutio ob dolum*, 1929; G. Maier, *Praetorische Bereicherungsklagen*, 1932, 17; 35; G. Longo, *Contributi alla dottrina del dolo*, 1937; F. Palumbo, *L'azione di dolo*, 1935; Coing, *Sem* 8 (1950) 12; *idem, Fschr Schulz* 1 (1951) 97.

Dolus bonus. Earlier jurists called shrewdness *dolus bonus,* "especially when anything was skillfully contrived against an enemy or a robber" (D. 4.3.1.3). *Dolus bonus* does not produce any legal consequences. Ant. *dolus malus.*—See DOLUS.

Dolus malus. Juristically syn. with *dolus*. *Malus* is in this connection a strengthening attribute but does not ·denote a higher degree of *dolus* to be treated otherwise than *dolus*.—See DOLO MALO, DOLUS, MACHINATIO.

Domestici. The court garrison in the imperial palace. —C. 12.17.—See DECEMPRIMI, COMITES DOMESTICORUM, PROTECTORES.

Seeck, *RE* 5; Braschi, *DE* 2; Babut, *Rev. Historique* 114 (1913) 226.

Domestici iudices. The staff in the office of provincial governors.—C. 1.51.

Domesticum furtum. See FURTUM DOMESTICUM.

Domesticum imperium. See IMPERIUM DOMESTICUM.

Domesticum iudicium. See IUDICIUM DOMESTICUM.

Domesticum testimonium. See TESTIMONIUM DOMESTICUM.

Domi. The area within the city of Rome and a radius of a mile from its walls. Ant. *militiae* = the territory beyond that area. The terms refer to the *imperium* of the magistrates and to their territorial criminal jurisdiction.—See LEX CORNELIA DE IMPERIO.

Domicilium. The domicile of a person, the place where he permanently (not temporarily) lives. *Domicilium* is sometimes identified with *domus* "where a man has his abode, his documents (*tabulae*) and the establishment of his affairs (*business*)" (D. 50.16.203). Other criteria of *domicilium* are: where one "is always acting in the municipality, when ·he buys, sells and concludes contracts there, when he makes use of its *forum*, baths, theaters and its other institutions, when he celebrates there the holidays" (D. 50.1.27.1). It was controversial whether a man might have two domiciles. Some jurists hold that he had no domicile at all; a contrary opinion prevailed in Justinian's law. Senators had their *domicilium* both in Rome and in their community of origin. Several rules concerning *domicilium* are referred to Hadrian. Even a longer sojourn in a city, for the purpose of studies is not considered a *domicilium* unless it lasted more than five years. *Domicilium collocare* = to establish one's domicile; syn. *larem collocare, constituere* (literally = to set a shrine for the tutelary deity of the household). A person who had a *domicilium* in a community was an *incola* thereof. *Domicilium* was important in civil procedure since, as a matter of rule, a debtor might be sued only where he had his *domicilium* (*forum domicilii*). The domicile also was decisive for the municipal charges (*munera*) since a person was obliged to perform them only where he was resident. On the other hand, only an *incola* could obtain an honorary post in his community.—D. 50.1; C. 10.40.—See INCOLA, ORIGO, TRANSFERRE DOMICILIUM.

Leonhard, *RE* 5; Berger, *RE* 9 (*s.v. incola*); Baudry, *DS* 2; Lechat, *DS* 3 (*s.v. incola*); V. Tedeschi, *RISG* 7 (1932) 213; *idem*, *Del domicilio*, 1936; Visconti, *Scr Ferrini* 1 (Univ. Catt., Milan, 1947) 429.

Dominicus. Refers to the master's (*dominus*) power over his slave (*dominica potestas*). *Dominicus* = connected with the private property of the emperor; See RES DOMINICA, DOMUS DIVINA.

Dominium. Ownership. Unknown in Cicero (although *dominus* is not rare in his works) the term appears for the first time at the end of the Republic. It denotes full legal power over a corporeal thing, the right of the owner to use it, to take proceeds therefrom, and to dispose of it freely. The owner's *plena potestas in re* (= full power over a thing) is manifested by his faculty to do with it what he pleases and to exclude any one from the use thereof unless the latter has acquired a specific right on it (a servitude, an usufruct) which he might obtain only with the owner's consent. Limits to private ownership may be imposed on account of public order or in the interest of the community (*utilitas publica*) which under certain circumstances may lead to an expropriation (taking away one's property through a compulsory purchase, *emptio ab invito*, the owner being compensated for the loss of his property). Under the later Empire expropriation was practiced in various instances. Restrictions of the unlimited utilization of immovable property were admitted when a neighbor was hindered in the free use of his property. Special restrictions concerning the owner's right to transfer his property by sale or in another way (*alienatio*) might be imposed on him by contract or by a testamentary disposition; in exceptional situations they were ordered by law, as for instance, by the LEX IULIA DE FUNDO DOTALI, which forbade the husband to sell the land pertaining to his wife's dowry, or the prohibition to alienate a thing which is the object of a pending suit (see RES LITIGIOSA). Finally, the owner's rights are limited when he has a thing in common ownership with another (see COMMUNIO).—Syn. *proprietas*, apparently a later creation. A fundamental feature of the Roman doctrine of ownership is the distinction between the legal power over a thing and the factual holding of a thing (*possessio*) which do not always meet together in the same person. Hence, conflicting situations might arise between the owner (*dominus, proprietarius*) and the possessor.—D. 41.1.—See DOMINIUM DUPLEX, MANCIPIUM, IN BONIS HABERE, POSSESSIO. For the acquisition of ownership see MANCIPATIO, IN IURE CESSIO, TRADITIO, USUCAPIO, LONGI TEMPORIS PRAESCRIPTIO, SPECIFICATIO, COMMIXTIO, CONFUSIO, OCCUPATIO, THESAURUS. For the protection of *dominium*, see REI VINDICATIO, ACTIO PUBLICIANA, OPERIS NOVI NUNTIATIO, CAUTIO DAMNI INFECTI, IMPETRATIO DOMINII, HASTA.—See also the following items.

Leonhard, *RE* 5; Baudry, *DS* 2; Anon., *NDI* 5; Berger, *OCD*; Di Marzo, *NDI* 10 (*s.v. proprietà*); C. H. Monro, *De adquirendo rerum dominio*, D. 41.1, Cambridge, 1900; Bonfante, *Scritti* 2 (1918); V. Scialoja, *Teoria della proprietà*, 1-2 (Lezioni, 1928, 1931); De Francisci, *Translatio dominii*, 1921; H. H. Pflüger, *Erwerb des Eigentums*, 1937; G. Cornil, *Du mancipium au dominium, Fschr Koschaker* 1 (1939); Kaser, *ibid.* 445; Koschaker, *ZSS* 58 (1938) 255; J. G. A. Wilms, *De wording van het Romeinsche dominium, Gent*, 1939/40; Biscardi, *StSen* 56 (1942) 275; Wieacker, *Entwicklungsstufen des röm. Eigentums*, in *Das neue Bild der Antike* 2 (1942) 156; Brasiello, *Studi Ferrara* 1 (1943); M. Kaser, *Eigentum und Besitz im älteren röm. R.*, 1943; E. Weiss, *Zwei Beiträge zur Lehre vom geteilten Eigentum, Pragmateiai tes Akademias Athenon* 14, fasc. 3, 1948; Monier, *St Solazzi*, 1948, 357; B. Biondi, *Le servitù prediali*, 1946, 58; F. de Zulueta, *Digest 41, 1 and 2* (translation and commentary) 2nd ed. 1950; E. Levy, *West Roman Vulgar Law*, 1951 (*passim*); P. Voci, *Modi di acquisto di proprietà (Corso)*, Milan, 1952.

Dominium duplex. Occurs when one person had *dominium ex iure Quiritium* over a thing, and another had ownership, recognized by praetorian law (*in bonis*), of the same thing, an ownership which was often in a basic contrast with the rules of the quiritary law (*ius civile*). See the following item.

Di Marzo, *BIDR* 43 (1936); Riccobono, *Scr Ferrini* (Univ. Pavia, 1946) 34; Ciapessoni, *St su Gaio*, 1943, 93; La Rosa, *AnCat* 3 (1949); Solazzi, *SDHI* 16 (1950) 286.

Dominium ex iure Quiritium. Ownership which a Roman citizen has acquired according to the principles of *ius civile* (*ius Quiritium*) of things which under that law could be in private ownership. The pertinent action for the recovery of such things was the REI VINDICATIO. Ant. *in bonis habere* = ownership which was recognized by, and under the protection of, the *ius honorarium.*—C. 7.25.—See IN BONIS ESSE, DOMINIUM DUPLEX, NUDUM IUS QUIRITIUM.

Sinaiski, *St Riccobono* 4 (1936) 39.

Dominium iustum. Ownership legally acquired.—See HASTA.

Dominus. The owner of a thing. He is opposed to the possessor and usufructuary thereof, who have no ownership but hold a thing. In a broader sense "the term *dominus* comprises also the usufructuary" (D. 42.5.8 pr.). *Dominus* = the master of a slave. In contractual and particularly in commercial relations, *dominus* is the principal (*dominus negotii*) for whom another is acting on mandate or without authorization (*negotiorum gestor*).

Lugli, *DE* 2.

Dominus. A title of the emperor in the later Empire. Hence the period of Roman history from the fourth century is called Dominate.

Neumann, *RE* 5; Lugli, *DE* 2, 1952; Dumas, *RHD* 10 (1931) 35.

Dominus litis. The person in whose name a trial is conducted by a representative (*procurator*) appointed by him.

Dominus navis (navium). The owner of a transport ship (or fleet). Syn. *navicularius*. The latter term is usually applied to owners of smaller vessels.

Dominus negotii. See NEGOTIORUM GESTIO, RATIHABITIO, DOMINUS.

Dominus proprietatis. An owner. The term is less used in a general sense; it serves to stress the contrast to another person who has an usufruct or another right (*ius in re aliena*) on the same property.—Syn. *proprietarius, dominus.*

Kaser, *Fschr Koschaker* 1 (1939) 465.

Domninus. A Byzantine jurist of the fifth century, probably a professor in the law school in Beirut.

Kübler, *RE* 5, 1521.

Domus. A house. The house where one is living is considered "his most secure shelter and retreat" (D. 2.4.18). Therefore summons to a trial (*in ius vocatio*) could not take place in the residence of the defendant. As a matter of rule, "no one should be taken (by force) from his home" (D. 50.17.103). *Domus* has sometimes the significance of *familia, gens,* or of a temple.—See DOMICILIUM, IUS REVOCANDI DOMUM, INSTRUCTUM, INSTRUMENTUM FUNDI, INTROIRE DOMUM.

Calza, *DE* 2, 2060; Polak, *The inviolability of the house, Symbolae van Oven* (1946) 251.

Domus augusta (divina, dominica, regia). The imperial household or the private property of the emperor or the empress.—C. 11.72; 77; 3.26.

Seeck, *RE* 4, 651; Neumann, *RE* 5; Calza, *DE* 2, 2061.

Domus divina. See DOMUS AUGUSTA.—C. 3.26; 7.56.

Lécrivain, *DS* 3, 961; Calza, *DE* 2, 2062; Ensslin, *SbMünch* 1943, Heft 6, pp. 37, 71.

Donare. To make a gift. "It is held to be donated what is given without any legal obligation" (D. 39.5.29 pr.). See DONATIO. The gift = *donum, munus.* The first term is broader, the latter refers rather to customary gifts, given on certain occasions or as a voluntary compensation for services rendered.

Donarium. A votive offering.

Donatio. An act of liberality by which the donor (*donator*) hands over or promises a gift to the donee with the intention to make a gift (*animus donandi*) and without expecting any reciprocal performance. The donor, however, may express the wish that the recipient fulfill a certain act or render a service; see DONATIO SUB MODO. A donation may be made also in the form of a release of a debtor from his debt by the creditor (*acceptilatio*). The promise of a gift to be given in the future required the form of a *stipulatio* in classical law; it was formless in Justinian's law. A *donatio* must bring about an enrichment of the donee in any form, not only in money, for instance, when the right to dwell in the donor's house is gratuitously granted. Hence the payment of a debt which is not actionable (*obligatio naturalis*) is not a *donatio*. For restrictions concerning both the amount of gifts and the group of persons to whom unlimited gifts could be given, see LEX CINCIA. A distinction is made between donations *inter vivos* (becoming effective during the lifetime of donor and donee) and donations *mortis causa,* made conditionally and effective when the donee survived the donor.

In the later Empire certain donations had to be made before public officials and registered in public archives (*insinuatio actis*). Justinian made the *insinuatio* obligatory for donations over 500 solidi, but various types of donations were exempt from that formality. Donations of a smaller amount were valid when made in a formless agreement, *pactum donationis*.—Inst. 2.7; D. 39.5; C. 8.53; 54.—See ANIMUS DONANDI, LEX CINCIA, COLLATIO DONATIONIS, CONTRACTUS IUDICUM, EXCEPTAE PERSONAE, MODUS DONATIONIS, REVOCARE DONATIONEM, CONFIRMARE DONATIONEM, NEGOTIUM MIXTUM, USUCAPIO PRO DONATO, STIPULATIO DONATIONIS, and the following items.

Leonhard, *RE* 5; Baudry, *DS* 2; Ascoli, *NDI* 5; Riccobono, *Mél Girard* 2 (1912) 415; *idem, ZSS* 34 (1913) 159; Perozzi, *Scr giur.* 2 (1948, ex 1897) 655; J. Stock, *Zum Begriff der donatio*, 1932; A. Ascoli, *Trattato delle donazioni*, 2nd ed. 1935; Bussi, *La donazione,* in *CristDirPriv,* 1935; H. Krüger, *ZSS* 60 (1940) 80; Arangio-Ruiz, *FIR* 3 (1943) nos. 93 ff.; B. Biondi, *Successione testamentaria,* 1943, 631; *idem, Scr Ferrini* 1 (Univ. Sacro Cuore, 1947) 102 (Bibl.); J. R. Lévy, *RIDA* 3 (= *Mél De Visscher* 2, 1949) 91; Archi, *St Solazzi,* 1948, 740; *idem, La donazione,* 1950; E. Levy, *West Roman Vulgar Law,* 1951, 137.

Donatio ante nuptias. A gift given to the fiancée by the fiancé. If marriage did not follow, the gift could not be claimed back unless it was made under such condition. In Justinian's law such condition is self-understood. Justinian's predecessor, Justinus, permitted donations between spouses which under classical law were forbidden (see DONATIO INTER VIRUM ET UXOREM). Such donations (*donatio propter nuptias*) were considered a counterpart to the dowry and subject to analogous rules. Hence the name *antipherna* (= counterdowry). The provisions concerning the restitution of a *donatio propter nuptias* in the case of divorce or of the husband's death were equally applied as in the case of a dowry.—C. 5.3; 14. —See DOS, COLLATIO DONATIONIS ANTE NUPTIAS.

Holldack, *Fg Güterbock,* 1910, 505; Scherillo, *RStDIt* 2, 3 (1929, 1930); F. Brandileone, *Scritti* 1 (1931) 117; Vismara, *CristDirPriv,* 1935; Vaccari, *CentCodPav,* 1933, 251; L. F. Re, *De donationibus ante nuptias,* Rome, 1935; L. Anne, *Le rite de fiançailles et la donation pour cause de marriage sous le Bas-Empire,* Louvain, 1941; L. Caes, *Le status juridique de la sponsalicia largitas,* Courtrai; 1949.

Donatio inter virum et uxorem. A gift made by the husband to his wife or *vice versa*. They were originally valid and not subject to the restrictions of the LEX CINCIA since the spouses belonged to the category of persons exempt from the restrictions of the statute (*personae exceptae*). Such donations were later prohibited. The prohibition was sanctioned by the legislation of Augustus who seemingly confirmed what customary law had introduced before (*moribus receptum est*). An oration of the emperors Severus and Caracalla restored the validity of such donations in A.D. 206 in case of the donor's death before that of the other spouse if the marriage was still existing at the time of his death.—D. 24.1; C. 5.16.—See RETENTIONES DOTALES.

Baudry, *DS* 2; De Medio, *Divieto di donare tra i coniugi,* 1902; F. Dumont, *Les donations entre époux,* 1928; J. B. Thayer, *On gifts between husband and wife,* Cambridge, Mass., 1929; Siber, *ZSS* 53 (1933) 99; J. G. A. Wilms, *Schenkingen tusschen Echtgenooten,* Gent, 1934; De Robertis, *AnBari* 1936, 37; Lauria, *St Albertoni* 2 (1937) 513; L. Aru, *La donazione fra coniugi,* 1938; C. Stoicesco, *La date de la prohibition de donations i. v. et u., Revista Clasica* (Paris-Bucharest) 1939–1940; Scherillo, *St Solmi* 1 (1941) 169; B. Biondi, *Successione testamentaria,* 1943, 649.

Donatio inter vivos. See DONATIO MORTIS CAUSA.

Donatio mortis causa. A gift made by a donor in the assumption that he would die before the donee. It was effective after the donor's death. The donation was invalidated if the donee died when the donor was still living. Donations made by a man seriously ill or in a time of a particular danger, might expressly be connected with the condition that they become void if the donor recovered or remained safe. A *donatio mortis causa* has a similar function as a legacy. It differs from the latter in that it is not made in a testament. In the later development it was assimilated to the legacy in many respects and some rules governing the law of legacies were extended to *donatio mortis causa*. Ant. *donatio inter vivos,* which is effective when the donor and the donee are alive.— D. 39.6; C. 8.56.—See DONATIO, REVOCARE DONATIONEM.

E. F. Bruck, *Schenkung für den Todesfall,* 1909; F. Senn, *Études sur le droit des obligations, 1. La donation à cause de mort,* 1914; Haymann, *ZSS* 38 (1918) 209; B. Biondi, *AnPer* 1914, 188; *idem, Successione testamentaria,* 1943, 703.

Donatio perfecta. A gift is accomplished (and consequently cannot be invalidated) when the thing presented entered irrevocably into the patrimony of the donee, as, for instance, when a *res mancipi* was transferred by *mancipatio* or *in iure cessio,* or a *res nec mancipi* was delivered over to the donee. Generally a *donatio* is considered *perfecta* when the donor had no action for demanding back the gift of which the donor had acquired full ownership.

B. Biondi, *Successione testamentaria,* 1943, 641; S. di Paola, *D. m. c.,* (Catania, 1950).

Donatio propter nuptias. See DONATIO ANTE NUPTIAS, ANTIPHERNA.—C. 5.3.

Donatio sub modo. A donation in which the donor imposed on the donee a certain performance (for instance, the erection of a monument in his honor). The term *modus* was unknown to the classical language in such connection. The beneficiary was only morally obliged to fulfill the donor's wish, unless it was expressed in the form of a condition (*"si . . ."*) of the validity of the *donatio* or the donee assumed the pertinent duty by a *stipulatio*. Imperial and Justinian's legislation gave the donor and his heirs means to enforce the fulfillment of the *modus* or to annul the donation.—C. 8.54.—See NEGOTIUM MIXTUM, MODUS.

F. Haymann, *Schenkung unter einer Auflage,* 1905; Schulz, *Fschr Zitelmann,* 1923; Giffard, *ACDR,* Roma, 2 (1935) 135; B. Biondi, *Successione testamentaria,* 1943, 710; G. Wesenberg, *Verträge zu Gunsten Dritter,* 1949, 29.

Donativum. A donation in money given to soldiers by the emperor on special occasions (a triumph, accession to the throne, birthday).

Fiebiger, *RE* 5.

Donator. See DONATIO.

Donum. See DONARE, DONATIO.

Dorotheus. A law professor in Beirut in Justinian's time. He was a member of the commission which compiled the Digest and the second edition of Justinian's Code. Together with Theophilus he edited the Institutes (see INSTITUTINONES IUSTINIANI) as a part of the emperor's legislative work. He wrote a summary (*index*) of the Digest.

Jörs, *RE* 5, 1572, no. 22.

Dos. A dowry, i.e., goods given to the bridegroom by the bride or somebody else, primarily her father, for her, in view of the marriage to be concluded. Syn. *res uxoria.* Normally the dowry was bestowed before the conclusion of the marriage, but it could also be given afterwards. According to the classical law the husband was the legal owner of the dowry; he was, however, limited in the disposal since it was meant as a contribution to the maintenance of the common household and had to be returned at the end of the marriage to the wife, her heir, or another person. The husband's ownership was therefore rather formal which found its expression in the opinion that the *dos* is only *in bonis mariti.* He had, however, full administration of the dowry which he had to manage as a *bonus pater familias* and he could use the proceeds thereof. He could not alienate landed property belonging to the dowry as a matter of principle (see LEX IULIA DE FUNDO DOTALI), except with the wife's consent. The same principle applied to the manumission of slaves that formed part of the dowry. The husband was liable for the value of slaves manumitted without the wife's approval. "There is no dowry where there is no marriage" (D. 23.3.3). Hence a dowry constituted before the conclusion of a marriage was held to have been made under the tacit condition that the marriage would follow (*si nuptiae fuerint secutae*). The restitution of the dowry could be claimed by *actio ex stipulatu* if the provisions concerning the restitution were set in the husband's *stipulatio (cautio rei uxoriae).* Formless agreements regulating the problems connected with the restitution of the dowry, in particular in the case of a divorce, were later admitted (*pactum nuptiale, pactum dotale, instrumentum dotale*). Generally a specific action for the recovery of the dowry lay against the husband (*actio, iudicium rei uxoriae*) independently of a particular agreement on the matter. It is not certain whether the action was *bonae fidei,* but the judge, no doubt, had to consider *ex aequo et bono*

the questions connected with the restitution. The rules concerning the restitution made a distinction as to whether the marriage came to an end by the death of one of the consorts or by divorce, and, in case of divorce whether the husband or the wife was at fault. The husband was granted the BENEFICIUM COMPETENTIAE and had the right to keep some parts of the dowry for various reasons (see RETENTIONES, IMPENSAE DOTALES). Justinian's law introduced important reforms. The problem of the husband's rights over the *res dotales* was solved simply by granting him only an usufruct; the *actio rei uxoriae* was declared an *actio bonae fidei.*—D. 23.3; 4; 5; 24.3; 25.1; C. 5.12; 13; 14; 15; 18; 19; 20; 22; 23; 7.74.— See COLLATIO DOTIS, DATIO DOTIS, DICTIO DOTIS, PROMISSIO DOTIS, FAVOR DOTIS, BENEFICIUM COMPETENTIAE, CONDICTIO CAUSA DATA, CONDICTIO SINE CAUSA, INSTRUMENTUM DOTALE, IMPENSAE DOTALES, EDICTUM DE ALTERUTRO, RETENTIONES DOTALES, USUCAPIO PRO DOTE, and the following items.

Leonhard, *RE* 5; Baudry, *DS* 2; Sacchi, *NDI* 5; Berger, *OCD* 540; S. Solazzi, *Restituzione della dote,* 1899; Gradenwitz, *Mél Gérardin,* 1907, 283; P. Noailles, *L'inalienabilité dotale (Ann. Univ. Grenoble)* 1919; Biondi, *AnPal* 7 (1920) 179; L. Tripiccione, *L'actio rei uxoriae e l'actio ex stipulatu nella restituzione della dote,* 1920; Capocci, *BIDR* 37 (1928) 139; Grosso, *RISG* 3 (1928) 39; Lémaire, *Mél Fournier,* 1929; Stella-Maranca, *AnBari,* 1928/I, 1929/I; Riccobono, *TR* 9 (1929) 23; Arnò, *St Bonfante* 1 (1930) 81; Albertario, *Studi* 1 (1933) 281 (several articles); Naber, *St Riccobono,* 3 (1936) 231; J. Sontis, *Digestensumme des Anonymus, 1. Dotalrecht,* 1937; Lauria, *ANap* 58 (1937) 219; C. A. Maschi, *Concezione naturalistica,* 1937, 313; Castello, *SDHI* 4 (1938); Orestano, *St Bonolis* 1 (1942) 9; Dumont, *RHD* 22 (1943) 1; Kagan, *TulLR* 20 (1946) 597; Lavaggi, *AG* 134 (1947) 24; Pflüger, *ZSS* 65 (1947); Wolff, *ZSS* 66 (1948) 31; Kaser, *RIDA* 2 (= *Mél De Visscher* 1, 1949) 511; Maschi, *AnTr* 18 (1948) 78; M. Ricca-Barberis, *La garanzia per evizione della dote,* 1950.

Dos adventicia. A dowry given for the woman not by her father (see DOS PROFECTICIA) but by another person, or constituted by herself when she was *sui iuris.*

Albertario, *Studi* 1 (1933) 283.

Dos aestimata. See AESTIMATIO DOTIS.

Dos fundi. See INSTRUMENTUM FUNDI.

Dos profecticia. A dowry given by the father of the bride or wife (*a patre profecta*). When the wife died before the husband, the father might claim the dowry back, but the husband was entitled to keep one fifth thereof for each child. Ant. DOS ADVENTICIA.

Dos recepticia. A dowry which after the death of the wife was to be returned to the person who had given it, according to a stipulatory promise of the receiver.

Solazzi, *SDHI* 5 (1939) 223.

Dositheanum fragmentum. See FRAGMENTUM DOSITHEANUM.

Dotalis. See FUNDUS DOTALIS, INSTRUMENTUM DOTALE, PACTA DOTALIA, IMPENSAE DOTALES, RETENTIONES DOTALES.

Dotare. To give a dowry. It was a moral duty of the head of a family to bestow a dowry upon his daughter (or granddaughter). To enter a marriage without a dowry (*indotata*) was considered humiliating to the woman. Clients (*clientes*) used to endow the daughter of their patron with a dowry. Justinian speaks explicitly of ancient laws which held the assignment of a dowry a *paternum officium*. Under his legislation it became a legal duty of the father and under certain circumstances also of the mother.— See FAVOR DOTIS.

> G. Castelli, *Intorno all'origine dell'obbligo di d., BIDR* 26 (1913, 164 = *Scritti*, 1923).

Dotis causa. As a dowry, in order to assign a dowry.

Dotis dictio. See DICTIO DOTIS.

Duae partes. Two-thirds. The presence of this majority of members of the municipal council (*ordo decurionum*) was required for the validity of its decisions.

Dubitare (dubitatio). To doubt. Various locutions with *dubitare* refer to controversial legal problems (*dubitationis est, dubitationem recipit*). Justinian calls attention to some controversial discussions of the classical jurists by using the phrase *apud veteres dubitatum est.*—See IUS CONTROVERSUM.

> A. B. Schwarz, *ZSS* 69 (1952) 349.

Dubius. See RES DUBIAE, PROCUL DUBIO.—D. 34.5.

Ducator navis. See GUBERNATOR NAVIS, MAGISTER NAVIS.

Ducatus. The rank of a DUX.

Ducenarius. An imperial official with a salary of 200.000 sesterces. See CENTENARIUS.

> Vulic, *DE* 2.

Ducentesima. (*Sc. usura.*) See CENTESIMA.

Ducere aquam. See AQUAE DUCTUS, SERVITUS AQUAEDUCTUS.

Ducere liberos. See INTERDICTUM DE LIBERIS EXHIBENDIS.

Ducere uxorem. To marry a woman. *Ducere in domum suam,* see DEDUCTIO IN DOMUM. For the *interdictum de uxore ducenda,* see INTERDICTUM DE LIBERIS EXHIBENDIS.

Duci (ferri) iubere. If the defendant in an *actio in rem* (a *rei vindicatio, for instance*) for a movable refused to "enter" the trial (to cooperate in the *litis contestatio*), the praetor might order that the thing in dispute be taken (*ferri*) by the plaintiff, or when the object of the controversy was a slave, that he be led off (*duci*). This was also the case when, sued for his slave's wrongdoing by an *actio noxalis,* the master refused to defend the slave. *Duci* or *ferri iubere* might be pronounced by the praetor when the thing or the slave was present before court. If the defendant denied having the thing (or the slave) in his possession, an *actio ad exhibendum* lay against him which he could not evade, this action being an *actio in personam. Duci iubere* also occurred when the defendant in a civil trial had been condemned (*con-*

demnatus), and refused to defend himself in a trial for the execution of the judgment (*actio iudicati*) and to pay the judgment-debt: the creditor was authorized by the praetor to "lead away" (*ducere*) the debtor.

> Leonhard, *RE* 4, 2244; Humbert, *DS* 2 (*s.v. debitoris ductio*); Pissard, *Ét Girard* (1912) 241. ___

Duciani. The retinue of a *dux; ducianus* (adj.) connected with office of a *dux.*

Dumtaxat. (In the procedural formula.) See CONDEMNATIO, TAXATIO.

Duo (or plures) rei promittendi. Two or more debtors owing the same sum as a whole (*in solidum*). Through the payment made by one of them the obligation of the other (or others) is extinguished. Syn. *correi.* Ant. *duo rei stipulandi* = two or more creditors to whom one debtor owes the same sum. Payment made to one of the creditors releases the debtor from his obligation to others. In such obligations for which modern terminology created the terms "correality" and "solidarity," one object (*una res, eadem pecunia*) is due, but there is a plurality of debtors or creditors. Obligatory relations *in solidum* arise through a *stipulatio* when in the case of a plurality of creditors the debtor gives only one answer to identical questions of all creditors, or when in the case of several debtors all of them give the same answer to the creditor's question. The characteristic feature of such obligations is "the whole is due to every one of the creditors, and every debtor is liable to the whole" (D. 45.2.2). Certain other acts, which generally produce the extinction of an obligation (e.g., *acceptilatio, novatio*), have an effect similar to that of a payment. If, however, one of the debtors is freed from his obligation owing to a personal reason (*capitis deminutio, confusio*) the other debtors are not released. Similarly a concession granted by the common creditor to one of the debtors (a *pactum de non petendo,* for instance) does not exclude the action against the others. The classical rule that a suit brought against one of the debtors and conducted until *litis contestatio* extinguished the obligation of the other debtors was abolished by Justinian. He permitted the creditor to sue one debtor after another until he received full payment. The question as to the rights of a debtor who paid the whole, against his co-debtors, or of a creditor against that of the creditors who received the full payment, depends upon the internal relation among the debtors or creditors, respectively.—Inst. 3.16; D. 45.2; C. 8.39.—See BENEFICIUM DIVISIONIS, BENEFICIUM CEDENDARUM ACTIONUM.

> Leonhard, *RE* 4 (*s.v. duo rei*); J. Kerr Wylie, *St in R Law, 1. Solidarity and correality,* Edinburgh, 1923; Bonfante, *Scritti* 3 (1926) 209, 368, 4 (1925) 568; Cuq, *Mél Cornil* 1 (1926); Collinet, *St Albertoni* 1 (1935); Grosso, *StSas* 16 (1938) 3; idem, *RDCom* 38 (1940) 224; Albertario, *St Besta* 1 (1939) 3; idem, *St Calisse,* 1939; idem, *Obbligazioni solidali (Corso),* 1944; idem, *Fschr Wenger* 1 (1944) 83; M. Lucifredi Peterlongo, *Intorno all'unità*

o pluralità di vincoli nella solidarietà contrattuale, 1941 (Bibl. p. 1); Archi, *ConfCast*, 1940, 241; *idem*, *SDHI* 8 (1942) 199; *idem*, *Obbligazioni solidali* (*Corso*), 1949.

Duodecim tabulae. See LEX DUODECIM TABULARUM.

Duovirales (duoviralicii). Persons who in a colony or *municipium* occupied the post of a *duovir*.

Duoviratus (duumviratus). The office of a *duovir*.

Duoviri (duumviri). Local magistrates in Rome, Italy and the provinces with varied functions. The principle of collegiality was observed in this magistracy too, since there were always two *duoviri* at least. —See DECURIONES, and the following items.

Liebenam, *RE* 5; Humbert, *DS* 2; Anon., *NDI* 5; Antonielli, *DE* 2.

Duoviri aedi dedicandae. Extraordinary magistrates who according to a decree of the senate, had to perform the dedication of a public area to a deity for the construction of a temple, or the dedication of a temple already constructed. A person who as a magistrate erected a temple at his own expenses might be later appointed a *duovir aedi dedicandae* in order to dedicate it when he was no longer in office.

Liebenam, *RE* 5, 1801; De Ruggiero, *DE* 1, 165.

Duoviri aedi locandae. Two magistrates appointed for the construction of a temple, if the matter was not managed by a higher magistrate (a consul, praetor, or censor). Sometimes they were identical with the *duoviri aedae dedicandae*.

Liebenam, *RE* 5, 1802.

Duoviri aediles. Two municipal officials with functions similar to those of the *aediles* in Rome. They had the right to impose fines.—See MULTA.

Kubitschek, *RE* 1, 460; De Ruggiero, *DE* 1, 244.

Duoviri iuri dicundo. Heads of the municipal administration and the highest judicial magistrates in Italian and provincial cities. Together with the DUOVIRI AEDILES they formed a board of four officials (*quattuorviri*). Several local statutes (*Lex Malacitana, Lex Rubria, Lex Iulia Municipalis, Lex Coloniae Genetivae Iuliae*) deal with the official activities of the *duoviri iuri dicundo*. They were elected by the local assemblies for one year. Each of them could exercise the right of INTERCESSIO against the other's acts. It often happened that the emperor was elected as a *duovir*; in that case another *duovir* was not elected and the emperor appointed in his place a *praefectus*. The functions of a *duovir* were similar to those of the consuls and praetors in Rome, with certain restrictions in the jurisdictional field, both civil and criminal.

Liebenam, *RE* 5, 1804; Kübler, *RE* 4, 2339.

Duoviri navales. Instituted in 311 B.C., they took care of the needs of the fleet and commanded a patrol for the defense of the coast.

Fiebiger, *RE* 5, 1800.

Duoviri perduellionis. In the time of the kingship they were appointed by the king to try cases of *perduellio* (high treason) when such crimes occurred. Under the Republic the consuls continued to appoint them (they are mentioned last in 63 B.C.) although since the middle of the third century B.C. the plebeian tribunes took cases of *perduellio* under their jurisdiction.

Liebenam, *RE* 5, 1799.

Duoviri quinquennales. Duoviri in municipalities and colonies, elected once in five years and charged with the census of the population.

Duoviri sacris faciundis. Priests, originally two (under the kings, later ten, *decemviri sacris faciundis*, and fifteen, *quindecimviri sacris faciundis*) whose particular function was to take care of, and interpret the Sibilline books of oracles (*libri Sibyllini*).— See LUDI SAECULARES.

Bloch, *DS* 2, 426; Boyce, *TAmPhilolAs* 69 (1938) 161.

Duoviri viis extra urbem purgandis. Lower magistrates charged with the maintenance of the roads outside of Rome. They belonged to the group of VIGINTISEXVIRI and were subordinate to the *aediles*.

Duplae (*sc.* pecuniae) **stipulatio.** See STIPULATIO DUPLAE.

Duplex dominium. See DOMINIUM DUPLEX.

Duplex iudicium. See IUDICIA DUPLICIA.

Duplicatio. See REPLICATIO. There is a confusion of terminology in the sources. What Gaius calls *duplicatio* (an objection made by the defendant to the plaintiff's *replicatio*) is called by Ulpian *triplicatio* which, however, to Gaius is the plaintiff's objection to the *duplicatio* of the defendant.

Duploma. See DIPLOMA.

Duplum. Double. *Actiones in duplum* = actions in which the defendant is condemned to pay double damages or price paid by the plaintiff when he purchased the object in dispute.—See ACTIONES IN SIMPLUM, INFITIATIO, REVOCATIO IN DUPLUM, STIPULATIO DUPLAE, USURAE ULTRA DUPLUM.

Dupondii. Students "of two asses"; a frivolous nickname given by advanced students to those of the first year (freshmen) of legal studies, because of their poor preparation in law.—See IUSTINIANI NOVI.

Cantarelli, *RendLinc*, ser. 6, vol. 2 (1926) 20; Kretschmar, *ZSS* 48 (1928) 559.

Dupondius (dupundius). Two asses. With regard to heirs instituted in a testament the term refers to the following case: if the testator exhausted the whole estate by distributing it among certain heirs and instituted besides them other heirs to some portions of the estate, the estate is reckoned not as one as (see AS) but as two asses, the former group receiving one-half of the inheritance, the latter group the second half.

Duumviri. See DUOVIRI.

Dux (duces). The head of a military district in the later Empire when the military power was taken from the provincial governors and transferred to the *duces*. They were commanders of a larger military unit on the frontiers of the Empire (*duces limitum*).—See DUCIANI, DUCATUS.

Seeck, *RE* 5; Vulic, *DE* 2; R. Grosse, *Röm. Militärgesetze*, 1920, 152.

E

Ea res agatur. "This shall be the object of the trial," an introductory clause in the part of the procedural formula called *praescriptio.*—See PRAESCRIPTIO.

Wlassak, *Mél Girard* 2 (1912) 615.

Eadem res. The same thing. The term is discussed by the jurists with regard to the rule: *bis de eadem re ne sit actio,* which excludes a second trial for the same claim. See BIS IDEM EXIGERE. Syn. *idem.;* ant. *alia res.*—See CONCURRERE.

E. Levy, *Konkurrenz der Aktionen* 1 (1918) 78; Cornil, *St Bonfante* 3 (1930) 45.

Ebrietas. Drunkenness. For crimes committed by drunken persons, see IMPETUS.

Ecclesia. The church both as a building and as the religious Christian community. The recognition of the Christian Church by Constantine was followed by a gradual recognition of Church property. Churches could be instituted as heirs and receive gifts under a will. Justinian admitted also monasteries and foundations for charitable purposes (*piae causae*) to property. He extended the time for *usucapio* to the detriment of ecclesiastic property to forty years. Testamentary gifts made to Christ, to an archangel or a martyr were considered to be in favor of the local church, or that dedicated to that archangel or martyr respectively.—C. 1.2; 12.—See CHRISTIANI, EPISCOPUS, OECONOMUS ECCLESIAE, PIAE CAUSAE, MINISTER, CONFUGERE AD ECCLESIAM.

G. Pfannmüller, *Die kirchliche Gesetzgebung Justinians,* 1902; W. K. Boyd, *The Ecclesiastical Edicts of the Theodosian Code,* New York, 1905; A. Knecht, *System des justinianischen Vermögensrechts,* 1905; A. S. Alivisatos, *Die kirchliche Gesetzgebung Justinians,* 1913; Roberti, *St Zanzucchi,* 1927, 89; Savagnone, *Studi sul dir. rom. ecclesiastico, AnPal* 14 (1930); Steinwenter, *ZSS, KanAbt* 50 (1930); P. G. Smith, *The Church in the Rom. Empire,* 1932; G. Krüger, *Die Rechtsstellung der vorjustinianischen Kirche,* 1935; P. W. Duff, *Personality in R. Law,* 1938, 174; G. Ferrari dalle Spade, *Immunità ecclesiastiche, AVen* 99 (1939–1940); G. Bovini, *La proprietà ecclesiastica la condizione giuridica della Chiesa,* 1949; Le Clercq, *Dictionnaire de dr. canon.* 4 (1947) 654.

Ecclesiasticus. (Adj.) Connected with the Church (*res, praedia, ius, dominium, negotia, canones*).

Ecclesiasticus. (Noun.) A person employed in the administration of Church property, a Church employee.—See PRIVILEGIUM FORI.

Ecloge. (The full Greek title is *Ecloge ton nomon.*) A selection of laws. It is a Byzantine compilation of excerpts from Justinian's legislative work and constitutions of later Byzantine emperors, written in Greek, and divided into eighteen titles. The work was prepared on the initiative of the emperor Leo the Isaurian and his son, Constantine Copronymos, about the middle of the eighth century. Several private compilations followed in later centuries, composed in a similar manner, for the use of practitioners, such as *Ecloge privata, Ecloge privata aucta, Ecloge ad Prochiron mutata* (early twelfth century) in which the later legislation is taken into consideration more or less.—See PROCHEIROS NOMOS.

Editions: *Zachariae v. Lingenthal, Collectio librorum iuris Graeco-Romani ineditorum,* 1852; Momferratos, *Ecloga Leonis et Constantini,* Athens, 1889; J. and P. Zepos, *Jus Graeco-Romanum* 2 (1931, p. VII, Bibl.).—Translation into English; E. H. Freshfield, *A Manual of R. Law, The Ecloga,* Cambridge, 1926.—Collinet, *Cambr. Med. Hist.* 4 (1923) 709; Diehl, *ibid.* 5; F. Dupouy, *Le droit civil romain d'après l'Ecloga,* Thèse, Bordeaux, 1902; Siciliano-Villanueva, *Dir. bizantino,* in *Enciclopedia giuridica italiana,* 1912, 41; Spulber, *L'Ecloga des Isauriens* (Cernauti, 1929); Grummel, *Echos' d'Orient,* 34 (1935) 327; Cassimatis, *La notion du mariage dans l'Eclogue, Mnem. Pappoulia,* 1934; Ferrari, *Enciclopedia Italiana* 7 (1930) 144. *For Ecloge privata aucta:* Editions: Zachariae v. Lingenthal, *Ius Graeco-Romanum* 4 (1865); Zepoi (see above), v. 6 (1931) 7.—E. H. Freshfield, *A Revised Manual of R. Law Founded upon the Ecloga,* Cambridge, 1927.—For the *Ecloge ad Prochiron mutata,* see Zachariae v. Lingenthal, *Jus Graeco-Romanum,* 4 (1865) 49; Zepoi (see above) 6 (1931) 217; E. H. Freshfield, *A Manual of the Later R. Law. The E. ad P. m.,* edited 1166, Cambridge, 1927; De Malafosse, *Archives d'Histoire du dr. Oriental* 5 (1950).

Edere actionem, formulam, iudicium. See EDITIO ACTIONIS.

Edere librum (libellum). To publish aᵗ booklet.— See EDITIO SECUNDA, LIBELLUS FAMOSUS.

Edicere. To make known by public announcement (*publice, publicitus*). For the praetor's announcements the phrase *praetor edicit* is used. With regard to private persons *edicere* = to make a promise publicly, see INDICIUM.

Edicta Augusti ad Cyrenenses. Five edicts issued by Augustus and published in Cyrene between 7 and 4 B.C. They are preserved in an inscription discovered there in 1926. The edicts, written in Greek, deal with various matters of criminal and civil procedure (actions between Greeks should be brought before Greek judges unless the defendant preferred judges of Roman origin), with public charges (*munera*) of Roman citizens, and other matters. The fifth edict known as a senatusconsult concerning extortion (*repetundae,* of 4 B.C.), see SENATUSCONSULTUM CALVISIANUM. The Augustan edicts are of great importance because they reveal the features of the earliest imperial edicts (see EDICTA IMPERATORUM) issued for the provinces.

Steinwenter, *RE* Suppl. 5, 352; Radermacher, *Anzeiger Akad. Wien,* 1928, 69; Stroux and Wenger, *ABayAW* 34 (1928) 2. Abhandlung; v. Premerstein, *ZSS* 51 (1931, Bibl.); Riccobono, *FIR* 1² (1941) no. 68 (Bibl.); Momigliano, *OCD* 250; Last, *JRS* 1945, 93; F. De Visscher, *Les édits d'Auguste,* Louvain, 1940; *idem, Nouvelles études,* 1949, 111; Oliver, *Memoirs Amer. Acad. Rome* 19 (1949) 105.

Edicta imperatorum (principum). Edicts issued by the emperors, containing general legal norms laid down both for officials and for private citizens. The *edicta* are based on the *ius edicendi* of the emperor which resulted from his *imperium proconsulare.* Unlike the edicts of the magistrates (see EDICTA MAGIS-

TRATUUM), which had only temporary validity the *edicta imperatorum* seem to have had unlimited validity. They were issued for one or more provinces or cities and were introduced with the formula: *imperator dicit* ("the Emperor says").—See CONSTITUTIONES PRINCIPUM.—C. 1.14.

Kipp, *RE* 5, 1947; Haberleithner, *Philologus* 98 (1909) 68; E. Weiss, *St. zu röm. Rechtsquellen*, 1914, 84, 119; Wilcken, *ZSS* 42 (1922) 132; Riccobono, *FIR* 1² (1941) no. 67 ff.; Orestano, *BIDR* 44 (1937) 219.

Edicta Iustiniani. Thirteen Justinian's constitutions preserved as an appendix in one of the two manuscripts of the collection of 168 Novels of the emperor, see NOVELLAE JUSTINIANI. Only ten of them were unknown, since three (1.5.6) were preserved in the other manuscript of the same collection (as nos. 8.111.122). Externally the *edicta* do not differ from the Novels; they have been called *"edicta"* to differentiate them from the Novels proper.

Edition: in the Schoell-Kroll edition of the Novels (see NOVELLAE IUSTINIANI) pp. 759–795.

Edicta magistratuum. Edicts issued by magistrates on the basis of their *ius edicendi,* at the beginning of their term of office, and containing rules by which they would conduct their judicial activity "in order to make the citizens know what law they would apply in the jurisdiction" (D. 1.2.2.10). See IUS EDICENDI. The right to issue edicts was held by consuls, praetors, dictators, aedils, quaestors, censors, plebeian tribunes; in municipalities by *duoviri* and *quattuorviri,* in the provinces by governors. The custom of issuing edicts was also followed by the prefects in imperial times. Of greatest importance in the development of Roman law were the edicts of the praetors and aedils. The creation of the *ius honorarium* was their work. There is no doubt, however, that the real authors of most praetorian edicts were the jurists, acting in their capacity as legal advisers of the magistrates and as initiators of new forms of action and creative ideas in daily legal life.—See IUS HONORARIUM, IUS PRAETORIUM, IUS EDICENDI, EDICTUM AEDILIUM, EDICTUM PRAETORIS.

Kipp, *RE* 5; Louis-Lucas and A. Weiss, *DS* 2, 456.

Edicta praefectorum praetorio. Edicts issued in the later Empire by the *praefecti praetorio* under various names (*edicta, programmata, formae, praecepta, praeceptiones, commonitoria*). They were concerned mostly with administrative matters.

Mommsen, *Hist. Schriften,* 3 (1906) 284; Zachariae (v. Lingenthal), *Anecdota* 1 (1843) 227.

Edicta praesidum. Edicts of the provincial governors.—See EDICTUM PROVINCIALE.

E. Weiss, *Studien zu den röm. Rechtsquellen,* 1914, 71; Wilcken, *ZSS* 43 (1921) 137.

Edicta principum. See EDICTA IMPERATORUM.

Edictales. Students in the second year of law studies, called so in pre-Justinian law schools because they studied the juristic commentaries to the pretorian edict.

Kübler, *RE* 5; Humbert, *DS* 2.

Edictalis bonorum possessio. See BONORUM POSSESSIO DECRETALIS.

Edictalis lex. A term which some late emperors (from the fifth century on) and Justinian applied to their enactments when promulgating them (*"haec edictalis lex"*).

Edictum. Either the whole edict published by the magistrate on the album when he assumed his office or a single clause thereof. A magisterial edict was one year's law (*lex annua*) since the magistrate was only one year in office.—See MAGISTRATUS, EDICTA MAGISTRATUUM, EDICTUM TRALATICIUM, IUS EDICENDI, CLAUSULA, NOVA CLAUSULA.

Kipp, *RE* 5; De Ruggiero, *DE* 2; v. Schwind, *Zur Frage der Publikation* (1940) 49.

Edictum aedilium curulium (aedilicium). The edict of the *aediles* who as supervisors of the market promulgated certain rules concerning the sale of slaves and domestic animals, and the liability of the seller for defects of the object sold. The aedilian norms were later extended to sales of other things.—D. 21.1.—See EMPTIO VENDITIO, EDICTUM DE FERIS.

H. Vincent, *Le droit des édiles,* 1922; Senarclens, *TR* 4 (1923) 384; *idem, RHD* 6 (1927) 385.

Edictum Augusti de aquaeductu Venafrano. (Between 18 and 11 B.C.) An edict by Augustus concerning the aqueduct in Venafrum.

Edition: Riccobono, *FIR* 1² (1941) no. 67 (Bibl.).

Edictum breve. Not a technical term; a brief edict issued with regard to another legal provision (a statute).

H. Krüger, *ZSS* 37 (1916) 303.

Edictum Carbonianum. See BONORUM POSSESSIO EX CARBONIANO EDICTO.

Edictum censorum. Against Latin rhetoricians (92 B.C.) It is known from literary sources.

Riccobono, *FIR* 1² (1941) no. 52.

Edictum Constantini de accusationibus. (Between A.D. 313 and 317.) Concerned the accusation in criminal matters. It is epigraphically preserved.

Riccobono, *FIR* 1² (1941) no. 94 (Bibl.).

Edictum de alterutro. A section in the praetorian edict granting a widow the right to claim restitution of her dowry after the husband's death, based either on her legal right to the dowry or on the husband's testament in which such restitution was ordered.

Lenel, *Edictum*³ (1927) 308.

Edictum de appellationibus. (Preserved on a papyrus.) Deals with appeals to the emperor and settles some pertinent procedural rules. The author of the edict is unknown (Nero?).

Riccobono, *FIR* 1² (1941) no. 91.

Edictum de feris. A part of the aedilian edict concerning the liability for damages done by non domestic animals (a dog, wolf, bear, panther, lion, etc.) held by a private individual.—See FERAE.

Lenel, *Edictum*³ (1927) 566; Scialoja, *Studi* 2 (1934) 142.

Edictum de violatione sepulcrorum (of Augustus?).
See VIOLATIO SEPULCRI.

   Riccobono, *FIR* 1² (1941) no. 69 (Bibl.).

Edictum Diocletiani de pretiis. An edict of Diocletian (A.D. 301) which established ceiling prices for a long list of goods, both necessary and luxurious, as well as for services rendered by professionals, such as advocates, physicians, shippers. Penalties were imposed on the violators who sold at higher prices or who hoarded merchandise. The prices were fixed in DENARII reduced to one twenty-fourth of their original value. The Edict had little success. It was published throughout the empire and is preserved epigraphically in considerable part.

   Blümner, *RE* 5; Ensslin, *RE* 7A (1949) 2469; Mommsen, *Jur. Schriften* 2 (1905) 323; Kübler, *Gesch. des röm. R.,* 1925, 361; Mickwitz, *Geld und Wirtschaft* (Helsingfors, 1932) 70; Balogh, *ACIVer* 2 (estr. 1951) 352 (Bibl.).

Edictum Domitiani de privilegiis veteranorum. (A.D. 88/89.) Granted certain privileges to veterans. —See VETERANI.

   Riccobono, *FIR* 1² (1941) no. 76 (Bibl.).

Edictum Hadriani de vicesima hereditatium. Concerned with the tax on estates. It was abolished by Justinian.—C. 6.33.—See VICESIMA HEREDITATIUM, MISSIO IN POSSESSIONEM EX EDICTO HADRIANI.

Edictum monitorium. The jurist Callistratus wrote a treatise in six books on *"edictum monitorium,"* but the meaning of the term is not clear in spite of the score of texts preserved in the Digest.

   Kotz-Dobrz, *RE* Suppl. 3, 227; F. Schulz, *History of R. legal science,* 1946, 193 (Bibl.).

Edictum novum. See NOVA CLAUSULA.

Edictum peremptorium. An official summons addressed to a defendant who refused to appear in court, warning him that the trial would be conducted even in his absence.—See EVOCATIO.

Edictum perpetuum. An edict issued by the praetor or another magistrate at the beginning of his year of service and valid for the entire year of his being in office. Ant. *edictum repentinum* = an *edictum* issued during the year of service. For another significance of *edictum perpetuum* see the following item.

   Guarneri-Citati, *NDI* 5, 296; Pringsheim, *Symbolae Friburgenses Lenel,* 1931, 1.

Edictum perpetuum Hadriani. A revision and codification of the praetorian and aedilian edicts, made by the jurist Salvius Iulianus at the initiative of the emperor Hadrian toward the end of his reign (after A.D. 132). The final codification of the edicts provoked an abundant commentatory activity of the jurists (Pomponius, Pedius, Furius Anthianus, Callistratus, and Gaius, the latter with regard to the provincial edict). The earlier commentaries were superseded by the extensive commentaries to the Edict by Ulpian and Paul (in 81 and 80 books, respectively) which were richly exploited by Justinian's compilers of the Digest. The edictal system was followed in Justinian's Digest and Code according to an express instruction of the emperor to keep in the compilations the order of presentation as systemized in the Edict. Thanks to this arrangement a reconstruction of Hadrian's Edict in its essential outlines was possible. In this final edition the Edict gives an extensive picture of the praetorian law, primarily of procedural legal institutions, such as *editio actionis, in ius vocatio,* representatives and securities in court, *in integrum restitutio,* execution of judgments, interdicts, exceptions, the formulae of actions (partly scattered through the whole work, partly reserved for the end). With the codification of the edict the edictal activity of the praetors was practically stopped.—See EDICTUM PRAETORIS.

   The standard work: Lenel, *Edictum perpetuum,* 3rd ed. 1927, was followed by the editors of *Fontes iuris romani,* recently by Riccobono 1² (1941) no. 65, p. 335 (Bibl.); Kipp, *RE* 5, 1945; Louis-Lucas and A. Weiss, *DS* 2; De Ruggiero, *DE* 2; Guarneri-Citati, *NDI* 5, 296; Girard, *Mélanges* 1 (1912); Pringsheim, *Sym. Friburgenses Lenel,* 1932; Riccobono, *BIDR* 44 (1937) 1; A. Guarino, *Salvius Julianus,* 1946, 26; Berger, *St Albertario* 1 (1950) 605; De Francisci, *RIDA* 4 (= *Mél De Visscher* 3, 1950) 319; D'Orgeval, *RHD* 27 (1948) 301; Kaser, *Fschr Schulz* 2 (1951) 21; Guarino, *St Albertario,* 625; idem, *ACIVer* 2 (estr. 1951) 169.

Edictum praetoris. Both the *praetor urbanus* and the *praetor peregrinus* issued edicts at the beginning of their term. See IUS EDICENDI, EDICTA MAGISTRATUUM. The praetorian edicts were a decisive factor of the development of the law (see IUS PRAETORIUM). They introduced new actions (*actiones praetoriae*) in order to protect legal situations and transactions which were deprived of judicial protection under the *ius civile.* They reformed the law of succession, both testamentary and intestate. Even before the final codification of the praetorian law (see EDICTUM PERPETUUM HADRIANI) many commentaries to the praetorian edict were written (by the famous Republican jurist Servius Sulpicius Rufus, then by Ofilius, Labeo, Sabinus, Vivianus). The announcements of the praetor in the edict are formulated, in the first person through such phrases as *iudicium dabo, cogam, permittam, restituam, iubebo, servabo* ("I shall grant an action, enforce, allow, restitute, order, protect") and similar. In this way he promised in his own name to apply certain rules or measures in his jurisdictional functions without directly ordering or prohibiting a certain behavior.—See KALENDAE, LEX CORNELIA DE EDICTIS.

   Kipp, *RE* 5; Brasiello, *NDI* 5; Wlassak, *Edikt und Klageform,* 1882; F. v. Velsen, *Beiträge zur Geschichte des e. praetoris urbani,* 1909; Weiss, *Über vorjulianische Ediktsredaktionen, ZSS* 50 (1930) 249.

Edictum provinciale. An edict issued by the governor of a province, chiefly on entering office. The governor had *ius edicendi* as the magistrates in Rome. The differences between the edicts in the various provinces and the edict of the Roman praetor seem not to have been very important. Only Gaius wrote a commentary on "the provincial edict" by which we must understand a typical provincial edict and not that of a specific province. To judge from the excerpts of that commentary as preserved in the Digest, we may assume that the provisions of the provincial edicts were modeled on the edict in Rome.

F. v. Velsen, *ZSS* 21 (1900); E. Weiss, *Studien zu den röm. Rechtsquellen*, 1914, 66; 109; L. Falletti, *Évolution de la jurisdiction du magistrat provincial*, 1926, 73; Reinmuth, The prefectural edict, *Aegyptus* 18 (1938) 3; Buckland, *RHD* 13 (1934) 82; F. v. Schwind, *Zur Frage der Publikation*, 1940, 70.

Edictum repentinum. An edict issued by a magistrate exceptionally during his term on a specific occasion, whereas the normal edict was promulgated at the time he took up his duties.—See EDICTUM PERPETUUM.

Edictum successorium. The section of the praetorian edict concerning BONORUM POSSESSIO. It contained the rules about persons entitled to claim the *bonorum possessio* if the person first entitled failed to do so within the prescribed period or refused to accept the estate. Syn. *caput successorium.*—D. 38.9; C. 6.16.—See BONORUM POSSESSIO INTESTATI.

Edictum Theodorici. A collection of 154 Roman legal provisions, compiled about A.D. 500 by order of Theodoric, king of the Ostrogoths, which had to be observed by both Roman citizens and Ostrogoths. The excerpts were taken from the three Codes, *Codex Gregorianus, Hermogenianus and Theodosianus,* from some post-Theodosian Novels, and from Paul's *Sententiae.*

Brassloff, *RE* 5; Brasiello, *NDI* 5, 595; Editions: Bluhme, *Monumenta Germaniae Historica* 5 (1875) 149; Baviera, *FIR* 2² (1940) 683 (Bibl.).—Schupfer, *Atti Accad. Lincei,* Ser. 4, T. 2 (1887–1888) 223; Patetta, *ATor* 28 (1893) 553; B. Paradisi, *Storia del dir. ital.* 1951, 103.

Edictum tralaticium. The part of a praetor's edict which he adopted from his predecessor's edict.

Weiss, *ZSS* 50 (1930) 253.

Edictum Vespasiani de privilegiis medicorum. (A.D. 74.) Epigraphically preserved; it granted physicians certain personal privileges and exemption from taxes (*immunitas*) and set penalties for violation of the enactment. Among the beneficiaries of the edict were also the teachers (*paideutai = magistri, praeceptores*). Similarly, a rescript by the emperor Domitian (A.D. 93–94) against certain abuses (*avaritia = greediness*) of physicians included *praeceptores* as well.—See MEDICI.

Edition: Riccobono, *FIR* 1² (1941), nos. 73, 77 (Bibl.).—S. Riccobono, Jr., *AnPal* 17 (1937) 50.

Editio actionis. The notification by the plaintiff to the defendant of the action he wanted to bring against the latter. First it had to be done extrajudicially. This *editio* had a preparatory character to let the defendant know the matter for which, and the type of action with which, he will be sued. This offered him the opportunity of settling the controversy before it came to trial. A second *editio* followed when both the parties appeared before the praetor, the plaintiff indicating exactly the action (formula) by which he was suing his adversary. There remained a possibility of changing or amending the proposed formula.—D. 2.13; C. 2.1.—See LITIS CONTESTATIO.

Wenger, *RE* 5; Humbert, *DS* 2.

Editio instrumentorum. The introduction of written documents by the parties to a trial as evidence either of the plaintiff's claim or of the defendant's denial.—See EXHIBERE, INSTRUMENTUM.

Wenger, *RE* 5, 1966.

Editio interdicti. A preliminary act in interdictal proceedings, analogous to the EDITIO ACTIONIS, when an ordinary process was initiated. *Edere interdictum* also refers to the issuance of an interdict by the praetor.—See INTERDICTUM.

Wenger, *RE* 5, 1965.

Editio iudicum. (In criminal trials, *quaestiones.*) The selection of one hundred jurors from the panel for *quaestiones,* proposed by the accuser for the appointment of a jury in a specific trial and communicated by him to the accused. From that number the latter might select (*electio*) fifty who then made up the jury. Later, this procedure was repeatedly modified.—See QUAESTIONES.

Editio rationum. (By a banker, *argentarius.*) A banker was obliged to produce his books in a trial in which not only his own interests were involved but also when those of his clients were at stake and the entries in the banker's book might serve to clarify the legal situation.—See ARGENTARII.

Editio rescripti. Mentioned only in the Theodosian Code in connection with the summons (*denuntiatio*) in the rescript procedure. It seems to be the modification of an imperial rescript to the adversary.

Andt, *La procédure par rescrit,* 1920, 13, 57; Fliniaux, *RHD* 9 (1930) 201.

Editio secunda. The second edition of a book. Second editions of juristic writings are mentioned by Justinian (*Cordi* 3) with the remark that in earlier times they were called *repetita praelectio.* A second edition of a monograph by Paul is noted in a later source (*Frag. Vat.* 247). There is no doubt that that some jurists have themselves prepared second editions. On the other hand we know that a few first editions (*editio prima*) of juristic works were reedited by other classical jurists, usually with a commentary or loose remarks (NOTAE). There is, however, a tendency in the recent Romanistic literature to ascribe to early postclassical times (end of the third and the first decades of the fourth century) a very vivid activity in anonymous reediting of classical juristic works which even if perhaps acceptable in very few instances, hardly can be proved and seems very unlikely when assumed to such extent as has been by some writers.

F. Schulz, *History of R. legal science,* 1946, 141, and *passim*; G. Riccobono, *Lineamenti della storia delle fonti,*

1949, 208; Berger, *Clas Journ* 43 (1948) 440; Sciascia, *BIDR* 49–50 (1947) 431; H. J. Wolff, *Scritti Ferrini* 4 (Univ. Sacro Cuore, Milan, 1949) 64; *idem, Roman Law* (Oklahoma, 1951) 130; *idem, Fschr Schulz* 2 (1951) 145; Wieacker, *ZSS* 67 (1950) 387; Berger, *Sem* 10 (1952) 95.

Educare (educatio). To educate, to rear, to bring up. The sources deal with *educare* with reference to wards (*pupilli*) being under the tutelage of guardians. The term is understood in a broader sense comprising not only the care for mental development but also nourishment and the necessities of physical development. Supervision of the pertinent duties of the guardians was exercised by the tutelary authorities.—D. 27.2; C. 5.49.—See TUTELA.

Effectus. The result, consequence of a legal transaction or of a trial. The term often appears in interpolated texts.

Volterra, *St Ratti,* 1933, 440; Guarneri-Citati, *Indice*² (1927) 32; *idem, Fschr Koschaker* 1 (1939) 133.

Efficax. Legally valid, efficient.

Effractor. (From *effringere.*) A burglar.—D. 47.18. —See CUSTOS.

Effusa. What has been poured out from a dwelling.—D. 9.3.—See ACTIO DE DEIECTIS ET EFFUSIS.

Egestas. Poverty, indigence. It served as a basis for exemption from certain duties (guardianship, public charges, and the like). It could also be the cause of the dissolution of a partnership.

Albertario, *Studi* 5 (1937) 435.

Egredi. To surpass, exceed, for instance, the terms fixed in an agreement (e.g., a mandate); with reference to the *condemnatio* in the procedural formula = to go beyond the limits fixed therein.

Egregiatus. The dignity of a *vir egregius.*—See the following item.

Egregius vir. The honorary title of an imperial *procurator* of equestrian rank.

Seeck, *RE* 5; O. Hirschfeld, *Kleine Schriften*, 1913, 652.

Eierare iudicem. See FERRE IUDICEM.

Eiuratio. A declaration made by a magistrate under oath at the end of his term to the effect that during his service he had observed the laws. *Eiuratio magistratus* = the renuntiation of a magistracy.

Neumann, *RE* 1, 25; Kübler, *RE* 14, 416; Staedler, *ZSS* 61 (1941) 81.

Eiusmodi. Of such a kind. Syn. *huiusmodi*. The latter word is preferred by Justinian in his constitutions, where it appears several hundred times while *eiusmodi* is used by him only once. *Huiusmodi* is, therefore, considered as a criterion of interpolation.

Guarneri-Citati, *Indice*² (1927) 44.

Electio. The right of the debtor to choose among the alternative things he owes if such a right was reserved to him in the pertinent agreement. Similarly, the creditor (or a legatee) might have been entitled to make the choice among alternative things owed (or bequeathed) to him.—D. 33.5.—See OPTIO, LEGATUM OPTIONIS.

Grosso, *RDCom* 38 (1940) 225.

Electio iudicum. See EDITIO IUDICUM.

Electio legata. See LEGATUM OPTIONIS.

Eleganter. In a correct, fine manner. The term is applied to express approval of another jurist's opinion with emphasis on the legal idea or doctrine rather than the style. It is a favorite expression of Ulpian's. Ant. *ineleganter.*

Radin, *LQR* 46 (1930) 311; Schulz, *History of R. legal science,* 1946, 335; Sciascia, *BIDR* 51–52 (1948) 372.

Elementa. Justinian called his Institutes *"Institutiones sive elementa"* and in the introductory constitution by which the work was promulgated (*Imperatoriam,* c. 4) he denotes the work as "the first elements of the whole of legal science (*totius legitimae scientiae prima elementa*)."

Elidere. In a civil trial, to repel the plaintiff's claim by an *exceptio* (*exceptione*) or the defendant's exception by a REPLICATIO.

Elocare. To let out, to lease.—See LOCATIO CONDUCTIO.

Elogium. An additional clause. *Elogium* is a testamentary clause, particularly when someone is disinherited. For *elogium* in the aedilian edict, see IUMENTUM. In criminal affairs *elogium* is the report transmitted to the competent military or civil authority about a criminal who has been arrested and questioned by the official who seized him.

Lafaye, *DS* 2; Braschi, *DE* 2.

Elogium ultimum. A testament.

Elugere virum. To mourn the husband.—See LUCTUS.

Emancipatio. The voluntary release of a son or daughter from paternal power by the father. Following a rule established by the Twelve Tables, "if a father sold his son three times, the son shall be free from his father" (Gaius, Inst. 1.132; Epit. Ulp. 10.1), a man would sell his son through *mancipatio* to a reliable person under fiduciary agreement that the latter would manumit him three times. Only after the third manumission did the son become free from paternal power because after each of the first two he returned to the *patria potestas*. Alternatively, the trustee could remancipate the son directly to the father; after the third *remancipatio,* the son did not come under *patria potestas* but became the father's *persona in mancipio* (see MANCIPIUM) to be freed by him through a simple *manumissio.* A third *remancipatio* by the trustee was necessary, because otherwise the trustee would have acquired certain rights of succession and of guardianship over the son which were generally not intended by the parties involved. With regard to daughters and grandsons, one *mancipatio* by the head of the family sufficed. The emancipated member leaves the family and becomes a head of a family himself. In Justinian's law, *emancipatio* is performed by a simple declaration before a competent official.—D. 1.7; C. 4.13; 8.48.— See DIVORTIUM, LEX ANASTASIANA, FIDUCIA REMANCIPATIONIS CAUSA, INGRATUS, PARENS MANUMISSOR.

Leonhard, *RE* 5; Kreller, *RE* 184, 1456; Baudry, *DS* 2;

Anon., *NDI* 5; Berger, *OCD*; Moriaud, *La simple famille paternelle*, 1910, 14; Mitteis, *Lat. Emancipationsurkunde, Festschrift Lauhn* (Univ. Leipzig, 1911); Solazzi, *AG* 86 (1921) 168; H. Lévy-Bruhl, *Novelles études* (1947) 80.

Emansio. See EMANSOR.

Emansor. A soldier who is absent without leave or who exceeds his furlough, but who intends to return to his unit unlike a deserter who quits for good or is absent for a longer time. Punishment for *emansio* depended upon the reason for the absence. In certain cases (illness, affection for parents and relatives, pursuit of a fugitive slave) the culprit was pardoned. Syn. *remansor.*

Emblemata Triboniani. A term used in Romanistic literature for interpolations by Justinian's compilers in texts taken from juristic writings of the classical period or in imperial constitutions.—See DIGESTA, TRIBONIANUS, GLOSSAE.

For bibl. see General Bibliography, ch. XIII.

Emendare. To correct, amend. It refers to legal reforms by which earlier law was improved, in particular to the activity of the praetors in this regard. —Syn. *corrigere.*

Emendare moram. See MORA.

Emendatio. A punishment, chastisement, especially correction administered by a father on the strength of his paternal power (*emendatio domestica*) or by a master to his slaves. See CORRECTIO. Imperial legislation of the fourth century restricted the formerly unlimited power of the father and master.—C. 9.14; 15.—See IUS VITAE NECISQUE.

Emere. See EMPTIO.

Emeritum. The pension of a soldier who had served out his time (*emeritus, veteranus*).

Emeritus. See the foregoing item. Syn. VETERANUS.
Lacour-Gayet, *DS* 2.

Eminentia. See EMINENTISSIMUS VIR.

Eminentissimus vir. An honorary title of the *praefectus praetorio,* and in third century after Christ also of the *praefectus vigilum.* The office of the *praefectus praetorio* is addressed by the emperor with the attribute *eminentia.*

Emittere. (With regard to written documents.) To write down and sign a document (*instrumentum, cautionem*) or a letter (*epistulam, litteras*) in which the writer makes a legally important statement.

Emittere rescriptum. To issue a rescript.

Emolumentum. An advantage, profit, primarily with regard to successional benefits (inheritance, legacies, *collatio,* Falcidian quarter). The term is common in the language of the imperial chancery and in Justinian's constitutions.

Emphyteusis. Long-term lease of an imperial domain or of private land for a rental in kind. The forerunner of this institution was the *ius in agro vectigali.* The *emphyteusis* gave the lease-holder (= *emphyteuta*) rights similar to those of a proprietor, although the real owner remained the person to whom the rent (*canon, pensio*) was paid. Under certain circumstances, the land returned to the owner (as in the case of the death of the *emphyteuta* without an heir, non-payment of the rent or taxes for three years, lapse of time if a term was fixed in the original agreement, *contractus emphyteuseos,* which was a specific contract and neither an ordinary lease nor a sale. The rights of the *emphyteuta* (*ius emphyteuticarium*) embraced the full use of the land and its products; they were alienable and transferable by testament or *ab intestato.*—C. 4.66; 11.63.—See AGER VECTIGALIS, IUS IN AGRO VECTIGALI, CANON.

Berger, *OCD* 314; Mitteis, *ASächsGW* 22 (1901); Macchioro, *AG* 75 (1905) 148; G. Baviera, *Scr giuridici* 1 (1909) 189; P. Bonfante, *Scr. giur.* 3 (1924) 141; W. Kamps, *Recueils de la Société J. Bodin,* 3 (1938) 67; Johnston, *Univ. Toronto LJ* 3 (1940) 323; A. Hajje, *Études sur la location à long terme,* 1926; E. Levy, *West Roman Vulgar Law,* 1951, 43, 90; S. O. Cascio, *AnPal* 22 (1951) 1.

Emphyteuta. See the foregoing item.

Emphyteuticarius (emphyteuticus). Encumbered (*ager fundus, praedium*) or connected with *emphyteusis (contractus, ius, canon).*

Emptio venditio. A purchase and sale, i.e., a contract by which a thing is exchanged for money. The terminology *emptio venditio* indicates the two elements of the contract: an *emere* by the buyer (*emptor*) and a *vendere* by the seller (*venditor*). The Roman sale was a consensual contract concluded when the parties by simple consent (*nudo consensu*) agreed upon the thing to be sold and the price (*pretium*) to be paid therefor, without further formality. The sale contract itself did not transfer ownership of the thing sold to the buyer. To accomplish that another legal act was necessary (*mancipatio, in iure cessio, traditio*). The vendor had only to hand over the thing to the buyer to make the latter possess and enjoy it peacefully (*ut rem emptori habere liceat*). The buyer had to pay the price in money, either immediately or later, according to the agreement. The exchange of one thing for another is not a sale, but a PERMUTATIO. Any thing may be the object of a sale (*merx*) except things excluded from private transactions (*res cuius commercium non est*). Non-corporeal things (a servitude, an usufruct) may be sold, as well as future things (see EMPTIO SPEI, EMPTIO REI SPERATAE). The price must be fixed in an unequivocal way (*pretium certum*) and be real, i.e., corresponding to the true value of the thing (*verum*), not fictitious (e.g., as a device to cover a prohibited donation). Sale was a contract *bonae fidei;* the pertinent actions were *actio venditi* (*ex vendito*) against the buyer for payment of the price and *actio empti* (*ex empto*) against the seller if he did not fulfill his obligations, failed to deliver the thing sold, for example, or to take care of it (*custodia*) in the period between the conclusion of the sale and delivery so that the thing perished or deteriorated. The seller was not liable for accident (*casus*). See PERICULUM REI VENDITAE. Special rules settled the liability of the vendor when the buyer was later evicted from the thing by a third person. See EVICTIO, STIPULATIO DUPLAE. Warranty against hidden defects in the thing sold was originally stipulated expressly by the seller; besides, the *actio empti,* as a *bonae fidei actio,* gave the opportunity to take into consideration defects fraudulently concealed by the seller. The edict of the *aediles curules,* as the supervisors of the markets established particular provisions for the sale of slaves and domestic animals. Above all, the seller had to inform the buyer of any defect or disease that was not apparent to the buyer. He was liable for all allegations (DICTA ET PROMISSA) he may have made about special qualities of the slave or animal or the lack of secret defects (even those unknown to himself). Two actions lay against him, either the *actio redhibitoria* for the rescission of the sale (the seller being obliged to return the price and the buyer to restore the thing with accessories) or the *actio quanti minoris* (named also *aestimatoria*) by which the buyer claimed restitution of a portion of the price paid, corresponding to the lesser value. The principles of the aedilian edict were later extended to all kinds of sale. Throughout the classical period no written document was required for the validity of a sale contract. When made, it served only for purposes of evidence. Justinian ordered some formalities for written sales, when according to the will of the parties, the written form was a requirement for the validity of the sale (*instrumentum emptionis, instrumentum emptionale*). Until the formalities were accomplished, with the assistance of a notary (*tabellio*), the parties could rescind the sale. Many reforms in the law of sale were introduced by Justinian.—Inst. 3.23; D. 18.1; 18.5; 19.1; C. 4.38; 40; 44; 45; 49; 54; 58.—See ACTIO DE MODO AGRI, ADDICTIO IN DIEM, ARRA, COMMISSORIA LEX, COMMODUM, EDICTUM AEDILIUM, EXCEPTIO REI VENDITAE, PACTUM DE RETROVENDENDO, PACTUM DISPLICENTIAE, PERFECTUS, PRETIUM, PERICULUM REI VENDITAE, VENDITIO, LAESIO ENORMIS, USUCAPIO PRO EMPTORE, REDHIBITIO, SIMPLARIA VENDITIO, VACUA POSSESSIO.

Leonhard, *RE* 5; Humbert, *DS* 2; Lécrivain, *DS* 4, 517 (*s.v. redhibitoria*); Pugliese, *NDI* 5 (*s.v. emptio*); Biondi, *NDI* 12, 880 (*s.v. vendita*); De Medio, *BIDR* 16 (1904) 5; Lusignani, *La responsabilità per custodia* 2 (1905); J. Mackintosh, *The Law of sale,* 2nd ed. 1907; E. Rabel, *Haftung des Verkäufers wegen Mangels im Recht,* 1912; F. Pringsheim, *Kauf mit fremdem Geld,* 1916; H. Vincent, *Le droit des édiles,* 1922; Ferrini, *Opere* 3 (1929) 49; R. Monier, *Mél Cornil* 2 (1926) 137; *idem, La garantie contre les vices cachés,* 1930; Pringsheim, *ZSS* 50 (1930); Meylan, *St Bonfante* 1 (1930); G. Longo, *ibid.* 3 (1930) 363; Senarclens, *ibid.* 91; Buckland, *LQR* 48 (1932) 217; Albertario, *Studi* 3 (1936) 401; Marianne Bussmann, *L'obligation de délivrance du vendeur,* 1933; Pringsheim, *ZSS* 53 (1933) 491; Flume, *ZSS* 54 (1934) 328; Beseler, *ACII* 1 (1935) 335; G. G. Archi, *Il trasferimento della proprietà nella compravendita romana,* 1934; Meylan, *St Riccobono* 4 (1936) 279; Biondi, *ibid.* 90; Pringsheim, *ibid.* 313; Haymann, *ibid.* 341; S. Romano, *AnPer* 10

(1934); *idem, Nuovi studi sul trasferimento della proprietà nella compravendita,* 1937; Meylan, *La vente, Annales de droit et de sciences polit. de Louvain,* 1938, 447; C. Longo, *BIDR* 45 (1938); Arnò, *ATor* 74 (1939) 570; Scarlata-Fazio, *RISG* 1939, 216; v. Lübtow, *Fschr Koschaker* 2 (1939) 113; Arangio-Ruiz, *ibid.* 141; F. De Zulueta, *The Roman Law of Sale,* 1945; Pflüger, *ZSS* 65 (1947) 205; Roussier, *Novation de l'obligation du vendeur, RHD* 1948, 189; W. Flume, *Eigenschaftsirrtum und Kauf,* 1948; Meylan, *Scr Ferrini* 4 (Univ. Sacro Cuore, Milan, 1949) 176; Coing, *Sem* 8 (1950) 6; Pezzana, *AG* 140 (1951) 53; E. Levy, *West Roman Vulgar Law,* 1951, 127; Pringsheim, *Actio quanti minoris, ZSS* 69 (1952) 234; V. Arangio-Ruiz, *La compravendita in dir. rom.* 1 (*Lezioni*) 1952.

Emptio ab invito. Used of an act of a magistrate by which an individual is compelled to sell his land to the state for the sake of public utility (construction of an aqueduct or a road) in return for a reasonable compensation. The term "expropriation" is unknown in juristic Latin.—See PUBLICATIO.

Jones, *Expropriation in R. law, LQR* 45 (1929); F. M. De Robertis, *La espropriazione per pubblica utilità,* 1936; U. Niccolini, *La proprietà, il principe e l'espropriazione,* 1940; Brasiello, *BIDR* 44 (1937) 475; *idem, Estensione e limiti della proprietà* (Corso, 1941) 58; De Robertis, *AnBari* 7–8 (1947) 153.

Emptio bonorum. See BONORUM EMPTIO.

Emptio familiae. See FAMILIAE EMPTOR.

Emptio hereditatis. The inheritance of a living person or a non-existent person could not be the object of a sale unlike the inheritance of a deceased person. Antoninus Pius granted the buyer of an inheritance an *actio utilis* against the debtors of the inheritance.—D. 18.4; C. 4.39.

Vassalli, *Miscellanea critica* 1 (1913); Cugia, *St Besta* 1 (1939) 514.

Emptio rei speratae. The sale of a thing which is expected to come into existence in the future (the sale of a crop, an unborn child of a slave = *partus ancillae*). The sale becomes void if the expected thing does not materialize.

F. De Visscher, *Vente des choses futures,* 1914.

Emptio spei. A sale of a future thing while it is quite uncertain whether it will come into existence at all (*ipsum incertum rei* is the object of the transaction), e.g., fish to be caught by a fisherman in his next catch. In such a sale, the buyer takes the full risk and the price has to be paid even if no fish are caught.—See IACTUS RETIS.

Brasiello, *NDI* 5; Vassalli, *AnPer* 1913 (*Miscellanea* 1); F. De Visscher, *Vente des choses futures,* 1914; Bartošek, *RIDA* 2 (= *Mél De Visscher* 1, 1949) 50.

Emptio sub hasta. See SUBHASTATIO, VENDITIO SUB HASTA.

Emptionale instrumentum. A written deed of sale.—See EMPTIO.

Emptor bonae fidei. A buyer of a thing who did not know that "the thing belonged to another (than the seller) or believed that the seller was entitled to sell it" (D. 50.16.109), for instance, as a guardian or curator or representative of the real owner.

Emptor bonorum. See BONORUM EMPTIO.

Emptor familiae. See FAMILIAE EMPTOR.

Enantiophanes. See ANONYMUS.

Enchiridium (enchiridion). An elementary handbook. A juristic writing so entitled appears in the Digest under the name of Pomponius. A long excerpt thereof containing a concise outline of legal history and a survey of jurisprudence until Julian is preserved (not free from later alterations) as frag. 2 in the title of the Digest 1.2 "on the origin of the law, all magistrates and the sequence (*successio*) of the jurists."

> Berger, *RE* 4A, 1907; Ebrard, *ZSS* 46 (1925) 117; Felgenträger, *Symb. Friburgenses Lenel* (1932) 369; Kretschmar, *ZSS* 59 (1939) 166; Schulz, *History of R. Legal Science*, 1946, 168; Guarino, *RIDA* 2 (= *Mél De Visscher* 1, 1949) 402; Weiss, *ZSS* 67 (1950) 503.

Enucleatum ius (antiquum). Law taken from older writings. Justinian calls the law collected in the Digest and in his Institutes by this term.

> Ebrard, *RIDA* 3 (= *Mél De Visscher* 2, 1949) 253.

Epanagoge (tou nomou). A collection of legal norms written between A.D. 879 and 886 at the initiative of the Byzantine emperor Basil the Macedonian but not officially published. The compilation, built up primarily on Justinian's codification, was to lead to an achievement similar to that of the BASILICA a few decades later. A similar compilation called *Epanagoge aucta* belongs to the tenth century.

> Editions: Zachariae, *Collectio librorum iuris Graeco-Romani ineditorum*, 1852; J. and P. Zepos, *Jus Gr.-Rom.* 3 (Athens, 1931) p. 23 (Bibl., p. XIV).—For *E. aucta: Zachariae v. Lingenthal, Ius Gr.-Rom.* 4 (1865) 171; J. and P. Zepos, *Ius Gr.-Rom.* 6 (1931) 49; De Malafosse, *Dictionnaire de dr. canonique* 5 (1951) 354.

Epidemetica. See METATUM.—C. 12.40.

Episcopalis audientia. The jurisdiction of bishops insofar as it was recognized by the State. Originally limited to spiritual matters and disputes among ecclesiastics, though also practiced by the bishops with regard to laymen in the capacity of arbitrators, it was later extended to controversies among laymen in various instances, operating concurrently with state courts. Fluctuating imperial legislation limited or increased the jurisdictional competence of the bishops until the whole matter was settled by Justinian.—C. 1.4; Nov. 123.

> Piacentini, *NDI* 1, 1154; Humbert, *DS* 2; Steinwenter, *RAC* 1; Siciliano-Villanueva, *Byzantion* 1 (1924) 139; Lammeyer, *Aeg* 13 (1933) 193; Volterra, *BIDR* 42 (1934) 453; G. Vismara, *E. a.* 1937 (Milan); Steinwenter, *Byzantinische Zeitschrift* 30 (1930) 660; Masi, *AG* 122 (1939) 86; Busek, *ACII* 1 (1934) 451; idem, *ZSS Kan. Abt.* 28 (1939) 453; Arangio-Ruiz, *FIR* 3 (1943) no. 183; Volterra, *SDHI* 13–14 (1948) 353.

Episcopus. A bishop. He had full control and administration of Church property, including the right to conclude contracts, such as leases, loans, pledges, emphyteuses. Property of his own acquired after consecration—except that from the next relatives—

belonged to the Church.—C. 1.3; 4.—See the foregoing item.

> Génestal, *NRHD* 32 (1908) 163; L. Galtier, *Du rôle des évêques dans le droit public et privé du Bas-Empire*, 1913; Leitner, *Die Stellung des Bischofs, Fschr Hertling*, 1913; Volterra, *BIDR* 42 (1934) 453; Declareuil, *RHD* 14 (1935) 33; Masi, *AG* 122 (1939) 86; Mochi Onory, *RStDIt* 4–6 (1931–1933); Ferrari, *AVen* 99, 2 (1939/40) 233.

Epistula. A private letter. "If I send you a letter, it will not be yours until delivered to you" (D. 41.1.65 pr.). Delivery of the letter to a secretary or messenger of the addressee makes the latter the owner thereof immediately. Certain agreements, primarily consensual contracts (a sale, for instance), might be concluded by letter (*per epistulam*). A letter might also be used by a testator in order to express some desires to his heir. It then had the legal value of a codicil (see CODICILLI). See EPISTULA FIDEICOMMISSARIA. An *epistula* might also serve for the acknowledgment of a debt; see CHIROGRAPHUM.—See DIVORTIUM, MANUMISSIO PER EPISTULAM, NUNTIUS.—For official letters, see EPISTULAE.

> Dziatzko, *RE* 3, 836 (*s.v. Brief*); L. De Sarlo, *Il documento oggetto di rapporti privati*, 1935, 37, 128.

Epistula fideicommissaria. A letter by which a person imposed on his heir, testamentary or intestate, a *fideicommissum* in favor of a third person.—See FIDEICOMMISSUM.

Epistula traditionis. See TRADITIO CHARTAE.

Epistulae. (In official matters.) Official letters written by magistrates and provincial governors to private individuals.—C. 7.57.

> De Ruggiero, *DE* 2.

Epistulae. (Of jurists.) Written legal opinions given by prominent jurists to magistrates, other jurists, or private persons at their request. Some jurists edited their *epistulae* in collections entitled *"Epistulae"* (Labeo, Proculus, Iavolenus, Neratius, Celsus, Africanus, Pomponius), works similar to *Quaestiones* or *Responsa*. Excerpts from *epistulae* often appear in the Digest in their epistolary form.

> Berger, *RE* 10, 1174.

Epistulae principum. Answers of the emperor given in a separate letter to enquirers or petitioners who addressed themselves directly to the emperor with a question or petition. The *epistulae* were issued by the imperial bureau AB EPISTULIS and primarily addressed to officials.—See RESCRIPTA.

> Brassloff, *RE* 6; De Ruggiero, *DE* 2, 2131; Riccobono, *FIR* 1² (1941) nos. 72, 74, 75, 78, 80, etc.; Lafoscade, *De epistulis imperatorum*, Paris, 1902; Haberleitner, *Philologus* 98 (1909).

Epitome Gai. An abstract of Gaius' Institutes, written in the Western Empire probably in the fifth century. It is a part of the LEX ROMANA VISIGOTHORUM under the title *"Liber Gaii."* Originally it may have served as a book for students.

> Editions: Seckel-Kübler in Huschke's *Iurisprudentia anteiustiniana*, 2, 2 (sixth ed. 1927) 395; Baviera, *FIR* 2²

(1940) 231; M. Conrat, *Die Entstehung des westgothischen Gaius*, 1905; Kübler, *RE* 7, 504; Albertario, *ACDR Roma I* 1933 (= *Studi* 5, 269); G. G. Archi, *Epitome G.*, 1937; Schulz, *History of R. Legal Science*, 1946, 302.

Epitome Iuliani. See NOVELLAE IUSTINIANI.

Epitome ton nomon. A private collection of laws divided into fifty titles, probably written about A.D. 930 in Greek, composed of excerpts from Justinian's codification and later imperial enactments. The original title of the compilation is "Ecloge of laws presented in an epitome."

Editions: Zachariae, *Ius Graeco-Romanum* 2, 265; J. and P. Zepos, *Ius Gr.-Rom.* 4 (1931) 263.—Mortreuil, *Hist. du droit byzantin* 2 (1844) 372.

Epitome Ulpiani. See ULPIANUS, TITULI EX CORPORE ULPIANI.

Equester. See EQUITES, AES EQUESTER, ORDO EQUESTER.

Equestris dignitas. In 'the later Empire the equestrian rank.—C. 12.31.

Equites. Knights, persons of equestrian rank. Originally *equites* were cavalrymen. Horses were provided either by the state (*equites equo publico*) or bought from a special allowance (AES EQUESTRE). Another allowance was granted for the maintenance of the horse (AES HORDIARIUM). Later, cavalrymen frequently provided their own horses (*equites equo privato*). Service in the cavalry was favored by the state and enjoyed various privileges. The *equites* were originally organized in eighteen equestrian units (CENTURIAE). Eventually they developed into a distinct social class, in particular when the LEX SEMPRONIA (122 B.C.) gave them the right to serve as jurors in criminal trials, with the exclusion of the senators. The *equites* became a nobility of rich men who obtained their wealth from commerce (forbidden to senators) and tax farming (see PUBLICANI), a capitalist nobility, lower in rank than the senatorial class but with gradually increasing influence in administration and politics. The connection with cavalry service was broken; the possession of a considerable wealth became decisive. The LEX ROSCIA (67 B.C.) fixed their patrimonial census at 400,000 sesterces. Augustus reorganized the equestrian body. Thereafter it played an ever increasing role in social and political life, since the high positions in the administration of the Empire were covered by persons of equestrian rank. The golden ring which in the time of the Republic was the distinguishing mark of senators and *equites* (*ius anuli aurei*) became an exclusively equestrian distinction. Through the occupation of the most important posts in the imperial chancery after the reform by Hadrian their influence grew still greater.—See CLAVUS LATUS, ANGUSTUS CLAVUS.

Kübler, *RE* 6; Cagnat, *DS* 2; Bartoccini, *DE* 2; De Robertis, *NDI* 5; Mattingly, *OCD*; C. W. Keyes, *The rise of the e. in the third century*, Princeton, 1915; R. H. Lacey, *The equestrian officials of Trajan and Hadrian*, 1917; A. Stein, *Der röm. Ritterstand*, 1927; B. Jenny, *Der röm. Ritterstand*, 1936; De Laet, *La composition de l'ordre equestre, Rev. Belge de Philol. et d'Hist.* 20 (1941)

509; Zwicky, *Die Verwendung des Militärs in der Verwaltung der röm. Kaiserzeit*, 1944, 54.

Equites legionis. Cavalrymen—normally 300— attached to a legion. They were divided into ten *turmae* (with 30 horsemen) and thirty *decuriae*.— See ALA, TURMA.

Kübler, *RE* 6, 279.

Equites singulares (principis, Augusti). Cavalrymen in the service of the emperor as his bodyguard.

Cagnat, *DE* 2, 789; Liebenam, *RE* 6, 312.

Ercisci (hercisci). See DIVIDERE, ACTIO FAMILIAE ERCISCUNDAE.

Ercto non cito. An ancient term for joint, not divided, ownership (familial community).—See CONSORTIUM.

Levy, *ZSS* 54 (1934) 276; De Zulueta, *JRS* 25 (1935) 19; Solazzi, *ANap* 57 (1935) 126; 58 (1937) 76; E. Schlechter, *Contrat de société*, 1947, 196 (Bibl.); Beseler, *Scr Ferrini* 3 (Univ. Sacro Cuore, Milan, 1948) 281; Weiss, *Fschr Schulz* 1 (1951) 84.

Eremodicium. The unexcused absence of a party to a trial in court. In later law, the proceedings were continued in favor of the party present in spite of the absence of the adversary. The contumacious procedure was thoroughly reformed by Justinian.—See ABSENS, CONTUMAX.

Kipp, *RE* 6; Humbert, *DS* 2; A. Steinwenter, *Versäumnisverfahren*, 1914; L. Aru, *Il processo contumaciale*, 1934.

Erepticium. See EREPTORIUM.

Ereptorium. An inheritance or legacy which is not given (*eripitur* = taken away) to an heir or legatee because of his unworthiness (*indignitas*), in certain instances of bad behavior towards the deceased. See INDIGNUS. The inheritance or legacy went to the fisc in most cases.

Leonhard, *RE* 3 (*s.v. bona e.*); Humbert, *DS* 2 (*s.v. ereptitium*).

Ergastulum. A workhouse into which lazy or untrustworthy slaves were put by their masters and forced to work. *Ergastularii* = either the watchmen or the inmates.—See VINCTUS.

Mau, *RE* 6.

Ergolabus. (In later imperial constitutions.) One who contracts to construct a building or to perform a work (*opus*) with his own materials and workers. The contract is a *locatio conductio operis faciendi*. Syn. (in classical language) *redemptor operis*.—C. 4.59.

Eripere. To take away something from another either by force (*vi*) or legally as when a person is deprived of illegal profits (*eripere hereditatem*).—See EREPTORIUM.

Erogare (erogatio). To expend, to lay out. In certain legal situations involving two or more persons, as, e.g., in a partnership, common ownership, or common inheritance, whatever one has expended in favor of all was computed with the gains which he made for himself without sharing with the others.

Erogatio. (In military administration.) Distribution of military supplies (of food = *erogatio annonae mili-*

taris, of clothes = *erogatio vestis militaris*). *Erogator* = the official who made the distribution.—C. 12.37.

Errare. To be mistaken, to ignore, not to know certain legally important facts, to believe in what is untrue and to act accordingly. A person acting in error = *errans. Errantis nulla voluntas* = "the (expressed) will of a person who is in error, has no (legal) force" (D. 3.20).—See ERROR.

Erhardt, *ZSS* 58 (1938) 167.

Erro. A vagrant slave who leaves his master's house in order to roam about, and who, after spending his money, returns to the master.

Error. A false knowledge or want of knowledge of legally important circumstances, factual or juridical (*error facti, error iuris*). Syn. *ignorantia.* An *error* may occur in unilateral (testaments) and bilateral acts (contracts). It creates a divergence between the will of a person and the manifestation of his will in spoken or written words. One thing is declared as wanted whereas another is really wanted. In a testament an *error* concerning the beneficiary (e.g., another name is written than that of the person to whom the testator wants to make a gift) or the bequest (another thing is mentioned as bequeathed than the one intended) renders the whole disposition void. In contractual relations *error* may invalidate the transaction under certain circumstances. Only an excusable error is taken into consideration in favor of the person acting in error, however, and then solely an *error* which concerns such an essential element of the transaction that it must be assumed that he would not conclude it at all had the *error* not occurred. These are problems which cannot be resolved in general terms, but must be judged individually in each concrete instance. The *error* of a person may serve in certain situations as an evidence of his acting in good faith (*bona fide*) and furnish the basis for a *restitutio in integrum,* or, when a payment was made in the erroneous assumption of a debt, for a *condictio indebiti.*—D. 22.6; C. 1.18.—See CAUSAE PROBATIO, CONDICTIO INDEBITI, DEMONSTRATIO FALSA.

R. Allain, *L'erreur,* Thèse, Paris, 1907; R. Leonhard, *Irrtum,* 1907; Schulz, *ZSS* 33 (1912); *idem, Gedächtnisschrift für Seckel,* 1927; Donatuti, *AG* 86 (1921) 223; Lauria, *RDCiv* 19 (1927) 313; Riccobono, *BIDR* 43 (1935) 1; P. Voci, *L'errore nel dir. rom.,* 1937; *idem, SDHI* 8 (1942) 82; Kaden, *Fschr Koschaker* 1 (1939) 334; Simonius, *ibid.* 359; P. F. Wilches, *De errore communi in iure rom. et canonico,* Rome, 1940; Riccobono, *Scr Ferrini* (Univ. Pavia, 1946) 35; Solazzi, *Condictiones e errore, ANap* 62 (1947/8); Flume, *Festschr. Schulz* 1 (1951) 209; Dulckeit, *ibid.* 175; F. Schwarz, *ZSS* 68 (1951) 266; *idem, Die Grundlage der condictio,* 1952, 65.

Error advocatorum. Mistakes or false allegations made by advocates in their written statements. "They do not prejudice the truth" (C. 2.9.3.).—C. 2.9.

Error calculi (computationis). An error in calculation. If it occurs in a judgment and is fully evident, no appeal is necessary. The judge himself may correct it. In public administration, *error calculi* is

without any legal effect. A reexamination and correction (*retractatio*) is admissible even after ten or twenty years.—C. 2.5.

Error facti. Ignorance or false knowledge of a fact. Syn. *ignorantia facti.* Ant. *error (ignorantia) iuris.* It is said that unlike *ignorantia iuris* an *error facti non nocet* (C. 1.18.7), to wit, it may be alleged as an excuse and in certain instances produce the nullity of the act. The rule was not generally applied.—See ERROR.

Error in corpore. An *error* concerning the thing to which a legal transaction refers (e.g., the buyer believes he is buying the slave Stichus while the seller means another).

Flume, *Fschr Schulz* 1 (1951) 244.

Error in corpore hominis. See ERROR IN PERSONA.

Error in iure. (*Error iuris.*) See IGNORANTIA IURIS.

Error in materia. See ERROR IN SUBSTANTIA.

Error in negotio. An *error* which concerns the transaction itself (e.g., one party believes he is buying an immovable while the other wants to lease it). Such an error makes the transaction void.

Error in nomine (nominis). A mistake made in the mention of a name (of an heir, a legatee, a slave bequeathed or a slave to be manumitted by the legatee).—See DEMONSTRATIO FALSA, NOMEN.

Flume, *Fschr Schulz* 1 (1951) 244.

Error in persona. An *error* concerning the person to whom a testator wants to make a gift or with whom one wants to conclude a transaction. The testamentary disposition or the transaction is void if in the concrete instance the identity of the person is of particular import. Syn. *error in corpore hominis.*

Error in substantia. Occurs when the mistake concerns the substance, nature or economic function of the thing involved (e.g., buying vinegar instead of wine). Syn. *error in materia.*

Thayer, *ACDR,* Rome, 2 (1935) 409; Flume, *Fschr Schulz* 1 (1951) 248.

Error iuris. See IGNORANTIA IURIS.

Erroris causae probatio. If a Roman woman who married a peregrine under the erroneous assumption that he was a Roman citizen, proved her error, the marriage remained valid, and the husband and children became Roman citizens.—See CAUSAE PROBATIO.

Erus. The owner, master of a household.

Eudoxius. A law professor in Beirut, about the beginning of the sixth century after Christ. He was the founder of a family of famous Byzantine jurists, among them his son, Leontius, and a grandson, Anatolius.

Kübler, *RE* 6, 927.

Eunuchus. Emasculated. See CASTRATIO. In Justinian law eunuchs were not allowed to marry or make an adoption. These restrictions did not exist in the classical law. Eunuchs were able to make a testament, however.—C. 4.42.

Hug, *RE* Suppl. 3, 449; Bonfante, *AG* 101 (1929) 3.

Eustathios. See PEIRA.

Evanescere. To vanish, to lose validity, to become void: The term is applied to testamentary dispositions and to contractual bindings. *Actio evanescit* an action which though originally available lost its applicability in a concrete case. The term is considered suspect as to its classicality.

Guarneri-Citati, *St Riccobono* 1 (1936) 719.

Evectio. An official permission to use the imperial post. Syn. *diploma.*—See TRACTORIA.

Seeck, *RE* 4, 1859; Humbert, *DS* 1, 1662.

Eventus. The legal effect of a transaction or a trial. With regard to wrongdoings, *eventus* (= the issue) is opposed to the intention (design) of the wrongdoer.—See EXITUS, ANIMUS.

Evictio. (From *evincere.*) Occurred when a seller sold a thing which did not belong to him and the buyer was later evicted by the real owner. When ownership over the thing sold was transferred by *mancipatio* the buyer had the *actio auctoritatis* against the seller in case of eviction. If there had been no *mancipatio* (the thing being a *res nec mancipi*, for instance), the seller used to promise by *stipulatio* to pay the buyer double the price (*stipulatio duplae*) or make a simple *stipulatio* (*stipulatio evictionis* or *de evictione*) by which he guaranteed the buyer peaceful use of thing sold (*habere licere*) and promised to pay the buyer any damages he incurred by eviction. In a later development the buyer could avail himself of the *actio empti* for damages independently of a preceding *stipulatio.* Liability for eviction, which became a legal element of the sale, could be excluded by a special agreement, *pactum de non praestanda evictione.*—*Evictio* might also occur when a thing belonging to another was given as a dowry or as a pledge (*fiducia, pignus*) by the debtor.—D. 21.2; C. 8.44; 45; 10.5.—See EMPTIO VENDITIO, EVINCERE, ACTIO AUCTORITATIS, LAUDARE AUCTOREM, DATIO IN SOLUTUM.

Humbert, *DS* 2; Pivano, *De evictione in iure rom.*, 1901; De Medio, *BIDR* 16 (1904) 5; De Francisci, *L'evizione della res data in solutum*, 1915; Guarneri-Citati, *AnPal* 8 (1921) 385; Girard, *Mélanges* 2 (1923) 1; Kamphuisen, *RHD* 16 (1927) 607; Ricca-Barberis, *St Riccobono* 2 (1930) 127; idem, *L'evizione nella datio in solutum*, 1931; Kaser, *ZSS* 54 (1934) 162; E. Albertario, *Studi* 3 (1936) 481; Erbe, *Pfandrecht und Eviction, Fschr Koschaker* 1 (1939) 479; Meylan, *RIDA* 3 (= *Mél De Visscher* 2, 1949) 193.

Evictionem praestare. To indemnify a buyer who was evicted by a third person from the thing sold.—See EVICTIO.

Evidens. Manifest, obvious, evident. The term is used with preference by Justinian and his compilers.

Guarneri-Citati, *Indice*[2] (1927) 36; E. Albertario, *Studi* 1 (1933) 322.

Evidentissimae probationes. Evidence which fully proves the truth of an alleged fact or right. It is a typical Justinian expression, frequently interpolated in classical texts.—See APERTISSIMUS, PROBATIONES.

Guarneri-Citati, *Indice*[2] (1927) 36 (Bibl.).

Evincere. See EVICTIO. *Evincere* occurs not only when a third person claims ownership of a thing from the buyer, but also when he claims an usufruct or a servitude. With regard to slaves *evincere* is used not only when the third person asserts that the slave is his, but also when he claims that the slave is a free person (*evincere in libertatem*).

Evocati. Persons who in case of emergency assumed military service for as long a time as the state remained in danger. Under Augustus they became a separate unit (*evocati Augusti, Caesaris*) of soldiers who had already served their time, under the command of the *praefectus praetorio.* Some of the *evocati* were appointed for special services in the imperial palace or in the office of the *praefectus praetorio,* others were distributed among the legions for special functions of a non-military character or were sent to the provinces on special missions. The purpose of the institution was to use able persons with military experience for further official service.

Fiebiger, *RE* 6, 1145; Cagnat, *DS* 2; De Ruggiero, *DE* 2.

Evocatio. The summons of a party or a witness to a trial by a magistrate in the proceedings *cognitio extra ordinem.* It could be made orally by *denuntiatio* when the person involved lived in the same city, otherwise by a letter (*litteris*) or by a public announcement (*edicto*) if his domicile was unknown. Syn. (in a few instances) *vocatio.*—See EDICTUM PEREMPTORIUM.

A. Steinwenter, *Versäumnisverfahren*, 1914, 8; L. Aru, *Procedura contumaciale*, 1934, 98.

Ex. Added as a prefix to the title of an imperial official who was no longer in service (e.g., *ex praefecto praetorio, ex comite, ex proconsule*).

Ex aequo et bono. See BONUM ET AEQUUM.

Ex asse heres. An heir to the whole estate. Ant. *ex parte. Ex semisse heres* = an heir to a half of the estate.—See DODRANS, SEMUNCIA.

Ex die. See DIES, MANUMISSIO SUB CONDICIONE.

Ex fide bona. In conformity with good faith, honesty. Ant. *ex iure Quiritium* = according to the strict law. —For *ex fide bona* in the procedural formula, see IUDICIA BONAE FIDEI.—See BONA FIDES.

Sinaiski, *St Riccobono* 4 (1936) 57 (for *ex i. Q.*).

Ex lege. According to a statute (law). It is to be understood "both according to the intention (*sententia*) and to the words of the law" (D. 50.16.6.1).

Ex post facto. From a later event. It refers to a fact or event subsequent to a legal situation, resulting from an agreement or a unilateral act (a legacy or donation). From (*ex*) that fact or event (for instance, the fulfillment of a condition), conclusions are drawn as to the validity of, or a change in, the former legal situation.—See PRAETERITA, INITIUM.

Berger, *Seminar* 7 (1949) 49.

Ex re alicuius. (Acquisitions made) from another's means. In particular *ex re patris* is applied to what a son acquired at the father's expense, apart from what the son acquired from other sources. A similar distinction separates what a slave acquired *ex re domini* (= from his master's means) from what he gained *ex opera sua* (= by his work).—*Ex re sua* = (acquisitions made) from one's own property.

Ex re usufructuarii. See SERVUS USUFRUCTUARIUS.
    Berger, *Philologus* 73 (1914) 69.

Exactio. (From *exigere*.) Taking legal measures against a debtor for the recovery of a debt, enforcing payment legally. With regard to payments owed to the state (taxes), *exactio tributorum* = the levy, collection by the competent officials or authorized persons. Enforcing payment of public debts in a higher measure than was legal = *superexactio*.—C. 10.19; 20.—See PRIVILEGIUM EXIGENDI.

Exactor. A collector of taxes and other payments due to the state.—In public administration *exactor* indicates an inspector, a superintendent of public buildings and works (*opera publica*).—C. 12.60.
    Louis-Lucas, *DS* 2; De Ruggiero, *DE* 2, Seeck, *RE* 6, 1542; Lammers, *RE* 4A, 973.

Exaequare (exaequatio). To make different legal institutions or enactments equal in their legal force. According to Justinian's statement, for instance, *fideicommissa exaequata sunt* to legacies (*legatis*) in all respects. By the LEX HORTENSIA DE PLEBISCITIS the plebiscites were declared equal to statutes passed by the assemblies of the whole people.

Exauctorare. To discharge a soldier from the service. The term is used of both honorable and dishonorable discharges.—See MISSIO.

Excantare fruges. To enchant the produce of another's field by magical formulae in order to deprive the land of its fertility and to transfer the fruits to the enchanter's plot. Such sorcery was punished as a crime according to the Twelve Tables.
    F. Beckmann, *Zauberei und Recht in Roms Frühzeit*, 1928, 5.

Excellentia. Excellency. An honorary title of the *praefectus praetorio*.

Excellentissimus (vir). A general title appearing in imperial constitutions of the late Empire in connection with high dignitaries.

Excelsa sedes. The office (court) of the *praefectus praetorio*.—C. 12.49.

Exceptae personae. Certain persons or groups to whom some legal prohibitions were not applied. There was no general rule establishing the persons thus privileged, the pertinent statutes designated the *exceptae personae* only within their own domain. Of particular importance were the rules concerning *exceptae personae* of the LEX CINCIA on donations. It admitted gifts—beyond the limitations established in the statute—in favor of the donor's fiancée, the wife, relatives until the fifth degree and some of the sixth degree, the patron, the ward, and some other persons. —See LEX CINCIA.
    Riccobono, *Mél Girard* 2 (1912) 415.

Exceptio. A defense opposed by the defendant to the plaintiff's claim to render it ineffective and exclude the defendant's condemnation as demanded by the plaintiff in the INTENTIO of the procedural formula. Formally the *exceptio* was a clause in the formula containing an assertion of the defendant who, without denying the plaintiff's claim in principle, opposed to it a legal provision (e.g., *exceptio legis Cinciae*, or *legis Plaetoriae*) or a fact not alleged by the plaintiff. Thus, for instance, the defendant asserts that he owes the sum claimed by the plaintiff, but according to a special agreement (*pactum de non petendo*) the plaintiff assumed the obligation not to sue for the money. The defendant's objection made during the proceedings *in iure*, is inserted into the formula as a negative condition, to wit, the judge may condemn the defendant "if there has not been an agreement that the plaintiff will not bring an action."—In the interdictal proceedings the *exceptio* is included in the interdict itself in the form of a negative conditional clause giving the defendant the right to disregard the praetor's order if the fact mentioned in the clause occurred. Some exceptions are an integral part of the interdict (e.g., *exceptio vitiosae possessionis, exceptio annalis*), others were inserted in a specific case by the praetor upon the request of the defendant. With the disappearance of the formulary procedure and the interdicts in their classical form, *exceptio* became any kind of defense applied by the defendant in order to paralyze, peremptorily or temporarily, the plaintiff's claim.—Inst. 4.13; D. 44.1; C. 7.40; 8.35.—Texts in which literal quotations of exceptions occur in the Digest are listed in *Vocabularium Iurisprudentiae Romanae* 2, 662 and 5, 450.—See OPE EXCEPTIONIS, DENEGARE EXCEPTIONEM, NOCERE. In the following presentation the different kinds of exceptions are treated under EXCEPTIONES, the specific exceptions under EXCEPTIO.
    Seckel, in Heumann's *Handlexikon zu den Guellen*[9] (1907) 180; Wenger, *RE* 6; Ferrini, *NDI* 5; Wlassak, *Ursprung der röm. Einrede, Fg L. Pfaff*, 1910; E. Weiss, *Fschr Wach* 2 (1913); J. Petrau-Gay, *Exceptiones et praescriptiones*, Paris, 1916; Biondi, *AnPal* 7 (1920) 3; Guarneri-Citati, *St Perozzi*, 1925, 245; Kipp, *ZSS* 42 (1921); R. Düll, *Der Gütegedanke*, 1931, 193; F. De Martino, *Giurisdizione*, 1937, 83; Ramos, *AHDE* 16 (1945) 720; Solazzi, *AG* 137 (1949) 3; Levy, *Iura* 3 (1952) 157.

Exceptio cognitoria. An *exceptio* by which the defendant denied the plaintiff's right to be a COGNITOR in the trial, either because the principal creditor was not able to appoint a representative, or because the *cognitor* had not the qualifications to represent another.—See COGNITOR, EXCEPTIO PROCURATORIA.
    Lenel, *Edictum perpetuum*[3] (1927) 502.

Exceptio conventionis. Functions the same way as EXCEPTIO PACTI and is based on a special agreement which excludes the plaintiff's claim. Analogous is *exceptio transactionis*.

Exceptio curatoria. An *exceptio* by which the defendant denies the plaintiff's right to act as a curator of the real creditor.

Exceptio doli. This was opposed by the defendant sued for the fulfillment of an agreement and based on the allegation that the plaintiff had acted fraudulently (*dolo*). The formulary wording of this *exceptio* was: *si in ea re nihil dolo malo Auli Agerii* (of the plaintiff) *factum sit* (= "if in this matter no fraud has been committed by the plaintiff"). The *exceptio doli* was strengthened by an additional clause, attached to the foregoing words, *"neque fiat"* which refers to the actual action of the plaintiff in the sense "nor is being committed by him," i.e., that his suit itself is not a fraud (inequitable). About this general applicability of the *exceptio doli* it is said: "he who makes a demand which may be broken down by an exception whatsoever, commits a fraud" (D. 44.4. 2.5). Therefore an *exceptio doli* can be opposed. Thus by the initiative of the praetor and the jurists the *exceptio doli,* originally a merely procedural measure, acquired a positive function, promoting the development of the substantive law through the protection of formless agreements not recognized by the *ius civile* (additional agreements connected with the transfer of property through *mancipatio,* constitution of servitudes, agreements attached to a *stipulatio,* and so on). A maxim gained currency that the *exceptio doli* is implied in the *bonae fidei iudicia* (D. 24.3.21), inasmuch as the judge has to decide on grounds of good faith, which gave him the opportunity to take into consideration all elements which might let the plaintiff's claim appear inequitable. To those elements belonged not only fraud committed at the conclusion of the transaction but also all circumstances which qualified the suit itself as being against good faith. Therefore, the insertion of an *exceptio doli* into the formula which contained already the clause *"ex fide bona"* was superfluous. The mechanism of the *exceptio doli* allowed the judge to consider counterclaims of the defendant (such as expenses he made on the thing claimed by the plaintiff) and condemn the defendant only for the balance (see COMPENSATIO).—D. 44.4.—See DOLUS, IUDICIA BONAE FIDEI, RETENTIO.

Kleinfeller, *RE* 5 (*s.v. dolus*); Vita, *NDI* 5, 144; E. Costa, *La e. d.,* 1897; Biondi, *AnPal* 7 (1920) 5; Beseler, *ZSS* 45 (1925) 245; Riccobono, *AnPal* 14 (1930) 405, 437; E. Protetti, *Contributi allo studio dell'efficacia dell'e.d.,* 1948.

Exceptio intercessionis. See SENATUSCONSULTUM VELLEIANUM.

Exceptio iurisiurandi. See IUSIURANDUM VOLUNTARIUM.

Exceptio iusti dominii. An exception of which the owner of a thing at *ius civile* could avail himself

against a plaintiff who based his claim for recovery of the thing on possession only (*actio Publiciana in rem*).

Exceptio legis Cinciae. See LEX CINCIA.

Exceptio legis Falcidiae. See LEX FALCIDIA.

Exceptio legis Plaetoriae. See LEX PLAETORIA.

Exceptio litis dividuae. This may be opposed when the plaintiff after having sued for a part of the debt, claims the remainder thereof in a second trial during the same praetorship. The exception is dilatory, the plaintiff having to expect the next praetor's term of office. A similar *exceptio* is the *exceptio litis residuae,* applicable when a plaintiff who has several claims against the same defendant sues only for one of them in order to vex the latter with another trial under the same praetorship.

Buckland, *RHD* 11 (1932) 311.

Exceptio litis residuae. See the foregoing item.

Exceptio metus (de metu, quod metus causa). An objection by the defendant that he assumed the obligation for which he is sued, under duress (*metus*). —D. 44.4.—See METUS.

Exceptio ne praeiudicium hereditati fiat. See HEREDITATIS PETITIO.

Exceptio non adimpleti contractus. The defendant's objection that the plaintiff did not fulfill his duties reciprocally assumed in the contract on which he based his claim.

R. Cassin, *De l'exception tirée de l'inexécution,* 1914.

Exceptio non numeratae pecuniae. This *exceptio,* analogous to the foregoing, is of later origin. The defendant objects that he did not receive the money from the plaintiff for the restitution of which he is being sued. Such things happened when the debtor issued a written document for a debt before receiving the money.—C. 4.30.—See QUERELA NON NUMERATAE PECUNIAE.

Platon, *NRHD* 33 (1909) 452; Suman, *AVen* 78, 2 (1919) 225; Kreller, *St Riccobono* 2 (1936) 285.

Exceptio pacti (conventi). An *exceptio* based on an additional agreement between creditor and debtor which modified the original obligation, as, for instance, not to claim the debt in a judicial trial at all, or within a certain time. In the latter case the exception was dilatory.

Biondi, *AnPal* 7 (1918) 50; Koschaker, *Abhandlungen zur antiken Rechtsgesch., Fsch Hanausek,* 1925, 139.

Exceptio pigneraticia. Mentioned in a specific case of an action brought for division of common property (*actio communi dividundo*) by a co-owner against his partner to whom the claimant had pledged his portion. The *exceptio* is opposed by the pledgee co-owner in order to be taken into consideration by the judge at the division.—See EXCEPTIO REI ANTE PIGNERATAE.

Last, *GrZ* 36 (1909) 457.

Exceptio procuratoria. The counterpart to the *exceptio cognitoria* in the case that the creditor is represented in a trial by a *procurator*. Through this *exceptio* the defendant objects that the plaintiff's representative has no right to act as a representative (*procuratorio nomine*). The *exceptio* is dilatory, the creditor having the opportunity to sue again either personally or through another representative.—See EXCEPTIO COGNITORIA, PROCURATOR (in a civil trial).

　　Solazzi, *RISG* 83 (1949) 60.

Exceptio quod metus causa. See EXCEPTIO METUS.

Exceptio rei ante pigneratae. This served the protection of the rights of a creditor to whom the debtor had pledged a thing, against another creditor to whom the same thing was hypothecated later.—See PIGNUS, HYPOTHECA.

Exceptio rei in iudicium deductae. See EXCEPTIO REI IUDICATAE.

Exceptio rei iudicatae. An exception opposed by the defendant and based on the fact that he had been sued for the same thing (*eadem res*) in a previous trial and a judgment had been passed in the matter. Identity of the plaintiffs was not necessary since the *exceptio* might be used against the successor of the claimant in the trial. There was a maxim: "Good faith does not permit that the same thing be claimed twice" (D. 50.17.57). The most important point in the application of this *exceptio* was the identity of the claims (EADEM RES). A similar *exceptio* was the *exceptio rei in iudicium deductae* which was available when in the first trial a judgment had not been rendered but the joinder of issue (*litis contestatio*) had been reached.—D. 44.2.—See BIS IDEM EXIGERE, RES IUDICATA, LITIS CONTESTATIO.

　　Eisele, *ZSS* 21 (1900); Leonhard, *Fg Dahn* 2 (1905) 65; Manenti, *BIDR* 21 (1909) 139; Weiss, *Fschr Wach* 2 (1913); Pflüger, *ZSS* 43 (1933); Guarneri-Citati, *BIDR* 33 (1923) 204; Siber, *ZSS* 65 (1947) 1.

Exceptio rei litigiosae. See RES LITIGIOSA.

Exceptio rei venditae et traditae. An *exceptio* opposed by the defendant sued for the delivery of a thing of which the plaintiff asserts to be the owner. The defendant, on his part, objects that he bought the thing and that it was delivered (*tradita*) to him by the seller.—D. 21.3.

　　Ferrini, *Opere* 3 (1929, ex 1891) 275; Last, *GrZ* 36 (1909) 490; J. Gonvers, *E. r. v.,* Thèse, Lausanne, 1939.

Exceptio restitutae hereditatis. Connected with FIDEICOMMISSUM HEREDITATIS. The heir who according to the testator's disposition handed over the whole estate to a *fideicommissarius* when sued for the testator's debts might oppose the *exceptio restitutae hereditatis,* and similarly he was exposed to this *exceptio* if he sued a debtor of the testator. In earlier law, when the rule SEMEL HERES SEMPER HERES was strictly observed, the heir could avoid any risk by demanding a *cautio* for indemnity from the real successor. The SENATUSCONSULTUM TREBELLIANUM established the liability of the *fideicommissarius* which made superfluous special agreements between the in-

stituted heir and the real beneficiary to whom he delivered over the inheritance.

Exceptio senatusconsulti Macedoniani. See SENATUSCONSULTUM MACEDONIANUM.

Exceptio senatusconsulti Trebelliani. See SENATUSCONSULTUM TREBELLIANUM, EXCEPTIO RESTITUTAE HEREDITATIS.

Exceptio senatusconsulti Velleiani. See SENATUSCONSULTUM VELLEIANUM.

Exceptio transactionis (transacti negotii). Has a similar function as the *exceptio pacti* or *exceptio conventionis*. It may be opposed by the defendant if the plaintiff sues for a debt on which he concluded a modifying transaction with the former.

Exceptio tutoria. An *exceptio* opposed to the plaintiff on the allegation that he is not the guardian of the person in whose name he is suing.—See EXCEPTIO CURATORIA.

Exceptio vitiosae possessionis. Applicable in possessory interdicts. The actual possessor of a thing is protected in his possession against anybody except the case that he himself acquired possession from his adversary (i.e., the claimant in the interdictal proceeding) in a defective way (*vitiose*).—See INTERDICTUM UTI POSSIDETIS, CLANDESTINA POSSESSIO, POSSESSIO INIUSTA.

Exceptiones annales. In actions which lie only for one year in favor of the claimant, the defendant may ask for an exception that the one-year period elapsed when the suit was brought after this period. In the domain of interdicts some of them contained a clause that the praetor's order is valid only if issued within a year after the fact against which the plaintiff remonstrates (*exceptio annalis*).—C. 7.40.—See ACTIONES TEMPORALES.

Exceptiones civiles—honorariae. Exceptions which are based on the *ius civile* (statutes, as, e.g., *excepiiones legis Cinciae, Plaetoriae,* or *senatusconsulta,* as, e.g., *exceptiones senatusconsulti Macedoniani, Velleiani*) are distinguished from exceptions of praetorian origin, introduced either in the praetorian edict or granted in a specific case, *exceptiones in factum*.

Exceptiones dilatoriae. Exceptions valid only for a certain space of time, for instance, the *exceptiones pacti* based on an agreement by which the plaintiff bound himself not to sue the debtor within a certain time. When the time fixed elapsed, the *exceptio* was without effect. Syn. *exceptiones temporales*. Ant. EXCEPTIONES PEREMPTORIAE (*perpetuae*).

　　Kipp, *ZSS* 42 (1921) 328; Solazzi, *AG* 137 (1949) 3.

Exceptiones in factum. Exceptions granted by the praetor in specific cases, although not established either by law (in statutes or *senatusconsulta*) or in the praetorian edict. The insertion into the formula was decided by the praetor after a thorough examination of the case (*causa cognita*).

　　Biondi, *AnPal* 7 (1918) 50.

Exceptiones in personam. A term not evidenced in the sources, but applied in literature as opposite to EXCEPTIONES IN REM.

Exceptiones in rem (scriptae). Exceptions which may be opposed to any claimant if the transaction on which the suit is founded was essentially defective, as, e.g., in the case of duress under which the defendant assumed an obligation. Therefore such *exceptio* was effective also against a plaintiff who did not take part in the act of force exercised on the debtor. Ant. *exceptiones in personam* (a term coined in literature) when the *exceptio* could be set forth against one plaintiff only for an action in which he participated, as the *exceptiones* for fraud (*exceptiones doli*). A counterpart to this distinction are the EXCEPTIONES PERSONAE COHAERENTES and *rei cohaerentes*.

Exceptiones peremptoriae. Exceptions which "are valid at any time and cannot be evaded" (Gaius, Inst. 4.120) when opposed by the defendant. Such exceptions, if sufficiently proved, make the plaintiff's claim void. Most *exceptiones* are peremptory; thus, e.g., *exceptio metus, exceptio rei iudicatae*, exceptions based on statutes or *senatusconsulta*. Syn. *exceptiones perpetuae;* ant. *exceptiones dilatoriae (temporales)*.

> Kipp, *ZSS* 42 (1921) 328; Devilla, *StSas* 19 (1942) 92; Solazzi, *AG* 137 (1949) 3.

Exceptiones perpetuae. See EXCEPTIONES PEREMPTORIAE.

Exceptiones personae cohaerentes. *Exceptiones* which only the defendant himself (not his sureties) may oppose, as, for instance, the *exceptio "quod facere possit"* available to a parent, patron or partner to the effect that he be condemned to an amount within his means (see BENEFICIUM COMPETENTIAE), the *exceptio* being strictly personal. Ant. *exceptiones rei cohaerentes*, which are available also to sureties for they impugn the matter of the controversy itself, such as, for instance, *exceptiones doli, iurisiurandi, rei iudicatae, metus,* etc.

Exceptiones quae minuunt condemnationem (damnationem). *Exceptiones* which do not wholly paralyze the plaintiff's claim but produce only the effect that the defendant is condemned to a sum smaller than originally claimed by the plaintiff. The existence of this type of exceptions in classical law is controversial. Those exceptions cover all cases where the defendant was permitted to invoke the so-called BENEFICIUM COMPETENTIAE.—See COMPENSATIO.

> Wenger, *RE* 6, 1557; Ferrini, *NDI* 5, 736; Arangio-Ruiz, *Exc. in diminuzione della condanna*, 1930; Solazzi, *BIDR* 42 (1934) 268.

Exceptiones rei cohaerentes. See EXCEPTIONES PERSONAE COHAERENTES.

Exceptiones temporales. See EXCEPTIONES DILATORIAE.

Exceptor. A scribe, short-hand writer, in court, in the senate, or the offices of higher officials. Their primary task was to keep the minutes of meetings or events which took place in the offices mentioned. In the imperial bureaucracy the number of *exceptores* increased considerably. They were employed also in the headquarters of military commanders.—C. 12.49.

> Fiebiger, *RE* 6, 1565; Cagnat, *DS* 2; Jones, *JRS* 39 (1949) 53.

Excipere. To oppose an exception against the claim of the plaintiff. In setting forth an exception (*excipiendo*) the defendant assumes the role of a plaintiff (*reus actor est*, D. 44.1.1) since he has to prove the facts alleged in his assertion (D. 22.3.9).

> R. Düll, *Der Gütegedanke*, 1931, 187; Levy, *Iura* 3 (1952) 157.

Excipere. (In transactions.) To insert a clause in favor of a party primarily of one who alienates something (e.g., excluding the liability of the seller of a slave for certain defects) or of the slave being sold (e.g., binding the acquirer to a certain behavior towards him).

Excipere mortem. To be condemned to death.

Excipere poenam (sententiam). To be sentenced in a criminal trial.

Excipere servitutem. To reserve a servitude or another right (*iter, usum, habitationem*, etc.) on behalf of the alienator when the ownership of an immovable is being conveyed.

Excipere usumfructum. See DEDUCTIO USUSFRUCTUS.

Excludere. To exclude a person from certain legal benefits or from the use of a procedural remedy.

Excusationes a muneribus. Exemption from public compulsory services (*munera*) were granted to women, men under twenty-five or over seventy, fathers of three children (four in Italy, five in provinces); it was limited, however, in these cases to exemption from personal services (*munera personalia*). Exemptions were also extended to certain professions (physicians, teachers), shippers, veterans, and members of municipal councils (*decuriones*). In granting exemption, poverty could be taken into consideration. After the time of Constantine, appeal (*querela, querimonia*) to the governor of the province was permitted.—D. 50.5; C. 10.48–59; 66.—See MUNERA, MEDICI, MAGISTER, PHILOSOPHI, POETAE.

> Kübler, *RE* 16, 648.

Excusationes a tutela. Persons called to guardianship by law or by testament were entitled to claim exemption (*excusatio*) because of certain circumstances, permanent or temporary, which made the fulfillment of their duties as guardians (*tutores* or *curatores*) impossible or very onerous to them. Among such grounds for exemption were age of seventy, high office, poverty, a certain number of children (three in Rome, four in Italy, five in the provinces) three tutorships already sustained, chronic illness, incapacity to manage another's property, and the like. Some grounds of exemption were available only with regard to specific guardianships, as, for instance, enmity against the ward's family.—Inst. 1.25; D. 27.1; C. 5.62–68; 10.48, 66.—See LIBELLUS CONTESTATORIUS.

Klingmüller, *RE* 6; Humbert, *DS* 2; Sachers, *RE* 7A, 1534; Albertario, *Studi* 1 (1933) 427.

Excussus. See EXCUTI.

Excutere rationes. To examine the accounts concerning the administration of property (e.g., of a ward by his guardian).—See ADMINISTRATIO.

Excuti. If a creditor has an action for the same claim against different persons, for instance, against the principal and a surety, he must sue them in a definite order, inasmuch as the action against a subsidiary debtor is admissible only when the trial against the debtor first sued has not resulted in the payment of the debt (because of the insolvency of the defendant or for other reasons). The defendant so fruitlessly sued was termed *excussus*.—See BENEFICIUM EXCUSSIONIS.

Executio, executor. See EXSECUTIO, EXSECUTOR.

Exemplar (exemplarium). The original of a document. Syn. *authenticum*. Ant. *exemplum*. Testators used to make testaments in two original copies; if one was lost or destroyed by accident, the other was valid. The opening of merely one original was considered the opening of the testament; see APERTURA TESTAMENTI.—See PARICULUM.

L. de Sarlo, *Il documento oggetto di rapporti giuridici*, 1935, 82; B. Biondi, *Successione testamentaria*, 1943, 66.

Exemplum. A copy of a document. Ant. *exemplar, authenticum*. In a few texts the term is used in the meaning of an original. Sometimes it is also used of a draft of a testament which is not valid if the testator dies before the formalities of a valid testament are accomplished.—*Exemplum* indicates a precedent, or what serves as a pattern.—Punishment in criminal matters is denoted an *exemplum* = serving as a deterrent warning.—*Exemplo* or *ad exemplum* is used when a legal remedy analogous to an existing one is granted (e.g., an *actio utilis*), or when a legal situation is dealt with in a similar way as another one, governed by a statute embracing similar legal situations (*exemplo legis Aquiliae*, for instance).—See RES IUDICATA.

Wünsch, *RE* 6; Kübler, *St Riccobono* 1 (1936) 435; L. de Sarlo, *Il documento oggetto di rapporti giuridici*, 1935, 82; F. v. Schwind, *Zur Frage der Publikation*, 1940, 137; H. Kornhardt, *Exemplum*, Diss. Göttingen, 1936; B. Biondi, *Successione testamentaria*, 1943, 67.

Exemptio (eximere). (From summons to court.) Taking away a person summoned to court (see IN IUS VOCATIO), by force or fraud to frustrate the summons and make impossible his appearance before the magistrate. The praetorian edict introduced an action against the wrongdoer.

Pugliese, *RIDA* 3 (= *Mél De Visscher* 2, 1949) 266.

Exercere. To carry on, practice, a profession. It is used not only of merchants, shipowners, bankers, innkeepers, etc., but also of ignominious professions (prostitutes, actors, matchmakers).

Exercere actionem. (*Iudicium, litem, exceptionem, appellationem.*) To use a judicial measure either in order to claim a right against another person or in defense against another's claim. See ACTIO. In criminal affairs *exercere accusationem, crimen* = to accuse. *Civiliter exercere* = to sue in a civil trial.

Exercere navem. See EXERCITOR NAVIS.

Exercere pecuniam (fenus). To lend money on interest. *Exercere pecuniam apud nummularios* = to invest money with a banker with profit.

Exercere vectigal. To levy, collect taxes.

Exercitator. A military instructor.

Bartoccini, *DE* 2.

Exercitor navis. A shipper, either the owner or lessee of a commercial ship used for the transportation of men and goods. "He is the man to whom the daily profit gained by shipping belongs" (Inst. 4.7.2). When he employs another as captain (*magister navis*), he is liable on the contracts concluded by the latter. The action lying against him was introduced by praetorian law, *actio exercitoria*. It belongs to the category of so-called *actiones adiecticiae qualitatis* (non-Roman term). These were "additional" actions (*actio adicitur*: D. 14.1.5.1) under which a person (a father, a slave's master, a principal, a shipper) under certain circumstances could be sued for acts done by his subordinate (a son, slave, employee) in the management of a *peculium* or a commercial business as his agent or on his order. The responsibility of the father and the other persons was additional to that of the subordinate although they did not participate in the latter's agreements or transactions.—D. 14.1; C. 4.25. —See ACTIO TRIBUTORIA, PECULIUM, IUSSUM, INSTITOR.

Humbert, *DS* 2 (*s.v. exercitoria a.*); Del Prete, *NDI* 5 (*s. eod. v.*); Valeri, *RDCom* 21 (1913) 14; Chialvo, *St F. Berlingieri*, 1933, 171; Ghionda, *RDNav* 1 (1935) 327; De Martino, *ibid.* 7 (1941) 5; Solazzi, *ibid.* 7 (1941) 185 and 9–14 (1943–1948).

Exercitus. The army. It is composed of *pedites* (= infantry) and *equites* (= cavalry). *Classis* = the navy. For the legal status of the soldiers, see MILITES. —See LEGIO, AUXILIA, COHORS, EQUITES, HASTATI, VELATI, MILITIA, MANIPULUS, DILECTUS, NUMERI, DIPLOMA, MISSIO, ALA, TURMA.

Liebenam, *RE* 6; Cagnat, *DS* 2, 912.

Exhauriri. To be expended wholly. It is used of inheritances which are exhausted by legacies to be paid by the heir.—See LEX FALCIDIA.

Exheredare. To disinherit. A son under paternal power (*filius familias*) must be disinherited by his father (*pater familias*) in the latter's testament by name (*nominatim*) or in any other way which admits of no doubt about the person meant. Syn. *exheredem facere*. Under *ius civile* a testament was void if the testator failed to institute his son (*heres suus*) as an heir or to disinherit him. Disinheritance of other persons, however, could be accomplished by a general clause ("all others shall be disinherited"). The jurists did not favor disinheritance in their opinions. Their principle was: "disinheritance must not be supported" (D. 28.2.19). The testator was not obliged to indicate the reason of the disinheritance. —Inst. 2.13; D. 28.2; C. 6.28.—See LEX IUNIA VELLAEA, PRAETERIRE, EXHERES.

Klingmüller, *RE* 6; Humbert, *DS* 2; Azzariti, *NDI* 5 (*s.v. diseredazione*); J. Merkel, *Justinianische Enterbungsgründe*, 1908.

Exheres. See EXHEREDARE. The term was used in the disinheriting clause ("*Titius exheres esto*" = Titus shall be disinherited).

Exhibere. To display, "to produce (a thing, a slave) in public (i.e., during a trial) in order to give the plaintiff the chance to proceed with his suit" (D. 10.4.2). The pertinent action to enforce the defendant to produce in court the movable thing in dispute when sued for its delivery (by REI VINDICATIO) he fraudulently denied having, was the *actio ad exhibendum*. In many cases the action served to prepare a future *rei vindicatio* which followed if the exhibited thing was in fact that very one which the plaintiff wanted to claim. This occurred, for instance, when a legatee was given by a testator the right to choose among the slaves of the inheritance, see OPTIO SERVI. The *actio ad exhibendum* was available when a plaintiff before suing the master of a slave for damages with an *actio noxalis* had to identify first which of the defendant's slaves was the wrongdoer. A specific application of the action was in a case of *accessio* when a person joined the plaintiff's thing to one of his own (e.g., set a gem belonging to the latter in a ring of his own). Through the *actio ad exhibendum* the plaintiff obtained the separation of his thing and its production in court, and might sue afterwards for recovery by a *rei vindicatio*. Even in cases when the thing to be claimed no longer existed (if, e.g., it was consumed by the defendant or destroyed or if the defendant intentionally gave up possession, *dolo desinere possidere*), the *actio ad exhibendum* was available for damages. The action was an *actio in personam* and had the advantage for the plaintiff, that the defendant could not refuse cooperation in the trial since in that case he was condemned to full indemnification.—D. 10.4; C. 3.42.— See ACTIONES ARBITRARIAE, ACTIONES IN PERSONAM, FURTUM NON EXHIBITUM, and the following items. Several interdicts are concerned with an *exhibere*, see INTERDICTUM DE HOMINE LIBERO EXHIBENDO, INTERDICTUM DE LIBERIS EXHIBENDIS, INTERDICTUM DE LIBERTO EXHIBENDO, INTERDICTUM DE UXORE EXHIBENDA, INTERDICTUM DE TABULIS EXHIBENDIS.

Ferrini, *NDI* 1 (*s.v. actio ad e.*); Aru, *NDI* 5; Humbert, *DS* 2; Last, *GrZ* 36 (1909) 433; Lenel, *GrZ* 37 (1910) 546; *idem*, *ZSS* 37 (1916) 116; *idem*, *Edictum perpetuum*³ (1923) 220; Beseler, *Beiträge* 1 (1910) 1; Last, *IhJb* 62 (1921) 120; Levy, *ZSS* 36 (1917) 1; Wlassak, *ZSS* 42 (1921) 435; G. Levi, *Studi M. d'Amelio* 2 (1933) 311.

Exhibere debitorem (reum). Refers to a guarantor who undertook to answer that a defendant in a civil trial would appear in court at a fixed date. His duty was to "produce" the defendant. See VINDEX. In a criminal trial *exhibere reum* = to submit to court a culprit of whom one had assumed the custody.—D. 48.3; C. 9.3.

Exhibere hominem liberum. In connection with the INTERDICTUM DE HOMINE LIBERO EXHIBENDO *exhibere* is defined "to produce in public (i.e., in court) and to make it possible to see and touch the man" (D. 43.29.3.8).—D. 43.29; C. 8.8.

Exhibere instrumenta. To produce documents for the purpose of evidence. It could be judicially enforced if it was in the interest of the adversary in the trial.—See EXHIBERE TABULAS.

Exhibere rationes. To produce accounts concerning the management of another's affairs (for instance, on the part of a guardian with regard to the ward's property).

Exhibere reum. See EXIBERE DEBITOREM.

Exhibere tabulas (testamenti). To produce a testament. It could be enforced by a person interested in the knowledge of the contents as a presumptive beneficiary.—D. 43.5; C. 8.7.—See INTERDICTUM DE TABULIS EXHIBENDIS.

Exhibere uxorem (familiam, patronum). To sustain, support one's wife (family, or patron). In another meaning *exhibere uxorem* is used in connection with the *interdictum de uxore ducenda*.—See INTERDICTUM DE LIBERIS EXHIBENDIS.

Exhibitio. See EXHIBERE.

Exigere. See EXACTIO.

Exilium (exsilium). A person involved in a criminal matter might voluntarily go into exile in order to escape a trial or a condemnation when the trial was already in course. *Exilium* also was a compulsory departure from the country if given as a punishment. Voluntary exile was tolerated in the case of a person sentenced to death in a criminal trial, but in such cases there followed an administrative decree which outlawed the fugitive (INTERDICERE AQUA ET IGNI). It deprived him of Roman citizenship (*capitis deminutio media*) and his property. Illicit return was punished by the death penalty. The consequences of a compulsory banishment varied according to the crime; they were fixed in the judgment. A milder form of banishment was RELEGATIO, while the severest one was DEPORTATIO. The terminology later became rather uncertain.—C. 10.61.—See IUS EXILII, VIATICUM.

Kleinfeller, *RE* 6; Humbert, *DS* 2; Berger, *OCD*; Braginton, *ClJ* 39 (1943-44) 391; U. Brasiello, *Repressione penale*, 1937, 272.

Eximere. To exempt, to free, to release a person from liability (*obligatione*), from special personal charges, such as guardianship (*a tutela*), or from penalty (*poena, damnatione*).—See EXEMPTIO.

Exire. When used of persons, to leave the family (*de familia*) by entering into another one or becoming *sui iuris*. Such steps were connected with *exire de (ex) potestate* (= to be released from the actual power of the head of the family). When referring to things (*exire de familia, de nomine*) *exire* = to depart from one property and enter another.

Existimare (existimatio). To assume, to consider (for instance, a thing belonging to another as one's own). An erroneous belief (thinking) is irrelevant from the juristic point of view. "More important is the truth (*res*) than the belief (*existimare*)" (D. 22.6.9.4). Exceptionally, however, as in the case of USUCAPIO a wrong opinion of the possessor of a thing may lead to his acquisition of ownership.—See ERROR.

Existimatio. The respect or esteem a person enjoys in society. "It is the state of undiminished dignity approved by law and custom" (D. 50.13.5.1). The *existimatio* of a person remains unharmed (*integra, illaesa*) as long as he does not commit a wrongdoing or a crime by which it "is diminished or extinguished under the authority of the laws" (D. *ibid.*).—See INFAMIA, TURPIS PERSONA, TURPITUDO.

U. Brasiello, *La repressione penale*, 1936, 546; Cicogna, *StSen* 54 (1940) 51.

Exitus. See EVENTUS.

Exonerare. To relieve, release (from a debt, or a public charge). Syn. *eximere*.

Expedire. To settle a controversy through a trial or extrajudicially; to accomplish a legal act (e.g., a manumission); to bear the expenses of a thing; to carry through as official matter.

Expellere. To dispossess a person by force from the use of his property. Syn. *deicere de possessione*.

Expellere uxorem (virum). To expel a wife (husband) from the common dwelling (*domo*) for the purpose of divorce.

Expendere. To pay out, to spend. *Rationes accepti et expensi* = a housebook for entries of income and disbursements.—See CODEX ACCEPTI ET EXPENSI, EXPENSILATIO.

Expensae. Expenses. Syn. IMPENSAE, SUMPTUS.

Expensae litis. Syn. *sumptus litis, impensae litis.*— C. 7.51.—See SUMPTUS LITIS.

Expensilatio. (From *expensum ferre*.) The making of an entry in a ledger, by which a person was charged with a debt in such fashion as if it were given to him as a loan. If made in the books of a banker, it created an obligation, *obligatio litteris contracta.*—See CONTRACTUS, NOMINA TRANSSCRIPTICIA.

Anon., *NDI* 5; Appert, *RHD* 11 (1932) 625.

Expensum ferre. See EXPENSILATIO.

Experiri actione (interdicto). To claim a right by a suit (or interdict). *Experiri ius* = to pursue a right. *Potestas experiundi* = the right to sue.

Beretta, *RISG* 85 (1948) 387.

Expilare hereditatem (expilatio). To purloin a thing belonging to an inheritance before the heir enters upon it. See CRIMEN EXPILATAE HEREDITATIS.—See USUCAPIO PRO HEREDE.

Expilator. A plunderer, a "more atrocious thief" (D. 47.18.1.1).

Explere. To fulfill (a mandate, a condition imposed by a testator, and the like). *Explere tempus usucapionis* = to possess a thing for the full time necessary for an *usucapio.*—See USUCAPIO.

Explorare (exploratio). In military service, to reconnoiter, to try to get information about enemy troops. *In exploratione esse* = to be put at a place to observe the enemy's movement. A soldier who leaves such a post, even though forced to do so under the pressure of the enemy, was punished by death.

Explorator. A scout, a spy.—See EXPLORARE, PRODITOR.

Bartoccini, *DE 2.*

Exploratus. In phrases like *explorati iuris est, exploratum est*, it is established, ascertained (law).

Exponere. With reference to written deeds, to write down (a donation, a security, *cautio*). The term belongs to the language of the later imperial constitutions.

Exponere filium (liberum). To expose, abandon a child in order to get rid of it. By doing so the father lost the *patria potestas* over the infant. The person who took him home and brought him up (*nutritor*) as of his own (*alumnus*) or as a slave, acquired power over him and might sell him as a slave. Later imperial legislation forbade the custom, but in vain. Parents were given the right to redeem a child that had been exposed, but were obliged to compensate the person who had raised him. The latter had to declare whether he would foster the child as free or slave, until Justinian ordained that any exposed child was to be considered free.—C. 8.51.

Mau, *RE 2* (*s.v. Aussetzung*); Weiss, *RE 11* (*s.v. Kinderaussetzung*); Albertoni, *Apokeryxis*, 1923; Carcopino, *Le droit rom. d'exposition*, Mémoires de la Société des Antiquaires en France, Sér. 8, vol. 7 (1924–27) 59; Fournier, *RHD* 5 (1926) 302; Radin, *CIJ* 20 (1925) 337; Volterra, *St Besta* 1 (1939) 455; Lanfranchi, *SDHI* 6 (1940); P. Delafon, *Droit d'exposition d'enfants à Rome*, Thèse, Montpellier, 1942; C. W. Westrup, *Introduction to Early R. Law*, I, 1 sect. 1 (1944) 248; Solazzi, *RISG* 86 (1949) 14.

Exponere servum (in insulam Aesculapii). Sick slaves abandoned by their masters (on the island of Aesculapius in the Tiber) to avoid expenses for medical cure became free under an edict of the emperor Claudius (A.D. 46–47).

Fasciato, *RHD* 27 (1949) 452.

Exportare. To send abroad (merchandise, slaves, etc.). Later imperial legislation forbade the export of certain commodities (such as wine or oil) to enemy countries. Export of weapons of any kind to an enemy state was punished by death and seizure of property.—C. 4.41.

Expositio filii. See EXPONERE FILIUM.

Expostulare. To address a complaint to a magistrate.

Expressa. "What was expressly stated is prejudicial, what was not expressed, is not prejudicial" (D. 50.17.195). The rule applies to statements concerning the object of a sale.—See DICTA.

Exprimere. To express. The term is frequently applied to testamentary dispositions or legal norms introduced by statutes, *senatusconsulta* and imperial constitutions.—See EXPRESSA.

Expromissio (expromissor). See the following item.

Expromittere (expromissio). To transfer an existing obligation into a *stipulatio* by which a stipulatory obligation replaced the original debt. On this occasion a change in the person of either the debtor or the creditor might occur when the debtor stipulated his debt to a new creditor (with the consent of the former creditor) or when a new debtor (*expromissor*) assumed another's debt towards the same creditor. Through such a transaction the former debtor was released if the creditor agreed to it. Sometimes *expromittere* has the same meaning as *promittere*.—See DELEGATIO.

De Villa, *NDI* 5.

Expugnare (navem, ratem). To subdue by force (a boat, vessel, *rates* = a bark, a raft).—D. 47.9.

Exrogatio legis. A partial repeal of a statute through the passage of a new one.—DEROGARE.

Exsecratio. A self-malediction. An oath was often combined with the imprecation of an evil or a curse upon oneself if one failed to carry out the terms of the oath. This made non-fulfillment a crime against the gods which resulted in exclusion from sacred rites.

Pfaff, *RE* Suppl. 4; De Ruggiero, *DE* 2, 2182.

Exsecrationes (defixiones). Maledictions written on metal tablets and directed against a personal enemy of the writer.

De Ruggiero, *DE* 2.

Exsecutio. (From *exsequi*.) With regard to criminal matters, prosecution of a criminal through accusation and trial; in civil matters = the claim on the part of a creditor of his right against a debtor, in particular against one who had been condemned in a civil trial and did not fulfill the judgment debt. The execution of a judgment in a civil trial was either personal (on the person of the judgment debtor) or real (on his property).—C. 7.53.—See IUDICATUM, LEGIS ACTIO PER MANUS INIECTIONEM, PIGNORIS CAPIO, ADDICTIO, DUCI IUBERE, MISSIONES IN POSSESSIONEM, BONORUM VENDITIO.

L. Wenger, *Actio iudicati,* 1902, 7; A. d'Ors, *AHDE* 16 (1945) 747.

Exsecutor (negotii, litis, litium). A court clerk serving as an official organ of summons in the proceedings of the later Empire. The defendant pays fees to the *exsecutor* and must give security (*cautio iudicio sisti*) that he will appear in court until the end of the trial. In the case of his refusal, the *exsecutor* may take him into custody. The *exsecutor* was also in charge of the execution of judgments. In Justinian's procedure the institution of *exsecutores negotii* underwent a radical change. They were private, influential individuals of high rank and their functions were enlarged as well as their financial profits.—C. 12.60; Nov. 96.—See SPORTULAE.

Arangio-Ruiz, *BIDR* 24 (1911) 226; Partsch, *Nachr. Götting. Ges. Wiss.,* 1911, 241; Rostowzew, *RE* 6; Thomas, *Études Girard* 1 (1912) 379; A. Steinwenter, *Versäumnisverfahren,* 1914, 131; Balogh, *St Riccobono* 2 (1916) 449; P. Collinet, *Procédure par libelle,* 1932, 79, 464, 480; Giffard, *RHD* 14 (1935) 732.

Exsecutor testamenti. The term and the institution are unknown to Roman classical law. According to the modern conception the *exsecutor testamente* is a person holding an estate in trust, and administering and distributing it according to the testator's wishes. The *familiae emptor* in the early Roman law fulfilled a similar task but the juristic structure of the two institutions is different. Later imperial legislation recognized the designation of a person in a testament for the fulfillment of specific dispositions of the testator connected with charitable purposes, such as ransom of prisoners of war, foundations (*piae causae*), and the like.

Kübler, *RE* 5A, 1013 (*s.v. Testamentsvollstrecker*); E. Caillemer, *Origine de l'exécution testamentaire,* 1901; Bruck, *GrZ* 40 (1914) 533; B. Biondi, *Successione testamentaria,* 1943, 607; Macqueron, *RHD* 24 (1945) 150.

Exsecutores. Officials in the late Empire authorized to enforce the payment of taxes and fiscal debts. Syn. *intercessores.*

Exsecutores rei iudicatae (sententiae). Officials charged with the execution of judgments.—See EXSECUTOR (NEGOTII).

Exsequi. To perform a legal act, to pursue a matter in court to its end (*actionem, litem*), to prosecute a crime in a penal trial until sentence, to execute a judgment debt (*sententiam, rem iudicatam*). Generally *exsequi* is applied to the activity of the various types of EXSECUTORES.

Exsilium. See EXILIUM.

Exsistere. *Condicio extitit,* see CONDICIO.

Exsolvere (exsolutio). See SOLVERE, SOLUTIO.

Exspirare. To become void, extinguished. Syn. *evanescere, exstingui.*

Exstare. To exist. *Exstat* = there is. The term is frequently used with reference to existing legal rules (*exstat edictum, senatusconsultum, rescriptum*) to point out "there is" a legal norm for the case under discussion.

Exstinguere. To annul, cancel (an agreement, a contractual clause, a condition, a legacy). *Exstingui* (syn. *evanescere, exspirare*) is applied to the extinction of rights and the obligations connected therewith (an action, a servitude, a usufruct, a stipulation, a legacy).

Exsul (exul). A man living in voluntary or compulsory exile.—See EXILIUM.

Exter, exterus. See EXTRANEUS.

Extorquere. To extort, to force a person to give or to do something, or to perform a legal act (to promise by *stipulatio,* to give security).—See METUS, VIS.

Extra iudicium. Outside the court, extrajudicially.

Extra ordinem. Beyond the normal order of things.
—See COGNITIO EXTRA ORDINEM, EXTRAORDINARIUS.
Wlassak, *Kritische Studien zur Theorie der Rechtsquellen,* 1884, 85; Lauria, *ANap* 56 (1934) 308; Orestano, *StCagl* 26 (1938) 170.

Extraneus (exter, exterus, extrarius). One who is outside; not belonging to a certain family or being no relative of a certain person (for instance, of the woman for whom one constitutes a dowry). *Extraneus* is also any third person not involved in a given transaction or situation, as, for instance, in possessory controversies between two persons, any one who never had possession of the thing under dispute. Syn. *persona extranea.*
Guarino, *ZSS* 61 (1941) 378.

Extraneus heres. An outside heir who is not subject to the testator's power at his death, and therefore is neither his *heres suus et necessarius* nor his *heres necessarius.* Such an *extraneus heres* is an emancipated son, or a slave appointed as an heir and freed in the testament who, however, had been manumitted by his master (the testator) when he was still alive, but after the testament was made. See NECESSARIUS HERES. An *extraneus heres* was given an opportunity to deliberate (DELIBERARE, *ius deliberandi*) whether to accept the inheritance or not. Therefore an explicit declaration of acceptance was required from him.—See VOLUNTARIUS HERES, PRO HEREDE GERERE, TEMPUS AD DELIBERANDUM.
Solazzi, *St Scorza,* 1940.

Extraordinarii. Selected army troops destined for particularly difficult tasks.
Liebenam, *RE* 6; Cagnat, *DS* 2.

Extraordinarius. What is *extra ordinem,* beyond the normal order of things. See EXTRA ORDINEM. The term is mostly applied to procedural institutions, both civil and criminal (*actio, iudicium, poena, cognitio, persecutio, crimen, remedium*).—D. 50.13; C. 47.11.
—See COGNITIO EXTRA ORDINEM, CRIMINA PUBLICA, IUS EXTRAORDINARIUM.

Extrarius. See EXTRANEUS.

Exul. See EXSUL.

Exurere, exurendum damnare. See CREMATIO.

F

Fabri. Workers, craftsmen, artisans, e.g., *fabri tignarii* (carpenters), *ferrarii* (forgers), *argentarii* (silversmiths), etc. *Fabri navales* = shipbuilders. Rich material on the various organizations (*collegia*) of craftsmen is found in inscriptions. So-called *cento-narii* (voluntary firemen) appear united with the *fabri* in one association (*collegium fabrorum et centonariorum*). In the earliest organization of the Roman army, attributed to the king Servius Tullius, there were two *centuriae* of *fabri* for all kinds of craftman's work.—See PRAEFECTUS FABRUM.
Kornemann, *RE* 6; Jullian, *DS* 2; Liebenam, *DE* 3; H. C. Maué, *Praefectus fabrum,* 1887, 50; idem, *Die Vereine der fabri centonarii,* Frankfurt, 1886; G. Kühn, *De opificum R. condicione,* Diss. Halle, 1910, 21; O. Hirschfeld, *Kleine Schriften,* 1913, 101; Schnorr v. Carolsfeld, *Gesch. der juristischen Person* 1 (1933) 281; Riccobono, *FIR* 2 (1941) no. 87.

Fabricenses. Workers in state factories (*fabricae*) for arms and military equipment. They had a privileged position in the later Empire, but were subject to very rigid discipline. Desertion from their posts was severely punished.—C. 11.10.
Seeck, *RE* 6.

Fabriles operae. See OPERAE.

Facere. "The term includes all kinds of doing, as to give, to fulfill an obligation, to pay money, to judge" (D. 50.16.218). With reference to contractual obligations *facere* = to do (or not to do) something.—OBLIGATIO, CONTRACTUS INNOMINATI.
Scherillo, *BIDR* 36 (1928) 29.

Facere aliquid alicuius. To make a thing enter into the ownership or possession of another.

Facere posse. To be able to pay one's debts, to be solvent. In certain civil actions the limit to which a defendant can be adjudicated is set by *in id quod facere potest* (= to as much as he can pay); see BENEFICIUM COMPETENTIAE.
Guarino, *SDHI* 7 (1941) 5; G. Nocera, *Insolvenza,* 1942, 40; F. Pastori, *Profilo dogmatico dell'obbligazione rom.,* 1951, 131.

Facinus. A general term for a criminal offense.
Del Prete, *AnMac* 11 (1937) 106.

Facti est. See RES FACTI.

Factio. A combination of persons, a plot for criminal purposes, in particular for organizing a sedition.

Factio testamenti. See TESTAMENTI FACTIO.

Factiones. Political unions for the purpose of the realization of the political ambitions of their members with the help of friends, clients and sympathizers.
Strasburger, *RE* 18, 788; Maricq, *Bull. Cl. Lettres, Acad. Royale de Belgique,* 36 (1950) 396.

Factum. A thing done by a human being, also an event, a happening independent of human influence. *Factum* is often opposed to *ius. Res facti—res iuris* = a matter of fact—a matter of law; *facti esse—iuris esse, questio facti—quaestio iuris. Condicio facti—condicio iuris* = a condition depending upon a fact—a condition imposed by the law. For the distinction *actiones in factum—actiones in ius conceptae,* see FORMULAE IN IUS CONCEPTAE; for the distinction *error facti—error iuris* (*in iure*), see ERROR FACTI, IGNORANTIA IURIS.
Vassalli, *AnPer* 28 (1914); Georgescu, *Scr Ferrini* 3 (Univ. Sacro Cuore, Milan, 1948) 144.

Factum alienum. Something done by another person. See NEMO FACTUM ALIENUM, etc. Ant. *factum suum* = something done by a person for which that same person is responsible. "Everybody bears the consequences of his doings, not his adversary" (D. 50.17.155 pr.).

Facultas. The legal ability to conclude an agreement or to accomplish a valid act (a testament).—See LIBERA MORTIS FACULTAS.

Facultates (facultates patrimonii). Property, wealth. The possession of a fixed fortune was a requirement for certain official positions. Thus, for instance, a *decurio* (= councilor) of a municipal council had to have one hundred thousand sesterces. The patrimonial census of a knight (see EQUITES) was 400,000 sesterces. Obligations of maintaining other persons (see ALIMENTA) are estimated according to the means (*pro modo facultatum*) of the person obligated.—See BENEFICIUM COMPETENTIAE.

Faenus. See FENUS.

Falcidia. Refers either to the statute *lex Falcidia* or to the so-called *quarta Falcidia*. See LEX FALCIDIA.
Vassalli, *BIDR* 26 (1913).

Falsa causa. An untrue, erroneous ground assigned by a testator or donor as the motive for a legacy or gift. Generally, it had no influence on the validity of the disposition.—C. 6.44.

Falsa demonstratio. See DEMONSTRATIO FALSA.

Falsa moneta. Counterfeit money, coins (*nummi*) made of tin or lead. Counterfeiters were punished under the *Lex Cornelia de falsis*.—C. 9.24.—See FALSUM.
Taubenschlag, *RE* 16, 1455 (*s.v. Münzverbrechen*).

Falsarius. One who commits a *crimen falsi,* such as a forger of documents, a counterfeiter of coins, measures, weights, and the like.—See FALSUM.

Falsum. A general definition says: "*falsum* is that which in reality does not exist, but is asserted as true" (Paul. Coll. 8, 6, 1). In the field of penal law *falsum* covers any kind of forgery, falsification or counterfeiting. The fundamental statute on *falsum* was the *Lex Cornelia de falsis* by Sulla (81 B.C.), also called the *Lex Cornelia testamentaria* or *nummaria* since it dealt with the forging of testaments and counterfeiting of coins as well. The statute was still in force in Justinian's Digest and was applied to crimes which originally were not mentioned in it and only through *senatusconsulta,* the interpretation by the jurists and the practice of the criminal courts became punishable under the statute. With regard to last wills the destruction or concealing thereof was a *crimen falsi* as well as the substitution of a forged testament or a fraudulent manipulation of the seals. See SENATUSCONSULTUM GEMINIANUM, LIBONIANUM, LICINIANUM. These decrees of the senate extended the penalties of the *Lex Cornelia* to forgery of documents other than wills, false testimony, producing forged imperial enactments (*epistulae, rescripta*).

With regard to coins the *Lex Cornelia* set penalties for various kinds of forgery and for knowingly bringing false money (see ADULTERINUS, FALSA MONETA) into circulation. Manifold crimes connected with jurisdictional activity were later subject to the penalties of the *Lex Cornelia,* as, for instance, the passing of an unjust judgment with the intention of violating existing laws, the giving of a bribe to a judge or the accepting of one by a judge, any kind of bribery in criminal matters to cause the dropping of an accusation or of the condemnation of a culprit, false testimony or subordination of witnesses; furthermore the refusal to accept state money, assuming false impersonation of an official, the counterfeiting of measures and weights, etc. Penalties of the *Lex Cornelia* were various, primarily *aquae et ignis interdictio* (see INTERDICERE AQUA ET IGNI), for graver crimes deportation and death.—D. 48.10; C. 9.22; 23; 24.— See QUAESTIONES PERPETUAE, PRODERE INSTRUMENTA, RESIGNARE.
Hitzig, *RE* 6; Humbert, *DS* 2, 967; H. Erman, *La falsification des actes dans l'antiquité, Mél Nicole,* 1905, 111; L. De Sarlo, *Repressione penale del falso documentale, Riv. di dir. e proc. penale* 14 (1937) 317; Levy, *BIDR* 45 (1938) 60; Archi, *Studi nelle scienze giur. e sociali* 26 (1941) 35; idem, *St Pavia* 26 (1941) 9.—On Lex Cornelia: Rotondi, *Leges publicae populi Romani,* 1912, 356; Cuq, *DS* 3, 1138.

Falsum testamentum. A forged testament. "It is no testament" (D. 50.16.221).

Falsum testimonium. See TESTIMONIUM FALSUM.

Falsus accusator. See CALUMNIA.

Falsus procurator. One who falsely assumes the role of another's representative (mandatary). He is considered a thief when he accepts money on behalf of his non-existing principal.
H. Fitting, *Sciens debitum accipere* (Lausanne, 1926) 19.

Falsus tutor. "A guardian who is not a guardian" (D. 50.16.221), a person who acts as a guardian (tutor or curator) without having been appointed as such.—See ACTIO PROTUTELAE, PRO TUTORE GERERE. —D. 27.6.
E. Levy, *Privatstrafe und Schadensersatz,* 1915, 84; idem, *Konkurrenz der Actionen* 2, 1 (1922) 243; Solazzi, *AG* 91 (1924) 133.

Familia. The term "has received different meanings, it is referred both to things and persons" (D. 50.16.195.1). Already in the Twelve Tables it appears in both senses: on the one hand embracing all persons who are under the same paternal power (the wife *in manu* included) and in a broader sense, all persons connected by blood through descent from the same ancestor, on the other hand referring to the whole property of a person, including all corporeal things and slaves. In a narrower meaning *familia* denotes all the servants (*in servitio*) in a household, in particular slaves and free men serving in good faith as slaves.—See ACTIO FAMILIAE ERCISCUNDAE, CAPITIS DEMINUTIO, EXIRE, FILIUS FAMILIAS, FILIA FAMI-

LIAS, MANCIPATIO FAMILIAE, PATER FAMILIAS, and the following items.

Leonhard, *RE* 6; Sachers, *ibid.* 184, 2124; Baudry, *DS* 2; De Ruggiero, *DE* 3; De Martino, *NDI* 5; C. W. L. Launspach, *State and Family in Early Rome*, London, 1908; P. Moriaud, *De la simple famille parternelle*, Genève, 1910; A. Baudrillart, *La famille dans l'antiquité*, 1929; Wlassak, *Studien zum altröm. Erb- und Vermächtnisrecht, SbWien* 215 (1933) 35; Cornil, *RHD* 16 (1937) 555; C. W. Westrup, *Introduction to Early R. Law. The Patriarchal Joint Family*, 1–3 (1934–1944); *idem, St Albertoni* 1 (1935) 143; Henrion, *Des origines du mot familia, AntCl* 10 (1941) 36; 11 (1942) 253; Burck, *Die altröm. Familie*, in *Das neue Bild der Antike* 2 (1942) 156; Paribeni, *Familia romana*, 3rd ed. 1947; C. Cosentini, *St sui liberti* 1 (1948) 27; B. Albanese, *Successione ereditaria* (= *AnPal* 20, 1949) 143; Volterra, *Sui 'mores' della 'familia' rom., RendLinc*, Ser. VIII, vol. 4 (1949–50) 516; M. Kaser, *La f. romana, AnTr* 20 (1950).

Familia castrensis. See CASTRENSIANI.

Familia pecuniaque. The whole property of a person.
Pierron, *Revue générale de droit* 19 (1895) 385; Pfaff, *Fschr Hanausek*, 1925, 94; M. F. Lepri, *Saggi sulla terminologia . . . del patrimonio*, 1 (1942); M. Kaser, *Das altröm. Ius*, 1949, 159; B. Albanese, *Successione ereditaria* (= *AnPal* 20, 1949) 134.

Familia rustica. Slaves working on a rural estate; ant. *familia urbana* = slaves attached to the household of their master in the city.—See VILICUS.

Familia urbana. See the foregoing item.

Familiae emptor. A trustee to whom a testator transferred his property through a *testamentum per aes et libram* and gave oral instructions (NUNCUPARE) as to the distribution of it after his death.—See MANCIPATIO FAMILIAE, NUNCUPATIO.

Familiares. The servants in a household.

Familiaris. Concerned with, belonging to the family. —See RES FAMILIARIS, SEPULCRUM FAMILIARE, SACRA FAMILIARIA.

Famosus. An action (*actio, iudicium, causa, delictum*) involving infamy for the defendants.—See ACTIONES FAMOSAE, CARMEN FAMOSUM, LIBELLI FAMOSI, FEMINA FAMOSA.

Far, farreum, farreus panis. See CONFARREATIO.

Fas. (As opposed to *ius.*) The moral law of divine origin, whereas *ius* is law created by men. The two terms appear together in the phrase *ius fasque. Fas* is what gods permit, *nefas* what they forbid. In its widest sense *fas* is what is permitted by law or custom.
Berger, *RE* 10, 1213; Kübler, *DE* 3; Ferrini, *NDI* 5; Beduschi, *RISG* 10 (1935) 209; F. Di Martino, *Giurisdizione*, 1937, 218; Orestano, *BIDR* 46 (1939) 194 (Bibl.), 276; Goidanich, *Atti Accad. d'Italia*, Ser. 8, v. 3 (1943) 499; M. Kaser, *Das altröm. Ius*, 1949, 29; Latte, *ZSS* 67 (1950) 56.

Fasces. A bundle of rods with an axe in the middle, carried by lictors before consuls and higher magistrates when they appeared in public or on other specific occasion. The axe symbolized the power to impose the death penalty (*ius gladii*) and was put into the *fasces* only when the magistrate exercised his military power (*imperium militiae*, see DOMI).
Samter, *RE* 6; De Ruggiero, *DE* 3; Treves, *OCD*; De Sanctis, *Riv. di filologia* 57 (1929) 1; Vogel, *ZSS* 67 (1950) 63.

Fasces. A list of tax-payers, in the later Empire.

Fasti. See DIES FASTI.

Fasti consulares (consulum). Lists of consuls in chronological order according to the years in which they were in office. There were also *fasti* of other higher magistrates, as dictators, censors (*fasti magistratuum*) and of high priests (*fasti sacerdotales*). *Fasti* is also used as the name of the official calendar of *dies fasti* and *nefasti*.
Edition: Degrassi, *Inscriptiones Italiae* 13, 1, 2 (1947); A. H. McDonald, *OCD*; Schön, *RE* 6; Bouché-Leclercq, *DS* 2; Liebenam, *F. c. von 30 v. Chr. bis 565 n. Chr.*, 1910; G. Costa, *I f. consolari*, 1910; E. Pais, *Ricerche sulla storia* 2 (1916); Cornelius, *Untersuchungen zur früheren röm. Geschichte*, 1940, 50; K. Hanell, *Das altröm. eponyme Amt*, Lund, 1946; A. Degrassi, *I fasti consolari dell'Impero romano dal 30 a.C. al 613 d.C.*, Rome, 1952.

Fatalis. See DIES FATALIS, DAMNUM FATALE.

Fateri. Syn. *confiteri.* See CONFESSIO.

Favor. (From *favere.*) A tendency in legislation, jurisprudence or jurisdiction in favor of certain legal institutions (testament, dowry, liberty). The intensity of such tendencies varied through the centuries and assumed particular strength in Justinian's law, but their origin goes back to classical ideas. The modern Romanistic literature inclines to ascribe these tendencies to Justinian's reforms, a doctrine which hardly can be true since in various instances the jurists reveal in their writings a favorable attitude in specific decisions even though they do not use the word *favor*. See the following items.
Guarneri-Citati, *Indice²* (1927) 39 (Bibl.).

Favor debitoris. The tendency to interpret contractual clauses in cases involving debt in favor of the debtor. With regard to *stipulatio* there was the following rule: "if it is doubtful what was agreed upon, the words are to be interpreted against the creditor" (D. 35.4.26). A larger application of the rule in civil trials is expressed in the saying: "defendants should be treated more favorably than plaintiffs" (D. 50.17.125). The legislation of the Christian emperors openly acted in favor of the debtors.

Favor dotis. The law of the dowry is governed by the tendency to favor the constitution of a dowry and its preservation during marriage so that, in the event of the restitution the dowry would remain undiminished, as far as possible. "It is in the public interest that dowries be preserved for the women" (D. 23.3.2). —See DOS.

Favor libertatis. "Whenever an interpretation regarding liberty is doubtful, the answer should be in favor of liberty" (D. 50.17.20). The simplification of the forms of manumission is an expression of this *favor libertatis* as well as the admission of cases in which a slave becomes free without manumission. Particularly obvious is the *favor libertatis* in decisions concerning testamentary manumissions which are declared valid where according to a strict interpretation of the law they would be void. Justinian called himself "a favorer of liberty" (*fautor libertatis*, C. 7.7.2.2).—D. 40.8.—See LIBERTAS, MANUMISSIO.

I. Pfaff, *Zur Lehre vom f. l.,* 1894; Schulz, *ZSS* 48 (1928) 197; Rotondi, *Scr giuridici* 3 (1930) 476; Albertario, *Studi* 1 (1933) 63; M. Nicolau, *Causa liberalis,* 1933, 174; 219; Orias, *ACII* 1 (1935) 153; Imbert, *RHD* 27 (1949) 274.

Favor testamenti. A tendency to declare a testament valid despite some doubts in this respect, in order to realize the will of the testator. Interpretation of ambiguous testamentary dispositions was governed by the desire to fulfill the wishes of the testator; hence, the frequent statements in juristic writings urging that his will (*voluntas*) be interpreted favorably (*benigne, plenius*).—See BENIGNA INTERPRETATIO, BENIGNE.

E. Costa, *Papiniano* 3 (1893); A. Suman, *Favor t.,* 1916; B. Biondi, *Successione testamentaria,* 1943, 7.

Felicissimus. An honorific title given to emperors in inscriptions.

De Ruggiero, *DE* 3.

Femina. A woman. "Women are barred from all civil and public office and therefore they cannot be judges, hold a magistracy, bring a suit, intervene for another, or be a representative in a trial" (D. 50.17.2 pr.). In many legal matters the position of women was inferior to that of men. Several restrictions on their capacity were imposed in the law of successions and obligations. As long as the guardianship over women was in force, they were not able to conclude legal transactions or manage their affairs without the consent of the guardian. A woman could not be a guardian; an exception was later introduced in behalf of a mother if there was no tutor appointed in a testament or by law. She had, however, to assume the obligation not to marry again. Postclassical development and Justinian law brought some reforms towards the equalization of the sexes under the law but some substantial differences remained even in Justinian's codification.—See TUTELA MULIERUM, LEX VOCONIA, SENATUSCONSULTUM VELLEIANUM, MULIERES.

Couch, *Woman in Early R. Law, Harvard LR* 8 (1894/5) 39; Wenger, *ZSS* 26 (1905) 449; Frezza, *Aeg* 11 (1931) 363; *idem, StCagl* 22 (1933) 126; Brassloff, *ZSS* 41 (1921); *idem, St zur rom. Rechtsgesch. I. Intestaterbrecht der Frauen,* 1925; Volterra, *BIDR* 48 (1941) 74.

Femina famosa (probrosa). See MERETRIX.

Nardi, *StSas* 16 (1938).

Femina stolata. See MATRONA.

Fenerator. Money-lender, usurer.—See FENUS, LEX MARCIA.

Fenus (faenus). Interest paid by the debtor to the lender. Syn. *usurae.* From the time of the Twelve Tables the legislation often intervened with the limitation of the rate of interest. See FENUS UNCIARIUM, FENUS SEMIUNCIARIUM, LEX GENUCIA, LEX MARCIA, LEX CORNELIA POMPEIA. Under the Empire the rate of twelve per cent was termed *fenus licitum, usurae legitimae.* A creditor who took higher interest could be sued for four times the amount exceeding the legal rate. Justinian considerably reduced the highest admissible rate, set different rates according to the nature of the loan and abolished the fourfold penalty.—See USURAE, PECUNIA FENEBRIS, EXERCERE PECUNIAM, and the following items.

Klingmüller, *RE* 6; Baudry, *DS* 2; G. Rotondi, *Leges publicae populi rom.,* 1912 (*Encicl. giuridica ital.*); Klingmüller, *ZSS* 23 (1902) 23.

Fenus licitum. See the foregoing item.

Fenus nauticum. A loan given in connection with the transportation of merchandise by vessel. The loan had to be repaid only when the ship arrived safely in port with the cargo. Because of the risk which the loan-giver assumed (shipwreck, piracy), the rate of interest was unlimited until Justinian fixed it at 12 per cent. Syn. *usurae maritimae.* The money loaned was called *pecunia traiecticia* as "money conveyed overseas," since either the money itself or the cargo bought by it was to be transported by boat.— D. 22.2; C. 4.33.

Klingmüller, *RE* 6, 2200; Cuq, *DS* 2; Heichelheim, *OCD* (*s.v. bottomry loan*); F. Pringsheim, *Kauf mit fremdem Geld,* 1916, 143; Nicolau, *Mél Jorga,* 1933, 925; De Martino, *RDNav* 1 (1935) 217; Biscardi, *St Albertoni* 2 (1937) 345; *idem, StSen* 60 (1948) 567; De Martino, *RDNav* 15 (1949) 19.

Fenus semiunciarium. A rate of interest amounting to one-half of the FENUS UNCIARIUM. It was introduced by a plebiscite of 347 B.C.—See the following item.

Fenus unciarium. The rate of interest established by the Twelve Tables. It was one *uncia* (one-twelfth of the sum loaned) per annum (8⅓ per cent), or when the year was reckoned as ten months, 10 per cent. Some scholars assume that such interest was paid monthly making 100 per cent per annum, which does not seem likely, although the other calculation appears too low for the primitive economy of the fifth century B.C.

G. Billeter, *Geschichte der Zinsfusses,* 1898, 157; Appleton, *RHD* 43 (1919) 467; Scialoja, *BIDR* 33 (1924) 240 (= *St giur.* 2, 287); Kübler, *Geschichte,* 1925, 47; Nicolau, *Mél Iorga,* 1933, 925; L. Clerici, *Economia e finanza dei Romani,* 1 (1943) 352; Arangio-Ruiz, *Istituzioni* (1947) 304; E. Weiss, *Institutionen²* (1949) 304; Kunkel, *Röm. Recht³* (1949) 182.

Fera (bestia). A wild animal. It was considered a *res nullius.* When caught (not merely wounded) it became the property of the captor and remained such as long as it was in his custody. After regaining its natural liberty it could be the object of another *occupatio.* A wild animal belongs to *res nec* *mancipi.*—See ANIMALIA, ANIMUS REVERTENDI, EDICTUM DE FERIS, OCCUPATIO, VENATIO.

Kaser, *RE* 7A, 684; Landucci, *NDI* 2, 588; *idem, AG* 29 (1882).

Ferendus non est. Said when the reasons (excuses) alleged in court by a person to justify his acting, are not to be taken into consideration.

Feriae (dies festi). Days on which agricultural, industrial and other kinds of labor, even that of slaves to a certain extent, were suspended, as well as all judicial activity (*vacatio a forensibus negotiis*). Such days were dedicated primarily to religious ceremonies and popular festivals. Any offence against such holidays was punished. There were also extraordinary *feriae publicae,* as on the occasion of a victory or an accession to the throne. *Feriae privatae* (anniversaries, commemorative days in associations, see COLLEGIA) considerably increased the number of holidays on which any labor ceased. At the beginning of the Principate the number of public holidays amounted to forty-eight. The whole matter was later regulated by a law of A.D. 389, which also took into consideration Christian holidays.—D. 2.12; C. 3.12.

Wissowa, *RE* 6; Jullian, *DS* 2; De Ruggiero, *DE* 2, 1782; Weinberger, *DE* 3; De Robertis, *Rapporti di lavoro,* 1946, 278; J. Paoli, *RHD* 30 (1952) 304.

Feriae Latinae. See PRAEFECTUS URBI.

Samter, *RE* 6; Jullian, *DS* 2.

Feriaticus (feriatus) dies. Holidays on which agricultural and industrial labor ceased. Work connected with the military service had to be done. Some acts of voluntary jurisdiction as, e.g., the appointment of a tutor or curator, were permitted.—See FERIAE.

Ferrariae. Iron mines.—See PROCURATOR FERRARIARUM.

De Ruggiero, *DE* 3.

Ferre. See FERENDUS NON EST.

Ferre expensum. See EXPENSILATIO.

Ferre iudicem. To propose to one's adversary in a trial a certain person from the panel of jurors (*album iudicum*) to be judge in the controversy. *Sumere iudicem* = to accept the proposal; *eierare* = to reject, to refuse (under oath).

Ferre legem. To propose (bring in) a law, to enact, to make a law.

Ferre opem. See OPE CONSILIO.

Ferre sententiam. To pass a judgment.

Ferre suffragium. To vote.

Ferre testimonium. To bear testimony.

Ferri iubere. See DUCI IUBERE.

Ferruminatio. The junction of two objects of the same metal, for instance, a bronze arm with a bronze statue. When the parts belonged to different owners, the owner of the principal part became owner of the whole. This was not the case when the soldering metal was different, as, for instance, when in the example above plumb was used (*adplumbatio*). If separation is possible without destruction of the whole, the owner of the part which was illegally joined could claim its restitution after having enforced its separation through *actio ad exhibendum.* —See CORPUS EX COHAERENTIBUS, PLUMBATURA, ACTIO AD EXHIBENDUM.

Leonhard, *RE* 1 (*s.v. adplumbatio*); Pampaloni, *Scritti* 1 (1941, written 1879) 9; Bozzi, *NDI* 5.

Festi dies. See FERIAE.

Festuca. A stalk of grass, later a rod, used in earlier law when a thing was claimed by *rei vindicatio* or in specific form of manumission (*manumissio vindicta*).

Nisbet, *JRSt* 8 (1918); Meÿlan, *La baguette, Mél F. Guisan* (Lausanne, 1950).

Fetiales. A group of twenty ·priests who from the earliest times were charged not only with religious functions, but also with public service, in particular in international relations with other states. Their duty was to observe whether or not the terms of international treaties were being fulfilled. They were involved in the concluding of treaties, in affairs of extradition, and were representatives of Rome in serving official declaration of war. In their missions abroad they were headed by one of them whose official title as the speaker of the delegation was *pater patratus.*

Samter, *RE* 6; A. Weiss, *DS* 2; De Ruggiero, *DE* 3; Ferrini, *NDI* 5, 928; Rose, *OCD*; Frank, *ClPhilol* 7 (1912); Volterra, *Scritti Carnelutti* 4 (1950) 248.

Ficta possessio (fictus possessor). See POSSESSOR FICTUS.

Fictio. (From *fingere.*) The assumption of the existence of a legal or factual element, although such an element does not exist. The purpose of a fiction is to cause certain legal consequences which otherwise would not occur. For *fictio* in the procedural formula, see ACTIONES FICTICIAE.

R. Dekkers, *La fiction juridique,* 1935.

Fictio legis Corneliae. See LEX CORNELIA DE CAPTIVIS.

Fideicommissaria hereditas. See FIDEICOMMISSUM HEREDITATIS.—Inst. 2.23.

Fideicommissaria hereditatis petitio. See HEREDITATIS PETITIO FIDEICOMMISSARIA.

Fideicommissaria libertas. Liberty granted through a *fideicommissum.*—D. 40.5; C. 7.4.—See MANUMISSIO FIDUCIARIA, SENATUSCONSULTUM DASUMIANUM, RUBRIANUM, VITRASIANUM.

Montel, *St Bonfante* 3 (1930) 633.

Fideicommissarius. (Noun.) Indicates sometimes a person awarded with a *fideicommissum,* sometimes an heir charged with one.

Fideicommissum. (From *fidei alicuius committere.*) Originally a request addressed by the testator to his heir ("*te rogo,*" "*peto a te*") to carry out a certain performance (payment of a sum of money, transfer of property) to the benefit of a third person. It created only a moral (not legal) duty. Augustus rendered the *fideicommissum* obligatory to the heir and made it enforceable by a new procedure (*cognitio extra ordinem*) before a special magistrate created for the purpose, the *praetor fideicommissarius*. *Fideicommissum* was formless and this advantage over legacies in the form of *legata* furthered its development. Anybody who received a gift *mortis causa* (not only an heir) might be charged with a *fideicommissum*. Not even a testament, without which a legacy could not be bequeathed, was necessary since a *fideicommissum* could be imposed on an heir at intestacy. The differences between *fideicommissa* and *legata* gradually disappeared and under Justinian both institutions were considered equal (*per omnia exaequata sunt*, D. 30.1).—D. 30; 31; 32; C. 3.17; 6.42–46.—See FIDEICOMMITTERE, SENATUSCONSULTUM PEGASIANUM, CODICILLI, ORATIO HADRIANI, ORATIO MARCI.

Leonhard, *RE* 6; Humbert, *DS* 2; Trifone, *NDI* 6 (1002); Kübler, *DE* 3; Milone, *Il fedecommesso romano*, 1896; Declareuil, *Mél Gérardin* (1907) 135; Riccobono, *Mél Cornil* 2 (1926) 310; R. Trifone, *Il fedecommesso* 1914; Lemercier, *RHD* 14 (1935) 443, 623; B. Biondi, *Successione testamentaria*, 1943, 289; F. Schwarz, *ZSS* 68 (1951) 266.

Fideicommissum a debitore relictum. A *fideicommissum* by which the testator ordered his debtor to pay the debt not to the heir but to a third person.

G. Wesenberg, *Verträge zu Gunsten Dritter*, 1949, 56.

Fideicommissum hereditatis. A *fideicommissum* concerning the whole estate or a part of it. A fideicommissary honored by such a *fideicommissum* became either successor to the entire inheritance or co-successor with the heir who had been charged with the *fideicommissum* (the fiduciary heir). The latter remained the heir (*heres*) but he had to transfer the pertinent portion to the fideicommissary; for the transfer of the testator's claims and debts reciprocal stipulations were made (*stipulationes emptae venditae hereditatis*) by which the fiduciary heir obligated himself to restitute the fideicommissary the payments received from the debtors of the deceased, whereas the fideicommissary assumed the liability to indemnify proportionally the heir for payments made to the creditors of the estate. For later reforms which directly gave the fideicommissary the legal situation of an heir and made the stipulations superfluous, see SENATUSCONSULTUM TREBELLIANUM and PEGASIANUM. Justinian simplified the whole matter and gave the fideicommissary the position of a universal successor (*heredis loco*).—Inst. 2.23.—See HEREDITATIS PETITIO FIDEICOMMISSARIA, COMMUNICARE LUCRUM, EXCEPTIO RESTITUTAE HEREDITATIS.

Lemercier, *RHD* 14 (1935) 462, 623; La Pira, *StSen* 47 (1933) 243.

Fideicommissum liberatatis. See MANUMISSIO FIDEICOMMISSARIA.

Fideicommittere. See FIDEICOMMISSUM. *Fideicommittere* was the term used by the testator when he addressed his request to his heir: "*fidei tuae committo*" (= I leave it to your faith, honesty). Other words could, however, be used as well (*peto, rogo, volo*, etc.).

Fideiussio, fideiussor. See ADPROMISSIO.

Fideiussor fideiussoris. A surety who assumes guaranty for another surety.

Fideiussor iudicio sistendi causa. See VINDEX, VADIMONIUM, SISTERE ALIQUEM.

Fideiussor tutoris (curatoris). A surety for a guardian (tutor or curator).—D. 27.7; C. 5.57.

Fideipromissio, fideipromissor. See ADPROMISSIO.

Fidem alicuius sequi. (Syn. *fidem habere alicui*.) To put faith in one's honesty, to trust.

Fidem praestare (conventioni, pacto). To perform the obligations assumed in an agreement. Syn. *fidem servare*; ant. *fidem fallere, fidem rumpere*.

Fides. Honesty, uprightness, trustworthiness. In legal relations *fides* denotes honest keeping of one's promises and performing the duties assumed by agreement. On the other side *fides* means the confidence, trust, faith one has in another's behavior, particularly with regard to the fulfillment of his liabilities. See FIDEM ALICUIUS SEQUI. For *fides* as the element of reciprocal confidence in contractual relations, see IUS GENTIUM; for *fides* in the promissory formulae by which one assumes guaranty for another, see ADPROMISSIO.—See BONA FIDES, CONTRACTUS BONAE FIDEI, IUDICIA BONAE FIDEI, EMPTOR BONAE FIDEI, LIBER HOMO, etc., USUCAPIO, POSSESSOR BONAE FIDEI, MALA FIDES.

De Ruggiero, *DE* 3, 77; Heinze, *Hermes* 64 (1929) 140; Fränkel, *Rheinisches Museum für Philol.* 71 (1916) 187; W. Flume, *Studien zur Akzessorietät*, 1932, 64; Beseler, *Fides, ACDR* Roma 1 (1934) 135; Hermesdorf, *ACII* 1 (1935) 161; F. Schulz, *Principles of R. Law* (1936) 223; Kunkel, *Fschr Koschaker* 2 (1939) 1; Dulckeit, *ibid.* 316; Condanari-Michler, *Scr Ferrini* 3 (Univ. Sacro Cuore, Milan, 1948) 90; Kaser, *Das altrömische Ius*, 1949 (*passim*); Frezza, *Nuova Riv. dir. com.* 2 (1949) 31.

Fides bona. See BONA FIDES.

Fides instrumentorum. The credibility, the conclusive force of documents as means of evidence. Similar applications of the term: *fides scripturae, fides tabularum*; with regard to witnesses and their testimony: *fides testimonii, testium*.—D. 22.4; C. 4.21.

Archi, *Scr Ferrini* 1 (Univ. Sacro Cuore, Milan, 1947) 15.

Fiducia. An agreement (*pactum fiduciae*) in addition to a transfer of property through mancipatio (or *in iure cessio*) by which the transferee assumes certain duties as to the property transferred or the later retransfer thereof to the transferor. The agreement is based on the transferor's trust (*fides, fiducia*) to the honesty of his partner. The transferor had an action (*actio fiduciae*) against the trustee if, contrary to the fiduciary agreement, the latter refused to retransfer the property. On the other hand, the trustee had an *actio fiduciae contraria* for the recovery of expenses and damages caused by the thing mancipated. *Fiducia* means sometimes the thing given *in fiduciam* or *fiduciae causa*. For the manifold applications of *fiducia*, see COËMPTIO FIDUCIAE CAUSA, and the following items.

Manigk, *RE* 6; Baudry, *DS* 2; Carrelli, *NDI* 5; Kübler, *DE* 3; Rotondi, *Scr giur.* 2 (1922) 137; Grosso, *AnCam* 3 (1929) 81; C. Longo, *CentCodPav* 1933; De Martino, *Giurisdizione*, 1937, 90; C. Longo, *Fiducia* (Corso) 1933; W. Erbe, *Die f. im röm. R.*, 1940; Collinet, *St Besta* 1 (1937) 91; Kaser, *ZSS* 61 (1941) 153; Kreller, *ZSS* 62 (1942) 143.

Fiducia cum amico. A fiduciary agreement concluded with a friend on the occasion of a transfer of ownership under specific circumstances for the purpose "that the thing be safer with him" (Gaius, Inst. 2.60). Such a transaction could serve for a deposit or a gratuitous loan of a thing (*commodatum*), the fiduciary assuming the duty to retransfer it to the depositor or *commodator*.

Fiducia cum creditore. A kind of pledge. The debtor transferred the ownership of a thing given as a real security to the creditor through *mancipatio* or *in iure cessio*. The latter assumed the obligation to retransfer the thing to the debtor after the debt was paid. For the pertinent actions, see FIDUCIA. An example of a *fiducia cum creditore* is epigraphically preserved in the so-called FORMULA BAETICA. This kind of pledge did no longer exist in Justinian's law. The term was canceled by the compilers of the Digest everywhere in classical texts and substituted by another term, primarily by *pignus*.—See FIDUCIA (Bibl.).

Hazeltine, in R. W. Turner, *The Equity of Redemption*, Cambridge, 1931, p. xiii; C. Longo, *CentCodPav* 1934, 795; Rabel, *Sem* 1 (1943) 39; A. Burdese, *St Solazzi*, 1948, 324; *idem, Lex commissoria e ius vendendi nella fiducia*, 1949.

Fiducia manumissionis causa. The conveyance of the ownership over a slave to a fiduciary under the agreement that the slave be manumitted. The purpose of such a transaction was to make the fiduciary the patron of the slave manumitted or to elude the legislation which restricted manumissions, see LEX FUFIA CANINIA, LEX AELIA SENTIA, LEX IUNIA NORBANA. Such transactions *in fraudem legis* (= to defraud the law) were void.

Grosso, *RISG* 4 (1929) 251.

Fiducia remancipationis causa. An agreement made with a third person by a father who wished to emancipate his son from paternal power, by which agreement the fiduciary assumed the duty to remancipate the son to the father until, after the third remancipation, the son was free from the paternal power.—See EMANCIPATIO.

Fiduciae causa. Refers to transactions (*mancipatio* or *in iure cessio*) creating a fiduciary relation between the contracting parties and imposing on the trustee the duty of performing under certain conditions a legal act entrusted to him.

Betti, *BIDR* 42 (1934) 299; Brasiello, *RIDA* 4 (1950) 201.

Fiduciaria res. A thing (a slave) transferred *fiduciae causa*. See FIDUCIA and the foregoing item.

Fiduciarius. (Adj.) See COËMPTIO, TUTELA FIDUCIARIA.

Filia familias. A daughter under the paternal power of her father or a paternal ascendant. She is *alieni iuris* and becomes *sui iuris* through *emancipatio* or marriage combined with in *manum conventio* by which she enters into the family of her husband where she is *filiae familias loco* under the paternal power of the head of her husband's family. In ancient law it was the father who promised his daughter into marriage through *sponsio* and who had the right to dissolve her marriage if she remained in his paternal power. Later only his consent was necessary for the daughter's betrothal and marriage but a tacit one sufficed. His right to dissent was limited in Justinian law, and so was his right to influence the daughter's divorce.—See PATRIA POTESTAS.

Moriaud, *Mél Girard* 2 (1912) 291; Solazzi, *BIDR* 34 (1925); *idem, St Albertoni* 1 (1935) 41; G. Longo, *BIDR* 40 (1932) 201; Brassloff, *St Riccobono* 1 (1936) 332; De Martino, *Giurisdizione* (1937) 328; Caes, *SDHI* 5 (1939) 122; Volterra, *RIDA* 1 (1948) 224.

Filii. Sons, children. In a broader sense the term also embraces descendants (*nepotes, pronepotes*).

Lanfranchi, *StCagl* 30 (1946) 23.

Filius adoptivus. An adopted son.—See ADOPTIO.

De Ruggiero, *DE* 3, 89.

Filius familias. A son under the paternal power (*in potestate*) of his father (*pater familias*) or paternal ascendant. Descendants (grandsons, great-grandsons have the same legal status as their father (or grandfather, respectively) who is under the *patria potestas* of the head of the family. A *filius familias* has no property of his own; all his acquisitions become property of his father. The introduction of a separate property of the son, *peculium*, brought a change in this regard. See PECULIUM. A major *filius familias* has full capacity to conclude legal transactions but he does not obligate his father unless he acts under his order or under specific circumstances; see PECULIUM, IUSSUM, ACTIO TRIBUTORIA. A *filius familias* could not marry without the explicit consent of his father. In Justinian's law the son could complain to the competent authority about an unjustified refusal. A *filius familias*, as a person *alieni iuris*, became *sui iuris* at the death of his father if he was under immediate paternal power of the deceased. With the consent of the father the son was freed from paternal power through EMANCIPATIO.—C. 2.22; 4.13; 10.62.—See PATRIA POTESTAS, PATER FAMILIAS, HERES SUUS ET NECESSARIUS, BONORUM POSSESSIO UNDE LIBERI, IUS VITAE NECISQUE, INTERDICTUM DE LIBERIS EXHIBENDIS, TESTAMENTI FACTIO, IUDICIUM DOMESTICUM, VINDICATIO FILII, NOXA, EX RE, EXHEREDARE, PECULIUM, OBLIGATIO NATURALIS.

Solazzi, *BIDR* 11 (1899) 113; *idem, RISG* 54 (1914) 17,

273; P. Moriaud, *La simple famille paternelle*, 1912; Declareuil, *Mél Girard* 1 (1912) 315; Philippin, *Mél Cornil* 2 (1926) 224; Kaser, *ZSS* 58, 59 (1938, 1939); *idem*, *SDHI* 16 (1950) 59; Volterra, *RIDA* 1 (1948) 213.

Filius iustus. A son born in a legally valid marriage (*iustae nuptiae*). In Justinian's language the term *filius legitimus* prevails.

Filius legitimus. See the foregoing item.

Filius naturalis. As an ant. to *filius adoptivus*, *filius naturalis* indicates a child born in a marriage. On the other hand, *filius naturalis* is a child born in a marriage-like union, *contubernium*, and from the time of Constantine a child issued in a concubinage. This latter significance predominates in Justinian's language where it comprises any illegitimate child. Children born in a concubinage may become *legitimi* in later law by a subsequent marriage of the parents (*legitimatio per subsequens matrimonium*, a term coined in literature). The emperor could grant an illegitimate child the position of a *filius legitimus* by a special privilege (*per rescriptum principis*).—C. 5.27.—See CONTUBERNIUM CONCUBINATUS, LEGITIMATIO.

Steinwenter, *RE* 16 (*s.v. naturales liberi*); De Ruggiero, *DE* 3, 85; Weiss, *ZSS* 49 (1929) 260; C. A. Maschi, *Concezione naturalistica*, 1937, 51; Wolff, *Sem* 3 (1945) 24; H. Janeau, *De l'adrogation des liberi naturales*, 1947, 15; Castello, *RIDA* 4 (= *Mél De Visscher*, 1948) 267; Lanfranchi, *StCagl* 30 (1946) 24.

Fines (finis). Boundaries of a landed (rural) property. Syn. *confinium*.—D. 10.1; C. 3.39.—See ACTIO FINIUM REGUNDORUM, AGRIMENSORES, CONTROVERSIA DE FINE.

Leonhard, *RE* 6; Anon., *NDI* 6; Schulten, *DE* 3.

Finge (fingamus). Suppose (let us suppose) that. The words are frequently suspected to be a compilatory addition introducing a hypothetical case which was not discussed by the classical jurist in his original work. Glosses or interpolations thus introduced do not prejudice, however, the classicity of the decision itself.

Guarneri-Citati, *Indice*² (1927) 40.

Finiri. To come to an end. A controversy is "considered finished when it was brought to an end by a judgment in court, settled by an agreement of the parties, or extinguished by silence (non-activity *sc.* of the claimant) through a longer time" (D. 38.17.1.12).

Fiscalis. (Noun.) An official concerned with fiscal administration.—See FISCUS.

Fiscalis. (Adj.) See IUS FISCI.

Fiscus (fiscus Caesaris). The treasury of the emperor. It was not property of the emperor; it was only entrusted to, and controlled by, him as a fund destined for public purposes. The emperor had the right, and the moral duty as well, to dispose of the fiscal revenues only for public welfare. The main revenues of the *fiscus* were derived from the imperial provinces; some income came from senatorial provinces. The creation of the *fiscus* under the Principate did not abolish the AERARIUM POPULI ROMANI which remained under the control of the senate. The *fiscus* was administered by imperial officials (*a rationibus*). *Procuratores fisci* appointed by the emperor decided controversies between the fisc and private individuals. The fisc gradually assumed a more privileged position towards private individuals who were its debtors (DEBITOR FISCI). In the course of time (first half of the third century) the *fiscus* absorbed other public funds, the *aerarium Saturni* (*populi Romani*) and the *aerarium militare*.—D. 49.14; C. 10.1; 8; 9; 2.17; 2.36; 3.26; 2.8; 7.73; 10.1–9.—See ADVOCATUS FISCI, ARCA, AERARIUM, IUS FISCI, LARGITIONES, FRAGMENTUM DE IURE FISCI, RES PRIVATA, MULTA FISCO DEBITA, A RATIONIBUS, HYPOTHECA OMNIUM BONORUM, DEFERRE FISCO, NUNTIARE FISCO, SENTENTIA ADVERSUS FISCUM, RETRACTARE CAUSAM, USURAE FISCALES, RES FISCI, PRAEDIA FISCALIA.

Rostowzew, *RE* 6; *idem*, *DE* 3; Humbert, *DS* 2; Stella-Maranca, *NDI* 6; Vassalli, *StSen* 25 (1908); L. Mitteis, *Röm. Privatrecht*, 1908, 349; Weiss, *ZSS* 53 (1933) 256; S. v. Bolla, *Die Entwicklung des F.*, 1938; P. W. Duff, *Personality in R. Law*, 1938, 51; B. Eliachevitch, *La personnalité juridique*, 1942, 33; Last, *JRS* 34 (1944) 51; Sutherland, *Amer. Jour. of Philology* 66 (1945) 151; Jones, *JRS* 40 (1950) 23.

Fiscus Iudaicus. A central fund in Rome for revenues from the poll-tax paid by the Jews in the whole empire.

Rostowzew, *RE* 6, 2403; T. Reinach, *DS* 3, 625; Ginsburg, *Jewish Quarterly Review* 21 (1930/31) 281; J. Juster, *Les Juifs dans l'Empire romain*, 2 (1914) 282.

Flagellum. See CASTIGARE.

Fougères, *DS* 2.

Flagitium. A crime against good customs, chiefly a military infraction. The term acquired later a more general meaning.

Reichenbecher, *De vocum scelus, flagitium, etc. apud priscoe scriptores usu*, Diss. Jena, 1913; Volterra, *AG* 111 (1934).

Flamines. Priests in early Rome. A *flamen* was assigned to the service of a specific deity, primarily for performing sacrifices. There were altogether fifteen *flamines* of whom three were *maiores* (patricians), all others (*minores*). The highest in rank was the *flamen Dialis* (of Jupiter) who during the period of kingship was appointed by the king. He had to be born in a marriage concluded in the form of *confarreatio* and could take a wife (*flaminica Dialis*) only by *confarreatio*. He was entitled to certain privileges (*sella curulis*, seat in the senate). Under the Empire special *flamines* were assigned to deified emperors.

Samter, *RE* 6; Jullian, *DS* 2; Anon., *NDI* 6; Espérandieu, *DE* 3; Rose, *OCD*.

Flamen curialis. See CURIA.

Flamen Dialis. See FLAMINES, LEX VOCONIA, FLAMINICA DIALIS.

Aron, *NRHD* 28 (1904) 5; Brassloff, *St Bonfante* 2 (1930) 365.

Flaminica Dialis. The wife of the *flamen Dialis.* She assisted her husband in his priestly functions.

Samter, *RE* 6, 2490; Espérandieu, *DE* 3.

Flavius, Gnaeus. See IUS FLAVIANUM.

Florentina. (*Sc. littera.*) The oldest and most authoritative manuscript of the Digest, written in the late sixth or early seventh century. The manuscript was preserved in Pisa during the twelfth and thirteenth centuries (hence it is named *Littera Pisana*). From the beginning of the fifteenth century it has been in Florence.

Kantorowicz, *ZSS* 30 (1909) 186.

Florentinus. A jurist of the second century after Christ, known only as the author of an extensive manual of Institutiones (in twelve books).

Brassloff, *RE* 6, 2755.

Flumen. See ALVEUS, INSULA.

Flumina privata. See FLUMINA PUBLICA.

Flumina publica. Rivers flowing the year through, perpetually (*flumen quod semper fluit, perenne*). Navigability is not decisive. See RES PUBLICAE. The public use of *flumina publica* is protected by special interdicts which serve to assure navigation, unloading boats, maintenance of navigable rivers, and the like. See INTERDICTA DE FLUMINIBUS PUBLICIS. The question whether water from public rivers could be diverted for private use is controversial.—D. 43.12–15.—See RIPA, AQUA PUBLICA, and the following item.

Berger, *RE* 9, 1634; Lauria, *AnMac* 8 (1932); G. Longo, *RISG* 3 (1928) 243; *idem, St Ratti,* 1934; Grosso, *ATor* 66 (1931) 369; *idem, Scr S. Romano* 4 (1940) 175; B. Biondi, *Categoria romana delle servitutes,*1938, 591; Albertario, *St* 2 (1941) 71; G. Segrè, *BIDR* 48 (1941) 17; Branca, *AnTriest* 12 (1941) 29, 71, 141; Scherillo, *Le cose,* 1945, 131.

Flumina torrentia. Rivers flowing during the winter only and regularly drying up during the summer. Later law treated them as *flumina publica.*

Costa, *BIDR* 27 (1914) 72.

Foederati. Citizens of a state which was tied to Rome by a treaty of alliance (*foedus*). "They enjoy their liberty in our country and retain their property in the same way as in their own land; we enjoy the same rights in their country" (D. 49.15.7 pr.).—See CIVITATES FOEDERATAE.

H. Horn, *Foederati,* 1930.

Foedus. A treaty of friendship, peace and alliance with another state. It bound the parties to reciprocal military aid in the case of a war (*foedus aequum*). If the treaty was not based upon equality and Rome only was granted military assistance from the partner, the treaty was a *foedus iniquum.*—See SOCII, AMICI POPULI ROMANI, CIVITATES FOEDERATAE, PAX.

Neumann, *RE* 6; Humbert, *DS* 2; Paribeni, *DE* 3; Frezza, *Le forme federative, SDHI* 4 (1938) 363, 5 (1939) 161; B. Paradisi, *Storia del dir. internazionale nel Medio Evo,* 1 (1940) 52; De Visscher, *Noxalité,* 1947, 97; A. Magdelain, *Origines de la sponsio,* 1943, 6.—For treaties concluded by Rome see L. Larivière, *Des traités conclus par Rome avec les rois étrangers,* 1892; R. v. Scala, *Staatsverträge* 1 (1898).

Fons. A source of water. Syn. *caput aquae.* It becomes juristically relevant when another has a right (servitude) to take water (see SERVITUS AQUAEHAUSTUS) from the source on neighbor's property or the right to drive his cattle thereto; see ADPULSUS PECORIS. Persons entitled to make use of another's *fons* are protected by an interdict *de·fonte.* On the other hand, the owner has an interdict against any one who prevents him from repairing or cleaning the spring.—D. 43.22.—See INTERDICTA DE FONTE, INTERDICTA DE REFICIENDO.

Berger, *RE* 9, 1637; G. Longo, *RISG* 3 (1928) 288.

Forensia negotia. See FERIAE.

Forensis. Connected with a judicial court, *forum* (e.g., *causa, res, negotium*).

Forma. A legal norm, established in a statute, an edict of a magistrate, a decree·of the senate, or an imperial enactment. With regard to certain contracts (a mandate, a lease) *forma* indicates the contents of the agreement. Sometimes *forma = formula.*

Falletti, *Mél Fournier,* 1929, 219; De Francisci, *RISG* 10 (1935) 102.

Forma censualis. Regulations issued for the performance of a CENSUS.

Schwahn, *RE* 7A, 63.

Forma idiologi. See GNOMON IDIOLOGI.

Forma iuris fiscalis. A rule of fiscal law.

Formae. Metallic tablets on which the boundaries of a plot of land are documentarily set.

Formare. (With regard to a written document.) To draw up.

Formula. (In the formulary procedure.) A written document by which in a civil trial authorization was given to a judge (*iudex*) to condemn·the defendant if certain factual or legal circumstances appeared proved, or to absolve him if this was not the case (*si paret . . . condemnato, si non paret, absolvito*). Introduced by the LEX AEBUTIA, and later extended by the Augustan LEX IULIA IUDICIORUM PRIVATORUM, the formulary procedure replaced almost completely the former procedure of *legis actiones.* See CENTUMVIRI. The formula consisted of several clauses. Some of them, the mention of the judge appointed to decide the case (. . . *iudex esto*) and two essential parts, INTENTIO and CONDEMNATIO, were included in each formula. (For prejudicial actions, see FORMULA PRAEIUDICIALIS.) Other clauses, such as DEMONSTRATIO and ADIUDICATIO, were inserted in order to specify more precisely the case at issue. Some circumstances alleged by the defendant, which, when verified, excluded his condemnation (see EXCEPTIO), might be inserted. The elasticity of the *formula* which made it adaptable to any case was its great advantage which explains its existence through centuries until it was gradually superseded by a new form of procedure, the COGNITIO EXTRA ORDINEM. In a concrete trial the *formula* was first proposed by the plaintiff (see EDITIO ACTIONIS) and became decisive for the continuation of the process through co-operation and consent of the defendant who, for his part, was entitled to ask for the insertion of exceptions and for other modifications of the *formula*. All this took place in *iure*, i.e., before, and under the supervision of, the praetor who had the right to grant new *formulae* hitherto not promulgated in his edict, if such an innovatory and unprecedented *formula* was proposed by the plaintiff or his legal advisers. Such new *formulae* in the development of which the jurists had an important role, either as consultants of the parties or counselors to the magistrates, played an important part in the development of the Roman private law (see IUS HONORARIUM). The term *formula* is used promiscuously with *actio* and was substituted in Justinian's codification by the latter since in his time the *formula* was only a historical reminiscence. Officially the *formulae* were abolished by an imperial constitution of A.D. 342 with the critical censure: "dangerous hair-splitting" (C. 2.57).—See besides the items mentioned above, PRAESCRIPTIONES, EA RES AGATUR, QUANTI EA RES EST, some entries under ACTIO, ACTIONES and the following items.

Wenger, *RE* 6; Lécrivain, *DS* 4, 227; Anon., *NDI* 6; Berger, *OCD* 487; Kübler, *ZSS* 16 (1895) 137; Partsch, *Schriftformel im röm Provincialprozess*, 1907; Huvelin, *Mél Gérardin*, 1907, 319; R. De Ruggiero, *BIDR* 19 (1907) 255; Arangio-Ruiz, *Les formules des actions*, in *Al Qanoun Wal Iqtisad* 4 (1934); Naber, *TR* 1 (1918) 230; Kocourek, *Virginia LR* 8 (1922) 337, 434; Wlassak, *Die klass. Prozessformel*, *SbWien* 202 (1924); Wenger, *Praetor und Formel*, *SbMünch* 1926; Betti, *CentCodPav* (1934) 451; O. Carrelli, *La genesi del procedimento formulare*, 1946; C. Gioffredi, *Contributi allo studio della procedura civile rom.*, 1947, 65; Biscardi, *RISG* 86 (1949) 444; G. Pugliese, *Il processo formulare*, 1–2 (*Lezioni Genova*, 1948–1949); Arangio-Ruiz, *Iura* 1 (1950) 15; G. I. Luzzatto, *La procedura civile rom.*, 3. *La genesi del procedimento formulare*, 1950.

Formula arbitraria. See ACTIONES ARBITRARIAE.

Formula Baetica. An epigraphically preserved example of a FIDUCIA as a pledge (*mancipatio fiduciae causa*) given to a creditor.

Edition: Arangio-Ruiz, *FIR* 3 (1942) no. 92; Gradenwitz, *SbHeid* 1915, 9, p. 12.

Formula census. See LEX CENSUI CENSENDO.

Formula certa—incerta. See ACTIONES CERTAE.

Formula Fabiana. See ACTIO CALVISIANA, FRAGMENTUM DE FORMULA FABIANA.

Formula ficticia. See ACTIONES FICTICIAE.

Formula in factum concepta. See FORMULA IN IUS CONCEPTA.—D. 19.5.

De Francisci, *StSen* 24 (1907); De Visscher, *RHD* 4 (1925) 193 (= *Études de dr. rom.* 1931, 359); Lévy-Bruhl, *Prudent et préteur*, *RHD* 5 (1916) 5; Lenel, *ZSS* 48 (1928) 1; Fabia, *Mél Huvelin*, 1938; Collinet, *La nature des actions*, 1947, 337; Philonenko, *RIDA* 3 (= *Mél De Visscher* 2, 1949) 237.

Formula in ius concepta. Ant. *formula in factum concepta*. The distinction is based on the contents of the *intentio* in the procedural formula. When a question of law is raised, as, for instance, when the plaintiff claims the ownership over a thing or another right, under Quiritary law, or when he sues for the performance of an obligation by the defendant under civil law (*dare oportere*), there is in the *intentio* a direct or indirect reference to a legal transaction or relation protected under *ius civile*. In a *formula in factum*, however, the *intentio* mentions the fact from which the plaintiff draws his claim and the judge is authorized to condemn the defendant if the fact in question is proved. The *formula in factum* is adapted to the particular circumstances of the case, for instance, when a freedman summons his patron to court, or when a person summoned to court does not appear or give a guaranty. The substantial difference between the two kinds of *formulae* is that in the *formula in factum* the condemnation of the defendant is connected with a fact from which his liability is derived, whereas in the *formula in ius* the establishment of a specific right of the claimant either over a thing or to a performance by the defendant effects the condemnation of the latter. In the creation of *formula in factum* the jurists and the judicial magistrates (the praetors) equally co-operated. Granted first in specific cases the *formula in factum* gradually entered into the praetorian edict in the form of an announcement of the praetor that he was willing to grant an action in certain situations, not protected hitherto by the law. The *formulae in factum* were an important factor in the development of the *ius honorarium*.—See FORMULA IN FACTUM CONCEPTA (Bibl.), INTENTIO.

Formula Octaviana. (*Actio quod metus causa*.) See METUS.

O. Carrelli, *La genesi della procedura formulare*, 1946, 200.

Formula petitoria (iudicium petitorium). The formula used in so-called ACTIONES IN REM by which the plaintiff claims a right over the thing at issue. The *formula petitoria* is applied in a REI VINDICATIO. It is opposed to another form of process when ownership of a thing is involved; see AGERE PER SPONSIONEM.

Formula praeiudicialis. The formula of the so-called prejudicial actions; see ACTIONES PRAEIUDICIALES. The *formula* has only an INTENTIO and no CONDEMNATIO, since the final statement by the judge establishes the existence of a legally important fact only.

Formulae. Formularies for last wills, contracts, actions, and the like. Collections of such forms were a favorite type of juristic writings in the early Republic. Such collections are known as IUS AELIANUM (see AELIUS PAETUS CATUS), IUS FLAVIANUM, *Monumenta Maniliana* (see MANILIUS). The last collection written by Manlius Manilius (consul 149 B.C.) was in use until the end of the Republic.

Fortasse, fortassis, forte. Perhaps, perchance, by accident. The words are used frequently by the compilers to introduce fictitious examples or, particularly by *nisi forte,* to add some restrictions to a legal norm expressed before.

Guarneri-Citati, *Indice*[2] (1927) 40 (Bibl.); *idem, St Riccobono* 1 (1936) 721.

Fortuitus casus. An accident "which cannot be foreseen by human mind" (D. 50.8.2.7).—See CASUS (Bibl)., TERRAE MOTUS.

Kübler, *Fg Gierke* (1911) 26.

Forum. (In procedural law.) The competent court (*forum competens*) before which one can be sued. Special courts had jurisdiction in specific cases; see DECEMVIRI STLITIBUS IUDICANDIS, CENTUMVIRI, RECUPERATORES. There were praetors with a special jurisdiction, as, e.g., the *praetor fideicommissarius, tutelaris,* and likewise the prefects in Rome were competent in particular controversies connected somewhat with their specific domain of administration. A general rule, *actor sequitur forum rei* (C. 3.13.2; 3.19.3; *Frag. Vat.* 326) established that the plaintiff could sue the defendant only where the latter had his judicial status either through origin (*origo*) or domicile (see DOMICILIUM, INCOLA). If the defendant is summoned (*in ius vocatio*) before a magistrate not competent to try the case, he must answer the summons, but the magistrate will refuse the action to the plaintiff (*denegare actionem*). The place where the defendant had to pay the debt, determined in certain cases the competent court. In Justinian's law trials concerning an immovable belonged to the court of the place where the immovable was situated. For delictual obligations the place where the offence was committed was decisive in the later law. For all these kinds of *fora* non-Roman terms were coined in literature (*forum domicilii, contractus, rei sitae, delicti*). Non-Roman is also the term *forum prorogatum* (*prorogatio fori*), when, by an agreement of the parties, a special court was selected. A change of the court after the joinder of issue (*litis contestatio*) was impossible. It was the duty of the judicial magistrate approached by the parties "to examine whether he was competent in the specific case" (*an sua est iurisdictio,* D. 5.1.5).—D. 5.1: C. 3.13.

Kipp, *RE* 7.

Forum. A market place, a small community (like VICUS).

Schulten, *RE* 7, 62 (no. 3); Thédenat, *DS* 2, 1278.

Fossa. A channel, a water way.—See LACUS, FLUMINA PUBLICA.

Fragmenta de iudiciis. Three brief excerpts from an unknown work, perhaps a commentary on the section *de iudiciis* of the praetorian edict. The manuscript is of the fifth or sixth century.

Editions in all Collections of *Fontes* (see General Bibliography, Ch. XII); the most recent one in Baviera *FIR* 2[2] (1940) 625.—Berger, *RE* 10, 1192.

Fragmenta de iure fisci. A few excerpts from a treatise on the rights of the fisc. Author and date are unknown. The manuscript is preserved on parchment; it was written in the fifth or sixth century.

Editions in all Collections of *Fontes*; the most recent one in Baviera, *FIR* 2[2] (1940) 627.—Brassloff, *RE* 7.

Fragmenta Vaticana. A collection of legal texts preserved in a Vatican manuscript. It contains excerpts from the works of Papinian, Ulpian, and Paul (*iura*) and imperial constitutions, primarily by Diocletian (*leges*). For the selection of the constitutions the *Codices Gregorianus* and *Hermogenianus* were probably used but not the *Codex Theodosianus.* The collection was compiled presumably in the second half of the fourth century.

Editions in all collections of *Fontes* (see General Bibliography, Ch. XII), recently Baviera, *FIR* 2[2] (1940) 463; Brassloff, *RE* 7; Volterra, *NDI* 12 (*s.v. Vat. Fr.*); Felgenträger, in *Romanistische Studien (Freiburger rechtsgeschichtliche Abhandlungen* 5, 1935) 27; Albertario, *Studi* 5 (1937) 551; F. Schulz, *Hist. of R. legal science,* 1946, 310; v. Bolla, *Scr Ferrini* 4 (Univ. Sacro Cuore, Milan, 1949) 91.

Fragmentum de bonorum possessione. A brief text on BONORUM POSSESSIO ascribed to Paul; it is preserved on a parchment sheet.

First edition: P. M. Meyer, *ZSS* 42 (1921) 42; Baviera, *FIR* 2[2] (1940) 427.

Fragmentum de formula Fabiana. A brief excerpt from a juristic writing (by Paul?), named in literature *"de formula Fabiana"* rather inappropriately in spite of three mentions of that formula. It is preserved in a parchment manuscript.—See ACTIO CALVISIANA.

Edition: Baviera, *FIR* 2[2] (1940) 429 (Bibl.).—Albertario, *Studi* 5 (1937) 571.

Fragmentum Dositheanum. This name is applied to a longer excerpt from a collection of passages used for translations from Latin into Greek and *vice versa.* It is commonly ascribed to the grammarian of the late fourth century after Christ, Dositheus, the author of *Ars grammatica.* The text preserved in both languages, is inaccurate and full of errors and contains some general conceptions and an extensive section on manumission which goes back probably to a classical elementary treatise.

Editions in all collections of *Fontes* (see General Bibliography, Ch. XII); lastly by Baviera, *FIR·* 2[2] (1940) 617.—Jörs, *RE* 5, 1603; Berger, *RE* 10, 1192; G. Lombardi, *Il concetto di ius gentium,* 1947, 246 (Bibl.).

Frangere. To break. The verb occurs in connection with the harmful wrongdoings in the LEX AQUILIA which may provide cause for an action for damages (*actio legis Aquiliae*) against the wrongdoer.—See OS FRACTUM.

Frater. A brother. Brothers (*fratres*) are the sons of the same parents (= *germani*) but also the sons of the same father only (*per patrem, fratres consanguinei*) or of the same mother (*per matrem, uterini*).

Under the *ius civile* brothers had a right to intestate succession in the group of the next agnates (*proximi agnati*), under the praetorian law (see BONORUM POSSESSIO INTESTATI) in the groups *unde legitimi* and *unde cognati*. The term *fratres* covers both brothers and sisters, unless a narrower sense is evident from the context. An adopted son is considered to be a brother of the other sons of the adoptive father (*per adoptionem quaesita fraternitas*). Prohibited, however, was *adoptio in fratrem* = adoption of a person as a brother of the adopting person (*fratrem sibi per adoptionem facere*) in order to institute him as an heir.

> Volterra, *BIDR* 41 (1933) 289; Koschaker, *St Riccobono* 3 (1936); Nallino, *ibid.* 321 (= *Raccolta di scritti*, 1942, 585).

Fratres Arvales. See ARVALES.

Fratres germani (uterini). See FRATER, GERMANI.

Fratres patrueles. See CONSOBRINI.

Fraudare. To defraud. "No one is held to defraud persons who know the matter and agree" (D. 42.8.6.9 = 50.17.145). *Fraudare creditores* (syn. *in fraudem creditorum agere*) = to act in order to defraud the creditors by diminishing one's property, e.g., through forbidden donations, manumissions of slaves, or alienations. Such fraudulent acts could be made by a freedman in order to deprive his patron of successional benefits (*fraudare patronum*).—See FRAUS.—C. 6.5.

Fraudare censum. See FRAUDARE VECTIGAL.

Fraudare creditores. See FRAUDARE.

Fraudare patronum. See FRAUDARE.—C. 6.5.

Fraudare legem. To evade a law by a fraudulent transaction, e.g., to sell a thing at a small fictitious price in order to cover up a forbidden donation. Syn. *in fraudem legis agere.*—See FRAUS LEGI FACTA.

Fraudare vectigal (**censum** and the like). To evade taxation or other payments due to the state.

Fraudatio. See FRAUDARE, FRAUS. *Fraudationis causa* = (an act accomplished) for the purpose of defrauding another.

Fraudator. A deceiver, in particular a debtor who is acting in order to defraud his creditors (*in fraudem creditorum*).—See FRAUDERE, FRAUS, INTERDICTUM FRAUDATORIUM.

> Solazzi, *Revoca degli atti fraudolenti* 1³ (1945).

Fraudatorium interdictum. See INTERDICTUM FRAUDATORIUM.

Fraudulosus. Using fraud, deceitful fraudulent. For *fraudulosus* in the definition of theft, see FURTUM.

Fraus. A detriment, disadvantage. The term means also evil intention, fraud (syn. DOLUS) and, consequently, any act or transaction accomplished with the intention to defraud another or to deprive him of a legitimate advantage. In contractual relations the term had a particular importance with reference to acts committed for the specific purpose to deceive the creditors through alienations (diminution of prop-

erty) performed in order to become insolvent and unable to pay one's debts to the creditors (*fraudare creditores, in fraudem creditorum agere*). Creditors thus deceived could obtain the rescission of such fraudulent alienations (donations, manumissions of slaves). Various remedies were introduced in the course of time. One of them was the INTERDICTUM FRAUDATORIUM. Under specific circumstances the praetor granted RESTITUTIO IN INTEGRUM by which the debtor's deceitful deeds (*fraudationis causa gesta*) were annulled. A specific action for the rescission of such alienations was an *actio in factum*, named *actio Pauliana* (the origin of the name is not clear). The action substituted in Justinian law the other remedies; the pertinent interpolations produced a certain obscurity in details as far as the classical law is concerned. The action was applicable against any third person who profited by the transaction with the insolvent debtor and knew of his fraud.—D. 42.8; C. 7.75.—See the foregoing items, CONSCIUS FRAUDIS, ALIENATIO, INTERDICTUM FRAUDATORIUM, REVOCARE ALIENATIONEM.

> Conforti, *NDI* 2 (*s.v. azione revocatoria*); G. Rotondi, *Gli atti in frode alla legge*, 1911; P. Collinet, *NRHD* 43 (1919) 187; Guarneri-Citati, *Mél Cornil* 1 (1926); Schulz, *ZSS* 48 (1928) 197; Radin, *Virginia L Rev* 18 (1931); F. Palumbo, *L'actio Pauliana*, 1935; Albertario, *Studi* 3 (1936) 523; H. Krüger and M. Kaser, *ZSS* 63 (1943) 117; Solazzi, *Revoca degli atti fraudolenti*, 1934 (3rd edition, 1, 1945).

Fraus legi facta. The Romans did not elaborate a real doctrine of *fraus legi facta*. There was a distinction between *contra legem facere* (= to do what the law forbids) and *in fraudem legis facere* ("who evades the intention of a statute but respects his wording," D. 1.3.29). In other words, a *fraus legi* occurs "when something is done what the law expressly did not forbid, but what it did not want to be done" (D. 1.3.30). Acting *in fraudem legis* was considered simply a violation of the law and it produced those consequences which were provided by the law.

> Rotondi, *Gli atti in frode alla legge*, 1911; *idem*, *BIDR* 25 (1912) 221 (= *Scritti* 3 [1922] 9); Lewald, *ZSS* 33 (1912) 586; Scheltema, *Rechtsgeleerd Magazijn* 55 (1936) 34 (Bibl.) 96; J. Bréjon, *Fraus legis*, Rennes, 1941; *idem*, *RHD* 22 (1949) 501.

Fraus patroni. Defrauding his patron by a freedman through the performance of alienations by which his rights of succession are impaired. See ACTIO CALVISIANA. As early as A.D. 4 the LEX AELIA SENTIA declared manumissions of slaves *in fraudem creditorum* void.—C. 7.75.

Fructuarius. Used of a person entitled to the usufruct of a thing (syn. *usufructuarius*) and of the thing itself being in usufruct (e.g., *servus fructuarius*).—See USUSFRUCTUS.

Fructus. Fruits, products, proceeds. The term comprises primarily the natural produce of fields and gardens, offsprings of animals, and proceeds obtained from mines (*fructus naturales*). Profits obtained through legal transactions (the rent from a lease) are also conceived as *fructus* (*fructus civiles*, non-Roman term). Children of a female slave (*partus ancillae*) are not considered *fructus*. As a matter of rule, the owner of a thing which produces fruits has the right of ownership over them. In certain specific legal situations, however, a person is given the right to the fruits from another's property (*ususfructus, bonae fidei possessio, emphyteusis*). The extension of such rights as to both the kind of fruits and the moment when they are acquired by the third person, is ruled by special provisions. Natural fruits become legally *fructus* after separation from the thing (land, tree, etc.) which produced them (*separatio fructuum, fructus separati*). Before separation (*fructus pendentes*) they are part of the principal thing and belong to the owner.—*Fructus* is sometimes identified with *ususfructus*.—D. 22.1; C. 7.51.—See the following items, IMPENSAE, USUSFRUCTUS, POSSESSOR BONAE FIDEI, VENATIO.

De Martino, *St Scorza*, 1940; Fabi, *AnCam* 16 (1942–44) 53; P. Ramelet, *L'acquisition des fruits par l'usufruitier*, Thèse, Lausanne, 1945; Kaser, *ZSS* 65 (1947) 248.

Fructus civiles (naturales). These are modern expressions. See FRUCTUS. For *fructus civiles* the Roman juristic language used the expressions *loco fructuum, pro fructibus*.

Fructus consumpti. Fruits already consumed; see PERCEPTIO FRUCTUUM. They are distinguished from *fructus exstantes* (*fructus non consumpti*) = fruits separated and gathered but not yet consumed.

Fructus dotis. The proceeds of a dowry. They belong to the husband.—See DOS.

Fructus duplio. See VINDICIAE FALSAE.

Fructus exstantes (stantes). Fruits still existing and not consumed; see FRUCTUS CONSUMPTI.

Fructus licitatio. A specific act in the procedure of possessory interdicts (INTERDICTUM UTI POSSIDETIS, UTRUBI). The temporary possession of the controversial property is assigned to the party who assumes the duty to pay a higher sum to the adversary in the case he would lose the claim for ownership in the trial to follow.

Berger, *RE* 9, 1697; Arangio-Ruiz, *DE* 4, 70; Siber, *Scr Ferrini* 4 (Univ. Sacro Cuore, Milan, 1949) 101.

Fructus naturales. See FRUCTUS, FRUCTUS CIVILES.

Fructus pendentes. Fruits not separated from the thing (land, tree, etc.) which produced them. They are considered a part of the land (*pars fundi*) until they are separated. Ant. *fructus separati*.—See USUSFRUCTUS.

Fructus percepti. Fruits of which one took possession by separating and gathering them.—See PERCEPTIO FRUCTUUM.

Fructus percipiendi. Products which the fruit-bearing thing would have produced if the holder of it had taken the necessary care. In exceptional cases they were taken into consideration when the restitution of a thing with all its proceeds was involved.—See POSSESSOR BONAE FIDEI.

Ratti, *Ann. Univ. Toscane* 47 (1930) 37.

Fructus rei pigneratae. The proceeds of a thing given as a pledge to the creditor. The question as to whether they are pledged too by virtue of a tacit agreement of the parties (so in Justinian law) or only when there was an explicit agreement to this effect, is controversial as far as the classical law is concerned. The sources deal primarily with the problem with reference to the offsprings of a female slave (*partus ancillae*).

Romano, *AnCam* 5 (1931); Carcaterra, *ibid.* 12 (1938); idem, *AnBari* 3 (1940) 123; Arnò, *ATor* 75 (1939–40); De Robertis, *AnBari* 9 (1948) 31.

Fructus separati. Fruits separated from the fruit-bearing thing. Only through separation the fruit becomes juristically *fructus*. Ant. *fructus pendentes*.—See FRUCTUS.

Fruges excantare. See EXCANTARE FRUGES.

Frui. Refers to the person who has the right to the proceeds (see FRUCTUS) of a thing.—See USUSFRUCTUS.

Frumentarii. Military officials charged with the care for provisions for the army.

Vaglieri, *DE* 3; Cagnat, *DS* 2; Paribeni, *Mitteilungen des kais. deutsch. Archaeol. Inst., Röm. Abt.* 20 (1905) 310.

Frumentationes. Doles of free corn distributed to the needy or sold them at a low price.—See LEX SEMPRONIA FRUMENTARIA, FRUMENTUM, TESSERAE FRUMENTARIAE.

Humbert, *DS* 2; Cardinali, *DE* 3; Rostowzew, *RE* 7, 172; D. Van Berchem, *Distribution de blé sous l'Empire*, Genève, 1939; Momigliano, *SDHI* 2 (1936) 374.

Frumentum. The administration of corn supply for Rome and the needs of the state (military provisions, *frumentationes*). *Frumentum* is used in the sense of free distribution of corn (e.g., *cura frumenti*, see FRUMENTATIONES).—C. 11.24; 28.—See ANNONA.

Rostowzew, *RE* 7.

Frumentum emptum. The corn which Rome bought from provinces with a rich agricultural production (e.g., Sicily) at a price fixed by herself. Sometimes the quantity of corn to be furnished and paid for was dictated by Rome (*frumentum imperatum*).

Humbert, *DS* 2; Schwahn, *RE* 7A, 30.

Frumentum imperatum. Compulsory supply of corn from a province against compensation when the FRUMENTUM EMPTUM did not suffice.

Rostowzew, *RE* 7, 165.

Frumentum in cellam. The provision of corn for the governor of a province and his staff to be furnished by the provincials at a price fixed by the senate.

Frumentum publicum. Corn distributed among the needy people by the state (FRUMENTATIONES). See LEX SEMPRONIA FRUMENTARIA, LEX CLODIA FRUMEN-

TARIA. Initiated under the Republic, the distribution was reformed by Augustus and continued by his successors. Nature and purposes of the action were not always the same.

Frustra. (With reference to a legal transaction, a donation, a sale. or a judicial action.) Indicates the legal non-validity or deficiency of the act accomplished.

Hellmann, *ZSS* 23 (1902) 428.

Frustrari (frustratio, frustrator). To obstruct the continuation and conclusion of a trial by resorting to tricks, such as evading summons to appear in court, hiding, or appealing without any chance of success. With regard to the payment of a debt *frustrari* = to fail to fulfill an obligation at the fixed date.—See MORA.

Fufidius. A little known jurist in the early Principate, author of a collection of *Quaestiones*.

Brassloff, *RE* 7, 201.

Fuga. A flight (of a slave). *Servus in fuga = servus fugitivus.* In the language of later imperial constitutions *fuga* = evasion of public charges (*fuga munerum, fugere munus*).

Fuga lata. See INTERDICTIO LOCORUM, EXILIUM.

Fugiens. In Justinian's constitutions refers to the defendant in a trial.

Fugitivarius. A man whose occupation was to catch fugitive slaves for a reward.—See SERVUS FUGITIVUS.

Daube, *JurR* 64 (1952) 12.

Fugitivus. A fugitive. See SERVUS FUGITIVUS. The term is also applied to fugitive COLONI and lessees of imperial estates.—C. 11.64.

Fulcinius Priscus. A little known jurist of the early Principate.

Brassloff, *RE* 7, 212 (no. 6).

Fullo. A fuller. He is responsible for taking care (CUSTODIA) of the customers' clothes accepted for fulling.—See LIS FULLONUM.

M. Maxey, *Occupation of the lower classes* etc., Chicago, 1938, 34; Rosenthal, *ZSS* 68 (1951) 260.

Fumus. A vaporous or odorous smoke. A disturbing smoke from the neighbor's house or factory (the sources mention the case of a cheese factory, D. 8.5.8.5) might be contested in court by the owners of the plots in the neighborhood, unless the adversary had a servitude which entitled him *fumum immittere* (= to let go the smoke to the neighbor's property, *servitus fumi immittendi*). Similar disturbances at a public place could be combated by an interdict.

Bonfante, *Corso* 2. 1 (1926) 309.

Functio. (From *fungi*.) The performance of official or other duties. *Functio* refers at times to public charges and payments. The term is frequently used by the imperial chancery.—See GENUS, FUNGI.

Savagnone, *BIDR* 55–56 (1952) 37.

Fundus. A plot of land. "By the term *fundus* any building and any plot of land, as well as land with buildings thereon are indicated" (D. 50.16.211).—

See DOS FUNDI, INSTRUMENTUM FUNDI, INTERDICTUM QUEM FUNDUM, LOCUS, PRAEDIUM, INSTRUCTUM, FRUCTUS PENDENTES.

Schulten, *RE* 7; *idem, DE* 3; Humbert, *DS* 2; E. Kaila, *L'unité foncière en dr. rom.*, 1927; Steinwenter, *Fundus cum instrumento, SbWien* 221, 1 (1942) 10; M. Kaser, *Eigentum und Besitz*, 1943, 259.

Fundus dotalis. Land constituted as a dowry.—See LEX IULIA DE FUNDO DOTALI.—D. 23.5; C. 5.23.

Fundus in solo Italico. A plot of land in Italy.—See PRAEDIA ITALICA, RES MANCIPI.

Fundus limitaneus (limitotrophus). A borderland of the Empire.

Fundus patrimonialis. Land belonging to the PATRIMONIUM PRINCIPIS in the later Empire. It was mostly exploited through emphyteutical leases.—C. 11.62–65.—See EMPHYTEUSIS.

Fundus provincialis (predium, solum provinciale). Provincial land. Quiritary ownership could not be acquired thereon because according to a Roman conception provincial soil was considered as belonging to the Roman people or to the emperor. Consequently, *usucapio* of such land was excluded. See LONGI TEMPORIS PRAESCRIPTIO. In later times provincial land was granted in exceptional cases to individuals.

Klingmüller, *Die Idee des Staatseigentums am Provinzialboden, Philologus* 69 (1910) 71; T. Frank, *JRS* 17 (1927) 141; Levi, *Ath* 7 (1929); Segrè, *ATor* 1936; Kaser, *ZSS* 62 (1942) 74; Bozza, *AnMac* 15 (1941) 83; *eadem, Ath* 20 (1942) 66, 21 (1943) 21; Ciapessoni, *Studi su Gaio*, 1943, 47 (Bibl.).

Fundus stipendiarius (tributarius). See PRAEDIA STIPENDIARIA, TRIBUTARIA.

Fundus uti optimus maximus. A clause in a sale of a land to the effect that it is in the best and perfect condition, i.e., free from servitudes. A similar clause was used in sales and legacies of buildings and land. In the case of a legacy also the necessary appurtenance (*instrumentum fundi*) was understood as bequeathed.

Fundus vectigalis. See AGER VECTIGALIS.

Fungi. To perform official functions (e.g., as a magistrate or judge). With regard to a trial *fungi* = to be a party to it (e.g., *fungi partibus actoris*). *Fungi vice (partibus) alicuius* = to act, operate in the place of another; see VICE.

Funerarius. See ACTIO FUNERARIA, PRIVILEGIUM FUNERARIUM.

Funus. A funeral. The disturbance of a funeral was punished under the LEX IULIA DE VI PRIVATA.—See ACTIO FUNERARIA, SUMPTUS FUNERUM.

Fur. A thief.—See the following items, FURTUM, MORA.

Fur balnearius. A thief who steals clothes and other things in a bathing establishment.—D. 47.17.—See BALINEUM.

Humbert, *DS* 2, 1409.

Fur diurnus. A thief who steals during the day. Ant. *fur nocturnus* = who steals during the night.

Fur manifestus (nec manifestus). See FURTUM MANIFESTUM.

Fur nocturnus. See FUR DIURNUS.

Furari. To commit a theft.—See ANIMUS FURANDI, FURTUM.

Furca. An instrument with two prongs used for the execution of the death penalty by hanging the criminal.

Furere. To be (or become) insane.—See FURIOSUS, FUROR.

Furiosus. An insane person, a lunatic. "A *furiosus* is considered to be absent" (D. 50.17.124.1). "He has no will" (D. 50.17.40) and therefore manifestations of his will are deprived of validity. He is not able to conclude a legal transaction except during a lucid interval (see INTERVALLA) when he regains a normal state of his mental faculties. During his insanity a *furiosus* is under control of a curator who manages his affairs. See CURATOR FURIOSI, BONORUM POSSESSIO FURIOSI NOMINE. The juristic sources apply several terms for insane persons, such as *demens, mente captus, insanus, non suae (sanae) mentis, non compos mentis*. No legal distinction was applied to the various kinds of lunatics.—See SUBSTITUTIO PUPILLARIS.

> A. Audibert, *Études d'hist. du droit.* 1. *La folie et la prodigalité*, 1892; De Francisci, *BIDR* 30 (1921) 154; Solazzi, *Mouseion*, 2 (1924); Lenel, *ZSS* 45 (1925) 514; Guarino, *AnCat* 3 (1949) 194; Renier, *RIDA* 5 (1950) 429.

Furius Anthianus. A jurist of the first half of the third century after Christ, seemingly the author of a commentary on the praetorian edict.

> Brassloff, *RE* 7, 319 (no. 22); F. Schulz, *History of the R. legal science* (1946) 201.

Furor. See FURIOSUS.

Furor intermissus. See INTERVALLA DILUCIDA.

Furtum. A theft. The classical conception of *furtum* included not only an actual removal of another's thing, but any intentional handling (see CONTRECTATIO) of another's thing with the view to derive a profit therefrom (*lucri faciendi, lucrandi causa*). This broad definition embraced not only simple stealing but also the most different acts of making use of another's thing without the knowledge of, or contrary to an agreement with, the owner, such as, for instance, selling another's thing, collecting money from another's debtor as a payment, without authorization by the creditor, and the like. The object of *furtum* could be only a movable though opinions to the contrary were not absent. Even a free person (a son or wife) could be "stolen." There was no *furtum* if there was not an owner of the stolen thing, as, e.g., if the thing was a *res nullius* or belonged to an inheritance not yet entered upon by the heir, since such a thing was considered (in earlier law) to be a *res nullius*. Only a fraudulent *contrectatio* could be qualified as *furtum* since "no one commits a theft without evil intention" (Inst. 4.1.7), which in the

sources is termed as *animus (affectus) furandi, furis, furti faciendi*. The terms may be of later coinage. There was no theft when one took another's thing in the erroneous belief that it was his or that he was making use of it with the owner's consent. *Furtum* was a private crime (*delictum*) prosecuted only by the person who suffered the loss. Two actions lay against the thief, first the *condictio furtiva* (available also against the heir of the thief) for the recovery of the stolen property (together with the proceeds) and second, the *actio furti* for a private penalty (*actio poenalis*) the amount of which depended upon the kind of the theft, see FURTUM MANIFESTUM, FURTUM NON MANIFESTUM. This action could not be brought against the heir of the thief. In certain legal situations it was not the owner but another person who was entitled to sue the thief (a *possessor bonae fidei*, a usufructuary; a creditor from whom the debtor's pledge was stolen). *Furtum* indicates sometimes the stolen thing itself.—D. 47.2; 5; 13.1; C. 4.8; 6.2.—See ANIMUS FURANDI, CONTRECTATIO, NATURALIS LEX, RES FURTIVA, OPE CONSILIO, MONETA, PECULATUS.

> Hitzig, *RE* 7; Humbert, *DS* 2; Brasiello, *NDI* 6; Berger, *OCD*; M. Pampaloni, *Scritti* 1 (1947, written 1894) 559, 653; Schulz, *ZSS* 32 (1911); P. Huvelin, *Le furtum*, 1915; Buckland, *NRHD* 41 (1917) 5; E. Levy, *Konkurrenz der Aktionen*, 2, 1 (1922) 90; Bossowski, *AnPal* 13 (1929) 343; Daube, *CambLJ* 1937, 217; Schepses, *SDHI* 4 (1938) 99, 5 (1939) 140; H. F. Jolowicz, *Digest 47.2, De furtis*, 1940; Tabera, *SDHI* 8 (1942); U. Baglivo, *Sul reato permanente nel dir. penale rom.*, 1943, 14; M. Kaser, *Das altröm. Ius*, 1949, 213; Niederländer, *ZSS* 67 (1950) 185; K. Olivecrona, *Three essays in R. law*, 1949, 43; De Robertis, *AnBari* 10 (1950) 55; Rosenthal, *ZSS* 68 (1951) 244.

Furtum balnearium. See BALINEUM, FUR BALNEARIUS.

Furtum conceptum. Occurs "when a stolen thing has been sought and found with somebody in the presence of witnesses" (Gaius, Inst. 3.186). The man could be sued by *actio furti concepti* for a threefold value of the thing stolen as a penalty, even if he was not the actual thief. In the latter case he himself had an *actio furti oblati* against the person who passed on to him the thing stolen even if the latter did not commit the theft. These actions disappeared in the law of the later Empire. The receivers of stolen things were liable for *furtum nec manifestum*.

> Daube, *TR* 15 (1937) 48; *idem, St in biblical law*, 1947, 260.

Furtum domesticum. A theft committed by a person pertaining to the household.

> M. Piques, *Vol à l'intérieur de la domus*, Dijon, 1938.

Furtum manifestum. A theft detected when being committed. Some jurists extended the qualification "manifest theft" to cases lying beyond the catching the thief in the very act. The opinions of the jurists varied as to the essential elements of *furtum manifestum* (capture of the thief on the spot, capture on the day of the theft with the thing stolen being still in his possession, seizure of the thing thrown away by the thief pursued). The Twelve Tables considered a *furtum manifestum* when the thief was convicted through an investigation LANCE ET LICIO. Capital punishment for *furtum manifestum,* ordained in that legislation, was later commuted into fourfold penalty. Ant. FURTUM NEC MANIFESTUM.—See DEPREHENDERE, DEICERE E SAXO TARPEIO.

F. De Visscher, *Études de dr. rom.,* 1931, 135; Arangio-Ruiz, *La repression du vol flagrant,* in *Al Qanoun Wal Iqtisad* 2 (1932) 109 (= *Rariora,* 1946, 197); Aru, *AnPal* 15 (1936) 128; Carrelli, *AnBari* 2 (1939).

Furtum nec manifestum. A theft which cannot be qualified as an open theft; see FURTUM MANIFESTUM. The private penalty was double the value of the thing stolen.

Furtum non exhibitum. Occurs when the stolen goods are not produced (see EXHIBERE). The thief who failed to produce them was liable in a praetorian action (*actio furti non exhibiti*) if they were found later on his premises.

Furtum oblatum. See FURTUM CONCEPTUM.

Furtum possessionis. The theft of a thing by its owner from the person who has the right to hold it (a usufructuary, a creditor holding the debtor's pledge).—See FURTUM REI SUAE.

C. Ferrini, *Opere* 5 (1930, written 1886) 107; M. Pampaloni, *Scritti giuridici* 1 (1947) 673 (written 1894); Sciascia, *Archivio penale,* 1947, 319.

Furtum prohibitum. An *actio furti prohibiti,* of praetorian origin, was granted against one who prevented another from searching a thing which had been stolen from him. The penalty was fourfold damages.—See LANCE ET LICIO.

D. Daube, *Studies in Biblical Law,* 1947, 276.

Furtum publicum. See PECULATUS.

Furtum rei suae. A theft committed by the owner of a thing who took it away from the person who had the right to keep it.—See FURTUM POSSESSIONIS.

Sciascia, *Archivio penale,* 1947, 319.

Furtum usus. A theft committed by an illicit use of a thing, which one obtained from the owner for a specific purpose, against the owner's will and beyond the limits imposed by the latter. Such a theft occurred, for example, when a depositary, a receiver of a *commodatum,* a creditor holding a pledge used the thing for other purposes than agreed upon. The classical origin of the term is rather doubtful.

C. Ferrini, *Opere* 5 (1930, written 1886) 107; M. Pampaloni, *Scritti giuridici* 1 (1947) 717 (written 1894).

Fustigatio, fustis. See CASTIGATIO, CRUX.

Fustuarium supplicium. The execution of a slave or a deserter condemned to death by beating him with clubs.—See CASTIGATIO, DESERERE.

Futura. See PRAETERITA.

G

Gaius. One of the most renowned Roman jurists of the middle of the second century after Christ (born under Hadrian). His origin, full name and personal whereabouts are unknown. For his standard work, the Institutes, see INSTITUTIONES GAI. Moreover, he wrote a series of works, among them a commentary on the Twelve Tables and commentaries on the Edict of the *praetor urbanus* and the provincial edict. No other jurist commented on the provincial edict, see EDICTUM PROVINCIALE. An elementary work, RES COTTIDIANAE (called also *Aurea*) is ascribed to him, but several scholars believe it to be a postclassical compilation of excerpts from Gaius' works. Monographs on legal institutions (on *fideicommissa,* on manumissions) appear under his name. In spite of this rich literary activity he is never cited by the classical jurists. Some sporadic mentions of a Gaius refer to the jurist Gaius Cassius Longinus (see CASSIUS). Later (A.D. 426) Gaius appears among the jurists whose opinions acquired official authority in the so-called Law of Citations (see IURISPRUDENTIA). Justinian considerably contributed to his fame by utilizing his Institutes as a basic source for the imperial *Institutiones* and speaking of him with great esteem (*"Gaius noster"*).—See INSTITUTIONES GAI, INSTITUTIONES IUSTINIANI.

Kübler, *RE* 7; Orestano, *NDI* 6; Berger, *OCD*; F. Kniep, *Der Rechtsgelehrte Gaius und die Ediktskommentare,* 1910; H. Kroll, *Zur Gaiusfrage* 1917; J. B. Nordeblad, *Gaiusstudien,* Lund, 1932; P. Meylan, *Le jurisconsulte Gaius,* 1923; Buckland, *Gaius and the liber singularis regularum, LQR* 40 (1924); C. Appleton, *RHD* 8 (1929) 197; Kocourek, *ACDR* Rome 2 (1935) 495 (Bibl.); Siber, *ibid.* 1 (1934) 424; Kreller, *ZSS* 55 (1935); Bizoukides, *Gaius, App. to vol.* 2 (1939, Bibl.); E. Weiss, *Fschr Schulz* 2 (1951) 79.

Gaius Cassius Longimus. See CASSIUS.

Gallus. See AELIUS GALLUS, AQUILIUS GALLUS.

Gemmae. Precious stones, gems. When mounted in gold or silver, included in a ring, or used as an ornament of vases they became part of the principal thing (*cedere*) and consequently the ownership of its owner, notwithstanding their great value. The same principle applies to pearls (*margaritae*).

Generalis (generaliter). General (generally). These terms frequently used by Justinian and his compilers served to formulate general rules, definitions, and to generalize (*"generaliter sancimus"*) earlier legal rules which had been applicable only to specific legal situations. The terms are therefore often suspect, but cannot be excluded from the classical juristic language.—See IUDICIA GENERALIA, HYPOTHECA GENERALIS.

Guarneri-Citati, *Indice*² (1923) 41; *idem, Fschr Koschaker* 1 (1939) 136.

Genius. The tutelary deity of a person. The *genius* of a *pater familias* was the deity of, and worshipped by, the whole family. Oaths were taken by invoking a *genius,* primarily that of the emperor (*per genium principis*). Slaves took an oath *per genium domini.* —See IUSIURANDUM.

Otto, *RE* 7, 1161; Steinwenter, *RE* 10, 1255; Wenger, *ZSS* 23 (1902) 251; L. Berlinger, *Beiträge zur inoffiziellen Titulatur der röm. Kaiser,* 1935, 10.

Gens. A major group (clan) of several families really or supposedly descending from a common ancestor. Originally a large plot of land was possibly assigned to the *gens* as a whole where its members lived together and formed a kind of a community. A surviving feature of this ancient organization is the right of succession on intestacy of the members of a *gens* (*gentiles*) in default of agnatic relatives. This principle, mentioned in the Twelve Tables, remained in force through the Republic and perhaps in the early Principate. The members of the *gens, gentiles,* were also entitled to guardianship if a member had neither a testamentary nor an agnatic tutor. An external sign pointing to the fact that the *gentiles* belonged to the same social unit was the common name (*nomen gentilicium*); to this must be added their common worship of a divinity as a special protector of the *gens* and common cult ceremonies (*sacra gentilicia*). They had also a common burial place. The *gens* had originally a political character and comprised patricians only; later plebeians had also their *gentes*. It is not quite certain whether the *stirpes* were smaller groups within the *gens;* many other elements in the organization of the *gentes* are likewise obscure. The smallest social unit within the *gens* was the family, *familia*. The clients (CLIENTES) had no membership in the *gens* but participated in its religious ceremonies.—See GENTILES, FAMILIA.

Kübler, *RE* 7; Siber, *RE* 21, 118; Humbert, *DS* 2; Orestano, *NDI* 6; De Ruggiero, *DE* 3; Treves, *OCD*; G. W. Botsford, *Political Science Quarterly* 22 (1907) 665; M. Radin, *ClasPhilol* 1914, 235; V. Arangio-Ruiz, *Le genti e la città,* 1914; G. I. Luzzatto, *Per una ipotesi sulle origini dell'obbligazione rom.,* 1934, 27; L. Zancan, *La teoria gentilizia, AVen* 95 (1935/6); C. Castello, *St sul diritto familiare e gentilizio rom.,* 1942; Coli, *SDHI* 17 (1951) 73.

Gentiles. Persons belonging to the same *gens* and using the same name, *nomen gentilicium.*—See GENS (Bibl.).

De Ruggiero, *DE* 3; Lenel, *ZSS* 37 (1917) 128.

Gentilicium nomen. See NOMEN GENTILICIUM.

Genus. A kind, sort, type. The term has manifold applications. It refers to actions (*genus actionis, iudicii*), to legal institutions (contracts, possessions = *genera possessionum*); the most important use is in the field of things: *genus* as opposed to *species*. Whereas the latter word refers to a specific, individual object, the other indicates fungibles, in which one thing can be replaced by another of the same quality since economically they exercise the same function (*quae in genere functionem recipiunt*), such as corn, oil, wine, money. See RES QUAE PONDERE NUMERO MENSURAVE CONSTANT. In obligatory relations the distinction *genus-species* becomes important when the thing due perished. In the case of a *species* the fulfillment of the obligation is impossible and the problem as to who is responsible becomes actual; in the case of *genus* the extinction of the obligation does not enter into consideration since things *in genere* can be replaced by others of the same quality and quantity unless they were specified by exact indications, e.g., wine which the debtor has in his cave.—*Genus* is sometimes synonymous to *gens.*—See LEGATUM GENERIS.

Scarpello, *NDI* 12, 2 (*s.v. species*); E. Albertario, *St 3* (1936) 375; Beretta, *Qualitas e bonitas nelle obbligazioni di genere, SDHI* 9 (1943); Savagnone, *La categoria delle res fungibiles, BIDR* 55–56 (1952) 18.

Geometra. Syn. AGRIMENSOR.—See STUDIA LIBERALIA.

Gerere. To administer (a patrimony), to manage his own or another's affairs (a business, *curam, tutelam, negotia aliena*), to exercise (a profession, a magistracy), to conclude a legal transaction (*negotium*).—See NEGOTIORUM GESTIO.

Gerere (gestio) pro herede. See PRO HEREDE GESTIO.

Gerere se. To conduct oneself; *gerere se pro . . .* = to impersonate, to assume falsely the character of another person, in particular of an official, or of a free person when one is a slave, or of a soldier without being one, etc., in order to obtain certain privileges illicitly.—See FALSUM.

Germani (fratres). Brothers born of the same parents. Similarly *sorores germanae* = sisters born of the same parents.—See CONSANGUINEI, FRATER, UTERINI.

Gesta. See ACTA, IUS GESTORUM.

Gestio. See GERERE, NEGOTIORUM GESTIO.

Gestio pro herede. See PRO HEREDE GESTIO.

Gestor. See NEGOTIORUM GESTIO.

Gestus. See GERERE. The term is primarily applied to the management of the ward's affairs by a tutor or curator. Syn. *gestio*.

Gladiatores. Gladiators. Condemnation to gladiatorial fights (*ludi gladiatorii*) was tantamount to the death penalty since the *gladiatores* generally lost their life in the fights. It happened, however, sometimes that the emperor abolished the death sentence by an act of mercy, particularly when a gladiator was successful in a fight.—C. 11.49.—See LUDI GLADIATORII.

Schneider, *RE* Suppl. 3; Lafaye, *DS* 2; Wright, *OCD*; L. Robert, *Les gladiateurs dans le monde grec,* 1940.

Gladius. A sword. It is the most characteristic symbol of the emperor's highest military command.—*Damnare ad gladium* = to condemn a culprit to the death penalty by decapitation with a sword.—See IUS GLADII, ANIMADVERSIO.

Glans. An acorn. See INTERDICTUM DE GLANDE LEGENDA. For the application of this interdict the term was extended to all kinds of tree-fruits.

Gleba. Earth, soil. For *glebae adscripti,* see ADSCRIPTICIUS.—*Gleba* was a land tax in gold imposed in the later Empire on senators (*gleba senatoria, glebatio*). Later it was levied even upon senators who were not landowners.—C. 12, 2.

Seeck, *RE* 4 (*s.v. collatio glebalis*); Thibault, *Rev. générale du droit* 24 (1900) 36.

Glebatio. See GLEBA.

Gloriosissimus. Under Justinian a title of the highest officers of the empire.

Koch, *Byzantinische Beamtentitel*, 1903, 58.

Glossa ordinaria. See ACCURSIUS.

Glossae. For glosses in juristic writings, called also (not quite properly) pre-Justinian interpolations, see DIGESTA.

Glossatores. Interpreters of Justinian's codification from the eleventh century until the middle of the thirteenth century. They were scholars and teachers in the school of Bologna under IRNERIUS (+ 1125) and his pupils. The name *glossatores* derives from the form of their exegetic remarks to texts, phrases or single words of Justinian's Corpus, written as marginal or interlineary glosses, in the order of Justinian's compilation. See ACCURSIUS. Systematic presentations in the form of summaries (*summae*) were rare. See AZO. Later commentators, from the middle of the fourteenth century, who worked in a somewhat different way, are termed by the collective denomination "postglossators." These post-Accursian commentators started from the *glossa ordinaria* of Accursius. They wrote commentaries and more extensive discussions on legal doctrines.—See BALDUS, BARTOLUS.

Anon., *NDI* 6; La Mantia, *RISG* 8 (1889) 3; F. v. Savigny, *Geschichte des röm. Rechts im Mittelalter*, 7 vol., 1850–1851; E. Seckel, *Distinctiones glossatorum*, 1911; P. Vinogradoff, *R. Law in Medieval Europe*, 2nd ed. by F. De Zulueta, 1939 (an Italian translation by Riccobono, *Diritto Rom. nell'Europa medievale*, 1950); Genzmer, *ACDR* Bologna 1 (1934); E. Albertario, *Introduzione storica allo studio del dir. rom. giust.* 1935, 236 (Bibl.); Kantorowicz, *TR* 16 (1938) 430; H. Kantorowicz and W. W. Buckland, *Studies in the Glossators of R. Law*, Cambridge, 1938; C. G. Mor, *Appunti sulla Storia delle fonti giur. rom. da Giustiniano a Irnerio* (*Lezioni*) 1937; Engelmann, *Die Wiedergeburt der Rechtskultur in Italien*, 1938; Genzmer, *Quare Glossatorum*, *Gedächtnisschrift für Seckel*, 1927; Koschaker, *Europa und das röm. Recht*, 1947, 55; Kuttner, *SDHI* 6 (1940) 275; B. Paradisi, *Stor. del dir. ital.* (Lezioni, 1951) 78; H. J. Wolff, *Roman Law*, Oklahoma, 1951, 187.—The *glossa ordinaria* is published in the earliest four volume editions of the *Corpus Iuris* in the sixteenth and sevententh centuries (last ed. 1627).

Gnaeus Flavius. See IUS FLAVIANUM.

Gnomon idiologi. A collection of imperial mandates (*liber mandatorum*) of Augustus and some of his successors. The text, written about the middle of the second century (probably under Antoninus Pius), is preserved in a papyrus. It contains instructions concerned with the administration of the private patrimony of the emperor (*res privata Caesaris = idios logos*). The provisions are primarily of fiscal character and deal with various matters, such as inheritances that fall to the fisc, taxes, fines, the capacity to make a testament, marriage between persons of different nationality. A few decisions of the praefects of Egypt are also added.

Editions: *Berliner Griechische Urkunden* 5, 1.2 (no. 1210) by Schubart (1919) and commented on by Uxkull-Gyllenband (1934); P. M. Meyer, *Juristische Papyri* no. 93 (1920); Riccobono, *FIR* 1² (1941) no. 99 (Bibl.).—Lenel-Partsch, *SbHeid* 1920, 1; Seckel-P. M. Meyer, *SbBerl* 1928, 424; T. Reinach, *NRHD* 1919, 583; 1920, 1; Besnier, *RIDA* 2 (= *Mél De Visscher* 1, 1949) 93; S. Riccobono, Jr., *Il g. dell'idios logos*, 1950 (Bibl.).

Gradatim. Gradually. In the law of successions the term refers to the admission of successors by degrees (see GRADUS) proceeding from a nearer degree, if there are not heirs (*heredes* or *bonorum possessores*), to the next degree, and so on.

Gradus (cognationis). Degrees of relationship. Their calculation is based upon the principle that "each procreation adds one degree" (Inst. 3.6.7, hence the formula: *tot gradus quot generationes*). *Inferior gradus* is applied to relatives in descendant line. Ant. *superior gradus*. See DE GRADIBUS COGNATIONUM, SUCCESSIO GRADUUM. In the official hierarchy *gradus* indicates the rank of a public (civil or military) officer.—Inst. 3.6; D. 38.10.

Humbert, *DS* 3; Guarino, *Pauli de gradibus cognationum e la compilazione del D. 38.10*, *SDHI* 10 (1944) 267.

Granius Flaccus. See PAPIRIUS.

Funaioli, *RE* 7, 1820.

Grassator. See LATRO.

Kleinfeller, *RE* 7, 1829; Düll, *RE* Suppl. 7, 1239.

Gratia. An act of grace by the emperor.—See INDULGENTIA, DIVORTIUM BONA GRATIA.

Gratis. Gratuitously, given without any recompense. —See GRATUITUS.

Gratuitus. Benefits conceded without any compensation are considered to be a donation and are subject to the same limitations as gifts. See DONATIO. Some contracts contain the element of gratuity (COMMODATUM, DEPOSITUM, PRECARIUM). A loan (*mutuum*) is gratuitous if interest is not paid (*gratuita pecunia*).

Gratulatio. See ABOLITIO.

Gravare. (In criminal matters) to incriminate, to charge with a crime as an accuser or witness, to cast suspicion upon another.

Gravis. Severe. The term is used of penalties inflicted on condemned criminals. When under specific circumstances a crime deserves a more severe punishment the sources speak of *gravior poena* (or *sententia*) without indicating precisely how the punishment is to be more severe. The choice is left to the judge. Ant. *levior poena*.

Gravis. With regard to contractual obligations, e.g., *aes alienum grave* a burdensome, heavy debt. Such a debt occurs when the debtor has to pay a penalty if he failed to fulfill his obligation at the fixed date. *Usurae graves* = high interest.

Gravitas. The dignity of a high office. The imperial chancery used this title in rescripts (letters) addressed by the emperor to official of a high rank.

Graviter loqui. To stutter. Stuttering was not considered a disease. Consequently the sale of a slave who stuttered could not be annulled for this reason.

Gregarii milites. Soldiers of the lowest rank, privates.

Gregatim. In herds, in flocks. Animals living *gregatim* = *greges* (see GREX), such as *equitium* (= a stud of horses), *armentum* (= plough-oxen). Such flocks are treated legally as units (*corpus ex distantibus*).—See CORPUS EX COHAERENTIBUS.

Gregorianus. See CODEX GREGORIANUS.

Grex. A herd. It is a collective thing (CORPUS EX DISTANTIBUS) which maintains its identity in spite of changes in the individual animals of which it is composed. A herd as a whole may be the object of a claim (*vindicatio gregis*) embracing all animals without regard to changes which therein or to single animals which do not happen to belong to the defendant. There is, however, no *usucapio* of a whole *grex* but only of single animals. It was held that at least ten sheep made a herd.—See GREGATIM.

Pampaloni, *RISG* 10 (1890) 268; Bossowski, *St Riccobono* 3 (1936) 357; O. Pallucchini, *L'usufrutto del gregge,* 1940.

Gromatici. Land-surveyors, writers on land-surveying.—See AGRIMENSORES.

Fordyce and Brink, *OCD.*

Gubernare (gubernatio). To govern, to administer. The term belongs to the language of imperial constitutions.

Gubernator navis. A steersman of a ship. He is liable for sinking another's ship through his fault and can be sued for damages under the *actio legis Aquiliae.*

H

Habere (rem). "Used in a double sense, since we say *habere* of a person who is the owner (*dominus*) of a thing and of one who without being its owner holds it. Finally we use to say *habere* of a thing which is deposited with us" (D. 45.1.38.9). In a still larger meaning *habere* is used of a person who has an action for the recovery of a thing held by another.

Habere licere. To enjoy full possession of a thing without being disturbed by another person.—See EMPTIO, VACUA POSSESSIO, STIPULATIO HABERE LICERE.

M. Kaser, *Eigentum und Besitz,* 1943, 14; Coing, *Sem* 8 (1950) 9.

Habitatio. As a personal servitude (*servitus personae*), this is in fact a type of the servitude *usus:* the right to use another's house for dwelling. It used to be granted primarily by legacy. It was strictly personal in classical law and could not be transferred to another person. Transfer was admitted, however, in Justinian's law. Quite different is the legal structure of the right of *habitatio* obtained through a contract of lease of a house (LOCATIO CONDUCTIO REI). The reciprocal rights and duties of the lessor and the tenant (*habitator, inquilinus*) are governed by the rules of *locatio conductio rei.*—Inst. 2.5; D. 7.8; 33.2; C. 3.33.—See HOSPES, USUS.

Leonhard, *RE* 7; De Villa, *NDI* 6; Ricci, *ibid.* 1 (*abitazione*); De Ruggiero, *DE* 3; Cicogna, *Fil* 1906; Berger, *Wohnungsmiete in den Papyri, ZVR* 29 (1913) 321; G. Grosso, *Uso, abitazione,* 1939.

Habitator. See HABITATIO.

Habitus. (Perfect passive participle of *habere.*) With reference to things done = concluded (e.g., *contractus, emptio*); pronounced, passed (*sententia* = a judgment); contained (in a document, in testimony).

Habitus corporis. The bodily appearance, constitution. In earlier times it was the basic element of puberty (see IMPUBES).

A. B. Schwarz, *ZSS* 69 (1952) 371.

Habitus matronalis. See MATRONA.

Haec quae necessario. These are the initial words of Justinian's constitution (of February 13, 528) in which he announced his plan of a code of imperial constitutions (the first edition of his Code).—See CODEX IUSTINIANUS.

Haeretici (haeresis). Heretics (heresy). The legislation of Christian emperors frequently dealt with heretics. The Codex title 1.5, which contains the pertinent enactments (from 326 until 521) starts with Constantine's statement that "Privileges which have been granted with regard to religion, are only in favor of those who observe the Catholic law (*Catholica lex*). We wish that heretics not only be excluded from those privileges but also be subject to various public charges" (C. 1.5.1). Heretics were excluded from public offices and had no political rights. Restrictions in the field of private law were manifold: inability to acquire landed property, to make a testament or to inherit under one. Certain types of heresy were prosecuted as a crime. The most severe penalties were inflicted upon Manichaeans.—See 1.15; 1.10; Nov. 45.109.132.—See APOSTATA, IUDAEI.

Th. Mommsen, *Röm. Strafrecht* (1899) 595; Volterra, *BIDR* 42 (1934) 453; Balan, *ACII* 1 (1935) 483; C. Pharr, *Codex Theodosianus,* 1951, 582.

Harena. Sand.—See IUS HARENAE FODIENDAE.

Harenarius. See ARENARIUS.

Harmenopoulos, Constantine. The author of a compilation of Roman law as it was about the middle of the fourteenth century (A.D. 1345) still in force in the Byzantine Empire. The collection contains excerpts from earlier Byzantine compilations (*Ecloge, Peira,* the two *Synopseis,* Novels of the emperor Leo, *Procheiros Nomos*). The title of the work is *Hexabiblos* (= in six books). It is also called *Prochiron tōn nomōn* (= *Manuale legum*).

Editions: G. E. Heimbach, *Manuale legum sive Hexabiblos,* 1851; Translation: H. E. Freshfield, *A manual of Byzantine law, compiled in the fourteenth century, Part VI: On torts and crimes,* Cambridge, 1930.—Mortreuil, *Histoire du droit byzantin,* 3 (1846) 349, 495; Maurocordato, *Rev. de législation et de jurisprudence,* 25 (1846) 193.

Haruspices. Diviners who interpreted abnormal phenomena in the inner organs of sacrificial animals, also celestial phenomena (lightning).

Thulin, *RE* 7; idem, *DE* 3; Pease, *OCD*; Bouché-Leclercq, *DS* 3; G. Wissowa, *Religion und Kultur der Römer*, 1902, 469.

Hasta. A spear, lance. It was considered a visible sign of ownership lawfully acquired (*signum iusti dominii*) since "the Romans primarily considered theirs what they had taken from an enemy (Gaius, Inst. 4.16). Public auctions were performed *sub hasta* (see SUBHASTATIO). When the centumviral court held its sessions, a spear was set before it.—C.10.3.—See LOCATIO SUB HASTA, PRAETOR HASTARIUS, CENTUMVIRI.

Hastati. See CENTURIO.

Haustus. Syn. *aquae haustus.*—See SERVITUS AQUAE HAUSTUS.

Hercisci (ercisci). See ACTIO FAMILIAE ERCISCUNDAE.

Heredis institutio. The designation of a person in a testament who as the testator's heir (*heres*), shall succeed as the owner of the whole estate (both corporeal things and rights). An heir may be instituted to a fraction of the inheritance and several heirs instituted in common without indication of their individual portions succeed in equal parts. The institution of an heir must be expressed in a prescribed form (*sollemni more*): "X shall be (my) heir" ("X *heres esto*"). The *heredis institutio* was the most important element of a testament. It had to be expressed at the beginning of the testament (*caput et fundamentum testamenti*). No testamentary disposition was valid if there was not a valid institution of an heir or if the heir did not accept the inheritance. In the later law the earlier rigid rules lost their strength. The requirement of solemn words was dropped. A testament with a not valid *heredis institutio* was efficient as a codicil and all dispositions of the testator were thus saved.—Inst. 2.14; D. 28.5; 7; C. 6.24; 25.—See CODICILLI.

Lenel, *Zur Gesch. der h. i., Essays, in legal history*, Oxford, 1913; S. Cugia, *L'invalidità totale dell'istituzione d'erede*, 1913; Tumedei, *RISG* 63–65 (1919–1921); Vismara, *St Besta* 3 (1939) 303; Sanfilippo, *AnPal* 17 (1937) 142; L. Cohen, *TAmPhilolA* 68 (1937) 342; B. Biondi, *Successione testamentaria*, 1943, 188.

Heredis institutio captatoria. See CAPTATORIUS.

Heredis institutio ex re certa. The institution of an heir to a specific thing (not to a fraction of the estate). Originally it was not valid and made the whole testament void. But already in the time of Augustus the jurist Sabinus expressed the opinion that an heir thus instituted should be considered an heir to the whole estate as if the specific thing were not mentioned. This doctrine, dictated by the tendency to save other testamentary dispositions (legacies, manumissions), prevailed in later law (*favor testamenti*).—See HERES.

Heredis institutio excepta re. The institution of an heir to the whole estate or a fraction thereof with the exception of one specific thing.

Sciascia, *Anais 1947–48 Pontif. Univ. Cat. de São Paulo* (Brazil) 223.

Hereditarius. Pertinent to, connected with, an inheritance.—See ACTIONES HEREDITARIAE, IUS HEREDITARIUM, RES HEREDITARIAE, SEPULCRA HEREDITARIA, PARS HEREDITARIA.

Hereditas. Used on the one hand in the sense of the complex of goods, rights, and duties of the deceased (the estate as a whole), and on the other hand of the legal position of the heir (*heres*) who after the death of another enters (*succedere*) into his legal situation and legal relations (*in universum ius, in locum defuncti*). "*Hereditas* is nothing else than the succession to the whole right (*universum ius*) which the deceased had" (D. 50.16.24). The fundamental distinction is between *hereditas testamentaria* = an inheritance of which the testator disposed by designating (*instituere*) the person or persons (*heres, heredes*), who should inherit his property, in a valid testament, and *hereditas legitima* = an inheritance which is given to heirs indicated by the law because the deceased did not leave a testament or his testament became later ineffective for specific reasons. The testamentary succession prevails over the intestate one. According to a legal rule both kinds of succession cannot apply simultaneously to the same estate; see NEMO PRO PARTE TESTATUS. *Hereditas* refers to successions under the *ius civile*; it is opposed to BONORUM POSSESSIO which is governed by norms of the praetorian law.—See ADITIO HEREDITATIS, DELATIO HEREDITATIS, EMPTIO HEREDITATIS, IN IURE CESSIO HEREDITATIS, HERES, HEREDITATIS PETITIO, SUCCESSIO, and the following items.

Baudry, *DS* 3; De Ruggiero, *DE* 3; Berger, *OCD* (s.v. inheritance); Rabel, *ZSS* 50 (1930) 295; Bonfante, *Scritti* 1 (1926), several articles; Bortolucci, *BIDR* 42 (1934) 150; 43 (1935) 128; Robbe, *StCagl* 25 (1937); La Pira, *StSen* 47 (1933) 243; Ambrosino, *SDHI* 10 (1944) 10; C. Sanfilippo, *St sulla hereditas* I (1936); idem, *Evoluzione storica dell'h., Corso*, 1946; Biondi, *Istituti fondamentali* 1 (1946) 24; B. Albanese, *La successione hereditaria, AnPal* 20 (1949) 228; Ambrosino, *SDHI* 17 (1951) 195; Solazzi, *Iura* 3 (1952) 21.

Hereditas damnosa. An estate in which the debts of the deceased exceed the value of the property he left.

Hereditas fideicommissa (fideicommissaria). An inheritance which in whole or in part was left to a person through a FIDEICOMMISSUM to be handed over by the heir instituted in a testament to the beneficiary (*fideicommissarius*), see FIDEICOMMISSUM HEREDITATIS. Syn. *hereditas fiduciaria.*

Hereditas fiduciaria. See the foregoing item.

Hereditas iacens. Corporeal things belonging to an estate (*res hereditariae*) during the time before the heir entered upon the inheritance (*aditio hereditatis*). From the time of the death of the person whose inheritance is involved until its acquisition by the heir the hereditas *"iacet"* (= lies). During this period the things to be inherited are considered to be *res nullius* (belonging to nobody). Taking away such things is not a theft (*furtum*) but a milder wrongdoing *crimen expilatae hereditatis.*—See USU-CAPIO PRO HEREDE.

Manigk, *RE* 8, 644; Di Marzo, *StScialoja* 2 (1905) 51; Scaduto, *AnPal* 8 (1921); A. d'Amia, *L'eredità giacente,* 1937; B. Biondi, *Istituti fondamentali di dir. ereditario,* 2 (1948) 102; *idem, Iura* 1 (1950) 150.

Hereditas legitima. (Or *quae iure legitimo obvenit.*) An inheritance which is conferred to an heir by the civil law (*ius civile*) in the case of intestacy.—Inst. 3.1; D. 38.6; 7; C. 6.58.—See HEREDITAS, INTES-TATUS.

La Pira, *La successione hereditaria intestata,* 1930.

Hereditas suspecta. See HERES SUSPECTUS.

Hereditas testamentaria. An inheritance which an heir obtains according to the testament of the deceased.—D. 37.2.—See TESTAMENTUM.

B. Biondi, *La successione testamentaria,* 1943.

Hereditatis aditio. See ADITIO HEREDITATIS.

Hereditatis petitio. An action by which an heir (*heres*), either the testamentary one (*heres testamentarius*) or one succeeding at intestacy (*heres legitimus, ab intestato*), claims the delivery of the whole estate, a portion of it or a single thing on the grounds of his right of succession. The action lies against any one who, holding things belonging to an estate claims either that he himself is an heir (*pro herede*), or simply denies the plaintiff's right of succession without giving any justification of his own possession (*pro possessore*). The *hereditatis petitio* is a kind of *rei vindicatio* based on a specific title of the plaintiff, i.e., the right of an heir. Therefore it is also termed *vindicatio hereditatis.* The rules concerning the restitution of *res hereditariae* are analogous to those of the *rei vindicatio.* See INTER-DICTUM QUEM FUNDUM. Special provisions were introduced by the *Senatusconsultum Iuventianum* which made an essential distinction between one who held the inheritance in good faith (*bona fide*) in the belief that he was the real heir, and one who knew that he had no rights of succession. A defendant sued under a *rei vindicatio* for the restitution of a single thing belonging to the estate might oppose an exception that the question of the plaintiff's rights of succession be not prejudged in that trial (*ne prae-iudicium hereditati fiat*). The exception compelled the plaintiff to sue with *hereditatis petitio* if he wanted to base his claim on his quality as an heir.—D. 5.3; 4; C. 3.20; 31.—See SENATUSCONSULTUM

IUVENTIANUM, VINDICATIO FAMILIAE, POSSESSOR BONAE FIDEI.

Degni, *NDI* 9, 1114; Di Marzo, *StSen* 23 (1906) 25; Messina-Vitrano, *BIDR* 20 (1908) 220; A. Marrel, *L'action en pétition d'hérédité,* Lausanne, 1915; Beseler, *Beiträge* 4 (1920) 5; Biondi, *AnPal* 7 (1920) 242; Lenel, *ZSS* 46 (1920) 1; Denoyez, *Fschr Koschaker* 2 (1939) 304; G. Longo, *La h. p.,* 1933; A. Carcaterra, *AnBari* 3 (1940) 35; Kaden, *ZSS* 62 (1942) 441.

Hereditatis petitio fideicommissaria. A ·*hereditatis petitio* granted to one who through a *fideicommissum hereditatis* obtained an estate or a fraction thereof. This *hereditatis petitio* was conceived of as an extension (*hereditatis petitio utilis*) of the normal HEREDITATIS PETITIO which originally was available only to an heir inheriting under *ius civile.*—D. 5.6. —See FIDEICOMMISSUM HEREDITATIS.

Hereditatis petitio possessoria. A *hereditatio petitio* granted the *bonorum possessor* (an heir inheriting according to the praetorian law). It was a later creation (by Justinian?) when the two systems of universal succession were unified. In the classical law the praetorian heir had the INTERDICTUM QUORUM BONORUM.—D. 5.5.

Hereditatis petitio utilis. See HEREDITATIS PETITIO FIDEICOMMISSARIA.

Heredium. A plot of land, including a garden, of the size of two Roman acres (*iugera*), allotted, according to a legendary tradition by the founder of Rome, Romulus, to the citizens. It was inalienable and indivisible, being reserved for the heir (*heredem sequi*).

Humbert, *DS* 3; Sacchi, *NDI* 6; Nap, *TR* 1 (1919) 390; Lenel, *Edictum perpetuum³* (1927) 180; Pöhlmann, *Gesch. der sozialen Frage* 1928, 334; H. Lévy-Bruhl, *Nouvelles études sur le trcs ancien droit romain,* 1947, 37; Kamps, *Archives d'histoire du droit oriental* 3 (1948) 262.

Heres. An heir, he "who enters in the rights and the place of the deceased" (D. 29.2.37). "No one leaves to his heirs more rights than he had himself" (D. 50.17.120). All advantages and disadvantages (charges, *commoda et incommoda*) resulting from the legal relations of the deceased are transferred to the heir. Hence he is liable for debts and duties of the defunct except those which are strictly personal and not transmissible to another person. Among the rights excluded from succession are, e.g., personal servitudes (*usus, ususfructus*). Possession (*possessio*) as a mere factual situation does not pass to the heir until he obtains physical holding of the things involved. Obligations originating from wrongdoings (*obligationes ex delicto*) are not binding on the heir, but he must return what he gained from such acts (the enrichment). Some contractual relations (partnership, mandate) are extinguished by the death of one party.—Inst. 2.14; 19; D. 28.5; C. 4.17; 6.24.—See the following items, and HEREDIS INSTITUTIO, SUUS HERES, SUUS ET NECESSARIUS HERES, PRO HEREDE GESTIO, EXHEREDARE, NEMO PLUS

COMMODI, EXTRANEUS HERES, USUCAPIO PRO HEREDE, UNCIA.

> Manigk, *RE* 9 (*s.v. hereditarium ius*) ; De Ruggiero, *DE* 3, 736; V. Korosec, *Erbenhaftung,* 1927; Wolff, *St Riccobono* 3 (1936) 460; Kamps, *Archives d'histoire du droit oriental* 3 (1948) 237; H. Lévy-Bruhl, *Nouvelles études,* 1947, 33 ; *idem, RIDA* 3 (= *Mél De Visscher* 2, 1949) 137 ; Kaser, *ADO–RIDA* 1 (1952) 507.

Heres extraneus. See EXTRANEUS HERES.

Heres fiduciarius. An heir, instituted in a testament, on whom the testator has imposed the duty to deliver the estate wholly or in part to a third person (FIDEICOMMISSUM HEREDITATIS, HEREDITAS FIDEICOMMISSA).

Heres legitimus. An heir who succeeds according to the order of succession established by the civil law, *ius civile* (the Twelve Tables, a statute), in the case of intestacy. Ant. *heres scriptus, testamentarius.*— See HEREDITAS LEGITIMA.

Heres necessarius. A slave manumitted and instituted as an heir in his master's testament. He acquires the estate immediately together with liberty without any formal acceptance of the inheritance, and he is unable to reject it.—Inst. 2.19; C. 6.27.—See HERES SUUS ET NECESSARIUS.

> Manigk, *RE* 4A, 672; Guarino, *SDHI* 10 (1944) 240.

Heres nuncupatus. See TESTAMENTUM PER NUNCUPATIONEM.

Heres scriptus. An heir appointed in a written testament. Ant. *heres legitimus.*

Heres secundus. See SUBSTITUTIO.

Heres suspectus. An heir who appears not to be able to pay the debts of the deceased. *Hereditas suspecta* = an inheritance overcharged with debts.—See SATISDATIO SUSPECTI HEREDIS.

Heres suus. An heir who at the death of a person was under his paternal power (*patria potestas*). This is a technical term to be distinguished from *suus heres* (= his heir) which refers to the heir of a specific person.—See Inst. 2.19; D. 38.16; C. 6.55.—See ADITIO HEREDITATIS, EXHEREDARE.

> Manigk, *RE* 4A, 664; 8, 629; Cuq, *DS* 4 (*s.v. suus*) ; Solazzi, *BIDR* 39 (1931) 5; Kirk, *ZSS* 58 (1938) 161; Lepri, *St Solazzi,* 1948, 299; Vogel, *ZSS* 68 (1951) 490.

Heres suus et necessarius. A person under the paternal power (or *manus*) of the deceased who after his death becomes SUI IURIS (head of a family). If appointed as an heir in a testament or succeeding at intestacy he has no power to refuse the inheritance and becomes heir at once after the testator's death whether he wishes or not. Such heirs are sons, daughters, and the widow of the deceased; grandsons and granddaughters are *heredes sui* only in the event that their father is dead or no longer under the paternal power of the deceased. The praetorian law granted the *heredes sui et necessarii* the right to refuse the acceptance of an insolvent inheritance (IUS ABSTINENDI).—See HERES SUUS.—Inst. 2.19.

> Manigk, *RE* 4A, 672.

Heres voluntarius. An heir who is neither *heres suus* nor *heres suus et necessarius.* He acquires the inheritance only through voluntary acceptance (see ADITIO HEREDITATIS).—See the foregoing items.

Hermaphroditus. Considered under the law to be of the sex which prevailed.

Hermogenianus. A Roman jurist of the late third century or the early fourth century after Christ. He is the author of a collection of excerpts (*Iuris epitomae*) in six books. His identity with the author of the *Codex Hermogenianus* cannot be established.

> Brassloff, *RE* 8; Riccobono, *ZSS* 43 (1922) 327; Pringsheim, *Symbolae Friburgenses Lenel,* 1931, 31; Felgenträger, *ibid.* 365 (Bibl.).

Hermogenianus Codex. See CODEX HERMOGENIANUS.

Hippocentaurus. A fabulous creature, half man half horse. *Hippocentaurum dare* is given as an example of an obligation which cannot be fulfilled because of the involvement of a thing which does not exist.— See IMPOSSIBILIUM NULLA OBLIGATIO.

Histrio. See SCAENICUS.

Hoc est. See ID EST.

Hodie. Today, nowadays. Some Justinian's innovations are referred to in his Institutes by *hodie* as well as in the Digest certain new legal rules are opposed to earlier ones through this word. Although the word appears in interpolated texts, it is not a reliable criterion of an interpolation.

> E. Albertario, *Hodie,* 1911; Beseler, *Beiträge* 2 (1911) 97; Berger, *KrVj* 16 (1914) 427; Guarneri-Citati, *Indice*² (1927) 43 (Bibl.).

Holographus. Written in full in one's own hand (e.g., a testament).

Homicida. A killer, manslayer.—See HOMICIDIUM.

Homicidium. An assassination, manslaughter. The term is of later origin; it appears twice in Cicero, but is rare in the writings of the classical jurists, although frequent in imperial constitutions. For earlier terminology, see PARRICIDIUM. The pertinent verbs are *necare, interficere, occidere.* After a period of self-vengeance, homicide in historical times became a *crimen publicum* (QUAESTORES PARRICIDII). Under specific circumstances killing a person is justified, as, e.g., in the case of self-defense against a thief during the night (*fur nocturnus*) or when a daughter and her accomplice have been caught in the very act of adultery. A person killed in such situations is considered *iure caesus* (= justly killed). The Twelve Tables inflicted the death penalty on a murderer of a free person. The *Lex Cornelia de sicariis* (by Sulla)—still in force under Justinian with various changes introduced by the imperial legislation—established the rules applicable to different kinds of murder, either fully executed or only attempted. There existed a principle of *dolus pro facto accipitur* (= malice, evil intention is considered as if the fact had been done, D. 48.8.7 pr.) ; see CONATUS. Participation in armed bands of murderers was punished as well as instigation of, or assistance in, the commission of the crime. Penalties for murder were differentiated according to the gravity of the crime under the Republic; under the Empire the social status of the culprit influenced the severity of the penalty, even in the death penalty distinctions being made (crucifixion, condemnation *ad bestias*, decapitation, burning = *crematio*). Not punished was the killing of a person exempt from the law (see INTERDICERE AQUA ET IGNI SACER). A master who killed his slave remained unpunished until Hadrian ordered that such a crime had to be treated as *homicidium*. Killing another's slave created civil responsibility only for damages done to his master; similarly a murder committed by a slave involved responsibility of his master for damages from which he was released by delivering the culprit to the family of the person killed (*in noxam dedere*, see NOXA). Accidental killing of a person was sued for by a private action for damages, an *actio utilis*, modeled on the *actio legis Aquiliae*.— D. 48.8; C. 9.16.—See PARRICIDIUM, SICARIUS, ADULTERIUM, IUS VITAE NECISQUE, LEX POMPEIA DE PARRICIDIO, SACER, TRANSFUGA.

> Pfaff, *RE* 8; Brunnenmeister, *Das Tötungsverbrechen im röm. Recht,* 1887.

Homo. A human being. "All human beings are either free or slaves" (D. 1.5.3). The word "*homo* (= man) includes both males and females" (D. 50.16.152). Very often *homo* is syn. with *servus* (a male slave).—*Homines* collectively denotes the subordinates of a high dignitary or the officials in the imperial household.

> Angelis, *DE* 3.

Homo alieni iuris (sui iuris). See ALIENI IURIS ESSE.

Homo integrae frontis. A blameless, honest person. The origin of the expression goes back to the custom of branding the forehead of a convicted *calumniator* (= slanderer) with the letter *K.*—See CALUMNIA.

Homo liber. A free man.—See INTERDICTUM DE HOMINE LIBERO EXHIBENDO, LIBER HOMO BONA FIDE SERVIENS, PLAGIUM.

Homo novus. A newcomer, who did not belong to the older aristocracy of birth and office (*nobiles*) but, despite the lack of a noble origin entered into the highest social class by obtaining a curule magistracy. The *homines novi* owed their official career to acknowledgment of their personal ability and proficiency (*per se cogniti*).

> Strasburger, *RE* 17, 1223; MacDonald, *OCD* (*s.v. novus h.*); J. Vogt, *H. n., ein Typus der röm. Republik,* 1926; Schur, *Bonner Jahrbücher* 134 (1929) 54.

Honesta missio. See MISSIO HONESTA.

Honestas. Respectability, an honorable reputation, an honest moral conduct.—See EXISTIMATIO.

Honestiores. See HUMILIORES.

Honestus. Honest, respectable, decent. "Not all that is permitted is honest" (D. 50.17.144 pr.).

> F. Klose, *Die Bedeutung von honor und h.,* Diss. Breslau, 1933; Carrelli, *AnBari* 2 (1939) 61; v. Lübtow, *ZSS* 66

(1948) 543; A. Carcaterra, *Iustitia nelle fonti,* Bari, 1949, 98.

Honor (honos). The dignity and privileges attached to the power of a magistrate, both in Rome and municipalities; hence also the reverence, consideration due to him (*honorem debere, tribuere*). *Honor* is frequently syn. with *magistratus*. When both terms occur together, *magistratus* refers to the power and its exercise, whereas *honor* covers the dignity, rank and privileges connected with a magistracy. *Honor* was extended later to any honorific position occupied by a person in a municipality. *Honor* denotes also a gift left in a testament to a person as a sign of respect and reverence. Finally *honor* is used in the meaning of an *honorarium* paid for services rendered (*remunerandi gratia*).—D. 50.4; C. 10.41.—See CURSUS HONORUM, DEBITOR CIVITATIS.

> Campanile, *DE* 3.

Honor matrimonii (maritalis). See CONCUBINATUS.

> R. Orestano, *Struttura giuridica del matrimonio rom.,* 1952, 314.

Honorarii. Persons who (in the later Empire) were given the title of a high official but who actually did not perform any official duties. They did not receive the distinction accorded to active officials (see CINGULUM).—See VACANTES, ILLUSTRIS.

> Kübler, *RE* 7A (*s.v. vacantes*).

Honorarium. A gift, an honorarium paid (under the Principate) to persons exercising liberal professions (lawyers, teachers, physicians, architects, etc.). For physical labor a *merces* was paid, *honorarium* indicated the compensation for higher, intellectual services. See ADVOCATI. The payment of an *honorarium* could be enforced through extraordinary proceedings (*cognitio extra ordinem*) in which gradually the principle was recognized that such kind of professional services should be recompensed. *Honorarium* (= *summa honoraria*) was also called the sum which municipal officials and senators in the Empire had to pay as a contribution to help defray the expenses of mounting public games.—See HONORARIA SUMMA, SPORTULAE, CONSUETUDO FORI, SENATUSCONSULTUM CLAUDIANUM.

> Kübler, *RE* 4A, 896; Klingmüller, *RE* 8; Cagnat, *DS* 3, 236.239; De Villa, *NDI* 6.

Honorarius. (Adj.) Based on, or originating from, the *ius honorarium* (*praetorium*), e.g., *actio, obligatio, successor*. Ant. *civilis* (based on the *ius civile*) or *legitimus* (based on a statute).

Honorati. In the later Empire, persons who occupy an honorific position, civil or military, in Rome or a municipality. They remain *honorati* even after leaving office and as such enjoy certain personal privileges.—C. 11.20.

Honoratus. In the law of succession, a person "honored" by a legacy in a testament. See HONOR. Syn. *legatarius*. Ant. *oneratus* = an heir appointed in a testament and charged with the payment of a *legatum* or *fideicommissum* to the beneficiary.

Honos. See HONOR.

Hordearium (hordiarium) aes. See AES HORDEARIUM.

Horrea. Storehouses, silos. *Horrea privata* = storehouses owned by private individuals and leased to private persons through *locatio conductio rei*. *Leges horreorum* = rules concerning the deposit of merchandise in storehouses. *Horrea publica* = large silos maintained by the government for the preservation of food (corn, oil, wine) for public use and distribution. They served also for the storage of food against emergency. The *horrea publica* were under the supervision of the *praefectus annonae*. Special *horrea* were provided for the needs of the army.— C. 10.26.—See HORREARIUS.

Fiechter, *RE* 8; Rostowzew, *DE* 3, 594; Romanelli, *DE* 3, 981; Thédenat, *DS* 3, 268; V. Scialoja, *St giur.* 1 (1933) 289.

Horrearius. The lessee of a storehouse leased from the owner (*dominus horrei*) for warehousing, i.e., the renting out of storage space to customers. Normally the *horrearius* assumed responsibility for the custody (*custodia*) of the things deposited, but he might publicly announce through a poster (*propositum*) the limits of the risk he assumed. The contractual relation between the *horrearius* and his customers is a lease of services (*locatio conductio operarum*), that between the *horrearius* and the owner a lease of a store (*locatio conductio rei*).—See HORREA.

Carrelli, *RBSG* 6 (1931) 608; Vazny, *AnPal* 12 (1929) 131.

Hospes. A guest in another's house. Ant. *habitator* = the tenant of a dwelling. See HABITATIO. Only the latter is responsible for damages done to third persons through things thrown or poured out from the abode by anybody.—See ACTIO DE DEIECTIS.

Hospites. Soldiers quartered on a private individual. *Hospites recipere* = to billet soldiers. Syn. *hospitium praebere*.

Cagnat, *DS* 3 (*s.v. hospitium militare*).

Hospitium. Hospitality granted by Rome to another nation in an international treaty. It comprised the right to sojourn in Rome, to conclude legal transactions with Roman citizens (*ius commercii*) and protection before Roman courts.—See TESSERA HOSPITALIS.

Leonhard, *RE* 8; Anon., *NDI* 6; Marchetti, *DE* 3; Lécrivain, *DS* 3; C. Phillipson, *International Law and Customs* 1 (1911) 217; Gallet, *RHD* 16 (1937) 265; Frezza, *SDHI* 4 (1938) 398.

Hospitium militare. See HOSPITES.

Hostia. A sacrificial animal. The seller of a *hostia* had a privileged right of execution (*legis actio per pignoris capionem*) against a buyer who failed to pay the price.

H. Meyer, *RE* 8; Krause, *RE* Suppl. 5.

Hostis. In ancient language (Twelve Tables) this was syn. with *peregrinus* = a stranger. Later *hostis* = the enemy with whom Rome was at war. "*Hostes* are those against whom we (the Roman people) have publicly declared war or those who have done so against us" (D. 50.16.118). The earlier term for an enemy was *perduellis*. *Hostis* also was used of an individual, citizen or stranger, who was declared to be an enemy of the state by a statute or by the senate. He might be killed on Roman territory by any citizen with full impunity.—See OCCUPATIO RERUM HOSTILIUM.

Cuq, *DS* 3; Vaglieri, *DE* 3; F. Vittinghoff, *Der Staatsfeind in der röm. Kaiserzeit*, 1936; O'Brien-Moore, *RE* Suppl. 6, 759.

Huiusmodi. See EIUSMODI.

Humanitas. The humane tendency as an ethical commandment, benevolent consideration for others. The term as well as the adjective *humanus* (*humanior*) appears both in juristic texts and imperial constitutions. The idea of humanity undoubtedly exercised a considerable influence on the development of the Roman law through interpretation and decisions of the jurists. In the Christian Empire its influence infiltrated various provinces of the law (family, marriage, succession, slavery, penal legislation). It is undeniable that many a decision introduced by phrases like *sed humanius est* or similar, is not of classical origin; on the other hand, however, it is not correct to ascribe every passage where the expression *humanitas* occurs and every decision based on humanitarian principles to postclassical (Christian) times or to Justinian. *Humanitas* and *humanus* cannot be completely eliminated from the juristic language and thinking. What appeared good (humane) to Cicero, could not appear contemptible to the jurists. The tendency to stigmatize the terms as scrupulously avoided by the jurists is an exaggeration similar to that one which condemns the expressions *benignitas, benignus,* and the like.—See INTUITU.

Heinemann, *RE* Suppl. 5; H. Krüger, *ZSS* 19 (1898) 6; Wolff, *ZSS* 53 (1933) 328; Harder, *Hermes,* 69 (1934) 64; Schulz, *Principles of R. Law,* 1936, 189; idem, *History of R. Legal Science,* 1946, 297; S. Riccobono, *Lineamenti della storia delle fonti,* 1949, 297; Maschi, *H. come motivo giuridico, AnTr* 18 (1949); idem, *Ius,* n. ser. 1 (1950) 266; S. Riccobono, Jr., *Il Circolo giuridico* (Palermo), 1950 (Bibl.); Berger, *ACIVer* 2 (1951) 194 (= *Sem* 9, 1951, 41).

Humanitas imperatoria (imperatoris). The later emperors liked to speak of themselves as "*humanitas nostra*." On the other hand, merciful acts of the emperors, particularly in criminal matters, are denoted as *humanitas*.

Humanus. See HUMANITAS. For decisions based on *humanitas* different phrases are used, e.g., *humanum, humanius, humanissimum est, humanius interpretari, humana (humanior) sententia*.

Humiliores. Lower classes of the Roman society. Syn. *tenuiores, humiliore loco nati, plebeii*. Ant. *honestiores* = citizens of the higher social classes distinguished by their official position, wealth or origin (*in aliqua dignitate positi, honestiore loco* *positi, nati*). The distinction between *humiliores* and *honestiores* had particular importance in the field of criminal law and procedure. Some kinds of punishment (capital punishment by crucifixion, by being thrown to wild beasts, torture, bodily punishment) were applicable only to *humiliores*. In certain cases where the *humiliores* were punished by death, the *honestiores* were merely sent into exile. In cases in which *relegatio* was applied to *honestiores, humiliores* were subject to *deportatio*.—See POTENTIORES, ALTIORES.

Jullian, *DS* 3; Brasiello, *NDI* 6; Berger, *OCD* (*s.v. honestiores*); Mitteis, *Mél Girard* 2 (1912); De Robertis, *RISG* 14 (1939) 65; E. Stein, *Gesch. des spät-röm. Reiches* 1 (1928) 44; Cardascia, *RHD* 28 (1950) 305, 461.

Hyperocha. The surplus over the amount of a debt which a creditor obtained from the sale of the debtor's pledge (*superfluum pretii, superfluum pignorum*). The creditor is obliged to restore such surplus to the debtor. The term *hyperocha* (of Greek origin) appears only once in the Digest. Ant. *residuum*.

Manigk, *SDHI* 5 (1939) 228.

Hypotheca. A form of real security. The thing pledged as a *hypotheca* was not handed over to the creditor, but remained with the debtor who might use it but could not alienate it. The Greek-termed institution originated in agreements under which tenants of dwellings or lessees of land hypothecated all the things they brought in (*invecta, illata, importata, introducta*) as security for the rent to be paid under the terms of the lease. The lessor could obtain possession of the things hypothecated through an interdict in the case of non-payment of the rent due (see INTERDICTUM SALVIANUM); later the praetor granted a special action, *actio Serviana*, for the same purpose; under this action the lessor could claim possession of the things hypothecated, even when they were held by a third person and not by the lessee himself. In a further development the *actio Serviana* was extended to other cases of hypothecation (*actio quasi Serviana*, called also *actio hypothecaria* and *pigneraticia in rem*) when the thing pledged had remained in the possession of the debtor. In Justinian's law manifold changes were introduced in order to unify the different forms of pledge and the terms *pignus* and *hypotheca* became synonymous.—D. 20.1; 3; 6; C. 8.13-35.—See PIGNUS.

Manigk, *RE* 9; 20, 1243; Cuq, *DS* 3; De Sarlo, *NDI* 6 (*s.v. ipoteca*); Herzen, *NRH* 22, 23 (1898, 1899); A. F. Sorrentino, *L'ipoteca delle servitù*, 1904; T. C. Jackson, *Justinian's Digest, Book 20*, 1908; Erman, *Mél Girard* 1 (1912); F. Ebrard, *Digestenfragmente ad formulam hypothecariam*, 1917; D. F. Vasilesco, *Successio hypothecaria*, Paris, 1931; Solazzi, *SDHI* 5 (1939) 228; Rabel, *Sem* 1 (1943) 44; Kreller, *ZSS* 64 (1944) 306.

Hypotheca generalis. An expression used by Justinian for the hypothecation of the whole property of the debtor.—See the following item.

Hypotheca omnium bonorum. An hypothecation embracing the whole property of a debtor at the time of the agreement (*res praesentes*); it could even cover things later acquired by the debtor (*res futurae*) if they were included in the hypothecary agreement. Justinian ordered that such things were automatically included in the hypothecation unless they were expressly excluded. Such general hypothecs were first introduced as a security for the fisc for its contractual claims and taxes. Later law granted a ward a general hypothec over the property of his guardian or curator for claims resulting from the administration of the ward's property. Claims connected with the restitution of a dowry also enjoyed this privilege under the law. No agreement of the parties was necessary (*hypotheca tacita*).

Hypotheca tacita. A general hypothec over the debtor's property in postclassical and Justinian's law. It is called *tacita* because an hypothecary agreement of the parties was not necessary since the *hypotheca* was established by the law.—D. 20.2; C. 8.14.—See the foregoing item, PIGNUS TACITUM.

Hypothecaria actio. See HYPOTHECA, PIGNUS.

I

Iacens hereditas. See HEREDITAS IACENS.

Iacobus. A glossator of the twelfth century, disciple of Irnerius.—See GLOSSATORES.

Berra, *NDI* 6, 515 (*s.v. Jacopo Bolognese*).

Iactura. A damage, loss. Syn. *damnum*.

Iactus lapilli. The throwing of a small stone on another's landed property as a symbolic act of protest against a new construction intended by the neighbor.—See OPERIS NOVI NUNTIATIO.

Berger, *RE* 9, 551; Lattes, *RendLomb* 47 (1914).

Iactus mercium. Jettison; the throwing of goods overboard from a ship in distress in order to lighten it (*navis levandae causa*).—See LEX RHODIA DE IACTU. —D. 14.2.

Berger, *RE* 9, 546; Arnò, *ATor* 76/II (1941) 290.

Iactus missilium. See MISSILIA.

Iactus retis. As the object of a sale, the catch made by a fisherman (syn. *captura piscium*). The sale is made before the fisherman leaves and the risk is assumed by the buyer who has to pay the agreed price even in the event that no fish was caught.—See EMPTIO SPEI.

Berger, *RE* 9, 555; F. Vassalli, *Miscellanea critica* 1 (*AnPer* 1913) 49.

Iavolenus (Octavius I. Priscus). A Roman jurist. Born about A.D. 60, he was still alive under Hadrian. He was the head of the Sabinian school and the teacher of the famous jurist Julian. His most important and original work, *Epistulae* (in fourteen books), fully reveals his juristic individuality. Other writings of Iavolenus are collections of excerpts from earlier jurists (*libri ex Cassio, ex Plautio*), frequently provided with his own comments. He edited also a collection of texts from Labeo's posthumous work POSTERIORES.

Berger, *RE* 17, 1830, no. 59; *idem, BIDR* 44 (1936/7) 91; Orestano, *NDI* 6 (*s.v. Giavoleno*); Di Paola, *BIDR* 49–50 (1948) 277.

Id est. To wit, namely, sometimes = for instance. Many explanatory remarks, introduced by *id est,* are postclassical glosses or interpolations by Justinian's compilers, mostly of a harmless nature. The locution cannot, however, be excluded, as a matter of rule, from classical texts. The same refers to expressions as *hoc est, scilicet,* and the like.

Guarneri-Citati, *Indice*² (1927) 49 (Bibl.); Chiazzese, *Contributi testuali, AnPal* 16 (1931) 149.

Id quod interest. "That what I have lost and what I would have gained" (D. 46.8.13 pr.). If a defendant was to be condemned *in id quod* (or *quanti*) *actoris interest,* the judge had to estimate the claimant's losses and his material situation which would have resulted if the fact for which the defendant was liable would not have occurred.—C. 7.47.—See DAMNUM EMERGENS, LUCRUM CESSANS, QUANTI EA RES EST.

Beretta, *SDHI* 3 (1937) 419; Giffard, *ConfInst* 1950, 61.

Idem est (erit). This and similar locutions, such as *idem dicendum est, observandum est, placet* (*placuit*), introduce a new legal situation but similar to the preceding one in order to state that the foregoing norm or opinion has to be applied to the new instance.

Ideo. In phrases *et ideo, ideoque* (= and therefore), this serves often—but not always—for the insertion of glosses or interpolations. In any case the conclusions introduced in this way have to be examined as to their genuineness since through such locutions a classical decision is sometimes introduced although in consequence of the omission of the preceding deliberations by the compilers the connection with the foregoing text is interrupted.

Guarneri-Citati, *Indice*² (1927) 45 (Bibl.); *idem, St Riccobono* 1 (1936) 723.

Idiologus. (From the Greek *idios logos.*) A fiscal administrator of the emperor's *res privata* in Egypt. —See GNOMON.

Plaumann, *RE* 9, 882; S. Riccobono, Jr., *Il gnomon dell'i.,* 1950, 11.

Idoneus. Used not only of the financial solidity and solvency of a person (a debtor, a surety, a guardian) but also of his honesty, trustworthiness, and moral reliability. In connection with security given by a debtor, *idonee cavere* = to give security either through suretyship or a pledge. "But if faith is given to the debtor's promise without any surety, it appears *idonee cautum*" (= the security is considered proper, sufficient), D. 40.5.4.8.

Kübler, *St Albertoni* 1 (1935) 506; G. Nocera, *Insolvenza,* 1942, 36.

Ignis. See INTERDICERE AQUA ET INGI, CREMATIO.
Ignobiles. See NOBILES.

Ignominia. A deprivation of one's good name as result of a blame expressed by the censors (*nota censoria*) or of a dishonorable discharge from the army.

Pfaff, *RE* 9, 1537.

Ignominiosus. One whose conduct is dishonorable; marked with IGNOMINIA.

Ignominiosa missio. See MISSIO IGNOMINIOSA.

Ignorantia facti. See ERROR FACTI.

Ignorantia iuris. Ignorance or an error concerning the existence or meaning of a legal norm. It is prejudicial (*nocet*), i.e., it does not afford an excuse and the person who acts from lack of knowledge of the law has to bear the consequences of his ignorance. Some persons, however, such as women, minors, soldiers, inexperienced rustic persons (*rustici*) may be excused.—D. 22.6; C. 1.18.

Vassalli, *StSen* 30 (1914); Volterra, *BIDR* 38 (1929) 75; De Martino, *SDHI* 3 (1937); Scheltema, *Rechtsgeleerd Magazijn* 56 (1937) 253; Guarino, *AnMac* 15 (1941/2) 166; *idem, ZSS* 63 (1943) 243; F. Schwarz, *Die Grundlage der Condictio,* 1952, 65.

Ignorare litteras (ignorantia litterarum). To be illiterate (syn. *nescire litteras*). An illiterate person may be excused from guardianship. In written declarations to be made for the authorities his signature could be written by another person.

Illata. (From *inferre.*) See INTRODUCTA.

Illatio. An installment, especially in the payment of taxes.

Illatio mortui. Burying a dead person either in a family grave or in one which belongs to another family on the ground of a *ius mortuum inferendi.* The *illatio mortui* makes the place a LOCUS RELIGIOSUS even when the dead was a slave.—D. 11.8.—See INTERDICTUM DE MORTUO INFERENDO, SEPULCRUM.

Taubenschlag, *ZSS* 38 (1917) 251.

Illegitimus. Illegal, unlawful, illegitimate. Ant. LEGITIMUS.

Illicitus. What is not permitted by law or custom, improper. Generally illicit acts are not valid. An illicit condition or testamentary disposition is considered *pro non scripta* (= as if it would not have been added, written). Ant. LICITUS.—See COLLEGIUM ILLICITUM, CONDICIO TURPIS.

Ferrini, *NDI* 6, 657; J. Macqueron, *L'histoire de la cause immorale ou illicite,* 1924.

Illustratus. The dignity of a *vir illustris.* Syn. *illustris dignitas.*

Berger, *RE* 9, 1071.

Illustris. (*Sc. vir.*) An honorific title of the highest officials of the later Empire. Frequent in imperial constitutions from the second half of the fourth century on, and in inscriptions, the title is connected with the prefects of the city of Rome and of the *praetorium,* with the *magister militum, comes sacrarum largitionum, quaestor sacri palatii,* etc. Although the title was normally attached to the office there were *illustres honorarii* upon whom it was bestowed by the emperor as a special privilege (through *codicilli honorariae dignitatis*). The wives of the *illustres* were *illustres,* too; similarly the office itself was called *illustris* (*illustris praefectura, administratio, sedes,* etc.). The *illustres* enjoyed special personal privileges, such as exemption from public charges (*munera*), a privileged position in civil and criminal trials and as witnesses, and the like.—C. 5.33.—See SPECTABILIS.

Berger, *RE* 9; Jullian, *DS* 3; Brasiello, *NDI* 6; De Ruggiero, *DE* 4, 55; A. Stein, *Bull. Acad. Belgique, Cl. Lettres,* 1937, 365.

Imaginarius. Used of a transaction (*contractus imaginarius, solutio imaginaria*) concluded by common consent of the parties *pro forma* in order to cover up another one intended by the parties but somewhat contrary to the law. Such a transaction was, e.g., one that looked on the surface like a sale but was in fact a donation prohibited by the law (between husband and wife). *Imaginarius* is called also a party to such a transaction, e.g., *imaginarius emptor.* In another sense *imaginarius* denotes the external resemblance of a transaction permissible under the law, to another legal transaction although substantially they are not identical. Thus *mancipatio* is called *imaginaria venditio,* an *acceptilatio—imaginaria solutio,* a *testamentum per aes et libram—imaginaria mancipatio.*—See the pertinent items, DICIS CAUSA, SIMULATIO.

Berger, *RE* 9; Rabel, *ZSS* 27 (1906) 300; G. Pugliese, *La simulazione nei negozi giuridici,* 1937, 147.

Imago. See IUS IMAGINUM.—C. 1.24.

M. Segrè, *Rend. Pontificia Accad. Archeologica* 19 (1942/3) 269.

Imagines. In the army, medallions with the portrait of the reigning emperor, used as insignia of military units (legions, urban cohorts).

Imbecillitas. Mental or physical weakness which may deprive a person of the ability to conclude a legal transaction. *Imbecillitas* is brought in connection with the age (*imbecillitas aetatis*) or sex (*imbecillitas sexus*), i.e., as *imbecillitas* of women.

Imitatio veteris iuris. See VETUS IUS.

Immiscere se. To meddle, to interfere in another's affairs (*negotiis alienis*). The term was primarily used when such an interference was done against the will or without authorization of the person involved. *Immiscere* creates the liability of the person so acting since "it is culpable to interfere in a matter which is not ours" (D. 50.17.36).

Berger, *RE* 9.

Immiscere (miscere) se hereditati (or bonis). See PRO HEREDE GERERE.

Berger, *RE* 9, 1108.

Immittere. To let into a place. It occurs when the owner of an immovable commits certain acts which do harm to the adjacent property (be it in private ownership or a public place or building), e.g., to let water or a sewer run into it, to disturb the neighbor by steam or smoke, to bring a beam (*tignum*) into the wall of the neighbor's house. Such acts normally can be inhibited by prohibitory or restitutory interdicts (*interdicta*).—See INTERDICTA DE VIIS PUBLICIS, FUMUS, STILLICIDIUM.

Pasquera, *NDI* 6, 723.

Immobilis. See RES IMMOBILES.

Immoderatus, immodicus. Excessive, immoderate, unreasonable. The terms are applied to acts or doings which exceed the normal or licit limits, e.g., to a donation, an obligation, the price of an object sold.

Immunes. Persons permanently exempt from military service (e.g., priests, persons over forty-six years of age, those who served ten years in cavalry or sixteen—later twenty-five—years in infantry). Temporarily relieved from service were the furnishers of the army, persons employed in lower official service (*apparitores*). Syn. noun *vacatio militiae.*—*Immunes* were also those who for any reason were exempt from public charges, taxes, and the like.—See IMMUNITAS, MUNERA.

De Ruggiero, *DE* 4; Fiebiger, *RE* 9; Jullian, *DS* 3; De Visscher, *Les édits d'Auguste,* 1940, 103; Welles, *JRS* 28 (1938) 41.

Immunitas. Exemption from taxes or public charges (MUNERA). It was granted as a personal privilege to individuals, as a privilege of a social group (public officials, soldiers) or of a community in Italy or in a province. The extension of *immunitas* was different; it varied according to the kind of the charges or the profession of the persons exempted (physicians, teachers, clergymen, etc.). *Immunitas* was granted by the senate through a decree (*senatusconsultum*) and under the Empire by the emperor through a general enactment (*edictum*) or a special personal privilege. Of particular importance were the exemptions in the domain of municipal administration.—D. 50.6; C. 10.25.

Ziegler, *RE* 9; Kübler, *RE* 16, 650; Messini, *NDI* 6, 727; Stevenson, *OCD*; Ferrari Dalle Spade, *Immunità ecclesiastiche nel dir. rom.,* *AVen* 99 (1939/40).

Impedire (impedimentum). To hinder (a hindrance, impediment). The terms are used of legal norms which impede the conclusion of certain legal acts, or to legal requirements which, when not complied with will produce the non-validity of the act done.

Impendere. To spend.—See IMPENSAE.

Impendium. See syn. IMPENSAE, DISPENDIUM.

Impensae. Expenditures made on a thing. They become juristically important when made in behalf of another's property (*in alienum*) or by one co-owner in behalf of a thing he owns together with others. Legal situations whereby one comes into the position to make expenditures for another are manifold. They may originate from a contract (*impensae* made by a depositee, or by one who received a thing as a gratuitous loan, *commodatum,* or as a pledge, by a husband with regard to the dowry) or from the possession of another's thing in good faith as one's own. For the various kinds of *impensae,* see the following items. The liability of the owner for the restitution of expenses could be established in a special agreement or by his consent to a specific expenditure. In the absence of a mutual understanding the legal rules were applied which settled the problem in various ways for specific legal situations. The proceeds derived from the thing held, are deducted from the *impensae* to be restituted.—D. 25.1.—See POSSESSIO BONAE FIDEI.

Guarneri, Citati, *NDI* 12 (*s.v. spese*); Riccobono, *AnPal* 3-4 (1917) 319; idem, *BIDR* 47 (1940); S. Riccobono, Jr., *AnPal* 17 (1937) 53; Daube, *CambrLR* 1945, 31.

Impensae dotales. Expenses made by the husband on the property he received as a dowry (*in dotem* [*res dotales*] *factae*). Specific rules determined the husband's right to recover his expenditures at the restitution of the dowry. They underwent various changes in the course of time. "Necessary expenses diminish the dowry by the force of law (*ipso iure*)" (D. 25.1.5 pr.).—D. 25.1.—See RETENTIONES DOTALES.

Guarneri-Citati, *NDI* 12, 1, 723; Schulz, *ZSS* 34 (1913) 57; E. Deter, *Impensae dotem minuunt,* Diss. Erlangen, 1935; J. P. Levy, *Les i. d.,* Thèse, Paris, 1937.

Impensae funeris. Expenses made for the funeral of a person. If made by a person not obliged to do it under the law, they can be recovered from the pertinent relatives.—See ACTIO FUNERARIA, SUMPTUS FUNERIS.

Impensae in fructus. (Or *fructuum precipiendorum causa.*) Expenses made to increase the produce of a land. They are taken into account when the person who laid out the money is sued for the restitution of the produce. "What remains after the deduction of expenses is considered a produce" (D. 5.3.36.5).—See FRUCTUS.

Riccobono, *AG* 58 (1897) 61; Riccobono, Jr., *AnPal* 17 (1937) 53.

Impensae litis. See SUMPTUS LITIS.

Impensae necessariae. Necessary expenditures made to prevent deterioration, destruction, or loss of a thing, e.g., repairing a building, medical attendance on a slave. They must always be made good except to the holder of a stolen thing. Ant. *impensae utiles, voluptariae.*

Impensae utiles. Useful, beneficial, expenditures made to promote the improvement of a thing, to increase its produce or selling value. Generally the improvements may be taken away by the person who made them to the profit of the owner if it is feasible without damage to the thing. *Impensae utiles* must be restored by the owner if they were made with his consent. Ant. *impensae necessariae, voluptariae.*—See IUS TOLLENDI.

Impensae voluptariae (voluptuosae). Expenditures made on a thing which serve only to increase its beauty or for ornaments. *Impensae voluptariae* are neither necessary (*necessariae*) nor beneficial (*utiles*). As a matter of rule, there is no liability on the part of the owner to refund them, but the person who made the ornament at his expenses has the right to take it away (IUS TOLLENDI).

Imperator. The commander (one who *imperat*) of the army. Under the Republic a high magistrate (*consul, praetor, proconsul*) who, by virtue of his *imperium,* commanded the troops, was hailed (*salutatio, acclamatio*) by them after the victory over an enemy as *imperator,* at the end of the battle or during his triumphant entrance in Rome. He used to be so addressed afterwards in public and private life. Augustus assumed the term *imperator* as a praenomen (*Imperator Caesar*) and so did his successors. Thus gradually the former honorific title became an appellative title of the *princeps,* the head of state ("the emperor").—See PRINCEPS.

Rosenberg, *RE* 9; Cagnat, *DS* 3; Orestano, *NDI* 6; De Ruggiero, *DE* 4, 41, 43; MacFayden, *The History of the title Imperator under the R. Empire,* Chicago, 1920; Stroux, *Die Antike* 13 (1937); Momigliano, *Bull. Comm. Archeol. Comunale di Roma* 53 (1930) 42; idem, *OCD*; De Sanctis, *St Riccobono* 2 (1936) 57.

Imperatoriam. The initial word of Justinian's enactment by which his Institutes were promulgated (November 21, 533).—See INSTITUTIONES IUSTINIANI.

Imperfectus. Not complete. A transaction is incomplete when one of its essential elements is not fulfilled or missing, e.g., if in a *stipulatio* the object of the promise or another essential element is not indicated. See TESTAMENTUM IMPERFECTUM. Imperfect acts or transactions lack legal validity.—See LEGES PERFECTAE, MINORES.

Aru, *AG* 124 (1940) 3.

Imperialis. Connected with, or originating from the emperor (e.g., *constitutio, statuta, praeceptum, liberalitas, auctoritas, maiestas,* etc.). *Imperialis* occurs as frequently as its syn. *principalis.*

Imperitia. The lack of professional skill, capacity (knowledge). It created liability of the person who through a contract (*locatio conductio operis,* or *locatio conductio operarum*) assumed the duty to render certain professional services, without having the necessary knowledge. It is considered as a form of CULPA (*culpae adnumeratur*). *Imperitia* is used of artisans and craftsmen as well as of persons exercising liberal professions (physicians, land-surveyors, etc.). Also the lack of knowledge of the law (inability) in a judge is qualified as *imperitia.*

Arangio-Ruiz, *Responsabilità contrattuale,* 2nd ed. 1933, 188.

Imperium. An order, command. A legal norm is called *imperium legis* when referring to a statute. *Imperium* means also the right to give orders (*ius imperandi*), the power over a smaller group such as a family (hence *imperium domesticum* is the *imperium* of the head of the family, *pater familias*). The supreme power of the Roman people, its sovereignty = *imperium populi Romani*. In a technical sense *imperium* = the official power of the higher magistrates (*magistratus maiores*) under the Republic, and of the emperor under the Empire. The magisterial *imperium* embraced various domains of administration, legislative initiative through proposals made before the popular assemblies (*ius agendi cum populo*), and military command. With regard to the administration of justice, *imperium* is sometimes opposed to, and distinguished from, IURISDICTIO, sometimes coherently connected with it. See IMPERIUM MERUM. The juristic sources do not agree as to the attribution of certain magisterial acts of jurisdictional character (*restitutio in integrum, missiones*, appointment of guardians) to *imperium* or *iurisdictio*. The confusion is doubtless the result of alterations of the texts or misunderstanding on the part of Justinian compilers for whom older distinctions lost their practical significance.—Finally *imperium* means the territory of the state.—See LEX DE IMPERIO, POTESTAS.

Rosenberg, *RE* 9; Toutain, *DS* 3; Lauria, *NDI* 6; De Ruggiero, *DE* 4; Balsdon, *OCD*; Nocera, *AnPer* 57 (1946) 145; F. Leifer, *Die Einheit des Gewaltgedankens im röm. Staatsrecht*, 1914, 68; Radin, *St Riccobono* 2 (1936) 21; Caspary, *St Albertoni* 2 (1937) 394; G. Pugliese, *Appunti sui limiti dell'imperium nella repressione penale*, 1939; Balsdon, *JRS* 29 (1939) 57; Rudolph, *Neue Jahrbücher für das klas. Altertum*, 1939, 145; H. Wagenwoort, *Roman dynamism*, 1947, 70; C. Gioffredi, *Contributi alla storia della procedura civ.*, 1947, 16; Vogel, *ZSS* 67 (1950) 62.

Imperium domesticum. The power of the *pater familias*.—See IMPERIUM.

Imperium domi. See DOMI.

Imperium maius. The *imperium* of a higher magistrate when compared with that of a magistrate lower in the hierarchy, e.g., the *imperium* of a consul was *imperium maius* when confronted with the praetor's *imperium*. Ant. *imperium minus*. *Par imperium* = the *imperium* of magistrates equal in rank (see COLLEGAE).—See INTERCESSIO.

Rosenberg, *RE* 9, 1209; Hugh Last, *JRS* 37 (1947) 157; M. Grant, *From imperium to auctoritas*, 1946, 411.

Imperium merum. The full magisterial power. As far as jurisdiction is concerned, it is limited only to criminal matters (*ius gladii, potestas gladii*) and does not include jurisdiction in civil matters. If, however, the latter was granted too, the *imperium* was termed *imperium mixtum*. The origin of this distinction is somewhat obscure.

Pfaff, *RE* 9; Rosenberg, *ibid.* 1210.

Imperium militiae. See DOMI.

Imperium mixtum. See IMPERIUM MERUM.

Imperium par. See IMPERIUM MAIUS.

Imperium proconsulare. See PROCONSUL.

Impetrare (impetratio). To obtain on request. The term is used of judicial and administrative measures which individuals succeeded to obtain by petitions (*petere, postulare, desiderare*), addressed to magistrates, imperial officials, or the emperor. The locution *impetrare actionem* belongs to the language of the imperial chancery.—C. 1.22; 2.57.

Naber, *RStDIt* 11 (1938) 5.

Impetratio dominii. A request of a creditor (*creditor pigneraticius*) addressed to the emperor to the effect that he be recognized as the owner of the thing, pledged to him by the debtor, for which he could not find a purchaser. Justinian ordained that if the value of the pledge exceeded the debt, the surplus had to be restored to the debtor. The latter had moreover the right to redeem the pledge within two years by paying the sum due with interest.—C. 8.33.—See HYPEROCHA.

A. Burdese, *Lex commissoria* (*Mem. Ist. giur. Torino* 63, 1949) 206.

Impetus. Mental impulse. A crime committed *impetu* is considered neither intentional nor casual. It is in the middle like *culpa* between *casus* and *dolus*. Acts committed in drunkenness (*ebrietas, per vinum, temulentia*) are punished mildly, especially when committed by soldiers. Imperial legislation considered violent excitement of the wrongdoer an extenuating circumstance. *Impetus doloris* was also taken into consideration (e.g., when one killed his wife caught in adultery) "since it is extremely difficult to master a justified grief" (D. 48.5.39.8).

F. De Robertis, *Studi di dir. penale rom.*, 1943, 140.

Implere. To fulfill (an agreement, an obligation, a condition), to satisfy legal requirements (e.g., of an usucapion), to complete, to bring to an end.

Impleri. *Condicio impletur*, see CONDICIO.

Implorare. To request a judicial remedy (e.g., an *in integrum restitutio*), to supplicate. The term occurs frequently in imperial constitutions.

Imponere. To impose (a duty, a charge, a penalty) upon a person. For *imponere festucam* (*vindictam*) in the *legis actio sacramento in rem*, see VINDICTA. *Imponere libertatem* = to grant freedom. *Imponere servitutem* = to impose a servitude upon an immovable by agreement or in a testament.

Gradenwitz, *ZSS* 23 (1902) 337.

Importata. See INTRODUCTA.

Impossibilium nulla obligatio. "An obligation to do impossible things is not binding" (D. 185.50.17). "Things which cannot be given (*impossibilia dari*) are considered not to be included (*sc.* in a transaction)" (D. 135.50.17). A condition is considered impossible when nature makes its fulfillment impossible.—See CONDICTIO IMPOSSIBILIS.

Rabel, *Mél Gérardin*, 1907, 473; idem, *Fg Bekker*, 1907, 193; Longo, *AnMac* 2 (1934) 213; F. Pastori, *Profilo dogmatico dell'obblig. rom.*, 1951, 171.

Impostura. See STELLIONATUS.

Improbare. To disapprove, to reject. The term is applied to agreements or contractual clauses (conditions) condemned (*improbari*) by law or custom. *Improbare* is also used of a disapprobation of a person who is considered to be unqualified for certain duties (e.g., a guardian) or works.—Ant. *adprobare, probare*.

Improbus. Dishonest, lacking in moral integrity. *Improbus* is a person who, for instance, knowingly sues for a debt which has been paid or who conducts a trial knowing that he is wrong (*improbus litigator*). "He who does not know how much he owes cannot be considered dishonest" (D. 50.17.99).—See NEMO DE IMPROBITATE.

Kleinfeller, *RE* 9.

Improbus et intestabilis. See TESTIS.

Improbus litigator. See IMPROBUS. Syn. *calumniator* (see CALUMNIA), *temere litigans*. According to Justinian's constitution he must pay his adversary all damages and expenditures caused by the trial (C. 3.1.14.1).

Imprudentia. Want of knowledge of law or facts, ignorance, inadvertence, imprudence. In legal matters it is treated like IGNORANTIA. On the other hand, however, "almost in all criminal trials assistance is given to youth and lack of prudence" (D. 50.17.108).—See IUDEX QUI LITEM SUAM FACIT, IMPERITIA.

Impubes. A person below the age of puberty, one who has not attained manhood. In earlier times no certain age was fixed for puberty (*pubertas*). Physical condition (*habitus corporis*) was decisive, both in men (*qui generare possunt* = who are capable to procreate) and women (*nubilis, viripotens* = fit for marriage). The beginning of puberty had its external distinction in the man's garment, *toga virilis,* hence the youth was called *praetextatus.* Later the age of fourteen years for boys, and twelve for girls, was established as the end of impuberty. An *impubes,* who is not under the paternal power (*patria potestas*) and is therefore *sui iuris,* must have a guardian (*tutor*), see TUTELA. An *impubes* under guardianship may conclude legal transactions only with the consent of his guardian, profitable transactions even without such consent. After completion of the age of fourteen, an *impubes* becomes *pubes* and enters the age of a *minor* which lasts until the completion of twenty-five years. Within the age of impuberty some distinctions are made (they are perhaps of later origin): *impubes infantiae proximus* = one who has somewhat exceeded the age of infancy (*infantia,* see INFANS) and *impubes pubertati proximus* = one who is near the age of puberty. The latter may be responsible for criminal wrongdoings if he is capable to understand the importance of his acts. A general classical rule was, however, that an *impubes* was not *capax doli,* i.e., he had no capacity of understanding the fraudulent (criminal) character of his actions.—

See CAPAX DOLI, CURATOR IMPUBERIS, TOGA PRAETEXTA.

Baudry, *DS* 2; S. Perozzi, *Tutor impubes, Scritti* 3 (1948, ex 1918) 127; Tumedei, *AG* 89 (1923); Albertario, *Studi* 1 (1933) 81; Di Marzo, *St Besta* 1 (1939) 111.

Impune. Without punishment, with safety. *Impune* is frequently used with a negative (*non impune, nemo impune,* and the like) and indicates that a person acting in a certain way may expect punishment. *Non impune* is sometimes syn. with *illicite.*

Impunitas. Freedom from punishment.—See ABOLITIO.

Impunitus. Unpunished, one who escaped punishment. The emperor Trajan made in a rescript the following statement: "It is better to leave a criminal unpunished than to condemn an innocent person" (D. 48.19.5 pr.).—See SUSPICIO.

Imputare. To reckon into (for instance, into expenses, a legacy, the *quarta Falcidia,* a debt), to make a deduction. *Imputare* is used also to mean charging one with fault or negligence (*culpa, neglegentia*).

In bonis esse (or rem habere). When a *res mancipi* was conveyed by a mere delivery (handing over, *traditio*), and not by one of the solemn acts required for the transfer of property of such things (*mancipatio, in iure cessio*), the transferee did not acquire ownership under Quiritarian law but he had the thing only *in bonis* (= among his goods, so-called bonitary ownership) which was protected by praetorian law. He might acquire Quiritarian ownership through USUCAPIO.—See ACTIO PUBLICIANA, DOMINIUM EX IURE QUIRITIUM, DOMINIUM DUPLEX.

A. Audibert, *Histoire de la propriété prétorienne,* 2 vol., 1889; P. Bonfante, *Scritti* 2 (1926) 370; M. Kaser, *Eigentum und Besitz,* 1943, 297.

In continenti. See CONTINENS.

In diem. Until, on, a fixed day.—See DIES.

In diem addictio. See ADDICTIO IN DIEM.

In domum deductio. See DEDUCTIO IN DOMUM.

In factum actiones (formulae). See FORMULAE IN IUS CONCEPTAE.

In integrum restitutio. See RESTITUTIO IN INTEGRUM.

In iudicio. Used (not correctly) in literature to denote the stage of a civil trial before the private judge. The correct expression is *apud iudicem.* Ant. IN IURE.—See IUDEX.

In iure. Before the judicial magistrate. The first stage of a civil trial in the proceedings of *legis actiones* and *per formulas* took place before the magistrate (the praetor), while the second, final stage, normally ended with a judgment, took place before the private judge (*iudex*), *apud iudicem.*—See FORMULA, IUS, IUDEX, CONFESSIO IN IURE, INTERROGATIO IN IURE, IUSIURANDUM NECASSARIUM.

R. Düll, *Der Gütegedanke,* 1931; F. De Martino, *Giurisdizione,* 1937, 41; Jolowicz, *ACDR* Bologna 2 (1935) 59; idem, *RIDA* 2 (= *Mél De Visscher* 1, 1949) 477; Kaser, *Fschr Wenger* 1 (1946) 106; Wenger, *St Solazzi* (1948) 47 (Bibl. 48).

In iure cessio. A fictitious trial in the form of a *rei vindicatio* before the magistrate (*in iure*) the purpose of which was the transfer of Quiritarian ownership. The plaintiff (the transferee) asserted that the thing was his (*vindicare*), the defendant (the transferor), interrogated by the praetor whether he wanted to make a countervindication (*contra vindicare*), remained silent or replied in the negative, whereupon the praetor assigned (*addictio*) the thing to the plaintiff. Thus the transfer was completed, without *litis contestatio,* or a procedure *apud iudicem.* The *in iure cessio* does no longer exist under Justinian.—See REI VINDICATIO.

Kipp, *RE* 3 (*s.v. cessio*); Baudry, *DS* 1 (*s.v. cessio*); De Villa, *NDI* 6 (*s.v. in iure c.*); S. Schlossmann, *In iure c. und mancipatio,* 1904; Rabel, *ZSS* 27 (1906) 309; H. Lévy-Bruhl, *Quelques problèmes du très ancien droit rom.,* 1934, 114; *idem, Nouvelles études,* 1947, 144; Pflüger, *ZSS* 63 (1943) 301; M. Kaser, *Das altröm. Ius,* 1949, 104; Meylan, *RIDA* 6 (1951) 103.

In iure cessio hereditatis. A cession of an inheritance in the form of *in iure cessio* to a third person by an heir on intestacy of the agnatic group. The *heredes sui* were not permitted to transfer the inheritance through *in iure cessio.* If the heir did it before taking over the estate, the cessionary became heir as if he were heir appointed by the law. If he did it after the acceptance of the inheritance (*aditio hereditatis*) he remained obligated to the creditors of the estate whereas the debts owed to the estate were extinguished since through *in iure cessio* only corporeal things were conveyed. The *in iure cessio hereditatis* disappeared together with the *in iure cessio.* It was absorbed by the sale of an estate; see EMPTIO HEREDITATIS.—See the foregoing item.

Garaud, *RHD* 1 (1922) 141; Cugia, *Alienazione dell'eredità, St Besta* 1 (1939); Ambrosino, *SDHI* 10 (1944) 3; Guarino, *St Solazzi,* 1948, 38; De Martino, *ibid.* 568; Betti, *ibid.* 594; B. Albanese, *Successione ereditaria, AnPal* 20 (1949) 285; Scherillo, *St Carnelutti* 4 (1950) 257; Ambrosino, *SDHI* 17 (1951) 203; Solazzi, *Iura* 3 (1952) 21.

In iure cessio servitutis. The constitution of a servitude through an *in iure cessio* in court, modeled on a trial for a servitude (*vindicatio servitutis*). It could be applied for predial servitudes and usufruct. —See IN IURE CESSIO.

In iure cessio tutelae. A guardian of a woman who under the law was entitled to assume the guardianship (*tutor legitimus*), could surrender the tutorship to another through an act before the magistrate, *in iure cessio.* The tutor thus appointed = *tutor cessicius.* At the latter's death the guardianship returned to the *tutor legitimus.* The *tutor cessicius* ceased to be tutor when the guardian under law died.

Sachers, *RE* 7A, 1594.

In iure cessio ususfructus. See IN IURE CESSIO SERVITUTIS.

In ius conceptae actiones (formulae). See FORMULAE IN IUS CONCEPTAE.

In ius vocatio. The summons of a debtor by the plaintiff to appear IN IURE (before the magistrate) where the plaintiff will claim his right. The defendant was bound to follow the summons according to a provision of the Twelve Tables: *si in ius vocat, ilo* (= if, *sc.* the plaintiff, summons to court the defendant shall go). The summoned defendant must not answer the plaintiff's summons immediately if he gives a surety (*vindex*) warranting that he (the summoned) would appear in court on a fixed day. Certain persons could not be summoned at all, such as consuls, praetors, and high provincial officials; others were exempt from *in ius vocatio* only when exercising a specific activity (a pontiff during a sacrifice, a judge or an advocate during a trial) or on specific occasions (wedding, funeral). Certain persons were prohibited from summoning other persons related to them by specific ties. Thus parents, patrons and their children and parents could not be summoned by children or freedmen, respectively, unless the latter obtained a special permission from the praetor. In later law a summons was performed by the plaintiff in writing in the presence of a clerk of the court; see DENUNTIATIO LITIS. In the later Empire the summons became an official act in which the plaintiff did not participate.—D. 2.4–7; C. 2.2.—See DOMUS, EVOCATIO, VINDEX, VADIMONIUM, MANUS INIECTIO, ORATIO MARCI, THEATRUM.

Cuq, *DS* 3, 743; Sacchi, *NDI* 6; Pugliese, *RIDA* 3 (= *Mél De Visscher* 2, 1949) 249.

In locum alicuius succedere. See SUCCEDERE IN LOCUM.

In manum conventio. See CONVENTIO IN MANUM, MANUS.

In mora esse. See MORA.

In personam actiones. See ACTIONES IN PERSONAM.

In pendenti esse. To be in suspense.—See CONDICIO, PENDERE.

In possessione esse. Syn. DETINERE. The term *possessio* is not used here with its technical meaning. —See POSSESSIO.

In procinctu. Before the troops gathered in face of the enemy. A testament made by a soldier *in procinctu* before a combat is one of the earliest forms of testament. Details are unknown.

In re sua. See RES SUA.

In rem actiones. See ACTIONES IN REM.

In rem agere per sponsionem. See AGERE PER SPONSIONEM.

In rem versum. See VERSUM IN REM, PECULIUM.

In summa. In conclusion, finally, generally. It was a favorite locution of some classical jurists (especially Gaius) to introduce a conclusive rule (*in summa sciendum est, dicendum est* = it must be said, understood).

Guarneri-Citati, *Indice*[2] (1927) 46; Sargenti, *AG* 122 (1939) 53; Solazzi, *La tutela delle servitù prediali,* 1949, 148.

In transitu. Used of official acts accomplished by a magistrate when passing by (e.g., when a praetor or a high provincial officer went to the theatre or into a bathing establishment). Only acts of voluntary jurisdiction (e.g., manumissions) could be performed on such occasion.

Inaedificatio. What was built on a land belongs to its owner, no matter who was the builder or to whom belonged the materials used. The maxim, "all that is built on soil goes with the soil" (D. 43.17.3.7; Gaius 2.73; Inst. 2.1.33), is an application of the rule *superficies cedit solo.* The owner of the materials remains their owner and may recover them by *vindicatio* only when the building for any reason comes down. However, one who knowingly built a house on another's land with his own materials, lost the ownership of them.—See TIGNUM, SUPERFICIES.

A. Suman, *Saggi minimi di dir. rom.,* 1919, 71; Guarneri-Citati, *AnPal* 14 (1930) 315; E. Nardi, *St sulla ritenzione,* 1947, 320.

Inanis. (When used of a legal transaction, obligation, action) void, of no legal effect.

Inauguratio. A religious ceremony celebrated by the augurs in republican Rome after the election of a high magistrate or the appointment of a high priest (*flamin*). A favorable result of the sacrifice was considered an approval by the gods.—See AUGURES.

Wissowa, *RE* 2, 2325; Richter, *RE* 9; Bouché-Leclercq, *DS* 3.

Incantare (incantatio). To enchant by a magic formula. According to the Twelve Tables *incantare* was punished as a crime. Syn. *excantare.*—See EXCANTARE FRUGES, MALUM CARMEN, OCCENTARE, MAGIA.

Pfaff, *RE* 9; F. Beckmann, *Zauberei und Recht in Roms Frühzeit,* 1928, 26, 45.

Incendere (incendium). To set fire, to burn (another's property). *Incendium* = arson.—See INCENDIARIUS.

Incendiarius. An incendiary, one guilty of arson (*incendium*). An *incendiarius* was punished with the death penalty (by burning) when he willfully had set fire to another's property within the city, either for reasons of enmity or for the purpose of committing a robbery. See CREMATIO. The burning of a country-house, outside the city, was punished less severely. Damage done to property by fire could be claimed by an *actio legis Aquiliae.* According to *Lex Cornelia de sicariis* an *incendiarius* was treated as a murderer when human life was destroyed by the fire. In minor cases arson was considered a *crimen vis* (violence). Syn. *incensor.*

Kleinfeller, *RE* 9; Humbert, *DS* 3; Condanari-Michler, *Scr Ferrini* 3 (Univ. Sacro Cuore, Milan, 1948) 74.

Incendium. A fire. The praetorian Edict granted a penal action for fourfold damages against a person who at a fire took things by violence or fraud or received goods stolen during a fire. After a year the action could be brought only for double the damages. Analogous actions were set in the Edict for robbery committed in a shipwreck (NAUFRAGIUM), when a house collapsed (RUINA) or during an attack against a boat (*expugnare navem*).—D. 47.9.

Lenel, *Edictum perpetuum*[3] (1927) 396.

Incensitus. Not registered in the tax payers' list. Ant. *censitus.*

Incensor. See INCENDIARIUS.

Incensus. One who abstained from registering in the census in order to avoid military service. According to ancient law he could be sold abroad losing liberty and citizenship (*capitis deminutio maxima*).

Pfaff, *RE* 9.

Incertae personae. See PERSONAE INCERTAE.

Incertum (incertus). See CERTUM, ACTIONES (FORMULAE) CERTAE, CONDEMNATIO INCERTA, DIES CERTUS.

Incestus (incestum). Incest, sexual union between persons tied by blood relationship. It was prohibited since the earliest times for physiological, ethical, and social reasons by *veteres mores* (old customs), undoubtedly under religious sanctions (*fas*). Later legislation was concerned only with the prohibition of marriages between persons closely related by blood (*nuptiae incestae*), without taking into account as a specific crime sexual intercourse outside a marital union, since such coition was punished under the law concerning related crimes (*stuprum, adulterium*). *Incestus* was always forbidden between descendants and ascendants (termed *incestus iuris gentium* as being prohibited with all nations). As to cognatic relationship the extension of the concept *incestus* (and the interdiction of marriage) varied in the course of time. As a matter of principle, "man commits *incestus* if he marries a woman among those whom by custom we are forbidden to marry" (D. 23.2.39.1). A marriage between brother and sister, uncle (or aunt) and niece (or nephew) always remained under ban. Legislation of Christian emperors dealt frequently with the matter. Punishment was originally the death penalty by throwing down the culprit from the Tarpeian rock; later *deportatio, relegatio,* and seizure of property were inflicted. At times penalties for the woman were severer than those for the man. Ignorance of the law or of the existing relationship was taken into consideration in setting the penalty. The marriage itself (*incestae nuptiae*) was null and the children were illegitimate. —C. 5.5.

Klingmüller, *RE* 9; Humbert, *DS* 3; Brasiello, *NDI* 6; Lotmar, *Mél Girard* 2 (1912); De Martino, *SDHI* 3 (1937) 405; Guarino, *St sull'i.,* 1942; idem, *ZSS* 63 (1943) 175 (Bibl. 177); G. Lombardi, *Ricerche in tema di ius gentium* (1946) 3.

Incestus superveniens. Adoption of his son's wife or his daughter's husband by a father dissolves the existing marriage as incestuous, the spouses being now in a relationship (although created artificially), which would exclude the conclusion of a valid marriage between them.

Inchoare actionem (iudicium, litem). When referring to the procedure *extra ordinem,* to initiate a lawsuit; when referred to the formulary procedure the term indicates the *litis contestatio.*

Solazzi, *ANap* 63 (1951).

Incidere. To become involved in a situation which makes a law (a statute) or a criminal or private action applicable against the person entangled, e.g., *incidere in legem Aquiliam, in edictum, in senatusconsultum.*—See COMMUNIO INCIDENS.

Incidere testamentum. To cut through a written testament (*tabulas testamenti*) in order to destroy the last will. If a testator in a state of insanity did so with the testament he had made when he had been mentally sane, the testament remained valid.

Incisus. (*Sc. aere*). One whose name was engraved on a bronze tablet containing a list of persons for a specific purpose, e.g., for participation in the gratuitous distribution of grain in Rome.

De Ruggiero, *DE* 4.

Incola. An inhabitant of a city or municipality, one "who conferred his domicile at a certain place" (D. 50.16.239.2). Hence syn. *qui domicilium habet.* See DOMICILIUM. An *incola* is distinguished from an *originarius,* i.e., a citizen of the community where he was born; see ORIGO.—"An *incola* has to obey the magistrates of the place where he is an inhabitant as well as those where he is citizen" (D. 50.1.29).—D. 50.1; C.10.40.—See CONSISTENTES.

Berger, *RE* 9; Lechat, *DS* 3.

Incolatus (ius). Rights and duties connected with the domicile, the quality of being an *incola* in a community.—See DOMICILIUM, INCOLA.

Incommodum. See COMMODUM.

Inconcussa possessio. Undisturbed possession of an immovable (*inconcusse possidere*). Unknown in the classical language, the term appears in later imperial constitutions.

Inconsiderate, inconsulte (inconsulto). Inconsiderately, thoughtlessly, without deliberation. One who is so acting must bear the consequences of his transactions or declarations made without deliberation.

Inconsultus. (Adj.) Not consulted. *Inconsulto praetore (principe)* = without asking the praetor (the emperor) for permission or advice.

Incorporalis. See RES INCORPORALES.

Incorporatio. The incorporation of confiscated property into the private property (*res privata*) of the emperor.—C. 10.10.

Incrementum. An increase, augmentation, produce. The term is applied to increases of a dowry, of an inheritance or legacy, of a *peculium,* and becomes juridically important when the restitution of such patrimonial units is involved.

Incubare (incubatio). To take and retain another's thing in unlawful possession. *Incubator* = an unlawful holder of a thing.

Daube, *CambLJ* 9 (1945) 37.

Inculpanter, inculpate. Free from fault, from culpability, without blame. Syn. *sine culpa.*—See CULPA.

Incursio, incursus (latronum, praedonum). An assault of bandits. An attack made by a group of robbers was considered a *vis maior.* It released the holder of another's things from responsibility.

Incusare. To accuse, to blame, to complain. The term appears only in the language of the imperial chancery.

Indebite. See INDEBITUM.

Indebitum (indebita pecunia). A debt which in fact does not exist. In a broader sense the term is used of an existing debt which may be repealed by a peremptory exception. What has been paid in discharge of a not existing debt may be recovered by a special action, *condictio indebiti.*—D. 12.6; C. 4.5.—See CONDICTIO INDEBITI.

F. Fitting, *Sciens indebitum accipere,* Lausanne, 1926; Van Oven, *Iura* 1 (1950) 21; J. G. Fuchs, *Iusta causa traditionis* (Basel, 1952) 163.

Indefensus. A defendant who by his negative attitude refused the cooperation necessary for the continuation of a trial. *Indefensus* is one who does not accept the formula (*accipere iudicium*) proposed by the plaintiff and approved by the magistrate, one who does not offer security ordered by the praetor, who does not answer when questioned by the praetor in court (*interrogatio in iure*), or who is hiding himself (*latitare*) so that he cannot be summoned by the plaintiff; see IN IUS VOCATIO. The sanction for the frustration of the process by the defendant was that the plaintiff was authorized by the praetor to enter into possession of the defendant's property, MISSIO IN POSSESSIONEM. In trials in which a right over a thing is involved, the thing itself is called *res indefensa* when the defendant assumed a passive attitude. In such a case the plaintiff was given possession of the thing. *Indefensus* is also one who being personally incapable to defend himself in court, is not properly represented by his tutor or curator.—See LATITARE, MISSIO IN POSSESSIONEM REI SERVANDAE CAUSA, DUCI IUBERE, DEFENSIO, DEFENDERE.

Wlassak, *Confessio in iure, SbMünch,* 1934, Heft 8.

Indemnis. Secure from loss, incurring no loss. *Indemnem praestare aliquem* = to indemnify either by reimbursement of the damages already done or by giving security against future losses.

Indemnitas. Security against loss, indemnification. See INDEMNIS, CAUTIO INDEMNITATIS.—C. 5.46.

Index. One who denounces a crime without being a formal accuser in a criminal trial; an informer. An *index* who had been an accomplice of a criminal frequently went unpunished if his information led to the discovery of the culprit. Both the denunciation and the award given to the *index* were termed *indicium.*

Kleinfeller, *RE* 9; Kaser, *RE* 5A, 1047.

Index. A summary of a juristic text or of a written document (*index scripturae*). In the Byzantine legal literature *indices* were résumés of older collections of legal texts in the form of concise formulations of legal norms with the omission of discussions, polemics, historical reminiscences, and the like. The most renowned Byzantine jurists (Theophilus, Dorotheus, Stephanus, Kyrillos) wrote *indices* of the Digest or of parts thereof. Authors of *indices* were designated as *indikeutai*.

> Berger, *Justinian's Ban, Bull. Polish Inst. of Arts and Sciences in America* 3 (1945) 676 (= *BIDR* 55–56, Post-Bellum, 1951, 148, Bibl.).

Index Florentinus. A list of juristic works which had been excerpted for Justinian's Digest. Justinian ordered that such a list be composed, but only the manuscript of the Digest of Florence (see FLOREN-TINA) contains such a list. However, some works of classical jurists are listed therein of which no excerpt is preserved in the Digest but on the other hand some works are excerpted in the Digest which are not mentioned in the *index Florentinus*.

> Peters, *Die oström. Digestenkommentare*, 1913, 75; Rotondi, *Scr. giur.* 1 (1922) 298.

Index rerum gestarum. (Of Augustus.) See RES GESTAE.

Indicere. To impose a duty. The term applies to both official orders (imposing public services, *munera* or other charges) and to testamentary dispositions by which an heir or a legatee was charged with the performance of services or with a moral duty (*indicere operas, indicere viduitatem*).—C. 6.40.

Indicere bellum. To declare war. Under the Republic the decision about a declaration of war depended upon the *comitia centuriata*.—See INDICTIO BELLI, LEX DE BELLO INDICENDO, FETIALES, CLARIGATIO.

Indicia. Circumstantial evidence. "*Indicia* have no less force of evidence than documents" (C. 3.32.19), provided they are not prohibited by law. The term appears in imperial constitutions (from the time of Diocletian) in connection with both criminal and civil matters.

Indicium. In criminal matters the denunciation of a crime and its perpetrator.—See INDEX, NUNTIATOR.

Indicium. The promise of a recompense for a certain service. It used to be announced publicly (*edicere*), as, for instance, the announcement of a reward for the return of a runaway slave. The award was promised to anybody who succeeded in fulfilling the action to be compensated.

> R. v. Mayr, *Die Auslobung*, 1905; R. Villers, *Remarques sur la promesse de récompense*, 1941; Düll, *ZSS* 61 (1941) 23.

Indictio. An imperial enactment ordaining an extraordinary requisition of corn from the owners of provincial land. From the beginning of the fourth century on, the *indictio* became a regular annual impost. The revision of the land taxes was carried out every fifteen years (= three censuses). These fifteen-year cycles came to serve afterwards as a new system of dating, the years being indicated by the number of the indiction and by one to fifteen according to their sequence in the given indiction. The first *indictio* cycle started in A.D. 297 and the beginning of an *indictio* was on September 1st.—*Indictio* (*indicere*) was the term for the imposition of public charges (*munera*).—C. 10.17; 43.—See SUPERINDICTIO.

> De Ruggiero, *DE* 4, 48; Humbert, *DS* 3; Seeck, *RE* 9; Ferrari dalle Spade, *Immunità ecclesiastiche, AV en* 99, 2 (1939–40) 149.

Indictio belli. A ceremonial act (throwing a blood-stained spear into the enemy's territory), performed by the FETIALES; it completed the declaration of war.—See INDICERE BELLUM, LEX DE BELLO INDICENDO, CLARIGATIO, FETIALES.

> Walbank, *ClPhilol* 1949, 15.

Indigena. A person living at his birth place. The term is used in imperial constitutions.—See ORIGO, DOMICILIUM.

Indignus. In the law of successions, a person who because of his (ungrateful) attitude towards the testator became unworthy to benefit by the latter's last will. He was deprived of the advantages granted therein. Generally it was the fisc which might claim the return (*eripere, auferre,* see EREPTORIUM) of the things already taken by the *indignus* under the testament. *Indignitas* (= the quality of being *indignus*) was primarily introduced by the imperial legislation. An *indignus* was one who killed the testator or did not take the necessary measures to revenge his assassination; one who impugned the last will as inofficious (see QUERELA INOFFICIOSI TESTAMENTI) or as forged and lost the trial; one who concealed the last will in order to avoid the payment of legacies, or who, appointed as a guardian, refused to accept the guardianship without any just reason, or the like.—D. 34.9; C. 6.35.—See INULTA MORS, NUBERE.

> E. Nardi, *I casi di indegnità*, 1937; idem, *SDHI* 6 (1940) 393; B. Biondi, *Successione testamentaria*, 1943, 155.

Indiscrete, indistincte. Without any distinction, without a specific indication which person or thing is meant, e.g., when a payment is made by a debtor liable for several debts without stating to which debt the payment refers.

Individuus. Indivisible. Things or rights which cannot be divided and things which cannot be separated into parts become the common property of the persons to whom they happen to be assigned. *Individuus* is sometimes syn. with *indivisus* (undivided). See the following item.

Indivisus. Undivided, not separated into parts. *Pro indiviso possidere* (*habere*) is used of owners who have a thing in common ownership (*communio pro indiviso*). In such instances the right of any one of them is expressed by a fraction and the thing itself remains undivided.—See COMMUNIO (Bibl.), PIGNUS.

Indotata mulier. A woman who entered a marriage without a dowry.—See DOTARE.

Inducere (inductio). To cross out, e.g., the institution of an heir or a legacy in a testament. See INTERLINERE, PERDUCERE.—*Inducere* with reference to a statute (e.g., *inducere legem Falcidiam*), a senatusconsult, or a legal remedy (an action, an exception) = to apply.—D. 28.4.

Inducta. See INTRODUCTA.

Indulgentia (indulgere). An act of grace (by the emperor = *indulgentia principis*), a benefit granted as a favor (*ex indulgentia*). The term occurs primarily in imperial constitutions concerned with acts of amnesty in criminal matters.

> Kleinfeller, *RE* 9; Cuq, *DS* 3; De Ruggiero, *DE* 4; P. Duparc, *Origine de la grâce dans le droit pénal rom.*, 1942, 25; Carrelli, *Restitutio i. principis*, AnBari 53, 2 (1934).

Indulgentissimus. A title given to emperors (after Hadrian).

> De Ruggiero, *DE* 4.

Indutiae. A truce, armistice.

> C. Phillipson, *The International Law and Custom of Ancient Greece and Rome*, 2 (1911) 287; E. Täubler, *Imperium Romanum* (1913) 29.

Inefficax. Deprived of legal effectiveness, ineffective. Ant. EFFICAX.

Inemptus. Not bought. Certain sales contained a clause to the effect that under specific circumstances the sale should be considered not valid and the object of the sale not bought (*res inempta*).—See LEX COMMISSORIA, PACTUM DISPLICENTIAE.

Inesse. To be contained in. It is used of clauses (conditions) inserted in an agreement by the will of the parties, or of essential elements of legal institutions or transactions, which are either fixed by law or self-evident. *Inesse officio iudicis* = to be part of the office of a judge.

Infamare. To defame, injure the good reputation of a person. The praetorian edict forbade the doing or saying anything (orally or by writing, see LIBELLI FAMOSI) *infamandi causa* (= for the purpose of defamation). The person injured could sue the offender by *actio iniuriarum*.—See INIURIA.

> Daube, *ACIVer* 3 (1952) 413.

Infamia. Evil reputation, the quality of being infamous (*infamis*). *Infamia* was not only connected with a diminution of the estimation of a person among his fellow citizens but produced also certain legal disabilities which differed according to the grounds for the infamy. In Justinian's law various groups of persons were added to those whose legal ability had been restricted already in earlier (primarily praetorian) law. The oldest measure to brand a person as dishonest was the *nota censoria* which was a moral punishment by the censors for misconduct in political or private life. See IGNOMINIA. The praetorian edict deprived certain persons for moral reasons of the right of appearance in court as advocates or representatives of a party to the trial, or of being represented by another. In particular, persons condemned for crimes or private wrongdoings (*delicta*) were struck by this measure. *Infamia* as it appears as a developed institution in Justinian's law originated either in the exercise of a dishonest profession (*personae turpes*) or in a condemnatory judgment in trials resulting from contractual relations which required a particularly honest behavior and in which the violation thereof appeared as a flagrant break of confidence (as, e.g., partnership, deposit, *mandatum, fiducia*). See ACTIONES FAMOSAE. Bankruptcy, a dishonest discharge from military service, misbehavior in family life, simultaneous betrothal with two persons, and many other wrongdoings made a person *infamis* (= *qui notatur infamia*, as Justinian says). Besides procedural disabilities *infamia* caused other disadvantages such as exclusion from tutorship and denial of the right to obtain a public office or to be an accuser in a criminal trial. Under specific circumstances, *infamia* was not without repercussion in the rights of succession.—D. 3.2; C. 2.11; 10.59.—See NOTA CENSORIA, IGNOMINIOSUS, INTESTABILIS, INUSTUS, TURPIS PERSONA, TURPITUDO.

> Pfaff, *RE* 9; Humbert and Lécrivain, *DS* 3; Sacchi, *NDI* 6; De Ruggiero, *DE* 4; Berger, *OCD*; A. H. J. Greenidge, *I. in R. law*, 1894; Schulz, *Fschr Zitelmann*, 1913, 11; E. Levy, *St Riccobono* 2 (1936) 77; L. Pommeray, *Études sur l'infamie*, 1937; U. Brasiello, *Repressione penale*, 1937, 152.

Infamis. (Adj.) See INFAMIA. Syn. *infamatus*.—C. 10.59.

Infans. *Qui fari non potest* (= one who cannot speak), a child who cannot express his ideas reasonably. "Children have no intellect" (Gaius 3.109). From the time of Justinian, or perhaps a little earlier, *infantia* (= childhood) comprehends children under seven completed years. An *infans* is completely incapable under the law. After the completion of seven years an *infans* becomes IMPUBES.—D. 37.3.

> Cuq, *DS* 3; Sciascia, *NDI* 6; Tumedei, *AG* 89 (1923); Solazzi, *BIDR* 49–50 (1947) 354.

Infantia. The age of an INFANS.—See IMPUBERES.

Infantiae (infanti) proximus. See IMPUBES.

Infanticidium. The term does not occur in juristic texts. A legal prohibition of infanticide is ascribed to the legendary founder of Rome, Romulus. The Twelve Tables permitted the killing of a new-born child that turned out a monster. Generally infanticide was punished as murder, both under the Republic (*Lex Cornelia de sicariis, Lex Pompeia de parricidiis*) and under imperial legislation, particularly that of Christian emperors. Syn. *necare infantem, partum*.—See EXPONERE FILIUM.

> Cuq, *DS* 3.

Infectum damnum. See DAMNUM INFECTUM.

Inferre. See ILLATA, INTRODUCTA, ILLATIO MORTUI.

Inferre. (With reference to account books.) To make an entry.—See RATIONES, CODEX ACCEPTI.

Inferre. (In procedural language.) To proceed with an action (*actionem, litem*) in a civil matter; to bring in an accusation (*accusationem, crimen*) against a person in a criminal matter.

Infirmare. To annul, to rescind, to revoke a unilateral act (a testament, legacy, donation). *Infirmare actionem* = to oppose an *exceptio* to the plaintiff's claim.

De Sarlo, *AG* 136 (1949) 102.

Infirmitas aetatis (or **sexus**). The weakness of an individual because of his age (or sex). It is given as a reason for guardianship or curatorship over a person under a certain age or over women.—See CURA IMPUBERIS, TUTELA MULIERUM.

Solazzi, *AG* 104 (1930).

Infitiae. *Ad infitias ire* = to deny the plaintiff's claim. Syn. *infitiari*.

Infitiari (infitiatio). To deny the plaintiff's claim. In certain actions (*actio legis Aquiliae, actio iudicati*, claim for a legacy left in the form of a LEGATUM PER DAMNATIONEM), a defendant who deliberately denied the claim although he knew that the claimant was right was judged liable to double the amount involved; see ACTIONES IN DUPLUM. Such an action is characterized as an *actio quae infitiando crescit in duplum* (*duplatur*).

Thomas, *NRHD* 27 (1903) 579; Betti, *ATor* 50 (1915); J. Paoli, *Lis infitiando crescit in duplum*, 1933; Kaser, *Das altröm. Ius*, 1949, 121.

Infligere. To impose (a penalty), to cause damage (*damnum*). Similar expressions are *imponere, iniungere*.

Ingenuitas. The status of a free-born person. See INGENUUS. In a trial as to whether a person was free-born, there had to participate an *adsertor ingenuitatis* whose role was analogous to that of the *adsertor libertatis* in a trial in which it was examined whether or not a person was free.—See ADSERTIO, VINDICATIO IN LIBERTATEM.

H. Krüger, *St Riccobono* 2 (1936) 227.

Ingenuus. Free-born. Ant. *servus* (= a slave) and *libertinus* (= a freedman, i.e., born as a slave and freed afterwards).—See INGENUITAS, NATALIUM RESTITUTIO.—Inst. 1.4; D. 40.14; C. 7.14.

Kübler, *RE* 9; Cuq, *DS* 3; Sciascia, *NDI* 6.

Ingenuus manumissus. A free-born person who erroneously served as a slave (*liber homo bona fide serviens*) and was manumitted by his "master" could initiate a trial for the recognition that he was born a free man. The restriction that he might do it only within five years after the manumission, was abolished by Justinian.—C. 7.14.—See INGENUITAS.

H. Krüger, *St Riccobono* 2 (1936) 234.

Ingratus. Ungrateful, ingrate. An emancipated son or daughter could in the later Empire be brought back under paternal power in case of ingratitude towards his father (e.g., a verbal offense, *convicium*). A freedman, ungrateful towards his former master (*libertus ingratus*), could be assigned to the latter as a slave. Non-fulfillment of his duties towards the patron, refusal of maintenance in the case of poverty, participation in a plot against the *manumissor*, treating him with contempt (*contumelia, convicium, castigatio fustibus*) and the like, were considered ingratitude of a freedman. *Accusatio liberti ingrati* = the complaint of a former master about an ungrateful freedman.—C. 8.49.—See OBSEQUIUM.

De Francisci, *Mél Cornil* 1 (1926) 304; C. Cosentini, *St sui liberti* 1 (1948) 96, 206; 2 (1950) 31.

Ingredi (ingressus). (With reference to an office.) To enter on official duties (a magistracy).

Ingredi in alienum fundum. To trespass upon another's land. The owner or possessor could oppose himself against such violation particularly when the trespasser committed it for hunting or catching birds. Possessory interdicts were available against the invader if he attempted to remain on the spot and keep it for good.—See INGREDI POSSESSIONEM.

Ingredi possessionem. To enter into another's immovable in order to take lawful possession thereof, e.g., after buying it or with the authorization by a magistrate (*missio in possessionem*). *Ingredi possessionem* may take place also unlawfully when the invader uses force (*vi*) or enters stealthily (*furtive*). The pertinent possessory interdicts (see INTERDICTUM QUOD VI AUT CLAM) serve for protection against such ingression.

Inhabilis militiae. Unfit for military service. A father who mutilated his son to make him *inhabilis* when a levy for war was ordered, was punished with deportation.

Inhabitare. See syn. HABITARE.

Inhibere. To check, to stop, e.g., another's act, a suit or transaction by a lawful countermove or with the help of a judicial authority. When used of a legal enactment *inhibere* = to forbid.

Inhibitio. See INHIBERE.

Inhonestus. Dishonest. Ant. *honestus*. The term is used of illicit or dishonest professions (prostitution, *lenocinium*) or of things forbidden by law or good customs.

Inhumanus, inhumanitas. See ant. HUMANUS, HUMANITAS.

Inicere condicionem. To add a condition to a transaction or to a testamentary disposition.

Inicere manum (iniectio manus). See MANUS INIECTIO, LEGIS ACTIO PER MANUS INIECTIONEM.

Iniquitas. See INIURIA IUDICIS.

Iniquus. Ant. of AEQUUS. *Iniquus* is frequently used of unjust judgment or arbitration.

Inire. (With regard to an office.) To enter on one's official duties. Syn. *ingredi*.

Inire consilium. (With reference to wrongdoings.) To take a decision, to form a design.—See CONSILIUM.

Initium. A beginning. *Initium* is used of the starting sentence of a written document (e.g., a testament, a contract, a letter) or of a statute. It refers also to the beginning of certain legal relations (partnership) or situations (*usucapio*) normally lasting for some time. *Ab initio* = from (at) the very beginning. A legal rule stated: "A legacy (an appointment of an heir) which is invalid (*nul*) at the beginning cannot become valid by a later event (*ex post facto*)," D. 30.41.2; 50.17.210.—See EX POST FACTO, TRACTUS TEMPORIS.

Iniungere. To impose upon a person a burden (guardianship) or a public charge (*munus*); to inflict a damage or a penalty.

Iniuria. A wrongful act, unlawfulness. Generally speaking, *iniuria* is "all that has been done *non iure*, i.e., against the law (*contra ius*)," Inst. 4.4 pr. On damages done *iniuria* (unlawfully) to another's property, *damnum iniuria datum*, see DAMNUM, LEX AQUILIA. Specifically *iniuria* embraces particular crimes, both bodily injuries (*iniuria re facta*) as well as offenses against the good reputation of a person, as defined in the Twelve Tables, in the praetorian edict, in the *Lex Cornelia de iniuriis*, and later in imperial constitutions. It was in particular the praetorian law which efficiently defended the honor of a Roman citizen against defamation by according a special action, *actio iniuriarum*. *Iniuria* was a private crime (*delictum*), prosecuted only at the request of the offended person. "There is no *iniuria* done to those who wished it (to be done)," D. 39.3.9.1. Penalties varied in the course of time from pecuniary reparation (fixed fines in the Twelve Tables)—the amount of which was set by the judge, who had great discretion in estimating the damage done to the reputation and the social rank and respectability of the individual injured—to more severe penalties, such as flogging, scourging, exile, according to the gravity of the injury and the social status of the culprit. In the *actio iniuriarum* the plaintiff made his own assessment of the extent of the damages in a sum of money and the judge sentenced the defendant to what seemed to him *bonum et aequum,* but not to a larger sum than demanded by the plaintiff. The *actio iniuriarum* was granted a father for *iniuria* done to a son under his paternal power, and the master of a slave for an injury done to the slave.—Inst. 4.4; D. 47.10; C. 9.35.—See CARMEN MALUM, LIBELLUS FAMOSUS, INFAMARE, OS FRACTUM, MEMBRUM RUPTUM, CONVICIUM, CONTUMELIA, OCCENTARE, PUDICITIA ADTEMPTATA, LEX CORNELIA DE INIURIIS, MANUS INFERRE, PERCUTERE, PUGNUS, THEATRUM.

Steinwenter, *RE* 9; Cuq, *DS* 3; De Villa, *NDI* 6; H. F. Hitzig, *Iniuria*, 1899; R. Maschke, *Persönlichkeitsrechte des röm. Iniuriensystems*, 1903; P. Huvelin, *Mél Appleton*, 1903; Thiel, *Iniuria und Beleidigung*, 1905; Audibert, *Mél Girard* 1 (1912) 35; Berger, *KrVj* 16 (1914) 77; L. Vos, *I. en de actio iniuriarum*, Amsterdam, 1913; P. F. Girard, *Mél de dr. rom.* 2 (1923) 385; Lenel, *ZSS* 47 (1927) 381·

De Visscher, *TR* 11 (1932) 39; Donatuti, *St Ratti*, 1934, 369; De Dominicis, *An Ferrara*, 1937; G. Pugliese, *St sull'iniuria*, 1941; Santi di Paola, *AnCat* 1 (1947) 268; Lavaggi, *SDHI* 13–14 (1948) 141; Kaser, *Das altröm. Ius*, 1949, 37, 207; Yvonne Bongert, in *Varia*, 1952, 131; Sanfilippo, *Il risarcimento del danno per l'uccisione di un uomo libero, AnCat* 5 (1951) 120; Dupont, *ADO-RIDA* 1 (1952) 423.

Iniuriā. (Abl.) Wrongfully, not lawfully. Syn. *non iure*.

Iniuria atrox. An atrocious, aggravated outrage. It occurred, e.g., when the victim was flogged or wounded, when the wrong was done in a public place (theatre, *forum*), when the offended person was a magistrate, or when a senator was insulted by a person of a lower social class. The atrocity (*atrocitas*) of the *iniuria* was thus distinguished according to the fact itself (*ex facto*), the place (*ex loco*), and the person (*ex persona*).—See PERCUTERE.

Iniuria cadaveri facta. See CADAVER.

Iniuria iudicis. An unjust judgment, condemnatory or absolutory, handed down by a judge or a magistrate in the exercise of his judicial functions, "when the praetor or a judge *non iure* (unlawfully) decides against a person" (Inst. 4.4 pr.). Other expressions used in such cases are *iniustitia, iniquitas* ("when one pronounced an unequitable or unjust judgment" = *inique vel iniuste sententiam dixerit*). *Iniuria* (*iniquitas sententiae*) can be corrected (*abolitio*) on appeal.

J. Dauvillier, *Iniuria iudicis dans la procédure formulaire, Rec. de l'Acad. de législation de Toulouse*, 13 (1937).

Iniussu. Without the order (IUSSUM) of the person whose order is required or presumed. *Iniussu populi* = without the order of the people. The term appears in connection with the prohibition against carrying out a death sentence without the approving order of the people.

Iniustitia. See INIURIA IUDICIS.

Iniustum—iustum sacramentum. It is generally assumed that the judgment in the LEGIS ACTIO SACRAMENTO stated whose (of the parties to the trial) *sacramentum* was just and whose unjust by which the decision on the claim itself was expressed implicitly. The distinction is based on Ciceronian texts (*pro Caec.* 33.97; *de domo* 28.78).

v. Mayr, *Mél Girard* 2 (1912) 177; Wenger, *ZSS* 59 (1939) 342 (Bibl.); v. Lübtow, *ZSS* 68 (1951) 322.

Iniustus. Unjust, unlawful.—See CONDICTIO EX INIUSTA CAUSA. For *iniusta sententia*, see INIURIA IUDICIS.—*Iniusta appellatio* (*iniuste appellare*) = an appeal not founded on legal grounds and rejected (*pronuntiata*) as unjust.—See TESTAMENTUM INIUSTUM.

Inl-. See ILL-.

Innocens. Innocent. A remarkable saying of the emperor Trajan in one of his rescripts states: "It is better to leave unpunished a crime of a guilty person than to condemn an innocent man" (D. 48.19.5 pr.).

The innocence of an accused person established after his condemnation could be ground for an appeal to the emperor and lead to the annulment of the condemnatory judgment. When the innocence of the accused has been established during the trial, he must be discharged even though he had admitted responsibility.—See IMPUNITUS, SUSPICIO.

Innocentius. A jurist of the time of Diocletian who allegedly had the *ius respondendi* "granted by the emperors." The notice goes back to a source of the late fourth century and is not fully reliable.

Seeck and Steinwenter, *RE* 9; Massei, *Scr Ferrini* (Univ. Pavia, 1946) 440.

Inofficiosus. One who disregards his natural duties to his next relatives or, in the case of a freedman, to his patron. A testament, a donation, or a dowry by which the rights of succession of the nearest relatives are violated is *inofficiosus.*—See QUERELA INOFFICIOSI TESTAMENTI, QUERELA INOFFICIOSAE DONATIONIS, DOTIS.—Inst. 2.18; D. 5.2; C. 3.28–30.

Inopia. Indigence, poverty, lack of necessary resources for living. It is ground for exemption from public charges and guardianship. A fine imposed on a person who is unable to pay it may be suspended or commuted into corporal punishment.

Inops (inopes). See LOCUPLETES.

Inp-. See IMP-.

Inquietare. To trouble, to vex a private individual or a magistrate with suits.

Inquilinus. A tenant living in a rented dwelling. Syn. *habitator.* In the later Empire *inquilinus = colonus.* There are two possibilities of living in another's house: either on a lease (*locatio conductio rei*) or on a personal servitude to use another's house, see HABITATIO.—See INTERDICTUM DE MIGRANDO.

Humbert, *DS* 3; Saumagne, *Byzantion,* 17 (1937).

Inquisitio. (From *inquirere.*) Investigation, inquiry in criminal trials, conducted in the form of *cognitio* proceedings. The *inquisitio* is made by subordinate official organs under the direction of a jurisdictional officer who is the prosecutor of the matter from the beginning to the end. *Inquisitio* is opposed to the ACCUSATIO in the earlier criminal procedure (see QUAESTIONES). In the *inquisitio* procedure an accuser was admissible, but his rights were rather limited in comparison with his position in the earlier procedure. *Inquisitio* in civil matters occurs primarily in the procedure concerning the appointment of tutors and curators. It was the inquiry by the magistrate to establish whether or not the individual to be appointed had the necessary personal and financial abilities (*idoneus*). In certain instances such *inquisitio* was obligatory, for instance, when the guardian was designated by a woman.

M. Lauria, *Accusatio—inquisitio, ANap* 56 (1934) 304.

Inquisitio localis. A local inspection in the case of a controversy between neighbors.

Inr-. See IRR-.

Insania (insanus). A general term for mental disease.—See FURIOSUS, DEMENS, MENTE CAPTUS.

Insciens, inscientia. Ant. of SCIENS, SCIENTIA.

Inscribere. To give a title (*inscriptio*) to a book; to write down (into a written document); to register in a list of persons or things (e.g., an inventory).

Inscribere operi publico. To engrave on a public building (or construction) the name of the emperor or the person at whose expense the building was erected.

Inscriptio (inscribere). In criminal trials, to enter in official records the accusation made against a person; see ACCUSATIO.—D. 48.2; C. 9.2.—See SUBSCRIPTIO, LIBELLUS INSCRIPTIONIS.

Pfaff, *RE* 9, 1561.

Inserere. To insert (a clause, a condition, a provision). The term is used with reference to statutes, last wills, agreements, etc.

Insidiae. An ambush, cheating, fraud.

Insidiari. To lie in wait to attack another by surprise; to bring into danger.

Guarino, *SDHI* 5 (1939) 457.

Insignia. Distinctive outward signs of high officials when they appeared in public. It was an old Roman custom to grant high officials the right to use certain insignia which varied according to the rank of the office. The Republic preserved most of the regal *insignia* for its high magistrates. The *insignia* were also differentiated according to the occasion; the most spectacular were on the occasion of a triumph (see TRIUMPHUS) when a victorious commander of the army entered the city of Rome after the end of a war. The use of improper *insignia* for the purpose of assuming the character of a higher official was severely punished as *crimen falsi* (see FALSUM).—See LICTORES, SELLA CURULIS, FASCES, GLADIUS, TOGA PRAETEXTA.

De Ruggiero, *DE* 4; Alföldi, *Insignien und Tracht der röm. Kaiser, Mitt. Deutsch. Archaeol. Instituts, Röm. Abt.* 50 (1935).

Insimulare (insimulatio). To accuse (in imperial constitutions of the third and later centuries).

Insinuare. To inform, to give notice.

Insinuare (insinuatio) actis. See ACTA.

M. Kroell, *Le rôle de l'écrit dans la preuve de contrat,* 1906, 129.

Insinuatio testamenti. (In Justinian's constitutions.) Syn. with APERTURA TESTAMENTI.

Inspector. An inspector, examiner (in private enterprises).

Schulz, *Haftung für das Verschulden der Angestellten, GrZ* 38 (1911) 10.

Inspector. In administrative law, an official in the later Empire charged with investigations in census matters.—C. 11.58.

Seeck, *RE* 5, 1184; 9, 1562.

Inspectio tabularum (inspicere tabulas, sc. testamenti). To inspect a testament. Any person who has an interest in knowing the content of a testament could obtain permission from the praetor to look into it and to examine the seals.—D. 29.3.—See INTERDIC-TUM DE TABULIS EXHIBENDIS, APERTURA TESTAMENTI.

Inspicere ventrem. To examine a woman as to whether she is pregnant or not. The measure was applied when there was a controversy between a man and his divorced wife about her pregnancy, in particular when the woman claimed to be pregnant, or denied it, contrary to the assertions of the husband. A similar situation occurred, when after the death of her husband, a widow declared that she was pregnant and there was a reasonable suspicion that the pregnancy was simulated. A similar institution is *custodire partum* = to watch the confinement in order to prevent the substitution of another child. The procedures, which were performed with the assistance of midwives, were precisely defined in the praetorian Edict.—D. 25.4.

Instantia. Perseverance, in particular of a claimant or defendant acting in court in claiming or defending his rights.

Instar. A resemblance, likeness. The term indicates that a legal act is to be dealt with like a certain definite legal institution (e.g., a donation, a sale, a legacy) with which it has some common features (*instar esse, instar habere*).—*Ad instar* is used by classical jurists to extend existing legal rules to new factual situations.—Syn. *ad exemplum*.

Instaurare. (With reference to trials.) To resume a civil or criminal prosecution, to re-open a controversy. The term appears frequently in imperial constitutions. As a matter of principle, controversies settled by a judgment cannot be resumed.—See BIS DE EADEM RE, RES IUDICATA.

Institor. The manager of a commercial or industrial business, appointed by its owner. For obligations contracted by an *institor* and connected with the business, the principal could be sued directly by an action called *actio institoria*. Later, but still in classical times the requirement that the business have a commercial character was dropped so that any one could be sued for obligations contracted by the manager of his affairs (*procurator*) under an action named *actio quasi institoria* (term not classical), modeled on *actio institoria*. These actions belong to the category of *actiones adiecticiae qualitatis* (see EXERCITOR NAVIS) because the manager was also liable. *Institor* could be a slave of the principal or of another person.—D. 14.3; C. 4.25.—See PRO-SCRIBERE.

Klingmüller, *RE* 9; Steinwenter, *RE* 9 (*s.v. institoria a.*); Humbert-Lécrivain, *DS* 3; E. Costa, *Actio exercitoria e institoria*, 1891; L. F. Dentraygues, *Ét. hist. sur l'actio institoria*, 1910; Rabel, *Ein Ruhmesblatt Papinians, die a. quasi institoria, Fschr Zitelmann*, 1913; P. Fabricius, *Der gewaltfreie institor im klass. röm. R.*, 1926; P. Huvelin, *Études d'hist. du droit commercial*, 1929, 160; Albertario, *Studi* 4 (1940, ex 1912) 189; E. Carrelli, *St Scorza*, 1940; Solazzi, *RDNav* 7 (1941) 185; Kreller, *Fschr Wenger*, 2 (1945) 73.

Instituere actionem (litem, querelam, accusatio-nem). To prosecute in court in a civil or criminal matter.

Instituere heredem (institutio heredis). See HERE-DIS INSTITUTIO.

Institutiones. Elementary law textbooks written primarily for students. *Institutiones* were written by Gaius (see INSTITUTIONES GAI), Florentinus, Callistratus, Paul, Ulpian and Marcian. Some of these works may have originated in the lectures of their authors. One part of Justinian's codification is also entitled *Institutiones;* see INSTITUTIONES IUSTINIANI.

Kotz-Dobrz, *RE* 9; Kübler, *RE* 1A, 396; De Villa, *NDI* 6; Kreller, *ZSS* 66 (1948) 572.

Institutiones Gai. An introductory textbook of legal institutions in four books (called *"commentarii"* by the author) written by Gaius about A.D. 161. The system adopted by Gaius is tripartite: law of persons, law of things (including succession), and law of actions (civil procedure). The work, discovered in 1816 in Verona (hence called *Gaius Veronensis*) in a manuscript of the (late) fifth century, is preserved nearly in full. Some of the lacunae have been filled by a few parchment sheets, found in 1933, seemingly of the late fourth century (now in Florence, hence named *Gaius Florentinus*). The new texts confirmed the reliability of the *Veronensis* to a large extent. Modern Romanistic literature has applied to the Institutes of Gaius the same critical (and hypercritical) method they used with regard to Justinian's Digest, a method which is often far from convincing, although it cannot be denied that the text preserved evokes sometimes serious doubts, hardly amazing in a manuscript written about three centuries later than the original. For many problems of the classical law, and primarily for the classical civil procedure, Gaius' Institutes remain the foremost authority the importance of which has not been lessened by the recent "purification" of the text.—See GAIUS.

Editions: in all collections of ante-Justinian sources (see General Bibl., Ch. XII), the best is by Seckel-Kübler in Huschke's *Iurisprudentia anteiustiniana*, 7th ed. 1935; Bizoukides, *Gaius*, 3 vol., Salonika, 1937–1939; Arangio-Ruiz and Guarino, *Breviarium iuris romani*, 1943; Alvaro d'Ors Perez-Peix, *Gaius Institutiones, Testo latino con una traduccion*, Madrid, 1943; F. de Zulueta, *The Institutes of Gaius*, 1 (transl.) 1946; 2, 1953; M. David, *Gai I.*, Leiden, 1948; J. Reinach, *Gaius Institutes* (with French translation, Collection Budé, 1950). Italian translation: P. Novelli, *Gaio, Elementi di dir. rom.*, 1914.—Kübler, *RE* 6, 494; Berger, *OCD* 376; Kniep, *Gai Institutionum commentarii*, 4 vol. incomplete (1911–1914); Beseler, *TR* 10 (1930) 161; Solazzi, *Glosse a Gaio*, 1 (*St Riccobono* 1, 1936); 2 (*CentCodPavia*, 1933); 3 (*SDIII* 6, 1940); 4 (*Scr Ferrini*, Univ. Pavia, 1947, 141); Albertario, *St* 5 (1937) 441; Schulz, *History of R. Legal Science*, 1946, 159; Bellinger, *AmJPhilol* 70 (1949) 394; Wieacker, *RIDA* 3 (1949) 577; idem, *Fschr Schulz* 2 (1951) 101; Maschi, *AnTr* 17 (1947) 77; idem, *ACIVer* 1 (1951) 9; H. J. Wolff, *St Arangio-Ruiz* 4 (1952) 171.—For Bibl. on the *Gaius Florentinus* (= *Papiri Società Italiana* 11, no. 1182, 1933) see Baviera, *FIR* 1² (1940) 195; Van Oven, *TR* 13 (1934) 248.—For the few fragments of the fourth book, preserved on a papyrus from Oxyrhynchos (*P. Oxy.* xvii no. 2103), see Baviera, *ibid.* p. 201; Wenger, *Scr Ferrini* 4 (Univ. Sacro Cuore, Milan, 1949) 268.

Institutiones Iustiniani. A part of Justinian's codification, compiled in 533 after the final draft of the Digest had been finished, and published on November 21, 533. It entered into force simultaneously with the Digest, published a few weeks later. The sources exploited for the composition of the Institutes are Gaius' *Institutiones* and his *Res cottidianae,* the Institutes of Florentinus, Marcianus, Ulpian, and Paul, and several imperial constitutions in some of which the reforms introduced by Justinian are emphatically stressed. The work was intended as an elementary manual—hence its title *Institutiones sive Elementa*—for law students in their first year. It was edited by the law professors, Theophilus and Dorotheus, under the supervision of Tribonian.

Editions: In P. Krüger-Mommsen, *Corpus Iuris Civilis* 1 (15th ster. ed., 1928); Girard, *Textes de droit romain,* 6th ed. by Senn, 1937; J. B. Moyle, *Imperatoris Iustiniani Institutiones,* 5th ed. 1913; V. Arangio-Ruiz and A. Guarino, *Breviarium iuris romani,* 1943. Vocabulary: G. Ambrosino, *Vocabularium Institutionum Iustiniani,* 1942.—Sacchi, *NDI* 6; Kotz-Dobrz, *RE* 9, 1566, 1583; Ch. Appleton, *Revue générale de droit* 15 (1891) 12, 97; A. Zocco-Rosa, *Iustiniani Institutionum Palingenesia, Annuario dell'Ist. di storia del dir. rom.* Catania, 9, 1–2, 10 (1901–1911); Ebrard, *ZSS* 38 (1917) 327; C. Ferrini, *Sulle fonti delle Ist., Opere* 1 (1929, ex 1901) 307; De Villa, *StSas* 17 (1939) 354; R. W. Lee, *Elements of R. law,* rev. ed. 1946.

Instructum domus (fundi). The necessary furnishings, equipment of a house (or a landed property); almost syn. with INSTRUMENTUM DOMUS (FUNDI), although some jurists assumed that *instructum* is the broader term. Both *instructum* and *instrumentum* are discussed casuistically by the jurists in connection with legacies of a land or house *cum instrumento* or a *fundus instructus (domus instructa).*—See LEGATUM INSTRUMENTI.—D. 33.7.

Instruere. To instruct, to teach; to impart knowledge (information) of a legal norm or legally important facts.

Instruere causam (litem). To support a judicial—civil or criminal—case with legal arguments and factual evidence.

Instruere domum (fundum). To provide a house (a land) with the necessary equipment (furnishings, utensils, implements).—See INSTRUCTUM, INSTRUMENTUM FUNDI.

Instrumentum. In a broader sense, this embraces all means of evidence (including the oral testimony of witnesses), but the regular meaning is that of a document; another word is often added to indicate the subject matter of the document, as *instrumentum donationis* (of a donation), *emptionis* (sale), *divisionis* (division of property), *instrumentum nuptiale* (concerning a marriage) or *dotale* (dowry). In later law documents acquired constantly increasing value as evidence, particularly when written with the assistance of a public or private notary (*instrumentum publice confectum*) or when signed by three trustworthy witnesses (*instrumentum quasi publice confectum*).—See EDITIO INSTRUMENTORUM, FIDES INSTRUMENTORUM.—D. 22.4; C. 4.21; Nov. 73.—PRODERE INSTRUMENTA, TRADITIO CHARTAE, RETRACTARE CAUSAM, SUBSCRIPTIO, STIPULATIO.

Steinwenter, *RE* 9; De Sarlo, *NDI* 6; Arangio-Ruiz, *DE* 4, 61; Riccobono, *ZSS* 35 (1914), 43 (1922); H. Lévy-Bruhl, *Témoignage instrumentaire,* 1910; A Steinwenter, *Beiträge zum öffentlichen Urkundenwesen der Römer,* 1915; Siegel, *Archiv für civilistische Praxis,* 113 (1915); L. De Sarlo, *Il documento oggetto di rapporti giuridici,* 1935; idem, *RendLomb* 1937–1938; idem, *Riv. di dir. proc. civ.* 14 (1937); J. P. Lévy, *Annales Fac. Droit, Aix-en-Provence* 43 (1950).

Instrumentum causae (litis). A document connnected with a judicial controversy.—See INSTRUERE CAUSAM.

Instrumentum domus. See INSTRUMENTUM FUNDI.

Instrumentum donationis. See INSTRUMENTUM.
Riccobono, *ZSS* 34 (1913) 159.

Instrumentum dotale. A written instrument concerning a dowry. It contained details of the dotal agreement (*pactum dotale*) concerning the objects constituting the dowry and its restitution at the end of the marriage by death or divorce. The *instrumentum dotale* came into use in the postclassical period.—See DOS, TABULAE NUPTIALES.
Kübler, *RE* 4 A, 1951; Riccobono, *ZSS* 34 (1913) 175; Castello, *SDHI* 4 (1938) 208.

Instrumentum fundi (domus). The equipment necessary for a reasonable management of rural (*instrumentum fundi*) or industrial property, or for the use of a house (*instrumentum domus*): furniture, tools, utensils, and all kinds of appurtenances needed for some specific use of the immovable. The interpretation of the term and its extension in the case of a lease or a legacy of a house or rural property *cum instrumento* is widely discussed in juristic works. It is pointed out that *instrumentum fundi* is not a part of the land; it may be therefore the object of special agreements.—D. 33.7.—See INSTRUCTUM, INSTRUERE DOMUM, FUNDUS, FUNDUS UTI OPTIMUS MAXIMUS, LEGATUM INSTRUMENTI, VENATIO.
Arangio-Ruiz, *DE* 4, 59; Riccobono, *St Brugi,* 1910, 173; Steinwenter, *Fundus cum instrumento, SbWien,* 221, 1 (1943) 24, 71.

Instrumentum nuptiale. See TABULAE NUPTIALES.

Instrumentum publice confectum. See INSTRUMENTUM.

Insula. A tenement house of a few stories, occupied by several families, chiefly of the indigent classes.
De Ruggiero, *DE* 4, 62; Lugli, *Rend. Pontif. Accad. di Archeologia,* 18 (1941–2) 191.

Insula in flumine nata. An island which came into being in a river. If located in the middle of the river, it belonged as a common property to the land-owners on both banks; if it arose nearer one bank it became property of the land-owners along that bank. Such an island in a public stream (*flumen publicum*) became public property.

Cogliolo, *St per l'ottavo centenario dell'Univ. di Bologna*, 1888; Pampaloni, *Scr giuridici* 1 (1941, ex 1885) 505; Herzen, *NRHD* 29 (1905) 561.

Insula in mari nata. An island which arose in the sea was *res nullius* (it belonged to nobody) and as such it became the property of the first occupant.

Insularius. A tenant in a rented dwelling in an INSULA. *Insularius* is also the guard or administrator of a tenement house.

Integer. Unchanged, untouched, whole. *Res integra* = an unchanged legal or factual situation. *Integer*, when used of the reputation of a person = blameless, irreproachable, upright.—See HOMO INTEGRAE FRONTIS, MORS, LOCARE EX INTEGRO, RETRACTATIO CAUSAE.

Integritas. Uprightness, integrity.—See INTEGER.

Intellectus. The power of understanding, of judging (*intellegere*). Insane persons have no *intellectus* (*intellectu carent*) and are therefore not able to conclude a legal transaction. With regard to dumb or deaf persons, the decisive element is whether they have *intellectus* or not.—See FURIOSUS, MUTUS, SURDUS.

Intellegere. To understand. With regard to persons having only physical (not mental) defects (deafness, blindness, muteness) and those acting with the assistance of their guardians, the requirement that they understand what is being done is imperative.—See INTELLECTUS.

Intellegi. Used primarily in impersonal form (*intellegitur* = it is considered) or in locutions such as *intellegendum est* (= it is to be considered), refers to instances in which a legal or customary rule prescribed a definite estimation of certain doings or in which a jurist recommends a certain interpretation of specific words or facts.

Intendere. Used of the plaintiff's claim in trial. *Intendere* is also a general term to indicate the activity of a person seeking justice in court, either in a civil (*intendere actionem, litem,* syn. *agere*) or in a criminal matter (*intendere accusationem,* syn. *accusare*).—See INTENTIO.

Intentare. Appears frequently in imperial constitutions with reference to criminal matters as syn. with INTENDERE (= to accuse).

Intentio. An intention, design. In criminal trials *intentio* = the accusation by an accuser (*accusator*) or an incrimination by an informer.

Intentio. In formulary procedure, "that part of the formula in which the plaintiff comprehends his claim" (Gaius 4.41). "If it appears that *X* (name of the defendant) ought to pay to *Y* (name of the plaintiff) the sum of . . ." is the wording of an *intentio certa* since the amount of the payment due is indicated precisely therein. An *intentio incerta* says instead: "Whatever (*quidquid*) it appears that the defendant ought to pay to the plaintiff." In an *actio in rem*

(for the recovery of a thing) the *intentio* says: "If it appears that . . . (designation of the thing, e.g., the slave *X*) belongs to . . . (the plaintiff) under Quiritary law." The *intentio* is expressed in the form of a condition "if it appears (*si paret*)," upon which the condemnatory judgment depends, because, if the condition does not materialize (*si non paret* = if it does not appear), the judge must absolve the defendant. In certain exceptional cases, the whole formula consists only of an *intentio,* as in *formulae praeiudiciales* in which no specific claim is expressed but only a question is posed (for instance, whether one is a freedman or what was the amount of the dowry), which is preliminary to a subsequent legal measure.—In postclassical procedure, *intentio* is any assertion of the plaintiff which must be proved by him.—See PRAEIUDICIA, SI PARET.

Audibert, *Formules sans i., Mél Girard* 1 (1912) 35; Berger, *KrVj* 16 (1914) 77; Juncker, *St Riccobono* 2 (1936) 325; Philonenko, *RIDA* 3 (1949) 231.

Inter absentes (praesentes). See ABSENTES.

Inter vivos. Refers to legal acts which have to produce legal effects while the interested parties are still alive. Ant. *mortis causa.*—See DONATIO MORTIS CAUSA.

Intercalare. See LEX ACILIA DE INTERCALANDO, MENSIS INTERCALARIS.

Intercedere. See INTERCESSIO.

Intercessio. (From *intercedere.*) To assume on oneself another's debt or a liability for another. For the interdiction of intercession of women, see SENATUSCONSULTUM VELLEIANUM. According to its terms, an *intercessio* embraced all kinds of assumption of an obligation for another, either primary or accessory one (suretyship, pledge, novation), in other words any obligation assumed by an agreement with another's creditor and concerning a third person's liability.—See SENATUSCONSULTUM VELLEIANUM (Bibl.).

Intercessio. In public law, a veto by a higher magistrate against an official act (decision) of his colleague (e.g., by one consul against an act of the other) or of a magistrate of a lower rank (e.g., by a consul against the act of a praetor). The performance of the act (the execution of the decision) was thus inhibited. Of greatest importance was the veto power of the plebeian tribunes over the official acts not only of other tribunes but of any magistrate. By vetoing the proposal of a bill made by any magistrate before a popular assembly or in the senate they could paralyze legislative activity, as well as any motion presented before the assemblies. The introduction of the tribunician *intercessio* was aimed at the protection of the interests of the *plebs* against abuses by magistrates, but in practice the institution turned out to be an important political weapon used by the tribunes for personal purposes. No *intercessio* was permitted against an act of a dictator.—See TRIBUNI PLEBIS, AUCTORITAS SENATUS.

Leonhard, *RE* 9, 1607; Siber, *RE* 21, 182; Cuq, *DS* 3; Lengle, *RE* 6 A, 2472; Anon., *NDI* 12, 2 (*s.v. tribunato*); Lécrivain, *DS* 5, 421; O'Brien, *RE* Suppl. 6, 684; 717; F. Leifer, *Die Einheit des Gewaltgedankens*, 1914, 182; 209.

Intercessio militaris. In imperial constitutions of the later Empire, the intervention of a public official to enforce the payment of taxes or other sums due to the state. Syn. *exsecutio.*

Cuq, *DS* 3, 556.

Intercessor. One who assumes an obligation on behalf of another.—See INTERCEDERE, INTERCESSIO.

Intercessores. See EXSECUTORES.

Intercidere. To perish, to be extinguished, to lose validity. The term is used of actions, obligations, legacies, and the like, which became void for one reason or another.

Interdicere (interdictio). Indicates any kind of prohibition, ban, or exclusion decreed by the competent magisterial or imperial authority.

Interdicere. In interdictal procedure (see INTERDICTUM) this is the procedural activity of a claimant who requests the issuance of an interdict. It is analogous to POSTULARE ACTIONEM in an ordinary process. Syn. *agere interdicto.* When applied to a magistrate, *interdicere* means his issuing an interdict.

Interdicere aqua et igni (interdictio aquae et ignis). The exclusion of a culprit from the common life with his fellow countrymen (= interdiction of fire and water). *Interdicere* was pronounced by the senate or a high magistrate when the accused left the community before the condemnatory sentence was passed and went into voluntary exile. Practically *interdicere* meant banishment connected with loss of citizenship and property. In case of return without permission the *interdictus* was deprived of legal protection and outlawed. He might be killed by anybody who met him within the boundaries of the country from which he was banished. *Interdicere* disappeared under the early Principate when the criminal procedure was reorganized.—D. 48.22.—See DEPORTATIO, EXILIUM, PATRIA.

Hartmann *RE* 2; U. Brasiello, *Repressione penale*, 1937, *passim*; Gioffredi, *SDHI* 12 (1946) 101; *idem, Archivio penale* 3 (1947) 426; DeVilla, *StSas* 23 (1950) 1.

Interdicere bonis (interdictio bonorum). The exclusion of a person from the administration of his property. According to the Twelve Tables it was applied to spendthrifts who were committed to the care of curators.—See PRODIGUS.

Kaser, *St Arangio-Ruiz* 2 (1952) 152.

Interdicere commercio. See COMMERCIUM.

Interdicere honore (honoribus). To deprive a person condemned in a criminal trial of the capacity to obtain an official or honorific position, or of the right to exercise a certain profession (e.g., advocacy) forever (*in perpetuum*) or temporarily.

Interdictio. See INTERDICERE.

Interdictio aquae et ignis. See INTERDICERE AQUA ET IGNI.

Interdictio bonorum. See INTERDICERE BONIS.

Interdictio locorum. An order issued by the competent authority, originally a popular assembly, excluding a person from a certain territory (Italy or a province) or from the whole state with the exception of a certain place (*lata fuga*).—See EXILIUM.

Interdictum. An order issued by a praetor or other authorized official (proconsul in the provinces) at the request of a claimant and addressed to another person upon whom a certain attitude is imposed: either to do something or to abstain from doing something. The interdictal procedure is more administrative than judicial in nature and differs from a normal trial in that there is no division of the proceedings into two stages inasmuch as the issuance of an *interdictum* depends upon the magistrate as an act of his *imperium*, not of jurisdiction. The *interdictum* is a provisory remedy with the purpose of protecting existing situations by a quick decision of the official. It fulfills its task—a speedy ending of a controversy—only when the adversary complies with the order. If he does not, the subsequent procedure which assumes the form of a normal trial, though not without certain particularities resulting from the fact that an interdict had been issued, is rather complicated and perhaps even slower than an ordinary process. The interdictal procedure is very summary; no long hearings of witnesses, no examination of evidence. What the plaintiff, i.e., the person who asks for the *interdictum* (*postulare interdictum*) affirms is taken for granted, if the authority considers that his claim deserves protection either in his interest or in public interest. If the assertions of the claimant are not true, the defendant will disregard the order and defend his right in the subsequent ordinary trial. Various interests are defended by interdictal protection. They are of both private and public character. In Justinian's law the differences between actions and interdicts are effaced. What was formerly proposed in the praetorian Edict as a form of interdict—an order or a prohibition—is in Justinian's law a legal rule. Acting against that rule may give rise to a judicial trial, just as in classical times a trial followed the transgression of an *interdictum* in a specific case, although the later procedure is quite different. Many interdicts lost their applicability entirely, however, and references to them were deleted or made unrecognizable by Justinian's compilers. The reconstruction of the formula of interdicts is therefore sometimes problematic. The law of interdicts is presented in the following items. The various types or groups of interdicts are specified below under INTERDICTA, particular interdicts under INTERDICTUM. Some interdicts took their name from the initial words of the pertinent form.—

Inst. 4.15; D. 43.1; C. 8.1.—See AGERE PER SPONSIONEM, PROPONERE ACTIONEM.

> Berger, *RE* 9 (Bibl. until 1915); Humbert—Lécrivain, *DS* 3; Riccobono, *NDI* 7; Arangio-Ruiz, *DE* 4; Berger, *ZSS* 36 1915, 176; *idem, Vol. delle onoranze Simoncelli,* 1915, 171; Gintowt, *St Albertoni* 2 (1937); Fabi, *AnCam* 15 (1941) 99; A. Biscardi, *La protezione interdittale nel processo rom.,* 1938; Albertario, *St* 4 (1946) 115; L. Beretta, *RISG* 2 (1948) 391; Daube, *RIDA* 6 (1951) 22.—For interdicts not mentioned below, see Berger, *RE cit.*; Lenel, *Edictum perpetuum,* 3rd ed. 1927, 446 ff.

Interdicta adipiscendae possessionis. These belong to the group of possessory interdicts serving for the protection of possession (POSSESSIO). The purpose of the possessory *interdicta* is either the acquisition of possession by a person who had not had it at all before, *interdicta adipiscendae possessionis* (such as, for instance, INTERDICTUM QUORUM BONORUM, INTERDICTUM QUOD LEGATORUM, INTERDICTUM SALVIANUM), retention of possession by the actual possessor, *interdicta retinendae possessionis* (INTERDICTUM UTI POSSIDETIS, INTERDICTUM UTRUBI) or resumption of possession (*interdicta reciperandae possessionis*) by the claimant who had been violently ejected from his land or house (INTERDICTUM UNDE VI).

> Berger, *RE* 9, 1615; Siber, *Scr Ferrini* 4 (Univ. Sacro Cuore, Milan, 1949) 98; Levy, *ibid.* 3 (1948) 109; *idem, West Roman vulgar law,* 1951, 243.

Interdicta annalia (annua, temporaria). Those *interdicta* which can be requested only within one year after the allegedly wrongful act was done against which the plaintiff remonstrates. Ant. *interdicta perpetua* which are not limited as to time.—See EXCEPTIO ANNALIS.

> Berger, *RE* 9, 1620; 1689; 1690.

Interdicta de cloacis. Several interdicts are granted for the maintenance of public and private sewers in good condition in the interest of public health. Any attempt to damage them or to prevent their repair could be frustrated by an appropriate *interdictum*.

> Berger, *RE* 9, 1633; Solazzi, *Tutela delle servitù prediali,* 1949, 79.

Interdicta de divinis rebus. Ant. *interdicta de humanis rebus.* This distinction of *interdicta* is based on that of RES DIVINI IURIS and RES HUMANI IURIS. Among the *interdicta de humanis rebus* there are some which serve for the protection of things which belong to nobody (RES NULLIUS) as the INTERDICTUM DE HOMINE LIBERO EXHIBENDO, of things which are in the private ownership of individuals (*res singulorum*) or of things used by the people (INTERDICTA DE FLUMINIBUS PUBLICIS, DE VIIS, DE LOCIS PUBLICIS). Some of them refer to single things, others to a *universitas rerum* (INTERDICTA DE UNIVERSITATE).

> Berger, *RE* 9, 1627.

Interdicta de fluminibus publicis. They are accorded for the protection of navigation on public rivers (FLUMINA PUBLICA). Any construction on the bank (see RIPA) or in the river proper which impedes the traffic of boats, the use of the harbors, the access to the river, etc., can be prevented by one of these interdicts which on the other hand were extended as *interdicta utilia* on similar wrongdoings on the seashore or harbor. When the construction has already been executed, the interdict orders its destruction and restoration of the former state.—D. 43.12; 13; 14; 15.

> Berger, *RE* 9, 1634; Branca, *AnTr* 12 (1941) 40, 177.

Interdicta de fonte. These serve for the protection of the SERVITUS AQUAE HAUSTUS.—D. 43.22.

> Berger, *RE* 9, 1637; Lenel, *Edictum perpetuum*[3] (1927) 480; Solazzi, *Tutela delle servitù prediali,* 1949, 77.

Interdicta de humanis rebus. See INTERDICTA DE DIVINIS REBUS.

Interdicta de itineribus publicis. These protect the use of public roads against any act which may hinder traffic. A specific *interdictum* is granted to anybody who is impeded in repairing a damaged public road.—D. 43.7; 11.

> Berger, *RE* 9, 1641; Lenel, *Edictum perpetuum*[3] (1927) 458.

Interdicta de locis publicis. These serve for the protection of public places against damage or harmful constructions which may impede their public use. Obstacles already constructed are interdictally ordered to be removed.—D. 43.8; 9.

> Berger, *RE* 9, 1643; 1654; Lenel, *Edictum perpetuum*[3] (1927) 459; Branca, *AnTr* 12 (1941) 169.

Interdicta de reficiendo. There are several interdicts which refer to particular situations between neighbors in connection with predial servitudes (SERVITUTES PRAEDIORUM). Using the neighbor's land for the exercise of a servitude (ITER, ACTUS, VIA) sometimes requires the possibility of entering it in order to repair the way if the owner is not bound to do so. To secure this right to a person entitled thereto an *interdictum* is proposed "for repairing" (*de reficiendo*), such as *interdictum de fonte reficiendo, de itinere actuque privato reficiendo, de sepulcro reficiendo, de cloaca privata reficienda, de rivis, de ripa munienda.* For similar *interdicta* with regard to public roads, see INTERDICTA DE ITINERIBUS PUBLICIS. All these *interdicta* are prohibitory since the order of the praetor, *vim fieri veto,* is addressed to anyone who prevents the claimant from doing the necessary work.—See RIPA, INTERDICTA PROHIBITORIA.

> Berger, *RE* 9, 1633 no. 4a; 1637 no. 6b; 1640; 1647 no. 24.

Interdicta de universitate. *Interdicta* the object of which is a complex of things, as, for instance, an inheritance (INTERDICTUM QUAM HEREDITATEM, INTERDICTUM QUORUM BONORUM).

> Berger, *RE* 9, 1627.

Interdicta duplicia. See INTERDICTA SIMPLICIA.

Interdicta exhibitoria. See INTERDICTA RESTITUTORIA.

Interdicta in praesens vel praeteritum relata. The distinction is based on the circumstance whether the actual situation at the moment when the *interdictum* is demanded or the situation which existed during a certain period before the *postulatio* of the *interdictum,* is decisive for the issuance of the interdict. The latter is the case in the INTERDICTUM UTRUBI.

Berger, *RE* 9, 1617.

Interdicta mixta. *Interdicta* of a mixed character being both *prohibitoria* and *exhibitoria.*

Berger, *Vol. onoranze Simoncelli,* 1915, 171; *idem, ZSS* 36 (1915) 198.

Interdicta ne vis fiat ei qui in possessionem missus est. Three interdicts are proposed to protect a person who by a praetorian MISSIO IN POSSESSIONEM is granted the right to take possession of another's property. They are prohibitory since the order forbids the use of force to prevent the claimant's entry. —D. 43.4.

Berger, *RE* 9, 1656.

Interdicta noxalia. See NOXA.

Interdicta perpetua. See INTERDICTA ANNALIA.

Interdicta popularia. See INTERDICTA PRIVATA.

Interdicta privata. Ant. *interdicta popularia.* The distinction is based on the same principle as that of actions in *actiones privatae* and *actiones populares.* *Interdicta popularia* are those *interdicta* which may be requested by "anyone from the people." Although most of the popular *interdicta* are introduced in the interest of public utility (*utilitas publica*), this element is not decisive for the distinction in question. In the interdictal form, the private character of the *interdicta* is recognizable by the reference to the claimant through the pronouns *ille* or *is,* lacking in the *interdicta popularia.*—See ACTIONES POPULARES.

Berger, *RE* 9, 1621.

Interdicta prohibitoria. Those *interdicta* in which the magistrate's order contains a prohibition (*aliquid fieri prohibet*). They impose upon the defendant the duty not to do the thing exactly indicated in the interdictal formula through *"ne . . . facias," "ne . . . immittas,"* or not to hinder the plaintiff in the exercise of his right. The prohibition is expressed by the words *vim fieri veto* (= I forbid the use of force), where *vis* is used in a broader sense and not precisely as force or violence. The *interdicta prohibitoria* constitute together with the *interdicta restitutoria* and *exhibitoria* the principal division of the *interdicta.*

Berger, *RE* 9, 1613.

Interdicta quae causam proprietatis habent. Ant. *interdicta quae possessionis causam habent.* The distinction appears only in one confused text and has given occasion to controversial interpretation. It may be of postclassical or Justinian origin and is based on the distinction whether the interdict takes into consideration the ownership of a thing or only possession.

Berger, *RE* 9, 1618; *idem, ZSS* 36 (1915) 183.

Interdicta reciperandae (recuperandae) possessionis. See INTERDICTA ADIPISCENDAE POSSESSIONIS.

Interdicta restitutoria. Order the restoration (*restituas*) of things to their former condition or of pos-

session to the plaintiff who has been deprived of it. They are distinguished from *interdicta exhibitoria,* which order the defendant to produce (*"exhibeas"*) a person (a free man, a slave, a child; see INTERDICTUM DE HOMINE LIBERO EXHIBENDO, INTERDICTUM DE LIBERIS EXHIBENDIS) or a thing (a testament, see INTERDICTUM DE TABULIS EXHIBENDIS) held by him, but do not impose the duty to deliver the person or the thing to the claimant. Both types of *interdicta* are also called *decreta.*—See INTERDICTA PROHIBITORIA.

Berger, *RE* 9, 1613.

Interdicta retinendae possessionis. See INTERDICTA ADIPISCENDAE POSSESSIONIS.

Interdicta simplicia. Ant. *interdicta duplicia.* The distinction is based upon the role of the parties in the interdictal proceedings. *Simplicia* are those in which one party is the plaintiff and the other the defendant to whom the prohibitory order is addressed or by whom things have to be restored or produced. In the *interdicta duplicia* both parties are at once defendant and plaintiff, as in the possessory interdicts UTI POSSIDETIS, UTRUBI. Here the praetor speaks "in an equal language" (*pari sermone,* Gaius 4.160) to both parties. In the terminology of Justinian's compilers, *interdicta duplicia* are those *interdicta* which exceptionally aim at acquiring and regaining possession; see INTERDICTUM QUAM HEREDITATEM, INTERDICTUM QUEM FUNDUM.

Berger, *RE* 9, 1616; *idem, Vol. di onoranze Simoncelli,* 1915, 186; *idem, ZSS* 36 (1916) 222; Arangio-Ruiz, *DE* 4 (1926) 69.

Interdicta temporaria. See INTERDICTA ANNALIA.

Interdicta unde vi. See INTERDICTUM DE VI.

Interdicta utilia. These are created by the extension of a normal interdictal formula beyond its limits. Thus a normal interdict becomes available to a larger group of persons and applicable to situations different from those protected by the original *interdictum.* The *interdicta utilia* are a creation analogous to ACTIONES UTILES, but the term *interdictum directum* is not to be found in the sources.

Berger, *RE* 9, 1623.

Interdictum de aqua. Issued for the protection of servitudes consisting in the use of water from another's property.—See SERVITUS AQUAE DUCTUS, CASTELLUM.—D. 43.20.

Berger, *RE* 9, 1630; Lenel, *Edictum perpetuum*[3] (1927) 479; Solazzi, *Tutela delle servitù prediali,* 1949, 66.

Interdictum de arboribus caedendis. Accorded to the owner of an immovable against a neighbor who does not remove tree branches hanging over the plaintiff's property. The latter may cut them and keep the wood if the tree owner does not obey the interdictal order.—D. 43.27.

Berger, *RE* 9, 1632.

Interdictum de glande legenda. Granted to protect the right of the owner of a tree to collect the fruits that fall on the neighbor's property.—D. 43.28.

Berger, *RE* 9, 1638; Lenel, *Edictum perpetuum*[3] (1927) 487.

Interdictum de homine libero exhibendo. A man who unlawfully holds (*retinere*) a free man as a slave is ordered by this popular *interdictum* to produce the man in court.—See LEX FABIA.—D. 43.29; C. 8.8.

Berger, *RE* 9, 1638; Lenel, *Edictum perpetuum*[3] (1927) 487.

Interdictum de itinere actuque privato. Serves for the protection of the servitudes ITER and ACTUS. The order is directed to the owner of the land on which the servitude is imposed, to the effect not to hinder the plaintiff in the exercise of his right.—D. 43.19.

Berger, *RE* 9, 1639; Lenel, *Edictum perpetuum*[3] (1927) 478; Biondi, *Actio negativa, AnMes* 3 (1929) 55; Solazzi, *Tutela delle servitù prediali* (1949) 57; Daube, *RIDA* 6 (1951) 40.

Interdictum de liberis ducendis. See the following item.

Interdictum de liberis exhibendis. When a person *alieni iuris* (*filius* or *filia familias*) is held by another, even by a member of the same family, against the will of his *pater familias,* the latter may request this *interdictum* which orders that the person withheld be produced (*exhiberi*). If through the exhibition the identity of the person involved was established, the magistrate issued a second interdict, *de liberis ducendis,* ordering his delivery to the *pater familias,* who then takes him home (*ducere*). Therefore the first *interdictum* is called *praeparatorium* with reference to the second. In later development analogous interdicts were introduced: *de uxore exhibenda* and *de uxore ducenda* in favor of a man whose wife was withheld by another, even her father.—D. 43.30; C. 8.8.

Berger, *RE* 9, 1641.

Interdictum de liberto exhibendo. This was issued in favor of a patron whose freedman, being held by another person, was not able to render the services due to the patron.

Berger, *RE* 9, 1643.

Interdictum de loco publico fruendo. A lessee of public land may request the issuance of this *interdictum* to secure his unimpeded use according to the lease agreement.—D. 43.9.

Berger, *RE* 9, 1643.

Interdictum de migrando. Granted to the tenant of a rented apartment against the landlord who retained his things under the pretext that the rent has not been paid. A distinction is made, on the one hand, between things which the tenant hypothecated to the landlord and those not hypothecated, on the other hand between things which were brought in by the tenant (*introducta, importata,* such as furniture, slaves) and those which were afterwards made by him or became his (slaves born in his house). The tenant who wants to move (*migrare*) to another place applies for this *interdictum* in order to release his property.

Berger, *RE* 9, 1646; Lenel, *Edictum perpetuum*[3] (1927) 490; Kreller, *ZSS* 64 (1944) 313.

Interdictum de mortuo inferendo. When somebody has the right to bury a deceased person in a certain place that belongs either to him or to someone else (*ius mortuum inferendi*), he is protected by this prohibitory interdict against any disturbance in so doing.—D. 11.8.

Berger, *RE* 9, 1646.

Interdictum de precario. See PRECARIUM.

Interdictum de ripa munienda. See RIPA.

Interdictum de rivis. The free access of the user of water-works, aqueducts, sluices, channels, cisterns, etc., for purposes of repair or cleaning is protected by this *interdictum* against anyone who attempts to prevent him from so doing. The *interdictum* is complementary to the *interdictum de aqua.*—D. 43.21.

Berger, *RE* 9, 1647; Lenel, *Edictum perpetuum*[3] (1927) 480; Solazzi, *Tutela delle servitù prediali,* 1939, 73.

Interdictum de sepulcro aedificando. This is connected with the INTERDICTUM DE MORTUO INFERENDO inasmuch as he who has the right to bury a corpse in another's property must be permitted to erect a tombstone on the grave.—D. 11.8.

Berger, *RE* 9, 1648.

Interdictum de superficiebus. See SUPERFICIES.—D. 43.18.

Berger, *RE* 9, 1647; Lenel, *Edictum perpetuum*[3] (1927) 476; H. Vogt, *Das Erbbaurecht,* 1950, 86.

Interdictum de tabulis exhibendis. Issued in the interest of a person to whom it is important to know the contents of a last will after the testator's death. The interdictal order compels the holder of the testament to produce it.—D. 43.5.

Berger, *RE* 9, 1648.

Interdictum de uxore ducenda (exhibenda). See INTERDICTUM DE LIBERIS EXHIBENDIS.

Berger, *RE* 9, 1642 (no. 12 c).

Interdictum de vi. This belongs to the group of *interdicta unde vi* which serve for regaining possession (*interdictum recuperandae possessionis*) on behalf of persons who have been deprived of possession by physical force (*vi deiecti*). He who gave order to others (family members, slaves) to dispossess, was also responsible. When the aggressor acted with the assistance of armed persons engaged for this purpose (*vis armata*), a special *interdictum de vi armata* was issued. Another *interdictum* was proposed for the case of rejection of a person by force from an immovable on which he had only an usufruct.—D. 43.16; C. 8.4.

Berger, *RE* 9, 1677; E. Levy, *Konkurrenz der Aktionen* 1 (1918) 285; G. Maier, *Praetorische Bereicherungsklagen* 1932 66; Lenel, *Edictum perpetuum*[3] (1947) 461; Aru, *AnPal* 15 (1936) 152; Biscardi, *Scr Solazzi,* 1948, 730.

Interdictum de viis publicis. There are several interdicts protecting the use of public roads and ways by private individuals. Analogous prohibitory interdicts are granted with regard to public areas (*loca publica*) such as squares, streets, islands, market places, etc., which "are intended for public use" (D. 43.8.2.5). These *interdicta* forbid any construction at a public place which might damage it or render it less available for use. Not only are constructions built on the road or place itself, e.g., a monument, hit by the prohibition but also works done on adjacent lands which directly or indirectly damage the place in question. Constructions permitted by law or by the local authorities are exempt from the prohibition. The demolition of a harmful work already done may be obtained by similar interdicts of restitutory character, by which restoration of the place to its original state, the removal of the obstacles, or reconstruction of what was damaged is ordered.—D. 43.8; 9.

Berger, *RE* 9, 1649; 1653 (no. 35); Lenel, *Edictum perpetuum*[3] (1927) 459.

Interdictum demolitorium. See OPERIS NOVI NUNTIATIO.

Interdictum ex operis novi nuntiatione. See OPERIS NOVI NUNTIATIO.

Interdictum fraudatorium. In classical law one of the measures to rescind any transaction (alienation) by which a debtor intentionally deprived himself of his rights or of his property to the detriment of his creditors (*fraudandi causa*). The purpose of the *interdictum* was the restoration of the legal situation which existed before the fraudulent act. Other means leading to the same effect were *actio Pauliana* and IN INTEGRUM RESTITUTIO. The relationship between these different expedients is rather obscure since the *interdictum fraudatorium* is effaced in Justinian sources.—D. 42.8; C. 7.75.—See FRAUS.

Berger, *RE* 9, 1650; Lenel, *Edictum perpetuum*[3] (1927) 495; G. Maier, *Praetorische Bereicherungsklagen*, 1932, 73; G. Segrè, *BIDR* 48 (1941) 38; Solazzi, *Revoca degli atti fraudolenti* 1 (1945).

Interdictum momentariae possessionis. See POSSESSIO MOMENTARIA.

Interdictum ne quid in loco sacro religioso fiat. A prohibitory *interdictum* serving for the protection of sacred and religious places (see RES RELIGIOSAE, RES SACRAE), similar to those which are granted for use of public roads and places (INTERDICTUM DE VIIS PUBLICIS). It is directed against all kind of wrongful doing (*facere*, such as constructions, and *immittere*, e.g., to let water run).—D. 43.6.

Berger, *RE* 9, 1655.

Interdictum ne vis fiat aedificanti. See AEDIFICATIO.

Interdictum possessorium. See BONORUM VENDITIO.

Berger, *RE* 9, 1657.

Interdictum quam hereditatem. An *interdictum* issued when in a trial for recovery of an inheritance (HEREDITATIS PETITIO) the defendant, i.e., the actual possessor of the estate, refused to cooperate in the manner prescribed for ACTIONES IN REM, e.g., to give security. In such a case he is considered INDEFENSUS, not defended as prescribed by the law, and his adversary could request the issuance of the *interdictum quam hereditatem* which was an *interdictum adipiscendae possessionis* since the claimant obtained possession of the estate. The new situation, although provisional, was of great advantage to him inasmuch as in any future process that might be brought against him by the former defendant in the interdictal controversy he had the favorable position of defendant. Some other interdicts are constructed on similar premises, such as *interdictum quem fundum* when the object of the claim is land, *interdictum quam servitutem,* when a praedial servitude is claimed, or *interdictum quem usufructum* when the claimant demands the delivery of an immovable on which he pretends to have the right of usufruct. In all these cases the victorious claimant obtains provisional possession of the controversial object.

Berger, *RE* 9, 1650; idem, *Vol. di onoranze Simoncelli*, 1915, 186; Lenel, *Edictum perpetuum*[3] (1927) 474.

Interdictum quam servitutem. See INTERDICTUM QUAM HEREDITATEM.

Berger, *RE* 9, 1659; Solazzi, *Mél De Visscher* 4 (= *RIDA* 5, 1950) 466.

Interdictum quem fundum. See INTERDICTUM QUAM HEREDITATEM.

Berger, *RE* 9, 1660.

Interdictum quem usufructum. See INTERDICTUM QUAM HEREDITATEM.

Berger, *RE* 9, 1661; Lenel, *Edictum perpetuum*[3] (1927) 475.

Interdictum quod legatorum. When somebody holds a thing under the pretext that it was bequeathed to him, he may be sued in interdictal proceedings by the heir under praetorian law (BONORUM POSSESSOR), who denies the legacy, for recovery. The claimant must give security for the return of the thing if there is a valid legacy.—D. 43.3; C. 8.3.

Berger, *RE* 9, 1661; Lotmar, *ZSS* 31 (1911); Perrot, *Ét. Girard* 1 (1913); Lenel, *ZSS* 52 (1932) 282.

Interdictum quod vi aut clam. A restitutory interdict issued against a person who forcibly (*vi*) or secretly (*clam*) did a "work" on the claimant's property. The work (*opus*) is here conceived in the broadest sense of any act done which changes the state of the land or its surface, such as cutting trees, ploughing, digging, demolition of existing constructions, etc. *Vis* (= force, violence) is also interpreted very broadly since any action taken against the prohibition by the owner is considered to be *vis*. The defendant is also liable for his slave's wrongdoings. The aim of the *interdictum* is restoration to the former state by the defendant himself or at his expense.—D. 43.2; C. 8.2.

Berger, *RE* 9, 1662; Cicogna, *I. quod vi aut clam*, 1910; E. Levy, *Konkurrenz der Aktionen* 1 (1918) 295; Lenel, *Edictum perpetuum*[3] (1927) 482; Marcel David, *Études sur l'i. q.v.a.c., Annales Univ. Lyon*, 3rd sér., 10 (1947).

Interdictum quorum bonorum. An *interdictum* available to a successor under praetorian law (BONORUM POSSESSOR) against anyone who holds things belonging to the estate and asserts to hold them as an heir or simply as a possessor without any title (*sine causa*). If he pretends to hold them as a legatee he is exposed to the *interdictum quod legatorum*. The *interdictum* belongs to the category of *interdictum adipiscendae possessionis.*—D. 43.2; C. 8.2.—See BONORUM POSSESSIO.

Berger, *RE* 9, 1666; Humbert and Lécrivain, *DS* 4 (*s.v. quorum b.*); De Martino, *ANap* 58 (1937) 348.

Interdictum Salvianum. An *interdictum* available to a landlord against his lessee for the latter's failure to pay the rent due. The *interdictum* is *adipiscendae possessionis,* since the claimant obtains possession of the tenant's things which were brought in (*invecta, illata*) and pledged for rent. It is prohibitory because the tenant is forbidden to impede the landlord in taking away the things.—D. 43.3; C. 8.9.

Berger, *RE* 9, 1667; Sacchi, *NDI* 7; Lenel, *Edictum perpetuum*[3] (1927) 490; Kreller, *ZSS* 64 (1944) 320; v. Bolla, *RE* 18[4], 2479; Daube, *RIDA* 6 (1951) 46.

Interdictum sectorium. See SECTIO BONORUM.

Interdictum secundarium. A second *interdictum* issued in a possessory controversy when one of the parties involved did not completely fulfill the order or refused to cooperate in the proceedings subsequent to the *interdictum* first issued in the matter. The details of this complicated procedure are not known since the sole pertinent text in Gaius' Institutes is not fully preserved.

Berger, *RE* 9, 1670; 1697; Gintowt, *AnPal* 15 (1934) 228.

Interdictum uti possidetis. Accorded in order to maintain an existing possessory situation at the request of the actual possessor who has been disturbed in the possession of an immovable by the adversary and is threatened with a suit over ownership. The order of the magistrate forbids any change in the actual situation. The *interdictum* is directed to both the parties; it is an *interdictum duplex* (see INTERDICTA SIMPLICIA) and inhibits the use of force (*vim fieri veto*) to dispossess the actual possessor. The plaintiff is protected only when his holding of the controversial immovable is not a defective possession (*possessio vitiosa*), to wit, acquired and kept by force (*vi*), secretly (*clam*) or through a gratuitous revocable loan (*precario*). In such cases the defendant avails himself of the so-called *exceptio vitiosae possessionis.*—D. 43.17; C. 8.6.

Berger, *RE* 9, 1682; Anon., *NDI* 12 (*s.v. uti p.*); Lenel, *Edictum perpetuum*[3] (1927) 469; Passerini, *Ath* 1937, 26; Ciapessoni, *St Albertoni* 2 1937 15; Kaser, *Eigentum und Besitz,* 1943, *passim.*

Interdictum utrubi. An *interdictum* based on the same principles as the foregoing, but limited to movables. It is an *interdictum duplex* and takes into account the *exceptio vitiosae possessionis.* Victorious in retaining or regaining possession is the party who,

during the year preceding the issuance of the *interdictum,* possessed the object for a longer period. Justinian extended the *interdictum uti possidetis* to movables; thus the *interdictum utrubi* lost its actuality in Justinian's law.—D. 43.31.

Berger, *RE* 9, 1684; Lenel, *Edictum perpetuum*[3] (1927) 488; Fraenkel, *ZSS* 54 (1934) 312; M. Kaser, *Eigentum und Besitz,* 1943, *passim*; Daube, *RIDA* 6 (1951) 32.

Interdictus. An individual punished by banishment, confinement, or any kind of INTERDICTIO LOCORUM. —See DEPORTATIO, RELEGATIO.—D. 48.22.

Interdum. Sometimes. The word is often inserted by Justinian's compilers to limit a general classical rule and to leave a way open for exceptions. Interpolation of the adverbs *plerumque* (= very often) and *nonnunquam* (= sometimes) has a similar function.

Guarneri-Citati, *Indice*[2] (1927) 48, 67.

Interesse. See the following items.

Interest. There is a difference; *multum interest* = there is a great difference; *nihil interest* = it makes (there is) no difference.

Interest alicuius. It is of interest (importance) to a person. If the phrase *is cuius interest* refers to a public authority, a magistrate, judge, or imperial functionary is meant. *Rei publicae* (or *publice*) *interest* = it concerns the welfare, the interests of the state (or the Roman people). The term *interest* is of particular importance in the cases involving payment of damages. There were no general rules for the evaluation of a person's interest when compensation was taken into consideration. It was the judge's task to estimate it in each instance according to the rules governing the extension of the liability of the defendant, in particular as to whether real damages only or also lost profit should be identified.—See ID QUOD INTEREST, QUANTI EA RES EST, VERITAS.

Steinwenter, *RE* 9; Fliniaux, *RHD* 7 (1928) 326; Beretta, *SDHI* 3 (1937) 419; Guarino, *Giurisprudenza comparata di dir. civile,* 6 (1941) 197.

Interim. Meantime. The adverb is used with reference to the time intervening between two legally important events, for instance, between the conclusion of a transaction or the bequeathing of a legacy and the fulfillment of a condition upon which the effectiveness of the agreement or legacy depends; or the time between a judgment and the appeal brought against it.

Interitus. (From *interire.*) Destruction, extinction. The term is used of the extinction of certain rights (a servitude, a usufruct) or of actions.

Interlinere. To efface, to obliterate a written document (a testament, an account book) wholly or in part. If a person did so illegally, he could be sued by any one who had an interest in the existence of the document, primarily through the *actio legis Aquiliae.*

Interlocutio. An order, a statement or preliminary decision issued by a magistrate, judge or chairman of a tribunal during a trial. *Interlocutio* is also an interlocutory statement or decision by the emperor in the course of a trial before the imperial court.— D. 42.1; C. 7.45.—See DEFINITIVA SENTENTIA, MULTA PRAEIUDICIALIS.

   Arangio-Ruiz, *RE* 4, 72.

Interminatio. In later imperial constitutions, threatening with punishment for a specific infraction.

Interna causae. In later imperial constitutions, the essential elements of a judicial affair.

Internuntius. (Syn. *nuntius*.) A messenger used for the oral transmission of a legally important decision (a declaration, a consent). Ant. of *per internuntium* is *per epistulam* (= by letter).

Interpellare (interpellatio). To press a debtor who had failed to pay on time, for payment. See MORA.— *Interpellare* is also used when one sues his adversary in court (hence *interpellatio* = an action, a suit) or when one forbids another to accomplish a certain act. With regard to usucaption (*usucapio interpellatur*), *interpellare* indicates that the *usucapio* is interrupted either through the loss of possession by the holder of the thing or through a successful action of the person who claims the recovery of the thing.

   Kaser, *RE* 16, 255; Biscardi, *StSen* 60 (1948) 607 (Bibl. on *interpellatio* in the case of default); Siber, *ZSS* 29 (1909) 47.

Interponere. Used of the conclusion of an obligatory transaction (*stipulationem, contractum, donationem,* giving security), of taking an oath (*interponere iusiurandum*), of writing down a document (*interponere instrumentum*), even of committing fraud (*interponere fraudem*).

Interponere aliquem. To appoint a person as a representative or mediator; see INTERPOSITA PERSONA.

Interponere auctoritatem. See AUCTOR, AUCTORITAS.

Interponere se. When said of a private individual, to interfere, meddle in a legal controversy between other persons; when said of a magistrate = to intervene officially, to take official measures.

Interposita persona. An intermediary, sometimes a straw man interposed in order to disguise an unlawful transaction (syn. *supposita persona*).

Interpositio decreti. In Diocletian's and later constitutions, the issuance of a *decretum* by the emperor or a high imperial official.

Interpres. An interpreter. References to the use of interpreters in judicial proceedings, in hearings before a magistrate or public corporate bodies (the senate, on the occasion of a reception of foreign envoys) are very scarce. In provincial administration the service of interpreters is better evidenced. Their use in imperial courts, in particular in the later Empire, is beyond any doubt (*interpretes diversarum gentium*). The jurist Paul defined the custom (*consuetudo*) as "the best interpreter of laws" (D. 1.3.37).

   De Ruggiero, *DE* 4, 72; Taubenschlag, *The interpreters in the papyri, Charisteria Sinko,* Warsaw, 1951, 361.

Interpretatio. The explanation of the significance of a legal norm or term. Originally the pontiffs who alone mastered the knowledge of the law and legal customs, accomplished the task on interpretation, later it was assumed by the jurists as the men "learned in the law." The interpretation of the law exercised a great influence on the development of the law from whatever source it originated. This refers not only to the *interpretatio* of the law of the Twelve Tables, which, being only a limited codification, was unable to satisfy the growing legal needs, but also to the *interpretatio* of legal customs. The *interpretatio prudentium* thus became a primary source of law, since it extended the norms of the decemviral legislation to new legal situations and problems and took into consideration customary practices which through the comprehensive activity of the jurists acquired a more perceptible expression. Hence the jurists were later designated as those who *iura condiderunt* (= established the law, see IURISPRUDENTIA) and their law as a law which "without writing was composed by the jurists and so became a *ius civile* proper consisting exclusively in the *interpretatio* of men learned in the law" (D. 1.2.2.12). The interpretative activity continued when legislative enactments were passed by the people (statutes = *leges*) and when the praetors began to create new legal rules in their edictal pronouncements. In the later Empire, the interpretation of law became a special province of the emperor and ultimately Justinian made the emphatic statement (*Tanta,* 21 *in fine*) that the emperor as the exclusive legislator had the exclusive right to interpret the law (*cui soli concessum est leges interpretari;* so-called authentic interpretation). The Roman jurists did not elaborate a specific theory of the interpretation of law, some rules of *interpretatio* are to be found, however, scattered through the Digest, such as: "Whenever a statute provides something there is a good opportunity to add further rules which aim at the same benefit (*utilitas* = utility) through interpretation or jurisdiction" (D. 1.3.13). "To know the laws (*scire leges*) means to adhere not to their words but to their force and sense" (D. 1.3.17). "The term *ex legibus* (= according to the laws) is to be understood according to both the sense and to the words" (D. 50.16.6.1). Several texts stress the importance of the intention and spirit of a statute. See BENIGNA INTERPRETATIO, HUMANITAS.—The *interpretatio* of the laws is to be distingushed from the interpretation of manifestations of will by private individuals in their legal acts, both unilateral (testamentary dispositions) and bilateral (agreements). Under the regime of strict formalism the ancient law gave no opportunity to differentiate between *verba* (what has been expressed) and *voluntas* (the intention) of the party or parties. In the later development, owing to the activity of the jurists, the evaluation of *voluntas* as against *verba* gradually increased, starting in the field of testaments and legacies and passing from there into other domains of the private law. Some interpretative directives given by the classical jurists appear in Justinian's legislative work, such as: "If ambiguous utterances occur, the intention of the person who used them should be taken into consideration" (D. 50.17.96). "Where there is ambiguity of words, what (in fact) was acted, is valid" (D. 34.5.21). "Where there is no ambiguity of words, the question of intention should not be admitted" (D. 32.25.1). The final two titles of the Digest contain a large number of interpretative suggestions concerning single words or locutions which are of importance for the understanding of juristic texts (D. 50.16) and a long series of general legal rules (*regulae iuris*, D. 50.17) of an interpretative nature.—See IUS RESPONDENDI, RESPONSA, VERBA, VOLUNTAS.

Kleinfeller, *RE* 9; Berger, *ibid.* 1167; Anon., *NDI* 7; R. Pound, *Harvard L R* 21 (1908) 383; Donatuti, *Dal regime dei verba al regime della voluntas, BIDR* 34 (1925) 185; J. Stroux, *Summum ius summa iniuria. Ein Kapitel aus der Gesch. der i. iuris,* 1926 (2nd ed. *Röm. Rechtswiss. und Rhetorik,* Potsdam, 1949); J. Himmelschein, *Symb. Frib. Lenel,* 1931; Biondi, *BIDR* 43 (1935) 139; C. A. Maschi, *St sull'i. dei legati, verba-voluntas,* 1938; Schiller, *Virginia LR* 27 (1941) 733; F. Schulz, *History of R. Legal Science* (1946) 24, 75, 132, 293; Riccobono, in several articles, see VOLUNTAS (Bibl.); Berger, *In dubiis benigniora, ACIVer* 2 (offpr. 1951) 187 (= *Sem* 9 [1951] 36).

Interpretatio duplex. The interpretation of a text in Justinian's codification (primarily in the Digest) from two points of view: on the one hand, what the text meant in the time and the language of the jurist who wrote it; on the other hand, the significance it acquired in Justinian's legislation. Many texts in the final title of the Digest (50.17: On various rules of the ancient law) offer instances for such an interpretation, since certain rules formulated by the classical jurisprudence on a specific occasion and for a specific legal situation were drawn out of their original context and settled as a general rule applicable at all times (*semper*) or at least "very often" (*plerumque*). The expression *interpretatio duplex* is of modern coinage.

Riccobono, *BIDR* 49–50 (1948) 6.

Interpretationes ad Codicem Theodosianum. Summaries or paraphrases of the constitutions collected in the Codex Theodosianus. They are preserved in the LEX ROMANA VISIGOTHORUM and frequently contain additional remarks and references to other sources. The *Lex Romana Visigothorum* contains also interpretations of some texts of Paulus' *Sententiae.* The *interpretationes* may originate from various private commentaries written to the sources mentioned.—See CODEX THEODOSIANUS.

Kleinfeller, *RE* 9, 1712; Berger, *RE* 12, 2400; Stouff, *Mél Fitting* 2 (1908) 165; M. Conrat, *Der westgothische Paulus,* Amsterdam, 1907; Checchini, *St sull'interpretatio*

al *Cod. Teodosiano, Scritti in memoria di Monticolo,* 1913; G. Ferrari, *Osservazioni sulla trasmissione diplomatica del Codice Teodosiano e sulla interpretatio Visigotica,* 1915; Wieacker, *Symb Frib Lenel,* 1931, 259; Chiazzese, *AnPal* 16 (1931) 301; Niccolai, *RendLomb* 75 (1942) 42; Buckland, *LQR* 60 (1944) 361.

Interpretatores (interpretes) legum, iuris. Justinian refers to the classical jurists by such terms as "the ancient interpreters of the law" or "the interpreters of the ancient law."

Interregnum. The interval between the death of a king and the election of his successor. At the beginning of the vacancy a senator elected by the senate was appointed *interrex* only for a period of five days. If this period expired without the election of a new king, the *interrex* designated his successor for the consecutive five days.—See INTERREX, PRODERE INTERREGEM.

Liebenam, *RE* 9; Ehrenberg, *RE* 13, 1498; Foligno, *NDI* 7; Giannelli, *DE* 4 (*s.v. interrex*); De Ruggiero, *DE* 2, 825; Heuss, *ZSS* 64 (1944) 79.

Interrex. See INTERREGNUM. Under the Republic an *interrex* selected from among the patrician senators was appointed by the senate when both consuls died or abdicated, for five days only. His principal function was to order the election of new consuls. The following *interreges* were consecutively designated by their predecessors for a five-day term as long as the election was not accomplished.

Giannelli, *DE* 4, 73.

Interrogatio. In a *stipulatio,* the question addressed by the future creditor to the debtor.—See STIPULATIO.

Interrogatio. In criminal trials, the question addressed by the court to the accused as to whether he pleads guilty or not. If he admits having committed the crime or if he is silent, which is considered an admission, the proceedings are quickly brought to an end. *Interrogatio* also means the questioning of a witness.

Berger, *RE* 9, 1729.

Interrogatio. In the senate, a request for opinion addressed to the senators by the presiding magistrate. The opinion given by a senator = *sententia.* Syn. *sententias rogare.*

Interrogatio in iure. Questioning the defendant in a civil trial. This was a specific institution for the purpose of establishing certain important points regarding the defendant's liability. In some *actiones in personam* the plaintiff was permitted to question the defendant during the first stage of the trial before the magistrate (see IN IURE) about certain circumstances that were decisive for the further progress of the trial. Thus, in a suit against the heir of his debtor, a creditor could ask the defendant whether he was in fact the heir (*an heres sit*) and of what share. In noxal actions (see NOXA) the plaintiff asked the defendant whether the son or slave for whose wrongdoings he was being sued was in his power legally and factually (*in potestate*). These were the two most practical uses of *interrogatio*. An affirmative answer by the defendant was binding even if it did not correspond to the truth. The fact of the affirmative answer was then inserted into the pertinent procedural formula; actions with formulae so modified were termed *actiones interrogatoriae*. The defendant's negative answer put an end to the trial. If the plaintiff was able to prove its untruth, the trial was continued and entailed considerable disadvantages for the defendant in case of condemnation. The *interrogatio* was not a general institution relieving the plaintiff of the burden of proof in any trial. There were also instances in which the magistrate might question the defendant *in iure* about some details which were prejudicial to further proceedings. The *actiones interrogatoriae* disappeared when the civil process ceased to be bipartite.—D. 11.1.

Berger, *RE* 9; Anon., *NDI* 6; Lautner, *Fschr. Hanausek, Abhandlungen zur antiken Rechtsgesch.*, 1925; Sanfilippo, *Circolo giuridico* 10 (1939).

Interrumpere (interruptio). To interrupt. With reference to possession, *interrumpere* is mentioned as a negative requisite of usucaption since the interruption makes impossible the usucaption.—C. 7.40.
—See USURPATIO, USUCAPIO, INTERPELLARE.

Interusurium. If the debtor pays the money due on a fixed day before that date, the creditor has the profit (*commodum*) of having the money at his disposal and of being able to lend it at interest for the remainder of the term (*interusurium medii temporis*). The debtor may deduct the *interusurium* from his payment only if the creditor consents, because the latter is not bound to accept a payment with a deduction before it is due.

De Dominicis, *NDI* 7, 87.

Intervalla dilucida (lucida). Periods during which an insane person regained full mental capacity and, consequently, legal capacity. Syn. FUROR INTERMISSUS.—See FURIOSUS, DEMENS.

De Francisci, *BIDR* 20 (1921) 154; Solazzi, *AG* 89 (1923) 80; Lenel, *BIDR* 33 (1923) 227, 45 (1925) 517.

Intervenire. A general term to indicate that a legally important event occurred, e.g., an agreement (*stipulatio, pactum*), a wrongdoing creating legal liability (*dolus, fraus, culpa*), a procedural measure (*cautio, accusatio*), and the like.

Intervenire (interventor, interventio, interventus). In obligatory relations syn. with INTERCEDERE. It is frequently used of sureties.

Intervenire. In judicial proceedings to intervene in a trial as a representative of a party, either as a general representative (*tutor, curator*) or as one appointed for a specific trial (*procurator*).

Interversio. An embezzlement.

Intestabilis. A person who is unable to be a witness at a solemn act requiring the presence of witnesses (e.g., *mancipatio, testamentum per aes et libram*) or to invite another to witness such an act to be made

by himself. *Intestabilis* was one who had been convicted of libel (*carmen famosum*) or who had refused to give testimony about an act in which he participated as a witness.—See IMPROBUS TESTIS.

Manigk, *RE* 9.

Intestato. (Adv.) Refers to a succession in which there is no valid testament. Syn. *ab intestato*.

Intestatus. A person who died without leaving a valid testament or whose testament, originally valid, became ineffective because the appointed heirs refused to accept the inheritance or by other reasons. Ant. *testatus*.—See TESTAMENTUM RUPTUM, TESTAMENTUM IRRITUM, NEMO PRO PARTE TESTATUS, etc.

Manigk, *RE* 9; Michon, *RHD* 2 (1921) 128; Daube, *RHD* 15 (1936) 341; La Pira, *La successione ereditaria intestata*, 1930.

Intexere. To interweave. The owner of a piece of cloth acquires ownership of whatever has been woven into it.

Arnò, *Textura, Mél Girard* 1 (1912) 27.

Intimare. In the language of the imperial chancery, to perform a legal act before an official or to register it in the official records; to announce official ordinances publicly; to send official instructions to the appropriate offices.

Intra. Within. With regard to a period of time, the word includes the last day, e.g., *intra centum dies* takes in the hundredth day. *Intra* with regard to years includes the last year in full. This kind of reckoning is applied to acts to be accomplished *intra* a certain lapse of time. In later imperial constitutions, *intra* connected with a number of days or months means exactly the last day of the term. For *intra miliarium*, see MILIARIUM.

Introducta. (Syn. *importata*.) Things brought into a rented apartment by the tenant (furniture, slaves, etc.). The analogous expressions in the lease of land are *invecta, illata* (furnishing, tools, instruments of husbandry, cattle, slaves, etc.).—See INTERDICTUM DE MIGRANDO.

Introductio actionis, litis (introducere actionem, litem). Starting a civil trial. In Justinian's language *introductio litis* is syn. with *litis contestatio* as conceived in the procedure of his time.—See LITIS CONTESTATIO.

Introire domum alicuius vi. To invade another's house by violence. It was punished under the LEX CORNELIA DE INIURIIS.—See DOMUS, INGREDI.

Introire fundum. To enter a landed property in order to take physical possession thereof. It sufficed to set foot on any part of it.—See POSSESSIO.

Introitus. The sum paid for obtaining a subaltern post in the civil service.—See MILITIA.

Marchi, *AG* 76 (1906) 319.

Intuitu. With regard to, in consideration of. The term is frequent in later imperial constitutions and those of Justinian in connection with *humanitas* or *pietas* (*intuitu humanitatis, pietatis*). In the Digest the word is rather suspect as to its classical origin.

Guarneri-Citati, *Indice*² (1927) 49.

Inulta mors. A murder which has remained unavenged (without prosecution) by the dead man's son. The latter was held unworthy (*indignus*) to benefit from the will of the father.

Inustus. (From *inurere*.) Stigmatized, branded by infamy (in the language of imperial constitutions). —See INFAMIA.

Inutilis. Legally ineffective. The term is used of acts (testaments, transactions, actions) which are void because of the non-fulfillment of a legal requirement. *Inutiliter* = without legal effect.—Inst. 3.19; C. 8.38.

Hellmann, *ZSS* 23 (1902) 422.

Invadere. To enter with violence another's immovable in order to take possession of it (*invadere bona, possessionem*).—See INGREDI, INTROIRE.

Invalidus. See VALIDUS.

Invasio (invasor). The act of committing an *invadere* (the person who does it).—See INVADERE.

Invecta (illata). See INTRODUCTA, INTERDICTUM DE MIGRANDO.

De Villa, *NDI* 7.

Inventarium. An inventory of property (e.g., belonging to a ward). An *inventarium* should be made by a guardian, when he assumed the tutorship, in his own interest since his liability for the administration is limited to the amount of the ward's property. Such an inventory became later obligatory. Syn. *repertorium.* An *inventarium* was also made by creditors who obtained *missio in possessionem* into the property of a bankrupt debtor. The *inventarium* had a particular importance in the law of succession; see BENEFICIUM INVENTARII.

Kaser, *RE* 7A, 1571.

Inventor thesauri. A person who finds a treasure-trove.—See THESAURUS.

Investigare (investigator). To search for a criminal or a fugitive slave; to investigate a crime. Syn. *inquirere* (see INQUISITIO), *quaerere.*

Invicem. Mutually, reciprocally. With regard to agreements, *invicem* denotes that both parties assume reciprocal obligations (*obligari, deberi*) and each party thus is both creditor and debtor.

Invitator. An imperial functionary charged with sending out invitations to appear before the emperor. He also assisted at the audiences in the imperial palace.

Invitus. One against whose will or without whose consent something is done. "An *invitus* is not only he who contradicts, but also someone of whom it is not proved that he has agreed" (D. 3.3.8.1). Generally, no legal effect is produced for or against a person by an act for the validity of which his consent was required but not given. Acquisitions, however, made by a slave for his master even without his will are

valid. The payment of another's debt releases him from it even against or without his will. Remarkable rules are the following: "No one can be forced to bring a suit or to accuse against his will" (C. 3.7.1). "No one is given a benefit, a favor, against his will" (D. 50.17.69).—See EMPTIO AB INVITO, NOLENS, NEMO INVITUS.

Fadda, *St Brugi*, 1910, 145.

Iocus. A joke. A stipulation made for the sake of a joke (*per iocum*) does not create an obligation.

Ipse. Used in Justinian's language in lieu of *is* (= he). It is an evident Grecism, and therefore considered a criterion of interpolation when it appears in classical texts in the Digest.

Guarneri-Citati, *Indice*² (1927) 49.

Ipso iure. By virtue of the law itself. The locution is opposed to *ope exceptionis* (= by virtue of an exception) or to *tuitione praetoris* (by the aid of a praetorian remedy).—See ADITIO HEREDITATIS.

Iracundia. Anger, irritation, indignation. "Whatever is done or said in the heat of anger is not considered binding, unless it appears through perseverance to have been an act (judgment) of the mind" (D. 50.17.48 = D. 24.2.3). A wife who had left her husband in a state of irritation and returns to him after a short time is not held to have been divorced (D. *ibid.*).

Ire. As a servitude, *ius eundi.*—See ITER, ACTUS, VIA.

Ire ad iudicem (iudicium). To proceed judicially; to go to court after having been summoned. *Ire ad arbitrum* = to appear before an arbitrator to settle a controversy.

Irenarcha. A provincial officer charged with the functions of a justice of the peace and with the maintenance of public order. He conducted criminal investigations.—C. 10.77.

Iri in bona (possessionem). To be granted possession of another's property through a decree of the praetor. Syn. *mitti in bona, mitti in possessionem.*— See MISSIO IN POSSESSIONEM, VACUA POSSESSIO.

Irnerius. (Also Guarnerius.) A famous jurist of the late eleventh and the first decades of the twelfth century. He was the founder of the law school in Bologna which became the center of legal studies in medieval Italy. He is often referred to as *lucerna iuris* (= the lantern of law) and is considered the initiator of the revival of the study of Roman law in Italy. As teacher of law he enjoyed great esteem and he was one of the most prominent, if not the first, of the so-called Glossators.—See GLOSSATORES.

Schupfer, *RISG* 1894, 346; H. Fitting, *Die Summa Codicis des I.,* 1894; idem, *Quaestiones de iuris subtilitatibus des I.,* 1894; E. Besta, *L'opera di Irnerio,* 1-2, 1896; Patetta, *StSen* 14 (1897); Chiappelli, *AG* 58 (1897) 554; H. Kantorowicz, *Studies in the Glossators of the R. Law,* 1938, 33; Zanetti, *AG* 140 (1951) 72.

Irreverens miles. A soldier who violated military discipline or offended his superior by lack of respect. —See DELICTA MILITUM.

Irritus. Invalid (a legal act or transaction), either from the beginning or by a later event. Ant. *ratus.* —See TESTAMENTUM IRRITUM.

Irrogare. To inflict a penalty (*poenam, multam*) either in a normal criminal proceeding or as an act of magisterial *coërcitio.*—See MULTA.

Is qui agit. Syn. ACTOR; *is qui agere vult* (*acturus*) = the plaintiff before the *litis contestatio; is cum quo agitur* = the defendant.—See REUS, AGERE, PETITOR.

Italicus. Italian, situated in Italy. Land in Italy (*praedia Italica, solum Italicum, terra Italica*) is distinguished from provincial land. Only a plot of land situated in Italy (not a provincial one) is a *res mancipi* and transferable by MANCIPATIO.—See IUS ITALICUM.

Iter. A rustic servitude (*servitus praediorum rusticorum*) which entitles the beneficiary "to pass (*ius eundi*), to walk (*ius ambulandi*), and to ride on horse-back through another's land" (D. 8.3.1 pr.). He has not the right to drive a draught animal.—See SERVITUTES PRAEDIORUM RUSTICORUM, ACTUS, VIA.

> De Ruggiero, *DE* 4, 120; Arangio-Ruiz, *St Brugi*, 1910; Saumagne, *Revue de philologie* 53 (1928) 320; Grosso, *St Albertario* (Estr., 1950) 596.

Iter ad sepulcrum. Access to a grave through another's property. Free access (*aditus*) to a family tomb is granted to persons interested therein either as a servitude or as a revocable concession given through a mediation of the competent official (*extra ordinem*). The right is not extinguished through non use.

Iter aquae. See SERVITUS AQUAE DUCENDAE.

Iter privatum. Indicates both a private road and a *servitus itineris* (see ITER) through another's land. —D. 43.19.—See INTERDICTUM DE ITINERE PRIVATO.

> Berger, *RE* 9, 1639; Maroi, *St Bonfante* 3 (1930), 619.

Iter publicum. A public road the use of which is permitted to all. For the protection of the public use of such roads, see INTERDICTA DE ITINERIBUS PUBLICIS. —D. 43.7; C. 12.44.

> Berger, *RE* 9, 1641, 1654.

Iteratio. Holding the same magistracy a second time. *Iteratio* was permitted only after an interval of ten years. The pertinent rules were often violated for political reasons. Syn. *iterum fieri* (e.g., *consul*).

> Mommsen, *Staatsrecht* 1³, 519; Kübler, *RE* 14, 404.

Iteratio. (In manumissions.) A second manumission was necessary when the first one was performed in a form not recognized by *ius civile,* or by a master who had only bonitary (*in bonis*) ownership over the slave. Since such defective manumissions gave the ex-slave restricted citizenship (see LATINI IUNIANI) a second manumission (*iteratio*) in a form prescribed by *ius civile* or a manumission by the quiritary owner gave the freedman full Roman citizenship.

> Steinwenter, *RE* 12, 921.

Iubere. To order, to command. By use of the word *iubeo* a testator instituted an heir (*heredem esse iubeo*) and formulated other dispositions, such as legacies, or manumissions(*"Servum meum Stichum liberum esse iubeo"*). *Iubere* is also applied to the right of magistrates to issue orders (*ius, potestas iubendi*), particularly in their jurisdictional activity. All commands issued by the praetor in the first stage of a civil trial, *in iure,* originate in a *iussum* (*praetor iubet*), e.g., *stipulationes praetoriae, cautiones, missiones.* Injunctions ordered by the judge (*iudex*) in the second stage of the bipartite trial are also covered by the term *iubere.* Precepts in written enactments are referred to by *iubere,* e.g., *lex* (*senatusconsultum, edictum*) *iubet. Iubere* is also the technical term for the vote of the Roman people when a statute is passed. —In domestic relations, *iubere* is applied to the orders given by a father to a son under his paternal power or by a master to his slave, as well to the authorization given by them to a son or slave to conclude a transaction with a third person which involved the responsibility of the father or master, respectively.— D. 15.4.—See IUSSUM (Bibl.), IUDICARE IUBERE, DUCI IUBERE.

Iudaei. Under the Principate, the Jewish religion was recognized by the state as a *religio licita* which gave its followers the right to build synagogues for religious gatherings, to perform there ceremonies in conformity with their religion, and to have cemeteries. These religious privileges were, however, not respected by all emperors (e.g., Tiberius, Caligula, Vespasian, Hadrian). Legally the Jews were aliens (see PEREGRINI), subject to taxation, except for groups and individuals who for one or another reason were granted Roman citizenship. As peregrines they were exempt from military service. After A.D. 49 they had the right of association. Jewish communities had their own courts for litigation between Jews. A Jew was admitted to tutorship over a non-Jew. Of Alexander Severus it is said: "He confirmed the privileges of the Jews (*Iudaeis privilegia reservavit*)." The policy of the Christian emperors varied from toleration and religious neutrality to the most severe restrictions. As a matter of principle, the Jewish religion remained a *religio licita,* and the synagogues were treated as *loca religiosa* and were exempt from billeting soldiers. From the beginning of the fifth century the Jews were excluded from public office, but they were subject to public charges (*munera*). Among the measures taken against the expansion of the Jewish religion were such as the interdiction of the construction of new synagogues (A.D. 415) and of the conversion of persons of other religions under threat of severe penalties. Manifold restrictions in private law were imposed in the later Empire on the Jews with regard to the acquisition of land, ownership of Christian slaves, last wills, marriage with Christions (forbidden and prosecuted as adultery), exclusion from public office and military service. After A.D. 415 Jews were excluded from arbitration in controversies in which one party was a Christian.—C. 1.9; 1.10.—See SENATUSCONSULTA DE IUDAEIS, CIRCUMCISIO, FISCUS IUDAICUS, UNIVERSITAS IUDAEORUM.

T. Reinach, *DS* 3; Jones, *OCD* (*s.v. Jews*); Heinemann, *RE* Suppl. 5 (*s.v. Antisemitismus*); Corradi, *DE* 4 (*s.v. Iudaea*); Mommsen, *Jur. Schriften* 3 (1907) 416; W. D. Morrison, *Gli Ebrei sotto la dominazione romana*, 1911; J. Juster, *Les Juifs dans l'Empire rom.*, 1–2 (1914); G. Costa, *Religione e politica nell'impero rom.*, 1923, 151; La Piana, *L'immigrazione a Roma, Ricerche religiose* 4 (1928) 193; A. Momigliano, *Ricerche sull'organizzazione della Giudea, Annali della Scuola Norm. Superiore Pisa*, ser. 2, vol. 3 (1934) 346; Browe, *Die Judengesetzgebung Justinians, Analecta Gregoriana* 8 (1935) 109; Solazzi, *BIDR* 44 (1936/7) 396; *idem, ANap* 59 (1938) 164; M. Brücklmeir, *Beiträge zur Stellung der Juden im röm. Reich*, 1939; A. Segrè, *Note sullo status civitatis degli Ebrei nell'Egitto, Bull. Soc. Royale Archéol. d'Alexandrie* 28 (1933) 143; *idem, Jewish Social Studies* 6 (1944) 375; V. Colorni, *Legge ebraica e leggi locali*, 1945; Ferrari Dalle Spade, *Fschr. Wenger* 2 (1945) 102; *idem, Giurisdizione speciale ebraica nell'Impero r. cristiano, Scr Ferrini* 1 (Univ. Cat., Milan, 1947) 239. For further bibl. see R. Marcus, *A Selected Bibliography of the Jews in the Hellen.-Rom. Period (1920–1945), Proceedings of the Amer. Acad. for Jewish Research*, 16 (1947) pp. 97–141, *passim*; S. W. Baron, *A Social and Religious History of the Jews, Ancient Times*, 1–2, Philadelphia, 1952.

Iudex. Originally a *iudex* was any magistrate who decided about a controversy by a judgment (*qui ius dicit*). In the bipartite civil procedure the rendering of a judgment (*iudicare*) was separated from *ius dicere,* and the *iudex* was the private judge. In the classical juristic language *iudex* was a private individual (judge) appointed as a judge in a specific trial. He was neither a magistrate nor a magistrate's subordinate, and he was bound solely by the instructions given in the formula. The right to serve as a judge was denied deaf (*surdi*), dumb (*muti*), and insane (*furiosi*) persons, to *impuberes,* and women. Senators removed from the senate were excluded from judgeship. The circumstance that one was under paternal power was no bar. A judge sitting in court (*cum de re cognoscat*) could not be summoned before the magistrate (*in ius vocatus*) by a creditor. Syn. *iudicans* (a term frequently interpolated in lieu of any jurisdictional official who did no longer exist in Justinian's times). In the later Empire and in Justinian's language *iudex* is any imperial official who has any jurisdiction at all, and *iudices* is a collective term for all administrative functionaries of the Empire.—See C. 1.45; 1.48; 7.49; Inst. 4.17; D. 11.2.—See the following items and ALBUM IUDICUM, DECURIAE IUDICUM, LEX PINARIA, LEX SEMPRONIA IUDICIARIA, LEX AURELIA, CONTRACTUS IUDICUM, POSTULATIO IUDICIS, IURARE SIBI NON LIQUERE, INIURIA IUDICIS, SUUS IUDEX, IUDICES.

Kübler, *RE* 6, 289; Steinwenter, *RE* 4 and Suppl. 5, 350; Humbert and Lécrivain, *DS* 3; Bozza, *DE* 4; Berger, *OCD*; Seckel, *Handlexikon*[9] (1914) 291; Wildenauer, *Richterwahl im röm. Privatprozessrecht*, 1919; J. Mazeaud, *La nomination du iudex unus dans la procédure formulaire*, 1933; Collinet, *Le rôle des juges, Recueil F.*

Gény, 1 (1934) 23; J. Dauvillier, *La théorie de l'iniuria iudicis, Rec. Acad. de législ. Toulouse* 13 (1937); Weiss, *BIDR* 49–50 (1948) 194; Jolowicz, *RIDA* 2 (= *Mél De Visscher*, 1, 1949) 477; Kaser, *Fschr. Wenger* 1 (1945) 122.

Iudex appellationis. A judge (jurisdictional official) vested with the power to decide on appeals from decisions of an inferior court.

Iudex competens. A judge competent in a specific matter, i.e., legally authorized to examine a judicial controversy and to pass judgment. The term *competens* is frequent in postclassical and Justinian's constitutions; the compilers substituted it frequently where a judicial magistrate was mentioned in the classical work.—C. 7.48.

Iudex compromissarius. An arbitrator selected by the parties to a controversy by virtue of a compromise; see COMPROMISSUM.

Iudex datus. In classical law, a private person appointed with the cooperation of the magistrate to be the judge in a specific trial. In postclassical law = a judge appointed by a higher official, primarily the provincial governor, to examine a controversy and to pass judgment. Syn. *iudex pedaneus.*

Iudex delegatus. A lower (auxiliary) judge whom a higher jurisdictional official appointed for a specific case to be examined and decided upon by him.

Iudex esto. The introductory part of the written procedural formula in which an individual person is authorized to be the judge in a specific litigation ("*Titius iudex esto*").

Steinwenter, *RE* 9, 2468.

Iudex extra ordinem datus. A judge appointed in a *cognitio extra ordinem* by a jurisdictional official to examine a case and deliver a judgment.

Iudex in re propria (sua). A judge in his own affair. No one may be judge in his own controversy with another (*sibi esse iudicem, sibi ius dicere*). "It is highly improper to give one the liberty to pass a judgment in a matter of his own" (C. 3.5.1).—See IURISDICTIO.

Iudex ordinarius. Refers to the governor of a province in his capacity as a judge.

Iudex pedaneus. A judge to whom as a *iudex delegatus* a judicial official assigned a case in the *cognitio* procedure. Provincial governors used to delegate minor cases (*negotia humiliora*) to a *iudex pedaneus* if governmental affairs made it impossible for them to act personally.—C. 3.3.

Wlassak, *RE* 3, 3102 (*s.v. chamaidikastes*).

Iudex privatus. A private individual selected by the parties with the cooperation of the judicial magistrate to serve as a judge under the regime of the *legis actiones* and the formulary procedure. He examined the evidence and rendered the judgment. Hence the second stage of a civil trial is termed *apud iudicem* (before the judge). In later imperial constitutions *iudex privatus* is syn. with *iudex compromissarius.*

Iudex quaestionis. The chairman of the jury in criminal trials in the *quaestiones*-procedure (also called *iudex quaestionis rerum capitalium*), primarily in capital matters. Normally a magistrate of a rank lower than the praetor or an ex-magistrate was charged with such function.

Iudex qui litem suam facit. A *iudex* who intentionally (*dolo malo*) gave a false judgment made himself liable ("he makes the trial his"). An action for damages lay against him. This was the case when the judgment exceeded the limits fixed in the written formula. The extension of the judge's responsibility to judgments delivered *per imprudentiam* (= by negligence, lack of knowledge) may have been a later innovation.—D. 50.13.

J. Bartoli, *Du juge qui l.s.f.*, These Paris, 1910; E. Levy, *Privatstrafe und Schadensersatz*, 1915, 48; P. De Francisci, *Synallagma* 2 (1916) 129; Kübler, *ZSS* 39 (1918) 215; G. A. Palazzo, *Obbligazioni quasi ex delicto* 1919, 31; J. Dauvillier, *Iniuria iudicis, Rec. Acad. législ. Toulouse*, 13 (1937) 163.

Iudex sacrarum cognitionum. See IUDICANS.

Iudex specialis. A judge assigned to a particular case by his superior. The term seems to be a postclassical (Justinian's?) creation.

Iudex suspectus. A judge whose impartiality is doubted. He may be rejected by the parties involved in a litigation. The term appears only in later imperial constitutions.

Iudex tutelaris (tutelae). A term interpolated for *praetor tutelaris*.

Iudex unus. One judge conducting the part of the trial called *apud iudicem*. See IN IURE, IUDEX. Ant. *decemviri, centumviri* as collegiate courts, and *recuperatores*, a tribunal of three judges.—See IUDICIUM LEGITIMUM.

J. Mazeaud, *La nomination du iudex u. dans la procédure formulaire*, 1933; Wenger, *ZSS* 55 (1935) 424.

Iudicans. See IUDEX.

Iudicans vice sacra. A judge appointed by the emperor to decide in his name as an appellate judge. Syn. *iudex sacrarum cognitionum*.

De Ruggiero, *DE* 2, 323.

Iudicare. The judicial activity, the rendering of a judgment, or decision by a person who is acting as a judge in civil or penal proceedings. In criminal matters, *iudicare* is opposed to *coërcere* (COËRCITIO) which is not preceded by an ordinary trial. In ancient law, *iudicare* is syn. with *adiudicare* = to adjudge a person to his creditor on account of an unpaid debt. —See RES IUDICATA, EXCEPTIO REI IUDICATAE, IUDICATUM.

Betti, *RISG* 56 (1915) 31; M. Kaser, *Das altröm. Ius*, 1949, 126.

Iudicare iubere (iussum iudicandi). The order given by the praetor to the private judge to pass judgment according to the terms of the written formula.

Steinwenter, *RE* 9, 2468; Wlassak, *SbWien* 197, 4 (1921); Lauria, *St Bonfante* 2 (1930) 506; E. Carrelli, *La genesi del procedimento formulare*, 1946, 121.

Iudicare vetare. To remove a *iudex* who is or has become unable to exercise his duties.

Iudicatio. See IUDICARE. In the language of later constitutions *iudicatio* = a judgment (syn. with *sententia*).

Iudicatum. The condemnatory judgment (*sententia*) as well as its contents, i.e., the sum of money which the defendant was condemned to pay to the victorious plaintiff, *iudicatum* = the judgment-debt. Under the classical law the defendant had to pay the judgment-debt within thirty days; otherwise he was sued by the plaintiff in a special action for the execution of the *iudicatum*, *actio iudicati*. The action was initiated in the same way as any other action; it was terminated in the *in-iure* stage through a decree of the praetor ordering fulfillment of the judgment-debt. See ADDICTUS. Only when the defendant contested the validity of the judgment or asserted that he had paid his debt, did the *actio iudicati* come before a private judge (*apud iudicem*), and if the allegations of the defendant proved untrue, he was condemned to pay double. In certain cases the defendant was bound to give security that the judgment-debt will be paid (*cautio, satisdatio iudicatum solvi*), e.g., when a representative appeared at the trial on his behalf. If the defendant appointed a COGNITOR, he had to provide the guaranty himself; if a *procurator* acted for him, however, the *procurator* gave the security *iudicatum solvi*. Other instances in which such a security was obligatory were when the defendant was a bankrupt (see DECOCTOR), when his property was seized by his creditors by virtue of a *missio in possessionem*, when an heir suspected of insolvency (see HERES SUSPECTUS) was sued, or when a debtor who had been condemned in a previous trial and did not pay the judgment-debt was sued by *actio iudicati*.—D. 46.7.—See CAUTIO IUDICATUM SOLVI, TEMPUS IUDICATI, DUCI IUBERE, MANUS INIECTIO, RES IUDICATA, EXCEPTIO REI IUDICATAE.

Steinwenter, *RE* 9; Cuq, *DS* 3; L. Wenger, *Die Lehre von der actio i.*, 1901; P. Gay-Lugny, *La cautio i. solvi*, 1906; Duquesne, *Mél Gerardin*, 1907, 197; *idem*, *Mél Fitting* 1 (1907) 321; Pflüger, *ZSS* 43 (1923) 153; Liebman, *St Bonfante* 3 (1930) 397; Biondi, *ibid.* 4 (1931) 35.

Iudicatus. A defendant in a civil trial against whom a judgment has been rendered.—See IUDICATUM.—Syn. *condemnatus*.

Iudices civiles—militares. In imperial constitutions, civil and military officials exercising special jurisdiction in fiscal and military matters.—C. 1.45; 46; 48.

Iudices decemviri. See DECEMVIRI STLITIBUS IUDICANDIS.

Iudices delecti. Jurors selected from the panel (see ALBUM) for a specific trial.

Iudices maiores—minores. A distinction made in the later Empire and by Justinian between superior and inferior courts.

Iudices sacri. Judges appointed by the emperor primarily for appellate matters.

Iudices selecti. Persons entered in the official panel of jurors (see ALBUM).

Iudicia. See IUDICIUM and the subsequent items.

Iudicialis. Connected with the functions of a *iudex* or the administration of justice.—See STIPULATIONES IUDICIALES.

Iudiciarius. Referring to judicial proceedings; see LEGES IUDICIARIAE.

Iudicio sistere (se sisti). See SISTERE ALIQUEM.

Iudicium (iudicia). Used in various technical senses. It is frequently syn. with ACTIO and comprises the whole process without regard to bipartition; at other times it indicates only the second stage, *apud iudicem,* i.e., the proceedings before the private judge. Not seldom *iudicium* refers to the written formula (*iudicium in rem, in factum*) and at times to the act which separates the two stages of the classical process, the LITIS CONTESTATIO (e.g., *ante iudicium, iudicium contestari*). The elasticity of the term diminishes in the cognitio proceedings in which the distinction *in iure*—*apud iudicem* no longer exists. There it denotes the whole trial and refers generally to any proceedings before an official acting in a jurisdictional capacity. Finally *iudicium* is used of the judgment itself (syn. *sententia*) by which the trial is brought to an end. This last use is hardly classical. Justinian's compilers frequently inserted the term *iudicium* to replace references to the bipartition of the classical process, in particular when the classical text alluded to the stage *in iure* or when mention of a classical institution obsolete in Justinian's time had to be deleted (see VADIMONIUM). In criminal matters *iudicium* refers to the trial as a whole as well as to its initial act (*accusatio*) and the process pending (see IUDICIA PUBLICA). The various meanings of *iudicium* are clarified by the context in which the word appears.—D. 5.1; C. 3.1.—See EXCEPTIO REI IN IUDICIUM DEDUCTAE and the following items (IUDICIA for various types of actions, IUDICIUM for specific actions, both civil and penal).

Leonhard, *RE* 9; Humbert and Lécrivain, *DS* 3; Flore, *DE* 4; Kübler, *ZSS* 16 (1895) 137; Jobbé-Duval, *Mél Cornil* 1 (1926) 532; Beseler, *ZSS* 46 (1926) 131, 52 (1932) 292; Lenel, *ZSS* 47 (1927) 29.

Iudicia absolutoria. See ABSOLUTORIUS.

Iudicia arbitraria. See ACTIONES ARBITRARIAE.

Iudicia bonae fidei. Contractual actions in which through the clause *ex fide bona* in the INTENTIO of the written formula the judge (*iudex*) was given full power to decide the controversial matter according to the principles of good faith, i.e., to estimate what should be paid by the defendant to the plaintiff. The pertinent clause does not refer to the actionability of the case but to the extension of the performance required of the defendant. All actions arising from consensual or real contracts (except *mutuum*), the *actio tutelae, rei uxoriae, negotiorum gestorum,* and some others were *bonae fidei*. The authority given

to the *iudex* was broad and it increased gradually; he might take into account formless pacts added to actionable contracts immediately after their conclusion and modifying their effects (*pacta conventa*). Ant. *iudicia stricta* (*actiones stricti iuris*), the formulae of which had no clause *ex fide bona*. There the judge could take into consideration only what was expressed in the formula.—See ACTIONES IN BONUM ET AEQUUM CONCEPTAE, CONDEMNATIO.

Longo, *StSen* 22 (1905); De Francisci, *ibid.* 24 (1907) 346; Biondi, *AnPal* 7 (1920) 3; *idem, BIDR* 32 (1922) 61; C. Zevenbergen, *Karakter en geschiedenis der i.b.f.,* Amsterdam, 1920; Grosso, *StUrb* 1927, 1928; *idem, RISG* 3 (1928); Koschembahr-Lyskowski, *St Riccobono* 2 (1936) 159; F. De Martino, *La giurisdizione,* 1937, 95; Daube, *ZSS* 68 (1948) 92.

Iudicia contraria. Syn. *actiones contrariae:* see ACTIONES DIRECTAE, IUDICIUM CONTRARIUM.

Iudicia directa. See ACTIONES DIRECTAE.

Iudicia duplicia. Actions in which each party is both plaintiff and defendant. This is the case in divisory actions for the partition of common property (*actio communi dividundo, actio familiae erciscundae*). The term *interdicta duplicia* is to be understood in the same sense.—See INTERDICTA SIMPLICIA.

Berger, *St Simoncelli* (1915) 185; Leone, *AnBari* 6 (1943) 187.

Iudicia extraordinaria. Trials conducted in the form of proceedings *extra ordinem.* See COGNITIO EXTRA ORDINEM. An interpolated text (D. 3.5.46.1) says: "In *iudicia extraordinaria* the use of written formulae (*conceptio formularum*) is not observed." Ant. *iudicia ordinaria.*

Iudicia generalia. Trials in which a complex of disputed matters is examined and decided upon. This occurs when a person (a guardian, a partner, or a *negotiorum gestor*) administers all or much of another's affairs. Ant. *iudicia specialia* in which the litigation concerns one specific matter, as in the case of *actio mandati, depositi, commodati,* etc. All actions *in rem* in which a specific thing (not a complex of things, *universitas*) is claimed are *actiones speciales*. The distinction is important in cases in which a special action concurs with a general one or when the settlement of a special controversy appears necessary before a general action can be brought against the adversary.

Peters, *ZSS* 32 (1911) 179.

Iudicia legitima. Trials between Roman citizens which took place in Rome or within the first milestone of the city, before one judge (IUDEX UNUS) only. Ant. *iudicia quae imperio continentur* (*iudicia imperio continentia*), in which any one of these requisites is missing. The former are governed by statutory law (see LEGITIMUS), the latter depend upon the *imperium* of the jurisdictional magistrate. A *iudicium legitimum* expires (*moritur* = "dies," see LIS MORITUR) if the trial has not been brought to an end within eighteen months from its beginning (LEX

IULIA IUDICIARIA), whereas a *iudicium quod imperio continetur* expires with the termination of the *imperium* of the magistrate before whom the trial began.

 Bonifacio, *St Arangio-Ruiz* 2 (1952) 207.

Iudicia ordinaria. Ant. of IUDICIA EXTRAORDINARIA.

Iudicia poenalia. In a broader sense, merely criminal trials. Syn. *poenales causae.* In a narrower sense (syn. with *actiones poenales*) = civil trials involving a penalty to be paid to the plaintiff.

Iudicia populi. Trials in criminal matters before the popular assembly (*comitia*) when a Roman citizen had been condemned by a magistrate to capital punishment or to a fine (see MULTA) exceeding the legal maximum (thirty oxen and two sheep or 3,000 asses). In the first case the *comitia centuriata* were competent, in the second the *comitia tributa.* The introduction of the *quaestiones* procedure diminished the role of the *iudicia populi.*

 Berger, *OCD*; E. E. Hardy, *JRS* 3 (1913) 25; Brecht, *ZSS* 59 (1939) 261.

Iudicia privata. See ACTIONES PRIVATAE. Ant. IUDICIA PUBLICA.

 Leonhard, *RE* 9.

Iudicia publica. Proceedings in criminal matters. Ant. *iudicia privata.* The distinction is clearly manifested in the Augustan legislation (*lex Iulia iudiciaria*) which deals separately with *iudicia publica* and *iudicia privata.*—Inst. 4.18; D. 48.1.

 Leonhard, *RE* 9; Humbert and Lécrivain, *DS* 3; Gatti, *AG* 113 (1935) 59, 115 (1936) 44; Pugliese, *Riv. dir. processuale civile,* N.S. 3, 1 (1948) 63.

Iudicia quae imperio continentur. See IUDICIA LEGITIMA.

 Nicolau, *Rev. de philologie* 9 (1935) 352.

Iudicia specialia. See IUDICIA GENERALIA.

Iudicia stricta. See IUDICIA BONAE FIDEI.

Iudicis postulatio. See POSTULATIO IUDICIS.

Iudicium accipere. Refers to the acceptance by the defendant of the procedural formula proposed by the plaintiff. Through such an agreement made under the supervision of the praetor, the object of the controversy is fixed (*lis contestata*) and the stage *in iure* of a civil trial comes to an end. *Post iudicium acceptum* = after *litis contestatio.*—See LITIS CONTESTATIO.

 Wlassak, *RE* 1 (*s.v. accipere i.*).

Iudicium calumniae (actio calumniae). An action for *calumnia* (see CALUMNIA). If a defendant was sued maliciously, the plaintiff having full knowledge that his claim was unjust, and was absolved, he could bring an action against his adversary for a tenth of the amount claimed in the former trial, but he had to prove that the latter acted *calumniae causa* (= with chicanery).—See IUDICIUM CONTRARIUM.

 Hitzig, *RE* 3, 1420.

Iudicium Cascellianum. A special trial (*iudicium secutorium*), when the defendant against whom the praetor issued a possessory interdict, did not obey

the order.—See INTERDICTUM, AGERE PER SPONSIONEM.

 Berger, *RE* 9, 1693; 1697.

Iudicium centumvirale. Refers to the second stage in a trial before the centumviral court. The first stage took place before the jurisdictional magistrate (the praetor).—See CENTUMVIRI.

Iudicium contrarium. A counter-action brought by a defendant against a plaintiff who had sued him inconsiderately and had lost the claim. Such a counter-suit was admissible only in a few specific cases, e.g., with regard to an *actio iniuriarum.* In a *iudicium contrarium* the former plaintiff was condemned for one tenth of his unsuccessful claim, even if he had acted without malicious intention. The *iudicium contrarium* concurs with *iudicium calumniae.*—See IUDICIUM CALUMNIAE.

 G. Provera, *Contributi alla teoria dei iudicia contraria, MemTor* 75 (1951).

Iudicium curationis. A term used by Justinian for the action which a ward under curatorship (see CURA) could bring against his curator for damages resulting from bad management of the ward's affairs. In classical law the pertinent action was the *actio negotiorum gestorum.*—D. 27.3.—See ACTIO CURATIONIS CAUSA UTILIS.

Iudicium de moribus. See ACTIO DE MORIBUS.

Iudicium de operis libertorum. See OPERAE LIBERTI.

Iudicium domesticum. A domestic court in which the head of the family (*pater familias*) exercised his jurisdiction over family members under his power. It was an ancient, customary institution in which his unlimited power (see IUS VITAE NECISQUE) found its most evident expression. In the case of major crimes he was assisted by the family council (*concilium propinquorum*) but the judgment lay with him. For women *sui iuris* and those under tutorship, the *iudicium domesticum* was composed of their nearest relatives.

 Humbert and Lécrivain, *DS* 3; Düll, *ZSS* 54 (1943); Volterra, *RISG* 85 (1948) 103.

Iudicium imperio continens. See IUDICIA LEGITIMA.

 Nicolau, *Revue de philologie* 9 (1935) 352.

Iudicium liberale. See CAUSA LIBERALIS.

Iudicium noxale. See NOXA.

Iudicium operarum. See OPERAE LIBERTI, IURATA PROMISSIO LIBERTI.

Iudicium petitorium. See FORMULA PETITORIA.

Iudicium quinquevirale. A tribunal in the later Empire, composed of five senators under the chairmanship of the *praefectus urbi,* for criminal offenses committed by senators.

 C. H. Coster, *The i.q.* (Cambridge, Mass., 1935); *idem, Byzantinische Zeitschr.* 38 (1938) 119.

Iudicium rectum. See ACTIONES DIRECTAE.

Iudicium restitutorium. See ACTIO RESTITUTORIA.

Iudicium secutorium. See AGERE PER SPONSIONEM.

Iudicium societatis. Syn. *actio pro socio;* see SOCIETAS.

Iudicium supremum (ultimum, testatoris). A last will (testament).

Iudicium triumvirale. See TRIUMVIRALE IUDICIUM.

Iugatio terrena. A tax paid on landed property. It is to be distinguished from the poll-tax, *capitatio humana.* The term *iugatio* comes from the land unit, *iugum,* which served as the basis for the assessment of the tax to be paid in natural products of the soil (*annona*).—See IUGUM.

> Thibault, *Revue générale du droit, de la législation* 23 (1899) 481.

Iugum (iugerum). A plot of land (three-fifths of an acre) "which two oxen can plow in one day."—See IUGATIO TERRENA.

> A. Déléage, *La capitation du Bas-Empire,* 1945, *passim.*

Iulianus, Salvius. A jurist of the second century, member of the imperial council under Hadrian, pupil of Iavolenus and teacher of Africanus, the last known head of the Sabinian school. In his official career he held many important posts from the tribunate to the governorship of several provinces as is testified by a well preserved inscription (CIL 8, 24094) found in North Africa, near Hadrumetum, where he may have been born. Iulianus was one of the outstanding Roman jurists, an original and independent thinker, whose works, in particular his DIGESTA, are among the most highly appreciated products of the Roman juristic literature. At Hadrian's initiative, he revised the praetorian edict; see EDICTUM PERPETUUM. His Digesta (in 90 books) were richly excerpted by the compilers of Justinian's Digest and frequently quoted by later classical jurists. It is a comprehensive collection of *responsa* on real and hypothetical cases; in general, it followed the edictal system. Julian also wrote commentaries on works of two earlier, little known jurists, Urseius Felix and Minicius, and a booklet *De ambiguitatibus* (= on doubtful questions). With Iulianus, the Roman jurisprudence reached its apogee.

> Pfaff, *RE* 1A, 2023; Orestano, *NDI* 6 (*s.v. Giuliano*); L. Boulard, *Salvius I.,* 1902; Rechnitz, *St zu S.I.,* 1925; Solazzi, *St Besta* 1 (1937) 17; A. Guarino, *S.I.,* 1946 (Bibl.); D'Orgeval, *RHD* 26 (1948) 301; Berger, *St in memoria di Albertario* 1 (1952) 605; Wolff, *Sem* 7 (1949) 69; Kunkel, *Iura* 1 (1950) 192; *idem, Herkunft und soziale Stellung der röm. Juristen,* 1952, 157; R. Reggi, *Studi Parmensi* 2 (1952) 105.

Iumentum. A beast of burden (horse, mule, ass). The edict of the aediles laid down certain rules concerning the sale of *iumenta,* and the liability of the seller for physical defects and diseases of the animal, similar to the provisions referring to the sale of slaves. Through an additional clause (*elogium*) the rules were expanded to other kinds of cattle (*pecus*) and domestic animals.—See EDICTUM AEDILIUM, ACTIO REDHIBITORIA, PECUS.

> H. Vincent, *Le droit des édiles,* 1922.

Iuniani. See LATINI IUNIANI.

Iuniores—seniores. Each *centuria* in the early military organization consisted of two groups, *seniores* (men from forty-six to sixty) and *iuniores* (men under forty-six). The *seniores* formed the reserve troops.—See TABULAE IUNIORUM.

Iungere. See ACCESSIO, TIGNUM IUNCTUM.—*Iungi* (= *se iungere*) = to be tied to another person by marriage or kinship.

Iura—leges. See LEX.

Iura praediorum. Rights attached to an immovable property, servitudes. For the various *iura praediorum,* see SERVITUTES PRAEDIORUM RUSTICORUM, SERVITUTES PRAEDIORUM URBANORUM, and the pertinent items.

Iuramentum. An oath. See IUSIURANDUM.

Iuramentum calumniae. See IUSIURANDUM CALUMNIA, ACCUSATIO.

Iurare (iurari). To take an oath.—See IUSIURANDUM.

Iurare bonam copiam. A rather obscure expression which appears in connection with the *Lex Poetelia Papiria* on *nexi* and is linked with an oath of the debtor, apparently about his pecuniary inability to pay his debts.

> Steinwenter, *RE* 10, 1259; Berger, *RE* Suppl. 7, 406; Humbert, *DS* 1 (*b.c. iurare*); G. Rotondi, *Leges publicae pop. rom.,* (*Encicl. giur. ital.* 1912) 231; P. Noailles, *Ius et fas,* 1948, 109; Berger, *St Arangio-Ruiz* 2 (1952) 117.

Iurare in leges. Taking an oath by a magistrate when entering office to the effect that he would observe the laws. The oath was administered by a *quaestor.*—See EIURATIO.

> Kübler, *RE* 14, 416; Steinwenter, *RE* 10, 1257; R. Maschke, *De magistratuum Romanorum iure iurando,* 1884.

Iurare sibi non liquere. A private judge (*iudex*) in a civil proceeding to whom the controversy did not appear sufficiently clarified, so that he felt unable to render a judgment, might take an oath that the matter "was not clear to him." He was released from the trial which was then submitted to another judge (*translatio iudicii*). For criminal cases, see AMPLIATIO.

> Leonhard and Weiss, *RE* 13, 726; Lemosse, *Cognitio,* 1944, 164.

Iurata promissio liberti. A promise under oath by which a manumitted slave assumed the duty of rendering certain services to his patron. In order to ascertain whether the slave would make such a promise after his manumission, it was usual to allow him to take the oath before he was freed, which created only a religious duty for him. After his manumission the *iurata promissio liberti* produced a civil, contractual obligation under oath. The pertinent action was *iudicium operarum.*

> Cuq, *DS* 3, 771; M. Chevrier, *Du serment promissoire,* 1921, 90.

Iuratores. Reliable persons who assisted the censors in their work of registering the citizens (see CENSUS) and who administered an oath to them on the truth of their declarations.

> Passerini, *DE* 4.

Iuratorius. See CAUTIO IURATORIA.

Iuratus. A person who upon assuming a public office, even a temporary one, took an oath before entering service.

Passerini, *DE* 4.

Iure. (Abl.) According to the law, legally, lawfully, in particular with reference to the solemn formalities prescribed by the law. '*Iure valere* = to be legally valid. *Non iure = iniuriā* (abl.).—See IPSO IURE, MERITO.

Riccobono, *ZSS* 34 (1913) 224.

Iure suo uti. See UTI SUO IURE.

Iure uti. (In phrases like *hoc* [*eo, quo*] *iure utimur.*) In this way the jurists used to refer to a legal norm still valid, particularly to one established in an imperial rescript, in order to stress the fact that it was still applicable. The phrases are not linked with *responsa*. Occasionally they were interpolated by Justinian's compilers when they wished to point out that the classical rule has remained unchanged. There is, however, no reason to exclude all such phrases from the classical juristic language.

Berger, *KrVj* 14 (1912) 440; Guarneri-Citati, *Indice²*, 1927, 51; Magdelain, *RHD* 28 (1950) 169.

Iurgium. Used of those kinds of legal controversies which are brought before an arbitrator, such as disputes on division of property or on boundaries between neighboring properties, or quarrels between family members. It is opposed in a certain measure to LIS. Later both terms were used rather indiscriminately.

Leonhard, *RE* 10; Cuq, *DS* 3; Brunelli, *NDI* 7; A. Magdelain, *Origines de la sponsio*, 1943, 192.

Iuri alieno subiectus. See ALIENI IURIS.

Iuridicatus. The office of a *iuridicus*. See IURIDICI in provinces.

Iuridici. In Italy, jurisdictional magistrates of senatorial rank, introduced by Marcus Aurelius with competence in civil and criminal matters. Territorially their competence was limited to one or more districts (REGIONES) into which Italy was divided. There were four *iuridici* altogether. In their jurisdiction in civil matters, fideicommissary and tutelary controversies were of particular importance. They also had jurisdiction in administrative disputes (e.g., *munera*, corn supply).—D. 1.20.—See DIOECESIS URBICA, REGIONES ITALIAE.

Rosenberg, *RE* 10; Jullian, *DS* 3; Samonati, *DE* 4; Berger, *OCD*.

Iuridici. In provinces, high officials of provincial administration with broad activity in judicial matters (*legati iuridici*) concurrent with that of the governor. The official title of the *iuridicus* in Egypt was *iuridicus Aegypti* with the frequent addition, *et Alexandreae*. —C. 1.57.

For bibl. see IURIDICI in Italy; Wlassak, *Zum röm. Provincialprozess*, *SbWien* 190, 4 (1919) 59; Balogh, *ACDR* Roma 2 (1935) 309; v. Premerstein, *RE* 10, 1151; Coroi, *Actes V-e Congrès Papyr. Oxford* (Brussels, 1938) 628.

Iuridici dies. See DIES IURIDICI.

Iuris auctor. See IURISPERITUS.

Iuris conditor. See CONDERE IURA.

Iuris est. (In such locutions as *id iuris est, certi, manifesti iuris est.*) "This is the law" in a specific question submitted to a jurist for opinion. *Quid iuris est* (= what is the law?) is the corresponding interrogatory phrase.—See IURE UTI, IUS CERTUM.

Iuris scientia. The knowledge of the law, jurisprudence.—See syn. IURISPRUDENTIA.

Iuris sui (or **alieni**) **esse.** See ALIENI IURIS.

Iurisconsultus. A jurist. The word alludes to the activity of the jurists as *qui consuluntur*, i.e., who are consulted for an opinion in a legal matter and who give *responsa* to the consultants (*consultator*). Other terms are *iurisperitus* (*iuris peritus*), *iuris prudens*, or simply *prudens*. The jurists "enjoyed the highest esteem among the Roman people" (Cic. *de orat.* 1.45.198). Their profession was considered one which "cannot be evaluated or dishonored by a price in money" (D. 50.13.1.5).—See IURISPERITUS, IURISPRUDENTIA, IUS RESPONDENDI, RESPONSA.

Berger, *RE* 10, 1164; Kübler, *Die klass. Juristen und ihre Bedeutung für die Rechtsentwicklung, ConfMil* 1931, 128; Massei, *Scr Ferrini* (Univ. Pavia, 1946) 42; Magdelain, *RHD* 28 (1950) 4; W. Kunkel, *Über Herkunft und soziale Stellung der röm. Juristen*, 1952.

Iurisdictio. (From *ius dicere*.) The power and activity of *ius dicere*, i.e., of settling legal principles which serve to adjust controversies. The term covers any judicial activity in civil matters, and in a broader sense, all activity connected with the administration of justice. With reference to the praetor, the jurisdictional magistrate *par excellence* of the classical times, it embraces all his acts and orders issued during the stage *in iure* of a civil trial, such as the appointment of a *iudex* (private juror), the grant of an action to the plaintiff as well as its denial (DENEGATIO), the order to the judge to decide the case in dispute, and so on. The power of *iurisdictio* is given to all magistrates with *imperium*; magistrates of lower rank (*magistratus minores*) had only a limited *iurisdictio* (see AEDILES). In a territorial sense, *iurisdictio* refers to the judicial district in which a magistrate may exercise his jurisdictional rights. The judicial activity of municipal magistrates is also covered by the term. Under the Empire, all higher officials are vested with *iurisdictio*. With reference to provincial governors the term comprehends the whole administration of the province, which is a sign of the extension in the significance of *iurisdictio* in later times. The classical *iurisdictio* refers only to the activity of judicial magistrates and imperial officials, and not to the activity of the private judge developed in the stage *apud iudicem* in a civil trial. The transition from the bipartite process to the *cognitio* procedure could not remain without influence on the content of *iurisdictio*, which was applied thereafter to any official acting as a *iudex* (*iudices*) in the broad sense which this term acquired in the later

Empire; see IUDEX. "A person provided with *iuris-dictio* shall not *ius dicere* in matters in which he himself, his wife or children, his freedmen or other persons of his household are involved" (D. 2.1.10).—D. 2.1; Cod. 3.13.—See the following items, FORUM, IUDEX IN RE PROPRIA.

> Steinwenter, *RE* 10; Cuq, *DS* 3; Lauria, *NDI* 5; Bozza, *DE* 4; F. Leifer, *Die Einheit des Gewaltgedankens* (1914) 68, 86; L. Falletti, *Evolution de la juridiction civile,* Thèse Paris, 1926; Lauria, *St Bonfante 2* (1930) 479; F. de Martino, *La giurisdizione nel dir. rom.,* 1937; C. Gioffredi, *Contributi allo studio del proc. civ. rom.* 1947, 9.

Iurisdictio contentiosa. Jurisdiction in cases involving a legal controversy between the parties to the trial. Ant. *iurisdictio voluntaria* = the intervention of a magistrate in matters in which there is no quarrel between the parties and the fictitious trial serves only as a way of performing certain legal acts or transactions (*in iure cessio, emancipatio, adoptio, manumissio*). *Iurisdictio voluntaria* also comprises cooperation of officials in guardianship matters and legal acts for the validity of which a permission of the competent authority is required. The distinction is important inasmuch as some magistrates who have no full *iurisdictio* may intervene in acts of *iurisdictio voluntaria* and as the personal interest of the magistrate is not a hindrance to the performance before him of such acts as adoptions, manumissions, emancipations in which he himself or his next relatives are involved.

> Solazzi, *AG* 98 (1927) 3; Gonnet, *RHD* 16 (1937) 193.

Iurisdictio delegata. The delegation of jurisdiction by the emperor to an official or a private person to examine a case (*delegatio causae*) and render judgment, either in the first instance or in appellate procedure. Such a jurisdictional delegate (*ex divina delegatione*) may subdelegate the matter to another judge. On the other hand, *iurisdictio delegata* occurs when a higher official (one of the prefects in Rome, a proconsul in the province) delegates another to act in a certain kind of judicial affair, or for a limited period or in a single case. The right of the provincial governors to delegate their jurisdiction was reduced to minor matters by imperial legislation of the fourth century or to exceptional situations when the governor was overburdened with jurisdictional duties, in order to relieve him to a certain extent. Through the delegation of jurisdiction a new instance arose because an appeal from the decision of the *iudex delegatus* to the *delegans* was admissible. In this important point the *iurisdictio delegata* differs from *iurisdictio mandata*. Ant. *iurisdictio propria.*—See IURISDICTIO, IURISDICTIO MANDATA.

> De Ruggiero, *DE* 2, 321; H. J. Conrad, *Die i.d. im röm. und kanon. Recht,* 1930 (Diss. Köln).

Iurisdictio extraordinaria. (In the language of the imperial chancery.) Jurisdiction in the *cognitio* procedure.

Iurisdictio iudicis. (Of postclassical origin.) After the disappearance of the bipartite civil procedure there was no further reason to distinguish between the functions of a magistrate and those of the private judge. Hence *iurisdictio iudicis* refers to the judicial activity of any public official.—C. 3.13.

> F. De Martino, *La giurisdizione nel dir. rom.,* 1937, 177.

Iurisdictio mandata. Jurisdiction transferred through mandate by a magistrate vested with *iurisdictio* to another person (magistrate or not). "He who assumes *iurisdictio mandata* has no right of his own but exercises the jurisdiction of his mandator" (D. 1.21.1.1). Therefore, he is not authorized to appoint another as a mandatary and his jurisdictional rights are extinguished when the mandator revokes his mandate or dies. An appeal from the decision of the mandatary goes not to the mandator but to his superior. The transfer of jurisdiction through mandate was widely practiced in the Republic. One of its most developed applications was the *iurisdictio mandata* of the *legatus proconsulis* in the provinces, who received his jurisdictional powers from the proconsul. There was a rule that "what is assigned to a magistrate by a statute, a senatusconsult or an imperial constitution as a special assignment, cannot be transferred to another as a *iurisdictio mandata*" (D. 1.21.1 pr.); only what belonged to the province of his magistracy (*ius magistratus*) might be entrusted to another through mandate. Ant. *iurisdictio propria.*—See IURISDICTIO DELEGATA.—D. 1.21.

> Steinwenter, *RE* 10, 1157.

Iurisdictio praetoria. The jurisdiction of the praetor. It embraces not only his activity in civil trials (in the stage *in iure*) but also his edictal creations (the issuance of new legal rules, formulae, interdicts, etc.).

> Betti, *St Chiovenda,* 1927.

Iurisdictio voluntaria. See IURISDICTIO CONTENTIOSA.

Iurisperitus. A man learned in the law, a professional jurist. The term alludes to his knowledge of the law, while *iurisconsultus* refers rather to a jurist consulted in legal matters. See IURISCONSULTUS. Syn. *iuris auctor, iuris prudens* (or simply *prudens*), *iuris conditor.*

> Massei, *AG* 133 (1946) 48; idem, *Scr Ferrini* (Univ. Pavia, 1946) 428.

Iurisprudens. See the foregoing item.

Iurisprudentia. Defined as "the knowledge of divine and human matters, the knowledge of what is just and what unjust" (D. 1.1.10.2). *Iurisprudentia* is syn. with *iuris scientia:* it is knowledge of the law in the broadest sense of the word, the science of the law. The Roman jurists were the most important element in the development of the Roman law, and with good reasons they are named *iuris auctores, iuris conditores;* see CONDERE IURA. This refers in particular to the classical period of Roman jurisprudence, i.e., in the last century of the Republic and the two centuries and a half of the Principate. The creative influence of their *responsa,* their literary and teaching activity, their participation in the councils of judicial magistrates and private judges as *assessores,* and later in the imperial *consilium* as legal advisers of the emperors furthered the development of the law through creative and progressive ideas based on the understanding of the necessities of the life, to which they adapted their opinions and doctrines taking into consideration the changes in the economic, political, and social development of the empire. They did not care for philosophical doctrines and conceptions, for precise definitions or etymologies, but they had a keen eye for the exigencies of everyday legal life with which they were constantly in touch in their various capacities. The high value of their works does not lie in theoretical deliberations and doctrinal speculations, but in the elaboration of a systematic structure of the law as a whole, in the gradual building up of a legal system composed of legal institutes with an admirable logical strength and guided by ideas which justify the conception of the law as *ars boni et aequi.* The juristic literature of the classical period acquired particular significance in the later Empire in spite of its completely different political, economic, and social structure, through the so-called Law of Citations, issued in 426 by Theodosius II. It laid down rules for the use of classical juristic writings as authorities in legal matters. The works of Papinian, Paul, Ulpian, Modestinus, and Gaius were established as the principal authorities. Their views had to be considered authoritative in legal disputes. Works of jurists other than the five mentioned might be taken into consideration only if they were quoted by the primary authorities and if those quotations could be strengthened by a comparison with the original works. In the case of divergent opinions of the jurists, the majority was decisive; if there was no majority, the opinion of Papinian prevailed. If none of these criteria was applicable the judge had free choice in rendering judgment. The greatest homage paid to the works of the classical jurists was Justinian's Digest, based as it was exclusively on excerpts from them.—D. 1.2; C. 1.17. For particular jurists, see the pertinent items; for their literary products, see DIGESTA, INSTITUTIONES, RESPONSA, QUAESTIONES, REGULAE, NOTAE, EDITIO SECUNDA.—See IUS EST ARS BONI ET AEQUI.

Jörs, *RE* 3, 2608 (*s.v. Citiergetz*); Solazzi, *NDI* 7 (*Legge delle citazioni*); Berger, *RE* 10; *OCD* 472; Riccobono, *NDI* 7; E. Seckel, *Das röm. R. und seine Wissenschaft,* 1920; F. Senn, *Les origines de la notion de jurisprudence,* 1926; Donatuti, *La definizione di Ulpiano,* *AG* 98 (1927) 51; Stella-Maranca, *Hist* 8 (1934) 640; F. Pringsheim, *Höhe und Ende der röm. Jurisprudenz,* 1933; La Pira, *La genesi del sistema nella giurisprudenza rom.,* *St Virgilii* 1935, *BIDR* 42 (1934) 336, *SDHI* 1 (1935) 319, *BIDR* 44 (1936–37); Biscardi, *StSen* 53 (1939); Riccobono, *Scr Ferrini* (Univ. Pavia, 1946) 17; Biondi, *ibid.* 201; Grosso, *ibid.* 251; Massei, *ibid.* 438 (on Law of Citations); Kagan, *Tulane Law Rev.* 21 (1946) 192; Schulz, *History of R.*

Legal Science, 1946; Schiller, *The Jurists and the Prefects of Rome,* RIDA 3 (= *Mél De Visscher* 2, 1949) 319; F. Wieacker, *Über das Klassische in der röm. Jurisprudenz,* 1950; Biondi, *Scr Carnelutti* 1 (1950) 97; idem, *St Arangio-Ruiz* 2 (1952) 79.

Ius (iura). In the Roman juristic language, *ius* has different meanings. In the broadest sense the term embraces the whole of the law, the laws (*iura populi romani*), without regard to the source from which they emanate. When used with a special attribute it applies to a bigger field of the law (*ius publicum, privatum, honorarium,* etc.) or to exceptional provisions (*ius singulare*). Even references to a single legal provision are not missing. The meaning of *ius* as *the* law in general is reflected in expressions like *iure* (abl.) = legally, in conformity with the law, or *ipso iure* = by virtue of the law itself. Allusions to specific legal provisions are in locutions such as "*idem* IURIS EST" or "*quid iuris est?*" when a question is put concerning the specific norm to be applied in a particular case. Conceived as the whole of the law originating from various sources—hence the distinction between *ius* and *lex* (a statute which is a source of *ius*)—the *ius* is defined by the jurist Celsus "IUS EST ARS BONI ET AEQUI" (see AEQUITAS) which is not far from another formula expressed by the jurist Paul, "what always is just and fair (*aequum et bonum*) is called *ius*" (D. 1.1.11 pr.). The fundamental principles (*praecepta*) of the *ius* are "to live honestly, not to do harm to anybody, to give any one what is his (*suum cuique tribuere*)" (D. 1.1.10.1). Along with the juxtaposition *ius—lex,* not always exactly distinguished by the jurists, there is another one, *ius—fas,* see FAS. Beside the use of the term in the objective sense as "the law," *ius* is applied to indicate the subjective right or rights (*iura*) of an individual, as the right to do something in a certain legal situation, to acquire a thing or to dispose of it, to claim something from another. In this sense the praedial servitudes are called *iura praediorum,* and the general term, *ius in re aliena,* is coined. Almost synonymous with *ius* in this meaning are the expressions *facultas* and *potestas* although the legal element is not explicit in them. The patrimonial rights of an individual as a whole are termed *iura* or simply *ius* (*universum*), as in the locution *successio in ius. Ius* also indicates the personal status of a person, as in the technical phrases, *sui* (or *alieni*) *iuris esse,* a distinction made according to whether a person is under the power of another or legally independent. With regard to landed property, *ius* may indicate the legal situation thereof including servitudes and liens (*ius fundi*). A specific meaning is attached to *ius* in procedural language. *Ius* is the place where the magistrate (praetor) administers the law. Hence the stage of a civil trial which takes place before him is named IN IURE. Here "the term is transferred from what is being done (*ius dicitur*) to the place where it is done" (D. 1.1.11). Hence some procedural institutions have their denomination, as *in ius vocatio, interrogatio in iure, confessio in iure.* Slight shades of difference in the meaning of *ius* will be found in the following entries, which deal with some more important expressions in which *ius* (or *iura*) is connected with either a noun or an adjective. In the language of the later imperial constitutions and of Justinian, *ius* appears in associations unknown in the classical juristic language.—Inst. 1.1; D. 1.1.— See IURE, IPSO IURE, IURISDICTIO, IURIS ESSE, AUCTORES, AUCTORITAS, IGNORANTIA, SOLLEMNIA, IN IURE, IN IURE CESSIO, INTERROGATIO, CONFESSIO, RIGOR IURIS, REGULA IURIS, and the following items.

> Leonhard, *RE* 10; Cuq, *DS* 3; Biondi, *NDI* 7; May, *Mél Gérardin,* 1907, 402; Clark, *Mél Fitting* 1 (1907) 241; Kamphuisen, *RHD* 11 (1932) 389; Villey, *Le droit subjectif et les systèmes juridiques rom., RHD* 24–25 (1946/7) 201; Goidanich, *Atti Accad. d'Italia,* Sez VII, vol. 3 (1943) 499; M. Kaser, *Das altrömische Ius* 1949, 29; D'Ors, *St Albertario* 2 (1952) 279.

Ius abstinendi. See ABSTINERE SE HEREDITATE.

Ius acta conficiendi (actorum conficiendorum). The right of magistrates and imperial officials to keep public records.—See ACTA.

Ius adcrescendi. The law of accrual under which the portion of a co-owner increases, as, for instance, if a co-owner manumits a common slave, the manumission being void, the other co-owner acquires full ownership over the slave (Justinian ordered the slave freed). In the law of succession, the share of a co-heir increases when the other co-heir fails to take his share under the will or on intestacy.

> Leonhard, *RE* 10; Humbert, *DS* 3; P. Bonfante, *Scritti giuridici* 3 (1926) 434; Macqueron, *RHD* 8 (1929) 580; Vaccaro-Delogu, *L'accrescimento nel dir. ereditario,* 1941; U. Robbe, *Ius a. e la sostituzione volgare,* 1947.

Ius adeundi. See ADITUS.

Ius adfinitatis. A relationship based on *adfinitas.*— See ADFINITAS.

Ius aedificandi. The owner of a plot of land has the right to construct a building on it, provided that his neighbor has no title under which to protest. In the case of a neighbor's unjustified protestation, the builder has an action against the neighbor in which he claims his right (*ius*) *sibi esse ita aedificatum habere,* i.e., to build the house in the way he wants to do it. On this occasion he also has the possibility of claiming some specific servitudes (e.g., *servitus altius tollendi, immittendi*) to which he is entitled. In the case of common property the *ius aedificandi* depends upon the consent of all the co-owners any one of whom may exercise the *ius prohibendi* (right of prohibition) against the partner who intends to build.—See AEDIFICATIO, OPERIS NOVI NUNTIATIO.

Ius Aelianum. See AELIUS PAETUS CATUS.

Ius aequum. See AEQUITAS.

> Pringsheim, *ZSS* 42, 643.

Ius agendi (iumentum). The right to drive draft animals through another's property.—See ACTUS, VIA.

Ius agendi cum populo (cum patribus, cum plebe). The right to convoke a popular assembly (*comitia*), primarily for legislative purposes. It was granted to the highest magistrates (consuls, praetors, dictators). A similar right of the plebeian tribunes to convoke the plebeian assemblies (*concilia plebis*) was the *ius agendi cum plebe.* The *ius agendi cum patribus* refers to the convocation of the senate which under the Principate was a prerogative of the emperor.

> Fadda, *NDI* 1, 238.

Ius agnationis. Rights deriving from the agnatic relationship. See AGNATIO.

Ius altius tollendi. See SERVITUS ALTIUS TOLLENDI.

Ius ambulandi. See ITER, VIA.

Ius anuli aurei. The right to wear a golden ring. It was a privilege of persons of equestrian rank.—D. 40.10; C. 6.8.—See EQUITES, RESTITUTIO NATALIUM.

Ius antiquum. The earlier law referred to for comparison with new legal provisions. In imperial constitutions of the later Empire and with Justinian, *ius antiquum* denotes the classical law, sometimes going as far back as the Twelve Tables. Syn. *ius vetus,* ant. *ius novum.*

Ius appellandi (appellationis). The right to appeal to a higher court. Syn. *auxilium appellationis.*—See APPELLATIO.

Ius applicationis. The relationship created through a voluntary placing of oneself under the protection of a powerful person (*patronus*) by a solemn act, *applicatio ad patronum.* The individual, a plebeian or a stranger (*peregrinus*), thus became a client (see CLIENTES) of the patron.

> Premerstein, *RE* 4, 32; Manigk, *RE* 10.

Ius aquaeductus (aquae ducendae). See SERVITUS ADQUAEDUCTUS.

Ius augurium. The sacral rules concerned with the activity of the augurs. They were collected in Books of the *augures* (*libri augurum* or *augurales*).—See AUGURES.

Ius auspiciorum. See AUSPICIA.

Ius auxilii. The right of the plebeian tribunes to assist a plebeian wronged by an official act of a patrician magistrate.—See TRIBUNI PLEBIS.

Ius (iura) belli. The rules which governed the conduct of war. They were observed by the Romans from the moment of the formal declaration of war.— See BELLUM INDICERE.

Ius caduca vindicandi. See CADUCA, CADUCORUM VINDICATIO.

Ius calcis coquendae. A praedial servitude of lime-burning on another's land.

Ius capiendi. The right to take under a will.—See CAPAX, CADUCA, LEGES CADUCARIAE.

Ius certum. Phrases like *certi iuris est* or *certo iure utimur* are used in juristic writings and imperial constitutions to indicate that the opinion of the jurist or the imperial decision is beyond question because it is based on a certain, doubtless legal rule. In the language of the imperial chancery, particularly in Justinian's time several analogous expressions occur as *certissimi, explorati, evidentissimi, indubitati, manifesti, manifestissimi iuris est* (or in the nominative *ius est*).

Ius civile. With regard to the sources from which the *ius civile* derives, a definition given by Papinian says "*ius civile* is the law which emanates from statutes (*leges*), plebiscites, decrees of the senate (*senatus-consulta*), enactments of the emperor and from the authority of the jurists" (D. 1.1.7). Ant. *ius praetorium (honorarium).* Etymologically *ius civile* denotes the law of a given *civitas* or of the citizens; with reference to Rome it is the *ius civile proprium Romanorum.* Syn. in earlier times IUS QUIRITIUM. To the republican jurists, *ius civile* was the law among the *cives,* applied in their mutual relations, therefore the private law. The earliest treatises on *ius civile,* entitled *Libri iuris civilis* or *Commentarii iuris civilis* (or *de iure civili*), therefore deal almost exclusively with the private law. In a narrower sense, the interpretation of the law by the men learned in law is called *proprium ius civile* (= *ius civile* proper). One of the most renowned textbooks on the *ius civile* was the LIBRI IURIS CIVILIS by the jurist Sabinus. His system was followed by later writers on the *ius civile,* who called their works "*ad Sabinum.*"—A counterpart of *ius civile* is *ius honorarium (praetorium)* on the one hand, the IUS GENTIUM on the other.—Inst. 1.2.—See the following item.

Weiss, *RE* 10; Pacchioni, *NDI* 2 (*diritto civile*); Berger, *OCD*; E. Ehrlich, *Beiträge zur Theorie der Rechtsquellen,* 1902; B. Biondi, *Prospettive romanistiche,* 1933; 40; Lauria, *Scritti Ferrini* (Pavia, 1946) 595; G. Segrè, *Interferenze, ravvicinamenti e nessi fra diritto civile e pretorio,* ibid. 729; De Francisci, *Scritti Ferrini* 1 (Univ. Sacro Cuore, Milan, 1947) 192; Gioffredi, *SDHI* 13–14 (1948) 12; M. Kaser, *Das altrömische Ius,* 1949.

Ius (iura) civitatis. The law of any state; with regard to Rome, *ius proprium civitatis nostrae* (*iura populi Romani, iura Romanorum*).—See IUS CIVILE.

Ius codicillorum. The law of codicils. It is considered as a special law (*ius singulare*).—D. 29.7.—See CODICILLI.

Ius coërcendi. See COËRCITIO.

Ius coëundi. The right of assembly granted to associations (*collegia*).

P. W. Duff, *Personality in R. law,* 1938, 94.

Ius cognationis. A relationship based on cognatic ties (*cognatio*).

Ius cognoscendi. See COGNOSCERE.

Ius commercii. A privilege granted to Latin colonies to have contractual relations, to trade with Roman citizens on equal terms, and to use the forms of contract available to Roman citizens. By a special act, the *ius commercii* could be conceded to other categories of foreigners, to communities, and even to individuals. The technical term for *ius commercii* is *commercium.*—See COMMERCIUM.

Ius commune. The general law common to all, the law which is binding on all peoples or all Roman citizens. Ant. *ius singulare, privilegium. Ius commune omnium hominum* (the law common to the whole of mankind) is opposed to the *ius proprium* (the law proper) of one nation, for all its citizens (*ius civile*).—See IUS SINGULARE, PRIVILEGIUM

Orestano, *AnMac* 11 (1937) 24.

Ius compascendi (compascui). See COMPASCERE.

Ius conubii. The right to conclude a marriage recognized by the law. Originally it was limited to patricians, until the passage of the LEX CANULEIA which permitted marriages between patricians and plebeians. Later, the *ius conubii* was extended to citizens of foreign communities, either generally or by special concession. The *ius conubii* of the parties was a necessary condition of the validity of the marriage. —See CONUBIUM (Bibl.).

Ius (iura) consanguinitatis. The reciprocal rights of persons who have the same father (brothers and sisters).—See CONSANGUINITAS.

Ius constitutum. A norm of the existing law without regard to the source from which it originates. Hence, customary law is *ius moribus constitutum.* Some legal decisions in the sources are proffered *iure constituto.*

Ius controversum. A concept familiar to rhetoricians and not to Roman jurists. It refers to legal norms which were controversial among jurists (*ambigitur inter peritissimos,* Cic. *de orat.* 1.57.242). Syn. *ius dubium, ambiguum* (in later imperial constitutions). Ant. *indubitatum ius.*

Schwarz, *Fschr Schulz* 2 (1951) 201.

Ius crediti. The creditor's right against the debtor.

Ius debiti. A debt. Syn. DEBITUM.

Ius deliberandi. See DELIBERARE.

Ius dicere (reddere, statuere). Refers to the jurisdictional activity of the magistrates, primarily of the praetor.—See IURISDICTIO.

F. De Martino, *Giurisdizione* 1937, 56.

Ius distrahendi. The creditor's right to sell the pledge (*fiducia, pignus*) if the debtor did not pay the debt due. Originally admitted only when it was agreed upon between debtor and creditor (*pactum de distrahendo pignore*), it was later considered to be self-understood unless expressly excluded by agreement (*pactum de non distrahendo pignore*).—Syn. *ius vendendi.*—D. 20.5; C. 8.27; 28.

Messina-Vitrano, *Per la storia del i.d.,* 1910; Ratti, *StUrb* 1 (1927); De Villa, *StSas* 10 (1938); Bartošek, *BIDR* 51–52 (1948) 238; A. Burdese, *Lex commissoria e ius vendendi,* 1949, 131.

Ius divinum (iura divina). Laws created by the gods and governing the relations of men to the gods. Ant. *ius humanum (iura humana).* A similar, but not identical distinction, is *fas—ius.*—See FAS, RES DIVINI IURIS.

Berger, *RE* 10, 1212; Orestano, *BIDR* 46 (1939) 195.

Ius dominii. The right of ownership. The term is rare in the Digest, more frequent in Justinian's Code. —See DOMINIUM.

Ius domum revocandi. See IUS REVOCANDI DOMUM.

Ius dotium. Legal provisions concerning the dowry.— D. 23.3; C. 5.12.—See DOS.

Ius ecclesiasticum. (With Justinian.) Church laws. *Ad ius ecclesiasticum pertinens* = governed by church laws.—See ECCLESIA.

Ius edicendi. The right of the higher magistrates to proclaim edicts (*edicta*) to the people. The contents of the edicts were manifold, according to the sphere of functions of the magistrate. The *ius edicendi* was an important element in the development of the law since the edicts dealt primarily with legal and procedural problems and introduced innovations into the existing law.—See EDICTA, EDICTUM, IUS HONORARIUM.

Kipp, *RE* 5, 1940; Louis-Lucas and A. Weiss, *DS* 2, 457.

Ius emphyteuticum (emphyteuticarium). See EMPHYTEUSIS.—C. 4.66.

Cascio, *AnPal* 22 (1951).

Ius est ars boni et aequi. "Law is the art of finding the good and the equitable." This unique definition of *ius* in the legal sources is expressed in the initial text of the Digest (D. 1.1.1 pr.).—See AEQUITAS, BONUM ET AEQUUM, IUS (Bibl.).

Arnò, *ATor* 75 (1939/40); Riccobono, *Quaderni di Roma* 1 (1947) 32; *idem, BIDR* 53–54 (1948) 5 and *AnPal* 20 (1949) Biondi, *Scr Ferrini* (Pavia, 1946) 209; v. Lübtow, *ZSS* 66 (1948) 578; P. Koschaker, *Europa und das röm. Recht*, 1947, 334; A. Carcaterra, *Justitia nelle fonti*, Bari, 1949, 42; Biondi, *Ius* 1 (1950) 107; F. Schwarz, *ArCP* 152 (1952) 214.

Ius eundi. See ITER, ACTUS, VIA.

Ius ex scripto (ex non scripto). See IUS SCRIPTUM.

Ius exilii (exulandi). The term in literature for the possibility given a person threatened by the death penalty in a criminal trial to avoid the capital sentence by voluntarily leaving Roman territory.—See EXILIUM.

Berger, *OCD* 353; Arangio-Ruiz, *Storia*⁵ (1947) 81; Gioffredi, *SDHI* 12 (1946) 191; *idem, Archivio penale* 3 (1947) 428.

Ius experiri. See EXPERIRI.

Ius extraordinarium. A rare term in the juristic sources (once in the Digest in a suspect text, D. 50.16.10, and once in the Code, 7.73.5). It is linked with the COGNITIO EXTRA ORDINEM. See IUS NOVUM. The expression *ius extra ordinem* used sometimes in literature does not occur in juristic sources.

Ius fetiale. The norms concerning primarily the solemn forms to be observed by the priests called *fetiales* in relations between Rome and other states.—See FETIALES.

De Ruggiero, *DE* 3, 71; C. Phillipson, *International Law of Ancient Greece and Rome* 2 (1911) 315.

Ius (iura) fisci. The state treasury (*fiscus*) occupied a privileged situation as creditor, with various advantages when acting as claimant in a trial or against an insolvent debtor, when taking a vacant inheritance or seizing private property for one reason or another. The complex of rules which determine the rights of the fisc is the *ius fisci* (*ius fiscale*).—"The norms of fiscal law cannot be overthrown by private agreements" (D. 2.14.42). Syn. *privilegia fisci.*—D. 49.14; C. 7.73; 10.1; 5; 9.—See FISCUS, BONA VACANTIA, CADUCA.

Wieacker, *Fschr Koschaker* 1 (1937).

Ius fruendi. See USUSFRUCTUS, FRUCTUS.

Ius Flavianum. A collection of forms of civil actions, compiled about 300 B.C. by Gnaeus Flavius, a freedman, secretary of the jurist Appius Claudius.

Danneberg, *RE* 10; Cuq, *DS* 3, 745; Gabrieli, *NDI* 6 (*s.v. Flavio Gneo*); Zocco-Rosa, *NDI* 7; E. Pais, *Ricerche sulla storia e sul dir. rom.* 1 (1915) 215.

Ius gentilicium. The law concerning the *gentiles* (members of a *gens*).—See GENS, GENTILES.

Bernhöft, *ZVR* 36 (1918), 99.

Ius gentium. Apart from the meaning, rather rare in the sources, that the *ius gentium* is the law governing the relations of Rome with other states (see IURA BELLI, LEGATI, FOEDUS, RECUPERATORES, etc.), the term appears frequently in juristic sources in a somewhat confused picture. On the one hand, it is linked with *ius naturale,* or at least with the *naturalis ratio* which dictates the same law to all peoples. This results from the definition given by Gaius, D. 1.1.9, "what *naturalis ratio* introduced among all men is observed by all peoples and called *ius gentium,* as the law applied by all peoples." Gaius thus gives the term the sense of *ius omnium gentium* which therefore is not opposed to the Roman law proper since the Romans are included among all peoples. Gaius' definition was fully adopted by Justinian in his Institutes (1.2.1) with a confusing introduction which treats *ius civile* and *ius gentium* as synonyms. The *ius gentium* is also linked with *ius naturale* in other texts, the genuineness of which is rather suspect, however. On the other hand, *ius gentium* appears in quite another shape as the product of the political and economic growth of the Roman state. Contact with foreign territories in the Mediterranean basin that were gradually conquered, commercial relations with those nations and the necessity of considering their legal customs in Roman courts when transactions were concluded in Rome, the jurisdictional activity of the *praetor peregrinus,* created expressly for the latter purpose and given the power to recognize transactions which the Roman *ius civile* did not recognize—all this promoted the development of a new legal system beside the formalistic *ius civile,* which was not accessible to peregrines. The formalism of the ancient law had to be sacrificed in favor of the development of international trade and the peregrines had to be admitted to Roman institutions. The admission of the Greek language in the thoroughly Roman STIPULATIO is one of the most characteristic examples of this development. That the new legal rules and institutions should be extended to transactions concluded between Roman citizens was a natural further step in the development, leading finally to a fusion of the two systems. It was particularly in the contractual field that the *ius gentium* exercised its influence, primarily by strengthening the element of reciprocal confidence (*fides*) without which relations with foreigners were hardly possible. The law of family and succession remained completely untouched. One common basis for all applications of *ius gentium* in the juristic sources could not be established. The intrusion of Greek philosophical ideas, *ius naturale* and *naturalis ratio*, brought in a certain confusion which makes it very difficult to separate what is classical from what is of later origin.—Inst. 1.2.—See IUS NATURALE NATURALIS RATIO, PEREGRINI.

Weiss, *RE* 10; Cuq, *DS* 3, 134; Longo, *RendLomb* 40 (1907); Bögli, *Beiträge zur lehre vom i.g.*, 1913; Clark, *Illinois Law Rev.* 14 (1919–1920) 243; Schönbauer, *ZSS* 49 (1929) 383; C. A. Maschi, *La concezione naturalistica*, 1937, 245; Lauria, *Fschr Koschaker* 1 (1939) 258; Kaser, *ZSS* 59 (1939) 67; Lewald, *Archeion Idiotikou Dikaiou* 13 (1946) 55; G. Lombardi, *Ricerche in tema di i.g.*, 1946; idem, *Sul concetto di ius gentium*, 1947 (Bibl. 3); De Martino, *AnBari* 7–8 (1947) 107; Riccobono, *AnPal* 20 (1949) 17; Kaser, *Das altrömische Ius*, 1949, 82; Frezza, *NuovaRDCom* 2 (1949) 26 (= *RIDA* 2, 259); Grosso, *RIDA* 2 (1949) 395; Solazzi, *ACIVer* 3 (1951) 307.

Ius gestorum. The right of certain higher officials in the Empire (the time of Constantine) to make an official record of declarations of private individuals or of documents presented to them. By this procedure the validity of the acts was officially strengthened. *Cf.* IUS ACTA CONFICIENDI.

H. Steinacker, *Die antiken Grundlagen der frühmittelalterlichen Privaturkunde*, 1927, 76.

Ius gladii. "The power to punish criminal individuals" (D. 2.1.3) with all kinds of punishment, the death penalty included. In Rome it was the emperor himself who exercises the right in capital trials. He could delegate it to the supreme officials in the provinces (governors, *legati*) and to the prefects in Rome, at first only in a specific case, later generally.—Syn. *potestas gladii.*

De Ruggiero, *DE* 3, 532; H. Pflaum, *Essai sur les procurateurs equestres*, 1950, 117.

Ius habitandi. The right to dwell in another's house. It may be based on a personal servitude (*habitatio*) or on a lease contract (*locatio conductio rei*).

Ius harenae fodiendae. The right (servitude) = to dig sand from another's sand-pit.

Ius hereditarium. The rights of an heir (HERES) as opposed to the rights of a legatee. *Iure hereditario* = by virtue of universal succession as heir.

Ius honorarium. The law introduced by the magistrates who had the right to promulgate edicts (*ius edicendi*) in order to support (*adiuvare*), supplement (*supplere*) or correct (*corrigere*) the existing law *propter utilitatem publicam* (in the interest of the community, D. 1.1.7.1), i.e., by taking into consideration the exigencies of the developed legal and economic life. A prominent jurist, Marcian, characterized the *ius honorarium* as the *viva vox iuris civilis* (= the living expression of the citizen's law, D. 1.1.8). The *ius honorarium* which consisted primarily of procedural remedies, developed into a legal system parallel to the *ius civile* in the strict sense (see IUS CIVILE). In practice, it gradually prevailed because of its more simplified forms and its accessibility to substantive and procedural innovations demanded by the changing economic and social necessities. Within the framework of the *ius honorarium* as a whole the *ius praetorium* is the larger portion by virtue of the edictal and jurisdictional activity of the praetors whereas the contribution of the *aediles* (*ius aedilicium*) is more modest. The *ius praetorium* was a decisive element in the development of the Roman law although it does not appear as a complete legal system covering the whole field of law and although it fluctuated somewhat dependent as it was upon the annual edicts of the praetors. In its final crystallization (see EDICTUM PERPETUUM) the *ius honorarium* assumed the shape of a complex of procedural measures which did not change the structure of the original legal institutions but which reformed their protective aspect in a way which sometimes produced essential changes in the existing law.

Cuq, *DS* 3, 244; Hruza, *Zum. röm. Amtsrechte*, 1908; Frese, *ZSS* 43 (1922) 466; Betti, *La creazione del diritto nella iurisdictio del pretore, St Chiovenda*, 1927, 67; Lauria, *Scr Ferrini* (Pavia, 1946) 639; G. Segrè *ibid.*; Steinwenter, *Anzeiger Akad. Wien*, 1946, no. 19; G. Grosso, *Premesse generali al corso di dir. rom.*, 1946, 82.

Ius honorum. The right of a Roman citizen to stand for office. Generally only free-born were admitted to magisterial offices.

Weiss, *RE* 10.

Ius humanum (iura humana). 'A counterpart to *ius divinum*. It is created by men and it is protected by sanctions imposed by men. Its field is the governance of relations between man and man. The distinction between *ius humanum* and *ius divinum* appears in the definition of marriage (see NUPTIAE) and in the division of things into *res divini et humani iuris.*

Berger, *RE* 10, 1212, 1238.

Ius imaginum. The privilege of a noble Roman family to have the portrait masks (*imagines*) of the ancestors of the family carried at the funeral of a deceased family member. Usually the masks were exhibited in a shrine in the atrium.

Schneider-Meyer, *RE* 9, 1097; Courbeaud, *DS* 3, 412; Bruck, *Sem* 7 (1949) 39.

Ius imperandi. See IMPERIUM. The term is used with regard to the father's (or master's) right to give orders to his son (or slave).

Ius in agro vectigali. The right of a lessee of an *ager vectigalis*. The lease of such a plot of land belonging to a public corporate body (*municipium, colonia*) is the classical precedent of EMPHYTEUSIS. —See AGER VECTIGALIS.

Cascio, *AnPal* 22 (1951) 27.

Ius in re (aliena). A right in the property owned by someone else, such as servitude, pledge, *emphyteusis, superficies*. Such rights impose restrictions on the exercise of the rights of ownership by the owner. The classical jurists do not use as technical either the term *ius in re* in the meaning of ownership (*dominium*) or the term *ius in re aliena* (familiar in the literature) in the meaning explained above.

Arangio-Ruiz, *AG* 81 (1908) 361, 82 (1909) 417; Viley, *RIDA* 2 (1949) 417.

Ius (iura) ingenuitatis (ingenui). The political rights of a freeborn, such as *ius suffragii, ius honorum*.

Ius iniquum. See AEQUITAS.

Ius intercedendi. See INTERCESSIO, TRIBUNI PLEBIS.

Ius Italicum. The privileges granted non-Italian provincial cities and communities by the emperor (from the time of Augustus) through a special law (*lex data*) by which they acquired the legal status of Italian cities as developed in the last century of the Republic. The *ius Italicum* comprised various rights both of public and private character, such as self-government, exemption from the supervision by the governor of the province, land ownership *ex iure Quiritium*, to which mere Roman institutions (*mancipatio, usucapio*) were applicable.

V. Premerstein, *RE* 10; Jullian, *DS* 3; Luzzatto, *RIDA* 5 (= *Mél De Visscher* 4, 1950) 79; Vittinghoff, *ZSS* 68 (1951) 465.

Ius (potestas) iubendi. See IUBERE.

Ius lapidis eximendi. See LAPIS.

Ius Latii. Rights connected with the legal position of colonies founded by the Romans as Latin colonies, and with the legal status of the citizens of such colonies. The *ius Latii* could be granted individually to foreigners (*peregrini*) the legal situation of a Latin having been more advantageous than that of other peregrines; it was, of course, less favorable than that of a Roman citizen.—See LATINI.

Steinwenter, *RE* 10; A. N. Sherwin-White, *The Roman Citizenship*, 1939, 30, 103; Vitucci, *DE* 4, 442; F. Vittinghoff, *Röm. Kolonisation und Bürgerrechtspolitik* (*Abh. Akad. Wiss. Mainz* 1951, no. 14) 43.

Ius legationis (legatorum). The rules governing the position of, and the relations with, the ambassadors of foreign countries. The *ius legationis* is "sacred (*sacrum, sanctum*) with all nations" (Cornelius Nepos, *Pelop.* 5.1; *cf.* D. 50.7.18).—See LEGATI.— *Ius legationis* is also the privilege granted to subjugated cities to send embassies to Rome.

G. Lombardi, *Il concetto di ius gentium*, 1947, 105.

Ius liberorum. Parents of several children enjoyed certain privileges, first introduced by the Augustan legislation (LEX IULIA ET PAPIA POPPAEA). Fathers might claim exemption (*excusatio*) from public charges and from guardianship to which they were called by law (*tutela legitima*). The most important application of *ius liberorum* concerned women. A freeborn woman with three children and a freedwoman with four children (*ius trium vel quattuor liberorum*) were freed from guardianship to which women were subject (*tutela mulierum*) and had a right of succession to the inheritance of their children. The women's *ius liberorum* was applied even when the children were no longer alive.—C. 5.66; 8.58.—See SENATUSCONSULTUM TERTULLIANUM.

Steinwenter, *RE* 10; Cuq, *DS* 3 (*s.v. liberorum ius*); Turchi, *Atene e Roma* 17 (1941) 333; Arangio-Ruiz, *FIR* 3 (1943) 71.

Ius mariti. Mentioned specifically in connection with adultery when the accusation of the wife is made by the husband *iure mariti*.—See ADULTERIUM.

De Dominicis, *SDHI* 16 (1950) 1.

Ius militare. Military law, applied to soldiers both in the field of criminal offences and military discipline, as well as with regard to some institutions of the private law (testament).—See MILITIA, MILITES, TESTAMENTUM MILITIS.

Ius militiae. See MILITIA.

Ius mixtum. A law originating from both a statute and a custom.

Ius mortuum inferendi. See IUS SEPULCRI, INTERDICTUM DE MORTUO INFERENDO, RES RELIGIOSAE.

Ius multae dicendae. See MULTA.

Ius naturale (ius naturae, iura naturalia). Natural law (laws). Unknown to Republican jurists, the *ius naturale* is not considered by those of the Principate a juristic conception denoting a special sphere of law, a particular category of law, or a system of legal norms. Nor do the occasional "definitions" of the *ius naturale*, found in the sources, give the picture of a certain uniformity of the conception, although the influence of Greek philosophy is evident. Striking by its peculiarity is the explanation of the term given by Ulpian: "that which nature taught all animals" (D. 1.1.1.4), followed by examples such as union of male and female, procreation and rearing of the young. The saying has no juristic content at all, and did not get any by the repetition in Justinian's Institutes (1.2 pr.). Quite different is the definition by Paul: "what always (at all circumstances) is just and right (*quod semper est bonum et aequum*)" (D. 1.1.11 pr.), but here the notion of an ideal law is expressed rather than what is the *ius naturale* within a legal system. The connection with *aequitas* is apparent also in several texts which speak of *naturalis aequitas*. Elsewhere, the *ius naturale* is identified with IUS GENTIUM as the law which all nations observe. Both *ius gentium* and *ius naturale* are linked with *naturalis ratio* (natural reason); nevertheless on another occasion, with reference to slavery, *ius naturale* is opposed to *ius gentium* inasmuch as *naturali iure* all men are born free, and it was the *ius gentium* which introduced slavery (*iure gentium servitus invasit,* D. 1.1.4 = Inst. 1.5. pr.). Although those definitions may be considered of classical and not of Byzantine origin (as has often been assumed in recent literature), no one of them was elaborated as a doctrine by the Roman jurists, whose practical sense was centered more on the positive law, its interpretation, and applicability or extension to the actual necessities of life. The mark *"iure naturali"* attached to a legal institution or a decision by a jurist means "by the natural order of things, by the reality of life," without any legal background. Combining an earlier idea with Christian doctrines, Justinian found a new formulation of *naturalia iura:* "they are those which are equally observed by all nations, and are somehow established by divine providence; they remain firm and unchangeable for ever" (Inst. 1.2.11). This Justinian doctrine produced in literature the tendency to ascribe many, if not all, sayings involving *ius naturale* or the related locutions, as *naturalis aequitas, naturalis ratio,* etc., to Justinian's compilers. As a matter of fact, in a few passages retouched by the compilers *naturalis ratio* was substituted by *ius naturale.* A great majority of the pertinent texts may be considered to be of classical origin, as recent, comprehensive studies on all the expressions mentioned have shown.—Inst. 1.2.—See AEQUITAS NATURALIS, IUS, RATIO, IUS GENTIUM, NATURALIS LEX.

Cuq, *DS* 3, 736; Longo, *RendLomb* 40 (1907); Goudy, *Trichotomy in Roman Law,* 1910; F. Senn, *De la justice et du droit,* 1927, 76; Arnò, *Atti Modena* 10 (1926) 127; E. E. Hoelscher, *Vom römischen zum christlichen Naturrecht,* 1931; Kamphuisen, *RHD* 11 (1932) 389; Albertario, *Studi* 5 (1937) 277; C. A. Maschi, *La concezione naturalistica del diritto e degli istituti giuridici romani* (Milan, Pubbl. Univ. Sacro Cuore, 1937); Orestano, *Riv. intern. di filosofia di diritto* 21 (1941) 21; G. Grosso, *Problemi generali del diritto,* 1948, 98; De Martino, *AnBari* 7–8 (1947) 107; L. Wenger, *Naturrecht und das röm. R., Wissenschaft und Weltbild* 1 (1948); E. Levy, *Natural law in the Roman period* (Univ. of Notre Dame Natural Law Institute Proceedings 2, 1949) 43 (reprinted in *SDHI* 15, 1949); H. Mitteis, *Über das Naturrecht,* 1948; Wenger, *Ius* 2 (1951) 1; Bartosek, *St Albertario* 2 (estr. 1950) 492; R. Voggensperger, *Der Begriff des i.n. im röm. R.* (Basel, 1952); Gaudemet, *ADO–RIDA* 1 (1952) 445.

Ius non scriptum (sine scripto). See IUS SCRIPTUM, CONSUETUDO.

Ius novum. A term which is more frequently used in the recent Romanistic literature than in the sources. Gaius uses it once in the meaning of the law which originates in *senatusconsulta* and imperial constitutions as opposite to the law of the Twelve Tables. In the literature *ius novum* is referred to the imperial law arising from imperial legislation and jurisdiction and the practice of the *cognitio extra ordinem.* The latter meaning is that of the term *ius extraordinarium* which occurs only once in a text not free from suspicion (D. 50.16.10). In Justinian's language *ius novum* is applied with regard to the emperor's own innovations.—See IUS EXTRAORDINARIUM.

Riccobono, *ACSR* 2 (1929) 235; *idem, Archiv für Rechts- und Wirtschaftsphilosophie* 16 (1922/3) 520; *idem, Mél Cornil* 2 (1926) 235; Chiazzese, *AnPal* 16 (1931) 31; G. Grosso, *Problemi generali,* 1948, 76; S. Riccobono, Jr., *Il Circolo giuridico* 20 (Palermo, 1949) 162.

Ius offerendae pecuniae. The right of a hypothecary creditor to offer the prior pledgee the sum due to him by the common debtor. Thus the later creditor gained the priority in the hypothecary degree which belonged to the pledgee whom he paid out.

Ius ordinarium. The normal law applied in regular proceedings. *Iure ordinario* = in the way of normal proceedings (*ordo iudiciorum*) as opposed to the *cognitio extra ordinem.*—See IUS EXTRAORDINARIUM.

Ius originis. See ORIGO.

Ius paenitendi (poenitendi). A term used in literature, but unknown in legal sources.—See PAENITENTIA.

Ius Papirianum. See PAPIRIUS.

Ius pascendi. The right (*servitude*) to pasture cattle on another's property.

Ius patris. The right of the father of the family. It is mentioned when the paternal power of the father over his children enters into account. A specific use of the term appears in connection with the father's right to accuse his daughter of adultery *iure patris.* —See IUS VITAE NECISQUE, ADULTERIUM, IUS MARITI.

Ius (iura) patronatus (patroni). The rights of a patron over the person and the inheritance of his freedman.—D. 37.14; C. 6.4.—See LIBERTUS, PATRONATUS, OPERAE LIBERTI, OBSEQUIUM.

Ius perpetuum. A right analogous to *ius emphyteuticarium,* based on an irrevocable grant of agricultural land (belonging to imperial domains) to individuals for a rent (*canon*). It is alienable.—*Cf.* EMPHYTEUSIS, IUS IN AGRO VECTIGALI.

E. Bassanelli, *La colonia perpetua,* 1933; Levy, *West Roman vulgar law,* 1951, 43.

Ius pignoris. See PIGNUS.

Ius piscandi. The right to fish in the sea, harbors and public rivers. It is free to all.

Ius pontificium. The laws governing the life and activity of the pontiffs of which they are both creators and guardians. Monographs were written on *ius pontificium* by Fabius Pictor and Fabius Maximus Servilianus. In their activity the pontiffs dealt often with questions of the *ius civile.* Therefore it was said: "No one can be a good pontiff without knowledge of the *ius civile*" (Cic. de leg. 2.19.47).—See PONTIFICES.

Berger, *RE* 10; Stella-Maranca, *AnBari* 1927.

Ius populi. The interest of the people.—See ACTIONES POPULARES.

Ius possessionis. Occurs in a few texts in which it denotes either the right to take possession of another's thing or the rights connected with the exercise of possession.

Vassalli, *AnPer* 28 (1914) 40; Solazzi, *BIDR* 49–50 (1947) 367.

Ius postliminii. See POSTLIMINIUM.

Ius praetorium. "The law which the praetors introduced in order to support, to supplement or to amend the *ius civile*" (D. 1.1.7.1). Its development intensified after the reform of the civil procedure initiated by the LEX AEBUTIA.—See IUS HONORARIUM.

> Riccobono, *Fusione del ius civile e praetorium, Archiv für Rechts- und Wirtschaftsphilos.* 16 (1922/3) 503; Frese, *ZSS* 43 (1923).

Ius privatum. The law which governs the relations among individuals and primarily concerns the benefit of private persons. Ant. IUS PUBLICUM.—See UTILITAS PRIVATA.

> Leonhard, *RE* 3; Cuq, *DS* 3, 732; E. Ehrlich, *Beiträge zur Theorie der Rechtsquellen,* 1902. For recent bibl. see IUS PUBLICUM.

Ius prohibendi. The right to prevent another from doing something. Its particular significance appears among co-owners or between neighbors when a praedial servitude entitles a person to prohibit a certain action on the neighbor's land.—See ACTIO PROHIBITORIA, COMMUNIO, IUS AEDIFICANDI. A group of interdicts serve for the protection of *ius prohibendi* in various situations; see INTERDICTA PROHIBITORIA, OPERIS NOVI NUNTIATIO.

> Pacchioni, *Riv. dir. commerciale* 10 (1912); P. Bonfante, *Scritti giuridici* 3 (1926) 382.

Ius publice respondendi. See IUS RESPONDENDI.

Ius publicum. The law which is concerned with the existence, organization (status) and functioning of the state. Ant. *ius privatum* which was concerned with the interest of private individuals. What is in the interest of the state or the people (*publice utilia*) belongs to field of *ius publicum*. The law dealing with sacred things (*sacra*), priests, and magistrates (government, administration) is *ius publicum*. The distinction between *ius publicum* and *ius privatum*, originating under the influence of Greek philosophy, is based on the juxtaposition of the state and the individual. Sometimes the law dealing with relations between private persons are attributed to *ius publicum*, when a general or social interest concurs with a private one (marriage, guardianship). The public law thus conceived in a larger sense "cannot be changed by agreements concluded between private individuals" (D. 2.14.38; 50.17.45.1). The law which emanates from legislative organs of the state, mainly from statutes passed by the people (*populus*) is also named *ius publicum* from which *senatusconsulta* and imperial constitutions are not excluded.—See IUS PRIVATUM.

> Leonhard, *RE* 10; Cuq, *DS* 3, 732; E. Ehrlich, *Beiträge zur Theorie der Rechtsquellen,* 1902; Stella-Maranca, *Le due positiones dello studium iuris, Studi Barillari, AnBari* 1936; S. Romano, *Scr Santi Romano* 4 (1940) 159; Coli, *Parallelismo del dir. pubblico e privato, SDHI* 4 (1938); Lombardi, *Il concetto di i.p. in Cicerone, RendLomb* 72 (1938/9) 465; G. Nocera, *Ius publicum* (D.2.14.38), Roma, 1946; De Francisci, *Scr Ferrini* 1 (Milan, 1947) 211; G. Grosso, *Problemi generali,* 1948, 84; Gioffredi, *SDHI* 13–14 (1948) 87; *idem, St Solazzi,* 1948, 461; Berger, *Iura* 1 (1950) 102; Kaser, *SDHI* 17 (1951) 267.

Ius Quiritium. The ancient national law of the Romans, a rigorous formalistic law of a primitive rural community. The term is used in the classical period as a contrast to the modernized law originating from other sources (*ius praetorium, ius gentium*).—For *ex iure Quiritium,* see EX FIDE BONA, DOMINIUM EX IURE QUIRITIUM.

> Weiss, *RE* 10; Moschella, *NDI* 7; C. L. Kooiman, *Fragmenta iuris Quiritium,* 1914 (Amsterdam); De Visscher, *Fschr Schulz* 2 (1951) 71; A. Guarino, *L'ordinamento giur. rom.* 1 (1949) 82; *idem, Iura* 1 (1950) 265.

Ius reddere. See IUS DICERE.

Ius respondendi (ius publice respondendi). The right granted by the emperor (from the time of Augustus) to prominent jurists to give answers (*responsa*) in juristic questions "on the personal authority of the emperor" (*ex auctoritate principis*). The Augustan reform produced the distinction between licensed (authorized) and not licensed jurists since many jurists continued the republican usage to give *responsa* without being authorized by the emperor. The imperial permission was a personal distinction; the jurists, thus authorized did not acquire any official character nor were their *responsa* legally binding on the magistrates or judges who had asked for them.—See RESPONSA PRUDENTIUM, AUCTORITAS PRINCIPIS.

> Berger, *RE* 10, 1166; De Visscher, 15 (1936) 615 (= *Nouvelles Études,* 1949, 296); Siber, *ZSS* 61 (1911) 397; Massei, *Scr Ferrini* (Pavia, 1946) 32; F. Schulz, *History of R. Legal Science,* 1946, 112; Kunkel, *ZSS* 66 (1946) 422; Guarino, *RIDA* 2 (1949) 401; *idem, AnCat* 4 (1949–1950) 209; Magdelain, *RHD* 28 (1950) 1, 157; Daube, *ZSS* 67 (1950) 511; Schönbauer, *Anzeiger Akad. Wiss. Wien* 87 (1950) 94; W. Kunkel, *Herkunft und soziale Stellung der röm. Juristen,* 1952, 281.

Ius retentionis. See RETENTIO.

Ius revocandi domum. A defendant who is not domiciled in Rome, when sued in Rome during his temporary sojourn, has the right to ask the praetor that his case may be sent to the court of his domicile (*revocare domum*).

> Kipp, *RE* 7, 58.

Ius sacrum. Strictly connected with IUS DIVINUM and IUS PONTIFICIUM. It embraces the legal principles and institutions which are connected with the relations of men to gods, with questions of cult, sacrifices, temples, consecration, graves, and sacerdotal functions, whenever they may occur. The jurists Servius Sulpicius and Trebatius wrote on the subject of the *ius sacrum*. In oldest times the *ius sacrum* exercised a considerable influence on private law, the knowledge of legal rules and their interpretation and applicability having been a monopoly of the priests.— See PONTIFICES, VOTUM, COMMENTARII SACERDOTUM.

> Berger, *RE* 10; Maroi, *Elementi religiosi nel dir. rom. AG* 109 (1933) 89; P. Noailles, *Du droit sacré au droit civil (Cours)* 1949; M. Kaser, *Das altröm. Ius,* 1949, 78.306.

Ius (iura) sanguinis. The rights of blood (blood ties = COGNATIO). They "cannot be destroyed by any civil law (*nullo iure civili,* D. 50.17.8)."

Ius scriptum. The written law, i.e., the law embodied in written form at its origin. It consists of statutes (*leges*), *plebiscita, senatusconsulta,* enactments of the emperors, edicts of the magistrates (*edicta*). Ant. *ius non scriptum* (*sine scripto*), "the law which usage (*usus*) has approved" (Inst. 1.2.9). The distinction which follows Greek concepts is based on the external form through which the legal rules are manifested. The *interpretatio prudentium* was considered *ius non scriptum,* but in Justinian's Institutes (1.2.3) the *responsa* of the jurists are listed among other forms of *ius scriptum.*

Leonhard, *RE* 10; Manenti, *StSen* 22 (1906) 209; Steinwenter, *St Bonfante* 2 (1926) 421; Scherillo, *RendLomb* 64 (1931) 1271; Schiller, *Virginia Law Rev.* 24 (1938) 270; Blatt, *ClMed* 5 (1942) 137.

Ius sententiae dicendae in senatu. See SENATUS.

M. S. De Dominicis, *Il i.s.d. nel Senato,* 1932.

Ius sepulcri. The right to bury a dead person in a grave (*sepulcrum*). The owner of a land may be buried therein unless he ordered otherwise in his last will. A *sepulcrum* was *familiare,* when it was designated by its owner in his testament as a grave for himself and the members of his family (household); it was *hereditarium* when it was destined only for the testator and his heirs (*heredes*).—See SEPULCRUM, RES RELIGIOSAE.

E. Albertario, *Studi* 2 (1941) 81; Biondi, *Iura* 1 (1950) 160; Düll, *Fschr Schulz* 1 (1951) 203.

Ius sine scripto. See IUS NON SCRIPTUM, IUS SCRIPTUM.

Ius singulare. A special law issued to the advantage of a certain class of persons (e.g., soldiers, minors) or of an individual. Ant. *ius commune* (*ius commune civium Romanorum*) which indistinctly concerns all Roman citizens.—See PRIVILEGIUM.

Orestano, *AnMac* 11 (1937) 39, 12–13 (1939) 89; Guarino, *ANap* 1939–40, 65; R. Ambrosino, *J.s.,* 1940; Guarino, *Annuario del dir. comparato* 18 (1946).

Ius soli. The legal situation of a piece of land. What is built on the soil (*superficies, aedificium*) *sequitur ius soli,* i.e., is in the same legal situation, as the land itself with all its charges (liens, servitudes).

Ius sollemne. Syn. *ius civile.* It is opposed to *ius praetorium.*

Ius statuere. See IUS DICERE.

Ius stillicidii (stillicidium avertendi, or non avertendi). Praedial servitudes connected with the water dripping from the roof.—See STILLICIDIUM.

Ius strictum. The rigid, stiff law. The term is not a technical creation of the classical jurisprudence. By a characteristic example Gaius (4.11) tries to explain how rigid was the law of the Twelve Tables. Nor is technical the meaning of the locution "*stricto iure*" (= strictly according to the law) which is used to stress the contrast with exceptional legal remedies, not deriving from the positive law but granted in specific cases by the praetor (*exceptio*) or the emperor. Seemingly a technical significance is attached to the term in the juxtaposition *actiones bonae fidei* and *actiones stricti iuris,* which occurs only once in Justinian's Institutes (4.6.28) and soon afterwards is substituted by *iudicia stricta.* The denomination *actiones stricti iuris* is apparently of Byzantine coinage since it is not to be found in juristic writings (in the Digest occurs another term: *actio stricti iudicii,* D. 12.3.5.4). Possibly it goes back to an earlier conception which started from the distinction that some actions were *bonae fidei* and others were not; therefore the judge had to pass his judgment strictly according to the law without making use of the liberties he had *ex fide bona* or *ex aequo et bono.* Thus the *ius strictum* is conceived as a counterpart of *ius aequum.*—See AEQUITAS.

Manigk, *RE* 10; Pringsheim, *ZSS* 42 (1921) 653.

Ius suffragii. The right to vote in the assemblies of the people. It was one of the most important political rights of the Roman citizens and of those to whom it was exceptionally granted.—See MUNICIPIUM, CIVITATES SINE SUFFRAGIO.

Rosenberg, *RE* 10.

Ius testandi. (Syn. *ius testamenti faciendi.*) See TESTAMENTI FACTIO.

Ius testamenti faciendi. See TESTAMENTI FACTIO.

Ius tigni immittendi. See SERVITUS TIGNI IMMITTENDI.

Ius tollendi. A person who possesses or holds a thing belonging to another, particularly an immovable, and makes some improvements thereon has, under certain conditions, the right to take them away (*tollere*) provided that the object suffers no damage by such an operation. Thus a husband has the *ius tollendi* with regard to his expenses made on objects constituted as a dowry, a tenant in a rented house with regard to the expenses spent on improvements. According to the classical law a possessor in bad faith (*possessor malae fidei*) had no right to avail himself of the *ius tollendi.* Justinian extended the applicability of the *ius tollendi.*—See IMPENSAE, IMPENSAE UTILES, IMPENSAE VOLUPTARIAE, TIGNUM IUNCTUM.

Pampaloni, *RISG* 49 (1911) 239; Riccobono, *AnPal* 3–4 (1917) 445; ibid. 20 (1949) 71.

Ius utendi. See USUS, USUSFRUCTUS.

Ius variandi. If parties had agreed in a contract that either the debtor (which was more frequent) or the creditor has the right to choose (*electio*) between two or more things which the debtor had to pay, the choice once made could be changed by the creditor as long as he did not claim judicially one of the things due, and by the debtor as long as he did not fulfill one of the alternative obligations. The *ius variandi* was also applicable in legacies and other testamentary dispositions when a right of selection was left to the beneficiary.—See LEGATUM OPTIONIS.

> Grosso, *StSas* 17 (1938) 161; *idem, RDCom* 38, 1 (1940) 224; Biondi, *Successione testamentaria,* 1943, 440; Sciascia, *Scr Ferrini* 2 (Univ. Sacro Cuore, Milan, 1947) 255.

Ius vectigalis. The right to collect the rents due from the lessees of public land.—See VECTIGAL.

Ius vendendi. For the right to sell a pledge, see IUS DISTRAHENDI; for the right of the *pater familias* to sell his son, see PATRIA POTESTAS.

Ius vetus. See IUS ANTIQUUM, VETUS IUS.

Ius vitae necisque. The power of life and death. Since the earliest times the head of a family had this right over persons under his paternal power (children and wife) and over his slaves. His right to punish them comprised also the death penalty. Before imposing a severe penalty the *pater familias* had to consult the council of relatives (*consilium propinquorum*) but its advice was not obligatory. An abuse of his rights was punished by infamy through a decision of the censors (*nota censoria*). Imperial legislation restricted considerably the *ius vitae necisque* until its complete abolishment by Valentinian I.

> Albanese, *Scr Ferrini* 3 (Milan, 1948) 343; Volterra, *RISG* 85 (1948) 139.

Iusiurandum. An oath. There were two kinds of oaths, one during a judicial trial (*iusiurandum in iure, iusiurandum necessarium, iusiurandum in litem*), the other sworn extrajudicially upon agreement of the parties engaged in a dispute (*iusiurandum voluntarium*). The promissory oath of a freedman was of a specific character. Syn. *iuramentum.*—See IURATA PROMISSIO LIBERTI, GENIUS, PERIURIUM, VADIMONIUM IUREIURANDO, SACRAMENTUM, CONDICIO IURISIURANDI, SENATUSCONSULTUM DE ADVOCATIONE, ABIURATIO, and the following items.

> Steinwenter, *RE* 10; Cuq, *DS* 3; Sacchi, *NDI* 7; M. Chevrier, *Du serment promissoire en dr. rom.,* Thèse Dijon, 1921; E. Seidl, *Der Eid im röm. Provinzialrecht,* 1933.

Iusiurandum calumniae. An oath demanded by the defendant from the plaintiff to the effect that he does not sue for mere chicanery (*non calumniae causa agere*) or by the plaintiff from the defendant that he does not deny the plaintiff's claim for a similar purpose. In Justinian's law both parties and their advocates had to take the *iusiurandum calumniae.*—C. 2.58.—See CALUMNIA.

> Hitzig, *RE* 3, 1420.

Iusiurandum in iure. See IUSIURANDUM NECESSARIUM.

Iusiurandum in litem. An oath taken by the plaintiff upon order of the judge (*apud iudicem*) and concerning the value of the object claimed. The judge may, however, condemn the defendant to an amount minor than assessed by the plaintiff's oath.—D. 12.3; C. 5.53.—See TAXATIO.

> Solazzi, *AG* 65 (1900); Marchi, *Il giuramento in litem, St Scialoja* 1 (1905); L. Chiazzese, *Iusiurandum in litem,* 1937.

Iusiurandum iudiciale. An oath taken by one of the parties to a trial in the proceedings before the judge. It was only a means of evidence the value of which depended upon the estimation of the judge.—D. 12.2.

> B. Biondi, *Il giuramento decisorio nel processo civile rom.,* 1913, 76.

Iusiurandum liberti. See IURATA PROMISSIO LIBERTI.

Iusiurandum magistratuum. See IURARE IN LEGES.

Iusiurandum minoris. An oath taken by a minor in order to confirm an obligation he assumed without the assistance of his curator. It produced the loss of the right to request a *restitutio in integrum* for the minor. —See MINORES.

Iusiurandum necessarium. (Syn. *iusiurandum in iure.*) Only in a few specific instances, when the debt was a fixed sum (*certa pecunia*) could the plaintiff tender the defendant an oath (*deferre*) to the effect that he denies the debt. The debtor was obliged to swear, because in the case of refusal he was exposed to an immediate execution on his property. He had, however, the right to retender (*referre*) the oath to the plaintiff which, too, was compulsory, since the plaintiff lost his claim if he refused. This oath procedure took place *in iure* before the magistrate and led to a quick end of the trial either in favor of the party who swore or against the party who declined to take the oath.—D. 12.2; C. 4.1.

> B. Biondi, *Il giuramento decisorio nel processo civile romano,* 1913; Debray, *NRHD* 32 (1908); see IUSIURANDUM (Bibl.); V. Joachimovici, *Le i.n. à l'époque classique,* Thèse Paris, 1912.

Iusiurandum voluntarium. An extrajudicial oath. It is opposed to the *iuramentum necessarium* since it is voluntary and is based on an agreement of the parties engaged in a controversy. "An oath contains a kind of a transaction and has a greater authority than a judgment" (D. 12.2.2). When the claimant swore to uphold his claim, he had a praetorian action (*actio ex iureiurando* or *iureiurandi*) against the debtor. When the debtor denied his debt under oath, he might oppose an *exceptio iurisiurandi* when sued by the creditor. The attribute *"voluntarium"* is a creation of Justinian.—D. 12.2.

Iussio. A postclassical term, syn. with IUSSUM.

Iussio sacra. An order of the emperor.

Iussu. By order or authorization. Ant. *iniussu.*—See IUSSUM, IUBERE.

Iussum. (In public law.) An order given by a magistrate within the limits of his power to issue an order (IUS IUBENDI). In private law = generally any act covered by the expression *iubere,* such as an order or authorization given by a father (or master) to a son under his power (or his slave) to conclude a transaction, to commit a licit or illicit act. All that has been accomplished *iussu patris* or *domini* is considered accomplished by themselves and on their own liability. Persons entering a contractual relation with a son or slave who negotiates with the authorization (*iussu*) of his father or master, have a praetorian action, called *actio quod iussu* ("whatever by order"), which lies directly against the father or master, "because the contract is concluded in a certain measure with the person who gives the authorization" (*qui iubet*, D. 15.4.1 pr.). A similar effect is connected with the subsequent ratification (*ratum habere, ratihabitio*) by a father or master.—D. 15.4; C. 4.26.—See IUBERE.

Steinwenter, *RE* 10; Humbert and Lécrivain, *DS* 10 (*s.v. quod iussu*); Accame, *DE* 4; Del Prete, *NDI* 7; G. Cicogna, *Iussus*, 1906; Lemosse, *RHD* 27 (1949) 171.

Iussum caveri. The order of the praetor in the *in-iure* stage of civil proceedings addressed to a party to give a CAUTIO.—See CAUTUM IUBERE.

Iussum iudicandi. See IUDICARE IUBERE.

Iusta causa. A just ground (cause). It is stressed as a requirement for some legal acts (adoption, manumission) or for the exemption from guardianship and public charges (*munera*). *Iusta causa* is particularly important in connection with *possessio, traditio* and *usucapio*.—See POSSESSIO, TRADITIO, USUCAPIO, REPUDIUM.

Collinet, *Mél Fournier*, 1929; J. Faure, *Justa causa et bonne foi*, Thèse Lausanne, 1936; J. G. Fuchs, *Iusta causa traditionis*, Basel, 1952.

Iustae nuptiae. See NUPTIAE.

Iusti dies. See DIES IUSTI.

Iusti liberi. Legitimate children born in a valid marriage (*iustae nuptiae*).

Iustiniani Institutiones. See INSTITUTIONES IUSTINIANI.

Iustiniani novi. A name introduced by Justinian for students in the first year of law schools. Simultaneously the nick-name DUPONDII was prohibited.

Kübler, *RE* 1A, 404; Steinwenter, *RE* 10, 1309.

Iustitia. Justice. A Roman definition of *iustitia* (D. 10.1.1) says: "it is a constant and perpetual desire to render every one his due." The sentence appears on the very beginning of Justinian's Institutes.—See Inst. 1.1; D. 1.1.—See IUS, IUS NATURALE, AEQUITAS.

F. Senn, *De la justice et du droit*, 1927; Donatuti, *AnPer* 33 (1921); Sokolowski, *Der Gerechtigkeitsbegriff*, *St Bonfante* 1 (1930); v. Lübtow, *ZSS* 66 (1948) 460; A. Carcaterra, *I. nelle fonti e nella storia del dir. rom.*, Bari, 1949.

Iustitium. The suspension of the judicial activity of the courts ordered by the highest magistrates with the approval of the senate because of an exceptionally critical situation of the state, such as a sudden menace of a war, violent riots (*tumultus*) or a grave national disaster. No statutes could be passed during *iustitium*. Therefore three plebiscites voted on proposal of a tribune Sulpicius (88 B.C.) during *iustitium* were annulled by the consuls.—See SENATUSCONSULTUM ULTIMUM.

Kleinfeller, *RE* 10; Cuq, *DS* 3, 779 and 2, 1407; De Ruggiero, *DE* 4; Berger, *RE* Suppl. 7, 413, no. 3; Lengle, *RE* 6A, 2484; Thomsen, *ClMed* 6 (1944).

Iustum matrimonium. Syn. *iustae nuptiae*; see NUPTIAE.

Iustum sacramentum. See INIUSTUM SACRAMENTUM.

Iustus. (Adv. *iuste*.) Conformable to the law (for instance, a judgment), justified, excusable (*iustus metus, error, iusta excusatio*).—See IUSTA CAUSA, NUPTIAE, IUSTI LIBERI, DOMINIUM IUSTUM, IUSTUM PRETIUM.

Donatuti, *AnPer* 33 (1921) 377; Albertario, *Studi* 3 (1936) 404.

Iustus titulus. See USUCAPIO.

Iuvenes. Organizations of youths (over fourteen) of senatorial and equestrian families for educational purposes and training in sports. Widespread in the Empire they were later recognized as *collegia*.

De Ruggiero and Lo Bianco, *DE* 4; Ziebarth, *RE* 10, Suppl. 7, 315; Balsdon, *OCD*; Mohler, *TAmPhilolAs* 68 (1937) 442; H. I. Marrou, *Histoire de l'éducation dans l'antiquité*, 1949, 398.

Iuvenis. A young man. The term has no technical meaning; it refers to both *impuberes* (under fourteen) and minors (under twenty-five), more frequently to minors in an advanced age. Syn. *adulescens*.

Berger, *RE* 15, 1862; Albertario, *RendLomb* 54 (1921) 303 (= Studi 1, 1933, 513); Axelson, *Mél Marouzeau*, 1948, 7.

K

K. Abbreviation for *Kalumniator*. See CALUMNIA.

Kalator. See CALATOR.

Kalendae. The first day of a month. *Kalendae* usually were fixed as the date for the payment of debts and interest. In the case of omission of the month whose *Kalendae* was set for payment (e.g., in a testament or *stipulatio*) the first day of the next month was understood. Omission of the year in a simple indication, such as *"Kalendis Januariis,"* the next January first was assumed unless the intention of the parties was apparent from other indications. January first was from 153 B.C., the day on which the magistrates elected several months before entered. On the same day the annual edicts of the magistrates whose terms expired lost their validity and those of their successors entered in force.

Kalendarium. A register of births in the form of a codex or a papyrus-roll where the declarations of birth were entered daily alongside the recording on the white board (*album*); see PROFESSIONES LIBERORUM.

Schulz, *JRS* 32 (1942) 88 and 33 (1943) 57; Montevecchi, *Aeg* 28 (1948) 151.

Kalendarium (calendarium). A debt-book of bankers and professional money-lenders in which they wrote the names of debtors and the sums and interest due. Municipalities had also their *kalendarium*, and a special official, *curator kalendarii*, was entrusted with the bookkeeping. There are some instances of the use of a *kalendarium* by private individuals.

Öhler, *RE* 10; Humbert, *DS* 1 (*calendarium*); De Ruggiero, *DE* 2 (*calendarium*); Kübler, *ZSS* 13 (1892) 156; R. Beigel, *Rechnungswesen und Buchführung der Römer*, 1904, 141.

Kyrillos. A famous professor in the law school of Beirut in the first half of the fifth century after Christ. Another jurist by the same name belongs to the epoch after Justinian's codification. He wrote a valuable *index* (summary) of Justinian's Digest.

Berger, *RE* Suppl. 7, 337.

L

L. Abbreviation for "*libero*" (= I acquit). See A.

Labeo, Marcus Antistius. One of the most famous Roman jurists, contemporary with Augustus, pupil of prominent republican jurists, among them Trebatius. He was both teacher and writer. Among his works, which altogether amounted to 400 books, were collections of cases (*Pithana, Responsa, Epistulae*), a commentary on the praetorian edict, a treatise on pontifical law. A progressive mind, original and courageous in his interpretations, he appears frequently as a keen innovator, although in his political ideas he was rather conservative. According to the tradition he was the founder of the "school" called later by the name of his follower, Proculus, *Proculiani*. Labeo is the only jurist whose works which remained unpublished during his lifetime were edited after his death (*Posteriores, sc. libri*) by an unknown writer and then in a shorter epitome by Javolenus. His father, Pacuvius Labeo, was also a jurist.

Jörs, *RE* 1, 2548, no. 34; Orestano, *NDI* 7; A. Pernice, *Labeo, Röm. Privatrecht im ersten Jahrh. der Kaiserzeit,* 1 (1873); Grosso, *Quaderni di Roma* 1 (1947) 335; Berger, *BIDR* 44 (1937) 96; Santi di Paola, *BIDR* 8–9 (1948) 277; Schulz, *History of Roman legal science* (1946) 207.

Lacus. A lake. "It has water permanently" (D. 43.14.1.3). Navigation on public stagnant waters, such as lakes, ponds (*stagna*), channels (*fossae*), is protected by the same interdicts as that on public rivers.—See FLUMINA PUBLICA, INTERDICTA DE FLUMINIBUS PUBLICIS.

Berger, *RE* 9, 1636; De Ruggiero and Mazzarino, *DE* 4.

Laedere. To injure, to hurt, to damage. "He who exercises his right injures no one (*neminem laedit*)." "Through agreements between private individuals rights of other persons cannot be impaired" (D. 2.15.3 pr.).—See AEMULATIO, UTI IURE SUO.

Laelius Felix. A jurist of the first half of the second post-Christian century, author of a little known commentary on the work of Q. Mucius Scaevola.

Berger, *RE* 12, 416.

Laesio enormis. A non-Roman term which refers to the sale of a thing for which the buyer paid less than half of its real value (*nec dimidia pars veri pretii*). In Justinian's (postclassical?) law such a sale could be rescinded at the request of the seller, but the buyer might keep the thing by supplementing the price paid to the full value.—See PRETIUM IUSTUM.

Brassloff, *ZVR* 27 (1912) 261; Meynial, *Mél Girard* 2 (1912) 201; Andrich, *RISG* 63 (1919); Solazzi, *BIDR* 31 (1921) 57; Levy, *ZSS* 43 (1922) 534; De Senarclens, *Mél Fournier* (1929) 696; Scheuer, *ZVR* 47 (1932); Nicolau, *RHD* 15 (1936) 207; Albertario, *St* 3 (1936) 401; Carrelli, *SDHI* 3 (1937) 445; R. Dekkers, *La l.e.*, Paris, 1937; Genzmer, *Die antiken Grundlagen der l.e., Ztschr. für ausländisches und intern. Privatrecht* 11 (1937); Jolowicz, *Recueil en l'honneur de E. Lambert*, 1 (1938); Leicht, *St Calisse* 1 (1940) 37.

Lance et licio. The search (*perquisitio*) for stolen things in the house of the accused person had to be made according to the Twelve Tables under certain formalities: the plaintiff was clothed only with a girdle (apron = *licium*) and he held a dish (*lanx*) with both hands. This measure excluded the possibility that the pursuer might bring in the stolen goods. The procedure took place in the presence of witnesses. It fell into disuse early.—See FURTUM, FURTUM CONCEPTUM, FURTUM OBLATUM.

F. De Visscher, *Études de droit rom.* 1931, 217; Rabel, *ZSS* 52 (1932) 477; Polak, *Symbolae van Oven*, 1946, 253.

Lanciarii. A military unit within the praetorian cohorts (see COHORS) instituted by Diocletian.

Mazzarino, *DE* 4.

Lapidicina. A stone quarry. Juristically relevant is the question of who owns a quarry discovered in a land after it had been sold without the seller's knowing of the quarry's existence. Generally stones are considered as proceeds (*fructus*) of the land.

Lapillus. See IACTUS LAPILLI.

Lapis. A stone of any kind (a building stone, a milestone, a boundary stone, see TERMINUS, even a gem, see GEMMA). IUS LAPIDIS EXIMENDI = the right (servitude) to take stones from another's land (stonepit).—See LAPIDICINA.

Laqueus. A rope.—See STRANGULATIO, SUSPENDERE.

Pfaff, *RE* 4.

Lares. Tutelary deities of a household; in a broader sense, the household itself.—*Lares collocare* see DOMICILIUM.

Vitucci, *DE* 4.

Largiri. To bestow, to donate, to give a liberal gift. The term is also applied to judicial remedies granted by the praetor, e.g., a *restitutio in integrum*.

Largitas. (Frequent in imperial constitutions.) Largess, giving a gift, granting a benefit. Syn. *largitio*.

Ensslin, *RE* 12.

Largitio imperialis. A benefit, privilege, grace bestowed by the emperor.—See COMES SACRARUM LARGITIONUM, LARGITIONES.

Largitionalis. Connected with the state treasury, *fiscus* (in the later empire). The term refers to all kinds of taxes and imposts paid to the treasury.

Largitiones. The state treasury (= *fiscus*) in the later Empire; it is also called *sacrae largitiones* as depending upon the control and disposal of the emperor, exercised by a staff of imperial officers (*palatini, comitatenses*) under the direction of the COMES SACRARUM LARGITIONUM.—C. 12.23.

Samonati, *DE* 4, 408.

Lascivia. Wantonness, lasciviousness, negligence. In certain situations it is considered as *culpa* and involves the responsibility of the person who neglected his duties *per lasciviam*.

Lata fuga. See INTERDICTIO LOCORUM, EXILIUM.

Laterculum. An official register of all public offices and officers in the later Empire. It was kept and supervised by special officials, *laterculenses*.

Laticlavius, laticlavus, latus clavus. See CLAVUS, TRIBUNI LATICLAVII.

Latifundia (lati fundi). Large estates owned by the state (*populus Romanus*), the emperor (*patrimonium principis*), members of the imperial family, or private individuals. Large private estates were the characteristic feature of the agricultural economy in the last two centuries of the Republic. They were cultivated by gangs of slaves who under the Empire were gradually replaced by free labor and later by tenants who practically became serfs.—See COLONI, PATROCINIUM VICORUM.

Lécrivain, *DS* 3; Heichelheim, *OCD*; N. Minutillo, *Latifondi nella legislazione dell'impero rom.*, 1906; P. Roux, *La question agraire en Italie. Le latifundium r.*, 1910.

Latina libertas. The legal status of LATINI IUNIANI. —C. 7.6.—See also LATINITAS.

Latini. The descendants of the population of ancient Latium (*Latini prisci*), which was organized as a federation of various smaller *civitates*. After its dissolution (in 338 B.C.), Rome entered into relations with the *civitates Latinae* on the basis of agreements by which they were given a rather privileged status, designated as *ius Latii*. Later, colonies were founded in Italy on the basis of *ius Latii* as *civitates Latinae*. The citizens of these colonies were *Latini coloniarii* (colonial Latins). The Latin colonies were granted internal autonomy, with their own legislative and jurisdictional organs, but they were subject to the Roman foreign policy, to financial obligations to Rome, and to military service in wartime. Although legally strangers (*peregrini*), they enjoyed some political rights in Rome, the right to vote in *comitia tributa*, acquisition of Roman citizenship through domicile in Rome, *ius commercii* with Rome, and the right to conclude marriages with Romans, when specifically granted. The charter issued on the occasion of the foundation of a Latin colony determined the rights of its citizens in each case. An important advantage of the *Latini coloniarii* was the opportunity to obtain Roman citizenship (either generally or individually) for services rendered to the Roman state. Latins who held offices in their own community easily became Roman citizens. The *ius Latii* was a particularly favorable legal status, in a sense, an intermediate status between Roman citizen-

ship and the status of *peregrini*.—See LATINI IUNIANI, LEX LICINIA MUCIA.

Steinwenter, *RE* 10 (*s.v. ius Latii*); Lécrivain, *DS* 3; Vitucci, *DE* 4 (*Latium*); A. N. Sherwin-White, *OCD*; idem, *The R. citizenship*, 1939; Wlassak, *ZSS* 28 (1907) 114.

Latini coloniarii. Citizens of Latin colonies founded by the Romans with the privileges of *ius Latii*. See LATINI. After the constitution of Caracalla on Roman citizenship, the status of *Latini coloniarii* ceased to exist.—See LATINI.

Kornemann, *RE* 4, 514; Steinwenter, *RE* 10, 1267; Lécrivain, *DS* 3, 978; Bernardi, *Studia Ghisleriana* 1 (1948) 237.

Latini Iuniani. Slaves manumitted in violation of the provisions of the LEX AELIA SENTIA and the LEX IUNIA NORBANA concerning manumissions or in a form which was not recognized by the *ius civile* (see MANUMISSIONES PRAETORIAE) became free but did not acquire Roman citizenship, only Latin status without political rights (*Latini Iuniani*). They had *ius commercii* and could acquire property by transactions or take it under a last will as heirs or legatees, but they had no right to make a testament, their property going to the patron after their death. Therefore their situation was characterized by the saying: "they live as free men, but they die as slaves." They had no *ius conubii* with Romans. The status of *Latini Iuniani* was abolished by Justinian.—See LATINITAS, ITERATIO in manumissions, SENATUSCONSULTUM LARGIANUM, CAUSAE PROBATIO, SENATUSCONSULTUM PEGASIANUM.

Steinwenter, *RE* 12; Kübler, *RE* 18, 799; Vitucci, *DE* 4, 446.

Latini prisci (veteres). See LATINI.

Latinitas. A term used by Justinian with regard to the status of *Latini Iuniani* which was abolished by him. Therefore he speaks of it as *antiqua Latinitas*. Syn. *Latina libertas*.—See IUS LATII, LATINI IUNIANI.

Latinum nomen. All peoples (*populi*) of Latin origin (from ancient Latium). *Socii nominis Latini* = Latin nations joined in alliance with Rome.

Latio legis. Making, enacting a law.

Latitare. To hide in order to escape a trial. *Latitans* is one who cannot be found and summoned to court. The praetorian edict dealt with persons who fraudulently withdrew from sight (*fraudationis causa latitare*) thus making impossible judicial proceedings against them. A remedy to enforce their appearance was the seizure of their property by the plaintiff, authorized by the praetor (*missio in possessionem rei servandae causa*).

G. Solazzi, *Concorso dei creditori* 1 (1937) 58.

Latium. Often syn. with *ius Latii*. Under the Principate there is a distinction between *Latium maius* and *Latium minus*. The former referred to the rights granted to colonies founded as *coloniae Latinae* outside Italy, combined with the concession of Roman citizenship to a larger group of individuals than

Latium minus, in which only the municipal magistrates and members of the municipal council (*decuriones*) were rewarded with Roman citizenship.

> Lécrivain, *DS* 3, 979; Vitucci, *DE* 4, 442; Mommsen, *Juristische Schriften* 3 (1907) 32.

Latro (latrunculus). A robber, bandit, highwayman. A person kidnapped by a *latro* remains free and does not become his slave. His legal situation remains unchanged, and the so-called *ius postliminii* which applies to Roman citizens who became prisoners of war, does not apply to him. In the earlier law a *latro* was treated like a thief unless his crime was combined with a graver one (murder or use of violence, *vis*). Later, robbery (*latrocinium*) committed by a group of armed bandits became a special crime involving the death penalty by hanging (see FURCA). —See GRASSATOR.

> De Ruggiero and Barbieri, *DE* 4; Düll and Mickwitz, *RE* Suppl. 7 (*s.v. Strassenraub*).

Latrocinari. To commit a *latrocinium.*

Latrocinium. Highway robbery.

> Pfaff, *RE* 12; Düll, *RE* Suppl. 7, 1239; Humbert and Lécrivain, *DS* 3.

Latrunculator. A military (police?) official charged with the running down of highwaymen (*latrones, grassatores*). The *latrunculatores* were stationed at posts (*stationes*) throughout the country.—See STATIONARII.

Latrunculus. See LATRO.

Latus. (With reference to relationship.) *Cognatio ex latere* = collateral relationship. Syn. *ex transverso gradu, ex transversa linea*; ant. *ascendentes, descendentes.*

Latus. (With reference to contracts and trials.) The party to a contract or to a trial.

Latus. (Adj.) Broad, wide. Adv. *late, latius, latissime.* The terms refer frequently to the meaning of words and their interpretation ("in a broader sense"). —See CULPA LATA, LATA FUGA.

Laudabilitas. An honorific title of a high official in the later Empire ("excellency").

> De Ruggiero and Barbieri, *DE* 4 (*s.v. laudabilis*); P. Koch, *Byzantinische Beamtentitel*, 1903, 117.

Laudare auctorem (laudatio auctoris). The buyer of a thing who was sued by a third person claiming the right of ownership in it, had to name the seller (*laudare auctorem,* syn. later *nominare auctorem*) as his predecessor in ownership. The latter was obliged to assist the buyer (*liti subsistere*) in the defense of his right against the claimant. A similar *laudare* took place when a non-owner of a thing (a depositee, a usufructuary) was sued by a third person for recovery of the thing. Here the defendant named the person in whose name he held the thing. It was the latter's task to defend his property.

> R. Thiele, *Die laudatio a. im r. R.,* 1900; M. Kaser, *Eigentum und Besitz*, 1943, 61.

Laudatio funebris. A funeral oration. Such orations, when delivered on behalf of a deceased official, were pronounced publicly (*pro contione*) by a magistrate authorized for the purpose (*laudatio publica*), whereas on behalf of a private person a *laudatio* was delivered by a family member.

> Vollmer, *RE* 12, 992; Cuq, *DS* 2, 1399; De Ruggiero and Barbieri, *DE* 4; E. Galletier, *Poésie funéraire romaine,* 1922; Crawford, *CIJ* 37 (1941) 17; Durry, *Revue de philologie* 16 (1942) 105.

Laudatio. (In a criminal trial.) See LAUDATORES.

Laudatio Murdiae. A funeral oration (or perhaps only a dedicatory inscription on a tomb?) of the first post-Christian century, preserved on a tombstone. It contains an important section concerned with the testament of the deceased woman, Murdia.

> Recent edition: Arangio-Ruiz, *FIR* 3 (1943) 218 (Bibl.); Weiss, *RE* 12; Fluss, *RE* 16, 659; De Ruggiero and Barbieri, *DE* 4, 474.

Laudatio Turiae. An extensive inscription half preserved with a *laudatio funebris* dedicated by a husband to his wife. The inscription contains precious details about marriage, divorce, and the administration of the spouses' property. The inscription was written between 8 and 2 B.C.

> Recent edition: Arangio-Ruiz, *FIR* 3 (1943) 209 (Bibl.); Weiss, *RE* 12; Arangio-Ruiz, *ANap* 60 (1941) 17; De Ruggiero and Barbieri, *DE* 4, 474; Van Oven, *RIDA* 3 (1949) 373; Lemosse, *RHD* 28 (1950) 251; Gordon, *Amer. J. of Archaeology* 54 (1950) 223; M. Durry, *Éloge funèbre d'une matrone rom.,* 1950; Van Oven, *TR* 18 (1950) 80.

Laudatores. Witnesses in a criminal trial who testified about the blameless life (*laudatio*) of the accused.

> Weiss, *RE* 12; Kaser, *RE* 5A, 1047; Messina, *Rivista penale* 73 (1911) 292.

Lectio. (E.g., *constitutionis.*) The text (of an imperial constitution). *Lectiones iuris* = legal texts. *Lectio Papiniani* (in Justinian) = a text taken from Papinian's writings.

Lectio senatus. Selection of the members of the senate. A *Lex Ovinia* (318–312 B.C.) vested the censors (see CENSORES) with the discretionary power of the selection of new members. Their first duty when they assumed the office was to establish a list of the senators. They started with the scrutiny of the list of the actual members (high magistrates and ex-magistrates) and excluded senators (*senatu movere*) they judged guilty of bad conduct. Then they filled any vacancies by appointing new senators chosen from among the prominent citizens (*optimi*) of the people. —See SENATUS.

> O'Brien-Moore, *RE* Suppl. 6, 686.

Legare. (In classical law.) To bequeath a legacy in the form of *legatum.* In the language of the Twelve Tables the term embraced all kinds of testamentary dispositions, the institution of an heir (see HEREDIS INSTITUTIO) included.—See LEGATUM.

Legatarius. A legatee, one to whom a legacy in the form of *legatum* is left.

Legatarius partiarius. A legatee who through a legacy (*legatum*) receives a fraction of the estate (not single things or a sum of money).—See PARTITIO LEGATA.

Legati. Ambassadors, both Roman *legati* sent abroad and those of foreign states in Rome. Foreign ambassadors in Rome were inviolable (*sancti*, D. 50.7.18); they remained so even after declaration of war against the country they represented. The Romans granted this privilege to other countries and claimed it also for their ambassadors. The maintenance of international relations lay with the senate; it received foreign ambassadors and sent official missions abroad. Under the Empire, however, the emperor assumed these tasks. Roman ambassadors were sent to perform special missions such as the declaration of war (see FETIALES), the conclusion of peace or of particular treaties, the settlement of a controversy between Rome and another state.—D. 50.7; C. 10.65.

V. Premerstein, *RE* 12; Cagnat, *DS* 3; De Dominicis, *NDI* 7; Jacopi, *DE* 4; O'Brien-Moore, *RE* Suppl. 6, 730; R. O. Jolliffe, *Phases of corruption in R. administration*, Diss. Chicago, 1919, 77; Krug, *Die Senatsboten der röm. Republik*, Diss. Breslau, 1916.

Legati. Members of provincial councils; see CONCILIA PROVINCIARUM.

Cagnat, *DS* 3, 1035.

Legati ad census accipiendos. Special delegates (of senatorial rank) sent by the emperor or the senate to senatorial provinces to conduct a census of the population.

Kubitschek, *RE* 3, 1919; v. Premerstein, *RE* 12, 1149; O. Hirschfeld, *Kaiserliche Verwaltungsbeamte*[2] (1905) 56.

Legati Augusti (Caesaris). Imperial ambassadors sent on a special mission. For *Legati Augusti pro praetore*, see LEGATI PRO PRAETORE.

V. Premerstein, *RE* 12, 1144; Solazzi, *AG* 100 (1928) 3.

Legati coloniarum. See LEGATI MUNICIPIORUM.

Legati decem. Ten delegates of the senate acting as a council for a commanding general in the concluding of a peace treaty or in the organizing of a conquered territory.

V. Premerstein, *RE* 12, 1141.

Legati iuridici. (In provinces.) Officials sent by the emperor to provinces to assist the governors in their judicial activity. Their competence was primarily in the field of *iurisdictio voluntaria* (as the appointment of guardians), but they might be delegated by the governor to examine and judge specific cases as his delegates.—See IURIDICI.

V. Premerstein, *RE* 12, 1149; Jullian, *DS* 3, 715.

Legati legionum. Legates of senatorial rank assigned regularly or only in war time to the *legati Augusti pro praetore* who were commanders of legions in the provinces, in order to assist them in military, administrative and judicial activity.

Liebenam, *RE* 6, 1641; v. Premerstein, *RE* 12, 1142, 1147.

Legati municipiorum (coloniarum). Delegations sent to Rome by provincial municipalities or colonies in order to present complaints against (or praise for) the provincial governor or against a magistrate of the colony. Such missions came to Rome also to express some particular wishes or to declare their loyalty to Rome or the emperor, on the occasion of a happy event. Generally they were composed of three persons.

Cagnat, *DS* 3, 1036.

Legati proconsulis. The provincial governor of a senatorial province, who had the rank of a proconsul, had a deputy, *legatus proconsulis*. The latter had jurisdiction only as far as it was delegated to him by the governor (*iurisdictio mandata*). His official title was *legatus pro praetore* and his *imperium* was of a degree lower (*pro praetore*) than that of the governor (*pro consule*). He replaced the governor in the case of absence or death. These legates are to be distinguished from the *legati Augusti pro praetore* in imperial provinces. All *legati pro praetore* had the right to be preceded by five lictors with *fasces*, hence they were named *quinquefascales*.—D. 1.16; C. 1.35.—See PROVINCIA, IURISDICTIO MANDATA and the following item.

V. Premerstein, *RE* 12, 1143; Lauria, *AnMac* 3 (1928) 92.

Legati pro praetore. See the foregoing item. *Legati Augusti (Caesaris) pro praetore* = governors of imperial provinces appointed by the emperor for an indefinite period. They were representatives of the emperor who himself had the proconsular *imperium* and therefore their *imperium* was only *pro praetore*. —*Legati Augusti pro praetore* could be sent by the emperor to senatorial provinces but only for a special task.

V. Premerstein, *RE* 12, 1144; Bersanetti, *DE* 4, 527; Solazzi, *AG* 100 (1928) 3.

Legatio. The office of an ambassador, a group of delegates entrusted with a mission. The head of the group = *princeps legationis*.—D. 50.7; C. 10.65.— See LEGATI, IUS LEGATIONIS, CONCILIA PROVINCIARUM.

Legatio gratuita. See LEGATIVUM.

Legatio libera. An ambassadorship granted by the senate to a senator to facilitate his travel abroad in personal matters. He did not assume any official duties.

A. v. Premerstein, *RE* 14, 1185; Jacopi, *DE* 4, 508.

Legativum. The expenses of an ambassador, primarily for traveling (*viaticum*). They were reimbursed unless the ambassador assumed the mission at his own expenses (*legatio gratuita*).

Legatum. A legacy. It is "a deduction from the inheritance" (D. 30.116 pr.) which according to the testator's wish is given some person other than the heir. The legatee (*legatarius*) is *legatarius partiarius* when a fraction of the inheritance is left to him (see PARTITIO LEGATA). Generally a legacy consisted of a sum of money or one or more objects individually designated (*res singulae*). A legacy in the form of *legatum* could be bequeathed only in a testament, and after the institution of an heir (*heredis institutio*) because it was the heir who was charged with the payment of the legacy, and all dispositions preceding the institution of an heir were void. A legacy termed "after the death of the heir" was null. For further details see the following items; for the form of a legacy called *fideicommissum,* see FIDEICOMMISSUM. D. 30. 31, 32; 37.5; Inst. 2.20; C. 6.37; 6.43.—See ACTIO EX TESTAMENTO, CAUTIO LEGATORUM NOMINE, ADEMPTIO LEGATI, TRANSLATIO LEGATI, COLLEGATARII, CONCURSU PARTES FIUNT, ANNUUM, ANNUA BIMA DIE, DIES CEDENS.

> Weiss, *RE* 12, Humbert and Cuq, *DS* 3; De Crescenzio, *NDI* 7; F. Messina-Vitrano, *L'elemento della liberalità e la natura del legato,* 1914; U. Coli, *Lo sviluppo della varie forme di legato,* 1920; Gioffredi, *DE* 4; Donatuti, *BIDR* 34 (1925) 185; P. Voci, *Teoria dell'acquisto del legato,* 1936; C. A. Maschi, *Studi sull'interpretazione dei legati. Verba e voluntas,* 1938; B. Biondi, *Successione testamentaria,* 1943, 267; M. Kaser, *Das altröm. Ius,* 1949, 147; v. Bolla, *ZSS* 68 (1951) 502.

Legatum alimentorum. See ALIMENTA LEGATA.

Legatum annuum. A legacy under which the legatee had to receive every year a certain sum or a quantity of things during a period of time or for life. The legatee must have the capacity of acquisition at each term when the payment is due.—D. 33.1.—See ANNUA BIMA DIE.

Legatum debiti. A legacy by which a testator bequeathed his debt to the creditor. Such a legacy was valid only if it contained an advantage for the creditor, by, for instance, rendering unconditional a debt that orginally was under a suspensive condition, or setting better terms of payment.

> B. Biondi, *Successione testamentaria,* 1943, 450.

Legatum dotis. A legacy concerning the dowry. A husband might bequeath the dowry to his wife; if so, after his death the dowry was restored immediately to the wife. A *pater familias* who held the dowry given to his married son might leave it to his son. —D. 33.4.

> B. Biondi, *Successione testamentaria,* 1943, 453.

Legatum generis. A legacy of fungibles (see GENUS) and not of some individually designated thing (*species*). The legacy of a slave, without any further indication, was such a legacy. Normally the testator set in his testament who had to make the choice from among the things of the same kind (slaves, horses) belonging to the estate: the heir, the legatee or a third person. The jurists did not agree about the solution in the case the testator did not entitle any person to make the selection. Apparently the rules varied according to the form in which such a legacy (*legatum*) was left. The Justinian law favored the choice by the legatee.

> B. Biondi, *Successione testamentaria,* 1943, 436.

Legatum instrumenti. A legacy of a house or land with all necessary appurtenances. See INSTRUMENTUM, INSTRUCTUM. It was held generally that there were two legacies, one of the house (land) and another of the appurtenances. Hence if the testator sold the house without the *instrumentum,* the legacy of the latter remained valid. There is in the Digest an abundant discussion about the extension of the term *instrumentum* in connection with legacies. The pertinent problems concern the interpretation of the term from the point of view of the social and economic connection of the accessories (even persons, slaves, professional craftsmen) with the principal thing. A *legatum* of a *fundus instructus* was the broadest type since it embraced all that served the owner's use (also food, provisions, furniture, and the like).—D. 33.7.

Legatum liberationis. A legacy by which a testator released a legatee who was his debtor, from the debt. —D. 34.3.

> De Villa, *La liberatio legata nel dir. classico e giustinianeo,* 1939; B. Biondi, *Successione testamentaria,* 1943, 457.

Legatum nominis. A legacy by which the testator bequeathed a debt due to him by a third person to the legatee.

> B. Biondi, *Successione testamentaria,* 1943, 448; Arias Bonet, *Rev. general legislacion y jurisprudencia* 187 (1950) 60.

Legatum optionis. A legacy naming several things among which, however, the legatee may select only one (*optare*). The choice was (until Justinian) a strictly personal right; accordingly, if the legatee died before making his selection, the legacy became void. Various innovations were introduced by Justinian. Syn. *optio (electio) legata.*—D. 33.5.—See EXHIBERE, IUS VARIANDI, ELECTIO.

> Ciapessoni, *ACSR* 1931, 3, 24; De Villa, *StSas* 11 (1934); Albertario, *St* 5 (1937) 345; B. Biondi, *Successione testamentaria,* 1943, 440; P. Bolomey, *Le legs d'option,* Lausanne, 1945.

Legatum partitionis. See PARTITIO LEGATA, LEGATARIUS PARTIARIUS.

Legatum peculii. A legacy of a slave's *peculium,* together with the slave or without him. The legacy was void if the slave was manumitted or sold by the testator or if he died before the legacy was available to the legatee. When the *peculium* alone was bequeathed, it was understood *deducto aere alieno,* i.e., with the deduction of what the slave owed to his fellow slaves, to his master, or to the latter's children. —D. 33.8.—See PECULIUM.

> B. Biondi, *Successione testamentaria,* 1943, 447.

Legatum penoris. A legacy of food provisions, of "what can be eaten or drunk" (D. 33.9.3 pr.). Such a legacy could involve the duty of furnishing the legatee a certain quantity of provisions continually through a longer period of time (every month or year). The interpretation of the term *penus* and related expres-

sions is extensively discussed by the jurists.—D. 33.9.
—See LEGATUM ANNUUM, ALIMENTA LEGATA.

Clerici, *AG* 73 (1904) 128; Guarneri-Citati, *AnPal* 11 (1923) 259; B. Biondi, *Successione testamentaria*, 1943, 463.

Legatum per damnationem. A legacy expressed by the testator with the words: "my heir shall be obliged to give (*damnas esto dare*). . . .'' Later other words were admitted (e.g., *dare iubeo* = I order my heir to give). This form of a *legatum* obligated the heir to fulfill the testator's wish. In the case of denial, the heir was condemned to double damages.
—See SENATUSCONSULTUM NERONIANUM, SOLUTIO PER AES ET LIBRAM.

Kübler, *RE* 18, 801; Thomas, *RHD* 10 (1931) 211; J. Paoli, *Lis infitiando crescit in duplum*, 1933, 135; Voci, *SDHI* 1 (1935) 48; Koschaker, *ConfCast* 1940, 97; M. Kaser, *Das altröm. Ius*, 1949, 123; 154.

Legatum per praeceptionem. A legacy expressed in the following form: "*X* shall take a thing beforehand." The nature of this kind of *legatum* was controversial among the jurists. The problem was whether it could be applied only in the case of an heir to whom the testator wanted to leave a specific thing over and above his share in the inheritance or whether it could be left to anyone with the effect of a *legatum per vindicationem*. The second view prevailed.

Legatum per vindicationem. A legacy left with the words: "I leave, I bequeath (*do lego*) to *X*" or (later) "let *X* take (*sumito, capito*)." A legatee thus rewarded could claim the thing with *rei vindicatio* as its owner. This type of a *legatum* also raised some doubts among the jurists, in particular as to the moment when the legatee acquired ownership over the thing bequeathed.—See USUCAPIO PRO LEGATO.

Wlassak, *ZSS* 31 (1941) 196; S. Romano, *Sull'acquisto del l.p.v.*, 1934; P. Voci, *Teoria dell'acquisto del legato*, 1936; Amirante, *Iura* 3 (1952) 249.

Legatum poenae nomine relictum. A legacy left with the purpose of compelling the heir to do or not to do something by charging him with a legacy to be given to a third person in the case of non-fulfillment. Formally it was a legacy under condition. In classical law such a legacy was void; Justinian made it admissible, but it was null if the thing to be done by the legatee was immoral, illicit or impossible.—D. 34.6; C. 6.41.

Marchi, *BIDR* 21 (1909) 7.

Legatum rei alienae. A legacy of a thing not belonging to the testator. If the testator knowingly bequeathed such a thing, the legacy was valid: the heir was obliged to acquire the thing from the third person and deliver it to the legatee. Decisions of the jurists were divergent if the third person did not want to sell the thing or demanded an exorbitant price. The opinion prevailed that the heir had to pay only the value of the thing to the legatee.

B. Biondi, *Successione testamentaria*, 1943, 421; Orestano, *AnCam* 10 (1936).

Legatum rei obligatae. A legacy by which the testator bequeathed the legatee a thing belonging to the latter which he (the testator) or the heir held under a specific right (as a pledge, or in usufruct).

Legatum servitutis. See SERVITUS.—D. 33.3.

Legatum sinendi modo. A legacy left with the following formula: "my heir shall be obliged to allow (*sinere*) that *X* take (e.g.) the slave Stichus and have him for himself." Such a legacy could involve even things which belonged to the heir at the time of the testator's death. The heir was obliged to fulfill the testator's order; in the case of refusal an *actio* (*incerti*) *ex testamento* lay against him.

Ferrini, *Opere* 4, 217 (ex 1900); N. O. D. Bammate, *Origine et nature du legs sinendi modo*, Lausanne, 1947; Cugia, *Scr Ferrini* 2 (Univ. Catt. Milano, 1947) 71; Kaser, *ZSS* 67 (1950) 320.

Legatum sub modo. A legacy combined with a request that the legatee perform a certain act.—D. 35.1; C. 6.45.—See MODUS.

Legatum supellectilis. A legacy of household goods (furniture, utensils). Gold and silver goods are excluded, as are domestic animals. The limits of such a legacy are widely discussed by the jurists.—D. 33.10.

Legatum ususfructus. A legacy of an usufruct.

F. Messina-Vitrano, *Legato d'usufrutto*, 1913; B. Biondi, *Successione testamentaria*, 1943, 346; Solazzi, *BIDR* 49–50 (1947) 393.

Lege agere. To conduct a suit under a procedure established by a statute (*lex*).—See LEGIS ACTIO.

Legere. To read. A written testament must be legible (= *legibile*). An illegible testament is void. A testator could annul his testament wholly or in part by making it or a part of it illegible.

Leges. Entries with the heading LEGES dealing with certain types or groups of statutes, concerned with the same subject matter (such as *leges caducariae, leges agrariae*, etc.), follow below, after the item LEX (LEGES).

Legibus solvere. See SOLUTIO LEGIBUS.

Legio. A military unit originally composed of 4200 footsoldiers and 300 cavalrymen. The number of soldiers increased in the last century of the Republic to 6000; under the Principate it dropped to 5000. In the third century there were 30 legions totalling 150,000 men. The service in a legion lasted twenty-five years.—See VETERANI, COHORS, CENTURIA, MANIPULUS, LEGATI LEGIONUM, TRIBUNI MILITUM.

Passerini, *DE* 4; Ritterling-Kubitschek, *RE* 12; H. M. D. Parker, *OCD*; idem, *The Roman legions*, 1928.

Legis actio. The earliest form of Roman civil procedure about which we are relatively well informed. Its characteristic feature was the use of prescribed oral formulae which were used in the stage of the trial before the magistrate (see IN IURE). Changes in the prescribed words by one of the parties might result in their losing the case. There were five *legis actiones: sacramento, per iudicis arbitri postulatio-*

nem, per condictionem, per manus iniectionem and
per pignoris capionem (see the following items).
This form of civil procedure was later superseded by
the formulary process with written formulae (see
FORMULA) which was the classical Roman procedure.
The fundamental source on *legis actio* is Gaius' Institutes, completed in part by a few parchment sheets
discovered in 1933, the so-called *Gaius Florentinus*
(see INSTITUTIONES GAI), which throws new light on
some problems connected with the procedure under
legis actio.

> Cuq, *DS* 3; Anon., *NDI* 7; Wlassak, *Gerichtsmagistrat
> im gesetzlichen Spruchverfahren, ZSS* 25, 28 (1904, 1907);
> E. Weiss, *Studien zu den röm. Rechtsquellen,* 1914, 9;
> *idem, BIDR* 49–50 (1948) 191; G. Luzzatto, *Procedura
> civ. rom.* 2.L.a. 1948.

Legis actio per condictionem. So termed from *condicere* = to give notice. At his first appearance before the magistrate the claimant made a formal statement that the defendant owed him a sum of money
or a specific thing. Two statutes (*leges*) of an
unknown date, *Lex Silia* and *Lex Calpurnia,* are
mentioned in connection with this *legis actio*; the
first established the procedure when a fixed sum of
money (*certa pecunia*) was claimed, the second introduced this *legis actio* for the recovery of any
specific thing(*de omni certa re*). After his formal
statement the plaintiff summoned the defendant to
confirm or to deny his statement. In the event of
denial the plaintiff "gave notice" to the defendant to
appear after thirty days before the magistrate in order
to have a judge appointed. It is likely that before
the appointment of the judge the parties bound themselves reciprocally to pay one third of the sum or
of the value of the object claimed, as a penalty in
case of defeat in the trial.

> Kipp, *RE* 4, 847; Humbert and Lécrivain, *DS* 4, 386;
> Jobbé-Duval, *Mél Cornil* 1 (1926) 548; Levy, *ZSS* 54
> (1934) 308; Robbe, *StUrb* 13 (1939); M. Kaser, *Das
> altröm. Ius,* 1949, 284.

Legis actio per iudicis arbitrive postulationem. Introduced by the Twelve Tables for claims originating
from a verbal contract (*sponsio—stipulatio*) and for
division of an inheritance among co-heirs. Later the
applicability of this *legis actio* was extended to other
litigations, in particular by a *Lex Licinnia* for the
settlement of controversies between co-owners (*actio
communi dividundo*). The procedure was very
simple: after the formal assertion of his claim by
the plaintiff and the denial by the defendant a judge
(*iudex*) or an arbitrator (*arbiter*) was appointed.
Whether a private judge or an arbitrator (an expert) was to be used, apparently depended upon the
nature of the claim. In the case of an *incertum* (an
uncertain claim, not expressed in a fixed sum of
money) and in divisory actions an arbitrator may
have been taken.

> Humbert, *DS* 4, 387; Levy, *ZSS* 54 (1934) 296; De
> Zulueta, *JRS* 26 (1936) 174; Frezza, *St Ferrara* 1 (1943)
> and *SDHI* 9 (1943); Kaser, *Das Altröm. Ius* (1949) 250.

Legis actio per manus iniectionem. This *legis actio*
was a form of a personal execution on the debtor for
specific claims. Its name comes from a symbolical
seizure of the debtor by the creditor by the laying of
a hand (*manum inicere*) upon him. This form was
applied against a debtor who within thirty days after
a judgment passed in a proceedings by *legis actio
sacramento, per condictionem,* or *per iudicis postulationem,* did not fulfill the judgment-debt. Summoned
by the plaintiff, the debtor was compelled to go to
court before the praetor where the plaintiff pronounced the solemn formula: "Inasmuch as you have
been adjudicated to pay the sum of . . . and you did
not pay, I lay my hand on you for that sum." If
nobody intervened for the debtor as a guarantor
(*vindex*), he was assigned to the creditor (see
ADDICTUS). The *vindex* had to pay the debt or
contest the judgment. The personal execution was
thus invalidated which was expressed by the locution *manum depellere* (= to push away the creditor's
hand).—See LEX POETELIA PAPIRIA, LEX MARCIA,
MANUS INIECTIO, VINDEX.

> Noailles, *RHD* 21 (1942) 9 (= *Fas et ius,* 1948, 157).

Legis actio per pignoris capionem. An extrajudicial
legis actio through which the creditor took a pledge
from the debtor's property. This way of execution,
reminiscent of an ancient form of self-help, could be
applied even in the absence of the debtor and on days
on which jurisdictional activity was in abeyance (see
DIES NEFASTI). In the presence of witnesses the
creditor pronounced a prescribed formula (*certa
verba*) and took the object to his house. Only certain privileged claims of a military (see AES EQUESTRE,
AES HORDEARIUM, AES MILITARE) or sacral (see
HOSTIA) nature were enforceable through this quick
form of execution.—See PIGNORIS CAPIO, PIGNUS.

> Lécrivain, *DS* 4 (*s.v. pignus*); Steinwenter, *RE* 20, 1235.

Legis actio sacramento. Qualified as general (*generalis*), i.e., it was available in any case for which no
other *legis actio* was provided by statute. The term
sacramentum reveals the sacral origin of the institution (an oath which, in the case that the assertion
of the party proved untrue, rendered the perjurer
outlaw, SACER). In the developed stage the *sacramentum* was a sum of money. The respective amount,
500 or 50 asses according to whether the object
under litigation was of the value of one thousand
asses or less, was deposited in cash (originally the
sacramentum was probably paid in cattle), but later
sureties were admitted who guaranteed the payment of the sum in the case of defeat. When the
controversy concerned the freedom of a man the
lower *sacramentum* of fifty asses was applied. The
defeated party forfeited the *sacramentum* as a penalty
paid to the treasury (not to the adversary) The
origin of the *sacramentum* remains obscure in the absence of any reliable source. Only in Gaius' Institutes
is some information on the procedure under the *legis*

actio sacramento preserved, but it concerns only *actiones in rem* (*vindicationes*). If the object was a movable, it had to be carried or led into court; if bigger things, land or a building, were involved, a small piece thereof was brought before the praetor. In controversies over a flock one animal sufficed or even a bunch of hair. Both the claimant and the defendant performed symbolic gestures over the thing, pronounced prescribed formulae asserting their right of ownership under Quiritary law (*ex iure Quiritium*), and challenged one another by the *sacramentum*. The judge's final decision concerned the question "whose *sacramentum* was *iustum* and whose *iniustum*" by which the litigation was settled.—See INIUSTUM SACRAMENTUM, LEX PINARIA, TRESVIRI CAPITALES, CENTUMVIRI, PRAEDES SACRAMENTI.

> Klingmüller, *RE* 1A, 1668; Cuq, *DS* 4, 952; Berger, *OCD* (*s.v. sacramentum*); v. Mayr, *Mél Girard* 2 (1912) 177; E. Weiss, *Studien zu den röm. Rechtsquellen,* 1914, 9; *idem, Fschr O. Peterka,* 1927, 67; Nap, *TR* 2 (1921) 290; Juncker, *Gedächtnisschr. für Seckel,* 1927, 242; H. Lévy-Bruhl, *Quelques problèmes du très ancien dr. rom.,* 1934, 174; F. De Martino, *La giurisdizione,* 1937, 44; Kaser, *Fschr Wenger* 1 (1944) 108; *idem, Das altröm. Ius,* 1949, *passim*; Meylan, *Mél F. Guisan,* Lausanne, 1950; Lévy-Bruhl, *RIDA* 6 (1951) 83.

Legislator. Justinian frequently refers to the classical jurists as legislators (also *legum latores*).

Legis vicem obtinere. To have the same legal force as a statute, to take place of a statute. A neat distinction is made between a statute (*lex*) and an enactment equal in force to a statute (*quod legis vicem obtinet*).

Legitimatio. (Term unknown in Roman juristic language.) The changing of the status of an illegitimate child into that of a legitimate one.

> Blume, *Tulane L R* 5 (1931); A. Weitnauer, *Die L. des ausserehelichen Kindes;* Basel, 1940.

Legitimatio per oblationem curiae. An illegitimate son was considered legitimate if his father gave him sufficient means to be a member of a municipal council (*decurio*). Likewise an illegitimate daughter was treated as legitimate if the father gave her a sufficient dowry to enable her to marry a *decurio*. The purpose of these provisions, introduced in the later Empire, was to find candidates for the decurionate with which considerable public charges were connected. The term *oblatio curiae* is also not Roman.—See CURIALES, ORDO DECURIONUM.

Legitimatio per rescriptum principis. A privilege granted by the emperor in the form of a rescript to the effect that a child born in concubinage was to be considered legitimate as if it were born in a valid marriage (*iustae nuptiae*). The institution is a creation of Justinian. The privilege was granted at the request of the father if the mother was already dead or not worthy to be married.

> De Sarlo, *SDHI* 3 (1937) 348; H. Janeau, *De l'adrogation des liberi naturales,* 1947.

Legitimatio per subsequens matrimonium. According to an innovation introduced by Constantine, an illegitimate child born in concubinage became legitimate through a subsequent marriage of the parents. The pertinent requirements were: the status of the mother as free-born, the consent of the child and the absence of legitimate children. The last restriction was dropped by Justinian.

> White, *LQR* 36 (1920).

Legitime, legitimo modo. In a way prescribed by the law, in the solemn form prescribed by the *ius civile*.

> Riccobono, *ZSS* 34 (1913) 224.

Legitimus. Lawful, legal, based on, or in accord with, the law, in particular with a statute (*lex*) or generally, with the *ius civile*. In a few connections *legitimus* directly refers to the Twelve Tables, as *hereditas legitima, tutela legitima*. In Justinian's language *legitimus* appears frequently in interpolated texts where it replaced another classical term; thus, e.g., *tempus legitimum* is used by the compilers to replace the terms which were fixed in earlier law and were changed by later imperial legislation. For similar reasons in the expression *usurae legitimae* the adjective is interpolated for the fixed rate of interest as established in Republican and later legislation.— See AETAS LEGITIMA, ACTUS LEGITIMI, IUDICIUM LEGITIMUM, PARS (PORTIO) LEGITIMA, FILIUS LEGITIMUS, HEREDITAS LEGITIMA, TUTELA LEGITIMA, USURAE LEGITIMAE, SUCCESSORES LEGITIMI, SCIENTIA LEGITIMA, PERSONA LEGITIMA.

> Heumann-Seckel, *Handlexikon,* 9th ed. 1914, 309; for interpolations see Guarneri-Citati, *Indice*[2] (1927) 52 (Bibl.).

Lena (leno). A person who exercises the profession of a pander (*lenocinium*), an owner of an ill-famed house. Juridically a *lena* (= *procuress*) who takes profit from other women's prostitution is treated as a *meretrix*. *Leno* is also used of the husband of a *lena* who profits by her profession or of the husband who profits by his wife's adultery, without taking steps for divorce. A man who married a woman condemned for adultery is considered a *leno*. Persons guilty of *lenocinium* were branded with infamy and severely punished.—C. 11.41.—See ADULTERIUM, MERETRIX, BALNEATOR.

> Kleinfeller, *RE* 12; Humbert and Lécrivain, *DS* 3; Accame, *DE* 4, 636; C. Castello, *In tema di matrimonio,* 1940, 117; Solazzi, *SDHI* 9 (1941) 193.

Lenocinium. See LENA.

Leonina societas. See SOCIETAS LEONINA.

Leontius. There were two Byzantine jurists by this name; one, a prominent law teacher in Beirut, son of Eudoxius and father of Anatolius, both renowned jurists; the other was the son of the famous Byzantine jurist, Patricius. The second Leontius was a member of the commission which compiled the first edition of Justinian's Code (see CODEX IUSTINIANUS). The two Leontii were often confused.

Berger, *RE* Suppl. 7, 373; 375; *idem, One or two Leontii?, Byz* 17 (1944–1945), 1 (= *BIDR* 55–56, *Suppl. Post-Bellum,* 1951, 259).

Levare. To levy, to collect and exact taxes.

Levis. Light, mild. Frequently used in connection with crimes and punishments (*crimen, delictum, poena, castigatio, coërcitio*) indicating the minor gravity. Analogous is the use of the adverbs *levius, leviter,* in particular when a milder punishment is recommended.

Levis culpa. See CULPA LATA.

Lex (leges). The primary meaning of *lex* is that of a statute, law, passed in the way legally prescribed by the competent legislative organs. According to an early definition *lex* is "a general order of the people (*populus*) or of the plebeians (*plebs*) passed upon the proposal of a magistrate" (Capito in Gell. *Noct. Att.* 10.20.2; Gaius Inst. 1.3). The definition embraces legislative acts of the popular assemblies (*comitia*) as well as those of the plebeian gatherings (*concilia plebis*) for the enactments of which a special term is coined, *plebiscita.* The distinction is still maintained by the jurist Gaius who (1.3) limits the term *lex* to "what the people order and decree," reserving *plebiscitum* to "what the *plebs* orders and decrees." These enactments by the whole people or by a part of it are covered by the term *leges publicae.* According to the Roman conception "the strength of a statute is commanding, forbidding, permitting, punishing" (D. 1.3.7). Statutes are designated by the gentile name of the proposer (either of the consuls, a praetor, a tribune of the *plebs*) or proposers (both consuls), which sometimes gives rise to doubts as in the case of such common names of *gentes* as *Cornelia, Julia, Sempronia.* A characteristic feature of the *leges publicae* is that they never cover a broad legal field. Thus there never was a law concerning the Roman constitution as a whole, or the private law or any division thereof, such as obligations, succession, etc. The *leges publicae* dealt with one single topic within any area of legal life. As the items immediately following and the subsequent selection of more interesting laws show, the statutory enactments were concerned with popular assemblies and voting, magistracies in Rome and the provinces, the senate and senatorial privileges, the priests and their duties, international relations, Roman citizenship, the provinces, municipalities and colonies, agrarian problems, food supply, luxury, associations, and select questions of private law like guardianship, slaves, succession, interest, civil procedure, and penal law and procedure, etc. With the progress in the development of the law, *lex* is also referred to laws emanating from other sources that have binding force for all, such as the edicts of the praetors, and decrees of the senate, although in discussions on the sources of law the *leges sensu stricto,* mentioned before, are distinguished from the others. With regard to imperial constitutions of which the jurist named above speaks of them as "standing in the place of a *lex*" (*legis vicem optinent,* Gaius 1.5), later classical jurists and imperial enactments call them *leges* directly. In the later Empire a new distinction arises. The imperial laws are opposed, as *leges* to *iura* (= the laws originating from other sources). But the term *leges* often refers to the law as a whole without respect to its sources. The study of law or the knowledge of law is expressed by *legum scientia, legum eruditio,* and of the jurists of the classical period Justinian speaks as *legum auctores, prudentes,* and the like. Even religious norms appear as *lex,* as *lex Judaica, lex Catholica.* The intrinsic idea of a *lex* as a binding rule for the whole people or the people of a smaller territory (*lex municipalis*) appears in the implication of *lex* as a legal provision created within the sphere of private relations between individuals. Their will, expressed either in a unilateral act or in bilateral agreements (contracts), gives rise to legal ties between the parties involved. With reference to transactions, as, e.g., *lex venditionis, locationis, donationis,* etc., *lex* is a particular clause of the transaction in question, a condition imposed upon the party who is interested in, or receives profit from, the transaction. The meaning of a condition appears clearly in phrases with *ea lege ut,* as, for instance, when somebody donates a slave on the condition *ea lege ut manumittatur,* i.e., that the slave be manumitted. In the following presentation types of statutes or groups of laws referring to the same subject matter are noted under "LEGES," while specific statutes appear under "LEX."—D. 1.3; C. 1.14.—See AUCTORITAS SENATUS, ROGATIO, SANCTIO, DEROGATIO, OBROGATIO, RENUNTIATIO LEGIS, ROGATORES, LEGITIMUS, FRAUS LEGI FACTA, MENS LEGIS, RATIO LEGIS, VOLUNTAS LEGIS.

Weiss, *RE* 12; Cuq, *DS* 3; G. Longo, *NDI* 7; Treves. *OCD*; Hesky, *Wiener Studien* 1902, 541; Rotondi, *Leges publicae populi romani* (*Enciclopedia giuridica italiana* 1912); Peterlongo, *Lex nel dir. rom. classico e nella legislazione giustinianea, St in memoria di R. Michels,* Padova, 1937; Arangio-Ruiz, *La règle de droit et la loi dans l'antiquité classique, L'Égypte contemporaine,* 1938 (= *Rariora,* 1946, 231); F. v. Schwind, *Zur Frage der Publikation* (1940) 21, 145; Cosentini, *Carattere della legislazione comiziale, AG* 131 (1944) 130. For statutes of lesser importance omitted in the following list see *Lex, RE* 12 (Weiss, Berger) and Suppl. 7 (Berger); Cuq, *DS* 3; Rotondi, *Leges publicae* (see above) and additions in *Scritti* 1 (1922) 411.

Leges agrariae. Statutes concerned with the distribution of public land (AGER PUBLICUS) which from the earliest times was considered state property. Through gratuitous assignment (ADSIGNATIO) plots of land were given to individuals or groups of citizens. The Roman agrarian legislation is as old as Roman history, since the earliest assignment of land to the people is referred to the founder of Rome, Romulus. More than forty agrarian laws of the time of the Republic are known, some of them with the name of their proposers, some simply as *lex* (*agraria*). A group of *leges agrariae* is connected with the foundation of new settlements (COLONIAE). Political considerations exercised a great influence on the agrarian legislation, radical agrarian reforms were often introduced at the expenses of the actual possessors who were deprived of their land, held through generations by inheritance, on behalf of poor citizens to whom it was assigned. Important agrarian legislation falls in the period of the tribunes Tiberius Sempronius Gracchus (133 B.C.) and Gauis Sempronius Gracchus (123–122 B.C.). Until 44 B.C. some twenty agrarian laws were passed, whereas only two laws are known from the first century after Christ, the *Lex Cocceia* (under the emperor Nerva, 96–98) being the last. In Justinian's Digest two citations of a *lex agraria* appear, both in connection with the removal of boundary stones (*termini motio*). The notices on the earliest agrarian legislation are often not reliable. In an inscription a LEX AGRARIA of 111 B.C. is preserved.

> Vancura, *RE* 12; De Ruggiero, *DE* 1, 733; Humbert, *DS* 1 (*agrariae l.*); Pasquali, *NDI* 1 (*agrariae l.*); A. Stephenson, *Public lands and agrarian laws of the R. Republic* (Baltimore, 1891); G. Rotondi, *Leges publicae populi romani*, 1912, 94 (Bibl.); Corradi, *St. ital. di filol. clas.*, 1927; Terruzzi, *AG* 97 (1927); J. Carcopino, *Autour des Gracques* 1928; Cardinali, *Hist* 7 (1933) 517; Balogh, *ACRVer* 2 (1951) 335.

Leges caducariae. Statutes which introduced incapacity of certain persons to take under a will and so-called *caduca* (inheritance becoming vacant because of the incapacity of the instituted heir). The most important *leges caducariae* are LEX JULIA ET PAPIA POPPAEA, and LEX IUNIA NORBANA.—See CADUCA (Bibl.).

> Besnier, *RIDA* 2 (1949) 93.

Leges censoriae. Conditions imposed by the censors in contracts concluded with tax-farmers (PUBLICANI) or collectors of other public dues as well as in sales or leases by auction through which state property was alienated or leased.—See LEGES CONTRACTUS, LEX VENDITIONIS.

> Cuq, *DS* 3, 1117; Plachy, *BIDR* 47 (1940) 91.

Leges censui censendo. See CENSUS.

Leges collegiorum. Statutes of associations to which all members are subject. The Twelve Tables already granted the members of COLLEGIA (*sodales*) the right to set internal rules.

> Kornemann, *RE* 4, 415; Cuq, *DS* 3, 1110; Waltzing, *DE* 2, 369.

Leges coloniarum, (de coloniis deducendis), municipales (municipiorum). Statutes concerning the constitutional organization of a colony (COLONIAE) or of a municipality in Italy or in a province.—See LEX COLONIAE GENETIVAE IULIAE, LEX MUNICIPALIS TARENTINA, MUNICIPIUM.

> Kornemann, *RE* 4, 577.

Leges comitiales. See LEGET ROGATAE.

Leges consulares. Statutes proposed by a consul.

Leges (lex) contractus. (In private law.) Applied to all transactions between private individuals with regard to particular provisions of a specific contract. According to a saying of the jurist Ulpian (D. 16.3.1.6) "contracts receive a law (*legem*) by agreement (*ex conventione*)," which means that what is agreed upon by the parties to the contract becomes law between them. In this meaning *lex* is applied to various types of transactions (*mancipatio, venditio, locatio, depositum, donatio*). In public administration *leges contractus* is used of contractual provisions set by the magistrates in transactions concluded with private persons in the interest of the state, such as leases (*leges locationis*), sales (*leges venditionis*), and the like. Since such transactions were primarily in the competence of the censors, literary sources often speak of a *lex censoria* (see LEGES CENSORIAE) with regard to rules imposed by the censors in such agreements. The term *lex dicta* also occurs on such occasions.

> Weiss, *RE* 12, 2317; Cuq, *DS* 3, 1113.1116; V. A. Georgescu, *Essai sur l'expression lex contr.*, Revista clasica 8 (Bucharest, 1936); idem, *Essai d'une théorie générale des leges privatae*, 1932; Buckland, *RHD* 17 (1938) 666.

Leges datae. Laws issued by higher magistrates under the Republic, later by the emperor, for communities on the occasion of their incorporation into the state. They are not voted in popular assemblies, unlike the *leges rogatae.*—See LEX MUNICIPALIS TARENTINA.

> Weiss, *RE* 12, 2317; Cuq, *DS* 3, 1119; De Villa, *NDI* 7; McFayden, *L.d. as a source of imperial authority*, Washington Univ. Studies, 1930.

Leges datae. (In the provinces.) Charters given to provincial cities making them free (CIVITATES LIBERAE). They were revocable by the authority which granted them or by the legislative bodies in Rome.

Leges de censoria potestate. Laws passed by the *comitia centuriata* every five years investing the censors with their magisterial power.—See CENSORES.

Leges de imperio. Under the Republic the investment of higher magistrates with the magisterial *imperium* was achieved by a statute passed in the curial assembly (*lex curiata*). Under the Principate the sovereign power is transferred to the emperor (*princeps*) by a similar act, *lex de imperio*, with the appropriate constitutional modifications. This was practiced at least during the first century. The statute conferring the sovereignty on Vespasian is preserved in a large part; see LEX DE IMPERIO.—See also IMPERIUM.

> Rosenberg, *RE* 9, 1206; Siber, *ZSS* 57 (1937) 234; Messina-Vitrano, *St Bonfante* 3 (1930) 253.

Leges decemvirales. See LEX DUODECIM TABULARUM.

Leges dictae. (From *legem dicere*.) A conception common to both private and public law. With reference to private persons they comprise dispositions settled in a last will or a contract by which a certain legal situation or character is imposed on a thing by its owner. One also speaks in such cases of *lex suae rei dicta*. *Leges dictae* is used also with regard to clauses settled in a contract concluded by the censors on behalf of the state; see LEGES CENSORIAE, LEGES CONTRACTUS. Finally, *leges dictae* are the rules imposed by the emperor in the administration of his private property.

Leges divinae (humanae). See IUS DIVINUM—HUMANUM.

Leges edictales. Laws emanating from imperial edicts. —See EDICTA PRINCIPUM.

Leges frumentariae. Laws concerned with the distribution of grain.—See FRUMENTUM, FRUMENTATIO, LEX SEMPRONIA FRUMENTARIA, LEX CLODIA FRUMENTARIA.

> Rostowzew, *RE* 7, 172; Cardinali, *DE* 3, 229; Humbert, *DS* 2 (*s.v. frum l.*); Van Berchem, *Les distributions de blé à la plèbe romaine sous l'Empire*, Genève, 1939.

Leges geminae (geminatae). In the literature the excerpts from juristic writings or imperial constitutions which are preserved twice in Justinian's codification are so called. Despite Justinian's order to avoid repetitions there is in the Digest a considerable amount of *leges geminae* derived from the works of the same author or different authors.

> May, *Mél Gérardin*, 1907, 399; F. Schulz, *Einführung in das Studium der Digesten*, 1916, 45.

Leges generales. In the later Empire imperial enactments of a general character.

Leges imperfectae. See LEGES PERFECTAE.

Leges iudiciariae. Statutes concerned with the organization of the courts and judicial procedure.—See LEX AURELIA.

> Lécrivain, *DS* 3 (*s.v. iudiciariae l.*); Fraccaro, *RendLomb* 52 (1919) 335.

Leges latae. See LEGES ROGATAE.

Leges lucorum. Sylvan statutes. Some of them are preserved in inscriptions.

> Arangio-Ruiz, *FIR* 3 (1943) 223.

Leges minus quam perfectae. See LEGES PERFECTAE.

Leges municipales (municipiorum). See LEGES COLONIARUM.

Leges perfectae. Statutes which forbid certain transactions with the sanction that acts performed in violation are void. Ant. *leges imperfectae* = laws without any sanction at all. There is also a category of *leges minus quam perfectae* which threaten only the violator with a penalty, but do not invalidate the act itself.—See SANCTIO.

> F. Senn, *Leges perfectae, etc.*, 1902; G. Baviera, *Scritti giuridici* 1 (1909); Gioffredi, *Archivio penale* 2 (1946) 177.

Leges publicae. Laws passed by the vote of the people in a popular assembly or by the plebs in a plebeian assembly. Syn. *leges comitiales, leges rogatae.*—See LEX, LEGES ROGATAE.

> Gioffredi, *SDHI* 13–14 (1948) 59.

Leges regiae. Laws attributed to the kings of Rome, Romulus, Numa Pompilius, and their successors. They are primarily concerned with sacral law. Their existence is highly questionable, although according to tradition the so-called *Ius Papirianum* is supposed to have been a collection of the *legis regiae*.—See PAPIRIUS.

> Steinwenter, *RE* 10, 1285; Bibl.; G. Rotondi, *Leges publicae pop. Rom.* 49; E. Pais, *Ricerche sulla storia e sul dir. pubbl. di Roma* 1 (1915) 243; Carcopino, *Mél. d'archéologie et d'hist. de l'École franc. de Rome* 54 (1937) 344; Kaser, *Das altrömische Ius* (1949) 43; C. W. Westrup, *Introduction to early R. law,* 4, 1 (1950) 57; Coli, *SDHI* 17 (1951) 111.

Leges rogatae. Statutes which are passed by vote of one of the popular assemblies upon the proposal (ROGATIO LEGIS) by a higher magistrate. Syn. *leges comitiales.* Ant. *leges datae.*

> G. Rotondi, *Scritti* 1 (1922) 1; Cosentini, *AG* 131 (1944) 130.

Leges Romanae barbarorum. Called in the literature the codifications made for the use of the Roman population in the territory of the former Western Roman Empire after its decay.

> Berger, *RE* 12, 1185.

Leges sacratae. Laws for the violation of which the offender is outlawed (SACER). The statutes on the inviolability of the plebeian tribunes fall in this category.—See LEX ICILIA, LEX VALERIA HORATIA, SACROSANCTUS, SACER.

> Lengle, *RE* 6A, 2461; Cuq, *DS* 3, 1173; Niccolini, *Hist* 2 (1928); Groh, *St Riccobono* 2 (1935) 5; T. Altheim, *Lex sacrata* (Amsterdam, 1940).

Leges saeculares. The term occurs only in the title of the so-called LIBER SYRO-ROMANUS.

Leges saturae (per saturam). Statutes dealing with heterogeneous subject matters. Such statutes were forbidden in the earlier law. The prohibition was renewed by the *Lex Caecilia Didia* of 88 B.C.

Leges sumptuariae. See SUMPTUS.

> E. Giraudias, *Études hist. sur les lois sumptuaires*, 1910.

Leges tabellariae. Statutes referring to voting in popular assemblies through tablets (TABELLAE).—See LEX CASSIA, GABINIA, MARIA, PAPIRIA.

> Humbert and Lécrivain, *DS* 5, 5.

Leges tribuniciae. Statutes proposed by plebeian tribunes.

> Weiss, *RE* 12, 2416; Cuq, *DS* 3, 1174.

Leges viariae. See VIAE.

Lex Acilia de intercalando. (Of 191 B.C. on intercalary days.) See INTERCALARE.

> Berger, *RE* Suppl. 7, 378; G. De Sanctis, *Storia dei Romani,* 4, 1 (1923) 378.

Lex Acilia repetundarum. (123 B.C.) This is one of the best known statutes on REPETUNDAE because it is preserved in large part in an inscription which is generally considered to be the *Lex Acilia*.

> Berger, *RE* 12, 2319 (Bibl.); Kleinfeller, *RE* 1A, 605; Riccobono, *FIR* 1² (1941) 74; De Ruggiero, *DE* 1, 41; E. H. Warmington, *Remains of ancient Latin* 4 (1940)

316; Fraccaro, *RendLomb* 52, 1919; Chroust and Murphy, *Notre Dame Lawyer* 24 (1948) 1; Sherwin-White, *JRS* 42 (1952) 47.

Lex Aebutia. (Of uncertain date, between 199 and 126 B.C. or even later.) Connected with the reform of the civil procedure. It abolished the LEGIS ACTIONES—except for the centumviral court and in the case of DAMNUM INFECTUM—and introduced the formulary procedure. The reform was completed by two statutes of Augustus (*leges Iuliae iudiciariae*). The Aebutian reform served to generalize the formulary procedure which was doubtless known earlier and practiced in trials between foreigners.—See FORMULA, CENTUMVIRI.

Berger, *RE* Suppl. 7 (Bibl.); G. Longo, *NDI* 7, 829; Radin, *TulLR* 22 (1947) 141; Kaser, *St Albertario* (1952) 3.

Lex Aebutia. (On extraordinary magistracies, about 150 B.C.?) Anyone who proposed the institution of an extraordinary magistrate could not himself be elected to that office. A later *lex Licinia* of unknown date dealt with the same matter.

G. Rotondi, *Leges publicae pop. Rom.*, 1912, 290.

Lex Aelia Sentia. (A.D. 4.) Completed the restrictions on manumissions introduced by the LEX FUFIA CANINIA. It prohibited any manumission to the detriment of the creditors of the slave's master and fixed minimum age limits both for the manumissor (twenty years) and the slave (thirty years). Exceptions were admitted when the reason for the manumission was particularly justified and was approved by a special commission (*consilium*) appointed for these matters. Slaves manumitted against the rules of the statute became LATINI IUNIANI, and in certain cases (previous conviction of a crime) they received the lowest degree of freedom, that of *dediticii*.—D. 40.9.—See MANUMISSIO, DEDITICII EX LEGE AELIA SENTIA.

Leonhard, *RE* 12, 2321; Cuq, *DS* 3, 1127; Longo, *NDI* 7, 830; Schulz, *ZSS* 48 (1928) 263; A. M. Duff, *Freedmen in the early Roman Empire* (1928); *Acta Divi Augusti* 1 (1945) 205 (Bibl.); Weiss, *BIDR* 51/2 (1948) 316.

Lex Aemilia. (On censorship, 367 B.C.) Limited the duration of the censor's activity to 18 months.

Kubitschek, *RE* 3, 1906; Humbert, *DS* 2, 992; G. Rotondi, *Leges publicae pop. Rom.* 1912, 211.

Lex Aemilia sumptuaria. (Of 115 B.C.) One of the most drastic statutes against luxury. It did not deal with expenses for banquets, but fixed "the kind and limits of meals" (*genus et modus ciborum*).—See SUMPTUS.

Kübler, *RE* 4A, 905.

Lex agraria. (Of 111 B.C.) Perhaps identical with *Lex Baebia agraria*, was an agrarian law concerning the distribution of the *ager publicus* in Italy and Africa. It is especially important because, partly preserved in an inscription it contains valuable information about the nature and structure of agrarian laws.—See AGER PRIVATUS VECTIGALISQUE.

Vancura, *RE* 12, 1182; Riccobono, *FIR* 1² (1941) 102; L. Zancan, *Ager publicus*, 1935; Bozza, *La possessio dell'ager publicus*, 1939, 33; E. H. Warmington, *Remains of ancient Latin* 4 (1940) 370; Kaser, *ZSS* 62 (1942) 6.

Lex Alearia. (204 B.C.?) Prohibited gambling with dice. The name of the proposer is unknown.—See ALEA.

G. Rotondi, *Leges publ. pop. Rom.* 1912, 261.

Lex Anastasiana (leges Anastasianae). Justinian uses the name *lex Anastasiana* for certain important constitutions of the emperor Anastasius (491–518). According to one of them the cessionary of a creditor could not demand from the debtor more than he himself paid to the creditor. See CESSIO. Another innovation of Anastasius was the emancipation of a person from paternal power by means of a rescript of the emperor and the admission of emancipated brothers and sisters to an intestate inheritance equally with those not emancipated.—See REDEMPTOR LITIUM.

Ferrini, *NDI* 7 (*legge A.*).

Lex Antia sumptuaria. (71 B.C.) Limited the sums that could be spent for banquets and prohibited (with some exceptions) magistrates and magisterial candidates from accepting invitations to banquets.—See SUMPTUS.

Weiss, *RE* 12, 2324; Kübler, *RE* 4A, 907; G. Rotondi, *Leges publ. pop. Rom.* 1912, 367.

Lex Antonia de Termessibus. (71 B.C.) Granted the citizens of Termessus (Pisidia) the privilege of being "free, friends and allies of the Roman people" as a reward for help in time of war. The law is epigraphically preserved.

Weiss, *RE* 12, 2325; Heberdey, *RE* 5A, 749; Riccobono, *FIR* 1² (1940) 135 (Bibl.); Kaser, *ZSS* 62 (1942) 63; D. Magie, *Rom. rule in Asia Minor* 2 (1950) 1176.

Lex Antonia. (On dictatorship, 44 B.C.) Issued on the proposal of the triumvir Antonius, abolished the institution of the dictatorship.—See LEX VIBIA.

Lex Apuleia de maiestate. (About 103 B.C.) The first statute on CRIMEN MAIESTATIS.

Berger, *RE* 12, 2325.

Lex Apuleia de sponsu. (Date not known exactly, after 241 B.C.) Introduced a kind of partnership among sureties (*sponsores, fideipromissores*). Any one of them had an action against the others for what he paid to the creditor more than his proper share. See ADPROMISSOR. Later statutes, *Lex Furia* and *Lex Cicereia*, made further provisions concerning these kinds of sureties.

Weiss, *RE* 12, 2325 and 3A, 1855; Cuq, *DS* 3, 1129; G. Rotondi, *Leges publ. pop. Rom.* 1912, 246; C. Appleton, *ZSS* 26 (1905) 3; E. Schlechter, *Contrat de société*, 1947, 290.

Lex Aquilia. (Of the second half of the third century B.C.) A statute concerned with the damage done to another's property. It abrogated the earlier legislation on the matter, including some specific cases which were mentioned in Twelve Tables. It set general rules of liability for damage caused by killing another's slave or domestic four-footed animal (*quadrupes pecus*) or by damaging his property by breaking, burning or spoiling. The loss inflicted on the owner must be the result of a wrongful act (*damnum iniuria datum*; *iniuria* is here synonymous with *non iure*), i.e., there must be no lawful excuse for what was done, as there would be, for instance, in the case of justifiable self-defense or of an order of a magistrate. The damage must be physical and result directly from a corporeal act (*corpore*). Mere omission creates no liability under the statute. The original provisions of the *lex Aquilia* were extended by the activity of the jurists and of the praetors to cases not considered by the law. The *actio legis Aquiliae* became available either as an *actio utilis* (*quasi ex lege Aquilia*) or as an *actio in factum* "following the model of the *actio legis Aquiliae*" (*ad exemplum legis Aquiliae*, D. 9.2.12) in cases lying far beyond the original statute. In Justinian's law it acquired a more general applicability, the strict rules of the *lex Aquilia* having been superseded by larger conceptions with regard to the persons to whom it became accessible (not only to the owner of the damaged property as in the original law), the kind of damage and the degree of negligence on the part of the wrongdoer. A characteristic feature of the *actio legis Aquiliae* was that the defendant who denied his liability had to pay double damages if condemned; see LIS INFITIANDO. The second chapter of the *lex Aquilia* had nothing to do with physical damage. It gave the primary creditor a remedy against a co-creditor (*adstipulator*) who fraudulently released the debtor from his debt. —Inst. 4.3; D. 9.2; C. 3.35.

Taubenschlag, *RE* 12; Ferrini, *NDI* 6, 680; Longo, *NDI* 7, 831; C. H. Monro, *Dig. 9.2 Ad legem Aquiliam* (1898); E. Levy, *Konkurrenz der. Aktionen* 2.1 (1922) 178; Rotondi, *Teorie postclassiche sull'actio l.A.* (= *Scritti* 2, 411); Jolowicz, *LQR* 38 (1922) 220; Kunkel, *ZSS* 49 (1929) 161; J. B. Thayer, *Lex A.*, Cambridge, Mass., 1929; v. Beseler, *ZSS* 50 (1930) 25; J. Paoli, *Lis infitiando crescit*, 1933, 84; Giffard, *RHD* 1933; Arnò, *CentCodPav* 1933; idem, *BIDR* 42 (1934) 195; Carrelli, *RISG* 9 (1934) 356; Daube, *LQR* 52 (1936) 253; Bernard, *RHD* 16 (1937) 450; De Visscher, *Symbolae Van Oven* 1946, 307; Condanari-Michler, *Scr Ferrini* 3 (Milan, Univ. Sacro Cuore, 1948) 95; Daube, *St Solazzi*, 1948, 93; Macqueron, *Annales Fac. Droit d'Aix-en-Provence*, 1950; F. H. Lawson, *Negligence in the Civil Law*, 1950; Albanese, *AnPal* 21 (1950); Sanfilippo, *AnCat* 5 (1951) 127.

Lex arae. See ARA.

Lex Aternia Tarpeia. (454 B.C.?) This and a later *Lex Menenia Sextia* (452 B.C.) established the highest limits for fines imposed by the magistrates; see MULTA: two sheep and thirty oxen. Another statute dealing with the same subject matter was the *lex Iulia Papiria*.

Lengle, *RE* 6A, 2454; Hellebrand, *RE* Suppl. 6, 1544.

Lex Atia. (63 B.C.) See LEX DOMITIA.

Lex Atilia. (Of the end of the third century B.C.?) Dealt with the appointment of a guardian by the competent praetor if no guardian was nominated in a last will or designated by the law. The appointment by the magistrate = *datio tutoris*. A guardian appointed in accordance with the *lex Atilia* was called TUTOR ATILIANUS.—Inst. 1.20.

Taubenschlag, *RE* 12, 2330; H. Krüger, *ZSS* 37 (1916) 290; Schulz, *St Solazzi*, 1948, 451.

Lex Atinia. On stolen things (second century B.C.), excluded RES FURTIVAE (= *subreptae*) from *usucapio*. —See SUBRIPERE.

Berger, *RE* 12, 2331; P. Huvelin, *Le furtum*, 1915, 255; Daube, *CambLJ* 6 (1938) 217; M. Kaser, *Eigentum und Besitz*, 1943, 95; Marky, *BIDR* 53–54 (1948) 244; F. De Visscher, *Nouvelles Études*, 1949, 183; v. Lübtow, *Fschr Schulz* 1 (1951) 263.

Lex Atinia. On plebeian tribunes (102 B.C.), was concerned with the admission of the plebeian tribunes to the senate.

G. Rotondi, *Leges publ. populi Rom.* 1912, 330.

Lex Aurelia de ambitu. (70 B.C.) Introduced the penalty of ten-year ineligibility for a candidate guilty of AMBITUS.

Berger, *RE* 12, 2336.

Lex Aurelia iudiciaria. (70 B.C.) Broadened the hitherto exclusive privilege of the senators to be judges in judicial trials by admitting persons of equestrian rank (*equites*) and TRIBUNI AERARII.

Weiss, *RE* 12, 2336; Girard, *ZSS* 34 (1913) 303.

Lex Aurelia. (On tribunes, 75 B.C.) Admitted former tribunes of the *plebs* to magistracies from which the dictator Sulla had excluded them; see LEX CORNELIA on tribunes.

G. Rotondi, *Leges publ. populi Rom.* 1912, 365.

Lex Caecilia Didia. Renewed the prohibition of LEGES SATURAE and the provision of *trinundinum* between the publication of a project of a statute and the vote on it.—See PROMULGARE, NUNDINAE.

Liebenam, *RE* 4, 695; G. Rotondi, *loc. cit.* 335.

Lex Caelia. See LEX CASSIA.

Lex Calpurnia de ambitu. (67 B.C.) See AMBITUS.

Lex Calpurnia de legis actione per condictionem. An early statute (later than LEX SILIA, after 204 B.C.) which made the procedure of *legis actio per condictionem* available for claims of a definite thing (*certa res*).—See LEX SILIA, LEGIS ACTIO PER CONDICTIONEM.

Lex Calpurnia de repetundis. (149 B.C.) See REPETUNDAE, QUAESTIONES PERPETUAE.

Berger, *RE* 12, 2338; Ferguson, *JRS* 11 (1921) 86.

Lex Canuleia. (445 B.C.) Permitted marriage (*iustum matrimonium*) between patricians and plebeians.

Berger, *RE* 12, 2339 (Bibl.); Longo, *NDI* 7, 832; H. Siber, *Die plebeischen Magistraturen*, 1936, 46.

Lex Cassia. (On plebeians, 45 B.C.) Conceded their admission (*adlectio*) to the patriciate. A similar statute was the *lex Saenia* of 30 B.C.

Schmidt, *RE* 1, 368; G. Rotondi, *Leges publ. populi Rom.* 1912, 426.

Lex Cassia. (On senators, 104 B.C.) Excluded from the senate individuals condemned or deprived of *imperium* by popular vote.

Lex Cassia tabellaria. (137 B.C.) Introduced the secret ballot in jurisdictional matters dealt with by the popular assemblies except for cases of treason. This exception was repealed by the *Lex Caelia* (107 B.C.).

Lex censui censendo. See CENSUS.

Lex Cicereia de sponsu. (Date unknown, second century B.C.?) A creditor taking *sponsores* or *fideipromissores* as sureties (see ADPROMISSOR) had to proclaim publicly certain details of the debt and the sureties.—See LEX APULEIA DE SPONSU.

> Weiss, *RE* 3A, 1855; G. Rotondi, *Leges publicae populi Rom.* 1912, 477; Appleton, *ZSS* 26 (1905) 34.

Lex Cincia. On donations. (A plebiscite of 204 B.C.) It limited gifts to a certain (unknown) amount. Larger donations were permitted only in favor of near relatives and certain privileged persons (*personae exceptae*). Gifts promised in violation of the statute were not void, but the donor could oppose the *exceptio legis Cinciae* if he was sued for payment. A special provision prohibited advocates from accepting gifts from their clients in payment for their professional activity.—See DONATIO, ADVOCATUS, REPLICATIO LEGIS CINCIAE, EXCEPTAE PERSONAE.

> Leonhard, *RE* 5, 1535; Ascoli, *NDI* 5, 188; Longo, *NDI* 7, 834; Rotondi, *loc. cit.* 261; Radin, *RHD* 7 (1928) 249; Appleton, *RHD* 10 (1931) 423; H. Krüger, *ZSS* 60 (1940) 80; B. Biondi, *Successione testamentaria*, 1943, 635; *idem, Scr Ferrini* 1 (Univ. Sacro Cuore, Milan, 1947) 110; Denoyez, *Iura* 2 (1951) 146.

Lex Claudia de tutela mulierum. A law passed under the emperor Claudius abolished the guardianship of the next relatives (*tutela legitima*) over women.

> Taubenschlag, *RE* 12, 2340; *idem, Vormundschaftsrechtliche Studien* (1913) 72.

Lex Claudia. (On senators, 218 B.C.?) Excluded them from maritime commerce by permitting them to possess vessels of a very small capacity only. The prohibition remained in force under the Principate.

> G. Rotondi, *Leges publ. populi Rom.* 1912, 249.

Lex Claudia. (On loans, A.D. 47.) Passed on the proposal of the Emperor Claudius, prohibited loans to *filii familias* on pain of a fine.

> Groag, *RE* 3, 2828; Weiss, *RE* 12, 2340.

Lex Clodia de collegiis. (58 B.C.) Permitted the foundation of associations prohibited a few years earlier by a decree of the Senate (64 B.C.).

> W. Liebenam, *Röm. Vereinswesen*, 1890, 24; Accame, *Bull. Commis. archeol. del Governorato di Roma* 70 (1942) 29.

Lex Clodia frumentaria. See LEX SEMPRONIA FRUMENTARIA.

Lex Cocceia agraria. See LEGES AGRARIAE.

Lex Cocceia. (On eunuchs, A.D. 96.) Under the emperor Nerva, prohibited castration.

> Berger, *RE* 12, 2341.

Lex Coloniae Genetivae Iuliae. Also called *Lex Ursonensis* (44 B.C.) = charter of the Roman colony Urso in Spain.

> Kornemann, *RE* 16, 613; Riccobono, *FIR* 1² (1941) 177 (Bibl.); Gradenwitz, *Die Stadtrechte von Urso, etc.*,

SbHeid 1920; *idem, ZSS* 42 (1921) 565, 43 (1922) 439; Alvaro d'Ors, *Emerita* (Madrid) 9 (1941) 138; Mallon, *ibid.* 12 (1944) 1; Le Gall, *Revue de philologie*, 20 (1946) 138; De Robertis, *AnBari* 7–8 (1947) 175; Schulz, *St Solazzi* (1948) 451; Wenger, *Anzeiger Akad. Wiss. Wien* 1949, 245.

Lex commissoria. See COMMISSORIA LEX.

Lex Cornelia (Leges Corneliae). The following entries, inasmuch as they refer to the legislation of the dictator Sulla (82–79 B.C.), deal only with some of his selected laws since several of the laws passed under his dictatorship were repealed by legislative enactments of the subsequent years. The attribution of some laws to the dictator Sulla is not always certain.

> For Cornelian laws not mentioned below, see Cuq, *DS* 3, 1137; Rotondi, *Leges publ. populi Rom.*, 1912, 349.

Lex Cornelia de adpromissoribus. (81 B.C.) Limited the sum for which a person could assume guaranty for the same debtor to the same creditor in any one year, to twenty thousand sesterces.—See ADPROMISSOR.

> Cuq, *DS* 3, 1138; Rotondi, *loc. cit.* 362.

Lex Cornelia de aleatoribus. (81 B.C.) Declared valid all bets made on athletic games in which competition was considered a bravery (*virtus*). Stipulations for gambling debts, however, were void.

> Cuq, *DS* 3, 1138; Rotondi, *loc. cit.* 363.

Lex Cornelia de ambitu. (81 B.C.) Sulla's law against bribery at elections.—See AMBITUS.

> Berger, *RE* 12, 2344.

Lex Cornelia de captivis. (82–79 B.C.) On last wills made before the testator became prisoner of war. They were valid if the testator died in captivity, and were treated "as if he died a free Roman citizen" (Epit. Ulp. 23.5). This is the so-called fiction of the Cornelian law (*fictio legis Corneliae*, also *beneficium legis Corneliae*).—See CAPTIVITAS, POSTLIMINIUM.

> V. Beseler, *ZSS* 45 (1925) 192; Balogh, *St Bonfante* 4 (1930) 623; Wolff, *TR* 17 (1939) 136; J. Imbert, *Postliminium*, Thèse Paris (1944) 149; L. Amirante, *Captivitas e postliminium*, 1950, 32.

Lex Cornelia de edictis. (67 B.C.) Ordered that "the praetors administer the law according to their perpetual edicts."

> G. Rotondi, *Leges publ. populi Rom.*, 1912, 371.

Lex Cornelia de falsis. See FALSUM.

Lex Cornelia de imperio. (81 B.C.) Separated the *imperium domi* (in the city of Rome with its environs) from *imperium militiae*.—See IMPERIUM, DOMI.

Lex Cornelia de iniuriis. (81 B.C.) Punished three kinds of injury committed by violence: *pulsare* (beating), *verberare* (striking, causing pains) and *domum introire* (forcible invasion of another's domicile).—See INTROIRE DOMUM.

> Polak, *Symb. van Oven*, 1946, 263.

Lex Cornelia de legibus solvendo. (76 B.C.) This plebiscite limited the right of the senate to exempt a person from the laws (*legibus solvere*). Such laws benefiting particular individuals had been passed in the past. The *lex Cornelia* set a quorum of two hundred senators and required subsequent approval by a popular assembly.—See SOLUTIO LEGIBUS.

G. Rotondi, *Leges publ. populi Rom.,* 1912, 371.

Lex Cornelia de magistratibus. (81 B.C.) Fixed the sequence of magistracies (*ordo magistratuum*), cf. LEX VILLIA. Quaestorship had to be held before praetorship, the latter before consulship. Likewise time intervals between tenures of office were set.

Humbert, *DS* 1, 270.

Lex Cornelia de maiestate. (Of the dictator Sulla, 81 B.C.) This was concerned with CRIMEN MAIESTATIS (high treason). It punished by exile any person who called in military forces, or began hostilities against another country without approval of the senate and the people.—See QUAESTIO DE MAIESTATE.

Lex Cornelia de praetoribus. (81 B.C.) Under the dictatorship of Sulla, increased the number of praetors to eight.

Cuq, *DS* 3, 1139.

Lex Cornelia de proscriptione. (82 B.C.) See PROSCRIPTIO.

G. Rotondi, *Leges publ. pop. Rom.,* 1912, 349.

Lex Cornelia de provinciis. (81 B.C.) See PROVINCIA.

Lex Cornelia de repetundis. (Of the dictator Sulla.) On extortion.—See REPETUNDAE.

Berger, *RE* 12, 2343.

Lex Cornelia de sicariis et veneficis. A Sullan enactment (81 B.C.) on murderers and poisoners was still in force under Justinian.—D. 48.8; C. 9.16.—See SICARII, VENEFICI.

Cuq, *DS* 3, 1140; G. Rotondi, *Leges publ. populi Rom.,* 1912, 357; Condanari-Michler, *Scritti Ferrini* 3 (Univ. Sacro Cuore, Milan, 1948) 70.

Lex Cornelia de tribunis plebis. (82 B.C.) This law of the dictator Sulla was inspired by the desire to deprive the plebeian tribunes of their power. Only senators could be elected to the tribunate; ex-tribunes were excluded from higher magistracies. Legislative proposals of the tribunes had to be previously approved by the senate, and their right of intercession was considerably restricted. Pompeius abolished the law and reinstated the former prerogatives of the tribunes.—See LEX POMPEIA LICINIA on tribunes.

Lengle, *RE* 6A, 2485; G. Rotondi, *Leges publ. populi Rom.,* 1912, 350.

Lex Cornelia de viginti quaestoribus. (81 B.C.) Raised the number of quaestors to twenty. Part of the law is epigraphically preserved; it deals with the subordinate personnel of the quaestorian office.—See QUAESTORES.

Riccobono, *FIR* 1² (1941) 131; E. H. Warmington, *Remains of old Latin* 4 (1940) 302.

Lex Cornelia nummaria. See FALSUM.

Lex Cornelia sumptuaria. (81 B.C.) The dictator Sulla used this law to combat excessive expenditures for banquets and pompous funerals.—See SUMPTUS.

Rotondi, *loc. cit.* 354; Kübler, *RE* 4A, 907.

Lex Cornelia testamentaria. See FALSUM.

Lex Cornelia Baebia de ambitu. (181 B.C.) One of the earliest statutes against bribery at elections.—See AMBITUS.

Berger, *RE* 12, 2344

Lex Cornelia Fulvia de ambitu. (159 B.C.) See AMBITUS.

Berger, *RE* 12, 2344.

Lex Cornelia Pompeia. (On *comitia tributa,* one or two laws passed under the consulship of Sulla in 88 B.C.) Imposed restrictions on the legislative and electoral activity of the *comitia tributa.*

G. Rotondi, *Leges publ. populi Rom.,* 1912, 343.

Lex Cornelia Pompeia. (On interest, 88 B.C.) A statute proposed by Sulla of uncertain content. Presumably it permitted loans at an annual interest of ten per cent. Higher interest payments may have been deducted from the principal.

Berger, *RE* Suppl. 7, 384.

Lex Crepereia. An earlier republican statute of unknown date, dealt with the proceedings before the centumviral court. The sum of the *sponsio* was fixed at 125 sesterces.—See CENTUMVIRI, IUDICIUM CENTUMVIRALE, AGERE PER SPONSIONEM, SPONSIO PRAEIUDICIALIS.

Berger, *RE* Suppl. 7, 384.

Lex Curiata de imperio. See COMITIA CURIATA, LEX DE IMPERIO.

Liebenam, *RE* 4, 1826; G. W. Botsford, *Pol. Sci. Quart.* 23 (1908); Latte, *Nachr. Goettingische Gesellschaft der Wissenschaften, Phil.-hist. Kl.* 1934; Heuss, *ZSS* 64 (1944) 70; Nocera, *AnPer* 51 (1946) 163.

Lex de bello indicendo. Decisions concerning the declaration of war were to be taken by the *comitia centuriata.*—See BELLUM, INDICERE BELLUM.

Liebenam, *RE* 696; Berger, *RE* Suppl. 7, 383 (with a list of the pertinent statutes); Siber, *ZSS* 57 (1937) 261.

Lex de flaminica Diali. (A.D. 24?) Provided that in a marriage of the FLAMEN DIALIS, concluded in the solemn form of *confarreatio,* his wife (*flaminica*) did not pass into his full power (*manus*). She was obliged to obey him only in sacral matters. The measure was designed to encourage marriages by *confarreatio,* which became very rare at the beginning of the Empire so that it was difficult to find candidates for the post of *flamen Dialis* who had to be born from such a marriage.

Berger, *RE* 12, 2353.

Lex de imperio. (Under the Empire.) A statute by which the emperor was vested with sovereign power by the people and the senate. Apparently this custom, practiced in the first century of the Principate, was a continuation of the old republican tradition, of the LEX CURIATA DE IMPERIO which conferred *imperium* on the higher magistrates. Several sections of a *lex* by which the emperor Vespasian received sovereignty, *lex de imperio Vespasiani* (A.D. 69–70) are epigraphically preserved. It is one of the most important epigraphical monuments. It enumerates various prerogatives of the emperor and describes their contents, primarily by reference to the same rights held by Vespasian's predecessors. The *lex de imperio* as a general institution is mentioned once in Gaius' Institutes and four times in Justinian's codification (once, C. 6.23.3, as *lex imperii*). The term applied to the *lex* by Justinian, *lex regia,* is doubtless not classical and corresponds to the Byzantine conception of the nature of kingship (*basileia*). In all these references there is certainly an element of truth and all efforts to eliminate them as spurious are futile. It remains questionable, however, how long this kind of investment of the emperor with *"omne suum imperium et potestas"* by the people continued in use.

Riccobono, *FIR* 1² (1941) 154 (Bibl.) ; Hellems, *L. de i. Vespasiani* 1902 (*Dissert. Americanae,* no. 1, Chicago) ; Cantarelli, *St. romani e bizantini,* 1915, 99 ; Beseler, *Juristische Miniaturen* 1929, 155 ; Messina-Vitrano, *St Bonfante* 3 (1930) 255 ; Last, *Cambr. Anc. History* 11 (1936) 406 ; S. Riccobono, Jr., *AnPal* 15 (1936) 501 ; Levi, *Ath* 16 (1938) 85 ; Magdelain, *Auctoritas principis,* 1947, 90.

Lex de imperio Vespasiani. See the foregoing item.

Lex de piratis. See LEX GABINIA.

Lex decemviralis (leges decemvirales). See LEX DUODECIM TABULARUM.

Lex dedicationis. See DEDICATIO.

Lex Dei. See COLLATIO LEGUM MOSAICARUM ET ROMANARUM.

Lex Didia sumptuaria. (143 B.C.) Extended the validity of the LEX FANNIA to all Italy and settled penalties for the guests who participated in banquets condemned by the statute.—See SUMPTUS.

Kübler, *RE* 4A, 295 ; G. Rotondi, *Leges publ. populi Rom.,* 1912, 295.

Lex Domitia. (103 B.C.) Reformed the system of election of pontiffs and augurs by introducing a combined method : election by a minor group of *tribus* from a list of candidates proposed by the *collegium* of priests in which the vacancy occurred. Abrogated by Sulla, the statute was later restored by the LEX ATIA.

Wissowa, *RE* 2, 2318 ; Münzer, *RE* 5, 1325 ; Weiss, *RE* 12, 2330 ; Rotondi, *loc. cit.* 329, 380.

Lex Duilia de provocatione. (449 B.C.) One of the earliest republican statutes. The plebiscite, proposed by the plebeian tribune Duilius to protect the institution of appeal (*provocatio*), provided the death penalty for anyone seeking to create a magistracy the decisions of which could not be checked by an appeal, or to leave the plebeians without tribunes.—See PROVOCATIO.

Weiss, *RE* 12, 2345 ; Rotondi, *loc. cit.* 203.

Lex Duilia Menenia (Maenia?). See FENUS UNCIARIUM.

Rotondi, *loc. cit.* 222 ; L. Clerici, *Economia e finanza dei Romani,* 1 (1943) 333.

Lex duodecim tabularum. (451–450 B.C.) The earliest Roman codification or rather collection of the fundamental rules of customary law was published on twelve tablets. The work was achieved by a commission of ten experts, *decemviri legibus scribundis,* hence the name *leges decemvirales* for the legislation. The decemviral laws were the outcome of a political struggle between the plebeians and the patricians. The principal grievances of the former were the fact that the law was administered exclusively by the patricians in their own interest, the uncertainty of the law, and the severity of the enforcement of debts (see NEXUM). Only a portion of the Twelve Tables is known partly from quotations (sometimes in their original archaic wording) preserved in juristic and literary sources, but chiefly, however, from scattered references to certain provisions appearing in a rather considerable number in Justinian's codification. The Twelve Tables contained a selection of rules from different provinces of the law. Starting with some procedural norms they comprised rules of private and penal law as well as of sacral law. (The more important statements of the law are noted in the present volume under the appropriate entries.) The decemviral legislation is the germ from which the ancient Roman *ius civile* arose and evolved but from which the Roman jurisprudence also developed. The interpretation of the Twelve Tables by the pontiffs and the professional jurists promoted the development of law and jurisprudence. Still in Cicero's boyhood the Roman youth learned them by heart. Several commentaries were written on the Twelve Tables, the last by the jurist Gaius about the middle of the second century after Christ (in six books). The excerpts from his work *"ad legem duodecim tabularum"* preserved in Justinian's Digest have contributed largely to the knowledge of the structure and nature of the whole codification. The high esteem the Twelve Tables enjoyed in Roman tradition for centuries is testified by many sayings of Roman writers (primarily Cicero) ; Livy did not hesitate to call them, not without a certain exaggeration, "the source of all public and private law" and "the body (*corpus*) of the whole Roman law (*omnis Romani iuris*)." This evaluation cannot be shattered by the outburst of modern criticism which has not only attacked their authenticity but has also not hesitated to pass an unfavorable judgment over them as a whole. —See ABSENS, ADDICTUS, ADSIDUI, AMBITUS, COLLEGIA, CONFESSIO IN IURE, DECEMVIRI LEGIBUS SCRIBUNDIS, DIES IUSTI, DEICERE E SAXO TARPEIO, DIFFINDERE, EMANCIPATIO, INIURIA, LEGARE, LEGITIMUS, LEGIS ACTIO PER IUDICIS ARBITRIVE POSTULATIONEM,

LEX VALERIA DE PROVOCATIONE, NEXUM, MANUS INIECTIO IUDICATI, OBVAGULATIO, SECARE PARTES, SUMPTUS, TALIO, TEMPUS IUDICATI, TESTES, TUTOR SUSPECTUS, TUTELA LEGITIMA, USUS AUCTORITAS, VINDICIAE FALSAE, VITES.

Berger, *RE* 4A (*s.v. Tabulae duodecim*, Bibl.); *idem, RE* Suppl. 7, 1275; Riccobono, *FIR* 1² (1941) 23; Girard, *La loi de Douze Tables*, London, 1914; E. Taübler, *Untersuchungen zur Gesch. des Dezemvirats und der Zwölftafeln*, 1921; Baviera, *St Perozzi*, 1924; Berger, *St Riccobono* 1 (1933) 587; *idem, St Albertoni* 1 (1933) 381; *idem, BIDR* 43 (1935) 195; *idem, Le Dodici Tavole e la codificazione giustinianea, ACDR* Roma 1 (1934) 39; E. Volterra, *Diritto rom. e diritti orientali*, 1937, 146, 175, 687; E. H. Warmington, *Remains of old Latin* 3 (1938) 424; Baviera, *St Riccobono* 1 (1936) p. XXXIII; R. Düll, *Das Zwölftafelngesetz, Übersetzung und Erläuterung*, 1944; Balogh, *Scr Ferrini* 3 (Univ. Sacro Cuore, Milan, 1948) 2; Gioffredi, *SDHI* 13–14 (1944) 33; C. W. Westrup, *Introduction to early R. law*, 4, 1 (1950) 79; P. Noailles, *Du droit sacré au droit civil*, 1950, 36; P. R. Coleman-Norton, *The Twelve Tables*³, (Princeton, 1950); *idem, Cicero's contribution to the text of the Twelve Tables, ClJ* 1950; Perrin, *RHD* 29 (1951) 383.

Lex Fabia. A statute of unknown date (second or first century B.C.) against kidnapping, treating a free man as a slave, or persuading another's slave to leave his master. The same crime (*crimen legis Fabiae, plagium*) is charged against anyone who helps the principal culprit in such undertakings (*socius*). In later development, making a free man the object of a transaction (sale, giving in dowry) was also considered to be a *plagium*. Both the giver and the receiver were subject to punishment but only if they had knowledge of the free man's status and acted fraudulently (*scientes dolo malo*). Severe penalties were provided for *plagium* in the *lex Fabia*; they were later aggravated by imperial enactments. Diocletian introduced the death penalty for *plagium*.—D. 48.15; C. 9.20.—See VINCULA.

Berger, *RE* Suppl. 7, 386; *idem, BIDR* 45 (1938) 267; Niedermeyer, *St Bonfante* 2 (1936); Lauria, *AnMac* 8 (1932).

Lex Falcidia. (40 B.C.) Provided that legacies (*legata*) should not exceed three quarters of the testator's estate. A minimum of a fourth part (*quarta Falcidia, Falcidia*) was reserved to the heir appointed in the testament. In the case of several heirs each of them had to receive at least one fourth of the share assigned to him. The part of the legacy exceeding three-quarters was void; an heir sued by the legatee for the surplus could oppose the *exceptio legis Falcidiae*. The value of the estate at the time of the testator's death was decisive. Later changes did not count. The tendency of the law was to prevent the refusal of an inheritance, charged with exorbitant legacies, by the testamentary heir. Imperial legislation introduced substantial reforms. Antoninus Pius extended the *quarta Falcidia* to intestate inheritance if the owner disposed in a codicil over more than three-fourths of the estate by *fideicommissa*. The application of the law was in some exceptional

cases excluded, as with regard to a soldier's testament or to legacies in favor of *piae causae* (for charitable purposes).—Inst. *2.22*; D. *35.2; 3*; C. *6.50*.—See BENEFICIUM COMPETENTIAE, CAUTIO EX LEGE FALCIDIA, DII, SENATUSCONSULTUM PEGASIANUM.

Steinwenter, *RE* 12, 2346 (Bibl.); Longo, *NDI* 7; Pampaloni, *BIDR* 21 (1909, = *Scr. giur.* 1, 1941, 347); Vassalli, *BIDR* 26 (1913) 52; F. Schwarz, *ZSS* 63 (1943) 314; B. Biondi, *Successione testamentaria*, 1943, 381; F. Bonifacio, *Ricerche sulla L.F.*, 1948; *idem, Iura* 3 (1952) 229; F. Schwarz, *SDHI* 17 (1951) 225.

Lex Fannia. (161 B.C.) One of the *leges sumptuariae;* it limited the expenditures for banquets and the number of persons would could be invited, particularly at the time of the great national games (*ludi*). —See SUMPTUS.

Weiss, *RE* 12, 2353; Kübler, *RE* 4A, 905.

Lex Fufia Caninia. (2 B.C.) Introduced restrictions on testamentary manumissions by fixing a ratio between the number of slaves belonging to the testator and the number of those he could enfranchise in his last will. The more he owned the smaller was the percentage of manumissions permitted. Manumissions ordered in violation of the exact provisions of the law (*in fraudem legis*) were void. The statute was abolished by Justinian whose legislation favored the liberation of slaves (*favor libertatis*).—Inst. *1.7*; C. *7.3*.—See SENATUSCONSULTUM ORFITIANUM.

Leonhard, *RE* 12, 2355; *Acta Divi Augusti* 1 (1945) 202.

Lex Furia de sponsu. (Of unknown date, probably later than the *lex Apuleia de sponsu*.) Dealt with suretyship contracted in Italy in the form of *sponsio* or *fideipromissio*.—See ADPROMISSOR.

Rotondi, *Leges publ. populi Rom.*, 1912, 475; Appleton, *ZSS* 26 (1905); *idem, Mél Gérardin*, 1907; Girard, *St Fadda* 2 (1905).

Lex Furia testamentaria. (Between 204 and 169 B.C.) Fixed the maximum amount of a legacy at one thousand asses except for legacies bequeathed to one's nearest relatives, spouse or bride. It is the earliest statute setting limits for legacies.

Steinwenter, *RE* 12, 2356 (Bibl.), 2421.

Lex Gabinia de piratis persequendis. (67 B.C.) Authorized Cn. Pompeius Magnus to combat piracy with an army of twenty legions and a navy of 500 ships. The identification of the statute with a Greek inscription found in Delos is not certain.

Riccobono, *FIR* 1² (1941) 121 (Bibl.).

Lex Gabinia. (139 B.C.) Forbade secret meetings (*clandestinae coitiones*) directed against the state.

Berger, *RE* Suppl. 7, 395.

Lex Gabinia tabellaria. (139 B.C.) Introduced the secret ballot in the election of magistrates in the popular assemblies.—See TABELLAE.

Lex Genucia. (342 B.C.) A plebiscite which prohibited loans at interest.

Klingmüller, *RE* 6, 2192; Stein, *RE* 7, 1207; Rotondi, *Leges publ. populi Rom.*, 1912, 226; L. Clerici, *Economia e finanza dei Romani*, 1 (1943) 334.

Lex Glitia. Known only from a commentary by Gaius *"ad legem Glitiam."* It dealt with the QUERELA INOFFICIOSI TESTAMENTI. Date is unknown.

　　Weiss, *RE* Suppl. 5, 577; Cuq, *DS* 3, 1145; Rotondi, *loc. cit.* 482.

Lex Hadriana. See LEX MANCIANA.

　　Kornemann, *RE* Suppl. 4, 253; Ch. Saumagne, *Tablettes Albertini*, 1952, 99.

Lex Hieronica. (Third century B.C.) Mentioned by Cicero in his orations against Verres, not a Roman law. Its author was Hiero II, tyrant and (later) king of Syracuse. It was an agrarian law, dealing with the lease of public land and land taxes and remained in vigor after the Roman conquest of Sicily.

　　Lenschan, *RE* 8, 1508; Schwahn, *RE* 7A, 15; Weiss, *RE* 12, 2361; Carcopino, *La loi de Hiéron*, 1914; Plachy, *BIDR* 47 (1940) 87.

Lex horreorum. See HORREUM.

Lex Hortensia de plebiscitis. (*Ca.* 286 B.C.) Provided that "the decrees of the plebeian assemblies shall be binding on the whole people" (Gaius, Inst. 1.3).—See PLEBISCITUM.

　　Lengle, *RE* 6A, 2471; Berger, *RE* Suppl. 7, 396; Siber, *RE* 21, 68; Humbert, *DS* 1, 546; Baviera, *St Brugi*, 1910, 367; Costa, *MemBol* 6 (1911–1912) 77; G. Rotondi, *Leges publ. pop. Rom.*, 1912, 238; H. Siber, *Die plebeischen Magistraturen* 1936, 43; Guarino, *Fschr Schulz* 1 (1951) 458.

Lex Hostilia. An early statute of unknown date, enabled a person who was in captivity or absent on official mission, to be represented in the trial against a thief for the theft committed in the absent person's property.

　　Rotondi, *loc. cit.* 480; P. Huvelin, *Furtum* (1915) 117; Nap, *TR* 13 (1934) 181.

Lex Icilia. (492 B.C.) Probably the earliest law on the inviolability of the plebeian tribunes.—See TRIBUNI PLEBIS.

　　Rotondi, *loc. cit.* 193.

Lex imperii. See LEX DE IMPERIO.

Lex Iulia (leges Iuliae). A statute passed on the legislative initiative of either Iulius Caesar or the emperor Augustus. The proposer cannot always be established with certainty.

Lex Iulia agraria. (59 B.C.) An agrarian law proposed by Caesar during his consulship. It completed the transfer of public land in Italy into private ownership.

　　Vancura, *RE* 12, 1184; Rotondi, *loc. cit.* 387.

Lex Iulia ambitus. (18 B.C.) A statute of Augustus against bribery in elections (AMBITUS). It was still in vigor under Justinian.—D. 48.14; C. 9.26.

　　Berger, *RE* 12, 2365; *Acta Divi Augusti* 1 (1945) 140.

Lex Iulia caducaria. Probably not a special statute concerning CADUCA, but a chapter of the Augustan legislation on marriage and related problems (LEX IULIA DE MARITANDIS ORDINIBUS).—See LEGES CADUCARIAE, CADUCA (Bibl.).

　　V. Bolla, *ZSS* 59 (1939) 546.

Lex Iulia de adulteriis. (18 B.C.) This Augustan statute, which some scholars consider to be a part of the LEX IULIA DE MARITANDIS ORDINIBUS, fixed the cases of adultery punishable as a crime, the penalties, the forms and terms of accusation, etc. See ADULTERIUM. The law also dealt with other crimes against chastity (STUPRUM, INCESTUM).—D. 48.5; C. 9.9.

　　Fitzler-Seeck, *RE* 10, 354; *Acta Divi Augusti* 1 (1945) 112.

Lex Iulia de annona. (18 B.C.?) An Augustan law against merchants raising the market prices of foodstuffs or committing other unfair practices in the sale or transportation of food.—D. 48.12.

　　Rotondi, *loc. cit.* 448; *Acta Divi Augusti* 1 (1945) 200.

Lex Iulia de cessione bonorum. (By Augustus.) Perhaps a part of the LEX IULIA IUDICIORUM PRIVATORUM.—See CESSIO BONORUM.

　　S. Solazzi, *Il concorso dei creditori* 4 (1943) 133; *Acta Divi Augusti* 1 (1945) 152.

Lex Iulia de civitate. (90 B.C.) Bestowed Roman citizenship on Latins (see LATINI) and a great number of the allies (*socii*) in Italy. All allies domiciled in Italy received citizenship in the following year by the *Lex Plautia Papiria* (89 B.C.), provided that they applied to the urban praetor in Rome within sixty days for enrollment on the list of citizens.

　　G. Rotondi, *Leges publ. populi Romani*, 1912, 338.

Lex Iulia de collegiis. An Augustan law; it is mentioned only once in an inscription (CIL 6, 4416 = 6, 2193).

　　Kornemann, *RE* 4, 408; 430; G. Rotondi, *loc. cit.* 442; Berger, *Epigraphica* 9 (1947) 44; G. Bovini, *La proprietà ecclesiastica*, 1949, 141.

Lex Iulia de fundo dotali. Not a specific Augustan law (although once mentioned as such) but a section of the emperor's legislation on adultery (LEX IULIA DE ADULTERIIS). It prohibited the husband to alienate land in Italy constituted as a dowry unless the wife gave her consent.—D. 23.5; C. 5.23.

　　Acta Divi Augusti 1 (1945) 127; Noailles, *Inalienabilité du fonds dotal*, *Annales Univ. Grenoble* 30–31 (1918–1919).

Lex Iulia de maritandis ordinibus. (18 B.C.) This law together with another one, also of Augustus, the *Lex Papia Poppaea* (A.D. 9) deals with several problems connected with marriage. In the writings of the Roman jurists the two laws appear both as two distinctive legislative acts and as one unified piece of legislation, sometimes called simply *"lex"* or *"leges."* The earlier law contained several prohibitions of marriage, such as between senators or their sons and their freedwomen, between free-born men and women of bad behavior or women convicted of adultery. Consorts married in violation of these provisions have no reciprocal rights of succession. Another tendency of the Augustan legislation was to promote marriage and the procreation of children in order to prevent a further decline of morality and family life, widespread in the last decades of the Republic. Various privileges were granted to married people and parents of children whereas on the other hand severe economic and social disadvantages were imposed on unmarried persons (*coelibes*) and childless married persons (*orbi*). A consul who had more children than his colleague had some preference over the latter. Fathers were excused from public charges (*munera*) and tutorship. Married women with three children (four, if they were freedwomen) were not submitted to guardianship (*tutela mulierum*). See IUS LIBERO- RUM. The second statute excluded unmarried men over twenty-five and under sixty and unmarried women over twenty and under fifty from succession under a will. For further provisions, see COELIBES, ORBI, CAPACITAS, PATER SOLITARIUS, CADUCA, DIES CEDENS LEGATI, EREPTORIUM, LEX IULIA MISCELLA, SENATUSCONSULTUM CALVISIANUM, SENATUSCONSUL- TUM MEMMIANUM, PRINCEPS LEGIBUS SOLUTUS.— C. 8.57.

> Fitzler-Seeck, *RE* 10, 354; Schiller, *RE* Suppl. 6, 227; Rotondi, *Leges publ. populi Rom.,* 1912, 443, 457; P. Cor- bett, *The Roman law of marriage,* 1930; Solazzi, *ANap* 59 (1939), 61 (1942); Siber, *Die Ehegesetzgebung des Augustus, Deutsche Rechtswissenschaft,* 4, 2 (1939); *Acta Divi Augusti* 1 (1945) 166 (Bibl.); Nardi, *SDHI* 7 (1941); B. Biondi, *Successione testamentaria* (1943) 136; Field, *ClJ* 1945, 398; Lavaggi, *StSas* 21 (1948); Weiss, *BIDR* 51/52 (1948) 323.

Lex Iulia de modo aedificiorum. A building regula- tion probably of Augustus (18 B.C.?); it set a maxi- mum for the height of houses and the thickness of walls.

> G. Rotondi, *Leges publ. pop. Rom.,* 1912, 447; *Acta Divi Augusti* 1 (1945) 198.

Lex Iulia de pecuniis mutuis. (49 B.C.) A statute passed under the dictatorship of Caesar, introduced some alleviation for debtors who had contracted a loan of money: deduction of interest already paid from the principal, cancellation of interest in arrears for two years, admission of payment in land instead of in cash. Some modifications of the law were made in a later Caesarean law of 46 B.C.

> G. Rotondi, *Leges publ. populi Rom.,* 1912, 415.

Lex Iulia de residuis. See PECULATUS, RESIDUA.

Lex Iulia de senatu habendo. (*Ca.* 10 B.C.) Con- cerned with the procedure of voting in the senate.— See DISCESSIO.

> Rotondi, *op. cit.* 452; *Acta Divi Augusti* 1 (Rome, 1945) 153.

Lex Iulia de vi privata and **Lex Iulia de vi publica.** It is more likely that there were two statutes on the topics indicated, not one, and that their author was Augustus rather than Caesar. For their contents, see VIS, RES VI POSSESSAE, TELUM.—D. 48.6; 7; C. 9.12 (*de vi privata*); D. 48.6; C. 9.12 (*de vi publica*).

> Rotondi, *loc. cit.* 457; Berger, *RE* Suppl. 7, 405; Girard, *ZSS* 34 (1913) 322; Coroi, *La violence en dr. rom.,* 1915; Berger, *Göttingische gel. Anzeigen* 1917, 336; Costa, *RendBol* 2 (1917/18) 23; Niedermeyer, *St Bonfante* 2 (1930) 400; Flore, *ibid.* 4 (1930) 335; G. Pugliese, *Ap- punti sui limiti dell'imperium nella repressione penale* 1939; *Acta Divi Augusti* 1 (1945) 129.

Lex Iulia de vicesima hereditatium. (A.D. 5?) The name Iulia is preserved, but Augustus' authorship is doubtful. The law introduced a tax of 5 per cent on estates and legacies except those left to parents and children and those of small value. The heir could deduct a proportional part of the tax from the legacies. The law also contained provisions concern- ing the opening of last wills (APERTURA TESTAMENTI) in connection with the taxes to be paid.—See VICE- SIMA HEREDITATIUM.

> Rotondi, *loc. cit.* 457; *Acta Divi Augusti* 1 (1945) 219; Stella-Maranca, *RendLinc* 33 (1924).

Lex Iulia iudiciorum privatorum. See the following item.

Lex Iulia iudiciorum publicorum. (17 B.C.?) This Augustan law and another procedural law concerning civil trials (*lex Iulia iudiciorum privatorum*) together constitute the *leges Iuliae iudiciariae.* They are men- tioned along with the LEX AEBUTIA as the statutes which completed the transition from the LEGIS AC- TIONES to the formulary procedure. The norms set in the statutes are known in part from references in Justinian's Digest, in part from juristic (Gaius' In- stitutes, Fragmenta Vaticana) and literary sources. They dealt with various questions about judicial magistrates and judges, the parties to a trial and their advocates, witnesses and the like. They were in a sense a procedural code.—See IUDICIA LEGITIMA.

> Girard, *ZSS* 34 (1913) 295; *Acta Divi Augusti* 1 (1945) 142 (Bibl.).

Lex Iulia maiestatis. There were two Julian statutes on the crime of *maiestas;* one by Caesar (46 B.C.), the other by Augustus (8 B.C.).—See CRIMEN MAIES- TATIS.—D. 48.4; C. 9.8.

> *Acta Divi Augusti* 1 (1945) 156.

Lex Iulia miscella. The name occurs twice in Jus- tinian's enactments. *"Miscella"* is not a proper name as sometimes assumed. It is an adjective, syn. with *saturus* (see LEGES SATURAE). The specific provi- sion referring to it (nullity of a legacy bequeathed by a husband to his wife on the condition that she remain unmarried after his death) is found in the LEX IULIA DE MARITANDIS ORDINIBUS, called *"mis- cella"* by Justinian because of its various intermingled provisions.—C. 6.40.

> Cuq, *DS* 3, 1157; *Acta Divi Augusti* 1 (1945) 173.

Lex Iulia municipalis. Known in modern literature as *Tabula Heracleensis* because the bronze tablet on which a part of the law is preserved was found near the site of ancient Heraclea. The text deals with different subjects and it is striking that a part of it refers to Rome itself, while another and larger portion is a general ordinance for municipalities and colonies. The topics dealt with are distribution of grain, building and traffic regulations, election of municipal magistrates, and administrative problems in munici- palities. Caesar's authorship and the date of the law are debatable, as is its basic character (a *lex data* or *lex rogata*). The law is a good illustration of a *lex satura* (see LEGES SATURAE), generally disliked in Roman legislation.

Ñap, *RE* 12; Kornemann, *RE* 16, 587.611; De Sanctis, *ATor* 45 (1908), 48 (1913); Legras, *La table latine d'Heraclée*, 1907; Gradenwitz, *SbHeid* 1916; v. Premerstein, *ZSS* 43 (1922) 45; Hardy, *Jour. of Philol.* 35 (1919–20); Sanchez Pequero, *Mél Cornil* 2 (1926) 383; D'Eufemia, *L'età della legge latina di Eraclea*, 1931; Cary, *JRS* 19 (1929) 116, 27 (1937) 51; Rudolph, *Stadt und Staat im röm. Italien*, 1935, 113, 176, 217; Riccobono, *FIR* 1² (1941) 140 (Bibl.).

Lex Iulia Papiria. (30 B.C.) On pecuniary fines. It fixed the equivalents 10 asses = one sheep, 100 asses = one ox.

Hellebrand, *RE* Suppl. 6, 545; G. Rotondi, *loc. cit.* 211.

Lex Iulia peculatus. A penal law of Augustus (or Caesar?), dealing with the crimes of PECULATUS and SACRILEGIUM.—D. 48.13; C. 9.28.—See RESIDUA, PRAEDA.

Brecht, *RE* Suppl. 7, 828; *Acta Divi Augusti* 1 (1945) 161.

Lex Iulia repetundarum. (59 B.C.) The last and most severe (*acerrima*) republican statute on *repetundae,* proposed by Caesar as consul. It was still in vigor under Justinian (D. 48.11; C. 9.27) and covered any act of bribery in which a person exercising a public office was involved, judges and arbitrators included. The generalization was so broad that any misdemeanor or violation by a public functionary might fall under the law.—C. 9.27.

Berger, *RE* 12, 2389.

Lex Iulia sumptuaria. (Of the dictator Caesar, 46 B.C.) Against luxury, containing, besides general prohibitions, some special interdictions such as those dealing with the use of litters, purple, luxurious clothing and pearl jewelry. Exceptions were admitted for special occasions and certain persons.—See SUMPTUS.

Kübler, *RE* 4A, 908.

Lex Iulia sumptuaria. (Of the emperor Augustus, 18 B.C.?) Reiterated various severe provisions against luxury in banquets. The law is to be distinguished from the law of the dictator Caesar (see the foregoing entry).

G. Rotondi, *Leges publ. populi Rom.*, 1912, 447; *Acta Divi Augusti* 1 (1945) 198.

Lex Iulia theatralis. (After A.D. 5.) An Augustan law, admitted only free-born persons whose fathers or grandfathers had a patrimony of at least 400,000 sesterces (the equestrian census) to seats in the first fourteen rows in the theater.—See LEX ROSCIA THEATRALIS, EQUITES.

G. Rotondi, *loc. cit.* 462; *Acta Divi Augusti* 1 (1945) 201.

Lex Iulia et Papia Poppaea. See LEX IULIA DE MARITANDIS ORDINIBUS.

Lex Iulia et Plautia. Cited in connection with the exclusion of things taken by force (RES VI POSSESSAE) from being acquired by USUCAPIO. Once (D. 41.3.33.2) the name *lex Plautia et Iulia* occurs. It is more likely, however, that two statutes are meant, *Lex Plautia de vi* and *Lex Iulia de vi.*

Berger, *RE* Suppl. 7, 405.

Lex Iulia et Titia. (Sometimes called simply *lex Titia.*) A law passed under Augustus (exact date unknown), a counterpart for the provinces to the LEX ATILIA on the appointment of tutors. The competent authority was the governor of the province. The term *tutor Titianus* is known from an inscription referring to a guardian appointed according to the *Lex Titia.*—Inst. 1.20.—See TUTOR DATIVUS.

Taubenschlag, *RE* 12; *Acta Divi Augusti* 1 (1945) 199; Solazzi, *Studi su tutela* 2 (1926) 17.

Lex Iunia. (126 B.C.) Ordered the expulsion from Rome of foreigners who pretended to be Roman citizens.

G. Rotondi, *loc. cit.* 304.

Lex Iunia Norbana. (A.D. 19.) Slaves manumitted informally or in violation of earlier laws which had set specific requirements or restrictions for manumissions, did not become full Roman citizens, but LATINI IUNIANI. The paramount disadvantage in their legal situation is that they were not able to make a will or to take under a will. Hence the person who manumitted them retained control over their property.

Steinwenter, *RE* 12, 910; Weiss, *RE* Suppl. 5, 578; Rotondi, *loc. cit.* 463; Wlassak, *ZSS* 26 (1905) 374; A. M. Duff, *Freedmen*, 1928, 75, 210; Biscardi, *Manumissio per mensam, StSen* 1939, 8.

Lex Iunia Petronia. (A.D. 19?) Introduced the rule that in the case of dissent among the jurors (CENTUMVIRI) in trials concerning the liberty of persons whose *status libertatis* is not clear because of lack of evidence, the decision should be in favor of liberty.

G. Rotondi, *loc. cit.* 464.

Lex Iunia Vellaea. (A.D. 26?) Introduced some rules on INSTITUTIO and on EXHEREDATIO of posthumous children.—See POSTUMI IUNIANI.

Weiss, *RE* 12, 2394; G. Rotondi, *loc. cit.* 465; Solazzi, *Ath* 18 (1930) 45.

Lex Laetoria. See LEX PLAETORIA.

F. Schulz, *Roman classical law*, 1951, 191.

Lex Latina tabulae Bantinae. (133–118 B.C.) A statute of unknown content; only the sanction is preserved containing penalties for non-observant magistrates. On the reverse side of the bronze tablet with the *Lex Latini* there is another inscription in the Oscan dialect (*lex Osca tabulae Bantinae*) with a partial text of the municipal charter of Bantia (South Italy).

E. H. Warmington, *Remains of old Latin* 4 (1940) 294; Riccobono, *FIR* 1² (1941) 82, 163; Zotta, *RendLinc* 98 (1939) 373 (on *lex Osca*).

Lex Licinia. On extraordinary magistracies, see LEX AEBUTIA on extraordinary magistracies.

Lex Licinia (Licinnia). (On the *actio communi dividundo.*) An early Republican statute introduced the proceedings by *legis actio per iudicis postulationem* for the division of common property.

Berger, *RE* Suppl. 7, 398.

Lex Licinia de sodaliciis. (55 B.C.) Directed against a special type of associations organized during the electoral period to support a candidate for a magistracy by unfair practices which were considered a special form of AMBITUS.

Weiss, *RE* 12, 2394, no. 3; Berger, *ibid.* 2395; Pfaff, *RE* 3, 785; Rotondi, *loc. cit.* 407; Accame, *Bull. Commissione archeologica del Governorato di Roma* 70 (1942) 32.

Lex Licinia Cassia. (172 B.C.) Gave consuls and praetors the right to appoint military tribunes; previously they were elected by the *comitia tributa*.

G. Rotondi, *loc. cit.* 282.

Lex Licinia Iunia. (62 B.C.) Ordered that the official text of statutes be deposited in the state archive in the *aerarium.*—See AERARIUM POPULI ROMANI.

Münzer, *RE* 10, 1090; Rotondi, *loc. cit.* 383; Landucci, *APad* 1896, 146; F. v. Schwind, *Zur Frage der Publikation* 1940, 27.

Lex Licinia Mucia. (95 B.C.) Established the conditions for the acquisition of Roman citizenship by Latins who had taken up residence in Rome, and fixed penalties for non-citizens in Rome who acted as if they were citizens.

Weiss, *RE* 12, 2395, no. 6.

Lex Licinia Sextia. On loans. (367 B.C.) Debtors received the right to pay in three annual installments and to deduct the interests paid from the sum due.

G. Rotondi, *loc. cit.* 217.

Lex Licinia Sextia. On the plebeian consulship and the creation of the praetorship. (367 B.C.) Granted the plebeians one of the two consulships and established the office of praetor accessible only to patricians.

G. Rotondi, *loc. cit.* 218; v. Fritz, *Historia* 1 (Baden-Baden, 1950) 3.

Lex Licinia Sextia agraria. (367 B.C.) Limited the dimensions of a plot of the *ager publicus* that could be assigned to individuals to 500 Roman acres (*iugera*) and settled the number of head of cattle to be held by the possessors.

Vancura, *RE* 12, 1164; Cuq, *DS* 3, 1153; Rotondi, *loc. cit.* 217; L. Clerici, *Economia e finanza dei Romani*, 1 (1943) 290; Tibiletti, *Ath* 26 (1948) 191.

Lex Licinia sumptuaria. (103 B.C.?) A statute against luxury which repeated provisions of earlier laws.—See SUMPTUS.

Rotondi, *loc. cit.* 327; Kübler, *RE* 5A, 905.

Lex Livia iudiciaria. (91 B.C.) Established a special court (*quaestio*) for trials of judges corrupted by bribery.

Rotondi, *loc. cit.* 337.

Lex Lutatia de vi. Probably identical with LEX PLAUTIA DE VI.

Berger, *RE* Suppl. 7, 399; Cousin, *RHD* 22 (1943) 88.

Lex Maenia de patrum auctoritate. (Of unknown date, probably not before the beginning of the third century B.C.) Ordered that candidates for office had to be approved by the senate before the people voted in the *comitia*. This provision of the statute is analogous to that of LEX PUBLILIA PHILONIS in legislative matters.

Weiss, *RE* 12, 2396; O'Brien-Moore, *RE* Suppl. 6, 677; Guarino, *Studi Solazzi*, 1948, 29.

Lex Malacitana. (A.D. 82–84.) See LEX SALPENSANA.

Lex Mamilia Roscia Peducaea Alliena Fabia. (Of uncertain date, after 111 B.C. and perhaps as late as 59 B.C.) Dealt with controversies over boundaries of landed property in colonies and *municipia*. Three chapters of the statute are preserved in the writings of land surveyors (*gromatici*). It is uncertain whether the law was a section of the LEX IULIA AGRARIA or a plebiscite proposed by a tribune Mamilius and his four colleagues. The appearance of five names in the denomination of the *lex* is unique.—See CONTROVERSIA DE FINE.

Vancura, *RE* 12, 1185; Kroll, *RE* 12, 2397; Cary, *Journ. Philol.* 35 (1920) 184; Fabricius, *SbHeid* 1924; Piganiol, *Comptes-Rendus Acad. des Inscriptions* 1939, 193; Riccobono, *FIR* 1² (1941) 138; Le Gall, *Revue de philologie* 20 (1946) 138; Herrman, *RIDA* 1 (1948) 113; L. R. Taylor, *Studies in honor of A. C. Johnson*, 1951, 68; Piganiol, *CRAI* 1949, 193.

Lex Manciana. (Under Vespasian?) Concerned with the administration of imperial domains in North Africa by imperial *procuratores* and the relations with the leaseholders (*conductores*). A similar law was the so-called *lex Hadriana*.

Kornemann, *RE* Suppl. 4, 251; A. Hajje, *Études sur les locations à long terme*, 1926; Haywood, in T. Frank, *An economic survey of ancient Rome* 4 (1938) 101; Riccobono, *FIR* 1² (1941) 484, 493; Toutain, *Mél F. Martroye* (*Société Nat. des Antiquaires de France*) 1941; Saumagne, *Tablettes Albertini*, 1952, 116.

Lex Manilia. (67 B.C.) Gave freedmen the right to vote in the *tribus* of their patrons.

G. Rotondi, *loc. cit.* 375.

Lex Manlia. (On manumission taxes, 357 B.C.) See VICESIMA MANUMISSIONUM.

G. Rotondi, *loc. cit.* 375.

Lex Marcia. (On usury, 104 B.C.) Protected the debtors who had paid the moneylenders interest at a rate higher than was legally permitted by granting them the privilege of recovering the sum unduly paid through the procedure of MANUS INIECTIO.

G. Rotondi, *loc. cit.* 326.

Lex Maria. (119 B.C.) Set general rules for secret voting by tablets in the popular assemblies.—See TABELLAE.

G. Rotondi, *loc. cit.* 318.

Lex Maria (Marcia) Porcia. (62 B.C.) See TRIUMPHUS.

Lex Menenia Sestia. (452 B.C.) See LEX ATERNIA TARPEIA.

Lex metalli Vipascensis. (Second century after Christ.) An ordinance for the administration of the mines in Vipasca (Spain) with instructions to the imperial *procurator metallorum* concerning the lease of the mines to private *conductores*.

Riccobono, *FIR* 1² (1941) 502; Schönbauer, *Beiträge zur Geschichte des Bergbaurechts*, 1929; Kübler, *ZSS* 49 (1929) 569; Schönbauer, *ZSS* 55 (1935) 212; U. Täckholm, *Bergbau in der röm. Kaiserzeit* (Uppsala, 1937) 101; D'Ors, *Iura* 2 (1951) 128.

Lex Minicia. (Date unknown, about 90 B.C.) Ordered that a child born of parents of a different *status civitatis* receives the lower status.

Weiss, *RE* 12, 2399; Rotondi, *loc. cit.* 338.

Lex municipalis Tarentina. (First century B.C.) A municipal charter (*lex data*) of Tarentum, preserved in part. It contains provisions about the responsibility of municipal magistrates, building regulations, and the like.—See LEGES DATAE.

G. Rotondi, *loc. cit.* 492; Rudolph, *Stadt und Staat im röm. Italien*, 1935, 132; Riccobono, *FIR* 1² (1941) 166; E. H. Warmington, *Remains of old Latin*, 4 (1940) 438.

Lex naturalis. See NATURALIS LEX.

Lex Ogulnia. (300 B.C.) Augmented the number of *pontifices* and *augures* from four to eight and nine, respectively, and established the rule that four *pontifices* and five *augures* were to be plebeians.

Riewald, *RE* 1A, 1639; Münzer, *RE* 17, 2065; Rotondi, *loc. cit.* 236.

Lex Oppia. (215 B.C.) Condemned luxury among women. It introduced restrictions on jewelry and prohibited many-colored dresses. The statute was abolished twenty years later by the *Lex Valeria Fundania.*—See SUMPTUS.

Kübler, *RE* 4A, 904.

Lex Orchia. (181 B.C.) Also a *lex sumptuaria.* See SUMPTUS. It limited the number of persons who could participate in a sumptuous dinner.

Rotondi, *loc. cit.* 276; Kübler, *RE* 4A, 905.

Lex Osca tabulae Bantinae. See LEX LATINA TABULAE BANTINAE.

Lex Ovinia. See LECTIO SENATUS.

Lex Papia. On foreigners. (65 B.C.) Introduced special proceedings against foreigners who unlawfully pretended to be Roman citizens. The penalty was expulsion from Rome.

Weiss, *RE* 12, 2399.

Lex Papia. On Vestal virgins. (65 B.C.) Established the procedure for the selection of Vestales by the high pontiff (PONTIFEX MAXIMUS).—See VESTALES.

Berger, *RE* Suppl. 7, 402.

Lex Papia Poppaea. See LEX IULIA DE MARITANDIS ORDINIBUS.

Lex Papiria. On TRESVIRI CAPITALES, of unknown date, third or second century B.C.

G. Rotondi, *loc. cit.* 312.

Lex Papiria de consecratione. (Date unknown.) Required the approval of the *plebs* for the validity of *consecratio* (*dedicatio*). The statute seems to have been one of the earliest plebiscites.

Berger, *RE* Suppl. 7, 402; Paoli, *RHD* 25 (1946/7) 176; Santi Di Paola, *St Solazzi* 1948, 631.

Lex Papiria tabellaria. (131 B.C.) Guaranteed secrecy in voting on legislative matters in the popular assemblies.—See TABELLAE.

Liebenam, *RE* 4, 692.

Lex Petronia de praefectis iure dicundo. (Before 32 B.C.) Regulated the election of *praefecti iure dicundo* in municipalities.

Cuq, *DS* 3, 1158; Rotondi, *loc. cit.* 439.

Lex Petronia. On slaves. (A.D. 61?) Prohibited masters from exposing their slaves to fight with wild beasts without permission from the competent magistrate. Approval was given when a slave deserved punishment for bad conduct.

Leonhard and Weiss, *RE* 12, 2401; Rotondi, *loc. cit.* 468.

Lex Pinaria. An early statute which fixed the term of thirty days for the reappearance of the parties in a trial conducted in the form of *legis actio sacramento.*—See LEGIS ACTIO SACRAMENTO.

G. Rotondi, *loc. cit.* 472.

Lex Pinaria Furia. (472 B.C.?) Reformed the calendar by the insertion of an intercalary month.

Berger, *RE* Suppl. 7, 403.

Lex Plaetoria (Laetoria?) de minoribus. (192/1 B.C.) Protected persons *sui iuris* under twenty-five years of age (*minores*) who had been defrauded in a transaction. The latter was valid in principle, but the minor, when sued for payment, had an exception, *exceptio legis Plaetoriae,* for his defense. Besides, an *actio legis Plaetoriae* was available to anyone (*actio popularis*) against the person who exploited the inexperience of a minor (*circumscriptio adolescentium*).—See MINORES.

Berger, *RE* 15, 1863, 1867; Weiss, *RE* Suppl. 5, 578; Rotondi, *loc. cit.* 271; Debray, *Mél Girard* 1 (1912) 265; Duquesne, *Mél Cornil* 1 (1926) 156; Nap, *TR* 13 (1934) 194.

Lex Plautia de vi. (78–63 B.C.?) The earliest law against the *crimen vis* (violence) committed either against the state or a private individual.—See VIS, RES VI POSSESSAE.

Berger, *RE* Suppl. 7, 403 (Bibl.); J. Coroï, *La violence en droit criminel rom.,* 1915, 31; Cousin, *RHD* 22 (1943) 88.

Lex Plautia iudiciaria. (89 B.C.) On the election of judges (fifteen for each *tribus*).

G. Rotondi, *loc. cit.* 342.

Lex Plautia Papiria de civitate. See LEX IULIA DE CIVITATE.

G. Rotondi, *loc. cit.* 340.

Lex Plotia de vi. See LEX PLAUTIA DE VI.

Lex Poetelia de ambitu. (358 B.C.) The earliest statute against unfair machinations for electoral purposes. In particular the statute forbade competition for votes in market places.

Berger, *RE* 12, 2407; Husband, *CIJ* 10 (1914/5) 376.

Lex Poetelia Papiria. (326 B.C.) The statute, called by Livy (VIII 28.1) "another beginning of the freedom of the Roman *plebs*," forbade the private imprisonment of the debtor by the creditor, which was a kind of enslavement since the debtor (*nexus*) had to work for the creditor like a slave. Many details about *necti* are doubtful as is the whole doctrine on *nexum,* owing to the discrepancies in the confusing reports in literary sources (Livy, Varro), especially about putting the debtor into fetters.—See NEXUM, IURARE BONAM COPIAM.

Huvelin, *DS* 4, 83; Berger, *RE* Suppl. 7, 405; Kleineidam, *Fg Dahn* 2 (1905) 1; Ausiello, *AnCam* 2 (1929); De

Visscher, *Mél Fournier* 1929 (= *Études de dr. rom.* 1934, 313); Kaser, *Das altröm. Ius* 1949, 247; v. Lübtow, *ZSS* 67 (1950) 154.

Lex Pompeia. On candidates for a magisterial post. (52 B.C.) It obliged them to be present in Rome during the electoral period.

Lex Pompeia. On provincial administration. (52 B.C.) Established the interval of five years between the holding of a magistracy in Rome and a subsequent pro-magistracy in a province.

G. Rotondi, *loc. cit.* 411.

Lex Pompeia de ambitu. (62 B.C.) A very severe statute against bribery at elections. It has interest because of its procedural provisions.

Berger, *RE* 12, 2403.

Lex Pompeia de culleo. (55 B.C.?) Abolished execution by drowning the condemned culprit in a leather sack (CULLEUS). The statute was perhaps a section of the *lex Pompeia de parricidio.*

Hitzig, *RE* 4 (s.v. *culleus*, no. 4).

Lex Pompeia de parricidio. (55 or 52 B.C.) Extended the term *parricidium* to the assassination of parents, grandparents, children, grandchildren, brothers, uncles, a consort or fiancé, and some other relatives. The law apparently substituted the penalty of AQUAE ET IGNIS INTERDICTIO for the ancient form of execution by CULLEUS. It is still in vigor under Justinian, D. 48.9.

Hitzig, *loc. supra cit.*; G. Rotondi, *Leges publ. populi Rom.,* 1912, 406; Radin, *JRS* 10 (1920).

Lex Pompeia de vi. (52 B.C.) A special statute on *crimen vis* (violence) the occasion of which was a great riot with fires and massacres at the *via Appia.* Severe penalties were set.—See VIS.

Berger, *RE* Suppl. 7, 409; Rotondi, *loc. cit.* 410; J. Coroï, *La violence en droit criminel rom.,* 1915, 93.

Lex Pompeia Licinia. On tribunes. (70 B.C.) Abolished the restrictions imposed on the plebeian tribunate by Sulla.—See LEX CORNELIA and LEX AURELIA on tribunes.

Lex Porcia (Leges Porciae). Three *Leges Porciae* of the second century B.C. are mentioned in connection with the right of appeal (PROVOCATIO) of persons condemned in a criminal trial. One of them dealt with the PROVOCATIO of soldiers.—See LEX VALERIA.

Cuq, *DS* 3, 1160; Rotondi, *loc. cit.* 268.

Lex praediatoria. See PRAEDIATOR.

Lex provinciae. A law concerning the organization of the administration of a conquered province. Originally it was issued by the commanding general with the assistance of a senatorial commission.—See LEX DATA, PROVINCIA, LEGATI DECEM.

Lex Publicia. (Earlier than *lex Cincia* of 204 B.C.) Limited the gifts of freedmen to their patrons who used to demand (*exigere*) excessive donations on the occasion of the feast of the Saturnalia.

Berger, *RE* Suppl. 7, 410.

Lex Publicia de aleatoribus. See LEX TITIA DE ALEATORIBUS.

Lex Publilia de sponsu. See ACTIO DEPENSI.

Lex Publilia Philonis. On admission of plebeians to censorship (339 B.C.) Henceforth, one of the censors had to be a plebeian.

Lex Publilia Philonis. On the *auctoritas* of the senate (339 B.C.). The law repealed the requirement that the senate approve (*auctoritas*) legislative enactments of the popular assemblies after their passage. From then on, approval was given in advance and thus became a mere formality. It is controversial whether the statute simply reiterated the provision of LEX VALERIA HORATIA to the effect that legal enactments voted by the plebeian assemblies (*concilia plebis*) were binding on all citizens, plebeians and patricians alike.—See AUCTORITAS SENATUS, LEX HORTENSIA, SENATOR.

Rotondi, *loc. cit.* 226; G. W. Botsford, *The R. assemblies,* 1909, 299; Guarino, *St Solazzi* 1948; *idem, Fschr Schulz* 1 (1951) 461.

Lex Publilia Voleronis. (471 B.C.) Based the plebeian assembly and the election of plebeian magistrates on a territorial, tribal division.

G. Rotondi, *loc. cit.* 197; Niccolini, *Hist* 2 (1928) 12, 3 (1929) 184.

Lex Pupia. (57 B.C.) Prohibited meetings of the senate on the days on which popular assemblies were convoked.

Rotondi, *loc. cit.* 399.

Lex Quinctia. On aqueducts. (9 B.C.) Settled penalties for damages to aqueducts and other constructions connected with the water supply of Rome. The statute is preserved in the monograph of the Roman writer Frontinus (first century after Christ) "On the Water Supply (*de aquis*) of Rome." The author was *curator aquarum* (= commissioner for water supply).

Riccobono, *FIR* 1² (1941) 152; *Acta Divi Augusti* 1 (1945) 154.

Lex regia. Justinian terms the so-called LEX DE IMPERIO by this name.—For the laws under the kingship, see LEGES REGIAE.

Lex Remmia. (80 B.C.) See CALUMNIA.

Hitzig, *RE* 3, 1415; Lindsay, *ClPhilol* 44 (1949) 241.

Lex Rhodia de iactu. Not a Roman creation. The Romans adopted it early from the Rhodians; at the end of the Republic it was already commented on by the Roman jurists. The law is based on the principle that when goods are thrown overboard to lighten a ship in distress, the loss is shared among all whose goods are saved. Robbery of merchandise by pirates does not come under the law.—D. 14.2.—See IACTUS.

Berger, *RE* 9, 545; Benedict, *Yale Law Jour.* 18 (1908/9) 242; Dareste, *NRHD* 29 (1905) 429; Kreller, *Ztschr. für das gesamte Handelsrecht* 85 (1921) 257; G. Hubrecht, *Quelques observations sur l'interprétation romaine de la l.R.,* 1934; De Martino, *RDNav* 1 (1935) 217, 3 (1937) 335, 4 (1938) 3.180; Léfèbvre d'Ovidio, *RDNav* 1 (1935) 36; R. Zeno, *Storia del diritto marittimo* 1946, 22; Osuchowski, *Iura* 1 (1950) 292; Wieacker, *St Albertario* 1 (1952) 515. For the Byzantine compilation of maritime law (eighth century), known as *Nomos Rhodion Nautikos,* see Ashburner, *The Rhodian Sea-law,* 1909; Perugi, *Roma e l'Oriente* 4 (1914) 9, 24, 140.

Lex Romana Burgundionum. (*Ca.* A.D. 500.) Belongs to the so-called LEGES ROMANAE BARBARORUM. It is a compilation of Roman legal rules for the use of the Roman citizens in Burgund. Its sources are the three *Codices, Gregorianus, Hermogenianus* and *Theodosianus,* some post-Theodosian Novels, and juristic writings of Gaius and Paul.

> Berger, *RE* 12, 2406; Baviera, *FIR* 2² (1940) 713; De Salis, *Monumenta Germaniae Historica, Legum sectio* 1, 2 (1892); H. Rüegger, *Einflüsse des röm. Rechts in der L.R.B.,* Diss. Berne, 1949.

Lex Romana canonice compta. A collection of constitutions from Justinian's Code, primarily concerned with ecclesiastical matters. It was compiled in Italy in the ninth century.

> C. G. Mor, *L.R.c.c.,* Pubbl. Univ. Pavia, 1927.

Lex Romana Raetica Curiensis. Also called *Utinensis.* (Of the late eighth or ninth century.) Built up on the pattern of the LEX ROMANA VISIGOTHORUM, for the use of Roman citizens in the Franconian state.

> Berger, *RE* 12, 2406; Edition: Zeumer, *Monumenta Germaniae Historica,* Leges, 5 (1889).

Lex Romana Visigothorum. By order of Alaric II, king of the Visigoths, a compilation of Roman Law was made for the use of Roman citizens in the Visigothic state. The sources excerpted in the collection are the three Codes, *Gregorianus, Hermogenianus* and *Theodosianus,* the post-Theodosian Novels, Gaius' Institutes and Paul's *Sententiae.* The excerpts from the *Sententiae* and the Theodosian Code are provided with paraphrastic and explanatory notes, *interpretationes,* of unknown origin, but not unimportant for they often contain additional details. The *Lex Romana Visigothorum* is called also *Breviarium Alaricianum* (*Alarici*).—See INTERPRETATIONES AD CODICEM THEODOSIANUM, EPITOME GAI.

> Edition: Haenel, *L.R.V.,* 1949; Baviera, *FIR* 2² (1940) 655 contains excerpts of the *Codex Gregorianus* and *Hermogenianus,* and two appendices of the *lex*; *Epitome Gai, ibid.* 231. Translation: S. P. Scott, *The Visigothic Code,* Boston, 1910.—Bibl.: Berger, *RE* 12, 2407; Baudry, *DS* 1 (*s.v. Breviarium A.*); Patetta, *AG* 47 (1891) 3; Calisse, *AG* 72 (1904) 143; M. Conrat, *Breviarium A.,* 1903; *idem, Die Entstehung des westgothischen Gaius,* 1905; *idem, Der westgothische Paulus,* 1907; G. G. Archi, *L'Epitome Gai,* 1937; Lear, *The public law in the Visig. Code, Speculum* 26 (1951) 1; Bruck, *St Arangio-Ruiz* 1 (1952) 202.

Lex Roscia. See EQUITES.

Lex Roscia theatralis. (67 B.C.) Contained some rules about the distribution of seats in the theaters. The *equites* were seated behind the senators.—See LEX IULIA THEATRALIS.

> Von der Mühll, *RE* 1A, 1126 no. 22.

Lex Rubria de Gallia Cisalpina. A charter for *Gallia Cisalpina,* issued before 42 B.C. when the territory

was still a Roman province. Only chapters 30–33 are epigraphically preserved. The inscription is of paramount importance for the knowledge of certain legal institutions, such as *operis novi nuntiatio* and *cautio damni infecti,* as well as of the jurisdiction of municipal magistrates and some procedural questions (execution against *confessi*).

> Edition: Riccobono, *FIR* 1² (1941) 169 (Bibl.); Gradenwitz, *Versuch einer Decomposition des Rubrischen Fragments, SbHeid* 1915; Berger, *RE* 12, 2412.

Lex Rupilia. (131 B.C.) Organized Sicily as a province. It is frequently referred to in Cicero's orations against Verres.

> Weiss, *RE* 12, 2413.

Lex Saenia. (30 B.C.) See LEX CASSIA of 45 B.C.
> *Acta Divi Augusti* 1 (1945) 107.

Lex Salpensana. (A.D. 82–84.) A municipal constitution of the Latin *municipium Salpensa.* A part of the text, together with the LEX MALACITANA, was found on a bronze tablet near Malaga in Spain. The sections of the two charters preserved inform us about municipal magistracies, manumission of slaves and appointment of tutors (*Lex Salpensana*), municipal assemblies, candidates in elections and voting, the administration of municipal funds, tax-farming, fines, and the like (*Lex Malacitana*). Some provisions are preserved in both charters.

> Kornemann, *RE* 16, 614; Riccobono, *FIR* 1² (1941) 202, 208; Schulz, *St Solazzi* (1948) 451.

Lex Scatinia (Scantinia). Against *stuprum cum masculo* (= pederasty, 149 B.C.). The penalty was a fine of ten thousand sesterces.

> Berger, *RE* Suppl. 7, 411; Weiss, *RE* 12, 2413.

Lex Scribonia. (About 50 B.C.) Excluded the acquisition of servitudes through *usucapio.*

> Leonhard, *RE* 2A, 1826; G. Rotondi, *Leges publ. populi Romani,* 1912, 414; Levy, *St Albertario* 2 (1950) 221.

Lex semiunciaria. (*De fenore semiunciario,* 367 B.C.) Reduced the *fenus unciarium* to half the former rate. —See FENUS UNCIARIUM.

> Berger, *RE* Suppl. 7, 394.

Lex Sempronia agraria. There were two agrarian laws under the name Sempronia: one of the tribune Tiberius Sempronius Gracchus of 133 B.C., the other of Gaius Sempronius Gracchus of 123 B.C.—See LEGES AGRARIAE.

> G. Rotondi, *loc. cit.* 298 (Bibl. on the Gracchi, see also Rotondi, *Scritti* 1, 1922, 421), 307; Vancura, *RE* 12, 1169; Terruzzi, *BIDR* 36 (1928) and *Ath* 5 (1928) 85.

Lex Sempronia de abactis. (123 B.C.) A magistrate forced to resign his office by a decision of the people could not obtain another office.

> Berger, *RE* Suppl. 7, 412.

Lex Sempronia de provocatione. (123 B.C.) Strengthened the rules regarding the appeal to the people (*provocatio*).

> Cuq, *DS* 3, 1164.

Lex Sempronia frumentaria. (123 B.C.) A plebiscite proposed by G. Sempronius Gracchus, introduced the distribution of grain (*frumentatio*) to all Roman citizens: five measures, *modii,* monthly at the fixed price of 6⅓ asses. A later statute, *lex Clodia* (58 B.C.), restricted the distribution to needy people.

Rostowzew, *RE* 7, 173; Cardinali, *DE* 3, 239; Van Berchem, *La distribution du blé à la plèbe rom.,* Genève, 1939.

Lex Sempronia iudiciaria. See EQUITES (123 B.C.).

Guénoun, *Ét Girard* 1 (1912); Fraccaro, *RendLomb* 52 (1919) 355.

Lex Sempronia. On interest. (193 B.C.) Provided that Roman statutes on interest in loan contracts should be also applied to transactions fictitiously (*via fraudis*) concluded with citizens of allied states (*socii*) in order to avoid the restrictions imposed on loan transactions among Roman citizens.

Berger, *RE* Suppl. 7, 412 (no. 5); Rotondi, *loc. cit.* 271.

Lex servilia de repetundis. (111 B.C.) More severe than the previous laws on the *crimen repetundarum.* It was the first statute to introduce the loss of political rights as a penalty for *repetundae.*

Berger, *RE* 12, 2414.

Lex Silia de condictione. An early statute of unknown date which established the *legis actio per condictionem* for claims of a fixed sum of money (*certum*).—See LEX CALPURNIA, LEGIS ACTIO PER CONDICTIONEM.

Nap, *TR* 9 (1929) 62.

Lex Silia de ponderibus. (Date unknown, third century B.C.?) Introduced penalties for magistrates who forged, or participated in a forgery of, weights or measures.

Riccobono, *FIR* 1² (1941) 79.

Lex Tarentina. See LEX MUNICIPII TARENTINI.

Lex Terentia. (189 B.C.) Gave the sons of freedmen citizenship *optimo iure* (with full rights).

Münzer, *RE* 5A, 652; Kübler, *RE* 9, 1545; Steinwenter, *RE* 13, 106.

Lex Thoria. An agrarian law of 119–118 B.C., often identified with the LEX AGRARIA of 111 B.C.

Vancura, *RE* 12, 1176; Rotondi, *loc. cit.* 318; Thompson, *Classical Rev.* 27 (1913) 23; Caspary, *Klio* 13 (1913) 84; Hardy, *Jour. of Philol.* 30, 32 (1909, 1912); D'Arms, *Amer. Jour. of Philol.* 56 (1935) 232.

Lex Titia de aleatoribus. A republican statute which allowed betting on sports in which the bravery (*virtus*) of the competitors was implied. The statute is mentioned (D. 11.5.3) together with a *Lex Publicia* and a *Lex Cornelia* the provisions of which are unknown.

Lex Titia. (43 B.C.) Introduced an extraordinary magistracy, a commission of three persons for the reorganization of the constitutional structure of the state, *tresviri reipublicae constituendae causa* (the first triumvirate was composed of Octavian, Antonius, and Lepidus). They were invested with full consular power for five years and with the right to appoint magistrates. The commission was apparently renewed by a statute of 37 B.C.

Lécrivain, *DS* 5, 412; De Villa, *NDI* 12, 1, 552; Strasburger, *RE* 7A, 519; Rotondi, *loc. cit.* 438.

Lex Titia. On tutorship (under Augustus, date unknown); see LEX IULIA ET TITIA.

Lex Trebonia. (448 B.C.) Introduced the election of ten plebeian tribunes in the *concilia plebis.*

Rotondi, *loc. cit.* 206.

Lex Tullia de ambitu. (63 B.C.) Proposed under the consulship of Cicero.—See AMBITUS.

Berger, *RE* 12, 2416.

Lex unciaria. See LEX CORNELIA POMPEIA.

Lex Ursonensis. See LEX COLONIAE IULIAE GENETIVAE.

Lex Valeria de provocatione. (509 B.C.) At the very beginning of the Republic, this established the rule that a Roman citizen sentenced to capital or corporal punishment by a consul had the right of appeal to the people. The rule was confirmed by the Twelve Tables, which provided that the appeal had to be submitted to the *comitia centuriata.* The rule, apparently violated in later times, was repeated with severe punishments by a *Lex Valeria Horatia* (449 B.C.), again by a *Lex Valeria* (300 B.C.) and a century later by the LEGES PORCIAE.—See PROVOCATIO.

G. Rotondi, *loc. cit.* 190; G. Pugliese, *Appunti sui limiti dell'imperium nella repressione penale,* 1939.

Lex Valeria. On the abolition of kingship. (509 B.C.) Threatened with the death penalty anyone who would endeavor to promote the restoration of kingship.

Berger, *RE* Suppl. 7, 414.

Lex Valeria. On debts, issued in a time of economic crisis. (86 B.C.) Permitted the debtors to pay only one-fourth of their debts and freed them from the remainder. The statute, criticized later as *turpissima lex* (= "a very bad law"), was in force only a few years.

Lex Valeria Cornelia. (A.D. 5.) See DESTINATIO.

Lex Valeria Fundania. See LEX OPPIA.

Lex Valeria Horatia. See LEX VALERIA DE PROVOCATIONE.

Lex Valeria Horatia. (449 B.C., on plebiscites.) Provided that "what the *plebs* assembled by tribes (*tributim*) ordered was binding on the whole people" (Livy 3.55).—See LEX PUBLILIA PHILONIS.

G. Rotondi, *loc. cit.* 203; Humbert, *DS* 1, 546; Guarino, *Fschr Schulz* 1 (1951) 461.

Lex Valeria Horatia. (449 B.C.) On the inviolability of the plebeian tribunes.—See SACROSANCTI.

Lex Valeria Horatia. (449 B.C.) On *senatusconsulta.* It ordered the deposition of *senatusconsulta* with the plebeian *aediles* in the temple of Ceres.

Lex Vallia. (Second century B.C.) Permitted the debtor in some cases of MANUS INIECTIO to resist immediate arrest by the creditor who laid hands upon him by repelling this gesture (*manum repellere*), and to defend himself without the aid of a guaranty (VINDEX).

Taubenschlag, *RE* 14, 1401; Berger, *RE* Suppl. 7, 416; G. Rotondi, *loc. cit.* 478.

Lex Varia. (90 B.C.) Punished for treason those who "by help and advice" (*ope et consilio*) induced an allied country to take up arms against Rome.

> G. Rotondi, *loc. cit.* 339.

Lex Vatinia. See REIECTIO IUDICIS.'

Lex venditionis. The conditions of sale in the case of BONORUM VENDITIO of an insolvent debtor. Generally *lex venditionis* indicates a specific clause in a sale which differs from the normal provisions of such a contract.—See LEX CONTRACTUS.

> Vazny, *BIDR* 40 (1932) 72.

Lex Vetti Libici. A statute of unknown origin and content. The name is preserved in an imperial constitution (C. 7.9.3.1) which notes the extension of that law to the provinces. The name is certainly corrupt. The law apparently dealt with the citizenship of freedmen, who before the enfranchisement were *servi publici*.

> Leonhard, *RE* 12, 2417; Cuq, *DS* 3, 1167; G. Rotondi, *loc. cit.* 471.

Lex Vibia. (43 B.C.) Renewed the abolition of the dictatorship.—See LEX ANTONIA.

Lex Villia. Called *annalis* (180 B.C.). Fixed the minimum age for Roman magistrates: for consuls forty-three years of age, for praetors forty, for *aediles curules* thirty-seven. The interval of time between the tenure of two offices was settled at two years.

> Humbert, *DS* 1, 270; Rotondi, *loc. cit.* 278; Fraccaro, *CentCodPav* (1934) 473; Afzelius, *ClMed* 8 (1947) 263.

Lex Visellia. On freedmen (A.D. 24). Freedmen of a lower degree of citizenship (LATINI IUNIANI) obtained full Roman citizenship as a reward for six years' service in the fire brigades (VIGILES) of Rome. Another provision of the law punished freedmen who falsely pretended to be free-born. Under the statute freedmen were excluded from municipal offices, especially from the decurionate.—C. 9.21.

> Leonhard, *RE* 12, 2418; Rotondi, *loc. cit.* 465; Schneider, *ZSS* 5 (1884) 245.

Lex Voconia. (169 B.C.) Contained several provisions concerned with the law of succession: (1) No woman could be heir (*heres*) to an estate having a value greater than a fixed amount on which the available historical sources do not agree (it was at least 200,000 asses). The restriction did not apply to intestate inheritance and to legacies, nor to testaments of Vestal virgins and of the *flamen Dialis*. (2) Admitted among female agnates only the sisters of the deceased to intestate succession. (3) No one person—male or female—could receive by legacy more than the heir (or all heirs together) instituted in the last will. This prohibition was also limited to larger estates, as above. The possibility remained of leaving the heirs very small portions in order to make numerous small legacies. The *lex Voconia* belongs, together with the former LEX FURIA TESTAMENTARIA and the later LEX FALCIDIA, to the statutes which by imposing limits on the amount of legacies, aimed at making inheritances more attractive to the heirs instituted and thereby discouraging their refusal of the testamentary inheritance, by which action all dispositions of the testator would be frustrated (*testamentum desertum, destitutum*). On the other hand, the *lex Voconia* had a purpose of more social character, namely to restrain the luxury of women inheriting big patrimonies. The rule, mentioned above under 3, was superseded by the LEX FALCIDIA. The incapacity of women to be instituted testamentary heirs was somehow alleviated by the Augustan legislation on marriage and lost its practical significance no later than the beginning of the second century. An allusion to the motivation of the *lex Voconia*, unfavorable to women's rights of succession is reflected in the term *Voconiana ratio*.

> Steinwenter, *RE* 12, 2418 (Bibl.); Kübler, *ZSS* 41 (1920) 23; Brassloff, *Studien zur röm. Rechtsgeschichte*, 1925, 70; Cassisi, *AnCat* 3 (1950).

Libellaticus. See LIBELLUS LIBELLATICI.

Libellensis. See SCRINIUM LIBELLORUM.

Libellus. A small booklet (*liber*), a pamphlet. The term is applied to all kinds of petitions or letters addressed to the emperor or a high official. Syn. *preces, supplicatio*. Written complaints in civil or criminal matters (accusations) as well as written declarations (attestations, issued by an official or a private person) are also termed *libellus*. In the Roman civil procedure of the later Empire a *libellus* (= petition, complaint) of the plaintiff was the start of proceedings called *per libellum*.—See A LIBELLIS, EPISTULA, and the following items.

> V. Premerstein, *RE* 13; Thédenat, *DS* 4; L. De Sarlo, *Il documento come oggetto di rapporti*, 1935, 57.

Libellus accusatorius. A written accusation, addressed to the competent official with the purpose of initiating a criminal trial against a person.—See ACCUSATIO.

Libellus appellatorius. See APPELLO.

Libellus contestatorius. A petition by which a person appointed as a guardian requests to be released on the grounds of a legal excuse.—See EXCUSATIO.

Libellus contradictionis (contradictorius). A written reply by which one party to a trial contradicts the claims or facts presented by his adversary. In the libellary procedure (*per libellum*) *libellus contradictionis* is the defendant's written reply to the *libellus conventionis* of the plaintiff.—See the next item.

> Betti, *ACDR* Roma 2 (1935) 152.

Libellus conventionis. A complaint addressed to the judicial magistrate (in provinces, to the governor) in which the writer presents the facts on which he bases his claim against the defendant. Thereupon the official authorizes the plaintiff to summon (with the assistance of a subordinate clerk of the court, *exsecutor*), the defendant communicating the *libellus conventionis* to him. The defendant either recognizes the plaintiff's claim or denies it in a written *libellus contradictorius* in which he assumes the obligation to appear before court.—See the foregoing item.

> V. Premerstein, *RE* 13, 49; Mitteis, *SbLeipz* 1910, 61; Steinwenter, *Fschr Hanausek* (*Abhandl. zur antiken Rechtsgesch.* 1925) 36; *idem, ZSS* 50 (1930) 373, 54 (1934) 373; *idem, SDHI* 1 (1935) 132; *idem, Fschr Wenger* 1 (1944) 180; P. Collinet, *Lo procédure par libelle* (*Ét historiques sur le droit de Justinien* 4), 1932; Betti, *ACDR* Roma 2 (1935) 145 (Bibl.); Balogh, *St Riccobono* 2 (1936) 453.

Libellus dimissorius. (Appears only in the plural, *libelli dimissorii.*) See LITTERAE DIMISSORIAE, APPELLO.—D. 49.6.

Libellus divortii. See DIVORTIUM.

Libellus familiae. (*Liber patrimonii.*) A book in which the whole property of the family (estate, slaves, valuable furniture, etc.) was recorded.

Libellus famosus. A pasquil, a lampoon. Syn. *libellus ad infamiam alicuius pertinens* (= defaming another person). According to the *Lex Cornelia de iniuriis* punishment was inflicted on the person who wrote (*scripserit*), composed (*composuerit*) or edited (*ediderit*) such a lampoon, even if the publication was made under another name or anonymously (*sine nomine*). *Libellus famosus* was also a letter addressed to the emperor or an official containing malicious accusations against another person. If the letter was anonymous, it had to be burnt, without any investigation against the person defamed.—D. 47.10; C. 9.36.—See CARMEN FAMOSUM, LEX CORNELIA DE INIURIIS.

> Pfaff, *RE* 13; v. Premerstein, *RE* 13, 29; Thédenat, *DS* 3, 1176; Anon., *NDI* 7.

Libellus inscriptionis. A written accusation of a crime brought against a person by an accuser (*accusator*). It contained a detailed description of the wrongdoing and was used by the competent office as the basis for the registering of the case in the official records (see INSCRIPTIO). This initiated the investigation and the criminal trial.—See LIBELLUS ACCUSATORIUS, INSCRIPTIO IN CRIMEN.

> *RE* 13, 59.

Libellus libellatici. A petition addressed to the commission instituted during the persecution of Christians by the emperor Decius, in which the petitioner (a Christian who, in fact, did not perform the pagan sacrifices) requested the issue of a certificate that he had made the appropriate sacrifices to the Roman gods. The certificate saved him from persecution.

> V. Premerstein, *RE* 13, 46; Wittig, *RE* 15, 1280; P. M. Meyer, *Die libelli der Decianischen Christenverfolgung, APrAW* 1910, Abh. 5; Faulhaber, *Zeitschr. für kath. Theologie* 43 (1919) 439, 617; Knipfing, *Harvard Theol Rev* 16 (1923) 345; Bludau, *Röm. Quartalschrift,* Suppl. Heft 27 (Freiburg i. Br., 1931); H. Schoenaich, *Die l. und ihre Bedeutung für die Christenverfolgung,* 1933.

Libellus refutatorius. See REFUTATIO, CONSULTATIO.

> V. Premerstein, *RE* 13, 59.

Libellus repudii. See DIVORTIUM.

Libellus rescriptorum. See LIBER LIBELLORUM RESCRIPTORUM.

Liber. A son. See LIBERI (children).

Liber. (In juristic writings.) A book as a division of a written work. The jurists used to divide their writings into books (*libri*). The average size of a *liber* was from 1500 to 2500 lines, each of approximately 35 letters. Gaius' Institutes are divided into *commentarii*. A writing consisting of one book only = *liber singularis.*

> P. Krüger, *ZSS* 8 (1887) 76.

Liber. (Adj.) Free. For *liber* in the sense of a free man, see LIBER (HOMO), LIBERTAS, STATUS LIBERTATIS. Generally, according to the connection in which it is used, *liber* means free from any legal or factual restrictions; with reference to immovables = free from charges (servitudes, hypothec).—See CIVITATES LIBERAE.

Liber (homo). A free man, either a free-born (*ingenuus*) or a freedman (*libertinus, libertus*). A person is free-born when born of free parents, legally married, even when they were not free-born themselves, but were free when the child was born. A child born of parents not married follows the condition of the mother. Ant. *servus.*

Liber Authenticorum. See NOVELLAE IUSTINIANI.

Liber beneficiorum. See COMMENTARII BENEFICIORUM.

> Baudry, *DS* 1, 688.

Liber Gaii. See EPITOME GAI.

Liber homo bona fide serviens. A free man who does not know his status as a free man and serves in good faith as another's slave. This might happen when a free-born child was exposed by his parents (see EXPONERE FILIUM) and was treated by the person, who took him into his home, as a slave, or when a slave manumitted in a testament by his master, had no knowledge of his being freed. What such a person acquired at his "master's" expense (*ex re domini*) or through his own labor belonged to the "master," all other acquisitions, donations, and testamentary gifts were his. Good faith on the part of the master is also presumed. Different is the situation of a free man who fraudulently (*dolose*) lets himself to be sold as a slave and shares the price with his accomplice who performed the sale. He loses freedom and becomes the slave of the buyer.—See INGENUUS MANUMISSUS, EX RE ALICUIUS.

> Berger, *Philologus* 73 (1914) 69; *idem, ZSS* 43 (1922) 398; G. Dulckeit, *Erblasserwille,* 1934, 12, 79; G. Ciulei, *L.h.b.f.s.,* Paris, 1941.

Liber libellorum rescriptorum. A collection of imperial rescripts issued in legal matters and publicly exhibited (see PROPONERE). Copies of single rescripts could be made by private individuals. On request they were provided with an official clause confirming their correctness (*descriptum et recognitum factum*).

F. v. Schwind, *Zur Frage der Publikation im röm. R.*, 1940, 169.

Liber patrimonii. See LIBELLUS FAMILIAE.

Liber populus. See CIVITATES FOEDERATAE.

Liber Syro-Romanus. An anonymous legal compilation of an unknown date (fifth century?) preserved in oriental versions (Syriac, Arabic and Armenian), presumably derived from a Greek translation of a Latin original. It deals primarily with laws of family, slavery, and inheritance and takes imperial legislation into account. The purpose of the compilation which in the various manuscripts shows different additions, is not quite clear. It would seem that it has been prepared for teaching rather than for the use of practitioners.

Editions: Bruns and Sachau, *Syrisch-röm. Rechtsbuch aus dem 5. Jahrhundert,* 1880; E. Sachau, *Syrisch-römische Rechtsbücher* 1 (1907). Latin translations: Ferrini, *Opere* 1, 397; Furlani in *FIR* 1² (1940) 753.—Seidl, *RE* 4A, 1779; Mitteis, *APrAW* 1905; Ducati, *BIDR* 17 (1905); *idem, Riv. di storia antica* 10 (1906); Nallino, *St Bonfante* 1 (1929) and in a series of articles, now republished in *Raccolta di scritti,* 5 (1942); Volterra, *RISG* 88 (1951) 153 (Bibl.); Taubenschlag, *Jour. of juristic papyrology* 6 (1952) 103.

Libera facultas mortis. Permission granted by the emperor to persons condemned to death to evade execution through suicide. Provincial governors did not have this right. Syn. *liberum arbitrium mortis.*
—See SUICIDIUM, MORTEM SIBI CONSCISCERE.

F. M. De Robertis, *St di dir. penale,* 1943, 89.

Liberalis. Concerning liberty. For *liberalis causa* (*liberale iudicium*), see CAUSA LIBERALIS.—See OPERAE LIBERALES, STUDIA LIBERALIA.

Liberalitas. Liberality, generosity. The term covers acts of liberality both by private individuals, magistrates, and by the emperor as well (donations, distribution of money among the people, *missilia, congiarium*; the coins or TESSERAE NUMMARIAE had the inscription *ex liberalitate Augusti* = by liberality of the emperor). *Liberalitas* occurs only when there is no reciprocal performance and no compensation. If a person is sued for the fulfillment of an obligation assumed by liberality, he could be condemned only to *id quod facere potest,* i.e., as far as his means allow, see BENEFICIUM COMPETENTIAE. Syn. *largitio.*—C. 10.14.

Berve, *RE* 13; Pringsheim, *St Albertario* 1 (1952) 661.

Liberare (liberatio). Applied in the field of private law in different meanings. With regard to slaves it is syn. with *manumittere* (= to free); with regard to contractual or other obligations = to release the debtor either after payment or through an act of liberality (see LEGATUM LIBERATIONIS); with regard to things = to release a thing from a legal tie, e.g., from a servitude or from being pledged. *Liberare creditorem* = to satisfy a creditor. *Liberare* also

indicates the release of a guardian from tutorship, or a curator from curatorship. *Liberare* refers to the emancipation of a son from paternal power, too. In criminal matters *liberare* = to absolve, to acquit the accused.—D. 46.3; 34.3; C. 8.42; 11.40.—See ACCEPTILATIO, SOLUTIO, MANUMISSIO, EMANCIPATIO, PER AES ET LIBRAM.

Cuq, *DS* 3; Meylan, *St Riccobono* 4 (1936) 287.

Liberi. Children, sons and daughters. In a broader sense the term embraces all descendants.—See IUS LIBERORUM, INTERDICTUM DE LIBERIS EXHIBENDIS, TESTAMENTUM PARENTIS INTER LIBEROS.

Lanfranchi, *StCagl* 30, 2 (1946) 15.

Liberi iusti. See FILIUS IUSTUS.

Liberi naturales. See FILIUS NATURALIS.—C. 5.27.

Liberorum quaerendorum (procreandorum) causa. Procreation of legitimate children was the aim of a Roman marriage. At the registration of citizens (see CENSUS) the head of a family was asked whether he was living with a wife *liberorum quaerendorum causa.* Hence a woman married *in iustae nuptiae* = *uxor liberorum quaerendorum causa.*

Libertas. Liberty, freedom, the status of a free (see LIBER) person as opposed to slavery (SERVITUS). In a broader sense *libertas* is "the power to live as you wish" (Cicero, *Parad.* 5.1.34). The following is the definition of the jurist Florentinus (D. 1.5.4 pr.): "*Libertas* is the natural liberty of doing whatever one pleases unless something is prohibited by force or law." This definition was literally repeated by Justinian in his Institutes (1.3.1). "Freedom is inestimable" (D. 50.16.106), it cannot be evaluated in money. Trials in which the *libertas* of a person is involved = *causa liberalis* (*iudicium liberale*).—C. 7.22.—See STATUS LIBERTATIS, FAVOR LIBERTATIS, VINDICATIO IN LIBERTATEM. *Libertas* with regard to immovables denotes freedom from servitudes.—See USUCAPIO LIBERTATIS, ADEMPTIO LIBERTATIS, POSSESSIO LIBERTATIS.

H. Kloesel, *Libertas,* Diss., Breslau, 1935; G. Lombardi, *Concetti fondam, del dir. pubblico,* 1942, 32; Wirszubski, *L. as a political idea at Rome during the late Republic and early Principate,* 1950; Wenger, *SDHI* 15 (1949) 60; Biondi, *Il diritto romano propagatore della libertà, Jus,* n. s. 3 (1952) 266.

Libertas directa. See the next item.

Libertas fideicommissaria. Freedom granted to a slave through a FIDEICOMMISSUM. The slave becomes free when the heir fulfilled a formal manumission. Ant. *libertas directa,* when a testator freed a slave directly (*"liber esto"* = he shall be free) in his testament; see MANUMISSIO TESTAMENTO.

Libertas Latina. See LATINI IUNIANI, LATINITAS.

Libertinitas. The status of a freedman (*libertinus*). A free-born considered erroneously a freedman might defend his *ingenuitas* (the status of a free-born) before court; see INGENUITAS.

Libertinus (libertina). A person born as a slave, but set free later by manumission (see MANUMISSIO), a freedman. Ant. *ingenuus* (= free born) and *servus* (= a slave). Freedmen were citizens, though enjoying fewer political rights than the free-born. They were excluded from magistracies and sacerdotal offices, and could not become members of the senate. Their right of voting in the popular assemblies was regulated to their disadvantage (exclusion from participation in *comitia centuriata* as long as they were based upon the organization of the army, since freedmen were not admitted to the service in the legions). Their social position, however, was not unfavorable because they were entrusted with confidential work in the household of their patrons. Their social esteem increased even under the Principate since many posts in the imperial chancery, in the general administration and in that of the imperial patrimony were confided to them, in particular to the emperor's freedmen (see LIBERTI CAESARIS). Hadrian introduced restrictions in the use of freedmen in important administrative positions in favor of persons of equestrian rank.—Inst. 1.5; C. 10.58.—See LEX VISELLIA, RESTITUTIO NATALIUM, LIBERTUS (Bibl.).

Steiner, *RE* 13; Lécrivain, *DS* 3; Sciascia, *NDI* 7; Barrow, *OCD* 371; A. M. Duff, *Freedmen in the Roman Empire*, 1928; Gordon, *The freedman's son, JRS* 21 (1931) 65.

Libertus. A freedman. The term is used of a freedman in relation to the person who manumitted him (*patronus, manumissor*). A freedman is *libertinus*, but *libertus* of his ex-master. In a few texts *libertus* is used in sense of *libertinus*. *Liberta* = a freedwoman. For the relations between a freedman and his patron, see PATRONUS, OPERAE LIBERTI, IUDICIUM OPERARUM, OBSEQUIUM, INGRATUS LIBERTUS, BENEFICIUM COMPETENTIAE, BONORUM POSSESSIO INTESTATI, IN IUS VOCATIO, ADSIGNATIO LIBERTI.—Inst. 1.5; 3.7; D. 38.2; 3; C. 4.13; 6.4; 7; 10.58.

De Francisci, *StSas* 1 (1921) 39; Buckland, *RHD* 2 (1923) 293; H. Krüger, *St Riccobono* 2 (1926) 229; Bellelli, *AG* 116 (1936) 65; Pergreffi, *Ricerche epigrafiche sui liberti, Epigraphica*, 2–3 (1940–41); Lavaggi, *SDHI* 12 (1946) 115; idem, *StCagl* 30 (1946), *StSas* 21 (1947); idem, *La successione nei beni dei liberti nel dir. postclassico*, 1947; C. Cosentini, *Studi sui liberti* 1 (1948), 2 (1950); idem, *AnCat* 2 (1948) 235.

Libertus Caesaris (principis). A freedman of the emperor. The manumission of a personal slave by the emperor was a sign of particular confidence. Imperial freedmen obtained normally important positions in the imperial palace and chancery and acquired at times great influence on state affairs and the imperial policy.

Libertus ingratus. See INGRATUS.

Libertus orcinus. A freedman manumitted in the testament of his master (see MANUMISSIO TESTAMENTO). In classical law he was free from patronage since his former master was dead. In Justinian's law, however, the manumitter's son became his patron with all the rights of patronage.

Loreti-Lorini, *BIDR* 34 (1925); Harada, *ZSS* 59 (1939) 498.

Libra. A balance. A *libra* was used in formal acts concluded *per aes et libram.*—See PER AES ET LIBRAM.

L. Michon, *Recueil F. Gény*, 1 (1934) 42.

Librarius. A slave who, in the service of a wealthy master, was charged with writing letters, copying books, and sometimes with bookkeeping. *Librarius* is also the technical term for a book-seller.—See SCRIBA.

Bilabel, *RE* 13; Lafaye, *DS* 3.

Libri. For some kinds of *libri* in the sense of records, registers, lists, see under LIBER, and the following items.

Libri ad edictum. Commentaries on the praetorian edict written by jurists. There were commentaries on the pre-Hadrian edict and after Hadrian on the *edictum perpetuum* as compiled by the jurist Julian; see EDICTUM PRAETORIS, EDICTUM PERPETUUM HADRIANI.

Libri ad Sabinum. See SABINUS.

Libri censuales. A land-register for taxation purposes.

Libri magistratuum. Lists of the annual magistrates (consuls, plebeian tribunes) were in use, seemingly, from the fifth century B.C. on.

Niccolini, *Atti della Società linguistica di scienze e lettere*, 5 (1926) 103.

Libri pontificum. See COMMENTARII PONTIFICUM.

Libripens. The man who held the balance when a legal act was performed in the solemn form PER AES ET LIBRAM.

Kübler, *RE* 13; Kaser, *RE* 5A, 1025; Foligno, *NDI* 7.

Licentia. Freedom; in a derogatory sense = boldness, licentiousness. With regard to magisterial power it is syn. with *potestas, facultas.*

Licere. To be permitted by law or custom. "Not all that is permitted (*licet*), is honest" (D. 50.17.144).

Licet. (Conj.) Although, even if. When used with a subsequent indicative, it is suspect as to its classicality, especially when followed by a concession, introduced with *attamen*. The incorrect indicative may, however, originate from a copyist's error or a wrong resolution of an abbreviation. Likewise, *quamvis*, followed by an indicative, is considered suspect.

Guarneri-Citati, *Indice*² (1927) 53, 72.

Licinnius Rufinus. A jurist of the third century, a pupil of Paul, author of an extensive work entitled *Regulae*.

Miltner and Berger, *RE* 13, 457 no. 151; H. Krüger, *St Bonfante* 2 (1930) 331; L. Robert, *Hellenica* 5 (1948) 28.

Licitari (licitatio). To bid at an auction.—See AUCTIO, SUBHASTATIO.

Licitatio fructuum. See FRUCTUUM LICITATIO.

Licitus. What is permitted by law or custom. Hence *licito iure* = lawfully, legally (= *licite*). *Licitus* is used at times instead of *legitimus, iustus.* Ant. ILLI-CITUS.

Licium. See LANCE ET LICIO.

Lictores. According to an old Roman custom (of Etruscan origin), the king was preceded in his official appearance by twelve lictors carrying bundles of rods (see FASCES) with a protruding axe-head as a symbol of the kind's sovereignty and power over his subjects' life and death. Under the Republic the use of lictors was preserved as a sign of magisterial power. A consul had twelve lictors, a dictator twenty-four, a praetor in Rome two, in the provinces six. The lictors were appointed by the higher magistrates and fulfilled lower official services, such as the convocation of popular assemblies, the citation of individuals to appear before a magistrate and the arrest of criminals by order of the competent magistrate. They assisted also at capital executions. Their principal duty was to escort the magistrate in public (marching before him = *anteire*) and to keep order wherever he appeared. Under the Principate they were organized in professional associations (*decuriae lictoriae*) with the addition of the office to which they were attached (e.g., *decuria lictoria consularis*).—See QUINQUEFASCALES.

　　Kübler, *RE* 13; Lécrivain, *DS* 3; Treves, *OCD*; De Sanctis, *Rivista di filologia,* 1929.

Lictores curiati. Lictors, attendants of priests of higher rank.

　　Kübler, *RE* 13, 516.

Lictores denuntiatores. See DENUNTIATORES.

　　Kübler, *RE* 13, 515.

Lignum. A wooden tablet, a testament written on a wooden tablet (*tabulae testamenti*).

Limes. The frontier of the state (sometimes specified by the name of the region, e.g., *limes Aegyptiacus*). *Limes* is also the free space between two neighboring landed properties, left for public use. In ancient times it had to be five feet wide (syn. *fines, terminus*).

　　Fabricius, *RE* 13.

Limitaneus. Connected with the state boundaries. *Milites limitanei* = troops stationed in a frontier garrison. *Agri limitanei* = land on the frontier of the state for the maintenance of *milites limitaneus.*—C. 11.60.—See FUNDUS LIMITANEUS.

Linea. The line of descent from a common ancestor on the paternal or maternal side (*linea paterna, materna*). *Linea transversa* = the collateral line.—See LATUS.

Linteum. See LANCE ET LICIO.

Linum. A thread with which the tablets of testament (*tabulae testamenti*) were bound and sealed. The testator's tearing the *linum* was considered tantamount to his destruction of the will.

　　De Sarlo, *AG* 136 (1949) 102.

Liquere. To be clear, evident.—See IURARE SIBI NON LIQUERE.

　　Leonhard and Weiss, *RE* 13, 726.

Lis. "Indicates any suit (*actio*), either *in rem* or *in personam*" (D. 50.16.36). The term refers both to the trial and to its object. The parties to a *lis* (*litigatores*) are "enemies" (*inimici*). IURGIUM is also a legal controversy but of a less inimical nature. Syn. *litigium.*—See the following items, IUSIURANDUM IN LITEM, LITIS CONTESTATIO, DECEMVIRI STLITIBUS IUDICANDIS, PRAEDES LITIS ET VINDICIARUM, CONSORTES LITIS.

　　Weiss, *RE* 13; Cuq, *DS* 3.

Lis deserta. See DESERERE, EREMODICIUM.

Lis dividua. See EXCEPTIO LITIS DIVIDUAE.

Lis fullonum. A trial before three *praefecti vigilum* (A.D. 226–244) in which the guild of fullers claimed the exemption from water rates on the ground of ancient privileges and some religious consideration. The record of the trial is preserved in an inscription.

　　Recent edition: Arangio-Ruiz, *FIR* 3 (1943) no. 165 (Bibl.); Waltzing, *DE* 2, 405; W. Liebenam, *Geschichte und Organisation des röm. Vereinswesens,* 1910, 239.

Lis infitiando crescit in duplum. See INFITIARI.

Lis moritur. See IUDICIA LEGITIMA. The term *mors litis* is a creation of Justinian's.—See LIS PERIT.

　　Kaser, *RE* 16; P. Tuor, *Die mors litis im röm. Formularproverfahren,* 1906; Beseler, *Beiträge* 4 (1920) 1; Bonifacio, *AG* 142 (1952) 34.

Lis pendens. See LITE PENDENTE.

Lite pendente. When a trial is still pending. During this time a supplication to the emperor concerning the object of the controversy was not admissible. The object of the trial = *res litigiosa.*—C. 1.21.

Lis residua. See EXCEPTIO LITIS DIVIDUAE.

Litem contestari. See LITIS CONTESTATIO.

Litem denuntiare. See LAUDARE AUCTOREM.

Litem suam facere. See IUDEX QUI LITEM SUAM FACIT.

Liti se offerre. To accept the part of a defendant in a trial involving the recovery of a thing (*rei vindicatio, hereditatis petitio*) by a person who does not possess it. Usually behind this acceptance was deliberate deception in order to cover the real possessor of the thing and to give him the opportunity to usucapt it in the meantime. The dishonest defendant was, of course, not able to restore the thing, but he was liable for damages on the ground of his CAUTIO IUDICATUM SOLVI which made him responsible for fraud.—See POSSESSOR FICTUS.

　　Lenel, *GrZ* 37 (1910) 532; Maria, *Ét Girard* 2 (1913) 237; Kaser, *ZSS* 51 (1931) 101.

Litigare. To be involved in a civil trial. The term refers particularly to the stage *in iure. Litigans* = the party to a trial. Syn. *litigator.*—D. 44.6; C. 8.36.

Litigator (litigans). See LITIGARE.

Litigiosus. See RES LITIGIOSA, LITE PENDENTE.—D. 44.6; C. 8.36.

Litis aestimatio. The evaluation in money of the thing claimed by the plaintiff to make possible a judgment in a sum of money (CONDEMNATIO PECU-

NIARIA). When in a *rei vindicatio* the defendant refused the restoration of the thing claimed, it remained with him when he paid the *litis aestimatio.* He could now acquire ownership thereon since he was protected against a new claim for the recovery of the thing by an *exceptio rei iudicatae.*—See ARBITRIUM LITI AESTIMANDAE, IUSIURANDUM IN LITEM.
　　Kipp, *RE* 1; Cuq, *DS* 3; Huvelin, *Mél Gérardin* 1903, 319; E. Betti, *Studi sulla litis a.,* 1–2, 1915; *idem, La l.a. in rapporto al tempo nelle varie specie di azioni,* 1919; O. Carrelli, *L'acquisto della proprietà per l.a.,* 1934; A. Erhardt, *L.a. im röm. Formularprozess,* 1934; *idem, ZSS* 55 (1935) 36; M. Kaser, *Quanti ea res est,* 1935; Russo-Spena, *RBSG* 10 (1935) 548.

Litis contestatio. The final act in the proceedings *in iure,* by which, after the appointment of the judge (*iudex*), the controversial issues are established and submitted to the latter for the examination of the facts and for judgment. In the procedure of *legis actiones* the end of the first stage of the process took place before witnesses summoned by the phrase *"testes estote"* (= be witnesses); hence the term *con-testatio.* In the formulary procedure the *litis contestatio* was achieved by agreement of the parties about the formula. The concept that the *litis contestatio* was of a contractual nature has been common opinion in the literature, since the parties gave their consent to surrender their controversy to the private judge. Among the manifold effects of the *litis contestatio* the most important is that the plaintiff's right to sue the defendant is "consumed" (*actio consumitur*) which excluded a second trial for the same claim; see BIS IDEM EXIGERE, EADEM RES. The defendant is protected, under specific circumstances, against a second suit by the law itself (*ipso iure*). In such cases the praetor could reject the second action (*denegare actionem*) immediately and, besides, the defendant might object to the identity of the second claim with that of the first trial. In other cases (*iudicia imperio continentia, actiones in rem, actiones in factum*) the defendant had to oppose a formal exception (in the formulary procedure) that the dispute at issue had been already the object of a *litis contestatio* (*exceptio rei in iudicium deductae*) or had been decided by a final judgment in a previous trial (*exceptio rei iudicatae*). After the *litis contestatio,* the plaintiff's claim became transmissible to his heir, even in those cases in which it was not hereditary before the *litis contestatio* being a strictly personal claim. Through *litis contestatio* the original obligation of the defendant was extinguished (*tollitur obligatio*) and transformed into an obligation, based on the *litis contestatio* itself, the substance of which was to fulfill the judgment debt (*iudicatum facere*) in case of condemnation. The legal situation at the time of the *litis contestatio* was decisive for the final judgment. With the disappearance of the bipartite procedure the *litis contestatio* lost not only its external aspect but also its material effects. The term,

however, occurs frequently in Justinian's legislative work where it refers to the *cognitio extra ordinem* and the postclassical procedure. What was later called *litis contestatio* resembled somewhat the classical *litis contestatio*; it was the moment when the jurisdictional officer "started" (*coeperit*) to hear the exposition of the case by the parties or their representatives: the *narratio* by the plaintiff, and the *contradictio* by the defendant. Legal consequences attached to the former *litis contestatio* became now connected with the final judgment itself.—C. 3.9.— See IUDICIUM ACCIPERE, ABSOLUTORIUS, EXCEPTIO, RES LITIGIOSA, EXCEPTIO REI IUDICATAE, PERIRE, SUSCIPERE ACTIONEM.
　　Weiss, *RE* 13; Humbert, *DS* 3; R. De Ruggiero, *BIDR* (1905) 149; Gradenwitz, *Fg Bekker* 1907; Wlassak, *SbWien* 184 (1917), 194 (1920); E. Betti, *Costruzione giuridica della consunzione processuale,* 1919; Guarneri-Citati, *BIDR* 34 (1925) 163; Riccobono, *ZSS* 47 (1917) 65; Meylan, *Mél Cornil* 2 (1926) 81; M. Kaser, *Restituere als Prozessgegenstand,* 1932; E. Carrelli, *La genesi del procedimento formulare,* 1946, 17; Lavaggi, *AG* 134 (1947) 24; C. Gioffredi, *Contributi allo studio del processo civ. rom.,* 1947, 65; Di Paola, *AnCat* 2 (1948) 253; Biscardi, *RIDA* 4 (= *Mél De Visscher* 3, 1950) 159; Bonifacio, *St Albertario* 1 (1952); Pugliese, *Riv. di diritto processuale* 6 (1951).

Litis denuntiatio. See DENUNTIATIO LITIS.

Littera Florentina. See FLORENTINA.

Littera Pisana. See FLORENTINA.
　　Naber, *St Bonfante* 2 (1930) 289.

Littera vulgaris. See VULGATA.

Litterae. A writing (opposed to spoken words, *oratio*), a letter (syn. *epistula*). A letter may be used for the conclusion of an agreement (*contrahere*) between persons not living at the same place. Illiterate persons (*ignarus litterarum, ignorans* or *qui nescit litteras*) are excluded from legal acts which require a written form. Justinian issued special rules for testaments of illiterate persons. "What has been written (*litterae*) on another's material (e.g., *charta* = paper, *membranae* = parchment), even if written with golden letters, becomes his property" (D. 41.1.9.1).—See COMPARATIO LITTERARUM, IGNARUS LITTERARUM, EPISTULA.

Litterae. (With reference to official correspondence.) A letter issued by a magistrate or an imperial official in an official matter. *Litterae* also indicates an imperial rescript; see RESCRIPTUM PRINCIPIS.

Litterae commendaticiae. A letter of recommendation.

Litterae dimissoriae. A written report of a judicial officer to a higher court in the case of an appeal (see APPELLATIO) concerning the controversy. It was to be presented to the appellate court by the appealing party. Syn. *libelli dimissorii, apostoli.*—D. 49.6.— See APPELLO.

Litterarum obligatio. (*Obligatio litteris contracta.*) An obligation which originates from a written document or from a written entry in an account-book.

The ancient forms of *litterarum obligatio* became obsolete already in classical times. In Justinian's law there is a new form of *obligatio litterarum*. A *scriptura* carried an obligation if the writer acknowledged by writing that he owed a sum of money to a certain person. He could, however, during two years, object that he actually had not received the money.—Inst. 3.21.—See NOMINA TRANSCRIPTICIA, CODEX ACCEPTI, CHIROGRAPHUM, SYNGRAPHE, EXPENSILATIO.

Steinwenter, *RE* 13; Messina-Vitrano, *AG* 80 (1908) 94; Binder, *St Brugi* 1910, 339; Riccobono, *ZSS* 43 (1922) 326; R. De Ruggiero, *St Perozzi* 1925, 369; Appert, *RHD* 11 (1932) 619; Gallet, *RHD* 21 (1942) 38; Erdmann, *ZSS* 63 (1943) 401; Brasiello, *SDHI* 10 (1944) 101; F. Bonifacio, *Novazione*, 1950, 53; Arangio-Ruiz, *St Redenti* 1 (1951) 12.

Litus maris. The seashore. It is a *res communis omnium*; consequently everybody may approach it and set his foot thereon. Its extension goes to the limits reached by the highest winter waves. Pearls, gems, etc., found on the seashore were subject to *occupatio* and became the property of the individual who found them. In some texts *litus maris* is listed among *res publicae*. A building constructed on a seashore belongs to the builder.—C. 12.44.—See MARE, OCCUPATIO.

Costa, *Riv. dir. intern.*, 5 (1916) 337; *idem, RendBol*, ser. II, vol. 10 (1925–26); Maroi, *RISG* 62 (1919) 164; Biondi, *St Perozzi* 1925; Scherillo, *Le cose* (*Lezioni*), 1945, 71; G. Lombardi, *Ricerche in tema di ius gentium*, 1946, 71, 90.

Locare ex integro. (Syn. *renovare locationem.*) To renew a lease, to prolong an existing lease.—See LOCATIO CONDUCTIO.

Locatio conductio. A general term which covers various types of lease and hire. The contracting parties are: the *locator* (*is qui locat* = he who gives his thing, immovable or movable, in lease, who gives his material of, or on, which a work has to be done, or who lets out his services to another) and the *conductor* (*is qui conducit rem, opus, operas* = the lessee of another's thing, the workman who engages himself to make a specific work, or he who hires another's services). The *locatio conductio* is a contract, concluded by mutual consent of the parties (see CONSENSUS) and governed by good faith, hence the actions resulting from a *locatio conductio, actio locati* (*ex locato*) for the *locator,* and *actio conducti* (*ex conducto*) for the *conductor* in the case of non-fulfillment of the reciprocal duties, are *actiones bonae fidei*. For the various types of the *locatio conductio* see the following items. The compensation for using another's thing or services (*merces*) was paid, as a matter of rule, in money, otherwise there was no *locatio conductio* but another kind of a contract (e.g., a sale or an innominate contract; see CONTRACTUS INNOMINATI). There are specific rules concerning the rights and duties of the parties and their responsibility in the case of non-fulfillment. The normal rules could be changed by a special agreement between the parties. It was held of *locatio conductio* that it was a contract similar to the sale (*proxima emptioni*); as a result many rules governing the sale were applied to *locatio conductio*.—Inst. 3.24; D. 19.2; C. 4.65; 11.71.—See LOCARE EX INTEGRO, RELOCATIO, RECONDUCTIO, MERCES.

Leonhard and Weiss, *RE* 13; Herdlitczka, *RE* Suppl. 6 (*s.v. Miete*); Cuq, *DS* 3; De Villa, *NDI* 7; C. H. Munro, *Locati Conducti*, D.19.2, 1891; E. Costa, *Locazione di cose*, 1915; Maroi, *Riv. ital. di sociologia* 20 (1916); Brasiello, *RISG* 2–3 (1927–28); Olivier-Martin, *RHD* 15 (1936) 419.

Locatio conductio operarum. Hiring another's labor, primarily manual work, since services rendered by intellectual professionals (physicians, lawyers, land-surveyors, teachers, architects, etc.), the so-called *operae liberales,* could not in classical law be the object of a *locatio conductio,* although under the Principate compensation for such professional services could be obtained in extraordinary proceedings (see HONORARIUM, ADVOCATI, MEDICI, AGRIMENSORES, OPERAE LIBERALES). Therefore, the expression *operae quae locari solent* (= which used to be hired) refers only to the labor of craftsmen, artisans and manual workers. The *locator* (the workman) has to perform the services as agreed upon by the parties and the wages must be paid to him if the performance of his services became impossible by a cause for which he was not liable (e.g., *vis maior*).—See IMPERITIA, MERCES.

Deschamps, *Locare operas, Mél Gérardin* 1907, 157; Berger, *A labor contract of 164 A.D., ClPhilol* 43 (1948) 231; F. M. De Robertis, *Rapporti di lavoro*, 1946; *idem, Organizzazione e tecnica produttiva*, 1946.

Locatio conductio operis (faciendi). A contract by which a person (*conductor, redemptor operis*) assumes the duty to perform a specific service or work on, or from, the material supplied by the employer. If the workman produces an *opus* out of his own material, it is a sale (*emptio*). Contracts of transportation of goods or persons is a *locatio conductio operis*; likewise building a house by a contractor on one's ground, no matter who furnishes the materials, the contractor or a third person; *locator* is the owner of the ground (*domum aedificandam locare*). Death of the *conductor* dissolves the contract when the services were strictly personal and had to be performed by the *conductor* himself. The employer has to pay the wages (*merces*) agreed upon when the work performed corresponds to the provisions of the agreement. Approval by the *locator* or by a third person (*adprobare*) is often settled as a condition of the employer's duty to pay the wages. The employer incurs the risk of the destruction of the work (even not yet approved) by an accident or when there was a delay in the approval by his fault.—See ADPROBARE, FULLO, RECEPTUM NAUTARUM.

Schulz, *GrZ* 38 (1911) 21; Huvelin, *RHD* 3 (1924) 322; M. Boitard, *Les contrats des services gratuits*, 1941; De

Robertis, *I rapporti di lavoro*, 1946, 153; Solazzi, *ACIVer* 3 (1951) 315.

Locatio conductio rei. A lease of a thing, movable or immovable (a house, a plot of land), to be used by the *conductor* according to its economic and social utility. A lease is concluded for a fixed period of time (a rural property normally for five years) or in perpetuity (*in perpetuum,* see EMPHYTEUSIS). Full or partial sublease is generally admitted unless prohibited by the agreement. The lessee has no possession of the thing let; he, therefore, has no possessory protection through interdicts. The rent is paid in money (*merces*); only in a lease of land it may consist in a part of the proceeds (*colonia partiaria*). The lessor is liable to the lessee (the tenant) if the latter is evicted by a third person. It was customary that the lessor, when selling the immovable, obliged the buyer to respect the lease and to leave the lessee on the spot until the lease expired. A renewal of the lease (*relocatio*) could be performed by an agreement of the parties to this effect or tacitly (*relocatio tacita*) when the lessee kept holding the immovable and the owner did not object.—See INQUILINUS, INSULA, MERCES, COLONI PARTIARII, LOCATIO CONDUCTIO (Bibl.), HABITATIO.

V. Bolla, *RE* 18, 4, 2474; Berger, *Wohnungmiete und Verwandtes in den Papyri, ZVR* 29 (1913) 321; E. Costa, *Locazione di cose,* 1915; Pflüger, *ZSS* 65 (1947) 193.

Locatio sub hasta. A lease performed through a public auction.—See AUCTIO, HASTA.

Voigt, *BerSächsGW* 1903, 19.

Loco. (Used adverbially.) In the place of, e.g., *heredis loco, domini loco,* in the same legal situation as an heir (HERES) or owner (DOMINUS), to be treated legally as an heir or owner (not to be an heir or owner).

Loco plus petere. See PLURIS PETITIO.

Locuples. The rich, the wealthy, chiefly in landed property. Originally the term was applied only to land-owners, even of small parcels. Syn. in earlier times ASSIDUI, ant. PROLETARII. Later it embraced all kinds of riches (slaves, cattle, movables, money). In procedural language, he who has sufficient means to satisfy the claims brought against him or to be an appropriate surety for the defendant is considered *locuples.*

Berve, *RE* 13.

Locupletari (locupletior fieri). To enrich oneself to the detriment of another. "Natural equity requires that no one should enrich himself to the detriment of another" (D. 12.6.14). Such enrichment can be reclaimed under specific circumstances by certain actions (CONDICTIONES) in which the defendant is condemned *in quantum* (*quatenus*) *locupletari factus est* (= to the extent of his enrichment) or *in id quod ad eum pervenit* (= of what were his earnings).— See PERVENIRE AD ALIQUEM.

F. Schulz, *Die actiones in id quod pervenit,* Diss., Breslau, 1905; Albertario, *Studi di dir. rom.* 4 (1947, several articles of 1913–1914); G. Maier, *Prätorische Bereicherungsklagen,* 1932; Frezza, *NuovaRDCom* 2 (1949) 47.

Locus. Distinguished from FUNDUS (= piece of land, estate) as a part of the whole. Both urban and rural lands are called *locus.* A plot of land in the city with no building on it = *arca,* in the country = *ager.* This terminology, however, is more strictly observed in juristic writings than in literary works and inscriptions.—See CONTROVERSIA DE LOCO, SUCCEDERE IN LOCUM, USUS LOCI.

Kübler, *RE* 13.

Locus profanus. See PROFANUM.

Locus publicus. (Pl. *loca publica.*) A parcel of public land. It is property of the Roman people and is protected by various interdicts (INTERDICTA) against violation by private individuals who might endanger its public character or its use by the people. —D. 43.7; 8; 9.—See INTERDICTA DE LOCIS PUBLICIS, INTERDICTUM DE LOCO PUBLICO FRUENDO.

Lécrivain, *DS* 3; G. Krüger, *Die Rechtsstellung der vorkonstantinischen Kirche,* 1935, 275.

Locus purus. A place which is neither *locus sacer,* nor *sanctus,* nor *religiosus,* and is consequently negotiable through all kinds of transactions.—See the following items.

Locus sacer. A land or a building dedicated to the gods with the authorization of the senate or by a statute. Interdicts (INTERDICTA) served the protection of *loca sacra.*—D. 43.6.—See RES SACRAE, INTERDICTUM NE QUID IN LOCO SACRO.

Locus sanctus. See RES SANCTAE.

Locus religiosus. A place where a dead person was buried by, or with the consent of, the owner. Ant. *locus profanus.*—D. 11.7; C. 3.44.—See RES RELIGIOSAE, PROFANUM, INTERDICTUM NE QUID IN LOCO SACRO.

Taubenschlag, *ZSS* 38 (1917) 245; Kobbert, *RE* 1A (*s.v. religiosa loca*).

Logographus. A bookkeeper in a public office.—C. 10.71.

Longa consuetudo. See CONSUETUDO.—D. 1.3; C. 8.52.

Longa possessio. In the language of Justinian's compilers = USUCAPIO.—See PRAESCRIPTIO LONGI TEMPORIS.

Longa praescriptio. See PRAESCRIPTIO LONGI TEMPORIS.

Longaevus usus. A usage, a custom, observed during a long period.—See CONSUETUDO.

Longi (longissimi) temporis praescriptio. See PRAESCRIPTIO LONGI TEMPORIS.

Longum silentium. See SILENTIUM.

Loqui. To speak. See GRAVITER LOQUI. With reference to statutes, *senatusconsulta,* and praetorian edicts ("*praetor loquitur*" = the praetor says) *loqui* is primarily used to introduce a literal quotation from the enactment. Syn. (*praetor, lex*) *dicit, ait.* Quotations from a testament are preceded by the statement that the testator *ita locutus est* (= has so disposed). Syn. *scribere.*

Luceres. See RAMNES.
> Berve, *RE* 13.

Lucra nuptialia. See NUPTIAE.

Lucrari. To gain, to derive a profit. Syn. *lucrifacere.* —See FURTUM.

Lucrativus. See CAUSA LUCRATIVA, RES LUCRATIVAE, USUCAPIO PRO HEREDE.

Lucrifacere. See LUCRARI.

Lucrosus. Profitable, advantageous. Ant. *damnosus.*

Lucrum. A gain, profit. Ant. DAMNUM. It is doubtful whether the wording of the saying "it does not conform to what is right and just (*bonum et aequum*) that one make a gain (*lucrum*) to another's detriment nor that one suffer a loss to the profit of another" (D. 23.3.6.2) is of classical origin.—C. 12.61.—See COMMUNICARE LUCRUM CUM DAMNO.
> Grünwald, *Ordnung der die Worte lucrum, lucrifacere etc. enthaltenden Stellen der Digesten,* Diss., Heidelberg, 1912.

Lucrum cessans. See DAMNUM EMERGENS.

Lucrum facere. (Syn. *lucrifacere.*) See FURTUM.

Luctus. Mourning. During the time fixed for mourning (*tempus lugendi*) after the death of her husband (ten months, later one year) the widow had to abstain from another marriage. One of the reasons was to avoid confusion about the paternity of a child born after the husband's death (*turbatio sanguinis* = confusion of blood). She might, however, become engaged or marry with the emperor's permission. If she had given birth to a child after the husband's death, there was no restriction in time for a second marriage. No marriage prohibition existed for widowers. Persons who violated the mourning duties, which were obligatory after the death of a near relative, were branded by infamy with all its procedural disadvantages (see INFAMIA). Later imperial legislation brought even more severe sanctions for widows transgressing the pertinent rules by excluding them from inheritance, legacies, and other testamentary gains from the deceased husband's estate.—See INSPICERE VENTREM, SUBLUGERE.
> Kübler, *RE* 13; Gachon, *DS* 3; Cuq, *DS* 2, 1401; Volterra, *RISG* 8 (1933) 171; Rasi, *Scr Ferrini* 1 (Univ. Sacro Cuore, Milan, 1947) 197.

Ludi. Public games, arranged on various occasions, of a spectacular character and of different nature (sportive, gladiatorial, theatrical = *ludi scaenici, circenses*). Some were organized by the state, on particularly solemn occasions, and were arranged by magistrates (*aediles curules,* later, from the end of the Republic on, by praetors) who were charged with the *cura ludorum* (*sollemnium*). The days on which public festivities (*ludi publici*) took place were considered as FERIAE (= *dies festi*) on which every kind of labor was suspended. There were also spectacles

of a more private character, arranged by high officials or candidates for magistracies in order to win the favor of the people.—C. 11.42.—See LEX FANNIA, HONORARIUM, SENATUSCONSULTUM DE SUMPTIBUS LUDORUM.
> Kubitschek, *RE* 1, 456, 462; Habel, *RE* Suppl. 5; v. Buren, *OCD.*

Ludi gladiatorii. For the condemnation to fight with gladiators as a penalty in criminal trials, see GLADIATORES. This kind of penalty for minor criminal offenses (*damnatio in ludum*) does not appear in Justinian's codification since it was abolished in the fourth century. Another kind of condemnation was *damnatio in* LUDUM VENATORIUM (a fight with wild animals) which existed still in Justinian's time. *Ludus gladiatorius* is used also of a school of gladiators.—See SENATUSCONSULTUM DE SUMPTIBUS.

Ludi saeculares. Extraordinary public festivals, combined with religious ceremonies, and arranged for the celebration of the end of a *saeculum* (century) and the beginning of a new one. They were organized by priests, *duoviri sacris faciundis.*—See SENATUSCONSULTA DE LUDIS SAECULARIBUS.
> Nilsson, *RE* 1A, 1696; Taylor, *OCD* (s.v. *secular games*); Diehl, *SbBerl* 1932, 762; J. B. Pighi, *De ludis saecularibus populi Rom.,* Milan, 1941; Wagenvoort, *Medelingen der Kon. Nederl. Akad. van Wetenschappen, Letterkunde* 14, no. 4 (1951) 163.

Ludi venatorii. See LUDI GLADIATORII.

Ludicra ars. Histrionic art. Actors and actresses (*qui ludicram artem exercent*) were branded with infamy. Members of senatorial families were prohibited to marry actresses or actors, or persons whose parents acted on the stage. The ban goes back to the Augustan legislation on marriage (see IULIA DE MARITANDIS ORDINIBUS).

Luere pignus. (Or *rem pignori datam.*) To redeem a pledge by paying the debt.—C. 8.30.

Lugendi tempus. See LUCTUS.

Luitio pignoris. See LUERE PIGNUS.

Lumen. See SERVITUS LUMINUM, SERVITUS NE LUMINIBUS OFFICIATUR.

Lustralis. Quinquennial, referring to a period of five years. Syn. *quinquennalis* (*census, lustrum*). For *collatio lustralis,* see AURUM ARGENTUMQUE.

Lustratio. See LUSTRUM.
> Böhm, *RE* 13; Bouché-Leclercq, *DS* 3.

Lustrum. The religious ceremony performed at the end of a census. It was called also *lustratio,* and was followed by a review of the army, assembled on the field of Mars. Later *lustrum* denoted the quinquennial period between two subsequent registrations of the citizens; see CENSUS, CENSORES.
> Berve, *RE* 13; Otto, *Rheinisches Museum für Philologie* 7 (1916) 17.

Lusus aleae. See ALEA.—C. 3.43.

Luxuriosus. Luxurious. Living luxuriously might be a reason of declaring a person a spendthrift (PRODIGUS) and of placing him under *cura prodigi.*

Lytae. Students in the fourth year of studies in the law schools. After Justinian's reform of the law curriculum, they studied ten books of the Digest concerned with family law, guardianship and law of inheritance.

Berger, *RE* 14; Cantarelli, *RendLinc* Ser. 6, vol. 2 (1926) 20.

M

Macer, Aemilius. A jurist of the first half of the third century, author of monographs on procedure, military law, and provincial governorship.

Jörs, *RE* 1 (*s.v. Aemilius,* no. 86).

Machinatio. (From *machinari.*) Appears in the definition of *dolus malus* as a "trick (ruse) used to deceive, to cheat, to defraud another" (D. 4.3.1.2).

Macula. A taint of infamy or of immoral behavior.

Maecianus, Volusius. A jurist of the middle of the second century, law teacher of Marcus Aurelius, and later, after a brilliant official career, member of the imperial council. His principal work was *Questiones de fideicommissis* (concerning *fideicommissa*), in 16 books. He wrote also on penal procedure and a monograph on the *Lex Rhodia.*

H. Krüger, *St Bonfante* 2 (1930) 314; Levy, *ZSS* 52 (1932) 352.

Magia. Sorcery, the exercise of magical arts. *Magia* was a crime when it was performed with an evil intention to harm or defraud another. The term covered various kinds of sorcery, such as the use of magic formulae, nocturnal sacrifices made in order to produce supernatural results, the use of magic liquids, and the like. Penalty for sorcery was death, for both the sorcerer and his associates. Possession of magic books was forbidden and punished by death or relegation; the books were burnt in public. Syn. *magica ars.*—See FRUGES EXCANTARE, OCCENTARE, MATHEMATICI.

Kleinfeller, *RE* 14; Hopfner, *ibid.* 301; Hubert, *DS* 3; P. Huvelin, *Magie et droit individuel, Année sociologique* 1905–6; Stoicesco, *Mél Cornil* 2 (1926) 455; Martroye, *RHD* 9 (1930) 669; C. Pharr, *TAmPhilolA* 63 (1932) 269; E. Massonneau, *La magie dans l'antiquité romaine,* 1934; V. A. Georgescu, *La magie et le dr. rom., Revista clasica* 1–2 (Bucharest, 1939–40); Cramer, *Sem* 10 (1952).

Magica ars. See MAGIA.

Magis. More. The term is applied in various phrases, such as *magis est, placet, videtur, dicendum est,* etc., to give preference to one legal opinion over another (= it is preferable, more correct, more proper to say that . . .). The compilers of the Digest often use such an expression to cut short a discussion on a controversial matter and to give a solution without any further reasoning.

Guarneri-Citati, *Indice*[2] (1925) 51 (Bibl.).

Magister. A general term (title) indicating a person who exercises high (or the highest) functions in an organization, association, or a public office. For the various *magistri,* whose particular function is nor-

mally indicated by the specification of the body in which they function as a *magister,* see the following items. *Magister* is also a teacher "in any field of learning (*cuiuslibet disciplinae praeceptor*)," D. 50.16.57 pr. The services of teachers were reckoned among *operae liberales* and could not be the object of contract of hire (see LOCATIO CONDUCTIO OPERARUM). Teachers enjoyed exemption (*immunitas, vacatio*) from certain public charges (*munera civilia*). The emperor Constantine considerably enlarged the privileges of *professores litterarum* and protected them against "vexation."—C. 10.53.—See IMMUNITAS, OPERAE LIBERALES, EDICTUM VESPASIANI.

Cagnat, *DS* 3; De Dominicis, *NDI* 8; A. E. R. Boak, *The R. magistri in the civil and military service, Harvard Studies in Class. Philology* 26 (1915); idem, *Univ. of Michigan Studies, Humanistic Ser.* 14 (1924) 123; Herzog, *Urkunden zur Hochschulpolitik der röm. Kaiser, SbBerl* 1935, 967; S. Riccobono, Jr., *AnPal* 17 (1937) 50; T. O. Martin, *Sem* 10 (1952) 60.

Magister admissionum. The master of ceremonies in the imperial court.—See ADMISSIONES.

Magister auctionis. The manager of a public auction. —See AUCTIO, BONORUM VENDITIO, MAGISTER BONORUM.

Magister bonorum. A man appointed by the creditors of an insolvent debtor to prepare and direct the sale of the debtor's property.—See BONORUM VENDITIO.

Solazzi, *Concorso dei creditori* 2 (1938) 70.

Magister census (censuum, a censibus). The highest officer among the CENSUALES. He was concerned with matters of taxation of the senators. He also intervened in the opening of a testament.—See APERTURA TESTAMENTI.

Seeck, *RE* 3, 1191.

Magister census. An official who kept a register of students of liberal arts who came to Rome for studies. He supervised their conduct and took care for their moral discipline. For bad behavior students were publicly flogged, expelled from Rome and sent back to their place of origin.

Seeck, *RE* 3, 1192.

Magister collegii. See CURATOR COLLEGII. He was the leading functionary of a *collegium* both in private associations and in colleges of public officials and priests. Some *collegia* had several *magistri* whose attributions in the management were different. They were elected for five years, hence their appellation *"quinquennales."*

Magister creditorum. See MAGISTER BONORUM.

Magister epistularum. The chief of the division of the imperial chancery concerned with the correspondence of the emperor.—See AB EPISTULIS, EPISTULAE, SCRINIUM EPISTULARUM.

Magister equitum. The commander of the cavalry. He was the deputy of the DICTATOR who appointed him. He was the first-in-command when the dictator was absent. For the *magister equitum* in the post-

Constantinian epoch, see MAGISTER MILITUM.—See MAGISTER POPULI.

> Westermayer, *RE* Suppl. 5, 631; Cagnat, *DS* 3; Momigliano, *Bull. Commissione archeol. comunale di Roma* 58 (1930) 35.

Magister iuvenum (iuventutis). The head of the organization of young men of noble families (*iuvenes*) in Italian cities. In some places his title was *praetor iuventutis.*—See IUVENES.

Magister libellorum. The chief of the bureau of the imperial chancery concerned with *libelli, scrinium libellorum.*—See A LIBELLIS.

> V. Premerstein, *RE* 13, 20.

Magister memoriae. The chief of the bureau *a memoria* of the imperial chancery. "He dictates all *adnotationes* and sends them out; he gives also answers to petitions (*preces, Notitia Dign. Occid.* XVII, 11).—See A MEMORIA, ADNOTATIO.

> Seeck, *RE* 2A, 896; Fluss, *RE* 15, 656.

Magister militum. From the time of Constantine the emperor as the supreme commander of the army was assisted by one *magister militum* or two *magistri* (*magister utriusque militiae*), one for the infantry (*magister peditum*), the other for the cavalry (*magister equitum*). The number of the *magistri* increased with the reform of the administration of the empire and its division into praefecturae (*magister militum per Orientem, per Illyricum, per Thraciam*, etc.).—C. 1.29; 12.4.

> Cagnat, *DS* 3, 1526; R. Grosse, *Röm. Militärgeschichte,* 1920, 180.

Magister navis. One "who is entrusted with the care of the entire ship" (D. 14.1.1.1). See EXERCITOR NAVIS. His agreement with the owner of the ship was either a contract of hire (*locatio conductio operarum*) or a *mandatum* when he assumed the duties gratuitously.

> A. E. R. Boak, *Univ. of Michigan Studies, Human. Ser.* 14 (1924) 134; Ghionda, *RDNav* 1 (1935) 327.

Magister officiorum. In the later Empire, the highest official among the court offices (*officia palatina*) with extensive and manifold functions. He was entrusted with the supervision of certain court bureaus and the secretariat.—C. 1.31; 12.6.—See OFFICIUM, OFFICIALES, SCRINIA.

> De Dominicis, *NDI* 8, 2; Boak, *RE* 17, 2048; *idem, The Master of the Offices, Univ. of Michigan Studies, Human. Ser.* 14 (1924).

Magister officiorum (operarum). In private service. Large private estates employing a great number of slaves were divided into units each with a separate management (*officium*) headed by a *magister.*—C. 1.31; 12.6.—See SCHOLAE PALATINAE.

Magister pagi. See PAGUS.

> Boak, *Univ. of Michigan Studies, Human. Ser.* 14 (1924) 136.

Magister peditum. See MAGISTER MILITUM.

> Cagnat, *DS* 3.

Magister populi. In the Republic, the title of a DICTATOR as the commander of the army, whereas the commander of the cavalry was the *magister equitum.*

> Westermayer, *RE* Suppl. 5, 633.

Magister rei privatae. See PROCURATOR REI PRIVATAE. From A.D. 340 his title is COMES RERUM PRIVATARUM.

Magister sacrarum cognitionum. The head of the imperial bureau concerned with judicial matters brought before the imperial court (from the end of the third century).—See A COGNITIONIBUS.

Magister scrinii. The head of any bureau in the imperial chancery in the later Empire. His deputy was *proximus scrinii.*—See SCRINIUM.—C. 12.9.

Magister societatis publicanorum. A leading personality in the association of tax farmers.—See PUBLICANI.

Magister universitatis. A *magister* in a corporate body.—See MAGISTER COLLEGII.

Magister utriusque militiae. See MAGISTER MILITUM.

Magister vici. The chief of the local administration of a village, or of a *vicus* in Rome.—See VICUS, REGIONES URBIS ROMAE.

> Boak, *Univ. of Michigan Studies, Human. Ser.* 14 (1924) 136; De Robertis, *Hist* 9 (1935) 247.

Magisterium (magisteria potestas). The office of a magister whatever his special functions were. The term is frequent in imperial constitutions. *Magisterium* refers also to the employment of a *magister navis* as well as of a teacher.—See the foregoing items.

Magistratus. Denotes both the public office and the official himself. Magistracy was a Republican institution; under the Principate some *magistratus* continued to exist but with gradually diminishing importance; in the post-Diocletian Empire some former magistracies still exist but reduced nearly completely to an honorific title. The magisterial power is based on two fundamental conceptions, IMPERIUM and POTESTAS, of which the first is the broader one. For the distinction between *imperium domi* and *imperium militiae*, see DOMI. The *imperium domi* was hampered by the right of intercession of magistrates of higher or equal rank, and primarily of plebeian tribunes (see INTERCESSIO). The most characteristic features of the Republican magistracy were the limited duration (one year) and colleagueship since each magistracy was covered by at least two persons (see COLLEGAE) with equal power. Colleagueship meant complete equality of competence and functions; colleagues in office could act in common or divide their functions by agreement. Unilateral action by one magistrate could be stopped by the veto of his colleague. Simultaneous holding of two ordinary magistracies was prohibited; iteration was admitted only after ten years; see ITERATIO. For the tenure of a magistracy later a minimum age was prescribed; likewise the periods, after which the tenure of another higher office was permitted, were fixed by statute; see LEX VILLIA ANNALIS. The magistrates were elected by the people, namely, those with *imperium* and the censors in the *comitia centuriata,* others in *comitia tributa.* The election of plebeian magistrates was directed by the plebeian tribunes, that of other magistrates by one of the consuls, in exceptional situations by a dictator, an *interrex,* or a military tribune. The candidates had to present themselves personally to the competent magistrate (*profiteri*) who was authorized to accept their candidacy or to reject it, see CANDIDATUS, AMBITUS. Non-citizens, freedmen, individuals branded with infamy, women, persons with certain physical (blindness, lameness) or mental defects were not eligible. During his year of service a *magistratus* could not be removed. Misdemeanor in office could be prosecuted only after the term, hence the tenure of an office for two consecutive years was prohibited. Specific crimes could be committed only by *magistratus* through violation of their official duties; see PECULATUS, REPETUNDAE. The tenure of a public office was considered an honor; for that reason the magistrates did not receive any compensation. Their political influence was, however, of greatest importance; membership in the senate and the possibility to continue the official career (for which a certain sequence was prescribed, see CURSUS HONORUM) and to obtain a high post in the administration of a province were attractive enough to assume the financial charges connected with a higher magistracy (as, e.g., the arrangement of public games, *ludi*). —D. 1.2; 27.8; C. 5.75; 11.35.—For the particular magistrates (consuls, praetors, quaestors, etc.), see the pertinent items; for the auxiliary personnel, see APPARITORES, LICTORES, PRAECO, SCRIBA, VIATORES. See also HONOR, ABACTUS, LEX CORNELIA DE MAGISTRATIBUS, KALENDAE, IUS AGENDI CUM POPULO, IURISDICTIO, POMERIUM, DESTINATIO, ACTIO SUBSIDIARIA, CREATIO, IURARE IN LEGES, EIURARE, NOMINATIO, PROFESSIO, LEX POMPEIA (on candidates), MULTA, COMPARATIO and the following items.

> Kübler, *RE* 14; Brassloff, *RE* 4, 1686 (*s.v. creatio*); Lécrivain, *DS* 3; De Dominicis, *NDI* 8; Treves, *OCD*; F. Leifer, *Die Einheit des Gewaltgedankens im röm. Staatsrecht,* 1914; Buckland, *Civil proceedings against ex-magistrates in the Republic, JRS* 37 (1937); H. Siber, *Die plebeischen Magistraturen,* 1938; Gonnet, *RHD* 16 (1937) 193; Nocera, *Il fondamento del potere dei magistrati, AnPer* 57 (1946) 145; T. R. S. Broughton and M. Patterson, *The magistrates of the R. Republic,* New York, 1951.

Magistratus curules. *Magistratus* who had the right to be seated on a folding ivory chair, *sella curulis,* when acting officially (dictators, consuls, praetors, censors, aedils). The *sella curulis* belonged to their official insignia and was carried about everywhere they had to perform an official act.—See SUBSELLIUM, SELLA CURULIS.

> Kübler, *RE* 2A (*s.v. sella curulis*); Chapot, *DS* 4 (*s.v. sella c.*).

Magistratus designati. Magistrates elected for the next term (normally in July) during the whole period which preceded their entering on the official duties (since 153 B.C., January first).—See KALENDAE, RENUNTIATIO.

Magistratus maiores—minores. The *magistratus maiores* were elected by the *comitia centuriata,* the *magistratus minores* by *comitia tributa* (see MAGISTRATUS). The *magistratus minores* were officials of minor importance, they had no *imperium* and were vested with a restricted jurisdiction and some functions in specific fields. The collective denomination for a group of *magistratus* of a lower degree was VIGINTISEXVIRI. The tenure of a minor magistracy opened the way for the quaestorship, the first step in the career of *magistratus maiores.*—See CURSUS HONORUM.

> Lécrivain, *DS* 3; Kübler, *RE* 14, 401.

Magistratus minores. See MAGISTRATUS MAIORES.

Magistratus municipales. Magistrates in municipalities (MUNICIPIA) who managed the local administration, finances, and jurisdiction. They were elected by the local assemblies, later by the *decuriones* and from among the members of the municipal council, *ordo decurionum.* The principles of colleagueship were also applied to them as well as the institution of INTERCESSIO. They had no *imperium.*—C. 1.56. —See DUOVIRI IURI DICUNDO, QUATTUORVIRI, QUAESTORES MUNICIPALES, DUOVIRI AEDILES, PRAEFECTI IURI DICUNDO, HONORARIUM, NOMINATIO.

> Lécrivain, *DS* 3; Kübler, *RE* 14, 434; E. Manni, *Per la storia dei municipii,* 1947.

Magistratus patricii—plebei. The distinction is based on the circumstance whether a magistracy was accessible only to patricians or to plebeians. In the course of time all magistracies which originally were reserved to patricians, could be obtained by plebeians. Specifically plebeian magistrates were the plebeian tribunes and the *aediles plebis.*—See TRANSITIO AD PLEBEM.

Magistratus populi Romani. Magistrates in Rome; ant. MAGISTRATUS MUNICIPALES.

Magistratus suffecti. Magistrates (chiefly consuls) elected when a magistracy became vacant by death or resignation of the magistrate in office.—See CONSULES ORDINARII.

Magna culpa. "Equal to *dolus* (*dolus est*)," D. 50.16.226.—See CULPA, CULPA LATA, DOLUS.

> De Medio, *St Fadda* 2 (1906).

Magnificus (magnificentia). A title of high imperial functionaries in the later Empire.

> P. Koch, *Byzantinische Beamtentitel,* 1903, 45; O. Hirschfeld, *Kleine Schriften,* 1913, 672.

Magnitudo. Occurs in the imperial correspondence as a term of address to the highest dignitaries of the Empire ("*magnitudo tua*").

Magus. See MAGIA.

Maiestas. Dignity, supremacy, the greatness of the state (*maiestas populi Romani*). *Maiestas* was also an honorific title of the emperor.—For *maiestas* in penal law, see CRIMEN MAIESTATIS, QUAESTIO DE MAIESTATE.

Maior. A person higher in official rank.—See MAGISTRATUS MAIORES.

Maior (natù). Older, in particular one who is over twenty-five years of age. Ant. MINOR. MAIOR AETAS = the age over twenty-five.—C. 2.53.

Maiores. Ascendants of a person, from the sixth degree. Generally *maiores* = ancestors, forefathers, when referring to their customs (*mos, mores maiorum*) or their legal opinions (*maiores putaverunt*) and institutions.

> H. Roloff, *Maiores bei Cicero,* Diss., Göttingen, 1938.

Mala fides. See BONA FIDES, FIDES. The term *mala fides superveniens* appears in the doctrine of USUCAPIO, i.e., bad faith of the holder of another's thing who at the beginning when he took possession thereof believed in good faith that it belonged to him, but later, before the usucaption was completed, became aware that he had no title to own the thing.

> Levet, *RHD* 12 (1933) 1; A. Hägerström, *Der röm. Obligationsbegriff* 1 (1927) 145; 2 (1940) 364.

Mala mansio. See MANSIO MALA.

Malae artes. Syn. *artes magicae.* See MAGIA.

Malae fidei possessio (possessor). See POSSESSIO BONAE FIDEI.

Male. (With reference to legal acts or transactions.) Unlawfully, inefficiently (e.g., to sue), unjustly (e.g., to pass a judgment).

Maleficium. A crime, wrongdoing. It is not a technical juristic term and is used as syn. with both *crimen* and *delictum.* At times it is syn. with *magia*; see MALEFICUS.—See OBLIGATIO EX DELICTO.

> Taubenschlag, *RE* 14; Lauria, *SDHI* 4 (1938) 182; Albertario, *Studi* 3 (1936) 197.

Maleficus. (Noun.) Commonly denotes a sorcerer. Syn. *magus,* see MAGIA. In similar connection *maleficus* (adj.) is syn. with *magicus.*—C. 9.18.

Malle. To prefer. The term is applied when a person has a choice between two or more things (in contractual relations or legacies). *Malle* in the meaning of to wish, want (= *velle*) is listed among the words suspected of interpolation since it frequently occurs in later imperial constitutions.

> Guarneri-Citati, *Indice*[2] (1927) 55.

Malum carmen. See CARMEN MALUM, INCANTARE.

Malum venenum. See VENENUM.

Manceps. One who at a public auction, conducted by a magistrate, through the highest bid obtained the right to collect taxes (a tax farmer) or custom duties, the lease of public land (*ager publicus*) or other advantages (a monopoly).—In postal organization *manceps* was a post-station master.

> Steinwenter, *RE* 14; M. Kaser, *Das altröm. Ius,* 1949, 140; P. Noailles, *Du droit sacré au droit civil,* 1950, 224.

Mancipare. See MANCIPATIO. Syn. *mancipio dare.*

Mancipatio. In historical times a solemn form of conveyance of ownership of a RES MANCIPI, accomplished in the presence of five Roman citizens as witnesses and of a man who held a scale (LIBRIPENS), with a prescribed ritual and the solemn utterance of a fixed formula by the transferee (the buyer when the *mancipatio* involved a sale). The formula was: "I declare that this slave (this thing) is mine under Quiritary law and be he (it) bought by me with this piece of bronze and the bronze scale." The assertion was not denied by the transferor. The transfer of ownership over a RES MANCIPI could be achieved only in this way, otherwise the transferee did not acquire Quiritary ownership, but only possession which might lead to such an ownership through USUCAPIO. The transaction was perhaps originally called *mancipium* (from *manu capere* = to grasp with the hand, which was one of the decisive gestures performed during the act). *Mancipatio* was also applied for other purposes as, e.g., to make a donation, to constitute a dowry, to hand over a thing to another as a trustee, *fiduciae causa* (see FIDUCIA). In all these instances the external aspect of the act was that of a sale although the "price" paid was fictitious, a small coin being given as compensation (*mancipatio nummo uno*). In the further development other legal transactions were performed in the form of *mancipatio* such as the transfer of power over the wife to the husband, emancipating a child (see EMANCIPATIO), making a testament *per aes et libram,* or constituting a servitude. Various clauses might be added to the oral formula of the *mancipatio,* except the restriction of the transfer by a condition or term (see ACTUS LEGITIMI). Such additional declarations of transferor were covered by the term *nuncupatio.* Later, specific duties of the parties were assumed by *stipulatio.* The increasing use of written documents deprived the *mancipatio* of its importance. In Justinian's law it does not appear any more. Mention of it in classical texts, accepted into Justinian's codification, was omitted and substituted by the formless TRADITIO; *mancipare* was replaced simply by *dare.*
—See ACTIO AUCTORITATIS, ACTIO DE MODO AGRI, SATISDATIO SECUNDUM MANCIPIUM, NUMMUS UNUS, RAUDUSCULUM.

> Kunkel, *RE* 14; Lécrivain, *DS* 3; Volterra, *NDI* 7; Berger, *OCD*; W. Stintzing, *Mancipatio,* 1904; S. Schlossman, *In iure cessio und m.,* 1904; A. Hägerström, *Röm. Obligationsbegriff* 1 (1927) 35, 372; 2 (1940) 301; Husserl, *ZSS* 50 (1930) 478; D. Hazewinkel-Suringa, *M. en traditio,* Amsterdam, 1932; De Visscher, *RHD* 12 (1933) 603; G. G. Archi, *Il trasferimento della proprietà,* 1934, 79; Leifer, *ZSS* 56 (1936) 136, 57 (1937) 172; S. Romano, *Nuovi studi sul trasferimento della proprietà,* 1937, 55; H. Pflüger, *Erwerb des Eigentums,* 1937, 97; v. Lübtow, *Fschr Koschaker* 2 (1939) 114; K. F. Thormann, *Der doppelte Ursprung der M.,* 1943; M. Kaser, *Eigentum und Besitz,* 1943, 107; idem, *Das altröm. Ius,* 1949, *passim*; Meylan, *Scr Ferrini* 4 (Univ. Sacro Cuore, 1949) 190; idem, *ConfInst* 1947 (1950) 173; P. Noailles, *Du droit sacré au droit civil,* 1950, 199.

Mancipatio familiae. The oldest form of a testament made by *mancipatio* through which the testator transfered his property to a trustee (a friend) with an oral instruction (*nuncupatio*) as to how the trustee, who formally was the buyer of the estate, *familiae emptor*, had to distribute it after the testator's death. Since the trustee was the immediate successor (*heredis loco*) and had to convey the single objects to the persons indicated by the testator, this kind of succession was a succession into specific things and not a universal one.—See FAMILIAE EMPTOR, NUNCUPATIO.

Kamps, *RHD* 15 (1936) 142, 413; Leifer, *Fschr Koschaker* 2 (1939) 227; Bruck, *Sem* 3 (1945) 11; C. Cosentini, *St sui liberti* 1 (1948) 24; Lévy-Bruhl, *RIDA* 2 (= *Mél De Visscher* 2, 1949) 163; idem, *Fschr Schulz* 1 (1951) 253; B. Albanese, *Successione creditaria*, *AnPal* 20 (1949) 164, 294.

Mancipatio fiduciae causa. See FIDUCIA.

Brasiello, *RIDA* 4 (= *Mél De Visscher* 3, 1950) 201.

Mancipatio nummo uno. The conveyance of property through *mancipatio* for a fictitious price (a piece of money) for various purposes (making a donation, constitution of a dowry).—See MANCIPATIO, NUMMUS UNUS.

Kunkel, *RE* 14, 1009; Rabel, *ZSS* 27 (1906) 327; G. Pugliese, *La simulazione* 1938, 76.

Mancipatus. The service of a postmaster (*manceps*) in the postal organization; see MANCEPS, CURSUS PUBLICUS.

Steinwenter, *RE* 14.

Mancipi res. See RES MANCIPI, MANCIPIUM.

Mancipio accipiens. The transferee of property in a MANCIPATIO. *Mancipio dans* = the transferor.

Mancipium. Belongs to the earliest juristic terminology. The original meaning (much discussed in literature) is rather obscure—it expressed the idea of power over persons and things—but its later applications show a considerable variance. For its synonymity with *mancipatio* (*mancipio dare, mancipio accipere*), see MANCIPATIO. In the technical term *res mancipi* (*mancipii*) there is a reminiscence of the original meaning (a thing taken with the hand in the formal act of *mancipatio*). *Personae in mancipio* (= *in causa mancipii*) are free persons who were conveyed through *mancipatio* to another (*adoptio, emancipatio, noxae deditio*). Finally *mancipium* is often syn. with *servus* (a slave).—C. 11.63.—See MANCIPATIO, SATIS-DATIO SECUNDUM MANCIPIUM.

Humbert and Lécrivain, *DS* 3; Volterra, *NDI* 8; Pampaloni, *Persone in causa mancipii*, *BIDR* 17 (1905); J. Ellul, *Études sur l'évolution de la notion juridique du m.*, 1936; Giffard, *Rev. de Philologie*, 1937, 396; Cornil, *Fschr Koschaker* 1 (1939) 404; J. G. A. Wilms, *De wording van het rom. dominium*, Gent, 1939–40, 13; Monier, *RHD* 19–20 (1940–41) 364; K. F. Thormann, *Der doppelte Ursprung der mancipatio*, 1943, 58, 175; Tejero, *AHDE* 15 (1945) 310; P. Noailles, *Fas et ius*, 1948, 144; M. Kaser, *Eigentum u. Besitz*, 1943, 107; idem, *Das altröm. Ius*, 1949, 136, 328; De Visscher, *Nouvelles études*, 1949, 193; M. David and H. L. Nelson, *TR* 19 (1951) 439.

Mandare. See MANDATA PRINCIPUM, MANDATUM.

Mandare actionem. See CESSIO.

Mandare iurisdictionem. See IURISDICTIO MANDATA.

Mandare tutelam. To appoint a guardian.

Mandata principum. Judicial and administrative rules or general instructions issued by the emperors to high functionaries of the empire, primarily to provincial governors to be applied by them in the exercise of their official functions. They were binding only in the province for which they were issued. When an imperial *mandatum* affected lower officials or the provincial population, it was made public by an edict of the governor. The jurists did not include the *mandata principum* into the imperial constitutions but mentioned them as a particular group of imperial enactments.—C. 1.15.

Finkelstein, *TR* 13 (1934) 150.

Mandatela. See CUSTODELA.

Mandator. One who orders, commissions another to do something. In the consensual contract *mandatum mandator* = is the person on whose order another assumes the duty to perform something without compensation. In penal law *mandator* is the person who orders another to commit a crime.

Mandator causae. One who orders another to denounce or to accuse a third person of a crime. He is responsible for malicious information or accusation made by a *delator* on his order.—See DELATORES.

Mandatum. A consensual contract by which a person assumed the duty to conclude a legal transaction or to perform a service gratuitously in the interest of the mandator or of a third person. The *mandatum* was based on a personal relationship of confidence (friendship) between the parties, it therefore ended by the death of one of them, by revocation by the mandator or renunciation of the mandatary. Gratuity of the service was essential, since if compensation was given, the agreement was a hiring of services (*locatio conductio operarum* or *operis faciendi*). The mandatary could not sue for an honorarium, but he might claim the reimbursement of expenses by an *actio mandati contraria*. The mandator's action against the mandatary for restitution of what the latter gained by executing the mandate or for damages caused by fraudulent acting was the *actio mandati* (*directa*). The actions were *bonae fidei* (see IUDICIA BONAE FIDEI), the condemnation of the mandatary involved infamy. Beyond the field of the contractual *mandatum, mandare* and *mandatum* are used in a broader sense of an order or authorization given by one person to another, as e.g., by a creditor to his debtor to pay the debt to a third person, or of a commission given to one's representative to administer his affairs or a specific affair (*negotium*, see PROCURATOR).—Inst. 3.26; D. 17.1; C. 4.35.—See ADSIGNATIO LIBERTI, RENUNTIARE MANDATUM.

Kreller, *RE* 14; Cuq, *DS* 3; Donatuti, *NDI* 8; Lusignani, *Responsabilità per custodia*, 2 (1905); Pampaloni, *BIDR*

20 (1908) 210; Donatuti, *AnPer* 39 (1927) 1; Kreller, *Arch. für civilistische Praxis* 133 (1931); Frese, *St Riccobono* 4 (1936) 397; Pringsheim, *St Besta* 1 (1937) 325; F. Bossowski, *Die Abgrenzung des m. und negotiorum gestio* (Lwów, 1937); Sachers, *ZSS* 59 (1939); Pflüger, *ZSS* 65 (1947) 169; Sanfilippo, *AnCat* 1 (1946–7) 167; *idem, Corso di dir. rom., Il mandato*, Catania, 1947; G. Longo, *Scr Ferrini* 2 (Univ. Sacro Cuore, 1948); Kreller, *ZSS* 66 (1948) 58; Arangio-Ruiz, *Fschr Wenger* 2 (1945) 60; *idem, Il mandato*, 1949; A. Burdese, *Autorizzazione ad alienare*, 1950, 57.

Mandatum generale. A general authorization concerning the administration of all affairs (*universa negotia*) of the mandator.

Peters, *ZSS* 32 (1911) 280.

Mandatum incertum. A *mandatum* in which the object of the mandate is not precisely defined.

Donatuti, *BIDR* 33 (1924) 168; G. Longo, *Scr Ferrini* 2 (Univ. Sacro Cuore, 1948) 138; Arangio-Ruiz, *Il mandato*, 1949, 110.

Mandatum mea (tua) gratia. A *mandatum* "to my (your) advantage," a distinction based on the circumstance whether the *mandatum* is in the interest of the mandator (*mea*) or the mandatary (*tua gratia*). *Mandatum aliena gratia* = a *mandatum* in the interest of a third person. A mandate in the exclusive interest of the mandatary is treated as an advice; see CONSILIUM.

F. Mancaleoni, *M. tua gratia*, 1899; Last, *AnPal* 15 (1936) 252; Rabel, *St Bonfante* 4 (1930) 283; Arangio-Ruiz, *Il mandato*, 1949, 120.

Mandatum pecuniae credendae. An order given a person to lend money to a third person (*mandare alicui ut credat*). It created on the part of the *mandator* the obligation to secure the mandatary against losses from such a transaction. Such a mandate (called by a non-Roman term *mandatum qualificatum*) made the mandator a surety to the mandatary. —C. 8.40; 5.20.

G. Segrè, *RISG* 28 (1900) 227 (= *Scr giur* 1, 1930, 267); Bortolucci, *BIDR* 27 (1914) 129, 28 (1915) 191; G. C. Müller, *Kreditauftrag als m. qualificatum*, Zürich, 1926; C. G. Constadaky, *Le mandat de crédit en dr. rom.*, Thèse Paris, 1932; Last, *AnPal* 15 (1936) 237; Arangio-Ruiz, *Il mandato*, 1949, 118.

Mandatum post mortem. An order which had to be fulfilled by the mandatary (normally the heir) after the death of the mandator. Such a *mandatum* is void, because an obligation could not arise in the person of an heir.

Sanfilippo, *St Solazzi* 1948, 554; Arangio-Ruiz, *Il mandato*, 1949, 142; Rouxel, *Annales Faculté de droit Bordeaux*, 3 (1952) 87.

Manere. To remain. The term is applied to legal situations or remedies (actions), to the status of a person or to a contractual relationship which remain valid as they were (*in sua causa*) in spite of some legal or factual changes which occurred therein.

Manifestare. To make public, manifest. *Manifestari* = to be made evident, apparent. The term is used of imperial constitutions by which a certain legal rule is settled. *Manifestare* and the adj. *manifestus* (*manifestissimus*) are frequent terms in the language of the imperial chancery of the later Empire and of Justinian.

Manifesti (manifestissimi) iuris est. See IURIS EST.

Manifestissimus (manifestissime). Most evident.— See EVIDENTISSIMAE PROBATIONES, PROBATIONES.

Guarneri-Citati, *Indice*² (1927) 55.

Manifestum furtum. See FURTUM MANIFESTUM.

Manilius, Manlius. A prominent jurist under the Republic, consul 149 B.C., author of a collection of juristic formularies (known under the name *Monumenta Maniliana, Actiones Manilianae*); see FORMULAE. He enjoyed high esteem among his contemporaries who consulted him on the forum and at home.

Münzer, *RE* 14, 1135.

Manipulus. A smaller unit within the legion, composed of one hundred and twenty to two hundred men. Originally there were thirty *manipuli*, each composed of two *centuriae*.—*Manipularius* = a common soldier.

Liebenam, *RE* 6, 1594; Cagnat, *DS* 3, 1051.

Mansio. A post station located on the principal post roads, with quarters for night's lodging of passengers. Syn. STATIO.—See MANCEPS.

Kubitschek, *RE* 14; Humbert, *DS* 1, 1655.

Mansio mala. An instrument of torture (see TORMENTUM) which immobilized the culprit who was bound to a board.

Taubenschlag, *RE* 14.

Mansuetudo. Mildness, clemency. The Christian emperors used to speak of themselves in their enactments *"mansuetudo nostra."*

Manu iniuriam (damnum) dare. To hurt, to inflict damage by the use of hands.

Manu militari. Through official organs. The term is applied to the execution of judicial orders and judgments in later civil procedure with the assistance of public functionaries.—See REI VINDICATIO.

Cagnat, *DS* 3.

Manubiae. Money obtained from the sale of war booty (see PRAEDA). The sale was directed by the military quaestors and was performed by auction.— See PECULATUS.

Lammert, *RE* 14; Brecht, *RE* Suppl. 7, 919; Vogel, *ZSS* 66 (1948) 408; L. Clerici, *Economia e finanza dei Romani*, 1943, 143, 153.

Manum inicere. See MANUS INIECTIO.

Manumissio. (From *manumittere*.) The release of a slave from the power (see MANUS) of his master by the latter, i.e., "giving freedom, *datio libertatis*" (D. 1.1.4). Originally the slave became not fully free (even as late as second century B.C. the term *servus* is applied to freedmen) and the rights of his former master, the manumitter, were more extensive than in historical times, when the manumitted slave became free, *sui iuris* (independent from paternal power) and a Roman citizen, except in certain specific cases in which his liberty was somewhat limited. For the forms of *manumissio,* see the following items; for limitations concerning the number of slaves to be manumitted by one master, the age of the slave owner and of the slaves themselves, see LEX FUFIA CANINIA, LEX IUNIA NORBANA, LEX AELIA SENTIA. The pertinent restrictions were abolished or, at least, considerably softened, by Justinian who also generally suppressed the distinctions in the legal status of freedmen which according to earlier statutes depended upon the kind of *manumissio* and the age of the slave. The *manumissio* did not tear all ties between the *manumissor* and his former slave. Even a restricted right of punishment remained from the former IUS VITAE NECISQUE. The freedman was materially independent but could be obligated to services on behalf of his former master (see IURATA PROMISSIO LIBERTI) who moreover, had the right of tutorship over his *libertus* and a right of succession when the latter died without leaving legitimate heirs. —Inst. 1.6; D. 40.1–9; C. 4.14; 7.10; 11; 15.—See LIBERTUS, LIBERTINUS, PATRONUS, TUTELA LEGITIMA, CAUSAE PROBATIO, CONCILIUM MANUMISSIONUM, IUS ACCRESCENDI, LATINI IUNIANI, FAVOR LIBERTATIS ITERATIO, ONERARE LIBERTATEM, INGRATUS, SERVUS DOTALIS.

Weiss, *RE* 14; Lécrivain, *DS* 3 (*s.v. libertas*); De Dominicis, *NDI* 8; S. Perozzi, *Scritti* 3 (1948, ex 1904) 511; F. Haymann, *Freilassungspflicht,* 1905; Lotmar, *ZSS* 33 (1912) 304; Kaser, *ZSS* 61 (1941); De Visscher, *SDHI* 12 (1946) 69 (= *Nouvelles Études,* 1949, 117); De Dominicis, *AnPer* 52 (1938), 57–58 (1947–48) 111; Cosentini, *AnCat* 2 (1947-8) 374; Lemosse, *RIDA* 3 (= *Mél De Visscher* 2, 1949) 39.

Manumissio censu. A manumission of a slave through his enrollment in the list of Roman citizens, with the consent of his master, during the operation of the CENSUS by the censors.

Daube, *JRS* 36 (1946) 60; C. Cosentini, *St sui liberti* 1 (1948) 14; Lemosse, *RHD* 27 (1949) 161; De Visscher, *SDHI* 12 (1946) 69; Danieli, *SDHI* 15 (1949) 198.

Manumissio fideicommissaria. A manumission ordered through a *fideicommissum:* a testator requested in his testament the heir or any person awarded by him in his last will to manumit a slave through a formal manumission. The slave did not become free until the manumission was performed and the fideicommissary manumitter became the patron of the slave freed. A senatusconsult under the Principate declared the slave free if the heir refused the acceptance of the inheritance or if for any other reason the performance of the *manumissio* became impossible. The *manumissio fideicommissaria* could be applied with regard to a slave of the heir or of a third person. In the latter case the heir was bound to buy the slave in order to manumit him. *Manumissio fideicommissaria* is termed also *manumissio fiduciaria.*—See LIBERTAS FIDEICOMMISSARIA, SENA-TUSCONSULTUM DASUMIANUM, SENATUSCONSULTUM RUBRIANUM, SENATUSCONSULTUM VITRASIANUM.

V. De Villa, *Liberatio legata,* 1939.

Manumissio fiduciaria. See the foregoing item.

Manumissio in convivio (convivii adhibitione). See MANUMISSIO INTER AMICOS.

Manumissio in ecclesia. A manumission performed in a church in the presence of the Christian congregation and priests, with consent of the master. It was introduced by Constantine. The slave manumitted became a Roman citizen.

De Francisci, *RendLomb* 44 (1911); Mor, *ibid.* 65 (1932); Gaudemet, *Rev. d'histoire de l'Eglise de France,* 1947, 38; Danieli, *StCagl* 31 (1947/1948) 263.

Manumissio in fraudem creditorum. A manumission performed by an insolvent debtor in order to defraud the creditors. The *manumissio* could be annulled at the request of the creditors.—See FRAU-DARE, FRAUS, LEX AELIA SENTIA.

Schulz, *ZSS* 48 (1928); Beseler, *TR* 10 (1930) 199.

Manumissio inter amicos. A formless manumission by the declaration of the master, made before witnesses, to the effect that the slave be free. If made at a banquet before the guests = *manumissio in convivio.*

A. Biscardi, *Manumissio per mensam,* 1939, 9.

Manumissio per epistulam. An enfranchisement of a slave by a letter of the master addressed to the slave. This form of *manumissio* could be applied to an absent slave.

Manumissio per mensam. An informal manumission of a slave through his admission to the master's table and a pertinent declaration of the latter.

Wlassak, *ZSS* 26 (1905) 401; Funaioli, *BIDR* 44 (1936–37); Paoli, *SDHI* 3 (1936) 369; A. Biscardi, *M. per mensam* (Florence, 1939); Henrion, *Rev. Belge de philol. et hist.,* 1943, 198.

Manumissio praetoria. A *manumissio* performed in a less formal act by the slave's master who had no quiritary ownership (*dominium ex iure Quiritium*) over the slave, but only possessed him IN BONIS (for instance, if the slave was not conveyed to him through *mancipatio,* but through an informal *traditio*). Other forms of *manumissiones praetoriae* were *manumissio per mensam, inter amicos* and *per epistulam.* They are called in the literature "praetorian" because they were not recognized by the *ius civile.* The freedom of slaves so manumitted was protected by the praetor (*in libertate tueri*) under certain conditions although they had no full rights of freedmen. Therefore their status is described as *in libertate morari* (= to live in freedom), or "to be in freedom through the protection of the praetor" (*tuitione praetoris*).

Wlassak, *ZSS* 26 (1905) 367; A. Biscardi, *M. per mensam e affrancazioni pretorie,* 1939.

Manumissio sacrorum causa. A manumission of a slave who assumed the duty to perform sacral rites in behalf of his patron.

Manumissio servi communis. A manumission of a slave owned by two or more masters in common. The classical law required manumission by all co-owners for the validity of the *manumissio* of such a slave.—See IUS ADCRESCENDI.

Manumissio sub condicione. A manumission under a condition, i.e., the liberty of the slave became effective only when the condition was fulfilled. Such a manumission could be made only in a testament. During the intermediary period the slave remained slave, his liberty being in suspense until the realization of the condition. Such a slave was sold as a slave, but the condition remained in force. Usually the condition consisted in the slave's payment of a sum to the heir. Such slaves were called during the period of suspense *statuliberi*. A child of a *statulibera* was a slave. A similar situation was a slave manumitted *ex die*, i.e., when the *manumissio* became valid at a fixed date. In the meantime, the slave continued to be a slave.—See STATULIBER.

G. Donatuti, *Statuliber*, 1940.

Manumissio testamento. A manumission through a testamentary disposition of the slave's master expressed in a traditional formula "my slave X shall be free (*liber esto*)" or "I order that my slave X be free (*liberum esse iubeo*)." The slave became free without any further formality, immediately after the acceptance of the inheritance by the heir. A slave thus manumitted could be instituted as an heir in the same testament. See HERES NECESSARIUS. In classical law the institution of a slave as an heir not combined with his manumission was void. In Justinian's law in such a case the manumission was assumed as self-understood and the slave instituted as an heir became automatically free.—D. 40.4; C. 7.2.—See REDDERE RATIONES.

Tumedei, *RISG* 64, 65 (1920); C. Cosentini, *St sui liberti* 1 (1948) 17.

Manumissio vindicta. A manumission before a magistrate, performed through a fictitious trial in which a third person, with the agreement of the slave's master, claimed that the slave was free. The process was similar to a REI VINDICATIO (suit for the recovery of a thing) in the *legis actio* procedure. The master did not oppose such affirmation whereupon the magistrate pronounced the slave free. The use of a rod (*vindicta*) with which the slave was touched by the claimant explains the name of this kind of *manumissio*.—D. 40.2.—See VINDICTA, ADSERTIO.

Ch. Appleton, *Mél Fournier* 1929; Lévy-Bruhl, *St Riccobono* 3 (1936) 1; Aru, *St Solmi* 2 (1941) 301; C. Cosentini, *St sui liberti* 1 (1948) 11 (Bibl.); Monier, *St Albertario* 1 (1952) 197; Kaser, *SDHI* 16 (1950) 72; Meylan, *RIDA* 6 (1951) 113.

Manumissor. See MANUMISSIO, MANUMITTERE.

Manumittere. To free a slave; see MANUMISSIO. *Manumittere* is also used with reference to the release of a person from the status of *mancipium* and of a son from paternal power.—See MANCIPIUM, EMANCIPATIO.

Manum depellere. See DEPELLERE MANUM.

Manupretium (manus pretium). Wages paid for handicraft, the value of an artisan's work.

Manus. Originally the term indicated the power of the head of a family over all its members and the slaves (MANUMISSIO = *de manu missio*). Later *manus* was only the husband's power over his wife, and that over his children was the PATRIA POTESTAS. The husband acquired *manus* through a special agreement (see CONVENTIO IN MANUM) which accompanied the conclusion of a marriage. The wife under the power (*in manu*) of her husband had the legal position of a daughter (*filiae familias loco*).—See MATRIMONIUM.

Manigk, *RE* 14; Lécrivain, *DS* 3; Anon., *NDI* 8; E. Volterra, *La conception du mariage* (Padova, 1940); *idem, St Solazzi* (1948) 675; Bozza, *Manus e matrimonio, AnMac* 15 (1942) 111; Düll, *Fschr Wenger* 1 (1945) 204; v. Schwind, *Scr Ferrini* 4 (Univ. Sacro Cuore, Milan, 1949) 131; Kaser, *Iura* 1 (1950) 64; Danieli, *StUrb* 1950; Volterra, *ACIVer* 3 (1951) 29.

Manus inferre. To lay hands upon a person, to hit. It is considered an *iniuria re facta*.—See INIURIA.

Manus iniectio (manum inicere). See LEGIS ACTIO PER MANUS INIECTIONEM (Bibl.)—*Manus iniectio* was also the symbolic act (touching the debtor's shoulder) performed by a plaintiff when he summoned the debtor into court (see IN IUS VOCATIO).—See LEX VALLIA, DEPELLERE MANUM.

Taubenschlag, *RE* 14; Lécrivain, *DS* 3; Noailles, *Revue des Études Latines* 20 (1942) 110; *idem, Fas et ius*, 1948, 147; *idem, Du droit sacré au droit civil*, 1950, 120; M. Kaser, *Das altröm. Ius*, 1949, 191.

Manus iniectio iudicati. Introduced by the Twelve Tables for the execution of judgment-debts.—See LEGIS ACTIO PER MANUS INIECTIONEM.

P. Noailles, *Du droit sacré au droit civil*, 1950, 110.

Manus iniectio pro iudicato. A *manus iniectio* "as if upon a judgment," i.e., an execution of certain kinds of debts in the form of *legis actio per manus iniectionem* as in the case of a *manus iniectio* for judgment-debts. In the oral formula pronounced by the plaintiff the words *pro iudicato* were added. There was, however, no preceding judgment.—See LEGIS ACTIO PER MANUS INIECTIONEM, ACTIO DEPENSI.

Manus iniectio pura. A *manus iniectio* which was neither *iudicati* nor *pro iudicato* but was introduced by special statutes for specific claims; see LEX FURIA TESTAMENTARIA, LEX MARCIA against usurers. The defendant was permitted to remove the plaintiff's hand (*depellere manum*) and defend himself personally (*pro se lege agere*).—See LEX VALLIA, and the foregoing items.

Manus sibi inferre. To commit suicide. Syn. CONSCISCERE SIBI MORTEM.

Marcellus, Ulpius. A jurist of the second half of the second century after Christ, author of an extensive work, *Digesta,* of a collection of *Responsa,* and of a commentary on the *Digesta* of Julian in the form of *Notae.*

Orestano, *NDI* 7; Sciascia, *BIDR* 49–50 (1948) 424.

Marcianus, Aelius. One of the last jurists of the classical period (later first half of the third century), author of *Institutiones* in 16 books, richly exploited by the compilers of the Digest. He also wrote a collection of *Regulae* and a few monographs, chiefly on criminal procedure.

Jörs, *RE* 1, 523 (no. 88); Ferrini, *Opere* 2 (1929, two articles of 1880 and 1901); H. Krüger, *St Bonfante 2* (1930) 312; Buckland, *St Riccobono* 1 (1936) 273; De Robertis, *RISG* 15 (1940) 220.

Mare. The sea is a *res communis omnium.* "By nature it is open to everyone" (D. 1.8.2.1; Inst. 2.1.1). Everybody has the right of fishing therein. —See LITUS.

Costa, *Rivista di dir. internazionale* 5 (1916) 337; Maroi, *RISG* 62 (1919); Biondi, *St Perozzi* 1925; Branca, *AnTr* 12 (1941) 5, 91; G. Lombardi, *Ricerche in tema di ius gentium,* 1946, 99.

Margarita. A pearl.—See GEMMA.

Maritalis affectio. See AFFECTIO MARITALIS, CONCUBINATUS.

Maritimus. See USURAE MARITIMAE.

Maritus. A husband. *Mariti* may sometimes refer to husband and wife.—See IUS MARITI.—C. 4.12.

Berger, *Amer. Jour. of Philology,* 67 (1946) 332.

Martinus. A glossator of the twelfth century (died 1166?), a disciple of Irnerius.—See GLOSSATORES.

Anon., *NDI* 6 (*s.v. Gosia Martino*); H. Kantorowicz, *St in the Glossators of R. Law,* 1938, 86.

Mater. "The mother is always certain" (*semper certa est,* D. 2.4.5), no matter whether the child was born in a legitimate marriage or not. The legal status (liberty, citizenship) of an illegitimate child depends upon that of the mother. A widow-mother was in postclassical times admitted to the guardianship over her children.—C. 4.12; 5.46.—See FEMINA, TUTELA, MANUS, and the following item.

Wenger, *ZSS* 26 (1905) 449; Frezza, *StCagl* 12 (1933–34); Sachers, *Fschr Schulz* 1 (1951) 327.

Mater familias. A woman, a Roman citizen, was either a *mater familias* (i.e., not under the power of another person, *suae potestatis*) or a FILIA FAMILIAS (i.e., under the paternal power of a *pater familias,* either as his wife, *uxor in manu,* or as his daughter, or daughter-in-law being *uxor in manu* of a *filius familias*). Originally *mater familias* was the wife of a *pater familias* married to him *cum manu.* In a broader sense, from a moral and social point of view, any woman who lived "not dishonestly" was a *mater*

familias whether she was married or a widow, free born or a freedwoman. Syn. *matrona.*

Kunkel, *RE* 14; Bickel, *Rhein. Museum für Philol.,* 65 (1910) 578; Carcaterra, *AG* 123 (1940) 113; C. Castello, *St sul dir. familiare,* 1942, 97; R. Laprat, *Le rôle de la femme mariée, Mél Gonnard* 1946, 173.

Mater tutrix. See TUTOR.

Materia (materies). The material, the substance of which a thing is made, in particular the materials used for the construction of a building. "He who is the owner of the material is also the owner of what has been made of it" (D. 41.1.7.7).—See SPECIFICATIO.

C. Ferrini, *Opere* 4 (1930, ex 1891) 103; S. Perozzi, *Scritti giur.* 1 (1948, ex 1890) 225.

Materna bona. See BONA MATERNA.

Mathematici. Astrologers, persons who exercise the *ars mathematica,* casting horoscopes. It was reckoned among *artes magicae* (see MAGIA) and prohibited as a condemnable (*damnabilis*) divination.— C. 9.18.

Matricula. An official list of public officials, primarily of military ones.

Ensslin, *RE* 14; Boak, *RE* 17, 2050.

Matrimonium. A marriage; in legal language syn. with *nuptiae.* According to a definition by the jurist Modestinus *matrimonium* was "a union between a man and woman, an association for the whole life, a community of human and divine law" (D. 23.2.1). The definition, which has not remained without heavy attacks as to its classicality, expresses, however, a basic truth about the moral and ethical elements of the Roman marriage, without saying anything about the legal aspect of the institution. The Roman marriage was a factual relation between man and woman, based on *affectio maritalis* (intention to be husband and wife) and cohabitation as husband and wife, i.e., with the social dignity of a legitimate marriage (see HONOR MATRIMONII, CONCUBINATUS). The aim of the *matrimonium* was the procreation of legitimate children (see LIBERORUM QUAERENDORUM CAUSA). The marriage was monogamic and the common living started with the DEDUCTIO IN DOMUM MARITI. Legal requirements of a valid marriage were IUS CONUBII and consent of the parties. "A marriage is concluded by consent" (= *consensus facit nuptias,* D. 50.17.30). "A marriage cannot be concluded between persons who do not want to conclude it" (D. 23.2.22). If the future spouses were under paternal power (*alieni iuris*), the consent of the heads of the family was necessary; likewise the consent of the guardian of a woman *sui iuris* was required. *Impuberes* (persons below the age of puberty) and lunatics were incapable of concluding a marriage. Soldiers were not permitted to marry; see MATRIMONIUM MILITUM. For the interdiction of marriage between persons related by blood, see INCESTUM, NUPTIAE INCESTAE. Adoptive relationship and affinity (see ADFINITAS) created incapability of inter-marriage to a certain degree. There were also specific prohibitions of marriage, as, for instance, senators and their sons were forbidden to marry freedwomen; persons of senatorial rank could not marry actors or actresses; a tutor or curator could not marry his ward; a high provincial official was forbidden to marry a woman living in his province. In the later Empire marriage between Christians and Jews was prohibited. The legal situation of the married wife depended upon the circumstance whether or not the marriage was accompanied by a *conventio in manum*; see MANUS, CONVENTIO IN MANUM. A *matrimonium* was dissolved—aside from divorce (see DIVORTIUM, REPUDIUM)—when one of the spouses lost the legal ability to conclude a marriage (see IUS CONUBII) through the loss of liberty (see SERVUS POENAE, captivity) or citizenship. The legislation of the Christian emperors and Justinian was considerably influenced by Christian doctrines, in particular by the dogma of the insolubility of marriage.—Inst. 1.10; D. 23.2; C. 5.4; 6; 7.—See AFFECTIO MARITALIS MANUS, CONFARREATIO, COËMPTIO, USUS, IUS CONUBII, LEX CANULEIA, LEX IULIA DE MARITANDIS ORDINIBUS, BINAE NUPTIAE, CONCUBINATUS, DOS, DONATIO INTER VIRUM ET UXOREM, DONATIO ANTE NUPTIAS, ACTIO RERUM AMOTARUM, SECUNDAE NUPTIAE, LUCTUS, ADULTERIUM, BENEFICIUM COMPETENTIAE, POSTLIMINIUM, CONCUBITUS, DIVORTIUM, REPUDIUM, SPONSALIA, ORATIO DIVI MARCI, and the following items.

Kunkel, *RE* 14; Erhardt, *RE* 17 (*s.v. nuptiae*); Lécrivain, *DS* 3; Piola, *NDI* 8; Berger, *OCD* (*s.v. marriage*); Weiss, *ZSS* 29 (1908) 341; Di Marzo, *Lezioni su matrimonio*, 1 (1919); P. G. Corbett, *The R. law of marriage*, 1930; Albertario, *Studi* 1 (1933, three articles); Vaccari, *St Pavia* 21 (1936) 85; Lévy-Bruhl, *Les origines du mariage sine manu*, TR 14 (1936) 453; M. Lauria, *Matrimonio e dote*, Naples, 1952; Lanfranchi, *SDHI* 2 (1936) 148; Koschaker, *RHD* 16 (1937) 746; Nardi, *StSas* 16 (1938) 173; H. J. Wolff, *Written and unwritten marriages in Hellenistic and postclass. R. law*, Haverford, 1939; R. Ballini, *Il valore giuridico della celebrazione nuziale cristiana dal primo secolo all'età giustinianea*, 1939; De Robertis, *AnBari* 2 (1939); C. Castello, *In tema di matrimonio e concubinato*, 1940; Nardi, *SDHI* 7 (1941); Orestano, *BIDR* 47 (1940) 159, 48 (1941) 88, 55–56 (1952) 185; the three articles published in a volume *La struttura giuridica del matrimonio rom.*, 1951; *idem, St Bonolis* 1 (1942); *idem, Scr Ferrini* (Univ. Pavia, 1946) 343; *idem, Scr Ferrini* 2 (Univ. Sacro Cuore, Milan, 1947) 160; Guarino, *ZSS* 63 (1943) 219; C. W. Westrup, *Recherches sur les antiques formes de mariage* (Danemark Akad. 30, 1943); P. Rasi, *Consensus facit nuptias*, 1946; Köstler, *ZSS* 65 (1947) 43; E. Volterra, *La conception du mariage d'après les juristes romains*, Padua, 1940; *idem, RISG* 1947, 399; *idem, RIDA* 1 (1948) 213; *idem, St Solazzi* 1948, 675; Wolff, *ZSS* 67 (1950) 288.

Matrimonium incestum. See INCESTUM, NUPTIAE INCESTAE.

Matrimonium iniustum. See MATRIMONIUM IUSTUM.

Matrimonium iustum. A marriage validly concluded between Roman citizens or by a Roman citizen with a non-Roman who was granted *ius conubii*. Ant. *matrimonium iniustum* (*non iustum*) between a Roman and a peregrine without *conubium*. It is not a *matrimonium iuris gentium*; the latter term occurs in the literature, but is unknown in Roman sources.

Corbett, *LQR* 44 (1928) 305; *idem, The R. law of marriage*, 1930, 96; Gaudemet, *RIDA* 3 (= *Mél De Visscher* 2, 1949) 309.

Matrimonium legitimum. In Justinian's language syn. with *matrimonium iustum*.

Matrimonium militis. Soldiers could not conclude a valid marriage. The influence of the husband's enlistment on the existence of the marriage is controversial. The sources do not give a precise answer as to whether the marriage became automatically null or only suspended. Children conceived and born during the soldier's service are illegitimate. The emperor Hadrian granted, however, such children rights of succession on intestacy (*bonorum possessio*) upon the father's death.

Tassistro, *SDocSD* 22 (1901); Stella-Maranca, *ibid.* 24 (1903); Marenti, *StSen* 33 (1917) 108; P. Corbett, *The R. law of marriage*, 1930, 41; Castello, *RISG* 15 (1940) 27; Menkman, *TR* 17 (1941) 311; Wenger, *Anzeiger Akad. Wiss. Wien*, 1945, 104; Berger, *Jour. of Jur. Papyrology* 1 (1945) 25, 32 (= *BIDR Suppl. Post-Bellum* 55–56 [1951] 109, 115).

Matrimonium subsequens. A marriage concluded between persons living in concubinage.—See LEGITIMATIO PER SUBSEQUENS MATRIMONIUM.

Matrona. An honorable wife of a Roman citizen even when he is not *pater familias* and is still under paternal power. See MATER FAMILIAS. When summoning a *matrona* into court (*in ius vocatio*), the plaintiff had to abstain from touching her body. In public a *matrona* appeared in dress reserved for married women (a *stola* with a purple border). Hence a *matrona*, particularly of a higher social rank = *femina stolata*, and the right to wear a *stola* = *ius stolam habendi*. *Matronalis habitus* = dignified behavior, the dress of a *matrona*.

Schroff, *RE* 14.

Mauricianus, Iunius. A jurist of the second half of the second century after Christ, author of an extensive commentary on the *Lex Iulia et Papia Poppaea*.

Kroll, *RE* 10 (no. 93).

Maxime si (or **cum**). Particularly, especially. The term is often interpolated in order to introduce a special case or a restrictive element to what was said by a classical jurist.

Guarneri-Citati, *Indice*[2] (1927) 51.

Maximus. See OPTIMUS MAXIMUS.

Mederi. To apply a legal remedy in order to "cure" an uncertain legal situation. The verb is frequently used by Justinian's chancery.

Medici. Physicians were considered to exercise a liberal profession (*ars liberalis*), for this reason their services were not compensated in earlier times. See HONORARIUM. They could, however, demand a payment if they assumed their duties by contract (*locatio conductio operarum*). The physician was responsible for inexpert (*imperite*) treatment or operation and could be sued either by a contractual action *ex locato* or by a delictual one, *ex lege Aquilia*. The latter was originally applicable only when a slave was the victim of an inexpert treatment. Later the action was available when a free man was involved. Physicians enjoyed exemption from public charges (*munera*).—C. 10.53.—See EDICTUM VESPASIANI, EXCUSATIONES A MUNERIBUS.

Heldrich, *IhJb* 88 (1940) 139; Herzog, *RAC* 1, 722.

Meditatio de pactis nudis. A Byzantine dissertation on simple pacts (the Greek title is *Melete Peri psilōn symfonōn*). The pamphlet, composed about the middle of the eleventh century, seems to be the opinion of a judge given in an actual trial. The unknown author reveals a considerable knowledge of the Digest.

H. Monier and G. Platon, *NRHD* 37–38 (1913–14).

Meditatum crimen. A crime committed with premeditation.

Medium tempus. The intervening time. *Medio tempore* (= *in medio*) = in the meantime, between two legally important events, as, for instance, between the making of a testament and the death of the testator; between setting a condition and its fulfillment (syn. *pendente condicione*); while an appeal is pending or when a man is in captivity.

Mela, Fabius. A little known jurist of the Augustan Age.

Brassloff, *RE* 6, 1830 (no. 117).

Melius est. Introduces a legal opinion which is preferable to another *melius est dicere, dici, probari, melius est ut dicamus* and the like). The locution is not free from suspicion of non-classical origin when used to cut short a discussion.

Guarneri-Citati, *Indice*[2] (1927) 56, 29; *idem, Fschr Koschaker* 1 (1939) 142.

Melius aequius. See BONUM ET AEQUUM.

Membranae. Appears only once as the title of a juristic work by NERATIUS (in 7 books). The meaning of the word is not quite clear. It refers either to the material (parchment) on which the manuscript was written, or it indicates the nature of the work as "short notes" which the author put down first in a rough draft on loose parchment sheets and of which he later made a collection.

F. Schulz, *History of R. legal science*, 1946, 228.

Membrum ruptum. See OS FRACTUM.

Binding, *ZSS* 40 (1920).

Memoria. See A MEMORIA, SCRINIUM MEMORIAE.

Memoria damnata. See DAMNATIO MEMORIAE.

Memoriales. Officials in the various bureaus of the imperial chancery (*scrinia*).

Ensslin, *RE* 15.

Memorialia. Things worthy to be remembered. It appears only once as a title of a juristic work by the jurist Sabinus (in eleven books). The work seems to have been more of an antiquarian than juristic nature.

Menander. See ARRIUS MENANDER.

Mens. Intention, volition (syn. *voluntas*), purpose, design. *Ea mente, ut* (syn. *eo animo, ut*) = with the intention that.—See ANIMUS, MENTE CAPTUS, COMPOS MENTIS.

Mens legis. The intention, the sense of a statute.

Mensa. See MANUMISSIO PER MENSAM.

Mensa. (In bankers' business.) A table (counter) at which money changing transactions were done (*mensa argentaria, nummularia*). This kind of banker was called *mensularius*. They accepted also deposits in cash.—See ARGENTARII, NUMMULARII.

Kruse, *RE* 15, 945.

Mensis intercalaris. An intercalated month (in February). "It consists of 28 days" (D. 50.16.98.2).—See LEX ACILIA DE INTERCALANDO.

Mensor. (In the later Empire.) A high imperial official who had to provide quarters for the emperor, his family and staff in Rome and during their travels, a quartermaster. High officials in the provinces and prefectures had also their *mensores*.

Fabricius, *RE* 15, 959; Albertario, *St* 6 (1953) 417.

Mensores aedificiorum. Experts in urban constructions.

De Ruggiero, *DE* 1, 206.

Mensores agrorum. See AGRIMENSORES.

Mensores frumentarii. Measurers, surveyors of transportation of corn in Italian ports. They assisted the *praefectus annonae* in the administration of the supply of corn for Rome.

Cardinali, *DE* 3, 301.

Menstruum. (Adj. *menstruus*.) A monthly pay (salary). Syn. *menstrua merces*. Alimony in money and sustenance in kind (*menstrua cibaria, menstruum frumentum*) were normally paid every month.

Mensularius. See MENSA, ARGENTARII.

Mensura. Mensuration, the activity of MENSORES (AGRIMENSORES). *Mensura* is also an instrument for measuring. The magistrate could order its destruction if it was false and used for fraudulent purposes.—See RES QUAE PONDERE NUMERO MENSURAVE CONSTANT, GENUS.

Mensura delicti. The gravity of a crime. It influenced the severity of the penalty.

Mente captus. A mentally disordered individual. He is subject to curatorship (*cura*).

Mercator. A tradesman, a merchant on a lower scale than a *negotiator*. Sometimes syn. with *emptor* (= a buyer).—See NEGOTIATOR.

Cagnat, *DS* 3; Brewster, *Roman craftsmen and tradesmen of the early Empire*, (Menasha, Wis.) 1917.

Mercennarius. A hired laborer who works for pay (*merces*). *Servus mercennarius* = a slave who is hired out by his master to another for money.—See LOCATIO CONDUCTIO OPERARUM.

Merces. A payment (wages, salary, rent) in money agreed upon in a lease or hire of services (see LOCATIO CONDUCTIO). A recompense paid for any kind of services, without a preceding agreement (e.g., for saving one's life) is called also *merces.*—See REMISSIO MERCEDIS.

  Longo, *Mél Girard* 2 (1912) 105.

Merere (mereri). To deserve. The verb is used in connection with favors granted to deserving persons (e.g., a judicial remedy, the emperor's grace). It is used also when a person deserves an unfavorable treatment (a punishment, a disinheritance). *Merere* occurs also in the meaning of earning through one's labor or under a testamentary disposition.

Meretrix. A prostitute. Syn. *mulier quae palam corpore quaestum facit* (= a woman who publicly earns money with her body). *Palam* means "in a house of ill-fame, in inn-taverns, without choice" (D. 23.2.43 pr. 1). A *meretrix* was branded with infamy even after she ceased to exercise her profession; a legal marriage freed her, however, from the stigma. *Meretrices* had to register with the *aediles.* They were excluded from testimony before court, from legacies and inheritance, from visiting public spectacles and were prohibited to wear garments reserved for honest women (*stola*). They paid a special tax, *vectigal meretricium.* Senators and their sons were prohibited from marrying *meretrices,* actresses, ill-famed women or those whose parents were connected with such professions. Relations with *meretrices* were not punished as STUPRUM. Syn. *femina famosa (probrosa).*—See MINUS, LUDICRA ARS.

  Schneider, *RE* 15; Navarre, *DS* 3; Nardi, *StSas* 16 (1938); Solazzi, *BIDR* 46 (1939) 49; C. Castello, *In tema di matrimonio,* 1940, 120; Wedeck, *Cl Weekly* 36 (1943); Grosso, *SDHI* 9 (1943) 289.

Merito. (Adv.) Justly, rightly, with good reason. *Merito* is frequently couped with *iure (iure ac merito*). Jurists used the term when they approved of another jurist's opinion.

Meritum. With reference to a high imperial office, dignity.

Meritum (merita) causae. The essential points of a litigation.

Merx. Merchandise, goods, which can be the object of a sale. Only movables (with the exclusion of slaves) are covered by the term.—See EMPTIO.

Merx peculiaris. Goods belonging to a son's or a slave's PECULIUM (primarily in a commercial business).

Messis. A harvest.—See ORATIO DIVI MARCI, VENDEMIA.

Messius. Probably a jurist. He is mentioned only once linked with Papinian. No further details about him are known.

  H. Krüger, *St Bonfante* 2 (1930) 331.

Metallarii. Miners. Their work was supervised by public officials.—C. 11.7.

Metallum. A mine. According to the principle that whatever is under the earth belongs to the owner of the land, mines were either in private ownership or belonged to the state. Public mines were exploited through the intermediary of tax-farmers (*publicani*) who paid the state a fixed sum. In the first century of the Principate the mines in Italy and the provinces came gradually under the imperial administration whose control was exercised through *procuratores* of equestrian rank. The system of leasing the mines to private farmers (*conductores*) was still in use but the more intensive supervision by imperial officials benefited both production and labor. The administration of stone-pits (*lapidicinae*) and quarries of marble was managed in a similar way.—C. 11.7.—See LEX METALLI VIPASCENSIS.

  Rostowzew, *DE* 3, 128; Orth, *RE* Suppl. 4, 145, 152 (*s.v. Bergbau*); Fiehn, *RE* 3A, 2280 (*s.v. Steinbruch*); Mispoulet, *Le régime des mines, NRHD* 31 (1907) 354. For further bibl. see LEX METALLI VIPASCENSIS. Another *lex metallis dicta* in Riccobono, *FIR* 1² (1941) no. 104 (Bibl.); L. Clerici, *Economia e finanza dei Romani,* 1 (1943) 466.

Metallum. In metallum (metalla) damnare. To condemn a criminal to work in a mine (or a quarry) for life. This was the severest punishment after the death penalty (*proxima morti* = nearest to death) since work in mines in addition to rigorous labor involved being kept in fetters. *Damnatio in metallum* implied loss of freedom (*servi poenae*). A milder degree of punishment was *damnatio in opus metalli.*

  U. Brasiello, *La repressione penale in dir. rom.,* 1937, 373.

Metatum. (In later imperial constitutions.) Quarters for soldiers. *Metator* = a quartermaster. The owner of an immovable on whom the duty of billeting soldiers was imposed could be released from the obligation paying a sum of money (*epidemetica*).—C. 12.40.

Metus. Fear. Use of duress in order to compel a person to conclude a transaction, to assume an obligation or to make a payment, is a private crime (*delictum*) which may be prosecuted by the person who acted under duress by a special action, *actio quod metus causa (sc. gestum est* = for what was done because of fear). If sued for the fulfillment of a promise given under duress, he might oppose the *exceptio metus.* Under certain circumstances a *restitutio in integrum* was granted. *Metus* is defined as "a trepidation of mind because of an imminent or a future danger" (D. 4.2.1), but not any fear, "only the fear of a greater evil" (D. 4.2.5). A groundless fear (*timor vanus, metus vani hominis*) is not taken into consideration. The original name of the action might have been *formula Octaviana* since it was introduced by a praetor Octavius (about 80 B.C.). Later it was called simply *actio metus causa.* The action was penal (*actio poenalis*). If brought within a year, the defendant (the extortioner) was condemned to a fourfold value of the property extorted. —D. 4.2; C. 2.19.—See COACTUS VOLUI, ACTIONES ARBITRARIAE, TIMOR.

L. Charvet, *La restitution des majeurs*, 1920, 27; Schulz, *ZSS* 43 (1922) 171; v. Lübtow, *Der Ediktstitel quod metus causa*, 1932; G. Maier, *Praetorische Bereicherungsklagen*, 1932, 44.91; Sanfilippo, *AnCam* 7 (1934); C. Longo, *BIDR* 42 (1934) 68; C. Castello, *Timor mortis*, *AG* 121 (1939) 195.

Meum. My property. "Mine is what I have the right to claim through *vindicatio*" (D. 6.1.49.1). *"Meum esse ex iure Quiritium"* (= it is mine under Quiritary law) was the assertion of the plaintiff in the *legis actio sacramento in rem* when he claimed a thing from the defendant.—See REI VINDICATIO.

Migrare. To move from one's dwelling.—D. 43.22.— See INTERDICTUM DE MIGRANDO.

Miliarium (milliarium). A milestone marking the distance of a thousand paces (*mille passus*). Civil trials within the first milestone of the city of Rome (*intra primum urbis Romae miliarium*) belong to the category of IUDICIA LEGITIMA.—The competence of the *praefectus urbi* embraced the territory within the hundredth milestone of the city.

Schneider, *RE* Suppl. 6; Lafaye, *DS* 3; O. Hirschfeld, *Kleine Schriften*, 1913, 703.

Militare. To serve as a soldier. In later times, to serve in a public office, civil or military.—See MILITIA, MILITES.

Militaris. (Adj.) Connected with, or pertaining to, soldiers or military service.—See MILITES, MILITIA, IUS MILITARE, MANU MILITARI, RES MILITARIS, AERARIUM MILITARIS, AES MILITARIS, INTERCESSIO MILITARIS, DELICTUM MILITARE, DIPLOMA MILITARE, VESTIS MILITARIS.

Militariter punire. To punish according to military penal law.

Milites. Soldiers enjoyed various privileges in the field of private law. They were allowed to make a testament without the observance of the formalities of the civil or praetorian law, see TESTAMENTUM MILITIS. The liability of a soldier instituted as an heir for the testator's debts was limited to the amount of the inheritance. The rights of succession on intestacy of a soldier's children born during his military service, which were denied by the *ius civile,* were recognized by the emperor Hadrian. Soldiers who were under paternal power (*filii familias*) were granted the right to have a PECULIUM CASTRENSE. A special privilege of soldiers was that under certain circumstances they could be excused on the ground of IGNORANTIA IURIS. On the other hand, however, various restrictions were imposed on *milites.* They had no *ius conubii* during the time of service and could not conclude a valid marriage; see MATRIMONIUM MILITIS. They were forbidden to belong to an association (*collegium*) *in castris* (see CASTRA),

and were not admitted to act as, or through, a *procurator* in a civil trial. In the field of criminal law there were special military crimes which were severely punished. Punishments were different from those applied to civilians; see DELICTA MILITUM. Soldiers were able to appear in court and to act for themselves. In the later Empire special military courts (*iudices militares*) assumed jurisdiction in civil matters when the defendant or both parties were soldiers. An imperial constitution of the later Empire (A.D. 458) prohibited soldiers from taking in lease another's land or from assuming obligations for others as sureties, agents or mandataries. "They should be busy with their military service (arms) and not with other people's affairs" (C. 4.65.31). Soldiers who were peregrines in auxiliary troops (*auxiliarii*) were granted Roman citizenship after their discharge.— C. 1.46.—See TESTAMENTUM IN PROCINCTU, BENEFICIUM COMPETENTIAE, AES MILITARE, COMMEATUS, EXPLORATIO, LEX PORCIA DE PROVOCATIONE, MISSIO, DIPLOMA MILITARE, NEMO PRO PARTE, MILITIA, SUICIDIUM MILITIS, DELICTA MILITUM.

D. Jacomet, *Les militaires en dr. rom.,* Lyon, 1882; A. Segré, *Il diritto dei militari peregrini, Rend Accademia Pontificia,* 1940–1941, 167.

Militia. Military service (sometimes the term refers to service in war time). *Militiae se* (or *nomen*) *dare* = to enlist in the army. Ant. *legi* (from *legere*) = to be compulsorily enrolled. Illegal enlistment of a person who was not permitted to serve in the army (a slave, a person who was condemned to fight with wild beasts, a former deserter) was punished with death. Voluntary enlistment in order to evade capital punishment or deportation did not offer release from the punishment. After Constantine *militia* acquired a broader meaning since it also covered employment in civil administration in the various imperial offices and in provincial government, militarily organized. At times in this period a distinction is made between the service in the army (*militia armata*) and the civil service (*militia cohortalis, palatina* or simply *militia*). The *militia* which already in classical times (second post-Christian century) appears as the object of a sale or legacy, may refer to a lower public service (in the fire-brigade, *apparitores*). In the later Empire the purchase of an official post was frequently practiced.—C. 12.33.— See MUTATIO MILITIAE, REICERE MILITIA, IRREVERENS.

Mommsen, *Röm. Staatsrecht* 3 (1887) 450; Marchi, *AG* 76 (1906) 291; G. Kolias, *Ämter und Würdenkauf im frühbyzantinischen Reich,* 1939.

Militia armata, cohortalis. See MILITIA.

Milita equestris. Military service of a high grade officer in the cavalry.

Militia palatina. See MILITIA.

Milliarium. See MILIARIUM.

Mimus. An actor in mimes, a dancer. A troupe of actors sold as an ensemble is considered a unit;

hence the sale of the whole can be rescinded because of defects in one of the group. The same rule applies to tragic actors (*tragoedi*). *Mimae* (= actresses, dancers) are socially equal to MERETRICES.

Wüst, *RE* 15, 1743.

Minicius. A jurist of the first century of the Principate, a disciple of Sabinus. His work is known by an extensive commentary of Julian.

Steinwenter, *RE* 15, 1809 (no. 3); Riccobono, *BIDR* 7 (1894) 225, 8 (1895) 169; A. Guarino, *Salvius Julianus,* 1946, 38; H. Krüger, *St Bonfante* 2 (1930) 332.

Minime. By no means, not in the least. The frequency of the adverb in late imperial constitutions, and particularly in those of Justinian, in the meaning of a simple negation (*non*) makes its authenticity in classical texts rather suspect when it appears there in the place of *non*.

Guarneri-Citati, *Indice*² (1927) 56.

Minister. A servant, a subordinate (assistant) of an official under the Empire. In exceptional instances it refers to higher officials, both civil and military. When mentioned in connection with a crime = an abettor, an accomplice. In the Christian Empire, when connected with ecclesiatical service = a Church servant, a minister (*ministeria ecclesiarum*).

Ensslin, *RE* Suppl. 6.

Ministeriales (ministeriani). Officials in the imperial palace of a rather subordinate rank. They had to take care of the imperial household (in the later Empire). They were appointed by the emperor and enjoyed exemption from humble public services (*munera sordida*). The MAGISTER OFFICIORUM exercised jurisdiction over them.—C. 12.25.—See CASTRENSIANI, MINISTRI CASTRENSES.

Ensslin, *RE* Suppl. 6; J. E. Dunlap, *Univ. of Michigan Studies, Human. Ser.* 14 (1924) 212; Giffard, *RHD* 14 (1935) 239.

Ministeriani. See MINISTERIALES.—C. 12.25.

Ministerium. The office (activity) of a MINISTER or of a MINISTERIALIS.—In criminal matters *ministerium* is the assistance in committing a crime, complicity.—See MINISTER.

Ministerium divinum (ecclesiae). A divine service.

Ministerium publicum. A public office. The term is also applied to municipal offices (*ministeria municipalia*).

Ministerium sacrum. Service in the imperial palace. Syn. *ministerium sacri palatii, sacri cubiculi.* The emperors speak of their palace staff as "*nostrum sacrum ministerium.*"

Ministerium servorum (servile, servitutis). Slaves' work, services rendered by slaves. Hence *ministeria* denotes all slaves in the service of the same master.—C. 3.33.

Ministri castrenses. See CASTRENSIANI. There were two kinds of *ministri castrenses: statuti* = members of the regular staff, and *supernumerarii* = additional members who were promoted to the rank of *statuti* to fill vacancies.

J. E. Dunlap, *Univ. of Michigan Studies, Human. Ser.* 14 (1924) 213.

Minor aetas. Minority. Syn. *adulta, imperfecta aetas.* Ant. *maior aetas.*—See AETAS, MINORES.

Berger, *RE* 15, 1769 (*s.v. Minderjährigkeit*), 1862.

Minores. An abridged expression for *minores viginti quinque annorum* (*annis*) or *minores annorum* (*annis*). *Minores* were persons who exceeded the age of IMPUBERES and were under twenty-five years of age. Similar expressions, although not technical in the juristic language, are *adultus, adulescens,* and *iuvenis.* Within the minority there is a special term for the age under eighteen, *plena pubertas,* the classicality of which is doubtful. It had no particular legal importance. A *minor sui iuris* (not under paternal power) was considered unable and not experienced enough to manage his affairs because of his juvenile light-heartedness and weakness of mind (*infirmitas animi, aetatis*). Until the curatorship of the minors, *cura minorum* (see CURATOR MINORIS) was introduced as a general institution, a minor was protected against fraud (see CIRCUMSCRIBERE) by the LEX PLAETORIA and the praetorian remedy of RESTITUTIO IN INTEGRUM which remained the most efficient protective measure during the classical period. Under Justinian the *cura minorum* became compulsory. The ability of a *minor* to appear in court was restricted by Constantine who ordered that the *minor* had to be assisted by a curator. In Justinian's codification the *cura minorum* appears completely assimilated to tutorship (TUTELA). This was performed through innumerable interpolations but not with consistency. Some details in the development of the *cura minorum* have remained therefore obscure and the nature of the duties of a *curator minoris* is still controversial. He certainly was something more than a simple adviser and was not excluded at all from the administration of the ward's property.—D. 4.4; C. 2.21–42; 5.71.—See CURATOR MINORIS, IUSIURANDUM MINORIS:

Berger, *RE* 15 (Bibl. p. 1889); Cuq, *DS* 3; Albertario, *Studi* 1 (1933, ex 1912) 407, 427, 475, 499; *idem, SDHI* 2 (1936) 170; G. Solazzi, *La minore età,* 1913; *idem, AVen* 75 (1916) 1599; Lenel, *ZSS* 35 (1915).

Minus. Less. "The *minus* is always included in what is greater (*plus*)" (D. 50.17.110 pr.). Therefore, "he who is allowed to do what is greater (*plus*) should not be prohibited from doing less" (D. 50.17.21).

Minus solvere. To pay less than one owes. "He who pays later pays less" (D. 50.17.12.1).

Minutio capitis (minui capite). See CAPITIS DEMINUTIO, CAPUT.

Miscere. See COMMISCERE, MIXTUS.

Miscere (se) hereditati. See IMMISCERE, PRO HEREDE GERERE.

Miserabilis persona. See PERSONA MISERABILIS.

Missilia. Money thrown as largesse to people in the theatre or on the street by emperors, high officials or wealthy individuals. The coins became the property of the persons who picked them up.—See TRADITIO IN INCERTAM PERSONAM, TESSERAE NUMMARIAE.

Berger, *RE* 9, 552 (*s.v. iactus*); Fabia, *DS* 3; Meyer-Collings, *Derelictio*, Diss. Erlangen, 1930, 2.

Missio. A discharge from military service. *Honesta missio* = an honorable discharge after the completion of twenty-five years of irreproachable service. Ant. *ignominiosa missio* when the dismissal was occasioned by the soldier's committing a common or military crime. *Missio causaria* (or simply *causaria*) = discharge because of mental or physical disability. For *missio* of peregrine soldiers, see AUXILIA.—See DIPLOMA MILITARE.

Lammert, *RE* 15, 1666; 4A, 1949; Rowell, *Yale Classical St* 6 (1939) 73.

Missio in bona. See MISSIONES IN POSSESSIONEM.

Missio in possessionem. See the entries below, after MISSIONES IN POSSESSIONEM.

Missio in rem. See MISSIONES IN POSSESSIONEM. The typical case of such *missio* by which a claimant was given possession of a single thing (an immovable) belonging to his adversary is MISSIO IN POSSESSIONEM DAMNI INFECTI NOMINE.

Missiones in possessionem (in bona). A coercive measure, applied by the praetor by virtue of his *imperium*, by which a claimant was authorized to enter into possession of his adversary's property, in whole or in a part (see MISSIO IN REM). The purposes of *missiones* were different and so were in the various cases their effects. The praetorian decrees concerning *missiones* were issued either in order to assure the normal progress of the trial and to prevent the defendant's attempts to sabotage it, or to secure the debtor's property for the satisfaction of his creditors, or to induce the debtor to assume a special obligation through *stipulatio* (*stipulationes praetoriae*) for security purposes if he refused to do it voluntarily. The legal situation of the *missus in possessionem* created by *missio* varied from real possession to simple custody and control (*custodia et observantia*) of the things the holding of which he obtained only to assure that the debtor's property would remain intact and be used exclusively for the benefit of the creditors. At times the situation of the *missus in possessionem* was comparable to that of a creditor who received a pledge (*pignus praetorium*, the term may be not classical), since the *missio* led finally to the sale of the debtor's property if he did not satisfy the creditors in the interim. Protection was given certain persons (such as *impuberes*, or those absent in the interest of the state) in that their property generally could not be sold. The edictal clause in which the praetor announced the issue of a *missio*-decree was in the most cases: "*bona possideri proscribi venirique iu-*

bebo" (= I shall order the property to be taken into possession, advertised for sale and sold"). The praetor's *missio*-decree was withdrawn and the *missus in possessionem* ordered to surrender possession (*decedere de possessione*) if the debtor came to an arrangement with the creditor. *Missiones* were acts designed to exert pressure on the debtor and were, if successful, of a temporary character. They were generally successful when the *missus* entered into a property occupied by the owner who had to suffer his continuous presence and control. In certain cases the *missus in possessionem* enjoyed interdictal protection; see INTERDICTA NE VIS FIAT EI QUI IN POSSESSIONEM MISSUS EST.—For the various *missiones in possessionem* or *in bona*, see the following entries.—D. 42.4.

Weiss, *RE* 15; Cuq, *DS* 3; S. Solazzi, *Concorso dei creditori* 1 (1937); M. F. Lepri, *Note sulla natura delle m.i.p.*, 1939; Branca, *St Solazzi* 1948, 483.

Missio in possessionem Antoniniana. Introduced by the emperor Caracalla, who admitted a *missio in possessionem legatorum servandorum causa* also into the property of the heir if, within six months after the presentation of a claim by a legatee, he did not give sufficient guaranty for the payment of the legacy. The legatee *missus in possessionem* might take the products (*fructus*) from the heir's property to satisfy his claim.—See MISSIO IN POSSESSIONEM LEGATORUM SERVANDORUM CAUSA.

Lepri, *op. cit.* 123; F. M. De Robertis, *Di una pretesa innovazione di Caracalla, AnBari* N.S. 1 (1938) 99.

Missio in possessionem bonorum (bona) pupilli. A *missio* into the property of an *impubes* if in a suit over a transaction concluded by his guardian the former (the *pupillus*) was not defended by his tutor. The *missio* was rescinded when the tutor or a relative of the *pupillus* assumed the defense.

Missio in possessionem damni infecti nomine. When the owner of a defective immovable refused to give CAUTIO DAMNI INFECTI for damages threatening the neighbor's property, the praetor allowed the latter to enter into possession (*missio in rem*) of the immovable. If the first decree (*missio ex primo decreto*) did not produce the desired effect (repairing of the building or giving the *cautio*) the praetor issued a second decree (*missio ex secundo decreto*) which put the *missus* in the position of a *possessor ad usucapionem*, i.e., he might usucapt the immovable.—See USUCAPIO.

Lepri, *op. cit.* 89; Branca, *Danno temuto*, 1937, 130.

Missio in possessionem dotis servandae causa. One of the cases of the MISSIO IN POSSESSIONEM REI SERVANDAE CAUSA. It was granted a divorced wife or a widow in order to secure her claim for the restitution of the dowry.

Solazzi, *Dote e nascituro, RendLomb* 49 (1916) 312.

Missio in possessionem ex edicto Hadriani. In order to assure the prompt payment of the estate-tax

(VICESIMA HEREDITATIUM) Hadrian ordered that an heir instituted in a testament apparently valid might take possession of the testator's estate immediately after the payment of the tax. This kind of *missio*, which differs essentially from the normal *missiones*, no longer existed in Justinian's time.—C. 6.33.

Missio in possessionem legatorum servandorum causa. If an heir refused to give a *cautio legatorum servandorum causa* for the payment of a legacy (or a *fideicommissum*) left under condition or to be paid at a fixed date (*ex die*), the legatee could ask for this *missio* in order to enter into possession of the estate (but not of the private property of the heir) and remain there, together with the heir, as long as the heir did not furnish security. He held the property *custodiae causa* (= for safekeeping).—D. 36.3; 4; C. 6.54.—See CAUTIO LEGATORUM NOMINE, MISSIO IN POSSESSIONEM ANTONINIANA.

> Lepri, *op. cit.* 113.

Missio in possessionem (bona) rei servandae causa. Decreed by the praetor in various circumstances during a trial: when the defendant was absent in court and was not defended by a representative, when he intentionally kept hiding (*latitare*) so as to avoid being summoned to court; or when he was considered *indefensus* because of his refusal to cooperate in the progress of the trial, as, for instance, when he refused to accept the procedural formula approved by the praetor. See INDEFENSUS. This *missio* is also the initial stage of the property execution against a defendant who has been condemned by judgment (*iudicatus*) or is considered as such (*pro iudicato*), as the *confessus in iure* was (see CONFESSIO IN IURE). The function of this *missio* was similar in the case of an insolvent debtor or an insolvent inheritance. The creditor or creditors could obtain possession of the debtor's property or estate which would eventually be sold; see VENDITIO BONORUM, CURATOR BONORUM.

> Weiss, *RE* 15; Cuq, *DS* 3; P. Ramadier, *Les effets de la m. in b.*, 1911; H. R. Engelmann, *Die Voraussetzungen der m. in b.*, 1911; Rocco, *Studi sulla storia del fallimento*, *RDCom* 1913 (= *Il fallimento*, 1917); S. Solazzi, *Il concorso dei creditori*, 1–4 (1937, 1938, 1940, 1943); Lepri, *op. cit.* 43.

Missio in bona suspecti heredis. See SATISDATIO SUSPECTI HEREDIS.

Missio in possessionem ventris nomine. A *missio* for the protection of the rights of an unborn heir. Its function was similar to the BONORUM POSSESSIO VENTRIS NOMINE when the father of the child was dead. —D. 25.5; 25.6; 37.9.

> S. Solazzi, *Il concorso dei creditori*, 1 (1937) 20.

Missus in possessionem (bona). A person who by the decree of the praetor was granted a *missio in possessionem* of the property of his debtor or adversary in a trial.—See MISSIONES IN POSSESSIONEM.

Mittendarii. Imperial officials sent to remote provinces with special imperial messages to the governor or in order to collect special taxes.

Mittere. To send (a letter = *epistulam*, a messenger = *nuntium*, a person to perform a specific official or private mission). For *mittere in possessionem*, see MISSIONES IN POSSESSIONEM. For *mittere repudium*, see REPUDIUM.

Mittere. (With reference to soldiers.) To discharge from military service (*ab exercitu*, *militia*).—See MISSIO, DIPLOMA MILITARE.

Mixtus. (From *miscere*.) With reference to legal institutions (*munera*, *condiciones*) or procedural remedies (*actiones*, *interdicta*) = of a hybrid, mixed nature. The term reflects more the Byzantine mentality than the exact legal thinking of the classical jurists and is suspect as being a late postclassical or Justinian creation.—See ACTIONES MIXTAE, IMPERIUM MERUM, INTERDICTA MIXTA, MUNERA.

> Berger, *Vol. onoranze Simoncelli*, 1915, 183; Guarneri-Citati, *Indice*[2] (1927) 57.

Mobiles res. See RES MOBILES.

Moderatio. (From *moderare*, *moderari* = to restrain, limit, rule.) The observing of reasonable limits, temperateness. When referring to their acts of grace, or indulgence the emperors used to speak of "*moderatio nostra.*"—A similar expression, *moderamen*, appears in late constitutions.

Moderator. A ruler. *Moderator provinciae* = the governor of a province.—See PRAESES PROVINCIAE.

Modestinus, Herennius. One of the last representatives of the classical Roman jurisprudence, a pupil of Ulpian, and a high official in the administration of Rome about A.D. 240. He wrote an extensive collection of *Responsa* (in 19 books), a work on *Differentiae* (= controversial questions) and *Regulae* (= legal rules). He was also the author of a Greek treatise on exemptions from guardianship (*excusationes*). Modestinus was one of the jurists distinguished in the Law of Citations (see IURISPRUDENTIA).

> Brassloff, *RE* 8 (*s.v. Herennius*, no. 31); H. Krüger, *St Bonfante* 2 (1930) 315.

Modicus. Moderate-sized, moderate, restrained. The term, applied to punishments, losses, expenses, lack of preciseness. *Modicum tempus* = a short time. *Modicus* appears in texts suspected of interpolation.

> Guarneri-Citati, *Indice*[2] (1927) 57.

Modus. A measure, a limit. In the meaning of a burden, a duty imposed in acts of liberality (donations, legacies, manumissions) on a beneficiary, the term is of late origin. It appears in the language of the chancery of later emperors, and in the language of Justinian and his compilers. Sometimes the term covers what was a CONDICIO (condition) in the classical language. In the classical law it was disputable whether a duty imposed as a *modus* created on the part of the beneficiary a binding obligation. The emperor Gordian set a general rule that the person interested in the fulfillment of a *modus* of pecuniary value could sue the heir or legatee for fulfillment.—D. 35.1; C. 6.45.—See DONATIO SUB MODO.

> Weiss, *RE* 15; Cuq, *DS* 3; F. Haymann, *Schenkung unter Auflage*, 1905; P. Lotmar, *Freilassungsauflage, ZSS* 33 (1912) 304; Messina-Vitrano, *St Riccobono* 3 (1936) 99.

Modus aedificiorum. A limit regulating height in the construction of buildings.—See LEX IULIA DE MODO AEDIFICIORUM.

> B. Biondi, *La categoria romana delle servitutes*, 1938, 23; Berger, *Iura* 1 (1950) 121.

Modus agri. The boundary of a plot of land.—See AGRIMENSORES, ACTIO DE MODO AGRI.

Modus donationis. Limits imposed on the amount of donations or with regard to the formalities to be accomplished to render a donation valid. See LEX CINCIA. In another sense *modus* is used with reference to gifts; see MODUS, DONATIO SUB MODO.

Modus facultatum. The financial situation of a person, mentioned in connection with the constitution of a dowry or with alimony which has to correspond to the financial means of the person obligated.—See FACULTATES, BENEFICIUM COMPETENTIAE.

Modus legatorum (or legis Falcidiae). The limits imposed on the amount of legacies by the LEX FALCIDIA. For *legatum sub modo,* see MODUS.

Modus servitutis. A modification of the typical content of a servitude limiting the rights the beneficiary has in the exercising of the servitude, for instance, the size of carriages he may use in the *servitus* ACTUS.

> S. Perozzi, *Scritti* 2 (1948, ex 1888) 29; Biondi, *Scr L. Barassi* 1943, 57; *idem, Le servitù prediali,* 1946, 46.

Modus usurarum. The limit of the rate of interest imposed by law.—See USURAE.

Moliri. To start the construction of a building.—See OPERIS NOVI NUNTIATIO.

Momentaria possessio. See POSSESSIO MOMENTARIA.

Momentum. Weight, importance. *Nullius momenti esse* = to be void, of no legal force. Syn. *inefficax, nullus, effectum non habere.* Ant. VALERE.

> Hellmann, *ZSS* 23 (1902) 421.

Momentum. An instant, a moment. When for legal effectiveness a certain period of time must elapse (as, e.g., for USUCAPIO) the time is reckoned in full completed days, not according to hours or specific moments (*a momento ad momentum*).

Monachi. Monks. They were in Justinian's law incapable of being guardians. Their property was inherited by their monastery if they died without leaving a testament and there were no near relatives. Several Justinian Novels (5.76.79.123.133) deal with monks and monastic life.—C. 1.3.

> Granic, *Byzantinische Ztschr.* 30 (1930) 669; Schaefer, *ACII* 1 (1935) 173; Tabera, *Professio monastica causa divortii, ibid.* 189.

Monachium. See MONASTERIUM.—C. 1.3.

Monasterium. A monastery. The ability of a monastery to own property was recognized in the fifth century. Legislation of the Christian emperors, par-

ticularly that of Justinian, dealt frequently with monasteries, their legal situation, and specifically with their ability to benefit by testaments as heirs or legatees.—See MONACHI.—C. 1.3.

> A. Ferradou, *Des biens des monastères à Byzance*, 1896; Branic, *Byzantinische Ztschr.* 29 (1929) 6; Schnorr v. Carolsfeld, *Geschichte der juristischen Person* 1 (1933) 394; P. W. Duff, *Personality in R. law*, 1938, 185; 196.

Moneta. Minted money. See FALSA MONETA. *Moneta* may also mean the mint itself. *Moneta sacra* = the imperial mint. The theft of coins from the mint is punished with work in mines (*metalla*) or exile.— See TRIUMVIRI MONETALES, NUMMULARIUS, TESSERA NUMMULARIA, OPTIO.

Monetarii. Workers in the imperial mint. They could leave their occupation only with difficulty.— C. 11.8.—*Monetarius* is also the counterfeiter of coins.

Monitor. (In the later Empire.) An official who reminded the tax-payers of taxes due.—In private enterprises = an overseer (over slaves).

Monitorium edictum. See EDICTUM MONITORIUM.

Monopolium. A monopoly, i.e., the exclusive right to sell and deal in a specific type of merchandise. An imperial constitution of the emperor Zeno (A.D. 483, C. 4.59.2) forbade the monopolization of the sale of certain commodities (clothes, foodstuffs) or items of common use, as well as of the performance of certain works. There were many other similar prohibitions carrying the penalty of confiscation of property and exile for life.—C. 4.59.

> Heichelheim, *RE* 16 (Bibl. 199).

Monstrum. An unnatural, monstrous creature (*monstruosum, prodigiosum, portentosum aliquid, ostentum*) which has not the shape of a human being (*contra formam humani generis*) is not considered a child. A law ascribed to Romulus allowed the killing of such an offspring immediately after birth. —See PORTENTUM.

> Kübler, *ZSS* 30 (1909) 159; Ambrosino, *RendLomb* 73 (1939/40) 70.

Montanus. See PAGANUS.

Monumenta. Written documents, records. *Publica monumenta* (= public records) offer a stronger evidence than the testimony of a witness, according to a decree of the senate.

> De Visscher, *AntCl* 15 (1946) 122.

Monumenta Maniliana. See MANILIUS, FORMULAE.

Monumentum. See SEPULCRUM.

Monumentum Ancyranum. Called a stone monument on which a great part of Augustus' autobiography (SEE RES GESTAE DIVI AUGUSTI) is preserved. *Monumentum Antiochenum* = fragments of the same work found in Antioch (Pisidia).

> Kornemann, *RE* 16; Momigliano, *OCD*; Robinson, *Amer. Jour. of Philology,* 47 (1926); W. M. Ramsay and A. v. Premerstein, *Klio*, Beiheft 19, 1924; H. Volkmann, *Bursians Jahresberichte* 279 (1949, Bibl. for 1914-1941); Luzzatto, *SDHI* Suppl. 17 (1952) 167.

Mora. Default. *In mora esse* = to be in default. "He from whom a payment cannot be demanded because of an exception (he has against the claim) in not in default" (D. 12.1.40). "A thief (*fur*) is always in default" (D. 13.1.8.1) with regard to the restoration of the thing stolen.—See MORA DEBITORIS.

Mora accipiendi. See the following item.

Mora debitoris—creditoris. There is a distinction between *mora debitoris,* an unjustified failure of a debtor to pay his debt, and *mora creditoris,* which occurs when the creditor refuses to accept the payment offered him by the debtor in due time, without any just reason or when he makes it impossible for the debtor to discharge his debt by, for instance, being absent. In the case of *mora debitoris (mora solvendi, solutionis)* the liability of the debtor is augmented: an accidental destruction of the thing due is at his risk, he has to pay interest (*usurae morae*) when the debt is of a sum of money, and he has to restore all proceeds he had from the time he has been in default (*in mora*). The debtor is not responsible, however, for a default caused by no fault of his own. The default of the debtor causes the obligation to become everlasting (*obligatio perpetuatur*). *Mora creditoris* involves also certain disadvantages to the creditor: the thing due is now at his risk and the debtor is responsible only for fraud (*dolus*), even if the original obligation imposed on him a larger responsibility. The debtor has the right to free himself from his obligation through a deposition of the sum due; see DEPOSITIO IN AEDE. The consequences of the *mora* come to an end (*purgare, emendare moram*) when, in the case of *mora debitoris,* the debtor offers full payment to the creditor, and, in the case of *mora creditoris* (syn. *mora accipiendi*), the latter accepts the payment. The usual expressions for *mora* are *stat per debitorem* (or *per creditorem*) *quominus solvatur* (= it is caused by the debtor or creditor that the payment is not being made). A general rule (D. 50.17.88) is "there cannot be a *mora* where there is no claim (*petitio*)."—See INTERPELLARE, MORA.—D. 22.1.

Kaser, *RE* 16; Cuq, *DS* 3; Montel, *NDI* 8; C. Scuto, *La mora del creditore,* 1905; Siber, *ZSS* 39 (1909); Gradenwitz, *ZSS* 34 (1913); Bohacek, *AnPal* 11 (1924) 341; Guarneri-Citati, *ibid.* 232; Genzmer, *ZSS* 44 (1924) 86; Arnò, *AG* 100 (1928) 443; A. Montel, *Mora del debitore,* 1930; Niedermeyer, *Fschr Schulz* 1 (1951) 399.

Mora solvendi, solutionis. See MORA DEBITORIS.

Morari. To delay, to defer (a payment); see MORA DEBITORIS.—*Morari* (= to stay, to abide at a place) is used of certain lasting legal situations of a person, e.g., *morari in possessione* (= to be in possession of a thing), *in libertate* (= to live as a free man).—*Morari* means also to detain. The formula by which the presiding magistrate dismissed the senators after the meeting, was *"nihil vos moramur"* (= I do not detain you any longer).

Morbus. A disease. The jurist deals with *morbus* (D. 21.1.1.7: "an unnatural state of the body which impairs its use") in connection with the liability of the seller of a sick slave. *Morbus* is distinguished from *vitium* inasmuch as *morbus* is "a temporary sickness of the body while *vitium* (a defect) is a perpetual impediment of the body" (D. 50.16.101.2).—See EMPTIO.

Morbus comitialis. Epilepsy. If a case of epilepsy occurred in a popular assembly an immediate interruption and postponement of the gathering took place, since the disease was considered a bad omen.

Seidl, *RE* 16.

Morbus perpetuus. A chronic disease. Ant. *morbus temporarius.*—See CURATOR MUTI.

Morbus sonticus. A grave, acute sickness. If incurred by a judge or one of the parties during a trial, an adjournment took place. A *morbus sonticus* of the debtor was considered a valid excuse for nonfulfillment of his obligation.

Lécrivain, *DS* 3.

More. (Abl.) According to usage (custom); in the way (fashion) of, e.g., *more iudiciorum* judicially, in court, by the normal procedure.

Mores (mos). Customs, "the common consent of all people living together; if observed for a long time (*mos inveteratus*) it becomes a *consuetudo.*" Certain legal institutions originate from *mores* (*moribus receptum, introductum est*), as, for instance, the interdiction of gifts between husband and wife (DONATIO INTER VIRUM ET UXOREM), or the management of the affairs of a spendthrift by a curator (CURA PRODIGI).—See DEDUCTIO QUAE MORIBUS FIT, CONSTITUERE IURA, IUS CONSTITUTUM, CONSUETUDO, and the following items.

Mores boni. See BONI MORES, CONTRA BONOS MORES.

Mores civitatis (provinciae, regionis). Customs of local character observed in a limited territory (city, province, district).

Mores diuturni. Customs observed during a long period and "approved by the consent of the people who apply them, are tantamount to a statute" (*legem imitantur,* Inst. 1.2.9).—See MORES, CONSUETUDO.

Mores (mos) maiorum. Customs of the forefathers, tradition of ideas, usages, customs. For *mores maiorum* as legal customs, see CONSUETUDO. For *mores* as norms of moral and social correctness, see BONI MORES, CONTRA BONOS MORES. An edict of the censors of 92 B.C. (Suetonius, *de rhet.* 1) said: "all new that is done contrary to the usage and customs of our ancestors, seems not to be right." In later imperial constitutions and those of Justinian references to ancient customs (*mos vetus, antiquus, veterum, antiquitatis,* and the like) are very frequent.—See MORES.

Steinwenter, *RE* 16; Cuq, *DS* 3; Rech, *M.m.,* Diss. Marburg, 1936; Schiller, *Virginia L Rev* 24 (1938) 271; Kaser, *ZSS* 59 (1939) 52; Volkmann, *Das neue Bild der Antike* 2 (1942) 246; Gioffredi, *SDHI* 13–14 (1948) 80; Volterra, *RendLinc* Ser. VIII, 4 (1949) 530.

Mores mulieris. Misconduct of a wife.—See ACTIO DE MORIBUS, RETENTIONES DOTALES.

Moris est. It is usual, customary.

Mors. Death. Certain contractual relations, as mandate (MANDATUM) and partnership (SOCIETAS) are dissolved by the death of one of the parties. Generally the death of a creditor has no influence on the further existence of the obligation; the death of the debtor extinguishes his obligation if it had to be fulfilled by him as a personal performance. The death of a legatee before the day on which he became entitled to claim the legacy (DIES CEDENS) makes the legacy void. Personal servitudes are extinguished with the death of the person entitled; see SERVITUTES PERSONARUM. A person accused of a crime who died before judgment was rendered, was considered blameless (INTEGER) since death effaced the crime, except in cases of MAIESTAS and REPETUNDAE. In these instances the heir was given the opportunity to defend the deceased, otherwise the latter's property was seized. Penal actions for private offenses (see ACTIONES POENALES) ceased to be available when the offender died.—See DIES MORTIS, POENA MORTIS, MORTIS CAUSA, CONSCISCERE SIBI MORTEM, COMMORIENTES, OBLIGATIO POST MORTEM, LIBERA MORTIS FACULTAS, MANDATUM POST MORTEM, STIPULATIO POST MORTEM, REUS (in a criminal trial).

Mors litis. See LIS MORITUR, IUDICIA LEGITIMA.

Mortalitas. Used in the meaning of MORS, this is of postclassical origin.

Guarneri-Citati, *Indice*[2] (1927) 57.

Mortis causa. In view of the death (e.g., dispositions made by a testator), because of the death (acquisitions made on the occasion of another's death).— D. 39.6.—See DONATIO MORTIS CAUSA, CAPIO.

S. Cugia, Indagini etc. *L'espressione mortis causa,* 1910; Brini, *RendBol* 6 (1912–1913).

Mos. See MORES, MORES MAIORUM.

Mos iudiciorum. See MORE.

Motio ex ordine. (From MOVERE.) Exclusion of a member from the municipal council (*ordo decurionum*). It was decreed when the member was guilty of a crime or bad behavior. The *motio* could be ordered for a certain time only, after which the member regained his position (*restitutio in ordinem*).— C. 10.61.

Kübler, *RE* 4, 2329.

Motus animi. An impulse, a motive which incites a person to do something, to conclude a transaction with another person (*in unum consentire*).—See CONSENSUS.

Motus iudicialis. (In imperial constitutions.) A court decision.

Motus terrae. See TERRAE MOTUS.

Moventia. See RES MOBILES, RES SE MOVENTES.

Movere. To set in motion, to initiate a judicial measure, to sue (*movere controversiam, litem. actionem,* interdictum, querelam*), to accuse (*movere accusationem*).

Movere. (A person.) To induce, to influence (a praetor, a judge). In juristic discussions *movere* = to bewilder, to confuse, to induce one to change his mind. *"Movet me* (or *moveor) quia"* a jurist used to say to introduce an objection against what was said before. Phrases like *"nec me movet"* or *"nec nos movere debet"* are used to introduce the rejection of an eventual objection.

Ratti, *RISG* 2 (1927) 53.

Movere (de) ordine. See MOTIO EX ORDINE.

Movere (de) senatu. To deprive a senator of membership in the senate. Under the Republic the exclusion was decreed by the censors through a NOTA CENSORIA, under the Empire by the emperor.

O'Brien-Moore, *RE* Suppl. 6, 688.763.

Movere terminum. See TERMINUS, ACTIO DE TERMINO MOTO.

Muciana cautio. See CAUTIO MUCIANA.

Mucius. There were three jurists by the family name of Mucius. The most prominent among them was Quintus Mucius Scaevola, a *pontifex maximus* who was consul in 95 B.C. and died in 82. He was an outstanding jurist; his treatise on *ius civile* is the most important juristic work written under the Republic. It was the first attempt of a systematic presentation of the private law and was commented on by later jurists (Gaius, Pomponius). The Mucian system was adopted by several writers on IUS CIVILE. See DEFINITIONES.—His predecessors were Publius Mucius Scaevola, consul in 133 B.C., also a *pontifex maximus* and Quintus Mucius Scaevola, consul in 117 B.C., an augur and teacher of law (Cicero attended his lectures). As jurists they are of lesser importance in the history of Roman jurisprudence.

Kübler and Münzer, *RE* 16, 437.442; Orestano, *NDI* 12, 1158; G. Lepointe, *Q. Mucius Scaevola,* Paris, 1926, Bruck, *Sem* 3 (1945) 16; Kreller, *ZSS* 66 (1948) 573; on P. M. Scaevola: Münzer 425, no. 17; on Q. M. Scaevola, the augur: Münzer *ibid.* 430, no. 21.

Mulier. Sometimes indicates any woman, whether married, or not, sometimes only a married woman (= *uxor*). Syn. FEMINA.—See TUTELA MULIERUM, SENATUSCONSULTUM VELLEIANUM, LEX VOCONIA, MUNERA.

P. Pierret, *Le sénatusconsulte Velléien,* 1947, 21.

Mulier quaestuaria. See MERETRIX.

Multa. A pecuniary penalty, a fine. Syn. *poena nummaria, pecuniaria.* In earlier times it was paid in cattle. The power of fining (*multam dicere, irrogare*) was a prerogative of magistrates, who used it as a measure of coercion (COËRCITIO). Some statutes fixed the maximum amounts of fines. *Multa* was the normal penalty for disobeying a magisterial order. It could be inflicted by a higher magistrate on a lower one for disciplinary offenses, by the presiding magistrate in the senate on senators for unjustified absence, by censors for untrue declarations made in the census proceedings, and the like. Pecuniary penalties were also established in penal statutes for offenses committed in ordinary criminal proceedings before a magistrate or before *comitia*. The final decision in cases involving fines lay with the *comitia* (*tributa*) as an appellate court. A *multa* could not exceed half of the defendant's property. Under the Empire *multae* were largely applied in the *cognitio* procedure and as a coercive measure. The right to impose fines (*ius multae dicendae, dictionis*) was granted all prefects in Rome, the provincial governors, and higher administrative officials. The fines were paid to the state. Condemnation to a *multa* did not involve infamy.—C. 1.54.—See LEX ATERNIA TARPEIA, LEX IULIA PAPIRIA, MULTA PRAEIUDICIALIS, and the following items.

Hellebrand, *RE* Suppl. 6; Lécrivain, *DS* 3; P. E. Huschke, *Multa und Sacramentum*, 1874; E. Mayer, *TR* 8 (1928) 35; U. Brasiello, *La repressione penale*, 1937, *passim*; L. Clerici, *Economia e finanza dei Romani*, 1 (1943) 491.

Multa. (For the violation of a grave.) A penalty settled in a testament of a Roman citizen for such a wrongdoing. The penalty was not paid to the heir but to the fisc, unless the testator made other disposition.

Pfaff, *RE* 2A (*s.v. Sepulcralmulten*); Lécrivain, *DS* 3, 2019; J. Merkel, *Sepulcralmulten, Fg Ihering* 1897; G. Giorgi, *Le multe sepolcrali*, 1910; A. Berger, *Strafklauseln in den Papyrusurkunden*, 1911, 96, 100; Arangio-Ruiz, *FIR* 3 (1943) 257.

Multa fisco debita. (In literature called *multa fiscalis*.) A fine to be paid to the fisc by one of the parties to a contract in the case of non-fulfillment of his obligation. The insertion of such a clause into a written contract was adopted from provincial practice.

Kübler, *RE* 4A, 157; A. Berger, *Die Strafklauseln in den Papyrusurkunden*, 1911, 34, 93; G. Wesenberg, *Verträge zugusten Dritter*, 1949, 56.

Multa testamentaria. A fine imposed by a testator on an heir or legatee for non-fulfillment of his wish.

Multae dictio. The imposition of a pecuniary fine by a magistrate in the exercise of his coercive power (COËRCITIO).—See MULTA.

Multare. (Syn. *multam dicere, multam irrogare*.) See MULTA.

Mundum. A fair copy (original) of a document.

Munera. Public services, charges, duties or offices which every individual living in the state is obliged to fulfill on behalf of the state or the city (*municipium*) in which he was born or has his domicile (see DOMICILIUM, INCOLA, ORIGO). The *munera* also embrace taxes whether paid in money or in kind. *Munera* have to be distinguished from public offices (*magistratus*) which are a privilege, a dignity (*honos*) and not a burden. There was one public office which, originally a *honos*, later became the most burdensome *munus*, the *decurionatus* (see ORDO DECURIONUM, DE-

CURIONES). The systematization of the various *munera* is a creation of later times and, forced on classical texts, obscured the earlier conceptions. Thus, for instance, the term *munera publica* is now far from being clear, since in one instance guardianship (*tutela*) is defined as *munus publicum*, in another it is not. More evident is the distinction between *munera personalia*, which are performed by personal work (among them is *tutela, cura*), and *munera patrimonii* which encumber property and are performed by the payment of money as a contribution to the costs of public works. Some *munera* are of a mixed, personal and pecuniary nature (*munera mixta*); see MUNERA POSSESSIONUM. The maintenance of public roads, buildings, waterworks, river banks, the contribution of means of transportation for public purposes (for corn supply), were among the *munera publica*. Exempt from *munera personalia* were persons over seventy and under twenty-five, women, fathers of several children, and individuals who for personal reasons (weakness, poverty) were unable to fulfill the pertinent duties; see EXCUSATIONES A MUNERIBUS. Exemptions from *munera patrimonii* were rarely granted.—D. 50.4; C. 10.41–56; 10.64.—See IMMUNITAS, VACATIO MUNERUM, NOTITIA, NOMINATIO POTIORIS, SUMPTUS MUNERIS, NAVICULARII, NEGOTIATORES, NOTITIA, OFFICIUM VIRILE, PALATINI, POETAE, QUERIMONIA, MAGISTRI, VETERANUS, VOCARI AD MUNUS.

Kübler, *RE* 16; Kornemann, *ibid.* 630; Lammert, *RE* 7A, 2028; F. Oertel, *Liturgie*, 1917, 62.

Munera civilia. All kinds of *munera* except those imposed on members of the military. Ant. *munera militaria*.

Munera militaria. Duties connected with, or in the interest of, the military service. Ant. *munera civilia*.

Munera municipalia. Services to be rendered by a citizen to his municipality.—See DOMICILIUM, ORIGO.

Munera patrimonii. See MUNERA.

Munera personalia. See MUNERA.

Munera possessionum. *Munera* which incumber immovable property (land and buildings) without regard to whether or not the owner has his *origo* or *domicilium* where the immovable is situated.

Munera sordida. Mean, humble services, such as working in mills, mines, limepits, constructing buildings, roads, bridges. Lists of such *munera* are given in imperial constitutions of the later Empire. The distinction as to what is a *munera sordidum* and what is not, was important because of exemptions from them which were granted to various categories of persons, such as those employed in imperial service, lessees of imperial property, philosophers, rhetoricians, grammarians, and the like.—See EXCUSATIONES A MUNERIBUS.

Ferrari Dalle Spade, *Immunità ecclesiastiche, AVen* 99 (1939–40) 122.

Munerarius. A private individual or an official who arranged public games, especially gladiatorial combats (*ludi gladiatorii*) or fights with wild animals.

Schneider, *RE* 16.

Municipalis. (Noun.) A member of the municipal council. *Municipalis* (adj.) connected with, or pertaining to *municipia*.—D. 50.1.—See DECURIONES, MUNERA MUNICIPALIA, LEX MUNICIPALIS TARENTINA, LEX IULIA MUNICIPALIS, MAGISTRATUS MUNICIPALES, and the following items.

Municipes. Citizens of a municipality (*municipium*). One became a *municeps* by birth (see ORIGO), adoption by, or manumission by a *municeps*. The etymology of the term (*munera capere, muneris participes*) indicates the principal duties of a *municeps* towards his municipality: rendering public services and assuming charges for the welfare of the community. The *municipes* have twofold citizenship, since they are Roman citizens and citizens of their *municipium*. In their first capacity they participated in the political life of the state when present in Rome, as citizens of a *municipium* they took part in the local administration. By a decree of the municipal council (*ordo decurionum*) municipal citizenship could be granted to individuals who were not entitled to it (*adlectio inter cives*).—D. 50.1; C. 10.39.—See ACTOR MUNICIPUM, CURIAE MUNICIPIORUM, INCOLA, ORIGO, MUNICIPIUM.

A. N. Sherwin-White, *The Roman citizenship,* 1939, 36; E. Manni, *Per la storia dei municipi fino alla guerra sociale,* 1947.

Municipium. Any town in Italy except Rome (= *urbs*). The term superseded gradually analogous expressions (*oppidum, colonia, praefectura*) and was later applied also to cities in the provinces. Syn. *civitas,* and, to a certain extent, *res publica.* Originally there were *municipia cum suffragio* (with the right to vote in popular assemblies) and *cum iure honorum* (the right of their citizens to be elected as magistrates in Rome), and *municipia sine suffragio* (deprived of such rights). The *municipia* had, however, the privilege of local autonomous government and jurisdiction. An attempt of a general regulation of the municipal organization was made in the so-called LEX IULIA MUNICIPALIS. Other municipal statutes, preserved in inscriptions, are LEX MUNICIPALIS TARENTINA, LEX RUBRIA DE GALLIA CISALPINA, LEX COLONIAE GENETIVAE IULIAE, LEX MALACITANA, LEX SALPENSANA. A uniform organization of the municipal administration was not fully established, and differences in the titles of the municipal magistrates, and their functions, as well as the functions of the municipal councils, were never completely eliminated. Under the Republic a *municipium* could not be instituted as an heir, but this situation improved in the course of time. First *fideicommissa* in favor of a *municipium* were admitted, then a *fideicommissum hereditatis* (see SENATUSCONSULTUM

APRONIANUM), and finally under Hadrian the full capacity of *municipia* to be instituted as an heir or legatee was recognized.—D. 50.1.—See DECURIONES, ORDO DECURIONUM, DUOVIRI IURI DICUNDO, DUOVIRI AEDILES, CURIAE MUNICIPIORUM, PATRONUS MUNICIPII, MAGISTRATUS MUNICIPALES, TABULAE COMMUNES.

Kornemann, *RE* 16; Toutain, *DS* 3; Sacchi, *NDI* 8; W. Liebenam, *Städteverwaltung in der Kaiserzeit*[2] (1900); L. Mitteis, *Röm. Privatrecht,* 1908, 376; J. Declareuil, *Quelques problèmes d'hist. des instit. municipales,* 1911; Ramadier, *Études Girard,* 1 (1912); J. S. Reid, *The municipalities of the R. Empire,* 1913; F. F. Abbott-A. C. Johnson, *Municipal administration in the Roman Empire,* 1927; H. Rudolph, *Stadt und Staat im röm. Italien,* 1935; B. Eliachevitch, *La personnalité juridique en droit privé rom.,* Thèse Paris, 1942, 57; E. Manni, *Per la storia dei m. fino alla guerra sociale,* 1947; Solazzi, *BIDR* 49-50 (1947) 393; Schönbauer, *Iura* 1 (1950) 124; Vittinghoff, *ZSS* 68 (1951) 455; idem, *Römische Kolonisations- und Bürgerrechtspolitik unter Caesar und Augustus, Abh. Akademie Wiss. Mainz,* 1951 (no. 14) 33.

Munire ripam. See RIPA.

Muniri. To be protected, supported by law (*ipso iure*) or by a legal remedy (*exceptiones, praescriptiones*). The term is frequent in the language of the imperial chancery.

Munus. See MUNERA.

Munus. A gift presented on a special occasion (on a birthday = *munus natalicium,* on a wedding = *munus nuptiale nuptalicium*).—See DONARE.

Munus. A public festival (game) arranged by a private person (*munus dare, edere*). It was customary to bequeath a legacy to a municipality in order that public festivities be made *ad honorem civitatis* (= to the honor of the city).

Munus nuptiale (nuptalicium). A wedding gift. Such a gift was customary but not obligatory. Therefore a guardian who gave his ward's mother or sister a wedding gift could not deduct the expense from the ward's property.

Murilegulus. A fisherman skilled in catching purplefish.—C. 11.8.

Murus. A wall. City walls were *res sanctae.* In Rome persons who lived in extramural buildings were considered inhabitants of Rome.—See RES DIVINI IURIS, ROMA, URBS, PARIES.

R. I. Richmond, *The city walls of the imperial Rome,* 1930.

Mutare causam possessionis. See NEMO SIBI IPSE CAUSAM POSSESSIONIS, etc.

Mutare testamentum. To change a last will. A testator had full power to do so, but if the motive for which he changed his mind and which was expressed in the later testament proved false, the former testamentary disposition might be taken into consideration. If, for instance, the testator believed that the heir first instituted was dead, the latter could claim the inheritance according to an imperial constitution.

Mutat. In the phrase *non mutat si* (*quod* or sim.) = it does not matter if. . . . The locution is used to state that a legal rule which was expressed beforehand, has to be applied to another legal situation.

Mutatio. In the postal service, see MANSIO.

Mutatio domini. A change in the person of the owner of a thing. It has no influence at all on the rights of a usufructuary or of a person who has a servitude over the thing.

Mutatio familiae. A change in the family status of a person. It takes place when a member of one family enters into another (marriage with *conventio in manum*) or when a person *sui iuris* comes under the paternal power of another through *adrogatio,* or *vice versa,* when a person *alieni iuris* becomes *sui iuris* and consequently the head of a new family (*emancipatio*). *Mutatio familiae* produces CAPITIS DEMINUTIO MINIMA because the ties with the former family are torn.—See ADOPTIO, STATUS.

Mutatio iudicii. See ALIENATIO IUDICII MUTANDI CAUSA.

Mutatio iudicis. A replacement of a judge after *litis contestatio,* when, for instance, the first judge died before rendering the judgment or became somehow unable to continue his activity.—See TRANSLATIO IUDICII.

> Steinwenter, *RE* Suppl. 5, 351; P. Koschaker, *Translatio iudicii,* 1905, 311; Wlassak, *Der Judikationsbefehl, SBWien* 197, 4 (1921) 232; Duquesne, *La translatio iudicii,* 1910, 221.

Mutatio militiae. The transfer of a soldier to another branch of service as a punishment for a minor offense. Syn. *in deteriorem militiam dare.*

Mutatio nominis. A change of name (*nomen, cognomen*). It was allowed if it was not intended for fraudulent purposes.—C. 9.45.

Mutatio rei. A change of the substance of a thing. It occurs when land became a pond or a marsh through inundation or when a forest was cleared and made into field. "Through *mutatio rei* an usufruct is extinguished" (D. 7.4.5.2).

> P. E. Cavin, *L'extinction de l'usufruit rei mutatione,* 1933.

Mutatio status. See STATUS.

Mutua pecunia. A sum of money given as a loan.—C. 10.6.—See MUTUUM.

Mutua substitutio. See SUBSTITUTIO.

Mutuae petitiones. Reciprocal claims between two persons who sue each other in separate actions. The claims could be united in one trial in order to be examined and decided by the same judge. Syn. *mutuae actiones.*

> De Francisci, *Synallagma* 2 (1916) 539; Levy, *ZSS* 52 (1932) 517; S. Solazzi, *Compensazione²* (1950) 107.

Mutuari (mutuare). To borrow, to receive a loan.—See MUTUUM.

Mutus. A mute person. If he is able to understand the meaning of the transaction he wants to conclude, he can express his will by signs (*nutu*).—D. 37.3.—See INTELLECTUS, NUTUS, CURATOR MUTI, TUTOR.

Mutuum. A loan. The creditor = *qui mutuam pecuniam* (*mutuo*) *dat, credit;* the debtor = *qui mutuum* (*mutuo*) *accipit.* A loan is concluded *re,* i.e., when its object (a sum of money, an amount of fungibles) was handed over to the debtor. The latter is obligated to return in due time the sum of money or the same quantity of fungibles of the same quality as was lent to him. He can be sued for return through the *actio certae creditae pecuniae,* when money was involved, or through *condictio triticaria* if fungibles were borrowed. The borrower becomes owner of the things given to him for consumption. Interest (*usurae*) must be promised by a special agreement (normally a *stipulatio*). The loan itself could also be vested in the form of a *stipulatio* if the debtor promised the payment through *stipulatio* (a verbal contract).—See RES QUAE PONDERE, etc., FENUS, USURAE.

> Kaser, *RE* Suppl. 6; Cuq, *DS* 3; G. Segrè, *St Simoncelli* 1917, 331; C. Longo, *Il mutuo (Corso)* 1933; P. E. Viard, *Mutui datio,* Paris, 1939; Robbe, *SDHI* 7 (1941) 35; P. Voci, *Il sistema rom. dei contratti²* (1950) 123; Seidl, *Fschr Schulz* 1 (1951) 373.

Mutuus dissensus. See CONSENSUS CONTRARIUS.

N

Narratio. (In postclassical language.) The oral presentation by the plaintiff or his advocate of the facts and legal arguments on which he based his claim. The reply of the defendant = *responsio, contradictio.*

> P. Collinet, *La procédure par libelle,* 1932, 208.

Nasci. To be born. "Those who are born dead are considered neither born nor procreated" (D. 50.16.129). *Nasci* is used of fruits (see FRUCTUS) which proceed from the soil (*in fundo*). With reference to legal institutions *nasci* is used of actions (*actio nascitur* = an action arises), interdicts, obligations, and the like, to which a legal situation under discussion gives origin.—See INSULA IN FLUMINE NATA.

Nasciturus. A child not yet born (unborn). Syn. *qui in utero* (in the womb) *est.* There was a rule that "a *nasciturus* is considered born when his interests are taken into account" (D. 1.5.26).—See CONCEPTUS.

> Anon., *NDI* 7; Stella-Maranca, *BIDR* 42 (1934) 238; Albertario, *Studi* 1 (1933, ex 1923) 1; C. A. Maschi, *Concezione naturalistica,* 1937, 66; Jonkers, *Vigiliae Christianae* 1 (1947) 240.

Natalium restitutio. The privileges of a free-born, granted by the emperor to a freedman. All official posts accessible to free-born persons were open to the individual thus privileged. He could enter the *ordo equester* (the equestrian class, see EQUITES) for which the status of a free-born was required.—D. 40.11; C. 6.8.

> A. M. Duff, *Freedmen in the R. empire,* 1928, 72.

Natura. Nature of things, natural order, natural reality. *Natura hominum (humana)* = human nature. *Natura* (abl.) = naturally, in a natural way. Ant. *contra naturam.*—With reference to legal institutions *natura* = the substance, the essential elements, the structure of an institution (*contractus, obligationis, negotii, stipulationis, emptionis*, etc.). Theoreticians among the law teachers coined this concept under the influence of philosophic ideas.—See the following items.

> Gradenwitz, *Fg Schirmer* 1900, 13; R. Bozzoni, *Sulle espressioni natura, naturalis . . .* , 1933; C. A. Maschi, *La concezione naturalistica del dir. e degli istituti giur. rom.*, 1937; Bartosek, *St Albertario* 2 (1952) 470.

Natura actionis. The juristic structure of a specific action with regard to its substantial functions. The term is probably of classical origin (Gaius), but it was expanded by Justinian's compilers into a general conception of the nature of actions without regard to a specific action.

> C. Longo, *St Scialoja* 1 (1905) 607; *idem, BIDR* 17 (1905) 34; Pringsheim, *SDHI* 1 (1935) 73; C. A. Maschi, *La concezione naturalistica*, 1937, 73.98; P. Collinet, *La nature des actions*, 1947; Solazzi, *BIDR* 49–50 (1947) 346.

Natura contractus. Generally or with regard to a specific contract (as, for instance, *natura depositi, societatis, mandati*), the juristic structure of a contract.

> Rotondi, *Scritti* 2 (1922) 159; C. A. Maschi, *La concezione naturalistica*, 1937, 73.92; Pringsheim, *SDHI* 1 (1935) 73.

Natura hominum (humana). The normal human nature, essential natural characteristics of mankind, moral or psychological attitudes of men. *Natura hominum* in specific circumstances may serve as a criterion for the juristic evaluation of an individual's acting in a given instance, i.e., whether his act was or was not in accordance with human nature.

> C. A. Maschi, *La concezione naturalistica*, 1937, 7.

Natura obligationis. The structure and function of an obligation in general or of a specific obligation.

> C. A. Maschi, *La concezione naturalistica*, 1937, 82.

Natura rerum. The reality (existence) of things, all that exists in nature. "What is prohibited by nature of things is not admitted by any law" (D. 50.17.188.1). *In rerum natura esse* = to exist.

> C. A. Maschi, *La concezione naturalistica*, 1937, 65.

Natura servitutis. The nature of a servitude. The *natura servitutis* is mentioned with regard to some servitudes, as, for instance, the indivisibility of the servitude ITER is explained by its nature.

> C. A. Maschi, *La concezione naturalistica*, 1937, 78.

Naturale ius. See IUS NATURALE.

Naturalis. Natural, by nature, connected with nature. For the various uses of the term which—not always for good reasons—have been supposed to have been introduced by the compilers, see the following items.

> Guarneri-Citati, *St Riccobono* 1 (1936) 730 (Bibl.).

Naturalis aequitas. See AEQUITAS, IUS NATURALE.

Naturalis cognatio. Blood relationship among slaves.

> Levy, *Natural Law*, in *Univ. of Notre Dame Natural Law Proc.* 2 (1949) 60 (= *SDHI* 15, 1949, 14).

Naturalis familia. The family to which one belongs by birth. Ant. *familia adoptiva* = the family into which one entered by adoption.

Naturalis filius. See FILIUS NATURALIS.

Naturalis lex. Only mentioned once in juristic sources, namely, with regard to the prohibition of theft (*furtum*) by natural law (*lege naturali*, D. 47.2.1.3, similarly Cicero, *de off.* 3.5.21: *contra naturam*).

> C. A. Maschi, *La concezione naturalistica*, 1937, 358.

Naturalis obligatio. See OBLIGATIO NATURALIS.

Naturalis possessio. See POSSESSIO.

Naturalis ratio. Natural foundation, conformity with nature, natural reason. The term is indicated as the basic component of IUS GENTIUM and appears at times as a ground of justification for certain legal institutions or decisions in specific cases (= reasonableness).

> Koschembahr-Lyskowski, *St Bonfante* 3 (1930) 467; C. A. Maschi, *La concezione naturalistica*, 1937, 236; De Martino, *AnBari* 7–8 (1947) 117; Kaser, *ZSS* 65 (1947) 219; Levy, *Natural Law, Univ. of Notre Dame Natural Law Proc.* 2 (1949, = *SDHI* 15, 1949); Bartosek, *St Albertario* 2 (1952) 474.

Naturaliter. By nature. Syn. *natura* (abl.). *Naturaliter possidere* = physical, corporeal possession.

Nauarchus. The captain of a vessel. *Nauarchus classis* = the commander of a fleet of the Roman navy; he had the privilege to make a formless testament according to the military law (*iure militari*), as all soldiers had.—See TESTAMENTUM MILITIS.

> Strack, *RE* 16, 1896.

Nauclerus. A shipmaster who effected the transportation of men and goods for the state.—C. 11.2.—See NAVICULARII.

> Kiesling, *RE* 16, 1937.

Naufragium. A shipwreck. It is considered as an unforeseeable accident; see CASUS, CASUS FORTUITUS. Pillage committed during a *naufragium* was punished with a penalty of the fourfold value of the goods robbed.—D. 47.9; C. 11.6.—See DEPOSITUM MISERABILE.

> Weiss, *RE* 16; Cuq, *DS* 4; Solazzi, *RDNav* 5 (1939) 253; De Robertis, *St di dir. penale rom.*, 1943, 77.

Nauta. A shipowner. His liability for goods taken for transportation by agreement (RECEPTUM) was regulated in the praetorian Edict which showed particular consideration for the interests of the owner of the transported goods. Syn. EXERCITOR. In the same section of the Edict was settled the responsibility of inn-keepers (*caupones*) and stable-keepers (*stabularii*).—D. 4.9; 47.5; C. 11.27.—See RECEPTUM NAUTARUM, NAVICULARII.

> Del Prete, *NDI* 7, 873, 875; Messina-Vitrano, *Note intorno alle azioni contro il nauta*, 1909; M. A. De Dominicis, *La clausola edittale salvum fore recipere*, 1933; Mackintosh, *JurR* 47 (1935) 54; Carrelli, *RDNav* 4 (1938) 323; Solazzi, *ibid.* 5 (1939) 35; Brecht, *ZSS* 62 (1942).

Nauticum fenus. See FENUS NAUTICUM. Syn. *nautica pecunia.*

Navicularii. Shipowners whose primary business was the transportation of men and goods over the Mediterranean Sea. The *navicularii* were organized in *collegia* (associations). Under the Empire they enjoyed a particular protection by the government because of their importance in supplying Rome with food. Owners of larger vessels (of at least ten thousand *modii* tonnage) were exempt from *munera*. Roman citizenship was granted to *navicularii* of Latin status, the sanctions of the *Lex Iulia et Papia Poppaea* were not applied to them, and women, owners of ships, were not subject to guardianship (*tutela mulierum*). The manifold privileges were strictly personal: they were granted the shipowners *propter navem* (because of the ship) and were denied to their sons and freedmen whether or not they were members of the professional association. In the later Empire, membership in the *collegium naviculariii* was compulsory. The organization as a whole and all its members were regarded as state employees, obliged to fulfill the orders of the government, under conditions dictated by the latter. Their services, frequently regulated by imperial enactments, became an *onus publicum* (a public charge), for the fulfillment of which they were responsible to the state with their whole property.—C. 11.2; 3; 4.—See DOMINUS NAVIS, NAUCLERUS.

> Stöckle, *RE* 16 (Bibl.); Besnier, *DS* 4; De Robertis, *Corpus naviculariorum, RDNav* 3 (1937) 189; L. Schnorr v. Carolsfeld, *Gesch. der juristischen Person,* 1 (1933) 283; Gaudemet, *St Solazzi* 1948, 657; Solazzi, *RDNav* 9 (1948) 45.

Navigium (navigatio). Navigation. For the protection of navigation on public rivers through interdicts, see FLUMINA PUBLICA. The protection was extended on anchoring- and landing-places (= *stationes*) and in the use of roads after landing (*iter*).

Navis. Any kind of a ship (boat, vessel) serving for the transportation of persons or goods on the sea, rivers and stagnant waters. A ship might be the object of a legacy and of a usufruct. For problems connected with the use of a ship, see EXERCITOR, GUBERNATOR, MAGISTER NAVIS, NAUTA, NAUFRAGIUM, NAVICULARII, IACTUS, NAVIGIUM, EXPUGNARE.—C. 11.4.

> E. Gandolfo, *La nave nel dir. rom.,* 1883; De Martino, *RDNav* 3 (1937) 41, 179.

Nec non. And also, and besides. The emphatic affirmation, often strengthened by an *et* (*etiam*), is somewhat suspected of being non-classical because it occurs frequently in Justinian's enactment.

> Guarneri-Citati, *Indice²* (1927) 58.

Necare. To kill. "One who refuses alimony, is similar to one who kills" (D. 25.3.4).

Necessarii (necessariae personae). Relatives, kinsmen.

Necessarius. See IMPENSAE, HERES NECESSARIUS, HERES SUUS ET NECESSARIUS.

Necessitas. Necessity, exigency, compulsion. The term is opposed to *libera voluntas* (the free will) of a person performing a legal act. *Ex necessitate* (*necessitate cogente*) = by the compulsion of the situation (circumstances), emergency. Ant. *nulla*

necessitate cogente. Syn. *necessitudo.*—See COACTUS VOLUI, METUS, VIS, SPONTE.

> Koschaker, *ConfCast* 1940, 180.

Necessitudo. The tie of relationship, kindred. *Necessitudo sanguinis* (*consanguinitatis*) = blood relationship.—See NECESSARII.

Necti. To be bound, e.g., a person bound by an obligation (*obligatione necti*), or involved in a crime (*crimine*); a thing pledged as a real security (*pignori, hypothecae*).

Nefas. See FAS.

Nefasti dies. See DIES NEFASTI.

Negare. To deny; in procedural language with reference to the defendant = to deny a claim; syn. *infitiari*. With regard to a magistrate who refused the plaintiff the action he demanded *negare* is syn. with *denegare* (*actionem, petitionem*).—See INFITIARI, DENEGARE ACTIONEM.

Neglegentia. Negligence, omission. In the sources *neglegentia* is tantamount to CULPA, and similarly graduated (*magna, lata neglegentia*). Precision in terminology is no more to be found here than in the field of *culpa*. One text declares (D. 50.16.226): "gross negligence (*magna neglegentia*) is *culpa*, *magna culpa* is *dolus*"; another (D. 17.1.29 pr., evidently interpolated) says: "gross negligence (*dissoluta neglegentia*) is near to *dolus* (*prope dolum*)." In the saying "*lata culpa* is exorbitant (extreme) negligence, i.e., not to understand (*intelligere*) what all understand" (D. 50.16.213.2) *neglegentia* is identified with ignorance. Some of these and other definitions concerning *neglegentia* are the result of interpolations by Justinian's compilers.—See DILIGENTIA, REMOVERE.

> F. H. Lawson, *Negligence in the civil law,* 1950.

Negotia. See NEGOTIUM.

Negotiari. To carry on a business of buying and selling.—See NEGOTIATOR.

Negotiatio. A commercial business (on a wholesale basis), the business of an inn-keeper, or a shipper.

Negotiator. A tradesman, a dealer who buys and sells merchandise, on a rather large scale. A slave, called *negotiator,* was the manager of his master's business.

Negotiatores. Under the Empire *negotiatores,* who provided food for the capital, enjoyed special personal privileges (exemption from *munera*). They had the right to be organized in associations (*collegia*) and were treated in much the same fashion as shipowners (see NAVICULARII) and other contractors of the government.—C. 12.34.—See CONSISTENTES.

> Kornemann, *RE* 4, 444; Cagnat, *DS* 3; H. J. Loane, *Industry and commerce in Rome,* 1938.

Negotiorum gestio. (From *negotia gerere.*) The management of another's affair or affairs without authorization by the person interested (*dominus negotii*). By such action the *negotiorum gestor* bound himself to conduct the matter to the end and to return to the *dominus negotii* all that he gained or acquired (proceeds, *fructus*) from the transaction; on the other hand the latter was bound to reimburse the *gestor* for his expenses. The *negotiorum gestio* arose from situations when a person acted in the interest of another during the latter's absence in order to defend the absent party's rights. The essential circumstance was that the *gestor* acted without a mandate. If the *dominus negotiorum* later gave his consent (*ratihabitio*) or did not protest against the gestor's meddling in his affairs, after he had knowledge thereof, the legal situation of the matter was considered a mandate. A further requirement on the part of the *gestor* was that he acted with the intention of serving the interests of another (*animus negotia gerendi*) and not of himself (*sui lucri causa*). Therefore there was no *negotiorum gestio* if he acted in order to execute a contractual duty of his own, fulfilled a moral duty, or made a donation. At any rate he had to abstain from acting *prohibente domino*, i.e., when the latter exactly forbade the gestor to act in his behalf. The *negotiorum gestio* created bilateral obligations although there was no agreement between the parties involved (*quasi ex contractu*). The *dominus negotii* might sue the *gestor* for recovery of the proceeds and for damages caused by an improper (fraudulent or culpable) management of the matter (*actio negotiorum gestorum*); on the other hand the *gestor* had an action for the reimbursement of his expenses (*actio negotiorum gestorum contraria*), even when his efforts reasonably made (*negotium utiliter coeptum*) remained unsuccessful. Postclassical development and Justinian's reforms obscured some details of the institution as they were in classical law; thus, in spite of an abundant literature some points are still controversial.—D. 3.5; C. 2.18; for *negotiorum gestio* in the interest of a guardian.—D. 27.5; C. 5.45.

Kreller, *RE* Suppl. 7 (Bibl. 551); Huvelin, *DS* 4; Scaduto, *NDI* 6 (*s.v. gestione d'affari*); G. Segrè, *StSen* 23 (1906) 289; Peters, *ZSS* 32 (1911) 263; Partsch, *St zur neg. g., SberMünch* 1913; *idem, Aus nachgelassenen Schriften*, 1931, 96; Riccobono, *AnPal* 3–4 (1917) 209, 221; Kübler, *ZSS* 39 (1918) 191; Frese, *Mél Cornil* 1 (1926) 327; *idem, St Bonfante* 4 (1930) 397; Bossowski, *BIDR* 37 (1929) 129; Haymann, *ACDR* Roma, 2 (1935) 451; Ehrhardt, *Romanistische Studien (Freiburger rechtsgesch. Abhandlungen* 5) 1935; G. Pacchioni, *Trattato della gestione d'affari*, 3rd ed. 1935; M. Morelli, *Die Geschäftsführung im klas. röm. R.*, 1935; Sachers, *SDHI* 4 (1938) 309; Kreller, *ZSS* 59 (1939) 390; *idem, Fschr Koschaker* 2 (1939) 193; V. Arangio-Ruiz, *Il mandato*, 1949, 28.

Negotium (negotia). Any kind of transaction or agreement. Acts involving transfer of property are also covered by this term. Less frequently *negotium* refers to trials, civil and criminal. *Negotia* may also connote the economic activity of a person, his commercial, banking, or industrial business. *Negotia gerere (administrare)* = to administer one's own (or another's) affairs. Some persons administer or cooperate in the management of affairs of others as his legally authorized representatives (*tutores, curatores*) or in virtue of a special agreement (*mandatum, locatio conductio operarum*) as his mandatary, agent, *institor*, etc.—See NEGOTIORUM GESTIO.

P. Voci, *Dottrina rom. del contratto*, 1946, 47; G. Grosso, *Il sistema rom. dei contratti²*, 1950, 43.

Negotium absentis. A matter which concerns an absent person.

Negotium alienum. A business matter (an affair) of another person. Ant. *negotium suum, proprium*.
Rabel, *St Bonfante* 4 (1930) 281.

Negotium civile. (In imperial constitutions.) A civil trial (litigation). Ant. *negotium criminale* = a criminal trial.

Negotium forense. A judicial matter, a trial.—See FERIAE.

Negotium mixtum cum donatione. A bilateral transaction with reciprocal but unequal performances, wherein one of the parties intending to make a donation gave the other party a thing of much greater value than he was receiving. Such a transaction was valid unless the parties thereby attempted to violate the laws concerning unlawful donations.—See DONATIO.

B. Biondi, *Successione testamentaria*, 1943, 717.

Negotium nullum (nullius momenti). A transaction which is legally invalid.

Negotium privatum. A private matter (transaction); ant. *negotium publicum* = a matter in which the state (*populus Romanus*) is concerned.

Nemini res sua servit. See SERVITUS.—D. 8.2.26.
Solazzi, *Requisiti e modi di costituzione delle servitù*, 1947, 13; *idem, SDHI* 18 (1952) 223.

Nemo. Nobody, no one. The phrase *nemo dubitat* (= nobody doubts) is frequently employed by the jurists to indicate that the opinion presented is beyond any doubt. Syn. *nullus.*—In the following items some legal rules starting with *nemo* are given.

Nemo alieno nomine agere potest. In the field of civil procedure: one cannot sue in the name of another. In the procedure under *legis actiones*, representation of a party (*lege agere*) was inadmissible (D. 50.17.123). A few exceptions were, however, recognized, e.g., in favor of persons who were held in captivity by an enemy or were absent in the interest of the state. For the formulary procedure, see COGNITOR, PROCURATOR. In the field of private law the rule disallows concluding a legal transaction for another. Under *ius civile* nobody could act for another, every one must act for himself in acquiring an obligation or a right over a thing (*per extraneam personam nobis adquiri non posse*, Gaius, Inst. 2.95). The exclusion of direct representation was compensated by the services rendered by persons under power (sons, slaves) as the organs acting for their father (the head of the family) or master. The praetorian law promoted the acknowledgment of obligations contracted or acquired by representatives (*actiones adiecticiae qualitatis, actiones utiles*).—Inst. 4.10.—See EXERCITOR NAVIS.

> Riccobono, *TR* 9 (1929) 33; *idem, AnPal* 14 (1930) 389.

Nemo alteri stipulari potest. No one can accept a promise by *stipulatio* on behalf of another" (D. 45.1.38.17; Inst. 3.19.19). This was a fundamental rule of the *ius civile.*—See the foregoing item.

Nemo damnum facit, nisi qui id fecit quod facere ius non habet (D. 50.17.151). No one inflicts a damage (*sc.* on another) unless he does something that he has no right to do.—See AEMULATIO, UTI IURE SUO, NEMO VIDETUR DOLO etc.

Nemo de improbitate sua consequitur actionem (D. 47.2.12.1). No one acquires an action through his dishonesty.

Nemo ex consilio obligatur. No one is obligated because of counsel (he gave another).—See CONSILIUM.

Nemo fraudare videtur eos qui sciunt et consentiunt. See FRAUDARE.

Nemo invitus ad communionem compellitur (D. 12.6.26.4). No one is forced to have common property with another.—See COMMUNIO.

Nemo invitus. For further analogous rules, see INVITUS.

Nemo plus commodi heredi suo relinquit quam ipse habuit (D. 50.17.120). No one leaves to his heir more rights than he had himself.—See HERES.

Nemo plus iuris in alium transferre potest quam ipse habet (D. 50.17.54). See TRANSFERRE.

Nemo pro parte testatus pro parte intestatus decedere potest (D. 50.17.7; Inst. 2.14.5). A decedent may not leave his property partly by testament, and partly by intestate succession. A testament must cover the whole estate. If the testator disposed in his last will of a part of his estate only, the rest does not pass on intestacy but the entire estate devolves to instituted heir or heirs. Exception to this rule was admitted in the case of a soldier's testament.

> Carpentier, *NRHD* 10 (1886) 1; P. Bonfante, *Scritti* 1 (1926, ex 1891) 101; E. Costa, *Papiniano* 3 (1896) 9; S. Solazzi, *Dir. ereditario rom.* 1 (1932) 212; Sanfilippo, *AnPal* 15 (1937) 187; *Meylan, Fschr Tuor* (Zürich, 1946) 179.

Nemo sibi ipse causam possessionis mutare potest (D. 41.2.3.19). See POSSESSIO.

Nemo (nullus) videtur dolo facere qui iure suo utitur (D. 50.17.55). No one who exercises his right is considered to act fraudulently.—See AEMULATIO, DOLUS.

Nepos. A grandson; *neptis* = a granddaughter. The term *filii* sometimes also comprises the *nepotes.*

> Lanfranchi, *StCagl* 30 (1946) 15.

Neratius, Priscus. A remarkable jurist of the first half of the second century after Christ; member of the councils of Trojan and Hadrian. He was the last known head of the Proculian school (*Proculiani*). He wrote casuistic works (*Responsa, Epis-*

tulae), one work with the unusual title MEMBRANAE, a collection of *Regulae,* and a monograph *De nuptiis* (On marriage).

> Berger, *RE* 16, 2549; G. Grosso, *ATor* 67 (1932).

Nerva, M. Cocceius. There were two jurists by this name, father (*Nerva pater*) and son (*Nerva filius*). The older (he died in A.D. 33) was head of the Proculian school (*Proculiani*) after Labeo. No specific work of his is known, but he is frequently quoted by later jurists. Little is known about his son, who was also of the Proculian school, and author of a monograph *De usucapionibus* (On usucaptions).

> Arnò, *TR* 4 (1923) 210 (on the father).

Nesennius Apollinaris. A disciple of the jurist Paul (third century).

> Berger, *RE* 17, 68.

Nex. A violent death.—See IUS VITAE NECISQUE.

Nexum. A legal institution of the ancient Roman law, mentioned in the Twelve Tables. Despite an extensive modern literature the character of *nexum* has remained somewhat obscure. The sources show that already about the end of the Republic the jurists had no precise knowledge about it. It seems clear, however, that *nexum* was a bilateral transaction accomplished like the *mancipatio* (with which it is sometimes identified because of the phrase *nexum mancipiumque* in the Twelve Tables) in the solemn form *per aes et libram* by which according to one opinion the debtor assumed an obligation (e.g., in the case of a loan) ; according to another view, the debtor sold himself or gave himself to the creditor as a pledge through self-mancipation as a guarantee for an existing or a future debt. Through an oral declaration (*nuncupatio*) the debtor settled his condition as *nexus,* i.e., though remaining free, he was bound to work for the creditor until the debt was paid and he remained with the creditor in a situation factually not very different from that of a slave. He gave his work or his labor power (*operas suas*), as Varro, *De lingua Lat.* 7.105 says, "into slavery (*in servitutem*)." The creditor had the right to put him in fetters. The *nexum* was abolished by the LEX POETELIA PAPIRIA.—See MANCIPATIO, PER AES ET LIBRAM.

> Düll, *RE* 17; Berger, *RE* Suppl. 7, 407; Huvelin, *DS* 4; Anon., *NDI* 8; Mitteis, *ZSS* 22 (1901) 96; Lenel, *ZSS* 23 (1902) 64; Kübler, *ZSS* 25 (1904) 254; H. H. Pflüger, *Nexum und mancipium,* 1908; Kretschmar, *ZSS* 29 (1908) 227; Pacchioni, *Mél Girard* 2 (1912) 319; A. Segrè, *AG* 102 (1929) 28; Popescu-Spineni, *ACDR* Roma 2 (1935) 545; Michon, *Rec Gény* 1 (1934) 42; v. Lübtow, *ZSS* 56 (1936) 239; S. Riccobono, Jr., *AnPal* 41 (1939) 45; De Martino, *SDHI* 6 (1940) 138; Noailles, *RHD* 19–20 (1940–41) 205 (= *Fas et ius,* 1948, 91) ; M. Kaser, *Eigentum und Besitz,* 1943, 154; *idem, Das altröm. Ius,* 1949, 233; H. F. Thormann, *Der doppelte Ursprung der mancipatio,* 1943, 176; Hernandez Tejero, *AHDE* 16 (1945) 296; J. Maillet, *Théorie de Schuld et Haftung,* Paris, 1944, 130; Westrup, *Note sur sponsio et nexum, Kgl. Danske Videnskab., Hist. Filol. Meddedelser* 31, 2 (1947) ; H. Lévy-Bruhl, *Nouvelles Études,* 1947, 97; v. Lübtow, *ZSS* 67 (1950) 112.

Nexus. (Adj.) Bound by an obligation; when used of a thing (*res pignori nexa, pignora nexa*) = pledged. —See NEXUM.

Nihil agere (agi). To perform an act which is legally invalid.

Hellmann, *ZSS* 23 (1902) 403.

Nisi. Except, unless, if not. Phrases introduced with *nisi* and used to complete a preceding legal rule were frequently inserted by the compilers to restrict the applicability of, or to admit an exception to, what had been said before. Many of such *nisi*-additions are of slight significance and do not represent any innovation upon earlier law. A large number of these additions refer to the requirement of precise evidence (see EVIDENTISSIMAE PROBATIONES, PROBATIONES) from which should certainly not be inferred that this requirement was introduced by Justinian. Similarly, restrictions of the following sort: *nisi aliud actum sit* (*convenerit,* and the like) by which an agreement of the parties, contrary to that one which had been discussed before, is admitted, in many instances did not differ from classical law. Therefore, in such instances it has to be ascertained whether what is included in the *nisi*-clause is in fact simply a repetition of what was already in force in the classical law, or a later innovation.

Guarneri-Citati, *Indice*[2] (1927) 60; Berger, *ClPhilol* 43 (1948) 241.

Nobilissimus. An honorific title of the emperor (*nobilissimus Caesar, imperator*) from the third century on. After Constantine, members of the emperor's family were also honored by this title.

Ensslin, *RE* 17.

Nobiles, nobilitas. There is no exact definition of these terms in ancient literature. Holders of the highest magistracies, their descendants and senatorial families formed a kind of an aristocratic social group, more in fact than in law. The distinction between *nobiles* and other people not belonging to the noble class (*ignobiles*) gradually superseded the earlier distinction between patricians and plebeians.

Strasburger, *RE* 17; Lécrivain, *DS* 4; Brasiello, *NDI* 8; Meynial, *St Fadda* 2 (1906); Gelzer, *Die Nobilität der röm. Republik, Hermes* 50 (1912) 395; Otto, *Hermes* 51 (1916) 73; A. Stein, *ibid.* 52 (1917) 564; Münzer, *Die röm. Adelsparteien und Adelsfamilien,* 1920; Afzelius, *ClMed* 1 (1938) 40, 7 (1945) 150; Moebus, *Neue Jahrb. für antike Bildung,* 1942, 275; K. Hanell, *Das altröm. eponyme Amt,* 1946, 19

Nocere. To do physical, economic, or moral harm, to be a hindrance. With regard to procedural measures, as e.g., to exceptions, *exceptio nocet* = an exception may be successful if opposed to the plaintiff's claim.

Nocturnus fur. See FUR DIURNUS, FURTUM.

Nolens. Unwilling. *Nolente* = without one's consent, against one's will. Syn. *invito.*

Nolle. To be unwilling, not to wish, to refuse (consent, acceptance, or to do something). Ant. *velle.*

"He who has the right to exercise his volition (*velle*) may refuse (*nolle*)," D. 50.17.3.—See NOLENS.

Nomen. A personal name. A free-born Roman citizen normally had three names: *praenomen* (first name), *nomen gentile* or *gentilicium* (the name of the *gens,* the family group, to which he belonged) and *cognomen* (a surname, the third name in the order of the full name). Sometimes, two or more first names appear in literary or epigraphic sources; sometimes, the *cognomen* is missing or two *cognomina* are given as a special distinction. The three-name-system begins to disappear in the third century in favor of the one-name-system.—In juristic works several typical names are employed to indicate fictitious persons in a legal case, where the parties are men, Titius, Lucius Titius, Gaius, Sempronius, Maevius, Seius, etc., where women, Titia, Gaia, Sempronia, Seia, etc., where slaves, Stichus or Pamphilus. A plaintiff often appears as AULUS AGERIUS, a defendant as NUMERIUS NEGIDIUS. In some texts the real names of the litigants appear which indicates that a real case is under discussion. Freedmen retained the name they had as slaves, but adopted the *nomen gentilicium* of their patron.

Fraenkel, *RE* 16, 1648 (*s.v. Namenwesen*); Morel, *DS* 3; Augustinus, *De nominibus propriis in Pandectis,* in Otto, *Thesaurus iuris R.,* 1 (1790) 259; Schultze, *Geschichte der röm. Eigennamen, Abh. Göttingische Gesellschaft der Wissenschaften,* 1904; B. Doer, *Untersuchungen zur röm. Namensgebung,* 1937.

Nomen. Refers to the name of an author of a book or pamphlet. Hence *sine nomine edere librum* = to publish a booklet (a defamatory pamphlet) anonymously. *Sub nomine* = a (true or false) name under which a book is published.

Nomen. With reference to things, the *nomen* (= denomination, appellation) is distinguished from the thing itself (*corpus*). "An error in the naming of a thing does not matter if the identity of the thing itself can be established" (D. 18.1.9.1).—See ERROR NOMINIS, DEMONSTRATIO FALSA. It was customary to denote a plot of land by a name (*nomen fundo imponere*). The jurists use for the specification of a land typical fictitious names, such as *fundus Cornelianus, Sempronianus, Titianus,* etc.

Nomen. In criminal procedure, see ACCUSATIO (for *nomen deferre*), NOMEN RECIPERE.

Nomen. In contractual relations, a demand, a claim. Syn. *creditum, res credita.* "The term *nomen* refers to any contract and obligation" (D. 50.16.6 pr.). *Collocare pecuniam in nomina (nominibus)* = to invest money in loans. See COLLOCARE.—See LEGATUM NOMINIS, NOMINA ARCARIA, NOMINA TRANSCRIPTICIA, NOMEN FACERE, PIGNUS NOMINIS.

Nomen actionis. The name of an action. "When commonly used names of actions are lacking, it must be sued *praescriptis verbis*" (D. 19.5.2).—See ACTIO PRAESCRIPTIS VERBIS.

Nomen alienum. See ALIENO NOMINE, NEMO ALIENO NOMINE. Ant. *nomen suum, nomen proprium.*

Nomen dare militiae. See MILITIA.

Nomen deferre. See ACCUSATIO.

Nomen facere. To make an entry in an account-book concerning a loan given to a person, hence to grant a loan.

> Erdmann, *ZSS* 63 (1943) 396.

Nomen falsum. A false name. Assuming a *nomen falsum* for fraudulent purposes (e.g., for claiming rights of succession) is punished as *crimen falsi.*—See FALSUM.

Nomen gentilicium. See GENS, NOMEN.

> Pulgram, *The origin of the Latin n.g., Harvard St Class Philol* 58 (1948) 163.

Nomen Latinum. See LATINUM NOMEN.

Nomen proprium. The proper name of a person; see NOMEN SUUM.

Nomen recipere. To enter the name of an accused person in the official record. Through such an act a criminal trial, initiated by a formal accusation of an accuser (*nomen deferre, nominis delatio*), was instituted after an investigation had been made by an official organ. Syn. (later) *inter reos recipere.*—See ACCUSATIO.

> Taubenschlag, *RE* 17; Eger, *RE* (*receptio nominis*) 1A; Wlassak, *Anklage und Streitbefestigung im Kriminalrecht, SbWien* 184 (1917) 6.

Nomen suum. *Suo (proprio) nomine agere* = to act (to sue) for one's own sake, on behalf of oneself. Ant. *alieno nomine.*

Nomenclator. A slave whose duty was to remind his master canvassing for electoral votes of the names of influential persons. He used to accompany his master· in public during the electoral period.—See CANDIDATI.

> Bernert, *RE* 17; Fabia, *DS* 4.

Nomina arcaria. Entries in the cash-book of a Roman citizen concerning payments made from or to the cash-box (*arca*), primarily connected with loans given or repaid. The entries served as evidence that a debt had been contracted (e.g., through *stipulatio*), but they were not as such considered to constitute a literal contract, i.e., to create an obligation by themselves.

> Weiss, *RE* 17.

Nomina trans(s)cripticia. Entries (*transcriptiones*) in the cash-book of a Roman citizen stating debts owed to him and payments made thereon. Usually *transcriptiones* were made to convert a pre-existing debt into a literal contract which relieved the creditor from the burden of proving the origin of the debt. The essential elements of a *transcriptio* are the discharging of an old debt and the contracting of a new one. There were *transcriptiones a re in personam* (from the thing to a person) when the receipt of an old debt is entered and the same debtor is charged with a new entry, and *transcriptiones a persona in personam* (= from one person to another) when a debt still due is entered as owed by another person who assumed the debt of the former debtor. The *nomina transcripticia* comprised only money debts, the entries being made under a special system of bookkeeping and with the consent of the debtor. A *transcriptio* created an *obligatio litteris* (= a "literal" obligation) which substituted an earlier obligation originating from a sale, a partnership or another contract. Cash-books ceased to be used· by private individuals in the third post-Christian century, but they remained in use by the bankers.—See CODEX ACCEPTI ET EXPENSI, OBLIGATIO LITTERARUM (Bibl.), NOVATIO, EXPENSILATIO.

> Steinwenter, *RE* 13, 787; Kunkel, *RE* 4A, 1887; Weiss, *RE* 17; Huvelin, *DS* 4; Aru, *NDI* 3, 223; Platon, *NRHD* 33 (1909) 325; Appert, *RHD* 11 (1932) 639; Arangio-Ruiz, *St Redenti* 1 (1951) 12.

Nominare. To appoint (a guardian, an heir in a testament), to mention by name (*nominatim enumerare*). In criminal matters = to denounce, to accuse a person of a crime.—See NOMINATIO.

Nominatim. By name (to indicate a person by his name), exactly.—See EXHEREDARE, CONVENIRE, TUTELA TESTAMENTARIA.

> U. Robbe, *I postumi*, 1937, 232; Grosso, *SDHI* 7 (1941) 147; Lepri, *Scr Ferrini* 2 (Univ. Sacro Cuore, Milan, 1947) 107.

Nominatio. (In public law.) The presentation of candidates for magistracies to the senate by the emperor. Subsequently, the senate completed the election formally by a confirmation of the emperor's proposals. In the election of municipal magistrates which was effected by the people and in later times by the municipal council, the candidates designated by the highest municipal magistrates might propose (*nominare*) another candidate. With reference to elections in colleges of pontiffs, augurs, etc., *nominatio* meant the proposal of candidates by the members of the college. The election was made by the *comitia tributa* among the candidates nominated.

> Kübler, *RE* 17.

Nominatio auctoris. See LAUDARE AUCTOREM.

Nominatio potioris. A guardian who was appointed by a magistrate (in the absence of a testamentary tutor and one called by law, *tutor legitimus*) might, in later classical law, propose (*nominare*) another in his place as better qualified (*potior*) to serve the interests of the ward either because of his relationship with the ward or in virtue of his better financial position. A *nominatio potioris* was also possible in the field of public charges (see MUNERA) to the effect that a person summoned to assume a public service (*munera civilia*) could propose in his place a better qualified one. Details are unknown.—C. 10.67.

> Kübler, *RE* 17, 828; Sachers, *RE* 7A, 1534; Solazzi, *RISG* 54 (1914) 23.

Nominatio tutoris. In later classical law syn. with *datio tutoris.*—See TUTELA.

Nominator. A person who exercised his right of NOMINATIO by proposing another for tutorship or a magistracy (particularly in municipalities).—D. *27.7*; C. 11.34.—See NOMINATIO POTIORIS.

Nomine. (Abl.) On account of, for the sake of. The use of the word is very frequent in juristic language. It is connected with a noun in the genitive (*filii, domini, pupilli, emptoris, absentis,* etc.) denoting the person for whom one is acting or with an adjective (*alieno, suo, proprio, meo nomine*). See ALIENO NOMINE. The phrases refer primarily to acting as another's representative in court. Such relationship is more explicitly expressed by locutions such as *cognitorio, procuratorio nomine*; see COGNITOR, PROCURATOR. *Nomine alterius* may sometimes mean "because of another, for the fact done by another," as in the case of *actiones noxales* or the so-called *actiones adiecticiae qualitatis* (see EXERCITOR NAVIS). With regard to things or rights (e.g., *hereditatis, pignoris, ususfructus, usurarum nomine*) *nomine* is syn. with *alicuius rei causa* and *propter aliquam rem* (= because of), and indicates the title under which a person claims anything from another.

Nominis delatio. See ACCUSATIO.

Nomocanones. Compilations of ecclesiastical canons collated with the pertinent imperial constitutions excerpted from Justinian's codification, including the Novels. An extensive collection of this kind is the *Nomocanon Quinquaginta Titulorum* (in 50 titles), compiled probably in the first half of the seventh century, and dealing with ecclesiastical matters, marriage, penal law, and some procedural institutions (witnesses, oath). A similar collection is the *Nomocanon Quattuordecim Titulorum* (in 14 titles) which was several times revised, the last edition being by Theodoros Balsamon in the twelfth century). These Greek collections are of importance for textual reconstruction of a number of imperial constitutions.—See ANONYMUS.

> Editions: Voellus and Justellus, *Bibliotheca iuris canonici veteris* 2 (1869) 603, for N. 50 tit.; Pitra, *Juris eccles. historia et monumenta* 2 (1868) 433.—Zachariae v. Lingenthal, *Die griechischen N.*, Mem. Acad. St.-Petersbourg, Ser. 7, vol. 23 (1877); De Clercq, *Dictionnaire de droit canonique* 3 (1935) 1171.

Nomos georgikos. An official Byzantine compilation (in Greek) of the agrarian law of about the middle of the eighth century, "selected from Justinian books."

> Mortreuil, *Histoire du dr. byzantin* 1 (1843) 393; Zachariae v. Lingenthal, *Gesch. des griechisch-röm. Rechts*, 3rd ed. 1892, 249. Editions: Ferrini, *Byzantinische Ztschr.* 7 (1898) 558 (= *Opere* 1, 1929, 376); Ashburner, *The farmers' law*, Jour. of Hellenic St 30 (1910) 85.—A. Albertoni, *Per una esposizione del dir. bizantino*, 1927, 50; Bach, *ClMed* 5 (1942) 70; Dölger, *Fschr Wenger* 2 (1945) 18; De Malafosse, *Recueil de l'Acad. de Législation* 19 (Toulouse, 1949).

Nomos Rhodion nauticos. The maritime law of the Rhodians, "selected from Book 14 of the Digest," as the title of this official codification of the eighth century indicates.—See LEX RHODIA DE IACTU.

> Pardessus, *Les lois maritimes* 1 (1828) 231; J. B. Mortreuil, *Histoire du droit byzantin* 1 (1843) 398; Zachariae v. Lingenthal, *Gesch. des griechisch-röm. Rechts*, 3rd ed. 1892, 313; Dareste, *Études d'histoire de droit*, 3. sér. 1906, 93; W. Ashburner, *The Rhodian Sea Law*, 1909; A. Albertoni, *Per una esposizione del dir. bizantino*, 1927, 51; Siciliano-Villanueva, *Enciclopedia giur. ital.* 4 (1912) 41.

Nomos stratiotikos. An official Byzantine compilation of military law in wartime, published about the middle of the eighth century based primarily on legal sources of Justinian's time.

> J. B. Mortreuil, *Histoire du droit byzantin* 1 (1843) 388; Zachariae v. Lingenthal, *Geschichte der griechisch-röm. Rechts*, 3rd ed. 1892, 17; idem, *Byzant. Ztschr.* 2 (1893) 606, 3 (1894) 437.

Non liquet. See IURARE SIBI NON LIQUERE, AMPLIATIO.

Non· usus (non uti). Making no use, not exercising one's rights. The failure of a person, entitled to a servitude or a usufruct, to exercise his right over another's property during a specified period, might produce the loss of said right. With regard to a usufruct the prescriptive time was one year for movables, two years for immovables.—See USUCAPIO LIBERTATIS.

> Grosso, *Il Foro ital.*, 62 (1937) part IV, p. 266; B. Biondi, *Servitù prediali*, 1944, 191; Branca, *Scr Ferrini* 1 (Univ. Sacro Cuore, Milan, 1947) 169.

Nonnumquam. See INTERDUM.

> Guarneri-Citati, *Indice*[2] (1927) 61.

Norma. (In the language of postclassical and Justinian's constitutions.) A legal principle, a norm.

> Wenger, *Canon*, SbWien 220, 2 (1942) 70.

Noster (nostrum). What belongs to "us," what is "ours." "What is ours cannot be transferred to another without an act of ours" (D. 50.17.11).

Noster. When connected with an emperor in a juristic writing (*princeps noster, imperator noster*) it refers to the still reigning emperor. Such allusions allow us to establish the date of composition of a juristic work. Ant. DIVUS, which refers to an emperor no more alive.

Nostra urbs (civitas). In the works of the jurists this means Rome.

Nota censoria. The disqualification of a citizen decreed by the censors for bad behavior in family life, blameworthy treatment of children, clients, or slaves, neglect of sacred duties, living in luxury, or offenses against good faith in the exercise of the duties of a guardian or a partner. Similarly, misdemeanor in office, bribery of judges or magistrates, and many other offenses could be stigmatized by the *nota censoria* with the result that the individual censured would be removed from the senate or from the centuriate or tribal organizations (*tribu moveri*) or reduced to the status of an AERARIUS. The *notatus* was branded with ignominy (IGNOMINIA), but not with infamy (see INFAMIA), and he was therefore not excluded from military service, from judgeship in a civil trial, and, indeed, in certain circumstances he might even compete for a magistracy.—See REGIMEN MORUM, CEN-SORES, TRIBUS, SUBSCRIPTIO CENSORIA.

Kübler, *RE* 17; C. Castello, *Studi sul diritto familiare,* 1942, 85.

Nota consularis. The decree of a consul excluding a person from the competition for a magistracy, after examination of his personal and moral qualifications.

Notae. Stenographic symbols, shorthand writing. A testament in shorthand writing is not valid, because "*notae* are not letters" (D. 37.1.6.2). Only a soldier was permitted to make such a testament.—See EX-CEPTOR.

Notae. Commentatory annotations to the edition of a work of an earlier jurist. Such more or less exten-sively annotated editions often contained not only remarks of the annotator which at times did not agree with the opinion commented on, but also citations from other jurists and imperial constitutions. *Notae* were richly excerpted by the compilers of the Digest and indicated as such ("*Paulus notat,*" or simply by the name of the annotator). On the other hand, however, the compilers often adopted only the opin-ion of the commentator disregarding the original opinion of the jurist commented on. Many promi-nent jurists contributed *notae* to the works of their predecessors; some of the latter have remained ob-scure. Thus, for instance, Julian wrote *Notae* to two little known jurists, Minicius and Urseius Ferox. Among the most important *Notae* are those of Mar-cellus to the *Digesta* of Julian, and of Scaevola to the *Digesta* of Julian and Marcellus. Paul annotated works of several earlier jurists. The imperial legis-lation treated the notes by Ulpian and Paul to the works of Papinian (*in Papinianum*) in a rather strange fashion: they were invalidated by Constantine as "depraving" the jurist's opinions. This was seem-ingly a tribute to the great jurist Papinian and his work. The ban was repeated in the so-called Law of Citations (see IURISPRUDENTIA) although both Ulpian and Paul appear there among the distinguished jurists. Justinian, however, declared the *notae* in question valid and permitted their acceptance into the Digest.

Berger, *RE* 10, 727, 1175; Balogh, *Ét Girard* 2 (1913) 422; H. Krüger, *St Bonfante* 2 (1930) 303; Massei, *Scr Ferrini* (Univ. Pavia, 1946) 43; Sciascia, *AnCam* 16 (1942–44) 87; *idem, BIDR* 49–50 (1947) 410.

Notae iuris. A collection of abbreviations (by initials) of legal formulae and phrases used in the *legis ac-tiones,* the praetorian Edict and documents. The collection is generally (but not unanimously) ascribed to Valerius Probus, a grammarian of the second half of the first post-Christian century.

Edition: Baviera, *FIR* 1² (1940) 453.—P. F. Girard, *Mélanges* 1 (1912) 177; P. Krüger, *Mél Girard* 2 (1912); Orestano, *BIDR* 43 (1935) 186.

Notare. Used in all the meanings of *notae;* see the foregoing items. Hence *notare* = to remark, to com-ment on, to correct, to blame, to reprimand.

Sciascia, *BIDR* 49–50 (1948) 429.

Notarius. A person, usually a freedman or slave, skilled in shorthand writing; in the later Empire *notarius* is syn. with *scriba.* In the imperial chan-cery of the later Empire there was a confidential secretariat of the emperor, called *schola notariorum,* headed by the *primicerius notariorum.* His deputy had the title *tribunus et notarius.* Both were among the highest functionaries of the state.

Lengle, *RE* 6A, 2452; Morel, *RE* Suppl. 7, 586; Lécrivain, *DS* 4.

Nothus. (From the Greek *nothos.*) See SPURIUS. The term appears in literary (non juristic) works.

Lanfranchi, *StCagl* 30 (1946) 30.

Notio. The examination (investigation) of a case. The term refers sometimes also to jurisdiction, but generally the phrase *is cuius de ea re notio est* means the official (magistrate) competent to examine the controversy in question.

Falletti, *Évolution de la jurisdiction civile,* 1916, 143.

Notitia. Knowledge. The word appears in the defini-tion of IURISPRUDENTIA as "the knowledge of divine and human matters" (*divinarum atque humanarum rerum notitia,* D. 1.1.10.2). Ulpian attributes to the jurists *notitia boni et aequi* (D. 1.1.1.2).—See IUS EST ARS BONI ET AEQUI.

Notitia. (In later imperial constitutions.) A list, a catalogue. To an imperial constitution of A.D. 337 (C. 10.66.1) a *notitia* (= *brevis*) was annexed enu-merating professionals who were exempt from public charges (*munera*).—See LATERCULUM.

Notitia dignitatum. A list "of all high offices, both civil and military, in the Eastern (*Oriens*) and West-ern (*Occidens*) parts" of the Empire. The list con-tains the titles of the high functionaries, those of their staff officers, an enumeration of military units and their garrisons, and besides, illustrations of civil and military insignia. The work is ascribed to the end of the fourth or the beginning of the fifth century.

Editions: O. Seeck, *N.d.,* 1876. E. Böcking, in two vol. (1839, 1853); Polaschek, *RE* 17; Mattingly, *OCD;* Bury, *JRSt* 10 (1920) 133; Lot, *Rev. des Études anciennes,* 25 (1923); Salisbury, *JRSt* 17 (1927) 192.

Notoria. A written denunciation of a crime, made by a police official or a private informer (*nuntiator*).—See INDICIUM, NUNTIATORES.

Novae clausulae. New rules added by a praetor to the edict of his predecessor. Such a new clause is ascribed to the jurist Julian inserted on the occasion of his codification of the praetorian Edict (see EDIC-TUM PERPETUUM). It is known as *nova clausula de coniungendis cum emancipato liberis eius,* and con-cerns the succession on intestacy of an emancipated son. If his children had remained under the paternal power of his father when he was emancipated, his share was divided into two halves of which he re-ceived one and his children the other.—D. 37.8.—See EMANCIPATIO.

Weiss, *RE* 17 (*s.v. nova clausula Iuliani*); Cosentini, *St Solazzi* 1948.

Novatio. The transformation and transfer of a former obligation into a new one (D. 46.2.1 pr.), i.e., an existing obligation is extinguished and substituted by a new one. *Novatio* was performed by the way of a *stipulatio* (later through *nomen transcripticium*, see NOMINA TRANSCRIPTICIA) comprising the same debt, *idem debitum*, although changes in persons and terms were admitted. It made no difference from what kind of a contract the previous obligation arose. An obligation originating in a testament could also be renewed by a *stipulatio*. The persons participating in a *novatio* could be different from those between whom the former obligation existed, since either a new creditor in the place of the former one, or a new debtor might intervene. See EXPROMITTERE, DELEGATIO. Through the extinction of the previous obligation the sureties therefor became released and securities ceased to be pledged unless they were extended by agreement of the parties to the new obligation. According to a widespread opinion it was Justinian's law which set the requirement that a *novatio* was valid only when the parties had the intention to make a *novatio* (*animus novandi*). The concept may have been frequently interpolated indeed, although it is hardly conceivable that in the developed classical law, when the abstract nature of the *stipulatio* was no more of its former strength, the intention of the parties might have been completely neglected. The term *novandi causa*, which appears in classical texts, alludes clearly to the intention of the contracting parties. The institution was profoundly reformed by Justinian and substantial interpolations obscured its development in the classical period.— D. 46.2; C. 8.41.—See ACCEPTILATIO, OBLIGATIO NATURALIS.

Weiss, *RE* 17; Last, *GrZ* 37 (1910) 450; Vassalli, *BIDR* 27 (1914) 222; Bohaček, *AnPal* 11 (1924) 341; Kaden, *ZSS* 44 (1924) 164; Koschaker, *Fschr Hanausek* 1925, 118; P. Nègre, *Les conditions d'existence et de validité de la n.*, Thèse Aix, 1925; Scialoja, *St Perozzi* 1925, 407; Guarneri-Citati. *Mél Cornil* 1 (1926) 432; Thorens, *La n. conditionnelle*, Thèse Lausanne, 1927; Cornil, *Mél Fournier* 1929, 87; Meylan, *ACII* 1 (1935) 281; A. Hägerström, *Der röm. Obligationsbegriff*, 2 (Uppsala, 1941) Beil., p. 199; B. Staehelin, *Die N.* (*Basler Studien zur Rechtsgesch.* 23, 1948); Daube, *ZSS* 66 (1948) 90; Sanfilippo, *AnCat* 3 (1948–49) 225; Beretta, *Scr Ferrini* 1 (Univ. Sacro Cuore, Milan, 1947) 77; F. Bonifacio, *La novazione nel dir. rom.,* 1950.

Novella constitutio (lex). A recent imperial constitution. The term appears already in the fourth century after Christ and is also applied to the constitutions issued by Theodosius II after the promulgation of his Code (see CODEX THEODOSIANUS) and by his successors until A.D. 472 ("Post-Theodosian Novels"). They generally are edited as an appendix to the Theodosian Code.—See NOVELLAE POSTTHEODOSIANAE.

Novellae Iustiniani. (*Sc. constitutiones.*) Justinian's constitutions (= Novels) promulgated after the sec-

ond edition of his Code (see CODEX IUSTINIANUS), in the period between A.D. 534 and 556. They were not edited by him as a supplement to the Code (what they really were) although he had the intention to do it (*alia congregatio novellarum constitutionum,* Const. *Cordi* 4). The Novels are known from three collections, (*a*) *Epitome Iuliani,* containing 122 Novels, until 555, (*b*) *Authenticum* (*liber Authenticorum*) with 134 Novels, from A.D. 535 until 556, and a Latin translation of the Novels written in Greek, and (*c*) a collection of 168 novels, compiled under Tiberius II (578–582) containing also four constitutions by Justin II and three by Tiberius II. Most Novels are issued in Greek, some in Latin and Greek, some only in Latin, in particular those which were addressed to the Western part of the Empire or contained supplementary provisions to earlier Latin constitutions.—See AUTHENTICUM.

Edition: Vol. 3 of the stereotype edition of the *Corpus Iuris Civilis* (by Mommsen-Krüger-Schoell), fifth ed. by Schoell-Kroll, 1928.—Steinwenter, *RE* 17, 1164; Anon., *DS* 4; Cuq, *NRHD* 28 (1904) 265; P. Noailles, *Les collections des Novelles de l'empereur Justinien. Origine et formation sous Justinien,* 1912; idem, *La Collection grecque de 168 Novelles,* 1914; E. Stein, *St Bizantini e Neoellenici* 5 (1930) 709; idem, *Bull. de l'Acad. de Belgique, Cl Lettres* 23 (1937) 383.

Novellae post-Iustinianae. (Of the Byzantine emperors after Justinian.) These are quite numerous. Of great importance are the Novels of the Emperor Leo the Wise (886–911).

Editions: Zachariae v. Lingenthal, *Ius Graeco-Romanum* 3 (1857); J. and P. Zepos, *Ius Graeco-Romanum,* 1 (1931); H. Monnier, *Les Novelles de Léon le Sage,* 1923; P. Noailles and A. Dain, *Les Novelles de Léon VI le Sage,* 1944.—A. Albertoni, *Per una esposizione del dir. bizantino,* 1927, 47, 57; G. Ferrari, *Il dir. penale nelle Novelle di Leone il Filosofo, Riv. penale,* 67 (1908).

Novelles post-Theodosianae. See NOVELLA CONSTITUTIO.

Steinwenter, *RE* 17, 1163; Anon., *DS* 4; Scherillo, *NDI* 8, 1139; idem, *St Besta* 1 (1939) 295.—Translation in C. Pharr, *The Theodosian Code* (Princeton, 1952) 487.

Novicius (servus). (Syn. *mancipium novicium.*) A young slave. Since he generally is more valuable than an older slave (*veterator, veteranum mancipium*) the aedilician edict provided that a fraudulent sale of an older slave to whom the appearance of a younger one was given could be rescinded by an action of the buyer who had also the choice to sue only for the restitution of a part of the price.

Novus. See IUS NOVUM, OPERIS NOVI NUNTIATIO, NOVAE CLAUSULAE, IUSTINIANI NOVI.

Noxa. Syn. both with *delictum* (hence a penalty, *poena,* is a revenge for a *noxa*) and *damnum,* damage (hence *noxam sarcire* = *damnum solvere, praestare,* to indemnify). Besides, *noxa* may indicate also the "body which inflicted the damage" (Inst. 4.8.1), and finally the indemnification itself. In these various meanings the term is used in a limited field of the liability of a master of a slave or a father of a son for offenses committed by the slave or the son. The liability was alternative, either to pay the damages or to surrender the offender to the person injured. The latter claimed reparation for the injury sustained through the pertinent action which lay for the offense committed (*actio furti, iniuriarum, legis Aquiliae, vi bonorum raptorum,* etc.) and which was termed *actio noxalis* when directed against the master or the father. In Justinian's law the noxal liability of the father did not exist any more. Since the son was able to possess property of his own, he could be sued directly. On the principle of noxal liability were also based *interdicta noxalia,* applicable only in the case of an INTERDICTUM DE VI and INTERDICTUM QUOD VI AUT CLAM. —Handing over a domestic animal which had caused damage to another is analogous to the cases mentioned beforehand; see ACTIO DE PAUPERIE.—See SCIENTIA DOMINI and the following items.—Inst. 4.8; D. 9.4; C. 3.41.

Lisowski, *RE* Suppl. 7, 587, 604; Cuq, *DS* 4; Biondi, *NDI* 8; Berger, *RE* 9, 1624; Biondi, *AnPal* 10 (1925); *idem, BIDR* 36 (1928) 99; Beseler, *ZSS* 46 (1926) 104; Lenel, *ZSS* 47 (1927); Branca, *StUrb* 11 (1937) 98; De Visscher, *RHD* 9 (1930) 411; *idem, Le régime romain de la noxalité,* 1947; *idem, Symb van Oven,* 1947, 306; G. I. Luzzatto, *Per una ipotesi sull'obbligazione romana* (1934) 64, 102; Daube, *CambLJ* 7 (1939) 23; M. Sargenti, *Contributo allo studio della responsabilità nossale (Pubblicazioni Univ. Pavia,* 104) 1949; M. Kaser, *Das altröm. Ius,* 1949, 223; Pugliese, *St Carnelutti* 2 (1950) 115.

Noxa caput sequitur (D. 9.1.1.12). Noxal liability (see NOXA) followed the person of the offender when his dependence upon another's power underwent a change. When after the wrong was committed, the slave or the son came under the power of another person, the liability of the master (or father), at the moment of the wrongdoing, was transferred to the master or father at the time when the noxal suit was brought in. Consequently, if the slave was manumitted in the meantime or the son became independent (*sui iuris*), there was no longer any noxal action, but a direct action against the wrongdoer himself.

Lisowski, *RE* Suppl. 7, 601; De Visscher, *Noxalité* (1947) 147.

Noxa solutus. Released from noxal responsibility.

Noxae datio, deditio (dare, dedere). Handing over (surrendering) the slave who committed the wrongdoing for which his master was liable, was achieved by the transfer of the ownership of the slave to the plaintiff of the noxal action. The *noxae datio* of a son was performed by the *mancipatio* of the son (*ex noxali causa mancipio dare*). The son became thus not a slave of the injured person, but a person *in mancipio* (*in causa mancipii*); see MANCIPIUM.—See NOXA (Bibl.), SCIENTIA DOMINI.

De Visscher, *RHD* 9 (1930) 411; Frezza, *SDHI* 5 (1939) 185.

Noxam committere. To inflict a damage, to commit a private crime (*delictum*).

Noxia. Syn. with NOXA. The rare term occurs a few times in the Twelve Tables.

Noxiam sarcire. See NOXA. Originally (in the Twelve Tables) = to repair the damage done by restitution in kind, not by compensation in money.

M. Kaser, *Das altröm. Ius,* 1949, 219; Daube, *St Solazzi* 1948, 7, 61.

Noxius. A slave or son who committed a wrongdoing for which his master or father bears the noxal liability; see NOXA. Generally, one who committed a crime.

Nubere. To marry. See MATRIMONIUM. *Nubere* is often mentioned as a condition upon which a liberality (a donation, a legacy) is depending, as, e.g., "if he (she) will marry" or "if he (she) will not marry X (a certain person)." The condition to marry a specific person was valid if the individual was an honest person. If he was *indignus* (= unworthy, despicable) the condition was considered not binding. This was also the case when a condition to remain unmarried was imposed.

Nubilis. A girl capable of marriage. Syn. *viripotens.* —See IMPUBES.

Nuda cautio. See CAUTIO. Ant. SATISDATIO.

Nuda conventio. An agreement by which a person assumes an obligation without giving a real security or a surety. A mere agreement is also an agreement which is not accompanied by the delivery of the thing involved.

Nuda pactio. See NUDUM PACTUM.

Nuda proprietas (nudum dominium). Mere ownership, i.e., when the owner has no right to use the object or to take the fruits thereof because these rights are vested in another either by a contract or through a personal servitude (see USUS, USUSFRUCTUS).—C. 7.25.

M. Pampaloni, *Mél Girard* 2 (1912) 337.

Nuda repromissio. See CAUTIO, SATISDATIO.

Nuda res. A thing itself, as opposed to proceeds and accessories thereof.

Nuda stipulatio. See CAUTIO.

Nuda traditio. A simple handing over of a thing to another without any just ground (*iusta causa*).—See TRADITIO.

Nuda voluntas. A mere, formless expression of will not accompanied by the delivery of the thing which is the object of a legal act.—See ADITIO HEREDITATIS.

Nudum dominium. See NUDA PROPRIETAS.

Nudum ius Quiritium. See DOMINIUM DUPLEX, DOMINIUM EX IURE QUIRITIUM. One who has a mere ownership *ex iure Quiritium* of a thing (e.g., of a slave) without holding it, because another is entitled to hold it, "has less right in it than a usufructuary or a possessor in good faith (POSSESSOR BONAE FIDEI)," Gaius 3.166. In a constitution of Justinian (C. 7.25.1) the term *nudum ius Quiritium* is qualified as "an empty and superfluous word."—See IN BONIS ESSE.

Nudum pactum (nuda pactio). A simple, formless agreement as opposed to *stipulatio* and *contractus*. A *nudum pactum* does not create an obligation but an exception (D. 2.14.7.4).—See PACTUM.

Nudus. Deprived of means.—For *nudus* with regard to certain legal institutions, see the foregoing and the following items.

Nudus consensus. See CONSENSUS.

Nudus usus. The right (a servitude) to use another's thing but not the proceeds (*fructus*) thereof.

Nullius momenti esse. See MOMENTUM.

Nullus. Nobody, no one (= *nemo*), not existing. With regard to legal acts or transactions *nullus* means invalid, void.—See RES NULLIUS.

Hellman, *ZSS* 23 (1902) 425.

Numen. Divinity. *Numen nostrum* ("our divinity") is often used by later emperors in their constitutions.

Ensslin, *Gottkaiser, SbMünch* 1943, 3rd issue.

Numerare pecuniam. To repay a debt in cash. *Pecunia numerata* = a cash payment. *Numerare pretium* = to pay the price of a thing purchased in cash.—See EXCEPTIO NON NUMERATAE PECUNIAE, QUERELA NON NUMERATAE PECUNIAE.

Numeratio pecuniae. A cash payment.

Numerarius. An accountant or auditor in higher imperial offices of the later Empire.—C. 12.49.

Ensslin, *RE* 17; 6A, 1870.

N(umerius) N(egidius). See A(ULUS) AGERIUS.

Numeri. Military units of infantry or cavalry, composed of soldiers recruited in provinces for service on the boundaries of the state. Their commander was the *tribunus numeri.*—See AUXILIA. *In numeris* = in military service.

Rowell, *RE* 17, 1327; Vittinghoff, *Historia* 1 (Baden-Baden, 1951) 390.

Numerus. See RES QUAE PONDERE NUMERO, etc.

Nummaria poena. A fine. See MULTA, POENA PECUNIARIA. Criminal matters in which the culprit was punished with a pecuniary fine = *nummariae res.*

Nummularius. The owner of a small bank, primarily for money-changing transactions. See ARGENTARII, MENSULARIUS, MENSA NUMMULARIA, TESSERA NUMMULARIA.—*Nummularii* were also officials of the mint (*officina monetae*) who were concerned with the test of coins.—See MONETA.—C. 11.18.

Herzog, *RE* 17; Laum, *RE* Suppl. 4, 75; Saglio and Humbert, *DS* 1 (*s.v. argentarii*); Voigt, *ASächGW* 10 (1880); Mitteis, *ZSS* 19 (1898) 203.

Nummus. A coin, a *sestertius*; in the later Empire the smallest copper coin. *In nummis* = in cash.—See FALSA MONETA, CORPUS.

Schwabacher, *RE* 17.

Nummus unus. A sale (or lease) in which the buyer (lessee) paid a fictitious price (rent) in the form of a small sum of money (*nummo uno* = for one piece of money) in order to disguise a donation prohibited by the law, was void.—See DONATIO, MANCIPATIO NUMMO UNO, SESTERTIUS.

Nuncupatio (nuncupare). A solemn oral declaration before witnesses. It was an essential part of the ancient acts (*negotia*) *per aes et libram* and had to be expressed in prescribed words. In a testament *per aes et libram* the *nuncupatio* contained the dispositions of the testator to be executed by a man worthy of his confidence, the FAMILIAE EMPTOR. The pertinent rule was expressed in the Twelve Tables (*uti lingua nuncupassit* = as one has disposed orally). —See MANCIPATIO, NEXUM, PER AES ET LIBRAM, TESTAMENTUM PER NUNCUPATIONEM.

Düll, *RE* 17; Anon., *NDI* 8; Cuq, *DS* 5 (*s.v. testamentum*); Sanfilippo, *AnPal* 17 (1937) 147; P. Noailles, *Du droit sacré au droit civil*, 1950, 300; Solazzi, *SDHI* 18 (1952) 213.

Nundinae. A market, a fair; the period of time (eight days) between two consecutive markets. *Nundinae* were frequently fixed as a term for the payment of money debts. According to one opinion such payment could be demanded by the creditor on the first day, while other jurists held that the payment could be made during the whole eight-day-period.—D. 50.11; C. 4.60.

Kroll, *RE* 17; Besnier, *DS* 4.

Nuntiare fisco. To denounce to the fisc a person holding property due to the fisc or obligated to make payments to the fisc. In a monograph on fiscal law by the jurist CALLISTRATUS there is a long list of cases which had to be denounced by private individuals to the fisc in its interest, primarily in matters of successions when the fisc might claim an inheritance. Other instances of such denunciations were the discovery of a treasure (see THESAURUS), fines to be paid to the fisc, etc. (D. 49.14.1 pr.). Such fiscal denunciations were frequently made in order to receive a reward (*praemii consequendi causa*). In criminal matters *nuntiare* = *denuntiare.*—See DELATORES, DEFERRE FISCO, DENUNTIATIO, CADUCA.

Berger, *RE* 17, 1475; Solazzi, *BIDR* 49–50 (1948) 405.

Nuntiatio operis novi. See OPERIS NOVI NUNTIATIO.

Nuntiator. (In criminal and fiscal matters.) A denouncer. Syn. DENUNTIATOR.—*Nuntiator* = one who protested against a new construction; see OPERIS NOVI NUNTIATIO.—*Nuntiator* also was the title of an official of a lower rank in the later Empire who publicly announced a felicitous event (e.g., the victorious end of a war). He was prohibited from accepting immoderate gifts.—C. 12.63.

Berger, *RE* 17, 1475; 18, 559.

Nuntius. A messenger. Declarations of will through the medium of a messenger were valid as were those made by letter (*per epistulam*) except in cases in which one had to give the declaration personally (as in a *stipulatio*, in acts concluded *per aes et libram*).

Carboni, *Sul concetto di n., Scr Chironi* 1 (1915); Düll, *ZSS* 67 (1950) 163.

Nuptiae. Almost completely syn. with *matrimonium* in juristic language. It is apparently the earlier term for marriage and is more related to the wedding ceremony than *matrimonium*.—Inst. 1.10; D. 23.2; C. 5.4; 8.—See MATRIMONIUM, VOTA MATRIMONII, CONCUBITUS.

Ehrhardt, *RE* 17. For further bibl. see MATRIMONIUM.

Nuptiae incestae. A marriage concluded between persons who are prohibited to marry because of near blood relationship or affinity. The marriage is not valid, the wife is no *uxor* and the children are illegitimate (*spurii*).—See INCESTUS.

Lombardi, *Ricerche in tema di ius gentium*, 1946, 25.

Nuptiae secundae. See SECUNDAE NUPTIAE.

Nuptialis. Pertinent to a marriage, e.g., *tabulae, instrumentum*.

Nutrire. To nourish, to rear.—See ALIMENTA.

Nutritor. A nourisher, a foster parent. The term refers primarily to persons who sustained with nourishment (and education) a child not of their own (a foundling). A *nutritor* "has no successorial rights of succession either under *ius civile* or *honorarium*" (C. 6.59.10).—See ALUMNUS.

Nutus. A wink, a sign. Under certain circumstances it might be considered as a valid expression of will, sufficient even for leaving a *fideicommissum*.—See MUTUS.

O

Obicere. To oppose a counter-claim to the claim of the plaintiff.

Obicere bestiis. To expose to wild beasts a criminal condemned to death *ad bestias* (= to fight with them). Syn. *subicere*.

Obicere crimen. To charge a person with a crime.

Obicere exceptionem. To oppose an exception in a civil trial.—See EXCEPTIO.

Oblatio. (From *offerre*.) An offer (to pay a debt, to give a security, to pay the estimated value of a thing). *Oblatio votorum*, see VOTA.

Oblatio curiae. See LEGITIMATIO PER OBLATIONEM CURIAE.

Obligare. To tie around, to bind, in a moral and legal sense.

Obligare rem. To "bind" a thing by the tie of a real security (*pignus, hypotheca*). Syn. *pignerare*, if the thing is given to a creditor as a PIGNUS. Hence *obligatus* (e.g., *fundus, ager, res, aedes*), with or without the addition of *iure pignoris* (*hypothecae*) = a thing given as a *pignus* or charged with a hypothec.

Brasiello, *RIDA* 4 (= *Mél De Visscher* 3, 1950) 203.

Obligari (se obligare). To assume an obligation. For *obligari civiliter* (*naturaliter*), see OBLIGATIO CIVILIS (OBLIGATIO NATURALIS). *Obligari actione* = to be suable by a specific action.—See OBSTRINGI ACTIONE.

G. Segrè, *St Bonfante* 3 (1930) 501.

Obligatio. (From *obligare*.) Refers to both legal obligations and moral duties. The definition of *obligatio* in the legal field, in Justinian's Institutes, which obviously goes back to a classical writing, says: "*obligatio* is a legal tie (*vinculum*) by which we are forcibly bound (*adstringimur*) to pay a certain thing (*alicuius solvendae rei*) according to the laws of our nation" (Inst. 3.13 pr.). "The substance of an *obligatio* consists in binding (*obstringere*) another person to give us (*dare*) something, to do (*facere*) or to perform (*praestare*) something" (D. 44.7.3). *Praestare* comprehends any performance by the debtor which is not a *dare* or *facere*, in particular, a payment of a penalty in the case of a private wrongdoing (*delictum*), an additional liability, as, e.g., that of a seller or a lessor in the case of eviction, the liability for *dolus* and *culpa*, etc. Both definitions are not fully satisfactory, but they reflect the essential element of the tie (binding) expressed in the term *ob-ligari* (= to be tied around, *obstringi, adstringi*). *Obligationes* arose from wrongdoings (*ex delicto*) the wrongdoer being obligated to pay a penalty to the injured person, and from contracts (*ex contractu*) when one party or both parties assumed obligations through agreement; see CONTRACTUS. To embrace other kinds of obligations which did not originate either in an agreement or in a crime, as, e.g., from the management of another's affairs without authorization (see NEGOTIORUM GESTIO), from the administration of a ward's property by a guardian, from the payment of a non-existing debt (see INDEBITUM), from a LEGATUM PER DAMNATIONEM, and the like, a comprehensive term *variae causarum figurae* (= various forms of causes, D. 44.7.1 pr.) was used, a vague expression without any juristic content. Nor much better are the two new categories created by Justinian (Inst. 3.13.2): obligations "which arise *quasi ex contractu*" and "*quasi ex delicto* (*maleficio*)," although the pertinent liabilities were known already in classical times. As to the object of an *obligatio* (*dare, facere, non facere*), the fundamental requirements were the natural possibility of its fulfillment (see IMPOSSIBILIUM NULLA OBLIGATIO), the absence of a content which was against good customs (*contra bonos mores*), illicit (*illicitus*) or immoral, and finally, a precise definition of the debtor's duties, either from the origin, through later events, or through the arbitration by a third person. An obligation, the determination of which was completely left to the debtor or to the creditor was not admissible. The terminology for the extinction of an obligation alludes again to the binding "tie"; see SOLUTIO (= loosing, unbinding), LIBERATIO (= setting free). For the various sources of obligations (contracts, delicts, etc.), see the pertinent items.—Inst. 3.13; 14; 21; 22; 27; 29; 4.5; D. 44.7; C. 4.10.—See MORA, ACTIONES IN PERSONAM, PERPETUATIO, NOVATIO, IUS VARIANDI, and the following items.

Radin, *RE* 17; Huvelin, *DS* 4; Brasiello, *NDI* 8 (Bibl. 1196); Perozzi, *Obbligazioni rom.*, 1903 (= *Scr.giur.* 2, 1948, 313); *idem, Obbligazioni ex delicto* (= *Scr.giur.* 2, 1948, 441, ex 1915–16); Marchi, *BIDR* 25 (1912), 29 (1916); Cornil, *Mél Girard* 1 (1912); *idem, St Bonfante* 3 (1930) 41; G. Pacchioni, *Concetto e origine dell'obbligazione rom.*, Append. to the Ital. translation of Savigny, *Das Obligationenrecht*, 1912; P. De Francisci, *Synallagma, Storia e dottrina dei contratti innominati*, 1–2 (1913, 1916); Betti, *St Pavia* 1920; *idem, AG* 93 (1925) 272; Arangio-Ruiz, *Mél Cornil* 1 (1926) 83; A. Hägerström, *Der röm. Obligationsbegriff* 1 (1927), 2 (1943); G. Segrè, *St Bonfante* 3 (1930) 499; Biondi, *ACSR* 1931, 3, 251; Leifer, *KrVj* 26 (1933); G. I. Luzzatto, *Per un'ipotesi sulle origini e la natura delle obblig. rom.*, 1934; Lauria, *SDHI* 4 (1938); Albertario, *Studi* 3 (1936) 1; De Martino, *SDHI* 6 (1940) 132; L. Maillet, *Le théorie de Schuld et Haftung en dr. rom.*, Thèse Aix-en-Provence, 1944; Arangio-Ruiz, *Fschr Wenger* 2 (1945) 56; Pflüger, *ZSS* 65 (1947) 121; G. Sciascia, *Lineamenti del sistema obligatorio rom.*, 1947; M. Kaser, *Das altröm. Ius*, 1949, 188; J. Macqueron, *Cours de dr. rom. 2. Les obligations* 1949; F. Pastori, *Profilo dogmatico e storico dell'obbligazione rom.*, 1951; Biscardi, *StSen* 63 (1951) 40; v. Lübtow, *Betrachtungen zum Gajanischen Obligationenschema, ACIVer* 3 (repr. 1951) 241; A. de la Chevalerie, *Observations sur la classification des obligations chez Gaius, ADO-RIDA* 1 (1952) 379.

Obligatio civilis. Used in a double meaning: (*a*) an obligation under *ius civile* as opposed to obligations recognized only by the IUS HONORARIUM (*obligatio praetoria, honoraria*); (*b*) an obligation suable by an action (civil or praetorian) as opposed to an *obligatio naturalis*, not enforceable by an action at all.—See OBLIGATIO NATURALIS.

Obligatio condicionalis. (Syn. *sub condicione.*) An obligation the existence of which depends upon the fulfillment of a condition. The obligation does not exist until the condition is materialized. The legal situation became complicated when the debtor died in the meantime or when the thing eventually due perished. Such cases are dealt with in the sources, but the decisions are not uniform.—See CONDICIO.

Vassalli, *RISG* 56 (1915) 195; Bohacek, *AnPal* 11 (1923) 329; Seckel-Levy, *ZSS* 47 (1927) 168; Riccobono, *St Perozzi* 1925, 349; Beseler, *TR* 10 (1930) 233; Flume, *TR* 14 (1936) 19.

Obligatio consensu contracta. See CONSENSUS.

Obligatio ex contractu. An obligation arising from a contract. The *obligatio* is unilateral when only one of the contracting parties assumes an obligation (as, e.g., in a *mutuum*, a loan). Bilateral obligations arise when both parties assume reciprocal, but different obligations.—See CONTRACTUS, CONTRACTUS INNOMINATI, and the entries dealing with the various contracts.

Obligatio ex delicto (maleficio). An obligation arising from a wrongdoing by which harm was done to a private person; see DELICTUM, FURTUM, RAPINA, INIURIA, DAMNUM INIURIA DATUM, LEX AQUILIA, ACTIONES POENALES.—Inst. 4.1.

Ferrini, *NDI* 6, 657; V. Meltzl, *Die Obligation im Zeichen des Delikts*, 1909; E. Costa, *Le obbligazioni ex de-*

licto, 1909; F. De Visscher, *Études* (1931) 255; F. Albertario, *Studi* 3 (1936) 88, 99; Lavaggi, *SDHI* 13–14, 1948, 141.

Obligatio honoraria. See OBLIGATIO CIVILIS.

E. Albertario, *Studi* 3 (1936) 31.

Obligatio in solidum. See DUO REI PROMITTENDI.

Obligatio iudicati. See IUDICATUM.

Obligatio litterarum (litteris contracta). See LITTERARUM OBLIGATIO, NOMINA TRANSCRIPTICIA.—Inst. 3.21.

Obligatio naturalis. An obligation, the fulfillment of which cannot be enforced by an action. The creditor has no means to compel the debtor to pay his debt. Ant. *obligatio civilis.* An *obligatio naturalis*, however, was not deprived of legal effects among which the most important was that the payment made by the debtor was valid and could not be claimed back by him through *condictio indebiti* because an *obligatio naturalis* was after all a *debitum* (a debt) and not an *indebitum*. An *obligatio naturalis* could be the object of a NOVATIO and a surety (FIDEIUSSOR) could guarantee the fulfillment thereof. *Obligationes naturales* were the obligations contracted by a slave (towards his master, another slave, or another person) or by a *filius familias* under paternal power (towards his *pater familias* or another *filius familias* under the same paternal power). A *filius familias* sued for the repayment of debt (a loan) could oppose an *exceptio Senatusconsulti Macedoniani*. New instances of *obligatio naturalis* were added in later and Justinian's law.—See DONATIO, SENATUSCONSULTUM MACEDONIANUM.

Gradenwitz, *Fg Schirmer* 1900, 137; H. Siber, *N.O., Leipziger rechtswiss. Studien* 11, 1925; Beseler, *TR* 8 (1928) 319; Lauria, *RISG* 1 (1926); Vazny, *St Bonfante* 4 (1931) 131; W. Flume, *Studien zur Akzessorietät der röm. Bürgschaftsstipulationen*, 1932, 70; Albertario, *St* 3 (1936) 55; *idem, SDHI* 4 (1938) 529; Maschi, *Concezione naturalistica*, 1937, 121, 348; De Villa, *StSas* 17 (1939) 85, 185; 18 (1940) 13; *idem, Le usurae ex pacto*, 1937; Di Marzo, *St Calisse* 1 (1940) 75; Levy, *Natural law* (*Univ. Notre Dame Natural Law Proceedings* 2, 1949, 62 (= *SDHI* 15, 1949, 15); G. E. Longo, *SDHI* 16 (1950) 86.

Obligatio post mortem. An obligation which had to become effective after the death of the promisor (e.g., a *stipulatio "post mortem meam"* creating an obligation on the part of the heir). Such a promise was not valid since according to an ancient rule "an obligation could not begin (*incipere* = to come into existence) in the person of an heir" (Gaius 3.100). Justinian admitted such obligations. An obligation *"cum moriar"* (= when I shall be dying), however, was valid because it was held that the obligation referred to the last moment of the debtor's life. See DIES MORTIS, MANDATUM POST MORTEM, STIPULATIO POST MORTEM, ADSTIPULATIO.

Scheltema, *Rechtsgeleerd Magazijn* 57 (1938) 380; G. Segrè, *BIDR* 32 (1922) 286; Solazzi, *Iura* 1 (1950) 49.

Obligatio praetoria. See OBLIGATIO CIVILIS.

Obligatio principalis. The obligation of a principal as opposed to that of a surety, or the obligation of a defendant which existed before LITIS CONTESTATIO as opposed to that after *litis contestatio* in a trial in which the creditor claimed the payment.

Obligatio quasi ex contractu. (I.e., *quae quasi ex contractu nascitur* = which arises as if from an agreement). An obligation arising from a situation which resembles one originating from a contract, but is not a contractual one because of the absence of an accord between the parties involved, as, e.g., in the case of NEGOTIORUM GESTIO, LEGATUM PER DAMNATIONEM, the payment of a non-existing debt (*indebitum*), *communio incidens,* guardianship, etc.—Inst. 3.27.—See OBLIGATIO.

　Riccobono, *AnPal* 3–4 (1917) 263.

Obligatio quasi ex delicto (maleficio). An obligation arising from an illicit act which is not qualified as a *delictum* (*quasi ex delicto debere, teneri*) but which nevertheless creates a liability, at times even for another's doings. Instances of such obligations are that of a IUDEX QUI LITEM SUAM FACIT, liability for *deiecta, effusa, posita, suspensa* from one's house or dwellings (see ACTIO DE DEIECTIS).—Inst. 4.5.

　G. A. Palazzo, *Obbligazioni quasi ex d.,* 1919; Y. Chastaignet, *La notion de quasi délit,* Thèse Bordeaux, 1927.

Obligatio re contracta. An obligation which originates from a contract concluded *re,* i.e., by handing over a thing to the future debtor.—See CONTRACTUS, COMMODATUM, DEPOSITUM, MUTUUM, PIGNUS.

　Brasiello, *St Bonfante* 2 (1930) 541.

Obligatio rei. See OBLIGARE REM.

Obligatio verborum (verbis contracta). An obligation assumed through the pronunciation of solemn, prescribed words.—Inst. 3.15; D. 45.1.—See CONTRACTUS, STIPULATIO, DICTIO DOTIS, IURATA PROMISSIO LIBERTI.

Obligationes mutuae. See MUTUAE PETITIONES.

Obligatus. (With regard to persons.) Bound by a contractual or delictual obligation; with regard to things (*ager, fundus, aedes, res, bona, fructus,* etc.) = given as a pledge (PIGNUS) to the creditor or hypothecated (see HYPOTHECA).—See OBLIGARE REM, OBLIGATIO.

Obnoxius. One who is responsible for damages (*damnum, noxa*) done to another; in a broader sense syn. with *obligatus.* With regard to criminal matters = one guilty of a crime (*obnoxius criminis*).

Obnuntiatio. Higher magistrates used to give notice (*obnuntiare*) to plebeian tribunes of unfavorable celestial signs which were considered as a bad prognostic for popular assemblies convoked or already commenced. Consequently, the gathering had to be revoked or interrupted.

　Weinstock, *RE* 17; Bouché-Leclercq, *DS* 1, 582.

Obreptio. (From *obrepere.*) Surreptitious concealing of true facts in order to obtain an advantage, in particular, to provoke a favorable decision (rescript) of the emperor. The term *subreptio* (*subrepere*) has a similar meaning and refers rather to telling a falsehood for the same purpose. If one succeeded in obtaining an imperial rescript based on false allegations made by himself, his adversary in the trial proves the untruth of the pertinent facts and the presence of an *obreptio,* which led to a dismissal of the plaintiff's claim.

Obrogare legem (obrogatio legis). Repealing in part an existing law by the substitution of a new provision.

Obscurus. Not clear, abstruse. Obscure expressions of will are to be interpreted in a way "which seems more likely or which mostly is being practised" (D. 50.17.114). In the case of unclear terms used in a manumission of a slave, the interpretation should be rather in favor of his liberty. Syn. *dubius, ambiguus. Obscuro loco natus* = born of low origin.

　Solazzi, *SDHI* 13–14 (1947–48) 276.

Obsequium. A respectful behavior of a freedman towards his patron. There is no juristic definition of *obsequium,* but it was taken to be customary (*consuetum*). A transgression of this duty (use of violence, audacity) exposed the freedman to the charge of ingratitude (see INGRATUS). A similar term is *reverentia* which was considered violated if the freedman sued his patron in court without permission of the competent magistrate.—D. 37.15; C. 6.6.

　C. Cosentini, *St sui liberti* 1 (1948) 239.

Observatio legis (legum). The observance of the law (laws).—See CONSUETUDO FORI.

Observatio rerum. The control (custody) of another's property. It is given to those who are put in possession of the debtor's property; see MISSIONES IN POSSESSIONEM.

Obses. A hostage. He can make a testament only with a special permission. Killing a hostage is treated as high treason (*crimen maiestatis*).

　E. Vassaux, *Des prisonniers de guerre et des otages en dr. rom.,* Thèse Paris, 1890.

Obsignare (obsignatio). To affix a seal (to a written document, to a testament). Money in a sealed bag could be the object of a deposit; the depositee had no right to use the money and was obligated to return it in the same condition as he received it. This kind of deposit of money was used by a debtor when the creditor was absent or unable to accept the payment; see DEPOSITIO IN AEDE.—See SIGNUM, SIGNARE.

　Radin, *RE* 17.

Obstare. To impede, to be a hindrance. The term refers to prohibitions or obstacles (*obstaculum*) resulting from legal provisions or from exceptions which may be opposed to a plaintiff's claim. *Nihil obstat* = nothing is in the way (there is no hindrance). With this phrase the jurists used to strengthen their opinions and advices as not being opposed by the law.

Obstringere rem (pignus). To give a thing as a pledge to a creditor.

Obstringi. To be bound by an obligation (see OBLI-GATIO); *obstringi actione (interdicto)* = to be exposed to, or to be sued by, a specific action (an interdict).

Obtemperare. To obey. During a judicial proceeding *obtemperare ius dicenti* = to obey the orders of the jurisdictional magistrate. The praetorian Edict started with a section "if one did not obey the jurisdictional magistrate (*ius dicenti non obtemperaverit*)," in which the praetor granted an action (*actio in factum*) against the recalcitrant party in a trial, both defendant and plaintiff. The action was of a penal nature, the disobedient party being condemned for the contempt of court to the full value of the object of litigation (*quanti ea res est*). The edict applied primarily to municipal (*municipia, coloniae, fora*) courts which had not the necessary auxiliary organs to enforce their orders.—*Obtemperare* is also used of the fulfillment of the testator's wishes (*obtemperare voluntati*) expressed in his testament.—D. 2.3.

Lenel, *Edictum perpetuum,* 3rd ed. 1927, 51.

Obtentus. A pretext alleged in order to evade the fulfillment of one's obligations. *Obtentu* = under the pretext. In imperial constitutions *obtentu* = with regard, in the face of.

Obtinere. To obtain (an inheritance, possession, a magistracy); *obtinere* in a trial = to win the case.—See OBTINUIT.

Obtinere legis vicem. See LEGIS VICEM OBTINERE.

Obtingere. To accrue to a person (e.g., an inheritance), to fall to a person's share when common property or an estate is divided. Syn. *obvenire*.

Obtinuit. (Syn. *placuit, receptum est.*) It is (has been) held. The phrase refers mostly to the reception of a legal principle, a juristic opinion or a legal custom, following the views of the jurists, judicial practice, or a common usage. Sometimes also the contrary opinion or principle is mentioned which was overruled by that which "prevailed (*praevaluit*)." *Placuit* often refers to an opinion of the jurists.

A. B. Schwarz, *ZSS* 69 (1952) 364.

Obvagulatio. According to the Twelve Tables one could force a stubborn witness who refused to testify on an act in which he had participated as a witness, by summoning him publicly (*obvagulatum ire*) before his house, to appear before court as a witness. Such a spectacular summons, if not justified, was regarded a personal insult (*convicium*) since the refusal of testimony by a person who was requested to witness an act, was considered a dishonest action. —See INTESTABILIS.

Huvelin, *DS* 4; Radin, *RE* 17, 1747; Mommsen, *Jur. Schriften* 3 (1907, ex 1844) 507.

Obvenire. See OBTINGERE.

Obventiones. Proceeds, profits (distinguished from natural products, *fructus*), income in rents from the lease of a house or a ship (*obventiones ex aedificiis, ex nave*).

Occasio. An event, a happening (a marriage, an inheritance) from which (*ex occasione*) one acquires or expects to acquire some gain. *Occasio usucapiendi* = a situation which affords the possibility of USUCAPIO.

Occasus solis. See SOLIS OCCASUS.

Occentare. To write or to recite a slanderous poem (*carmen famosum*); to affect by witchcraft or sorcery.

Brecht, *RE* 17; F. Beckmann, *Zauberei und Recht in Roms Frühzeit,* 1928; Hendricksen, *ClPhilol* 20 (1925) 289; Lindsay, *ibid.* 44 (1949) 240; R. E. Smith, *Cl Quarterly* 44 (1951) 169.

Occultare (occultatio). To conceal a person (a criminal); *se occultare* = to hide oneself to evade summons into court. Syn. *latitare.*—C. 9.39.

Occultator. A hider, a concealer (of thieves, of stolen goods or of a deserter).—C. 12.45.

Occupantis melior condicio est. "He who holds a thing is in a better position" (D. 9.4.14 pr.). The rule refers to the better procedural situation of the holder of a thing when other persons claim the same thing. When several persons sue the same defendant by *actiones noxales* or *actiones de peculio,* the claimant who first obtained a favorable judgment was in a better situation than the other claimants since his claim was first satisfied by *noxae deditio* or from the *peculium.*

A. Biscardi, *Il dogma della collisione alla luce del dir. rom.,* 1935, 115.

Occupatio. A profession, employment, both civil and military.

Occupatio. A mode of acquisition of ownership by taking possession of a thing which does not belong to anybody (see RES NULLIUS) and is capable of being in private ownership. Among such things are in the first place animals caught by hunting or fishing, things found on the seashore, things abandoned by their owner, and the like.—See VENATIO, PISCATIO, DERELICTIO, INSULA IN FLUMINE NATA, and the following items.

Kaser, *RE* Suppl. 7; Beauchet, *DS* 4; Romano, *O. delle res derelictae, AnCam* 4 (1930).

Occupatio a fisco. The seizure of private property by the fisc either for debts due (in particular by tax-farmers, see PUBLICANI) or as a penalty in criminal matters.

Occupatio rerum hostilium. (Called in literature *occupatio bellica.*) In addition to the occupation of the enemy's land after a victorious war (see AGER OCCUPATORIUS), things belonging to the enemy used to be seized in war time. When taken by a common action of the army as a booty (see PRAEDA), they became property of the Roman state, but, when seized during an isolated enterprise of a soldier, they became his property. Occupation of immovables was excluded from such kind of acquisition of private ownership, since they were always acquired for the state.

Kaser, *RE* Suppl. 7, 686; Beauchet, *DS* 4, 143; J. Bray, *Essai sur le droit pénal militaire des Rom.*, 1894, 126; De Francisci, *AVen* 82 (1923) 967; Vogel, *ZSS* 66 (1948) 394.

Occurrere. To help one by a procedural or another legal measure.

Octava. A special tax of one-eighth (12½ per cent) of the value of the merchandise imposed on sales on a market.

Millet, *Mél Glotz* 1932, 615.

Octavenus. A Roman jurist of the late first century after Christ.

Berger, *RE* 17, 1787; Ferrini, *Opere* 2 (1929, ex 1887) 113.

Octaviana formula. See METUS.

Octoviri. A group of eight functionaries in the earlier organization of municipal administration. They had no jurisidictional power.

Rudolph, *RE* 17; *idem, Stadt und Staat im röm. Italien,* 1935, 66; E. Manni, *Per la storia dei municipii,* 1947, 141.

Odofredus. A renowned postglossator in the thirteenth century (died in 1265).—See GLOSSATORES.

Kuttner, *NDI* 9.

Oeconomus ecclesiae. An administrator of Church property, assistant of the bishop in administrative matters. He acted also as *dispensator pauperum* (= the guardian of the poor).—See REVERENTISSIMUS.

Offendere. To offend, to insult. An offense (*offensa*) committed by a slave against his master was punished by the latter.—See INIURIA.

Offendere legem (legi). To violate, to commit a breach of a legal enactment (a statute, an edict, a *senatusconsultum*).

Offensa. See OFFENDERE.

Offerre. To make an offer. *Offerre pecuniam* = to offer the payment of a debt; *offerre satisdationem, cautionem* = to offer a security.—See IUS OFFERENDAE PECUNIAE, OBLATIO.

Offerre iusiurandum. (*Deferre iusiurandum.*) See IUSIURANDUM NECESSARIUM.

Offerre se liti. See LITI SE OFFERRE.

Officere lumini. See SERVITUS NE LUMINI OFFICIATUR.

Officiales. Officials of a lower grade in the imperial administration (clerks, assistants, even workmen), mostly freedmen and slaves.—C. 12.47.

Boak, *RE* 17, 2049; Lécrivain, *DS* 4.

Officinatores monetae. Officials of the imperial mint, mostly freedmen.—See NUMMULARIUS, MONETA.

Vittinghoff, *RE* 17, 2043.

Officium. A moral duty originating in family relationship or friendship (*officium amicitiae*); a duty connected with the defense of another's interests (*officium tutoris, curatoris, advocationis*). In public law *officium* denotes the official duties of any person employed in public service as well as the office (bureau) of a magistrate together with its personnel. The term is applied also to provincial offices and officials, in particular to the provincial governors. The first books of the Digest and of the Code contain a large number of titles dealing with the duties of various imperial officials in Rome and the provinces. Several jurists (Venuleius, Ulpian, Paul, Macer, Arcadius Charisius) wrote monographs *"De officio"* (= On the duties) of higher governmental officials. —*Ex officio* = by virtue of one's official duties. *In officio alicuius esse* = to be employed in one's services. —Inst. 4.17; D. 1.10–22; C. 1.40; 43–46; 48; 11.39. —See MAGISTER OFFICIORUM.

Boak, *RE* 17; E. Bernert, *De vi atque usu vocabuli o.,* Diss. Breslau, 1930.

Officium admissionum. See ADMISSIONES.

Officium iudicis. The complex of legal and customary rules (*mos iudiciorum, usus fori*) which the private judge (*iudex*) had to observe in his judicial activity in addition to the binding instructions of the formula imposed on him. Syn. *officium iudicantis, officium arbitri.* "What a judge has done which does not pertain to his duties, is not valid" (D. 50.17.170).— See USURAE QUAE OFFICIO IUDICIS PRAESTANTUR.

Officium ius dicentis. Comprises all rights and duties within the competence of a judicial magistrate. The term refers in the first place to the praetor (*officium praetoris*).—D. 1.14; C. 1.39.

Officium palatinum. An office in the imperial residence. The *officia palatina* became in the later Empire state offices. Their number increased considerably in the course of time and their holders enjoyed manifold privileges. *Princeps officii* = the head of an *officium palatinum.*—See PALATINI.

Officium pietatis. See PIETAS.

Officium praetoris. See OFFICIUM IUS DICENTIS.

Officium virile. Duties, services accomplished by men (*munera virilia*) from which women were exempt. An *officium virile* was representing another in a trial, guardianship, curatorship, and the like.—See MUNERA.

Ofilius, Aulus. A jurist of the last century of the Republic. He was a disciple of Servius Sulpicius Rufus and the author of the first commentary on the praetorian Edict.

Münzer, *RE* 17, 2040.

Olim. Once, formerly. Through *olim* jurists allude to earlier law to which they oppose the law being in force in their own times (*nunc, hodie, temporibus nostris* = nowadays, in our times).

Omissum legibus. What has been neglected in statutes (laws). "What has been omitted in the laws, will not be neglected by the conscience of those who render judgments" (D. 22.5.13).

Omittere. To fail to fulfill one's duty, or not to exercise one's right, e.g., to neglect the formal acceptance of an inheritance or the request of a *bonorum possessio,* to fail to bring a suit in due time. In certain cases the failure to make use of one's right might cause its loss (see NON USUS). D. 29.2.

Honig, *Fg Richard Schmidt* 1 (1932) 3.

Omittere. (In a testament.) To omit a person in a last will by neither instituting him as an heir nor disinheriting him. Syn. PRAETERIRE.

Omnem. A constitution of the emperor Justinian concerning the organization of legal studies. It was addressed to the teachers of law and issued on the same day as the Digest (December 16, A.D. 533). *Omnem* is the first word of the enactment.—See DIGESTA IUSTINIANI.

Omnes. All men, the whole people (*populus*).—See RES COMMUNES OMNIUM. *Omnes* often refers to all jurists (e.g., *inter omnes constat,* see CONSTAT).

Omnes (omnia). In certain phrases, as *per omnia* (= in every respect), *in omnibus casibus* (= in any case), *omnes omnino* (= all throughout), *omnimodo* (= at any rate), the word occurs frequently in interpolated sentences as an expression of the tendency of Justinian's collaborators toward generalizations.

> Guarneri-Citati, *Indice*² (1927) 63; *idem, Fschr Koschaker* 1 (1939) 144.

Omnia iudicia absolutoria sunt. See ABSOLUTORIUS.

Omnimodo. By all means, at any rate.—See OMNES.
> Guarneri-Citati, *Indice*² (1927) 62.

Omnino. (Combined with *omnes, omnia.*) See OMNES.

Onera hereditatis. Debts, liens, taxes, and all kinds of charges by which an estate is encumbered.

Onera matrimonii. Expenses connected with the common life of married persons. "There should be dowry where there are burdens of marriage" (D. 23.3.56.1).—See DOS, PARAPHERNA.

> Albertario, *Studi* 1 (1933) 295; Wolff, *ZSS* 53 (1932) 360; Dumont, *RHD* 22 (1943) 34.

Onerare libertatem. To aggravate the liberty of a freedman by imposing on him at the manumission heavy duties exceeding the normal obligations of a freedman towards his patron (*libertatis onerandae causa imposita*). A stipulation of the freedman, assuming such obligations in the event that he offended his patron, was void for the reason that he would always have lived in fear of being forced to pay the penalty (*metu exactionis*). However, a promise made by a slave to pay the patron a certain sum as a compensation for the manumission, and repeated by him after he was freed, was not regarded as a promise *libertatis onerandae causa.*

> C. Astoul, *Des charges imposées par le maître à la liberté,* Thèse Paris, 1890; Albertario, *Studi* 3 (1936) 397; C. Cosentini, *Studi sui liberti* 1 (1948) 95.

Onerari. To be burdened with debts and other charges or expenses. The term is applied primarily to an heir on whom the payment of legacies and *fideicommissa* was imposed. Hence *onerosa hereditas* an inheritance encumbered with excessive debts and legacies.

Oneratus. See HONORATUS, ONERARI.

Onerosa hereditas. See ONERA HEREDITATIS, ONERARI.

Onus. See ONERA, CADUCA, ACTIO ONERIS AVERSI, SERVITUS ONERIS FERENDI.

Onus probandi. The burden of the proof.—See PROBATIO.

> Levy, *Iura* 3 (1952) 171.

Ope consilio. By aid and counsel. The phrase is applied in criminal matters with reference to all kinds of accessories who help another in committing a crime. It occurs in connection with crimes against the state or the emperor, with adultery and, in the field of private *delicta,* with the theft. In the formula of *actio furti* the two words were attached to the name of the defendant whether he was the principal thief or an accessory. In the first case the words covered the doing of the thief himself (acting with design, intention, see CONSILIUM), in the second case they referred to abettors and instigators. *Ope* means physical help, *consilio* means no simple advice, but instructing and encouraging. "He who persuades and impels another to commit a theft and instructs him with advice, is held to give a *consilium,* one who gives him assistance and help in taking away the goods is acting *ope*" (D. 47.2.50.1).

> M. Cohn, *Beiträge zur Bearbeitung des röm. R.,* 1880, 10; R. Balougditch, *Étude sur la complicité en dr. pénal rom.,* 1920, 44.

Ope exceptionis. Through an *exceptio.* Syn. *per exceptionem.* Ant. IPSO IURE. The phrase is used to indicate that the defendant had to oppose an *exceptio* in order to repeal the plaintiff's claim.—See EXCEPTIO, COMPENSATIO.

Opera publica. Public constructions, such as buildings, bridges, harbors, roads. They were under the supervision of the censors (see CENSORES), or special functionaries who from the time of Augustus had the title of *curatores* and depended upon the *praefectus urbi.*—D. 50.10; C. 8.11(12).—See PROCURATORES OPERUM PUBLICORUM, EXACTOR.

> Lengle, *RE* 18; Humbert, *DS* 4; E. De Ruggiero, *Lo Stato e le opere pubbliche in Roma antica,* 1925.

Operae. (Pl.; rarely used in sing. *opera.*) Labor in all its manifestations, both manual and intellectual. Syn. *labor* (from the fourth post-Christian century). *Operae* applies also to the work of animals (*operae iumenti*). *Operas praestare* = to render services. To acquire *ex operis* (or *operis*) = by one's work; the phrase is opposed to acquisitions *ex re* = by means (money) taken from one's property.—See LOCATIO CONDUCTIO OPERARUM, and the following items.

> F. De Robertis, *Rapporti di lavoro,* 1946, 13.

Operae animalium. The right to use another's beasts of burden. Such right was a personal servitude (*usus iumenti, pecoris, ovium*), usually left by a legacy. It was perhaps a creation of the later (Justinian's?) law.

> G. Grosso, *Uso, abitazione,* 1939, 128.

Operae diurnae. Services (work) to be done in daytime.

Operae fabriles. Labor done by professional craftsmen (*fabri*).

> Mitteis, *ZSS* 23 (1902); C. Cosentini, *St sui liberti* 1 (1948) 125.

Operae liberales. (Termed also *artes liberales, ingenuae.*) Services rendered by persons exercising a profession worthy of a free (*liber*) man, primarily intellectuals (lawyers, physicians, architects, land-surveyors, etc.). The *operae liberales* could not be the object of contract of hire (*locatio conductio operarum*). But payment for such services could be claimed through proceedings of *cognitio extra ordinem*. Ant. *operae illiberales* (term unknown in the sources, but used in modern literature).—See HONORARIUM, STUDIA LIBERALIA.

> Heldrich, *IhJb* 88 (1940) 142; Siber, *ibid.* 161; M. Boitard, *Les contrats des services gratuits,* 1941, 9.

Operae liberti. Services rendered by a freedman to his patron. The duties assumed by the freedman could not be sued for by an action (*obligatio naturalis*) unless he promised his *operae* under oath (see IURATA PROMISSIO LIBERTI) or through a *stipulatio operarum*.—D. 38.1; C.6.3.—See ONERARE LIBERTATEM.

> Lécrivain, *DS* 3, 1215; G. Segrè, *StSen* 23 (1906) 313; Thelohan, *Ét Girard* 1 (1912); Biondi, *AnPer* 28 (1914); M. Chevrier, *Du serment promissoire,* Thèse Dijon, 1921, 153; O. Lenel, *Edictum perp.*³ (1927) 338; J. Lambert, *Operae liberti,* 1934; Giffard, *RHD* 17 (1938) 92; Lavaggi, *Successione dei liberi patroni nelle opere dei liberti, SDHI* 11 (1945) 236; E. Albertario, *Studi* 4 (1946) 3, 13; C. Cosentini, *St sui liberti* 1 (1948) 103, 2 (1950).

Operae officiales. Services of personal nature due by a freedman to his patron, such as to accompany him, to travel with him, to administer his affairs, and the like.

> Mitteis, *ZSS* 23 (1902) 143; C. Cosentini, *St sui liberti* 1 (1948) 125.

Operae quae locari solent. See LOCATIO CONDUCTIO OPERARUM.

Operae servorum. (As a personal servitude.) The right to use the services or labor of another's slave. Syn. *usus servi.* Such right used to be bequeathed by a legacy.—D. 7.7; 33.2.

> Cicogna, *Fil* 31 (1906); G. Grosso, *Uso, abitazione, opere dei servi,* 1939, 121.

Operarius. A workman, one who renders subordinate services.—See MERCENNARIUS.

Operis novi nuntiatio (denuntiatio). A protestation by the owner of an immovable (*is qui nuntiat*) against a neighbor starting a new construction (*opus novum*) on his realty which might prevent the former from the use of his property. A *nuntiatio* is justified when the objector acted to defend his right, to prevent a damage which might be caused by the *opus novum,* or when the construction endangered the use of a public place or road. In the last instance any Roman citizen was entitled to protest; in other cases, only the owner whose property was exposed to damages, the beneficiary of a servitude, or one who held the land on a right similar to ownership (an *emphyteuta,* a *superficiarius*). He to whom the protesting notice was given (*is cui nuntiatum est*) was bound to cease the construction or to give the objector security to the effect that he would not suffer any damages or that the former state would be restored (*satisdatio de opere restituendo*). If he failed to give such security, the objector might request an interdict (*interdictum ex operis novi nuntiatione,* named in literature *interdictum demolitorium*) by which the praetor ordered the demolition of what had been constructed. A refusal to comply with the interdict led to a normal trial (see INTERDICTUM). The builder of the *opus novum* had another remedy to evade the prohibition resulting from the *nuntiatio.* He might ask the praetor for the annulment of the *operis novi nuntiatio* (*remissio operis novi nuntiationis*) if he could prove that the objector had no right to oppose the projected construction. The *operis novi nuntiatio* was reformed by Justinian and various innovations were introduced through interpolations performed by the compilers on classical texts leaving, however, some details in obscurity.—D. 39.1.—See PATIENTIAM PRAESTARE, DEMOLITIO.

> Berger, *RE* 9, 1670; 18; Humbert, *DS* 4; Bruno, *NDI* 4, 713; Martin, *Ét Girard* 1 (1912) 123; R. Henle, *Unus casus,* 1915, 406; Niedermeyer, *St Riccobono* 1 (1936) 253; Branca, *SDHI* 7 (1941) 313; idem, *AnTriest* 12 (1941) 96, 128, 156; M. David, *Et sur l'interdit quod vi aut clam, AnnUniv Lyon* 3. ser. 10 (1947) 31; Gioffredi, *SDHI* 13–14 (1947/8) 93; Berger, *Iura,* 1 (1950) 102, 117; Cosentini, *AnCat* 4 (1949–50) 297.

Opinator. See OPINIO.

Opifex. A workman, an artisan.

> G. Kühn, *De opificum Rom. condicione,* Diss. Halle, 1910.

Opinio. (In administrative law.) An estimation of a provincial landed property (in the later Empire) for the assessment of the import in corn to be delivered by the landowner for the army. *Opinatores* = officials charged with the evaluation and collection of such corn contributions.

> Cagnat, *DS* 4.

Opiniones. Opinions on legal questions, expressed in *responsa* or elsewhere. There is only one work known under the title *Opiniones* which was excerpted for the Digest, namely, by Ulpian (in six books). The collection of Ulpian "Opinions" was perhaps compiled in postclassical times.

> Jörs, *RE* 5, 1450 (no. 12); G. Rotondi, *Scritti giur.* 1 (1922) 453; F. Schulz, *History of R. legal science,* 1946, 182.

Oportere. A legal obligation recognized and sanctioned by the *ius civile.* The verb appears in the INTENTIO of the procedural formula in *actiones in personam* and is there connected with another verb which describes the nature of the defendant's obligation: *dare* (= to give), *dare facere* (= to do), *damnum decidere*

(= to indemnify), *praestare* (= to perform) *oportere*. *Oportere* occurs also only in the so-called *actiones in ius conceptae;* see FORMULA IN IUS CONCEPTA, OBLIGATIO.

Paoli, *Rev. des ét latines,* 15 (1937) 326; Kunkel, *Fschr Koschaker* 2 (1939) 4.

Oppidum. A town (originally any place surrounded by walls). The term was later replaced, usually by *municipium.*

Kornemann, *RE* 18.

Opponere. To oppose. The term refers primarily to exceptions (*opponere exceptionem*) which the defendant opposed to the plaintiff's claim; see EXCEPTIO. It is also applied to counterclaims by which the defendant repeals the plaintiff's demand, as e.g., *opponere compensationem.*—See COMPENSATIO.

Opprobrium. An ignominious, disgraceful doing. Syn. *probrum.* "Some doings are ignominious by nature, as theft or adultery, some by the customs of the country" (D. 50.16.42), as, e.g., bad management of a ward's affairs by his guardian, followed by a condemnation in *actio tutelae.*

Optimates. A political group ("the best ones," the aristocrats) composed of wealthy and influential senators and senatorial families in the later Republic who controlled the public administration and finances as an oligarchy, eager to defend their privileged, monopolistic position against the opposing group, the *populares* who fought for the extension of the political rights of the people and the defense of its interests. The two groups were not political parties but assemblages of ambitious individuals and families struggling incessantly for the defense of the interests of their own and their members.

Strasburger, *RE* 18; L. R. Taylor, *Party politics in the age of Caesar* (Los Angeles, 1949) 11.

Optare. See OPTIO.

Optimo iure (optima lege). Refers to persons and things, free from legal restrictions and charges. A person *optimo iure* is one who has full legal capacity. A land *optimo iure* indicates a real property free from private charges (servitudes, pledge) and from taxes and public burdens as well.—See LEX TERENTIA.

Kübler, *RE* 18, 772; Ciapessoni, *St Bonfante* 3 (1930) 661; Beseler, *St Albertoni* 1 (1933) 432; Kaser, *ZSS* 61 (1941) 25.

Optimus (princeps). An attribute ("the best") given to the reigning emperor (*optimus princeps noster*), sometimes enhanced by the addition of *maximus* (*optimus maximusque princeps noster*).

Optimus maximus. These words were usually added in sales or legacies of immovables (e.g., *fundus uti optimus maximusque*) to indicate the legal and factual conditions of the land or building. Through this clause a seller assumed the liability that the immovable was free from easements (*optimus*) and had the size affirmed by him (*maximus*).

Kübler, *RE* 18, 803; E. Rabel, *Haftung des Verkäufers für Mängel im Recht,* 1912, 92.

Optinere, optingere. See OBTINERE, OBTINGERE.

Optio. A title of military and civil officials. In the army *optio* = a substitute of a *centurio.* There were also *optiones* in specific military services as well as in the civil administration, as, for instance, in the staff of the *praefectus urbi. Optio* was the leading official in the imperial mint.

Lammert, *RE* 18; Vittinghoff, *RE* 17, 2044.

Optio. A selection. Syn. *electio.* A selection between two or more things could be granted the legatee in a testament (see LEGATUM OPTIONIS) or established in an agreement in behalf of a contractual party, as, e.g., in a stipulation to give either the slave Stichus or Pamphilus.—See OPTIO SERVI.

Optio legata. See LEGATUM OPTIONIS.—D. 33.5.

Optio servi. The election of a slave. It was granted a legatee as the right to select one slave among those who belonged to the estate. The legatee had the choice also when "a slave" was generally bequeathed without any precise indication, and there were several slaves in the estate. If the testator did not fix a date for the choice, the heir might ask the praetor to settle a term. Non-execution of the selection by the legatee within the term fixed resulted in the loss of the right and the heir might offer the legatee a slave of his own choice.—See LEGATUM OPTIONIS.

Optio tutoris. The choice of a guardian (*tutor*). A husband under whose power (see MANUS) his wife was, could in his testament dispose that she might freely choose her guardian. The guardian appointed at the widow's request = *tutor optivus.* The pertinent disposition of the husband could not be restricted by the addition of a condition.—TUTELA MULIERUM.

Sachers, *RE* 7A, 1592.

Opus. See LOCATIO CONDUCTIO OPERIS, ADPROBARE, INTERDICTUM QUOD VI AUT CLAM.

Opus metalli. See METALLUM.

Opus novum. See OPERIS NOVI NUNTIATIO.

Opus publicum. See OPERA PUBLICA, INSCRIBERE OPERE PUBLICO.

Opus publicum. (In criminal law.) Forced labor on a public construction or a public work as a punishment for crimes (*damnatio in opus publicum*) committed by persons of the lower classes of the population. Working in an *opus publicum* comprised the construction or restoration of roads, cleaning of sewers, service in public baths, bakeries, weaving-mills (for women) and the like. Condemnation for lifetime involved loss of Roman citizenship; in other cases the status of the condemned person remained unchanged.

Lengle, *RE* 18, 828; Lécrivain, *DS* 4; Brasiello, *Repressione penale,* 1937, 361.

Oraculum. An imperial enactment (in the language of the imperial chancery of the later Empire).

Orare causam. See CAUSAS DICERE, CAUSAM PERORARE.

Oratio (principis in senatu). A speech of the emperor made in the senate by himself or by his representative (a *quaestor*) in order to propose a *senatusconsultum* which alone became the law. This procedure was observed in the first century of the Principate alongside the other form of proposing *senatusconsulta* by high magistrates. From the time of Hadrian the proposals of magistrates fell into disuse and the emperor's discourse in the senate, even made by his representative in his absence, became the normal way leading to a *senatusconsultum*. The emperor's proposal was approved by the Senate without discussion; the approval became a simple formality. Hence *oratio principis* as a technical term replaced that of *senatusconsultum* which from the end of the second century was applied only to earlier *senatusconsulta*. Thus, in the last analysis, the *oratio principio* turned out to be an imperial law, promulgated in the senate. For more important *orationes*, see the following items.—See CONSTITUTIONES PRINCIPUM.

> Radin, *RE* 18; Pottier, *DS* 4; Orestano, *NDI* 9; Volterra, *NDI* 12, 29; Cuq, *Le consilium principis, Mémoires Acad. Insc. et Belles Lettres,* Sér. 1, v. 9 (1884) 424.

Oratio (orationes) Claudii. (On *recuperatores,* and on *accusatores* in criminal matters, A.D. 42–51). The oration of the Emperor Claudius (there may have been two orations), confirmed by a decree of the senate, set the age of twenty-five completed years for RECUPERATORES, and declared guilty of *calumnia* those accusers in a criminal trial who without any just reason abandoned an accusation in a trial already in course.—See ACCUSATIO, SENATUSCONSULTUM TURPILLIANUM, CALUMNIA.

> Editions: in all collections of *Fontes* (see General Bibl., Ch. XII), the most recent in Riccobono, *FIR* 1², no. 44 (Bibl.); L. Mitteis, *Grundzüge und Chrestomathie der Papyruskunde* 2, 2 (1912) no. 370; Stroux, *SbMünch* 1929, fasc. 3.—Woess, *ZSS* 51 (1931) 336.

Oratio Hadriani. Prohibited an appeal from the decisions of the senate to the emperor.

Oratio Hadriani. (On *fideicommissa.*) Confirmed by a *senatusconsultum,* ordained that a FIDEICOMMISSUM left to peregrines be confiscated by the fisc.

Oratio Marci. (On APPELLATIO.) The Emperor Marcus Aurelius ordered that terms fixed for *appellatio* had to be reckoned as TEMPUS UTILE.

Oratio Marci. On *crimen expilatae hereditatis.*—See CRIMEN EXPILATAE HEREDITATIS.

Oratio Marci. (On IN IUS VOCATIO.) Prohibited from summoning one's adversary into court during the harvest (*messis*) or vintage (*vindemiae*) except in urgent cases, as, for instance, when the plaintiff would lose his action through the lapse of time.

Oratio Marci. (Of the Emperor Marcus Aurelius.) Admitted children to intestate succession of their mother.—See SENATUSCONSULTUM ORFITIANUM.

Oratio Marci. (Of the Emperor Marcus Aurelius.) Protected slaves manumitted in a testament of their master who had been assassinated. According to SENATUSCONSULTUM SILANIANUM in such a case the testament could not be opened (see APERTURA TESTA-MENTI) before the discovery of the murderer. The *oratio* settled that, if a slave was manumitted in the testament, his child born in the meantime, i.e., before the opening of the will, was free, and profits which would have come to the slave if he were freed immediately after the testator's death, belonged to him although the testament entered in force much later.

Oratio Marci. (Of the Emperor Marcus Aurelius.) On *confessio in iure.* The contents of this *oratio* is not quite clear; it is mentioned in connection with CONFESSIO IN IURE.

> Giffard, *RHD* 29 (1905) 449; W. Püschel, *Confessus pro iudicato est,* 1924, 156; Wlassak, *Konfessio, SbMünch* 1934, 42.

Oratio Marci. (Of the Emperor Marcus Aurelius.) On marriages, forbade marriage between a senator's daughter and a freedman, and between a *tutor* (or *curator*) and his ward. In a monograph of Paul the latter prohibition appears as introduced by an *oratio "divorum Marci et Commodi"* (of the late Emperors Marcus and Commodus).

Oratio Marci. (On transactions concerning alimony.) Ordered that they had to be confirmed by the praetor.

Oratio principis. See ORATIO.

Oratio Severi. (Of A.D. 195.) Prohibited tutors (and curators?) from alienating or pledging real property of their wards unless the transaction was allowed by the praetor.

> Sachers, *RE* 7A, 1550; G. Kuttner, *Fschr Martitz* 1911, 247; Peters, *ZSS* 32 (1911) 299; E. Albertario, *Studi* 1 (1933) 477; Brasiello, *St Solazzi* 1948, 691; *idem, RIDA* 4 (= *Mél De Visscher* 3, 1950) 204.

Oratio Severi et Caracallae. Concerning donations between husband and wife, see DONATIO INTER VIRUM ET UXOREM.

Orator. (In judicial proceedings.) One who assists a party to a civil trial by advice and speech both before the magistrate (*in iure*) and the judge (*apud iudicem*), or who defends the accused in a criminal trial. See ADVOCATUS, PATRONUS CAUSAE. Although trained in law, the *orator* needed the help of a professional jurist in a difficult case; in particular in civil matters such help in the first stage of the trial before the praetor might be necessary to write down the formula and its complicated parts or when a new kind of action was requested. Therefore the activity of the *orator* as an assistant of the party has to be distinguished from that of the jurists. See IURISPRUDENTIA. Some lawyers combined both professions, but instances of a transition from one profession to the other are also known. Under the Principate the two professions are neatly separated. In the second stage of a civil trial before the private judge the eloquence of the *orator* might exercise a greater influence on the final decision since the proceedings were closed after a recapitulation of the legal arguments and the results of the proofs by the representatives of the parties. Rhetoric had an important role in judicial oratorship inasmuch as the rhetoricians in their capacity as teachers dealt with legal problems on the ground of real or fictitious cases.—See RHETORES (Bibl.), CAUSAM PERORARE, CAUSAS DICERE.

Himmelschein, *Symb. Frib. Lenel,* 1931, 373; Steinwenter, *ZSS* 65 (1947) 106; J. Stroux, *Röm. Rechtswissenschaft und Rhetorik,* Potsdam, 1949; F. Schulz, *History of R. legal science,* 1946, 108.

Orbi. Married persons who have no children.—See LEX IULIA DE MARITANDIS ORDINIBUS, SENATUSCONSULTUM MEMMIANUM.

Orbis Romanus. The Roman Empire.

J. Vogt, *O.R. Zur Terminologie des röm. Imperialismus,* 1922.

Orcinus libertus. See LIBERTUS ORCINUS.

Orbitas. The state of being married and childless. See ORBI. In imperial constitutions *orbitas* means the loss of either a child or a parent.—C. 8.57.

Ordinare. (In the language of the imperial chancery.) To appoint (a *tutor,* a *curator,* a *procurator*).

Ordinare iudicium (ordinatio iudicii). Comprises the whole activity of the magistrate (the *praetor*) in the proceedings *in iure* in a civil trial.—See the following item.

Hölder, *ZSS* 24 (1903) 201; Lenel, *ibid.* 335.

Ordinare litem (ordinatio litis). Apparently a special act in a trial concerning the status of a person as a free man (*causa liberalis*), in particular of a defender of the liberty of the person involved and the acceptance of a security (*cautio*) offered by him. The act is of importance since after *litis ordinatio* (*lite ordinata*) the person whose liberty was under examination was considered free until the final decision was rendered. With regard to other trials the phrase *ordinare litem* seems to be of postclassical origin.—See CAUSA LIBERALIS, ADSERTIO.

Wlassak, *ZSS* 26 (1905) 395; Partsch, *ZSS* 31 (1910) 424; M. Nicolau, *Causa liberalis,* 1933, 116.

Ordinare testamentum (ordinatio testamenti). To make a testament. *Ordinare* refers also to codicils. —Inst. 2.10; 6.23.

Ordinarius. Normal, regular. With reference to procedural institutions *ordinarius* indicates all those which are connected with the normal organization of the courts and the procedure before them (*ordo iudiciorum*). Ant. *extra ordinem, extraordinarius.* With regard to officials and offices a distinction is made between *dignitates ordinariae* (officials in active service) and *dignitates honorariae* which are only honorific titles.—See IUDEX ORDINARIUS, IUS ORDINARIUM, IUDICIA EXTRAORDINARIA, HONORARII.

Born, *RE* 18.

Ordo. Generally means a sequence, an order or rather a right order. Hence *ordine* = in a proper order. In the law of successions *ordo* refers to the order in which a group (a class) of successors under praetorian law (*bonorum possessores*) are admitted to the inheritance, see BONORUM POSSESSIO INTESTATI, EDICTUM SUCCESSORIUM.—*Ordo* is also the order in which

citizens are called to fulfill public services (*munera*). —See the following items.

Kübler, *RE* 18; Sachers, *RE* Suppl. 7, 792.

Ordo. (With reference to a group of persons.) The senate (*ordo amplissimus*). For the municipal council, see ORDO DECURIONUM. For *ordo* in the meaning of a social class, see ORDO EQUESTER (persons of equestrian rank) and ORDO SENATORIUS (persons of senatorial rank). *Ordo* is also used of professional groups, as, for instance, *ordo publicanorum* (tax-farmers, see PUBLICANI), or of persons in subordinate service of the state (*ordo scribarum, apparitorum,* and the like), who were organized as associations.—C. 10.61.

Ordo amplissimus. The senate.—See SENATUS.

Ordo collegii. Indicates either an association, a guild (see COLLEGIUM) or its administrative board.

Kübler, *RE* 18, 931.

Ordo decurionum. The municipal council. See MUNICIPIUM. The *ordo decuriorum* was the center of the municipal administration and functioned also as a superior instance for the decisions of municipal magistrates in all administrative and certain judicial matters. The decisions of the *ordo* were passed by a simple majority, in more important matters by two-thirds or three-fourths of the votes. Members of the council were appointed by the highest magistrates of the municipality (see MAGISTRATUS MUNICIPALES), in some *municipia* by their citizens or by the council itself (see ADLECTIO). The new members paid a fee of admission to the council (*summa honorarii,* see HONORARIUM). The membership in the *ordo decurionum* was considered a dignity, and the families of the *decuriones* constituted the local nobility. From the middle of the third post-Christian century the situation of the *decuriones* changed radically to their detriment as a result of the interference of the emperors in the municipal administration, especially in financial and taxation matters. Heavy financial burdens were imposed on the *decuriones;* the former local nobility became in the later Empire the most vexed group of the municipal population. The membership in the *curia* (this was the new name for the *ordo decurionum,* the *decuriones* being termed ever since *curiales*) became hereditary. The few personal privileges (as, for instance, to be judged by the governor of the province or to be exempt from the most severe penalties or torture in criminal matters) meant very little in face of the financial and personal burdens they had to bear. They were liable for the amount of taxes imposed on the citizens of the *municipium.* An extensive imperial legislation, of which a considerable portion is preserved in the Theodosian and Justinian Codes, dealt with the *curiales,* their duties and the penalties inflicted for violation of the pertinent laws and attempts to evade the obligations imposed. Under Justinian the *curia* became a kind of a penitentiary since the assignment to the *curia* was applied as a punishment.—D. 50.2; C. 10.32–35; 12.16.—See DECURIONES, ALBUM CURIAE, QUINQUENNALES, DUAE PARTES, MOTIO EX ORDINE.

Kübler, *RE* 4 (*s.v. decurio*); Kornemann, *RE* 16, 621.

Ordo dignitatum. See DIGNITAS.

Ordo equester. See EQUITES.

Ordo iudiciorum privatorum. The ordinary civil, bipartite proceeding in the classical period, to be distinguished from proceedings *extra ordinem*. The term was coined in literature as a counterpart to the extraordinary procedure, see COGNITIO EXTRA ORDINEM.

Sachers, *RE* Suppl. 7, 793; Lécrivain, *DS* 4.

Ordo iudiciorum publicorum. The normal criminal procedure (see QUAESTIONES PERPETUAE) in the last centuries of the Republic and under the Principate, distinguished from *cognitio extra ordinem* in criminal matters which gradually superseded the *quaestiones* procedure owing to the imperial legislation and the transfer of the criminal jurisdiction to the emperor and bureaucratic officials.—See ACCUSATIO, INQUISITIO.

Sachers, *RE* Suppl. 7, 797; Lécrivain, *DS* 4.

Ordo magistratuum. See CURSUS HONORUM.

Ordo senatorius. A privileged social group from the times of Augustus, composed of the members of the senate and their families (agnatic descendants until the third degree with their wives) and of persons to whom the emperor granted the senatorial rank (see CLAVUS LATUS). Possession of property of the value of at least one million sesterces was required. The *ordo senatorius* enjoyed various privileges both in civil and criminal matters. The highest civil and military offices in the state (*praefectus urbi, praefectus aerarii, legati iuridici,* commanders of legions, governors of provinces, etc.) were accessible only to persons of senatorial rank. Lower in social rank was the *ordo equester* (see EQUITES). Persons of equestrian rank could obtain the admission to the senatorial rank from the emperor (see ADLECTIO). Both these privileged classes were referred to as *uterque ordo* when a legal norm applied to both of them.

Kübler, *RE* 18, 931.

Oriens. The Eastern part of the Empire.—See COMES ORIENTIS, DIOECESIS.

Originalis. One who belongs to a social group or community by birth (*originalis colonus*).

Originarii. Citizens of a community by birth (*origo*). —C. 10.39.—See INCOLA.

Origo. The birth place. A person acquired the local citizenship in his *origo* if he was the son of a citizen of the same locality (*municeps*). He became a *civis suae civitatis* (= a citizen of his city). *Origo* was different from the *domicilium* of a person, if he took domicile in another municipality than in that of his birth. A manumitted slave acquired *ius originis* in the *origo* of his patron, an adopted person in that

of his *pater adoptivus*. Municipal citizenship could be granted by the municipal council to a person who was born elsewhere. A person who had *origo* in a given community was subject to public charges there without regard to the circumstance whether or not he had his domicile there.—C. 10.39.—See INCOLA, MUNICIPIUM, DOMICILIUM, MUNERA.

Berger, *RE* 9, 1252; Cuq, *DS* 4; A. Visconti, *Note preliminarie sull'o. nelle fonti imper. rom.*, St Calisse 1940.

Ornamenta. Distinctive titles and insignia of high magistrates (*ornamenta consularia, praetoria, quaestoria*) or of senators (*ornamenta senatoria*). *Ornamenta* were granted under the Principate as a personal distinction to persons who had never been magistrates or had held a magistracy of a lower rank than the *ornamenta* bestowed on him. See ADLECTIO, HONORARII. Municipal magistrates and *decuriones* had also *ornamenta* (*ornamenta decurionalia, duoviralia*).—See INSIGNIA.

Borcsák, *RE* 18; Lécrivain, *DS* 4.

Ornamenta (ornatus) aedium (domus). Things which serve to adorn a building. They are distinguished from *instrumentum domus* since the latter "pertain to the protection of a house, and the ornaments serve for pleasure" (D. 33.7.12.16). To *ornamenta* belong pictures, sculptures, and other things which embellish a house.—See INSTRUMENTUM.

Ornamenta iumentorum. An ornamental equipment (caparison, trappings) of beasts of burden which they used to wear when sold at the market. According to the aedilician edict which dealt with the sale of domestic animals, the *ornamenta* were considered sold together with the animals, and the buyer could claim them by a specific action.—See EDICTUM AEDILIUM CURULIUM.

Biondi, *Actiones arbitrariae, AnPal* 1 (1911) 153.

Ornamenta mulierum. Women's ornaments (jewelry). The term is discussed by the jurists in connection with legacies of *ornamenta mulierum*.—D. 34.2.—See SUMPTUS.

Ornamenta triumphalia. Ornaments worn by a military commander during his triumphal entrance in Rome after a victorious war.—See TRIUMPHUS.

Borzsák, *RE* 18, 1121.

Ornatio provinciae. The assignment of military units to a province for its security, together with the necessary provisions of food and money for the expenses of administration. The senate was the competent authority.

O'Brien-Moore, *RE* Suppl. 6, 728.

Os fractum. An injury inflicted on a person and consisting in the fracture of a bone. It is mentioned already in the Twelve Tables as a punishable crime by the side of *membrum ruptum* which comprises major damages to a human body.

Binding, *ZSS* 40 (1919) 106; Appleton, *Mél Cornil* 1 (1926) 51; Di Paola, *AnCat* 1 (1947) 268.

Osculum. A kiss. If a man kissed his fiancée at the conclusion of the betrothal (*osculo interveniente*) and died before the marriage, the woman might keep one-half of the gifts he had given her; the other half had to be returned to the heirs of the deceased, according to postclassical law.

M. B. Pharr, *CIJ* 42 (1947) 393.

Ostendere. To prove. It is a favorite term in Justinian's constitutions; it occurs also in some interpolated texts.

Guarneri-Citati, *Indice*², 1927, 63.

Ostentatio. A display, an exhibition. Consumable things (see RES QUAE USU CONSUMUNTUR) could be the object of a gratuitous loan (COMMODATUM) if they were used only for an ostentatious show (*ostentatio*) and a vain display (*pompa*).

Ostia. A house door. A lease of a house or a dwelling could be unilaterally dissolved by the lessee if the landlord refused to restore doors (and windows, *fenestrae*) which were in a bad condition. On the other hand the tenant who provided the house with doors at his own expense had the right to take them away (see IUS TOLLENDI) after restoring the entrances to their former condition.

Ostiarius. A janitor, normally a slave.

Otiosus. Idle, unemployed, free from charges. *Otiosa pecunia* = money not lent out on interest.

Ovatio. See TRIUMPHUS.

Rohde, *RE* 18.

Ovile. An enclosure on the *Campus Martius* (= the field of Mars in Rome) where the *comitia centuriata* gathered and voted (*suffragia ferre*). The term became a popular expression for a voting place. The official term was *saeptum*. *Saepta* were also termed the enclosed places assigned to the single *tribus* or *centuriae* for the purpose of voting.

Rosenberg, *RE* 1A (*s.v. saepta*).

P

Pabulatores. Military units sent out to provide forage for horses.

Lambertz, *RE* 18.

Pacisci. See PACTUM, TALIO.

Pacisci de crimine. An agreement with a wrongdoer to the effect that one would not bring an accusation against him (*de non accusando*) or would accuse him but conduct the accusation in a way to make the culprit be absolved.—See PRAEVARICATIO, TERGIVERSATIO, SENATUSCONSULTUM TURPILLIANUM.

Kaser, *RE* 6A, 2416; Levy, *ZSS* (1933) 186; Bohacek, *St Riccobono* 1 (1936) 343.

Paconius. An unknown Roman jurist of whom only one text is preserved in the Digest. He is probably identical with Pacunius, also represented by a single text in the Digest.

Berger, *RE* 19 (no. 6).

Pactio. See PACTUM.

Pactio collegii. The by-laws of an association (see COLLEGIUM) voted on and passed by the members to deal with the internal organization of the association (*pactionem ferre, constitutere*). Syn. *lex collegii*.

Pactio libertatis (pro libertate). An agreement with the master of a slave under which money was given to him in advance (or promised) in order that the slave be manumitted.

Pactiones et stipulationes. Pacts and stipulations between the interested parties served for the constitution of praedial servitudes or of a usufruct on provincial soil by agreement, since *mancipatio* and *in iure cessio*, the civil ways of the constitution of such rights, were not applicable to provincial land.—See SERVITUTES PRAEDIORUM, USUSFRUCTUS.

Condanari-Michler, *RE* 18, 2150; P. Krüger, *Die praetorische Servitut*, 1911; Frezza, *StCagl* 22 (1935) 98; B. Biondi, *Servitù prediali*, 1946, 215; S. Solazzi, *Requisiti e modi di costituzione delle servitù prediali*, 1947, 109.

Pactum. "The agreement (*placitum*) and consent of two or more persons, concerning the same subject (*in idem*)" (D. 2.14.1.2). Since the earliest times the term applied to any agreement. Even in international relations an agreement between two states (such as a peace treaty) or between the commanders of two armies engaged in a fight, was termed *pactum*. In the law of obligations *pactum* (*pacisci*) is used in the broadest sense, both with regard to contractual and delictual obligations. With regard to the latter, *pactum* referred to a composition between the offender and the person injured by the wrongdoing (*delictum*) and still in classical law a transaction with the person damaged excluded the availability of the pertinent penal action (e.g., in the case of a theft the *actio furti*, or in the case of INIURIA the *actio iniuriarum*). In such cases the *pactum* produced the extinction of an obligation. In the province of contractual obligations the development of *pacta* (formless agreements) was due to the praetorian Edict in which the praetor proclaimed: "I shall protect *pacta conventa* (agreements, mutual understandings) which were concluded neither by fraud, nor contrary to statutes, plebiscites, *senatusconsulta*, imperial decrees, or edicts, nor with the intention to evade fraudulently one of those enactments" (D. 2.14.7.7). The protection was granted in the form of an EXCEPTIO if one party was sued contrary to the agreement reached in a formless *pactum*. In IUDICIA BONAE FIDEI, governed by good faith, an exception was superfluous inasmuch as the judge had to pass the judgment according to the principles of *bona fides* which implied that any reasonable agreement between the parties be taken into consideration.—D. 2.14; C. 2.3.—See CONTRACTUS, EXCEPTIO PACTI, and the following items.

Condanari-Michler, *RE* 18; Beauchet, *DS* 4; *NDI* 9 (Anon.); Ferrini, *Opere* 3 (1929 ex 1892) 243; Manenti, *StSen* 7 (1890) 85, 8 (1891) 1, 31 (1915) 203; G. Platon, *Pactes et contrats en droit romain et byzantin*, 1917; Stoll,

ZSS 44 (1924) 1; Koschaker, *Fschr Hanausek* 1925, 118;
P. Bonfante, *Scritti* 3 (1926) 135; Grosso, *Efficacia dei
patti nei bonae fidei iudicia, MemTor* 3 (1928); idem,
StUrb 1, 2 (1927, 1928); Riccobono, *St Bonfante* 1 (1930)
125; idem, *Stipulationes, contractus, pacta, Corso,* 1934/5;
V. De Villa, *Le usurae ex pacto,* 1937; Boyer, *Le pacte
extinctif d'action, Recueil de l'Acad. de législation de Toulouse,* Sér. 4, v. 13 (1937); G. Lombardi, *Ricerche in tema
di ius gentium,* 1946, 200; G. Grosso, *Il sistema romano
dei contratti,* 2nd ed. 1950, 186.

Pactum adiectum. (A non-Roman term.) An additional agreement to a contract involving a change of
the typical content thereof. Thus, for instance, a
pactum adiectum in a sale was the ADDICTIO IN DIEM,
or LEX COMMISSORIA.

Condanari-Michler, *RE* 18, 2142; P. E. Viard, *Les pactes
adjoints aux contrats,* 1929; Stoll, *ZSS* (1930) 551.

Pactum conventum. A term which seemingly was
used as a technical one in the praetorian Edict (*pacta
conventa,* see PACTUM). It is uncertain whether the
expression is to be understood as two nouns (= pact
—agreement) or as a "pact agreed upon."—See
IUDICIA BONAE FIDEI.

Pactum custodiae. An agreement by which one party
assumed the duty of custody of the other party's
things. Such a duty could be the object of a special
contract (*locatio conductio operarum*) or of an additional clause to another contract.—See CUSTODIA.

Pactum de constituto. See CONSTITUTUM.

**Pactum de .distrahendo (vendendo) or de non dis-
trahendo pignore.** An agreement between debtor
and creditor concerning the sale (or non-sale) of the
pledge in the case of the debtor's default. See IUS
DISTRAHENDI. If in the sale of the pledge the creditor
obtained a sum bigger than the debt was, he had to
restore the surplus (SUPERFLUUM) to the debtor.

Manigk, *RE* 20, 1557.

Pactum de emendo pignore. An agreement between
debtor and creditor that the thing given as a pledge
(*pignus*) might be bought by the creditor or by the
surety who guaranteed the payment.—C. 8.54.

Manigk, *RE* 20, 1557.

Pactum de non petendo. A formless agreement between creditor and debtor by which the former assumed the obligation not to sue the debtor in court
for the payment of the debt or for the fulfillment of
his obligation. Such an agreement could be limited
to a specific action, e.g., *ne depositi agatur* (= not to
proceed with the *actio depositi*) or not to sue for
execution of a judgment-debt (*actio iudicati*); it could
be also limited in time, i.e., not to sue within a
certain space of time. A creditor who contrary to
such an agreement brought an action against the
debtor could be repealed by an *exceptio pacti.* The
benefit involved in a *pactum de non petendo* could
be strictly personal, i.e., granted solely to the debtor
alone, or extended to all persons engaged in the given
obligation (sureties, co-debtors, co-creditors). This
distinction is the basis of the terminology *pactum de*

non petendo in personam and *in rem,* which seems to
be of postclassical origin. A *pactum de non petendo*
could be modified or annulled by a later agreement
ut petere liceat giving the creditor the right to sue
the debtor.

Condanari-Michler, *RE* 18, 2142; De Villa, *NDI* 9; Segrè,
RDCom 12 (1915) 1062; Rotondi, *Scr giuridici* 2 (1922,
ex 1913) 307; Koschaker, *Fschr Hanausek* 1925, 118; Albertario, *St Calisse* 1 (1940) 61; Guarino, *St Scorza* 1940,
443.

Pactum de non praestandā evictione. See EVICTIO.

Pactum de retro emendo (vendendo). An additional
clause in a sale by which the seller is granted the
right to buy back the thing sold, within a certain
time at a fixed price. A contrary agreement was in
favor of the buyer to the effect that he might sell
back the thing purchased to the seller. The terms
de retro emendo (vendendo) were coined in the literature.

Pactum de vendendo pignore. See IUS DISTRAHENDI,
PACTUM DE DISTRAHENDO PIGNORE.

Pactum displicentiae. An additional clause in a sale
to the effect that the buyer is entitled to return the
thing to the seller and to annul the sale within a
certain time if the thing does not suit him. Such a
sale is conditional, its validity depends upon the approval by the buyer. The term *pactum displicentiae*
is not Roman.—See EMPTIO.

Pactum donationis. See DONATIO.

Pactum dotale. An agreement concerning the dowry,
in particular its restitution in the case of dissolution
of the marriage by divorce or death of one of the
spouses.—D. 23.4; C. 5.14.—See DOS, INSTRUMEN-
TUM DOTALE.

Pactum ex continenti. An additional clause (*pactum
adiectum*) to a contract agreed upon by the parties
at the conclusion of the contract. Ant. *pactum ex
intervallo* = an agreement, reached afterwards, primarily in favor of the debtor.—See CONTINENS.

Pactum ex intervallo. See the foregoing item.

Pactum fiduciae. See FIDUCIA.

Pactum in favorem tertii. See CONTRACTUS IN FA-
VOREM TERTII.

Pactum legitimum. (In the later Empire.) A formless agreement protected by an action.

Pactum ne dolus praestetur. A clause attached to a
contract governed by *bona fides* (see CONTRACTUS
BONAE FIDEI) to the effect that the debtor is not
responsible for fraud (see DOLUS), for instance, in a
contract of a deposit (see DEPOSITUM). Such a
clause was not admissible; it was considered as being
against good faith (*contra bonam fidem*) and good
customs (*contra bonos mores*) and as such it was
void. On the other hand, however, the extension of
the liability of the debtor for *culpa* (see CULPA) in a
contract under which he normally was answerable
for *dolus* only (as in the case of a deposit), was valid
(*pactum ut et culpa praestetur*).—See DOLUS MALUS.

Pactum nudum. See NUDUM PACTUM.

Pactum praetorium. A formless agreement the fulfullment of which could be enforced by a praetorian action (*actio in factum*).—See FORMULAE IN IUS CONCEPTAE, RECEPTUM.

Pactum ut minus solvatur. An agreement concluded with an heir by which the creditors of the estate declared to be satisfied with the payment of a portion of the debts if the inheritance was insolvent.

> Guarino, *St Scorza* 1940, 443; *idem, AnCat* 4 (1949–50) 196; see Solazzi, *Concorso dei creditori* 4 (1943) 96.

Pactumeius Clemens. A jurist of the first half of the second century after Christ; he made a brilliant official career (consul A.D. 135). He was frequently employed by Hadrian and Antoninus Pius for official missions into provinces.

> Hanslik, *RE* 18, 2154 (no. 3).

Pacuvius Labeo. A jurist at the end of the Republic, father of the famous jurist LABEO, disciple of the prominent Republican jurist, Servius Sulpicius Rufus.

> Berger, *RE* 18, 2176 (no. 9).

Paedagogium. An educational institution where boys were trained for service as pages in the imperial palace.

> Ensslin, *RE* 18, 2204; Navarre, *DS* 4.

Paedagogus. A slave who escorted the master's children to school and took care of them in school and at home. A *paedagogus* enjoyed a privileged position in the master's house and usually was manumitted sooner than other slaves.—In the later Empire *paedagogus* was the director of the PAEDAGOGIUM.

> Schuppe, *RE* 18 (*s.v. paidagogos*); Navarre, *DS* 4.

Paelex (pelex, pellex). A mistress of a married man; a woman who lived with a man as his wife without being married to him. "She is named by the true name 'a friend' (*amica*) or by the name 'concubine' which is a little more honorable" (D. 50.16.144).—See CONCUBINA.

> Erdmann, *RE* 18; C. Castello, *In tema di matrimonio e concubinato* (1940) 9.

Paenitentia. (From *paenitere*.) A change of one's mind concerning a transaction already concluded or concerning the omission of the performance of a legal act within a fixed term (e.g., non-acceptance of an inheritance when the solemn form of CRETIO was prescribed). Generally *paenitentia* is without any legal effect. However, in Justinian's law there were some specific cases in which a person could unilaterally withdraw from a legal transaction by a simple change of mind, if the other party had not as yet fulfilled his obligation, and through an action *condictio* (termed in literature *condictio propter paenitentiam, ex paenitentiam*) recovered what he had already paid. Thus, for instance, one who had made a donation to a slave's master to have the slave be manumitted, could revoke the donation before the manumission was performed.—See ARRA, IUS PAENITENDI.

> F. Manns, *Pönitenzrecht*, 1879; O. Gradenwitz, *Interpolationen in den Pandekton* 1887, 146; N. Verney, *Ius*

poenitendi, Thèse Lyon, 1890; J. Bendixen, *Das ius poenitendi*, Diss. Göttingen, 1889; W. Felgenträger, *Antikes Lösungsrecht*, 1933, 27.

Paganus. (Adj.) See PECULIUM PAGANUM.

Paganus. (Noun.) Used in different meanings: the inhabitant of a PAGUS; the inhabitant of a lower situated place, a valley, as opposed to an inhabitant of a mountain or a hill, *montanus*; a civilian person (non-soldier), ant. *miles*, hence the distinction *peculium paganum—peculium castrense;* a heathen, a pagan.—C. 1.10; 11.

> Kornemann, *RE* 18; Gilliam, *Amer. Jour. of Philol.* 73 (1952) 75.

Pagus. In oldest times, an ethnic or tribal group comprising several settlements, an arrangement found in the primitive organization of peoples (*populi*) in Italy. According to a not quite reliable source, Rome under the last kings consisted of 26 *pagi*. A minor unit was the VICUS (= village). Under the Republic *pagus* denotes a rural territory, an administrative district. For larger territories with a larger population terms such as *civitas, urbs, oppidum*, etc., were used. "To indicate a piece of land one should say in which *civitas* and *pagus* it is situated" (D. 50.15.4 pr.). The inhabitants of a *pagus = pagani*. In Italy and the provinces the head of the administration of a *pagus* is called *magister, praefectus, curator* or *praepositus pagi*.

> Kornemann, *RE* 18; Toutain, *DS* 4.

Palam. Publicly, before witnesses, "in the presence of many persons" (D. 50.16.33).—See PROSCRIBERE.

Palam est. It is obvious, there is no doubt. The locution occurs frequently in the language of the jurists when they want to stress that the opinion expressed is beyond any doubt.

Palam facere. To announce publicly.

Palatini. All persons in civil or military service in the imperial palace. All functionaries in the financial imperial administration which was concentrated in the office of the COMES SACRARUM LARGITIONUM and of the COMES RERUM PRIVATARUM, were among the *palatini*. The *palatini* in the higher positions enjoyed exemption from public charges (*munera*), sometimes even after leaving their official post.—C. 12.23; 30.

> Ensslin, *RE* 18; Cagnat, *DS* 4.

Palatini largitionum. See LARGITIONES.—C. 12.23.

Palatium. The imperial palace (*sacrum palatium*). *Qui in sacro palatio militant* = persons employed in the imperial palace.—C. 11.77; 12.28.—See ARCHIATER SACRI PALATII.

Palmarium. A compensation given (or promised) to an advocate after a successful trial.—See HONORARIUM.

Paludamentum. A scarlet military cloak, part of the insignia of a magistrate commanding troops outside Rome.

Pandectae. (From Greek = an all embracing work.) It was the second title given by Justinian to the Digest (*"Digesta seu Pandectae"*) ; see DIGESTA IUSTINIANI. The term is not an invention by Justinian, since it was previously used as a title of comprehensive juristic works by Ulpian (in 10 books) and by Modestinus (in 12 books).

Pangere. To agree. Syn. *pacisci. Pangere ne petatur* is syn. with PACTUM DE NON PETENDO.

Panis. (From the fourth century after Christ.) Bread from the state bakeries gratuitously distributed in Constantinople and other cities to meritorious persons or to proprietors of houses in order to stimulate the construction of buildings (*panis aedium, aedificiorum*). *Panis popularis* (*civilis, civicus*) = bread distributed to the poor.—See ANNONA CIVILIS.

Kübler, *RE* 18, 3, 606; *idem, St Bonfante* 2 (1930) 351; D. Van Berchem, *Distribution de blé* (Genève, 1939) 102.

Panis farreus. See CONFARREATIO.

Pantomimus. A pantomine, a stage-dancer. The profession was considered an ARS LUDICRA (dishonest). A *pantomimus* could be killed on the spot when caught by the husband of an adulterous wife.

Papinianistae. The third year students in Byzantine law schools, so called because the chief subject of their studies was the works of Papinian.

Papinianus, Aemilius. A Roman jurist of the second/third century after Christ. He was *praefectus praetorio* from 203 until 205. He died in A.D. 212, executed by order of the Emperor Caracalla. His language shows some peculiarities which, however, do not suffice for the assumption of his Syrian or African origin, but his style is a model of conciseness and precision. Papinianus is one of the most remarkable figures among the Roman jurists. His opinions prove an independent mind, his solutions are based on a profound understanding of the necessities of life, on equity, and, at times, on ethical more than merely technical juristic arguments. See AEQUITAS. His principal works were not comprehensive treatises but collections of cases (*Quaestiones* in 37 books, *Responsa* in 19 books) in which other jurists' *responsa*, court decisions and imperial constitutions were often taken into consideration. Other works include: *Definitiones* (in two books) and a monograph on adultery. Papinianus was appreciated by subsequent writers and Justinian more than any other classical jurist. The so-called Law of Citations (see IURISPRUDENTIA) which attributed a particular importance to Papinian's works, is an eloquent evidence of the loftiness of his reputation in postclassical times.—See NOTAE.

Jörs, *RE* 1, 572 (*s.v. Aemilius*, no. 105) ; Orestano, *NDI* 9; Berger, *OCD*; W. Kalb, *Roms Juristen*, 1890, 111; Leipold, *Über die Sprache des Juristen Papinian*, 1891; E. Costa, *Papiniano*, 1 (1894) ; H. Fitting, *Alter und Folge²*, 1908, 71; Solazzi, *AG* 133 (1946) 8; Schulz, *Scr Ferrini* 4 (Univ. Sacro Cuore, Milan, 1949) 254; W. Kunkel, *Herkunft und soziale Stellung der röm. Juristen*, 1952, 224.

Papirius. (First name uncertain.) A *pontifex maximus* about 500 B.C., author of a collection (called *Ius Papirianum*) of rules of sacral law, generally ascribed to the LEGES REGIAE. The existence of such a collection is based on the mention of a commentary thereon written by a certain Granius Flaccus in the time of Caesar or Augustus, entitled *De iure Papiriano.*

Steinwenter, *RE* 10; 18, 3, 1006; Cuq, *DS* 3, 745; Zocco-Rosa, *NDI* 7; *idem, RISG* 39 (1905) ; Oberziner, *Hist* 1 (1927) ; Di Paola, *St Solazzi* 1948, 634; Paoli, *RHD* 24–25 (1946/7) 157; C. W. Westrup, *Introd. to early R. law* 4, 1 (1950) 47.

Papirius Fronto. A little known Roman jurist of the late second post-Christian century, author of a collection of *Responsa.*

Berger, *RE* 18, 3, 1059.

Papirius Iustus. A jurist of the second half of the second post-Christian century, known only as the author of a collection of imperial constitutions in 20 books, of which only eighteen excerpts were accepted into the Digest. He was the only jurist who edited imperial constitutions in their original text. The edition was without any commentary ·or criticism. His official career is unknown.

Berger, *RE* 18, 3, 1059; Scarlata Fazio, *SDHI* 5 (1939) 414.

Papirius, Sextus. A jurist of the early first century B.C., disciple of Quintus Mucius Scaevola.

Münzer, *RE* 18, 3, 1012 (no. 25).

Par causa (condicio). A legal situation in which several persons (creditors, sureties) have equal rights. "Among several persons in the same legal situation that one who is in possession (of the thing in dispute) is in the better case" (D. 50.17.128 pr.).

Par imperium. The equal power (*imperium*) of magistrates who are colleagues in office.—See COLLEGAE, IMPERIUM.

Par ratio. *Parem rationem adscribere* = the entry in a banker's ledger by which a debt is noted as paid. *Parem rationem facere* = to settle the balance of reciprocal claims; syn. *paria facere.*

Parangariae. Carriages used for the transportation of goods on by-roads.—C. 12.50.—See ANGARIA. ·

Seeck, *RE* 4, 1852; Humbert, *DS* 1, 1659.

Parapherna. "Things which belong to the wife beyond the dowry (*extra dotem*)" (C. 5.14.8). The wife might dispose thereof as she pleased and entitle her husband with the administration. When the marriage was dissolved, the *parapherna* had to be restored to the wife or her heirs. In the later Empire, the *parapherna* were held in defraying the burdens of the marriage (ONERA MATRIMONII) and certain legal rules concerning the dowry were extended to the *parapherna*, as, e.g., the wife was granted a general hypothec on the husband's property as a guaranty for the restitution of the *parapherna*.—C. 5.14.

P. Bonfante, *Corso di dir. rom.* 1 (1925) 373; Pampaloni, *RISG* 52 (1912) 162; G. Castelli, *I p. nei papiri e nelle fonti rom.,* 1913 (= *Scr giuridici* 1, 1923) ; A. Ehrhardt, *Iusta causa traditionis,* 1931, 96.

Paraphrasis Institutionum Theophili. A Greek paraphrase of Justinian's Institutes (see INSTITUTIONES IUSTINIANI) by the Byzantine jurist Theophilus in which the author, one of the compilers of Justinian's Institutes himself, used in a considerable measure the Institutes of Gaius. He added some remarks (not always reliable) of an historical nature.—See THEOPHILUS, INSTITUTIONES GAI.

> Edition: C. Ferrini, *Institutionum graeca paraphrasis, Theophilo vulgo tributa,* 1–2 (1884, 1897) ; J. and P. Zepos, *Ius Graeco-Romanum* 3 (Athens, 1931).—Kübler, *RE* 5A, 2142; Ferrini, *Opere* 1 (1929) 1–228 (several articles of 1884–1887); Riccobono, *BIDR* 45 (1938) 1; Nocera, *RISG* 12 (1937) 251; Maschi, *Punti di vista per la ricostruzione del dir. classico, AnTr* 18 (1946) ; *idem, Scr Ferrini* (Univ. Pavia, 1946) 321; Wieacker, *Fschr J. v. Gierke* 1950, 296.

Parare (paratio). To acquire either by purchase (for money) or otherwise. Syn. *comparare.*

Paratus. Ready, prepared, willing. The term is used primarily of a debtor ready to pay his debt or to give security, or of a debtor summoned to court and willing to assume the role of a defendant in the trial and to cooperate in the continuation of the process (see LITIS CONTESTATIO).

Paratitla. (In Byzantine juristic literature.) Supplementary appendices to single titles of Justinian's codifications (Digest and Code), edited, summarized, or commented on by a Byzantine jurist. The *paratitla* might contain references to additional texts from other titles, connected with the topic dealt with in a given title as well as references to parallel texts. Justinian specifically excluded such kind of commentatory remarks from his ban concerning the commentaries on the Digest.

> Berger, *Bull. Polish Inst. of Arts and Sciences* 3 (New York, 1945) 661 (= *BIDR* 55–56, Post-Bellum, 1951, 129).

Parens. A father, in a broader sense "not only the father, but also the grandfather, the great-grandfather and all ascendants, as well as the mother, grandmother, and great-grandmother" (D. 50.16.51). *Parentes* = parents. *Parentes* also includes the slaves who are parents of a child born in slavery.

Parens binubus. A man who married a second time. If he had children from the first marriage, he could not dispose of his property by testament without taking them into consideration.

Parens manumissor. A father who released a child (a son or daughter) from his paternal power; see EMANCIPATIO. He was entitled to be the guardian of the emancipated child and had a certain right to the intestate inheritance of the child.

> Kreller, *RE* 18, 4, 1456; Solazzi, *Ath* 5 (1927) 101; Grosso, *RISG* 4 (1929) 251; W. Erbe, *Fiduzia,* 1929, 170; Buckland, *JRS* 33 (1943) 11.

Parere (pario). To bring forth, to produce. The term refers to legal transactions or situations from which

an obligation, an action or an exception arises for one or both parties involved.

Parere. See SI PARET.

Paria facere. See PAR RATIO.

Pariculum. See PERICULUM.

Paries communis. A party wall which separates two adjoining buildings. It is held in common ownership by the owners of the two buildings. The situation is governed according to the principles of *communio* except for such measures which are physically impossible, as, for instance, a division.—See DEMOLIRE.

> Fougères, *DS* 4; Brugi, *RISG* 4 (1887) 161, 363; Voigt, *BerSächGW* 1903, 179, 185; G. Branca, *Danno temuto,* 1937, 79.107; Arangio-Ruiz, *FIR* 3 (1943) no. 107.

Parricidas. A term the origin and primitive meaning of which are uncertain. It occurred allegedly in a law attributed to the king Numa Pompilius (Festus p. 221) in the following provision: "If somebody knowingly and with evil intention killed (literally: delivered to death) a free man, let him be a *parricidas* (PARICIDAS ESTO)." It is not certain whether the term means here simply a murderer.—See PARRICIDIUM.

> Leifer, *RE* 18, 4, 1472; Riccobono, *FIR* 1² (1941) 13 (Bibl.) and p. XVI; E. Costa, *Crimini e pene,* 1915, 20; Pasquali, *St Besta* 1 (1939) 69; De Visscher, *Études de dr. rom,* 1931, 466; Gernet, *Rev. de philologie* 63 (1937) 13; Henrion, *Rev. belge de philol. et histoire* 20 (1941) 219; Leroy, *Latomus* 6 (1947) 17; Londres da Nobrega, *ibid.* 9 (1950) 3.

Parricidium. The assassination of a (one's own?) *pater familias* (the head of a family group). The identification of *parricidium* with homicide belongs to a later development. *Parricidium* was one of the first public crimes (*crimina publica*) prosecuted by the state.—D. 48.9; C. 9.17.—See PARRICIDAS, HOMICIDIUM, QUAESTORES PARRICIDII, LEX POMPEIA DE PARRICIDIO, POENA CÚLLEI.

> Lécrivain, *DS* 4; Berger, *OCD*; Danieli, *Archivio penale,* 1949, 315.

Pars. A part, a portion of a whole. *Pro parte* (= for a part) is opposed to *in solidum* (= for the whole) with regard to the liability of a person or to the release of a debtor from an obligation.

Pars. (With reference to state territory.) A province, a large administrative district.

Pars. (In judicial proceedings.) A party to a trial. *Pars actoris* = the plaintiff; *pars rei* = the defendant. —See VICTOR.

Pars dimidia. A half.—See LAESIO ENORMIS, SPONSIO TERTIAE PARTIS.

Pars diversa. The adversary in a trial.

Pars (portio) hereditaria (hereditatis). The share one has in an inheritance.

Pars (portio) legitima. The share of an inheritance due to an heir who would succeed under the law on intestacy (*heres legitimus, ab intestato*). The fourth part of the *pars legitima* (*quarta legitimae partis*) had to be left certain heirs among the next relatives (descendants, ascendants, and later, consanguineous brothers and sisters) in àny form. Otherwise, i.e., if the share left to them was less than the required fourth, or if they were not mentioned in the testament at all or were unjustly disinherited, they had the QUERELA INOFFICIOSI TESTAMENTI which might lead to the rescission of the whole testament.

G. La Pira, *La successione ereditaria ab intestato e contro il testamento*, 1930.

Pars maior. A majority in a public or private corporate body. "What is done by the majority concerns all" (D. 50.17.160.1).

Pars pro indiviso. A part of a thing expressed through a fraction, when the thing cannot be physically divided into parts. Syn. *pars indivisa;* ant. *pars pro diviso.*—See COMMUNIO, INDIVISUS.

Pars virilis. See VIRILIS, PORTIO HEREDITARIA.

Partes. (With reference to an official or a judge.) The official functions (activity) or duties of a magistrate or a judge. *Partes sustinere* = to assume the part or functions, primarily in a civil or criminal trial, such as that of a plaintiff, a defendant, a representative, an accuser, etc. Syn. *partibus fungi.*—See VICE.

Partes formulae. The parts of a formula in the formulary procedure.—See FORMULA, INTENTIO, DEMONSTRATIO, ADIUDICATIO, EXCEPTIO, PRAESCRIPTIO.

Partiarius. See COLONIA PARTIARIA, PARTITIO LEGATA.

Particeps fraudis. See CONSCIUS FRAUDIS.

Participare. To partake, to share in common with others (in profits or losses). The term is used also in a bad sense, to participate in a wrongdoing (fraud, theft).

Partitio legata. A legacy by which a fraction of an estate is left to the legatee (*legatarius partiarius*) who shares the inheritance with the heirs instituted in a testament. The pertinent disposition of the testator runs as follows: "my heir shall divide my estate with . . . ." A *legatarius partiarius* is not a universal successor, therefore he cannot be sued directly by the creditors of the estate. His proportional liability was settled through a special arrangement with the heirs, namely, through reciprocal stipulations (*stipulationes partis et pro parte*) which at the same time guaranteed the legatee the appropriate portion of the sums paid by the debtors of the testator. Syn. *legatum partitionis.*—See SENATUSCONSULTUM PEGASIANUM.

Wlassak, *ZSS* 31 (1910) 200; B. Biondi, *Successione testamentaria*, 1943, 442.

Partus. An embryo in the womb. Before birth it is considered a part of the woman and not a human being. *Partus* can also mean a new-born child (see PARTUS PERFECTUS).—See NASCITURUS, INSPICERE VENTREM, INFANTICIDIUM, AGNOSCERE LIBERUM, SENATUSCONSULTUM PLANCIANUM, and the following items.

Ambrosino, *RISG* 15 (1940) 3.

Partus abactus (partum abigere). Abortion. A woman guilty of criminal abortion was punished with exile. A person who gave a woman a poisonous liquid (*poculum amatorium*) to cause abortion was punished with death if the woman died, otherwise with deportation or, when the woman was of a lower social class, with compulsory labor in mines (*metalla*).

Brecht, *RE* 18, 4, 2046; Humbert, *DS* 1 (*s.v. abortio*).

Partus ancillae. A slave child. Such children were not considered proceeds (see FRUCTUS). If the mother was given as a pledge, the child (*partus ancillae pignoratae, partus pignoris*) shares the legal situation of the mother.—C. 8.24.—See FRUCTUS REI PIGNERATAE.

Brini, *MemBol* 4 (1909/10); V. Basanoff, *P.a.,* Thèse Paris, 1929; Carcaterra, *AnCam* 12, 2 (1938) 51.

Partus perfectus. A child born after a full time of pregnancy. A seven-months' child was held to be a *partus perfectus.*

Partus suppositus. A fraudulently substituted (suppositious) child. Syn. *partus subiectus, subditicius.* —See EDICTUM CARBONIANUM, INSPICERE VENTREM, SUBDITICIUS.

Kleinfeller, *RE* 4A, 952 (*s.v. suppositio partus*); Brecht, *RE* 18, 4, 2048; Saglio, *DS* 4, 1570.

Pascuum. A pasture. The owner of a private pasture land could allow the cattle of others to graze thereon either by a contract of lease (*locatio conductio rei*) or by constituting a servitude (*servitus pecoris pascendi, ius pascui;* see COMPASCERE). He is liable if poisonous grass injured or killed the others' animals. —C. 7.41; 11.60; 61.

Kübler, *RE* 18, 4, 2052.

Pascuum publicum. Public pasture land. The use of such a land by the citizens of a community was originally free. From the fourth century B.C. a fee (*scriptura*) had to be paid to the treasury of the community.—C. 11.61.

Kübler, *RE* 18, 4, 2054.

Passim. Simply, without any further examination of the case under decision. The term is used in the juristic language as ant. to CAUSA COGNITA, i.e., after a scrupulous examination.—See CAUSAE COGNITIO.

Passus. A pace. A Roman mile = one thousand paces (about 1620 English yards). Twenty miles were counted as one day's journey when a magistrate ordered a party to appear in court.

Pastus. (In later imperial constitutions.) The supply and distribution of provisions (primarily for the army).

Pastus pecoris. Pasturing cattle.—See ACTIO DE PASTU PECORIS, SERVITUS PASCUI, PASCUUM, IUS PASCENDI.

Cuq, *DS* 4, 340.

Pater civitatis. Syn. with CURATOR CIVITATIS in the later Empire.

Pater. A father. "Father is he whom the marriage indicates (as such)" D. 2.4.5. The term refers also to a grandfather.—See PATER FAMILIAS, PARENS.

Pater familias. The head of a family, without regard as to whether or not a person so designated has children, whether he is married or is below the age of puberty. A *pater familias* must be a Roman citizen and not under paternal power of another. By the death of a *pater familias* all sons (and grandsons whose father was dead or had been emancipated) who were directly under his paternal power, became *patres familias*. The *pater familias* was the first in the family (*princeps familiae*) and was the master of the "house" (*in domo dominium habet*). His power lasted as long as he lived, without regard to the age of the persons under his paternal power (*patria potestas*) or their official position. His power was boundless and limited only by custom and social tradition. He alone has the right to dispose of the family property.—C. 4.13; 43.—See PATRIA POTESTAS, FILIUS FAMILIAS, BONUS PATER FAMILIAS, DILIGENS PATER FAMILIAS, EMANCIPATIO, INTERDICTUM DE LIBERIS EXHIBENDIS.

Sachers, *RE* 18, 4, 2121 (Bibl.); Anon., *NDI* 9; Longo, *BIDR* 40 (1932) 201; C. Castello, *Studi sul diritto famaliare*, 1942, 69; Volterra, *RIDA* 1 (1948) 213; *idem*, *RISG* 85 (1948) 103; Daube, *St Albertario* 1 (1952) 435; Sachers, *Fschr Schulz* 1 (1951) 319.

Pater naturalis. An illegitimate father, sometimes the father of an emancipated son or of one who has been adopted by another.

Lanfranchi, *StCagl* 30 (1946) 47.

Pater patratus. The head of the group of *fetiales* who as representatives of the Roman people declared war upon an enemy or acted in the proceedings of *deditio* (extradition of persons or things.)—See FETIALES, DEDITIO, BELLUM, BELLUM INDICERE.

De Ruggiero, *DE* 3, 68; Muller, *Mn* 55 (1927) 386; Krahe, *Arch. für Religionswissenschaft* 34 (1937) 112.

Pater patriae. The first emperor who was granted the title of the "father of the fatherland" was Augustus. Before him the title had been conferred on Caesar, shortly before his death. After Augustus several emperors were honored by this title.

L. Berlinger, *Beiträge zur inoffiziellen Titulatur der röm. Kaiser*, 1935, 77; M. Grant, *From imperium to auctoritas*, 1946, p. 444 (Bibl.).

Pater solitarius. A widower and father of legitimate children who after the death of his wife remained unmarried. The *Lex Iulia et Papia Poppaea* contained a provision concerning the *pater solitarius* as a COELEBS, but its content is unknown.—See LEX IULIA DE MARITANDIS ORDINIBUS.

Solazzi, *ANap* 61 (1942) 184.

Pati. To suffer, to bear (a loss, an injury, damages); with regard to civil judicial matters = to be involved in a controversy or a trial (*pati controversiam, actionem, interdictum, exceptionem*); in criminal matters to incur a punishment (*poenam*).

Patientia servitutis. Occurred when the owner of land tolerated the exercising by another (a neighbor) of certain rights (*usus servitutis*) on his property, such as ITER, ACTUS, and the like. This toleration was not understood as a simple passive attitude but as a tacit expression of the will of the owner and a recognition as if the other were entitled to exercise an easement on account of a previous agreement (the constitution of a servitude). In classical law the beneficiary could use the ACTIO PUBLICIANA, in Justinian's law the *patientia* is identified with a voluntary concession of a servitude (*traditio servitutis*).

See Perozzi, *Scritti 2* (1948, ex 1897); Rabel, *Mél Girard* 2 (1912) 394; Guarneri-Citati, *Indice²* (1927) 64; B. Biondi, *Servitù prediali*, 1948, 229; S. Solazzi, *Requisiti e modi di costituzione di servitù pred.*, 1947, 149.

Patientiam praestare. To tolerate another's (a neighbor's) entering into one's property and performing there certain acts (such as the demolition of a construction which was harmful to a neighbor's property and which the owner was obligated to carry out but failed). This occurred usually when a person other than the owner of a landed property (his lessee, slave, or predecessor in title) built a construction which caused or threatened to cause damage to a neighbor's property. Such construction could be averted by a protesting action on the part of the neighbor (see OPERIS NOVI NUNTIATIO, ACTIO AQUAE PLUVIAE ARCENDAE). If the harmful construction was not destroyed by the owner or his lessee, the neighbor might do it at his own expense (which, of course, had to be reimbursed by the owner) and the owner had to tolerate such action on his land.—See the foregoing item.

Patres. The oldest term denoting the members of the king's senate which presumably was composed of the "fathers," i.e., the heads of the *gentes* (see GENS) and prominent families. Livy says that the earliest senators were called *patres* for dignity's sake (*propter honorem*). The relatives of the *patres* and their descendants formed the class of *patricii* (patricians). Hence *patres* was used as syn. with *patricii*, as, e.g., in the norm of the Twelve Tables which forbade marriage between plebeians and patricians (*patres*).—See AUCTORITAS PATRUM.

Kübler, *RE* 18, 4, 2222.

Patres conscripti. Originally the plebeian members of the senate when, about the middle of the fourth century B.C., the plebeians were admitted to the senate, their selection being determined by the censors. Later, the term *patres conscripti* was applied to senators without distinction as to whether they were patricians or plebeians.

Brassloff, *RE* 4; De Ruggiero, *DE* 2, 604; O'Brien-Moore, *RE* Suppl. 6, 674; Meurs, *Mn* 55 (1927) 377.

Patria. The native country, the fatherland. "Rome is our common native country" (D. 50.1.33: *Roma communis nostra patria est*). For *patria* in the meaning of the entire Roman state, see PATER PATRIAE.

E. De Ruggiero, *La patria nel dir. pubblico*, 1921; L. Krattinger, *Der Begriff des Vaterlandes im republ. Rom,* Zürich, 1944.

Patria potestas. The power of the head of a family (see PATER FAMILIAS) over the members, i.e., his children, natural and adoptive (see FILIUS FAMILIAS), his wife, if the conclusion of the marriage was combined with *conventio in manum,* the wives of those sons who remained under his power (under the same condition as with regard to his wife). Originally unlimited in the judicial, economic, and moral fields, the *patria potestas* gradually became a power in the interest of the persons subject to it and was conceived as embracing moral duties (*officium*), such as protection, maintenance, and assistance. The IUS VITAE NECISQUE of the earliest law became more and more restricted under imperial legislation, and in the law of Justinian it was only an historical reminiscence. Restrictions were also imposed on the father's right to expose a child (see EXPONERE FILIUM). Only the *ius vendendi,* i.e., the right to sell a child which made him a *persona in mancipio* in Rome, and a slave when he was sold abroad, remained in force for a longer period; in Justinian's law selling a child was admitted in the case of extreme poverty of the parents, but the child could redeem himself and become free by paying the buyer the price that he had paid to his father. For surrendering a member of the family for damages done to a third person, see NOXA, NOXAE DEDITIO, ACTIONES NOXALES. The institution was abolished by Justinian. For the legal situation of a person under paternal power as far as property, legal capacity in transactions, the conclusion of a marriage are concerned, see FILIUS FAMILIAS, FILIA FAMILIAS, PECULIUM. The head of a family acquired *patria potestas* over his children born in a legitimate matrimony or through adoption of another's offspring (see ADOPTIO, ARROGATIO). The *patria potestas* was extinguished through CAPITIS DEMINUTIO of the father, or through release from the paternal power, see EMANCIPATIO. Without regard to the will of the family's head, the extinction of the *patria potestas* occurred when the son became a priest (*flamen Dialis*) or the daughter a Vestal virgin. In the law of Justinian a person who obtained a high governmental post or became a dignity in the Church hierarchy, was free from paternal power.—Inst. 1.9; D. 1.7; 12; C. 8.46.—See moreover ALIENI IURIS, ALIMENTA, INTERDICTUM DE LIBERIS EXHIBENDIS, PATER FAMILIAS.

Beauchet, *DS* 4; Berger, *OCD*; Cornil, *NRHD* 21 (1897) 416; Costa, *MemBol* 1909/10, 117; Bonfante, *Scritti* 1 (1926, ex 1906) 64; Wenger, *Hausgewalt im röm. Altertum, Miscellanea F. Ehrle* 2 (Rome, 1924); H. Stockar, *Entzug der väterlichen Gewalt,* Zürich, 1903; C. W. Westrup, *Introduction to the early R. law,* 3 (1939); C. Castello, *St sul diritto familiare e gentilizio* 1942, 63; Cicogna, *StSen* 59 (1945) 44; Kaser, *ZSS* 58 (1938) 62, 59 (1939) 31; *idem, Das altröm. Ius,* 1949, *passim; idem, ZSS* 67 (1950) 474.

Patricii. The earliest patricians were the descendants of the PATRES, i.e., the members of the senate in the regal period. The patrician families and groups of families (see GENS) were the privileged class in the citizen body (originally perhaps the only Roman citizens), while the lower class, the plebeians (*plebeii*) were deprived of political rights and lived in economically unfavorable conditions. During a long period the *patricii* were the exclusive holders of magistracies and priestly offices; the assignment of public land (*ager publicus*) was almost exclusively to their benefit; voting in the *comitia* was arranged to their advantage; and intermarriage between them and the plebeians was not permitted. The struggle between these two social classes of the Roman people lasted more than two centuries (until the early third century B.C.); it had some dramatic episodes (three secessions of the plebeians), but it brought the plebeians a gradual admission to the magistracies and, in the last analysis, political equality. Among the political conquests of the plebeians were: the creation of TRIBUNI PLEBIS (in 494 B.C.?), the legislation of the Twelve Tables (see LEX DUODECIM TABULARUM, in 451/50 B.C.), intermarriage with patricians (see LEX CANULEIA, 445 B.C.), admission to the military tribunate (see TRIBUNI MILITUM CONSULARI POTESTATE), the LEGES LICINIAE SEXTIAE (admission to the consulship, 367 B.C.), admission to the highest pontificate (LEX OGULNIA), election of the first plebeian censor (in 356 B.C.), the first plebeian dictatorship (in 351 B.C.), the LEX PUBLILIA PHILONIS (339 B.C.), election of the first plebeian praetor (in 337 B.C.), and finally, the LEX HORTENSIA (287 B.C.) which made the plebiscites (see PLEBISCITUM) of equal legal force with the *leges* voted in the popular assemblies (*comitia*). Only some sacerdotal posts, the office of the INTERREX, the honor of being a PRINCEPS SENATUS and some other minor privileges remained reserved for the *patricii.* Patriciate was acquired through birth in a legal marriage (*iustae nuptiae*) when the father was a patrician, through adoption by a patrician, through marriage with a patrician, concluded in the form of CONFARREATIO which remained a patrician form of marriage with *manus.* Under the Principate meritorious persons were granted the patriciate by the emperor. The patricians as a hereditary nobility lost much of their significance through the rise of a new nobility based on wealth (see EQUITES) or the holding of high imperial office. The Emperor Constantine created the patriciate (*patriciatus, patricia dignitas*) as a personal (not hereditary) honorific title to be conferred by the emperor on high dignitaries for life (= "highness"). Justinian extended the patriciate to all persons who had the right to the title ILLUSTRIS. This involved exemption from *patria potestas.*—C. 12.3.—See CURIAE, TRANSITIO AD PLEBEM.

Kübler, *RE* 18, 4, 2222; Lécrivain, *DS* 4; Di Marzo, *NDI* 9; Momigliano, *OCD*; Oberziner, *Patriziato e plebe, Pubbl. dell'Accad. Scientifico-Letteraria*, Milan, 1 (1913); Rose, *JRS* 12 (1922) 106; Picotti, *Arch. storico ital.*, Ser. 7, vol. 9 (1928) 3; Fruin, *TR* 9 (1929) 142; Ensslin, *Der Konstantinische Patriziat, Annuaire de l'Institut de Philol. et d'Hist. orient. et slaves, 2* (1934) 361; Bernardi, *Rend Lomb* 1945/6, 3.

Patricius (Patrikios). A prominent jurist and teacher in the Law School of Beirut in the second half of the fifth century after Christ. Excerpts of his writings, mostly devoted to imperial constitutions, occur in the scholia to the BASILICA.

Berger, *RE* 18, 4, 2244 (under no. 2).

Patrimonialis. See PATRIMONIUM CAESARIS.

Patrimonium. The whole property of a person; in a narrower sense, the property inherited from one's father (ancestor).—See MUNERA PATRIMONII, RES EXTRA PATRIMONIUM.

Pfaff, *Zur Lehre vom Vermögen, Fschr Hanausek* 1925, 89; M. F. Lepri, *Saggi sul patrimonio* 1 (1942); Albanese, *Successione ereditaria, AnPal* 20 (1949) 135; Scherillo, *Lezioni I. Le cose* (1945) 4.

Patrimonium Caesaris (principis). Under the Principate the crown property of the emperor, inherited from his predecessor and left by him to his successor. It gradually assumed larger and larger dimensions through inheritances, purchases, and confiscations (see BONA DAMNATORUM) and was administered by *procuratores patrimonii*. Transfer of objects belonging to the *patrimonium* through sale or donation was admitted. In the later Empire the official term was *sacrum patrimonium*. A *comes sacri patrimonii* was at the head of the administration. The distinction between the *patrimonium principis* and the privy purse of the emperor (RES PRIVATA PRINCIPIS) was in the later Empire not so precisely observed as it was before and revenues of the *patrimoniam principis* went to the private property of the emperor. Many details are still doubtful and the frequent changes in the administration of the pertinent funds and lands do not facilitate a neat distincton. The general tendency was to attribute as much as possible to the emperor. The adj. *patrimonialis* refers in the later Empire to persons and land pertaining to the *sacrum patrimonium* (*coloni, fundi, agri, patrimoniales*).—C. 1.34; 11.62–65.—See RES PRIVATA PRINCIPIS, RATIO PRIVATA, FUNDI PATRIMONIALES.

Lécrivain, *DS* 4 and 3, 961; Orestano, *NDI* 9, 515; O. Hirschfeld, *Kaiserliche Verwaltungsbeamte*² (1905) 1; L. Mitteis, *Röm. Privatrecht* 1 (1908) 358.

Patrocinari. To give protection, to defend by legal remedies.

Patrocinium. Patronage, protection, a relationship between two persons in which one, the *patronus*, grants protection to the other. *Patrocinium* is also used of the legal assistance given to a party in a trial by an advocate.

Kornemann, *RE* Suppl. 4.

Patrocinium vicorum (colonorum). Possessors of small landed property in the later Empire (fourth century), vexed by tax collectors and public charges, used to render themselves under the protection of wealthy and influential men (POTENTIORES) as their *patroni*. The latter exploited this situation for tax evasion. Imperial legislation tried to abolish these practices but in vain. The land taken under protection by the patrons remained in their possession and the former small land-proprietors became the serfs of their protectors.—C. 11.54.—See COLONI, LATIFUNDIA.

Kornemann, *RE* Suppl. 4, 265; M. Gelzer, *Studien zur byzantinischen Verwaltung Aegyptens*, 1909, 69; F. De Zulueta, *De patrociniis vicorum, Oxford St in Social and Legal History* 1, 1909; Lewald, *ZSS* 32 (1911) 473; G. Rouillard, *L'administration civile de l'Égypte rom.*, 1928, '10; Martroye, *RHD* 7 (1928) 201.

Patrona. A woman who manumitted her slave, a patroness of a freedman. See PATRONUS. Marriage between a freedman and his patroness was prohibited.

Patronatus. The relationship between the former master and his freedman. See PATRONUS, IUS PATRONATUS. In a broader sense, *patronatus* refers to any relationship between a person (*patronus*) who protects (defends) another and the protected person. It refers also to a legal adviser (lawyer) of a party to a trial (*patronus causae*).—D. 37.14; C. 6.4.—See PATROCINIUM, CLIENTES, IUS APPLICATIONIS.

Patronus. The master of a slave became after manumitting him the *patronus* of the freedman (*libertus*). The freedman had various duties towards his manumissor; see OBSEQUIUM, REVERENTIA. "The person of a patron should always appear honorable and sacred to the freedman and his son" (D. 37.15.9). The freedman had to abstain from accusing the patron of criminal doings and from suing him with actions which involved infamy (*actiones famosae*). He could, however, sue him by permission of the praetor. For the obligation of the freedman to render certain services to the patron, see OPERAE LIBERTI, IURATA PROMISSIO LIBERTI. Between the patron and his freedman there was a reciprocal obligation of maintenance in the case of poverty. The patron had certain rights of succession to the inheritance of his freedman (see BONORUM POSSESSIO INTESTATI) and he could demand the rescinding of alienations and other dispositions made by the freedman with the purpose of defrauding the patron of his rightful inheritance (see ACTIO CALVISIANA). If a freedman who had no children or had disinherited them, did not in his will reward his patron or his patron's sons, the praetor granted the patron a *bonorum possessio contra tabulas* of one half of the freedman's property. Marriage between a freedman and his patroness (*patrona*) or with his patron's daughter was prohibited. After the death of the patron, the patronate went to his heirs, the patron might, however, assign the freedman to one of the heirs, see ADSIGNATIO LIBERTI.—D. 37.14; 38.1–3; C. 6.3–7.—See IUDICIUM OPERARUM, INGRATUS LIBERTUS, BENEFICIUM COMPETENTIAE, LIBERTUS (Bibl.).

La Pira, *St ital. di filol. clas.* 7 (1929) 145; J. Lambert, *Les operae liberti,* 1934; A. A. Schiller, *Legal Essays in tribute to O. K. McMurray,* 1935, 623; Kaser, *ZSS* 58 (1938) 88; K. Harada, *ibid.* 138; C. Cosentini, *St sui liberti* 1 (1948) 69, 2 (1950) 11.

Patronus causae. Syn. ADVOCATUS.

Patronus clientis. See CLIENTES.

Patronus civitatis (coloniae). See PATRONUS MUNICIPII.

Patronus collegii. An honorary protector of an association, usually a magistrate or an imperial official. In the later Empire associations concerned with the provision of food for Rome were supervised by *patroni* who were members of the associations.

Lécrivain, *DS* 4, 359; W. Liebenam, *Geschichte und Organisation des röm. Vereinswesens,* 1910, 212.

Patronus fisci. See ADVOCATUS FISCI.

Patronus municipii (civitatis). Municipalities used to place themselves under the protection of one or more powerful persons (senators, ex-magistrates) who were selected (*adoptare,* later *cooptare*) by the municipal council and given the title *patronus.* The pertinent decree was engraved on a bronze tablet (*tabula patronatus*) in two copies, one for the *patronus,* the other for the municipality. The patronage was hereditary. The *patronus* defended the interests of the municipality in public and private matters, subsidized the construction of monuments and public buildings, etc. The patronage of a colony was similar.

Kornemann, *RE* 16, 625; Lécrivain, *DS* 3, 299; Mommsen, *Jurist. Schriften* 1 (1905) 237, 345; Thouvenot, *CRAI* 1941, 133; 1947, 485.

Patronus provinciae. Some provinces had a protector, *patronus,* who in case of abuse by a provincial official intervened with the Roman authorities in order to obtain the prosecution of the wrongdoers. The patron was a distinguished and influential person of the Roman nobility, often a descendant of the conqueror of the province.

Pauliana actio. See FRAUS.

Paulus, Iulius. A famous jurist whose prolific literary activity (about 320 *libri*) gave Justinian's compilers the opportunity to excerpt his writings very extensively for the Digest. The dates of his birth and death are unknown. He was a member of the imperial council under Septimius Severus and Caracalla, and *praefectus praetorio* under Alexander Severus. His works were written in the first decades of the third century. He was the author of an extensive commentary on the praetorian Edict (in 80 books) and a treatise on *ius civile* (*ad Sabinum,* in 16 books). Among his writings are also commentaries on works of some earlier jurists and a great number of monographs on various topics of public, fiscal, private, and criminal laws. There is in recent litera-

ture a tendency to deny Paulus' authorship of a number of writings, a tendency which is not free from exaggeration. For his *Sententiae,* see SENTENTIAE PAULI. Paulus was not an uncritical compiler; he often expressed opinions of his own and some of his critical remarks, in particular on the decisions of earlier jurists, give evidence of the sagacity of his juristic thinking.

Berger, *RE* 10, 690 (*s.v. Iulius*); idem, *OCD;* Orestano, *NDI* 9 (*s.v. Paolo*); Kübler, *Lehrbuch der Gesch. des r.R.,* 1925, 283; C. Sanfilippo, *Pauli Decretorum libri tres, Pubbl. Fac. Giur. Catania,* 1939; De Robertis, *RISG* 15 (1940) 205; Scherillo, *St Solazzi* 1948, 439.

Pauperes. Poor people. From the time of Nerva Roman emperors ordered that public care be taken of children of poor parents and that nourishment be provided them from public funds.—See PAUPERTAS.

J. J. Esser, *De pauperum cura apud Romanos,* 1903; A. Müller, *Jugendfürsorge in der röm. Kaiserzeit,* 1903; Biondi, *Ius* 3 (1952) 233.

Pauperies. See ACTIO DE PAUPERIE.

Paupertas. Poverty. It was an acceptable excuse from guardianship and also ground for exclusion from being an accuser in a criminal matter.—See PAUPERES.

Pax. Peace. A state of war between Roman and another state was normally ended by an armistice (*indutiae*). Peace, *pia et aeterna pax* (= a pious and eternal peace), was achieved by a special, solemnly enacted treaty, *foedus,* which might not only establish peaceful relations between the former belligerants but also *amicitia* (= friendship) and even a community of political interests (*societas,* see SOCII). The conclusion of a peace treaty was in the competence of FETIALES or special embassies; the consent of the people and the senate was required. Under the Empire it was the emperor who concluded peace. Gaius (Inst. 3.94) mentions as the form for the conclusion of peace the *sponsio,* an exchange of a question (*pacem futuram spondes?*) and answer (*spondeo*) between the emperor and the sovereign of the other state.—See SPONSIO, AMICITIA, AMICUS POPULI ROMANI.

De Ruggiero, *DE* 2, 767; H. Lévy-Bruhl, *Quelques problèmes du très ancien dr. rom.,* 1934, 40.

Peccatum. In classical law a violation of a somewhat criminal nature of a legal norm. A neat distinction between the term and *crimen* or *delictum* can hardly be established. In Justinian's law *peccatum* is not only a violation of human laws but also that of an ethical norm.

G. Segrè, *St Bonfante* 3 (1930) 515; Roberti, *St Calisse* 1 (1940) 161.

Peculatus. Misappropriation of things belonging to the state, embezzlement of public money. Hence *peculatus* is also named *furtum pecuniae publicae, furtum publicum.* A commanding general who appropriates the booty taken from the enemy or the money obtained from its sale (*manubiae*) to his own profit was guilty of *peculatus.* Augustus' *Lex Iulia* *peculatus,* still in force in Justinian's time, was the basic statute on the matter: "No one should intercept or appropriate any sacred, religious, or public money for his own profit unless he is permitted to do so by law" (D. 48.13.1). The statute also defined *peculatus* as a case in which a person "added anything to (alloyed) or mixed with, gold, silver, or copper belonging to the state" (*D. ibid.*), to the detriment of the state. A particular form of embezzlement occurred when a person who had received money from the treasury for a specific purpose did not spend the money thereon (*pecuniae residuae*). Later imperial legislation increased the penalties for *peculatus*; Justinian ordered deportation or the death penalty, according to the gravity of the case.—D. 48.13; C. 9.28.—See QUAESTIONES PERPETUAE, LEX IULIA PECULATUS, RESIDUA, PRAEDA.

Brecht, *RE* Suppl. 7; Cuq, *DS* 4.

Peculiaris. Connected with, or pertaining to, a PECULIUM. *Res peculiares* = things belonging to a *peculium,* such as money, claims, goods, business equipment, and the like. *Peculiari nomine, peculiariter* = (to hold a thing) as belonging to a *peculium,* or (to buy one) from the means of the *peculium.*—See MERX PECULIARIS.

Peculium. A sum of money, a commercial or industrial business, or a small separate property granted by a father to his son or by a master to his slave, for the son's (or slave's) use, free disposal, and fructification through commercial or other transactions. The origin of the institution is to be found in the increase in the economic need of the Roman citizens to use the services and activity of the persons under their paternal power and of their slaves able to develop independent business activity in the interest of the family group and its head. The *peculium* remained the father's (master's) property, but was separate from his own property; the son (the slave), however, had the right to administer the separate fund or business and dispose thereof through various transactions (not by donations). In Justinian's law the free administration of the *peculium* (*libera administratio peculii*) had to be conceded expressly. An existing *peculium* could be increased (*augeri*) by additional funds or goods, diminished (*minui*) or fully withdrawn (*adimi*) by the grantor. The concession of a *peculium* by a father (master) created on the part of the grantor a civil liability for debts and obligations contracted by the son (slave) in transactions concluded with third persons. This liability was, however, restricted to the pecuniary value of the *peculium* (*dumtaxat de peculio*), after deduction of whatever the son (slave) owed to his father (master). The creditors of the *peculium* had a direct action against the father (master), *actio de peculio;* or, when the father (master) had a special profit from the transaction concluded with the manager of the *peculium,* an action called *actio de in rem verso* (for his enrichment). Both these actions, which were introduced by the praetor, belong to the so-called *actiones adiecticiae qualitatis* (see EXERCITOR NAVIS). —D. 15.1; 2; C. 4.26; 7.23.—See ACTIO TRIBUTORIA, LEGATUM PECULII, MERX PECULIARIS, and the following items.

V. Uxkull, *RE* 19; Anon., *NDI* 9; L. Lusignani, *Consumazione processuale dell'actio de peculio,* 1899; *idem, Ancora intorno alla consumazione, etc.,* 1901; Solazzi, *StSen* 23 (1905) 113; *idem, St Fadda* 1 (1906) 347; *idem, St Brugi* (1910) 203; *idem, BIDR* 17, 18, 20 (1905–1908); Seckel, *Fg Bekker* 1907; L. Lemarié, *De l'actio tributoria,* Thèse Paris, 1910; Buckland, *LQR* 31 (1915); G. Longo, *AG* 96 (1928) 184; *idem, BIDR* 38 (1930) 29; *idem, SDHI* 1 (1935) 392; G. Micolier, *Pécule et capacité patrimoniale,* Thèse Lyon, 1932; E. Albertario, *Studi* 1 (1933) 139; Biscardi, *StSen* 60 (1948) 580; G. E. Longo, *SDHI* 16 (1950) 99.

Peculium adventicium. Used in the literature for everything that a *filius familias* acquired through his own labor or the liberality of a third person (a donation, a legacy). According to Justinian's law such acquisitions remained the son's property, the father having only a usufruct on it. Ant. *peculium profecticium* ('term not Roman), the normal *peculium* granted by a father to his son (*a patre profectum* = coming from the father).

Peculium castrense. Everything that a *filius familias* earned or acquired from, or during, his military service (*in castris*). From the time of Augustus he was permitted to dispose of it by testament. Hadrian extended this privilege to soldiers discharged from service and veterans. The *peculium castrense* embraced the gifts which the soldier received when he entered service and inheritances received from fellow soldiers. Later, a *filius familias* might freely dispose of his *peculium castrense* since "with regard to it he acts as a head of a family (*pater familias*)," D. 14.6.2.—D. 49.17; C. 1.3; 12.30; 12.36.

Cagnat, *DS* 4; v. Uxkull, *RE* 19, 15; H. Fitting, *Das p.c. in seiner gesch. Entwicklung,* 1871; Appleton, *NRHD* 35 (1911) 593; E. Albertario, *Studi* 1 (1933) 159; A. Guarino, *BIDR* 48 (1941) 41; Daube, *St Albertario* 1 (1952) 435.

Peculium paganum. The name given by Justinian to an ordinary *peculium,* as distinguished from *peculium castrense* and *peculium quasi castrense.*

Peculium profecticium. See PECULIUM ADVENTICIUM.

Peculium quasi castrense. Everything that a *filius familias* earned as a public official, as a lawyer, in the service of the Church, or by the liberality of the emperor or empress. The legal situation of a *peculium quasi castrense* was the same as that of a *peculium castrense.*

Uxkull, *RE* 19, 16; Orestano, *AnMac* 11 (1937) 118; Archi, *St Besta* 1 (1939) 121.

Pecunia. Money. Originally the term denoted property in cattle (*pecus*), as distinguished from other kinds of property; see FAMILIA. In classical language "the term *pecunia* comprises all things, both movables and immovables, both corporeal things and rights" (D. 50.16.222).—See CREDERE, OTIOSUS.

> Mickwitz, *RE* 19; Sachers, *RE* 18, 3, 2125; Lenormant, *DS* 4; Pfaff, *Fschr Hanausek* 1925, 94 (Bibl.); M. Wlassak, *Erb- und Vermächtnisrecht, SbWien* 215 (1933) 5; M. F. Lepri, *Saggi sul patrimonio* 1 (1942); K. F. Thormann, *Der doppelte Ursprung der mancipatio*, 1943, 155; Mattingly, *Numismatic Chronicle* 1953, 21.

Pecunia compromissa. See COMPROMISSUM.

Pecunia constituta. A money debt reaffirmed by a CONSTITUTUM.

Pecunia credita. See CREDERE, ACTIO CERTAE CREDITAE PECUNIAE, MUTUA PECUNIA.

Pecunia fenebris. Money lent on interest.—See FENUS.

Pecunia (or summa) honoraria. A sum of money (not less than ten thousand sesterces), paid by municipal magistrates (*duoviri iuri dicundo*) when they entered service. On such occasions also other kinds of gifts were also offered to the municipality (a statue or the arrangement of spectacular games, *ludi*).

> Liebenam, *RE* 5, 1814.

Pecunia indebita. See INDEBITUM, CONDICTIO INDEBITI, SOLUTIO INDEBITI.

Pecunia mutua. See MUTUA PECUNIA.

Pecunia numerata. See NUMERARE PECUNIAM.

Pecunia publica. Money belonging or owed to the state treasury (see AERARIUM). *Pecunia publica* could be lent to private individuals only on interest and with real security.—See PECULATUS.

Pecunia residua. See PECULATUS.

Pecunia sacra. Money belonging to a temple or destined for divine cult and sacrifices. Embezzlement or robbery of such money was qualified as a *crimen* PECULATUS.

Pecunia traiecticia. See FENUS NAUTICUM.

Pecuniarius. Expressed or evaluated in a sum of money; concerning a payment in money (*causa, lis, res pecuniaria*).

> G. Pacchioni, *La pecuniarietà dell'interesse nelle obbligazioni.* 1st app. to the translation of C. F. Savigny's *Obbligazioni,* 2 (1915) 305.

Pecus. A domestic four-footed animal, normally living in a herd (*gregatim,* see GREX), such as "sheep, goats, oxen, horses, mules, donkeys" (D. 9.2.2.2) and pigs. Dogs are excluded. The term appears in the LEX AQUILIA, which dealt with damages done to animals (*pecudes*). Ant. *animalia quae pecudes non sunt.*—See ANIMALIA QUAE COLLO DORSO DOMANTUR, IUMENTUM.

Pedaneus iudex. See IUDEX PEDANEUS.

Pedarii. See SENATORES PEDARII.

Pedes (pedester). An infantryman. *Militia pedestris* = infantry.

Pedius, Sextus. A jurist of the late first century and the early second. His original and independent ideas are known only from quotations by later jurists, primarily by Ulpian and Paul, because his works were not directly excerpted in the Digest. He is the author of an extensive commentary on the praetorian and aedilian edicts.

> Berger, *RE* 19, 41 (no. 3); La Pira, *BIDR* 45 (1938) 293.

Pegasus. A jurist of the second half of the first post-Christian century.—See SENATUSCONSULTUM PEGASIANUM.

> Berger, *RE* 19, 64.

Peira. A collection of juristic decisions, written in Greek about the middle of the eleventh century by a judge, Eustathios Romaios (Romanus).

> Editions: Zachariae v. Lingenthal, *Ius Graeco-Romanum* 1 (1856); J. and P. Zepos, *Ius Graeco-Romanum* 4 (Athens, 1931).—Mortreuil, *Histoire du droit byzantin* 2 (1844) 474; Zachariae v. Lingenthal, *Krit. Jahrbücher für die deutsche Rechtswissenschaft,* 1847, 596.

Pellex. See PAELEX.

Penates. Deities protecting the household of a Roman citizen.—See LARES.

> Weinstock, *RE* 19, 423.

Pendente condicione. When the condition is still pending. During the time of uncertainty as to whether a condition would be fulfilled or not, the legal situation varies according to the nature of the conditional obligation and the contents of the condition.—See CONDICIO.

Pendēre (pendeo). To hang. See FRUCTUS PENDENTES.—*Pendere* as syn. with *in pendenti esse* = to be uncertain, in suspense. The term refers to legal situations, rights, or duties which are uncertain until (*donec*) a specific event or fact happens or until a fixed day arrives upon which the suspended validity of a legal act or transaction depends. "What is in suspense is not considered as existing" (D. 50.17. 169.1).—See CONDICIO PENDET, IN PENDENTI ESSE, LITE PENDENTE, PENDENTE CONDICIONE.

Pendēre (pendo). To pay out (a fine, interest, taxes).

Penes. (Prep.) In the power (or possession or house) of a person.

Pensatio (from pensare). A recompense.—See COMPENSATIO.

Pensio. Payment by installment, either of a part of a sum due or of a sum due at fixed intervals (such as rents for the lease of a house or a farm, in the case of EMPHYTEUSIS, or alimony). *Pensio* also refers to payments of taxes or other sums due to the fisc. Syn. *pensitatio.*

> Wenger, *Canon, SbWien* 220 (1942) 35.

Pensitatio. See PENSIO.

Penus. See LEGATUM PENORIS.

Per aes et libram. Some legal acts of early origin were performed with the use of copper and scales (such as MANCIPATIO, NEXUM, a specific form of testament, COËMPTIO, SOLUTIO PER AES ET LIBRAM) and the pronunciation of prescribed solemn formulae. The acts (*gesta, negotia*) thus performed required the presence of five Roman citizens as witnesses and of a *libripens* (the man who held the scales). Acts *per aes et libram* went out of use in the later law.

—See MANCIPARE, LIBRA, LIBRIPENS, FAMILIAE EMPTOR, TESTAMENTUM PER AES ET LIBRAM.

Kunkel, *RE* 14, 999; 1006; Severini, *NDI* 9; Popescu-Spineni, *ACDR* 2 Bologna (1935) 553; H. Lévy-Bruhl, *Nouvelles études* 1947, 97 (= *LQR* 1944, 51); W. Geddes, *Per aes et libram,* Liverpool, 1952.

Peraequatio. (In fiscal administration.) An equitable adjustment of taxes through an increase or reduction of the last year's taxes. The operation was performed by a special officer, a supervisor in tax assessments (in the later Empire), *peraequator.*—C. 11.58.

Seeck, *RE* 5, 1184; Ensslin, *RE* 19, 564.

Peragere. To accomplish, to perform a legal act completely, e.g., *peragere testamentum*; with regard to judicial proceedings to continue one's activity therein until the defendant in a civil trial, or the accused in a criminal case, is condemned.

Perceptio fructuum. Gathering the fruits after their separation from the soil which produced them. See SEPARATIO FRUCTUUM. The *perceptio fructuum* normally coincides with *separatio* by the same person, unless a third person has a right over the separated fruits.—See FRUCTUS PERCEPTI, FRUCTUS PERCIPIENDI.

Percipere. To gather, collect (proceeds of any kind, revenues, interest, rents, wages).—See PERCEPTIO FRUCTUUM.

Percutere. To strike a person with the fist or a stick. Such an action constitutes an offense (see INIURIA). If the person beaten was gravely hurt, the wrongdoer was guilty of *iniuria atrox.*

Perducere. (With regard to testaments.) To cancel, to erase a testamentary disposition or the name of a beneficiary (an heir or legatee). The disposition is considered not written even if the name is still legible. Syn. *inducere.*

Perducere ad libertatem. To bring a slave to liberty, to make a slave free, either directly through manumission or indirectly by imposing on another the duty to free the slave.—See MANUMISSIO, MANUMISSIO FIDEICOMMISSARIA.

Perduellio. Treason. One is guilty of *perduellio* who "is inspired by a hostile mind against the state and the emperor" (D. 48.4.11). The Twelve Tables set the death penalty for treason. *Perduellio* embraced various criminal acts, such as joining the enemy, rousing an enemy against the Roman state, delivering a Roman citizen to the enemy, desertion on the battlefield, and the like. Later, *perduellio* was gradually absorbed by the CRIMEN MAIESTATIS.—See MAIESTAS, DUOVIRI PERDUELLIONIS, CONSCIENTIA, LEX VARIA, DESERERE.

Brecht *RE* 19; Lécrivain, *DS* 4; Berger, *OCD*; E. Pollack, *Majestätsgedanke im röm. Recht,* 1908; Robinson, *Georgetown LJ* 8 (1919); P. M. Schisas, *Offences against the state in R. law,* London, 1926; Renkema, *Mn* 55 (1927) 395; F. Vittinghoff, *Der Staatsfeind in der röm. Kaiserzeit,* 1926; A. Mellor, *La conception du crime politique sous la Rép. rom.,* 1934; C. Brecht, *Perduellio,* 1938; idem, *ZSS* 64 (1944) 354.

Perduellis. See HOSTIS.

Peregrinus. A foreigner, a stranger, a citizen of a state other than Rome. A great majority of the population of Rome were peregrines, subjects of Rome after the conquest of their country by Rome. With the increase of the Roman state the number of peregrines grew constantly without being compensated by the number of new citizens to whom Roman citizenship was granted. Within Roman territory the peregrines enjoyed the rights of free persons unless a treaty between Rome and their native country granted them specific rights. Generally, the legislation under the Republic, both statutes and *senatusconsulta,* applied to peregrines only when a particular provision extended their validity to them. Peregrines had no political rights, they could not participate in the popular assemblies, and were excluded from military service. A *peregrinus* might conclude a valid marriage (*iustae nuptiae*) only when he had the IUS CONUBII (see CONUBIUM), either granted to him personally or acquired through his citizenship in a *civitas* which obtained this right from Rome. A peregrine could not make a testament in the forms reserved for Roman citizens nor act as a witness thereto. He could not be instituted an heir of a Roman citizen nor receive a legacy (*legatum*) except in a testament of a soldier. He was able to conclude a commercial transaction with a Roman citizen if he had the IUS COMMERCII, which was granted in the same ways as *ius conubii.* Though excluded from the proceedings by LEGIS ACTIO, a peregrine had the benefit of protection in Roman courts, in particular before that praetor who had jurisdiction *inter peregrinos* (see PRAETORES) from the middle of the third century B.C. Certain actions were gradually made available to peregrines and against them by the means of a fiction "as if he were a Roman citizen"; see ACTIONES FICTICIAE. Foreigners from the same state concluded transactions in accordance with the laws of that state and litigations among them were settled according to their own laws. A peregrine who obtained Roman citizenship (see CIVITAS ROMANA) ceased to be a peregrine whether he obtained it as a personal grant or within a large group. The sharp distinction between *cives* and *peregrini* lost its emphasis in the legal field in the course of time as a result of the development of commercial relations between Romans and peregrines. On the other hand the extension of Roman citizenship which at the end of the Republic was conferred on the entire population of Italy, furthered the disappearance of the once very sensible differences. The CONSTITUTIO ANTONINIANA did the rest. In Justinian's law the only peregrines were the barbarians (see BARBARI). —For the exceptional status of the Latins, see LATIUM, IUS LATII, LATINI. For the influence of the commercial relations between Romans and peregrines

on the development of the Roman private law, see
IUS GENTIUM.—See DEDITICII, IUS CIVILE.

> Kübler, *RE* 19; Humbert and Lécrivain, *DS* 4; Severini,
> *NDI* 9; Sherwin-White, *OCD*; G. Moignier, *Les pérégrins
> déditices,* Thèse Paris, 1930; Taubenschlag, *St Bonfante* 1
> (1930) 367; Lewald, *Archeion Idiotikou Dikaiou* 3 (1946)
> 59; Volterra, *St Redenti* 2 (1951) 405.

Peremptorius. See EDICTUM PEREMPTORIUM, EXCEP-
TIONES PEREMPTORIAE.

Perendinus (dies). See COMPERENDINUS.

Perennis. See FLUMINA PUBLICA.

Perennitas. Perpetuity, perennity. The term was an
honorific title of the Roman emperors in the later
Empire.

Perfectissimus (vir). A title of high officials of
equestrian rank. From the time of Marcus Aurelius
all *praefecti* (except the *praefectus praetorio,* who had
the title *eminentissimus*), high officials in the financial
administration and in the imperial chancery, and
certain military commanders belonged to the group
of *perfectissimi.* Under Diocletian and his successors
the circle of *viri perfectissimi* was greatly extended.
Perfectissimatus = the dignity of a *vir perfectissimus.*
—C. 12.32.

> Ensslin, *RE* 19; Anon., *DS* 4; O. Hirschfeld, *Kleine
> Schriften,* 1913, 652.

Perfectus. Fully accomplished. A sale (EMPTIO) is
considered *perfecta* when the parties agreed upon the
object sold, its quantity and quality, and the price,
and the agreement was unconditional. A testament
was regarded *perfectum* (*iure perfectum*) when all
formalities required by the law were fulfilled.—See
DONATIO PERFECTA, PERFICERE, AETAS PERFECTA,
LEGES PERFECTAE.

Perficere. To conclude a legal transaction (to accomplish a legal act) in a form prescribed by the law.
See PERFECTUS (with regard to sales and testaments). *Perficere* refers also to the fulfillment of
an obligation or to a donation effectively given; see
DONATIO PERFECTA.

> Seckel and Levy, *ZSS* 47 (1927) 150.

Perfuga. (From *perfugere.*) A deserter who went
over to the enemy.—See DESERERE.

Periclitari. To run a risk (e.g., of being liable from
a procedural *sponsio* or *cautio* if one loses a case
in court).

Periculum (pariculum). A written draft of a judgment to be read by the judge to the parties.—See
SENTENTIAM DICERE, RECITARE.

> Kübler, *ZSS* 54 (1934) 327.

Periculum. A risk, a danger. The term is used of
the risk incurred by a party to a trial, plaintiff or
defendant, not only of losing the case but also of
being subject to an increased liability arising from
specific procedural measures (*sponsio, cautio*). See
PERICLITARI. In contractual relations *periculum* indicates the risk of a loss incurred by one party who
expressly assumed a more extensive liability, as, for

instance, for damages caused by an accident (*casus*),
periculum praestare, or by suffering such loss under
special circumstances. *Periculo alicuius esse* = to be
at one's risk, to be responsible for, or to suffer damages.—C. 5.38; 10.63; 11.34; 35.—See the following
items.

Periculum emptoris. See PERICULUM REI VENDITAE.

Periculum rei venditae. The risk of deterioration or
destruction of a thing which was sold and not immediately delivered to the buyer. As a matter of rule
such risk was with the buyer from the moment the
sale was concluded (*emptio perfecta*), if the loss was
caused by accident. He, therefore, had to pay the
sale price for the thing perished or deteriorated before the delivery. Exceptions in favor of the buyer
were introduced in some cases, in particular if the
vendor assumed responsibility in specific events or
neglected his duties of custody. Details are controversial in the literature, but it is probable that some
attenuations of the principle *"periculum est emptoris"*
were favored by the classical jurists in view of the
bona fide character of the contract of sale.—D. 18.6;
C. 4.48.—See EMPTIO, PERFECTUS.

> Arnò, *St Brugi* (1910) 153; Haymann, *ZSS* 40 (1919)
> 254; 41 (1920) 44; 48 (1928) 314; Rabel, *ZSS* 42 (1922)
> 543; M. Konstantinovitch, *Le p.r.v.,* Thèse Lyon, 1923;
> Huvelin, *RHD* 3 (1924) 318; Ch. Appleton, *RHD* 5
> (1926) 375; 6 (1927) 195; Seckel and Levy, *ZSS* 47
> (1927) 117; H. R. Hoetink, *Periculum est emptoris,* Haar-
> lem, 1928; Beseler, *TR* 8 (1928) 279; Vogt, *Fschr Ko-
> schaker* 2 (1939) 162; Krückmann, *ZSS* 59 (1939) 1, 60
> (1940) 1; Meylan, *RIDA* 3 (= *Mél De Visscher* 2, 1949)
> 193; idem, *Iura* 1 (1950) 253; idem, *ACIVer* 3 (1952) 389.

Periculum tutelae (tutorum). A general term for
the responsibility of guardians (*tutores*) connected
with their management of the ward's affairs and the
administration of his property. The term *periculum*
is also applied to *curatores.*—D. 26.7; C. 5.38.—See
TUTELA.

Perimere. To make void, to annul, to annihilate.
Perimi = to become inefficacious, extinguished, void
(*actio, obligatio, pignus perimitur*).

> M. F. Peterlongo, *Pluralità di vincoli,* 1941, 32.

Perinde (proinde) ac si (atque). Just as if. Although
the locutions occur beyond question in some interpolated texts, they may at times refer to cases which
were already treated in classical law as analogous to
other legal situations, protected by the law, to which
the praetor extended his protection by praetorian
actions (see ACTIONES UTILES, ACTIONES FICTICIAE).

> Riccobono, *TR* 9 (1929) 13; Guarneri-Citati, *Indice*[2]
> (1927) 65; idem, *Fschr Koschaker* 1 (1939) 145.

Perire. To perish. *Actio perit* = an action (the right
to sue) gets lost, is extinguished. See LIS MORITUR.
All actions which are extinguished by the death of
one party or by the lapse of a fixed time, survive if
they were introduced before court and brought to
LITIS CONTESTATIO before the death of the plaintiff
or before the term elapsed.

Peritus. See IURIS PERITUS.

Periurium. (From *periurare*.) Perjury. It was not generally punished as a *crimen publicum* since *periurium* was considered an offense to the gods which was revenged by them. It produced, however, a social dishonor (Cicero: *humanum dedecus*) which might be branded by the censors with a *nota censoria*. For false testimony, see TESTIMONIUM FALSUM. Perjury committed in order to obtain a pecuniary profit was qualified as *crimen* STELLIONATUS. Perjury committed under an oath taken *per genium principis* (see GENIUS) was treated as *crimen maiestatis* and, generally, it was severely punished. In pecuniary matters, if one swore that he did not owe money to another or that another owed him money, the punishment was beating (*castigatio fustibus*) with the admonition "do not swear inconsiderately."

Latte, *RE* 15, 353 (*s.v. Meineid*).

Perlusorium iudicium. See COLLUSIO.

Permissum. Permission, leave. The term refers to what is allowed by a statute (*permissu legis*) or by a magistrate (*permissu praetoris*), e.g., when a freedman wished to sue his patron, he had to ask the praetor for special permission.

Permutatio. The exchange of one thing for another, a barter. It differs from sale in that instead of money a thing is given as compensation. *Permutatio* is an innominate contract (see CONTRACTUS INNOMINATI) of the type *"do ut des"* (= I give you in order that you give me) and it is not concluded by mere consent of the parties, as sale, but by an actual, real (*re*) transfer of ownership of a thing from one party to another.—See ACTIO PRAESCRIPTIS VERBIS.—D. 19.4; C. 4.64.

M. Ricca-Barberis, *La garenzia per evizione, Mem. Ist. giur. Univ. Torino*, Ser. II, 40 (1939).

Permutatio. (In banking business.) A transaction between two banking firms to make payments from Rome to Italy and the provinces, and *vice versa*.

Kiessling, *RE* Suppl. 4, 700 (*s.v. Giroverkehr*).

Permutatio status. See STATUS.

Perorare causam. See CAUSAM PERORARE.

Perpetua causa servitutis. The natural conditions of a piece of land involved in a servitude must be such that the exercise of the servitude is permanently (not only temporarily) possible.

S. Perozzi, *Scr giur* 2 (1948, ex 1892) 85; C. Ferrini, *Opere* 4 (1930, ex 1893) 145; B. Biondi, *Le servitù prediali*, 1946, 156.

Perpetuari. See PERPETUATIO.

Perpetuarius. (Noun.) *Emphyteuta, emphyteuticarius.—Ius perpetuarium = ius emphyteuticum, ius emphyteuticarium.* See EMPHYTEUSIS.

Perpetuatio actionis. After the LITIS CONTESTATIO in a civil trial *actio perpetuatur*, i.e., the action, though temporally limited (see ACTIONES TEMPORALES), is no longer subject to a limitation of time.

Perpetuatio obligationis (obligatio perpetuatur). See MORA.

Gradenwitz, *ZSS* 34 (1913) 255; Genzmer, *ZSS* 44 (1924) 102; F. Pastori, *Profilo dogmatico e stor. dell'obbligazione rom.*, 1951, 173.

Perpetuus. Everlasting, perpetual, unlimited in time. Ant. *temporarius* (= temporary). *In perpetuum =* forever, for life (e.g., banishment).—See ACTIONES PERPETUAE, PERPETUA CAUSA, EDICTUM PERPETUUM, EXCEPTIONES PEREMPTORIAE.

Hernandez Tejero, *AHDE* 19 (1948–49) 593.

Perquisitio lance et licio. See LANCE ET LICIO.

Persecutio. Indicates an action by which "a thing is sued for" (D. 44.7.28: *rei persequendae gratia*). Hence *persecutio* connected with the object claimed (*persecutio hereditatis, legati, pignoris*) alludes to the pertinent specific action. *Persecutio poenae =* an action by which one sues for a private penalty (see ACTIONES POENALES). *Persecutio extraordinaria* refers to trials conducted in the form of COGNITIO EXTRA ORDINEM when the claim cannot be sued in ordinary proceedings, as for instance, in the case of a FIDEICOMMISSUM.—See PERSEQUI, PETITIO.

Persequi. To claim one's right through a judicial proceeding (*iudicio, actione*), to sue for a thing or a private penalty.—See PERSECUTIO.

Persolvere. In the meaning of *solvere* (= to pay a debt) this occurs frequently in interpolated passages.

Guarneri-Citati, *Indice*[2] (1925) 65.

Persona. A person, an individual, a human being. "The principal division of persons is that into free men (*liberi, ingenui*) and slaves (*servi*)," Gaius, Inst. 1.9. The law concerning persons (*ius quod ad personas pertinet*) is—according to Gaius (1.8)—one of the three groups of legal rules, the other two of which concern things (*res*) and actions (*actiones*). The law of persons (*ius personarum*) consists of those portions of the law which deal with liberty and slavery (*status libertatis*), citizenship (*status civitatis*), family (*status familiae*), marriage, guardianship and curatorship (*personae sui iuris, alieni iuris*). The law of persons embraces all institutions which have an influence on the legal condition of a person and his capacity to have rights and assume obligations. *Persona* is also used of slaves to denote them as human beings (*persona servi, servilis*) although legally they are treated as things (*res*) and therefore legal personality is denied them. There are also collective entities which, although not human in nature, "function" as persons (*personae vice fungi*), such as *hereditas* (= inheritance), a municipality, a *decuria* or an association of individuals. In postclassical and Justinian's language the use of *persona* (in Greek *prosopon*) became more extensive and was occasionally inserted into classical texts.—Inst. 1.3.—See ACTIONES IN PERSONAM, EXCEPTIONES IN PERSONAM, EXCEPTIONES PERSONAE COHAERENTES, NASCITURUS, STATUS, CAPUT, CAPITIS DEMINUTIO.

Düll, *RE* 19, 1040; Cuq, *DS* 4, 416; De Martino, *NDI* 9, 928; S. Schlossmann, *Persona und Prosopon*, 1905; Rheinfelder, *Das Wort p., Beihefte zur Ztschr. f. romanische Philologie* 77 (1928); L. Schnorr v. Carolsfeld, *Gesch. der juristischen Person,* 1 (1932) 52; P. W. Duff, *Personality in R. private law,* 1938, 1.—For p. in interpolated texts: Guarneri-Citati, *Indice²* (1927) 65, *St Riccobono* 1 (1936) 733, *Fschr Koschaker* 1 (1939) 145; Nédoucelle, *Revue des sciences réligieuses,* 1948, 277.

Persona extranea. See EXTRANEUS.

Persona miserabilis. A person deserving pity (because of age or sickness). Such persons were granted certain personal privileges in proceedings before the imperial court.—C. 3.14.

Persona turpis. See TURPIS PERSONA.

Personae exceptae. See EXCEPTAE PERSONAE.

Personae in mancipio. See MANCIPIUM.

Personae incertae. (In a testament.) Persons who are not precisely designated, whose existence is uncertain (see POSTUMI ALIENI) or of whom the testator had no precise idea (e.g., a legacy left to the person who would first come to the testator's funeral). Such testamentary dispositions in favor of *personae incertae* were void. Postclassical and Justinian's law permitted some exceptions.—C. 6.48.

Personae legitimae. The term occurs in later imperial constitutions in various meanings, primarily in that of a person capable to conclude a legal transaction or to act personally in court.

P. W. Duff, *Personality in R. private law,* 1938, 9.

Personalis. Pertaining to persons or to an individual. See CONSTITUTIONES PERSONALES, MUNERA PERSONALIA. The term occurs frequently in later imperial constitutions and was often interpolated in classical texts, as, for instance, *actio personalis* for *actio in personam.*—See PERSONA.

Guarneri-Citati, *Indice²* (1927) 65.

Personam alicuius sustinere. To represent (to replace) another person. With regard to an inheritance it is said (D. 41.1.34) that "it represents the person of the defunct, not of the heir."

Perterritus. Frightened. The term is used of a person who acted *metu* (= under fear).—See METUS.

Pertinere ad aliquem. To belong to a person as his property. The verb is used "in a very broad sense . . . it applies also to things which we possess under any title, although we have no ownership over them; we also say *pertinere* of things which are neither in our ownership nor possession but may become such" (D. 50.16.181), as, e.g., an inheritance *"pertinet"* to the heir although he did not yet enter it. The phrase *"is ad quem ea res pertinet"* may indicate a person who is interested in, or concerned with, a certain matter. *Pertinere ad aliquem* denotes sometimes a legal or moral duty of a person; when connected with a magistrate or a judge, it refers to his official duty.

Pervenire ad aliquem. What someone has obtained, gained (from another's property or to another's detriment). The term is important in the law of succession since, in certain instances, the liability of the heir (*teneri*) does not go beyond what he received from the estate. Syn. *in quantum quis locupletior factus est.* See ACTIONES IN ID QUOD PERVENIT. Ant. *in solidum teneri* = to be liable for the whole without regard to what the defendant had in fact received. —See LOCUPLETARI, BENEFICIUM INVENTARII.

F. Schulz, *Die actiones in id quod pervenit,* Diss. Breslau, 1905; P. Voci, *Risarcimento e pena privata,* 1939, 193.

Pervenire ad (in) aliquid. To obtain, to reach, to come to; *pervenire in senatum* = to become a senator; *pervenire ad libertatem* = to become a free person; *pervenire ad pubertatem* = to reach puberty.

Petere. See PETITIO, PACTUM DE NON PETENDO, and the following items.

De Sarlo, *Causa petendi,* BIDR 51/52 (1948).

Petere bonorum possessionem. To demand BONORUM POSSESSIO from the praetor. *Bonorum possessio* was granted only at the request of the person entitled to it.

Petere tutorem. See POSTULATIO TUTORIS.—D. 26.6; C. 5.31; 32.

Petitio. (In private law.) *Actio.* The term generally refers, however, to *actiones in rem* (see ACTIONES IN PERSONAM). A neat technical distinction between *actio* and *petitio* seemingly never existed nor can a substantial differentiation be found between the two terms and PERSECUTIO; the three words occur sometimes together without any indication whatsoever of the distinctions among them. In the language of the imperial chancery of the later Empire *petitio* is used of a petition addressed to the emperor or a high official.—See PLURIS PETITIO.

Schnorr v. Carolsfeld, *RE* 19.

Petitio hereditatis. See HEREDITATIS PETITIO.

Petitor. The plaintiff. See *actor, is qui agit.*

Petitoria formula. *Petitorium iudicium,* in Justinian's language, *actio petitoria.*—See FORMULA PETITORIA.

Peto. (In the formula of a *fideicommissum.*) See FIDEICOMMISSUM.

Philosophi. Philosophers were exempt from the duty of assuming a guardianship. They were not reckoned among the professors and therefore they could not sue for a salary (see HONORARIUM); "they despise mercenary services" (D. 50.13.1.4).

Piaculum. (In later imperial constitutions.) A crime which required expiation (punishment). *Piaculum* is also an expiatory sacrifice.

Piae causae. Pious, charitable purposes. Gifts to charitable institutions (foundations), such as orphanages, hospitals, poorhouses, almshouses for old people, and the like, were favored by Justinian's legislation. Such institutions were administered by directors who were considered temporary and limited owners and were authorized to appoint their own successors.— See LEX FALCIDIA.—C. 1.3.

Saleilles, *Mél Gérardin* 1907, 513; Cugia, *St Fadda* 5 (1906) 229; A. Sarrazin, *Études sur les fondations,* Thèse Paris, 1909; P. W. Duff, *Charitable foundations of Byzantium, Cambridge Legal Essays presented to Bond, Buck-*

land, 1926, 83; *idem, Personality in R. private law*, 1938, 203; L. Schnorr v. Carolsfeld, *Gesch. der juristischen Person*, 1 (1933) 15; J. M. Casoria, *De personalitate juridica piarum causarum*, (Naples) 1937; Bruck, *Sem* 6 (1948) 18; Philipsborn, *RIDA* 6 (1951) 141.

Pictura. A picture, a painting. The controversial question whether a painting made on another's material (*tabula*) became the property of the owner of the material or of the painter was later decided in favor of the latter. He had, however, to compensate the owner for the material used.

Bortolucci, *BIDR* 33 (1923) 151; *idem, Pubbl. Univ. Modena* 30 (1928) 14; Nardi, *AG* 121 (1939) 129; *idem, St sulla ritenzione*, 1947, 339.

Pietas. Dutifulness, respectful conduct, sense of duty, affection towards gods, parents, or near relatives; in general noblemindedness, honest way of thinking. "It is to be held that we are unable to commit acts which injure our dutiful conduct (*pietas*), our reputation (*existimatio*), our moral way of thinking, and generally speaking, are contrary to good customs." This saying is by Papinian (D. 28.7.15). Although heavily criticized and frequently ascribed to Justinian's compilers, it expresses a late classical idea. —See INTUITU.

Koch, *RE* 20; H. Krüger, *ZSS* 19 (1898) 6; Guarneri-Citati, *Indice²* (1927) 66 (Bibl. for interp.); Rabel, *St Bonfante* 4 (1930) 295; Th. Ulrich, *P. als politischer Begriff*, 1930; E. Renier, *Ét sur l'histoire de la querela inofficiosi testamenti*, 1942, 61; Riccobono, *Lineamenti* (1949) 71.

Pietas. An honorific title of the emperors. From the time of Diocletian they used to speak of themselves as *"pietas nostra"* (*mea*).

Pigneraticius creditor. A creditor who accepted a pledge from his debtor as a security. *Pigneraticius fundus* = land given as a security (*pignori datus*). For *actio pigneraticia* (*iudicium pigneraticium*), see PIGNUS.—See EXCEPTIO PIGNERATICIA.

Pigneratio, pignoratio (pignerare). Handing over a thing to one's creditor as a pledge.—See PIGNUS.

Pignoris capio. (By a magistrate.) Taking a pledge from a person who did not obey the magistrate's command. This was one of the means of the coercive power of a Roman magistrate (COËRCITIO). Originally the thing was destroyed (*pignus caedere*), later it was kept by the magistrate as pressure on the disobedient citizen. This might finally lead to the sale of the thing or to restoration to the owner in case he submitted. Syn. *pignoris captio*.

Steinwenter, *RE* 20, 1234.

Pignoris capio. (Through judicial proceeding.) A way of executing a debt due, see LEGIS ACTIO PER PIGNORIS CAPIONEM, PIGNUS. Tax-farmers had the right to take a pledge from a tax-debtor through this *legis actio*. In the provinces they could do so in simpler extrajudicial proceedings.

Steinwenter, *RE* 20, 1235; Carcaterra, *AnBari* 5 (1942); Hill, *AmJPhilol* 67 (1946) 60; M. Kaser, *Das altrömische Ius*, 1949, 205.

Pignoris causa indivisa est. A thing given a creditor as a pledge remains pledged until the debt is paid in full.—See PIGNUS.

Pignus. Both the thing given as a real security (pledge) to the creditor by the debtor and the pertinent agreement under which the security was given (*pignerare, pignori dare, pignus obligare*). The agreement was a contract concluded *re*, i.e., by the delivery of the pledge to the pledgee. *Pignus* implies the transfer of possession (not ownership) of the thing pledged to the creditor (*creditor pigneraticius*) who held it until his claim was fully satisfied, see PIGNORIS CAUSA. During this time he was protected in his possession of the pledge by possessory interdicts; see INTERDICTUM. For the rights of the pledgee, see IUS DISTRAHENDI, HYPEROCHA, LEX COMMISSORIA, IMPETRATIO DOMINII. As a matter of rule, the creditor had no right over the proceeds (fruits, rents, etc.) of the thing pledged unless it was agreed that he might take them as interest (see ANTICHRESIS). Nor could the pledgee use the thing pledged. "A creditor who makes use of the pledge commits a theft" (Inst. 4.1.6). The pledger could sue the creditor for restoration of the pledge when he had fulfilled his obligation or when the debt was extinguished (for instance, when the proceeds of the thing had been taken by the creditor, in accordance with an agreement with the debtor, and they exceeded both interest and the principal). The same action, *actio pigneraticia*, lay against a creditor through whose fault the thing perished or deteriorated. On the other hand, the pledgee had an action against the pledger (*actio pigneraticia contraria*) for damages caused by the thing pledged through the fault (*culpa*) of the pledger, and for reimbursement of necessary expenses (*impensae necessariae*) incurred in the care of the pledge. *Pignus* differed from other types of security, FIDUCIA and HYPOTHECA, in that by *fiducia* ownership was transferred to the creditor, and by *hypotheca* the thing was not handed over at all, whereas through *pignus* only possession of the *res pignorata* was conveyed to the creditor. In Justinian's law the differences between *pignus* and *hypotheca* were abolished.—D. 20.1; 3; 6; C. 8.13–32. For *actio pigneraticia* D. 13.7; C. 4.24.—See PRIOR TEMPORE, VINCULUM PIGNORIS.

Manigk, *RE* 20; Humbert and Lécrivain, *DS* 4; Pagge, *NDI* 9 (*s.v. pegno*); Berger, *OCD* (*s.v. security*); T. C. Jackson, *Justinian's Digest Book XX with Engl, translation*, 1909; E. Rabel, *Die Verfügungsbeschränkungen des Verpfänders*, 1909; E. Weiss, *Pfandrechtliche Untersuchungen*, 1–2 (1909, 1910); F. Messina-Vitrano, *Per la storia del ius distrahendi nel pegno*, 1910; M. Fehr, *Beiträge zur Lehre vom Pfandrecht*, Uppsala, 1910; Biondi, *AnPal* 7 (1920) 233; U. Ratti, *Sull'accessorietà del pegno*, 1927; Grosso, *ATor* 65 (1929–30) 111; E. Volterra, *Pegno di cosa altrui*, 1930; S. Romano, *Appunti sul pegno dei frutti*, *AnCam* 5 (1931); La Pira, *StSen* 47 (1933) 61; *idem, St Cammeo* 2 (1933) 1; *idem, St Ratti* 1934, 225; E. Carrelli, *St sull'accessorietà del pegno*, 1934; Carcaterra,

AnCam 12, 2 (1938) 51; Arnò, *ATor* 75 (1939–40); Rabel, *Sem* 1 (1943) 33; Kreller, *ZSS* 64 (1944) 306; Bartošek, *BIDR* 51–52 (1948) 238; Provera, *St Solazzi* 1948, 346; Koschaker, *Scr Ferrini* 3 (Univ. Sacro Cuore, Milan, 1948) 232.

Pignus Gordianum. According to a reform of the emperor Gordian (A.D. 239) a creditor who had several claims against the same debtor only some of which were secured by a pledge, was allowed to retain the pledge until all debts were paid.

E. Nardi, *Ritenzione e pegno Gordiano*, 1939; *idem, St sulle ritenzione. 1. Fonti e casi*, 1947.

Pignus in causam iudicati captum. A pledge taken from a debtor by order of a magistrate in execution of a judgment-debt adjudicated in a *cognitio extra ordinem*. The step was accomplished by official organs (*apparitores*). In Justinian's law this kind of execution was extended to all condemnatory sentences if the defendant refused to fulfill the judgment voluntarily.

Manigk, *RE* 20, 1273; P. Dienstag, *Die rechtliche Natur des p.i.c.i.c.,* 1908; Sanfilippo, *St Riccobono* 2 (1936) 521.

Pignus nominis. A pledge the object of which is the debtor's claim (*nomen*) against a third person. The *utilis.*—See ACTIONES UTILES.

creditor might sue the debtor's debtor by an *actio*

Pignus pignori datum. Named in literature by the non-Roman term *subpignus,* this occurs when a creditor who received a pledge from his debtor gave it in turn to his own creditor as a pledge.

Pignus praetorium. A pledge taken by the creditor upon order of a magistrate; see PIGNUS IN CAUSAM IUDICATI CAPTUM. The MISSIONES IN POSSESSIONEM had a similar function. In Justinian's language *pignus praetorium* is "a pledge which is given by the *iudices.*" By this phrase the *missiones* are meant. —C. 8.21.

S. Solazzi, *Concorso dei creditori* 1 (1937) 208; Branca, *StUrb* 1937, 105; M. F. Lepri, *Note sulla natura giuridica delle missiones,* 1939.

Pignus publicum. (A non-Roman term.) A pledge constituted in a document (*instrumentum*) made before a public official (*publice confectum*). It was recognized as valid in a late imperial constitution (A.D. 472). Justinian permitted setting up a pledge in a private document, signed by three witnesses (*instrumentum quasi publice confectum*).

Pignus rei alienae. A pledge of a thing which does not belong to the debtor.

Pignus tacitum (tacite contractum). See HYPOTHECA TACITA. Certain specific claims involved a right of pledge (*ius pignoris, hypotheca*) under the law over the property of the debtor. An agreement between the parties was not necessary. Thus, for instance, a person who lent money for the construction or repair of a building or of a ship had the right of pledge on the building or ship; from the time of Constantine the property of a tutor or curator was charged with a general hypothec in favor of the

ward's claims. Justinian granted legatees and fideicommissaries the same right over the things belonging to the estate. The privileged position of the fisc with regard to its debtors from contracts or for taxes is designated as *velut iure pignoris, pignoris vice.*— D. 20.2; C. 8.14.

Wieacker, *Fschr Koschaker* 1 (1939) 239.

Pilleus. A close fitting cap of liberty worn by freedmen on special occasions (e.g., the patron's funeral). Hence *pilleare* = to put a cap on a slave's head as a sign of manumission.

Paris, *DS* 4.

Pillius. A glossator of the twelfth century.—See GLOSSATORES.

Gabrieli, *NDI* 9.

Pirata. A pirate. There was no special law concerning robbers on the high sea. They were punished with death by the naval commander who was engaged in a fight against them or by the provincial governor to whom they were handed over. A theft committed during an attack of pirates was subject to a fourfold penalty.—See LEX GABINIA DE PIRATIS.

Kroll, *RE* 2A, 1042 (*s.v. Secraub*); Cary, *OCD*; Lécrivain, *DS* 4, 487; Ormerod, *Piracy in ancient world,* 1924; Levi, *Riv. di filol. ed istr. classica,* 2 (1924) 80; Riccobono, *FIR* 1², 1941, 121 (Bibl.); Jones, *JRS* 16 (1926) 155.

Piscari (piscatio). Fishing in the sea and in public streams (see FLUMINA PUBLICA) was free; the fisherman acquired ownership of the fish caught as of a *res nullius* (see OCCUPATIO), unless a special and exclusive right of fishing was conferred by the competent authorities to individuals or groups (*conductores piscatus*) through a lease. There was apparently a tendency to protect the rights of professional fishermen. Fishing in private lakes or fish-ponds (*piscina*) depended upon the permission of the owner. —See PORTUS, PISCATORES.

Kaser, *RE* Suppl. 7, 684; Lafaye, *DS* 4; Longhena, *NDI* 11, 107; Rostowzew, *DE* 2, 593; Bonfante, *Corso* 2, 2 (1928) 61; Lombardi, *BIDR* 53–54 (1948) 339.

Piscatores. Fishermen.

Stöckle, *RE* Suppl. 4, 460 (*s.v. Fischereigewerbe*); M. Maxey, *Occupation of the lower classes in Roman society,* Chicago, 1938, 12.

Pistores. Bakers. Under the empire the bakers of Rome were organized in an association. Their profession enjoyed particular protection by the authorities; occasionally its exercise for a few years was the ground for granting Roman citizenship to a foreigner (a Latin). Bakers were exempt from the duty to assume guardianship. Bakeries were under the supervision of the office of the *praefectus annonae.* The introduction of gratuitous distribution of bread to poor people by the emperors, and later, the sale of bread at a low price contributed to giving the bakers the character of public servants. Later imperial legislation (C. Theod. 14.3) dealt frequently with the *pistores* and their legal status and privileges. Their union was called *corpus* or *ordo pistorum* and their task comprised the baking of bread and its distribution and sale.—C. 11.16.

Hug, *RE* 20; Besnier, *DS* 4; G. Gandi, *Pistores. Note storico-corporative sui panificatori,* 1931.

Pithana. Plausible, persuasive topics. This was the title of a collection of decisions in individual cases by Labeo. The work is known only from an epitome by Paul.

Jörs, *RE* 1, 2551; Berger, *RE* 10, 723.

Pittacium. A term of Greek origin used in later imperial constitutions. A tablet, a short note. It was used in the administration of food supply for the army.

Placentinus. A glossator of the twelfth century. He died in 1192. He was the founder of a law school in Montpellier.—See GLOSSATORES.

Kuttner, *NDI* 9, 1118; P. De Tourtoulon, *Placentin,* 1876; H. Kantorowicz, *Jour. Warburg Inst.* 2 (1938) 22; Zanetti, *AG* 140 (1951) 72.

Placere. *Placet,* when referring to an individual jurist, is used for introducing his personal opinion. *Placet mihi* = in my opinion. *Placuit,* without reference to a specific jurist or jurists, indicated the opinion of several jurists which prevailed over the opinion of other jurists. Syn. *obtinuit. Placuit principi* refers to an imperial decision or enactment.—See CONSTITUTIONES PRINCIPUM.

Placitum. What private individuals agreed upon, an agreement. The term is less frequently used than its syn. PACTUM. With reference to legislative provisions *placitum* denotes either a statutory norm (*placitum legis*) or that of an imperial constitution (*placitum principis*).

Plagiarius. One who committed the crime of *plagium,* a kidnapper. Syn. *plagiator.*—See PLAGIUM, LEX FABIA DE PLAGIARIIS.

Plagium. The legal rules concerning the *crimen plagii* were settled in the LEX FABIA *de plagiariis* which remained in force in Justinian's legislation, with some alterations introduced by the legislation of the emperors and the interpretation of the jurists.—D. 48.15; C. 9.20.—See LEX FABIA, VINCULA, SUPPRIMERE, SUSCIPERE SERVUM.

Berger, *RE* Suppl. 7, 386; Brecht, *RE* 20; Lécrivain, *DS* 4; Niedermeyer, *St Bonfante* 2 (1930) 381; Lardone, *Univ Detroit Law J* 1 (1932) 163; Lauria, *AnMac* 8 (1932); Berger, *BIDR* 45 (1938) 267.

Plane. Certainly, to be sure, of course. The particle was often used by the compilers to introduce an explanatory or restrictive remark, mostly of a harmless nature.

Guarneri-Citati, *Indice*² (1927) 66 (Bibl.).

Planta. A plant put in another's ground became property of the land-owner, provided that it had taken root there.

Plantare (plantatio). See PLANTA, SUPERFICIES CEDIT SOLO, SATIO.

Planum. See DE PLANO.

Plautius. A jurist of the first post-Christian century. He is known only from commentaries written by later jurists (Neratius, Pomponius, Javolenus, Paulus) on his work which apparently dealt primarily with the praetorian law. The attention paid by the classical jurists to Plautius (Paul's commentary had no less than 18 books) is evidence of the great esteem Plautius enjoyed with the later jurisprudence.

Berger, *OCD; idem, RE* 10, 710; 17, 1835; Siber, *RE* 21 (no. 60); Orestano, *NDI* 9; Riccobono, *BIDR* 6 (1893) 119; Ferrini, *Opere* 2 (1927, ex 1894) 205.

Plebeii. See PLEBS, PATRICII.

Plebiscitum. A decision, decree or legislative measure passed by the assembly of the plebeians (*concilia plebis*). Originally the gatherings of the plebeians dealt only with matters which concerned the plebeians. The most important matter was the election of plebeian magistrates (*tribuni, aediles plebis*). Later, the competence of the *concilia plebis* were extended on legislative enactments. For the historical development which finally made the legal force of *plebiscita* equal to that of *leges* (statutes passed by *comitia* of the Roman people), see LEX VALERIA HORATIA, LEX PUBLILIA PHILONIS, LEX HORTENSIA, EXAEQUARE, LEX, CONCILIA PLEBIS, and the following item.

Siber, *RE* 21; Fabia, *DS* 4; Tilman, *Musée Belge,* 1906; Baviera, *St Brugi* 1910; Guarino, *Fschr Schulz* 1 (1951) 458; Biscardi, *RHD* 29 (1951) 153.

Plebs. The great "bulk of the people" (*multitudo*) opposed to the noble families. In the technical meaning *plebs* denotes a social class (group, "order") of the free population of Rome, distinguished from the patricians (see PATRICII). The uncertainty of the sources made of the origin of the *plebs* one of the most controversial questions of early Roman history. Originally the *plebs* probably consisted of various elements, such as the population of the surrounding territories conquered by Rome, clients (see CLIENTES) of patrician families, who lost the protection of a noble *gens,* and foreigners who came to Rome as workers or to exercise a small commerce. In historical times the plebeians appear already as Roman citizens although not enjoying full political and civil rights of the privileged social group, the patricians. The plebeians were excluded from magistracies and priesthood, and marriage between patricians and plebeians was prohibited. During the first two centuries of the Roman Republic there was a continuous struggle between the two classes during which the *plebs* gradually obtained the right to have magistracies of their own (*tribuni plebis, aediles plebis*) and the admission to magistracies and positions formerly reserved for the patricians. For details, see PATRICII. See also PLEBISCITUM and the related items. Under the Empire the distinction *plebeii—patricii* acquired a quite different significance. *Plebs* generally refers to the lower classes of the population without specific connotations and is opposed to persons of senatorial or equestrian rank, to the classes of officials or wealthy and influential persons; see HONESTIORES, HUMILIORES, POTENTIORES.—See PATRICII (Bibl.), TRANSITIO AD PLEBEM.

Siber and Hoffmann, *RE* 21 (Bibl. 102); Lécrivain, *DS* 4; Di Marzo, *NDI* 9; Momigliano, *OCD*; Vassalli, *StSen* 24 (1907) 131; J. Binder, *Plebs*, 1909; Bloch, *La plèbe rom., Rev. Historique* 106–7 (1910–11); Giorgi, *St storici per l'antichità clas.* 5 (1912) 249; Rosenberg, *Hermes* 48 (1913) 359; G. Oberziner, *Patriciato e plebe* (*Pubbl. Accad. Scientif.-Lett.,* Milan, 1913); V. Arangio-Ruiz, *Le genti e la città,* 1914, 64; Piganiol, *Essai sur les origines de Rome,* 1917, 53, 247; Rosè, *JRS* 12 (1922) 106; Hoffmann, *Neue Jahrbücher für das klas. Altertum* 1938, 82; F. Altheim, *Lex sacrata. Die Anfänge der plebeischen Organisation* (Amsterdam, 1940); Last, *JRS* 35 (1945) 30; A. Dell'Oro, *La formazione della stato patrizio-plebeo,* 1950, 59.

Plecti. To inflict a penalty. The term occurs in imperial constitutions.—See CAPITE PUNIRE.

U. Brasiello, *La repressione penale,* 1937, 223.

Plena pubertas. See MINORES.

Plenus. Full, complete, undiminished. The term is often connected with *ius, proprietas, dominium,* and similar words. It is a favorite adjective in the language of the imperial chancery; particularly frequent are the superlatives *plenissimus* and *plenissime.*

Plerumque. See INTERDUM.

Guarneri-Citati, *Indice*[2] (1927) 67.

Plumbatura. Soldering two pieces of metal with lead. The parts thus joined remain distinct and may be separated when belonging to two different owners. Syn. *adplumbatio.*—See FERRUMINATIO.

Plures rei promittendi (stipulandi). See DUO REI.

Plures tutores. See CONTUTORES.

Pluris petitio. See PLUSPETITIO.

Plus. See MINUS.

Pluspetitio (pluris petitio). Claiming more than is due, an excessive claim. A plantiff may overclaim (*plus petere*) in substance (*re*) when he claims a bigger amount than is due to him; in time (*tempore*) when he claims before the payment is due; in place (*loco*), when he claims at a place (in a city) other than that where the payment had to be performed (see ACTIO DE EO QUOD CERTO LOCO); or in cause (*causa*) when he claims a certain thing although the debtor had the right to chose between two or more things. According to the classical law, a plaintiff who claimed in the INTENTIO of the formula more than he was entitled to, lost the case definitely. His claim could be restored, however, by a RESTITUTIO IN INTEGRUM in circumstances in which this remedy was available. An overstatement in the part of the formula called DEMONSTRATIO did not produce the loss of the case for the plaintiff. After the abolition of the formula-regime the *pluspetitio* lost its actuality. Imperial legislation modified the severe provisions against overclaims; the plaintiff was allowed to change or limit his claim during the trial, but he incurred some losses because of the unnecessary delay of the trial. In Justinian's law the plaintiff lost the case only if he maliciously persisted during the whole trial in his overclaim.—C. 3.10.

Schnorr v. Carolsfeld, *RE* 21; P. Collinet, *La procédure par libelle,* 1932, 483; Solazzi, *SDHI* 5 (1939) 231.

Pluvia aqua. Rain water.—See ACTIO AQUAE PLUVIAE ARCENDAE, SERVITUS STILLICIDII.

Poena. Punishment, penalty. *Poena* is both punishment for public crimes (CRIMEN) and pecuniary penalty to be paid to the person wronged by a private wrongdoing (see DELICTUM). The Roman system of penalties was built up on the conception that punishment was of an expiatory and vindictive nature and had to serve as a deterrent measure; correction of the criminal was not taken into consideration. Hence the death penalty was threatened in most cases. For the various kinds of execution, see CRUX, ANIMADVERSIO GLADII, FURCA, CULLEUS, CREMATIO, OBICI BESTIIS, DEICERE E SAXO TARPEIO, STRANGULATIO, DECOLLATIO, METALLUM. The death penalty was one of the capital punishments (*poena capitalis, poena capitis*) which involved either loss of life or only loss of liberty or citizenship (see CAPUT). The loss of liberty (see SERVUS POENAE) was connected with compulsory labor in mines for life (*damnatio ad metalla,* see METALLUM) or in public works (see OPUS PUBLICUM). For the loss of citizenship see DEPORTATIO, RELEGATIO, EXILIUM, INTERDICERE AQUA ET IGNI. Another group of penalties embraced pecuniary penalties (*poena pecuniaria, nummaria*) such as seizure of property (see ADEMPTIO BONORUM, PUBLICATIO, CONFISCATIO) and fines (see MULTA). Corporal punishment was not strictly a *poena* but a coercive measure (*coërcitio*) or an aggravation of another kind of punishment (sometimes even applied before the capital execution); see CASTIGARE, FLAGELLUM, FUSTIS, VERBERA. Imprisonment (see CARCER) was applied as a measure of coercion to enforce obedience to an order of a magistrate. Penalties to be inflicted for specific crimes were fixed in the statute which declared the pertinent wrongdoings as a crime to be prosecuted and punished as a *crimen publicum,* or in imperial constitutions which dealt with criminal matters. Under the Empire penalties were differentiated according to the social status of the person convicted (*honestiores—humiliores*), persons of lower classes being exposed to severer penalties; in certain cases in which the *honestiores* (*potentiores*) were punished only by banishment, the *humiliores* suffered the death penalty. Later imperial legislation introduced manifold reforms both in the system of penalties and their applicability. Some of those reforms were of a short duration since the emperors often modified the innovations of their predecessors. Private penalties which superseded private vengeance and retaliation of the earliest law (see TALIO), consisted in the payment of a sum of money to the person injured by a private crime (*delictum*); see FURTUM, RAPINA, INIURIA. The condemnation for a crime involved certain other consequences for the culprit although they were not considered a *poena* in the strict sense of the word; see POENA EXISTIMATIONIS, INTESTABILITAS, INFAMIA, IGNOMINIA.—D. 48.19; C. 9.47.—See moreover IUDICIA PUBLICA, QUAESTIONES, COGNITIO, ACTIONES POENALES, LEGATUM POENAE NOMINE RELICTUM, COËRCITIO, GRAVIS, and the following items.

Lécrivain, *DS* 4; Brasiello, *NDI* 12 (*sistema délle pene*); Buonamici, *Il concetto della pena nel dir. giust.*, *St Pessina* 2 (1899) 187; E. Costa, *Crimini e pene da Romolo a Giustiniano*, 1921; Jolowicz, *The assessment of penalties in primitive law*, *Cambridge Legal Essays in honor of Bond, Buckland, etc.*, 1926, 203; Ciulei, *Rhein. Museum für Philologie* 91 (1942) 32; U. Brasiello, *La repressione penale*, 1937; Levy, *BIDR* 45 (1938) 57; F. M. De Robertis, *ZSS* 59 (1939) 219; *idem*, *RISG* 14 (1939) 30; *idem*, *AnBari* 4 (1941) 17, 9 (1948) 1; *idem*, *St in dir. penale rom.*, 1943, 101; *idem*, *St Solazzi* 1948, 168; *idem*, *La variazione della pena nel dir. rom.*, *Parte generale*, 1950.

Poena. (In the law of obligations.) A penalty agreed upon by the parties, to be paid by the debtor in the case of non-fulfillment of his obligation in due time. A penalty clause could be added to any agreement either in the form of a *stipulatio* (*stipulatio poenae*) or of a formless *pactum* attached to a *contractus bonae fidei*. A penalty clause could be inserted in a testament to compel the heir to fulfill the testator's orders. —See STIPULATIO POENAE.

Brassloff, *ZSS* 25 (1904); Guarneri-Citati, *BIDR* 32 (1922) 241; P. Voci, *Risarcimento e pena privata*, 1939, 185.

Poena capitalis (capitis). Denotes not only the death penalty but also a penalty connected with the loss of *caput* (*capitis deminutio maxima* and *media*, see CAPUT), to wit, of liberty or citizenship. Locutions such as *capite plecti, puniri*, and the like usually refer to the death penalty. Syn. *poena mortis*. For the various forms of execution, see POENA. The death penalty was normally executed in public, unless execution in prison was ordered. The execution of a woman was not public. Execution was performed after the final judgment without delay; the execution of a pregnant woman was postponed until after delivery.

Latte, *RE* Suppl. 7 (*s.v. Todesstrafe*); U. Brasiello, *La repressione penale*, 1937, 215 and *passim*.

Poena cullei. See CULLEUS.

Poena dupli. See LIS INFITIANDO.

Düll, *Scr Ferrini* 3 (Univ. Sacro Cuore, Milan, 1948) 218.

Poena exilii. See EXILIUM.

Poena existimationis. A penalty by which the esteem which a person enjoyed in society was destroyed.— See EXISTIMATIO, INFAMIA, IGNOMINIA.

Poena metalli. See METALLUM.

Poena mortis. See POENA CAPITIS.

Poena nummaria. See NUMMARIA POENA, POENA PECUNIARIA.

Poena pecuniaria. A fine, a penalty consisting in the payment of a sum of money. The amounts were originally fixed in the penal statutes, often in proportion to the injury caused. The severest form of a pecuniary penalty was the seizure of the whole or of a part of the wrongdoer's property.—See MULTA, ADEMPTIO BONORUM, CONFISCATIO, PUBLICATIO.

U. Brasiello, *La repressione penale*, 1937, 131.

Poena sanguinis. See SANGUIS.

Poenae temere litigantium. Penalties imposed on reckless litigants, both plaintiff and defendant, who initiated or continued a trial inconsiderately.—Inst. 4.16.—See INFITIATIO, CALUMNIA, INFAMIA, ACTIONES FAMOSAE, IMPENSAE LITIS, IUDICIUM CONTRARIUM.

Poenalis. Connected with (involving) a penalty. See ACTIONES POENALES, IUDICIA POENALIA. *Causa poenalis* = a criminal matter (trial).

Poenitentia. See PAENITENTIA.

Poetae. Poets. An imperial constitution of the middle of the third century (C. 10.53.3) stated: "Poets are not granted any privileges of immunity" (from public charges), contrary to teachers and physicians.—See MAGISTRI, MEDICI.

Politio. A contract with a cultivator (*politor*) who assumed the task of improving the productivity of land. He was rewarded with a portion of the proceeds. The agreement was a combination of a hire and a partnership.

Polliceri. To promise. The term refers to promises made both in a solemn form (*stipulatio*) and in a formless agreement. In his Edict the praetor used the term to announce that in certain legal situations he would grant protection (*auxilium*) through a procedural remedy (*actio, iudicium, restitutio in integrum*), or in cases of succession, a BONORUM POSSESSIO.

Düll, *ZSS* 61 (1941) 28.

Pollicitatio. A promise of a gift in money made to a municipality by a person who obtained or sought to obtain an official post in the municipal administration. Such a promise was considered binding and could be sued for. Another kind of *pollicitatio* was a promise made by a person to a municipality to erect a construction on a public place (a monument, a building for public purposes). The promisor was obligated by such a promise if the construction had been commenced. He had to finish the work or to provide the sum necessary for that purpose.—D. 50.12.

Anon., *NDI* 9; Brini, *MemBol* 1908; Ascoli, *St Salandra* 1928, 215; Archi, *RISG* 8 (1933) 563; E. Albertario, *St* 3 (1936) 237; Villers, *RHD* 18 (1939) 1; Düll, *ZSS* 61 (1941) 19; Biondi, *Scr Ferrini* 1 (Univ. Sacro Cuore, Milan, 1947) 131; Roussier, *RIDA* 3 (1949) 296.

Pollicitatio dotis. The constitution of a dowry trough, a formless promise. A constitution of the emperor Theodosius II (C. 5.11.6, A.D. 428) introduced the *pollicitatio dotis* and made thus the solemn forms (*dictio dotis, stipulatio dotis*) superfluous.—C. 5.11. —See PROMISSIO DOTIS.

Riccobono, *ZSS* 35 (1914) 270; Landucci, *AG* 94 (1925) 39.

Pomerium. The territory of Rome within the original boundaries (walls) of the city. The *pomerium,* which from the beginning was somewhat connected with sacral rites, and, later, the territory within the first milestones (see MILIARIUM) was the domain of the magisterial *imperium domi* (see DOMI). The *comitia curiata* could gather only within the boundaries of the *pomerium* (*intra pomerium*), the *comitia centuriata* only outside of it (*extra pomerium*). The emperors had the power to extend the *pomerium* beyond its former limits.

Besnier, *DS* 4; Severini, *NDI* 9; Richmond, *OCD*; O. Karlowa, *Intra p. und extra p.,* 1896; v. Blumenthal, *RE* 21, 2 (1952) 1867.

Pompa. See OSTENTATIO.

Bömer, *RE* 21, 2 (1952) 1978.

Pomponius, Sextus. A prominent jurist of the time of Hadrian and Antoninus Pius (around the middle of the second century). He is the author of three treatises on civil law written as commentaries on works of earlier jurists (*ad Quintum Mucium, ad Plautium, ad Sabinum*), of an extensive commentary on the praetorian Edict (known only from citations by later jurists), and of a series of monographs on various topics (on *fideicommissa,* on stipulations, on *senatusconsulta*). For his brief history of Roman jurisprudence, see ENCHIRIDIUM. Two extensive collections of casuistic material (*Epistulae* and *Variae lectiones*) complete the picture of his literary activity which was abundantly exploited by Justinian's compilers of the Digest.

Berger, *OCD*; Di Marzo, *Saggi critici sui libri di Pomponio Ad Q. Mucium,* 1899; Wesenberg, *RE* 21, 2 (1952) 2415.

Ponderator. An official weigher who ascertained the weight of money (primarily of gold coins) contributed by taxpayers (in the later Empire).—C. 10.73.

Pondus. The weight.—See RES QUAE PONDERE, NUMERO, etc.

Pone. (Imperative.) Let us suppose, assume. The locution frequently occurs in juristic writings to introduce a specific, imaginary instance ("for instance" = *verbi gratia*) for a better understanding of what was said before.

Ponere. Sometimes syn. with *deponere* (*pecuniam, magistratum*), sometimes with *opponere* (e.g., *exceptionem*).

Ponere. (With reference to agreements or testaments.) To settle, to order, to dispose.

Ponere diem. To fix a date for the fulfillment of an obligation or for certain procedural acts in a trial.

Pons. A bridge. A bridge over a public river (*flumen publicum*) built up by the owner or owners of the opposite banks remained private property of the builders.

G. Segrè, *BIDR* 48 (1941) 26.

Pontifex maximus. The chief pontiff among the pontifices, the head of the pontifical college. He was "considered the judge and arbitrator over divine and human matters" (Festus). The *pontifex maximus* was appointed for life and could not be removed. He was, in fact, the executor of the pontifical power in all more important actions, the other pontiffs (see PONTIFICES) generally acted as his council. He convoked and presided over the *comitia curiata.* He had the power of punishing the members of the pontifical college and other priests, as well as the Vestal Virgins (see VESTALES). The dignity of a *pontifex maximus* was for a long period the privilege of the patricians; the first plebeian *pontifex* was Tiberius Coruncanius (253 B.C.); see CORUNCANIUS. Under the Principate the emperors held the position of the *pontifex maximus.*—See LEX PAPIA, REGIA.

G. Wissowa, *Religion und Kultus der Römer,* 1902, 437; M. F. Martroye, *Le titre de p.m. et les empereurs chrétiens, Bull. de la Société des Antiquaires de France,* 1928, 192; Leifer, *Klio,* Beiheft 23 (1931) 122; Zmigryder-Konopka, *Eos* 34 (1933) 361; L. R. Taylor, *ClPhilol* 1942, 427; Gioffredi, *Bull. Commissione archeol. Comunale* 71 (1945) 129.

Pontifices. High priests who took care of all matters connected with religion and public cult. They constituted a body (*collegium*) originally of three, later of six members (among them was perhaps the king). In further development the college of pontiffs had nine members (according to *Lex Ogulnia* four patricians and five plebeians); their number increased to fifteen and more. The pontiffs were creators, guardians of, and experts in, divine and pontifical law (*ius divinum, pontificium*) and settled the rules for sacred rites (*ius sacrum*). The close connection between religion and law in the early Roman state gave the pontiffs a particular position in legal matters. They alone knew the law, divine and human (*fas—ius*), and the legal forms, which, being preserved in the archives of the pontifical college, were accessible to them only. In view of the fact that formalism was the basic element of early law, the *pontifices* acquired a kind of monopoly in the knowledge of legal forms and rules, which through the first two centuries of the Republic remained their exclusive possession. Their activity in legal life was similar to that of the jurists in later centuries. They advised the magistrates in legal matters and gave answers (*responsa*) to juridical questions put before them by private individuals and helped them in drafting written documents and in the use of procedural and other forms. The Roman calendar was organized by the pontiffs; they fixed the days on which trials could not take place. The popular assemblies, *comitia curiata,* were convoked and presided by the highest priest among the *pontifices,* the *pontifex maximus,* and since several acts connected with the family organization were performed there (such as *adrogatio,* or a testament), the pontiffs, although primarily interested in the sacral rites (*sacra*) of the family, acquired a considerable influence in the province of family law. The contribution of the pontiffs to the development of the Roman law was considerable. As late as the third century after Christ, the jurist Ulpian in the definition of jurisprudence mentions in the first place the *divinarum rerum notitia* (see IURISPRUDENTIA).—In the enactments of the Christion emperors *pontifex* = bishop.—See PONTIFEX MAXIMUS, DIES FASTI, COMMENTARII SACERDOTUM, LEX DOMITIA, LEX OGULNIA.

Berger, *RE* 10, 1159; Bouché-Leclercq, *DS* 4; Frezza, *NDI* 9; Rose, *OCD*; A. Coqueret, *De l'influence des pontifes sur le droit privé à Rome*, Thèse Caen, 1895; O. Tixier, *Influence des pontifes sur le développement de la procédure civile*, 1897; G. Wissowa, *Religion und Kultus der Romer²*, 1912; C. W. Westrup, *R. pontifical college*, 1929; Sogliano, *Hist* 5 (1931); G. Rohde, *Kultsatzungen der röm. P.*, 1936; F. De Martino, *La giurisdizione*, 1937, 13; Bruck, *Sem* 3 (1945) 2; F. Schulz, *History of R. legal science*, 1946, 6; M. Kaser, *Das altröm. Ius*, 1949, *passim*; idem, *Religione e diritto in Roma arcaica*, *AnCat* 3 (1949) 77; Latte, *ZSS* 67 (1950) 47; P. Noailles, *Du droit sacré au droit civil*, 1950, 24.

Pontifices minores. Secretaries (*scribae*) of the pontifical college. They assisted the pontiffs in their functions.

Pontificium. Used in later imperial constitutions in the meaning of power, right (even in the domain of private law).

Populares. See OPTIMATES.

Popularis. (Adj.) See ACTIONES POPULARES, INTERDICTA PRIVATA.

Popularis. (Noun.) A member of the *populus* (population) of a city.

Populus. Cicero (*Rep.* 1.25.39) gives the following definition of *populus:* "it is not any assemblage of men brought together in some way, but an assemblage of a crowd associated by law agreed upon and by common interests." The term *populus* embraces all citizens, and in a narrower sense, all men gathered together in a popular assembly.

G. I. Luzzatto, *Epigrafia giuridica greca e romana*, 1942, 45.

Populus Romanus (or populus Romanus Quiritium). The whole citizenry of the Roman state, including both patricians and plebeians (orginally only patricians). The *populus Romanus* was a collectivity of physical persons which had its own rights, its existence; it might be owner, debtor, creditor, legatee, heir, manumitter of slaves, vendor or buyer, etc. Its acts and legal transactions, however, were not equal to those of individual citizens and did not give origin to normal trials as between individual citizens, but to measures and remedies of an administrative nature. The Roman jurists did not elaborate a theory of the state as a juristic personality; they dealt with the pertinent problems from the practical point of view in order to protect the social and eco-

nomic interests of the state.—See AERARIUM POPULI, RES POPULI, SENATUS POPULUSQUE ROMANUS.

Volterra, *StSas* 16 (1938); G. Nocera, *Il potere dei comizi*, 1940, 15; idem, *AnPer* 51 (1946) 153; G. Lombardi, *AG* 126 (1941) 198; idem, *Concetti fondamentali del ius gentium*, 1942, 11; Cousin, *Rev. Ét Latines*, 1946, 66.

Portae. The gates of a city. They are considered as RES SANCTAE.

Portentum (portentosum). A monstrous offspring; see MONSTRUM. It was not considered a human being, but was reckoned in favor of the mother for the IUS LIBERORUM and to the advantage of its parents in connection with the sanctions of the *Lex Iulia et Papia Poppaea* against childless parents; see ORBI, LEX IULIA DE MARITANDIS ORDINIBUS.

Portio. In the language of later imperial constitutions, an office, an official post.

Portio hereditaria (hereditatis). The portion of an inheritance to which an heir was instituted by the testator. *Porto virilis* = a fraction of the inheritance which an heir on intestacy receives equally with other heirs of the same degree of relationship.

Portoria. Custom (export and import) duties, paid primarily in harbors (*portus*).—See DEFERRE FISCO.

Rostowzew, *DE* 3, 126; Bonelli, *StDocSD* 21 (1900) 40; Clerici, *Economia e finanza dei Romani* 1 (1943) 485; S. J. De Laet, *Portorium. Étude sur l'organisation douanière chez les Romains* (Recueil de travaux de la Fac. de Philosophie de l'Univ. de Gand, 1950).

Portus. A harbor. A *portus* belongs to the category of RES PUBLICAE. Fishing therein is allowed as in public rivers (*flumina publica*).

Poscere. To ask, to demand. Used of requests made to public officials (magistrates), in particular, to applications addressed to the praetor in matters of voluntary jurisdiction (*iurisdictio voluntaria*, see IURISDICTIO CONTENTIOSA), as, e.g., appointment of a *tutor* or *curator*.

Posita. *Res positae.* See ACTIO DE DEIECTIS.

Posse. Indicates both physical and legal possibility (i.e., what the law permits).—See FACERE POSSE.

Possessio. The factual, physical control of a corporeal thing (*possessio* or *possidere corpore*) combined with the possessor's intention to hold it under physical control, normally as the owner (*animus possidendi, animus domini*). The first element, a material one, gives the possessor the opportunity to exercise his power over the thing, the second is a psychical one, based normally on a legal ground (*causa possessionis*) by which the thing came under the power of the possessor. *Possessio* is distinguished from the mere physical holding of a thing (*tenere, in possessione esse*, see DETENTIO) on the one hand; on the other, it differs from ownership (*proprietas, dominium*) since at times one person may be the owner and another the possessor of the same thing. *Posessio* is qualified as a *res facti*, a factual situation, although it produces legal effects and is protected by the law inasmuch as public order and social interests and security require that the existing possessory situations be protected against any one and any disturbance. In certain circumstances the possessor is even protected against the owner if he is entitled under the law or an agreement with the owner to have the factual control over the thing. Hence the saying, D. 21.2.12.1: "Ownership (*proprietas*) has nothing in common with *possessio.*" *Possessio* is acquired when its basic elements, i.e., *possidere corpore* and *animo* are materialized, to wit, when the possessor obtains physical power over a thing and has the intention to keep it under his power. Acquisition of *possessio* is either original when a thing which was not possessed before by another person is taken into possession (see OCCUPATIO, RES NULLIUS) or derivative, when one obtains *possessio* of a thing from its last possessor (see TRADITIO). *Possessio* as a factual situation is not transferred to an heir or legatee automatically; physical things belonging to an estate must be taken into material *possessio* by the beneficiaries. The specific protection of *possessio* is achieved through *interdicta* (see INTERDICTUM), in particular the possessory interdicts which serve both for the protection of existing possessory situations (*interdicta retinendae possessionis*), for the recovery of lost *possessio* (*interdicta recuperandae possessionis*) and for obtaining possession (*interdicta adipiscendae possessionis*). An owner who has *possessio* of the thing belonging to him may use all measures available for the protection of possession. The advantageous position of the possessor found its expression in the saying: "He who has possession has through this very fact that he is possessor, a better right than he who does not possess" (D. 43.17.2). One of the most important consequences of *possessio* is that the possessor of a thing who for certain reasons did not acquire ownership (for instance he bought *bona fide* a thing from a non-owner) might become legal owner after a certain time through usucaption (see USUCAPIO). There was a legal rule concerning *possessio: nemo sibi ipse causam possessionis mutare potest* (D. 41.2.3.19) = no one can change by himself the ground on which he obtained possession, which means that one who acquired possession under a specific title, e.g., by sale or donation, cannot assert later that he acquired the thing as an heir or legatee; nor can one who holds another's thing, e.g., as a depositee or lessee transform the detention into possession simply by having the intention to possess it for himself (*animus possidendi*).—D. 41.2; C. 7.32.—See ANIMUS DOMINI, ANIMUS POSSIDENDI, DOLO DESINERE POSSIDERE, ACTIO PUBLICIANA, ACCESSIO POSSESSIONIS, TRADITIO BREVI MANU, CONSTITUTUM POSSESSORIUM, CONDICTIO POSSESSIONIS, and the following items.

Beauchet, *DS* 4; Rossi, *NDI* 10; Berger, *OCD*; Schlossmann, *ZSS* 24 (1903) 13; Riccobono, *ZSS* 31 (1910) 321; idem, *Scr Chironi* 1 (1911) 377; G. Rotondi, *Scr giur* 3 (1922 = *BIDR* 30, 1920) 94; see Brassloff, *P. in den Schriften der röm. Juristen*, 1928; G. Longo, *BIDR* 42 (1934) 469; Bozza, *AnMac* 6 (1930); Grimm, *St Riccobono* 4 (1936) 173; Rabel, *ibid.* 203; Kunkel, *Symb. Friburgenses Lenel*, 1931; A. Carcaterra, *Possessio. Ricerche di storia e dogmatica*, 1938; idem, *AnBari* 4 (1941) 128; E. Albertario, *Studi* 2, 2 (1941, several articles); B. Fabi, *Aspetti del possesso rom.*, 1946; Riccobono, *BIDR* 49–50 (1947) 40; Branca, *St Solazzi* (1948) 483; Lauria, *ibid.* 780; K. Olivecrona, *Three essays in R. law*, 1949, 52; J. De Malafosse, *L'interdit momentariae possessionis*, Thèse Toulouse, 1949; Monier, *St Albertario* 1950, 197; Kaser, *Detentio, Deutsche Landesreferate zum 3. intern. Kongress für Rechtsvergleichung*, 1950, 85 (Bibl.); Branca, *St Carnelutti* 4 (1950) 369; E. Levy, *West Roman Vulgar Law*, 1951, *passim*.

Possessio ad interdicta. Possession which is protected by *interdicta*. Interdictal protection was granted also to those who held another's thing according to an agreement with the owner and although they had no intention of possessing it as their own, they could not be disturbed in their right over the thing. Thus a creditor holding a pledge (*creditor pigneraticius*), one who received the thing as a PRECARIUM, a possessor of an *ager vectigalis* or *emphyteuticarius*, a sequester, all these might ask for an interdict in the case of disturbance by a third person. Other holders of another's things had either special interdicts introduced by the praetorian law for their protection (as the *superficiarius*, see INTERDICTUM DE SUPERFICIEBUS* or the usufructuary, to whom an interdict was granted as *interdictum utile*, see INTERDICTA UTILIA) or had no interdictal protection at all as in the case of *depositum* or *commodatum.*

Kaser, *ZSS* 64 (1944) 389.

Possessio civilis. See POSSESSIO NATURALIS.

Possessio clandestina. See CLANDESTINA POSSESSIO, CLAM.

Possessio corporalis (corpore). The factual control over a thing; see POSSESSIO, POSSESSIO NATURALIS.

Possessio ficta. See POSSESSOR FICTUS.

Possessio iniusta. Possession of a thing obtained either *vi* (by force), *clam* (secretly, *clandestina possessio*) or *precario* (upon request, see PRECARIUM). Syn. *possessio vitiosa.* Ant. *possessio iusta* = possession which is not affected by one of the defects mentioned. *Possessio iniusta* could be objected only by the person who was deprived of its possession by the *possessor iniustus.* Against third persons the latter enjoyed the same protection as a *possessor iustus.*—See EXCEPTIO VITIOSAE POSSESSIONIS, INTERDICTUM UTI POSSIDETIS.

Possessio iuris (quasi possessio). Possession of a right, as, for instance, of an usufruct. In such cases the classical terminology used the expression *usus iuris.* Since in classical law possession was limited to corporeal things, the terms *possessio iuris* and *quasi possessio* are obviously a postclassical or Justinian's creation.

Di Marzo, *StSen* 23 (1906) 23; Riccobono, *ZSS* 34 (1913) 251; Albertario, *Studi* 2 (1941, ex 1912) 307, 337, 359,

369; G. Segrè, *BIDR* 32 (1922) 293; Denoyez, *Fschr Ko-schaker* 2 (1939) 304; A. Carcaterra, *Il possesso dei diritti,* 1942; Sargenti, *Scr Ferrini* 2 (Univ. Pavia, 1947) 226; S. Solazzi, *La tutela delle servitù,* 1949, 139.

Possessio iusta. See POSSESSIO INIUSTA.

Suman, *AVen* 76 (1917) 1607; E. H. Seligsohn, *Iusta p.,* 1927.

Possessio libertatis. The term *possessio* is sometimes applied with reference to the personal status of a person, e.g., to his liberty (*possessio libertatis*), citizenship (*possessio civitatis*) or to his being a slave (*possessio servitutis*).

Peterlongo, *St Albertoni* 2 (1937) 195, 213.227.

Possessio momentaria. A vague, non-technical, postclassical term referring to a temporary, provisional possession settled through a possessory remedy (*interdictum*). The *possessio momentaria* is opposed to possession definitely decided upon in a trial (*actio in rem*) in which the question of ownership (*causa proprietatis*) of the thing in dispute was involved. The confusion in the terminology of imperial constitutions of the fourth and fifth centuries (the use of *momentum* for *possessio momentaria,* of *quaestio momenti* for *interdictum momentariae possessionis*) does not permit a clear picture. The *interdictum momentariae possessionis* which generally has been identified with the INTERDICTUM UNDE VI, perhaps served originally to protect possession held through a representative (a friend, relative or slave) in the absence of the true possessor, as a provisory arrangement until the absent person returned.

Levy, *Scr Ferrini* 3 (Univ. Sacro Cuore, Milan, 1948) 111; *idem, West Roman Vulgar Law,* 1951, 244; J. De Malafosse, *L'interdit momentariae possessionis,* Thèse Toulouse, 1949.

Possessio naturalis (naturaliter possidere). A simple holding of a thing. The holder had no intention *rem sibi habendi* (= to have the thing for himself) and there was no *iusta causa possessionis* for his holding the thing. Ant. *possessio civilis* which is based on a *iusta causa* (= a just legal title) for the acquisition of possession and which, under *ius civile,* might lead in certain circumstances to the acquisition of property through USUCAPIO. *Possessio civilis* is protected by the ACTIO PUBLICIANA. In Justinian's law a confusion was brought into the classical distinction *possessio civilis—possessio naturalis* inasmuch as certain possessory situations which in the classical law were not covered by the term *possessio civilis* were so qualified by Justinian. In classical law persons with mental defects, and infants could not have a legally valid will (*animus*) and consequently no *possessio civilis.* Other cases of *possessio naturalis* were those of a lessee, depositee and a *commodatarius* since they are considered holding the thing for the owner; therefore they can not claim interdictal protection.

Riccobono, *ZSS* 31 (1910) 321; *idem, Scr Chironi* 1 (1915) 377; Scherillo, *RendLomb* 63 (1930) 507; Bonfante, *Scr giur* 3 (1926) 534; Kunkel, *Symb Frib Lenel,*

1931, 40; Maschi, *La concezione naturalistica,* 1937, 112; Peterlongo, *AnPer* 50 (1938) 169; M. Kaser, *Eigentum und Besitz,* 1943, 169; *idem, Detentio,* in *Deutsche Landesreferate zum Dritten Intern. Kongress für Rechtsvergleichung,* 1950.

Possessio vacua. See VACUA POSSESSIO.

Possessio vitiosa. See POSSESSIO INIUSTA.

Possessiones. Great landed property, big estates.

Possessor (possidens). See POSSESSIO, PAR CAUSA, AGER OCCUPATORIUS.

Possessor bonae fidei (possidere bona fide). One who possesses a thing belonging to another, and believes in good faith that he is the owner; for instance, one who bought a thing from a non-owner. When sued by the real owner for restitution of the thing, he loses the case; when he sues the owner who succeeded in obtaining the thing back, the latter will oppose the *exceptio iusti dominii* claiming that he is the right owner. Against third persons the *possessor bonae fidei* is protected by *interdicta* and may also use the ACTIO PUBLICIANA. The *possessor bonae fidei* becomes owner under *ius civile* through possession during a certain period; see USUCAPIO. Ant. *possessor malae fidei (possidere mala fide)* = one who knows that he is not the owner of the thing he holds unlawfully. The distinction between *possessores bonae fidei* and *malae fidei* was of importance; when sued by the owner and condemned they had to return the proceeds (see FRUCTUS) to the owner. The *possessor bonae fidei* was liable only for the *fructus extantes* (still existing) and the *fructus* he gathered (*percepti*) after the joinder of issue (*litis contestatio*), whereas the *possessor malae fidei* was liable for all *fructus,* even FRUCTUS PERCIPIENDI. Analogous rules were applied in the case of the restitution of an inheritance (see HEREDITATIS PETITIO); the extension of the responsibility of the possessor of the estate depended upon the circumstance whether he was in good or in bad faith.

Aru, *BIDR* 45 (1938) 191; De Martino, *St Scorza* 1940, 275; Fabi, *AnCam* 16 (1942–44) 53; Daube, *CambLJ* 9 (1945) 31; P. Ramelet, *L'acquisition des fruits par l'usufruitier et par le p.b.f.,* 1945; Henrion, *RIDA* 4 (= *Mél De Visscher* 3, 1950) 579; Albanese, *AnPal* 21 (1950) 91.

Possessor fictus (possessio ficta). In literature a person who in reality does not possess the thing which is the object of a dispute but who maliciously feigns to possess it in order to deceive the plaintiff.—See LITI SE OFFERRE, DOLO DESINERE POSSIDERE.

Arnò, *Mem. Accad. Torino, Scienze morali,* 70, 2 (1939-40) 39.

Possessor malae fidei (possidere mala fide). See POSSESSOR BONAE FIDEI.

Possessor pro herede. One who holds an estate in the belief that he is the heir.—D. 41.5.

Possessor pro possessore. One who holds an estate and does not assert that he is the heir but when questioned by the praetor about the title of his possession, he has no other answer than: "I possess because I possess." He is considered a *possessor malae fidei* and treated as a PRAEDO.—D. 41.5.

Possessorius. Connected with BONORUM POSSESSIO. See HEREDITATIS PETITIO POSSESSORIA. For *interdictum possessorium,* see BONORUM VENDITIO.

Possidere. See POSSESSIO.

> Carcaterra, *AG* 115 (1936) 168.

Post. (Adv.) Syn. *postea.* See EX POST FACTO.

Posteri. Descendants. Syn. *descendentes,* sometimes syn. with *postumi.* In a broader sense *posteri* = more distant relatives.

Posterior lex. A statute later than another one referring to the same matter. "A later statute is related to a former one unless it is contrary to it" (D. 1.3.28).—See PRIOR LEX.

Posteriora (libri posteriores). A posthumously edited work. In Roman juristic literature, one such work only is known, the *Posteriora* of Labeo, allegedly in forty books. A compilation of excerpts from this work (an epitome) was prepared by the jurist IAVOLENUS.

> Berger, *RE* 17, 1836; idem, *BIDR* 44 (1937) 91; Di Paola, *BIDR* 49/50 (1947) 277; F. Schulz, *History of Roman Legal Science,* 1946, 207.

Postliminium. A Roman citizen who had been caught by an enemy as a prisoner of war became a slave of the enemy, but he regained freedom and "all his former rights through *postliminium (iure postliminii),*" when he returned to Roman territory. His marriage, however, which was dissolved through his captivity, did not revive; the same applied to possession, which was a factual situation (*res facti,* see POSSESSIO); hence his things had to be taken into possession anew.—D. 49.15; C. 8.50.—See REDEMPTUS AB HOSTIBUS (Bibl.), CAPTIVUS, LEX CORNELIA DE CAPTIVIS, ACTIO RESCISSORIA, DEPORTATIO, TRANSFUGA.

> Berger, *OCD;* Anon., *NDI* 10; Lécrivain, *DS* 4; L. Sertorio, *La prigionia di guerra e il dir. di postliminio,* 1916; Solazzi, *RendLomb* 1916, 638; Beseler, *ZSS* 45 (1925) 192; Ratti, *Alcune repliche in tema di postliminio,* 1931; Ambrosino, *SDHI* 5 (1939) 202; Orestano, *BIDR* 47 (1940) 283; Guarino, *ZSS* 61 (1941) 58; A. D'Ors, *Revista de la Faculdad de derecho de Madrid,* 1942, 200; G. Faiveley, *Redemptus ab hoste,* Thèse Paris, 1942; J. Imbert, *Postliminium,* Thèse Paris, 1944; P. Rasi, *Consensus facit nuptias,* 1946, 107; Solazzi, *Scr Ferrini* 2 (Univ. Catt. Sacro Cuore, 1947) 288; Bartošek, *RIDA* 2 (1949) 37; De Visscher, *Fschr Koschaker* 1 (1939) 367 (= *Nouvelles Études* 1949, 275); L. Amirante, *Captivitas e p.,* 1950; Imbert, *RHD* 27 (1949) 614; Gioffredi, *SDHI* 16 (1950) 13; Kreller, *ZSS* 69 (1952) 172.

Postliminium rei. When certain things (slaves, ships, horses) and not their owner, were taken by an enemy, they returned after the war, when recovered from the enemy, to the owner.

> Solazzi, *RISG* 86 (1949) 1.

Postrema voluntas. In imperial constitutions a last will.

Postulare. (In a civil trial.) "To expound one's claim or that of one's friend in court (*in iure*) before the magistrate who has jurisdiction or to contradict the adversary's claim" (D. 3.1.1.2). *Postulare* refers to the request addressed to a magistrate for granting an action, an interdict, an exception, an *in integrum restitutio,* or a *bonorum possessio.* The parties usually acted personally, with the assistance of advocates (see ADVOCATUS) or through representatives (see COGNITOR, PROCURATOR). The praetorian Edict contained precise rules as to who might or might not legally act in court. There were three categories of persons in this respect, first persons totally or partially excluded from *postulare* (such as minors under seventeen years, deaf persons). They might act through an advocate who was assigned by the praetor if they had none by their own choice. The second group were excluded from *postulare* (acting) for other persons, but not from *postulare* for themselves (such as women, blind persons, persons condemned for a capital crime, gladiators). The third group included persons permitted to postulate for themselves; among them were persons dishonorably discharged from military service, condemned for certain crimes or in civil trials for acts committed against good faith in contractual relations with other persons. Persons enumerated in this group could act in court also in behalf of their nearest relatives, patrons, and the like.—D. 3.1; C. 2.6.—See INFAMIA.

> Solazzi, *BIDR* 37 (1929) 1.

Postulare. (In criminal matters.) Syn. *accusare.*

Postulare interdictum. See INTERDICTUM.

Postulare pro aliis. To act in court in behalf of other persons.—See POSTULARE.

Postulatio iudicis (arbitri). See LEGIS ACTIO PER IUDICIS ARBITRIVE POSTULATIONEM, IUDICES.

Postulatio simplex. In the later civil procedure the initial act of the plaintiff or his lawyer presenting the case against his adversary and asking for the start of a trial.—See LIBELLUS CONVENTIONIS.

> P. Collinet, *La procédure par libelle,* 1932, 239; Steinwenter, *ZSS* 54 (1934) 377; Fliniaux, *RHD* 9 (1930) 94; Betti, *ACDR* Roma 2 (1935) 149; Balogh, *St Riccobono* 2 (1936) 473.

Postulatio suspecti tutoris. See TUTOR SUSPECTUS.

Postulatio tutoris. A request addressed to the competent authority (a consul or praetor in Rome, a municipal magistrate, a governor of a province) for the appointment of a guardian. The request (*petere tutorem*) had to be made by a relative, a friend or a creditor of the ward.—See TUTOR DATIVUS.—D. 26.6; C. 5.31; 32.

> Sachers, *RE* 7A, 1518.

Postumus. A child born after the death of the testator within ten months or after the will was made. For the various kinds of posthumous children some of whom had a right of succession to the inheritance of the person whose *postumi* they were, see the following items. In the developed classical law certain *postumi* should be instituted as heirs since otherwise the testament was void.—C. 6.29.

Cuq, *DS* 4; Robbe, *NDI* 10; *idem, I postumi nella successione testamentaria romana,* 1936; B. Biondi, *Successione testamentaria,* 1943, 114.

Postumus alienus. A child born after the death of the testator, who would not have come under his power had he lived at the time of the birth. Syn. *postumus extraneus.* Ant. *postumus suus.*

Postumus Aquilianus. A grandchild, born after the death of his grandfather (the testator), whose father (a son under paternal power of the testator) was alive when the testament was made but died before the grandfather. The jurist Aquilius Gallus invented a formula by which such a *postumus* had to be taken into consideration in the grandfather's testament in order to avoid its nullity. Such a *postumus* had to be conceived at the time of his father's death (not at the time when the testament was made).

Postumus extraneus. See POSTUMUS ALIENUS.

Postumus Iulianus. A grandchild born after the testament of his grandfather had been made, who became the grandfather's *heres suus* before his death through the previous death of his own (i.e., the *postumus'*) father. The term *postumus Iulianus* was coined in literature after the name of the jurist Julian who admitted the institution of such as *postumus* as an heir or his disinheritance in the grandfather's testament.

Postumus Iunianus. A posthumous child born after a testament was made by his father, but before the latter's death. The term *Iunianus* (also *Vellaeianus*), given to such a *postumus* in literature, originates in the LEX IUNIA VELLAEA which settled the rules concerning his rights of succession.

Postumus legitimus. A posthumous child born after the death of his father or a grandchild born after the death of his grandfather when his father was no longer alive.

Postumus suus. A posthumous child who would have come under the paternal power of his father if the latter had not died before the child's birth. The child had to be conceived at the time of the making of the testament by the father. A *postumus suus* was also any person who became HERES SUUS of the testator, i.e., came under his paternal power, after the testament had been made, in a way other than by birth (by adoption, *arrogatio, conventio in manum*). *Postumi sui* had to be either instituted as heirs or disinherited. Ant. *postumus alienus.*—See PRAETERIRE.

Postumus Vellaeianus. See POSTUMUS IUNIANUS.

Potentiores. In the later Empire persons who because of their official position or wealth (great landowners) exercised a more influential economic and social power over their fellow citizens. Their powerful influence in society gave them the opportunity of abusing their privileges to the disadvantage of the poor classes (see HUMILIORES). In order to prevent such abuses, in particular in civil trials, imperial legislation prohibited the cession of claims as well as the alienation of a controversial thing to a *potentior* made in order to aggravate the situation of one's opponent in the trial.—C. 2.13; 2.14.—See DEFENSOR CIVITATIS, HONESTIORES.

Mitteis, *Mél Girard* 2 (1912) 225; R. Paribeni, *Potentiores.*

Potestas. A term in both public and private law. In the first domain it generally indicates the power of a magistrate whether he is vested with IMPERIUM or not. *Potestas* embraces all the rights and duties connected with a particular magistracy (*ius edicendi,* rights of an executive nature, such as *ius multae dictionis, ius coërcendi,* and the like). Colleagues in office had equal power (*par potestas*), whereas the *potestas* of magistrates of a different rank in the magisterial hierarchy was differentiated in *maior* and *minor potestas* (= greater and lesser power). See MAGISTRATUS, IMPERIUM. At times *potestas* denotes the office, the official employment itself (similarly as *magistratus*). *Potestas* in the field of private law refers either to the power of a head of a family over its members (see PATRIA POTESTAS), or the power over a thing (*res,* among which are also the slaves, hence the expression *dominica potestas* is applied to the master's power over his slaves, although in the Roman juristic language the expression is not found). *Potestas* is also used in the sense of physical power; in particular, with regard to slaves, the master is not considered to have *in potestate* a slave who runs away or cannot be found. In its broadest sense *potestas* means either the physical ability (= *facultas*) or the legal capacity, the right (= *ius*) to do something.— D. 1.12.

De Villa, *NDI* 10; L. Wenger, *Hausgewalt und Staatsgewalt, Miscellanea Ehrle* (Rome, 1924) 1; A. Caspary, *St Albertoni* 2 (1937) 384; De Visscher, *Il concetto di potestà, ConfCast* 1940; *idem, Nouvelles Études,* 1950, 265; Hernandez Tejero, *AHDE* 17 (1946) 605.

Potestas dominica. See POTESTAS, DOMINICUS.

Potestas gladii. See IUS GLADII.

Potestas legis. The sphere of effectiveness of a statute, the strength of a law.

Potestas patria. See PATRIA POTESTAS.

Potestas regia. The sovereign power of the king.— See REX.

Potestas vitae necisque. See IUS VITAE NECISQUE.

Potestativa condicio. See CONDICIO POTESTATIVA.

Potior. See PRIOR TEMPORE.

Potior in pignore. If a thing was successively pledged to several creditors, the creditor to whom it was pledged first, had priority before the later creditors. If, however, a debtor pledged the same thing as a whole (*in solidum*) to two creditors simultaneously, the legal situation of the creditor to whom the pledge was handed over was more advantageous (*melior*

condicio possidentis, D. 20.1.10).—D. 20.4; C. 8.17.
—See PIGNUS, SUCCESSIO IN LOCUM PRIORIS CREDI-
TORIS, IUS OFFERENDI PECUNIAM, POSSESSIO.

Potiores. Persons in a prominent social position.
　　Biondi, *Ius* 3 (1952) 235.

Potioris nominatio. See NOMINATIO POTIORIS.

Potius est. It is better (preferable) to say. In
juristic language the phrase serves to introduce an
opinion which should be given preference.

Pp. Abbreviation for *proposita* (*sc. constitutio*), i.e.,
promulgated, officially published. The abbreviation is
applied in Justinian's Code to indicate the place and
date of the promulgation of an imperial enactment.
The indications are given at the end of the text of
the constitution. The normal place was the locality
where the emperor had actually resided, unless another place was specified.

Praecellens, praecellentissimus. An honorific title
of high dignitaries in the later Empire. Syn. *excellentissimus.*

Praeceptio. See LEGATUM PER PRAECEPTIONEM.

Praecepta iuris. Legal norms.—See IUS.
　　E. Levy, *Univ. of Notre Dame, Natural Law Inst. Proc.*
　　2 (1949) 67 (=*SDHI* 15, 1949, 18); A. Carcaterra, *Iu-
　　stitia nelle' fonti*, Bari, 1949, 81.

Praeceptor. A teacher. See MAGISTER, EDICTUM VES-
PASIANI, PROFESSORES, HONORARIUM, STUDIA LIBE-
RALIA.

Praecipere. With reference to statutes, the praetorian
Edict, or imperial constitutions = to ordain, to decree,
to set a legal rule.—See PRAECEPTA IURIS.

Praecipere. To take beforehand, in advance (*prae-
capere*). The term applies to cases in which several
claims of various persons occur (as, e.g., in the
division of a common property or of an inheritance
among the co-heirs, or when several creditors have
to be satisfied from the debtor's property) and one
of the claimants had to be satisfied before the others.
See LEGATUM PER PRAECEPTIONEM. The amount or
share which one of the claimants receives before the
others is termed *praecipuum.*

Praecipitare de saxo Tarpeio. See DEICERE DE SAXO
TARPEIO.

Praecipuum. See PRAECIPERE.

Praecones. Criers, heralds. They belonged to the
auxiliary staff of higher magistrates whose orders
they announced publicly, e.g., the convocation of a
popular assembly. They also made public events
which interested the population and assisted in public
auctions.—See APPARITORES, LEX CORNELIA DE VI-
GINTI QUAESTORIBUS.
　　Saglio, *DS* 4, 609.

Praeda. The booty taken from the enemy in a war
through an operation of the army. It became property of the Roman state. The appropriation of such
things by an individual soldier was considered as a
crime of embezzlement (see PECULATUS) to be punished according to the LEX IULIA PECULATUS. In
earlier times such appropriation was allowed.—See
RES HOSTILES.
　　Cagnat, *DS* 4; Vogel, *ZSS* 66 (1948) 396.

Praedecessor (prodecessor). A predecessor in office.
Certain rules regulated the question as to how long
a magistrate or an imperial official remained in office
until his successor arrived. The question was of
particularly practical significance in provincial administration; a governor might quit his post when
his successor arrived in the province.

Praedes. (Sing. *praes.*) In the earlier law of the
Republic sureties who assumed guaranty for a person
who concluded a contract with the state (e.g., a lease,
a *locatio conductio operarum*, etc.).
　　Humbert and Lécrivain, *DS* 4; Schlossmann, *ZSS* 26
　　(1905) 285; P. Viard, *Le praes*, 1907; Mitteis, *Aus röm.
　　und bürgerl. Recht, Fschr Bekker* 1907, 120; Partsch,
　　ASächGW 32 (1920) 659; Gradenwitz, *ZSS* 42 (1921)
　　565; v. Mayr, *ibid.* 205; J. Maillet, *Theorie de Schuld et
　　Haftung*, Thèse Aix-en-Provence, 1944, 99.

Praedes litis et vindiciarum. Sureties assuming guaranty for a thing being the object of a trial (*lis =res*)
and for the proceeds (*fructus*) from it. Such *praedes*
had to be given in the procedure through *legis actio
sacramenti* by the party to a trial concerning the
ownership of a thing to whom the praetor assigned
possession of it during the trial. The *praedes* war-
ranted through *stipulatio* the restitution of the thing
and its *fructus* in the case of defeat of the party to
whom possession was assigned. In the later procedure for the recovery of a thing, connected with a
sponsio (see AGERE PER SPONSIONEM), it was the
defendant who stipulated a certain sum for such
event; see CAUTIO PRO PRAEDE LITIS ET VINDICIARUM.
—See REI VINDICATIO, PRAEDES (Bibl.), VINDICIAE.
　　V. Lübtow, *ZSS* 68 (1951) 338.

Praedes sacramenti. Sureties for the payment of the
sacramentum in the procedure by LEGIS ACTIO SACRA-
MENTI. In the later development the amount of the
sacramentum was not deposited by the parties at the
beginning of the trial; it was only promised and the
payment was guaranteed by sureties.

Praedia. Plots of land (estates) together with the
buildings erected on them. Syn. *fundus.*—See the
following items.
　　Humbert and Lécrivain, *DS* 4.

Praedia curialium (decurionum). Land belonging to
CURIALES (DECURIONES) in the provinces could not
be alienated in the later Empire without permission
of the provincial governor which was given only
when the necessity of the sale was proved.—C. 10.33.

Praedia fiscalia. Land owned by the fisc (see FISCUS).
In the later Empire it was administered by a *pro-
curator praediorum fiscalium.*—C. 11.72-74.—See
ACTOR PRAEDIORUM FISCALIUM.

Praedia Italica. Plots of land in Italy. Syn. *fundus
in Italico solo. Praedia Italica* were among *res mancipi* and consequently were transferable only through

mancipatio or *in iure cessio*. They are distinguished from PRAEDIA PROVINCIALIA (= provincial land) which were *res nec mancipi*. In the later Empire there was no longer any difference between Italian and provincial landed property.—See RES MANCIPI, SOLUM ITALICUM.

Praedia provincialia. Plots of provincial land. They were *res nec mancipi* and therefore not transferable through *mancipatio* or *in iure cessio*. The owners of provincial land were obliged to pay taxes, *tributum* (*soli*) in imperial provinces, *stipendium* in senatorial provinces.—See PRAEDIA TRIBUTORIA, PRAEDIA STIPENDIARIA, PRAEDIA ITALICA, PRAESCRIPTIO LONGI TEMPORIS.

Praedia rustica. Landed property situated on the outside of cities and exploited for agriculture. Syn. *fundus, ager, locus*. Ant. *praedia urbana*.—See SERVITUTES PRAEDIORUM RUSTICORUM.—D. 8.4; C. 11.70.
   Guarneri-Citati, *BIDR* 43 (1935) 78.

Praedia stipendiaria. "Land in those provinces which are held to be property of the Roman people" (Gaius, Inst. 2.21), i.e., the senatorial provinces. The owners of such land paid the fisc a tax called STIPENDIUM. Ant. PRAEDIA TRIBUTARIA.—See PROVINCIAE POPULI ROMANI.
   Solazzi, *AnBari* 5 (1942) 7.

Praedia subsignata. Land pledged to a public body (the state or a municipality) as a security for a debt assumed. The land was not handed over but could be afterwards seized by public authorities when the debt was not paid in due time.—See SUBSIGNARE.

Praedia tributaria. "Landed property in the provinces regarded as a property of the emperor" (Gaius, Inst. 2.21), i.e., the imperial provinces. The owners paid a land-tax called TRIBUTUM.—See PROVINCIAE CAESARIS, PRAEDIA STIPENDIARIA.

Praedia urbana. Buildings, even when located in the country. Syn. *aedes, aedificium*. Ant. *praedia rustica*.—See SERVITUTES PRAEDIORUM RUSTICORUM. Gardens connected with buildings are considered *praedia urbana*, except when they are exploited for commercial purposes, for instance, for viticulture (D. 50.16.198).—D. 8.4; C. 11.70.—See SUBURBANUM PRAEDIUM.
   Guarneri-Citati, *BIDR* 43 (1935) 73.

Praediator. The purchaser of a plot of land which had been pledged to the state by a debtor and forfeited. The sale (*praediatura*) was performed by a public auction the conditions of which were fixed in a *lex praediatoria*.
   Liebenam, *RE* 5, 1824; O. Karlowa, *Röm. Rechtsgeschichte* 2 (1901) 5.

Praedicere (praedictio). An oral declaration made at the conclusion of a transaction, for example, by the seller of a slave about the latter's defects. For *praedicere* in an auction, see AUCTIO.

Praedo. A robber, pillager; in a broader sense, any possessor in bad faith (*possessor malae fidei*) who seized another's property without legal grounds. (D. 50.17.126 pr.).—See POSSESSOR PRO POSSESSORE.

Praeesse provinciae. To govern a province. *Is qui praeest provinciae = praeses provinciae.*

Praefectorius. (Adj.) Connected with, or pertaining to, the office of a *praefectus*.

Praefectianus. A subordinate official in the bureau of the PRAEFECTUS PRAETORIO.

Praefectorius. (Noun.) An ex-praefect.

Praefectura. Indicates either the official position of a *praefectus* or the territory subject to his authority. For *praefectura* as an administrative unit after Constantine's reform of the administration of the Empire, see DIOECESIS.—See the following items.
   Cagnat, *DS* 4; Belloni, *NDI* 10.

Praefectura morum. The supervision of public morals. The term is applied to the activity of the censors, see CENSORES.

Praefecturae municipales. In earlier municipalities which were not granted political rights (*sine suffragio*) jurisdiction over the municipal citizens (*municipes*) was vested in a *praetor* in Rome who, however, exercised it by a special delegate, *praefectus iuri dicundo*. Hence the municipalities without *ius suffragii* were termed *praefecturae*.—See SUFFRAGIUM.
   Sherwin-White, *OCD* 725; Fabricius, *SbHeid* 1924/5, 1, 29; E. Manni *Per la storia dei municipii*, 1947, 69.

Praefectus. (From *praeficere* = to place a person at the head of an office.) The chief of an office in any branch of administration. Commanders of military and naval units also had the title *praefectus* (*alae, castrorum* = of a military camp, *centuriae, classis, cohortis, legionis*). In sacral matters there were *praefecti* of a more local character (*praefectus rebus divinis, sacrorum, sacris faciendis*). Some *praefecti* were also called *praepositi*.—The following items deal with the more important praefectural offices.
   Liebenam, *RE* 6, 1644.

Praefectus Aegypti (also **praefectus Alexandreae et Aegypti**). The governor of Egypt. He was the chief of the administration, and was appointed and recalled by the emperor. In the provincial administration Egypt occupied a unique position, being more tied with the person of the emperor than any imperial province. Hence the *praefectus* was considered a personal representative of the emperor. In jurisdictional matters he was assisted by a special official, the *iuridicus Aegypti* (*et Alexandreae*), in financial matters by the IDIOLOGUS.—D. 1.17; C. 1.37. —See PRAEFECTUS AUGUSTALIS, GNOMON, IURIDICI.
   De Ruggiero, *DE* 1, 278; O. W. Reinmuth, *The Prefects of Egypt, Klio, Beiheft* 34, 1935; H. F. K. Hübner, *P. Aeg. von Diokletian bis zum Ende der Röm. Herrschaft*, Diss. Erlangen, 1948; A. Stein, *Die Präfekten von Aegypten in der röm. Kaiserzeit*, Bern, 1950.

Praefectus aerarii militaris. See AERARIUM MILITARE.

Praefectus aerarii Saturni. See AERARIUM POPULI ROMANI.

Praefectus alimentorum. An official of senatorial rank charged with distribution of provisions (*alimenta*) among poor people and children.—See ALIMENTARIUS.

Praefectus annonae. The head of food administration, instituted by Augustus (A.D. 6). His was the task to bring in sufficient supplies of corn to the market in Rome; moreover, he supervised the prices. He also had jurisdiction in matters connected with the food administration (see CURA ANNONAE) and punished offenses committed by criminal machinations in the corn trade. The *praefectus annonae* was assisted by subordinate officials (*procuratores*) in the provinces and in Italy as well as by guilds of professionals active in the corn trade and transportation (NAVICULARII).—C. 1.44; 12.58.—See MENSORES FRUMENTARII.

> De Ruggiero, *DE* 1, 477; De Robertis, *La repressione penale nella circoscrizione dell'urbe*, 1937, 35; idem, *St di dir. penale romano*, 1943, 35; Schiller, *RIDA* 3 (1949) 322.

Praefectus Augustalis. (Or simply *Augustalis*.) The title of the *praefectus Aegypti* from the late fourth century on.—D. 1.17; C. 1.37.—See PRAEFECTUS AEGYPTI.

> De Ruggiero, *DE* 1, 824.

Praefectus Caesaris (quinquennalis). See PRAEFECTUS MUNICIPUM.

Praefectus civitatis (gentis, nationis). A military administrator of a newly conquered territory on the frontiers of the Empire, before it was organized as a province.

> H. Zwicky, *Die Verwendung des Militärs in der Verwaltung der Kaiserzeit*, 1944, 11.

Praefectus castrorum. The commander of a military camp.

> Liebenam, *RE* 6, 1642.

Praefectus classis. The commander of a fleet.

Praefectus collegii. The chairman of an association connected with military service.

Praefectus collegii fabrum. In municipalities the title of a person who, being a member of the municipal council (*ordo decurionum*), directed the service of firemen and was, normally, also the protector of their association (*patronus*).—See PRAEFECTUS FABRUM, FABRI.

> Kornemann, *RE* 6, 1920; Jullian, *DS* 2, 956; Liebenam, *DE* 3, 14; Bloch, *Musée Belge* 7 (1903); 9 (1905).

Praefectus fabrum. The head of the body of technicians in the army in earlier times. In the last centuries of the Republic and under the Principate the *praefectus fabrum* was an officer appointed by a praetor or proconsul, and later by the emperor, and employed by his superior for confidential missions (an adjutant). The connection with *fabri* is not quite clear. From the time of Augustus the service of a *praefectus fabrum* was the beginning of an equestrian

career; later it assumed the character of a mere honorary post.—See the foregoing item (Bibl.).

> H. C. Maue, *Der p.f.*, 1887.

Praefectus frumenti dandi. (Called also *curator frumenti*.) An official in charge of the distribution of corn (see FRUMENTATIO) among the population of Rome.

> Rostowzew, *RE* 7, 176; Mommsen, *Hist. Schriften* 1 (1906, ex 1870) 192.

Praefectus iuri dicundo. A deputy jurisdictional official in a municipality or one who was temporarily assigned there to judicial matters when the post of the permanent jurisdictional magistrate was vacant. —See LEX PETRONIA (of 32 B.C.).

> Kornemann, *RE* 16, 623; Cagnat, *DS* 4, 611.

Praefectus legionis. The commander of a legion, of equestrian rank (*eques*). In the development of the Roman army, he was the successor of the LEGATUS LEGIONIS.

Praefectus municipii. If a municipality elected the emperor for its highest magistrate (*duovir*)—this happened frequently—the emperor delegated a *praefectus* as his substitute who administered the office alone, without any colleague. A *praefectus municipii* was also appointed when a member of the imperial family was appointed and did not enter the office but in this case the *praefectus municipii* had a *duovir* as a colleague. Such *praefecti* were called *praefectus Caesaris quinquennales* because they served five years.

Praefectus orae maritimae. A military official, assisted by a military detachment and appointed for the control and defense of an important sector of the seashore, primarily in provinces. He also had jurisdiction over crimes committed during a shipwreck.

> Barbieri, *Rivista di filologia classica* 69 (1941) 268; 74 (1946) 166.

Praefectus praetorio. The commander of a military unit in the imperial residence serving as a body-guard of the emperor (*cohors praetoria*, see PRAETORIUM). The number of *praefecti praetorio* varied from one to four. The *praefecti praetorio* acquired high political influence being steadily in personal touch with the emperor. Their military command was extended over the troops in Italy. They were assigned administrative and jurisdictional functions, the latter also in criminal matters, from the third century on. Some of the prominent jurists (Papinian, Ulpian, Paul) were *praefecti praetorio*. Although only of equestrian rank, the *praefectus praetorio* were the highest governmental officials and the chief advisers of the emperors in military and civil matters. After the division of the territory of the Empire into four *praefecturae*, each *praefectura* had its *praefectus praetorio*.—D. 1.11; C. 7.42; 12.4; for *praefectus praetorio Africae* C. 1.27; for *praefectus praetorio Orientis et Illyrici* C. 1.26.—See EMINENTISSIMUS, EXCELLENTISSIMUS, EDICTA PRAEFECTORUM PRAETORIO, DIOECESIS.

Cagnat, *DS* 4; Cuq, *NRHD* 23 (1899) 393; idem, *Mél Boissier* 1903; E. Stein, *Untersuchungen über das officium des Prätorianerpräfekten seit Diocletian*, 1922; idem, *Bull. Comm. archeol. com. di Roma*, 52 (1924) 9; idem, *Her* 60 (1925) 94; idem, *Rhein. Museum* 74 (1925) 347; Baynes, *JRS* 15 (1925) 204; J. Palanque, *Essai sur la préf. du prét. du Bas-Empire*, 1933; De Robertis, *La repressione penale nella circoscrizione dell'urbe*, 1937, 13; idem, *St di dir. pen. rom.*, 1943, 19; G. Lopuszanski, *La transformation du corps des officiers supérieurs de l'armée rom.*, *Mél. Ecole Franc. Rome*, 1938, 131; L. L. Howe, *The Praetorian Prefect* A.D. 180–305, 1943; De Laet, *Rev. Belge de Philol. et d'hist.* 22 (1943), 25 (1947); Pastori, *StUrb* 19 (1950–1951) 37.

Praefectus sociorum. See SOCII.

Praefectus urbi(s). The prefect of Rome. During the period of kingship the *praefectus urbi* was the representative of the king in his absence. In the early Republic the practice of appointing a *praefectus urbi* was continued when all higher magistrates were absent. Since the creation of the urban praetorship (367 B.C.) the *praefectus urbi* practically disappeared. On one occasion only, when the national feast of the Latins (*feriae Latinae*) was celebrated in the presence of all Roman magistrates, a special *praefectus urbi feriarum Latinarum* was instituted. Augustus also reestablished the office of a *praefectus urbi*, only for the time of his absence from Italy; Tiberius, however, transformed it into a permanent one. Originally the *praefectus urbi* exercised criminal jurisdiction when he was delegated by the emperor, but later his jurisdictional power increased constantly and when the QUAESTIONES PERPETUAE ceased to function under Septimius Severus, the competence of the *praefectus urbi* in criminal matters was almost unlimited not only in Rome but also in the territory within one hundred miles from the city. In the later Empire the *praefectus urbi* was the head of the administration and jurisdiction in both civil and criminal matters. In the first instance he was the exclusive judge in matters in which persons of senatorial rank were involved. Appeals from judgments of the *praefectus annonae*, the *praefectus vigilum*, and other officials of civil jurisdiction (*cognitio extra ordinem*) went to his court as far as the public order in the city was affected. A small armed unit (*cohortes urbanae*) for the maintenance of order was under his command.—D. 1.12; C. 1.28; 12.4.—See MILIARIUM, CUSTOS URBIS, ZENONIANAE CONSTITUTIONES.

Cagnat, *DS* 4; De Ruggiero, *DE* 2, 780; Lambrechts, *Philologische Studiën*, 1937, 13; P. E. Vigneaux, *Essai sur l'histoire de la praefectura u.*, 1896; Brancher, *La jurisdiction civile du p.u.*, 1909; F. M. De Robertis, *Origine della giurisdizione criminale del p.u.*, 1935; idem, *La repressione penale nella circoscrizione dell'urbe*, 1937; idem, *St di dir. pen. rom.*, 1943, 3; Schiller, *RIDA* 3 (1949) 322.

Praefectus vehiculorum. The postmaster of the imperial post in Rome (from the time of Hadrian an official of equestrian rank). Later, larger districts in Italy and the provinces had also their *praefectus vehiculorum*.—See CURSUS PUBLICUS.

Humbert, *DS* 1, 1651.

Praefectus vigilum. One of the highest officials in the administration of the city of Rome. He was the commander of the fire brigade (*vigiles*) and exercised the functions of chief of the police. He had to take care of the security in the capital and had jurisdictional power in such criminal matters as arson, robbery, burglary, and the like. His function in civil trials involved controversies arising from leases of houses.—D. 1.15; C. 1.43.—See VIGILES (Bibl.).

O. Hirschfeld, *Kleine Schriften*, 1913, 96; F. M. De Robertis, *La repressione penale nella circoscrizione dell'urbe*, 1937, 35; idem, *St di dir. rom. penale*, 1943, 35; Schiller, *RIDA* 3 (1949) 322.

Praegnans. The protection of a pregnant woman after her divorce from the father of the child to be born (*nasciturus*) was regulated by a special *senatusconsultum de agnoscendis liberis*.—D. 23.5.—See AGNOSCERE LIBEROS, SENATUSCONSULTUM PLANCIANUM.

Praeiudicare. To prejudice, to impair, to damage. "A judgment which settled a controversy between certain persons does not cause prejudice to others" (D. 42.1.63). There were, however, some exceptions from this rule. In Justinian's language *praeiudicare* is syn. with *nocere*.

Praeiudicialis. See ACTIONES PRAEIUDICIALES, FORMULAE PRAEIUDICIALES, PRAEIUDICIUM.

Praeiudicialis multa. In later civil procedure a fine imposed on a party to a trial who appealed from an interlocutory judgment; see INTERLOCUTIO.

Praeiudicium. A judicial proceeding for the examination of a preliminary question upon which the decision of a controversy depends. See ACTIONES PRAEIUDICIALES. Since a negative solution of the prejudicial question may eliminate the availability of an action for the principal claim, *praeiudicium* is used in the sense of prejudice, damage. For the use of an exception by a defendant in order to prevent that the trial be not extended on questions which may be prejudicial to him for future claims (*exceptio ne praeiudicium hereditati fiat*) see HEREDITATIS PETITIO. For *praeiudicium* with regard to interlocutory judgments, see INTERLOCUTIO. When in a trial the question arose as to whether a party therein involved was a free person (*praeiudicium an liber sit*), this question was taken into examination before all.—D. 44.1; C. 3.8; 7.19; 9.31.

Humbert and Lécrivain, *DS* 4; Weiss, *RE* 3A, 2234; H. Pissard, *Les questions préjudicielles en droit rom.*, 1907; M. Nicolau, *Causa liberalis*, 1933, 156; Siber, *Fschr Wenger* 1 (1944) 46; idem, *ZSS* 65 (1947).

Praelegare (praelegatio). To make a legacy in favor of an heir who, in addition to his share in the inheritance, receives a specific thing as a legacy. The term *praelegatum* used in the literature, is not of Roman coinage.—See LEGATUM PER PRAECEPTIONEM.

C. Ferrini, *Opere* 4 (1930 ex 1895) 237; Scuto, *RISG* 45 (1910) 3; Gangi, *RISG* 47 (1912) 315; Beseler, *ZSS* 49 (1929) 155; B. Biondi, *Successione testamentaria*, 1943, 466 (Bibl.); v. Lübtow, *ZSS* 68 (1951) 511.

Praemature. Before a fixed term. A creditor who asks for payment *praemature* asks for more than is due; see PLUSPETITIO (*tempore*).

Praemium. See NUNTIARE FISCO, DEFERRE.

Praenomen. See NOMEN. Under the Empire, foreigners who were granted Roman citizenship by a decree of the emperor took as a *praenomen* the first name of the emperor. Hence the great number of *Aurelii* among the new citizens naturalized by the emperor Caracalla who bore the name *Aurelius* among his *praenomina.*—See CONSTITUTIO ANTONINIANA, IMPERATOR.

Rosenberg, *RE* 9, 1148 (for *p. imperatoris*).

Praeponere (alicui rei). To put a person at the head (*praepositus*) of a commercial enterprise (see INSTITOR), of the bookkeeping service in a bank, or of a ship (see MAGISTER NAVIS). Syn. *praeficere*. In public law the term *praepositus* is used of the chiefs (commanders) of an office, a public institution or a military unit. In some instances it appears in the title of the official who directs the office; see the following items.

Praepositura. The office of a *praepositus*.

Praepositus. See PRAEPONERE. *Praepositus* is the chief of subaltern officers in certain branches of administration, such as, for instance, the imperial post (*praepositus cursorum, tabellariorum*), the archives (*praepositus tabulariorum*). In the military organization *praepositus* is the commander of a detachment of a limited, territorial nature, for instance *praepositus castrorum* = the commander of a military camp.— See SCHOLAE.

Cagnat, *DS* 4; Severini, *NDI* 10; J. E. Dunlap, in Boak and Dunlap, *Two studies in later R. and Byzantine administration*, 1924, 189.

Praepositus sacri cubiculi. The chamberlain of the imperial household.—C. 12.5.—See CUBICULUM.

Dunlap, *loc. cit.* 160.

Praerogativa. In postclassical period, syn. with PRIVILEGIUM.

Orestano, *AnMac* 12–13 (1939) 29, 69.

Praerogativa centuria. See CENTURIA PRAEROGATIVA.

Praes. See PRAEDES.

Praescripta verba. See ACTIO PRAESCRIPTIS VERBIS.

Praescriptio. In the procedural formula an extraordinary part of the formula preceding the INTENTIO (*prae-scribere*) and serving for a preciser delimitation of the claim. Originally there were *praescriptiones* in favor of the defendant (*praescriptio pro reo*) and of the plaintiff (*praescriptio pro actore*). The former fell early into disuse and were replaced by exceptions, as, e.g., the *praescriptio ne praeiudicium hereditati fiat* (see HEREDITATIS PETITIO, PRAEIUDICIUM). A *praescriptio pro actore* was applied, for instance, in the case when the plaintiff sued for an installment of a debt. In order to save his right to sue later for further installments, a *praescriptio* was inserted at the beginning of the formula: "Let the action be (*ea res agatur*) only for what is already due." In postclassical juristic language *praescriptio* often replaced the former *exceptio* and became a general term for any kind of defense opposed by the defendant.—D. 44.1; C. 7.40; 8.35.—See DENEGATIO ACTIONIS, EA RES AGATUR, FORMULA, EXCEPTIO.

Beauchet, *DS* 4, 626; Bortolucci, *NDI* 10; see Schlossmann, *P. und praescripta verba*, 1907; Wlassak, *ZSS* 33 (1912) 81; J. Petrau-Gay, *Évolution hist. des exceptiones et praescriptiones*, Thèse Lyon, 1916; Steinwenter, *ZSS* 65 (1947) 98.

Praescriptio longi temporis. An institution similar to *usucapio* and applied to provincial land which could not be usucapted under *ius civile*; see USUCAPIO. A possessor of a provincial land might oppose this *praescriptio* to a claimant who sued him for the delivery of the land if he was in possession of it for ten or twenty years. The period of ten years sufficed *inter praesentes*, i.e., if both parties lived in the same locality (later, in the same province); uninterrupted possession through twenty years was required when the parties lived in different cities (provinces). The possession of the defendant had to be based on a just cause (*iusta causa*) and acquired *bona fide* (see USUCAPIO). Originally the *praescriptio* was a way of defense against a *rei vindicatio* (*praescriptio* = *exceptio*), but in later development such a qualified possession gave the possessor the right to claim the recovery of the land if he lost possession. Thus the *praescriptio longi temporis* became a mode of acquisition of property. In Justinian's law the two institutions, *usucapio* and *praescriptio longi temporis* were fused into one. The new terminology was: *usucapio* for movables, *praescriptio longi temporis* for immovables. Numerous interpolations became necessary to eliminate any connection between *usucapio* and immovables; the terms *usucapio* (*usucapere*) were substituted by *longum tempus, longa possessio* (*per longum tempus capere*).—C. 7.33–36; 40; 22.—See ABSENTES, BONA FIDES, and the following items.

Bortolucci, *NDI* 10, 203 (*s.v. prescrizione*); Partsch, *Die longi temporis p.*, 1906; Wenger, *Hist. Jahrb.*, 1940, 359; Levy, *BIDR* 51/52 (1948) 352; idem, *West Roman Vulgar Law*, 1951, 180; Schönbauer, *Anzeiger Akad. Wiss. Wien* 88 (1951) 431.

Praescriptio longissimi temporis. See PRAESCRIPTIO QUADRAGINTA ANNORUM.

Praescriptio quadraginta annorum. The Emperor Constantine ordered that any one who held another's thing for forty years could not be sued for its restitution no matter what the origin of his possession might have been (*praescriptio longissimi temporis*). Excluded from this kind of acquisition were the lessees of an immovable. Uninterrupted possession through forty years was also required for the usucaption of things belonging to the emperor, the fisc, the church and charitable foundations.—C. 7.39.

Riccobono, *FIR* 1² (1941) no. 96; Arangio-Ruiz, *ibid.* 3 (1943) no. 101 (Bibl.); idem, *Aegyptus* 21 (1941) 261 and *ANap* 61 (1942) 311.

Praescriptio quadriennii. The emperor, the empress and the fisc could validly sell things belonging to private individuals. The owners, however, could claim indemnization within four years.—C. 7.37.

Praescriptio triginta annorum. According to an enactment of Theodosius II (A.D. 424), any action was extinguished if the plaintiff did not sue the debtor within a period of thirty years from the time he could sue him except in those cases in which an action expired in a shorter time.—C. 7.39.—See ACTIONES PERPETUAE, ACTIONES TEMPORALES.

Praescriptio viginti annorum. In Justinian's language the normal PRAESCRIPTIO LONGI TEMPORIS of immovables which required uninterrupted possession for twenty years *inter absentes*.

Praescriptum (praescriptio) legis. A legal rule, a norm settled in a statute. Syn. *praecepta legis*.

G. Rotondi, *Leges publ. populi Romani,* 1912, 150.

Praesens (praesentes). See ABSENTES, STIPULATIO INTER ABSENTES.

Praesentalis. A person who was employed in the imperial palace.

Praesenti die. Immediately, at once, without delay (e.g., *debere, solvere, dare*). Syn. *praesens.* "In all obligations in which a date was not fixed for payment, the debt is due at once" (D. 45.1.41.1).

Praeses provinciae. (Or simply *praeses.*) The governor of a province. Originally only governors of imperial provinces (*legatus Augusti pro praetore*) had the title *praesides,* later the term referred to all governors of provinces, both imperial and senatorial, and without distinction whether they were of senatorial or equestrian rank. "The title of *praeses* is a general one. Proconsuls, legatees of the emperor and all who govern provinces are called by the name *praesides*" (D. 1.18.1). In newly acquired provinces the governor was regarded as a military commander who had to subjugate the territory and take care there for order, until a normal provincial administration was introduced. The *praeses* was the highest official in the province. "His functions embrace those of all magistrates in Rome" (D. 1.18.12). He had the jurisdiction of the praetors in Rome, full *imperium,* and after the emperor, the greatest authority in his province. During his term of office a governor could not be removed. No one could become governor of his native province without permission of the emperor. Outside his province the governor was considered a private person. Syn. *is qui praeest provinciae, rector provinciae* (in later times).—D. 1.18; C. 1.40; 5.2.—See PROVINCIA (Bibl.), EDICTUM PROVINCIALE, EDICTA PRAESIDUM, VICE.

Chapot, *DS* 4; Orestano, *NDI* 10; F. Leifer, *Einheit des Gewaltgedankens,* 1914, 305; H. E. Mierow, *The R. provincial governor as he appears in the Digest etc.,* Colorado Springs, 1926; Solazzi, *SDHI* 16 (1950) 282.

Praesidalis. Connected with, or pertaining to the office of a provincial governor.

Praesidium. A military garrison.—See CURATOR PRAESIDII.

Praestantia. An honorific title of certain higher officials in the later Empire. The emperors addressed them in their letters with *"praestantia tua."*

Praestare. (From *praes stare.*) To be a guarantee, to be responsible for certain duties which arise from contractual obligations in specific circumstances as, for instance, for *dolus, culpa,* eviction, and the like (e.g., *dolum, culpam, damnum, custodiam,* etc., *praestare*). The verb appears in the definition of *obligatio* and covers any liability of the debtor beyond the principal obligations of *dare* or *facere.* See OBLIGATIO. The term is elastic and is applied in the classical language in a broad sense in various legal situations even those arising from delictual obligations and sometimes in connection with performances in which no legal duty is involved.—See CUSTODIA, DOLUS.

V. Mayr, *ZSS* 42 (1921) 198; F. Pastori, *Profilo dogmatico e storico dell'obligazione romana,* 1951, 143.

Praestare actionem. To cede an action to another.— See CESSIO.

Praestare patientiam. See PATIENTIAM PRAESTARE.

Praestatio. The performance, fulfillment of a duty. See PRAESTARE. For *praestationes personales* in actions for division of common property, see ACTIO COMMUNI DIVIDUNDO.

Praestituere. To fix a date or a space of time (e.g., *annum, diem, tempus*) for the fulfillment of legal or procedural duties. It is primarily used of terms fixed by legal enactments or by jurisdictional authorities.

Praestituere aliquem. To put a person at the head of an office or a private enterprise. Syn. *praeponere, praeficere.*

Praesumptio. (From *praesumere* = to presume.) A presumption occurs when a fact is deemed proved although it is not directly proved and its existence is only logically inferred from another fact established through evidence. Such kind of presumption is termed in literature *praesumptio facti* or *praesumptio hominis.* E.g., a child born to a married woman is presumed to be the husband's child and consequently a legitimate child. A counterproof is admissible. Such presumptions are often introduced by phrases like *credi debet, creditur* (= it is presumed). In later (Justinian's) law there were some presumptions legally imposed to the effect that a fact had to be considered proved in court as long as no counterproof was offered (*praesumptio iuris*). Thus, for instance, a presumption was fixed for the event that several persons died simultaneously (e.g., in a shipwreck) to the effect that children below the age of puberty were presumed to have died before their parents, whereas the elder children were presumed to have died after them. In certain exceptional cases a counterproof was not admitted (*praesumptio iuris et de iure*).—

D. 22.3.—See COMMORIENTES.

> Donatuti, *NDI* 10; idem, *Le praesumptiones iuris in dir. rom.*, 1930; idem, *Riv. dir. priv.* 1933, 161.

Praesumptio Muciana. The jurist Quintus Mucius Scaevola is considered the author of the presumption that everything that a married woman possessed, was given to her by her husband unless she was able to prove the contrary.

> Kübler, *RE* 16, 445; G. Donatuti, *Le praesumptiones iuris in dir. rom.*, 1930, 15; G. Balis, *Die p.M., Mél Streit* Athens, 1939.

Praetendere. To bring forward an excuse (a true or a false one), to pretend, for instance, the ignorance of the law.

Praeterire. See SENATU MOVERE.

Praeterire. To pass over in silence a person in a last will. The so-called *heredes sui* (see HERES SUUS), natural or adoptive, had to be instituted or disinherited (see EXHEREDATIO); otherwise if they were not mentioned in the testament at all (*praeteriti*) the latter was void and the testator was deemed *intestatus*. —C. 6.28.—See POSTUMUS SUUS.

> Beseler, *ZSS* 55 (1925) 1; Sanfilippo, *AnCam* 12 (1938) 265.

Praeterita (scil. **facta, negotia**). Events which happened in the past, such as crimes committed before the issuance of a pertinent penal statute, legal acts and transactions concluded at a former time. Ant. *futura* = future events. The antithesis is connected with the problem of the retroactivity of legal enactments. Non-retroactivity is the rule, but in a few exceptional cases some later imperial enactments, even of penal character, admitted retroactivity. Most of them are in the Theodosian Code.—See EX POST FACTO.

> Siber, *Analogie und Rückwirkung im Strafrechte, ASächGW* 43 (1936); Berger, *Sem* 7 (1949) 63; Marky, *BIDR* 53–54 (1948) 241.

Praetextatus. See TOGA PRAETEXTA, IMPUBES.

Praetextus. See TOGA PRAETEXTA.

Praetor. In the earliest times (before the introduction of the consulship) the *praetor* was the highest official (*prae-itor* = one who goes in the front of the people). As a magistracy (see MAGISTRATUS) the praetorship was created by the *Lex Licinia Sextia* (367 B.C.). It was assigned the civil jurisdiction which it took over from the consuls. The office of the *praetor urbanus* was first created. Originally a patrician post, the praetorship was made accessible to plebeians since 337 B.C. The *praetor urbanus* had jurisdiction (*ius dicebat*) in Rome; later (242 B.C.) a second praetor was instituted and vested with jurisdictional power in civil matters between foreigners (*inter peregrinos*) and between foreigners and Roman citizens (*praetor peregrinus*). Since the government of provinces was originally directed by praetors their number constantly increased (up to 16). Later, it became customary to send ex-praetors after their year of service in Rome to provinces as governors. When the permanent criminal courts (see QUAESTIONES PERPETUAE) were established, their chairmen were taken among the praetors. The praetors were the highest magistrates in the Republic after the consuls and were vested with full *imperium* and far-reaching authority in military, administrative and judicial matters. But their principal domain was jurisdiction; for their creative activity in the development of the law, see IUS HONORARIUM, IUS PRAETORIUM, IUS EDICENDI, EDICTUM PERPETUUM. They were obliged to reside in Rome and were not allowed to leave the capital for more than ten days. Under the Principate the activity of praetors was almost exclusively jurisdictional. Afterwards, when the jurisdiction was taken over by bureaucratic officials, the praetorship became an office without any important activity. Its functions were limited to the arrangement of public games and spectacles.—D. 1.14; C. 1.39; 12.2.—See IURISDICTIO, STIPULATIONES PRAETORIAE, IN IURE, MANUMISSIO PRAETORIA, and the following items.

> Lécrivain, *DS* 4; Anon., *NDI* 10; Treves, *OCD*; F. Leifer, *Die Einheit des Gewaltgedankens*, 1916, 196; H. Lévy-Bruhl, *Prudent et préteur*, 1916; G. T. Sadler, *The R. praetors*, London, 1922; Wenger, *Prätor und Formel, SbMünch* 1926; E. Betti, *St Chiovenda* 1927; Riccobono, *TR* 9 (1929) 6; F. Wieacker, *Vom röm. Recht*, 1944, 86; Gioffredi, *SDHI* 13–14 (1948) 102.

Praetor aerarii. See AERARIUM POPULI ROMANI.

Praetor de liberalibus causis. A praetor with a special jurisdiction in matters concerning the liberty of an individual, in particular, in controversies between slaves and their masters involving the liberty of the slaves. The office was still in existence in Justinian's times.

> M. Nicolau, *Causa liberalis*, 1933, 67.

Praetor fideicommissarius. A praetor instituted in the early Principate with jurisdiction in matters concerned with *fideicommissa*.—See FIDEICOMMISSUM.

> Kübler, *DE* 3, 75.

Praetor fiscalis. A special praetor with jurisdiction in controversies between the fisc and private individuals. The office was instituted by the emperor Nerva (A.D. 96–98).

Praetor hastarius. A praetor who, in the later Principate presided over the centumviral court.—See CENTUMVIRI, HASTA.

> Wlassak, *RE* 3, 1937.

Praetor iuventutis. See MAGISTER IUVENUM.

Praetor liberalium causarum. See PRAETOR DE LIBERALIBUS CAUSIS.

Praetor maximus. A controversial office; seemingly the highest among three officials who at the beginning of the Republic had the sovereign governmental power (*dictator? magister populi?*).

> Heuss, *ZSS* 64 (1944) 68; Wesenberg, *ZSS* 65 (1947) 319.

Praetor peregrinus. See PRAETOR. For the influence of the judicial activity of the *praetor peregrinus* on the development of the so-called *ius gentium,* see IUS GENTIUM (Bibl.).

> Nap, *TR* 12 (1933) 170; Gilbert, *Res Iudicatae* 2 (Melbourne, 1939) 50; Daube, *JRS* 41 (1951) 66.

Praetor populi (plebis). An official instituted by Justinian (Nov. 13, A.D. 535) for criminal jurisdiction, with a competence similar to the former PRAEFECTUS VIGILUM.

Praetor tutelarius (tutelaris). A praetor (from the time of Marcus Aurelius) charged with the appointment of guardians and with jurisdiction in controversies between guardians and their wards.

> Preisendanz, *RE* 7A, 1608.

Praetor urbanus. See PRAETOR.

Praetoriani. Soldiers of the imperial body-guard, see PRAETORIUM. Syn. *cohors praetoria.*

> Cagnat, *DS* 4, 632.

Praetorianus. (Adj.) Pertaining to the office of the *praefectus praetorio.*

Praetorium (cohors praetoria). A military unit serving as the body-guard of the emperor under the command of the PRAEFECTUS PRAETORIO.

> Cagnat, *DS* 4, 632; Parker, *OCD*; H. Zwicky, *Die Verwendung des Militärs in der Verwaltung,* Zürich, 1944, 64; M. Durry, *Les cohortes prétoriennes,* 1938; A. Passerini, *Le coorti pretorie,* 1939; H. Lorenz, *Untersuchungen zum Praetorium,* Diss. Halle, 1936.

Praetorium. The residence of a provincial governor; the headquarters of a commanding general. *Praetorium* is also used of any luxurious mansion. Even when situated in the country (a country-seat) it is considered a *praedium urbanum.*

> Cagnat, *DS* 4, 640; Richmond, *OCD*; Domaszewski, *Bonner Jahrbücher* 117 (1908) 97.

Praetorius. (Noun.) A retired praetor.—See ADLECTIO.

Praetorius. (Adj.) Connected with, or pertaining to, the office of a praetor (*ius, iurisdictio, actio, stipulatio,* etc.).

Praetura. The office of a praetor.—See PRAETOR.

Praevaluit. See OBTINUIT.

Praevaricatio (praevaricator). A collusion between the *prosecutor* (accuser) and the accused in a criminal trial to obtain the latter's acquittal. The second trial against an accused who had been absolved in a first trial, took place before the same court the first duty of which was to examine whether or not in the first proceedings there had been a *praevaricatio.* The *praevaricator,* i.e., the accuser whose guilt was established, was severely punished and branded with infamy. See ACCUSATIO. *Praevaricatio* was also a collusion between a lawyer and the adversary of his client to the detriment of the latter.—D. 47.15.

> Kaser, *RE* 6A, 2146; Lécrivain, *DS* 4; Levy, *ZSS* 53 (1933) 177.

Pragmatica sanctio. In the later Empire an imperial enactment of a particular importance and of a general and permanent validity. It concerned the general administration, privileges granted larger groups of persons, orders given to officials of a larger administrative body or corporations, etc. Letters by which the emperors of the Eastern and Western parts of the Empire reciprocally exchanged their enactments to be published in the other part of the Empire, were also termed *pragmatica sanctio.* Syn. *pragmatica iussio, pragmatica lex,* or simply *pragmatica,* or *pragmaticum.* Special functionaries of the imperial chancery, *pragmaticarii,* were entrusted with the drafting of such enactments.—C. 1.23.—See SANCTIO PRO PETITIONE VIGILII.

> Cuq, *DS* 4, 642; H. Dirksen, *Hinterlassene Schriften* 2 (1871) 54; Mommsen, *ZSS* 25 (1904) 51 (= *Jur. Schr.* 2, 426); Dell'Oro, *SDHI* 11 (1945) 314; Renier, *RHD* 22 (1943) 208.

Pragmaticarius. See the foregoing item.

Pragmaticus. A person skilled in legal matters, primarily in the composition of legal documents.

Precario (precariis verbis). By begging, by entreaty, by request. The typical expressions (*precaria verba*) were *rogo, peto;* they were used in a testament for a *fideicommissum* and addressed to the heir as a request to fulfill the testator's wish. Syn. *precative, precativo modo.*—See PRECARIUM.

Precarium. "What is given gratuitously a person at his request to be used by him as long as the grantor permits" (D. 43.26.1 pr.). The latter is *precario dans,* the grantee = *precario accipiens.* The grantee is liable for fraud only; he has possession of the thing given *precario* and interdictal protection, but his possession does not count for usucaption. On the other hand the grantor demands the restitution of the *precarium* by INTERDICTUM DE PRECARIO.—D. 43.26; C. 8.9.

> Beauchet, *DS* 4; Anon., *NDI* 10; Lenel, *Edictum perpetuum*[3] (1927) 486; Ciapessoni, *ACSR* 6 (1928); Scherillo, *RendLomb* 62 (1929) 389; Bozza, *AnMac* 6 (1930) 213; V. Scialoja, *St* 1 (1931, ex 1888) 341; Albertario, *St Solmi* 1 (1941) 337 = *St* 2 (1941) 14; Silva, *SDHI* 6 (1940) 233; Caracaterra, *AnBari* 4 (1941) 115; Branca, *St Solazzi* 1948, 498; Levy, *ZSS* 67 (1948) 1; Roels, *RIDA* 6 (1951) 177.

Precator. A petitioner, particularly one who addresses himself to the emperor with a petition (PRECES).

Preces. (Sing. *prex.*) A petition addressed to the emperor by a private person. Since the petition normally was not accompanied by a piece of evidence, the imperial answer (decision, rescript) was given with the reservation "provided that your allegations are based on truth" (*si preces veritate nituntur*). See LIBELLUS, SUBSCRIPTIO.—In relations between private individuals *preces* mean a request, entreaty. The term appears in the definition of PRECARIUM.—C. 1.19.

Preces refutatoriae. Syn. *libelli refutatorii.* See REFUTATIO, CONSULTATIO.

Prensio. (From *prendere*.) The arresting of delinquents by magistrates with *imperium* and plebeian tribunes. The right to arrest = *ius prensionis*.

Pretium. The price fixed in a sale and paid (or to be paid) by the buyer to the seller. See EMPTIO VENDITIO. The price is an essential element in a contract of sale, since "there is no sale without a price" (Inst. 3.23.1). The price had to be established in money, otherwise the agreement was not a sale but PERMUTATIO (an exchange, a barter). The fixing of the price may be left to a third person. The classical jurists did not agree as to the moment when in such a case the sale was concluded. Justinian decided that the sale was concluded after the third person established the price. See LAESIO ENORMIS.—*Pretium* sometimes indicates the sum paid by the lessee in a lease or by the employer to a workman for the work done; see MERCES.

Pretium iustum. An adequate, just price. In the classical law there was no requirement of a just price. For the later development, see LAESIO ENORMIS.

Prex. See PRECES.

Pridianum. A military record concerning the strength of a unit and the changes therein (accessions and losses).

> Fink, *Trans. Amer. Philol. Assoc.*, 63 (1942) 61; Gilliam, *Yale Clas St* 11 (1950) 222.

Primas. In later imperial constitutions a person who holds the first place in an office, in a public administrative body (a city, a village) or in professional associations (*primus advocatorum*).—C. 11.29.

Primatus. The rank of a PRIMAS.—See the foregoing item.

Primicerius. In the later Empire the chief, the highest official, first in rank, in an imperial bureau or the superintendent over several bureaus (e.g., *primicerius scriniorum, officiorum*). Similar expressions: *primas, magister*. His deputy = *secundocerius*. The dignity of a *primicerius* = *primiceriatus*.—C. 12.7.

> Cagnat, *DS* 4.

Primicerius notariorum. See NOTARIUS.—C. 12.7.

Primipilarius. See the following item.

Primipilus. The first among the centurions of a legion. After retiring from service a *primipilus* received the title *primipilarius* and was granted certain distinctions and privileges, primarily of a financial nature. *Primipili* were entrusted by the emperor with special military missions or a honorary position, at times with a magistracy in the community of residence.—C. 12.57; 62.—See CENTURIO.

> Cagnat, *DS* 4; v. Domaszewski, *RE* 3 (*s.v. centurio*); De Laet, *Le rang social du p., AntCl* 9 (1940) 13.

Primiscrinius. The first official in an imperial bureau (SCRINIUM).

Princeps. The emperor. The title was first assumed by Augustus in the period between 27 and 23 B.C. not as an official one but in the sense simply of "the first citizen." Hence the period of the Roman history from that date on is termed the Principate (until Diocletian). The term *princeps* does not appear among the titles of the emperor in official documents. In these his position is stressed instead by the words *Imperator, Caesar, Augustus*. Other distinctive attributes were *Pius* and *Felix* or, referring to victorious enterprises, *Germanicus, Arabicus,* and the like. The basic elements of the *princeps'* power was on the one hand the tribunician power (*tribunicia potestas*) established by Augustus as a symbol of the restoration of the Republic, which gave him the inviolability of the tribunes (*sacrosanctitas*), the right of INTERCESSIO, but no colleagueship of other tribunes, and re the right to summon the senate and the people; on the other hand he held the *imperium maius* of a proconsul for life which strengthened his position with regard to the provinces and vested him with the highest military command in the whole empire. The emperor's consulship and censorship (the latter assumed by some successors of Augustus) completed the external aspect of the power of the *princeps*. Through the duration of the Principate the rights of the emperor were gradually extended without any substantial change in their legal bases. See LEX DE IMPERIO VESPASIANI, PRINCEPS LEGIBUS SOLUTUS. The control of the foreign policy and the right to decide about war and peace as well as to conclude treaties with foreign countries and to receive and send ambassadors belonged to the prerogatives of the *princeps*. In the field of legislation the emperor's wishes were originally (under Augustus) submitted for ratification by the people, an act which in the course of the first post-Christian century became a simple formality and afterwards disappeared. In the jurisdictional domain the emperor was the supreme judge both in criminal and civil matters, either as a first or an appellate instance. The emperor was also *pontifex maximus*. The influence of the emperor on the composition of the senate constantly increased (see ADLECTIO) and so did his interference in the election of magistrates (see COMMENDATIO). Moreover, he had the exclusive right to appoint officials of the imperial chancery, for his personal service and for the imperial household as well. He alone chose the delegates to carry out some of his governmental duties in his name. The imperial service became gradually a state service, at the expenses of the magistracies which under the Principate continued to exist but with responsibilities which continually diminished. For the various imperial offices, the imperial chancery, the administration of the imperial patrimony, and the imperial household, see the pertinent entries; for the role of the senate under the Principate, see SENATUS; for the legislative activity of the *princeps*, see CONSTITUTIONES PRINCIPUM; ORATIO PRINCIPIS; for his judicial activity, see DECRETA, RESCRIPTA. Succession to the throne was not fixed by law. It was not hereditary but elective; election by the senate as representatives of the people was the rule. There was, however, at times a hereditary succession, in fact, when an emperor indicated his successor (a natural or adoptive son, or a near relative) by designating the latter as his heir thereby implying the wish that his heir might be also his successor as the *princeps*. A similar designation of a successor might be expressed by the appointment of a co-regent. The juridical structure of the Principate has remained controversial in spite of a tremendous literature in recent times on the occasion of Augustus' bimillenary. The Principate can hardly be classified as a uniform constitutional system. It started from the tendency of Augustus to keep in force certain Republican institutions, but in the course of time some authoritarian features were added at the expense of earlier democratic elements, so that the constitutional aspect at the beginning of the Principate was gradually disappearing in later times, particularly under Hadrian and in the late first half of the third century. With the reign of Diocletian a new epoch started in the Roman constitutional development with an autocratic monarch at the head of the empire (no more *princeps*, but *imperator*). This period is termed (perhaps not very appropriately) Dominate, the emperor being now (from the time of Aurelian, A.D. 270–275) the master, *dominus*, over the territory and the population of the state. See, moreover, LEGATI CAESARIS, PROCURATOR CAESARIS, RES PRIVATA CAESARIS, CONSILIUM PRINCIPIS, FISCUS, MAGISTRATUS, DIVUS, GENIUS, DAMNATIO MEMORIAE, EPISTULAE PRINCIPIS, DOMUS DIVINA, MAIESTAS, CONSORTES IMPERII, RES GESTAE DIVI AUGUSTI, AUCTORITAS PRINCIPIS, MANDATA PRINCIPUM.—For the legislative activity and legal policy of the individual emperors, see General Bibliography, Ch. VI.

Cagnat, *DS* 4; Lécrivain, *ibid.* (*s.v. principatus*); Balsdon, *OCD*; O. Th. Schulz, *Wesen des röm. Kaisertums der ersten zwei Jahrhunderte*, 1916; Domaszewski, *Die Consulate der röm Kaiser*, *SbHeid* 1918, 6; Schönbauer, *ZSS* 47 (1927) 264; Gagé, *Rev. historique* 177 (1927) 264; E. Kornemann, *Doppelprinzipat und Reichsteilung*, 1930; L. R. Taylor, *The divinity of the R. Emperor*, 1931; H. Siber, *Zur Entwicklung der röm. Prinzipatsverfassung*, *ASäch GW* 42 (1933), 44 (1940); A. Gwosdz, *Der Begriff des röm. P.*, Diss. Breslau, 1933; M. Hammond, *The Augustean Principate*, 1933; L. Berlinger, *Beiträge zur inoffiziellen Titulatur der röm. Kaiser*, 1935; Hohl, *Herm* 70 (1935) 350; F. De Martino, *Lo stato di Augusto*, 1936; Wagenvoort, *Philologus* 91 (1936) 206, 323; W. Weber, *Princeps*, 1936; S. Riccobono, Jr., *Augusto e il problema della nuova costituzione*, *AnPal* 15 (1934) 363; Arangio-Ruiz, *SDHI* 1 (1935) 196, 2 (1936) 466, 5 (1939) 570; A. v. Premerstein, *Wesen und Werden des Prinzipats*, *ABayAW* 1937; Sickle, *Changing bases of the R. imperial power*, *AntCl* 8 (1939) 153; Beranger, *L'hérédité du Principat*, *Rev. Ét Lat* 17 (1939) 171; R. Syme, *The R. revolution*, 1939, 313; P. De Francisci, *Genesi e struttura del principato augusteo*, *Mem. Accad. d'Italia*, Ser. VII, 1941; idem, *Arcana imperii*, 3 (1948) 169; Kolbe, *Klio* 36 (1943) 22; Ensslin, *SbMünch* 1943, 6 Heft; Wickert, *Klio* 36 (1943) 1; De Laet, *AntCl* 14 (1945)

145; Schönbauer, *SbWien* 224, 2 (1946) 75; J. Magdelain, *Auctoritas principis*, Paris, 1947; Rogers, *TAmPhilolA* 78 (1947) 140; Dell'Oro, *SDHI* 13–14 (1947–1948) 316; F. De Visscher, *Nouvelles Études*, 1949, 3; Beranger, *Museum Helveticum* 5 (1949) 178; De Robertis, *RIDA* 4 (1950) 409.

Princeps. (Generally.) An outstanding personage, a chief, in civil or military service.

Princeps agentium in rebus. The chief of the AGENTES IN REBUS.—C. 12.21.

Giffard, *RHD* 14 (1935) 239.

Princeps centurio. See CENTURIO.

Princeps civitatis. A leading man in the state.

Princeps coloniae (municipii). Not an administrative official but an outstanding personage in a colony (*municipium*), usually an ex-magistrate of a higher rank.

Kornemann, *RE* 16, 626.

Princeps iuvenum (iuventutis). The title of the emperor's son when he put on the *toga virilis* and entered service in the cavalry. He was the head of the young men of equestrian rank.

Weinstock, *RE* 6A, 2184; Cagnat, *DS* 4; Balsdon, *OCD*.

Princeps (principes) legionis. Soldiers of the second line in the legion, older than the first line infantry men (*hastati*) and sent into combat after them. The commander of a centuria composed of *principes* also had the title *princeps* (*centurio*).

Princeps legibus solutus. This principle stating that the emperor is above the law appears in Justinian's Digest as a general one. It is clear, however, that in the source (D. 1.3.31) from which it was taken the rule originally referred only to the exemption of the emperor from the restrictions imposed by the *Lex Iulia et Papia Poppaea*. Under the Principate the rule had the meaning that the emperor might abolish or change the laws as he pleased.—See LEX IULIA DE MARITANDIS ORDINIBUS.

De Francisci, *BIDR* 34 (1925) 321; Schulz, *Engl. Hist. Rev.* 60 (1945) 155; A. Magdelain, *Auctoritas principis*, Paris, 1947, 109.

Princeps officii. See OFFICIUM PALATINUM. Any head of an administrative office, civil or military, used the title *princeps*, e.g., *princeps agentium in rebus*.—C. 12.57.

Marchi, *St Fadda* 5 (1906) 381; E. Stein, *ZSS* 41 (1920) 195.

Princeps scrinii. The head of an imperial bureau in the later Empire. The *principes scriniorum* were subject to the *magister officiorum*.

Princeps senatus. A distinguished, leading member of the senate. In the list of senators his name was at the head. Augustus and his successors assumed this Republican title.

O'Brien-Moore, *RE* Suppl. 6, 699.

Principales. (Noun.) In military service officers of a lower rank, technicians, musicians, etc., in the army. They were organized in associations (*collegia*).

Waltzing, *DE* 2, 367; Drake, *Univ. of Michigan Studies, Human. Ser.* 1 (1904) 261.

Principalis. (Adj.) Connected with, pertaining to, or originating from the emperor, as, e.g., *principalis constitutio, iussio, cognitio, beneficium.*

Principalis. (Adj.) First in place, degree, or importance, as opposed to another person or thing of minor or secondary importance. Thus *res principalis* (= the principal thing) is distinguished from ACCESSIO; *heres principalis* (= the principal heir) is opposed to the substituted heir (see SUBSTITUTIO).

Principalis. (Noun.) The highest official in the municipal administration or in a specific office. Syn. *princeps.*

Principatus. The high position of the emperor (see PRINCEPS); the highest rank in an office.

Principi placuit. See CONSTITUTIONES PRINCIPUM.

Principia. In military terminology the center of a military camp, the area about the tent of the commanding general (*praetorium*). In the *principia* were the tents of higher officers and commanders of minor units. There was also the place where the higher officers gathered to receive orders.

　　Lécrivain, *DS* 4, 640; Saglio, *DS* 1, 945.

Principium. The initial words of an interdictal formula. Some interdicts are denoted by their first words, as, e.g., *interdicta uti possidetis, utrubi, quorum bonorum, quam hereditatem.* In citations of texts of Justinian's legislation *principium* (= *pr.*) indicates the introductory passage of a text where numbered sections follow.

Prior. Prior in degree, rank, or time. Ant. *posterior.* *Lex prior* = an earlier law. *Prior heres* (syn. *principalis*) = an heir first instituted, before the heir substituted to him; see SUBSTITUTIO.

Prior. In the election of magistrates, when a candidate for a higher magistracy received a majority of the *centuriae* voting in the *comitia centuriata,* the voting was not continued further. The magistrate so elected was designated as *prior,* e.g., *prior (consul) factus est.*

　　Liebenam, *RE* 4, 693.

Prior tempore potior iure. "He who is first in time has a better (stronger) right" (C. 8.17.3). The rule refers to a thing pledged successively to several creditors by the same debtor. The creditor to whom the thing was pledged first had to be satisfied before those to whom the thing was pledged subsequently.— D. 20.4; C. 8.17.—See PIGNUS, HYPOTHECA, POTIOR IN PIGNORE.

　　A. Biscardi, *Il dogma della collisione,* 1935, 49; *idem,* *SDHI* 4 (1938) 484.

Priscus. Some jurists had the surname (*cognomen*) Priscus, among them Iavolenus and Neratius. Therefore, when a text appears under the name of Priscus, the authorship may be doubtful. The jurist Fulcinius (Priscus) enters also into consideration.

　　Berger, *RE* 16, 2549; 17, 1832.

Privatiani. Officials subordinate to the COMES RERUM PRIVATARUM.

Privatim. Privately, in a private capacity. Ant. *publice* = in public, publicly. The distinction is parallel to that between *publicus* and *privatus.* *Privatim* refers also to official acts of the praetor when, in exceptional cases, he performed them (as, for instance, manumissions) at home (*in villa*).—See DE PLANO, IN TRANSITU.

Privatus. (Noun.) A private person as opposed to a public official, a corporate body, the fisc, or a member of the military.—See UTILITAS PUBLICA.

Privatus. (Adj.) Connected with, or pertaining to, a private person. Ant. *publicus* = all that concerns the Roman people (*populus Romanus* = the state).— See RES PRIVATAE, RES PRIVATA CAESARIS, ACTIONES PRIVATAE, DELICTUM, UTILITAS, INTERDICTA PRIVATA, ITER PRIVATUM.

Privignus. A stepson, i.e., a son of one's wife by a former marriage or a son by concubinage. *Privigna* = a stepdaughter.

Privilegium. A legal enactment concerning a specific person or case and involving an exemption from common rules. Originally *privilegium* might indicate unfavorable treatment of the person involved. The Twelve Tables ordered that "privileges should not be imposed" (*privilegia ne irroganto*). Later, however, the term assumed the meaning of an exceptional favor granted an individual or an indefinite number of persons, as, for instance, a certain category of creditors (called *privilegiarii*) to whom a better legal position was assigned than other creditors of the same debtor. There is a distinction between *privilegia causae* and *privilegium personae,* the first being connected with the matter itself, as with certain specific claims, the latter being attached to a person or a group of persons with regard to their profession or social position. Only the first were transferable to the heir of the privileged person. Privileged claims were, for instance, the claims of a ward against his guardian or curator, or the claim of a wife against her insolvent husband for the restitution of a dowry. Under the Empire *privilegium* is used sometimes as syn. with IUS SINGULARE.

　　Beauchet, *DS* 4; Anon., *NDI* 10; Legras, *NRHD* 32 (1908) 584, 650; Ramadier, *NRHD* 34 (1910) 549; E. Pais, *Ricerche sulla storia* 1 (1915) 401; R. Orestano, *Ius singulare e p., AnMac* 12–13 (1939) 5.

Privilegium exigendi. A right granted certain categories of creditors against an insolvent debtor under which they had to be satisfied before other creditors.

　　Orestano, *AnMac* 13 (1939) 24; S. Solazzi, *Il concorso dei creditori* 3 (1940) 132.

Privilegium fisci. See IUS FISCI.—C. 7.73; 10.1; 5; 9.

Privilegium fori. The privilege granted in the later Empire to ecclesiastical persons to have recourse to ecclesiastical jurisdiction.

　　Genestal, *NRHD* 32 (1908) 162.

Privilegium funerarium. The expenses for the funeral of an insolvent person had to be covered from his property first, before the satisfying of the claims of his creditors.

Privilegium (privilegia) militum. The privileges of soldiers in the field of private law, as, for instance, their right to make a testament without observance of the forms prescribed for civilians.—See MILITES.

Pro. (Connected with the title of a high magistrate, *proconsul, propraetor, proquaestor,* or separately written *pro consule, pro praetore, pro quaestore.*) Originally indicated a magistrate who acted as a substitute for the magistrate involved. Under the Republic a pro-magistrate was either a former magistrate whose functioning was extended beyond the year of service for special reasons (see PROROGATIO) or an official who was temporarily appointed (not elected by the people) as a substitute for another magistrate. At the end of the Republic *proconsul* was the title of the governor of a province who had been previously a consul (or even only a praetor). Pro-magistracies became later dissociated from former service and were a separate type of office without regard to the fact whether or not the person holding it had been a consul or praetor.

　　Kübler, *RE* 14, 430; W. F. Jashemski, *The origin and history of the proconsular and propraetorian imperium,* Chicago, 1950.

Pro. (In connection with possession as a title, *iusta causa,* for usucaption; see USUCAPIO.) There were various titles which led to usucaption when the holder of a thing erroneously, but in good faith, assumed he was entitled to keep it as his. Thus the title *pro emptore possidere* means that one held a thing which he acquired by purchase; *pro legato* was used when one received a thing in fulfillment of a legacy; *pro donato,* when one received a thing as a gift from a non-owner; *pro dote,* when a husband received a thing in a dowry; *pro soluto,* when a thing was given in fulfillment of an obligation; *pro derelicto* when one took a thing abandoned by a person whom he considered the owner. In all these cases the holder (*possessor*) of the thing was regarded as *possessor pro suo* since he possessed it in the belief that he was its owner whereas in actual fact, he was not the owner because the transferor himself (the seller, the donor, etc.) had not been the owner or the legacy or donation were invalid.—D. 41.4–10.—See TRADITIO, USUCAPIO, POSSESSIO, POSSESSOR PRO HEREDE, POSSESSOR PRO POSSESSORE.

　　Banmate, *RIDA* 1 (1948) 27 (for *pro legato*).

Pro herede gerere (gestio). To act intentionally as an heir (to use the deceased man's property, to sell or to lease things belonging to the estate, to pay the debts of the deceased, to sue another with *hereditatis petitio,* and the like). Such doings were considered as an acceptance of the *hereditas* and had the legal consequences of an ADITIO HEREDITATIS in cases in which an explicit declaration of acceptance of the heir was required, i.e., when the heir was an outside heir

(see HERES EXTRANEUS, VOLUNTARIUS). When a *heres suus* or *heres suus et necessarius* acted in the way mentioned, his doings were qualified as *se immiscere (miscere) hereditati* and resulted in his losing the right to refuse the inheritance (*ius abstinendi,* see ABSTINERE SE HEREDITATE). In order to avoid such consequences the person so acting could declare before witnesses (*testatio*) that his acts did not imply the acceptance of the inheritance.

　　Berger, *RE* 9, 1108 (*s.v. immiscere*); Sanfilippo, *AnCat* 2 (1947–48) 166.

Pro herede usucapio. See USUCAPIO PRO HEREDE.

Pro nihilo esse (haberi). To be (considered) legally void.

　　Hellmann, *ZSS* 23 (1902) 426.

Pro socio actio. See SOCIETAS.

Pro·tribunali. In front of the TRIBUNAL, in court. Ant. *de plano, in transitu.*

　　Düll, *ZSS* 52 (1932) 174.

Pro tutore gerere. To act as if a guardian. "One acts as if a guardian (*tutor*) when he fulfills the duties of a guardian in the ward's affairs, no matter whether he does so in the belief that he is the guardian or he knows that he is not, but falsely pretends to be the guardian" (D. 27.5.1.1). He could be sued by *actio protutelae* for damages caused during his acting.—D. 27.5; 6; C. 5.45.—See FALSUS TUTOR, ACTIO PROTUTELAE.

　　Sachers, *RE* 7A, 1525, 1585.

Probare. To approve. The term is used to indicate the approval of one jurist's opinion by another jurist. Syn. *adprobare.*

Probare. In court or extrajudicially, to prove, to ascertain through evidence.—See ONUS PROBANDI, PROBATIO.

Probare opus. In connection with a *locatio conductio operis faciendi,* see ADPROBARE.

　　Samter, *ZSS* 26 (1905) 125.

Probatio. Proof, evidence, the act of proving. In civil trials there was the rule: *ei incumbit probatio qui dicit, non qui negat* (he who affirms has to prove, not he who denies, D. 22.3.2). The plaintiff therefore, has to prove the facts on which his claim is founded, the defendant those facts which serve as a basis for his denial of the plaintiff's claim or for his exception opposed thereto. Each party has free choice of the means of evidence he wishes to offer. In the classical law the value of the various means of evidence (documents, witnesses) was equal and the judge had full liberty in the evaluation of the proofs presented. In postclassical and Justinian's law the tendency prevailed to give preference to written evidence and to debase that of a witness, if not to declare a testimony of the latter in certain cases insufficient. Under the influence of Christianity the oath became more and more predominant as a means of evidence.—D. 22.3; C. 4.19.—See ONUS PROBANDI, TESTIS, INSTRUMENTUM.

Riccobono, *ZSS* 34 (1913) 231; De Sarlo, *AG* 114 (1935) 184; Tozzi, *Riv. dir processuale civile,* 17 (1940) 125, 212; M. Lemosse, *Cognitio,* 1944, 233; J. P. Levy, *La formation de la théorie des preuves, St Solazzi* 1948, 418; Levy, *Iura* 3 (1952) 155.

Probatio anniculi causae. See CAUSAE PROBATIO.

Probatio erroris causae. See CAUSAE PROBATIO.

Probatio operis. See ADPROBARE, PROBARE, LOCATIO CONDUCTIO OPERIS FACIENDI.

Probationes apertissimae, evidentissimae, manifestissimae. The most evident conclusive proofs. Terms frequently used by Justinian and his compilers, primarily with reference to proofs concerning the interpretation of wills.

Probatores. Approvers, professional experts who approved of a work done by a contractor.

Probitas (probus). Honesty (honest).

Probatoria. In the later Empire = an imperial decree by which an official of the imperial administration was appointed.—C. 12.59.

Procedere. To occur, to take place. *Quod ita procedit, si* (= this occurs if) is a favorite phrase of Justinian's compilers which they used to restrict a legal principle previously expressed.

Guerneri-Citati, *Indice*² (1927) 50 (*s.v. ita*).

Probus (Valerius Probus). See NOTAE IURIS.

Proceres. The highest officials in the service of the later emperors.

Procheiros nomos. A succinct official compilation of laws (similar to the ECLOGE) based primarily on Justinian's codification and published under the emperor Basile Macedo about A.D. 879. A revised edition, enriched by additions from the later legislation and called *Prochiron Auctum* was made four centuries later, about 1300.

Anon., *NDI* 10, 643; Editions: Zachariae v. Lingenthal, *P.N.,* 1837; idem, *Jus Graeco-Romanum* 6 (1870); J. and P. Zepos, *Jus Graeco-Romanum* 2 (Athens, 1931) 3, 107 (Bibl. p. XII); E. H. Freshfield, *A manual of Eastern R. law, P.N.,* Cambridge, 1928; idem, *A provincial manual of later R. law, the Calabrian Procheiron,* 1931; F. Brandileone and V. Pusitoni, *Prochiron legum, pubblicato secondo il Cod. Vat. Gr. 845. Fonti per la storia d'Italia,* 1895.

Procinctus. The army in fighting order.—See IN PROCINCTU.

Proclamare (proclamatio) ad (in) libertatem. To assert and defend one's liberty. Syn. *in libertatem adserere.*—See ADSERTIO, CAUSA LIBERALIS.—D. 40.13; C. 7.18.

Lécrivain, *DS* 4; M. Nicolau, *Causa liberalis,* 1933, 105.

Proconsul (pro consule). Ex-consuls and ex-praetors (*pro praetore*) whose magisterial power, *imperium* (not the consulship or praetorship itself), was prolonged (see PROROGATIO IMPERII), were entrusted with the administration of provinces. The titles *proconsul* and *propraetor* later were applied even when a certain time elapsed between leaving the office in Rome and embarking on the administration of a province. The provinces ruled by the senate were either *consulares* (as Asia and Africa) when the rank requested for the governor was that of an ex-consul, or *praetoriae* when they were governed by an ex-praetor. The *imperium* of a proconsul (*imperium proconsulare*) comprised jurisdiction, civil and criminal, and the general administration of the province. —D. 1.16; C. 1.35.—See PRO, PROVINCIA, LEGATI PROCONSULIS, IURISDICTIO MANDATA.

Chapot, *DS* 4; Severini, *NDI* 10; De Ruggiero, *DE* 2, 855; Siber, *ZSS* 64 (1944) 233; W. F. Jashemski, *The origins and history of the proconsular and propractorian imperium to 27 B.C.,* Chicago, 1950.

Proconsularis. Connected with, or pertaining to, the office of a proconsul (*imperium, insignia*).—See PROCONSUL.

Proconsulatus. The office of a proconsul as a governor of a senatorial province.

Procreare (procreatio). See LIBERORUM QUAERENDORUM CAUSA.

Procul dubio. Beyond any doubt. The locution is frequently used by Justinian's compilers to stress the certainty of a legal norm whether of classical or later origin.

Guarneri-Citati, *Indice*² (1927) 32.

Proculiani. See SABINIANI.

Proculus. A jurist and law teacher of the middle of the first century after Christ. He is known more from citations by other jurists than by works of his own, of which only his *Epistulae* are certain. They were highly estimated by later jurists. Proculus was the head of the so-called Proculian group (*Proculiani*).—See SABINIANI.

Berger, *BIDR* 44 (1937) 120.

Procurare (procuratio). To manage another's affairs, to act for another as his representative in a civil trial. *Procuratio* refers also to the office of a *procurator* in administrative law.—See the following items.

Procurator. (In a civil trial.) A representative of the plaintiff or of the defendant. See COGNITOR. He was informally appointed by his mandator, without notification necessarily being given to the adversary. Even a person without a mandate of the party or in his absence could be admitted to represent him in a trial and to defend his interests. Such a voluntary representative (*negotiorum gestor*), however, had to offer guaranty that his principal (*dominus negotii*) would approve of what he as the latter's *procurator* has done in the course of the trial; see CAUTIO DE RATO. When such a *procurator* appeared before court for the defendant, he had to offer the *cautio iudicatum solvi;* see IUDICATUM. In the later development, the procurator in a process, acting under a mandate of his principal was assimilated to the former *cognitor;* the *procurator* became the only representative of a party to a trial and the term *cognitor* was completely eliminated from the classical sources accepted into Justinian's compilation.—D. 3.3; C. 2.12.—See CAU-

TIO AMPLIUS NON AGI, DOMINUS LITIS, PROCURATOR AD LITEM, INTERVENIRE, NEGOTIORUM GESTIO.

F. Eisele, *Cognitur und Procuratur,* 1882; Heumann-Seckel, *Handlexikon*[9] (1907) 463 (*s.v. procurator*); Orestano, *NDI* 10, 1092; Solazzi, *ANap* 58 (1937) 19, 62 (1948) 3; idem, *BIDR* 49–50 (1947) 338; Arangio-Ruiz, *Il mandato,* 1949, 12.

Procurator. (In private law.) "One who administers another's affairs under his authorization (*mandatu*)" (D. 3.3.1 pr.). Wealthy people used to have a general manager (*administrator*) of their property, a *procurator omnium bonorum,* whose activity for his principal was practically unlimited (alienations were excluded), unless specific restrictions were imposed on him concerning certain kinds of transactions. He was designated as a general agent *ad res administrandas datus* (= appointed for the administration of the property). Normally such an agent was a freedman (sometimes even a slave). Procuratorship was distinguished from MANDATUM (in a technical sense) which referred to an authorization to perform a certain act whereas the *procurator omnium bonorum* acted either under a general authorization or, at times, as a *negotiorum gestor* and for an absent principal. The *procurator unius rei* (= for one affair) is a later creation.—Inst. 4.10; D. 3.3; C. 2.12; 48.—See ADSTIPULARI, MANDATUM, NEGOTIORUM GESTIO.

Bouché-Leclercq, *DS* 4; G. Le Bras, *L'évolution du procurateur,* Thèse Paris, 1922; Donatuti, *AnPer* 36 (1922); idem, *AG* 89 (1923) 190; Solazzi, *RendLomb* 56 (1923) 142, 735; 57 (1924) 302; idem, *Acg* 5 (1924) 3; Bonfante, *Scritti* 3 (1926) 250; B. Frese, *Procuratur u. negotiorum gestio,* Mél Cornil 1 (1926) 327; idem, *St Bonfante* 4 (1931) 400; idem, *St Riccobono* 4 (1936) 399; De Robertis, *AnBari* 8 (1935); F. Serrao, *Il procurator,* 1947 (Bibl.); Düll, *ZSS* 67 (1950) 168; Dumont, *Un nouvel aspect du procurator,* Bourges, 1949; Rouxel, *Annales de la Faculté droit Bordeaux, Sér. juridique* 3 (1952) 94.

Procurator (procuratores). (In the imperial administration.) Augustus was the first to appoint *procuratores* as officials of the administration. He entrusted them with the management of the imperial property. With the increase of the imperial patrimony, the exploitation of the provinces for the imperial purse, and the introduction of new taxes and sources of income, *procuratores* were put at the head of all branches of the administration, even those which were not directly connected with the emperor's property. Thus, beside the *procuratores Augusti* (*procuratores* in service of the emperor) there were *procuratores* active in the interest of the state. Moreover, some offices which in the past were covered by officials with the title of *curatores* or *magistri,* were later granted the official title of *procurator.* Many *procuratores* were originally freedmen, but, from the time of Hadrian on, only persons of equestrian rank were appointed as *procurator.* Most of the procuratorial offices were concerned with the financial administration; there were, however, various *procuratores* with a different and limited competence. The *procurator* received a salary and four categories were distinguished according to the amount of their salary; see CENTENARIUS, DUCENARIUS. The highest salary was 300,000 sesterces (*trecenarius*), the lowest was 60,000 (*sexagenarius*). *Procuratores* were used in the imperial household, chancery, and in special capacities in Rome, in the administration of the fisc in imperial provinces, for the management of specific taxes and revenues, etc., and finally as governors of certain provinces, primarily on the boundaries of the Empire. The more important procuratorships are mentioned among the following items.—See LEX MANCIANA.

Cagnat, *DS* 4; Orestano, *NDI.* 10; Mattingly, *OCD;* Horovitz, *Rev. Belge de philologie et d'hist.* 17 (1938) 53, 775; idem, *Rev. de philol.* 13 (1939) 47, 218; Besnier, *Rev. Belge de philol. et d'hist.* 28 (1950) 440; H. G. Pflaum, *Essai sur les procurateurs equestres sous le Haut Empire,* 1950.—A list of imperial *procuratores* who occur in inscriptions in Dessau, *Insc. Lat. sel.* 3, 1 (1914) 408, 426.

Procurator a censibus. See A CENSIBUS.
Oliver, *Amer. Jour. Philol.* 67 (1946) 311.

Procurator a rationibus. A later title of the chief of the central financial administration, previously called A RATIONIBUS.
Rostowzew, *DE* 3, 133.

Procurator absentis. A person who assumed the defense of the interests of a party to a trial in his absence (with or without his authorization). He was obliged to give the pertinent guaranties; see PROCURATOR in a civil trial. Ant. *procurator praesentis.*

Procurator ad annonam Ostiis. A grain controller, stationed in Ostia.

Procurator ad litem. See PROCURATOR in a civil trial.
Solazzi, *ANap* 62 (1948).

Procurator apud acta. A representative in a litigation who was appointed by his principal through a declaration made in the office of a magistrate. An official record was made of the appointment.

Procurator aquarum. An official instituted by the Emperor Claudius for the administration of the water installations and water supply in Rome.
De Ruggiero, *DE* 1, 551.

Procurator Augusti. A procurator appointed by the emperor as his representative in administrative functions, primarily in financial matters, but sometimes also in military affairs.—D. 1.19.
Sherwin-White, *Papers of the Brit. School at Rome* 15 (1939) 11.

Procurator bibliothecarum. The supervisor of the administration of public libraries in Rome (from the time of Claudius). The director of a particular library = *procurator bibliothecae.*
Dziatzko, *RE* 3, 422; De Ruggiero, *DE* 1, 1003.

Procurator Caesaris. See PROCURATOR AUGUSTI, RATIONALIS.—D. 1.19.

Procurator castrensis. See CASTRENSIS.

Procurator falsus. See FALSUS PROCURATOR.

Procurator ferrariarum. An imperial *procurator* appointed for the administration of iron mines.

De Ruggiero, *DE* 3, 63.

Procurator gynaecii. An imperial official appointed for the management of an imperial garment factory. —C. 11.8.

A. W. Persson, *Staat und Manufaktur im röm. Reiche*, Lund, 1923, 70.

Procurator hereditatium. A *procurator* concerned with the fiscal revenues from inheritance taxes and estates which were taken by the fisc or were left to the emperor by private persons.—See VICESIMA HEREDITATIS, BONA VACANTIA, CADUCA.

De Ruggiero, *DE* 3, 734.

Procurator in rem suam. A fictitious representative. —See COGNITOR IN REM SUAM, CESSIO.

Procurator metallorum. An imperial delegate appointed for the administration of mines. His official titles is sometimes more specified, as, for instance, *procurator argentariarum* (silver mines), *procurator ferrariarum* (iron mines), *procurator marmorum* (marble quarries). His activity is referred to by the word *cura*, the mines being *sub cura procuratoris*. —C. 11.7.—See LEX METALLI VIPASCENSIS.

Cuq, *NRHD* 32 (1908) 668; U. Täckholm, *Bergbau in der röm. Kaiserzeit*, Uppsala, 1937, 101; 117; 148.

Procurator monetae. See TRESVIRI MONETALES.

Procurator omnium bonorum (rerum). A person who administers another's property as his representative (agent).—See PROCURATOR.

Arangio-Ruiz, *Il mandato*, 1949, 8, 49; Düll, *ZSS* 67 (1950) 170; A. Burdese, *Autorizzazione ad alienare*, 1950, 26.

Procurator operum publicorum. At the end of the second century after Christ an imperial superintendent of public buildings was instituted. He replaced the former *curator operum publicorum*.—See OPERA PUBLICA, CURATORES.

Procurator patrimonii (Caesaris). The administrator of the PATRIMONIUM CAESARIS. Originally his functions embraced also the RES PRIVATA of the emperor, but from the time of Septimius Severus the private property of the emperor was administered by a *procurator rei privatae*.

Procurator praediorum fiscalium. See PRAEDIA FISCALIA.

Procurator praesentis. A *procurator* in a civil trial acting in the presence of the party whom he represents. Ant. *procurator absentis*.

Procurator rationis privatae. See PROCURATOR REI PRIVATAE.

Procurator regionum urbis Romae. See REGIONES URBIS ROMAE, CAESARIS.

Procurator rei privatae. The administrator of the emperor's private property. This high ranking official had also the title *procurator rationis privatae* or, in the provinces, *magister rei privatae*. From the time of Constantine his official title was *rationalis*, and later, *comes rerum privatarum*.—See RES PRIVATA, RATIONALIS, PROCURATOR PATRIMONII.

Procurator summarum rationum. A deputy administrator of fiscal matters, subordinate to the *procurator a rationibus*.

Procurator unius rei. An agent of a private person instituted for the management of one specific affair. The institution is probably a later creation.—See PROCURATOR (in private law).

Frese, *Mél Cornil* 1 (1926) 327; E. Albertario, *Studi* 3 (1936) 495; V. Arangio-Ruiz, *Il mandato*, 1949, 17.

Procuratores. (In the imperial chancery.) The chiefs of the various divisions in the imperial chancery (*ab epistulis, a cognitionibus, a memoria, a studiis, a libellis*) received in the later Principate the title *procuratores*.

Prodere instrumenta. To deliver documents which one received from another in deposit (e.g., an agent, *procurator*, from his principal), secretly to the adversary of the depositor, against the interest of the latter. The wrongdoer was punished for *crimen falsi* (see FALSUM).

Prodere interregem. To designate an *interrex* when both consulships became vacant. The first *interrex* was appointed by the senate; after five days of *interregnum*, he himself designated his successor in office for the next five days, and so did his successors until new consuls were elected.—See INTERREGNUM, INTERREX.

Liebenam, *RE* 9, 1716; O'Brien-Moore, *RE* Suppl. 6, 676.

Prodigium. See MONSTRUM.

Prodigus. A spendthrift. According to Justinian's definition (D. 27.10.1 pr.) a *prodigus* is "one who does not regard time or limit in his expenditures, but lavishes (*profundere*) his property by dissipating and squandering it." After he was interdicted from the administration of his affairs, the *prodigus* was not able to make a last will. However, a testament made before remained valid.—D. 27.10; C. 5.70.—See CURATOR PRODIGI, INTERDICERE BONIS.

Beauchet, *DS* 4; A. Audibert, *NRHD* 14 (1890) 521; idem, *Ét. sur l'histoire du dr. r. I. La folie et la prodigalité*, 1892, 79; I. Pfaff, *Zur Gesch. der Prodigalitätserklärung*, 1911; F. De Visscher, *Ét de dr. rom.* 1931, 21; Collinet, *Mél Cornil* 1 (1926) 149; Solazzi, *St Bonfante* 1 (1930) 47; Kaser, *St Arangio-Ruiz* 2 (1952) 152.

Proditio. High treason, in particular the delivery of Roman territory or of a Roman soldier or citizen to the enemy. See PRODITOR.—*Proditio* is also the denunciation of a crime to the authorities.—See MAIESTAS, PERDUELLIO.

C. Brecht, *Perduellio*, 1938, 91; 191.

Proditor. A traitor, a denouncer. A military *proditor* was an *explorator* (= a soldier assigned to the reconnoitering service) who betrayed military secrets to the enemy. He was punished with death. Syn. *renuntiator*.

Proditus. (From *prodere.*) Originating from, introduced by (a statute or a praetor in his jurisdictional capacity, as, e.g., an action or exception).

Profanum. A profane thing. Ant. *sacrum*; see RES SACRAE. *Profanus locus* is the ant. of *religiosus locus.* See RES RELIGIOSAE. A place in which a dead person was buried temporarily, merely to be transferred later into a grave remained *locus profanus.*

Profecticius. See DOS PROFECTICIA, PECULIUM ADVENTICIUM.

Proferre. To produce a document (a testament) in court, to present witnesses (*testimonia, testes*); to produce in public.

Proferre diem. To prolong, to defer (the term of a payment).

Proferre sententiam. To pronounce a judgment in a trial. Hence *sententia prolata* = a judgment pronounced by a judge.

Professio. (From *profiteri.*) A declaration (return) made before an official authority (*apud magistratum, apud acta* = for the records). The *professiones* concerned different matters, primarily personal connotations of a person (such as age, liberty, family status), the birth of children, and the like. The *professiones* could be made personally by the individuals involved, by a representative of an absent person or by a guardian for persons under guardianship.—See the following items.
     Cuq, *DS* 4; Elmore, *JRS* 5 (1915) 125; Reid, *ibid.* 207.

Professio. Candidates for a magistracy had to declare their willingness to compete for a certain magistracy before the magistrate who convened the popular assembly and later presided over the particular election (consul, praetor, plebeian tribune). A statute of the late Republic required a personal appearance on the part of the candidate before the competent magistrate, who in case of acceptance, put the candidate's name on the list to be announced in public before the election. The magistrate had the power to refuse a candidate's admission, if the latter seemed to him ineligible for a specific reason.—See CANDIDATUS, MAGISTRATUS.
     Brassloff, *RE* 4, 1697.

Professio censualis. A declaration concerning his family and property made by a citizen before the censors during the CENSUS. These *professiones* served military and taxation purposes. Under the Empire a perfected census system was set up by the imperial bureaucratic machinery. Fraudulent returns were severely punished.
     Schwahn, *RE* 7A, 55; Cuq, *DS* 4, 674.

Professio frumentaria. A return made by persons who requested the admission to the list of those who received gratuitous distribution of corn.—See FRUMENTATIO.
     Mitteis, *ZSS* 33 (1912) 171; Elmore, *JRS* 5 (1915) 125; Gittardy, *Clas Quarterly* 11 (1915) 27; v. Premerstein, *ZSS* 43 (1922) 59.

Professio liberorum (natorum). A declaration made before competent authority by the father (mother or grandfather) concerning a new-born child. These returns served as the basis for entries into an official register of births of legitimate children of Roman citizens. The registration was ordered by Augustus.
     Cuq, *DS* 4, 675; *idem, Mél Fournier* 1929, 119; F. Lanfranchi, *Ricerche sul valore giuridico delle dichiarazioni di nascita,* 1942; Weiss, *BIDR* 51/52 (1948) 317; Schulz, *JRS* 32–33 (1942, 1943 = *BIDR* 55–56, *Post-Bellum,* 1951, 70); Montevecchi, *Aeg* 28 (1948) 129.

Professor. Syn. *magister, antecessor. Professores iuris civilis* = law teachers. Teaching law (*civilis sapientia*) "should not be estimated nor dishonored by a price in money," since "the wisdom of law is a very sacred thing (*civilis sapientia est res sanctissima,*" D. 50.13.1.5).—C. 10.53; 12.15.—See MAGISTER, ANTECESSOR, HONORARIUM.

Proficere. To be useful. *Proficit* is said when a legal transaction or act serves the purpose for which it was done. Ant. *non proficere* = to be of no legal effect (use).

Proficisci (a, ab, ex). To originate, to arise from (e.g., the praetorian edict, praetorian jurisdiction, a testament).

Profiteri. See PROFESSIO.

Profundere bona. To dissipate one's property.—See PRODIGUS.

Progenies. Descendants. The term occurs only in imperial constitutions.

Programma. A proclamation, a manifesto of the emperor or of a provincial governor. When addressed to a private person, the term denotes an edictal (public) summons of an absent person.—C. 7.57.
     F. v. Schwind, *Zur Frage der Publikation,* 1940, 114.

Prohibere. To prohibit, to forbid. The term is used of prohibitions issued in certain situations by a private individual (e.g., by a co-owner or a neighbor) and of prohibitive orders of a magistrate or of a statute. See IUS PROHIBENDI, COMMUNIO. ACTIO PROHIBITORIA, INTERDICTUM, OPERIS NOVI NUNTIATIO, IUS AEDIFICANDI. With reference to criminal offenses *prohibere* = to impede, to prevent. Generally no one is bound to intervene in order to prevent a crime except when the crime is directed against the state or in certain specified cases, such as counterfeit of coins, abduction, or murder of a near relative. In such cases one had to prevent the wrongdoer from committing the crime if he could do it (*cum prohibere potuit*); otherwise he risked being treated as the criminal's accessory.—See FURTUM PROHIBITUM.
     Honig, *Fschr Heilfron* 1930, 63.

Prohibitorius. See ACTIO PROHIBITORIA, INTERDICTA PROHIBITORIA.

Proiectio (proiectum). A part of a building projecting over a neighbor's property. The construction of a *proiectio* could be prohibited by the neighbor.—See PROTECTUM. OPERIS NOVI NUNTIATIO.

Proinde. See PERINDE.

Proles. Syn. with PROGENIES.

Proletarii. Men without property. Originally the term was applied to persons not registered in the classes of the centuriate organization (see CENTURIA) because they had not even the minimum property required for the lowest class. Their sole possession was their children, *proles*; hence the name. The *proletarii* were the poorest stratum of the population. Ant. *classici* = those registered in the first class according to their property, see CLASSICUS.—See ADSIDUI, CAPITE CENSI.

Lécrivain, *DS* 4; Gabba, *Ath* 27 (1949) 175; *idem, Riv. di filologia classica* 1949, 173.

Prolytae. Fifth-year students in the Eastern law schools.—See LYTAE.

Promercium. See COMMERCIUM.

Promiscua condicio. See CONDICIO MIXTA.

Promissio, promissum. (From *promittere*.) A promise which created an obligation on the part of the promissor. It is a general term applied to both contractual and unilaterally assumed obligations, to written and oral, formal and formless promises. But the specific application of the term is to obligations arising from a STIPULATIO, either by the principal debtor or by a surety.—See REUS PROMITTENDI, ADPROMISSIO, CAUTIO. In Justinian's legislative work the terms *promittere* and *promissio* were substituted for obligations which in earlier law had to be contracted through *stipulatio*.

Promissio dotis. The constitution of a dowry by a formless promise. It replaced both the formal DICTIO DOTIS and the *stipulatio dotis* in later times and was substituted therefor in classical texts by Justinian's compilers.—C. 5.11.—See POLLICITATIO DOTIS.

Promissio operarum. See IURATA PROMISSIO LIBERTI.

Promissio post mortem. See OBLIGATIO POST MORTEM.

Promittere. See PROMISSIO.

Promovere (promotio). To confer a higher rank or an honorific title on an imperial official. The term occurs only in imperial constitutions.

Promulgare (promulgatio). To publish, to promulgate a law. In the Republic, the text of a bill submitted to a popular assembly was promulgated in the form of an edict by which the magistrate who proposed the law publicly announced its text. Alterations were not permitted. Between the *promulgatio* and the gathering of the assembly convoked for the purpose a lapse of time called *trinundinum* (presumably twenty-four days) was obligatory.—See PP.

G. Rotondi, *Leges publicae populi Romani*, 1912, 123; v. Schwind, *Zur Frage der Publikation*, 1940.

Pronepos (proneptis). A great-grandson (a great-granddaughter).—See NEPOS.

Pronuntiare (pronuntiatio). General terms for legally important pronouncements (declarations) made by officials, and on rare occasions by private persons. With reference to judicial trials (primarily civil), the terms are used of declarations by both the magistrate and the judge in the bipartite procedure as well as by the jurisdictional magistrate in the *cognitio extra ordinem*. *Pronuntiare secundum actorem (reum)* = to pass a judgment in favor of the claimant (the defendant); *pronuntiare adversus* (or *contra*) *actorem (reum)* = to pass a judgment against the plaintiff (the defendant). *Pronuntiatio* is often used of a judicial decision concerning the status of a free man or slave, the validity of a testament or marriage, etc. In so-called ACTIONES ARBITRARIAE and in the procedure before the emperor (in either the first or the appellate instance) *pronuntiatio* is used in the sense of an interlocutory decision.—See SENTENTIA, ARBITER EX COMPROMISSO, SENTENTIAM DICERE (PRONUNTIARE).

G. Beseler, *Beiträge zur Kritik* 2 (1911) 139, 3 (1913) 3; E. Betti, *L'antitesi di iudicare (p.) e damnare nello svolgimento del processo rom.*, 1915; M. Wlassak, *Judikationsbefehl, SbWien* 197, 4 (1921) 77; Siber, *ZSS* 65 (1947) 3.

Pronuntiatio sententiarum. In the senate the announcement by the presiding magistrate of opinions expressed by individual senators on a topic on which a vote was to be taken.

O'Brien-Moore, *RE* Suppl. 6, 715.

Prope (propius) est. It is proper, adequate, easy to understand. The locution is frequent in the juristic language.

Propinqui (propinquitas). Near relatives, neighbors.—See CONCILIUM PROPINQUORUM.

Proponere. To submit a case (*proposita species, quaestio*) to a jurist for an opinion. The respondent jurist gave his view on the basis of the facts as alleged by the questioning party (*propositum, in proposito*). Some jurists, therefore, used to give their opinion with the reservation, "according to what has been alleged," or with a clause excluding or restricting a certain decision (*nihil proponi cur* . . . = nothing has been alleged as to why or why not . . .).

Proponere (propositio). (With regard to magisterial edicts and imperial enactments.) To expose to public view. From the time of Hadrian, imperial rescripts could be made public by *propositio*.—See PROSCRIBERE LEGEM, PP.

F. v. Schwind, *Zur Frage der Publikation*, 1940, 167.

Proponere actionem (interdictum). To announce in the praetorian Edict an action and its formula or an interdict to be granted in specific circumstances by the praetor acting in his jurisdictional capacity.

Propositio (propositum). A case presented for a juristic opinion.—See PROPONERE.

Propositum. A poster.—See HORREARIUS, PROPONERE.

Propositum. Intention. The term is used with reference to good or (more frequently) to evil intention (e.g., to commit a crime, to steal).—See IMPETUS.

Propositus. E.g., *proposita causa*, species.—See PROPONERE.

Propraetor (pro praetore). An ex-praetor as a governor of a senatorial province (*provincia praetoria*); a praetor whose term was prolonged for exceptional reasons on advice of the senate.—See PRO, PROROGATIO IMPERII, LEGATI PROCONSULIS, LEGATI PRO PRAETORE, PROCONSUL.

Lécrivain, *DS* 4; W. F. Jashemski, *Origins and history of the proconsular and propraetorian imperium*, Chicago, 1950.

Proprietarius. See DOMINUS PROPRIETATIS.

Proprietas. Ownership. Syn. DOMINIUM.—See NUDA PROPRIETAS, DOMINUS PROPRIETATIS.

Proprio (suo) nomine. (E.g., *agere.*) To act, to sue on one's own behalf. Ant. ALIENO NOMINE.

Proprius. Belonging to a certain person as his own. Ant. *alienus, communis.* With regard to *iurisdictio propria*, the ant. is *iurisdictio mandata, delegata.*

Propter. See DONATIO PROPTER NUPTIAS.

Proquiritare legem. The announcement of the vote on a proposed statute passed by a popular assembly.
Weiss, *Glotta* 12 (1923) 83.

Prorogare (prorogatio). To postpone, to defer, to prorogue (e.g., the date a payment is due, a contractual relation); sometimes *prorogare* = to pay in advance.

Prorogatio imperii. The prolongation of the magisterial *imperium* of a high magistrate (consul, praetor) as a *pro consule* or *pro praetore* beyond the end of his year of office. The *prorogatio* applied either to his last post or to taking a governorship in a province.
—See PRO, PROCONSUL, PROPRAETOR.

Proscribere (proscriptio). To announce publicly (*palam*) by a poster, easily accessible to the public, containing information which concerned a larger number of people, for instance, the appointment of an *institor* in a business.

Proscribere bona (proscriptio bonorum). To announce publicly that the property of a person (e.g., of a bankrupt debtor) will be sold by auction. During the period of *proscriptio* (normally thirty days in the case of bankruptcy, fifteen days when an inheritance was involved), creditors had the opportunity to join in the proceedings which led to the sale of the bankrupt estate. See MISSIO IN POSSESSIONEM REI SERVANDAE CAUSA.—*Proscribere bona* is also used of the confiscation of a private person's property by the state. See PUBLICATIO BONORUM. For *proscribere bona* in the praetorian Edict, see MISSIONES IN POSSESSIONEM.—C. 9.49.

S. Solazzi, *Concorso dei creditori* 1 (1937) 171; S. v. Bolla, *Aus röm. und bürgerl. Recht*, 1950, 25.

Proscribere legem. To make a statute public. The text was written on boards publicly displayed in the forum so that "it could be plainly read from level ground" (*de plano*, D. 14.3.11.3).—See PROPONERE.
F. v. Schwind, *Zur Frage der Publikation*, 1940, 26.

Proscriptio. (In public law.) Inscribing the name of a person upon a list of outlaws. Simultaneously, a reward was offered for his head. The ill-famed proscriptions by the dictator Sulla were ordered by the *Lex Cornelia de proscriptione* (82 B.C.). In later imperial constitutions *proscripti* (*proscriptio*) is used of persons sent into exile.—C. 9.49.
Humbert, *DS* 4.

Proscriptio albi. Listing a person in the publicly exposed ALBUM DECURIONUM. Entry in the list without a preceding election is without any legal effect.

Proscriptio bonorum. See PROSCRIBERE BONA.

Proscriptio debitorum. Making public the names of insolvent debtors through an inscription on a wall or on a column in a public place. The publication was by the creditors.
Weiss, *RIDA* 3 (1950) 501.

Proscriptio locationis. An advertisement, through an inscription on a building, of an apartment to rent under conditions specified in the notice.
Arangio-Ruiz, *FIR* 3 (1943) 453; Maiuri, *La parola del passato* 3 (1948) 153.

Prosecutor annonae. An agent appointed for the transportation of food supplies for the army. His duty was a liturgy (*munus*) and entailed responsibility for the safety of the goods convoyed. The term *prosecutor* was also used of escorts conveying (*prosecutio*) arrested persons or gold belonging to the state (*prosecutor auri publici*), C. 10.74.

Prosecutoria. (*Sc. epistula.*) An imperial letter of commendation.

Prospectus. See SERVITUS NE PROSPECTUI OFFICIATUR.

Prospicere. To foresee, to provide beforehand, to take precautions. The term refers both to precautionary measures introduced by the praetor in his edict in order to prevent illegal or harmful acts, and to those taken by private persons through such legal remedies as *cautio* or *satisdatio* in order to be saved from eventual losses that might result from a transaction concluded.

Prostituere. To prostitute. If a female slave (*ancilla*) was sold under the condition that she should not be delivered to prostitution (*ne prostituatur*) by her new master, a clause was usually added that in the case of a breach she would be free. In such an event she became a freedwoman of the vendor. Under the later imperial legislation, a slave became free if her master forced her into prostitution.—C. 4.56.
W. Buckland, *The R. law of slavery*, 1908, 70; 603.

Protectores. In the later Empire an infantry unit for the protection of the emperor, his family and the imperial palace. They accompanied the emperor in public ceremonies. The term *protectores domestici* refers to cavalrymen in the entourage of the emperor.—C. 12.17.—See DOMESTICI.
Besnier, *DS* 4; Braschi, *DE* 2, 1938; Babut, *Recherches sur la garde impériale*, *Rev. Historique* 114, 116 (1913, 1914); B. Grosse, *Röm. Militärgeschichte*, 1920, 13; E. Stein, *Gesch. des spätrömischen Reichs* 1 (1928) 187; Gigli, *RendLinc* 1949, 383.

Protectum. A roof or balcony projecting onto a neighbor's property. The latter could prohibit such a construction unless the builder had a servitude, *servitus protegendi.*—D. 39.2.—See PROICERE.

Protestari. To make an announcement in public (in court or by a placard), for instance, to the effect that a person is not one's representative, agent, or business manager.

Protutela. See PRO TUTORE, ACTIO PROTUTELAE.

Prout quidque contractum est, ita et solvi debet. "In the same way in which an obligation was contracted, it should be discharged" (D. 46.3.80).—See SOLUTIO.

Providere (providentia). To foresee, to procure beforehand, to provide for. The terms refer to statutes, senatusconsults, imperial enactments, and orders of high officials (e.g., provincial governors). The verb *providere* was used by the imperial chancery with great frequency to stress the duty of an official to take specific measures in a given situation.

> Charlesworth, *Harvard Theol. Rev.* 29 (1936) 107; Albertario, *Ath* 6 (1928) 165, 325 (= *St di diritto rom.* 6 [1953] 165).

Provincia. The original meaning of the term was that of the sphere of action of a magistrate with *imperium,* distinguished from the sphere of action of his colleague (see COLLEGA). *Provincia* was also used of a district under the ruling of a military commander. Later, territories outside Italy conquered and annexed by Rome were assigned as a *provincia* to a Roman magistrate (a consul or a praetor) or a high pro-magistrate vested with *imperium* and representing there the authority of the Roman state. The first instances in which the term *provincia* was applied to a conquered and incorporated territory were Sicily and Sardinia (241 and 238 B.C.). The organization of a new province was regulated by a *lex provinciae,* but there were no general rules for the administration of provinces. Within 'the territory organized as a province there were territorial units, cities and municipalities, which were granted a special status of CIVITATES FOEDERATAE or CIVITATES LIBERAE ET IMMUNES. The *Lex Cornelia de provinciis ordinandis* (on the organization of provinces, 81 B.C.) set some rules for the administration of provinces by ex-praetors who, after their year of service in Rome, assumed the governorship of a province as pro-magistrates with a prorogated *imperium* (see PROROGATIO IMPERII). Ex-consuls were admitted to governorship under the same circumstances. Later, however, the *Lex Pompeia* (52 B.C.) fixed a delay of five years between the tenure of a high magistracy in Rome and that of a governorship in a province. From the time of Augustus the governors received a fixed salary. The legal status of the population of a conquered province was that of *peregrini* or of *peregrini dediticii* when the conquest resulted from a victorious war and a surrender of the enemy (see DEDITICII, DEDITIO). See TRIBUTUM. Roman citizenship was granted either to individual provincials or to larger groups, until the CONSTITUTIO ANTONINIANA bestowed citizenship on all inhabitants of the Empire. The investment of the *princeps* with *imperium proconsulare maius* (qualified also as indefinite, *perpetuum*) gave the emperor in theory the highest power over all the provinces. It was granted for the first time to Augustus by the senate in 23 B.C., but very early—already under Augustus—a distinction was made between imperial (*provinciae principis, Caesaris*) and senatorial provinces (*provinciae senatus*). The latter were the pacified, long annexed provinces, while the imperial provinces were those which had been recently acquired and in which revolts still occurred or were to be expected. The shift of a province from one category to the other could be ordered by the emperor. Under Diocletian the provincial administration acquired a different aspect. The division of the Empire into *praefecturae* and *dioeceses* (see DIOECESIS) was connected with the creation of new provinces, smaller in territory than under the Principate. The military command was separated from the civil administration; the governors retained their jurisdictional power, which was subject to an appeal to the VICARII and eventually to the emperor. In imperial legislation, provincial matters were among the topics to which the emperors devoted their greatest attention. The terms *provincia* and *provincialis* are among the most frequent in Justinian's Code. For details concerning the administration, officials, jurisdiction, etc., in the provinces, see the pertinent items, e.g., ARCA PROVINCIALIS, CONVENTUS, CONVENTUS CIVIUM ROMANORUM, CONCILIA PROVINCIARUM, LEGES DATAE, LEGATI DECEM, LEGATI AD CENSUS ACCIPIENDOS, LEGATI IURIDICI, LEGATI LEGIONUM, LEX RUPILIA, LEX POMPEIA, ORNATIO PROVINCIARUM, REPETUNDAE, FUNDUS PROVINCIALIS, PEREGRINI, and the following items.

> Chapot, *DS* 4; Severini, *NDI* 10; De Ruggiero, *DE* 2, 847; Stevenson, *OCD*; C. Halgan, *Essai sur l'administration des provinces senatoriales,* 1898; T. Mommsen, *Die Provinzen von Caesar bis Diokletian,* 6th ed. 1909 (Engl. translation, 1909); W. T. Arnold, *The R. system of provincial administration,* 3rd ed. 1914; L. Falletti, *Évolution de la jurisdiction civile du magistrat provincial sous le Haut Empire,* 1926; Anderson, *The genesis of Diocletian's prov. admin., JRS* 22 (1932); Gitti, *L'ordinamento provinciale dell'Oriente sotto Giustiniano, Bull. Comm. Archeol. Comunale di Roma, Bull. del Museo* 3 (1932) 47; Pisani, *RendLomb* 74 (1940–41) 148; Duyvendak, *Symb. v. Oven,* 1946, 333; A. Solari, *l'impero rom.,* 4. *Impero provinciale* (1947) 193; G. H. Stevenson, *Rom. provincial administration, till the age of the Antonines,* 2nd ed. 1949; D. Magie, *Rom. rule in Asia Minor to the end of the third cent.* 1–2 (1950).

Provinciae Caesaris (principis). Provinces ruled by the emperor, who administered them through governors appointed by himself (*legati Augusti pro praetore*). They were assisted by special imperial

PROCURATORES (primarily for the financial administration) who were subordinate not to the governor but directly to the emperor. On occasion, the emperor sent special delegates in a specific mission who, too, were directly responsible to him. The soil of imperial provinces (*praedia tributoria*) was considered property of the emperor and all imposts and revenues from these provinces went to the imperial fisc. See TRIBUTUM. Some provinces annexed to the empire were governed by imperial *procuratores* of equestrian rank. The emperor exercised his power over those territories not by virtue of the *imperium proconsulare* vested in him by the people, but as the successor of their former sovereigns (kings or princes).—See PROVINCIA.

Provinciae consulares. Provinces assigned to ex-consuls by the Senate under the Republic.—See SENATUSCONSULTUM DE PROVINCIIS CONSULARIBUS.

Provinciae populi Romani. See PROVINCIAE SENATUS.

Provinciae praetoriae. Provinces governed by ex-praetors as governors.

Provinciae principis. See PROVINCIAE CAESARIS.

Provinciae procuratoriae. Provinces of the emperor governed by *procuratores.*—See PROVINCIAE CAESARIS.

W. E. Gwatkin, *Cappadoeia as a R. procuratorian province, Univ. of Missouri Studies* V, 4 (1930); P. Horowitz, *Le principe de création des provinces procuratoriennes, Rev. Belge de philol. et d'hist.,* 1939.

Provinciae senatus. Provinces under the control of the senate. In the Republic the senate directed the administration of the provinces through governors selected from among former consuls and praetors (hence the distinction between *provinciae consulares* and *praetoriae*). From the time of Augustus there were two categories of provinces, imperial (see PROVINCIAE CAESARIS) and senatorial. Henceforth the senate had full control only over the senatorial provinces. The governors of these provinces were proconsuls appointed by the senate and subject to its orders and instructions. From the second century on it became customary for imperial functionaries (CORRECTORES, CURATORES CIVITATIS) to supervise the financial administration, which in these provinces was confided to special officials, *quaestores,* subordinate to the governor. The soil was considered the property of the Roman people (see PRAEDIA STIPENDIARIA). An impost (see STIPENDIUM) was levied on communities; they in turn assessed it on the inhabitants.

O'Brien-Moore, *RE* Suppl. 6, 793; McFayden, *The princeps and the senatorial provinces, ClPhil* 16 (1921); J. M. Cobban, *Senate and provinces (78–49 B.C.),* Cambridge, 1935.

Provincialis. (Adj.) Refers to different matters (*res provincialis*), both to persons somehow connected with a province and its administration and to provincial soil (*fundus provincialis, praedium provinciale*).—See EDICTUM PROVINCIALE.

Provincialis. (Noun.) An inhabitant of a province "who has his domicile there, not one who is born in a province" (D. 50.16.190).—See DOMICILIUM.

Provisio. In the sense of a legal enactment (provision), the term prevails in the language of the imperial chancery of the later Empire.

Provocare. To challenge, to provoke (a jurisdictional measure in a trial). The term is primarily used of appeals from judgments of a lower instance to a higher one; see PROVOCATIO.

Provocare ad populum. See PROVOCATIO.

Provocare sacramento. To challenge the adversary by a *sacramentum*; see LEGIS ACTIO SACRAMENTO.

Provocare sponsione. To challenge one's adversary in a trial by a *sponsio* in order to make him promise to pay a certain sum in case of defeat, e.g., "Do you promise to pay me . . . if the slave is mine under Quiritary law?"—See AGERE PER SPONSIONEM.

Provocatio (provocare). An appeal by a citizen condemned by a magistrate in a criminal trial, to the popular assemblies (*provocatio ad populum, a magistratu, adversus magistratum*) under the Republic. An appeal from capital punishment went to the *comitia centuriata,* from a pecuniary fine (MULTA) to the *comitia tributa.* Several Republican statutes regulated the procedure of *provocatio: Lex Valeria de provocatione, Lex Valeria Horatia, Lex Duilia, Lex Porcia, Lex Sempronia.* There was no *provocatio* from a decision of a dictator, from a judgment of the DECEMVIRI, or from that of the criminal courts, *quaestiones.* Under the Empire an appeal was addressed to the emperor (*provocatio ad imperatorem, ad Caesarem*). In civil matters *provocatio* is syn. with *appellatio.*—C. 7.64; 70.—See ANQUISITIO.

Lécrivain, *DS* 4; Strachan-Davidson, *Problems of R. criminal law* 1 (1912) 127; Düll, *ZSS* 56 (1936) 1; G. Pugliese, *Appunti sui limiti dell'imperium,* 1939, 62; Brecht, *ZSS* 59 (1939) 261; Siber, *ZSS* 62 (1942) 376; Heuss, *ZSS* 64 (1944) 104.

Provocator. He who appeals through PROVOCATIO.

Proxeneta. A broker, an agent. He could sue his client for compensation for his services in a *cognitio extra ordinem. Proxeneticum* = a broker's (factor's) commission.—D. 50.14; C. 5.1.

Siber, *IhJb* 88 (1939–40) 177.

Proximi. (In the administration.) Lower officials, assistants to the head of an office and his substitutes during his absence. Generally they succeeded their superiors when the office became vacant. The various divisions of the imperial chancery each had their *proximi (proximi ab epistulis, a libellis, a memoria, a studiis, proximi scrinii*).—C. 12.19.

Proximus agnatus. See AGNATUS PROXIMUS.

Proximus infantiae (infanti), pubertati. See INFANS, IMPUBES.

Prudentes (prudentiores). In the sense of *iuris prudentes,* see IURISCONSULTUS, IURISPERITUS.

Prudentia. Used in imperial constitutions for *iuris-prudĕntia*.

Pubertas. See IMPUBES, MINORES, HABITUS CORPORIS.

Pubertas plena. See MINORES.

Pubertati proximus. See INFANS.

Pubes. See IMPUBES.

A. B. Schwarz, *ZSS* 69 (1952) 345.

Pubescere. To become capable of procreation (*pubes*, see IMPUBES). Ant. *qui pubescere non potest* = impotent; see SPADO.

Publicani. Farmers of public revenues (taxes, salt and metal mines, chalk pits, etc.). They were organized in financial companies (*societates publicanorum*) which at the public auctions arranged by the state for the lease of the pertinent rights acted collectively through their representative (*manceps*). Senators were prohibited from participating in collection of taxes or other imposts. The *publicani* were businessmen of equestrian rank. During the Punic wars they acquired great fortunes and, subsequently, also a great influence in political life. The affairs of the association of *publicani* were managed by a *magister societatis publicanorum*, assisted by a staff of subordinates throughout the territory (province) in which the society had leased the particular revenues involved. The provincials suffered much under that system of tax-collecting. The *societas* was not dissolved by the death of a member; his heir could be accepted in his place. Tax-farming was also practiced in municipalities.—D. 39.4.—See CONDUCTORES VECTIGALIUM, REDEMPTOR VECTIGALIUM, SOCII, EDICTUM DE PUBLICANIS.

Cagnat, *DS* 4; De Villa, *NDI* 10; Stevenson, *OCD*; F. Kniep, *Societates publicanorum*, 1896; M. Rostowzew, *Gesch. der Staatspacht in der röm. Kaiserzeit, Philologus*, Suppl. 9, 1903; O. Hirschfeld, *Die kais. Verwaltungsbeamten*, 2nd ed., 1905, 81; L. Mitteis, *Röm. Privatrecht*, 1908, 403; F. Messina-Vitrano, *Sulla responsabilità dei p., Circolo guiridico* (Palermo) 1909; Arangio-Ruiz, *St Perozzi* 1925, 231; Lotz, *Studien über Steuerverpachtung, SbMünch* 1935; Reinmuth, *ClPhilol* 31 (1936) 146; B. Eliachevitch, *La personnalité juridique en droit privé rom.*, 1942, 305; E. Schlechter, *Le contrat de société*, 1947, 320; Arias Bonet, *AHDE* 19 (1948–49) 218.

Publicatio bonorum (publicare bona). Confiscation of the property of a person convicted of a crime against the state. The confiscated wealth became the property of the state (*res publica*). See CONFISCATIO, PROSCRIBERE BONA. *Publicatio* is also called the act of expropriation for reasons of public utility (see EMPTIO AB INVITO).—See SECTIO BONORUM.

Humbert and Lécrivain, *DS* 4; U. Brasiello, *Repressione penale*, 1937, 112.

Publicatio legis. The making public of a statute. Under the Republic the publication of a statute passed by the competent *comitia* was not obligatory. The magistrate who proposed a bill could make it public, if he wished, by posting the text in the *forum* or on the walls of a temple (PROSCRIBERE). Some statutes contained clauses concerning their publication. Trea-

ties concluded with other states were engraved on two bronze tablets, one of which was posted on the Capitol in Rome. For the publication of edicts of magistrates (praetors), see ALBUM. *Senatusconsulta* acquired legal force when deposited in the *aerarium*; public exposition was not compulsory. As for imperial legislation, enactments of general import, binding throughout the whole empire or in a larger part of it (all *edicta* and *decreta* of special significance), were sent to the provincial governors who took care of making them public in the cities.—See PP., PROPONERE, PROMULGARE.

Landucci, *Atti Accad. Padova*, 2 (1896); G. Rotondi, *Leges publicae populi Rom.*, 1912, 167; F. v. Schwind, *Zur Frage der Publikation im röm. R.*, 1940.

Publice. In public, in the public interest, in a public place (in court). Syn. *in publico*.—See INTEREST ALICUIUS, UTILIS PUBLICE.

Publice venire. To be sold at a public auction. Ant. *privatim venire*.

Publiciana in rem actio. See ACTIO IN REM PUBLICIANA.

Publicum (publica). Public property (of the Roman people), public treasury (see AERARIUM). *In publico = publice*.

Publicus. Connected with, pertinent to, available to, or in the interest of the Roman people. "Public property (*bona publica*) is what belongs to the Roman people" (D. 50.16.15). The adjective *publicus* is applied to various concepts in contrast to *privatus*, such as *ius, iudicia, res, leges, causa, utilitas, crimina, officium*, etc.—See also RES PUBLICA, DELICTUM, LOCUS PUBLICUS, INTERDICTA DE LOCIS PUBLICIS, AGER PUBLICUS, ITER, VIA, MUNERA, MONUMENTA, VIS, ABOLITIO, SERVI PUBLICI, PASCUUM, NEGOTIA PRIVATA, OPERA PUBLICA, USUS, DISCIPLINA, SACRA, SUMPTU PUBLICO.

Kaser, *SDHI* 17 (1951) 274.

Pudicitia. Chastity, a crime against chastity. The LEX IULIA DE ADULTERIIS is also called *de pudicitia*. *Pudicitia adtemptata* = an offense against the reputation of an honest woman committed in public (on a street) by pursuing her constantly or making indecent proposals. It was considered an INIURIA and persecuted accordingly.

Puella. See PUER.

Puer. Used in various senses: (*a*) a slave. Some names of slaves were combined with *puer*, as, e.g., *Marcipor = Marci puer*; (*b*) a boy, ant. *puella* (= a girl); (*c*) syn. for *puerilis aetas, pueritia* = youth. The term *puer* is not technical and does not indicate a specific age.

Pueritia. See PUER. In D. 3.1.1.3 *pueritia* is used of the age of persons under seventeen. They were excluded from acting in court.

Pugnus. A fist. *Pugno percutere* = striking a person with the fist. Such an action was considered a corporal injury (*iniuria*); it was not, however, an outrage to the master of a slave when the latter was struck by a third person, although generally an injury to a slave was treated as an outrage to the master himself.—See INIURIA.

Pulsare. To strike a person. That is the typical case of *iniuria,* as in the LEX CORNELIA DE INIURIIS.—See INIURIA.

Pulsari actione (lite). To be persecuted by an action in court, both in civil and criminal cases; the term is used only in the language of the imperial chancery.

Punire. To punish. *Punire* is mentioned as one of the tasks and forces of the laws (statutes, see LEX). The term refers to all kinds of punishment (capital, corporal, and pecuniary) imposed on wrongdoers for crimes and delictual offenses, public and private.— See CAPITE PUNIRI.

Punitio. Syn. POENA.

Pupillaris. Concerning, or belonging to, a ward (*pupillus*) under guardianship (TUTELA).—See RES PU-PILLARES, TESTAMENTUM PUPILLARE, SUBSTITUTIO PUPILLARIS, USURAE PUPILLARES.

Pupillus (pupilla). "One below the age of puberty (*impubes*) who ceased to be under the power of his father by the latter's death or through emancipation" (D. 50.16.239 pr.). An *impubes* who became *sui iuris* was under guardianship (*tutela impuberum*). In a broader sense *pupillus* is used of all who are below the age of puberty, hence *aetas pupillaris* = the age below puberty. A *pupillus* could not alienate property or assume an obligation without the consent of his guardian (*auctoritas tutoris*). The opinions of the jurists were divergent as to whether a *pupillus* could acquire possession; some required the guardian's cooperation. Justinian declared the acquisition valid when the *pupillus* was beyond the age of infancy. In Justinian's Law, the property of a *pupillus* was not accessible to usucaption.—D. 26.8; 27.2; C. 5.49; 50.—See TUTELA IMPUBERUM, IMPUBES, FILIUS FAMILIAS, OBLIGATIO NATURALIS, INFANTIA.

Solazzi, *BIDR* 22–25 (1910–1912); Suman, *L'obbligazione naturale del pupillo, Fil* 1914; De Villa, *StSas* 18 (1940) 13.

Purgatio morae. See MORA.

Purpura. Purple. In the later Empire the private fabrication of purple materials and garments was prohibited, the production being reserved as a monopoly of the state. Likewise, wearing purple cloths (*holovera vestimenta*) and even possession were prohibited.—See TOGA PURPUREA, ADORATIO PURPURAE.

Purus. Free from charges, unconditional (ant. *condicionalis, sub condicione,* see CONDICIO), not limited by a fixed date (*sine die,* ant. *in diem, ex die,* see DIES). A similar distinction exists between the adverbs *pure* and *condicionaliter.*—See STIPULATIO PURE FACTA.

Puta. See UTPUTA.

Putare. To believe, to think. The term is also used of persons who erroneously assume something to exist which is not true, e.g., that one is an heir or

a guardian (*se heredem, tutorem esse,* see USUCAPIO PRO HEREDE, FALSUS TUTOR), and act accordingly. Opinions of jurists are introduced in juristic writings with *putare,* e.g., *ego puto, X putat.*

Puteolanus. An unknown Roman jurist, cited once by Ulpian, author of a work *Libri adsessioriorum.*—See ADSESSORIUM.

Q

Qua de re agitur. A clause in the procedural formula by which the object of the controversy, already defined in the foregoing part of the formula, was pointed out once more for better identification (= "that which is the object of the trial").—See FORMULA.

H. Krüger, *ZSS* 29 (1908) 378.

Quadragesima litium. A tax amounting to one-fortieth of the value of the object of litigation (2½ per cent) imposed in civil trials. It was in force for only a brief period in the first century after Christ.

R. Cagnat, *Étude hist. sur les impôts indirects chez les Romains,* 1882, 235; Bonelli, *StDocSD* 21 (1900) 323.

Quadriga. A team of four horses regarded as a unit. Killing one horse is considered a destruction of the whole, and, according to the LEX AQUILIA, the wrongdoer is liable for the value of all four.

Quadrupes. A four-footed animal.—Inst. 4.9; D. 9.1. —See ANIMAL, ACTIO DE PAUPERIE, LEX AQUILIA.

Quadruplatores. Informers (see DELATORES) who received one-fourth of the property seized from culprits denounced by them, in case of condemnation. *Quadruplatores* also were the accusers of persons who if convicted had to pay a four-fold penalty (such as gamblers, *aleatores,* and usurers).

Quaerere. In the sense of to acquire, to obtain, to earn, syn. with *adquirere. Quaerere* in the sense of to investigate, to inquire, to search after, is used in both civil and criminal matters. Syn. *inquirere.*

Quaerere liberos. PROCREARE.—See LIBERORUM QUAE-RENDORUM CAUSA.

Quaeritur (quaesitum est). The jurists used these locutions to introduce doubtful cases in which "a question arises" ("it has been questioned") about the legal solution of the situation presented. The terms occur not only in collections of so-called QUAESTIONES, but also in other writings of the casuistic type. Similar phrases were: *quaestio (quaestionis) est, quaestio in eo consistit* (= the question consists in that).

Quaesitor. An investigator in a criminal matter.—See TORTOR.

Quaestio. As a form of criminal proceedings, see QUAESTIONES PERPETUAE.

Quaestio de maiestate. A Sullan statute, LEX COR-NELIA DE MAIESTATE (81 B.C.), established a permanent court for criminal offenses qualified as CRIMEN MAIESTATIS.

Cramer, *Sem* 10 (1952) 3.

Quaestio Domitiana. A case presented to the jurist Celsus by a certain Domitius Labeo who inquired whether a person who wrote a testament for another might be a witness thereto (D. 28.1.27). The case became famous because of the rude answer of the jurist who called the query "very stupid and ridiculous." The name *Quaestio Domitiana* was coined in the literature.—See SCRIPTOR TESTAMENTI, TESTIS AD TESTAMENTUM ADHIBITUS.

C. Appleton, *Mél Girard* 2 (1912) 1; Kretschmar, *ZSS* 57 (1937) 52.

Quaestio facti. See RES FACTI.

Quaestio per tormenta. Inquiry under torture. Slaves were interrogated in criminal trials under torture until they confessed to the crime of which they were accused, in particular when their masters were the accusers. Citizens could not be tortured except those of the lower classes (*humiliores*).—See TORMENTA.

Lecrivain, *DS* 4.

Quaestio status. An examination (investigation) concerning the personal status of a person (citizenship, liberty).—See STATUS, ACTIONES PRAEIUDICIALES, LIBERTINITAS.

Quaestionarius. (Syn. *a quaestionibus*.) A military official attached to a military court for criminal matters.

Cagnat, *DS* 4.

Quaestiones. (As a type of juristic writing.) Collections of cases, true or fictitious, discussed by the jurists. Many of the cases might originate in the jurists' discussions in the classroom with their pupils. Other material for the *Quaestiones* came from cases with which the jurists dealt in their capacity as respondents (*responsa*). *Quaestiones* which arose from real discussions are identified by the introductory term *quaeritur, quaesitum est* (= it is [has been] asked). Several jurists published *Quaestiones* (Celsus, Africanus, Scaevola, Papinian, Paul, Callistratus, and Tertullianus). In the juristic literature the *Quaestiones* are among the most instructive works; they reveal the acumen of juristic thinking of their authors and the strength of their criticism of divergent opinions.

Riccobono, *NDI* 10; Berger, *RE* 10, 1173.

Quaestiones perpetuae. Permanent criminal courts, composed of persons of senatorial and (later) equestrian rank. The first *quaestio* was established by the LEX CALPURNIA (149 B.C.) to try extortions (see REPETUNDAE) committed by provincial governors. Later statutes introduced additional tribunals for other crimes: treason (MAIESTAS), sacrilege (SACRILEGIUM), embezzlement (PECULATUS), forgery of wills, documents, coins, weights, etc. (FALSUM), bribery and other corrupt practices at elections (AMBITUS), and the like. The courts consisted of thirty or more jurors and were normally presided over by a praetor. For the personal qualifications of the jurors (*iudices*) and the proceedings before the *quaestiones*, see LEX SEMPRONIA IUDICIARIA, LEX AURELIA, ALBUM IUDICUM, SORTITIO, REIECTIO. Some of the statutes which instituted the *quaestiones perpetuae* had particular provisions concerning the jurors and the procedure. The trial started with an ACCUSATIO by a citizen. Penalties were fixed in the pertinent statutes. The judgment of a majority of the jurors was final; there was no appeal. There was, in criminal matters, another kind of procedure, *cognitio extra ordinem,* in which bureaucratic officials exercised jurisdiction through the whole process from the investigation to the final judgment.—D. 48.18; C. 9.41; 44.—See AMPLIATIO, IUDICIA PUBLICA, LEX IULIA IUDICIORUM PUBLICORUM, ORDO IUDICIORUM PUBLICORUM.

Berger, *OCD* (*s.v.* quaestio); Belloni, *NDI* 10; A. H. J. Greenidge, *The legal procedure of Cicero's time*, 1901, 415; H. F. Hitzig, *Die Herkunft des Schwurgerichts im röm. Strafprozess*, 1909; Fraccaro, *RendLomb* 52 (1919) 344; Lengle, *ZSS* 53 (1933) 275.

Quaestores. The quaestorship was established at the beginning of the Republic although certain sources place its origin in the period of kingship. Originally two *quaestores* were assistants of the consuls and were appointed by them; later they were elected by the *comitia tributa*. The activity of the *quaestores* was concentrated on the financial affairs of the state. During the Republican period their number constantly increased and reached twenty under Augustus (from 45 B.C. there were forty). The large number is to be explained by the fact that several *quaestores* accompanied the army commanders on expeditions to administer the finances of the military units. The *quaestores* also managed the finances of the provinces. Those *quaestores* who remained in Rome (*quaestores urbani*) supervised the treasury and the financial administration of the state; see QUAESTORES AERARII. The quaestorship was the initial office in the magisterial career. Under the Republic the *quaestores* had no *imperium*, no lictors, no *sella curulis,* but from the time of Sulla they were eligible to a seat in the Senate. In the later Empire the *quaestores* functioned as city officials with less important functions; their principal task was to organize public games.—D. 1.13; C. 1.30; 12.6.—See IURARE IN LEGES, LEX CORNELIA DE VIGINTI QUAESTORIBUS and the following items.

Kübler, *RE* 14, 406; Lécrivain, *DS* 4; Anon., *NDI* 10; Stevenson, *OCD*; Latte, *TAmPhilolAs* 67 (1936) 24.

Quaestores aerarii. Two quaestores in Rome charged with the supervision of the treasury; see AERARIUM, with all its extended tasks. They made agreements with contractors for the construction of public works (*opera publica*) and with the tax-farmers (*publicani*); they executed payments requested by other high magistrates (primarily the consuls). Under the Principate the activity of the *quaestores* suffered considerable restrictions because of the interference of imperial officials, but the nature of the office remained unchanged. Two *quaestores* were assigned to the emperor for his personal service; see QUAESTORES CANDIDATI PRINCIPIS. One *quaestor* accompanied the emperor on his travels and functioned as a paymaster.

De Ruggiero, *DE* 1, 204.

Quaestores aquarii. Quaestors entrusted with the supervision of the aqueducts.

Quaestores candidati principis. Two quaestors appointed on the proposal of the emperor (*candidati principis*) to act as his private secretaries. They read the addresses of the emperor in the senate.

Quaestores militares. Quaestors assigned to generals in the field for the administration of the legions.— See MANUBIAE.

Quaestores municipales. The quaestorship was also a municipal office in some *municipia,* charged with the financial administration.

Quaestores Ostienses. One quaestor was obliged to live in Ostia, the port of Rome, in order to supervise the grain supply for the capital.

Quaestores parricidii. Mentioned in the Twelve Tables. Possibly they had already been instituted in the regal period for the prosecution of the crime of PARRICIDIUM.

Quaestores pro praetore. Either governors of small provinces or officials assigned to provincial governors (proconsuls) as their assistants and substitutes.— See the following item.

Quaestores provinciales. Only in senatorial provinces; see PROVINCIAE SENATUS. They had the rank of propraetors and a limited jurisdiction corresponding to that of *aediles curules* in Rome. They supervised the financial administration of the provinces. Small provinces had quaestors for governors, but generally the provincial quaestors assisted the governors and acted in their place when one died or left the province.

Quaestores sacri palatii. The *quaestor sacri palatii* was one of the highest civil functionaries in the later Empire, concerned with the preparation of enactments and legal decisions to be issued by the emperor. He was the principal legal adviser of the emperor and he was therefore chosen from among persons with considerable legal training.

Quaestores urbani. Quaestors acting in Rome as *quaestores aerarii.* Ant. *quaestores municipales* and *quaestores provinciales.*

Quaestores urbis. The office of a *quaestor urbis* was created by Justinian for the control of foreigners, beggars, and other suspected elements in Constantinople.

Quaestorius. (Adj.) Connected with, or pertinent to, the office of a quaestor.

Quaestorius. (Noun.) A former quaestor.—See ADLECTIO.

Quaestuaria mulier (mulier quae corpore quaestum facit). A prostitute.—See MERETRIX.

Quaestura. The office, the rank, of a quaestor. In the later Empire = the office of the QUAESTOR SACRI PALATII.

Quaestus. A profit, a gain. With regard to the contract of partnership (SOCIETAS) the term is defined as the profit which is derived from a partner's work (industry).—See LUCRUM, QUAESTUARIA MULIER.

Quamvis. See LICET.

Quanti ea res est. What is the value of the thing. This clause, connected with the object of a pending civil trial, occurred in the part of the procedural formula called CONDEMNATIO. It referred to the evaluation of the object of the controversy. In certain formulae the clause referred to the past (*quanti ea res fuit*), i.e., to the time when the wrong was committed (e.g., in *actio furti* or *actio legis Aquiliae*), in others to the present (*est*), i.e., to the time of the *litis contestatio* (which was the normal case), or to the future (*quanti et res erit*), i.e., when the evaluation was to be made at the time of the judgment.

Steinwenter, *RE* 9, 1707; M. Kaser, *Quanti ea res est,* 1935; P. Voci, *Risarcimento del danno,* 1938, 16.

Quanti minoris. See ACTIO QUANTI MINORIS.—D. 21.1.

Quarta pars. One-fourth of the whole. One-fourth (*quarta*) of an estate (*hereditatis*) refers to the so-called *quarta Falcidia* (see LEX FALCIDIA) unless another meaning, a simple fourth part of the inheritance, is evident.

Quarta Afiniana. See SENATUSCONSULTUM AFINIANUM.

Quarta Antonina. See QUARTA DIVI PII.

Quarta debitae portionis. See QUERELA INOFFICIOSI TESTAMENTI.

Quarta Divi Pii. (Called in literature *quarta Antonina.*) A person below puberty (see IMPUBES) who had been adopted (see ADOPTIO), had the right to a fourth part of the inheritance of his *adrogator,* after being emancipated without just reason or unjustly disinherited by the latter. This rule has been set by an enactment of Antonius Pius.

Beseler, *Subsiciva,* 1931, 2; David, *ZSS* 51 (1931) 528.

Quarta Falcidia. See LEX FALCIDIA.

Quarta legitimae partis. See PARS LEGITIMA.

Quarta Pegasiana. See SENATUSCONSULTUM PEGASIANUM.

Lemercier, *RHD* 14 (1935) 646.

Quarta Trebelliana. The term used in the literature for the quarter of an inheritance analogous to the *Quarta Pegasiana* after the reform of the law of *fideicommissa* by Justinian on the basis of the *Senatusconsultum Trebellianum.*—See FIDEICOMMISSUM, SENATUSCONSULTUM PEGASIANUM.

Quasi. As if, as it were. The word is often used by classical jurists when applying recognized institutions or rules to similar relations and situations (analogy). This type of adaptation is accomplished by such phrases as: *perinde* (*pro eo*) *est quasi* (*ac si*), and the like. Such locutions allude at times to situations in which an *actio ficticia* (see ACTIONES FICTICIAE) might be given, since the situation was dealt with "as if." On the other hand, however, it cannot be denied that *quasi* is one of those elastic expressions which fit into the mentality of the Byzantine jurists. The adverb occurs frequently in Justinian's constitutions and is therefore suspect in many texts. But its presence cannot be considered a decisive criterion of interpolation.—See LEX AQUILIA, ACTIO QUASI INSTITORIA, PECULIUM QUASI CASTRENSE.

> Guarneri-Citati, *Indice²* (1927) 73; *idem, St Riccobono* 1 (1936) 735; Berger, *ZSS* 36 (1915) 186, 212, 220; Riccobono, *Scr Ferrini* (Univ. Pavia) 1946, 54.

Quasi contractus—quasi delictum. These terms, often used in modern literature, are not Roman. The Roman jurists speak of *quasi ex contractu* (*quasi ex delicto*) *nascitur obligatio, debere, teneri, obligari*, which means an obligation arises, to be obligated, to owe "as if from a contract (as if from a delict)." In these locutions *quasi* is to be connected with the verb, and not with *contractus* or *delictum* (*maleficium*). The Roman idea was that from certain situations or doings obligations arise analogous to those which originate from contracts or wrongdoings; the jurists did not create a category of "almost contracts" or "almost wrongdoings."

> Vizioz, *La notion de quasi-contrat*, Thèse Bordeaux, 1912; Radin, *Virginia Law Rev.* 23 (1937) 241.

Quasi possessio. See POSSESSIO IURIS.

> Riccobono, *ZSS* 34 (1913) 251; De Sarlo, *StCagl* 29 (1942) 155.

Quasi ususfructus. An exceptional form of a usufruct of things which are consumed in use. Such things were generally not susceptible of *ususfructus*. The usufructuary is bound to return the same quantity of things of the same quality. The term *quasi ususfructus* was coined in Justinian law. If a usufruct of a complex of things was bequeathed and among them were consumable things (*res quae usu consumuntur*), the usufruct was valid, according to a decree of the senate under Tiberius on the condition that security was given to the heir to the effect that the same quantity of goods would be returned after expiration of the usufruct.—D. 7.5.—See USUSFRUCTUS.

> Beauchet and Collinet, *DS* 5, 613; Pampaloni, *BIDR* 19 (1907) 95; P. Bonfante, *Corso* 3 (1933) 86; Grosso, *BIDR* 43 (1935) 237.

Quattuorviri aediles (or quattuorviri iuri dicundo). A board of four officials in Italian and provincial cities in colonies and municipalities appointed for administrative and judicial functions.—See DUOVIRI IURI DICUNDO.

> Del Prete, *NDI* 10; Rudolph, *Stadt und Staat im röm. Italien*, 1935, 87; E. Manni, *Per la storia dei municipii*, 1947, 171; Degrassi, *Atti Lincei*, Ser. 8, Vol. 2 (1950), 281; Vittinghoff, *Römische Kolonisation und Bürgerrechtspolitik*, *Abh. Akad. Wiss. Mainz* 1951, no. 14, *passim*.

Quattuorviri praefecti Capuam, Cumas. See VIGINTISEXVIRI.

Quattuorviri viis purgandis. See VIGINTISEXVIRI.

Querela inofficiosae donationis (dotis). A complaint made by an heir entitled to a legitimate share of the estate (see PARS LEGITIMA, QUERELA INOFFICIOSI TESTAMENTI), asking the rescission of an excessive donation which the testator made when still alive with the purpose of diminishing the heir's legitimate share. See INOFFICIOSUS. The action for restitution of the gift was permissible against the donee and his heirs provided it was brought within five years. An analogous remedy was the *querela inofficiosae dotis* when the estate was diminished to the disadvantage of such an heir by an excessive dowry constituted by the testator.—C. 3.29; 30.

> Donatuti, *St Riccobono* 3 (1936) 427; H. Krüger, *ZSS* 60 (1940) 83.

Querela inofficiosae dotis. See the foregoing item.

Querela inofficiosi testamenti. A complaint of an heir who would be legitimate in intestacy but who was omitted (see PRAETERIRE) or unjustly disinherited in the testator's will (see EXHEREDATIO). The complaint was based on the ground that the testament was *inofficiosum* (= *contra officium pietatis*, see INOFFICIOSUS), the testator having disregarded his natural duties towards his nearest relatives. If the plaintiff succeeded in his *querela*, the whole testament was declared null (*testamentum rescissum*) since it was assumed that the testator was not mentally sound when he made his will (see COLOR INSANIAE), and a succession in intestacy took place. The *querela inofficiosi testamenti* could be brought by the descendants of the testator, or, when there were none, by ascendants; and later (from the time of Constantine) by consanguineous brothers and sisters in the absence of descendants and ascendants. The *querela* was excluded when the heir received through the testator's disposition (a legacy or a *donatio mortis causa*) one-fourth of what he would have received as his share in intestacy (*quarta legitimae partis*). If the testator left less than a quarter of the *legitima pars* to the heir entitled to it, the latter had the right to sue for the completion of the *pars legitima*. Under this action he obtained what was missing up to the legitimate share (*actio ad supplendam legitimam* which probably was available from the fourth century after Christ). Justinian reformed thoroughly the *querela* and the action mentioned to the benefit of the heirs.—Inst. 2.18; D. 5.2; C. 3.28; Nov. 115.—See CENTUMVIRI, SEPTEMVIRALE IUDICIUM, PARS LEGITIMA, BONORUM POSSESSIO CONTRA TABULAS, PERSONA TURPIS, TESTAMENTUM MILITIS.

> Düll, *RE* 17, 1062 (*s.v. Noterbrecht*); De Crescenzio, *NDI* 10, 1032; C. Chabrun, *Essai sur la q. i. t.*, Thèse Paris, 1906; Brugi, *Mél Fitting* 1 (1907) 113; Jobbé-Duval, *ibid.* 437; *idem, Mél Gérardin* 1907, 355; *idem, NRHD* 31 (1907) 755; Naber, *Mn* 34 (1906) 365, 40 (1912) 397; A. Suman, *Saggi romanistici*, 1919, 3; G. La Pira, *Suc-*

cessione testamentaria intestata, 1930, 412; F. v. Woess, *Das röm. Erbrecht und die Erbanwärter*, 1930, 207; E. Racz, *Les restrictions à la liberté de tester en dr. rom.*, Thèse Neufchatel, 1934; Donatuti, *St Riccobono* 3 (1936) 427; H. Krüger, *ZSS* 57 (1937) 94; *idem, Fschr Koschaker* 2 (1939) 256; *idem, BIDR* 47 (1940) 63; Lavaggi, *SDHI* 5 (1939) 76; Nardi, *ibid.* 450; E. Renier, *Étude sur l'hist. de la q. i. t.*, Liège, 1942; Siber, *ZSS* 65 (1947) 25.

Querela non numeratae pecuniae. The complaint of a debtor who had issued a promissory note in advance and then did not receive the money which he had acknowledged to owe. Through the *querela* he might obtain the annulment of the note, if he sued within a certain time (in Justinian law within two years). The *querela* is a counter-part to the EXCEPTIO NON NUMERATAE PECUNIAE with which the defendant could oppose the plaintiff when the latter sued for payment.—C. 4.30.

Collinet, *Atti del IV. Congr. Intern. di Papirologia*, 1936, 89; Kreller, *St Riccobono* 2 (1936) 285; H. Krüger, *ZSS* 58 (1938) 1; Archi, *Scr Ferrini* (Univ. Pavia) 1946, 702; Lemosse, *St Solazzi* 1948, 470.

Querella. See QUERELA.

Queri. To complain, to make a charge about a person to a magistrate (for instance, when a slave complains about bad treatment by his master, a patron about his freedman, or a ward or his relatives about a guardian). *Queri* is also used of all kinds of *querelae* (see the foregoing items) and of a complaint against an order of a magistrate.

Querimonia. A complaint made to a public official; an appeal from the assignment of a public service (see MUNERA). The term is used by the imperial chancery.

Quid enim (tamen) si? What, however, if? This rhetorical question occurs often in juristic works as an introduction to a case slightly different from the case discussed immediately before. Some of these, and similar, rhetorical questions may be of later origin (interpolations) but certainly not all of them.

Guarneri-Citati, *Indice*[2] (1927) 33, 75; G. Beseler, *Beiträge zur Kritik* 1 (1910) 61; Berger, *KrVj* 14 (1912) 434; Ambrosino, *RISG* 1940, 18.

Quidem. In phrases such as *si quidem . . . si vero* (*sin autem, quod si*), this occurs in juristic writings when two different legal situations are taken into consideration: if . . . ; if, however. . . . Such juxtapositions in classical texts are branded with the suspicion of non-classical origin; but they are not fully reliable as criteria of interpolation.

Guarneri-Citati, *Indice*[2] (1927) 74.

Quiescere. *Actio quiescit* = an action which temporarily cannot be brought. In the language of the imperial chancery *quiescere* frequently means to become void, inefficient.

Quilibet ex populo. Any Roman citizen. In the so-called ACTIONES POPULARES and INTERDICTA POPU-LARIA any one of the Roman people might act as a plaintiff.

Quincunces usurae. Five per cent interest *per annum* (i.e., five-twelfths of *usura centesima*, 12 per cent). —See USURAE CENTESIMAE.

Quincunx. Five-twelfths of a whole (an AS or an inheritance, hence *heres ex quincunce* = an heir who receives $5/12$ of the estate).

Quindecimviri sacris faciundis. See DUOVIRI SACRIS FACIUNDIS. They supervised the foreign cults in Rome.

Bloch, *DS* 2, 428; Rose, *OCD*; M. W. Hoffmann, *AmJPhilol* 1952.

Quingenarium sacramentum. A *sacramentum* of 500 asses; *quinquagenarium sacramentum* = a *sacramentum* of fifty asses.—See LEGIS ACTIO SACRAMENTO.

Quinquaginta decisiones. Fifty constitutions issued by Justinian after the publication of the first Code A.D. 529 but before the start of the work on the Digest, i.e., during 529 and 530. No collection of these constitutions, which seemingly were separately published, is preserved.—See CODEX IUSTINIANUS.

Jörs, *RE* 4, 2275; Anon., *NDI* 4, 593; P. Krüger, *Fg Bekker, Aus röm. und bürgerlichem Recht*, 1907; S. Di Marzo, *Le Q. D.*, 1–2 (1899–1900); G. Rotondi, *Scritti giur.* 1 (1922) 227; P. Bonfante, *BIDR* 32 (1922) 278; Pringsheim, *ACDR* Roma 1 (1934) 457.

Quinquefascales. Governors of imperial provinces (*legati Augusti pro praetore*), so-called because they were each assigned five lictors (see LICTORES).—See LEGATI PROCONSULIS.

Quinquennalis (quinquennalicius). A municipal magistrate appointed for five years; he was also called *quinquennalis perpetuus.*—See MAGISTER COLLEGII, DUOVIRI QUINQUENNALES.

R. Magoffen, *The q., Johns Hopkins Univ. Studies*, Baltimore, 1913; Larsen, *ClPhilol* 1931, 322.

Quinquevirale iudicium. See IUDICIUM QUINQUEVIRALE.

Quinqueviri. A group of five officials who served as the night police in Rome.

Quinqueviri agris dandis assignandis. See TRIUMVIRI COLONIAE DEDUCENDAE.

De Ruggiero, *DE* 2, 430.

Quirites. The earliest name for the Romans. According to an explanation given by Justinian (Inst. 1.2.2), the name originates from Quirinus, a surname of Romulus, the legendary founder of Rome. —See IUS QUIRITIUM, DOMINIUM EX IURE QUIRITIUM, NUDUM IUS QUIRITIUM.

Severini, *NDI* 10; Kretschmer, *Glotta* 10 (1920) 147.

Quivis ex populo. See QUILIBET EX POPULO.

Quodammodo. To some extent, to a certain degree. This vague, elastic term is used by the Byzantines with predilection and is not rare in interpolated texts. It is not unknown, however, in the classical language and is applied by the jurist to underscore an analogy.

Guarneri-Citati, *Indice*[2] (1927) 76.

R

Ramnes. One of the three tribes (see TRIBUS) into which the population of Rome was divided at the time of the foundation of the city. The other two were *Tities* and *Luceres.* The names are probably of Etruscan origin.

Rosenberg, *RE* 1A.

Rapere. See RAPINA, RAPTUS.

Rapina. Robbery. *Rapina* was considered a form of *furtum* (theft) committed with the use of violence (*vis*). Only movables (*vi bona rapta*) could be the object of *rapina.* *Rapina* was a private wrongdoing (*delictum*), prosecuted only at request of the person injured, under a praetorian, penal action, *actio vi bonorum raptorum,* which if brought within one year of the time of the robbery, could lead to the condemnation of the convicted defendant to a four-fold value of the things stolen as a penalty to be paid to the plaintiff. After a year the condemnation was only *in simplum* (see ACTIONES IN SIMPLUM). The condemned robber was branded with infamy.—Inst. 4.2; D. 47.8; C. 9.34.—See INTERDICTUM DE VI, TURBA.

Kleinfeller, *RE* 1A; Lécrivain, *DS* 5; Brasiello, *NDI* 10; E. Levy, *Konkurrenz der Aktionen* 2, 1 (1922) 194.

Raptor. See RAPTUS.

Raptus. The abduction of a woman against the will of her parents. The abductor (*raptor*) was punished with death from the time of Constantine, under whom *raptus* became a *crimen publicum,* and so was the woman (until Justinian) when she had consented. Justinian's enactment (C. 9.13.1) extended the penalties for *raptus* (death and seizure of property) on *raptores* of widows and nuns (*sanctimoniales*).

Eger, *RE* 1A; Lécrivain, *DS* 4.

Ratihabitio. (From *ratum habere.*) Ratification, approval. *Ratihabitio* occurs when a person on whose behalf another had concluded a transaction or accomplished a legally important act (e.g., by appearing for him in court and defending his interests) without authorization, approved of what had been done for him. "*Ratihabitio* is equivalent to a mandate" (D. 46.3.12.4). Hence, by his approval the principal party (*dominus negotii*) assumed any liability which resulted from the act done in his favor.—D. 46.8; C. 5.74.—See NEGOTIORUM GESTIO, MANDATUM.

C. Bertolini, *La ratifica degli atti giuridici,* 1–2 (1889, 1891); G. Bortolucci, *R. mandato comparatur,* 1916; Donatuti, *AnPer* 36 (1922); Arangio-Ruiz, *Il mandato,* 1949, 197.

Ratio. Reason, a ground, a motive, consideration. *Rationem habere alicuius rei* = to take into consideration. See RATIO IURIS. *Ratio* in the writings of the Roman jurists is not a philosophical concept and has no universal value. It is invoked only where it seems opportune for a specific reason. Hence the saying: "It is impossible to give reasons for all that our ancestors laid down" (D. 1.3.20, Julian) and "therefore it should not be inquired into the reasons for what is being ordained (*quae constituuntur*), otherwise much that is secure would be undermined" (D. 1.3.21).—Another group of meanings of *ratio* is connected with *rationes* = an account book. Thus *ratio* may indicate an account, a calculation, a computation. See EXPENDERE (*ratio accepti et expensi*). —*Rationes* refer to the complex of financial matters of the emperor, of a public corporate body or of a private individual, and to its financial management.— See ACTIO DE RATIONIBUS DISTRAHENDIS, A RATIONIBUS, CODEX RATIONUM DOMESTICARUM, REDDERE RATIONES, and the following items.

Lécrivain, *DS* 4.

Ratio accepti et expensi. See EXPENDERE.

Ratio aequitatis. See AEQUITAS.

Ratio Caesaris. Syn. with *res privata Caesaris, ratio privata* (*sc. Caesaris*).—See PATRIMONIUM CAESARIS. PROCURATOR REI PRIVATAE.

Ratio castrensis. A part of the administration of the imperial court, particularly concerned with the military treasury of the emperor and his residences in the provinces.

Rostowzew, *DE* 3, 106; Lécrivain, *DS* 4, 812.

Ratio domus Augustae. The management of the financial matters of the imperial palace.—See DOMUS AUGUSTA.

Ratio Falcidiae. The deduction (computation) made with regard to a legacy according to the LEX FALCIDIA.

Ratio (rationes) fisci. The financial administration of the fisc, fiscal funds (property). Syn. *rationes imperii.*—See RATIONES.

Ratio iuris. The reasonableness (rationality) of a legal provision, the logic of the law. The Roman jurists stress the *ratio iuris* as a means of interpretation of the law (*ratio suadet, efficit,* and the like).

Ratio legis. The reason (ground) of a written law (a statute), the spirit to be drawn from the law itself (not from external elements), the purpose, the motive which inspired the promulgation of a specific law, as, e.g., *ratio legis Falcidiae.*—See RATIO VOCONIANA.

Biondi, *NDI* 10; Gaudemet, *RHD* 17 (1938) 141.

Ratio naturalis. See NATURALIS RATIO, IUS NATURALE.

Ratio privata Caesaris (principis). See RATIO CAESARIS, RES PRIVATA CAESARIS.

Ratio Voconiana. The motives which led to the issuance of the *Lex Voconia.*—See LEX VOCONIA.

Kübler, *ZSS* 41 (1920) 24.

Ratiocinator. A bookkeeper, an accountant.

Ratiocinia. (In financial administration.) Keeping accounts, concerning the financial management of public institutions, works and buildings (*ratiocinia operum publicorum*).—C. 8.12; 3.21.

Rationalis. (Noun.) The title *rationalis* first appears in the third century after Christ for provincial pro-curators and for the head of the fisc. Later, it became more frequent, being used in both the fiscal administration and that of the *res privata* of the emperor. *Rationalis* was substituted for the former *magister* and *procurator* (*a rationibus*) and was afterwards replaced by a *comes*. Thus the *rationalis summae rei* (the chief of the fiscal administration) became between A.D. 340 and 345 *comes sacrarum largitionum* and the *rationalis privatae* (*rei*) *comes rei privatae*. Both these high officials had representatives also called *rationales* (*summarum* or *rerum privatarum* respectively) whose competence embraced the territory of a *dioecesis* of a *provincia*. The frequent changes in official titles in the postclassical bureaucracy makes a precise delimitation of their competence extremely difficult.—D. 1.19.—See the following item.

Liebenam, *RE* 1A; Lécrivain, *DS* 4; O. Hirschfeld, *Kais. Verwaltungsbeamte*[2] (1905) 34; E. Stein, *Gesch. des spätröm. Reiches* 1 (1928) 58.

Rationes. Various branches of the imperial financial administration. Some had local divisions (*stationes*) at important places. There were *rationes metallorum* (for mines), *rationes operum publicorum* (for public buildings and enterprises), *rationes bibliothecarum* (for libraries), etc. In all these offices, functionaries called *rationales* fulfilled the tasks of accountants.— See A RATIONIBUS.

Liebenam, *RE* 1A (*s.v. ratio*).

Rationes. Account books of a banker.—See ARGENTARII, RATIO.

Ratum habere. See RATIHABITIO.—C. 5.74.

Ratus. Legally valid (e.g., *ratum testamentum, legatum*). Ant. *irritus*.

Raudusculum. A small rod of bronze used during the performance of a MANCIPATIO. The man who held the scale (*libripens*) handed over the *raudusculum* to the transferee who touched the scale with it, thereby indicating that he acquired the object mancipated.

Reatus. The state of being accused in a criminal trial. —See REUS, ACCUSATIO, NOMEN RECIPERE, INSCRIBERE.

Eger, *RE* 1A.

Recedere. To withdraw, to retreat, to recede. "There is no doubt that with the consent of the persons who assumed reciprocal obligations, one may withdraw from a sale, a lease and other similar obligations provided that everything remained unchanged" (D. 2.14.58).

Receptaculum aquae. See CASTELLUM.

Receptator (receptor). One who hides a thief or who receives stolen goods to be concealed. He is subject to the same penalties as the principal wrongdoer. Only hiding near relatives was punished more mildly. A man who received money or a part of the stolen things and dismissed the robber when he could have

apprehended him, was himself treated as a *receptor*. —D. 47.16.

Eger, *RE* 1A; Humbert and Lécrivain, *DS* 4; Saviotti, *AG* 55 (1895) 353; H. Balougditch, *Complicité en droit rom.*, Thèse Montpellier, 1920, 83.

Recepticia actio. See RECEPTUM ARGENTARII.

Recepticia dos. See DOS RECEPTICIA.

Recepticius servus. A term known only in literary (non juristic) sources and already a subject of controversy among the ancient grammarians. It probably indicated a slave who was returned to the seller because of physical or mental defects.—See REDHIBITIO.

De Senarclens, *TR* 12 (1933) 390; Kornhardt, *ZSS* 58 (1938) 162; Solazzi, *SDHI* 5 (1939) 222.

Receptor. See RECEPTATOR.

Receptum. The term covers different transactions (see the following items) which have in common the sole point that they originated in so-called praetorian pacts (see PACTUM PRAETORIUM) recognized by, and enforceable under, praetorian law. It is likely that the pertinent obligations were assumed by the use of the word *recipio* (= "I accept").

Klingmüller, *RE* 1A; Partsch, *ZSS* 29 (1908) 403.

Receptum arbitrii. An agreement by which a person elected as arbitrator by the common consent of the parties involved in a dispute assumed the duty to settle their controversy by an arbitration (*arbitrium*). —D. 4.8; C. 2.55.—See ARBITER EX COMPROMISSO, COMPROMISSUM.

Wenger, *RE* 1A; Lécrivain, *DS* 4; Frezza, *NDI* 11.

Receptum argentarii. A formless promise to pay another's debt (see CONSTITUTUM DEBITI ALIENI) by which a banker (*argentarius*) assumed the obligation to pay a client's debt at a fixed date. The action against the banker to enforce payment = *actio recepticia*. Justinian abolished the action, primarily for the reason that under it the banker was liable even when the original obligation was not valid. In Justinian's law the *receptum argentarii* was subjected to the general (reformed) rules concerning the CONSTITUTUM DEBITI ALIENI.

Wenger, *RE* 1A; Frezza, *NDI* 11; Partsch, *ZSS* 29 (1908) 412; Platon, *RHD* 33 (1909) 157, 289; De Dominicis, *APad* 49 (1933); G. Astuti, *St intorno alla promessa del pagamento* 2 (*Il constituto*), 1941, 282.

Receptum est. See OBTINUIT, USUS.

Receptum nautae (cauponis, stabularii). An agreement by which a shipowner (the keeper of an inn or of a stable) assumed goods for transportation or custody, with the addition of a specific proviso *salvum fore* (*recipere*), i.e., that the things confided them will be safe. The responsibility of such persons was greater than in a simple LOCATIO CONDUCTIO. They were not liable for *vis maior* (shipwreck or a major assault of robbers which could not be resisted) but they had to make good damages or destruction caused by themselves or their personnel and they were answerable if the goods were stolen. Inn-keepers were even responsible for any persons living permanently in their inns. The extended responsibility of those persons was established in the praetorian Edict with the justification that the "dishonesty (*improbitas*) of this kind of persons" required such measures (D. 9.4.3.1).

Klingmüller, *RE* 1A; Humbert and Lécrivain, *DS* 4; Severini, *NDI*; L. Lusignani, *Responsabilità per custodia*, 1 (1902); Schulz, *GrZ* 38 (1911) 41; H. Vincent, *Res recepta*, Thèse Montpellier, 1920; P. Huvelin, *Ét d'hist. du droit commercial rom.*, 1929, 138; Partsch, *ZSS* 29 (1928) 403; Bonolis, *Scritti Zorli*, 1929, 477; De Dominicis, *APad* 49 (1933); Carrelli, *RDNav* 4 (1928) 323; De Martino, *ibid.* 201; De Robertis, *AnBari* 12 (1952).

Recidere. To come back, to return into a former legal situation, e.g., to the same paternal power (*in potestatem*) under which one had been previously. *Recidere* sometimes has the sense of *cadere*, e.g., when said of an inheritance = to come, to accrue to a person, to fall to a person's share.

Reciperatio (recuperatio). A treaty between Rome and another state under which reciprocal protection of the citizens of one state in the territory of the other was established, in particular in case of litigation for the recovery of property. The judges in the pertinent procedure were the *reciperatores* (*recuperatores*) who later might also function as judges in trials between Roman citizens.—See RECUPERATORES.

Wenger, *RE* 1A; Lécrivain, *DS* 4; Severini, *NDI* 11.

Recipere. To receive (e.g., an inheritance), to receive back what one has given, lent, or lost. *Recipere* means also to assume an obligation for oneself or for another (as a surety, see RECEPTUM ARGENTARII). When syn. with *excipere*, *recipere* = to reserve a certain right or advantage for oneself on the occasion of the transfer of property (e.g., an easement, a usufruct).

Wenger, *RE* 1A; De Robertis, *AnBari* 12 (1952) 15.

Recipere arbitrium. To assume the function of an arbitrator.—See RECEPTUM ARBITRII.

Recipere nomen. See ACCUSATIO.

Recipere usu. See USURECEPTIO.

Recitare (recitatio). To recite, to read out in court (a written testimony of an absent witness, any document), in the senate (an *oratio principis*) or in public (a proclamation of a magistrate). *Recitatio sententiae* = the reading by the judge of the final judgment in a trial. In postclassical proceedings the judge had to read it from a written draft.

Recitatio testamenti. See APERTURA TESTAMENTI.

Recludere. To shut up (*in carcere* = in a prison).

Recognoscere. (With regard to written documents.) To examine the authenticity, to control the exactness, of a copy by comparison with the original. The clause confirming the fact that a copy was made in an office and its exactness verified was: *descriptum et recognitum factum* (D. 10.2.5; 29.3.7). *Recognoscere* was also used to indicate that the written text

of a document agreed with the dictated text. The acknowledgment of the authenticity of a seal on a document = *recognoscere signum* (see SIGNUM). *Recognovi* = I have verified.

Mommsen, *Jur. Schriften* 2 (1905 ex 1892) 179; F. Preisigke, *Die Inschrift von Skaptoparene* (*Schriften der wissensch. Gesellschaft in Strassburg* 30, 1917) 26.

Reconciliare matrimonium. See REDINTEGRARE.

Reconductio. The renewal of a lease (*locàtionem renovare*). A tacit *reconductio* is assumed when the tenant holds the thing (immovable) rented after the expiration of the first lease. Securities given for the original lease remain pledged for the following one.

Recte (rectius, rectissime). With these terms the jurists used to express their approval of other jurists' opinions (= correctly, rightly). Sometimes Justinian and his compilers manifested their approval of earlier legal norms in the same way.—*Recte*, when referring to the performance of a legal act, indicates that it was accomplished in conformity with the law being in force, in particular, that the prescribed solemn forms were observed.

Guarneri-Citati, *Indice²* (1927) 77; Riccobono, *ZSS* 34 (1913) 224.

Rector provinciae. The governor of a province. The title is not used in juristic writings but is frequent in later imperial constitutions.—C. 1.40.

Recuperatio. See RECIPERATIO.

Recuperatores. A court composed of at least three judges for civil trials in various matters (*actio iniuriarum, quaestiones status*), acting under a somewhat accelerated procedure. Originally established in international treaties, the court later became competent in disputes between Romans and peregrines and between Roman parties alone. The procedure was *per formulas* (see FORMULA) and the *recuperatores* were private jurors acting as *iudices* in the second stage of the trial (see IN IURE). Apparently there was no precise delimitation of their competence; according to a prevailing opinion the parties to the trial had the right of choice whether to put their dispute before *recuperatores* or before a single judge (*unus iudex*). *Recuperatores* also appears in post-interdictal trials. In postclassical law there is no trace of *recuperatores*. No mention of them occurs in Justinian's legislation. —See ORATIO CLAUDII, VADIMONIUM RECUPERATORIBUS SUPPOSITIS.

P. F. Girard, *Mél* 2 (1923) 391; Wenger, *RE* 1A, 418; Bozza, *DE* 4, 159; Poggi, *Riv. ital. di dir. internazionale privato* 2 (1932) 525; Wlassak, *Judikationsbefehl, SbWien* 197, 4 (1921) 51, 131; M. Nicolau, *Causa liberalis*, 1933, 52; M. Lemosse, *Cognitio*, 1944, 175; Y. Bongert, in *Varia. Ét. de dr. rom.*, Paris, 1952.

Recuperatorium iudicium. A trial before the court of RECUPERATORES.

Reddere. "Although the term *reddere* means to give back (to return), it has, however, in itself the meaning of giving" (D. 50.16.94). *Reddere* = to pay back a loan or whatever one owes to another; in a broader sense = *dare*.

Reddere actionem (iudicium). When referring to the judicial activity of a magistrate, syn. with DARE ACTIONEM.

Reddere interdictum. To issue an interdict.—See INTERDICTUM.

Reddere iudicium. See DARE ACTIONEM.

Reddere ius. Indicates the jurisdictional activity of the praetor.

Reddere pignus. To return the pledge to the debtor when the debt was paid. Syn. *restituere* with regard to FIDUCIA.

Kreller, *ZSS* 62 (1942) 170.

Reddere rationes (rationem). To render an account of management of another's affairs, and to pay the remainder to the person entitled to it. It was customary to free a slave in a testament under the condition *"si rationes reddiderit"* (= if he paid what remained over from the administration of the master's business to the latter's heir).

Redemptor. (With references to taxes.) A tax-farmer (*redemptor vectigalium*). Syn. *conductor vectigalium, manceps, publicanus.*

Redemptor litium (causarum). One who buys creditors' claims against third persons. Transactions of this kind were made in the form of CESSIO, chiefly by speculators who acquired the claims at a low price in order to sue later the debtors for the whole. The LEX ANASTASIANA (A.D. 506) made such speculative activity unprofitable.

Severini, *NDI* 11.

Redemptor operis. A contractor. Syn. *conductor operis.*—See LOCATIO CONDUCTIO OPERIS FACIENDI.

Humbert, *DS* 4.

Redemptor vectigalium. See REDEMPTOR.

Redemptus ab hoste. A prisoner of war who was redeemed from the enemy by a ransomer. The redeemed prisoner was bound to repay the ransom and the ransomer had a lien on him until the debt was discharged by payment or by services. During this time the *redemptus* had no *ius postliminii* (see POSTLIMINIUM). In postclassical law the period of service to the ransomer was limited to five years. If a slave was redeemed from the enemy not by his master, the latter might regain him by repayment of the amount to the ransomer.—D. 49.15; C. 8.50.— See CAPTIVUS, VINCULUM PIGNORIS.

Pampaloni, *BIDR* 17 (1905) 125; Albertoni, *Riv. di dir. internazionale* 17 (1925) 358, 500; Romano, *RISG* 5 (1930) 3; H. Krüger, *ZSS* 51 (1930) 203; 52 (1931) 351; W. Felgenträger, *Antikes Lösungsrecht*, 1933, 95; G. Faiveley, *R. a. h.*, Thèse Paris, 1942; Levy, * ClPhilol* 38 (1943) 159 (= *BIDR* 55–56, 1951, Post-Bellum, 70).

Redemptus suis nummis (*sc.* servus). A slave redeemed from his master by a third person, a fiduciary, through payment of a sum of money. The money either came from the slave's *peculium* or was given to the redeemer by a person who acted in the slave's interest (for instance, one to whom the slave promised services in the future or repayment of the loan after manumission). The redeemer was obliged to free the slave but only a rescript of Marcus Aurelius and Verus entitled the slave to seek a remedy in court (in a *cognitio extra ordinem*) for enforcing the manumission (D. 40.1.5 pr.). Syn. *emptus suis nummis.*

Seuffert, *Loskauf von Sklaven mit ihrem Geld, Fschr Univ. Giessen*, 1907; W. W. Buckland, *Law of slavery*, 1908, 636.

Redhibere. See the following item.

Pezzana, *RISG* 88 (1951) 274.

Redhibitio. The restitution of a purchased thing (e.g., a slave) to the seller because of its essential defects, while the seller returned the price to the buyer. Such rescission of a sale was obtained by the buyer under the *actio redhibitoria*; see EMPTIO. The term *redhibitio* comes from *redhibere* = "to have the seller get back what he had before" (D. 21.1.1 pr.).—D. 21.1.

Redigere. To bring a person (e.g., a slave) or a thing back into its former legal situation.

Redigere pecuniam. To obtain money, to gain a pecuniary profit from a transaction.

Redintegrare. To renew (syn. *renovare*, e.g., a lease), to restore to integrity or to former legal status. *Matrimonium redintegratum* = a second marriage concluded between persons who had been married to each other and divorced. Syn. *reconciliare.* Such a marriage abolished a pending *actio rerum amotarum* of the husband against the wife.

Reditus. Income, proceeds; often syn. with *fructus.* —*Reditus civilis* = revenues of the state from taxes, etc.—C. 11.70.

Redundare. To devolve (e.g., a risk, liability, charges, losses) from one person to another.

Referendarius. See REGERENDARIUS.

Referre. To enter (in public records, in census lists, in account books). In juristic writings *referre* is used to introduce a citation or a literal quotation from another jurist's work (*X refert hoc, apud Labeonem relatum est [refertur] Sabinum existimasse* = it is related by Labeo that Sabinus' opinion was, and the like). *Referre* is also used when a jurist relates the contents of an imperial rescript or senatusconsult.

Referre. (In judicial matters.) To make a report in postclassical procedure to a higher judge or to the emperor on substantial circumstances of the matter in dispute.—D. 49.1; C. 7.61.

Referre iusiurandum. See IUSIURANDUM NECESSARIUM.

Refert. It is of importance. *Multum (maxime) refert* = it is of great (greatest) importance. Ant. *nihil (parvi) refert* = it does not matter. The locutions are used by the jurists to stress (or exclude) the importance of a factual or legal element in the decision of a case.

Reficere. To restore an injured thing to its former condition. See INTERDICTA DE REFICIENDO. Repairing (*reficere*) a building is considered a kind of *aedificare*; accordingly, it is exposed to a protestation by a neighbor (see OPERIS NOVI NUNTIATIO) in the same way as a new building.

Reficere testamentum. To make a new testament.

Refragari. To be opposed to, to be contrary to, to be a hindrance. The term is applied to legal acts or opinions which are contrary to a law, to *ratio iuris*, to *auctoritas iuris*.

　　Seckel in Heumann's *Handlexikon*[9], 1907, 499; Berger, *KrVj* 14 (1912) 436; Guarneri-Citati, *Indice*[2] (1927) 77.

Refuga. A runaway, one who escaped from prison or custody.

Refundere. To repay, to reimburse, to refund (expenses, proceeds lost).

Refutatio (refutare). In later civil procedure a written refutation by one party to a trial of the appeal made by the adversary. The *refutatio* was sent to the emperor's court, either in an appeal procedure or together with the lower judge's *consultatio* (*relatio*) by which the emperor was requested for an opinion in a specific case; see CONSULTATIO. In the latter instance both parties could oppose the judge's statement by written presentations *preces refutatoriae, libelli refutatorii*.

Regens exercitum. A military commander. "His duty was not only to order military discipline but also to observe it" (D. 49.16.12 pr.). He was forbidden to use a soldier for his private service or for his advantage (hunting or fishing).

Regens provinciam. See RECTOR PROVINCIAE.

Regere fines. To draw the boundaries between two neighboring lands.—See ACTIO FINIUM REGUNDORUM.

Regerendarius (referendarius). An auxiliary official in the office of a PRAEFECTUS PRAETORIO, DUX, or other high official in the provinces. In Justinian's times there were several *referendarii palatii* = officials of the imperial court charged with tasks of a more confidential nature. Their functions were established in Justinian's Nov. 10.

Regesta. A collection (register, list) of imperial enactments or other official documents of lasting importance (*regesta officii*). The institution was introduced in the later Empire.

Regia (*sc.* domus). The king's house. In historical times *regia* was the official building in which the *pontifex maximus* had his office. The pontiffs gathered there for their meetings and solemn religious ceremonies.

　　Rosenberg, *RE* 1A.

Regia lex. See LEX REGIA.

Regiae leges. See LEGES REGIAE.

Regimen morum. The control and supervision of public morals. The *regimen morum* was a domain of the censors' activity; see CENSORES. They exercised this control when selecting worthy persons for the senate (see LECTIO SENATUS) or when excluding from that body those senators whose moral life was blemished (see SENATU MOVERE). The censors had to qualify certain persons as unfit for public service by the NOTA CENSORIA which branded them with ignominy for the current five-year period (*lustrum*). Syn. *cura morum*.

Regio. A territory of an indefinite extent, a locality. —See CONSUETUDO REGIONIS, TRACTUS.

Regiones Italiae. Eleven administrative districts into which Italy was divided probably by Augustus, simultaneously with the division of Rome into fourteen regions; see REGIONES URBIS ROMAE. There were no changes in this administrative organization until Constantine.

　　R. Thomsen, *The Italic regions from Augustus to the Lombard invasion*, Copenhagen, 1947; v. Gerkan, *Bonner Jahrbücher* 149 (1949).

Regiones iuridicorum. See IURIDICI, DIOECESIS URBICA.

Regiones urbis Romae. The first division of the city of Rome into four districts (*regiones* or *tribus urbanae*) is attributed to the king Servius Tullius. Augustus divided Rome into fourteen administrative *regiones*, each under the supervision of a magistrate (praetor, tribune, aedil). Under Hadrian each *regio* had two *curatores urbis Romae* who by the end of the second century were called *procuratores regionum*. In the regional organization established by Augustus, the *regiones* were subdivided into *vici*, each of which was under the control of four *magistri vicorum* (*vicomagistri*).—See VIGILES, REGIONES ITALIAE.

　　Graffunder, *RE* 1A, 480; Thédenat, *DS* 4; Richmond, *OCD*.

Regius. Either connected with the kings of the period of Roman kingship or with the emperors of the Empire. Similarly *regnare* (= to reign) refers both to the kings and the emperors.—See LEX REGIA, LEGES REGIAE.

Regnum. Kingship, government by kings. *Regnum* refers to the earliest period of Rome's history, from the foundation of Rome (753 B.C.) until the constitution of the Republic (the beginning of the sixth century B.C.) See REX. In a broader sense *regnum* = sovereignty. *Regnum* refers also to foreign kingdoms (*regnum alienum*).

　　Fustel de Coulanges, *DS* 4, 824; Westrup, *Archives d'hist. du droit oriental* 4 (1949) 85; Coli, *SDHI* 17 (1951) 2.

Regradare (regradatio). To regrade an official in rank, in particular one in the emperor's service (*domestici*) for a longer unjustified absence from office.

Regressus. (From *regredi*.) A recourse, making use of a legal remedy (a suit), in particular for recovery of damages (e.g., *in* [or *ad*] *venditorem* in a case of eviction, *ad mandatorem* = for the reimbursement of expenses).

Regula (iuris). An abstract legal principle of a more general nature whether originating in jurisprudence or in an imperial enactment. "A rule is that which briefly expounds a matter" (*rem breviter enarrat*, D. 50.17.1). The legal rules are concise formulations drawn from the law which is in force; "the law is not derived from rules (*regulae*) but a rule is derived from the existing law" (D. *ibid.*). Therefore the rule itself does not create law. Syn. (in the language of imperial constitutions) *norma* (not used by classical jurists). The legal maxims set up in earlier law were at times criticized by the classical jurists inasmuch as they were no longer applicable to the developed economic relations and necessities of everyday legal life. The final title of the Digest (D. 50.17), entitled "on various rules of the ancient law" contains a collection of legal rules of the *ius antiquum*. Some of them are a repetition of texts inserted in former titles of the Digest; many of them drawn out from the context in which they were expressed in the original juristic writings, were thus made applicable as general rules although originally they referred only to specific situations. Other legal rules of classical origin are to be found in the Digest beyond the title 50.17, but some of them were limited in their general application through words like *plerumque* (= often), *interdum* (= sometimes), inserted by the compilers.—See CANON, NORMA, DEFINITIO, the following items and some legal rules quoted under NEMO, etc.

Riccobono, *NDI* 11; Leonhard, *RE* 1A; Pringsheim, *Fschr Lenel* 1921, 244; Brugi, *St Del Vecchio* 1 (1930) 38; Stella-Maranca, *Rec Gény* 2 (1934) 91; Arangio-Ruiz, *La règle de droit dans l'antiquité classique, Égypte Contemporaine*, 1938; Wenger, *Canon, SbWien* 220, 1 (1942) 47; Riccobono, *Scr Ferrini* (Univ. Pavia, 1946) 22; G. Nocera, *Ius publicum* (D.2.14.38), Rome, 1946; Berger, *ACIVer* 2 (1951) 193 (= Sem 9 [1951] 42).

Regula Catoniana. (Also *sententia Catoniana.*) A rule concerning legacies. "A legacy which would have been void if the testator died at the time of making the testament, is invalid whenever he shall have died" (D. 34.7.1 pr.). This rule, whose author was one of the two Catones (see CATO), was in later classical law not fully valid.—D. 34.7.

Ferrini, *NDI* 2; 1143; Clerici, *AG* 77 (1906) 441; G. Borgna, *Origine e fondamento della r. C.*, 1909; Cicala, *StSen* 31 (1915) 21; J. Lambert, *La règle Catonienne*, Thèse Lyon, 1925; Appleton, *TR* 11 (1931–32) 19; B. Biondi, *Successione testamentaria*, 1943, 416.

Regulae. A type of juristic writing. Under this title collections of rules were written by Neratius, Pomponius, Gaius, Scaevola, Marcian, and Modestinus; Ulpian and Paul wrote even two compilations of *Regulae*. Excerpts from juristic collections of "rules" show, however, a picture different from the title

50.17 of the Digest, *De regulis iuris* (see REGULA). The texts in the collections of *Regulae* are by far not so concisely formulated as generally *regulae* were.

Berger, *RE* 10, 1174.

Regulae Ulpiani. See ULPIANUS, TITULI EX CORPORE ULPIANI.

Regulariter. Regularly, normally. *Regulariter definire* = to establish in the form of a rule.

Rei vindicatio. An action which served for the protection of quiritary ownership. Under this action the owner of a thing sued the possessor of his thing for its recovery. The victorious plaintiff regained possession of the object claimed. If the defendant denied the plaintiff's ownership, the plaintiff had to prove the acquisition of it under the rules of the *ius civile* from its previous quiritary owner. Such proof might be difficult in certain circumstances and, if so, the plaintiff could avoid it by using another action, ACTIO PUBLICIANA IN REM, in which he had only to prove that, before having been deprived of the possession of the thing in dispute, he possessed it under conditions which normally led to usucaption (*in condicione usucapiendi*). The defendant, when defeated, had to return the thing *cum sua causa* (see CAUSA), i.e., with all that the plaintiff would have had if the thing were delivered at the time of the *litis contestatio* (proceeds, *fructus*) and was liable for damages done to the thing after the *litis contestatio*. The liability of the defendant for *fructus* and damages in the period before *litis contestatio* depended upon whether he held the thing in good faith (in the belief to be its owner) or in bad faith; see POSSESSOR BONAE FIDEI. If the defendant refused to deliver the thing claimed, the plaintiff could estimate under oath (*iuramentum in litem*) the value which the actual restitution represented to him (*litis aestimatio*). The defendant was adjudicated to pay the sum but he retained the thing. Only Justinian admitted an execution on the thing itself, which was performed with the assistance of public officials (MANU MILITARI).— D. 6.1; C. 3.32; 7.38.—See ACTIONES IN PERSONAM, ACTIONES ARBITRARIAE, LEGIS ACTIO SACRAMENTO, EXHIBERE, IUS TOLLENDI, IMPENSAE, QUANTI EA RES EST, LITIS AESTIMATIO, AGERE PER SPONSIONEM, FORMULA PETITORIA, LAUDARE AUCTOREM, POSSESSOR FICTUS, DOLO DESINERE POSSIDERE, INTERDICTUM QUEM FUNDUM, DUCI VEL FERRI IUBERE, ADPREHENDERE, LITI SE OFFERRE, HEREDITATIS PETITIO, RESTITUERE, UNUS CASUS.

Leonhard, *RE* 1A; Beauchet, *DS* 4; Cuq, *DS* 5, 902; Sternheim, *NDI* 11; Berger, *OCD* (*s.v. vindicatio*); H. Siber, *Passivlegitimation bei der r. v.*, 1907; Last, *GrZ* 36 (1909) 433; Lenel, *GrZ* 37 (1910) 515; Maria, *Ét Girard* 2 (1913) 223; Betti, *Fil* 1915, 321; *idem, Rend Lomb* 48 (1915) 503; E. Abgarowicz, *Essai sur la preuve dans la r. v.*, Thèse Paris, 1916; Herdlitczka, *ZSS* 49 (1929) 274; Kaser, *ZSS* 51 (1931) 92; *idem, Restituere als Prozessgegenstand*, 1932; *idem, Eigentum und Besitz*, 1943 (*passim*); *idem, Das altröm. ius*, 1949 (*passim*);

Lévy-Bruhl, *RHD* 11 (1932) 205 (= *Quelques problèmes*, 1934, 95); Düll, *ZSS* 54 (1934) 101; Senn, *RHD* 15 (1936) 401; F. Thormann, *Der doppelte Ursprung der mancipatio*, 1943, 29.

Rei vindicatio utilis. A *rei vindicatio* extended to cases lying beyond its normal applicability. Some of these cases were introduced by praetorian jurisdiction, some by imperial legislation of a later period. A *rei vindicatio utilis* was granted, for instance, when the action concerned a thing not identical with that which the owner originally possessed, e.g., a garment that had been made by the defendant from the plaintiff's wool, or a picture painted on the plaintiff's tablet.—See SPECIFICATIO.

Cuq, *DS* 5, 904; Mancaleoni, *StSas* 1 (1900) 11; v. Mayr, *ZSS* 26 26 (1906) 83; Bortolucci, *BIDR* 33 (1923) 151; F. Pringsheim, *Kauf mit fremdem Geld*, 1916, 123.

Reicere. See REIECTIO.

Reiectio civitatis. Giving up Roman citizenship through the acquisition of the citizenship of another state.

Reiectio iudicis. Rejection of a judge. A party to a civil trial had the right to reject a judge who was inacceptable to him for personal reasons. See ALBUM IUDICUM, SORTITIO. Rejection was also permitted in criminal trials in the procedure through QUAESTIONES. It was executed by the accuser and the accused, each having the right to reject the same number. In the year 59 B.C., a *Lex Vatinia* settled the rules for the rejection procedure.

Liebenam, *RE* 1A, 514; Steinwenter, *RE* 9, 2467; Mommsen, *Röm. Strafrecht*, 1899, 214; G. Rotondi, *Leges publicae populi R.*, 1912, 391; Sage, *AmJPhilol* 39 (1918) 367; Gelzer, *Hermes* 63 (1928) 113.

Reiectio militia. Dismissal from military service as a punishment for a minor military offense. Syn. *exauctorare*.

Reicere rem. To throw away a thing. Syn. *relinquere, derelinquere*.—See DERELICTIO.

Relatio. (From *referre*.) See REFERRE.

Relatio. In civil procedure of the later Empire, see CONSULTATIO.—D. 49.1; C. 7.61.

Lécrivain, *DS* 4.

Relatio. In the senate (*referre ad senatum*), a report made by the magistrate, who convoked the senate, to the gathered senators concerning the subject matter which had to be discussed and voted on.

O'Brien-Moore, *RE* Suppl. 6, 707, 768.

Relatio criminis. The bringing in of a counter-accusation by the accused against the accuser in a criminal trial. Such a manoeuver did not impede the proceedings.

Relatum est. See REFERRE.

Relegare pecuniam. To order one's banker (*argentarius*) to make a payment from one's deposit. Syn. *delegare ab argentario*.

Laum, *RE* Suppl. 4, 77.

Relegatio. The expulsion of a citizen ordered either by an administrative act of a magistrate or by judg-ment in a criminal trial. In the latter case the *relegatio* was sometimes combined with additional punishments, such as confiscation of the whole or of a part of the property of the condemned person, loss of Roman citizenship, confinement in a certain place. A milder form of *relegatio* was the exclusion of the wrongdoer from residence in a specified territory. Illicit return was punished with death penalty.—D. 48.22.—See EXILIUM, DEPORTATIO.

Kleinfeller, *RE* 1A; Berger, *OCD*; J. L. Strachan Davidson, *Problems of R. criminal law*, 2 (1912) 64; E. Levy, *Röm. Kapitalstrafe*, 1931, 30; U. Brasiello, *Repressione penale*, 1937, 279; Zmigryder-Konopka, *NRH* 18 (1939) 307.

Relegatio dotis. Leaving on the part of the testator the amount of the dowry to the person to whom he had to restore it in the event of a dissolution of his marriage.

Relevare. To relieve a person from his duties, obligations or charges.

Religio. When used with reference to public officials, judges, etc., conscientiousness, scrupulousness in the fulfillment of official duties.

Kobbert, *RE* 1A; idem, *De verborum religio atque religiosus usu*, Königsberg, 1910; W. Fowler, *The Latin history of the word r.*, Transactions of the third intern. Congress for the History of Religion, 2 (Oxford, 1908).

Religiosus. See LOCUS RELIGIOSUS, RES RELIGIOSAE. In the constitutions of the Christian emperors *religiosus* (and *religiosissimus*) is used of ecclesiastical persons (bishops) and institutions (churches, cemeteries).

Relinquere (rem). Syn. DERELINQUERE.—See DERELICTIO.

Relinquere. In the law of succession, to leave. Refers either to the person (*relinquere heredem* = to leave an heir) who after the death of another is his heir (either instituted in his testament or by intestacy), or to an inheritance (*relinquere hereditatem*), a legacy (*relinquere legatum, fideicommissum*) or freedom (*relinquere libertatem*).

Reliquatio. (From *reliquari*.) An unpaid remnant of a debt.—See RELIQUUM, RESIDUUM.

Reliquator. A person in arrears who owes a part of his debt. A person who owed the fisc or a municipality some money from the management of public matters was excluded from honorific positions until he repaid the rest. This measure did not apply to those who were debtors through private transactions with the fisc or municipalities.

Reliquator vectigalium. A tax-farmer who owed the fisc a part of the rent. He was not admitted to a new lease until he had fully discharged his debt.

Reliquum (reliqua). The balance one owes to a private person or a public body (tax-arrears).

Relocatio (relocare). A renewal of a lease or a hire (see RECONDUCTIO). *Relocatio operis* = hiring another to finish a work which the first contractor failed to complete by the day fixed.—See LOCATIO CONDUCTIO.

Remancipatio (remancipare). A retransfer of a thing through *mancipatio* to the person from whom one acquired it by *mancipatio*, or to a third person. *Remancipatio* also was the retransfer of a son through *mancipatio* to his father from whom the transferor had acquired him through *mancipatio* and had held him as *persona in mancipio* (see MANCIPIUM).—See EMANCIPATIO, DIVORTIUM, COEMPTIO FIDUCIAE CAUSA.
Kaser, *ZSS* 67 (1950) 492.

Remansor. See EMANSOR.

Remedium. Legal procedural measures introduced by praetorian law, *senatusconsulta* or imperial legislation, such as *actio, interdictum, exceptio, restitutio in integrum, appellatio,* etc.
Guarneri-Citati, *Indice*[2] (1927) 78.

Remissio. See REMITTERE.

Remissio mercedis. A reduction of the rent, granted to the lessee of a land in the case of a lean crop (*sterilitas*). The abatement could be conceded with the condition that it would be made good if next year's crop was abundant.

Remissio operis novi nuntiationis. See OPERIS NOVI NUNTIATIO.
Berger, *RE* 9, 1671; 17, 573; *idem, IURA* 1 (1950) 106; 117.

Remittere. Sometimes syn. with *mittere, permittere.*—See the following items, REMISSIO.

Remittere. With reference to wrongdoings and criminal offenses, to forgive, to condone (*remittere crimen, dolum, iniuriam*).—See REMITTERE POENAM.

Remittere actionem. To renounce an action; also to renounce an exception (*remittere exceptionem*) or a servitude (*remittere servitutem*).

Remittere causam (cognitionem). To assign, to allot a civil or criminal case to a judicial magistrate (a praetor, à provincial governor, a *praefectus*) or to transfer a case to the imperial court.

Remittere condicionem. To release a beneficiary of a testament from the necessity of fulfilling a condition imposed in the will.—See CONDICIO TURPIS, CONDICIO IURISIURANDI.

Remittere debitum (obligationem). To release a person from an obligation.

Remittere pignus. To release a pledge (*pignus*) given to a creditor by the debtor.—C. 8.25.

Remittere poenam (multam). To remit a penalty (a fine).

Remotio suspecti tutoris. See TUTOR SUSPECTUS.

Removere. To remove a senator from the senate (see MOVERE SENATU), to remove a guardian from the administration of his ward's property because of negligence or incapacity (see TUTOR SUSPECTUS). *Removere officio* = to remove a public official from office (*propter neglegentiam* = because of negligence in fulfillment of his duties). *Removere* is also applied to the denial of a right of succession (to an inheritance

or legacy). In judicial proceedings *removere* = to exclude from acting in court (*postulatio*).

Remunerare. To give a reward to a person for a service gratuitously rendered. To give such a reward is a kind of liberality since it is not a fulfillment of a legal duty and not even of an *obligatio naturalis,* the only motive being to recompense another for a meritorious performance to which he was not obligated to do.
P. Timbal, *Les donations rémunératoires en dr. rom.,* 1925.

Remuneratio. See REMUNERARE. The noun occurs in later imperial constitutions. *Remuneratio sacra* = a remuneration (liberality) by the emperor.

Renovare locationem. See RELOCATIO, RECONDUCTIO. Syn. *locare ex integro.*

Renuntiare. To renounce (a right, a privilege, an inheritance or a legacy, a legal remedy such as an action, a *querela*).—*Renuntiare* is often syn. with *denuntiare.*

Renuntiare mandatum. A unilateral withdrawal of a mandatary from the mandate. It was admissible only at a time when the mandator notified of the withdrawal could manage the matter himself or by another mandatary.
V. Arangio-Ruiz, *Il mandato,* 1949, 136.

Renuntiare societatem. See SOCIETAS.
Solazzi, *Iura* 2 (1951) 152.

Renuntiatio. (In military law.) Treason. A person (a soldier or a civilian) who betrayed to an enemy important military information (*renuntiatio consiliorum*) was punished with death (by *crematio*).—See PRODITOR.

Renuntiatio. (In public law.) The announcement of the names of the magistrates elected by the *comitia*. From that moment the magistrate was considered *designatus*; see MAGISTRATUS DESIGNATI.
Klingmüller, *RE* 1A.

Renuntiatio legis. An official announcement that a statute was decreed by a popular assembly (*comitia*). After the *renuntiatio* an INTERCESSIO (protestation, veto) was no longer admissible.
Klingmüller, *RE* 1A.

Reparatio temporum. In late postclassical procedure. A plaintiff who did not appear in court before the end of a four-months' period after DENUNTIATIO LITIS lost the case. He could, however, obtain a restoration of the term and permission to appear in court at a later date if his non-appearance was excusable.—C. 7.63.

Renuntiator. See PRODITOR.

Repellere. In civil trials the verb is used of exceptions entered by the defendant against the plaintiff's claim which, when successful, effected the loss of the case by the plaintiff (see EXCEPTIO). When used of a magisterial decision, *repellere* denotes that a petitioner's claim was denied. Sometimes *repellere* = *renuntiare, repudiare* (= to refuse the acceptance of an inheritance or legacy).—See VIM VI REPELLERE LICET.

Repertorium. See INVENTARIUM.

Repetere (repetitio). To claim back, to reclaim what one gave to another (e.g., paying an *indebitum*). "What one received as his property, cannot be claimed back" (D. 12.6.44).—See CONDICTIONES.

Repetere accusationem. To renew an accusation against the same person and for the same crime. A renewed accusation by the same accuser occurred when the judicial magistrate concerned with the matter died or retired from office while the trial was still pending. A new accuser could *repetere accusationem* when the first accuser died or withdrew his accusation. Syn. *repetere reum.*

Repetere actionem. To sue a second time for the same claim. Such repetition was generally excluded according to the rule *bis de eadem re ne sit actio*; see BIS IDEM EXIGERE. The defendant could oppose the plaintiff with the *exceptio rei iudicatae,* when the matter had been decided by a judgment, or the *exceptio rei in iudicium deductae,* when the action under which the claim was brought to court, had been conducted until *litis contestatio.* Only when the first trial was interrupted before *litis contestatio,* a *repetere actionem* was admissible.

Repetere reum. See REPETERE ACCUSATIONEM.

Repetita die. To refer a claim to a former date, to antedate, to compute according to an earlier date.

Repetita praelectio. See EDITIO SECUNDA.

Repetitio. See REPETERE.

Repetitio rerum. In international relations. The formal declaration of war by the *fetiales* had to be preceded by *repetitio rerum,* i.e., a demand for redress of the injury inflicted.—See CLARIGATIO.

　　C. Philippson, *The intern. law and custom of ancient Greece and Rome* 2 (1911) 331.

Repetundae. Literally the term indicates things (*res*) or money (*pecuniae*) which could be claimed back (*repetere*) by the person who gave them to an official person (a magistrate, a provincial governor) under extortion as a bribe. Hence *crimen repetundarum* = the crime of extortion. A series of Republican statutes from the *Lex Calpurnia* (149 B.C.) to the *Lex Iulia* (by Caesar, 59 B.C.) dealt with *repetundae*; the last statute was still in Justinian's legislation the foundation of the penal repression of extortion. Jurisprudence and imperial legislation contributed to the development of the concept of *repetundae* to be punished under the statute. According to later legislation any person who "exercising a magistracy, a power (*potestas*), a curatorship (*curatio*), an embassy, or any other public office, charge or ministry accepted money" (D. 48.11.1 pr.) was liable under the statute. The *Lex Iulia* declared guilty of *repetundae* a judge who took a bribe for rendering (or not rendering) a judgment, a witness for refraining from testimony,

even a senator who received money for expressing a certain opinion in the senate. Sons of officials were also guilty of *repetundae* when taking money with the understanding that they would influence the activity of their fathers. Manifold misdemeanors of officials and persons not embraced by the definition quoted above (which in its general formulation may contain non-classical elements) were subject to the penalties for *crimen repetundarum.* Originally the giver could claim the recovery of the sum he paid under extortion; later, he could claim a double or fourfold amount, within a year after retirement of the official from service. In extreme instances, seizure of the whole property of the condemned person took place. Persons who had a share in the bribe money (*ad quos pecunia pervenit*) were liable as well. A person condemned for *repetundae* could not obtain a magistracy or membership in the senate; he would not be a witness or representative of another in court, or function as a judge. More drastic infractions were punished with exile. Penalties became more and more severe in the course of time. The *Lex Acilia* (of 123 B.C.) contained detailed provisions concerning the procedure in trial for extortion.—D. 48.11; C. 9.27.—For the statutes on *repetundae:* see LEX ACILIA, CALPURNIA, CORNELIA, IULIA, SERVILIA; see also SENATUSCONSULTUM CLAUDIANUM, CONCUSSIO.

　　Kleinfeller, *RE* 1A; Lécrivain, *DS* 4; Berger, *OCD*; *idem, RE* 12, 2390; R. O. Jolliffe, *Phases of corruption in Roman administration in the last half century of the R. Republic,* Chicago, 1919; Blum, *Revue gén. de droit* 46 (1922) 197; v. Premerstein, *ZSS* 48 (1928) 505; J. P. Balsdon, *History of the extortion court at Rome, PBritSR* 14 (1938); F. De Visscher, *Les édits d'Auguste découverts à Cyrene,* 1940, 138; Sherwin-White, *PBritSR* 17 (1949) 5; *idem, JRS* 42 (1952) 43; Henderson, *JRS* 41 (1951) 71.

Repignerare. To redeem a thing given as a pledge (*pignus*) to a creditor by paying the debt.

Replicatio. An exception (see EXCEPTIO) opposed by the plaintiff to an exception of the defendant. Through *replicatio* the plaintiff rejects what the defendant's exception asserted. To a *replicatio* the defendant may again reply by an exception called *duplicatio* by Gaius, once *triplicatio* by Ulpian. An example of a *replicatio* is as follows: if the defendant opposed to the claim of the plaintiff the *exceptio pacti de non petendo,* i.e., that the plaintiff had agreed not to sue the defendant in court, the plaintiff might oppose a *replicatio* to the effect that by a later agreement (*pactum*) the first had been annulled or limited to a certain time.—Inst. 4.14.

　　Leonhard, *RE* 1A.

Replicatio legis Cinciae. See REPLICATIO, LEX CINCIA. If a donor claimed back the thing he had given as a gift, as contrary to the provisions of the *Lex Cincia,* and the donee opposed an exception that the thing had been donated and delivered (*exceptio rei donatae et traditae*) and therefore could not be claimed back, the donor might reply by *replicatio legis Cinciae,* to the effect that the ownership of the thing donated was not acquired by the donee, e.g., because the thing, a *res mancipi,* was conveyed through *traditio,* and not by MANCIPATIO, which was necessary for the transfer of ownership of the thing donated.

Reposcere. To claim a thing which had to be returned to the claimant, e.g., a deposit or a thing given as a PRECARIUM or COMMODATUM.

Repraesentare. To pay, to perform an obligation, which is owed on a condition or at a fixed date, before the condition is materialized or before the due time. *Commodum repraesentationis* = the profit a creditor has in such a case, when the debtor pays the debt in advance before it is due.—In a more general sense *repraesentare = praestare, solvere, reddere* (post-classical use).

Schnorr v. Carolsfeld, *Fschr Koschaker* 1 (1939) 103.

Reprehendere (reprehensio). To blame, to reprove, to find fault with a person.

Reprehensa Mucii capita. (Also entitled *Notata Mucii.*) A collection of critical notes written by the jurist SERVIUS SULPICIUS RUFUS on the work of his predecessor Quintus Mucius Scaevola, see MUCIUS.

Reprobare. To disapprove, to reject (another's opinion). Ant. PROBARE.

Reprobus. False, forged. *Reproba pecunia (reprobi nummi)* = false money (coins). Syn. *adulterinus.* "Payment made with bad money does not discharge the payer" (D. 13.7.24.1).

Repromissio. (From *repromittere.*) A kind of CAUTIO by which a debtor promises through *stipulatio* the performance of an already existing obligation or of an obligation not suable under the law.

Repromissio secundum mancipium. A stipulation by which the seller of a thing guarantees the buyer against eviction.—See EVICTIO, SATISDATIO SECUNDUM MANCIPIUM.

Repudiare. To refuse to accept, to reject. The most frequent use of the verb is with reference to acquisitions to be made under a testamentary disposition (an inheritance, a legacy) or under the law (on intestacy) from another's estate.—C. 6.19; 31.—For *repudiare matrimonium, uxorem,* see REPUDIUM.—In procedural language *repudiare* = to reject (an appeal).

Repudiatio hereditatis (bonorum possessionis). See REPUDIARE.

H. Krüger, *ZSS* 64 (1944) 394.

Repudium. A unilateral breaking up of a betrothal; see SPONSALIA. The term refers also to the dissolution of a marriage existing made by one of the spouses either by an oral declaration before witnesses, by a letter, or through the intermediary of a messenger (*per nuntium*) who transmitted to the other party the wish that the marriage be solved (*mittere, remittere repudium,* or *nuntium*). The actual interruption of common living as husband and wife had to accompany such declarations. The written form

(*libellus repudii*) became mandatory in the later Empire. A *repudium ex iusta causa* caused pecuniary losses (the loss of the dowry or nuptial denations) to the party whose bad behavior justified the divorce. The term *repudium* occurs also in cases of a divorce of the spouses.—D. 24.2; C. 5.17.—See DIVORTIUM.

Klingmüller, *RE* 1A; E. Levy, *Hergang der röm. Ehescheidung,* 1925, 55; Solazzi, *BIDR* 34 (1925) 312; Basanoff, *St Riccobono* 3 (1936) 175.

Reputare (reputatio). To calculate, to compute, in particular to take into account the counterclaims of the debtor. Syn. *computare, imputare.*—C. 2,47.

Requirere. To inquire after, to search for somebody (e.g., a runaway slave) or anything (e.g., a stolen thing), to investigate. A particular application of the term occurs with reference to persons absent (fugitives) against whom a criminal trial was to be instituted, the so-called *requirendi* (the searched for ones). Their names were publicly announced in posters and their property was seized unless they appeared in court within a year from the public summons.—D. 48.17; C. 9.40.

Res. Used in the juristic language in various senses; it applies to both corporeal things and incorporeal, abstract conceptions. See RES CORPORALES. For the division of things, see the items below.—D. 1.8; Inst. 2.1.—*Res* (in sing.) also refers to the entire property of a person (see EX RE ALICUIUS ADQUIRERE, IN REM VERSIO) and in this sense it is syn. with BONA, PATRIMONIUM. *Res* is often syn. with HEREDITAS. The use of the term *res* by the jurists ranges from the most general meaning of "everything that exists" (*in rerum natura, in rebus humanis esse*) to specific objects. An interpretative rule by Ulpian says: "the term *res* comprises both *causae* (legal relations, judicial matters, see CAUSA) and *iura* (rights)," D. 50.16.23. The inclusion of the vague term *causae* renders this saying likewise indefinite. With reference to judicial trials, *res* means both the object of the controversy (see QUANTI EA RES EST, QUA DE RE AGITUR) and the litigation itself; see RES IUDICATA, RES IN IUDICIUM DEDUCTA, ACTUS RERUM. In the law of contracts *res* indicates the physical delivery of a thing to another person which was the decisive element in the so-called real contracts (*contractus re factus, obligatio re contracta, re contrahere,* see CONTRACTUS).—See OBLIGARE REM.

Leonhard, *RE* 1A; Beauchet, *DS* 4; S. Di Marzo, *Le cose e i diritti sulle cose,* 1922; Grosso, *St Besta* 1 (1939) 33; G. Scherillo, *Lezioni. Le cose* 1, 1945; Kreller, *ZSS* 66 (1948) 572.

Res amotae. See ACTIO RERUM AMOTARUM, RETENTIONES DOTALES.

Res capitalis. See CAUSA CAPITALIS.

Res castrenses. Things belonging to a PECULIUM CASTRENSE; also things used by a soldier during his military service.

Res communes. Things belonging to two or more owners (co-owners, co-heirs) as a common property. —See COMMUNIO, ACTIO COMMUNI DIVIDUNDO.—C. 4.52; 8.20.

Res communes omnium. Things which "by natural law are the common property of all men" (D. 1.8.2 pr., 1), such as air, flowing water, the sea and its shores, etc. They could not be appropriated by a private individual.—See RES PUBLICAE, AËR, AQUA PROFLUENS, MARE, LITUS.

> Pernice, *Fg Dernburg*, 1900; Debray, *Rev. générale de droit* 45 (1921) 1; Branca, *AnTr* 12 (1941) ; G. Lombardi, *Ricerche in tema di ius gentium*, 1946, 90.

Res corporales. Physical things which "by their nature can be touched" (D. 1.8.1.1). Ant. *res incorporales.*

> Naber, *RStDIt* 13 (1940) 379; Villey, *RHD* 25 (1946–47) 209; Pflüger, *ZSS* 65 (1947) 339; Monier, *RHD* 26 (1948) 374; *idem, St Solazzi* 1948, 360; Albanese, *AnPal* 20 (1949) 232.

Res cottidianae. The title of a work (in seven books) ascribed to the jurist Gaius, "the everyday legal matters." It is of a rather elementary nature. The authenticity of the work which appears in the sources also under the title *"Aurea"* (= Golden words, rules) is not beyond doubt.

> Arangio-Ruiz, *St Bonfante* 1 (1929) 495; Albertario, *Studi* 3 (1936) 95; Felgenträger, *Symb Frib Lenel,* 1931, 365 (Bibl.) ; Di Marzo, *BIDR* 51–52 (1948) 1.

Res creditae. Things (money) given as a loan.—D. 12.1; C. 4.1.—See CREDERE, MUTUUM.

Res cuius (quarum) commercium non est. Generally in literature called by the non-Roman term *res extra commercium* = things which cannot be the object of exchange or of any legal commercial transaction between private individuals, such as RES DIVINI IURIS, RES COMMUNES OMNIUM.—See COMMERCIUM.

> Scherillo, *loc. cit.* 29; G. Longo, *St Bonfante* 3, 1930; Biondi, *St Riccobono* 4, 1936; W. G. Vegting, *Domaine public et res extra c.* (Alphen a. d. Rijn, 1950) ; Kaser, *St Arangio-Ruiz* 2 (1952) 161.

Res derelictae. See DERELICTIO.

Res divini iuris. Things under divine law, as RES RELIGIOSAE, SACRAE, SANCTAE. They are not negotiable and excluded from any legal transaction. Ant. RES HUMANI IURIS.

> Scherillo, *loc. cit.* 40; Archi, *SDHI* 3 (1937) 5.

Res dominica. The private property of the emperor. C. 7.38; 11.67.—See RES PRIVATA CAESARIS.

Res dubiae. Doubtful legal questions arising from ambiguous expressions used, e.g., by a testator in his last will. In such cases, broadly discussed in D. 34.5, "always preference should be given to the more benevolent (benign, liberal, *benigniora*) interpretation" (D. 50.17.56). The solution should be in favor of the act and avoid its annulment.

> Berger, *ACIVer* 2 (1951) 187 (= *Sem* 9 [1951] 36).

Res extra commercium. See RES CUIUS COMMERCIUM NON EST.

Res extra patrimonium (nostrum). Things which cannot be in private ownership (see RES PUBLICAE, RES COMMUNES OMNIUM), nor the object of any legal transaction between private individuals; see RES CUIUS COMMERCIUM NON EST. Ant. *res in patrimonio nostro* = all things not expressly excluded from private ownership.

> Scherillo, *loc. cit.* 29; Branca, *AnTr* 12 (1941).

Res facti. A matter of fact, a factual situation. Syn. *quaestio facti, est facti.* Ant. *res iuris* = a matter of law.

Res familiaris. Private property, patrimony.

Res fiscales. Things belonging to the fisc (FISCUS). "They are in some way private property of the emperor" (D. 43.8.2.9).—C. 10.4.

> Vassalli, *StSen* XXV (1908) 232 (= *St giuridici* 2 [1939] 5).

Res furtivae. Things taken by theft (FURTUM) from the owner or from whoever holds them in his name. They could not be acquired by USUCAPIO either by the thief himself or by any one who got them from him, according to a rule of the Twelve Tables, and a later statute, the LEX ATINIA. Syn. *res subreptae*; in earlier times the stolen thing was called also *furtum.*—See USUCAPIO.

> Berger, *RE* 12, 2331; v. Lübtow, *Fschr Schulz* 1 (1951) 263.

Res gestae divi Augusti. An autobiography of the emperor Augustus, written in the last months of his life (finished probably in A.D. 13). It contains a record of the emperor's achievements, political and military. The original, written in Latin was read after his death in a solemn session of the senate; Greek translations were made and sent to Greek-speaking provinces where they were engraved on bronze tablets and set up publicly. Extensive fragments in both languages are known (see MONUMENTUM ANCYRANUM). Augustus presents himself in this *"Index rerum a se gestarum"* (= a register of things achieved by himself) as a head of the state who governed it, authorized and supported by the confidence of the senate and of the people.—See AUCTORITAS PRINCIPIS.

> Momigliano, *OCD*; J. Gagé, *R. g. d. A.,* Paris, 1935; Arangio-Ruiz, *SDHI* 5 (1939) 570; Volkmann, *Bursians Jahresberichte über die Fortschritte der klass. Altertumswissenschaft,* Suppl. 276 (1942, Bibl.) ; Städler, *ZSS* 62 (1942) 120 (Bibl.) ; *Acta Divi Augusti* 1 (*Regia Academia Italica,* Rome, 1945) ; P. De Francisci, *Arcana imperii* 3, 1 (1948) 220; E. Schönbauer, *SbWien* 224, 2 (1946) ; Levi, *Rivista di filologia,* 1947, 209; A. Guarino, *R. g. d. A., Testo, traduzione e commento,* 1947; Pugliese Carratelli, *Imp. Caesar Augustus, Index rerum a se gestarum,* 1947; Chilver, *Augustus and the Roman Constitution, Historia* 1 (Baden-Baden, 1951) 408.

Res hereditariae. Things belonging to an inheritance HEREDITAS. Syn. *corpora hereditaria.* Together, all *res hereditariae* of one estate are also called UNIVERSITAS (*bonorum*). *Res hereditariae* are considered as belonging to no one until someone qualifies as heir (HERES).

Res hominum. See RES PRIVATAE.

Res hostiles. Things belonging to an enemy of the Roman state, see HOSTIS. If at the outbreak of war they are on Roman soil, they become property of the occupants, and not public property (RES PUBLICAE). —See OCCUPATIO RERUM HOSTILIUM.

Res humani iuris. All things which are not *res divini iuris*. They are governed by human law. The distinction between *res humani iuris* and RES DIVINI IURIS is the main division of things (*summa divisio rerum*). *Res humani iuris* are either public (RES PUBLICAE) or private property (RES PRIVATAE).

    Branca, *AnTr* 12, 1941.

Res immobiles. Immovables: land (FUNDUS) and buildings (AEDES, AEDIFICIA). Syn. *res soli,* or *res quae solo continentur* (= which consist in land). Ant. RES MOBILES. As early as the Twelve Tables, a differentiation was introduced with regard to the acquisition through USUCAPIO, and the interdictal protection was built up on the distinction between *res immobiles* and *res mobiles*. The distinction acquired particular importance in Justinian's law when the division of things into RES MANCIPI and RES NEC MANCIPI became insignificant.

    Schiller, *ACDR*, Rome 2, 1935; Kübler, *St Bonfante* 3, 1930; Naber, *RStDIt* 14, 1941; Di Marzo, *BIDR* 49–50 (1948) 236.

Res in iudicium deducta. A judicial controversy which after the joinder of issue (LITIS CONTESTATIO) passed to the second stage of the trial, before the private judge (*iudex*). The defendant is protected against a reiterated claim in the same matter by an exception that the claim has already been the object of a trial (*exceptio rei in iudicium deductae*). This exception is similar to the EXCEPTIO REI IUDICATAE. The difference is that the latter could be applied when a judgment has already been rendered.—See LITIS CONTESTATIO.

    M. Kaser, *Restituere als Prozessgegenstand*, 1932.

Res in publico usu. Things belonging to the state, the use of which is allowed to all people, as streets, theatres.

    W. G. Vegting, *Domaine public et res extra commercium* (Alphen a. d. Rijn, 1950) 52; H. Vogt, *Das Erbbaurecht*, 1950, 22.

Res in patrimonio nostro. See RES EXTRA PATRIMONIUM.

Res incorporales. Things "which cannot be touched, such as those consisting in rights, e.g., an inheritance, a usufruct, obligations" (D. 1.8.1.1), immaterial things. Ant. RES CORPORALES.—Inst. 2.2.

Res integra. See INTEGER.

Res iudicata. "A controversy which was concluded by the judgment of a judge" (D. 42.1.1). *Res iudicata* creates a new legal situation between the parties to the trial thus finished and "is considered as truth"

(*pro veritate accipitur,* D. 1.5.25). The sources speak of an *auctoritas* (authority, validity, legal power) *rei iudicatae*, whereas *auctoritas rerum similiter iudicatarum* (= authority of identical judgments) is referred to as reflecting the judicial practice of courts constantly (*perpetuo*) manifested through identical judgments in similar legal controversies (D. 1.3.38). Justinian ordered (C. 7.45.13) that "judgments should be rendered not according to precedents (*exempla*) but in conformity with the laws."—D. 42.1; C. 7.52.—See IUDICATUM.

    Esmein, *Mél Gerardin* 1907, 229; Weiss, *Fschr Wach* 2 (1913); E. Betti, *Limiti soggettivi della cosa iudicata,* 1922; Guarneri-Citati, *BIDR* 33 (1924) 204; Dauvillier, *Iniuria iudicis, Recueil Acad. Législ. Toulouse* 13 (1937) 147; Jolowicz, *BIDR* 46 (1939) 394; Vazny, *BIDR* 47 (1940) 108; Siber, *ZSS* 65 (1947) 1.

Res iuris. See RES FACTI.

Res litigiosa. The object of a pending suit after *litis contestatio*. Its alienation was void and so was its dedication to a god in order to make it a RES SACRA. The defendant holding the thing was protected against any claim by a third person through an exception (*exceptio rei litigiosae*).—D. 44.6; C. 8.36.

    Gradenwitz, *ZSS* 53 (1933) 409.

Res lucrativae. Things which one acquired without any compensation, EX CAUSA LUCRATIVA (e.g., an inheritance, a legacy, a donation). Such things were in later law charged with a special tax, *descriptio*.— C. 10.36.

Res mancipi. Things the ownership of which is transferable only by the solemn act of MANCIPATIO (hence the name) or by IN IURE CESSIO. *Res mancipi* included buildings and land on Italian soil, rustic (not urban) servitudes connected with such land, slaves, and farm animals of draft and burden, such as "oxen, horses, mules, asses" (Gaius, Inst. 1.120). All these things and rights (servitudes) represented the highest value in a primitive rural economy, and the wealth of a Roman peasant consisted primarily in them. The distinction lost its importance in the later Empire; officially it was not abolished until Justinian who destroyed its basic idea by abrogating the requirements of solemn formalities in the transfer of ownership of *res mancipi*. Ant. RES NEC MANCIPI.— See MANCIPATIO.

    Marchi, *AG* 85 (1921); Bonfante, *Scr giuridici* 3 (1918); De Visscher, *SDHI* 2 (1936) 263 (= *Nouvelles Études,* 1949, 236); Ferrabino, *SDHI* 3 (1937); Cornil, *RH* 1937, 555; Clerici, *Economia e finanza di Roma* 1 (1943) 311; Hernandez Tejero, *AHDE* 16 (1945) 290.

Res militaris. Military matters, legal rules concerning soldiers and their legal situation, military discipline, and organization, and particularly military penal law. Several jurists (Tarruntenus, Arrius Menander, Macer, and Paul) wrote monographs on military law.—D. 49.16; C.12.35(36).

Res mobiles. Movables. Syn. *mobilia*. Ant. RES IMMOBILES, *res soli*. The distinction is of importance in various institutions of Roman private law and procedure (POSSESSIO, USUCAPIO, MANCIPATIO, DOS, INTERDICTA, etc.). A special category of *res mobiles* (syn. *res moventes, moventia*) consists of RES SE MOVENTES.

Res nec mancipi. See RES MANCIPI.

G. Segrè, *ATor* 1936; Solazzi, *ACNSR* (2. Congr.) 1931; Tejero, *AHDE* 16 (1945) 290.

Res nullius. Things belonging to nobody. He who takes possession of them (OCCUPATIO) acquires ownership by this very act provided that they are accessible to private ownership since some *res nullius,* such as RES DIVINI IURIS, are excluded from it.—See HEREDITAS IACENS, FURTUM, SERVUS SINE DOMINO.

Riccobono, *NDI* 11.

Res nummariae. See NUMMARIUS.

Res peculiares. Things belonging to the *peculium* of a slave or a *filius familias,* or affairs connected with the management of a *peculium.*—See PECULIUM.

Res praesentes. See HYPOTHECA OMNIUM BONORUM.

Res principalis. See PRINCIPALIS.

Res privata Caesaris (principis). The purely private property of the emperor. From the time of Septimius Severus it was neatly separately from the PATRIMONIUM CAESARIS. Syn. RATIO PRIVATA.

Liebenam, *RE* 1A; Lécrivain, *DS* 3, 961; L. Mitteis, *Röm. Privatrecht* 1 (1908) 358; Haijje, *Histoire de la justice seignoriale 1. Les domaines des Empereurs,* 1927.

Res privatae. Private property, things "belonging to individuals" (D. 1.8.1 pr.). Syn. RES HOMINUM, ant. RES PUBLICAE.

Res propria. See RES SUA.

Res publica (respublica). The term corresponds in a certain measure to the modern conception of the State, but is not synonymous with it. It comprises the sum of the rights and interests of the Roman people, *populus Romanus,* understood as a whole. Therefore it often means simply the Roman people and is separate from the emperor, the Roman empire, the fisc as well as from other public bodies, such as *municipia,* or *coloniae* which are sometimes also called *res publicae,* but different from the Roman one. The meaning of *res publica* is particularly manifest when the sources speak of services rendered to the *res publica,* of holding a high office in the *res publica* or of a man's being absent in the interest or for the benefit of the *res publica (rei publicae causa abesse)* which saved him from detrimental consequences his absence might otherwise bring him.—See ABSENTIA, SENATUSCONSULTUM ULTIMUM, INTEREST ALICUIUS.

Rosenberg, *RE* 1A; R. Stark, *R. p.,* Diss. Tübingen, 1937; Lombardi, *AG* 126 (1941) 200; idem, *Ricerche in tema di ius gentium,* 1946, 49; De Francisci, *SDHI* 10 (1944) 150; Guarino, *RIDA* 1 (1948) 95; Nocera, *AnPer* 58 (1948) 5.

Res publicae. Public property, such as theatres, market places, rivers, harbors, etc. *Publicum* is all that "belongs to the Roman people" (D. 50.16.15). Therefore the *res publicae* may be used by every one, e.g., fishing in public rivers; see FLUMINA. On the contrary RES COMMUNES OMNIUM were not considered property of the Roman people although their use was accessible to all citizens.—D. 50.8; C. 11.31.

Vassalli, *StSen* 25 (1908) = *St giuridici* 2 (1939); G. Scherillo, *Lezioni. Le cose* 1 (1945) 89; G. Lombardi, *Ricerche in tema di ius gentium,* 1946, 49; Branca, *AnTr* 12 (1941) 78; idem, *St Redenti* 1 (1951) 179.

Res pupillares. The property (the affairs) of a ward (*pupillus*).—D. 27.9; C. 5.37.

Res quae pondere numero mensurave constant. Things which are weighed, counted or measured, such as wine, oil, grain, coined money, etc. When given in loan, the debtor returns things of the same kind, and not the same things *in specie.*—See MUTUUM.

Brassloff, *Wiener Studien* 36 (1919) 348; Savagnone, *BIDR* 55-56 (1952) 18.

Res quae usu consumuntur. Things the normal use of which consists in full or partial consumption. Such things, as e.g., articles of food, cannot be the object of transactions in which the restitution of the things given in use is involved, as USUS, USUSFRUCTUS, COMMODATUM.—D. 7.5.—See QUASI USUSFRUCTUS.

Res religiosae. Things "dedicated to the gods of lower regions" (*diis Manibus,* Gaius Inst. 2.4), such as tombs or burial grounds. They belong to the category of RES DIVINI IURIS. A piece of land being in private ownership became LOCUS RELIGIOSUS when the owner or another person acting with his permission, buried a human body in it. A burial by an unauthorized person did not render the soil *religiosus.* With the permission of the pontiffs, the owner could remove the corpse, and had a praetorian action against the wrongdoer for damages. *Res religiosae* could not be the object of a legal transaction. The owner who legally made a *res religiosa* of his land, especially when the funeral of the deceased person was his duty, had no ownership on the place, but he acquired a special right on the grave, IUS SEPULCRI, which implied various duties, such as taking care of the tomb, observing sepulcral cult, sacrifices, and the right to bury other dead there (*ius mortuum inferendi*).—D. 11.7; C. 3.44.—See SACRILEGIUM.

Leonhard, *RE* 1A (*s.v. religiosa*); Toutain, *DS* 4; C. Fadda, *St. e questioni di dir.* 1 (1910); Cuq, *RHD* 9 (1930) 383; G. Scherillo, *Lezioni. Le cose* 1 (1945) 48.

Res sacrae. Sacred things, i.e., consecrated to the gods in heaven by virtue of a statute "through the authority of the Roman people, by a decree of the Senate" (Gaius, Inst. 2.4; 5), or by the Emperor. They belong to the RES DIVINI IURIS. In Justinian's law *res sacrae* were also gifts "duly dedicated to the service of God" (Inst. 2.1.8).—See SACRILEGIUM.

A. Galante, *Condizione giuridica delle cose sacre,* 1903; G. Hertling, *Konsekration und r. s.,* Diss. München, 1911; Brassloff, *Studien zur röm. Rechtsgesch.,* 1925; G. Scherillo, *Lezioni. Le cose* 1 (1945) 40.

Res sanctae. Hallowed things, such as city walls and gates. Any wrong done to them was punished by death.—See RES DIVINI IURIS.

Res se (sese, per se) moventes (or moventia). Things moving by themselves, such as slaves and animals. This type of things (mentioned first in the fifth century) was added to the twofold classification: RES IMMOBILES and RES MOBILES.

Res singulae (singulares). Single, individual things, not composed of several things, but made up as a whole from one substance (*corpus quod uno spiritu continetur*). Ant. CORPUS EX COHAERENTIBUS, a complex of things, such as an inheritance (HEREDITAS), the whole property of a person (BONA).

Bianco, *NDI* 4, 371 (*s.v. cose semplici*).

Res soli. See RES MOBILES.

Res sua (propria). One was excluded from certain activities in affairs of one's own, e.g., from being judge (see IUDEX IN RE PROPRIA) or witness (see TESTIS IN RE PROPRIA), or from giving consent as a guardian to his ward's transaction when his own interests were involved. The affairs of one's father, wife, children, and freedmen were also considered *res sua.* Syn. *causa propria.*—See COGNITOR IN REM SUAM, PROCURATOR IN REM SUAM.

Gonnet, *RHD* 16 (1937) 196.

Res subreptae. See RES FURTIVAE, LEX ATINIA.

Berger, *RE* 12, 2331.

Res turpis. Syn. *turpis causa.*—See CONDICTIO OB TURPEM CAUSAM.

F. Schwarz, *Die Grundlage der condictio,* 1952, 169.

Res universitatis. Things belonging to a corporate body, primarily of public law as *civitates, municipia. Res universitatis* include, e.g., theatres and stadia.

Res uxoria. Dowry.—See DOS.

Res vi possessae. Things taken by force from the owner or from whoever possessed them for him. They were barred from USUCAPIO to the same extent as stolen things (RES FURTIVAE).—See LEX IULIA ET PLAUTIA, VIS LEX ATINIA.

Berger, *RE* Suppl. 7, 405.

Resarcire. To restore, to make good (losses, damages). Syn. *sarcire.*

Rescindere (rescissio). To annul, to make void, to repeal. The verb applies to judicial judgments (*sententiae*), agreements between private persons, legal effects resulting from certain situations (e.g., *usucapio*), wills, etc., annulled either by law, a magisterial order, a judicial judgment or another remedy (e.g., *in integrum restitutio*) at request of a person interested in the rescission.—D. 49.8; C. 7.50.

Hellmann, *ZSS* 24 (1903) 94.

Rescindere venditionem. To annul a sale.—D. 18.5; C. 4.44.—See EMPTIO VENDITIO, REDHIBITIO.

Rescindere usucapionem. See ACTIO RESCISSORIA, USUCAPIO.

Rescissio. See RESCINDERE.

Rescissoria actio. See ACTIO RESCISSORIA.

Rescribere. To answer by writing. The verb is used both of written answers given by jurists to questions on which they were asked for an opinion (see RESPONSA PRUDENTIUM) and of written answers (decisions) of the emperors (see RESCRIPTA PRINCIPUM).

Rescripta principum. Written answers given by the emperor to queries of officials (*relatio, consultatio, suggestio*) or to petitions of private persons (*preces. libellus, supplicatio*). The rescripts were issued either on the petition itself in the form of a SUBSCRIPTIO or in a separate letter (EPISTULAE PRINCIPUM). A rescript expressed the emperor's opinion upon a legal question or a decision in a specific case. It often gave rise to a legal innovation when the emperor's view introduced a new legal rule which, although in principle binding only in the case for which it was issued, nevertheless, because it emanated from the emperor's authority, easily could acquire a general binding force. In particular, when a specific rule was repeatedly expressed by various emperors (phrases like *imperatores saepe rescripserunt, saepe [saepissime] rescriptum est,* and the like, occur frequently in juristic writings), it became law in fact. For the development of a special proceeding in civil matters by imperial rescript, see CONSULTATIO.—C. 1.23.—See CONSTITUTIONES PRINCIPUM, LEGITIMATIO PER RESCRIPTUM PRINCIPIS, LIBER LIBELLORUM RESCRIPTORUM.

Klingmüller, *RE* 1A, 1668; Cuq, *DS* 4, 952; Lécrivain, *DS* 4; Berger, *OCD*; Wilcken, *Hermes* 55 (1920) 1; Sickle, *ClPhilol* 23 (1928) 270; W. Felgenträger, *Antikes Lösungsrecht,* 1933, 3; F. v. Schwind, *Zur Frage der Publikation,* 1940, 167; De Robertis, *AnBari* 4 (1941) 281; L. Vinci, *AnCat* 1 (1947) 320; De Dominicis, *I destinatari dei rescritti imperiali, Ann. Univ. Ferrara* 8, parte 3 (1950); Wolff, *ZSS* 69 (1952) 128.

Rescriptio. RESCRIPTUM. See the foregoing item.

Rescriptum Domitiani de medicis. (On physicians.) See EDICTUM VESPASIANI.

Residua (residuae pecuniae). Sums embezzled by public officials. The LEX IULIA PECULATUS contained some specific provisions concerning *residua,* hence the statute was named also *Lex Iulia de residuis.*—D. 48.13.—See PECULATUS.

Acta Divi Augusti 1 (Rome, 1945) 165.

Residuum. A remainder. The noun refers in particular to the sum which remained due because the amount obtained by a creditor from the sale of his debtor's pledge (*pignus, hypotheca*) did not cover the whole sum owed.—See HYPEROCHA.

Manigk, *RE* 20, 1257.

Resignare. To unseal a document, primarily a sealed testament either for the official opening (see APERTURA TESTAMENTI) or by a private person for purposes of a forgery. Illegal removing the seals from a testament was punished under the *Lex Cornelia de falsis.*—See FALSUM.

Resistere. To oppose, to resist. The term is primarily used of physical resistance to another's force (*vis*) in self-defense.

Resolvere. To annul, to rescind a transaction either by mutual consent of both contracting parties (*contrario consensu*) or, in specific circumstances, by a unilateral act of one of the persons involved. *Resolvi* to be rescinded, to become void (e.g., a mandate, *mandatum,* by the death of one party).

Resolvi sub condicione. A conditional transaction or testamentary disposition became null through the fulfillment of the condition if the act had contained a clause providing for its rescission in the event of fulfillment.

Respicere. To take into consideration, to have regard to. The jurists used the verb in calling attention to specific points which were decisive for the juristic evaluation of the case under discussion.

Respondere. See RESPONSA PRUDENTIUM, IUS RESPONDENDI, PROPONERE.

Responsa. A type of juristic writing. The jurists used to publish their answers (see RESPONSA PRUDENTIUM) in collections entitled *Responsa.* We know of *responsa* of Labeo, Sabinus, Neratius, Marcellus, Scaevola, Papinian, Paul, Ulpian, and some other jurists. The adaptation of the original *responsa* for publication required sometimes the addition of specific argumentation, particularly when opinions of other jurists were being rejected. Some jurists dealt with the cases, on which they had given opinions (*responsa*) as respondent lawyers, in other works, such as *Quaestiones,* or *Digesta* (Celsus, Julian, Marcellus) and *vice versa,* they inserted some real or fictitious cases they discussed as teachers in the works published as *Responsa.*

Berger, *RE* 10, 1173.

Responsa pontificum. Opinions of the pontiffs on questions concerning sacral law, in particular, whether an intended sacral act was admissible or an act already performed was legal. *Responsa pontificum* were given also at the request of magistrates.

F. Schulz, *History of R. legal science,* 1946, 16.

Responsa prudentium. Oral or written answers (opinions), given by the jurists when they were queried by persons involved in a legal controversy or in litigation. *Responsa* were given also to magistrates or judges if they addressed themselves to a jurist for opinion on a legal problem. The giving of *responsa* was an old Roman custom, going back to the times when the pontiffs were the exclusive experts in law (see RESPONSA PONTIFICUM). *Responsa* are given in writing when they had to be presented in court. "The answers of the jurists are the views and opinions of those to whom it was permitted to lay down the laws (*iura condere*). If the opinions of all of them agree, that which they so hold stands in the place of a statute. However, if they disagree,

the judge is free to follow the opinion he pleases." These rules are attributed by Gaius (Inst. 1.7) to a reform by the emperor Hadrian. See CONDERE IURA, IUS RESPONDENDI, OPTINERE LEGIS VICEM. The term *responsa* does not cover opinions of the jurists expressed in theoretical discussions or in their literary products. The importance of the responding activity of the jurists suffered somewhat after the codification of the praetorian Edict under Hadrian (see EDICTUM PERPETUUM) and the granting of *ius respondendi* became certainly rarer (if practiced at all), while on the other hand, the authority of those jurists who participated in the emperor's council (CONSILIUM PRINCIPIS) became predominant. Some problems in the field of the *ius respondendi* have remained still controversial despite the copious recent literature. As a matter of fact, collections of *responsa* (see RESPONSA), reflecting the responding activity of the jurists, appear through the century after Hadrian. For the influence of the *responsa prudentium* on the development of the law, see IURISPRUDENTIA.

Berger, *RE* 10, 1167; Wenger, *RE* 2A, 2427; Cuq, *DS* 4 (*s.v. prudentium r.*); Anon., *NDI* 10 (*s.v. prudentium r.*); Pringsheim, *JRS* 24 (1934) 146; Wieacker, in *Romanistische Studien, Freiburger rechtsgesch. Abhandlungen* 5 (1935) 43; Arangio-Ruiz, *StSas* 16 (1938) 17; De Zulueta, *TulLR* 22 (1947) 173; for earlier literature, see Massei, *Scr Ferrini* (Univ. Pavia, 1946) 430; for further recent literature, see IUS RESPONDENDI.

Responsio (responsum). As a part of the STIPULATIO, the answer of the debtor assuming an obligation to the question (*interrogatio*) of the creditor.

Responsio (respondere). In a trial the reply of the defendant or his representative to the presentation of the case by the plaintiff; see NARRATIO. *Responsio* comprises all means of defense (*defensio*) used by the defendant for the denial of the plaintiff's claim.

Responsio in iure. The answer given by a party to a trial questioned *in iure* by the magistrate; see INTERROGATIO IN IURE.

Betti, *ATor* 50 (1914–15) 389.

Responsitare. A rare term indicating the responding activity (*respondere*) of the jurists.—See RESPONSA PRUDENTIUM.

Restipulatio. (In interdictal procedure.) See AGERE PER SPONSIONEM, INTERDICTUM.

Restipulatio tertiae partis. See SPONSIO TERTIAE PARTIS.

Restituere. To reinstate (a building, a construction, a road, and the like) to its former condition (*in pristinum statum*). *Restituere* = "to take away what one did (constructed on another's property) or to restore on its place what was taken away" (D. 43.8.2.43). In this sense *restituere* is used in the formulae of INTERDICTA RESTITUTORIA ("*restituas*"), i.e., restoration into such condition as to enable the plaintiff to regain the full utility (*omnis utilitas*) he had before the destruction or damage caused by the defendant. *Restituere* also involved the compensation for all losses and irreparable damages.

Restituere (rem, hereditatem, bona). To return, to restore (a thing, an inheritance) with all fruits and proceeds derived therefrom. "When the words 'you are to restore (*restituas*)' are used in a law, the proceeds also are to be restored although nothing expressly has been said thereof" (D. 50.7.173.1). *Restituere* with reference to guardianship or curatorship (*restituere tutelam, curam*) = to render accounts concerning the management of the ward's property and affairs by the guardian (curator) when the guardianship (curatorship) came to an end.

Levy, *ZSS* 36 (1915) 30; G. Maier, *Prätorische Bereicherungsklagen*, 1931, 160; M. Kaser, *R. als Prozessgegenstand*, 1932.

Restitutio in integrum. A reinstatement into the former legal position. This was an extraordinary praetorian remedy (*auxilium*) granted at the request of a person who had suffered an inequitable loss or was threatened by such a loss. A thorough investigation of the case (*causae cognitio*) preceded the *in integrum restitutio* as a result of which the praetor could annul through a decree (*decretum*) a transaction, valid according to the *ius civile*. He passed such a decree when reasons of equity appeared to him sufficient enough to treat legally important events or transactions as non-existing and thereby to deprive them of the consequences which were prejudicial to the person involved. Granting a *restitutio in integrum* was rather an act of the praetor's IMPERIUM than of his *iurisdictio*. The reasons and situations in which this remedy could be applied, were manifold; the most typical are dealt with in the items below. The praetor could also save a party from unjust losses in another way; he might grant him an action, as if nothing had happened before and the legal situation had remained unchanged, or, in the case of a person who was sued under a transaction deserving annulment, grant him an exception. The reforms in the civil procedure and the regime of bureaucratic jurisdiction gave the *restitutio in integrum* a different aspect: from the extraordinary procedural remedy depending on the discretion of the praetor, it became in the later Principate and the Empire a "*beneficium*" (a legal benefit) and other measures made it in certain cases superfluous. —D. 4.1; C. 2.21–41; 43; 46; 47; 49; 52; 53.—See USUCAPIO, ALIENATIO IUDICII MUTANDI CAUSA.

Klingmüller, *RE* 1A; Lécrivain, *DS* 4; Sciascia, *NDI* 11; L. Charvet, *Évolution de la restitution des majeurs*, Diss. Strassbourg, 1920; Lauria, *St Bonfante* 2 (1930) 513; Jobbé-Duval, *St Bonfante* 3 (1930) 183; W. Felgenträger, *Antikes Lösungsrecht*, 1933, 101; Gallet, *RHD* 16 (1937) 407; Carrelli, *SDHI* 4 (1938) 5, 195; *idem, AnBari* 1 (1938) 129; Beretta, *RISG* 85 (1948) 357; Archi, *St Solazzi* 1948, 740; Levy, *ZSS* 68 (1951) 360.

Restitutio in integrum militum. Granted to soldiers; see the following item.—C. 2.50.

Restitutio in integrum propter absentiam. Granted to persons who because of their absence had incurred damages, as, for instance, the loss of an action through *praescriptio*, usucaption of the absent person's property by a third person. Absence in the interests of the state, captivity, or absence enforced by duress, was considered absence which justified a *restitutio in integrum*. A request for *restitutio* had to be brought within a year from the end of the period of absence —C. 2.50.—See ABSENTES.

Gallet, *RHD* 16 (1937) 407.

Restitutio in integrum propter aetatem. Granted to minors (see MINORES) who had concluded a prejudicial transaction. In the praetorian Edict there was a section which concerned this kind of *restitutio*: "If a transaction will be said to have been concluded with a minor below twenty-five years of age, I shall give attention to the case according to its particular circumstances" (D. 4.4.1.1): Therefore this *restitutio in integrum* was not conceded in just any case; the injured minor had to prove that it was only because of lack of experience due to his age that he had concluded the transaction, since the minor's right to be protected by *restitutio* was considered a privilege of age (*beneficium aetatis*). There were several cases in which a *restitutio* was refused. The request for annulment of the harmful transaction had to be made within a year after the minor attained the age of majority.

Solazzi, *BIDR* 27 (1914) 296.

Restitutio in integrum propter capitis deminutionem. A creditor who lost his claim against a debtor because of the latter's CAPITIS DEMINUTIO (when, e.g., he was adopted by *arrogatio*, or when a female debtor concluded a marriage with *conventio in manum*) might request *restitutio in integrum* from the praetor.

Carrelli, *SDHI* 2 (1936) 141.

Restitutio in integrum propter dolum. See DOLUS.

Duquesne, *Mél Fournier* 1929, 185.

Restitutio in integrum propter metum. Reestablished the legal situation which existed before a transaction was concluded (or an act was done, e.g., the refusal of the acceptance of an inheritance) under duress. The annulment of the pertinent transaction or act was decreed at the request of the person who had acted under duress. In his Edict the praetor proclaimed: "I shall not approve of what has been done because of fear" (D. 4.2.1).—See METUS.

Restitutio in ordinem. See MOTIO EX ORDINE.

Restitutio indulgentia principis. The restoration of a person, who had been condemned to deportation for a crime, into his former rights through an act of grace by the emperor. Such *restitutio* is also called *restitutio in integrum*. The result was that the one so restored (*restitutus*) was regarded as if he never had been condemned. Some restrictive clauses might be added to the emperor's decree and the return of confiscated property had to be expressly granted. The imperial *restitutio* was also applied in cases when a person was condemned to forced labor in mines (see METALLUM).—See ABOLITIO, INDULGENTIA.

Carrelli, *AnBari* 2 (1937) 55; Dessertaux, *TR* 7 (1927) 281.

Restitutio natalium. See NATALIUM RESTITUTIO.

Restitutorius. See ACTIO QUAE RESTITUTIT OBLIGATIONEM, INTERDICTA RESTITUTORIA.

Retentio. (From *retinere*.) The retaining of a thing by a person who normally is obligated to return it to its owner. This kind of self-help could occur in various situations, especially when a person had to bear expenses on another's thing (see IMPENSAE), which he was temporarily holding. When sued by the owner for recovery he might oppose an *exceptio doli* which, when proved justified, liberated him from the restoration of the thing until his claims were satisfied. *Retentio* was admitted also when an heir claimed the *quarta Falcidia* (see LEX FALCIDIA) before paying a *legatum* or a *fideicommissum* to the beneficiary. It seems that the *retentio* was applicable in classical law in various legal situations which because of alterations made by the compilers on the pertinent texts are no longer recognizable. The *ius retentionis* (= the right to retain another's thing) was, however, not admitted in any instance in which one who claimed a payment from another person, was holding the latter's property under a specific title (for instance, as deposit or a gratuitous loan). Generally, there had to be a relationship between the thing retained and the claim.—The more important cases of *retentio* are dealt with in the following items.

Leonhard, *RE* 1A; Cuq, *DS* 4; D'Avanzo, *NDI* 11, 834; Last, *GrZ* 36 (1909) 505; Riccobono, *AnPal* 3–4 (1917) 178; E. Nardi, *Ritenzione e pegno Gordiano*, 1939; idem, *AG* 124 (1940) 74, 139; idem, *Scr Ferrini* 1 (Univ. Cattolica Sacro Cuore, Milan, 1947) 354; idem, *St sulla ritenzione, 1. Fonti e casi*, 1947; E. Protetti, *Contributo allo studio dell'efficacia dell'exc. doli a fine di ritenzione*, 1948.

Retentio pignoris. See PIGNUS GORDIANUM.

Retentio propter res donatas. See RETENTIONES DOTALES.

Siber, *St Riccobono* 3 (1936) 241.

Retentiones dotales (ex dote). In certain cases a husband had the right to retain a portion of the dowry when the restitution thereof was to be performed. *Retentiones propter liberos* (= retention in favor of children): in the event of the wife's death, the husband could retain one-fifth of the dowry for each child, in the case of divorce by fault of the wife one-sixth, but in neither case more than a half altogether. *Retentiones propter mores* = retention in case of divorce arising from a misconduct of the wife: one-sixth when she was guilty of adultery (*mores graviores*), one-eighth when her improper conduct was less grave (*mores leviores*). *Retentiones propter res donatas* = retention because of

donations which the husband had made to the wife under violation of the prohibition of such donations (see DONATIO INTER VIRUM ET UXOREM). *Retentiones propter impensas* = retention because of expenditure made on the objects constituted as dowry. *Retentiones propter res amotas* = retention because of the husband's things which were taken away by the wife (see ACTIO RERUM AMOTARUM). In the last three instances the heirs of the husband also had the *ius retentionis*. The *retentiones* was materialized through an *exceptio doli* opposed by the husband (or his heir) when he was sued for the restitution of the dowry under the ACTIO REI UXORIAE. Justinian's reform of the dowry law abolished the *retentiones*. The claims of the husband were partly suppressed, partly (as those for *impensae*) made suable under specific actions or allowed to compensate for the reciprocal claim for the restoration of the dowry. The compilers replaced the term *retentio* with the terms *exactio* and *compensatio*.—See RETENTIO.

E. Nardi, *St sulla ritenzione 1* (1947) 146.

Retinere. See RETENTIO.

Retractare (retractatio). To revoke, to rescind a juristic act, to deny the validity (e.g., of a testament).

Leonhard, *RE* 1A.

Retractare causam. To try in court anew (*ex integro*) a case which had already been decided in a previous trial. This was possible only inasmuch as the rule *bis de eadem re ne sit actio* (see BIS IDEM EXIGERE) was not applicable and an EXCEPTIO REI IUDICATAE could not be opposed. *Retractare causam* was admissible only in exceptional cases, for instance, if it could be proved that the former judge had been bribed or new documents were found (*nova instrumenta*) which reversed the evidence presented in the first trial. Imperial constitutions were particularly innovating in this respect. The fisc was especially privileged in *retractare causam* if it could offer new evidence on its behalf, but only within three years from the first decision.—C. 10.9.

Biondi, *St Bonfante* 4 (1930) 96.

Retractare sententiam. To change a judgment from which a party had appealed.—See RETRACTARE CAUSAM, ERROR CALCULI.

Hellman, *ZSS* 24 (1903) 87.

Retro agere. To rescind a transaction (a sale, a donation).

Retro dare. To return, to repay a debt. Syn. *solvere*.

Reus. A defendant in a civil trial. Syn. *is cum quo agitur*. Ant. *actor*. There was a rule on behalf of the defendant: "Defendants are regarded as deserving more favorable treatment than plaintiffs" (D. 50.17.125). Another rule defined: "That which is not permitted to the defendant should not be allowed to the plaintiff" (D. 50.17.41 pr.). By opposing an exception to the plaintiff's claim the defendant assumed the role of a plaintiff; see EXCIPERE, EXCEPTIO.

In the so-called divisory actions (*actio familiae erciscundae, actio communi dividundo, actio finium regundorum*) each party to the trial is both plaintiff and defendant.—See IUDICIA DUPLICIA.—*Reus* is also the accused in a criminal trial. In connection with a specific crime (*reus homicidii, falsi, maiestatis*) = guilty. The death of the accused produced the discontinuance of the trial.—C. 9.6.

Eger, *RE* 1A; Lécrivain, *DS* 4.

Reus. (In obligatory relations.) Refers both to the debtor (primarily) and to the creditor. See REUS CREDENDI, REUS PROMITTENDI, REUS STIPULANDI, DUO REI. With reference to suretyship *reus* is applied both to the principal debtor (see REUS PRINCIPALIS) and to the surety (*fideiussor*).

Reus credendi. A creditor. Ant. *reus debendi* = a debtor.—See CREDITOR.

Reus culpae. Guilty of negligence. Syn. *reus ex culpa*.—See CULPA.

Berger, *KrVj* 14 (1912) 436.

Reus debendi. See REUS CREDENDI, DEBITOR.

Reus excipiendo actor est. The rule applies to the defendant in a civil trial: by opposing an exception to the plaintiff's claim the defendant acts as a plaintiff.—See EXCIPERE, EXCEPTIO, REUS.

Reus principalis. The principal debtor as opposed to a surety (*fideiussor, adpromissor*). Syn. *principalis debitor*.

Reus promittendi. One who becomes a debtor by assuming an obligation through *stipulatio* (*qui promittit, promissor*). Ant. *reus stipulandi*.

Reus stipulandi. One who becomes a creditor through *stipulatio* (*qui stipulatur*). Syn. *stipulator*. Ant. *reus promittendi*.

Revendere. To sell back. The term is applied to the sale of a freedman's services (*operae liberti*) to the freedman himself by the patron. Through such a transaction the freedman was released from the obligation of performing further work for the patron. Passive *revenire* (*re-veneo*) = to be sold back.

Reverentia. Respect due by children to their parents or by a freedman to his patron.—See OBSEQUIUM.

Kaser, *ZSS* 58 (1938) 117; C. Cosentini, *St sui liberti* 1 (1948) 251.

Reverentissimus. A title given to high ecclesiastical dignitaries (archbishops, bishops, *oeconomus ecclesiae*).

Reverti. To return. See ANIMUS REVERTENDI. *Reverti* is used of persons (slaves) who reverted under the power of the same person under whom they had been before, and of things which returned to the same owner to whom they had belonged.

Revocare (revocatio). To revoke unilaterally a legal act (a donation, a testamentary disposition), to annul it by a manifestation of will to the effect that the previous legal situation be restored.—See REVOCARE ALIENATIONEM, REVOCARE DONATIONEM.

Leonhard, *RE* 1A; Cuq, *DS* 4.

Revocare alienationem. To rescind an alienation. Used of a creditor who called into question an alienation made by his debtor with the purpose of defrauding the creditors.—C. 7.75.—See FRAUS.

Revocare domum. See IUS REVOCANDI DOMUM.

Revocare donationem. In classical law a donation already accomplished (see DONATIO PERFECTA) was irrevocable. In certain specific cases, however, the postclassical law admitted the revocability of a donation, as in the case of a flagrant ingratitude of the donee or of donations made to villainous or irreverent children. A donation could also be revoked (from the third century after Christ on) if the donee did not fulfill the duty (see MODUS) imposed on him by the donor. The revocation was allowed to the donor alone, not to his successors. A patron might revoke a donation made to his freedman if the latter proved ungrateful, see INGRATUS LIBERTUS. In the later law (from the time of Constantine) a gift made to a freedman by a childless patron could be revoked if the donor begot a child afterwards. A DONATIO MORTIS CAUSA was always revocable according to Justinian's law.—C. 8.55.—See PAENITENTIA.

B. Biondi, *Successione testamentaria*, 1943, 695; C. Cosentini, *St sui liberti* 1 (1948) 223; S. Di Paola, *Donatio mortis causa*, 1950, 66.

Revocare in patriam potestatem. From the time of Constantine a father could recall an emancipated son under his paternal power because of the latter's ingratitude.

Revocare in servitutem. To revoke a manumission. A patron might *revocare in servitutem* an ungrateful freedman (see INGRATUS LIBERTUS) in a case of particular gravity.

De Francisci, *Mél Cornil* 1 (1926) 295.

Revocare legatum. See ADEMPTIO LEGATI.

Revocare mandatum. See MANDATUM.

Revocare Romam. To call a judicial matter into a Roman court. Already in the later Republic the senate or the consuls could order important judicial matters transferred from a province to Rome.

Revocare testamentum. To revoke a testament by making another valid one or by annulment or destruction (e.g., by removing the seals, see LINUM). This was a fundamental principle of the Roman law on testaments: "the will of a testator is changeable until the very end of his life" (D. 34.4.4). This was in conformity with the conception of the testament as the "last will" (*suprema, ultima voluntas*) of the deceased. A testator could not relinquish that right by inserting in his testament a clause invalidating any future testament. Such a clause was not binding; Justinian, however, required that the testator when making a new testament should expressly declare that he was acting against his previous decision.

R. Bozzoni, *Il testamento r. primitivo e la sua revocabilita*, 1904; De Francisci, *BIDR* 27 (1915) 7; Bohacek, *St Bonfante* 4 (1930) 307; B. Biondi, *Successione testamentaria*, 1943, 591.

Revocari per legem. To be declared ineffective by a legal enactment (a statute, the praetorian edict, an imperial constitution).

Hellmann, *ZSS* 24 (1903) 104.

Revocatio. See REVOCARE.

Revocatio in duplum. A defendant condemned in a trial could without awaiting the plaintiff's action for execution (ACTIO IUDICATI) challenge the judgment as invalid. Such a complaint was called *revocatio in duplum* since in the case of failure he had to pay double the amount of the previous judgment.

Biondi, *St Bonfante* 4 (1930) 92.

Rex. During the period of kingship, which lasted about 250 years from the foundation of Rome, a king (*rex*) was at the head of the Roman people as the holder of the highest military and judicial power. The king was also the highest priest and presided over the sacred ceremonies; his religious duties were the most important in peace time. Tradition preserved the names of seven kings from the legendary founder of Rome, Romulus, to the last king, Tarquinius Superbus, whose expulsion (in 509 B.C.) marked the end of the regal regime. The constitutional structure of the state and the legal institutions of this period are obscure in many details. Later historical sources are not fully reliable because of their tendency to retroject the origin of certain Republican institutions back to the times of the kings. The power of the *rex* was not hereditary; he was elected by the people for life, the election being confirmed by the senate. The composition, election (nomination by the king?) and activity of the senate are also obscure. Its principal role might have been that of an advisory council of the king. The number of the senators (*patres*), originally one hundred, was increased to three hundred. Popular assemblies (*comitia curiata*) also existed already in the regal period.—See REGNUM, CURIA, LEGES REGIAE, IUS PAPIRIANUM.

Treves, *OCD*; Fustel de Coulanges, *DS* 4, 824; De Robertis, *NDI* 11; F. Bernhöft, *Staat und Recht der röm. Konigszeit,* 1882; F. Leifer, *Die Einheit der Gewaltgedankens,* 1914, 147; idem, *Klio, Beiheft* 23 (1931) 77; Gioffredi, *Bull. Commissione Comunale archeol. di Roma,* 1943–1945; Nocera, *AnPer* 57 (1946) 171; S. Mazzarino, *Dalla monarchia allo stato repubblicano,* 1947; P. Noailles, *Du droit sacré au dr. civil,* 1950, 32; Westrup, *Archives d'hist. du dr. oriental* 4 (1950) 85; Coli, *SDHI* 17 (1951) 54.

Rex sacrorum (sacrificulus). A priest who officiated at certain religious observances. The office was created at the beginning of the Republic; the *rex sacrorum* first assumed the sacral functions of the king, hence the title of *rex* was conferred on him. He was, however, lower in rank than the PONTIFEX MAXIMUS, who was his superior. The *rex sacrorum* existed still in the Empire.

Rosenberg, *RE* 1A.

Rex socius. The king of a foreign country with whom Rome had a treaty of alliance.—See SOCII.

Rhetor. A rhetorician. See ORATOR. A *rhetor* giving instruction in rhetoric was reckoned among teachers (*magistri*), and his discipline among the *artes liberales*. A rhetorician was at his request exempt from the duties of a judge in a civil trial. For the privileges granted to the rhetoricians, see MAGISTRI. The problem of the influence of rhetoric on Roman jurisprudence is the subject of controversy. Attempts to deny any influence are futile; but it is hardly possible to delimit this influence with any certainty. There is also in the literature a tendency to exclude certain words and phrases from the juristic language although they occur frequently in the language of the rhetoricians. Such a method applied in the search for interpolations is erroneous. After all, the jurists studied rhetoric in their youth like all well educated Romans, and it would be quite natural for them to use words and locutions they heard from their teachers.

Ziebarth, *RE* 2A, 765; Pasquali, *Riv. di filologia e d'istruzione classica* 10 (1927) 228; F. Lanfranchi, *Il diritto nei retori rom.,* 1938; Kübler, *SDHI* 5 (1939) 285; Steinwenter, *Rhetorik und röm. Zivilprozess, ZSS* 65 (1947) 69; S. F. Bonner, *Rom. declamation in the late Republic and early Empire,* 1949; J. Stroux, *Röm. Rechtswissenschaft und Rhetorik* (Potsdam, 1949; contains a new ed. of the author's *Summum ius summa iniuria,* 1926; Italian translation of the first ed. by Riccobono, *AnPal* 12, 1928).

Rhopai. A Byzantine juristic writing of the seventh century composed in Greek by an unknown author and published under the title "On spaces of time from one moment (rhope = a moment) to one hundred years." It is an exact collection of the various extents of time which occur in Justinian's legislation, the Novels included.

Edition: K. E. Zachariae, *Rh. oder die Schrift über Zeitabschnitte,* 1836; J. and P. Zepos, *Ius Graeco-Romanum* 3 (Athens, 1931) 273.—J. A. B. Mortreuil, *Hist. du droit byzantin* 1 (1843) 40; Tamassia, *AG* 54 (1895) 175; Scheltema, *TR* 17 (1941) 415.

Rigor iuris. The severity, inflexibility, rigidity of the law. A rule defined by the late classical jurist, Modestinus (D. 49.1.19) recommended: "If a judgment is rendered clearly against the *rigor iuris,* it shall not be valid, and therefore the matter should be brought again into court even without an appeal."

Ripa. The bank of a river. If the bank of a public river was in private ownership, its use was accessible to all for navigation, transportation, fishing, etc. The owner's right to repair or strengthen the bank (*munire ripam*) was protected by a special interdict, *interdictum de ripa munienda,* against any interference with the necessary repairs or improvements provided they did not impair navigation. On the other hand the demolition of constructions which impeded navigation (*quo navigatio deterior fit*) could be enforced by another interdict.—D. 43.12; 15.—See INTERDICTA DE FLUMINIBUS PUBLICIS, INTERDICTA DE REFICIENDO.

Berger, *RE* 9, 1634 (no. 5 a), 1637 (no. 5 f); D'Amario, *AG* 77 (1906) 3; Lenel, *Edictum perpetuum*³, 1927, 461; G. Lombardi, *Ricerche in tema di ius gentium*, 1947, 81; Branca, *AnTr* 12 (1941) 76.

Rite. In due, solemn form, prescribed by law.
Riccobono, *ZSS* 34 (1913) 224.

Rivales. Persons using water from the same stream. —See RIVUS.

Rivus. A brook, a stream, a minor flowing of water. *Rivus* is also a ditch (a channel) through which water runs from one man's property to another's in the case of a *servitus aquaeductus.*—D. 43.21.—See INTERDICTUM DE RIVIS, INTERDICTA DE REFICIENDO.
Berger, *RE* 9, 1674; Longo, *RISG* 3 (1928) 243.

Rixa. An affray, a brawl, a tumultuous quarrel. A man who died as a result of a *rixa* was presumed to have been killed by accident rather than by intent, and a milder penalty was accordingly inflicted on the culprit.
F. M. De Robertis, *St di dir. rom. penale*, 1943, 145; 205.

Rogare. To request, to ask another for a service, as, e.g., to be a witness (see TESTIS ROGATUS) or surety, or for the permission to use his property (see COMMODATUM, PRECARIUM).—See ROGO.

Rogatio legis. Proposal of a statute to the people gathered in a popular assembly (*comitia*). Literally *rogatio* means a question; here it refers to the formulaic request for approval by which the proposer addressed to the voters: *"Velitis, iubeatis haec ita, ut dixi, ita vos, Quirites, rogo"* (= will and order as I proposed, I beg you, *Quirites*). See VELITIS, IUBEATIS, U.R., A.—Sometimes the term *rogatio* (*lex rogata*) indicates a statute approved by vote. The right of the highest magistrates (consuls, praetors) to propose a statute to the *comitia* = *ius rogationis.* —See LEGES ROGATAE.
Liebenam, *RE* 1A; Lengle, *RE* 6A, 2463; 2479; G. Rotondi, *Leges publicae populi Rom.*, 1912, 14.

Rogator legis. One who proposed a statute to a popular assembly.—See ROGATIO LEGIS.

Rogatores. Tellers who collected and counted the votes in a popular assembly. Syn. *diribitores* since their activity was called *diribitio.*
Liebenam, *RE* 1A, 5 (*s.v. diribitio*); G. Rotondi, *Leges publicae populi Rom.*, 1912, 142.

Rogatu. At request.—See ROGO.

Rogerius. A glossator of the second half of the twelfth century.—See GLOSSATORES.
Kuttner, *NDI* 11, 906; H. Kantorowicz and W. W. Buckland, *Studies in the Glossators of the R. Law*, 1938, 122.

Rogo. Used in the formula of a FIDEICOMMISSUM.

Rogus. A funeral pile.—See BUSTUM, USTRINA.
Ziegler, *RE* 1A; Cuq, *DS* 2, 1394.

Roma. Rome. *"Roma* is our common fatherland" (D. 50.1.33). Syn. *urbs.* After Constantinople became the capital of the Empire, Rome was denoted in imperial constitutions as the "ancient Rome" (*vetus Roma*) while the new capital was termed *nova Roma.* Both cities were designated as *utraque Roma.*—See

URBS, CONTINENTIA, MILIARIUM, MURUS, REVOCARE ROMAN, REGIONES URBIS ROMAE.

Rubrica. The superscription of a section in the praetorian Edict. In the literature, *rubrica* indicates the superscription of titles in the various parts of Justinian's codification. The classical jurists who commented on the praetorian Edict accepted in their commentaries the rubrics of the Edict, as did the compilers of the Digest, following the juristic commentaries. The rubrics of the titles of the Code of Justinian are concordant in part with those of the Digest, in part with those of the Theodosian Code, but many of them were composed by the compilers of the Code themselves, primarily where new topics were involved.
Solazzi, *SDHI* 2 (1936) 325.

Rufinus. See LICINNIUS RUFINUS.

Ruina. The collapse of a building. Appropriation of things belonging to a person struck by such an accident was severely punished; for a deposit given on the occasion of a *ruina,* see DEPOSITUM MISERABILE. Looting in the case of *ruina* was punished severely in the same manner as in the case of shipwreck.— See NAUFRAGIUM.—D. 47.9.

Rumpere. To damage, to injure, to deteriorate. The term is among the kinds of damages inflicted on another's property enumerated in the LEX AQUILIA. For *membrum ruptum,* see OS FRACTUM.

Rumpere testamentum. See TESTAMENTUM RUPTUM.

Rustici. Peasants, simple men lacking experience, particularly in legal matters. *Rustici* might be excused for ignorance of the law and errors, a privilege which citizens normally could not claim.—See IGNORANTIA IURIS.

Rusticitas. Simplicity, quality of being rustic, inexperienced.—See RUSTICI.

Rusticus. (Adj.) Rural, connected with, or pertaining to, life and work in the country.—See PRAEDIA RUSTICA, SERVITUTES PRAEDIORUM RUSTICORUM, FAMILIA RUSTICA, VILLA.

Ruta et caesa. Things taken out of the soil (= *eruta,* such as sand, clay, quarry-stones) or cut down (such as trees). If separated from the soil, they could be reserved for the seller (*excepta*) on the occasion of selling the land. According to another opinion, they always remained in the ownership of the seller unless they were expressly sold together with the land.

Rutiliana actio, constitutio. See ACTIO RUTILIANA, CONSTITUTIO, RUTILIUS RUFUS, USUCAPIO EX RUTILIANA CONSTITUTIONE.

Rutilius Maximus. A jurist of the third post-Christian century, author of a one-book-dissertation on the LEX FALCIDIA.

Rutilius Rufus (Publius). A jurist of the first half of the first century B.C., a disciple of the famous republican jurists, Manilius, Brutus, and P. Mucius Scaevola. He was in great demand for juristic opinions (*responsa*). He was the creator of the ACTIO RUTILIANA, and perhaps also of the actions granted the patron for services due by his freedmen (see IUDICIUM OPERARUM) which are attributed to a praetor Rutilius.—See CONSTITUTIO.

Münzer, *RE* 1A, 1269 (no. 34); Orestano, *NDI* 11, 948.

S

Sabiniani. The name of a school (*schola, secta*) of legal thought in the first and the early second centuries after Christ. The name refers to the famous jurist Massurius Sabinus (see SABINUS), a prominent leader of the group. The "school" is called also *Cassiani* after the name of the jurist C. Cassius Longinus, Sabinus' successor. The origin of the *Sabiniani* as well as that of the rival school of Proculians (*Proculiani, Proculeiani*), so-called after the name of their leader PROCULUS, goes back to the time of Augustus. The founders may have been Labeo and Capito (the latter was predecessor of Sabinus). A considerable number of controversial questions, on which the opinions of the leading representatives of the two groups differed, is known but it is difficult to find a common basis—a political, philosophical, or economic background—that will explain the differences in their opinions. According to a recent view the distinction between the two schools is based on the real existence of two legal educational institutions. Among the prominent Sabinians after Sabinus and Cassius were Iavolenus, Gaius, and Julian, among the Proculians Pegasus, Celsus the Younger, and Neratius.—See SCHOLA.

Kübler, *RE* 1A (*s.v. Rechtsschulen*); Berger, *OCD* (*s.v. Sabinus*); G. Baviera, *Le due scuole dei giureconsulti rom.*, 1898; Di Marzo, *RISG* 63 (1919) 109; Ebrard, *ZSS* 45 (1925) 134; P. Frezza, *Metodi ed attività delle scuole rom. di diritto*, 1938; F. Schulz, *History of R. legal science*, 1946, 119; 338.

Sabinus, Caelius. See CAELIUS SABINUS.

Sabinus, Massurius. A famous jurist of the early first century after Christ, head of the school of Sabinians (see SABINIANI), author of an extensive, systematic treatise on *ius civile* which was commented on by later jurists until the third century in works entitled "*Ad Sabinum.*" The system adopted by Sabinus in his fundamental work followed this scheme: law of successions (testamentary and on intestacy), law of persons, law of obligations and law of things. Sabinus wrote also a commentary to the praetorian Edict, a collection of *responsa*, and a monograph on theft.

Steinwenter, *RE* 1A, 1600; Berger, *OCD*; O. Lenel, *Das Sabinussystem (Fg Ihering*, Strassburg, 1896); F. Schulz, *Sabinusfragmente in Ulpians Sabinuskommentar*, 1906; P. Frezza, *Osservazioni sopra il sistema di Sabino, RISG* 8 (1933) 412.

Saccularius. One who steals money from another's purse, a pick-pocket. A *saccularius* was more severely punished than an average thief.

Saccus (sacculum). A sack, a money-purse. A deposit of a sealed purse containing money was treated as a normal deposit (*depositum*).—See DEPOSITUM IRREGULARE.

Sacer. (In sacral law.) Sacred, consecrated to gods. —See LOCUS SACER, RES SACRAE, CONSECRATIO, DEDICATIO, PECUNIA SACRA, IUS SACRUM.

Ganschinietz, *RE* 1A, 1626.

Sacer. (In earlier penal law.) Some of the oldest provisions of the Roman criminal law established as a punishment for certain crimes the *sacratio* of the wrongdoer by proclaiming "*sacer esto*" (= that he be consecrated to gods, be outlawed). This involved exclusion from the community, from divine and human protection. The death penalty was not inflicted directly, but killing a *sacer homo* was not considered murder. *Sacratio* was decreed for crimes against institutions which were under divine protection, for removing boundary stones (see TERMINUM MOVERE), for fraud committed by a patron against his client, and from the middle of the fifth century B.C. for an injury done to a plebeian tribune. In addition to the *sacratio capitis* the property of the *sacer* was forfeited to gods (*consecratio* or *sacratio bonorum*).—See INTERDICERE AQUA ET IGNI, LEGES SACRATAE, SACROSANCTUS, SACRAMENTUM, TERMINI MOTIO.

Ganschinietz, *RE* 1A, 1627; Lécrivain, *DS* 4 (*s.v. sacratio capitis*); J. L. Strachan-Davidson, *Problems of the R. criminal law* 1 (1912) 3; W. W. Fowler, *Roman essays*, 1920, 115; Groh, *St Riccobono* 2 (1936) 5; M. Kaser, *Das altröm. Ius*, 1949, 45.

Sacer. (With reference to the emperor.) Sacred, imperial. Imperial enactments are termed *sacrae constitutiones*. The term *sacer* is very frequent in later imperial constitutions and is applied to everything connected with the emperor (*sacrae sententiae, sacra oratio, sacrum auditorium*, etc.)—See PRAEPOSITUS SACRI CUBICULI, LARGITIONES SACRAE, COMES SACRARUM LARGITIONUM, COGNITIO SACRA, IUDICANS VICE SACRA.

Sacerdotes. A general term for priests. See PONTIFICES, FLAMINES, AUGURES, FETIALES, FRATRES ARVALES, DUOVIRI (DECEMVIRI, QUINDECIMVIRI) SACRIS FACIUNDIS, COLLEGIA SACERDOTUM. Under the Christian emperors *sacerdotes* = ministers of the Church; sometimes *sacerdos* indicates a bishop (*episcopus*). In Justinian's legislative work the term *sacerdotes* as well as *sacerdotium* (= priesthood, the office of a priest), even when quoted from the work of a pagan jurist, is to be understood in the new sense.

Riewald, *RE* 1A; Chapot, *DS* 4; Rose, *OCD* (*s.v. priests*); E. Pais, *Ricerche sulla storia* 1 (1915) 27; Carter, *The organization of the Roman priesthoods at the beginning of the Republic, Mem. Amer. Academy in Rome* 1 (1916).

Sacerdotes municipales. Priests in municipalities. The *municipia* had their *pontifices, augures, flamines, Vestales*, and also priests whose sacral service was connected with a specific municipal deity. The appointment of *sacerdotes municipales* was made by the *ordo decurionum* (= the municipal council).

Riewald, *RE* 1A, 1651.

Sacerdotes provinciales. Priests in provinces. Their service was dedicated not only to gods, but also to the worship of the emperor.

Sacerdotium. Priesthood.—See SACERDOTES.

Sacra. All kinds of relations between men and gods. The most important domain of the *sacra* were the sacrifices performed by bodies of public character (including communities) and by private persons. Hence the division into *sacra publica* and *sacra privata*. The former were carried out at the expense of the state or other public body (*sumptu publico*) and on behalf of the people (*pro populo*) by priests and high magistrates without active participation of the people; the latter were a private affair which concerned an individual or a group of individuals (*familia, gens*). Within the family group the *sacra familiaria* included worship of a special deity, protector of the family (see LARES, PENATES), as well as of the ancestors of the family. These religious rites were celebrated by the heirs, not only the descendants of the last head of the family, but also by heirs appointed in a testament even when they were strangers to the family. Thus the continuity of the *sacra familiaria* was intimately connected with the succession to the family property. Of an analogous nature but on a larger scale were the *sacra* of a *gens* (*sacra gentilicia*), i.e., the common worship and religious rites celebrated by the members of a *gens*. This community of *sacra* (*communio sacrorum*) of the members of a *gens* was a strong tie uniting them (the *gentiles*). The pontiffs assisted private persons with advice as to rites and forms to be applied in the performance of sacred ceremonies and exercised a certain supervision of the pertinent activities.—See IUS SACRUM, IUS PONTIFICIUM, REX SACRORUM, DETESTATIO SACRORUM, MANUMISSIO SACRORUM CAUSA.

Geiger, *RE* 1A; Toutain, *DS* 4; Severini, *NDI* 11; G. Wissowa, *Religion und Kultus der Römer*, 2nd ed. 1912; Bruck, *Sem* 3 (1945) 4; *idem, Scr Ferrini* 4 (Univ. Sacro Cuore, Milan, 1949) 6; Biondi, *Iura* 1 (1950) 155.

Sacra familiaria (familiae). *Sacra* performed on behalf of a family (*sacra pro familiis*).—See SACRA FAMILIA, SACRA PRIVATA.

Sacra gentilicia. See SACRA, GENS. Syn. *sacra pro gentibus*. Some of the more influential *gentes* were assigned the performance of sacred rites on behalf of specific gods usually honored by *sacra publica*.

G. Castello, *St sul diritto familiare e gentilizio*, 1942, 25.

Sacra nocturna. Sacrifices and religious ceremonies performed at night. They were not prohibited, but were generally regarded as undertaken for evil purposes (*sacra impia*). The use of magical arts (see MAGIA) on such occasions was punished by death.

Sacra popularia. Religious festivals arranged for the whole people.

Sacra privata. Sacrifices and religious rites performed "on behalf of individuals, families, and *gentes*" (Festus 245).—See SACRA.

A. De Marchi, *Il culto privato di Roma antica*, 1896; R. Lefèvre, *Des s. p. en droit romain*, 1928; Bruck, *Scr Ferrini* 4 (Univ. Sacro Cuore, Milan, 1949) 6; 35.

Sacra publica. See SACRA, IUS SACRUM, IUS PONTIFICIUM, SACRA GENTILICIA.

Sacrae largitiones. See LARGITIONES SACRAE.

Sacramentum. An oath. For oaths in civil trials, see IUSIURANDUM, IURAMENTUM, IURARE.

P. Noailles, *Du droit sacré au dr. civil*, 1950, 275.

Sacramentum. In the procedure through *legis actiones*; see LEGIS ACTIO SACRAMENTO, INIUSTUM SACRAMENTUM.

Lévy-Bruhl, *Revue des Études latines* 30 (1952).

Sacramentum. In military and civil service, *sacramentum* = the soldier's oath of allegiance to the standards. In the Empire the soldiers were sworn in by an oath to the emperor. The violation of the *sacramentum* rendered the offender an outlaw; see SACER. Magistrates and imperial officials (*militia civilis*) took a similar oath to observe the laws.—In later imperial constitutions, *sacramentum* = an official post.—C. 10.55.

Klingmüller, *RE* 1A; Parker, *OCD*; Cuq, *DS* 4, 951; A. v. Premerstein, *Wesen und Werden des Prinzipats*, *ABayAW* 15 (1937) 73.

Sacrarium. In Justinian's language, a court-hall.

Sacratio. See SACER, CONSECRATIO, RES SACRAE, LEGES SACRATAE.

Sacratissimus. Most sacred. This epithet was applied to the emperors and institutions connected with them (see PALATIUM, AERARIUM) already during the Principate. *Sacratissima constitutio* = an imperial enactment. In the later Empire churches and ecclesiastical institutions were termed *sacratissimae*.

Sacrificium. A sacrifice. See SACRA. *Malum sacrificium* = a sacrifice in which a human being was the victim (*hominem immolare*). The offender was punished by death. Heathen sacrifices were forbidden by the emperor Constantius (A.D. 354, C. 1.11.1). Imperial legislation of the fourth and fifth centuries concerning pagan religious institutions and customs (temples, sacrifices) is found in Justinian's Code, 1.11.—See SACRA, SUPPLICATIONES.

Latte, *RE* 9 (*s.v. immolatio*); Toutain, *DS* 4, 972; G. Wissowa, *Religion und Kultus der Römer²*, 1912; Eitrem, *OCD*.

Sacrilegium. Theft of sacred things (*furtum sacrorum*) or of RES RELIGIOSAE. Stealing things used for divine service from a temple was punished with death. See QUAESTIONES PERPETUAE. The offender who committed such a crime = *sacrilegus* (*fur sacrorum*). In the later Empire the conception of *sacrilegium* was somewhat distorted and those "who through ignorance or negligence confound, violate and offend the sanctity of a divine law" (C. 9.29.1) were considered guilty of *sacrilegium.* "Divine" is here used in the sense of imperial, issued by the emperor; see DIVINUS. Thus *sacrilegium* and *sacrilegus* became rather general terms applied to the neglect or violation of imperial orders or enactments.—D. 48.13; C. 9.29.—See LEX IULIA PECULATUS.

Pfaff, *RE* 1A; Cuq, *DS* 4.

Sacrilegus. See SACRILEGIUM.

Sacrorum detestatio. See DETESTATIO SACRORUM.

Sacrosanctus. The term was applied to plebeian tribunes (see TRIBUNI PLEBIS) in indication of their inviolability and sanctity of person. This distinct quality was proclaimed by the plebeians at the very creation of the office and sanctioned solemnly by their oath to the effect that any one who attacked a tribune and hindered him in the performance of his official duties would be considered an outlaw (see SACER) and might be killed by anyone at will. The patrician statute, *Lex Valeria Horatia* (449 B.C.) confirmed the inviolability of the tribunes. The *potestas sacrosancta* of the tribunes was opposed to the *imperium* of the magistrates. In the later Empire and by Justinian *sacrosanctus* is applied to the Christian Church and its institutions.—C. 1.2.—See LEX IULIA, SCRIPTURAE SACROSANCTAE.

Kübler, *RE* 1A; Lengle, *RE* 6A, 2460; Ronzeaud, *Rev. des Ét latines*, 1926, 218; Groh, *St Riccobono* 2 (1936) 3; Gioffredi, *SDHI* (1945) 37.

Saeculares ludi. See LUDI SAECULARES.

Saepta. See OVILE.

Rosenberg, *RE* 1A.

Sagittarii. Archers, light-armed troops recruited primarily among soldiers who came from countries where archery was in use. They were organized in *cohortes* and *alae.*

Fiebiger, *RE* 1A.

Salariarius. A person who received pay for his services (*salarium*).—See the following item.

Fiebiger, *RE* 1A.

Salarium. An honorarium given to persons exercising a liberal profession (*ars liberalis*), such as physicians, teachers, and the like, who enjoyed high esteem in society. In municipalities the municipal council could grant such persons a yearly salary. Augustus introduced a fixed salary for public officials serving in Italy and overseas. The sum was understood to be an allowance for covering living expenses (*salarium* = money for salt). See CIBARIA. A similar allowance, called *vasarium* = furniture money, could be assigned by a provincial governor to members of his staff. In the army *salarium* was paid to so-called EVOCATI; the regular soldier's pay = *stipendium.*—C. 10.37.—See VASARIUM, HONORARIUM, MAGISTER, STUDIA LIBERALIA.

Rosenberg, *RE* 1A; Lécrivain, *DS* 4; Marchi, *AG* 76 (1906) 303; Siber, *JhJb* 88 (1939–40) 179.

Salarius. See SALINAE.

Salinae. Salt-works. They were property of the state and were exploited through lease to private persons (*conductores salinarum, salarii*). The condemnation of a criminal to compulsory work in salt-mines was equal to *damnatio in metalla.*—See METALLUM.

Blümmer, *RE* 1A, 2097; L. Clerici, *Economia e finanza dei Romani* 1 (1943) 463; 472.

Saltuarius. A person charged with the service as guard of a SALTUS, being in either private or public ownership.—See the following item.

Saltus. Woodland-pasture, mountainous place, unconducive to agricultural exploitation. Later (in the early Principate) the term was used of large estates, public and private (primarily in Africa). Large landed property belonging to the emperor or the imperial family was also called *saltus* (*saltus divinae domus, saltus dominici*). Syn. *fundus saltuensis.*—C. 11.62–64; 66; 67.

Kübler, *RE* 18, 3, 2053 (*s.v. pascua*); Kornemann, *RE* Suppl. 4, 255; Lécrivain, *DS* 3, 958; Cicogna, *AG* 74 (1905) 273, 382; 75 (1905) 59.

Saltus aestivi (hiberni). Pasture lands used only during a part of the year (in winter = *saltus hiberni,* in summer = *saltus aestivi*). The lands were considered to be in the continuous possession of the person who used them only during the appropriate season.

Salva rerum substantia. See USUSFRUCTUS.

Salvianum interdictum. See INTERDICTUM SALVIANUM.

Salvum fore recipere. See RECEPTUM NAUTARUM.

Salvus. Safe, uninjured. *Salvo iure* = without prejudice, without detriment to one's right (e.g., *salva Falcidia*).

Sancire. To ordain (by a statute = *lege,* by an edict = *edicto,* by custom = *moribus*), to enact (e.g., *principes sanxerunt*). *Sanciri* = to be established, sanctioned (by law, etc.).

Sanctimonialis. A nun.—C. 9.13.—See RAPTUS.

Sanctio (legis). A clause in a statute which strengthens its efficacy by fixing a penalty for its violation, by forbidding its derogation through a later enactment, or by releasing from responsibility any one who by acting in accordance with the statute violated another law. The purpose of the sanction clause was to settle the relation between the new statute and former and future legislation. Thus the *sanctio* could also state that a previous statute remained fully or partially in force without being changed by the new one.—See LEX, LEGES PERFECTAE, SANCTUS.

Kübler, *RE* 1A; Rotondi, *Leges publicae populi Rom.,* 1912, 151; Gioffredi, *Archivio penale* 2 (1946) 166.

Sanctio pragmatica. See PRAGMATICA SANCTIO.

Sanctio pragmatica pro petitione Vigilii. An enactment by Justinian, issued in 554 at request of Pope Vigilius, on the legal order in Italy (after the liberation of Rome from the Goths). By this enactment Justinian ordered that his existing legislative work (the Institutes, the Digest and the Code) and all his later enactments should be in force in Italy.

Edition: App. VII in the edition of Justinian's Novels (*Corpus iuris civilis*, 3) by Schöll and Kroll (fifth ed. 1928); M. Conrat (Cohn), *Gesch. der Quellen und Literatur des röm. R. im Mittelalter*, 1891, 131.

Sanctus. "What is defended and protected against injury by men" (D. 1.8.8) and "what is neither sacred (*sacrum*) nor profane, but is confirmed by a kind of sanction (*sanctio*) without being consecrated to a god" (D. 1.8.9.3). See RES SANCTAE. Laws are called *sanctae* since they are supported by a *sanctio*.

Sane. Certainly, of course, to be sure. The word occurs in texts suspected of interpolation.

Guarneri-Citati, *Indice*[2] (1927) 79.

Sanguis. Blood. *Poena sanguinis* = the death penalty, hence *in sanguine* = in a criminal matter in which the accused is threatened by the death penalty.—See COGNATIO, IUS SANGUINIS, CONSANGUINEUS.

Sapiens. See SEMPRONIUS.

Sarcinator. A mender of clothes. He was liable for CUSTODIA of the clothes which had been given him for repair.

Sarcire. To repair. See *damnum* (*noxiam*) = to make good damages, losses, to indemnify.

Satio. Sowing seed. The product belongs to the owner of the land even when another's seed was used.—See PLANTA, SUPERFICIES CEDIT SOLO.

Satis. Enough, sufficient, satisfactory. When connected with a verb (see the following items), *satis* refers primarily to security given by the debtor and accepted by the creditor. In connection with *dare* (*datio*) and *facere* (*factio*) *satis* is written either separately (*satis dare, satis facere*) or joined with the pertinent verbs or nouns (*satisdare, satisfacere, satisdatio, satisfactio*).

Satis accipere. Used of a creditor who is satisfied with a debtor's performance, with his formal promise (*stipulatio*) or with the securities or sureties offered by him (*satisdationem accipere*). The corresponding term for the debtor is *satisfacere*.

Satis desiderare. To demand a security from a debtor; syn. *satis exigere, postulare, petere*.

Satis facere (satisfacere). See SATIS ACCIPERE, SATISFACTIO.

Satis offerre. To offer sufficient security to one's creditor.

Satisdatio (satisdare). Security given to the creditor by a debtor through a personal guaranty assumed by a surety (*sponsor, fideiussor*). *Satisdatio* is opposed to a simple promise (*nuda promissio, repromissio*) by the principal debtor and to a security given in the form of a pledge. The usual *satisdationes* which were a form of a *cautio*, are dealt with under CAUTIO;

see also the following items.—Inst. 4.11; 1.24; C. 2.56.

Steinwenter, *RE* 2A; Severini, *NDI*; R. De Ruggiero, *Satisdatio e pigneratio nelle stipulazioni pretorie, St Fadda* 2 (1906) 101.

Satisdatio de opere restituendo. See OPERIS NOVI NUNTIATIO.

Berger, *Iura* 1 (1950) 117.

Satisdatio legatorum. See CAUTIO LEGATORUM CAUSA.

Satisdatio pro praede litis et vindiciarum. See CAUTIO PRO PRAEDE LITIS ET VINDICIARUM.

Satisdatio rem pupilli salvam fore. See CAUTIO REM PUPILLI SALVAM FORE.

Satisdatio secundum mancipium. A guarantee connected with MANCIPATIO, probably a formal promise (*stipulatio*) by the seller to deliver the immovable alienated with all proceeds and profits he had derived therefrom in the time between the *mancipatio* and the effective delivery.

Meylan, *RHD* 26 (1948) 1 (Bibl.).

Satisdatio suspecti heredis. A security by sureties, required by the creditors of an heir who was thought to be unable to pay the debts of the deceased. In case of refusal the creditors might obtain possession (*missio in possessionem*) of the heir's whole property.—See HERES SUSPECTUS.

S. Solazzi, *Concorso dei creditori* 1 (1937) 98.

Satisdatio usufructuaria. See CAUTIO USUFRUCTUARIA.

Satisdationem accipere. See SATIS ACCIPERE.

Satisdato cavere (defendere, promittere). SATISDARE (= to give a surety).

Satisdator. A surety.—See SATISDATIO, FIDEIUSSOR.

Satisfacere (satisfactio). Generally to fulfill another's wish, to gratify the desire of a person; when used of a debtor = to carry out an obligation whatever is its origin (a contract, a testament, a statute). At times *satisfacere* is opposed to the effective fulfillment (payment, *solutio*) of an obligation and refers to other kinds of extinction of an obligation, in particular to giving security (in any form). Hence the saying: "*satisfactio pro solutione est*" (*satisfactio* takes the place of *solutio*, D. 46.3.52) and: "under the term *solutio* any kind of satisfaction (of the creditor) is to be understood" (D. 50.16.176).—See SOLUTIO, SATISDATIO.

Grosso, *Remissione del pegno e s., ATor* 65 (1930); Brasiello, *StSen* 52 (1938) 41.

Saturninus, Claudius. A jurist of the second half of the second century after Christ, author of a monograph on penalties of which a long excerpt is preserved in the Digest (48.19.16). His identification in the INDEX FLORENTINUS with Venuleius Saturninus is not reliable.

Jörs, *RE* 3, 2865 (n. 333).

Saturninus, Quintus. A jurist mentioned twice by Ulpian, once as the author of a commentary on the

Edict. He is perhaps to be identified with Venuleius Saturninus.

H. Krüger, *GrZ* 41 (1915) 318.

Saturninus, Venuleius. See VENULEIUS.

Saxum Tarpeium. See DEICERE.

Scaenicus. An actor; *scaenica* = an actress. Syn. *histrio*. See ARS LUDICRA, MINUS, PANTOMIMUS. *Ludi scaenici* (= theatrical performances) played an important part among the LUDI PUBLICI under the Republic.

Habel, *RE* Suppl. 5, 610.

Scaevola, Quintus Cervidius. A famous and most original jurist of the second half of the second post-Christian century. He was a legal adviser of Marcus Aurelius and teacher of the jurist Paul and perhaps of Papinian. His works (*Quaestiones* in 20 books, *Responsa* in 6 books, and *Digesta* in 40 books) are predominantly of casuistic nature. Many of his *responsa* deal with provincial cases. A sagacious and independent mind, Scaevola wrote his opinions in a very concise and dogmatic manner, often without any argumentation. He wrote also *Notae* to the *Digesta* of Julian and Marcellus.—See QUAESTIO DOMITIANA.

Jörs, *RE* 3 (*s.v. Cervidius*, no. 1); Orestano, *NDI* 11, 1158; Berger, *OCD* 798 (no. 5); Samter, *ZSS* 27 (1906) 151; Schulz, *Überlieferungsgesch. der Responsen des C. S.*, *Symb Lenel*, 1931, 143; Sciascia, *Le annotazioni ai Digesta e Resp. di S., AnCam* 16 (1942–44) 87.

Scaevolae. For Scaevolae of the *gens Mucia*, see MUCIUS.

Scheda. A written draft of a document to be copied for the original document. It was binding when written by a notary (see TABELLIO).

Schola. Used with reference to the schools of Sabinians and Proculians; see SABINIANI. Syn. *secta*. It is only Gaius who frequently speaks of the Sabinians as his school (*nostrae scholae auctores*) and of the Proculians as *diversae scholae auctores*. The two schools of legal thought are mentioned as *scholae* only by one other jurist (Venuleius), and Justinian follows Gaius' terminology sporadically in his Institutes.

Scholae. (In the later Empire.) From the fourth century on the term *scholae* is applied to larger groups of persons in military service or officials organized in military fashion (see MILITIA) under the command of a *tribunus* or a *praepositus*. In particular, officials of the imperial palace or attached to the person of the emperor as his bodyguards and the AGENTES IN REBUS were united in *scholae* (see SCHOLAE PALATINAE). *Scholares* = members of such *scholae*.—C. 12.29.—See SCHOLAE PALATINAE.

Cagnat, *DS* 4, 1122; E. Stein, *ZSS* 41 (1920) 194.

Scholae palatinae. Military units or militarily organized groups in the service of the emperor, stationed either in the imperial palace or in its neighborhood. They stood under the supervision of the MAGISTER OFFICIORUM and were commanded by a *tribunus* or

a *comes*. The members of the *scholae palatinae* received a higher stipend. than ordinary soldiers did, and they enjoyed special privileges. They replaced the earlier *praetoriani* as bodyguards of the Emperor.

Seeck, *RE* 2A; Babut, *Rev. historique* 114 (1913) 230.

Scholares. See SCHOLAE.

Babut, *Rev. historique* 114 (1913) 258; P. Collinet, *La procédure par libelle*, 1932, 415.

Scholasticus. (In the later Empire.) An advocate, a lawyer who assisted a party during a trial or served as a legal counselor of a high officer. Sometimes he assumed an official function, such as of a *defensor civitatis* or judge.

Preisigke, *RE* 2A, 624.

Scholia Sinaitica. A collection of brief comments on some parts of Ulpian's work *Ad Sabinum*. A manuscript thereof was discovered on the Mount Sinai. It is a pre-Justinian work, containing quotations from the latest classical jurists (Ulpian, Paul, Modestinus, and others) and from the three Codes (Gregorianus, Hermogenianus, Theodosianus). The unknown author might have been a teacher in one of the law schools in the Eastern Empire. Some additions were perhaps inserted after the publication of the Digest.

Editions: Kübler in Huschke's *Iurisprudentia anteiustiniana* 2, 2 (sixth ed., 1927, 461); Baviera, *FIR* 2 (second ed. 1940) 461; Girard, *Textes de droit rom.* (sixth ed. by Senn, 1937) 609.—Winstedt, *ClPhilol* 2 (1907) 201; Riccobono, *BIDR* 9 (1896) 217; *idem, AnPal* 12 (1929) 550; Peters, *Die oström. Digestenkommentare, BerSächGW* 65 (1913) 90.

Scholia. To the Basilica, see BASILICA.

Sciendum est. It should be understood. This is a favorite locution of many jurists to introduce an important, general legal rule. The locution is frequently strengthened by *in summa* (= generally speaking on the whole), *generaliter,* and the like.

Sciens. One who has knowledge, one who does something knowingly (that it is forbidden or invalid). At times, *sciens* is syn. with *conscius* (see CONSCIENTIA).—See SCIENTIA.

Sciens dolo malo. See DOLUS MALUS.

Scientia. Knowledge. The term refers both to a professional knowledge (as, e.g., *scientia iuris, scientia artis*) and to the knowledge of a fact, of another's doing, of a specific legal provision, etc. Ant. *ignorantia.*

Scientia domini. The master's knowledge of a wrongdoing about to be committed by his slave. In certain circumstances *scientia domini* could be considered as complicity and the master could not free himself from responsibility by delivering the slave (*noxae deditio*).

H. Lévy-Bruhl, *Nouvelles études sur le très ancien dr. rom.*, 1947, 128.

Scientia iuris (civilis). Knowledge of the law. *Scientiam iuris profiteri* = to exercise the profession of a jurist. For the lack of knowledge of legal norms involved in a specific case, see IGNORANTIA IURIS.

In order to avoid the harmful consequences of the ignorance of the law, one had to consult a professional lawyer, since "*scientia iuris* is the knowledge one has by himself or may acquire by consulting persons more learned in law (*prudentiores*)," D. 37.1.10.

Scientia iusti et iniusti. The knowledge of what is just and what unjust. Appears in the definition of IURISPRUDENTIA by Ulpian (D. 1.1.10.2).

Scientia legitima. See SCIENTIA IURIS.

Scilicet. Of course, certainly, evidently, to be sure. See ID EST. Some phrases introduced by *scilicet* may have originated in marginal, explanatory glosses which later copyists inserted in the text of a juristic writing, and which subsequently were copied by the compilers of the Digest.

Guarneri-Citati, *Indice*[2] (1927) 80.

Scipio Nasica (Gaius). A highly estimated jurist of the second century B.C. According to a (not fully reliable) remark by Pomponius he was offered a house at public expense in order to make him readily accessible for consultation.

Münzer, *RE* 4, 1501 (no. 353).

Scire. See SCIENTIA, SCIENS, SCIENDUM EST.

Scire leges. See INTERPRETATIO.

Scitum. A decree, an ordinance, a generally recognized legal rule.—See PLEBISCITUM.

Scriba. A clerk in a court or in an office, a secretary (in an association, *collegium*). The *scribae* in a magisterial office (*scribae aedilicii, tribunicii, quaestorii*) belonged to the subordinate personnel, the *apparitores*. Municipal magistrates had also their *scribae*. A *scriba* is to be distinguished from a *librarius* who was simply a copyist. When a *scriba* performed the tasks of a *librarius,* his title was *scriba librarius.*—C. 10.71.—See APPARITORES.—See PONTIFICES MINORES.

Kornemann, *RE* 4, 423; 4A; Lécrivain, *DS* 4; Jones, *JRS* 39 (1949) 38.

Scriba quaestorius (or ab aerario). A clerk in the office of a quaestor. Among the magisterial clerks the *scribae quaestorii* were the most important; they were the bookkeepers of the treasury (see AERARIUM) and, in view of the many tasks they had to fulfill in connection with the financial administration, the most numerous (6).

Kornemann, *RE* 2A, 850.

Scribendo adesse. When a record of the passing of a *senatusconsultum* was written, several senators were present ("*scribendo adfuerunt*") to assure the accuracy of the written text.

Scribere. To write. Used of all kinds of public and private announcements or declarations made in writing. *Scribere* refers both to what the praetor promulgated in his edict or a provincial governor in his ordinances and letters, and to what the emperor ordained in his enactments. *Scribere* is used of all written legal documents (*testamentum, instrumentum,*

chirographum, etc.). Quotations from juristic writings are also introduced by *scribere* ("*Labeo scribit*") with or without indication of the work from which the quotation was taken.—See the following item, SCRIPTURA.

Klingmüller, *RE* 1A.

Scribere heredem (tutorem, exheredem). To institute an heir (to appoint a guardian, disinherit a person) in a testament. Hence *heres scriptus* = an heir instituted in a testament. Ant. *heres legitimus.*

Scrinia. Subdivisions of the bureaus of the imperial chancery in the later Empire. Literally the term indicates the buckets in which the official papers were stored. The chiefs of those offices, which were called also *sacra scrinia,* the *magistri, proximi, comites,* were subject to the MAGISTER OFFICIORUM. The various *scrinia* were indicated by an additional term as to their specific functions, e.g., *scrinia epistularum, libellorum.*—See the following items.—C. 12.9.

Seeck, *RE* 2A; Lécrivain, *DS* 4.

Scriniarii. Officials employed in the SCRINIA.—C. 12.49.

Seeck, *RE* 2A, 894; Jones, *JRS* 39 (1949) 54.

Scrinium a memoria (memoriae). A bureau in the imperial chancery which, under the direction of the *magister (sacrae) memoriae,* performed the secretarial work on all decisions in writing, letters, appointments, and orders issued by the emperor.

Seeck, *RE* 2A, 897.

Scrinium dispositionum. See COMES DISPOSITIONUM.

Seeck, *RE* 2A, 909.

Scrinium epistularum. Under the direction of a *magister epistularum,* in the later Empire this replaced the former office AB EPISTULIS.

Seeck, *RE* 2A, 898; Rostowzew, *RE* 6, 210.

Scrinium libellorum. An office in the imperial chancery in the later Empire concerned with all kinds of petitions (*libelli*) addressed to the emperor. *Libellensis* = an official in this bureau.

Seeck, *RE* 2A, 899.

Scrinium memoriae. See SCRINIUM A MEMORIA.

Scripta. Things written (e.g., a testament, document, juristic writing). A legal transaction (act) is termed *sine scriptis* when concluded only orally, without a written instrument.—See SCRIPTURA, INSTRUMENTUM.

Scriptor testamenti. The person who wrote a testament for a testator. He might also serve as a witness to the will.—C. 9.23.—See QUAESTIO DOMITIANA, TESTIS AD TESTAMENTUM ADHIBITUS.

Scriptura. A written document (a receipt, an acknowledgment of a debt, a testament, a contract, etc.). Syn. *in scriptis,* INSTRUMENTUM. Ant. *sine scriptura, sine scriptis.* Generally a *scriptura* was made for the purpose of evidence. In postclassical times written acts became more and more usual. In Justinian's law certain transactions had to be concluded in writing to be valid. *Scriptura* is also used of a single disposition of a written last will. For *scriptura* in Justinian's language, see LITTERARUM OBLIGATIO.

M. Kroel, *Du rôle de l'écrit dans la preuve des contrats*, Thèse Nancy, 1906; L. De Sarlo, *Il documento come oggetto di rapporti*, 1935, 63; Archi, *Scr Ferrini* 1 (Univ. Sacro Cuore, Milan, 1947) 19.

Scriptura. (With reference to a jurist.) An opinion expressed by a jurist (*scriptura Sabini, Iuliani*) in a published work.

Scriptura. (In administrative law.) A fee paid for the use of public pasture land.

Kübler, *RE* 2A; Rostowzew, *DE* 2, 582; L. Clerici, *Economia e finanza dei Romani*, 1 (1943) 453.

Scriptura exterior—interior. See DIPTYCHUM.

Scriptura legis (senatusconsulti). The written text, or a single proviso of a legal enactment (a *senatusconsultum*).

Scripturae Sacrosanctae. Holy Writ. Justinian ordered (C. 3.1.14.1) that in all kinds of courts the judges (*omnes omnino iudices Romani iuris disceptatores* = all judges who decided according to Roman law) should not start the proceedings until a copy of the Scriptures was deposited in court, where it had to remain until the end of the proceedings.

Scripturarius ager. See AGER SCRIPTURARIUS.

Burdese, *St sull'ager publicus, MemTor* Ser. II, 76 (1952) 36, 90.

Scutarii. Heavily armed bodyguards of the emperor in the later Empire. They were among the *scholares* of the SCHOLAE PALATINAE.

Seeck, *RE* 3A, 621.

Secare partes. This expression occurred in the Twelve Tables in connection with the creditors' right of execution on the person of a debtor in default. The pertinent provision as related by Gellius (*Noctes Att.* 20.1.52) ordained: "on the third market day they (*scil.* the creditors) might cut [the debtor] to pieces; cutting more or less [of the body of the debtor] would not be a fraud." The meaning of the phrase is not beyond any doubt; it seems to allude to an old custom of bringing an insolvent debtor to the market on three consecutive market days and pronouncing publicly what he owed, in order to give his relatives and friends an opportunity to pay for him. If they did not, the creditors were authorized to kill him. Whatever the meaning of this provision, literary sources note that no instance of such a cruelty on the part of creditors was known.

Riccobono, *FIR* 1² (1941) 33 (ad Table 4.6; Bibl.); F. Kleineidam, *Die Personalexecution der Zwölf Tafeln*, 1904, 224; J. Kohler, *Shakespeare vor dem Forum der Jurisprudenz* (1919) 50; Radin, *AmJPhilol* 43 (1922) 32; H. Lévy-Bruhl, *Quelques problèmes du très ancien dr. rom.*, 1934, 152; Düll, *ZSS* 56 (1936) 289; G. I. Luzzatto, *Procedura civile rom.*, 2 (1948) 36; Georgescu, *RIDA* 2 (1949) 367; Kaser, *Das altröm. Ius*, 1949, 187.

Secretarium. A closed court-hall (in the later Empire) in which trials were held and judgments ren-

dered. Syn. *secretum*. These terms allude to a time when proceedings were held in secret and the public was separated from the court by a curtain (*velum*) which was lifted only in specific cases. Constantine ordered that proceedings be public.

Seeck, *RE* 2A, 279; Mommsen, *Röm. Strafrecht*, 1899, 362.

Secretum. See SECRETARIUM.

Secta. A group of followers of a school of thought (*secta studiorum*). Syn. SCHOLA. See SABINIANI.— *Secta* means also a religious sect, primarily with reference to heretics. See HAERETICI. The followers of a sectarian religious doctrine = *sectatores*.

Sectatores. In religious matters, see SECTA.

Sectatores. Adherents of a candidate to a magistracy who used to accompany him in public during the campaign period in order to impress the voters. The custom was condemned by some statutes against AMBITUS, as an unfair practice.

Fluss, *RE* 2A.

Sectio bonorum. The purchase of confiscated property sold by the fisc at public auction in a lump. The purchaser = *sector bonorum*. The institution is not well known; in Justinian's time it no longer existed. If some items among the confiscated property were still held by a private individual, the *sector* was granted a special interdict, the so-called *interdictum sectorium* under which he obtained possession of the things in question.

Leonhard, *RE* 3 (*s.v. bonorum s.*); Berger, *RE* 9, 1669 (no. 50); Humbert, *DS* 1 (*s.v. bonorum s.*); Klingmüller, *RE* 2A, 892; O. Lenel, *Edictum perpetuum³* (1927) 456; Rotondi, *CentCodPav.* 1934, 103; Solazzi, *Concorso dei creditori* 1 (1937) 242.

Sector. See SECTIO BONORUM, AUCTIO.

Secundae nuptiae. A second marriage. The conclusion of a second marriage after the dissolution of the previous marriage through death or divorce, was generally permitted—to men without restrictions, to women (originally only widows, and later also divorced women) after ten months (later one year). See LUCTUS, TURBATIO SANGUINIS. Augustus' legislation (see LEX IULIA DE MARITANDIS ORDINIBUS) fostered even second marriages by inflicting financial disadvantages to unmarried and childless persons. Under the influence of Christianity the later imperial legislation became unfavorable to second marriages. From the fourth century on, it imposed upon men and women married a second time various restrictions of a financial nature in favor of children born of the first marriage.—C. 5.9; Nov. 22.—See UNIVIRA.

Secundae tabulae. See TESTAMENTUM PUPILLARE.

Secundarium interdictum. See INTERDICTUM SECUNDARIUM.

Secundocerius. See PRIMICERIUS.—C. 12.7.

Secundum. In favor of, according to, e.g., to render a judgment in favor of the plaintiff (*secundum actorem*), to decide according to the testament (*secundum tabulas*) in favor of the heir. Ant. *contra*.

Secundum tabulas (*sc.* **testamenti**). According to the testament. Ant. *contra tabulas.*—See BONORUM POSSESSIO SECUNDUM TABULAS.

Securitas. Security, guaranty. *Securitas rei publicae* (*publica*) = the security of the state, public safety.

Securitates. In the meaning of receipts, syn. with *apochae.* They attested the debtor's discharge of his debts. Official *securitates* were issued for the discharge of compulsory public services (*munera*).

Securus. Irresponsible, free from responsibility, not exposed to an action or exception. Juristic decisions to the effect that a person is *securus* (= secure) meant that he need not fear a suit or judicial prosecution. *Securus* was also used of a creditor who received sufficient securities (pledge, sureties) from his debtor.

Secutores. Soldiers, attendants (orderlies) assigned to the personal service of high military commanders, military tribunes, etc. Naval commander had also their *secutores.*
    Fiebiger, *RE* 2A.

Sedes. With reference to private persons, residence. Syn. *domicilium.* With reference to imperial offices (in the language of the imperial chancery), the office itself. *Sedes urbana* (or *urbicaria*) = the office of the *praefectus urbi. Sedes praetoriana* = the office of the *praefectus praetorio.* The emperors, in addressing high government officials, used to call their office "*sedes vestra.*"—See EXCELSA SEDES.

Seditio. Open resistance, an uprising of a rather large group of persons with the use of—armed or unarmed —force against magistrates; a violent disturbance of a popular assembly or of a meeting of the senate. Leaders and instigators (*auctores*) were punished by death. The participants (*seditiosi*) were tried under the *Lex Iulia de vi,* or for *crimen maiestatis.* A sedition in the army (mutiny) was treated with particular severity. Vociferous demonstrations or complaints of soldiers, although called also *seditio,* were milder punished.
    Pfaff, *RE* 2A; Humbert and Lécrivain, *DS* 3, 1558.

Seditiosi. Those who participated in a sedition (see SEDITIO) and, according to imperial constitutions, those who incited the lower class of the people (*plebs*) against "the public order" (C. 9.30.1).— C. 9.30.

Seius. See NOMEN.

Sella curulis. See MAGISTRATUS CURULES, SUBSELLIUM.

Semel heres semper heres. "Once an heir always an heir." One who at law or by entry into an inheritance (see ADITIO HEREDITATIS) became an heir of a deceased person, remained his heir (see HERES) forever. Therefore an heir could not be appointed for a limited period.   .
    C. Sanfilippo, *Evoluzione storica dell'hereditas,* 1946, 93; Ambrosino, *SDHI* 17 (1951) 222.

Semenstria. See COMMENTARII PRINCIPUM.

Semenstris pensio. Payments (e.g., rents) in six-month-installments.

Semis. See EX ASSE, USURAE SEMISSES.

Sempronius. See NOMEN.

Sempronius. An unknown jurist of the third century B.C. (consul 305 B.C.?), popularly known by the Greek epithet *Sophos* (= *Sapiens*) because of his profound knowledge of the law.—A similar case is that of the also unknown jurist, Publius Atilius (he appears in Cicero as Lucius Acilius), of the second century B.C., who was honored with the title of *Sapiens.*
    Münzer, *RE* 2, 1437 (no. 85); Klebs, *RE.* 1, 252; W. Kunkel, *Herkunft und soziale Stellung der röm. Juristen,* 1952, 6, 10.

Semuncia. One twenty-fourth part of a whole (e.g., of an inheritance).—See AS, EX ASSE.

Senaculum. The place where the senate gathered. Originally, it was an open place in the forum, later a building (a *curia* or temple).
    Klotz, *RE* 2A.

Senatores. Members of the senate. See PATRES. After the admission of plebeians to the senate (the time cannot be exactly fixed, probably at the beginning of the Republic), a distinction between the patrician and plebeian members of the senate was reflected in the expression *patres* (*et*) *conscripti* by which the senators were addressed, the term *conscripti* seemingly referring to the plebeian senators (*conscripti* = enrolled in the list of senators, see PATRES CONSCRIPTI). The LEX PUBLILIA PHILONIS (339 B.C.) abolished the differentiation between patrician and plebeian senators. In the later Republic a kind of hierarchy among the senators came into existence, based on the magistracies the senators (ex-magistrates) had held before. Those who had been MAGISTRATUS CURULES (ex-consuls, ex-praetors, ex-aedils) preceded those who had held other offices (ex-tribunes, ex-aedils of the *plebs*) or none at all. Before the LEX OVINIA (318–312 B.C.) senators were nominated by the consuls or by the extraordinary magistrates (dictators) temporarily replacing the consuls. According to an early custom, ex-magistrates of high rank became automatically members of the senate; after the *Lex Ovinia,* by which the censors were entrusted with the selection of the senators, that custom became a fixed rule. Eligible for membership in the senate were only Roman citizens who were free-born or sons of free-born fathers. Excluded were women, persons condemned in an *actio famosa* and branded with infamy, persons who practiced an ignominious profession, and bankrupts. The age of a newly-appointed senator varied according to the magistracy he had held; see MAGISTRATUS. The youngest were the ex-quaestors (over thirty-one). Under Augustus the minimum age was lowered to twenty-five. The financial independence of the senators who generally came from the wealthiest families, was guaranteed by the requirement of a minimum property which was fixed by Augustus at one million sesterces. Senators were forbidden to participate in a business enterprise; see LEX CLAUDIA.—D. 1.9; C. 3.24.—See SENATUS (Bibl.), ORDO SENATORIUS, SENATUM COGERE.

Senatores. (In municipalities.) Members of the municipal council (*ordo decurionum*). Syn. *decuriones*.
> Kübler, *RE* 14, 2321.

Senatores ab actis senatus. Senators entrusted by the emperor with the edition and custody of the ACTA SENATUS.

Senatores nondum lecti. Ex-magistrates not yet selected by the censors for the senate.

Senatores pedarii. The term is not quite clear; its origin was obscure to ancient writers, as related by Gellius (*Noct. Att.* 3.18). *Senatores pedarii* were either senators who had held a lower, non-curule magistracy or ex-magistrates who had not yet been enrolled into the list of senators by the censors. The term *pedarii* was perhaps connected somehow with the senate's way of voting by a division of the voters (*pedibus in sententiam ire*, see DISCESSIO). The *senatores pedarii* could participate only in this form of voting and were excluded from taking part in discussion.—See MAGISTRATUS CURULES, LECTIO SENATUS.
> O'Brien-Moore, *RE* Suppl. 6, 680; M. A. De Dominicis, *Il ius sententiae nel senato rom.*, 1932.

Senatorius. Connected with, or pertaining to, senatorial rank (e.g., *nuptiae, ornamenta, dignitas, ordo*, etc.).—See ORDO SENATORIUS.

Senatu movere. See MOVERE (DE) SENATU, NOTA CENSORIA, LECTIO SENATUS. The censors could refuse the admission of an ex-magistrate who according to his rank was eligible to the senate, by omitting his name (*praeterire*) from the list of senators.
> O'Brien-Moore, *RE* Suppl. 6, 763.

Senatum cogere (convocare, vocare). To convoke the senate. See SENATUM HABERE. Senators were required to reside in Rome and to attend the meetings. They were subject to fines for unjustified absence.

Senatum consulere. See SENATUSCONSULTUM.

Senatum dare. To give persons (e.g., foreign embassies, delegations from provinces, provincial governors) the opportunity of being heard by the senate by convoking it for this purpose.

Senatum habere. To convoke the senate in order to present an important matter to the senators (e.g., to propose a law, to ask for an opinion). The convoking magistrate presided over the meeting.—See SENATUM DARE.

Senatum mittere (dimittere). To declare a meeting of the senate adjourned.

Senatus. The senate was one of the earliest Roman constitutional institutions; it remained in existence throughout the entire history of the Roman state, not, of course, without fundamental changes in its structure and its legal and political importance. For the *senatus* in the regal period, see REX. In the Republic, the senate became the most important organ of foreign and internal policy. Its activity was not fixed by a written law; in particular, its rights with respect to the popular assemblies (*comitia*) on the one hand, and to the magistrates on the other, were not defined by statutes. The pertinent rules were customary law. In the field of foreign relations the senate received foreign ambassadors and appointed embassies for missions abroad. Decision concerning war and peace lay with the people (see LEGES DE BELLO INDICENDO), but a previous opinion of the senate was binding. In case of war the senate appointed the commanders for the various fronts and designated the armed and naval forces therefor. Incompetent generals were removed by the senate. Treaties with foreign countries were concluded by the Senate but had to be ratified by a popular assembly. In financial matters the senate decided about taxes, the sale of public land (*ager publicus*), expenses for conducting a war, for sacred institutions, and the like; it supervised the administration of public funds (see AERARIUM POPULI ROMANI). The senate also had the control of the religious life, and could institute the cult of new deities. In matters of internal policy the senate functioned as an advisory body (*sententiam dicere*) to the high magistrates (consuls, praetors). The magistrates who had the right of convoking the senate (*ius agendi cum patribus*, in the Republic consuls, praetors, dictators, and later the plebeian tribunes) submitted to the senators for their opinion proposals for new laws, administrative measures of major importance, problems concerning the political life of the state, and the like, but such consultation was only customary, not mandatory. Nor was the advice of the senate binding upon the magistrates. A clause *"si magistratibus videbitur"* (= if the magistrates deem it right) made compliance with the senate's advice officially optional. Normally, however, the advice was followed, since it was not in the interest of the magistrate to provoke a conflict with the senate. For the administration of provinces, see PROVINCIAE SENATUS. Only members of the senate (originally 300, later 600, under Caesar 900, in the Empire 600 again) were admitted to the meetings of the senate, which took place with the doors of the meeting house open but with the public excluded. In the Principate the senate obtained legislative functions (see SENATUSCONSULTA) and jurisdiction in criminal matters, primarily in crimes involving the state. Formally the senate elected the emperor (see PRINCEPS, LEX DE IMPERIO). It also obtained the right to appoint the magistrates, but this right in the course of time lost its importance since the emperors used to nominate candidates (see CANDIDATI CAESARIS) and the senate's approval became a mere formality. Gradually the senate was compelled to give up much of its independence, and its powers and activity depended, in fact, upon the attitude of the reigning emperor. In the late Empire the importance of the senate declined continuously with the increase in the autocratic power of the emperor. Its functions, as far as they were exercised at all, became a pure formality, as did also the election of the emperor, which was performed to carry out the wishes of the army leaders. The supreme authority being vested in the emperor, the senate with its exorbitant number of members (2,000) was nothing more than a municipal council of Rome (and Constantinople, since Constantine created a second senate there), with a specific competence in conferring honorific titles and distinctions.—See SENATORES, SENATUSCONSULTA, AMPLISSIMUS ORDO, ORDO SENATORIUS, PATRES, AUCTORITAS PATRUM, INTERREGNUM, PRONUNTIARE SENTENTIAM, PLEBISCITA, LECTIO SENATUS, SENTENTIAM ROGARE, CLARISSIMUS, ACTA SENATUS, ACCLAMATIO, ALBUM SENATORUM, ADLECTIO, MOVERE DE SENATU, COMMENDARE, IUSTITIUM, IUS ANULI AUREI, LEX MAENIA, LEX PUPIA, PRODITIO, SOLUTIO LEGIBUS, SOLIS OCCASUS, DISCESSIO, INTERROGATIO, RELATIO, LEGATI DECEM, VERBA FACERE, DECURIA, and the foregoing and following items.

O'Brien-Moore, *RE* Suppl. 6; Lécrivain, *DS* 4; Volterra, *NDI* 12; Momigliano, *OCD*; P. Willems, *Le sénat de la Rép. rom.* 1–3 (1883–1885); Th. A. Abele, *Der Senat unter Augustus*, 1907; Homo, *Rev. Historique* 137 (1921) 161, 138 (1922) 1; P. Lambrechts, *La composition du Sénat rom. 117–192 de l'accession au trône d'Hadrien*, 1936; idem, *La composition du Sénat rom. de Septime Sévère à Dioclétien*, 1937; idem, *Studien over Romeinsche instellingen, I. De Senaat*, 1937; S. J. De Laet, *La composition du Sénat rom. 193–284 A.D.*, Budapest, 1937 (*Dissert. Pannonicae* I, 8); idem, *La composition du Sénat rom. 28 B.C.–68 A.D.* (*Travaux Fac. Philos. Gand*, no. 92), 1941; E. Stein, *Disparition du Sénat à la fin du sixième siècle, Bull. Acad. Belg.* 25 (1939) 308; G. Nocera, *Il potere dei comizi*, 1940, 243; De Francisci, *Rend. Accad. Pontificia di Archeologia*, 1946–47, 275.

Senatus legitimi. Regular meetings of the senate, normally twice in a month. Extraordinary sessions were frequently convoked, especially by the emperors.

Senatus municipalis (municipii). See ORDO DECURIONUM.

Kübler, *RE* 4, 2319; Lécrivain, *DS* 4; H. U. Instinsky, *S. im Gemeinwesen peregrinen Rechts, Philol* 96 (1944).

Senatus populusque Romanus (abbr. S.P.Q.R.). A traditional formula, applied in official acts to indicate the government of the Roman state (in the Republic and even in the early Principate). It stresses the part of the Roman people in the organization of the government as a constitutional organ equal to the role of the senate. The abbreviation is preserved in many inscriptions.

Mommsen, *Röm. Staatsrecht* 3, 2 (1888) 1257; H. Dessau, *Inscriptiones Latinae Selectae*, 3, 1 (1914) 589; G. Nocera, *Il potere dei comizi*, 1940, 244.

Senatusconsulta. Decisions, decrees of the senate issued in response to requests for advice (*senatum consulere*) from one of the high magistrates (consul, praetor, *tribunus plebis,* under the Principate the *praefectus urbi*) who after presenting the matter (*verba facere*) asked the senators for their individual opinions. From the very beginning a *senatusconsultum* was what the name expresses: an advice to the magistrate requesting it. The magistrate normally followed the advice in exercising his functions or incorporated it into his edict giving a more binding character thereto. Some of the republican *senatusconsulta* made reference to previous statutes and plebiscites. For the indirect influence of the senate on the legislative activity of the popular assemblies, see AUCTORITAS SENATUS. As to the legislative force of the *senatusconsulta,* there is no doubt that about the middle of the second century after Christ the *senatusconsulta* acquired the legal force of statutes, as attested by Gaius (Inst. 1.4): "*Senatusconsultum* is what the senate orders and decrees; it has the force equal to that of a statute (*legis vicem optinet*) although this has been questioned." This remark suggests that under the Republic and the early Principate the senate had no legislative power. Accordingly, one century later, Ulpian stated (D. 1.3.9): "it is beyond doubt that the senate can make the law." From the third century B.C. it became customary to write the decrees of the senate and to deposit a copy in the AERARIUM SATURNI where they were preserved under the supervision of the aedils. More important *senatusconsulta* were inscribed on bronze tablets posted in public. Under the early Principate the *senatusconsulta* superseded the comitial legislation, but were later in turn superseded by imperial enactments. The *senatusconsulta* were usually named after the proposer (a magistrate or imperial official). The *senatusconsulta* concerned various matters; a considerable number of them dealt with private law. —D. 1.3.—See ORATIO PRINCIPIS, SENATUS, LEX VALERIA HORATIA, IMMUNITAS, CENSERE, SCRIBENDO ADESSE, PUBLICATIO LEGIS, and the following items.

O'Brien-Moore, *RE* Suppl. 6 (1935); Lécrivain, *DS* 4; Volterra, *NDI* 12; Momigliano, *OCD*; Loreti-Lorini, *St Bonfante* 4 (1930) 377.

Senatusconsultum Acilianum. Forbade legacies of things which were joined to buildings as their ornaments (e.g., statues, sculptures, vases). The purpose of the *senatusconsultum* was to protect buildings from loss of their embellishment. In practice the *senatusconsultum* was also applied to sales of such things. The name Acilianum is not preserved in the sources; it was coined in the literature from the name of one of the consuls, Acilius Aviola, under whose consulship the *senatusconsultum* was passed (A.D. 122).

Bachofen, *Ausgewählte Lehren*, 1848, 209; Voigt, *Die röm. Baugesetze, BerSächGW* 1903, 195; Bonfante, *Corso* 2, 1 (1926) 266; M. Pampaloni, *AG* 30 (1883) 260 = *Scr. giur.* 1 (1941) 225.

Senatusconsultum Afinianum. (Of unknown date.) Dealt with the rights of succession of a child who being one of three brothers was adopted by a third person. He had a right to a quarter of the adoptive father's estate, even after his emancipation by the latter.

> G. Bergman, *Beiträge zum rom. Adoptionsrecht* (Lund, 1912) 76.

Senatusconsultum Apronianum. (Under Hadrian.) Permitted awarding *fideicommissa hereditatis* to cities (*civitates*).

Senatusconsultum Articuleianum. (A.D. 123.) Concerned fideicommissary manumissions in provinces.

Senatusconsultum Calvisianum. (4 B.C.) Dealt with penal procedure in trials for *crimen repetundarum* held in provinces.

> Riccobono, *FIR* 1² (1941) p. 409; Stroux and Wenger, *ABayAW* 34, 2 (1928) 112; Arangio-Ruiz, *Riv. di filologia*, N.S. 6 (1928) 321; v. Premerstein, *ZSS* 48 (1928) 428; 478 and 51 (1931) 446; La Pira, *St ital. di filol. clas.* 8 (1929) 59; I. G. Luzzatto, *Epigrafia giuridica* (1942) 239 (Bibl.), 278; J. H. Oliver, *Mem. Amer. Acad. Rome,* 1949, 105.

Senatusconsultum Calvisianum. (A.D. 61.) Ordained that a marriage of a man over sixty with a woman over fifty did not exempt them from the sanctions of the LEX IULIA DE MARITANDIS ORDINIBUS.

Senatusconsultum Claudianum. 1. (A.D. 47.) Forbade advocates to claim more than 10,000 sesterces as an honorarium on pain of being prosecuted for *crimen repetundarum*; see SENATUSCONSULTUM DE ADVOCATIONIBUS. 2. (A.D. 49.) Permitted marriage with a niece (to make possible the marriage of the emperor Claudius with his niece). 3. (A.D. 52.) Contained among other things the provision that a free woman living in a conjugal union with a slave (*contubernium*) became a slave (and her children as well) if after three warnings by the slave's master she continued her relation with the slave. She was then attributed to the slave's master as his slave. Later legislation gradually modified the penalties of this *senatusconsultum.*—There were still some other *senatusconsulta* in the times of Claudius.—Inst. 3.12; D. 29.5; C. 7.24; 9.11.

> Brecht, *RE* 18, 4, 2049; (Volterra) *NDI* 12, 36; Rossello, *StSen* 11–12 (1894, 1896); Albanese, *Il Circolo giuridico* 22 (Palermo, 1951) 86; Biondi, *Iura* 3 (1952) 142.

Senatusconsultum Dasumianum. (*Ca.* A.D. 119.) Provided remedies for fideicommissary manumissions when through absence or impuberty of the beneficiary the manumission ordered by the testator could not be performed.

> H. Krüger, *ZSS* 48 (1928) 178; Besnier, *RHD* 19 (1930) 836.

Senatusconsultum de advocationibus. (A.D. 55.) Prohibited the payment or promise of an honorarium to advocates before the trial. "All who have a lawsuit will be ordered before proceeding to take an oath that they have not given, promised, or guaranteed by a *cautio* any sum to anybody with regard to his activity as an advocate (*advocatio*) in the trial" (Pliny, *Ep.* 9.4). They could, however, after the conclusion of the trial pay an honorarium not exceeding the amount of 10,000 sesterces; see SENATUSCONSULTUM CLAUDIANUM (under no. 1).

Senatusconsulta de aedificiis non diruendis. (A.D. 44 and 56.) Prohibited the acquisition of buildings with the intention of destroying them for profit (*diruendo plus adquirere*). Such a transaction was void and the buyer had to pay double the price to the fisc as a penalty. The two *senatusconsulta* are called Hosidianum and Volusianum after their proposers.

> Riccobono, *FIR* 1² (1941) no. 45 (Bibl.); Grupe, *ZSS* 48 (1928) 572; May, *RHD* 14 (1935) 1.

Senatusconsultum de agnoscendis liberis. See AGNOSCERE LIBEROS, SENATUSCONSULTUM PLANCIANUM.

Senatusconsultum de aquaeductibus. (11 B.C.) See AQUAEDUCTUS.

> Riccobono, *FIR* 1² (1941) no. 41; Kornemann, *RE* 4, 1784; De Robertis, *La espropriazione per pubblica utilità,* 1936, 95; *idem, AnBari* 7–8 (1947) 177.

Senatusconsultum de Asclepiade. (78 B.C.) Granted various privileges (e.g., exemption from all taxes and requisitions) to the captains of three Greek ships for the help given Rome in the Social War time. It is preserved completely in Greek, partly in Latin.

> Riccobono, *FIR* 1² (1941) no. 35; Gallet, *RHD* 1937, 242; 387; E. H. Warmington, *Remains of ancient Latin* 4 (1940) 444; Pietrangeli, *BIDR* 51–52 (1948) 281.

Senatusconsultum de Bacchanalibus. (186 B.C.) Instituted proceedings against the participants in the so-called Bacchanalian conspiracy who committed various crimes. In order to suppress the orgiastic outrages performed under the cover of Dionysiac festivities the consuls were authorized to conduct the trials in an extraordinary procedure (*quaestio extra ordinem*) without regard to the rules of appeal, and beyond the walls of the city of Rome. The text of the *senatusconsultum* is preserved.

> Riccobono, *FIR* 1² (1941) no. 30 (Bibl.); E. H. Warmington, *Remains of old Latin* 4 (1940) 254; Volterra, *NDI* 12, 31; De Ruggiero, *DE* 1 (*s.v. Bacchus*); Wissowa, *RE* 1; E. Massonneau, *La magie dans l'antiquité rom.,* 1934, 151; F. M. De Robertis, *Diritto associativo,* 1937, 52; Arangio-Ruiz, *SDHI* 5 (1939) 109; Bequignon, *Rev. archéologique,* 1941, 184; Frezza, *AnTr* 17 (1946–47) 205.

Senatusconsultum de collegiis. A decree of the senate of unknown date (Augustus?) concerning the foundation of *collegia* (associations) and ordering their dissolution in the case of an activity against the state. The relation of the *senatusconsultum* to the *Lex Iulia de collegiis* is not quite clear. Doubtful also is the question of whether a portion of a *senatusconsultum* preserved epigraphically belongs to this *senatusconsultum.*—See COLLEGIA.

> Riccobono, *FIR* 1² (1941) 291; Arangio-Ruiz, *FIR* 3 (1943) 101; Volterra, *NDI* 12, 34; F. M. De Robertis, *Diritto associativo romano,* 1938, 244; 292; *Acta Divi Augusti* 1 (1945) 266; Berger, *Epigraphica* 9 (1947) 44.

Senatusconsultum de collusione detegenda. See
SENATUSCONSULTUM NINNIANUM.

Senatusconsultum de Iudaeis. (132 B.C.) An answer to the Jewish state concerning its complaints against Antiochus, king of Syria. The knowledge of this *senatusconsultum* as of several others dealing with Jewish matters, comes from Flavius Josephus.
J. Juster, *Les Juifs dans l'Empire Rom.* 1 (1914) 133.

Senatusconsulta de ludis saecularibus. (17 B.C. and A.D. 47.) Partly preserved, concern the national games called LUDI SAECULARES, in the arrangement of which the *quindecim viri sacris faciundis* played an important role.
Riccobono, *FIR* 1² (1941) no. 40; *Acta Divi Augusti* 1 (1945) 240; Nilsson, *RE* 1A, 1696; Pighi, *De ludis saecularibus,* 1941.

Senatusconsultum de nundinis saltus Beguensis. (A.D. 138.) Granted market privileges to a locality in the province of Africa.
Riccobono, *FIR* 1² (1941) no. 47.

Senatusconsultum de pago Montano. (Of the first century B.C.?) Prohibited the dumping of refuse in certain zones outside of Rome.
Riccobono, *FIR* 1² (1941) no. 39; Philipp, *RE* 16, 204.

Senatusconsultum de philosophis et rhetoribus. (161 B.C.) Forbade Greek philosophers and rhetoricians to reside in Rome.

Senatusconsultum de provinciis consularibus. (51 B.C.) Settled the rules for the relations between the senate and the magistrates of consular provinces.

Senatusconsultum de sumptibus ludorum gladiatoriorum minuendis. (A.D. 176.) Issued provisions in order to diminish the expenses connected with gladiatorial games.—See LUDI GLADIATORII.
Riccobono, *FIR* 1² (1941) no. 49; L. Robert, *Les gladiateurs dans l'Orient grec,* 1940, 284.

Senatusconsultum de Thisbensibus. (170 B.C.) Concerned the relations with the city of Thisbae in Boeotia.
Riccobono, *FIR* 1² (1941) no. 31.

Senatusconsultum de Tiburtinis. (159 B.C.) Granted a general amnesty to the city of Tibur.
Riccobono, *FIR* 1² (1941) no. 33.

Senatusconsultum Geminianum. Extended the penalties of the *Lex Cornelia de falsis* on persons who accepted money for a false testimony.—See FALSUM.

Senatusconsultum Hosidianum. (A.D. 44.) Directed against speculation in house property.—See SENATUS-CONSULTA DE AEDIFICIIS NON DIRUENDIS.
De Pachtère, *Mél Cagnat* 1912; May, *RHD* 14 (1935) 1.

Senatusconsultum Iuncianum. (A.D. 127.) Established again (see SENATUSCONSULTUM DASUMIANUM) some rules concerning a fideicommissary manumission of slaves in the case of absence of the person who for any reason (*ex quacumque causa*) had to free them.

Senatusconsultum Iuventianum. (Decreed under Hadrian on the proposal of the jurist Iuventius Celsus.) Dealt with claims of the *acrarium populi*

Romani against private individuals for the recovery of vacant inheritances. The rules of the *senatusconsultum* appear extended to *hereditatis petitiones* among private persons, but apparently a good part of this extension belongs to later development, if not to postclassical and Justinian's law. The *senatusconsultum* established the liability of an illegal holder of an estate who fraudulently sold objects belonging to the inheritance or gave up possession thereof (*dolo desiit possidere*) as well as the duty of restitution of products and profits (interest) which the unlawful possessor of the estate derived therefrom. Distinction was made between possessors in good faith and such in bad faith.—See HEREDITATIS PETITIO.
Beseler, *Beiträge* 4 (1920) 13; Fliniaux, *RHD* 2 (1923) 82; J. Denoyez, *Le S. I.,* 1926; Lewald, *ZSS* 48 (1928) 638; C. Appleton, *RHD* 9 (1930) 1, 621; Fliniaux, *ibid.* 110; Huber, *Die Ausdehnung der Normen des sc. J.,* Diss. Erlangen, 1933; Carcaterra, *AnBari* 3 (1940) 104; A. Guarino, *Salv. Iulianus,* 1946, 82; B. Biondi, *Istituti fondamentali del dir. ereditario* 2 (1948) 193; Santi Di Paola, *AnCat* 2 (1948) 275; A. Carcaterra, *L'azione hereditaria* 2 (1948) 37.

Senatusconsultum Largianum. (A.D. 42.) Established the order of succession for inheritances of LATINI IUNIANI.

Senatusconsultum Libonianum. (A.D. 16.) Declared testamentary dispositions in favor of the writer of the testament to be void. By an enactment of the Emperor Claudius the writer was in such a case subject to the penalties of the *Lex Cornelia de falsis.*—D. 48.10.—See FALSUM.
De Martino, *Scr in memoria di E. Massari,* 1938, 331.

Senatusconsultum Licinianum. (A.D. 27? 45?) Dealt with conspiracy to forge a testament and false testimony concerning a testament.

Senatusconsultum Macedonianum. (Under Vespasian.) Forbade loans to sons under paternal power (*filii familias*). The transaction was not void, but the son was protected by an *exceptio* (*exceptio senatusconsulti Macedoniani*) against the claim of the lender even after the father's death.—D. 14.6; C. 4.28.—See STUDIUM.
Volterra, *NDI* 12, 38; Devilla, *StSas* 18 (1941) 255; Daube, *ZSS* 65 (1947) 261.

Senatusconsultum Memmianum. (A.D. 63.) Contained the provision that childless persons (*orbi*) could not evade the disadvantages introduced by the LEX IULIA DE MARITANDIS ORDINIBUS by a fictitious adoption of children.

Senatusconsultum Neronianum. (A.D. 57?) Extended the provisions of the *senatusconsultum Silanianum* on the slaves of the widow of an assassinated master.

Senatusconsultum Neronianum de legatis. (Between A.D. 60 and 64.) Abolished the distinction among the various forms of legacies (*legata*). It decreed that a legacy expressed in less appropriate terms should be as valid as if it had been made in the most favorable form (*optimo iure*, i.e., *per damnationem*).—See LEGATUM, LEGATUM PER DAMNATIONEM.—There were several other *senatusconsulta* decreed under Nero.

> Volterra, *NDI* 12, 37; Ciapessoni, *St Bonfante* 3 (1930) 649; Piaget, *Le S. N.* (Lausanne, 1936); C. A. Maschi, *St sull'interpretazione dei legati*, 1938, 104; B. Biondi, *Successione testamentaria* (1943) 282.

Senatusconsultum Ninnianum de collusione detegenda. (Under Domitian.) Contained provisions against collusion between patron and freedman with a view to having the latter declared free-born.—See COLLUSIO.

Senatusconsultum Orfitianum. (A.D. 178.) Gave a woman's children preference as to her inheritance over her brothers, sisters, and other agnates.—Another *senatusconsultum* (of the same year) declared testamentary manumissions of slaves valid when their identity could be established beyond doubt, even if they were not indicated in the testament by name, as the LEX FUFIA CANINIA required.—Inst. 3.4; D. 37.17; C. 6.57.

> G. La Pira, *La successione ereditaria intestata*, 1930, 293, Lavaggi, *SDHI* 12 (1946) 174; Sanfilippo, *Fschr Schulz* 1 (1951) 364.

Senatusconsultum Pegasianum. (About A.D. 73.) Granted an heir the right to keep a fourth part of the *fideicommissa* he had to deliver according to the testator's will. This provision is analogous to that of the LEX FALCIDIA with regard to legacies. The initiative for the *senatusconsultum* was apparently taken by the jurist Pegasus. In Justinian's legislation the *senatusconsultum Pegasianum* does not appear, references to it having been replaced by those to the SENATUSCONSULTUM TREBELLIANUM.—Another *senatusconsultum Pegasianum* (A.D. 72) extended the privilege of *anniculi causae probatio* to LATINI IUNIANI over thirty years of age; see CAUSAE PROBATIO.

> Solazzi, *RISG* 86 (1949) 30.

Senatusconsultum Pisonianum. (A.D. 57.) Concerned the sale of a slave who might be subject to torture and the penalties provided in the SENATUSCONSULTUM SILANIANUM because his master was found assassinated. The sale was null and the seller had to return the purchase price to the buyer.

Senatusconsultum Plancianum. (Before the reign of Hadrian.) Ordered that a pregnant woman had to notify (*denuntiare*) her divorced husband of her condition within thirty days after divorce. The husband had either to send attendants (*custodes*) to watch the woman until the child was born or to deny (*contra denuntiare*) his paternity.—D. 25.3.—See AGNOSCERE LIBERUM.

> Weiss, *RE* 3A, 1889; P. Tisset, *Présomption de paternité* (Montpellier, 1921) 180.

Senatusconsultum Rubrianum. (After A.D. 100.) Ordered the praetor to declare a slave free when the person who had to perform the manumission according to the testator's will refused to do so.

Senatusconsultum Silanianum. (A.D. 10.) When a master of slaves was assassinated and the murderer could not be found, all slaves who lived with him "under the same roof" were subjected to torture and eventually condemned to death. A slave who revealed the murderer was declared free by the praetor's decree.—See SENATUSCONSULTUM NERONIANUM, PISONIANUM, ORATIO MARCI, TECTUM, VINDICARE NECEM.

> Luzzatto, *St Ratti* (1934) 545; Aru, *ibid.* 211; *Acta Divi Augusti* 1 (1945) 258; Herrmann, *ADO-RIDA* 1 (1952) 495.

Senatusconsultum Tertullianum. (Of the time of Hadrian.) Granted a mother who had the IUS LIBERORUM a right of succession on intestacy to her children's inheritance, but it gave priority to the children's children, their father and some agnates. Later imperial legislation improved the rights of succession of the mother. Justinian abolished the requirement of *ius liberorum*.—Inst. 3.3; D. 38.17; C. 6.56.

> G. La Pira, *La successione ereditaria intestata*, 1930, 277; G. Goutelle, *De la lutte entre agnation et cognation à propos du S. T.*, 1934; Sanfilippo, *Fschr Schulz* 1 (1951) 364.

Senatusconsultum Trebellianum. (A.D. 56.) Ordered that "if an inheritance was delivered over to anyone on account of a *fideicommissum*, the actions which would lie at *ius civile* for, or against, the heir, should also be given in favor of, or against, him to whom the inheritance has been made over" (Gaius, Inst. 2.253). The pertinent actions were proposed in the praetorian edict as *actiones utiles*.—D. 36.1; C. 6.49.—See EXCEPTIO RESTITUTAE HEREDITATIS, HEREDITATIS PETITIO FIDEICOMMISSARIA.

> Lemercier, *RHD* 14 (1935) 623; B. Biondi, *Successione testamentaria* (1943) 477; Bartošek, *Scr Ferrini* 3 (Milan, 1948) 308.

Senatusconsultum Turpillianum. (A.D. 61.) Contained provisions against TERGIVERSATIO.—D. 48.16; C. 9.45.

> Volterra, *StCagl* 17 (1929) 114; Levy, *ZSS* 53 (1933) 213; Bohaček, *St Riccobono* 1 (1936) 361.

Senatusconsultum ultimum. A decree of the senate in times of extreme emergency (*ultima necessitas*) ordering "that the consuls see to it that the state (*res publica*) suffered no harm" (*Cic. pro Mil.* 26.70) or, in other words, to defend the *res publica*. By virtue of such a decision the consuls (or the highest magistrate available) were authorized to apply any extraordinary measures required by the situation (*tumultus*, war), even a temporary suspension of certain constitutional institutions (see IUSTITIUM). The first application of this exceptional remedy was during the Gracchan movement (121 B.C.; it was proposed for the first time in 133 B.C., but was rejected owing to resistance of the then consul, the jurist P. M. Scaelova).

> O'Brien-Moore, *RE* Suppl. 6, 756; Momigliano, *OCD*; C. Barbagallo, *Una misura eccezionale dei Romani, il S. U.,*

1900; *idem, RendLomb* 35 (1902) 450; De Marchi, *ibid.* 224, 464; Plaumann, *Kl* 13 (1913) 321; Antonini, *S. U.,* 1914; Last, *JRS* 33 (1943) 94; Wirszubski, *Libertas* (Cambridge, 1950) 55.

Senatusconsultum Velleianum (or Vellaeanum). (About A.D. 46.) Forbade women to assume liability for other persons (*intercedere, intercessio*). The transaction was not void, but lost its efficacy if the woman when sued by the creditor opposed the *exceptio senatusconsulti Velleiani.* She could also claim the return of what she had paid in fulfillment of her obligation. In certain instances the exception was inadmissible (e.g., against a minor, or when the transaction was in the interest of the woman). Sureties and heirs of the woman might use the exception too. Justinian reformed the whole institution of women's intercession by requiring a public act before witnesses, and excluding the benefits of the *senatusconsultum Velleianum* if the woman renewed the intercession after two years and in certain other specific cases.—See INTERCESSIO, ACTIO QUAE RESTITUIT (INSTITUIT) OBLIGATIONEM.—D. 16.1; C. 4.29.

> Leonhard, *RE* 9 (*s.v. intercessio*); Cuq, *DS* 3 (*s.v. intercessio*); Volterra, *NDI* 12, 35; Carrelli, *RISG* 12 (1937) 63; *idem, SDHI* 3 (1937) 305; P. Pierret, *Le s. Velléien,* 1947; Vogt, *Studien zum s.V.,* Bonn, 1952.

Senatusconsultum Vitrasianum. (Before or during the reign of Hadrian). Concerned the case of the fideicommissary manumission of a slave when one of the co-heirs was a child.

Senatusconsultum Volusianum. (A.D. 56.) See SENATUSCONSULTA DE AEDIFICIIS NON DIRUENDIS.

> May, *RHD* 14 (1935) 1.

Senectus (senex). Old age (an old man). There was no legal definition as to when a person had to be considered old. Senility, however, was taken into consideration as an excuse from guardianship, for exemption from *munera personalia,* and the like, as well as in certain agreements, for instance, concerning alimony. A guardian who could not fulfill his duties because of old age might ask for the assignment of a curator for the administration of the ward's property.

Seniores. In military centuriae, see IUNIORES.

Sensus. In the legal field the capacity of understanding the significance of one's doings, in particular, whether they are wrong or right. Children in infancy (see INFANTES) have no *sensus;* likewise lunatics, except during INTERVALLA DILUCIDA. *Sensus* also means the intention, the desire of a testator; syn. *voluntas.*

Sententia. (With reference to a jurist.) The opinion of a jurist expressed either in his writing or in a RESPONSUM.

Sententia. (In judicial proceedings.) The final judgment in a civil trial, rendered by a judge (*iudex*) in the bipartite procedure or by a judicial official in the *cognitio extra ordinem.* The *sententia* put an end to the controversy between the parties and the matter in dispute became now a *res iudicata.* The judgment was either condemnatory (*condemnatio, damnatio*) or absolutory (*absolutio*). In the formulary procedure the condemnatory judgment was always for a sum of money (see CONDEMNATIO PECUNIARIA) without regard to the object of the controversy. In the procedure through *cognitio* a *condemnatio pecuniaria* was no longer exclusive. A judgment once pronounced could not be changed or revoked by the judge who passed it. See ERROR CALCULI. The execution of a judgment was achieved by a second action; see ACTIO IUDICATI. The judgment was pronounced orally, without indication of motives; in the later law a written judgment was required in addition to the oral pronouncement; see SENTENTIAM DICERE. *Sententia* is also the judgment of an arbitrator; see ARBITER, COMPROMISSUM.—The terminology in criminal trials was also *condemnatio (damnatio)* for condemnatory sentences, *absolutio* for an acquittal.—D. 42.1; C. 7.43–47; 55; 10.9; 50.—See RES IUDICATA, IUDICATUM, RETRACTARE CAUSAM, APPELLATIO, PROVOCATIO, PERICULUM, SENTENTIAM PROFERRE, LITIS AESTIMATIO.

> Wenger, *RE* 2A; Leonhard, *RE* 2A, 1503; Kleinfeller, *RE* 2A, 1505; Delaunay, *Mél Boissier* (Paris, 1903) 161; G. Kuttner, *Fschr Martitz* 1911, 235; Biondi, *St Bonfante* 4 (1930) 29; H. Appelt, *Die Urteilsnichtigkeit im röm. Prozess,* 1937; F. Vassalli, *Studi* 1 (1939) 405; Vazny, *BIDR* 47 (1940) 108.

Sententia adversus fiscum. A sentence rendered against the fisc.—C. 10.9.—See RETRACTARE CAUSAM.

Sententia contra constitutiones. A judgment rendered contrary to imperial constitutions. The judge who rendered such a judgment was guilty of *crimen falsi.*—See FALSUM.

> Biondi, *St Bonfante* 4 (1930) 69; Levy, *BIDR* 45 (1938) 138; De Robertis, *ZSS* 62 (1942) 255.

Sententia definitiva. See DEFINITIVA SENTENTIA, INTERLOCUTIONES.

Sententia iudicis. See SENTENTIA.

Sententia legis (edicti, senatusconsulti). The intention, the purpose, the spirit of a legal enactment (a statute, an edict, a *senatusconsultum*).—See EX LEGE.

> Wenger, *RE* 2A, 1502.

Sententia Minuciorum. See TERMINARE.

Sententia senatus. See SENTENTIAM ROGARE, PRONUNTIARE SENTENTIAM.

> Wenger, *RE* 2A, 1496.

Sententiae Pauli. A work by the jurist Paul in five books, entitled *Sententiarum ad filium libri quinque.* Excerpts of this work are to be found in the Digest, *Fragmenta Vaticana, Collatio,* and *Consultatio,* and probably one-sixth of the whole work in an Epitome appended to the *Lex Romana Visigothorum.* It is assumed (not without opposition) that the work was not written by Paul himself, but was an anthology compiled about A.D. 300 from various works of Paul's by an unknown hand. The work as is preserved undoubtedly contains postclassical additions, and the more important problem is to determine what in the work is classical and what not. As a matter of fact, Constantine, less than a century after Paul's death (*C. Theod.* 1.4.2, A.D. 327 or 328), extolled the value of the work in glowing terms and ordered that it should have full authority when produced in court. The Law of Citations (see IURISPRUDENTIA) of A.D. 426 reiterated the validity of Paul's Sentences.

Editions in all collections of *Fontes Iuris Rom.* (see General Bibl., Ch. XII), the most recent by Baviera, *FIR* 2² (1940).—Berger, *RE* 10, 731; M. Conrat, *Der westgothische Paulus,* Amsterdam, 1907; G. Beseler, *Beiträge zur Kritik* 1 (1910) 99; 3 (1913) 6; 4 (1920) 336; B. Kübler, *Gesch. des röm. R.,* 1925, 284; Schulz, *ZSS* 47 (1927) 39; Levy, *ZSS* 50 (1930) 272; Lauria, *AnMac* 6 (1930) 33; Volterra, *ACDR* 1 (Roma, 1934) 35; *idem, Riv. Storia dir. ital.* 8 (1935) 110 (Bibl.); Scherillo, *St Riccobono* 1 (1936) 39; E. Levy, *Medievalia et Humanistica* 1 (1943) 14; *idem, Pauli S., a Palingenesia of the opening titles* (Ithaca, 1945); *idem, BIDR* 55/56 (1951) 226; F. Schulz, *History of R. legal science,* 1946, 176.

Sententiam dare. See SENTENTIAM DICERE.

Sententiam dicere. (In judicial proceedings.) To pronounce judgment. The judge had to do it orally, in later law reading the decision from a written draft. Syn. *sententiam dare, pronuntiare, proferre.*—See PERICULUM.

Sententiam dicere. (In the senate.) See SENTENTIAM ROGARE.

Sententiam rogare. To ask the senators for their opinions. It was the presiding magistrate who requested the senators to express their opinion by vote (*sententiam dicere*). Hence *sententia* often means the result of the vote, the final decision (*ex sententia senatus*).—See VERBA FACERE.

Sentire aliquid (or de aliqua re). To have in mind, to wish, to intend, to understand. The term occurs frequently in texts dealing with the intention of a testator when the expressions he used in his will were not fully clear.—See SENSUS, VOLUNTAS.

Sentire damnum. To suffer damage (loss). Ant. *sentire commodum, lucrum* = to gain a profit.

Separare. To divide, to separate, to disjoin. See FRUCTUS SEPARATI. With reference to a marriage = to divorce; hence *separatio = divortium.*

Separatio bonorum. The separation of the heir's property from the estate he inherited. The *separatio bonorum* served to protect the creditors of the deceased by reserving the estate for them and excluding the creditors of the heir, who might be insolvent. The institution, called *beneficium separationis,* was extended to the benefit of the legatees, but not of the creditors of the heir when the inheritance was insolvent. See BENEFICIUM INVENTARII. The *separatio bonorum* comprised the estate at the time of death, together with subsequent products and accretions which occurred afterwards.—D. 42.6; C. 7.72.

Ferrini, *Opere* 4 (1930, ex 1899–1901) 167; 175; 183; G. Baviera, *Il commodum separationis,* 1901; Solazzi, *BIDR*

(1901) 247; Milani, *StDocSD* 25 (1904) 5; C. Tumedei, *La s. dei beni ereditari,* 1927; Guarino, *ZSS* 60 (1940) 185; *idem, SDHI* 10 (1944) 240; Solazzi, *Il concorso dei creditori* 4 (1943) 1.

Separatio fructuum. Separation of fruits from the thing which produced them.—See FRUCTUS, FRUCTUS SEPARATI.

Separatim. See CONIUNCTIM. Syn. *disiunctim.*

Septemvirale iudicium. A court composed of seven persons competent (presumably) to judge complaints concerning undutiful testaments; see QUERELA INOFFICIOSI TESTAMENTI.

Leonhard, *RE* 2A (*s.v. septemviri*); Eisele, *ZSS* 35 (1914) 320.

Sepulcri violatio. See VIOLATIO SEPULCRI.

Sepulcrum (sepulchrum). A grave, a burial place "where a corpse or bones are laid down" (D. 11.7.2.5). A *sepulcrum* is a *locus religiosus,* also when a slave has been buried, but not the grave of an enemy. A monument (*monumentum*) erected "in order to preserve the memory of a dead person" (D. 11.7.2.6) is not a *locus religiosus* if the person is not buried there.—D. 11.8; 47.12; C. 9.19.—See ITER AS SEPULCRUM, IUS SEPULCRI, ILLATIO MORTUI.

C. Fadda, *St e questioni di diritto* 1 (1910) 147; Taubenschlag, *ZSS* 38 (1917) 244; M. Morel, *Le s.* (*Annales Univ. Grenoble*) 1928; E. Albertario, *Studi di dir. rom* 2 (1941) 1, 29, 39; Arangio-Ruiz, *FIR* 3 (1943) no. 80; F. De Visscher, *AntCl* 15 (1946) 123; *idem, SDHI* 13–14 (1947–48) 278; *idem, RIDA* 1 (1948) 199; *idem, Le régime jurid. des plus anciens cimetières chrétiens, Analecta Bollandiana* 69 (1951) 39; Crichton, *JurR* 60 (1948) 138; Biondi, *Iura* 1 (1950) 160; Düll, *Fschr Schulz* 1 (1951) 191.

Sepulcrum familiare (hereditarium). See IUS SEPULCRI.

Sequela. (With reference to an obligation.) A secondary obligation, as distinguished from the principal obligation of a debtor.

Sequester. "One with whom the parties to a controversy deposit the object of the dispute" (D. 50.16.110). The *sequester* was a depositee and his liability was the same as in the case of a normal deposit; see DEPOSITUM. The recovery of the thing deposited could be claimed by an action, called *actio (depositi) sequestraria.* Unlike the normal depositee, the *sequester* was considered possessor of the thing and was protected by possessory interdicts.

Weiss, *RE* 2A; Beauchet, *DS* 4; Arangio-Ruiz, *AG* 76 (1906) 471; 78 (1907) 233; Albertario, *St Solmi* 1 (1941) 349; Düll, *Fschr Schulz* 1 (1951) 203.

Sequestrare (sequestratio). To deposit a controversial thing with a third person as a *sequester.* Syn. *in sequestre deponere.*—C. 4.4.—See SEQUESTER.

Sequestre. *In sequestre,* see SEQUESTRARE.

Sequi. Used of rights and obligations which are devolved, after the death of a person, on his heir, as well as of rights connected with an immovable (such as servitudes) which in the case of its transfer pass to the acquirer.

Sequi caput alicuius. See NOXA CAPUT SEQUITUR.

Sequi condicionem alicuius. To follow a person in his personal status (freedom, citizenship). Legitimate children share the status of the father; children born out of wedlock follow that of the mother.—See VULGO CONCEPTI.

Sequi fidem alicuius. To put one's trust, to have confidence (faith) in another's promise or good faith, to confide.

Serenissimus (serenitas). An honorific title of the emperor in the later Empire (from the fourth century on). The emperors used to speak of themselves in their enactments *serenitas nostra* ("our serenity").

Serva. A female slave. Syn. *ancilla*.

Servare. To take care of, to protect. The praetor used the term in his edict when he promised to protect certain transactions or agreements (e.g., *"pacta conventa servabo"*).—See MISSIO IN POSSESSIONEM DOTIS (REI) SERVANDAE CAUSA, MISSIO IN POSSESSIONEM LEGATORUM SERVANDORUM CAUSA.

Servare (ab aliquo). To obtain by a suit what is due, to recover (e.g., expenses made for another, indemnification).

Servari. In locutions such as *servandum est, servabitur,* syn. with *observari* (= to be observed, to be acted according to the law).

Servi. Slaves.—See SERVUS.

Servile supplicium. See CRUX.

Servilis. Connected with slavery or pertaining to slaves. *Servilis condicio* = the legal and social condition of a slave. *Servilis cognatio,* see SERVUS.

Servire. Refers to the legal situation of a slave (see SERVUS) or to that of an immovable encumbered by a servitude (*praedium quod servit*). The terms *praedium serviens* and *praedium dominans,* used in the literature, are unknown in Roman sources.

Servitium. Comprised all persons who were in the service of another. They constituted his *familia* (see FAMILIA). In the language of imperial constitutions *servitium* was used in the sense of any kind of service.

Servitus. Slavery. "We compare slavery almost with death" (D. 50.17.209). "Slavery is an institution of the law of all nations (*ius gentium*) under which one is subject to the mastership (*dominium*) of another, contrary to nature" (D. 1.5.4.1).—See SERVUS (Bibl.), SERVITUTEM SERVIRE, REVOCATIO IN SERVITUTEM, VINDICATIO IN LIBERTATEM.

Servitus (servitutes). A servitude, an easement. *Servitutes* were classified among *iura in re aliena* (= rights over another's property) since their substance consisted in a right of a person, other than the owner, primarily the proprietor of a neighborly immovable, to make a certain use of another's land. This right was vested in the beneficiary not as a personal one, but as a right attached to the immovable (land or building) itself, regardless of the person who actually happened to own it. These servitudes

are *servitutes praediorum* (also *servitutes rerum, iura praediorum*). Among them there is a distinction between *servitutes praediorum rusticorum* and *servitutes praediorum urbanorum* according to the economic exploitation of the benefiting immovable, i.e., either for agricultural production or for urban utilization (housing, commercial or industrial buildings) regardless of the location of the immovable in a city or in the country. Later (postclassical or Justinian's) law added to the servitudes a new category, the personal servitudes (*servitutes personarum, hominum*), in which the beneficiary was a specific person. But only the term, *servitutes personarum,* was a later creation, the pertinent rights to use another's property (*iura in re aliena*) were known in the classical law and discussed and developed by the classical jurisprudence. At the death of the beneficiary a personal servitude was extinguished, whereas in predial (rustic or urban) servitudes the death of the actual beneficiary was without any effect on the existence of the servitude which as connected with the immovable passed to the successor of the owner. Predial servitudes were of a very different nature. Some of them were more typical and the extension of the pertinent rights vested in the owner of the dominant land were determined by law or custom. Modifications were, however, admitted in specific cases; see MODUS SERVITUTIS. There was a legal rule: *"Nemini (nulli) res sua servit"* (D. 8.2.26, no one can have a servitude on a property of his own), since ownership as such implied all kinds of utilization of the thing. Another rule was that a predial servitude could not impose on the owner of the servient immovable the duty of doing something. His liability went only so far as to abstain from doing something to the deriment of the beneficiary of the servitude or to tolerate the latter using his property in some way. A predial servitude, being strictly connected with the dominant immovable, could not be transferred to another person unless the immovable itself was alienated. By the alienation the new owner became the beneficiary of the servitude. A servitude was constituted through MANCIPATIO or IN IURE CESSIO when it was reckoned among RES MANCIPI, as the rustic servitudes were, or on the occasion of the division of a common landed property in favor of the owners of the shares. In a last will a servitude could be granted only in the form of a LEGATUM PER VINDICATIONEM. Praetorian law introduced the establishment of a servitude by an agreement; see PACTIONES ET STIPULATIONES. In Justinian's law the stipulation became usual for this purpose. A predial servitude was extinguished when one of the two immovables, the servient or the dominant, was destroyed, or when the owner of one acquired the other; see CONFUSIO. —*Servitus* in the language of Justinian indicates at times restrictions imposed by the law on owners of immovables, as, for instance, in the buildings regulations set in a constitution of the Emperor Zeno. See ZENONIANAE CONSTITUTIONES. The following items deal with typical predial servitudes, both rural and urban. Some of them appear in the sources as *ius* (*iura*). For the so-called personal servitudes, see USUS, USUSFRUCTUS, HABITATIO, OPERAE SERVORUM. —Inst. 2.3; D. 8.1–3; C. 3.34.—See USUCAPIO SERVITUTIS, USUCAPIO LIBERTATIS, NON USUS, PATI, VINDICATIO SERVITUTIS, PERPETUA CAUSA SERVITUTIS, INTERDICTUM QUAM HEREDITATEM.

> Leonhard, *RE* 2A; Beauchet, *DS* 4; Ciccaglione, *NDI* 12; Berger, *OCD*; Longo, *BIDR* 11 (1899) 281; Buckland, *LQR* 42 (1928); *idem, St Riccobono* 1 (1936) 277; Bonfante, *St Ascoli* (1931) 179; Arangio-Ruiz, *Foro Ital.*, 59 (1932); Frezza, *StCagl* 22 (1934); Grosso, *In tema di costituzione tacita di servitù*, *BIDR* 42 (1934) 326; *idem, SDHI* 3 (1937) 274; *idem, Riv. di dir agrario* 17 (1938) 174; *idem, Problemi di diritti reali* (1944) 26; Guarneri-Citati, *BIDR* 43 (1935) 19; Ciapessoni, *StPav* 22 (1937) 107; B. Biondi, *La categoria rom. delle servitutes*, 1938; *idem, Le servitù prediali* (*Corso*) 1946; E. Albertario, *Studi* 2 (1941) 339; S. Solazzi, *Requisiti e modi di costituzione delle servitù prediali*, 1947; *idem, Specie e estinzione delle servitù prediali*, 1948; *idem, La tutela e il possesso delle servitu prediali*, 1949; E. Levy, *West Roman vulgar law*, 1951, 55.

Servitus actus (ius agendi). See ACTUS, INTERDICTUM DE ITINERE ACTUQUE.

Servitus altius non tollendi (*sc.* aedes). An urban servitude which imposed on the owner of a building the duty not to build higher over a certain limit. A counterpart was a servitude *ius altius tollendi* which gave the beneficiary the right to build higher.

> Buonamici, *Annali Univ. Toscane*, 32 (1913); A. Perret, *Ius a. tollendi*, Thèse Paris, 1924; Grosso, *St Albertoni* 1 (1935) 453; Branca, *St A. Cicu* 1 (1951) 105.

Servitus aquaeductus (aquae ducendae). A rural servitude consisting in the right of the owner of the dominant land to conduct water from, or across, another's land through pipe or canals. The *servitus* was protected by interdicts granted against any one who prevented the beneficiary from exercising his right or who tried to render the water or the necessary constructions useless.—See INTERDICTUM DE AQUA, CASTELLUM.

> Manigk, *RE* 10; Berger, *RE* 9, 1630; Gianziano, *NDI* 1 (*s.v. acque private*); Orestano, *BIDR* 43 (1935) 217; De Robertis, *AnBari* 1 (1938) 61; Maschi, *BIDR* 46 (1939) 313; Solazzi, *Fschr Schulz* 1 (1951) 380.

Servitus aquae haustus. The right to take water from a fountain, a pond, or a spring located on another's property. This easement implied free access (*iter*) to the place. Syn. *servitus aquae hauriendae.*—See FONS, INTERDICTA DE FONTE.

> Leonhard, *RE* 2; Grosso, *BIDR* 40 (1932) 401.

Servitus arenae fodiendae. The right to dig for sand in a land belonging to another.

Servitus calcis coquendae. The right to burn lime on another's land.

Servitus cloacae immittendae. The right to have a drain through a neighbor's land.—See CLOACA.

Servitus cretae eximendae. A rural servitude which entitled one to take chalk from another's soil.

Servitus eundi. See ITER.

Servitus fumi immittendi. See FUMUS.

Servitus itineris. See ITER.

Servitus itineris ad sepulcrum. See ITER AD SEPULCRUM.

Servitus lapidis eximendi. A rural servitude to take stones from a quarry belonging to another.

Servitus luminis. The right to profit by the light from a neighbor's land.

Servitus ne luminibus officiatur. An urban servitude which entitled the beneficiary to prevent his neighbor from building a house which might shut him off from the light. A counterpart to this servitude was the right *ius officiendi luminibus vicini* which gave the beneficiary the right to build on his land as he pleased, regardless of the neighbor's suffering a limitation or loss of light.—See SERVITUS ALTIUS NON TOLLENDI.

Servitus ne prospectui officiatur. This servitude gave the owner of an immovable the right to prevent his neighbor from building a house or planting trees which might impede the beneficiary's pleasant view. —See SERVITUS NE LUMINIBUS OFFICIATUR.

Servitus oneris ferendi. An urban servitude involving the right of the beneficiary to have his building supported by the neighbor's wall. The latter was bound to keep his wall in good condition.

> Ciccaglione, *NDI* 12, 1, 165; Riccobono, *ibid.* 218; Scialoja, *St giur.* 1 (1933, ex 1881) 84; G. Segrè, *BIDR* 41 (1932) 52; *idem, St Ascoli* (1931) 681.

Servitus pascui (pecoris pascendi). See IUS PASCENDI.

Servitus praetoria. A servitude constituted in a form introduced by praetorian law.—See SERVITUS, PACTIONES ET STIPULATIONES.

> H. Krüger. *Die prätorische Servitut*, 1911; Rabel, *Mél Girard* 2 (1912) 387; Berger, *GrZ* 40 (1913) 299; Maschi, *BIDR* 46 (1939) 274; B. Biondi, *Le servitù prediali* (1946) 213.

Servitus proiciendi. See the following item.

Servitus protegendi. An urban servitude which entitled the beneficiary to project a roof on the neighbor's property. A similar servitude was *servitus proiciendi* concerning a balcony projected over the neighbor's land.—See PROTECTUM.

Servitus servitutis esse non potest. A servitude cannot be imposed on a servitude. There was no possibility to transfer the exercise of a servitude wholly or in part to another.

> Perugi, *BIDR* 29 (1916) 181.

Servitus silvae caeduae. The right to cut wood on another's property.

Servitus stillicidii. There were different servitudes connected with the use of dropping rain-water: (*a*) *servitus stillicidii immittendi* = the right to discharge the dropping rain-water from the eaves or spouts of one's building on the property of a neighbor; the latter was obliged to receive it; (*b*) *servitus stillicidii avertendi* = the right to divert the rain-water from the roof of a neighbor's building to make it run on the beneficiary's land; (*c*) *servitus stillicidii recipiendi* = the right to receive·the rain drip from a neighbor's property.

Anon., *NDI* 12, 1, 905; Grosso, *St Albertoni* 1 (1935) 465; Guarneri-Citati, *RendLomb* 59 (1926); B. Biondi, *La categoria rom. delle servitutes* (1938) 129.

Servitus tigni immittendi. An urban servitude which entitled the beneficiary to introduce a beam serving for his building into the wall of a neighbor's building. —See TIGNUM IUNCTUM.

Servitus viae. See VIA.

Servitutem debere. Used of a land which is encumbered with a predial servitude. *Fundo servitus debetur* is used of a land the owner of which is the beneficiary of a predial servitude.

S. Solazzi, *Tutela della servitù prediali,* 1949, 163.

Servitutem servire. Denotes a factual (not legal) condition of a person who although being free performed services of a slave.—See LIBER HOMO BONA FIDE SERVIENS.

J. Ellul, *Évolution et nature jurid. du mancipium* (1936) 282.

Servitutes personarum. See SERVITUS.

C. Sanfilippo, *S. p. (Corso),* 1944; Ciapessoni, *CentCod Pav* (1934) 879; B. Biondi, *Le servitù prediali,* 1946, 50.

Servitutes praediorum (rusticorum, urbanorum). See SERVITUS.

Servius Sulpicius Rufus. A prominent jurist of the second half of the first century of the Republic, consul in 51 B.C., orator and a famous legal teacher. His writings amounted to 180 books; among them was the first commentary on the praetorian Edict. According to Cicero, he furthered the application of equity (see AEQUITAS) in settling legal disputes.

Münzer. *RE* 4A, 851 (no. 95); E. Vernay, *Servius et son école,* 1909; Peters, *ZSS* 32 (1911) 463; Kübler, *ACDR* Roma 1 (1934) 96; Stroux, *ibid.* 130; Di Marzo, *BIDR* 45 (1938) 261; P. Meloni, *S. S. R. e i suoi tempi, Annali Fac. Lettere e Filosofia Univ. Cagliari,* 13 (1946).

Servus. A slave. Syn. terms: *homo, mancipium, ancilla* (a female slave), *puer.* Although a human being, legally a slave was considered a thing (*res*) without any legal personality. He belonged to his master as a RES MANCIPI, and therefore the transfer of ownership of a slave was to be performed through *mancipatio.* All that the slave acquired belonged to his master and he could not assume an obligation for 'his master. Hence there was no action against the latter from transactions concluded by the slave. Exceptions from this rule were introduced by the praetorian law; see PECULIUM, ACTIO TRIBUTORIA, INSTITOR. Aside from these specific cases a general rule was that the legal situation of a master might be improved by a contractual activity of his slave, but

could not be made worse. The master was, however, liable for delictual offenses of the slave (see DELICTUM), but when sued with an *actio noxalis* for the slave's wrongdoing (see NOXA), he might free himself from liability by handing over (surrendering) the slave to the person injured (*noxae deditio*). A slave could not be sued nor could he be plaintiff in a trial. In the earlier law the master had IUS VITAE NECISQUE over the slave, and even during the period of the Republic a slave had no protection against his master's cruelty. See LEX PETRONIA. The law of the Empire brought several restrictions to the master's power. A master who killed his slave without just grounds was punished, and in the case of ill-treatment of a slave he could be compelled to sell him. The pertinent provisions were frequently changed in the later Empire in favor of the slaves under the influence of Christianity. A slave had no family; his marriage-like union was not considered a *matrimonium*; see CONTUBERNIUM. Blood tie created through a servile union (*cognatio servilis*) was later regarded as an impediment to a marriage between persons thus related, after their manumission. Specific rules were in force in criminal law and procedure as far as slaves were concerned. Penalties inflicted on slaves were generally severer than those to which free men were exposed. A slave was not allowed to testify in a criminal trial against his master, except in the case of *crimen maiestatis.* A testimony contrary to this rule was capitally punished. Usually, a slave as a witness in criminal matters was subject to torture;·see QUAESTIO PER TORMENTA. Slavery arose by birth from a slave mother. A foreigner of an enemy country became a slave in the Roman state when taken as a prisoner of war. The same happened to a stranger belonging to a country, not allied with Rome with a treaty of friendship, even when he was caught not in time of war. Other causes of enslavement were: *venditio trans Tiberim* (= the sale of a free man beyond the Tiber, i.e., abroad, see ADDICTUS), the case sanctioned by the SENATUSCONSULTUM CLAUDIANUM, the case of an INGRATUS LIBERTUS (= a freedman ungrateful towards his patron), and the case of a fraudulent sale of a free man (over twenty) as a slave who gave his consent to such a transaction in order to participate in the price. For enslavement as a result of a condemnation for a crime, see SERVUS POENAE. For the specific rules governing the sale of a slave and the liability of the master for physical and mental defects of the slave sold, see EDICTUM AEDILIUM CURULIUM, DICTA, REDHIBITIO. —D. 11.3; 18.7; C. 6.1; 2; 7.7–9; 13.—See moreover, ACTIO SERVI CORRUPTI, OPERAE SERVORUM, ANCILLA, PARTUS ANCILLAE, HOMO, NOMEN, EVINCERE, MANUMISSIO, DEDITICII EX AELIA SENTIA, PECULIUM, LIBER HOMO BONA FIDE SERVIENS, EXPONERE SERVUM, CAPTIVITAS, SENATUSCONSULTUM SILANIANUM, FAMILIA,

STATULIBER, PACTIO LIBERTATIS, INIURIA, and the following items.

Westermann, *RE* Suppl. 6 (*s.v. Sklaverei*); Weiss, *RE* 3A (*s.v. Sklaverei*); Beauchet and Chapot, *DS* 4; W. W. Buckland, *The Roman law of slavery*, 1908; Berger, *Streifzüge durch das röm. Sklavenrecht, I. Philologus* 73 (1914) 61; II. *ZSS* 43 (1922) 398; Tumedei, *RISG* 64 (1920) 55; B. W. Barrow, *Slaves in the R. Empire*, 1928; H. Lévy-Bruhl, *Quelques problèmes du très ancien dr. rom.*, 1934, 15; Jonkers, *De l'influence du Christianisme, Mn* 1934, 241; Juret, *Rev. des études Latines*, 1937, 30; Del Prete, *Responsabilità penale dello schiavo*, 1937; De Manaricua, *El matrimonio de los esclavos, Analecta Gregoriana*, 23 (1940); E. Ciccotti, *Il tramonto della schiavitù nel mondo antico*, 2nd ed. Udine, 1940; Kaser, *SDHI* 6 (1940) 357, 16 (1950) 59; L. Clerici, *Economia e finanza dei Romani* 1 (1943) 128; Solazzi, *SDHI* 15 (1949) 187; Imbert, *Christianisme et esclavage, RIDA* 2 (1949) 445; G. E. Longo, *SDHI* 16 (1950) 86.

Servus actor. See ACTOR.

Servus alienus. A slave belonging to another. If another's slave was instituted as an heir in a testament, his master acquired the inheritance. Freedom given to another's slave in a will was without any effect unless the testator ordered his heir to buy the slave from his master and to manumit him, or the testator rewarded the slave's master on condition that he would free the slave.—See SUPPRIMERE SERVUM ALIENUM.

Desserteaux, *RHD* 12 (1933) 35; G. Dulckeit, *Erblasserwille und Erwerbswille* (1934) 94.

Servus Caesaris. A slave belonging to the emperor either as *servus patrimonialis* (see PATRIMONIUM CAESARIS) or a *servus rei privatae Caesaris* (see RES PRIVATA CAESARIS).

Servus communis. A slave who belongs to more than one master as a common property.—C. 7.7.—See MANUMISSIO SERVI COMMUNIS.

Servus corruptus. See ACTIO SERVI CORRUPTI.

Servus derelictus. A slave whom his master abandoned (*servus quem dominus pro derelicto habet*). Such a slave was a *servus sine domino* (= a slave without a master, a *res nullius*). His former master had no claim for his recovery. In Justinian's law a *servus derelictus* was considered free.—See DERELICTIO (Bibl.), EXPOSITIO SERVI.

Fasciato, *RHD* 27 (1949) 458; Philipsborn, *RHD* 28 (1950) 402.

Servus dotalis. A slave among things constituted as a dowry. The husband was permitted to manumit the slave, even without the consent of the wife, and he became patron of the slave freed. He had to account, however, for the loss which through the manumission resulted to the *dos*, unless his wife assented to the manumission with the intention to make a gift to her husband. Such a gift *manumittendi causa* (= with the purpose of manumission) was not banned by the prohibition of donations between husband and wife.—See DONATIO INTER VIRUM ET UXOREM.

Berger, *Philologus* 73 (1914) 96; Cosentini, *SDHI* 9 (1943) 291.

Servus fiscalis (fisci). A slave employed in the business of the fisc. Slaves came under the mastership of the fisc when the master died without an heir, or when the heir instituted in a testament refused to enter the inheritance (see CADUCA), or when the fisc seized the property of a person condemned for a crime (see CONFISCATIO, PUBLICATIO).—See FISCUS.

Servus fructuarius. A slave on whom a person other than the owner had a usufruct (see USUSFRUCTUS). All that such a slave acquired *ex re* of the usufructuary (i.e., from his money or other property, or from the *peculium* granted by him to the slave), or *ex operis suis* (= from the slave's labor), belonged to the usufructuary; other acquisitions, such as an inheritance or legacies went to the profit of the slave's master. A *servus fructuarius* freed by his master without the fructuary's consent, became a *servus sine domino* (= a slave without a master); under the law of Justinian he became free.—See EX RE ALICUIUS.

Berger, *Philologus* 73 (1914) 61, 91; *idem, ZSS* 43 (1922) 398; Pringsheim, *ZSS* 50 (1930) 408; G. Dulckeit, *Erblasserwille und Erwerbswille* (1934) 26, 101; Solazzi, *BIDR* 49–50 (1947) 373.

Servus fugitivus. A slave who ran away from his master with the intention not to return to him. A *servus fugitivus* also was a slave who ran away from his master's creditor, to whom he had been given as pledge (*creditor pigneraticius*), or from a teacher, and did not return to his master. When caught by a public organ or a private individual, a *servus fugitivus* had to be delivered to the master. Concealing a fugitive slave or helping a slave to escape from his master was considered a theft; see LEX FABIA DE PLAGIO. Syn. *in fuga esse, fugitivus* (noun). A fugitive could be usucapted if the man who held him was in good faith (e.g., he believed to hold a masterless slave).—See CAUTIO DE SERVO PERSEQUENDO.— D. 11.4; C. 6.1.

Arnò, *St Perozzi* 1925, 259; Carcaterra, *AG* 120 (1938) 158; M. Roberti, *La lettera di San Paolo a Filemone e la condizione del servo fugitivo*, 1933; E. Albertario, *St di dir rom.* 2 (1941) 273; Pringsheim, *St Solazzi* 1948, 602; *idem, Fschr Schulz* 1 (1951) 279; Coleman-Norton, *St in honor of A. C. Johnson* (Princeton, 1951) 172.

Servus hereditarius. A slave belonging to an inheritance. Such a slave was interrogated under torture when the authenticity of the testament was questioned, without regard to whether he was freed therein or not.

Servus ordinarius. A slave who had in his *peculium* a slave (see SERVUS VICARIUS).

Servus peculiaris. A slave who was a part of a PECULIUM. A slave in a soldier's *peculium* (PECULIUM CASTRENSE) was the soldier's slave. A *filius familias* endowed with a *peculium* could not manumit a slave belonging to the *peculium* without his father's authorization.

Servus poenae. A free man who became a slave through condemnation with capital punishment (death penalty, fight with wild beasts, forced labor in mines).

He was considered a slave *sine domino* (not belonging to anybody). If a slave was condemned to capital punishment, the ownership of his master was destroyed and did not revive any more. A *servus poenae* could not be freed. In certain cases, a sentence, even when not involving capital punishment, could impose on the condemned slave the additional penalty *"ne manumittatur"* which meant that he could not be manumitted and remained slave for life.

Pfaff, *RE* 2A; Lécrivain, *DS* 4, 1284; Donatuti, *BIDR* 42 (1934) 219; U. Brasiello, *St Virgilii* (1935) 41; *idem, Repressione penale* (1937) 416.

Servus publicus (servus populi Romani). A slave owned by the state (the Roman people). Public slaves were employed in the offices of magistrates, in Rome and municipalities, in temples, pontifical offices and the like, for minor auxiliary work and servant duties. They were granted some personal privileges and, if they had a *peculium*, they might dispose thereof in part. Better qualified slaves were employed in accounting and secretarial service; they obtained at times influential positions and were soon rewarded by their masters with liberty. In the later Empire there was a tendency to exclude slaves from civil service. The manumission of a *servus publicus* was performed by a pertinent declaration of a magistrate with the previous authorization of the senate; in the Empire the emperor granted liberty to a *servus publicus*. In municipalities the manumission was decreed by the municipal council.—C. 7.9.

De Ruggiero, *DE* 2, 750; L. Halkin, *Les esclaves publics chez les Rom.,* 1897.

Servus recepticius. See RECEPTICIUS SERVUS.

Servus redemptus. See REDEMPTUS AB HOSTE.

Servus redemptus suis nummis. See REDEMPTUS SUIS NUMMIS.

Servus sine domino. A slave without a master, not owned by anybody. His legal situation was that of a RES NULLIUS.—See SERVUS POENAE, SERVUS DERELICTUS, SERVUS FRUCTUARIUS.

F. X. Affolter, *Die Persönlichkeit des herrenlosen Sklaven,* 1913.

Servus usuarius. See USUARIUS (adj.), USUS.

Servus vicarius. The slave of a slave, a slave in another slave's *peculium*. He is *servus peculiaris* while his superior is *servus ordinarius*. A *servus vicarius* could have a *peculium* for himself, *peculium vicarii*. The manumission of a *servus vicarius* could be performed by the master of the *servus ordinarius*.

Lécrivain, *DS* 5, 823; H. Erman, *S.v. (Recueil publié par la Faculté de droit de l'Univ. de Lausanne,* 1896) 391; Düll, *ZSS* 67 (1950) 173.

Servus. (Adj.) Used both of persons (slaves) and of immovables encumbered with a servitude (see SERVITUS), as *servus fundus, servum praedium.* Syn. *praedium quod servit.*

Sessio. (From *sedere*). A praetor's sitting in court (*praetor sedit*) whether he is acting PRO TRIBUNALI or DE PLANO.

Sestertium. One thousand sesterces (*sestertii*).—See SESTERTIUS, SOLIDUS.

Lenormant, *DS* 2, 95.

Sestertius (*scil.* nummus). A silver coin in the Republic, a brass coin in the Principate. It was first equivalent to two and a half asses, later to four asses (see AS). Abbreviation: HS. *Sestertio nummo uno* occurs in inscriptions for *nummo uno*; see NUMMUS UNUS.—See SOLIDUS.

Regling, *RE* 2A; Babelon, *DS* 4; Lenormant, *DS* 2, 94; Mattingly, *OCD* (*s.v.* coinage).

Sestertius pes. See AMBITUS.

Severus Valerius. See VALERIUS SEVERUS.

Seviri (sexviri) Augustales. See AUGUSTALES.

Sexagenarius. See PROCURATORES in public law.

Sexprimi. The "first six." They were the chairmen of the association of subordinate officials (see APPARITORES).

Si paret. See INTENTIO (a part of the procedural formula).

Si quidem . . . , si vero. . . . If . . . , if, however. Sentences in which two or more contrasting legal situations are taken into consideration occur in interpolated passages. This and similar constructions are, however, not an absolutely reliable criterion of interpolation.

Guarneri-Citati, *Indice²* (1927) 81; *idem, Fschr Koschaker* 1 (1937) 152.

Si quis. See SIGNIFICATIO VERBORUM.

Sicarius. A murderer. Sulla's *Lex Cornelia de sicariis* introduced a *quaestio perpetua* (a permanent court) for murderers (*sicarii*) and poisoners (*venefici*). In classical law a *sicarius* was also one who was going around armed with the intention to assassinate someone or to commit a theft, furthermore one who in his capacity as a magistrate or chairman of a criminal court induced a witness to make false testimony in order to prosecute and convict an innocent person of a crime, and a magistrate or judge who received a bribe to accuse a person of a capital crime. "It makes no difference whether one killed a man or caused his death" (D. 48.8.15). Under the influence of jurisprudence and imperial legislation the mentioned *Lex Cornelia,* which remained in force still under Justinian, was applied to various kinds of offenses which resulted in the death of a man. Death penalty was inflicted on the criminal and his property was seized. In many cases the accuser was rewarded.—D. 48.8; C. 9.16.—See LEX CORNELIA DE SICARIIS, HOMICIDIUM, PARRICIDIUM.

Pfaff, *RE* 8, 2249; Cuq, *DS* 3, 1140; Hitzig, *Schweizerische Ztschr. für Strafrecht* 9 (1896) 28; Condanari-Michler, *Scr Ferrini* 3 (1948, Univ. Sacro Cuore, Milan) 70.

Sigillum. A seal affixed to a written document. Syn. SIGNUM.

Siglae. Abbreviations. Justinian forbade the use of *sigtae* in manuscripts of the Digest and the Code.

Bilabel, *RE* 2A; Berger, *BIDR* 55–56 Post-Bellum (1951) 158; 166.

Signare. To subscribe a document (a last will); syn. *subscribere. Signare* denotes also to seal with a *signum* (with a seal ring = *anulus signatorius*), e.g., wax-tablets on which a testament was written. In a wider sense *signare* = to provide a thing with a sign or a mark to indicate the owner.—See SIGNUM, ANULUS.

Signare pecuniam. To seal a little bag (*sacculum*) containing money to be deposited with a banker or a friend. The depositary was obliged to restore the bag untouched. If the depositor died special precautions were prescribed when one of the heirs demanded the delivery of his share.

Wenger, *RE* 2A, 2377.

Signatores testamenti. Those who signed and sealed a testament as witnesses. When a testament had to be opened after the death of the testator (see APERTURA TESTAMENTI), the *signatores* had to be convoked to acknowledge their seals.

Archi, *StPav* 26 (1941) 84; Macqueron, *RHD* 24 (1945) 164.

Signifer. A standard-bearer in a legion.

Kubitschek, *RE* 2A.

Significatio verborum. The meaning of words. The title 50.16 of the Digest (*De significatione verborum*) gives explanations of several hundreds of terms, both juristic and non-juristic. The definitions were collected from various juristic works in which almost all classical jurists were represented. The collection was prepared for furthering a better understanding of terms and locutions used in the Digest. The title starts with the explanation of the phrase *"si quis"* (= if anybody . . .) which is interpreted to the effect that it "comprises both men and women" (D. 50.16.1).—C. 6.38.

Signum. (With reference to military units.) A standard, a banner.

Kubitschek, *RE* 2A, 2349.

Signum. (On written documents.) A seal (a stamp) put on to close a document in order to make its contents inaccessible to unauthorized persons and protect it against forgery, or at the end of it after the written text. In the latter case the seal (without or with a signature) indicated that the sealer recognized the written declaration as his (*subscriptio, subsignatio*). *Signum* is also the seal of a witness who was present at the making of a document. In certain specific instances sealing a document was legally required. See TESTAMENTUM SEPTEM SIGNIS (SIGILLIS) SIGNATUM. Sealing a forged testament or an illicit removing of a seal from a testament was punished under the *Lex Cornelia de falsis.*—See OBSIGNATIO, SIGNARE, ANULUS.

Wenger, *RE* 2A; Chapot, *DS* 4; Erman, *ZSS* 20 (1899) 181; Wenger, *ZSS* 42 (1921) 611.

Signum agnoscere. To acknowledge a seal as one's own. Syn. *recognoscere.*

Silentiarii. A body of thirty officials in the later Empire, to maintain order in the imperial palace and at court-meetings in the imperial *consistorium.* They also had their assignment in the court ceremonial. Created in the fourth century, they acquired later some military functions. Their commanders (*decuriones*) were considered among the highest functionaries of the imperial palace.—C. 12.16.

Seeck, *RE* 3A; Lécrivain, *DS* 4; J. E. Dunlap, *Univ. of Michigan Studies, Humanistic Ser.* 14 (1924) 220.

Silentium. Silence. Generally, *silentium* is not considered a manifestation of will. Sometimes, however, the silence of a person who in a given situation had to speak, was regarded as non-opposition (*non contradicere, non dissentire*) and as such as a tacit consent, e.g., the silence of a father with regard to a marriage of his son (*filius familias*).—*Silentium* was used also of the inaction on the part of a person who was entitled to act as a plaintiff. *Longum silentium* = such inaction during a longer time; it might produce the loss of an action; see LONGI TEMPORIS PRAESCRIPTIO. For *silentium* of a party during a trial, see TACERE, INTERROGATIO in criminal trials.

G. Borgna, *Del silenzio nei negozi giuridici,* 1901; P. Bonfante, *Scr giur* 3 (1926) 150; Donatuti, *St Bonfante* 4 (1930) 459; Perozzi, *Scr* 2 (1948, ex 1906) 599.

Siliqua. A small silver coin equal to one twenty-fourth of a *solidus aureus.*

Regling, *RE* 3A; Seeck, *ibid.* 65.

Siliquaticum. A sales tax in the later Empire, reckoned in *siliquae.*

Ferrari, *AVen* 99, 2 (1939–40) 202.

Silva. A wood, a woodland. There was a distinction between a *silva caedua* (exploited by cutting trees for timber) and *silva pascua* (used as pasture for cattle). The usufructuary of another's woodland should use it in an economically reasonable way ("as a father of a family," D. 7.1.9.7) and not abuse it to the detriment of the owner.

Burdese, *St sull'ager publicus, MemTor ser.* II, 76 (1952) 117.

Similitudo. Resemblance, analogy. *Ad similitudinem* is syn. with *ad instar, ad exemplum.*—See INSTAR, EXEMPLUM.

Steinwenter, *St Arangio-Ruiz* 2 (1952) 172.

Simplaria venditio. A sale in which the seller did not specify any particular quality or defect of the thing sold (for instance, a slave sold as "no good, no bad"). Such sales which normally concerned ordinary things of no great value, could not be rescinded by REDHIBITIO.

Bruns and Sachau, *Syrisch-röm. Rechtsbuch,* 1880, 207.

Simplicia interdicta. See INTERDICTA SIMPLICIA.

Simplicitas. Simplicity, clearness. "Simplicity (clarity) in laws seems to us more desirable than intricacy" (Justinian, Inst. 2.23.7).

Simpliciter. Simply, plainly. The adverb is used in different meanings, depending on with what it is contrasted. Thus, for instance, to promise (to give a donation, to bequeath a legacy) *simpliciter* = unconditionally (when opposed to *sub conditione*); to assume an obligation *simpliciter* = without giving security (when opposed to *cum satisdatione*); to stipulate *simpliciter* = without a penalty (when opposed to a *stipulatio* under penalty). With reference to judicial measures to be granted by a magistrate *simpliciter* is opposed to *causa cognita* (after investigation of the case, see CAUSAE COGNITIO).

Simplum. See ACTIONES IN SIMPLUM.

Simulare (simulatio). To feign, to simulate, to pretend. In contractual relations a *simulatio* occurred when the parties with mutual understanding concluded a transaction while their intention was to conclude another or none at all. The purpose of such fictitious transactions was either to give thereto the appearance of a legal act, while in fact the transaction was illicit (e.g., the parties covered a prohibited donation with a fictitious sale) or to feign that a legal situation existed which in fact did not exist (e.g., an imaginary marriage, *nuptiae simulatae,* to avoid the disadvantages imposed on unmarried persons by the Augustan legislation on marriages, see LEX IULIA ET PAPIA POPPAEA). Acts concluded *simulate* (simulated acts) were not valid since they were not intended by the parties; nor was the act which the parties wanted to conclude valid if it was contrary to the law. The rubric of the title 4.22, of the Code, defines: "More valid is what is being done than what is being expressed in simulated terms." The rule lay stress in particular on the "truth of the mätter" (*veritas rei*) and not on what had been feigned in a written deed.—C. 4.22.—See IMAGINARIUS, DICIS CAUSA.

> Berger, *RE* 9, 1094 (*s.v. imaginarius*); Rabel, *ZSS* 27 (1906) 290; Partsch, *ZSS* 42 (1921) 122; *idem, Aus nachgelassenen Schriften,* 1931, 122; G. Longo, *St Riccobono* 3 (1936) 113; *idem, AG* 115 (1936) 117; 116 (1937) 35; Betti, *BIDR* 42 (1934) 299; *idem, Fschr Koschaker* 1 (1939) 297; *idem, ACSR,* IV Congr., 1938; G. Pugliese, *La simulazione nei negozi giuridici,* 1938.

Sinceritas. A complimentary title used by the emperors in official letters (rescripts) addressed to higher officials of the Empire (*"sinceritas tua"* = your sincerity).

Sine die. Refers to obligations for the fulfillment of which a term was not fixed. "What is due without a date being fixed, has to be paid immediately" (D. 45.1.41.1).

Sine die et consule. Without indication of the day and the consul, i.e., without a date. Constantine ordained that undated imperial constitutions were not valid.

> Niedermeyer, *ACDR* Roma 1 (1934) 366.

Sine domino. See SERVUS SINE DOMINO.

Sine re. See BONORUM POSSESSIO SINE RE.

Sine suffragio. When a juror did not indicate on his voting tablet whether he was for the acquittal or condemnation of the defendant, the tablet was *sine suffragio* (= without any vote).—See CIVITATES SINE SUFFRAGIO.

Sinere. See LEGATUM SINENDI MODO.

Singulare ius. See IUS SINGULARE.

Singuli. Individual citizens (as opposed to the whole people, *populus Romanus*); members of an association (as opposed to the whole body, *universitas*).

Sistere aliquem. To assume the obligation by giving security (to guarantee) that a certain person engaged in a lawsuit (primarily the defendant) will appear in court (*iudicio sistere*) at a fixed date.—See CAUTIO IUDICIO SISTI, VADIMONIUM, VINDEX.

Sisti (se) iudicio. To appear in court.—D. 2.10.

Societas. A contract of partnership concluded between two or more persons with the purpose to share profits and losses. The contractual relationship among the partners (*socii*) arose through simple consent (consensus) of the partners. The intention to conclude a *societas* is termed *affectio societatis*; it certainly makes no difference whether the term is a classical or later creation since, in fact, it does not denote more than *consensus*. The partners contributed to the common business money, goods, rights, claims against third persons, or their personal professional skill and labor. Funds and things collected became joint ownership of all partners, normally in equal shares unless different shares were established at the conclusion of the *societas,* when the contributions of the partners were not equal or when their parts in labor or personal services were of a different value. Accordingly, the share of each partner in profits and losses was fixed by agreement. The *societas* had no legal personality; the partners were liable for the debts of the *societas,* without regard to its funds, on the other hand the claims of the *societas* against its debtors were claims of the partners. A *societas* was dissolved by a mutual agreement of the partners (*dissensus*), by the death of one partner, his *capitis deminutio* or bankruptcy, or by *renuntiatio* of one partner, i.e., his unilateral withdrawal from the *societas.* Controversies among the partners were settled in an action, *actio pro socio,* brought by one partner against the other. The action was an *actio bonae fidei*; the defendant could be condemned only *in id quod facere potest* (see BENEFICIUM COMPETENTIAE), but the condemnation involved infamy. The division of the common property of the partners was achieved through ACTIO COMMUNI DIVIDUNDO. The origin of *societas* goes back to the community of property (see CONSORTIUM) among *filii familias,* heirs of their father, which served as a model for common ownership and common management of affairs among persons not tied by the origin from a common ancestor.—The term *societas* occurs at times in the sense of an association (= *collegium, corpus*).—Inst. 3.25; D. 17.2; C. 4.37.—See COMMUNIO, CONSORTIUM

ERCTO NON CITO, ACTIO COMMUNI DIVIDUNDO, COM-
MUNICATIO LUCRI ET DAMNI, ACTIO PRO SOCIO,
QUAESTUS, VIATICUM.

Manigk, *RE* 3A; Lécrivain, *DS* 4; Rodino, *NDI* 12, 1
(*s.v. società civile*); C. H. Monro, *Digest 17.2. Pro socio*
(Cambridge, 1902); E. Levy, *Konkurrenz der Aktionen*
2, 1 (1922) 139; E. Del Chiaro, *Le contrat de société en
dr. privé rom.*, 1928; A. Poggi, *Il contratto di società*, 1–2
(1930, 1934); Guarneri-Citati, *BIDR* 42 (1934) 166; F.
Wieacker, *ZSS* 54 (1934) 35; *idem, Societas, Hausgemein-
schaft und Erwerbsgesellschaft*, 1936; Arangio-Ruiz, *St
Riccobono* 4 (1936) 357; Daube, *CambLJ* 6 (1937) 381;
C. Arnò, *Il contratto di società* (*Lezioni*) 1938; Di Marzo,
BIDR 45 (1938) 261; Condanari-Michler, *St Besta* 3
(1939) 510; Pflüger, *ZSS* 65 (1947) 188; E. Schlechter,
Le contrat de société en Babylon, en Grèce et à Rome,
1947; Frezza, *St Solazzi* (1948) 529; V. Arangio-Ruiz,
La società in dir. rom. (*Corso*), 1950; Weiss, *Fschr Schulz*
2 (1951) 86; Solazzi, *Iura* 2 (1951) 152; Van Oven, *TR*
19 (1951) 448; *idem, St Arangio-Ruiz* 2 (1952) 453;
Wieacker, *ZSS* 69 (1952) 302.

Societas leonina. A *societas* in which one partner
participates only in the losses and is excluded from
sharing the profits. Such a contract was not valid.

V. Arangio-Ruiz, *La società in dir. rom.*, 1950, 110.

Societas maleficii. A group of persons intent to commit a crime together.

Societas negotiationis. See SOCIETAS UNIUS NEGOTII.

Societas omnium bonorum. A partnership embracing the whole property of all partners. Such a kind
of *societas* was the earliest form of joint ownership
of an estate among the heirs; see CONSORTIUM.

V. Arangio-Ruiz, *La società in dir. rom.*, 1950, 16; Van
Oven, *TR* 19 (1951) 448.

Societas publicanorum. See PUBLICANI.

Societas quaestus. A partnership which comprises
gains obtained from the economic activity and legal
transactions (sales, leases) of the partners. Excluded from the community are donations, legacies
and inheritances.

Societas re contracta. A *societas* existing independently from the consent of the parties. This occurred
when one or more things came into common ownership of several persons. The notion of *societas re
contracta* is a postclassical creation.

Arangio-Ruiz, *St Riccobono* 4 (1936) 357; *idem, La società in dir. rom.*, 1950, 35.

Societas unius negotii (societas negotiationis). A
partnership concerning a commercial or industrial
business. All juristic and economic operations connected with it are covered by the partnership.

Arangio-Ruiz, *La società in dir. rom.*, 1950, 141.

Societas unius rei. A partnership concerning one,
commercial or non-commercial, transaction (a sale,
a lease, etc.)—See POLITOR.

Societas vectigalium. See SOCIETAS PUBLICANORUM.
—See PUBLICANI.

Socius. (In private law.) A partner in a company
(see SOCIETAS), a co-owner, a member of an association (*collegium*).

Socius. (In penal law.) An accomplice, an accessory,
an abettor, one who gives assistance (*iuvat, adiuvat,
adiutorium praebet*) to a criminal before, during, or
after the crime. Syn. *conscius, consors, particeps*.
As a matter of rule, the *socius* was punished by the
same punishment as the principal wrongdoer; exceptions from this rule were introduced later in favor
of the accessory.—See OPE CONSILIO, LEX FABIA.

Pfaff, *RE* 3A; R. Balougditch, *Étude sur la complicité*
(Thèse Montpellier, 1920); K. Poetzsch, *Begriff und Bedeutung des s. im röm. Strafrecht* (Diss. Göttingen, 1934).

Socius. (In public law and international relations.)
An allied state with which Rome had a treaty of
alliance (*foedus*) delimiting the ally's rights and
duties towards Rome. In internal administration
an allied state was autonomous in retaining its constitution, its government, its control of finances and
its legal system. Among its duties that of furnishing a contingent of troops under Roman command
(*praefecti sociorum*) was the most burdensome.
The privileges granted an ally were not uniform;
their extension depended upon the closeness of his
attachment to the Roman state. An ally had no
right to conclude a treaty with another state or to
make war independently of Rome. During the third
and second centuries B.C. restrictions were gradually
imposed on the autonomy of the allies. The situation
of the allies in Italy (*socii Italici*) turned to the
worse; after the Social War (91–88 B.C.) Roman
citizenship was granted to all cities in Italy which
brought the expansion of Roman law and jurisdiction over the whole peninsula. There were also
socii beyond Italy, more or less dependent on Rome.
Their number increased after the Roman victory over
Carthage. After various modifications the provin-
cialization of the former allies was achieved and the
Roman rule expanded over territories in which the
autonomous institutions fell soon into oblivion giving
place to Roman power and governors.—See FOEDUS,
CIVITATES FOEDERATAE, FOEDUS, AMICUS POPULI
ROMANI.

Lécrivain, *DS* 4, 1367; Sherwin-White, *OCD*; Matthaei,
Class. Quarterly Rev., 1907, 182.

Sodales. Members of an association (*collegium, sodali-
tas*). In a more specific sense the term refers to colleges of a religious character, primarily to minor
priesthoods.

Bailey, *OCD*.

Sodales Augustales. A college of priests instituted by
the emperor Tiberius after the death of Augustus and
charged with the cult of the late emperor. Later,
similar groups of priests were entrusted with the cult
of the emperors Titus, Hadrian, and Antoninus Pius
(*sodales Flaviales, Hadrianales, Antoniniani*).

Cagnat, *DS* 4.

Sodalicia. See the following item.

Sodalitates (sodalicia). Groups of persons organized
under the chairmanship of a *magister* as a body for

specific purposes. In the political life the *sodalitates* were a union of individuals who illegally worked for a candidate during the electoral campaign; see LEX LICINIA DE SODALICIIS.

> Pfaff, *RE* 3A; Ziebarth, *RE* 3A; Riewald, *RE* 1A, 1640; U. Coli, *Collegia e sodalitates*, 1913.

Solacium. An indemnification, a compensation for damages. In imperial constitutions the term is used in the meaning of a stipend or a salary.

Solarium. See SUPERFICIES.

Solere. To use to do something. Used of customs and usages, practiced in legal and commercial life as well as in courts.

Solidare. In imperial constitutions to confirm, to strengthen (a legal transaction).

Solidum. (Noun.) A thing in its entirety, a whole, a sum due as a whole. *Solidum* occurs primarily in locutions *in solidum* and *pro solido,* e.g., to acquire or to sell a thing as a whole, to sue one of more debtors for the whole debt. See DUO REI PROMITTENDI. For *solidum* in the law of successions, see CAPACITAS, CAPAX, LEGES CADUCARIAE.—See PERVENIRE AD ALIQUEM.

Solidus. (Adj.) *Actiones solidae* = lawsuits for the whole debt. *Solida successio* = the whole inheritance.

Solidus. (Noun.) AUREUS (syn. *aureus solidus, solidus aureus*), a gold coin containing from the time of Constantine 1/72 of a Roman pound (*libra*) of gold. Justinian's compilers interpolated the *solidus* in juristic writings for the former one thousand sesterces (see SESTERTIUM); thus both *sestertium* and *sestertius* disappeared in Justinian's codification.

> Regling, *RE* 3A; Babelon, *DS* 4; S. Bolin, *Der S., Acta Instituti Rom. Regni Sueciae,* 2 ser. 1 (1939) 144; Cesano, *Bull. Comm. Archeol. di Roma,* 58 (1930), *Bull. del Museo,* p. 42.

Solis occasus. Sunset. According to the Twelve Tables a trial in court had to be closed before sunset by the pronouncement of a judgment by the judge. Meetings of the senate, which normally started early in the morning, were to be ended at sunset.

Solitarius. See PATER SOLITARIUS.

Solitus. Customary, usual.—See SOLERE.

Sollemne ius. Opposed to the law created by the praetor (*ius praetorium, ius honorarium*). *Sollemne ius* is syn. with IUS CIVILE and refers primarily to the solemn formalities prescribed by that law.

Sollemnia (iuris). Legal formalities prescribed by the law for certain acts, such as the acts *per aes et libram,* testaments, *legis actiones, stipulatio,* etc. Syn. *sollemnitates iuris.* Praetorian law and imperial legislation gradually alleviated and partly abolished the formalities of the earlier law. In a rescript issued in a particular case Emperor Marcus Aurelius stated: "Although in solemn legal formalities changes should not easily be made, yet where obvious equity (*aequitas*) requires help must be granted" (D. 4.1.7 pr.).

This rule was accepted by Justinian as a general one through its repetition in the final title of the Digest, *De diversis regulis iuris antiqui* (D. 50.17.183). In the language of the imperial chancery the *sollemnia* found a wide application, being connected with any act for which certain formalities were prescribed (e.g., *sollemnia accusationis, adoptionis, appellationis, iurisiurandi,* etc.).

> Riccobono, *L'importanza e il decadimento delle forme sollenni, Miscellaneous Vermeersch* 2 (1935).

Sollemnia testamenti. Formalities required for the validity of a testament.

Sollemnia verba. See VERBA CERTA ET SOLLEMNIA.

Sollemnis. Prescribed by law, human or sacral, or observed through tradition. See SOLLEMNIA (IURIS). Hence *sollemniter* indicates any act performed under observance of the prescribed formalities.

Sollemnitas, sollemniter. See SOLLEMNIA (IURIS), SOLLEMNIS.

Sollicitator. A seducer.—See ACTIO SERVI CORRUPTI.

Solum. See SUPERFICIES, RES MOBILES.

Solutio. In a broader sense *solutio* indicates any kind of liberation of the debtor from his debt. Obligations contracted in a specific form (*litteris, verbis*) had to be extinguished in a similar form; see PROUT QUISQUE. Thus a literal obligation (*litterarum obligatio*) was extinguished by EXPENSILATIO, a *stipulatio* by a parallel oral form, the ACCEPTILATIO. In a narrower sense *solutio* denotes the payment, the fulfillment of an obligation. Payment could be made by anyone, not only by the debtor himself, but even without his knowledge and against his will. The creditor was not obliged to accept a part of the debt nor another thing in lieu of that which was actually due (*aliud pro alio*). Failure to pay at the term fixed produced for the debtor the disadvantages of a default (see MORA DEBITORIS). A creditor who refused the acceptance of the payment could also be in default (*in mora*); see MORA CREDITORIS.—D. 46.3; C. 8.42; 11.40.—See OBLIGATIO, SATISFACTIO, ADIECTUS SOLUTIONIS CAUSA, BENEFICIUM COMPETENTIAE, DATIO IN SOLUTUM, APOCHA, USUCAPIO PRO SOLUTO.

> Huvelin, *DS* 4; Leonhard, *RE* 3A; P. Kretschmar, *Die Erfüllung,* 1906; P. Thermes, *Le paiement* (Thèse Toulouse, 1934); S. Solazzi, *L'estinzione dell'obbligazione,* 2nd ed. (1935) 9.

Solutio imaginaria. The solemn acts of liberation of the debtor, the ACCEPTILATIO, and the SOLUTIO PER AES ET LIBRAM, are qualified as *solutio imaginaria,* see IMAGINARIUS. Through these acts the debtor was liberated from his obligation whether or not he effectively paid the debt.

Solutio indebiti. The payment of a debt which in fact did not exist.—See INDEBITUM, CONDICTIO INDEBITI.

> P. Voci, *La dottrina rom. del contratto* (1946) 98.

Solutio legibus. In the Republic the senate could decree in exceptional cases that a law being in force should not be applied in a specific case. Normally such a decree of the senate had to be followed by a confirming vote of a popular assembly. Such dispensations of magistrates from a strict application of a law, or of an individual person from a legal requirement, were issued as an exceptional measure in case of urgency. This rule was not always observed and abuses were not rare. See LEX CORNELIA DE LEGIBUS SOLVENDO (of 67 B.C.). The right of the senate to grant a *solutio legibus* was still exercised in the early Principate.

O'Brien-Moore, *RE* Suppl. 6, 746; Mommsen, *Röm. Staatsrecht* 3, 2 (1888) 1229; G. Rotondi, *Leges publicae populi Rom.* (1912) 165; 520.

Solutio per aes et libram. The payment of a debt which arose from a transaction concluded in the solemn form PER AES ET LIBRAM. The liberation of the debtor had to be performed in the same form, with the assistance of five witnesses and a balance-holder (*libripens*). This form of *solutio* was applied also with regard to judgment-debts (see IUDICATUM) and legacies bequeathed in the form of LEGATUM PER DAMNATIONEM.—See SOLUTIO IMAGINARIA.

Michon, *Recueil Gény* 1 (1934) 42.

Solutionis causa adiectus. See ADIECTUS SOLUTIONIS CAUSA.

Solutum. See DATIO IN SOLUTUM.

Solutus. See VINCTUS.

Solvendo esse. To be solvent. "No one is considered solvent unless he is able to pay the whole debt" (D. 50.17.95). The term is applied both to persons and estates. Ant. *solvendo non esse.* An insolvent person was exempt from the duty to assume a guardianship. Insolvency of a debtor which was effected by fraudulent acts of his own (donations, manumissions) performed *in fraudem creditorum*, could be rescinded by the creditors; see FRAUS, INTERDICTUM FRAUDATORIUM, IDONEUS, FACERE POSSE.

Pringsheim, *ZSS* 41 (1920) 252; Schulz, *ZSS* 48 (1928) 214; Kübler, *St Albertoni* 1 (1935) 493; G. Nocera, *Insolvenza e responsabilità sussidiaria* (1942) 19.

Solvere. To pay a debt. "We say *solvere* when somebody did what he had promised to do" (D. 50.16.176). See SOLUTIO. In a broader sense *solvere* means to dissolve a legal (contractual) relationship by mutual agreement of the parties involved. For the rule that an obligation assumed by a contract should be discharged (*solvi*) in the same way, see PROUT QUISQUE, etc. Hence verbal contracts had to be dissolved orally, through the use of prescribed words, and literal contracts (see OBLIGATIO LITTERARUM) by written forms (*litterae*). *Solvi* = to be liberated from an obligation or any legal binding, to be dissolved (e.g., *matrimonium*).

Solvere legibus. See SOLUTIO LEGIBUS.—See LEX CORNELIA DE LEGIBUS SOLVENDO.

Sonticus morbus. A serious disease which prevented a person from the fulfillment of his duties. It was a justified excuse for non-appearance in court.

Sordida munera. See MUNERA SORDIDA.

Soror. A sister. *Soror* was also a mother or step-mother who acquired in the family the legal situation of a daughter through marriage with the father of the family combined with CONVENTIO IN MANUM and thus became a sister of the latter's children.—See FILIA FAMILIAS, MANUS.

Sors. A lot. When two co-owners or co-heirs applied to a court for the division of the common property (inheritance) under *actio communi dividundo* or *actio familiae erciscundae,* it used to be determined by lot which of the parties had to institute the trial as the plaintiff.—See SORTITIO.

Sors. A sum lent at interest, the principal.—See USURAE.

Sors. A plot of AGER PUBLICUS assigned to a member of a colony.

Sortitio. Determination by lot.—See ALBUM IUDICUM, SUBSORTITIO.

Ehrenberg, *RE* 13, 1495 (*s.v. Losung*); Lécrivain, *DS* 4, 1417.

Sortitio. (In public law.) In centuriate assemblies (*comitia centuriata*) the *centuria* which had to vote first (*centuria praerogativa*) was determined by lot (*sortiri*). If in an election of magistrates two candidates received an equal number of votes, it was decided by lot which of the two was to obtain the magistracy. In some other instances (of minor importance) designation by lot was alternative with the decision by a superior magistrate.

Ehrenberg, *RE* 13, 1493 (*s.v. Losung*).

Sortitio. Among colleagues in office, see the following item.

Sortitio provinciarum. Drawing by lot for the assignment of the various spheres of activity (*provinciae*) to colleagues in office (see COLLEGA), as consuls, praetors, municipal magistrates, etc. The division of functions concerned primarily military command and jurisdiction. It could be settled by common agreement which made the drawing of lots superfluous (*sine sorte*). *Sortitio* was mandatory with regard to the functions of praetors.

Spado. Incapable of procreation, either by nature or through castration. A *spado* was permitted to marry and adopt.—See PUBESCERE, CASTRATI, EUNUCHI.

Pfaff, *RE* 2A.

Spatium. Indicates both space in room (e.g., an interval between two buildings, see AMBITUS) and in time (a period of time within which a legal act had to be accomplished).

Spatium deliberandi. See DELIBERARE, TEMPUS AD DELIBERANDUM.

Specialis. Special; *specialiter* = especially, expressly, in particular. The words occur frequently in Justinian's constitutions and, together with ant. *generalis* and *generaliter,* are among his favorite expressions. They are generally considered as criteria of interpolations; their occurrence, however, in works of rhetoricians does not permit their definite exclusion from the language of the jurists. In particular, the adverb *specialiter* often occurs in connection with specific clauses inserted in an agreement.—See GENERALIS, IUDICIA GENERALIA, IURISDICTIO MANDATA, NISI.

Guarneri-Citati, *Indice*[2] (1927) 83; Peters, *ZSS* 32 (1911) 183; E. Albertario, *Studi* 4 (1946) 79.

Species. An individual thing, to be distinguished from *genus* = a kind, sort of things, with common qualities. The distinction is of importance in obligatory relations; see GENUS. *Species* is also used of a specific legal problem submitted for a decision or discussion. When connected with a legal institution (e.g., *species legati, fideicommissi) species* means the legal form in which an act was performed (a legacy). *Speciem novam facere* = to make a new thing from a raw material; see SPECIFICATIO. In later imperial constitutions *species* (in plur.) indicates natural, agricultural products; hence *in speciebus* = in kind, *in natura. Sub specie* = under the pretext of.

Scarpello, *NDI* 12, 2; S. Perozzi, *Scritti* 1 (1948, ex 1890) 241; Ferrini, *Opere* 4 (1930, ex 1891) 103; A. Hägerström, *Der röm. Obligationsbegriff* 1 (1927) 236; Savagnone, *BIDR* 55–56 (1952) 241.

Specificatio. Making one thing from another (raw material). The term is not of Roman coinage; its origin is to be traced to the locution *novam speciem facere;* see SPECIES. Juristically *specificatio* becomes important if a person makes a thing from another's material without the latter's authorization; the problem as to who is the owner of the *nova species,* the owner of the material or the worker (the maker), was largely discussed by the jurists and not always decided according to the same principle. The opinions of the two schools, the Sabinians and Proculians, differed in this respect. Justinian solved the problem from the point of view of the reducibility of the new thing (*nova species)* to its former shape. If the new thing was made partly from the maker's material, it became property of the maker. For the various types of *specificatio,* see COMMIXTIO, CONFUSIO, CONIUNCTIO, TEXTURA, TABULA PICTA, ACCESSIO, PLANTA, SATIO.

Weiss, *RE* 3A; Lécrivain, *DS* 4; R. Piccard, *Recherches sur l'hist. de la s.* (Thèse Lausanne, 1926); De Martino, *RDNav* 3 (1937) 179; Kaser, *ZSS* 65 (1947) 242.

Speciosa persona. A person (man or woman), primarily of senatorial rank, who was entitled to be distinguished by the appellative CLARISSIMUS. Syn. *spectabilis.*

Spectabilis. An honorific title of higher officials in the later Empire. The *spectabiles* formed the second rank after the ILLUSTRES. They enjoyed various personal privileges similar to those of the *clarissimi;* exemption from the decurionate (see ORDO DECURIONUM) was their most important right. After a period of nearly two centuries, during which the honorific titles were fluctuating, from the beginning of the fifth post-Christian century a strict distinction was made among the three high-ranking groups, *illustres, spectabiles* and *clarissimi.*

Ensslin, *RE* 3A; Chapot, *DS* 4; P. Koch, *Byzantinische Beamtentitel* (1903) 22; O. Hirschfeld, *Kleine Schriften* (1913) 664; 670.

Spectaculum. A show. See LUDI. It is characteristic that the title 11.41 of Justinian's Code deals with *spectacula* together with actors and *lenones* (matchmakers).

Spectare. Through *spectandum est* the jurists used to call attention to specific circumstances which should be taken into consideration at the examination of a case. *Spectare aliquem* = to concern a person (for instance, a debt, a risk).

Spectator. A mint official who tested coins. Syn. *nummularius.*—See TESSERAE NUMMULARIAE.

Regling, *RE* 13.

Spectio. The activity and the right to observe celestial or other signs during the AUSPICIA. They were a prerogative of the highest magistrates.

Marbach, *RE* 3A.

Speculatores. Soldiers or cavalrymen in the intelligence service of the army (normally ten in a legion). *Speculatores* were also particularly qualified soldiers who served as bodyguards of the emperor. They were also employed as military couriers. At times *speculator* indicates an executioner.

Lammert, *RE* 3A; Cagnat, *DS* 4, 637; Jones, *JRS* 39 (1949) 44; O. Hirschfeld, *Kleine Schriften* (1913) 585; 598.

Spes. See EMPTIO SPEI, EMPTIO REI SPERATAE.

Bartošek. *RIDA* 2 (1949) 20.

Splendidiores personae. See HONESTIORES.

Spernere. To repudiate (e.g., an inheritance, a legacy), to reject, to condemn (the decision of an arbitrator in order to sue one's adversary before an ordinary court).

Spolia. Weapons and armor taken from an enemy in time of war. They became the property of the victorious soldier who killed him. *Spolia* was also used of what a person condemned to death had on himself before his execution. He was stripped of them and the executioner had the right to claim them.—See SPECULATORES.

Lammert, *RE* 3A; Cagnat, *DS* 4; Vogel, *ZSS* 66 (1948) 394.

Spoliatio cadaveris. Larceny of property committed on a dead body.—See CADAVER.

Spondere. The decisive expression in the formula of *stipulatio* by which a person promised to pay a sum of money or assumed any obligation (*spondesne ? spondeo*). In lieu of *spondere,* later other words were admitted. See STIPULATIO. The term *spondere* also indicates the obligation assumed by a surety; see SPONSIO, FIDEIUSSIO.

Sponsa. A fiancée.—See SPONSALIA.

Sponsalia. A betrothal. "*Sponsalia* are the promise (*mentio*) and the counterpromise for a future marriage" (D. 23.1.1). In ancient law the father of the fiancée promised his daughter to the future husband or to his father in the solemn form a *sponsio* (question and answer). Later, a simple consent sufficed for a betrothal. *Sponsalia* were not binding and even a penalty clause attached to the pertinent agreement was void since "it was considered dishonest that marriage be enforced by the tie of a penalty" (D. 45.1.134 pr.). *Sponsalia* had nevertheless some legal effects, though of minor importance. Thus the conclusion of a new betrothal before the former was dissolved, involved infamy. A personal offense (*iniuria*) of the fiancée could be prosecuted by her fiancé. A fiancé could not be compelled to testify against his future father-in-law and *vice versa*. A fiancé could accuse his fiancée of adultery. In the fourth century after Christ earnest money (*arra sponsalicia*) served as a guarantee for the fulfillment of *sponsalia* since the party which broke off the betrothal without any just ground lost the *arra* given or had to return double the amount received. *Sponsalia* could be dissolved by mutual consent or by a simple declaration of one party; see REPUDIUM. Gifts between betrothed persons are termed *sponsalia* in imperial constitutions. —D. 23.1; C. 5.1.—See MATRIMONIUM, ARRA SPONSALICIA (Bibl.), DONATIO ANTE NUPTIAS, FILIA FAMILIAS, PATRIA POTESTAS, OSCULUM, REPUDIUM.

Weiss, *RE* 3A; Lécrivain, *DS* 3, 1654; Koschaker, *ZSS* 33 (1912) 392; Solazzi, *ATor* 51 (1916) 749; *idem, St Albertoni* 1 (1935) 42; Volterra, *BIDR* 40 (1932) 87; *idem, RISG* 10 (1935) 3; *idem, SDHI* 3 (1937) 135; E. Herman, *Die Schliessung des Verlöbnisses im Rechte Just., Analecta Gregoriana* 8 (1935); Massei, *BIDR* 47 (1940) 148; Beseler, *ConfCast* 1940, 38; L. Anné, *Les rites des fiançailles* (Diss. Louvain, 1941); A. Magdelain, *Les origines de la sponsio* (1943) 98; Gaudemet, *RIDA* 1 (1948) 79; R. Orestano, *La struttura giuridica del matrimonio rom.*, 1952, 339 (= *BIDR* 55–56, 1952, 221).

Sponsalicia largitas. Gifts given to a fiancée by her fiancé. Syn. *donatio sponsalicia*.—See DONATIO ANTE NUPTIAS.

L. Caes, *Le statut juridique de la s. l. echue à la mère veuve*, 1949.

Sponsio. (From *spondere*.) The earliest form of an obligation under *ius civile* assumed through an oral answer ("*spondeo*") to the future creditor's question ("*spondesne?*"). The *sponsio*, conceived in this broader sense, was in the course of time absorbed by the STIPULATIO. In a narrower sense *sponsio* denoted the obligation of a surety who equally through exchange of question and answer obligated himself to pay what another had promised; see ADPROMISSIO. This function of the *sponsio* was probably the earlier

one.—See LEX APULEIA, LEX FURIA DE SPONSU, PROVOCARE SPONSIONE, ACTIO DEPENSI, AGERE PER SPONSIONEM, SPONDERE, and the following items.

Weiss, *RE* 3A; Anon., *NDI* 12; Mitteis, *Fg Bekker* (1907) 109; E. Levy, *Sponsio, fidepromissio, fideiussio*, 1907; *idem, ZSS* 54 (1934) 298; Wenger, *ZSS* 30 (1909) 410; Partsch, *ASächGW* 32 (1920) 659; W. Flume, *Studien zur Akzessorietät der röm. Bürgschaftsstipulationen*, 1932; G. Segrè, *BIDR* 42 (1934) 497; Ph. Meylan, *Acceptilation et paiement* (Lausanne, 1934) 69; Leifer, *BIDR* 44 (1936–37) 160; F. De Martino, *Studi sulle garenzie personali*, 1–2 (1937, 1938); *idem, SDHI* 6 (1940) 132; A. Magdelain, *Essai sur les origines de la s.* (Thèse Paris, 1943); J. Maillet, *La Théorie de Schuld et Haftung* (1944) 144; Westrup, *Noté sur sponsio, Kgl. Danske Videnskab, Hist.-Filol. Meddedelser* 31, 2 (1947); Pastori, *SDHI* 13–14 (1948) 217; Seidl, *Scr Ferrini* 4 (Univ. Sacro Cuore, Milan, 1949) 168; M. Kaser, *Das altröm. Ius* (1949) 256; Düll, *ZSS* 68 (1951) 209.

Sponsio. (In interdictal procedure.) See AGERE PER SPONSIONEM, INTERDICTUM.

Sponsio. (In international relations.) An arrangement concluded by the commanding Roman general with the enemy concerning an armistice. The commander acted on his own responsibility. The reciprocal duties were established through the exchange of questions and answers.—See PAX.

Neumann, *RE* 6, 2821; De Visscher, *St Riccobono* 2 (1936) 11; H. Lévy-Bruhl, *RHD* 17 (1938) 533 (= *Nouvelles Études*, 1947, 116); Frezza, *SDHI* 5 (1939) 191; F. La Rosa, *Iura* 1 (1950) 283.

Sponsio. (In trials concerning ownership.) See AGERE PER SPONSIONEM (under 2).

Sponsio dimidiae partis. See SPONSIO TERTIAE PARTIS.

Sponsio poenalis. A promise in the form of a *sponsio* (*stipulatio*) to pay a sum of money as a penalty in the case of non-fulfillment of an obligation or of a magisterial command (*interdictum*).—See POENA (in the law of obligations).

Sponsio praeiudicialis. See AGERE PER SPONSIONEM (under 2), LEX CREPEREIA.

Sponsio tertiae (or dimidiae) partis. In certain specific trials any party could demand that his adversary promised through *sponsio* (*stipulatio*) to pay one-third (*tertia pars*) or one-half (*dimidia pars*) of the amount claimed as a penalty in the case of defeat. In return the party who made such a promise could demand a similar counterpromise (*restipulatio dimidiae* or *tertiae partis*) from the other party. The reciprocal promises were given in the first stage of the lawsuit before the praetor (*in iure*) and under his supervision. The purpose of these procedural *sponsiones* was to restrain inconsiderate litigation.—See CONSTITUTUM, ACTIO CERTAE CREDITAE PECUNIAE.

A. Palermo, *Il procedimento cauzionale* (1942) 13.

Sponsor. One who assumed an obligation as a surety. The term was in earlier times probably applied to any person who through *sponsio* assumed an obligation as a principal debtor.—See SPONSIO.

Daube, *LQR* 62 (1946) 266.

Sponsus. (Noun.) SPONSIO.—See LEX APULEIA, LEX fiancé (fiancée).—See SPONSALIA. FURIA DE SPONSU.

Sponsus (sponsa). A betrothed man (woman), a

Sponte. (With or without **sua**.) Spontaneously, freely, of one's free will. The expression refers to the opposite of situations in which one is bound to do something by law, agreement, order of a magistrate or of the person under whose power he is, or by necessity (*necessario, necessitate cogente*).

Sportellarius (sportellaria). An exposed child.—See EXPONERE FILIUM.

Sportulae. In the later Empire fees to be paid to subaltern officials for their activity in judicial matters. —C. 3.2.—See EXSECUTOR NEGOTII.

Wlassak, *RE* 4, 217; Hug, *RE* 3A; Lécrivain, *DS* 4; Jones, *JRS* 39 (1949) 51.

Sportulae decurionum. See HONORARIUM.

Hug, *RE* 3A, 1886 (under 2).

Spurius. A child whose father is unknown ("a child without a father, as it were," Inst. 1.10.12). See VULGO CONCEPTUS. If the mother was a Roman citizen, the *spurius* was also a Roman citizen. A *spurius* became immediately *sui iuris* (free from *patria potestas*) and *proximus agnatus* of his mother. He was reckoned in favor of her IUS LIBERORUM.— C. 5.12.—See FILIUS NATURALIS.

Weiss, *RE* 3A, 1889; *idem, ZSS* 49 (1929) 260; Kubitschek, *Wiener Studien* 47 (1929) 130; Lanfranchi, *StCagl* 30 (1946) 33.

Stabularius. A stable-keeper. The liability of a *stabularius* for the custody of horses assumed by agreement with the owner (*receptum stabularii*) was settled in the praetorian Edict, in the section concerning similar agreements with shipowners and innkeepers (*receptum nautarum, cauponum*).—D. 4.9; 47.5.—See RECEPTUM NAUTARUM.

De Robertis, *AnBari* 12 (1952) 125.

Stagnum. A pond.—See LACUS, FLUMINA PUBLICA.

Stare (alicui rei). To cling to, to hold on firmly to (e.g., to an agreement), to fulfill exactly (e.g., a testator's will).

Stat per aliquem. It is one's fault, one is the cause of.—See MORA.

Statim. Immediately. In certain situations the jurists admitted a rather liberal interpretation of the term if a payment had to be made *statim*. "It is understood, of course, with a moderate extension of the time if something is to be paid immediately" (D. 46.3.105).—See SINE DIE.

Statio. A public place (at a forum or market) or an office where a TABELLIO exercised his notarial activity.

Statio. See NAVIGIUM. *Statio* is also a station of the state postal service; syn. MANSIO, STATIVA.

Humbert, *DS* 1, 1655.

Statio. In military service. A station of military guards.—See STATIONARII.

Lammert, *RE* 3A, 2211, 2213.

Statio vicesimae hereditatium. A fiscal office concerned with the inheritance taxes.—See APERTURA TESTAMENTI, VICESIMA HEREDITATIUM.

Stationarii. Military police officers assigned to posts throughout the country for the purpose of public security.—See LATRUNCULATOR.

Lammert. *RE* 3A; Lécrivain, *DS* 4.

Stationes fisci. Divisions of the fisc for the administration of revenue in fixed districts.

Weiss, *RE* 3A, 2212.

Stationes ius docentium et respondentium. Public places (state buildings?) where jurists taught law and gave opinions (*responsa*) in legal matters.

Hug, *RE* 3A, 2210; S. Riccobono, *Lineamenti della storia delle fonti*, 1949, 65.

Stativa. A station of the state post. Syn. *mansio, statio.*—C. 12.52(52).

Statores. Subordinate officials in the service of the emperor (*statores Augusti*) or high officials (provincial governors). They exercised police functions and were authorized to arrest private persons. They were in part successors of the VIGILES.

Kübler, *RE* 3A, 2228; Lammert, *ibid.* no. 2.

Statua. A statue erected in public for the embellishment of a place. It was withheld from the disposal of the person who offered it. A person who was honored by a public statue might act through the *interdictum quod vi aut clam* against anyone who removed it by force or stealth.—D. 34.2; C. 1.2.4.

Brassloff, *St Riccobono* 1 (1936) 323.

Statua Caesaris. See CONFUGERE AD STATUAM CAESARIS.

Statuere. To ordain, to enact (e.g., *lex, imperator statuit*), to settle by an agreement.—See TEMPUS STATUTUM.

Statuliber. A slave manumitted in a testament by his master upon a suspensive condition. He remained a slave as long as the condition was not fulfilled. If the condition consisted in an act of the slave himself (e.g., he had to pay a certain sum to the heir, or to render accounts of his administration of the master's property), it was considered satisfied if the heir or another person prevented the fulfilling of the condition, and the slave became free despite the nonfulfillment of the testator's wish.—D. 40.7.—See MANUMISSIO SUB CONDICIONE.

Weiss, *RE* 3A; G. Donatuti, *Lo s.*, 1940; Bartošek, *RIDA* 2 (1949) 32.

Status. Generally indicates a legal situation or condition. With regard to an individual, the term refers either to his official rank or to his position as a free Roman citizen and head of a family. In the latter sense it is syn. with CAPUT. In the distinction *status libertatis, status civitatis*, and *status familiae* only the first occurs in the sources. A change in one of these three fundamental elements of the legal *status* of an individual, liberty, citizenship, and headship of a family (*mutatio, permutatio status*), could either improve his legal condition (when a slave became free, a foreigner became a Roman citizen, a person *alieni iuris* became *sui iuris*) or make it worse (loss of freedom, of citizenship or of the position as head of a family). When the *status* of a person was doubtful (*quaestio, controversia status*), in particular when it was uncertain whether he was free, free-born or a slave, his condition was examined in a trial; see CAUSA LIBERALIS.—D. 1.5; C. 3.22.—See CAPUT, CAPITIS DEMINUTIO.

Weiss, *RE* 3A, 2433; Lécrivain, *DS* 4; Orestano, *NDI* 12; Cicu, *St Simoncelli* 1917, 61; Allen, *LQR* 46 (1930) 277.

Status civitatis. The legal status of a person as a Roman citizen. Ant. the *status* of a stranger (PEREGRINUS).—See CIVES, CIVITAS ROMANA.

Status controversia (quaestio). See STATUS.

Status defuncti. The legal status of a person before his death, primarily the question of whether he was free or a slave. It could not be the object of a trial if five years elapsed after his death.—D. 40.15; C. 7.21.

Status familiae. The legal connection of a person with a family either as its head (*pater familias*) or member.—See SUI IURIS.

Status legitimus. The age of majority.

Status libertatis. The legal status of a person of being free, and not a slave. With regard to a free person the question might arise as to whether he was free-born or a freedman.—See LIBERTAS, MANUMISSIO, CAPITIS DEMINUTIO, STATULIBER, CAUSA LIBERALIS, LIBERTINITAS, INGENUITAS.

Status pristinus. The former factual or legal state (condition, situation) of a thing or a person.—See RESTITUERE, RESTITUTIO IN INTEGRUM.

Status rei publicae. The existence, organization, welfare of the state. The expression occurs in the definition of *ius publicum* by Ulpian (D. 1.1.1.2).—See IUS PUBLICUM.

E. Kostermann, *S. als politischer terminus in der Antike*, *Rheinisches Museum* 86 (1937) 225; Lombardi, *AG* 126 (1941) 206; Berger, *Iura* 1 (1950) 109.

Statuti. See MINISTRI CASTRENSES.

Statutum. A law, an enactment. *Statuta imperialia* = imperial constitutions.

Statutum tempus. A term fixed either by an agreement of the parties involved concerning the date on which a certain act (a payment) was to be performed, or by law (a statute, the praetorian Edict, an imperial constitution) for certain legal achievements, such as *usucapio,* for actions or exceptions, *cretio, longi temporis praescriptio*, etc. In Justinian's legislation, in many classical texts the general, indefinite term, *statutum tempus* (*statuta tempora*) replaced the former exact indications of periods of time if the latter had been changed by postclassical or Justinian's legislation.

Seckel, in Heumann's *Handlexikon*⁹ (1909), *s.v. statuere*, p. 553; Stella-Maranca, *AnBari* 1929/II, 76.

Stellionatus. A crime committed by fraud, trickery, deception, or cheating, if such a wrongdoing in specific circumstances is not qualified as another crime (*si alium crimen non sit*), for instance, a theft (*furtum*) or forgery (*falsum*). There is no definition of *stellionatus* in the sources. The formula defining that "what in private controversies gives origin to an *actio* is in criminal matters prosecuted as *stellionatus*" (D. 47.20.3.1), is not precise enough to permit an exact delimitation of the elements of *stellionatus*. Evil intention, deceit, shrewdness (*calliditas*), imposture (*impostura*) are mentioned in the various cases of *stellionatus,* which seemingly primarily applied to fraud in commercial relations. Perjury could also be punished as *stellionatus. Stellionatus* was not a *crimen publicum.* If an accusation of *stellionatus* was brought before the competent magistrate (*praefectus urbi*, a provincial governor), it depended upon his decision whether or not a criminal proceeding (*extra ordinem*) would be started against the accused. The penalty was differentiated according to the social status of the culprit, temporary banishment for HONESTIORES, forced labor for HUMILIORES.—D. 47.20; C. 9.34.

Pfaff, *RE* 3A; Beauchet, *DS* 4; Brasiello, *NDI* 12; Volterra, *StSas* 7 (1929) 107.

Stemma cognationum. A genealogical tree. A picture containing the names of relatives (ascendants in six generations and descendants) of a person was found in some manuscripts of the LEX ROMANA VISIGOTHORUM.

Editions: in all collections of pre-Justinian legal sources, see General Bibl. Ch. XII; the most recent one in *FIR* 1 (1940) 633.—Ferrini, *Opere* 1 (1926, ex 1900) 224; Poland, *RE* 3A.

Stephanus. A Byzantine jurist, law professor in Constantinople (or Beirut?) under Justinian. He was, however, not the emperor's collaborator in the compilation of the Digest, nor is he mentioned among the compilers of the Code. He wrote an annotated summary (see INDEX) of the Digest and was highly thought of by later Byzantine jurists. His work was extensively exploited for scholia to the Basilica.

Kübler, *RE* 3A, 2401; Heimbach, *Basilica* 6 (1870) 13, 49, 78; J. A. B. Mortreuil, *Histoire du droit byzantin* 1 (1843) 132, 148; Zachariae v. Lingenthal, *ZSS* 10 (1889) 270.

Sterilis pecunia. Money not loaned at interest. Syn. *nummi steriles.* The adj. *sterilis* is used also of a dowry (*dos*) from which the husband had no profit.

Stillicidium. See SERVITUS STILLICIDII.

Adren, *Eranos* (*Acta Philol. Suecana*) 43 (1945) 1.

Stipendiarius. See CIVITATES STIPENDIARIAE, PRAEDIA STIPENDIARIA, STIPENDIUM (in public law).

Stipendium. The soldier's pay. From the fourth post-Christian century on the soldiers received the *stipendium* in kind (see ANNONA) which in times of shortage was replaced by money.—See ADAERATIO, DONATIVUM.

Lammert, *RE* 3A, 2537; v. Domaszewski, *Neue Heidelberger Jahrbücher,* 1900, 218 ff; Schlossmann, *Archiv für lat. Lexikographie* 14 (1906) 211.

Stipendium. (In public law.) A contribution imposed on the defeated enemy; it served to cover the expenses of war. During the armistice the enemy had to pay the Roman soldiers' salary (*stipendium*). This may explain how the term came to mean contribution. In later times *stipendium* was the term for land-taxes paid by provincials. The rate of the *stipendium* was fixed whereas the so-called TRIBUTUM depended upon the value of the proceeds from the soil.—See PRAEDIA STIPENDIARIA.

Lammert, *RE* 3A, 2538 (under no. 2); Cagnat, *DS* 4, 1515; Schlossmann, *Arch. für lat. Lexikographie* 14 (1906) 211; Ciapessoni, *Studi su Gaio,* 1943, 52.

Stips menstrua. A monthly fee paid by members of an association (*collegium*) for common purposes (e.g., banquets, celebrations of religious nature).

Kornemann, *RE* 4, 437; Hug, *RE* 3A, 2540.

Stipulari. To accept a promise made in the form of *stipulatio*. It is the creditor who *stipulatur* (*reus stipulandi*), i.e., who pronounced the question to be answered accordingly by the debtor (*reus promittendi*). Only in exceptional cases *stipulari* is used of the debtor (= to promise).—See STIPULATIO.

Stipulatio. An oral, solemn contract concluded in the form of a question (*interrogatio* by the creditor: "*spondesne centum dare?*" = "do you promise to pay one hundred?") and an affirming answer (*responsio*) of the debtor ("*spondeo*" = "I promise"). The answer had to agree perfectly with the question; any difference or restriction (addition of a condition) made the *stipulatio* void. Presence of both parties was required, and any interruption between question and answer was inadmissible. *Stipulatio* was used for any kind of obligation, from the payment of a sum of money to the most complicated performances. It was employed for the promise of marriage (see SPONSALIA), the constitution of a dowry (see DOS), the various kinds of promises in the course of a civil trial (*cautiones, stipulationes praetoriae*), a NOVATIO and DELEGATIO, the assumption of a guaranty for another's debt (sureties), the constitution of certain rights on another's property (see PACTIONES ET STIPULATIONES), etc. The *stipulatio* was abstract in content, to wit, the cause (*causa*) for which the debtor assumed an obligation was not indicated in the *stipulatio* (e.g., whether it was for a loan or an unpaid price of a thing purchased). A promise made through *stipulatio* was suable if the oral exchange of question and answer was performed, without regard as to whether there was a ground for the obligation or not. Any obligation, contracted otherwise, could be transferred into a *stipulatio* (*stipulatio Aquiliana,* see ACCEPTILATIO). This brought the creditor the advantage in case of a controversy that he had to prove only the fact that a *stipulatio* had taken place. In the course of time, however, the praetorian law granted an *exceptio doli* to the debtor if the obligation he had assumed was not based on a just cause. Witnesses at the conclusion of a *stipulatio* were not necessary. The elasticity of the *stipulatio* together with its simple formality made it the most common instrument for providing any promise with legal efficacy. Originally accessible only to Roman citizens (see SPONSIO), the *stipulatio* was later made available to foreigners, and not only the realm of permissible Latin words was extended (in lieu of *spondeo* the use of *dare* [*facere*] *promittere,* and, for sureties: *fideipromittere, fideiubere*) but also Greek, and perhaps other languages, were admitted in order to respond to the needs of commercial relations with other nations. In further development, written "stipulations" came into use under the influence of the practice observed by other peoples. Provisions of the agreement were written and the oral promise embraced in one phrase the promise "to give all that had been written down above" (*ea omnia quae supra scripta sunt dari*), which in the opinion of the Roman jurists contained in fact as many stipulations as there were provisions. The written document was in origin only a piece of evidence, but later the importance of the written agreement prevailed so that in postclassical times it could be stated: "if it was written in a document (*instrumentum*) that one made a promise, it is considered as if an answer were given to a preceding question" (Paul. *Sent.* 5.7.2; Inst. 3.19.17). Thus, through a fiction, which normally excluded a counter-proof, it was held that a *stipulatio* had taken place (STIPULATIO INTER ABSENTES). In Justinian law the *stipulatio* appears as a written act, without any formal requirements. For an oral stipulation *certa verba* were no longer a condition of its validity; the debtor's answer could be expressed by signs and after a brief interval, even some slight discrepancies between question and answer were not harmful. The intervention of an interpreter was permitted if one party did not understand the language used by the other. The actions from a *stipulatio* available to the creditor in the classical law were: *actio certae creditae pecuniae* (*condictio certae pecuniae*), when the *stipulatio* concerned the payment of a fixed sum of money, *condictio certae rei* when the object was a *certa res* (an individual thing), *condictio triticaria* when things were indicated generically (as a GENUS), and, finally, *actio ex stipulatu,* when the object was not precisely defined in a way mentioned above and the stipulatory obligation concerned a certain performance by the debtor. The classical origin of some denominations of these actions is not beyond doubt. —Inst. 3.17–19; D. 45.3; 46.5; C. 8.37; 38.—See besides the following items, ACCEPTILATIO, CAUTIO, SPONSIO, NOVATIO, NEMO ALTERI STIPULATUR, FAVOR

DEBITORIS, EXPROMISSIO, DONATIO, DIES MORTIS, TRANSACTIO.

Weiss, *RE* 3A; Cuq, *DS* 4; Riccobono, *NDI* 12; Carrelli, *ibid.* 904; Berger, *OCD*; Mitteis, *Aus röm. und bürgerl. Recht, Fg Bekker* (1907) 107; Collinet, *Mél Gérardin* 1907, 75; Riccobono, *ZSS* 35 (1914) 214, 43 (1922) 262; idem. *BIDR* 31 (1921) 28; idem, *AnPal* 12 (1929) 540; idem, *Stipulationes, contractus, pacta. Corso*, 1935; idem, *ACDR* Roma 1 (1934) 338; G. Segrè, *St Simoncelli* 1917, 331; Scherillo, *BIDR* 36 (1928) 29; idem, *St Bonfante* 4 (1930) 203; H. Steinacker, *Die antiken Grundlagen der frühmittelalterlichen Privaturkunde* (1927) 83; V. De Gautard, *Les rapports entre la stipulatio et l'écrit stipulatoire* (Thèse Lausanne, 1931); F. Brandileone, *Scritti* 2 (1931) 419 (= *RStDIt* 1, 1928); A. Segrè, *AG* 108 (1932) 179; idem, *Annuaire de l'Inst. de Philol. et d'Hist. orientales et slaves* 7 (1944) 243; D. Ochsenbein, *La transmissibilité hereditaire de l'obligation conditionnelle ex stipulatu* (Thèse Lausanne, 1935); Leifer, *BIDR* 44 (1936–37) 160; A. Hägerström, *Der röm. Obligationsbegriff* 2 (1941); Archi, *Scr Ferrini* (Univ. Pavia, 1946) 688; G. Lombardi, *Ricerche in tema di ius gentium*, 1946, 175; M. Kaser, *Das altröm. Ius*, 1949, 267; Dekkers, *RIDA* 4 (= *Mél De Visscher* 3, 1950) 361; Düll, *ZSS* 68 (1951) 191; Nicolas, *LQR* 69 (1953) 63.

Stipulatio aedilicia. A *stipulatio* imposed by an aedile to a party in a trial which took place under his jurisdiction.—See, for analogy, STIPULATIO PRAETORIA.

Stipulatio aliquem sisti. The promise of a person who assumed the guaranty that a defendant in a trial would appear in court on a fixed date.—See VINDEX, VADIMONIUM, SISTERE ALIQUEM.

Stipulatio amplius non agi. See CAUTIO AMPLIUS NON AGI.

Stipulatio Aquiliana. See ACCEPTILATIO.

Stipulatio argentaria. A promise made by a banker, in charge of a public auction, to the owner of the object to be sold, to the effect that the latter would receive the full proceeds from the sale, after deduction of the banker's fees and expenses.

F. Kniep, *S. a., Fg. der jur. Fakultät Jena*, 1911; Platon, *NRHD* 33 (1909) 142, 314.

Stipulatio certa. A stipulation in which the thing promised (*quid* = what), its quality (*quale*) and quantity (*quantum*) were precisely fixed. Ant. *stipulatio incerta*.

Stipulatio communis. A stipulation which could be imposed during a civil trial either by the jurisdictional magistrate (praetor, aedile) *in iure* or by the judge in the second stage of a civil trial (*apud iudicem*).—See STIPULATIO PRAETORIA, STIPULATIO IUDICIALIS. In a different sense the phrase *communiter stipulari* is used. It refers to a stipulation on behalf of two or more creditors.

Stipulatio condicionalis (or sub condicione). A promise whereby one assumes an obligation depending on whether a certain event will happen or not.—See CONDICIO.

Stipulatio conventionalis. A *stipulatio* based on an agreement of the parties, as opposed to a *stipulatio* ordered by a magistrate (*stipulatio praetoria, aedilicia*) or a judge (*stipulatio iudicialis*).

Stipulatio cum moriar. A *stipulatio* for payment at death ("when I shall be dying") of either party was valid since it was held that a man was alive at the moment of his death. However, a *stipulatio* concerning a payment *"pridie quam moriar"* (= a day before my death) or several days before the death either of the debtor or the creditor was void since until the actual death it could not be told when the obligation was due. Justinian declared such a *stipulatio* valid.

Stipulatio de dolo (or cautio de dolo). A *stipulatio* imposed by the judge on the defendant in specific circumstances, particularly in suits concerning claims for a thing (*actiones in rem*). Under such a *stipulatio* the defendant stipulated that he had not committed, nor would commit fraud in the matter under controversy. This *stipulatio* was a form of a *stipulatio iudicialis*. Such a *stipulatio* could take place extrajudicially as when a creditor demanded a promise from the debtor to abstain from any fraud in the fulfillment of the obligation.—See DOLUS.

Stipulatio donationis. A promise of a donation made in the form of a *stipulatio*. The *stipulatio* created an obligation of the donor to transfer the promised thing (to pay the promised sum) to the donee.—See DONATIO.

Stipulatio dotis. A promise of a dowry made in the form of a *stipulatio*.—See DOS, PROMISSIO DOTIS.

Stipulatio duplae (sc. pecuniae). A stipulation by the seller to pay the buyer double the price of the thing sold in the event of eviction of the thing by a third person.—D. 21.2.—See EMPTIO VENDITIO, EVICTIO.

P. F. Girard, *Mél de droit rom.* 2 (1923) 78, 113; H. Vincent, *Le droit des édiles*, 1922, 154; Kamphuisen, *RHD* 16 (1927) 610; Coing, *Seminar* 8 (1950) 9.

Stipulatio emptae et venditae hereditatis. See FIDEICOMMISSUM HEREDITATIS.

Stipulatio evictionis (or de evictione). See EVICTIO.

Stipulatio habere licere. A guaranty made in the form of a *stipulatio* by the seller to the buyer, to the effect that the latter would peacefully possess and use the thing sold and take proceeds from it (*habere, uti frui licere*).—See EMPTIO, EVICTIO.

Stipulatio in diem. A *stipulatio* in which payment on a fixed date is promised.

Stipulatio in faciendo. A promise through *stipulatio* to do something, to render certain services to the creditor. *Stipulatio operis faciendi* = a *stipulatio* concerning the construction (accomplishment) of a work. Ant. *stipulatio in non faciendo* = a *stipulatio* to abstain from doing something.

Stipulatio incerta. See STIPULATIO CERTA.

Stipulatio inter absentes. A *stipulatio* between persons who were not together. Such a *stipulatio* was void in classical law since the stipulatory question and answer were to be exchanged without interruption (*inter praesentes*, see STIPULATIO). Justinian modified the rule in that if a written document stated that the parties were present, a counterproof was permitted only when both parties were in different localities on the day when the *stipulatio* allegedly took place.

Stipulatio iudicialis. A compulsory *stipulatio* imposed by the judge in a civil trial on one or both parties during the second stage (*apud iudicem*), in order to assure the normal continuation of the trial.

Stipulatio operarum. See OPERAE LIBERTI.

Stipulatio partis et pro parte. See PARTITIO LEGATA.

Stipulatio poenae. A *stipulatio* concerning the payment of a penalty by a debtor if he failed to perform his obligation as agreed upon. The penalty settled in the *stipulatio* might serve either as a substitute for the losses suffered by the creditor (in such a case he might sue the debtor for the payment of the penalty without proving the amount of his actual losses) or as a mere penalty (*poenae nomine*) to be paid beside the indemnification for effective losses.—See POENA (in the law of obligations), SPONSIO POENALIS.

> Debray, *Revue générale du droit* 32 (1908) 97, 217, 289; Donatuti, *SDHI* 1 (1935) 299; Biscardi, *StSen* 60 (1948) 589.

Stipulatio post mortem. A *stipulatio* under which one promised the payment of a debt after the death of the creditor (*"post mortem meam dari spondes?"*) or after his own death by his heir (*"post mortem tuam dari spondes?"*). Such stipulations were null since neither could an heir be obligated before entering the inheritance nor could an obligation arise in his behalf. Consequently, a *stipulatio* by which the debtor assumed an obligation to the benefit of the heir of the creditor ("do you promise to pay my heir?") was without any legal effect. Justinian permitted such stipulations.—See OBLIGATIO POST MORTEM, MANDATUM POST MORTEM, ADSIGNATIO LIBERTI, ADSTIPULATIO, DIES MORTIS.

> Rouxel, *Annales Faculté droit Bordeaux, Sér. jurid.* 3 (1952) 7.

Stipulatio praepostera (or praepostere concepta). A *stipulatio* under which one assumed an immediate obligation but made it depend upon the fulfillment of a condition in the future (e.g., a promise to give today when a certain event will happen afterwards). In the classical law such a *stipulatio* was null, but Justinian recognized its validity; payment could be demanded after the fulfillment of the condition.

> L. Mitteis, *Röm. Privatrecht,* 1908, 180; Archi, *RISG* 88 (1951) 225.

Stipulatio praetoria. A *stipulatio* ordered by the praetor in his capacity as a jurisdictional magistrate. Such a compulsory *stipulatio* could be imposed on one or both parties to a trial in order to ascertain the normal continuation of the trial and to prevent an interruption as well as to assure a certain behavior of the parties by making them assume the duty of doing or refraining from doing something. If the promise embodied in the *stipulatio* was not fulfilled,

an ordinary action lay against the contravening party. A refusal of the praetor's order or the absence of the party on whom the *stipulatio* was to be imposed led to a MISSIO IN POSSESSIONEM in favor of his adversary. If the plaintiff refused to make the stipulatory promise ordered by the praetor, he lost the case through DENEGATIO ACTIONIS by the praetor. The praetorian stipulations were primarily applied for procedural purposes (see CAUTIO). They could, however, be ordered beyond a judicial trial at the request (*postulatio*) of the interested party. In such a case the adversary was summoned before the praetor.—D. 46.5.—See CAUTIO AMPLIUS NON AGI, CAUTIO DE RATO, CAUTIO IUDICATUM SOLVI, CAUTIO PRO PRAEDE LITIS ET VINDICIARUM.

> Cuq, *DS* 4, 1520; Anon., *NDI* 12; Jobbé-Duval, *St Bonfante* 3 (1930) 178; v. Woess, *ZSS* 53 (1933) 407; A. Palermo, *Il procedimento cauzionale,* 1942; Guarino, *SDHI* 8 (1942) 316.

Stipulatio pridie quam moriar. See STIPULATIO CUM MORIAR.

Stipulatio pro praede litis et vindiciarum. See CAUTIO PRO PRAEDE LITIS ET VINDICIARUM.

Stipulatio pure facta. A *stipulatio* not limited by a fixed date or a condition. Ant. *stipulatio in diem, stipulatio sub condicione (condicionalis)*.

Stipulatio rei uxoriae. See CAUTIO REI UXORIAE.

Stipulatio sortis et usurarum. A *stipulatio* in which the payment of both principal and interest is promised. Normally the promise of interest was made in a separate *stipulatio* (*stipulatio usurarum*).

Stipulatio sub condicione. See STIPULATIO CONDICIONALIS.

Stipulatio turpis. See TURPIS STIPULATIO.

Stipulatio usurarum. See STIPULATIO SORTIS ET USURARUM.

Stipulator. The creditor in a *stipulatio*. Syn. *reus stipulandi.* "Ambiguous stipulations should be interpreted against the creditor" (D. 34.5.26; 45.1.38.18).

> Stella-Maranca, *AnBari* 3 (1929/II) 20.

Stipulatum. (Noun.) See STIPULATIO.

Stirps. Descendants in a straight line from a common ancestor. When an inheritance is divided in *stirpes,* each son of the same father receives an equal part. All descendants of a son who died before his father receive together as much as any other son alive; if they are all of the same degree of relationship with the deceased, e.g., all are grandchildren. The share of a *stirps* (i.e., the descendants of one son) is divided in *capita* (in the example mentioned among the grandchildren) in equal portions.

Stola. A garment of an honorable, married woman. —See MATRONA, TOGA.

> Bieber, *RE* 4A; Leroux, *DS* 4.

Strangulare (strangulatio). To strangle a person with a rope (*laqueus*) to death. This form of execution was forbidden under the Principate.

> Pfaff, *RE* 4.

Stratores. In the late Empire, subaltern officers in the imperial palace who took care of the emperor's horses. The *stratores* were subordinates of the *comes stabuli* (the equerry). There also were *stratores* in the service of the *praefectus urbi* and provincial governors in imperial provinces. Superintendents of prisons were also called *stratores*.—C. 12.24.—See CUSTOS.

Lammert, *RE* 4A.

Strena. A gift donated on the occasion of a festivity, in particular on New Year's Day (*quod Kalendis Januariis dari solet* = what is used to be given on Kalends of January), e.g., to physicians.

Strepitus. A noise, a din. In the language of the later imperial constitutions the term refers to voices of the audience in a court-room during a criminal trial. Hence it denotes sometimes a criminal proceeding.

Strictus. Rigorous, governed by precise rules.—See IUS STRICTUM, IUDICIA BONAE FIDEI.

Pringsheim, *ZSS* 42 (1921) 65.

Structores. Workers (such as masons, carpenters, etc.) active in building a house or a ship. Primarily freedmen and slaves, they were organized in associations (*collegia*).

Hug, *RE* 4A; Saglio, *DS* 5.

Studium (studia). Study, learning. *Studiorum causa* = for the purpose of learning. Absence for such a reason was taken into consideration as an excuse when a person was obliged to appear before a public authority (*iustissima causa* = the most just cause). In a trial against a person absent for studies the praetor had to protect his interests. A stay in Rome for studies was not decisive for establishing a domicile (*domicilium*) since a sojourn there was considered temporary. A loan given to a *filius familias* for studies was not subject to the provisions of the SENATUSCONSULTUM MACEDONIANUM.

Studium liberale. Studies (occupations) befitting a free man, "worthy of a noble-minded man" (as Cicero, *Acad.* 2.1.1, defined it) were reckoned among *studia liberalia*. Among such professions were those of rhetorician (*rhetor*), grammarian (*grammaticus*) land-surveyor (*geometra*), physician (*medicus*), and the like. Teachers of *studium liberale* (*praeceptores*) could demand an honorarium only in a trial through *cognitio extra ordinem*.—D. 50.13; C. 11.19.—See PRAECEPTORES, MAGISTRI, PROFESSORES, HONORARIUM, OPERAE LIBERALES, EDICTUM VESPASIANI.

Studiosus iuris. A person devoted to the study of law, a practicing lawyer (not a *iurisconsultus* endowed with *ius respondendi*), a juristic writer.

Stuprare. To commit a STUPRUM. The term refers only to men (= *stuprator*).—See the next item.

Stuprum. Illicit intercourse with an unmarried woman or a widow of honorable social conditions. *Stuprum* is distinguished from adultery (*adulterium*) where a married woman is involved. Both parties were punished by seizure of half of their property; the woman was acquitted if the man had used violence.—C. 9.9. —See MERETRIX.

Pfaff, *RE* 4A; Lécrivain, *DS* 4; Guarino, *ZSS* 63 (1943) 184.

Stuprum cum masculo (puero). Pederasty. Originally it was punished by death, later only with a fine of money. In the later Empire the death penalty was inflicted again.—See LEX SCANTINIA.

Pfaff, *RE* 4A, 424; Lécrivain, *DS* 4, 1547.

Suadere. To give advice. The term is used of the activity of lawyer's when consulted by clients for legal advice.—See CONSILIUM.

Suae aetatis fieri. Not a precise technical term. It may mean to become either *maior* (over twenty-five years of age) or *pubes* (over fourteen, see IMPUBES).

Berger, *RE* 15, 1862.

Suae mentis esse (fieri). To be (become) mentally sound. Ant. *suae mentis* (or *suus*) *non esse* = to be insane.

Suae potestatis esse. See SUI IURIS.

Suarii. Swine dealers. In the later Empire they were compulsorily organized in associations, as other food merchants.—C. 1.17.

Hug, *RE* 4A, 469; 12, 689; Baudrillart, *DS* 4, 923.

Sub. (When prefixed to the title of an official.) An assistant official, subordinate to the head of an office (e.g., *subcurator operum publicorum, subcurator aedium sacrarum, subpraefectus, subprocurator*).

Sub modo. See DONATIO SUB MODO, LEGATUM SUB MODO.

Sub potestate esse. To be under paternal power; see PATRIA POTESTAS.

Subcurator. An official of equestrian rank acting as an assistant (*adiutor*) of a *curator*, e.g., *subcurator aedium sacrarum* (see AEDES), *subcurator operum publicorum* (for the administration of public buildings), *subcurator aquarum* (for the water administration), and others.—See CURATORES AEDIUM SACRARUM, CURATORES OPERUM PUBLICORUM, CURATORES AQUARUM.

Kubitschek, *RE* 4A.

Subditicius filius. A fraudulently substituted (suppositious) son. Syn. *partus suppositus, subiectus*. If a person instituted as his heir one whom he falsely believed to be his son and who in fact was supposititious, the institution was null if it could be proved that the testator would not have appointed him, had he known the truth.

Subdole. Deceitfully, deceptively. Syn. *dolose*.—See DOLUS.

Subducere. To take away by stealth, to hide. In another sense *subducere* = to take into account, to deduct (e.g., the proceeds one had from a thing, the *quarta Falcidia*).

Subhastarius. Sold at a public auction.

Subhastatio (subhastare). A public auction.—See HASTA, AUCTIO. Syn. *venditio sub hasta.*
> Voigt, *BerSächGW* 1903, 13.

Subicere. To add to an agreement, a clause, e.g., concerning the liability of a party for fraud (*clausula doli*), or a penalty clause. In another meaning *subicere* = to substitute one thing or person for another (*persona subiecta,* see SUBDITICIUS). *Subicere* is used of a forged testament being substituted for the real one; see FALSUM.

Subicere falsum partum. See PARTUS SUPPOSITUS, SUBDITICIUS.

Subici. To be subject (*subiectus*) to one's jurisdiction (*iurisdictioni*); to be exposed to a penalty (*poenae*); to be liable for taxes or public charges (*vectigalibus, muneribus*).

Subiectum nomen. A false name, the name of another person assumed for fraudulent purposes (e.g., when one buys or takes a lease under another's name).

Subiectus partus. See SUBICERE PARTUM, PARTUS SUPPOSITUS.

Subiectus iuri alieno (or alicuius). Subject to paternal power; see PATRIA POTESTAS, ALIENI IURIS.

Subire. To undergo, to assume, to risk (condemnation in a civil trial, duties, charges [= *onera*], a guaranty). *Subire poenam* = to suffer, to endure a penalty.

Sublimissimus (vir). An honorific epithet of the highest officials in the late Empire (e.g., *praefectus praetorio, magister officiorum*). They were addressed by the emperor under the title *"sublimitas tua"* ("your excellency"). Syn. *magnificentia, eminentia.*

Sublimitas. See the foregoing item.

Sublugere. Refers to a lower degree of mourning (e.g., after the death of a child below three years).—See LUCTUS, TEMPUS LUGENDI.

Submittere. To substitute one thing for another. With reference to an usufruct of a herd = to replace a dead head of cattle by a new one when the herd was to be returned to the owner.—See GREX.
> Kübler, *RE* 4A, 483.

Subnotare (subnotatio). To sign (a signature).—See SUBSCRIBERE.

Subornare. To bribe a witness to bear false testimony, to suborn, to instigate a person by bribery to commit a crime.

Subpignus. (Non-Roman term.) See PIGNUS PIGNORI DATUM.

Subpraefectus annonae. An assistant (*adiutor*) of the *praefectus annonae.*
> O. Hirschfeld, *Kais. Verwaltungsbeamte*[2] (1905) 246.

Subpraefectus classis. A deputy commander of a fleet, subordinate to the PRAEFECTUS CLASSIS.
> O. Hirschfeld, *Kais. Verwaltungsbeamtc*[2] (1905) 228.

Subpraefectus vigilum. A deputy commander of the VIGILES, subordinate to the *praefectus vigilum.*
> O. Hirschfeld, *Kais. Verwaltungsbeamte*[2] (1905) 256.

Subprocurator. An assistant *procurator* in an imperial province designated by the emperor for a special branch of administration (e.g., for the management of mines).
> O. Hirschfeld, *Kais. Verwaltungsbeamte*[2] (1905) 400.

Subreptio (subrepere). See OBREPTIO.

Subripere. To take away secretly, to steal.—See LEX ATINIA. *Res subreptae = res furtivae.*
> Berger, *RE* 12, 2331.

Subripere instrumentum. To remove fraudulently a document (a testament) in order to make it impossible to produce it in court or to put a forged one in its place.

Subrogare legem. To add a supplementary provision to an earlier law.

Subscribendarius. A lower ranking official in the later Empire charged with the preparation of the draft of a decision to be made by his superior.
> Ensslin, *RE* 4A; Humbert, *DS* 4; Henne, *ConfInst* 1947 (1950) 117.

Subscribere. To sign.—See TESTAMENTUM TRIPERTITUM, SUBSCRIPTIO.

Subscriptio. (From *subscribere.*) A signature. With regard to private documents (*subscriptio instrumenti, subscriptio chirographi*) there were signatures of both parties who concluded an agreement, or only of the party who assumed an obligation, and eventually of his surety. The *subscriptio* consisted of the name of the subscriber and a brief summary of the content of the document or of the nature of the obligation the subscriber assumed. The signatures of witnesses (TESTIS) contained the indication that they acted as witnesses. With the increase of the use of written documents the imperial legislation issued detailed provisions concerning the signatures of the parties, the notary involved, and the witnesses. The subscription of the party became an important element in a document when its body was written by another person. —See SUBSCRIPTIO TESTAMENTI, SUPERSCRIPTIO.
> Kübler, *RE* 4A; Lécrivain, *DS* 4.

Subscriptio. (In a criminal trial.) A written accusation (see INSCRIPTIO) or an oral accusation written down in the records of the competent office and signed by the accuser. The accuser and those who signed the accusation together with him to support the accusation = *subscriptores.*—C. 7.57.
> Kübler, *RE* 4A, 490; Kleinfeller, *ibid. (s.v. subscriptores);* Riccobono, *ZSS* 34 (1913) 246; Wlassak, *Anklage und Streitbefestigung, SbWien* 184, 1 (1917) 89.

Subscriptio. (In military administration.) The signing of documents concerning the distribution of food among soldiers by the officer involved.—See SUBSCRIBENDARIUS.

Subscriptio censoria. See NOTA CENSORIA.
> Kübler, *RE* 4A, 490.

Subscriptio principis. A signature of the emperor. When written at the foot of a petition addressed to him, it was a kind of an imperial rescript (*rescriptum* *principis*) since it was the emperor's answer to the petition (*preces, libellus*). The petition provided with the answer and the emperor's signature was publicly exposed. The petitioner received a copy at request.

> Premerstein, *RE* 13, 39; Kübler, *RE* 4A, 399; De Dominicis, *RendLomb* 83 (1950).

Subscriptio testamenti. The signature of the testator on a written testament, which was valid under praetorian law, was not necessary when the will was sealed by seven witnesses. However, when the testator rewarded the writer of the testament, he had to confirm the pertinent disposition with his own hand. See SENATUSCONSULTUM LIBONIANUM. Forgery of a signature in a testament or another document was under pain of the penalties of the LEX CORNELIA DE FALSIS.—See SUPERSCRIPTIO.

> Kübler, *RE* 4A, 493; Macqueron, *RHD* 24 (1945) 160.

Subscriptor. One who subscribed (a document, a testament).—See SUBSCRIPTIO, in a criminal trial.

> Kleinfeller, *RE* 4A.

Subsellium. A bench used in court or in certain offices. It was lower than the SELLA CURULIS, which was the privilege of higher magistrates only. Judges in criminal trials (*quaestiones*) were seated on *subsellia* and so were also the accuser and the lawyers. Hence *subsellium* is used sometimes to mean a court. Plebeian tribunes and aediles had no right to a *sella curulis* and could use only a *subsellium*.

> Hug, *RE* 4A; Chapot, *DS* 4.

Subsidere. To remain. Used of legacies which the legatee refused to accept and which therefore remained with the heir.

Subsidiarius. See ACTIO SUBSIDIARIA.

Subsidium. Help, assistance. The term is used of legal remedies granted to a person in order to save him from a loss (e.g., an action, an exception, an interdict, a *restitutio in integrum*).

Subsignare. To sign, to subscribe (syn. *subscribere*), to seal (syn. *signare*).—In another meaning *subsignare* = to give a landed property to the state or a municipality as security for obligations owed them (e.g., to collect taxes, to construct a building). In constitutions of the later Empire, *subsignare* is used for setting up real securities in general.—See PRAEDIA SUBSIGNATA.

> Hardy, *Three Spanish charters*, 1912, 78.

Subsistere. To defend oneself or another in a trial against an adversary. See LAUDARE AUCTOREM. When used of a legal act (e.g., a testament, a judicial judgment) = to be valid.

Subsortitio. A supplementary selection of a juror in a criminal trial if after the selection (SORTITIO) of jurors for a specific trial a seat became vacant by death or election of a juror to a magistracy).—See ALBUM IUDICUM.

> Kübler, *RE* 4A; Ehrenberg, *RE* 13, 1495.

Substantia. The substance, the essential nature or function, social or economic, of a thing (*substantia rei*) or of a legal transaction (*substantia emptionis, obligationis*). In several constitutions by Diocletian the word is strengthened by the addition of *veritatis* (= the true nature of a legal transaction). *Substantia* also refers to the entire property of a person (e.g., *substantia paterna* = the father's property) or to an inheritance as a whole (*substantia hereditatis, substantia defuncti*). *Substantia* was a favorite term of the imperial chancery and occurs in interpolated passages.—See ERROR IN SUBSTANTIA, USUSFRUCTUS.

> Guarneri-Citati, *Indice²* (1927) 84; *idem, Fschr Koschaker* 1 (1939) 153; Scheltema, *Rechtsgeleerd Magazijn* 55 (1936) 60.

Substituere. To appoint, to substitute one person in the place of another (e.g., a representative in a trial, a guardian, a curator). The term was of particular importance in the law of successions.—See the following items.

Substitutio. The appointment of another heir by a testator in the event that the heir first instituted did not take the inheritance either because he would not or could not do so. The heir instituted in the second place = *heres substitutus, heres secundus*. Several heirs could be substituted to the heir first appointed, and one person to two or more heirs. Likewise the heirs first instituted could be reciprocally substituted one to the other (*substitutio mutua, reciproca*) and a *heres tertius* (a third heir) to the *heres secundus*. Through a *substitutio* the testator saved the validity of the testament which would have become void if the heir first appointed did not accept the inheritance. Syn. *substitutio vulgaris* (= ordinary *substitutio*), to be distinguished from *substitutio pupillaris*.—Inst. 2.15; D. 28.6; C. 6.25; 26.

> Weiss, *RE* 4A; Beauchet, *DS* 4; G. Segrè, *Scritti giur.* 2 (1938) 348; B. Biondi, *Successione testamentaria* (1943) 245; Solazzi, *SDHI* 16 (1950) 1.

Substitutio duplex. A *substitutio vulgaris* (see SUBSTITUTIO) combined with a SUBSTITUTIO PUPILLARIS. It occurred when a testator appointed a third person as a substitute to a child in his power and below the age of puberty (*impubes*) for the event that the child might die before him (i.e., the testator) or before puberty after becoming heir. In the later development (still in classical law) it was held that a pupillary *substitutio* implied automatically an ordinary *substitutio* (*substitutio vulgaris*) unless the testator disposed otherwise. Ant. *substitutio simplex* = a *substitutio* limited by the testator to one of the two basic forms of *substitutio*.—See SUBSTITUTIO, SUBSTITUTIO PUPILLARIS.

Substitutio mutua. See SUBSTITUTIO.

Substitutio pupillaris. The appointment of a substitute by the father for his child instituted as an heir in his testament. The substitute became heir if the child, after the acceptance of the inheritance, died before reaching puberty, i.e., before being able to make a testament. Through *substitutio pupillaris* the father provided in his testament for a successor to his child. *Substitutio pupillaris* was permitted only in the father's testament, and then only along with the institution of the child as heir in the first place. See, however, TESTAMENTUM PUPILLARE. Justinian introduced a new form of *substitutio*, modeled on the *substitutio pupillaris* (*ad exemplum pupillaris substitutionis*, C. 6.26.9) for use with insane descendants. The father could appoint an heir for his insane descendant to succeed in the event that the latter did not recover sanity. This form of *substitutio* is called in the literature *substitutio quasi pupillaris*. The testator (father or mother) had, however, to appoint first a nearest relative of the insane, and only in the absence of relatives could he appoint an heir of his own choice.—Inst. 2.16; D. 28.6; C. 6.26.—See CURIANA CAUSA.

La Pira, *St Bonfante* 3 (1930) 271; Wolff, *St Riccobono* 3 (1936) 437; Vazny, *BIDR* 46 (1939) 68, 47 (1940) 31; B. Biondi, *Successione testamentaria* (1943) 252; Cosentini, *Ann. di dir. comp. e di st. legislativi* 22 (1946) 152; Perrin, *RHD* 47 (1949) 335, 518; *idem, in Varia, Ét de droit rom.* (*Publications de l'Institut de droit rom. de l'Univ. de Paris*, 9, 1952) 267.

Substitutio quasi pupillaris. See SUBSTITUTIO PUPILLARIS.

Substitutio reciproca. See SUBSTITUTIO.

Substitutio simplex. See SUBSTITUTIO DUPLEX.

Substitutio vulgaris. See SUBSTITUTIO.

Subtilitas legum. In the language of Justinian's constitutions, severity, rigorous formalities of the earlier law. The expressions *subtilis, subtilitas,* and *subtiliter* when used with regard to ancient law to stress its rigidity, are frequently interpolated.

Seckel, in *Heumann's Handlexikon*[9] (1907), *s.v. subtilis*; Guarneri-Citati, *Indice*[2] (1927) 84.

Subtrahere. To take away, to remove. The term is used in connection with theft. *Se subtrahere* = to withdraw illegally from public services (*munera, military service*).

Suburbanum praedium. A plot of land located in the vicinity of a city. Its possibilities for economic exploitation decided whether it qualified as urban (*praedium urbanum*) or rustic land (*praedium rusticum*). *Praedia suburbana* were among the landed properties the sale of which by a guardian was prohibited by the ORATIO SEVERI.

Suburbicariae regiones. Territories bordering on Rome. They are mentioned in a few constitutions of the Theodosian Code. They are not specific administrative units.—See VICARIUS IN URBE.

Subvas. See VAS.

Subvenire. To come to the aid. Used of judicial remedies granted primarily to persons who in particular situations or for specific reasons deserve such help. The term refers to *restitutiones in integrum* and exceptions.

Succedere (successio). To succeed, to take the place of a person either as his successor in office or as his heir. In the latter case a person (*successor*) enters into the legal situation of a defunct person (*succedere in ius, in locum, in ius et locum defuncti*) both as creditor and debtor in all his legal relations except those which are extinguished by death (as, e.g., *mandatum, societas*) or are merely factual, as *possessio*. In postclassical and Justinian's law the terms *succedere* and *successio* were extended to cases in which one succeeded in one specific relationship of the deceased (*succedere in rem, in singulas res, in rei dominium* = in the ownership of one thing) which is opposed to *successio in universum ius* (*in universum dominium, in universa bona* = in the whole property). It is generally accepted that the definition of successors, preserved in the Digest (39.2.24.1a): "successors are not only those who succeed to a whole property, but also those who succeeded in the ownership of one thing are covered by this term," is an interpolation by Justinian's compilers. *Succedere hereditario iure* = to succeed as an heir. *Successio* indicates at times the right of succession, and it is used as a collective term embracing all heirs (descendants) of a person.—Inst. 3.2.; 5; 7; C. 6.59. —See UNIVERSITAS, SUCCESSOR, HEREDITAS, BONORUM POSSESSIO, HERES, SUCCESSIO IN UNIVERSUM IUS.

Beauchet, *DS* 4; Longo, *BIDR* 14 (1902) 127, 224; 15 (1903) 283; Bonfante, *Scr giuridici* 1 (1926) 250; Ambrosino, *SDHI* 11 (1945) 65; 94; B. Biondi, *Istituti fondamentali* 1 (1946) 9; B. Albanese, *La successione ereditaria in dir. rom. antico, AnPal* 20 (1949).

Successio graduum. See BONORUM POSSESSIO INTESTATI, EDICTUM SUCCESSORIUM.

De Crescenzio, *NDI* 12, 960.

Successio in locum prioris creditoris. Succession into the place of a prior creditor. It happened when the same thing was hypothecated successively to several creditors; see HYPOTHECA. A creditor earlier in date had priority over creditors to whom the thing was hypothecated later. Renunciation by one creditor or extinction of his claim (e.g., by payment) caused the creditor next in order to enter in his place. Such a succession could also be agreed upon between two creditors.—D. 20.4; C. 8.18.—See IUS OFFERENDI PECUNIAM, POTIOR IN PIGNORE.

Successio in possessionem (possessionis). Succession into the possession of a thing. In the case of succession through inheritance an heir did not automatically succeed in possession through the acceptance of the inheritance (see ADITIO HEREDITATIS). He had to take physical possession of all things belonging to the estate (*res hereditariae*). This gave him the opportunity to continue and complete the usucaption of individual things if their possession by the defunct person satisfied the conditions of *usucapio*. —See ACCESSIO POSSESSIONIS, USUCAPIO.

Successio in universum ius. See SUCCEDERE, UNIVERSITAS.—For universal succession in the property of a living person, see ADROGATIO, BONORUM VENDITIO, CONVENTIO IN MANUM.

Catalano, *AnCat* 1 (1947) 314.

Successio ordinum. See BONORUM POSSESSIO INTESTATI, EDICTUM SUCCESSORIUM.—D. 38.15.

De Crescenzio, *NDI* 12, 960.

Successio in usucapionem. See SUCCESSIO IN POSSESSIONEM, USUCAPIO.

Successor. One who succeeded another in office or as his heir.—See SUCCEDERE.—C. 10.63.

Successor honorarius. A person who inherited another's property according to praetorian law, either under a testament valid according to praetorian law or according to the order of succession on intestacy established in the praetorian edict.—See BONORUM POSSESSIO, EDICTUM SUCCESSORIUM.

Successor legitimus. An heir inheriting under *ius civile*. Ant. *successor honorarius, praetorius*.

Successor praetorius. See HONORARIUS.

Successores ceteri. All other successors who inherit beside *heredes* and *bonorum possessores*. Wherever the *successores ceteri* appear along with *heredes* or with *heredes* and *bonorum possessores* the expression *successores ceteri* is interpolated. Through this addition the compilers wished to extend certain legal rules applicable to heirs, to other persons who under any title acquired another's property.

Longo, *BIDR* 14 (1902) 150; Guarneri-Citati, *Indice²* (1907) 17.

Successorium edictum. See EDICTUM SUCCESSORIUM.

Succidere. See ACTIO ARBORUM FURTIM CAESARUM.

Succurrere. To help. The term is used of procedural measures (exceptions, *restitutio in integrum*) by which the praetor saved persons who for special reasons (e.g., minor age) deserved protection from losses. Syn. *subvenire*.

Suffectus. A magistrate (e.g., a consul) elected to fill a vacancy which occurred during the service year.

Kübler, *RE* 4A.

Sufferre. To bear, to undergo, to suffer (losses or penalties) either a pecuniary fine through a decision of a magistrate (see MULTA) or a penalty to be paid in accordance with an agreement for default in fulfillment of an obligation (see POENA) or, in a civil trial, the disadvantage of a LITIS AESTIMATIO.

Sufficere. To suffice. Often used of an action or another procedural remedy available to a person for putting forward his claim.

Suffragator. One who used his influence to support another in an electoral campaign for a magistracy, or one who intervened with the emperor in favor of another person. Any such action = *suffragatio*.—See SUFFRAGIUM.

Kübler, *RE* 4A.

Suffragium. A vote, the right to vote. *Suffragium* refers to both the vote in popular assemblies (*comitia*) and in criminal courts (*quaestiones*). For abbreviations used see A, C, U.R. To start voting = *suffragium inire, ferre*.—C. 4.3.—See CIVITATES SINE SUFFRAGIO, TABELLAE, IUS SUFFRAGII, LEGES TABELLARIAE, ROGATOR, DIRIBITIO.

Kübler, *RE* 4A; Saglio, *DS* 4; De Marchi, *La sincerità del voto nei comizi rom.*, *RendLomb* 1912, 653; G. Rotondi, *Leges publicae populi Rom.* (1912) 19; Fraccaro, *La procedura del voto nei comizi*, *ATor* 49 (1913/14) 600.

Suffragium. (In the later Empire.) Recommendation of a person to the emperor or a high official for an official position or a special privilege. The person on behalf of whom the *suffragator* intervened usually promised an honorarium for the service rendered; the pertinent agreement = *contractus suffragii*. An imperial constitution of A.D. 394 ordered that such a promise had to be made in the solemn form of a *sponsio* (C. 4.3.1). *Suffragium* is also used of gratuitous recommendations or interventions on behalf of another.—C. 4.3.—See SUFFRAGATOR.

Kübler, *RE* 4A, 657.

Suggerere. To advise, to prompt, to suggest. The verb occurs in texts suspected of interpolation. It is rare in classical language, but frequent in imperial constitutions.

Guarneri-Citati, *Indice²* (1927) 84.

Suggestio. A query or a report presented by a lower official to a higher one or to the emperor. The term is used primarily in imperial constitutions.

Sui. (In a general meaning.) The next relatives of a person; persons living in the same household under the one head of the family.—See SUUS.

Sui iuris (esse). To be legally independent, not under the paternal power (*patria potestas*) of another. Syn. *suae potestatis esse*. Ant. ALIENI IURIS.—See SUUS.

Suicidium. A suicide. See CONSCISCERE SIBI MORTEM, LIBERAE MORTIS FACULTAS. "A soldier who attempted to commit suicide and did not succeed, is to be punished by death unless he wanted to die because of unbearable pains, sickness, affliction (mourning), or for another reason; in such cases he is to be dishonorably discharged" (D. 48.19.38.12).

Sumere arbitrum (iudicem). To take an arbitrator or judge by common agreement of the parties involved in a controversy.—See COMPROMISSUM, IUDEX.

J. Mazeaud, *La nomination du iudex unus*, 1933, 121.

Sumere poenam (supplicium). To exact punishment (e.g., the death penalty).

Summa. An enactment by Justinian through which the first Code (see CODEX IUSTINIANUS) was promulgated (April 16, 529). The constitution starts with the words *Summa rei publicae*.

Summa. See IN SUMMA.

Summa (pecuniae). A sum of money; the term is frequently connected with a noun indicating the origin or nature of the obligation (*summa debiti, sacramenti, sponsionis, dotis, condemnationis*, etc.).

Summa honoraria. See HONORARIUM.

Kübler, *RE* 4A.

Summa Perusina. A summary of imperial constitutions from the first eight books of Justinian's Code, entitled *Adnotationes Codicum Domini Iustiniani.* The author of the *Summa* which was written in the seventh or eighth century and is preserved in one manuscript (now in Perugia), is unknown.

Editions: Heimbach, *Anecdota* 2 (1840); Patetta, *BIDR* 12 (1900).—Monti, *NDI* 12, 1; M. Conrat, *Gesch. der Quellen und Literatur des röm. R. im frühen Mittelalter* (1891) 182; Besta, *Atti Accad. Palermo* 1908.

Summa res. See SUMMAE RATIONES.

Summae. Called in the literature brief abstracts (summaries) of Justinian's Digest and the Code which were written in Greek by Byzantine jurists soon after the publication of Justinian's codification to make the large legislative works more easily accessible to practitioners.—See INDEX.

Summae rationes. The general fiscal administration of the Roman state. The officials charged with the pertinent duties = *tabularii summarum rationum.* Syn. *summa res.*

O. Hirschfeld, *Kais. Verwaltungsbeamte*[2] (1905) 32.

Summatim cognoscere. A summary, simplified procedure applied in the COGNITIO EXTRA ORDINEM in specific civil cases when a speedy investigation of the matter (e.g., when alimony was sought) was desirable. With the cooperation of the parties the course of the proceedings was hastened. *Summatim rem exponere* is used of lawyers who briefly summarized the case in court.

Wlassak, *RE* 4, 213; Biondi, *BIDR* 30 (1921) 220; H. Krüger, *ZSS* 45 (1925) 39; Wenger, *Institutes of the R. civil procedure* (1940) 324.

Summovere. To exclude (e.g., from an inheritance or guardianship). The principal application of the term is with reference to procedural exceptions (see EXCEPTIO) when the plaintiff's claim is successfully opposed by the defendant's *exceptio.*

Summum supplicium. The death penalty. Syn. *ultimum supplicium.*—See SUPPLICIUM.

Summus. The highest. The superlative is primarily used of institutions and things that pertained to, or were connected with, the emperor.

Sumptu publico. At the expense of the state or a municipality.—See SUMPTUS.

Sumptuariae leges. See the following item.

Sumptus. Generally all kinds of expenses (syn. IMPENSAE), also those which one incurs for another in contractual relations or other legal situations. See NEGOTIORUM GESTIO, POSSESSOR BONAE FIDEI. In a specific sense *sumptus* = expenses connected with a luxurious life. In the Republic a series of statutes were issued in order to suppress the increasing luxury in Roman life (*leges sumptuariae*). They prohibited luxurious clothes for women, the excessive use of jewelry, and prodigality in banquets and feasts. The

legislation apparently was not successful since the prohibitions, combined with high taxes, were frequently repeated. See LEX AEMILIA, FANNIA, OPPIA, ORCHIA. Luxurious funerals were also repeatedly prohibited, first by the Twelve Tables. Later on, the censors frequently intervened with prohibitions. The last *lex sumptuaria* was LEX IULIA SUMPTUARIA by Augustus.

Kübler, *RE* 4A; Lécrivain, *DS* 4; G. Longo, *NDI* 7 (*s.v. leges sumptuariae*); Richter, *NDI* 12, 1 (*s.v. sumptuariae leges*); E. Giraudias, *Études historiques sur les lois sumptuaires* (Thèse Poitiers, 1910); G. Rotondi, *Leges publicae populi Rom.* (1912) 98.

Sumptus funeris (in funus). See SUMPTUS, ACTIO FUNERARIA, IMPENSAE FUNERIS.—D. 11.7; C. 3.44.

Cuq, *DS* 2, 1408.

Sumptus litis (in litem). The emperor Zenon (C. 7.51.5, A.D. 487) introduced a general rule that any one who was defeated in a trial, plaintiff or defendant, whether he was in good or bad faith, had to pay the victorious adversary the expenses connected with the trial. Syn. *expensae litis.*—C. 7.51.—See CALUMNIA, POENA TEMERE LITIGANTIUM.

Chiovenda, *BIDR* 7 (1894) 275; idem, *RISG* 269 (1898) 3, 161; H. Erman, *Restitution des frais de procès en dr. rom.*, Lausanne, 1892.

Sumptum ludorum. Expenses connected with the arrangement of public games.—See LUDI, SENATUS-CONSULTUM DE SUMPTIBUS LUDORUM MINUENDIS.

Sumptus muneris. Expenses connected with the fulfillment of public charges (MUNERA). If a person was assigned a certain public service together with others, but he alone fulfilled the duties imposed, the others who failed to cooperate had to reimburse him for the expenses he incurred on their behalf.—C. 11.38; 10.69.

Suo nomine. See NOMINE.

Supellex (suppellex). Household goods.—See LEGATUM SUPELLECTILIS.—D. 33.10.

Super. When followed by an ablative it is syn. with *de.* A Grecism frequently occurring in the language of the imperial chancery and in interpolated passages.

Guarneri-Citati, *Indice*[2] (1927) 85.

Superare aliquem. (When referring to a civil trial.) To be victorious over one's adversary, to win the case. With reference to a criminal trial = to establish the guilt of the accused, to convict.

Superexactio (superexigere). See EXACTIO.—C. 10.20.

Flore, *St Bonfante* 4 (1930) 345.

Superficiariae aedes. A building built on leased land. It belongs to the owner of the land.

Superficiarius. (Noun.) One who has the right of SUPERFICIES on another's land.

Superficiarius. (Adj.) An immovable, land or building, encumbered with the right of *superficies* on behalf of a person other than the owner.—See SUPERFICIES.

Superficies. All that is connected with the soil whether it comes out from it (trees, plants, etc.) or is built upon it. All this "goes with the soil" (*superficies cedit solo,* Gaius, Inst. 2.73, D. 43.17.3.7), i.e., it becomes property of the owner (see INAEDIFICATIO, PLANTATIO, SATIO) even if the material used for constructions, plants, seed, etc., belongs to another person.—*Superficies* as a right over another's property = the right to use all that is on the surface of another's land. The origin of *superficies* as far as buildings are concerned, arose from arrangements made between the owner of a given piece of land and the constructor of the building thereon (first on public land, later on private property). Under such agreements the builder acquired a right similar to that of a lessee (see LOCATIO CONDUCTIO REI), but perpetual and hereditary. The *superficiarius* (= the person entitled to *superficies*) had a specific legal situation not only with regard to the owner of the land (to whom he paid an annual rent, *solarium*) but also to third persons against whom he was protected by a special interdict (*interdictum de superficiebus*). In later development certain other actions were granted the *superficiarius,* actions which normally were available to owners only. In Justinian's law the *superficies* appears as a fully developed institution, as a strong right on another's property, protected by legal means analogous to those which were granted to the owner. The development of the *superficies,* though doubtful in details, shows the transformation of the institution from a merely obligatory relationship to a real right (*ius in re aliena*) over another's property endowed with nearly all advantages which resulted from ownership.—D. 43.18.
—See AEDES, USUSFRUCTUS, POSSESSIO AD INTERDICTA.

Kübler, *RE* 4A; Lécrivain, *DS* 4; Simoncelli, *NDI* 12; Berger, *RE* 9, 1647; idem, *Teilungsklagen,* 1912, 32; Beseler, *Beiträge zur Kritik* 1 (1911) 100, 3 (1913) 169; G. Baviera, *Scritti giur.* 1 (1909) 177; Arangio-Ruiz, *AG* 81 (1908) 436; Rabel, *Mél Girard* 2 (1912) 307; Buckland, *RHD* 17 (1938) 666; B. Biondi, *La categoria romana delle servitutes* (1938) 443; idem, *Le servitù prediali* (1946) 70; E. Albertario, *Studi* 2 (1941, ex 1911, 1912) 409, 459; Pugliese, *Temi Emiliana* 20, 4 (1943) 119; Solazzi, *SDHI* 3–14 (1947/8) 307; idem, *RISG* 86 (1949) 23; Branca, *RIDA* 4 (1950) 189; M. Vogt, *Das Erbbaurecht des klas. röm. R.,* 1950; E. Levy, *West Roman Vulgar Law,* 1951, 49, 80.

Superficies cedit solo. See SUPERFICIES, INAEDIFICATIO, ACCESSIO.

Riccobono, *AnPal* 3–4 (1917) 508; Wenger, *Philologus* 42 (1933) 254; C. A. Maschi, *La concezione naturalistica* (1937) 284; idem, *St Arangio-Ruiz* 4 (1953) 135.

Superficium. See SUPERFICIES.

Superflua non nocent. See SUPERFLUUS.

Superfluum. What remains from a sum of money after deductions have been made, e.g., from the price of a pledge sold if the price exceeded the debt for which the pledge had been given.—See PACTUM DE DISTRAHENDO, HYPEROCHA.

Superfluus. Unnecessary, superfluous. An imperial constitution (C. 6.23.17) pointed out the distinction between necessary and unnecessary clauses in a contract or testament. The omission of necessary clauses which are required for the validity of the act invalidated it whereas the addition of superfluous details because of exaggerated cautiousness did not since *"superflua non nocent"* (= superfluous additions do no harm).

Superindictio (superindictum). In the later Empire an extraordinary additional charge or tax levied when the normal taxes or public charges (*munera*) did not suffice. A *superindictio* was primarily decreed in war time. The owners of large estates (*possessores*) were the first to be charged with *superindictio.*—C. 10.18.—See INDICTIO.

Ensslin, *RE* 4A; Lécrivain, *DS* 4; Thibault, *Rev. générale du droit, de la législation* 24 (1900) 112.

Superior. In the official hierarchy higher in rank. *Superius imperium* = the power of a magistrate higher in rank; see IMPERIUM. Ant. *inferior.*

Superiores. Relatives in ascendant line.—See GRADUS.

Supernumerarii. In the later Empire, see MINISTRI CASTRENSES.

Superscriptio. The signature of a person placed on a document alongside its seal (*nomen adscribere*). Such an additional signature was required in testaments.—See SUBSCRIPTIO.

Supersedere. To neglect, to omit. The term is used of failure in fulfilling one's duties and of omission of certain required procedural measures in due course.

Honig, *Fg R. Schmidt* 1 (1932) 21.

Superstitio. Used of religions other than the Roman. Thus the emperors Severus and Caracalla spoke of *superstitio Iudaica* (D. 50.2.3.3). To Christian emperors any non-Christian religion was *superstitio* (*haeretica, paganorum, Iudaica,* etc.).—In the later Principate the profession of new religious doctrines "by which human minds are perturbed" (Paul. *Sent.* 5.21.2) was treated as a capital crime for which persons of higher social classes (HONESTIORES) were punished with deportation.—*Superstitio* also occurs in the meaning of an excessive, superstitious fear of a divinity in a rescript of the emperor Marcus Aurelius (D. 48.19.30) by which a person who "made weak-minded individuals terrified by a superstitious fear of a deity" was to be punished with deportation to an island.—See APOSTATA, CHRISTIANI, HAERETICI, IUDAEI.

Pfaff, *RE* 4A; Mommsen, *Religionsfrevel, Jurist. Schriften* 3 (1907, ex 1890) 389; Martroye, *RHD* 9 (1930) 669.

Superveniens. See MALA FIDES.

Supervivere. To survive.—See COMMORIENTES.

Supplere. To complete, to make full (e.g., *usucapionem, fideicommissum, aetatem, tempus, numerum*).

Guarneri-Citati, *SDHI* 1 (1935) 153.

Supplere ius civile. See IUS HONORARIUM.

Guarneri-Citati, *SDHI* 1 (1935) 157.

Supplicatio. A petition directly addressed to the emperor with a request for his decision in a judicial matter. Syn. *libellus, preces.* The *supplicatio* developed in later times into an appeal when a petitioner asked the emperor for a renewed examination in a matter in which normally no appeal was permitted (e.g., from judgments passed by praetorian prefects). —C. 1.19.

Arangio-Ruiz, *BIDR* 49/50 (1947) 55.

Supplicationes. Bloodless sacrifices performed by private persons at home. *Supplicationes* also were sacrifices celebrated by the whole nation and arranged by public authorities in order to ask aid of the gods in times of national calamity or to thank them in the case of a happy event.

Wissowa, *RE* 4A; Toutain, *DS* 4; Rose, *OCD*.

Supplicium. Death, death penalty, penalty in general. For the kinds of execution, see POENA.

Pfaff, *RE* 4A; Lécrivain, *DS* 4; Heinze, *Archiv für lat. Lexikographie* 15 (1908) 98; V. Brasiello, *La repressione penale,* 1937, 246; Vergote, *Les principaux modes de supplice, Bull. Inst. Hist. Belge de Rome* 10 (1939) 141.

Supplicium fustuarium. See FUSTUARIUM SUPPLICIUM.

Supplicium servile. See SERVILE SUPPLICIUM, CRUX.

Supplicium summum. See SUMMUM SUPPLICIUM.

Supplicium supremum. See SUPREMUM SUPPLICIUM.

Supplicium ultimum. The death penalty. Syn. *summum supplicium, supremum supplicium.*

Supponere. In later imperial constitutions to give a creditor a thing as a pledge.

Supponere partum. See PARTUS SUPPOSITUS. Syn. *subicere partum.*—See SUBDITICIUS.

Supposita persona. See INTERPOSITA PERSONA.

Suppressio. See SUPPRIMERE.

Suppressor. See SUPPRIMERE SERVUM ALIENUM.

Supprimere (suppressio). To conceal, to hide a thing in order to defraud another (a creditor, the fisc), to embezzle.

Supprimere servum alienum. To conceal another's slave. The wrongdoer was guilty of PLAGIUM and was punished under the LEX FABIA.

Supprimere tabulas (testamentum). To conceal a testament (or a codicil) to the detriment of the heir instituted therein (or a legatee). See INTERDICTUM DE TABULIS EXHIBENDIS. A slave who believed himself to have been manumitted in a testament concealed by the heir in order to frustrate the manumission, was permitted to accuse the latter on that charge (*accusatio suppressi testamenti*).

Supremum supplicium. The death penalty.

Supremus. Last, final. When connected with a noun referring to the will of a person (*suprema voluntas, supremum iudicium, supremae tabulae, supremae preces*) or simply *suprema* (plur. neut.) = a testament.—See IUDICIUM SUPREMUM, VOLUNTAS SUPREMA.

Surdus. Deaf. A deaf person could not promise by *stipulatio* nor accept a stipulatory promise because he was unable to hear the question or the answer. He was excluded from personal participation in oral transactions and from being a witness thereto. A person hard of hearing (*tarde exaudire*) is not considered *surdus.*—See CURATOR MUTI, TUTOR.—D. 37.3.

Susceptor (susceptio). (From SUSCIPERE.) In the financial administration of the later Empire = a collector of taxes in money or in kind (grain, wine = *susceptor vini,* clothes = *susceptor vestium*).—C. 10.72; 11.17.

Lammert, *RE* 4A.

Suscipere. In financial administration of the later Empire, see SUSCEPTOR.

Suscipere. In contractual and obligatory relations, to assume a unilateral obligation (e.g., *mandatum, depositum, commodatum*), to incur a debt (*suscipere mutuum, suscipere aes alienum*). *Suscipere obligationem* = to assume an obligation as one's own or for another (*suscipere obligationem alienam*) by releasing the principal debtor or as his surety (*fideiussor*).

Suscipere actionem (iudicium, litem). In civil trials, when referring to the formulary procedure, this is synonymous with *accipere iudicium* (see LITIS CONTESTATIO). With reference to the procedure through *cognitio extra ordinem* the term indicates that the defendant assumed the role of the plaintiff's adversary in the trial. *Suscipere defensionem* = to assume the defense of a defendant.

Suscipere filium (liberum). To beget a child. *Suscipi* = to be born (*susceptus*). *Suscipere filium alienum* = to adopt another's child.

Berger, *Jour. of juristic papyrology* 1 (1945) 30 (= *BIDR* 55–56, Post-Bellum [1951] 113).

Suscipere servum alienum. To give harbor to a slave who had left his master. Keeping the slave secretly (*celare, supprimere*) against the will of his master was considered a crime (see PLAGIUM) and punished under LEX FABIA.—See SUPPRIMERE SERVUM ALIENUM.

Suspectus. See HERES SUSPECTUS, SATISDATIO SUSPECTI HEREDIS, TUTOR SUSPECTUS, IUDEX SUSPECTUS, SUSPECTUS REUS.

Suspectus reus. A person suspected of having committed a crime. A slave suspected of a crime could be submitted to torture in order to obtain his confession if other evidence was not available.—See TORMENTA, SUSPICIO.

Suspendere (laqueo). To hang a person with a rope. See LAQUEUS, FURCA. This kind of punishment was practiced on slaves by some masters. The death of the slave was treated as homicide (*homicidium*).— C. 9.14.

Suspensa. Syn. *res suspensae.* See ACTIO DE DEIECTIS.

Suspensus sub condicione. See CONDICIO, IN SUSPENSO ESSE.

Suspicio. Suspicion. The emperor Trajan ordered that "no one should be condemned on the ground of suspicion alone" (D. 48.19.5).

Sustinere. To undergo (an accusation or a punishment), to suffer (losses), to be liable (for a debt, expenses, etc.).

Sustinere actionem (iudicium). To suspend proceedings and judgment in a trial until a preliminary (prejudicial) question was cleared up. If, e.g., a noxal action (see ACTIO NOXALIS, NOXA) was brought against a master for a wrongdoing committed by his slave while a proceeding concerning the slave's liberty was pending, the noxal trial was to be suspended until the status of the slave was established.—See DILATIO.

Sustinere partem actoris (rei). To assume the role of the plaintiff (or defendant) in a trial. *Sustinere personam alicuius* = to represent a person. Thus, a *tutor* or a *curator* represents the ward; an inheritance represents the personality of the defunct (*personam defuncti sustinet*).

Suum. All that belongs to a person, his whole property. The plural *sua* is also used in the same sense. *Suum* sometimes means only what is due to a person (*suum petere*). *Suum facere aliquid* = to acquire ownership of a thing.

Suum aes. See AES ALIENUM.

Suum cuique tribuere. See IUS.

Suus. See SUI, SUI IURIS, SUAE POTESTATIS, SUAE AETATIS, SUAE MENTIS. *Suus* is often used for HERES SUUS.

Suus et necessarius heres. See HERES SUUS ET NECESSARIUS.

Suus heres. See HERES SUUS.

Suus iudex. In the language of the imperial chancery a judge designated by law to decide upon a specific case.

Symbolum. A sign of recognition (è.g., a ring = *anulus*), a proof of authorization (a document, provided with a seal). A messenger of a creditor had to prove by a *symbolum* to the debtor that he was authorized to receive payment.

　　Bickermann, *RE* 4A, 1088.

Synallagma. Indicated in Greek law any agreement from which an obligation arose. In Roman sources it acquired a somewhat different meaning, referring only to agreements from which reciprocal (bilateral) obligations of both parties originated (D. 2.14.7.2; 50.16.19); the authenticity of the two texts is, however, controversial. In postclassical and Justinian's law *synallagma* is synonymous with *contractus*.

　　Seidl, *RE* 4A; P. De Francisci, *Synallagma. Storia e dottrina dei cosidetti contratti innominati,* 1–2 (1913, 1916); J. Partsch, *Aus nachgelassenen Schriften* (1931) 16.

Syndicus. A representative of a public or private corporate body (*civitas, municipium, collegium*). The term is of Greek origin. Syn. *actor.*

　　Seidl, *RE* 4A, 1333; Chapot, *DS* 4; Albertario, *Studi* 1 (1933) 121.

Syngraphe. In classical law a form of literal obligation (see LITTERARUM OBLIGATIO) contracted between peregrines (Greeks) or between a Roman and a peregrine. The term and the institution came into Roman legal life early through the commercial relations between Rome and Greece. A *syngraphe* was written in two copies and signed by both parties; each kept one copy. It is doubtful whether a *syngraphe* was valid if the obligation assumed therein by a party was not based on a real transaction.

　　Kunkel, *RE* 4A, 1384; Beauchet, *DS* 4; Moschella, *NDI* 12, 1, 1240.

Synopsis Basilicorum. A collection of brief abstracts from the BASILICA, composed in alphabetical order by an unknown author in the tenth century. The text is preserved in several manuscripts which suggests that the collection was widely used. The *Synopsis* is important for the knowledge of the missing parts of the Basilica. The title of the collection is "Ecloge and Synopsis of the sixty books of the Basilica with references thereto, arranged alphabetically." From this *Synopsis*, termed in the literature *Synopsis Maior,* a lesser abstract, also in alphabetical topical order was composed about the beginning of the thirteenth century under the title *Nomimon kata stoicheion* (= a legal book in alphabetical order). The latter is called *Synopsis Basilicorum Minor.*

　　Editions: *S. B. Maior:* Zachariae, *Jus Graeco-Romanum* 5 (1869); J. and P. Zepos, *Jus Graeco-Romanum* 5 (Athens, 1931).—*S. B. Minor:* Zachariae, *op. cit.* 2 (1851); Zepos, *op. cit.* 6 (Athens, 1931).—J. A. B. Mortreuil, *Histoire du droit byzantin* 2 (1844) 435, 3 (1846) 315.

T

Tabellae. Wax covered wooden tablets on which the voters in a popular assembly recorded their vote in legislative and jurisdictional matters through appropriate abbreviations, such as A, C, U.R. In elections of magistrates votes also were made on tablets on which the names of the candidates were inscribed. The pertinent rules concerning the use of tablets in voting = *leges tabellariae.*

　　Liebenam, *RE* 4, 692; Lafaye, *DS* 5, 5.

Tabellariae leges. See TABELLAE, LEGES TABELLARIAE.

Tabellarius. A messenger (courier) charged with the delivery of private letters (*tabellae*). The term seems to have been applied also to officials of the CURSUS PUBLICUS (post service) concerned with the movement of the official correspondence.—See STATIO.

　　Schroff, *RE* 4A; Lafaye, *DS* 5.

Tabellio. A private, professional person who drew up written documents for private individuals. The jurists and lawyers advised their clients about legal problems; the *tabelliones* assisted them in writing legal documents (testaments, transactions) and applications (*libelli, preces*) to be addressed to the emperor or higher officials. The *tabelliones* exercised their profession on public places (*fora,* markets) or in offices (*stationes*) assisted by clerks and secretaries (*scribae, notarii*). Their activity was controlled by governmental officials who were authorized to inflict penalties for fraud or negligence or for cooperation in illicit transactions. Justinian required every *tabellio* to obtain official permission (*auctoritas*), and settled rules about the formalities to be observed by a *tabellio* in his work (C. 4.21.17, A.D. 528, Nov. 44). In the case of a dispute between the parties, the *tabellio* was obliged to testify about the conformity of the document with the transaction concluded with his cooperation.—The ceiling-price schedule issued by Diocletian (see EDICTUM DIOCLETIANI DE PRETIIS) fixed the fees to be paid to a *tabellio*, by the lines of the written document.—See INSTRUMENTUM, TABULARIUS.

Sachers, *RE* 4A; Lécrivain, *DS* 5; Rota, *NDI* 12; M. Tardy, *Les tabelliones romains* (Thèse Bordeaux, 1901); T. Pfaff, *Tabellio und Tabularius*, 1905; H. Steinacker, *Die antiken Grundlagen der frühmittelalterlichen Privaturkunde* (1927) 79; A. Segrè, *BIDR* 35 (1927) 87; J. C. Brown, *Origin and early history of the office of notary* (Edinburgh, 1936) 17; Berger, *Jour. of Juristic Papyrology* 1 (1945) 37 (= *BIDR* 55–56, Post-Bellum [1951] 120).

Taberna. A shop used for the sale of merchandise or for an industrial or commercial activity. *Taberna argentaria* = a banker's shop. Usually, *tabernae* were built by private individuals on public ground along streets and roads or in the vicinity of marketplaces, with the permission of local authorities. The builder was permitted to transfer the use of the *taberna* to another person.

Schneider, *RE* 4A, 1864; Kübler, *ibid.* 929; Chapot, *DS* 5.

Tabernarius. The owner of a TABERNA. *Tabernarius* (or *tabernaria*) was also the keeper of an inn-tavern.

Schneider, *RE* 4A.

Tabula (tabulae). A tablet used for writing, in both public and private life. See TABULAE CERATAE. The administration used *tabulae* of bronze or of wood covered with white paint (see ALBUM) for public announcements, such as publication of laws, the praetorian Edict, and imperial enactments (see PROMULGATIO) and in public offices for records, registration, accounting books, documents, etc. See TABULAE PUBLICAE. In private life the use of *tabulae* (in the plural, since normally two tablets were joined together, see DIPTYCHUM) was widespread: in the household for notes on income and expenses (see CODEX ACCEPTI ET EXPENSI), for records of the family history, in banking for account books, and generally for all kinds of transactions and legal acts. Thus the term *tabula* occurs in connection with the pertinent contractual relation (*tabula emptionis, tabula cautionis, tabula contractus, tabula chirographi,* and the like). The most frequent use is *tabulae testamenti* = a testament.—See TESTIMONIUM PER TABULAS.

Sachers, *RE* 4A; Lafaye, *DS* 5; H. Steinacker, *Die antiken Grundlagen der frühmittelalterlichen Urkunde* (1927) 82.

Tabula Bantina. See LEX LATINA TABULAE BANTINAE.

Tabula Hebana. See DESTINATIO.

Coli, *Parola del Passato* 6 (1951) 433; *idem, Iura* 3 (1952) 90; Staveley, *AmJPhilol* 74 (1953) 1.

Tabula Heracleensis. See LEX IULIA MUNICIPALIS.

Tabula picta. See PICTURA.

Tabulae censoriae. Registers made by the censors during the registration of the population (see CENSUS). The *tabulae censoriae,* also called *libri censorii,* were first preserved in the censors' office, but were later transferred to the state archive (see AERARIUM). *Tabulae censoriae* actually comprised all documents connected with the activity of the censors, in particular the contracts concluded by them with private persons (contractors) concerning professional services rendered to the state.—See CENSORES, TABULAE IUNIORUM.

Tabulae ceratae. Wooden tablets covered with wax on which writing was done with a stylus. Syn. *tabulae ceraeque.* On the use of such tablets for documents, see TABULA, DIPTYCHUM, TRIPTYCHUM. Many such tablets have been preserved in the mines of Transylvania Pompei, and in Herculaneum.

Lafaye, *DS* 5, 12; Editions: in the *Corpus Inscriptionum Latinarum* and in the collections of pre-Justinian sources (*Fontes,* see General Bibliography, Ch. XII), the most recent one by Arangio-Ruiz, *FIR* 3 (1943). For the wax tablets of Herculanum: Maiuri, *La parola del passato* 1 (1946/7) 373, 8 (1948) 165; Pugliese-Carratelli, *ibid.* 1, 379; Arangio-Ruiz, *ibid.* 8 (1948) 129; *idem, RIDA* 1 (1948) 9.—P. Krüger, *Gesch. der Quellen*[2] (1912) 267.

Tabulae communes municipii. Account books concerning the administration of municipalities. They also contained records of contracts concluded with private persons.

Tabulae dotales (dotis). See INSTRUMENTUM DOTALE, TABULAE NUPTIALES.

Tabulae duodecim. See LEX DUODECIM TABULARUM.

Tabulae honestae missionis. See MISSIO, DIPLOMA MILITARE.

Lammert, *RE* 4A.

Tabulae iuniorum. Registers of young men to be called to military service. The *tabulae* were a part of the TABULAE CENSORIAE.—See IUNIORES.

Tabulae nuptiales. A written marriage contract. Its usage appears as early as the beginning of the Principate. The contract was not a requisite for the validity of the marriage. It contained among other things provisions concerning the dowry, its constitution, and restitution when the marriage would be dissolved. The *tabulae nuptiales* acquired particular importance in Justinian's law (C. 5.27.10, A.D. 529) inasmuch as children born of a non-marital union of two persons who later made an *instrumentum dotale* (generally considered a proof of the existence of a marriage), were regarded as legitimate. Justinian also made a written marriage contract mandatory for some marriages (e.g., with a slave [Nov. 22.11; 78.3], with actresses or their daughters). Syn. *tabulae* *matrimoniales, instrumentum nuptiale.*—See INSTRUMENTUM DOTALE.

> Kübler, *RE* 4A, 1949; Castelli, *SDHI* 4 (1938) 208; J. P. P. Levy, *RDH* 30 (1952) 468.

Tabulae patronatus. See PATRONUS MUNICIPII.

Tabulae primae. See TESTAMENTUM PUPILLARE.

Tabulae publicae. Tablets used in public administration, in particular records of the official activities of the magistrates. When the year of service of a magistrate was over, his official *tabulae* were transferred to the AERARIUM POPULI ROMANI which served as a general state archive under the supervision (*cura tabularum publicarum*) of the quaestors. In the Principate the archive was under the control of *curatores tabularum publicarum* who later were replaced by *praefecti*.

> Kornemann, *RE* 4A.

Tabulae quaestoriae. The account books of the quaestores, concerning financial administration.

Tabulae secundae. See TESTAMENTUM PUPILIARE.

Tabulae signatae (septem sigillis). A written testimony signed and sealed by (seven) witnesses to serve as evidence that a transaction was concluded or that a legally important event happened.—See TESTIMONIUM PER TABULAS, TESTATIO.

> Sachers, *RE* 4A, 1885; Kaser, *RE* 5A, 1027; Lécrivain, *DS* 5, 155; Brassloff, *ZSS* 27 (1906) 217.

Tabulae testamenti. (Or simply *tabulae*.) A written testament.—D. 37.2; 38.6.—See TESTAMENTUM, BONORUM POSSESSIO SECUNDUM TABULAS, BONORUM POSSESSIO CONTRA TABULAS.

> Archi, *StPav* 26 (1941) 63.

Tabulae triumphales. See TRIUMPHUS.

Tabularium. An archive in which documents (*tabulae*) were kept. The central archive was the AERARIUM POPULI ROMANI. See TABULAE PUBLICAE. In addition, there were several special *tabularia*, as, e.g., one in the temple of Ceres for *plebiscita* and *senatusconsulta*. *Tabularium Caesaris* = a general archive for the imperial administration, the emperor's correspondence, reports from provincial governors, and the like. In the provinces there were a special *tabularium* for the records of the provincial administration and a *tabularium principis* (*Caesaris*) chiefly concerned with the financial administration the imperial domains included. The latter was called also *tabularium publicum*. The municipalities had a *tabularium civitatis*.

> Sachers, *RE* 4A; Lafaye, *DS* 5; Del Prete, *NDI* 12, 1; Richmond, *OCD*.

Tabularium castrense. A special archive for military administration. In the Empire it was a part of the imperial archive. *Tabularium legionis* = the archive of a legion.

Tabularius. A subordinate official in the fiscal administration, chiefly concerned with taxes. Originally slaves (*servi publici*), later freedmen, occupied the posts of *tabularii* who were active in the various branches of the general and financial administration (*rationes*) and subject to a chief, *praepositus tabulariorum*. They were organized as a *collegium*. *Tabularii* were also found in provincial and municipal administration as well as in the army. Their connection with the archives and public records in the various offices (hence their official title), their collaboration in drawing up public documents in the different domains of public administration, and their experience in such work led in the later Empire to their being permitted to assist private persons in writing documents. The activity of *tabularii* in the private field became similar to that of private notaries (TABELLIONES). In post-Justinian times there was no difference between *tabelliones* and *tabularii*.—C. 10.71.

> Sachers, *RE* 4A; Lafaye, *DS* 5; I. Pfaff, *Tabellio und tabularius*, 1905; H. Steinacker, *Die antiken Grundlagen der frühmittelalterlichen Privaturkunde*, 1927, 78.

Tacere. To be silent, to give no answer. In classical law there were no strict rules about the significance of the silence of a person who gave no answer in court when questioned by a magistrate or judge. With regard to CONFESSIO IN IURE the jurists assumed that "he who is silent does not confess at all, but it is true that he does not deny" (D. 11.1.11.4). In Justinian's Digest the compilers promoted this opinion to a general rule by placing it in the final title "On legal rules" (D. 50.17.142). Only with reference to INTERROGATIO IN IURE was silence on the part of a person interrogated by the magistrate considered a contempt of court and interpreted in his disfavor.—In certain contractual relations the silence of a party could be regarded as consent in particular when the renewal of an agreement was at issue; see SILENTIUM, TACITE.

Tacite. Secretly, not expressly stated, self-understood. Some clauses are assumed to be agreed upon (*tacite inesse*) if the parties do not exclude them. Thus, e.g., in a pledge of rustic lands it is self-understood that the proceeds (*fructus*) are also pledged.—See TACERE, SILENTIUM, and the following items.

Tacitum fideicommissum. A *fideicommissum* based on a secret agreement between the testator and the heir to the effect that after the testator's death the heir was to deliver the legacy to an incapable person. Such an agreement, concluded in order to defraud the law, was void, the thing involved was seized by the fisc, and the heir became INDIGNUS and was excluded from any benefit under the testament.

Tacitum pignus (or tacite contractum). See HYPOTHECA TACITA.—C. 8.14.

Taciturnitas. See SILENTIUM.

Tacitus. See HYPOTHECA TACITA, RECONDUCTIO, CONSENSUS, and the foregoing items.

Tacitus consensus omnium (or populi). Alleged as the foundation of customary law.—See CONSUETUDO, MORES.

Talio. Retaliation, infliction of the same injury on the delinquent as that done by him. *Talio* was a kind of private vengeance which was permitted under the earliest law. The institution is already established in the Twelve Tables (VIII 2) as a sanction in the case of MEMBRUM RUPTUM. Retaliation was carried out by the injured person himself or in the case of his inability by his nearest relative. The parties might, however, agree on a pecuniary compensation to be paid by the offender (*pacisci de talione redimenda*), according to the Twelve Tables; in this case the application of *talio* was excluded. In the penal law of the later Empire penalties for certain crimes are somewhat reminiscent of the ancient idea of retaliation, e.g., in case of arson the culprit was punished by death through burning; see CREMATIO.

Herdlitczka, *RE* 4A; Jolowicz, *The assessment of penalties in primitive law*, in *Cambridge Legal Essays* (1926) 203; Genzmer, *ZSS* 62 (1942) 122.

Talis. When used with reference to someone or something (*tale*) mentioned before, instead of *is* (*id*), this is not classical Latin. It occurs frequently in interpolated passages.

Guarneri-Citati, *Indice*[2] (1927) 86.

Tangere. To touch. The verb appears in the definition of corporeal things: *quae tangi possunt* (= which can be touched upon).—See RES CORPORALES.

Tanta. Justinian's enactment of December 16, 533, by which the Digest was promulgated. The Greek version (not a literal translation) of this constitution is called DEDOKEN (from the initial word). Both constitutions are very instructive for the understanding of the emperor's intentions and the nature of his legislative work, made up of excerpts taken from the writings of the classical jurists.—See DIGESTA IUSTINIANI, DEDOKEN.

Ebrard, *ZSS* 40 (1919) 113.

Tarruntenus Paternus. A Roman jurist of the second half of the second century after Christ. He wrote a treatise *De re militari* (= on military matters) which dealt with tactics and with legal problems connected with the military service. From one excerpt of the work (D. 50.6.7) we know of a long list of professionals who worked for the army and were therefore exempt from public services (*munera*).

Berger, *RE* 4A, 2405; W. Kunkel, *Herkunft und soziale Stellung der röm. Juristen*, 1952, 219.

Taxatio. The establishment of a maximum to which the defendant in a civil trial could be condemned. The limit was expressed in the part of the procedural formula called CONDEMNATIO through a clause starting with the word *dumtaxat* (= not exceeding, only) followed by the indication of the amount which the condemnation could not exceed. The limit could be determined otherwise, by a specification of the fund from which the plaintiff was to be satisfied, e.g., the defendant's *peculium* (*dumtaxat de peculio*). See BENEFICIUM COMPETENTIAE.—Another kind of *taxatio* was in the case of IUSIURANDUM IN LITEM. The judge could impose on the plaintiff as the utmost limit his estimation of the value of the object in litigation.

Kaser, *RE* 5A; Levy, *ZSS* 36 (1915) 64.

Tectum. A roof. *Tectum praestare* (*exhibere*) *alicui* = to grant someone a dwelling. *Sub eodem tecto* = under the same roof, in the same household. The last expression was broadly interpreted by the jurists in connection with the SENATUSCONSULTUM SILANIANUM which submitted to investigation and torture all slaves, living *sub eodem tecto* when their master was assassinated and the murdered not discovered.— *Tecta sarta* (from *sarcire*) = roofs well repaired, buildings in good condition. The question as to who is obliged to repair the roof of a house is discussed by the jurists with regard to a usufruct and use (*usus*) (agreed upon or bequeathed) of the house.

O. Karlowa, *Röm. Rechtsgeschichte* 1 (1885) 247.

Telum. A missile, a weapon of any kind. The meaning of the term is discussed by the jurists in connection with the LEX IULIA DE VI PUBLICA, under which an aggressor who used a *telum* against the victim or an armed thief was guilty of violence of a higher degree. There the term was interpreted in the broadest sense; *telum* was anything by which a man could hurt another, "a stone, a piece of wood or iron thrown by hand" (D. 50.16.233.2).—See VIS ARMATA, TURBA.

Temere litigare. See POENAE TEMERE LITIGANTIUM, TEMERITAS.

Temeritas. Rashness, lack of caution, of reflection, in starting a lawsuit or accusing a person of a crime. —See CALUMNIA, POENAE TEMERE LITIGANTIUM.

Chiovenda, *RISG* 26 (1898) 26.

Temo. A recruit-tax, levied primarily on landowners to be used for wages for mercenary soldiers and for payments to be made as commutation for actual service in the army.—See AURUM TIRONUM. *Temonarii* = collectors of the tax.

Kubitschek, *RE* 5A; Humbert, *DS* 1, 579.

Temperare. To moderate, to apply moderation. In the language of the imperial chancery the term is frequently used of the activity of jurisdictional officials in moderating the consequences of a strict application of the law.

Tempestas. A storm. A *tempestas* is among those unforeseen accidents (*casus fortuiti*), like inundation (*vis fluminis* = flood) which were accepted as an excuse for non-appearance in court.

Templa. Places (edifices) in which solemn sacrifices (e.g., *auspicia*) were celebrated. The establishment and surveyance of *templa* were duties of the AUGURES. —See SACRIFICIUM.—*Templa* in the later Empire = churches.—C. 11.70; 71; 79; 7.38.

Wissowa, *RE* 2, 2337; Dorigny, *DS* 5; Blumenthal, *Klio* 27 (1934) 1.

Templa pagana. Pagan temples. They were ordered closed by Constantine (C. 1.11.1, A.D. 354).

Tempora. When referring to certain procedural institutions, terms fixed by law, within which certain remèdies are available to parties involved in a legal controversy (e.g., for an action, an appeal, an interdict, a *restitutio in integram*).—C. 2.52; 7.63.

Temporalis (temporarius). Limited in time (*quod tempore finitur*), continuing for a limited time. Ant. PERPETUUS.—See ACTIONES TEMPORALES, EXCEPTIONES DILATORIAE.

Tempus. Time, a period. *Certum tempus* = a fixed day (*dies*) or a fixed interval of time within which (*intra certum tempus*) certain legal acts were to be performed in order to avoid loss. *Ad (certum) tempus* = for a fixed time. Ant. *in perpetuum* = forever. Justinian's compilers in many instances replaced the terms established for certain legal acts in earlier law by colorless expressions, such as *tempus legitimum, statutum, constitutum* (= legal, established time) thereby adopting the older texts to later legislation by which the pertinent terms were changed.— See PRIOR TEMPORE POTIOR IURE, ACCESSIO TEMPORIS, STATUTUM TEMPUS, TEMPORALIS, PLUSPETITIO, and the following items.

Pagge, *NDI* 12, 258 (*s.v. termini*); Milone, *Dottrina romana del computo del tempo, ANap* 1912; Guarneri-Citati, *Indice²* (1927) 87.

Tempus ad deliberandum (deliberationis). At the request of the creditors of an inheritance, the praetor could impose on the heir (*heres voluntarius*) a fixed term, normally one hundred days in which to decide whether or not to accept the inheritance.—See DELIBERARE.—D. 28.8; C. 6.30.

Tempus continuum. A period of time computed according to the calendar without the omission of any days. Ant. *tempus utile.*—See DIES CONTINUI, ANNUS CONTINUUS.

Tempus iudicati. The period of time granted to a defendant to comply with the judgment-debt (*iudicatum*). The Twelve Tables fixed the term at thirty days (*triginta dies*); see DIES IUSTI. In the *cognitio extra ordinem* the official who rendered the judgment could settle another period. In Justinian law the *tempus iudicati* was extended to four months.—See IUDICATUM.

Tempus legitimum. See LEGITIMUS, TEMPUS.

Tempus lugendi. See LUCTUS, SUBLUGERE.

Tempus statutum (tempora statuta). See STATUTUM TEMPUS, TEMPUS.

Tempus utile. An interval of time in which certain days are not computed, to wit, days in which the action which had to be accomplished during a fixed time could not be taken. The reasons were either personal (captivity of the person who had to perform the action, his absence in the interest of the state, sickness, and the like) or official when judicial activity of the courts were suspended (see DIES NEFASTI) or the magistrate before whom the action was to be performed could not be reached. Ant. *tempus continuum.*—See ANNUS UTILIS, DIES UTILES, IUSTITIUM.

Kübler, *RE* 5A; *NDI* 12, 1; Ubbelohde, *Berechnung des t. u. bei honorarischen Temporalklagen*, 1891.

Temulatio. Drunkenness.—See IMPETUS.

Tenere (aliquid). To hold a thing, to have physical power over a thing.—See DETENTIO.

Tenere. (Intransitive.) To be legally valid (e.g., *obligatio, stipulatio tenet*).

Teneri. To be liable (under a statute = *lege,* under a *senatusconsultum* = *senatusconsulto*), to be suable (*actione, interdicto*).

Frese, *ACDR* Roma 2 (1935) 241.

Tenor. The content, text of a statute or a senatusconsultum, a legal rule.

Tenuiores. See HUMILIORES. Ant. HONESTIORES.— See COLLEGIA FUNERATICIA.

Cardascia, *RHD* 28 (1950) 308.

Terentius Clemens. A little known jurist of the second century after Christ, author of an extensive treatise on the LEX IULIA ET PAPIA (in 20 books). He is not cited by later jurists, but his work was used by Justinian's compilers.

Berger, *RE* 5A, 650.

Tergiversatio. (From *tergiversari.*) The withdrawal of the accuser from a criminal trial. The accused could demand that the trial be brought to an end so that he could sue the accuser for *calumnia*. The *Senatusconsultum Turpillianum* (A.D. 61) fixed a fine and declared the accuser who deserted the accusation (*tergiversator*) to be infamous. The accuser's withdrawal could be declared expressly during the trial or manifested by his non-appearance in court. He might, however, justify his withdrawal by a reasonable excuse. Syn. *deserere, desistere, destituere accusationem.*—D. 48.16.—See CALUMNIA.

Taubenschlag, *RE* 5A; Lécrivain, *DS* 5; M. Wlassak, *Anklage und Streitbefestigung im Kriminalrecht der Römer, SbWien* 184, 1 (1917) 199; Levy, *ZSS* 53 (1933) 211; Lauria, *St Ratti* 1934, 124; Bohacek, *St Riccobono* 1 (1936) 361.

Terminare. To fix the boundaries of a municipality or of landed property belonging to a public corporate body or a private person through boundary stones (*terminus, cippus, lapis*). The judgment of arbitrators in a boundary dispute between two communities in the district of Liguria is preserved in an inscription, called *Sententia Minuciorum.*

Fabricius, *RE* 5A; Toutain, *DS* 5; for *Sent. Minuciorum:* Arangio-Ruiz, *FIR* 3 (1943) no. 163 (Bibl.).

Terminare litem. To end a controversy by judgment in a trial or by arbitration.

Termini. Boundary stones indicating the borders of a landed property. Syn. *cippus, lapis.*—D. 47.21.— See TERMINARE, ACTIO FINIUM REGUNDORUM, TERMINARE.

Toutain, *DS* 5, 121; Holland, *Amer. Jour. of Archeology* 37 (1933) 549.

Terminum movere (termini motio). To remove a boundary stone in order to change the existing ownership situation of landed property. According to an ancient provision (attributed to King Numa Pompilius), destruction or disarrangement of such stones which were considered as being under religious sanction, made the wrongdoer an outlaw (see SACER). An agrarian law by Caesar and enactments by the emperors Nerva and Hadrian ordered severe penalties for *terminum movere*. Syn. *terminum avellere, auferre*.—D. 47.21.—See ACTIO DE TERMINO MOTO.

Taubenschlag, *RE* 5A; Lécrivain, *DS* 5.

Terrae motus. An earthquake. It is reckoned among the cases of *vis maior;* see CASUS FORTUITUS.

Terrenus. See IUGATIO TERRENA.

Terribiles libri. The "terrible books," Justinian's term for books 47 and 48 of the Digest (*Tanta,* 8c) which contain rules on crimes and penalties.

Territorium. The territory of a community or the whole land assigned to a colony; see UNIVERSITAS AGRORUM. *Territorium* is also the territory in which a magistrate exercised his jurisdictional activity. "A magistrate who exercises jurisdiction beyond his territory may be disobeyed with impunity" (D. 2.1.20).

Toutain, *DS* 5.

Terror. See METUS.

Tertullianus. A little known jurist represented in Justinian's Digest by five texts, author of *Quaestiones* and a monograph on *Peculium castrense*. His identification with the contemporaneous Church Father, Tertullianus (middle of the third century), often assumed, is very doubtful.

Steinwenter, *RE* 5A, 844; Koch, *ibid.* 822; Kübler, *Lehrbuch der Gesch.,* 1925, 278 (Bibl.); De Labriolle, *Tertullien jurisconsulte, NRHD* 30 (1906) 5; W. Kunkel, *Herkunft und soziale Stellung der röm. Juristen,* 1952, 236.

Tessera. A square tablet, a token used as a proof of identity, a ticket. *Tesserae* for public spectacles (*ludi*) were distributed to poor people by the *curatores ludorum*.—See the following items.

Lafaye, *DS* 5, 134; Rostowzew, *Röm. Bleitesserae,* 1905.

Tessera frumentaria. A token for a certain quantity of grain (five *modii* monthly) which gratuitously was distributed to needy people by the government.—See FRUMENTATIO.

Rostowzew, *RE* 7, 179; Regling, *RE* 5A, 852; Cardinali, *DE* 3, 271; Lafaye, *DS* 5, 133; Rota, *NDI* 12, 2; Van Berchem, *Distributions de blé à la plèbe romaine* (1939) 85.

Tessera hospitalis. A token of identity which permitted recognition of a stranger (*hospes*) to whom as an individual or to whose nation Rome granted HOSPITIUM.

Tessera militaris. A token of identity given to soldiers of a military unit through which they could be distinguished from the enemy and recognized as members of the Roman army. The *tessera* were provided with a catchword. An officer of lower rank charged with the distribution of the *tessera = tesserarius.*

Lafaye, *DS* 5, 135; Lammert, *RE* 5A.

Tessera nummaria. Similar to the TESSERA FRUMENTARIA. It gave the right to a sum of money which some emperors used to distribute to the people as a gift.—See MISSILIA.

Cardinali, *DE* 3, 271.

Tessera nummularia. A tablet, attached to a sealed bag with coins, certifying that the coins are genuine. The statement was issued by a mint officer; see NUMMULARIUS, SPECTATOR.

Regling, *RE* 13; Laum, *RE* Suppl. 4, 78; Herzog, *Abhandlungen der Giessener Hochschulgesellschaft* 1 (1919); Cary, *JRS* 13 (1923) 110.

Tesserarius. See TESSERA MILITARIS.

Testamentarius. (Adj.) Pertaining to, connected with, or established in, a testament (e.g., *hereditas, libertas, manumissio, tutor, tutela*). *Lex testamentaria =* a statute which was concerned with the making of a testament; see LEX FURIA, FALSUM (for *Lex Cornelia*).

Testamentarius. (Noun.) One who wrote a testament for another. Syn. *scriptor testamenti.*—See SENATUSCONSULTUM LIBONIANUM, QUAESTIO DOMITIANA.

Testamenti apertura. See APERTURA TESTAMENTI.

Testamenti factio. The legal capacity of a person to make a testament (*ius testamenti faciendi*). This *testamenti factio* (called in the literature by the non-Roman term, *testamenti factio activa*) is to be distinguished from the capacity to be instituted heir in a testament or to be rewarded with a legacy (*testamenti factio passiva*). For active *testamenti factio* the Roman juristic language used the expression *testator habet testamenti factionem cum aliquo (cum herede, cum legatario*) for the so-called *testamenti factio passiva: heres (legatarius) habet testamenti factionem cum testatore*. *Testamenti factio* also refers to the ability to witness a testament of a specific person. *Testamenti factio* was required on the part of the testator both when the testament was being made and at the time of his death. A testament made by a person without capacity did not become valid if he later acquired it. See FICTIO LEGIS CORNELIAE. Those unable to make a testament were slaves (except public slaves, *servi publici,* who could dispose of half their *peculium* by a last will), persons *alieni iuris* as long as they were under paternal power, persons below the age of puberty, lunatics (see FURIOSUS), spendthrifts (see PRODIGUS) and women (see COËMPTIO FIDUCIAE CAUSA). From the time of Hadrian women were permitted to make a testament with the consent of their guardians (see TUTELA MULIERUM). In later postclassical law apostates and heretics were excluded from making a testament (see APOSTATA, HAERETICI) and from taking under one. Only Roman citizens could be instituted heirs in the testament of a Roman citizen. For restrictions concerning women, see LEX VOCONIA. Persons *alieni iuris* could be heirs and legatees, but whatever they acquired went to their *pater familias*. A testator's slave could be instituted as an heir only *cum libertate,* i.e., if he was freed in the same testament. Another man's slave acquired all that he received from a testament for his master, provided that the latter had *testamenti factio passiva.* The institution of "uncertain persons" (see PERSONAE INCERTAE) was not permitted. Exceptions in favor of the state, municipalities, charitable institutions (see PIAE CAUSAE) and *collegia,* were gradually admitted. See also POSTUMI, DII, ECCLESIA. For the ability to witness a will, see TESTIS AD TESTAMENTUM ADHIBITUS.—Inst. 2.12; D. 28.1.

De Crescenzio, *NDI* 12, 1, 964; Schulz, *ZSS* 35 (1914) 112; H. Krüger, *ZSS* 53 (1933) 505; Volterra, *BIDR* 48 (1941) 74; B. Biondi, *Istituti fondamentali 2* (1948) 6.

Testamentum. A solemn act by which a testator instituted one or more heirs to succeed to his property after his death. The appointment of an heir was the fundamental element of a testament (see INSTITUTIO HEREDIS); a last will in which an heir was not appointed was not valid. A testament could contain other dispositions, such as legacies (*legata, fideicommissa*), manumission of slaves, appointment of a guardian. Since a testament "derived its efficiency from the institution of an heir" (Gaius, Inst. 2.229), all dispositions made in the testament prior to the institution of the heir were null under the classical law. This principle was abolished by Justinian. For the various forms and types of testaments, see the following items. A will could be revoked by a later one; see REVOCARE TESTAMENTUM. The later *testamentum* invalidated the first since nobody could leave two testaments. See CODICILLI. The existence of a valid testament excluded the admission of heirs on intestacy. Syn. *tabulae testamenti, tabulae.*—Inst. 2.10; 17; D. 28.1; 29.3; 35.1; C. 6.23. —See TESTAMENTI FACTIO, CONTEXTUS, SUPPRIMERE TABULAS, SENATUSCONSULTUM LIBONIANUM, QUERELA INOFFICIOSI TESTAMENTI, LEX VOCONIA, BONORUM POSSESSIO SECUNDUM TABULAS, NUNCUPATIO, MANCIPATIO FAMILIAE, FAVOR TESTAMENTI, VOLUNTAS DEFUNCTI, LINUM, MANUMISSIO TESTAMENTO.

Kübler, *RE* 5A; Cuq, *DS* 5; Arangio-Ruiz, *FIR* 3 (1943) no. 47 ff.; C. Appleton, *Le testament romain,* 1903 (= *Rev. gén. de droit* 27, 1902/3); Liebenthal, *Ursprung und Entwicklung des röm. Testaments,* 1914; A. Suman, *Favor testamenti e voluntas testantium,* 1916; Lévy-Bruhl, *NRH* 44 (1920) 618; 45 (1920) 634; Goldmann, *ZSS* 51 (1931) 223; David, *ZSS* 52 (1932) 314; F. Wieacker, *Hausgenossenschaft und Erbeinsetzung. Über die Anfänge des röm Testaments, Fschr Siber* 1940; Volterra, *BIDR* 48 (1941) 74; B. Biondi, *Successione testamentaria,* 1943; Van Oven, in the collective work *Het testament* (Arnhem, 1951) 9.

Testamentum apud acta conditum. A *testamentum* made before a judicial or municipal authority. An

official record was made and entered in the archives of the office.

Testamentum calatis comitiis. See COMITIA CALATA. The solemn performance before the popular assembly was a kind of adoption to have an heir in the event of the testator's death; its primary purpose was to secure his own and his ancestors' worship.

B. Biondi, *Successione testamentaria,* 1943, 47; C. Cosentini, *St sui liberti* 1 (1948) 17; M. Kaser, *Das altröm. Ius* (1949) 148 (Bibl.).

Testamentum caeci. The testament of a blind man. Under the classical law he could make a testament *per aes et libram.* In later law a written *testamentum* was permitted in the presence of an additional eighth witness (or a city official, *tabularius*) who wrote down the testament as dictated by the testator before seven witnesses.

Testamentum desertum. See TESTAMENTUM DESTITUTUM.

Testamentum destitutum. A testament, all the heirs of which died before the testator or before the acceptance of the inheritance, or refused to accept it. Syn. *testamentum desertum* (= an abandoned testament). In such a case succession on intestacy took place.—See LEX VOCONIA.

Testamentum duplex. See TESTAMENTUM PUPILLARE.

Testamentum falsum. A forged testament. It is null since it does not express the will of the testator.— See FALSUM, SENATUSCONSULTUM LIBONIANUM.

B. Biondi, *Successione testamentaria* (1943) 590.

Testamentum holographum. A testament written by the testator in his own hand. In classical law such a testament was subject to all the requirements of a written testament. Only an imperial constitution (Nov. 21.2 of Theodosius II and Valentinian III of A.D. 446) recognized the validity of such a testament without witnesses. The constitution was, however, not accepted into Justinian's Code.—See TESTAMENTUM PARENTIS INTER LIBEROS, TESTAMENTUM MUTI.

Testamentum imperfectum. A testament in which the rules of form were not fully satisfied, in particular when the witnesses did not sign or seal it. It was void.

Testamentum in procinctu. A testament made by a soldier when a battle was imminent or, at least, when the army was in a permanent camp.

Zocco-Rosa, *RISG* 35 (1903) 302; *idem, Il t. i. p.,* 1910; C. Cosentini, *St sui liberti* 1 (1948) 21.

Testamentum iniustum. A testament made by a person who backed TESTAMENTI FACTIO or one in which an heir (*heres*) was not appointed. Ant. *testamentum iustum.*—D. 28.3.

Testamentum inofficiosum. See QUERELA INOFFICIOSI TESTAMENTI, TESTAMENTUM RESCISSUM.

Testamentum inutile. An invalid testament.—See TESTAMENTUM RUPTUM, TESTAMENTUM NULLUM.

Testamentum irritum. A testament which was valid when the testator made it, but which became void because he lost his capacity (TESTAMENTI FACTIO) later (e.g., through *capitis deminutio* when he lost liberty or citizenship).—D. 28.3.

Testamentum iure factum. A testament made by a testator able to make a will (see TESTAMENTI FACTIO) with all the formalities prescribed for its validity observed.

Testamentum iure praetorio factum. See TESTA-MENTUM PRAETORIUM.

Testamentum iustum. See TESTAMENTUM INIUSTUM.

Testamentum militis. A soldier's testament. It was exempt from all formalities. Soldiers might make a testament "in any way they want and can" (D. 29.1.1 pr.). Even a will written by a soldier, dying in battle, with his blood on the scabbard of his sword or with the point of the sword on the sand, was valid. Several legal rules which were binding with regard to all other testaments were not applicable to a *testamentum militis*. A soldier could make two testaments, and he could dispose of a part of his property while the remainder went to his heirs on intestacy. Neither *querela inofficiosi testamenti* nor *Lex Falcidia* were applicable to a soldier's testament. A *testamentum militis* was the testament the soldier made during his service. It was valid for one year after his discharge. Justinian made, however, an important change, restricting the privileges to soldiers engaged in a battle with the enemy. Syn. *testamentum iure militari factum.*—Inst. 2.11; D. 29.1; 37.13; C. 6.21. —See TESTAMENTUM IN PROCINCTU.

Cuq, *DS* 5, 140; Kübler, *RE* 5, 1000; Arangio-Ruiz, *BIDR* 18 (1906) 157; Calderini, *Atene e Roma*, 1915, 259; Tamassia, *AVen* 85 (1927); Weiss, *ZSS* 45 (1934) 567; Guarino, *RendLomb* 72, 2 (1938/9) 355; A. Haegerstroem, *Der röm. Obligationsbegriff* 2 (1943) Beil. 52; B. Biondi, *Successione testamentaria* (1943) 73; S. v. Bolla, *Aus röm. und bürgerlichem Erbrecht* (1950) 1.

Testamentum muti (surdi). A testament of a dumb (or deaf) man. It should be written in his own hand according to an enactment by Justinian.

Testamentum nullum. A testament which is void from the beginning, e.g., when the testator lacked TESTAMENTI FACTIO, when the prescribed forms were not observed, or when there was no appointment of an heir (see HEREDIS INSTITUTIO).

Testamentum parentis inter liberos. A testament by which a father (*pater familias*) disposed of his property in favor of his children alone. Such a testament could be made without witnesses if the testator wrote it in his own hand and gave the exact names of the heirs and their shares. It was a different act when a father ordered the way in which his property was to be divided among his children on intestacy (*divisio inter liberos*). This was no testament at all and the document had to be signed by the father and the children.

Rabel, *Elterliche Teilung. Fschr zur 49. Versammlung deutscher Philologen*, Basel, 1907; B. Biondi, *Successione testamentaria* (1943) 70; Solazzi, *SDHI* 10 (1944) 356.

Testamentum per aes et libram. See MANCIPATIO FAMILIAE, FAMILIAE EMPTOR, NUNCUPATIO, PER AES ET LIBRAM, TESTIMONIUM DOMESTICUM.

Kamps, *RHD* 15 (1936) 142; Amelotti, *SDHI* 15 (1949) 34.

Testamentum per nuncupationem. See NUNCUPA-TIO. According to the civil law (*ius civile*) the oral declaration made before seven witnesses should be pronounced in a prescribed formula (Gaius, Inst. 2.204) in which the testator referred to his detailed written dispositions. The praetor, however, granted BONORUM POSSESSIO SECUNDUM TABULAS even when the prescribed formula was not pronounced. Later imperial legislation recognized a merely oral testament (*testamentum per nuncupationem*), without any written document, when the testator announced his will and appointed heirs in the presence of witnesses. An heir thus appointed = *heres nuncupatus.*—See TESTAMENTUM PER AES ET LIBRAM.

Solazzi, *SDHI* 17 (1951) 262, 18 (1952) 212.

Testamentum (iure, rite) perfectum. See PERFEC-TUS, TESTAMENTUM IMPERFECTUM.

Testamentum pestis tempore. A testament made in time of pestilence. The witnesses were not bound to be present simultaneously.

Testamentum posterius. A later testament made by a testator in order to revoke an earlier one. See REVO-CARE TESTAMENTUM. The first testament was "broken" (TESTAMENTUM RUPTUM).

Kübler, *RE* 5A, 1008.

Testamentum praetorium. A testament valid according to the praetorian law (but invalid under civil law). The praetorian Edict granted BONORUM POSSESSIO SECUNDUM TABULAS if some of the formalities required by *ius civile* (*mancipatio familiae, nuncupatio*) had not been observed and a written will was made in the presence of seven witnesses and sealed by them. —See TESTAMENTUM PER NUNCUPATIONEM.

B. Biondi, *Successione testamentaria* (1943) 49.

Testamentum principi oblatum. A testament consigned to the emperor. Later, deposition in a public archive sufficed.

Testamentum pupillare. That part of a father's testament in which he made a testament for a child then under his paternal power and below the age of puberty for the event that the child died before reaching puberty. See SUBSTITUTIO PUPILLARIS. Later, it became customary to write down the child's testament (*testamentum filii, testamentum pupillare*) in a second, separate document (*tabulae secundae*) in order to avoid the child's heir becoming known when the father's testament was opened upon his death. The prospective heir of the child who would inherit only if the child died before reaching puberty, might be interested in the child's premature death and therefore it was advisable to keep secret the content of the *testamentum pupillare*. In the case of a separate document for the *substitutio pupillaris* the father's testament is called *testamentum duplex,* the *tabulae secundae* being only a supplement to the real testament which dealt with the succession to the father's property (*tabulae primae*).

B. Biondi, *Successione testamentaria* (1943) 254.

Testamentum rescissum. A testament rescinded as *inofficiosum* as a result of a QUERELA INOFFICIOSI TESTAMENTI.—See RESCINDERE.

Testamentum ruptum. A testament which was "broken" by a later event (e.g., by the birth of a posthumous child who was omitted in the father's testament, see POSTUMUS SUUS) or was revoked by the testator through a later testament; see TESTAMENTUM POSTERIUS.—D. 28.3.

Kübler, *RE* 5A, 1008; Sanfilippo, *AnPal* 17 (1937) 73; De Sarlo, *AG* 142 (1952) 69.

Testamentum ruri conditum. A testament made in the country by a rustic person. In Justinian law such a testament was valid if only five persons were present. If some of the witnesses were illiterate others might sign for them.

Testamentum surdi. See TESTAMENTUM MUTI.

Testamentum tripertitum. A particular type of testament the requirements for which were fixed in a late imperial constitution (C. 6.23.11, A.D. 429): it had to be made without interruption (*uno contextu,* see CONTEXTUS), in the presence of seven witnesses (who had to subscribe and seal it), and, in addition, the testator had to sign it (*"subscripsi"* = "I signed"). If he was illiterate, another could sign for him. The term *tripertitum* (= tripartite), used by Iust., Inst. 2.10.3, derives from the fact that in the formalities mentioned three sources of law are combined: *ius civile, ius praetorium* and imperial legislation.

Riccobono, *Archiv für Rechtsphilosophie* 16 (1922) 503.

Testari. To be a witness to a legal act or transaction, to testify, to make a legally important declaration before a witness. Hence *testari* also means to invite another person to be a witness, and consequently to let the witness sign a written document to be used as evidence (*in testatum redigere*). In some texts *testari* is syn. with *testamentum facere.*—See TESTATIO, TESTIS, TESTIMONIUM.—D. 29.6; C. 6.34.

Wenger, *RE* 2A, 2427; Schulz, *JRS* 33 (1943) 61; Kunkel, *ZSS* 66 (1948) 425.

Testatio. A document containing a declaration made in presence of, and signed by, witnesses for the purpose of evidence. *Testatio* is also the oral or written testimony of a witness.—See TESTIS, CONTESTATIO.

Kaser, *RE* 5A, 1030; Vazny, *AnPal* 8 (1921) 481; Taubenschlag, *ZSS* 38 (1917) 255; Weiss, *BIDR* 51/52 (1948) 316; Arangio-Ruiz, *RIDA* 1 (1948) 18; J. P. P. Levy, *RHD* 30 (1952) 453.

Testato. (Adv.) In the presence of a witness or witnesses (e.g., to notify someone of something legally important to another, to summon, to make a declaration). *Testato decedere (mori)* = to die after having made a testament. Ant. *intestato.*

Testator (testatrix). One who has made a testament. The wishes of a testator are referred to by expressions like *velle, nolle, scribere, iubere, mandare.*

Testificari (testificatio). To testify, to prove through witnesses.—See TESTATIO.

Testimoniales. (*Sc. litterae.*) A written official certificate (in later imperial constitutions).

Testimonium. In a broader sense, any kind of evidence; in a narrower sense, the testimony of a witness; see TESTIS. *Testimonium* of a witness was given in person, normally under oath.—See TESTIMONIUM PER TABULAS.

Kaser, *RE* 5A; Lécrivain, *DS* 5; Berger, *OCD.*

Testimonium domesticum. The testimony of a witness who lived in the household of the person on whose behalf he was testifying. In a *testamentum per aes et libram* persons subject to the paternal power of the testator were excluded from acting as witnesses. In general a *testimonium domesticum* was not considered a probatory evidence.

Testimonium falsum. False testimony. A witness who knowingly gave false testimony in a capital trial was considered a murderer and punished under the *lex Cornelia de sicariis.* The Twelve Tables fixed the death penalty for *testimonium falsum;* the accused was executed by being thrown from the Tarpeian rock (see DEICERE DE SAXO TARPEIO). Under the later law the penalty was exile.—See FALSUM.

Kaser, *RE* 5A, 1053; Taubenschlag, *RE* 5A; Lécrivain, *DS* 5; Pringsheim, *RIDA* 6 (1951) 161.

Testimonium unius. (*Sc. testis.*) The testimony of a single witness. It is without any probatory value. An imperial constitution of A.D. 334 (C. 4.20.9) ordered that the testimony of a sole witness should not be heard at all.

Testimonium per tabulas. A voluntary testimony given extrajudicially in writing. Normally it had little authority except if the witness could not appear in court personally because of age, absence, or bad health.

Testis. A witness. There were witnesses whose presence was necessary for the validity of an act or transaction (e.g., a testament, *mancipatio,* acts *per aes et libram,* etc.) and witnesses in a trial, civil or criminal, who testified about facts. Only Roman citizens above the age of fourteen could witness solemn legal acts. Excluded were persons with certain physical defects which made it impossible for them to perceive actions or words, lunatics, and individuals convicted of crime. The Twelve Tables already contained the rule that a witness to a legal transaction could not afterwards refuse to testify if his testimony was required in a trial. Should he do so, he became unable to serve as a witness in the future and could not ask others to witness his acts (*improbus et intestabilis*). Thus, he lost the ability to make a testament. For solemn acts the number of witnesses was prescribed (usually seven), for other acts, in which their presence was not required by law but was requested by a party for the purpose of evidence, two witnesses were sufficient. Near kinship with a person involved in the transaction, living with him in the same household (see TESTIMONIUM DOMESTICUM), close friendship or open enmity barred a witness from giving testimony. Descendants were not admitted to testimony in matters concerning their ascendants and *vice versa*; similarly freedmen and their descendants with regard to their manumitters. There were no strict rules for the evaluation of the testimony of witnesses and of other means of evidence. The judges were advised to "explore exactly whether a witness was worthy of confidence" (D. 22.5.3 pr.) through examination of his social situation, his financial condition, his moral reliability (e.g., whether he would do anything for profit) and the like. The directive given by the emperor Hadrian to a high official is characteristic: "you should estimate through the judgment of your mind (*ex sententia animi tui*) what you should assume to be true and what to be no more than barely proved" (D. 22.5.3.3).—D. 22.5; C. 4.20).—See TESTIMONIUM, TESTATIO, SUBSCRIPTIO, INTESTABILIS, VACILLARE, SENATUSCONSULTUM SILANIANUM (concerning testimony of slaves), TORMENTA, ANTESTATUS, LITIS CONTESTATIO, and the following items.

Kaser, *RE* 5A; Lécrivain, *DS* 5, 152; Berger, *OCD* (*s.v. testimonium*); Messina, *Riv. penale* 73 (1911) 278.

Testis ad testamentum adhibitus. A witness present at the making of a testament. The capacity of a person to be a witness to a specific testament is also termed TESTAMENTI FACTIO. The witness had to be invited (see TESTIS ROGATUS)—not forced—to serve and to be present near the testator during the entire act. He should know that it was a will which he witnessed, but the contents could remain unknown to him. At the opening of the testament (see APERTURA TESTAMENTI) he had to recognize the authenticity of his seal. Specific restrictions were imposed with regard to witnesses belonging to the immediate family of the testator. See TESTAMENTUM DOMESTICUM. Women and slaves were excluded. The rules concerning the admission of a person (or persons subject to his paternal power) to witness a testament in which he was instituted as an heir were finally settled by Justinian who excluded them all. Legatees, however, were admitted.—See TESTAMENTUM, QUAESTIO DOMITIANA, SCRIPTOR TESTAMENTI.

Kaser, *RE* 5A, 1041; B. Biondi, *Successione testamentaria* (1943) 59.

Testis idoneus. A person legally able to be a witness. There were general reasons for excluding a person from being a witness in all cases (see TESTIS) and specific reasons which applied only in particular cases, the hindrance being a special relationship between the proposed witness and the acting person or the act itself. See TESTIS, TESTIMONIUM DOMESTICUM, TESTIS

AD TESTAMENTUM ADHIBITUS. No one could be a witness if forced or ordered to do so by the acting person.—See TESTIS ROGATUS.

Testis in re propria (sua). "No one is a proper witness in his own matter" (D. 22.5.10).

Testis rogatus. A witness who was requested (not forced or ordered) to be a witness. He had to be informed only about the nature of the act he was to witness.

Texere (textura). For weaving one's wool or another material into another man's cloth, see INTEXERE.

Thalelaeus. A law teacher (probably in Beirut), contemporary with Justinian, author of an extensive commentary on Justinian's Code. His work was abundantly excerpted for the BASILICA, their scholia and for later Byzantine legal works.

Kübler, *RE* 5A (*s.v.* Thalelaios, no. 4); Berger, *BIDR* 55–56 (1952) 124.

Theatrum. Theatres were public property (*res publicae, res universitatis*) and could not be in private ownership. Admission was free. A person who was prevented from entering a theatre could sue the opponent by *actio iniuriarum* (see INIURIA). An outrage inflicted on a person in a theatre was treated as *iniuria atrox*. But a creditor could summon his debtor to court in a theatre (IN IUS VOCATIO).—See LEX ROSCIA, LEX IULIA THEATRALIS.

Navarre, *DS* 5, 204; A. Guichard, *De la législation du théâtre à Rome* (Thèse Douai, 1880).

Theodorus Scholasticus. Born in Hermoupolis in Egypt (hence he is called *Hermopolitanus* or *Thebanus*), a juristic writer of the second half of the sixth century. He wrote a summary (*index*) of Justinian's Code and an abridged edition of the emperor's Novels (*Epitome, Syntomos Nearon*).

Kübler, *RE* 5A, 1863 (no. 43); Zachariae, *Anecdota* (1843) p. XXII and 7 (edition of the *Syntomos ton nearon diataxeon*); Heimbach, *Basilica* 6 (1870) 80, 88; J. A. B. Mortreuil, *Histoire du droit byzantin* 1 (1843) 306.

Theophilus. A law teacher in Constantinople, one of the most active collaborators of Justinian in the codification of the laws. He was a member of the commission which compiled the first Code and the Digest, and together with Dorotheus he composed the Institutes (INSTITUTIONES IUSTINIANI). He wrote a summary of the initial part of the Digest and a paraphrase of Justinian's Institutes, a work which despite some occasional errors is instructive from different points of view.—See PARAPHRASIS INSTITUTIONUM.

Kübler, *RE* 5A, 2138 (no. 14).

Thesaurensis. An official of the later Empire charged with the administration of public (imperial) storehouses.—See THESAURUS.

Dorigny, *DS* 5, 224; O. Hirschfeld, *Kaiserliche Verwaltungsbeamte*[2] (1905) 308.

Thesauri. (In the Empire.) The treasury of the emperor. It was administered by the *procurator thesaurorum,* in the later Empire by the *comes thesauro-*

rum who was among the high officials in charge of the imperial household.

O. Hirschfeld, *Kaiserliche Verwaltungsbeamte*² (1905) 307.

Thesaurus. A treasure-trove, a valuable movable (primarily money) which had been hidden for so long a time so that its actual owner was unknown and his identity could no longer be established. The finder of a *thesaurus* (*inventor thesauri*) could keep it for himself if he found it on his own land or in a sacred place (*locus sacer* or *religiosus*). If he found it in another's land by accident, only one-half belonged to him and the other half to the landowner. If the *thesaurus* was found in ground which was a *locus publicus*, the finder shared the *thesaurus* with the fisc. A finder who did not report his find to the fisc when the latter was entitled to a half, lost his share and had to pay the entire amount of the *thesaurus* to the fisc. Finding a *thesaurus* in another's land through deliberate search gave the finder no right at all.—C. 10.15.

Kübler, *RE* 6A; Dorigny, *DS* 5; Ravetta, *L'acquisto di tesoro*, 1910; Bonfante, *Mél Girard* 1 (1912) 123 (= *Scritti* 2 [1926] 904); Schulz, *ZSS* 35 (1914) 94; Appleton, *St Bonfante* 3 (1930) 1; G. Hill, *Treasure-trove in law and practice* (1936) 5; Biscardi, *StSen* 54 (1940) 297; Düll, *ZSS* 61 (1941) 19; Hubaux and Hicter, *RIDA* 2 (1949) 425.

Thesaurus. (In administrative law.) A storehouse. —See HORREUM, THESAURI.

Tiberis. The river Tiber. For *venditio trans Tiberim* (= selling a free person beyond the Tiber), see SERVUS, ADDICTUS, TRANS TIBERIM.

Tignum iunctum. A beam used for the construction of a house; in a broader sense, any material used for that purpose. According to the rule, *superficies cedit solo* (see SUPERFICIES) the owner of the building became owner of the material used even if it originally belonged to another. The latter could not sue the owner for the recovery of the material as long as the house stood firm; if it collapsed or if the material was separated in some other way, he might then claim his property. He had an action, however, the *actio de tigno iuncto*, against the owner for double the value of the material if the latter was used in bad faith (e.g., if it was stolen). A claim for separation of the material was not permissible. Justinian introduced the IUS TOLLENDI in favor of the owner of the material.—D. 47.3.—See SERVITUS TIGNI IMMITTENDI.

Chapot, *DS* 5; Ehrhardt, *RE* 6A; E. Heilborn, *T. i., plantatio und accessio* (Diss. Breslau, 1907); Riccobono, *AnPal* 3–4 (1917) 445; E. Levy, *Konkurrenz der Aktionen* 1 (1918) 420; R. Monier, *Le t. i.*, 1922; Berger, *St Riccobono* 1 (1936) 623; Pampaloni, *Scritti giur.* 1 (1941, ex 1883, 1885) 217, 485; *idem*, *BIDR* 21 (1909) 205.

Timor. Fear, anxiety. "A groundless fear is no just excuse" (D. 50.17.184).—See METUS.

Tingere. To dye. If one dyed another person's fabric (wool) by applying a product (e.g., purple) of his own, the owner of the material remained owner of the colored stuff.—See FULLO.

Tipoukeitos. A peculiar Byzantine juristic product of the late eleventh century, a repertory, or kind of "table of contents," indicating all the topics dealt with in the BASILICA, in the order of their titles and sections. The origin of the name is the Greek phrase "*ti pou keitai*" (= what is where, *sc.* in the Basilica). The author was a judge, Patzes.

Recent edition: M. *Kritou tou Patze Tipoukeitos sive Librorum 60 Basilicorum Summarium* 1 (books 1–12, 1914) by Ferrini and Mercati, 2 (books 13–23, 1929) by Doelger, 3 (books 24–38, 1944) by Seidl and Hoermann, in *Studi e Testi*, vol. 25, 51, 107 (Città del Vaticano).—Noailles, *Mél Cornil* 2 (1926) 177; Seidl, *Die Basiliken des Patzes, Fschr Koschaker* 3 (1939) 294; H. Müller, *Der letzte Titel des XX. Buches der Basiliken des Patzes* (Diss. Greifswald, 1940); Berger, *Trad* 3 (1945) 394 (= *BIDR* 55–56 [1951] 277); Wenger, *ibid.* 10 (Bibl.); Seidl, *Byzantinische Ztschr.* 44 (1951) 534.

Tiro. In military service a recruit, a soldier newly enlisted, without sufficient training. The *tirones* were mostly 17 to 20 years of age.—C. 12.43.—DELICTA MILITUM.

Lammert, *RE* 6A; Cagnat, *DS* 5.

Tiro. A beginner in a profession, also in that of a lawyer. *Tiro* was also a young man solemnly introduced in the *forum* by his parents for the first time. On this occasion he wore the TOGA PRAETEXTA (*toga civilis*).

Tirocinium. The state of being a TIRO (a beginner in military service, in a profession or in political life). Hence *tirocinium* is used in the sense of lack of experience.

Regner, *RE* 6A, 1450; S. Cugia, *Profili del tirocinio industriale*, 1922.

Tironatus. See TIROCINIUM.

Tities. See RAMNES.

Schachermeyr, *RE* 6A.

Titii sodales. A college of priests charged with special religious duties (sacrifices), the nature of which is not quite clear.

Weinstock, *RE* 6A; Cagnat, *DS* 5.

Titius (Lucius Titius). A fictitious name frequently used in juristic writings to indicate a party involved in the case under discussion.—See NOMEN.

Tituli ex corpore Ulpiani. (Also called *Epitome Ulpiani* or *Regulae Ulpiani* in the literature.) An apocryphal collection of legal rules, attributed until recent times to Ulpian. It was perhaps written by a later unknown jurist about the end of the third century or shortly thereafter. Many rules of the collection remind one of the Institutes of Gaius.

Edition: F. Schulz, *Die Epitome Ulpiani des Cod. Vat. Reg.* 1128 (1926).—E. Albertario, *Studi* 5 (1937) 491; Volterra, *RStDIt* 8 (1935) 390 (Bibl.); F. Schulz, *History of R. legal science*, 1946, 180.

Titulus. A dedicatory or honorary inscription on a temple, gravestone, or building; a placard placed on a house to indicate that there is an apartment for rent; a tablet hung on a slave offered for sale in the market. *Titulus* is also the title of a book, of a chapter in a juristic work, or of a section in the praetorian Edict (e.g., *titulus de in ius vocando*).— The word has a specific meaning in connection with the acquisition of ownership, predominantly in the field of USUCAPIO.

Schulz, *ZSS* 68 (1951) 21.

Toga. The outer garment (robe, cloak) of a Roman citizen when he appeared in public (at the *forum*); hence it was called *vestis forensis* (garment for the *forum*). The use of a *toga* was prohibited to soldiers, foreigners, and persons condemned to exile. Originally women also wore a *toga,* but it was soon replaced by the *stola*, the *toga* being reserved for women of ill fame condemned in a criminal trial (*iudicium publicum*) or for adultery, and for prostitutes. The normal *toga* of a Roman citizen (of white wool) was also called *toga pura* or *libera*.—See TRABEA, CLAVUS.

Courby, *DS* 5; Wright, *OCD*; L. Wilson, *The R. toga* (1924).

Toga candida. See CANDIDATUS.

Toga picta. A purple robe embroidered with gold. It was one of the insignia of higher Republican officials, worn only on the occasion of a triumph (see TRIUMPHUS) or other solemn celebration. The custom was adopted by the emperors. Syn. *toga palmata*.—See TOGA PURPUREA.

Ehlers, *RE* 7A, 505; Courby, *DS* 5, 349.

Toga praetexta. A white robe with a purple border stripe. It was one of the insignia of consuls, praetors, and priests. In the Principate the emperor wore a *toga praetexta* when he appeared within the walls of Rome in public. Young men over fourteen wore the *toga praetexta* as a sign of manhood before they put on the *toga virilis*. Hence *togatus* (*praetextatus*) = a youth in the age of manhood.—See IMPUBES.

Goethert, *RE* 6A, 1659; Regner, *ibid.* 1451.

Toga pura. See TOGA.

Toga purpurea. A *toga* of purple color. It was the *toga* of the kings. Later it was used by a triumphant army commander when he entered Rome after a victorious war; see TRIUMPHUS.—See TOGA PICTA.

Toga sordida. A dark grey *toga* worn when one was mourning or appeared in court as an accused.

Toga virilis. The normal white toga of a Roman citizen. There was no fixed age for wearing the *toga virilis*; normally young men between sixteen and eighteen put on the *toga virilis*. After a solemn ceremony which usually took place at a religious feast, dedicated to Bacchus, the youth wearing the white toga was introduced to the forum accompanied by his parents and relatives, after which he ceased to wear the *toga praetexta*.—See IMPUBES.

Regner, *RE* 6A, 1451; Hunziker, *DS* 5.

Togatus. A Roman citizen wearing (or having the right to wear) the *toga virilis*. In later juristic language *togatus* was any state official wearing the *toga* as his official robe. The term was also applied to lawyers pleading in court (*togatus fori*).

Steinwenter, *RE* 6A, 1666; Philipp, *ibid.* 1662; Ehlers, *RE* 7A, 505.

Tollere. See IUS TOLLENDI.

Tollere altius. See SERVITUS ALTIUS NON TOLLENDI.

Tollere legem. To abolish a statute by promulgating a new one.

Tollere liberum. To lift a child. According to an ancient custom when a married woman bore a son, the father (*pater familias*) lifted him up from the earth, thus denoting symbolically that he was accepting him in the family as his son. The act had no legal significance; the omission of this gesture was without legal effects.

Declareuil, *Mél Girard* 1 (1912) 326; Perozzi, *St Simoncelli* (1917) 213 (= *Scritti* 3 [1948] 93; Berger, *Jour. of Juristic Papyrology* 1 (1945) 30 (= *BIDR* 55–56 [1951] 114); Volterra, *Fschr Schulz* 1 (1951) 388; *idem, Iura* 3 (1952) 216.

Tolli. With reference to legal acts and transactions, to be annulled, to become void (e.g., a testament, an agreement, an obligation, a stipulation). *Actio tollitur* = the right to sue a person is abolished.

Tormentum. Torture. It was applied in Roman criminal procedure as a means to extort (*torquere*) from a person suspected of a crime a confession or a testimony from a witness. On the other hand, *tormentum* was applied as a penalty, in particular as an aggravation of the death penalty, in the Republic only to slaves, in the Empire also to free citizens, as, e.g., in the case of *crimen maiestatis* or murder through poisoning. From the late second century on, distinction was made between *honestiores* and *humiliores* inasmuch as with regard to the former torture was applied only in the case of heinous crimes (*maiestas, magia*). In the later Empire torturing became more frequent.—The use of torture in questioning witnesses (*tormentum* became almost synonymous with *quaestio*) was severely criticized by jurists and by some emperors. "Many persons undergo torture through endurance so that by no means can the truth be extorted from them; others instead are so unable to suffer pains that they prefer to lie than to be tormented. It so happens that they confess in different ways incriminating not only themselves but also others" (D. 48.18.1 pr.). A slave could not be compelled by torture to testify against his master. Torture as a penalty for crimes committed by slaves was practiced in a large measure. Masters were permitted to torture their slaves if the crime was directed against the masters themselves (until the third century). In other cases permission to torture had to be secured from the authorities. For the torture of slaves suspected as murderers of their master, see SENATUSCONSULTUM SILANIANUM. Torture was applied as a penalty against an accuser who initiated a criminal trial against another for treason (*crimen maiestatis*) and was not able to prove his accusation. —*Tormentum* is also the instrument used for torturing.—D. 48.18; C. 9.41.—See QUAESTIO PER TORMENTA, TALIO, FUSTIS, SUPPLICIUM FUSTUARIUM, FLAGELLUM, VERBERA, MALA MANSIO.

Ehrhardt, *RE* 6A; Lafaye, *DS* 5; Berger, *OCD*.

Torquere. See TORMENTUM.

Torrentia flumina. See FLUMINA TORRENTIA.

Tortor. One who executed the torture, the torturer. He is to be distinguished from the *quaesitor*, the official who questioned the accused or a witness.— See TORMENTUM, CARNIFEX.

Trabea. A toga with purple and scarlet worn by the kings and in the Republic by consuls on specific solemn occasions. Hence *trabea* is used in the meaning of consulship, and the adj. *trabeatus* is syn. with CONSULARIS. Certain high priests, as the *flamen Dialis,* and persons of equestrian rank also wore the *trabea.*

Schuppe, *RE* 6A; Courby, *DS* 5.

Tractare. To treat. The term refers to the treatment to be applied to certain categories of criminals. The verb is also used of the administration of property or the management of one's own or another's affairs (*tractare bona, negotia, pecuniam*). With reference to juristic discussions (oral or written) *tractare* = to deal with, to discuss a problem (*quaestionem, materiam*). Hence *tractatus* = a juristic dissertation.

Tractatores. Officials in the financial administration (in the later Empire) subordinate to the *praefectus praetorio.*

Tractatus. See TRACTARE.

Tractatus de gradibus cognationum. See DE GRADIBUS COGNATIONUM.

Tractatus de peculiis. See DE PECULIIS.

Tractoria. A written official permission for the use of the state post. The *tractoria* implied also board and lodging at the expense of the state for travelers in official mission. From the second half of the fourth century on the *tractoria* were signed by the emperor.—C. 12.51(52).

Ensslin, *RE* 6A; Humbert, *DS* 5; Ganshof, *TR* 8 (1928) 69.

Tractus. A larger tract of land (a district) in the emperor's domain, administered by a *procurator* who also exercised certain jurisdictional functions in the name of the emperor in disputes between the principal lessee of the domain (*conductor*) and the sublessee (*colonus*). Syn. *regio.*

Tractus temporis. A lapse (a period) of time. A legal rule (D. 50.17.29) stated: "what is invalid at the beginning cannot become valid through lapse of time (*tractu temporis*)."—See INITIUM.

Tradere. To teach. Justinian used frequently the term in his constitution OMNEM as syn. with *docere,* when he dealt with the courses which the teachers of law

had to offer in the law schools.—See TRADITUR, TRADITIO.

Traditio. (From *tradere.*) The transfer of ownership over a *res nec mancipi* (see RES MANCIPI) through the handing over of it to the transferee by the owner. A simple delivery of *res mancipi* did not transfer ownership (see MANCIPATIO), the transferee acquired only the so-called bonitary ownership (see IN BONIS ESSE) which could be converted in quiritary ownership (under *ius civile*) through USUCAPIO. The classical *traditio* required a just cause (*iusta causa*) since, being only a transfer of possession of a thing from one person to another, it had, in order to transfer ownership, to be based on a special legal relationship of an obligatory or another nature between transferor and transferee. "A simple delivery of a thing never transfers ownership, unless a sale or another just cause preceded the delivery" (D. 41.1.31 pr.). A *iusta causa* also was a donation. There was, however, no just cause if the transaction, which was followed by *traditio,* was prohibited by law, as, e.g., a gift between husband and wife (see DONATIO INTER VIRUM ET UXOREM). Transfer of ownership could be performed only by the owner of the thing or by a person authorized by him or by the law (see ALIENATIO). Normally *traditio* was a material act: the effective delivery of the thing to be transferred from hand to hand which, when movables (money) were concerned, was very simple. The delivery of an immovable (a piece of land) was executed through introduction of the acquirer on the land and his walking around the boundaries of the property. In later development the acquirer's entering on the premises or even a more simplified formality sufficed; see TRADITIO LONGA MANU, TRADITIO FICTA, CLAVES, CUSTOS. *Traditio* was an institution *iuris gentium* which arose from relations with foreigners. It was therefore available to peregrines. With regard to provincial land (*fundus provincialis*) it was the only mode of acquisition of ownership. In Justinian's law the distinction between *res mancipi* and *res nec mancipi* having been abolished, the *traditio* served as a general means for the transfer of ownership. The compilers substituted in many texts *traditio* for *mancipatio* which was no longer actual, and *tradere* for *mancipio dare* (or *accipere*).—D. 21.3; 41.1; 41.2; C. 7.32.—See EXCEPTIO REI VENDITAE ET TRADITAE.

Ehrhardt, *RE* 6A; Beauchet and Collinet, *DS* 5; Aru, *NDI* 12; P. De Francisci, *Il trasferimento della proprietà* (1924); Betti, *St Bonfante* 1 (1930) 305; *idem, BIDR* 41 (1933) 143; H. Lange, *Das kausale Element im Tatbestand der klass. Eigentumstradition,* 1930; Monier, *St Bonfante* 3 (1930) 219; A. Ehrhardt, *Iusta causa traditionis,* 1931; D. Hazewinkel-Suringa, *Mancipatio en t.* (Amsterdam, 1932); G. G. Archi, *Il trasferimento della proprietà,* 1934; H. H. Pflüger, *Zur Lehre vom Erwerb des Eigentums,* 1937; Thayer, *BIDR* 44 (1937) 439; S. Romano, *Nuovi studi sul trasferimento della proprietà,* 1937;

C. A. Funaioli, *La tradizione*, 1942, 5; M. Kaser, *Eigentum und Besitz* (1943) 195; Voci, *SDHI* 15 (1949) 141; J. G. Fuchs, *Iusta causa traditionis und romanist. Wissenschaft* (Diss. Basel, 1949); Levy, *West Roman vulgar law*, 1952, *passim*; van Oven, *TR* 20 (1952) 441.

Traditio brevi manu. Occurred when the transferee held already the thing, the ownership of which had to be transferred, but not as its owner, as, e.g., when a depositee or *commodatarius* of a thing acquired the ownership of it through sale or donation. A handing over of the thing in such a case was superfluous.—See CONSTITUTUM POSSESSORIUM.

Stella-Maranca, *NDI* 2, 544; Schulz, *Einführung in das Studium der Digesten* (1916) 62; Arnò, *StPav* 16 (1931).

Traditio chartae (per chartam). The delivery of an immovable through the handing over of a written deed of conveyance of property to the transferee. This form of *traditio* was practiced in the later Empire. The document was termed also *epistula traditionis*. Syn. TRADITIO INSTRUMENTI.

Brandileone, *St Scialoja* 1 (1905) 3; Riccobono, *ZSS* 33 (1912) 277; H. Steinacker, *Die antiken Grundlagen der frühmittelalterlichen Urkunde* (1927) 88.

Traditio clavium. See CLAVES.

Traditio ficta. (A non-Roman term.) A symbolic handing over of a thing which was to be delivered to the transferee. There was no physical delivery thereof but other acts, performed instead, manifested the transfer of the thing beyond any doubt. The typical case of such a *traditio* was the delivery of keys of a shop, or of a house, to the transferee.

Biermann, *T. f.*, 1891; Riccobono, *ZSS* 33 (1912) 259, 34 (1913) 159; C. A. Funaioli, *Traditio*, 1942, 29.

Traditio in incertam personam. Called in the literature a form of *traditio* in which the transferee was not a certain individual but any one of the people. Such a case was the so-called *iactus missilium;* see MISSILIA.

Berger, *RE* 9, 553; *idem*, *BIDR* 32 (1922) 154; F. Pringsheim, *Kauf mit fremdem Geld* (1916) 66; Kaden, *ZSS* 53 (1933) 613.

Traditio instrumenti. See TRADITIO CHARTAE.

Traditio longa manu. A form of *traditio* in which the thing to be transferred to the acquirer was placed with his knowledge and consent in his sight (*in conspectu*) so that he might take possession thereof whenever he pleased. The handing over of a thing to a person other than the real acquirer with the consent of the latter or in his presence, had the same legal effect.

F. Schulz, *Einführung in das Studium der Digesten* (1916) 66.

Traditio nuda. See NUDA TRADITIO.

Traditio possessionis (tradere possessionem). Handing over possession. The expression correctly stresses the external aspect of *traditio*.—See TRADITIO, VACUA POSSESSIO.

Traditio servitutis. The "delivery" of a servitude could hardly be an institution of the classical law since *traditio* was applicable only to corporeal things and not to rights. The meaning of the expression was to put the beneficiary of the servitude in the position of being able to exercise his right (e.g., an usufruct = *traditio ususfructus*).

Riccobono, *ZSS* 34 (1913) 208.

Traditur (traditum est). It is taught, held, handed down. The expression is used of doctrines which have been prevailing among jurists for a long period of time (through tradition).

Tragoedus. See MIMUS.

Traiecticia pecunia. See FENUS NAUTICUM. *Traiecticius contractus*, an agreement concerning a maritime loan (FENUS NAUTICUM).

Trans Tiberim. Beyond the river Tiber, i.e., beyond the boundaries of the city of Rome (*urbs*), abroad.—See ADDICTUS, SERVUS, TIBERIS.

Sautel, in *Varia, Études de droit romain* (*Publications de l'Inst. de dr. rom. de l'Univ. de Paris*, 9) 1952, 86.

Transactio. (From *transigere*.) An extrajudicial agreement between two parties involved in a controversy in order to settle it in a friendly way and avoid a trial in court. *Transigere* = "to settle a doubtful matter, an uncertain and unfinished controversy" (D. 2.15.1). Usually the parties made reciprocal concessions, the claimant renouncing his action, the debtor recognizing his liability and either paying immediately his debt or promising to do so in the future, normally through *stipulatio* to make the claim easily suable. From the juristic point of view the *transactio* was a pact (*pactum*). A *transactio* over a controversy already decided by a judgment was not permissible unless (under later law) an appeal from it was brought. Postclassical and Justinian's legislation favored the *transactio* as a friendly settlement of controversies. The *transactio* became an autonomous legal institution similar in type and effect to innominate contracts (see CONTRACTUS INNOMINATI).—D. 2.15; C. 2.4.

Kaser, *RE* 6A; C. Bertolini, *Transazione*, 1900; M. E. Peterlongo, *La transazione*, 1936; G. Boyer, *Pacte extinctif d'action en dr. civil rom.*, *Recueil de l'Acad. de législation de Toulouse*, 13 (1937); Riccobono, *Miscellanea G. Mercati*, 5 (1946) 24.

Transcripticia nomina. See NOMINA TRANSCRIPTICIA.

Transcriptio. See NOMINA TRANSCRIPTICIA.

Transferre. To transfer to another (a right, a thing, possession, etc.). There was a fundamental rule concerning the transfer of property or rights to another: "No one can transfer to another more rights (*plus iuris*) than he has himself" (D. 50.17.54). Another rule stated: "What belongs to us cannot be transferred to another without an action of ours (*sine facto nostro*)," D. 50.17.11.

Transferre. (When referred to a legal norm.) To apply a legal principle to an analogous case.

Transferre actionem (translatio actionis). See CESSIO.

Transferre domicilium. To transfer the domicile. The transfer was to be real and factual (*re et facto*, D. 50.1.20), not simply by a declaration before witnesses.

Transferre possessionem. See TRADITIO.

Transfuga. (From *transfugere*.) A soldier who runs over to the enemy (*ad hostem transit, transfugit*). In war time he was punished by flogging to death. *Transfuga* also was a soldier who when taken by the enemy as a prisoner did not escape although he had the opportunity to do so. A *transfuga* was regarded as an enemy and had no *ius postliminii*. Syn. *perfuga*.

Schnorr v. Carolsfeld, *RE* 6A.

Transfusio. See the definition of NOVATIO.

Transigere. See TRANSACTIO.

Transire. To pass over, to devolve to, to be transferred to another (e.g., an inheritance, a right or an obligation, ownership, a legal remedy such as an *actio, exceptio* or *querela*).

Transire ad hostem. To desert to the enemy. Syn. *transfugere.*—See TRANSFUGA.

Transitio ad plebem. Transition from the patrician order to the plebeian. This brought the new plebeian the advantage of his eligibility to the plebeian tribunate. The transition was achieved through adoption by a plebeian performed in an assembly of the plebeians (CONCILIUM PLEBIS).

Kübler, *RE* 6A; Siber, *RE* 21, 125; Humbert, *DS* 2, 1509.

Transitus. See IN TRANSITU.

Translatio dominii. See TRANSLATIO IURIS.

Translatio iudicii. An alteration in the procedural formula in a specific trial after the issue was framed (LITIS CONTESTATIO). Such alteration became necessary when a change of a person involved in the trial occurred, e.g., the death of the judge, appointed in the procedural formula, or of one of the parties or his representative (death of a COGNITOR, withdrawal of, or loss of citizenship by, the *cognitor*). Minor complications were caused if the change concerned other representatives of a party, a *procurator* (see PROCURATOR in a civil trial), a guardian or a curator. The technical side of the *translatio iudicii* in the events mentioned is not quite clear, in particular, whether a new *litis contestatio*, a *restitutio in integrum,* or a specific agreement between the parties, confirmed by the competent magistrate, was necessary. It is likely that all instances of *translatio iudicii* were technically not treated in the same way.

Kaser, *RE* 6A, 2160; P. Koschaker, *T. i.* (1905); J. Duquesne, *T. i.* (Paris, 1910); Wlassak, *Judikationsbefehl, SbWien* 197, 4 (1921) 234.

Translatio iuris. The transfer of a right from one person to another either by an act *inter vivos* (an agreement, a donation) or *mortis causa,* through succession. See TRANSFERRE. *Translatio rei (dominii)* = the transfer of ownership.—See CESSIO, DOMINIUM.

Kaser, *RE* 6A, 2158.

Translatio legati. See ADEMPTIO LEGATI.—Inst. 2.21; 34.4.

Kaser, *RE* 6A, 2168; Sanfilippo, *AnPal* 17 (1937) 120.

Translatio rei. See TRADITIO, TRANSLATIO IURIS.

Kaser, *RE* 6A, 2159 (Bibl.).

Transmittere (transmissio). Primarily used of the transfer of a right from one person to another through inheritance or legacy (*mortis causa*). In a specific, technical sense, *transmitti* (pass.) refers to a transfer of the right to accept an inheritance by the appointed heir to his successors. Under the classical law, when an heir upon whom an inheritance was conferred (*delata,* see DEFERRE HEREDITATEM) died before the acceptance of the inheritance (see ADITIO HEREDITATIS), the latter was not "transmitted" to another. Some exceptions from this rule, however, were admitted in the later law. Two cases of *transmissio* are particularly important. First, the so-called *transmissio Theodosiana* (C. 6.52.1), which occurred when a testator appointed his descendant as an heir and the latter died before the testament was opened (see APERTURA TESTAMENTI). In such an event the heir's nearest descendant had the right to accept the inheritance. In a much larger measure the classical rule was superseded by the so-called *transmissio Iustiniana* (C. 6.30.19): if an heir (a testamentary one or on intestacy) died before a year elapsed from the time he had notice of the *delatio* or before the time for deliberation (see DELIBERARE, TEMPUS AD DELIBERANDUM) expired, his heirs could accept the inheritance during the rest of the time. If an heir died without having knowledge of the inheritance conferred upon him, the pertinent terms (one year or the *tempus ad deliberandum,* respectively) ran fully in favor of his heirs.—C. 6.50; 52.

P. Bonfante, *Corso di dir. rom.,* 6 (1930) 243; B. Biondi, *Successione testamentaria* (1943) 251.

Transversus. See LINEA, LATUS.

Trebatius, Caius T. Testa. One of the last Republican jurists, contemporary with, and friend of, Cicero, teacher of Labeo. No direct excerpt from his works is preserved in the Digest, nor is a title of a writing of his cited. Literary sources make it clear that he wrote a treatise on civil law (*de iure civili*) and an extensive work on divine law. He enjoyed high esteem with the classical jurists.

Sonnet, *RE* 6A, 2251; Berger, *RE* Suppl. 7, 1619; *idem, OCD.*

Trecenarii. Imperial officials receiving the highest annual salary of 300,000 sesterces. Lower groups were *ducenarii* (with a salary of 200,000 sesterces), *centenarii* (100,000) and *sexagenarii* (60,000).—See PROCURATORES (IN PUBLIC LAW).

Kubitschek, *RE* 3; Seeck, *RE* 5 (*s.v. ducenarii*); A. Segrè, *TAmPhilolAs* 74 (1943) 102.

Trecenarius. In the army, the highest officer (*centurio*) in the PRAETORIUM.

Lammert, *RE* 6A.

Tres faciunt collegium. The minimum number of members of an association was three (D. 50.16.85). —See COLLEGIUM.

Tres partes. In some manuscripts of the Digest a part of the second (middle) portion (see INFORTIATUM), to wit, from D. 35.2.82 until the end of book 38, appears as a separate volume starting with the words *"tres partes."* The division has no essential significance at all; it might be a jest of the scribe who saw in these two words an allusion to the division of the Digest into three volumes.—See VULGATA.

Kantorowicz, *TR* 15 (1937) 40.

Tresviri (triumviri). A body of three officials associated in the same official functions. Additional words indicate the office and functions for which they were appointed. They acted in common or separately if they agreed upon the division of their functions among themselves.—See the following items.

Strasburger, *RE* 7A (*s.v. triumviri*); Lécrivain, *DS* 5.

Tresviri aediles. (In municipalities.) In some MUNICIPIA there were three *aediles* instead of two (DUOVIRI AEDILES).

E. Manni, *Per la storia dei municipi* (1947) 159.

Tresviri (triumviri) agris dandis (or dividundis). See TRESVIRI COLONIAE DEDUCENDAE.

Tresviri aere argento auro flando feriundo. See TRESVIRI MONETALES.

Tresviri capitales. Magistrates of a lower rank (*magistratus minores*) belonging to the group of VIGINTISEXVIRI. They exercised police functions in Rome and fulfilled certain tasks in criminal and civil jurisdiction (arresting suspect persons, castigating thieves and slaves, supervising executions of persons condemned to death). They also collected pecuniary fines (*multae*), the sum of *sacramentum* from the party defeated (see LEGIS ACTIO SACRAMENTI), if the sum was not deposited before. A *Lex Papiria* of an unknown date (between 242 and 122 B.C.) ordered their election by *comitia tributa*, presided over by the *praetor urbanus*. The *tresviri capitales* still existed in the third century after Christ but most of their functions were performed under the Principate by the VIGILES.

Strasburger, *RE* 7A, 518; Lécrivain, *DS* 5, 413; G. Rotondi, *Leges publicae populi Romani* (1912) 312.

Tresviri (triumviri) coloniae deducendae. Three commissioners appointed for the foundation of a colony and the distribution of plots of land among the colonists. Their number increased in the course of time (*quinqueviri, septemviri, decemviri*) and their official title was enlarged through the addition of words such as *agris dandis, assignandis, iudicandis.*

Strasburger, *RE* 7A, 511; Schulten, *DE* 2, 429; Bayet, *Rev. des Études Latines* 6 (1928) 270.

Tresviri monetales. Masters of the mint. They were magistrates of lower rank (*magistratus minores*) and belonged to the group of officials called by the collective name VIGINTISEXVIRI. Under the Republic their names were impressed on the coins. From the time of Augustus their official title was *tresviri aere argento auro flando feriundo* (= the officials to blow and coin bronze, silver and gold). From the third century the masters of the mint bore the title *procuratores monetae*; from the time of Diocletian they were appointed for each dioecesis.

Strasburger, *RE* 7A, 515.

Tresviri nocturni. See VIGINTISEXVIRI. They were probably predecessors of the TRESVIRI CAPITALES.

Strasburger, *RE* 7A, 518.

Tria verba. See DO DICO ADDICO.

Paoli, *NRH* 30 (1952) 297.

Triarii. See CENTURIO.

Lammert, *RE* 7A; H. M. D. Parker, *The Roman legions* (1928) 10.

Tribonianus. Justinian's principal collaborator and adviser in his legislative work. He was a member of the commission appointed by the emperor for the compilation of the first Code and presided over the commissions which composed the Institutes, the Digest, and the second Code. Hence the changes made by the compilers on the texts of classical juristic writings and imperial constitutions, collected for Justinian's codification, are termed in the literature *emblemata Triboniani* ("Tribonianisms"). During the work on the codification he was—with a brief interruption—QUAESTOR SACRI PALATII and temporarily MAGISTER OFFICIORUM. He probably also was the author of Justinian's earlier Novels. He died about A.D. 545. In spite of some critical remarks about his character by a contemporary writer (Procopius of Caesarea) the reliability of which are not beyond doubt, Tribonianus was the most prominent personality of Justinian's epoch. The emperor speaks of him with the highest praise. His collection of rare juristic works which served the compilers in the preparation of the Digest, is particularly emphasized by Justinian (*Tanta* c. 17).

Kübler, *RE* 6A; Berger, *OCD*; E. Stein, *Bull. de la Classe des Lettres, Acad. Royale de Belgique,* 23 (1937) 365.

Tribu moveri. See NOTA CENSORIA.

Tribuere. To grant, to concede. The term refers to legal remedies granted both by law (a statute) and a jurisdictional magistrate. *Tribuere* appears in the classical definition of justice (see IUSTITIA): *ius suum cuique tribuere* (= to render everyone his due).— See TRIBUTIO, ACTIO TRIBUTORIA, ULTRO TRIBUTA.

Tribunal. A platform for a court, in the open air or (under the Principate) in a basilica. The jurisdictional magistrate, his secretary, and his council (*consilium*) were seated on the *tribunal*. The seat of the presiding magistrate was in the middle on the front of the tribunal (*pro tribunali*). The magistrate acted *pro tribunali* when he decided about *bonorum possessio, missiones, restitutio in integrum,* appointment of guardians, adoptions, manumissions, and the like.

Ant. DE PLANO. *Tribunal* was later used in the sense of a court.—See IN TRANSITU, CENTUMVIRI.

Weiss, *RE* 6A; Chapot, *DS* 5; Severini, *NDI* 12, 2; Pernice, *ZSS* 14 (1893) 135; Kübler, *Festschrift für O. Hirschfeld* (1903) 58; H. D. Johnson, *The R. tribunal*, Baltimore, 1927; Düll, *ZSS* 52 (1932) 174; Wenger, *ZSS* 59 (1939) 376.

Tribunal. (In a military camp.) A higher platform on which a military commander and his retinue were seated.

Lammert, *RE* 6A, 2430.

Tribunatus. The office of a tribune in military service (in the army or in the imperial guard).

Tribuni. The following items deal with the more important officials bearing the title of *tribunus*. There were some more functionaries called *tribuni*, during the whole period of Roman history, for some specific functions of subordinate nature. Several of them were involved in the administration of military supplies.

Lengle, *RE* 6A.

Tribuni aerarii. Originally they were officials of the TRIBUS charged with the payment of stipend to soldiers, collection of the necessary means for this purpose (*tributum*) imposed on the members of the TRIBUS, and the management of contributions and booty taken from the enemy. Since these functions were assigned to financially reliable persons, the term *tribuni aerarii* was later applied to persons classified in higher classes of the *census*. A *lex Aurelia* (70 B.C.) ordered that one-third (300) of the jurors in criminal courts (*quaestiones*) be selected among the *tribuni aerarii*, but a statute issued under the dictator Caesar abolished that privilege. Although the census of *tribuni aerarii* was lower than that of persons of equestrian rank (see EQUITES), they belonged to the well-to-do group of the society.—See LEX AURELIA IUDICIARIA, TRIBUS.

Lengle, *RE* 6A, 2432; Treves, *OCD*; Hill, *AmJPhilol* 67 (1946) 61.

Tribuni celerum. See CELERES.

Tribuni civitatis. Military commanders and high officials of the civil administration in larger cities in the later Empire (particularly in Egypt).

Lengle, *RE* 6A, 2435.

Tribuni classis. Commanders of navy units, probably of a lower rank than the *praefectus classis*.

Lengle, *RE* 6A, 2436.

Tribuni cohortis. Military commanders of *cohortes praetoriae*, subordinate to the *praefectus praetorio*. Later the title was given to specific (voluntary) units of the military forces in the field.

Lengle, *RE* 6A, 2436.

Tribuni laticlavii. Among all military tribunes who normally were of equestrian rank, they ranked highest since they belonged to the senatorial class.

Tribuni militum. The highest officers in the legions, normally of equestrian rank (see TRIBUNI LATICLA-

VII). There were six *tribuni militum* in a legion; one of them assumed in times of war the command of the whole legion. In peace time their activity was manifold, as described by the jurist Macer, in his work "On military matters" (*de re militari*): "to hold the soldiers in the camps, to make them exercise for training, to keep the keys of the gates, to make sometimes the rounds of the watch, to supervise the distribution of the food, to examine the grain, to restrain frauds attempted by the furnishers of food, to punish offenses, to be frequently present in the headquarters, to hear the complaints of the legionnaires, to inspect their healthy conditions," etc. (D. 49.16.12.2). Under the Principate the title *tribuni militum* was conferred on commanders of other units of a more or less military character and on officials of the imperial administration.—See LEX LICINIA CASSIA.

Liebenam, *RE* 6, 1639; Parker, *OCD*.

Tribuni militum consulari potestate. Military tribunes with consular power. The *tribuni militum consulari potestate* were created first in 444 B.C. in the place of consuls. Their number varied from three to six, and they were appointed as extraordinary magistrates by a decree of the senate. They disappeared as a constitutional institution in 367 B.C. when the praetorship was established.

Lengle, *RE* 6A, 2448; Bernardi, *RendLomb* 79 (1945–46) 3.

Tribuni numerorum. See NUMERUS.

Tribuni plebis. Plebeian tribunes. The office was created in 494 B.C. after the first secession of the plebeians to the Sacred Mount (*Mons Sacer*). The *tribuni plebis* were originally not magistrates of the state but officials of the plebeian order (see PLEBS). Their number increased gradually from two to ten. The development of the plebeian tribunate reflects the development of the rights and social situation of the plebs. The primary function of the *tribuni* was the defense of the plebeians against illegal acts and abuses of the patrician magistrates (*ius auxilii*, see AUXILIUM, INTERCESSIO TRIBUNICIA). The house of the *tribuni* had to be accessible even during the night; a *tribunus* could not be absent from Rome longer than one day. Originally the tribunes were elected by the plebeian assemblies (see CONCILIA PLEBIS), later by *comitia tributa*. The office and the person of a *tribunus* were sacrosanct (see SACROSANCTITAS); one who violated the sacrosanctity of a *tribunus* became an outlaw (see SACER, LEGES SACRATAE). For the right of the tribunes to protest against the administrative acts and legislative proposals of the magistrates (*ius intercedendi*), see INTERCESSIO IN PUBLIC LAW. A *tribunus* had the right to convoke a gathering of the plebs (CONCILIA PLEBIS), to preside over it, and to make proposals of bills to the plebeian assembly on which the plebs voted (see PLEBISCITA). The tribunes obtained the greatest success in the field of legislation when they were admitted to the meetings of the senate and were granted the right to make legislative proposals which after approval by the senate were transmitted to the *comitia tributa* for a vote. Later, the *tribuni* were authorized to convoke the senate and under the *Lex Atinia* (149 B.C.) they obtained a seat in the senate after their term of service. Tribunes had *ius coërcendi* (see COËRCITIO) over persons who offended their dignity or opposed their orders. They could order the arrest of the wrongdoer which was made by the *aediles plebis* or the subordinates of the *tribuni,* the *viatores.* In the field of jurisdiction the tribunes assumed the competence of the former DUOVIRI PERDUELLIONIS in cases qualified as PERDUELLIO and decided upon offenses against their person. Generally they inflicted fines (*multae*), but they had the power to pronounce even the death penalty. The latter and higher fines (over 3020 sesterces), however, had to be confirmed by the *comitia centuriata* or *tributa* (for fines). Only a plebeian could be a tribune (see TRANSITIO AD PLEBEM). The *tribuni* had no IMPERIUM, but their legal position became in the later Republic very similar to that of magistrates. The great importance of the plebeian tribunate is evidenced by the fact that Augustus based his sovereign power primarily on *tribunicia potestas,* against which no *ius, intercedendi* (either by tribunes or by magistrates) could be applied. Consequently, the tribunes lost much of their prestige although their *ius intercedendi* against the orders of magistrates, the *ius auxilii,* and some minor rights as well as their honorific privileges remained undiminished. Mention of *tribuni plebis* still occurs in the fifth century, but only as an honorary title.—See moreover, IUS AGENDI CUM PLEBE, LEX AURELIA, LEX CORNELIA (on tribunes), LEX HORTENSIA, LEX PUBLILIA PHILONIS, LEX POMPEIA LICINIA, LEX ICILIA, LEX PUBLILIA VOLERONIS, LEX VALERIA HORATIA, TRIBUNICIA POTESTAS.

Lengle, *RE* 6A, 2454 (Bibl.); Lécrivain, *DS* 5; Anon., *NDI* 12, 2 (*s.v. tribunato*); Momigliano, *OCD*; *idem, Bull. Comm. archeol. comunale di Roma,* 59 (1932) 157; F. Stella-Maranca, *Il tribunato della plebe dalla Lex Hortensia alla lex Cornelia* (1901); B. Kübler, *Privatrechtliche Kompetenz der Volkstribunen in der Kaiserzeit* (Fschr O. Hirschfeld, 1903); E. Meyer, *Kleine Schriften,* 1910, 351; E. Cocchia, *Tribunato della plebe* (1917); E. Pais, *Ricerche sulla storia* 3 (1918) 3 (on *Fasti tribunicii*), 227; G. Niccolini, *I tribuni e il processo capitale, Atti della Soc. Linguistica Ligure di Scienze e Lett.* 3 (1924); *idem, Historia* 3 (1929) 181; *idem, I fasti dei trib. della plebe,* 1934; H. Siber, *Die plebeischen Magistraturen bis zur lex Hortensia,* 1936; Brecht, *ZSS* 59 (1939) 271; G. De Sanctis, *Miscellanea G. Mercati,* 5 (1946); C. W. Westrup, *Introduction to early R. law,* 4, 1 (1950) 91; Siber, *RE* 21, 169.

Tribuni scholarum. See SCHOLAE.

Tribuni vigilum. See VIGILES.

Tribuni voluptatum. Police officers in the later Empire who had the supervision of public games and theatrical spectacles, and the control of public morals.

Tribunicia potestas. The fullness of power conferred on plebeian tribunes. Caesar and Augustus had the title *tribunicia potestate* conferred on them in order to be inviolable (*sacrosanctus*).—See TRIBUNI PLEBIS.

Mattingly, *JRS* 20 (1930) 78; Strack, *Klio, Neue Folge* 14 (1939); De Visscher, *SDHI* 5 (1939) 101 (= *Nouvelles Études,* 1949, 27); Gioffredi, *SDHI* 11 (1945) 37; M. Grant, *From imperium to auctoritas,* 1946, 446.

Tribunicius. (Adj.) Connected with the office of a *tribunus plebis.*

Tribunicius. (Noun.) A retired tribune.—See ADLECTIO.

Tribunus et notarius. See NOTARIUS.

Tribus. A tribe. The original three tribes, Ramnes, Tities, and Luceres (see RAMNES) were of ethnic character. The later division of the territory of Rome into four *tribus* (ascribed to King Servius Tullius) was a local one and superseded the ethnic division. In 495 B.C., sixteen country *tribus* were added to the former urban ones and after 241 B.C. there were thirty-five *tribus* altogether, the original four urban *tribus* (*tribus urbanae*) and thirty-one "rustic" (*tribus rusticae*) covering the whole country. In the *tribus rusticae* the landowners were concentrated, whereas the city-*tribus* embraced (since 304 B.C.) the non-owners of land. The *tribus rusticae* became thus more distinguished and the assignment to an urban *tribus* was implied in a *tribu moveri* (expulsion from a *tribus rustica*) through a NOTA CENSORIA. Each Roman citizen had to be registered in a *tribus* during the CENSUS. The registration gave him the right to vote in the popular assembly of the *tribus* (*comitia tributa*). The division in *tribus* served for calling to military service and taxation within the *tribus* (*tributim*). The TRIBUNI AERARII functioned as chairmen of the *tribus.* Their principal duty was to pay off the soldiers of the *tribus* (*aes militare*) and to collaborate in the assessment of the landed property for taxation purposes. In the later Republic the territorial basis for the enrollment into a *tribus* was not strictly observed. Under the Principate the *tribus* became an organization for relief of its poor members who were entitled to some help in grain and food from the state. See TESSERAE FRUMENTARIAE.—See CURIAE MUNICIPIORUM.

Kubitschek, *RE* 6A; Chapot, *DS* 5; Momigliano, *OCD*; O. Hirschfeld, *Kleine Schriften* (1913) 248; Niccolini, *St Bonfante* 2 (1930) 235; E. Täubler, *SbHeid* 1929/30, Heft 4; Last, *JRS* 35 (1945) 30; Gintowt, *Eos* 43 (1948/9) 198.

Tribus municipiorum. See CURIAE MUNICIPIORUM.

Tributarius. (Noun.) A taxpayer. The term refers to payers of taxes of any kind. *Tributarius* (adj.) = connected with, or pertinent to, the payment of TRIBUTUM.—See PRAEDIA TRIBUTARIA.

A. Segrè, *Trad* 5 (1947) 103.

Tributim. By *tribus,* e.g., voting *tributim* in the *comitia tributa.*—See TRIBUS, LEX VALERIA HORATIA.

Tributio. (From *tribuere.*) Distribution of an insolvent commercial *peculium* belonging to a slave or *filius familias* among its creditors (see ACTIO TRIBUTORIA).—See TRIBUTUM.

Tributoria actio. See ACTIO TRIBUTORIA.

Tributum. In earlier times an extraordinary charge in kind imposed (*indicere*) on citizens, non-soldiers, in war time in order to secure equipment and nourishment for the army. After a victorious war the *tributum* was sometimes reimbursed to the payers if the booty and contribution taken from the enemy was large enough to cover the expenses of the war. Syn. *tributio.* Later, *tributum* became a general term for taxes; see the following items. For *tributum* in the provinces, see TRIBUTUM SOLI, STIPENDIUM, PRAEDIA TRIBUTARIA.—C. 10.16; 21.

Schwahn, *RE* 7A; Lécrivain, *DS* 5; Schlossmann, *Arch. für lateinische Lexicographie* 14 (1906) 25; Ciapessoni, *St su Gaio* (1943) 52; L. Clerici, *Economia e finanza dei Romani,* 1 (1943) 440; Van Oven, in *Tractatus tributarii, offered to P. J. A. Adriani* (Haarlem, 1949) 29.

Tributum capitis. A tax imposed on the population of certain provinces. The tax was not uniform. It was either a tax from property other than land or a poll-tax levied as a *capitatio plebeia* (*humana*) which was paid by certain groups of the population subjugated.—See CAPITATIO in the provinces.

Schwahn, *RE* 7A, 68; E. H. Stevenson, *Roman provincial administration,* 2nd ed. 1949, 151; Tcherikover, *Jour. of Juristic Papyrology* 4 (Warsaw, 1950) 193.

Tributum soli. A land tax, the most important impost in the provinces paid either in kind or in money. It was based on a survey of the land and an evaluation by experts. Originally there was no difference between *stipendium* and *tributum*; under the Principate distinction was made depending upon the circumstance whether the province was imperial or senatorial: *tributum* was paid in imperial provinces, *stipendium* in senatorial.—See PRAEDIA STIPENDIARIA, PRAEDIA TRIBUTARIA.

Schwahn, *RE* 7A, 10; 62; 70; Anon., *NDI* 12, 2.

Tributum temerarium. A general extraordinary tax paid voluntarily in times of urgent necessity (emergency) by well-to-do persons in order to save the state from financial calamity. The money given was considered a loan to be repaid by the state when its financial situation would improve. The *tributum temerarium* was practiced only in the Republic.

Schwahn, *RE* 7A, 58.

Triginta dies. A period of thirty days. It was applied in both criminal and civil procedure on various occasions. Its origin was perhaps in sacral law (armistice) from which it was by statute or custom transferred into legal procedural practice.—See DIES IUSTI, TEMPUS IUDICATI, LEX PINARIA, LEX CICEREIA.

F. Kleineidam, *Personalexecution der Zwölf Tafeln* (1904) 130; Düll, *Fschr Koschaker* 1 (1939) 27.

Trinoctium. Three consecutive nights. Through a wife's intentional absence for three nights from the common dwelling with her husband, the acquisition of *manus* (power) over her through USUS was interrupted. The marriage concluded through cohabitation remained valid and could be continued when the wife returned to the common home.—See USURPARE.

Lévy-Bruhl, *TR* 14 (1936) 452 (= *Nouv. Études* [1947] 72); Wolff, *TR* 16 (1938) 145; Kaser, *Iura* 1 (1950) 72.

Trinundinum. See NUNDINAE, PROMULGARE, LEX CAECILIA DIDIA. Syn. *trinum nundinum.*

Kroll, *RE* 17, 1471; Treves, *OCD*; G. Rotondi, *Leges publicae pop. Rom.* (1912) 125.

Tripertita. The title of the earliest Roman juristic treatise, written by the jurist Sextus Aelius Petus Catus; see AELIUS.

Tripertitum ius. See TESTAMENTUM TRIPERTITUM.

Triplicatio. See DUPLICATIO, REPLICATIO.

Triptychum. Three wooden, wax covered, square tablets bound together like a booklet with six pages. Pages one and six were left blank, pages from two to five contained the text of the document (*scriptura interior* on pages two and three was sealed by the witnesses on page four, *scriptura exterior* was written on pages four and five).—See TABULAE, TABULAE CERATAE, DIPTYCHUM.

P. Krüger, *Gesch. der Quellen²* (1912) 267.

Triticaria condictio. See CONDICTIO TRITICARIA.

Triumphator. A military commander (an emperor or a high magistrate entering Rome under an imposing ceremonial (see TRIUMPHUS) after a victorious war. As an honorific title the term was applied to emperors in the later Empire.

Triumphus. The solemn entrance of a military commander in Rome after a victorious war. Under the Republic it was only a dictator, a consul, or a praetor (magistrates with *imperium*) who had the right to celebrate the victory of his troops (or the navy, *triumphus navalis, maritimus*) in this way, if they were still in office (*in magistratu*) and a previous decision of the senate granting the *triumphus* was passed before they returned to the city of Rome (*pomerium*). Only a victory over the enemy obtained by bloodshed (at least five thousand enemies killed) gave the right to a *triumphus,* according to a *lex Maria Porcia* of 62 B.C., which fixed penalties for commanders who gave false information about the number of enemies killed in war. In the Empire, the *triumphus* was a prerogative of the emperor. The triumphator had the right to certain special insignia (*ornamenta triumphalia*) such as a chariot richly ornamented with gold, ivory, and laurels (*currus triumphalis*), a TOGA PICTA (*vestis triumphalis*), a laurel crown (*corona triumphalis*) on his head, while another crown (made of gold) was held over his head by a public slave, etc. A lesser *triumphus* (*minor triumphus*), called *ovatio,* was also granted by the senate in cases in which the military success did not justify a full triumph or when the campaign was of lesser importance.—See ACCLAMATIO.

> Ehlers, *RE* 7A; Borzsák, *RE* 18, 1122; Rohde, *RE* 18, 1890 (*s.v. ovatio*); Cagnat, *DS* 5; Cuq, *DS* 3, 1155; G. Rotondi, *Leges publicae populi Rom.* (1912) 382.

Triumvirale iudicium. In postclassical times three arbitrators chosen by the parties to settle a controversy between them.

Triumviri. See TRESVIRI.

Triumviri rei publicae constituendae causa. See LEX TITIA.

Tryphoninus, Claudius. A jurist of the first half of the third century, member of the council of the emperor Septimius Severus, a disciple of the famous jurist Cervidius Scaevola. He wrote notes (*notae*) to his teacher's work and an extensive casuistic collection, *Disputationes* (in 21 books).—See CLAUDIUS.

> Jörs, *RE* 3, 2882; W. Kunkel, *Herkunft und soziale Stellung der röm. Juristen,* 1952, 231.

Tubero, Quintus Aelius. A jurist of the second half of the last century of the Republic. He wrote on constitutional law (on the senate) and on the duties of a judge. Of another jurist of the same name, who was consul in 118 B.C., very little is known. He was highly praised by Cicero.

> Klebs, *RE* 1, 535 (no. 155), 537 (no. 156); Grosso, *ATor* 78 (1942/3) 180.

Tuditanus, Caius Sempronius. Consul 129 B.C., the first jurist who wrote on public law, author of a treatise on magistracies (at least in 13 books).

> Münzer, *RE* 2A, 1441.

Tueri. To defend, to protect, to take care, to administer carefully (one's property, affairs). The term is frequently applied to legal institutions and procedural remedies (actions, exceptions, interdicts) by which a person could defend his rights and interests in court or be granted protection by the praetor; see TUITIO PRAETORIS.

Tuitio praetoris. Protection, defense, granted by the praetor in specific cases in which, under *ius civile,* such a protection was not available.—See IPSO IURE, MANUMISSIO PRAETORIA, SERVITUTES PRAETORIAE, IUS HONORARIUM.

> S. Solazzi, *Requisiti e modi di costituzione delle servitù prediali* (1947) 137.

Tumultus. A riot, an uproar, a violent agitation (revolt) of the people against public authorities (*adversus rem publicam*) when an internal critical situation was threatening. In such circumstances exceptional measures were taken, as, e.g., calling all citizens to arms and suspension of exemptions from military service. The state of *tumultus* was publicly proclaimed by the senate. With regard to contractual obligations the impossibility of their fulfillment caused by accidents during a *tumultus* were considered a *vis maior.*—See IUSTITIUM, SENATUSCONSULTUM ULTIMUM, DEPOSITUM MISERABILE, TURBA, SEDITIO.

> Sachers, *RE* 7A, 1345.

Tunc enim (or **autem, etenim, certe, deinde**). Occurs in interpolated texts, in particular when the locutions follow a negative conditional phrase (*nisi* . . .) and serve to define precisely the exceptional case (*tunc* = in that case). The locutions, however, are not an absolutely reliable criterion of interpolation, as often has been assumed.

> E. Albertario, *Fil* 36 (1911) 801; Berger, *KrVj* 14 (1912) 419; Guarneri-Citati, *Indice*² 1927, *s.vv. enim, tunc.*

Turba. A riot, a turmoil. Robbery committed during a riot in which many persons ("not three or four," D. 47:8.4:3) were engaged was more severely punished than a simple RAPINA. *Turba* also refers to a multitude of persons whom a man gathered in order to enter with violence another's house for the purpose of plundering. If the accomplices were armed (*turba cum telis*), the culprit was punished by death.—D. 47.8.—See TUMULTUS.

> Esmein, *Mél Girard* 1 (1912) 458.

Turbatio. A tumultuous disturbance of public order and peace.—See TURBA.

Turbatio sanguinis. See LUCTUS.

Turma. A small cavalry unit, normally of thirty cavalrymen, one-tenth of all horsemen attached to a legion. See EQUITES LEGIONIS. Commander of a *turma* was the *decurio* commanding the first *decuria* (= ten cavalrymen) of the *turma.* The *decuria* was the smallest cavalry unit. In the Empire a larger unit was the ALA which consisted of sixteen or more *turmae.*

> Lammert, *RE* 7A; Cagnat, *DS* 5.

Turmarii. Imperial officers in the later Empire concerned with the enlistment of recruits for the cavalry.

Turpis. See CONDICIO TURPIS, CONDICTIO OB TURPEM CAUSAM, ACTIONES FAMOSAE, RES TURPIS, and the following items.

Turpis persona. A person whose occupation or conduct was disreputable. Among *personae turpes* were actors (see SCAENICUS), gladiators (see HARENARII), prostitutes (see MERETRIX), owners of houses of lewdness (see LENA, LENO). A *turpis persona* was excluded from guardianship and could not contest a testament through QUERELA INOFFICIOSI TESTAMENTI. —See TURPITUDO.

> Sachers, *RE* 7A, 1435.

Turpis stipulatio. A *stipulatio* under which a person assumed an obligation to commit a crime. The promise was null. *Stipulatio ex turpi causa* = a *stipulatio* in which the ground of the promise was immoral although the object was not (e.g., a promise made to prevent a crime intended by another). In such a case the promisor when sued for payment, could oppose the *exceptio doli*; on the other hand the magistrate could refuse the plaintiff the *actio* (*denegatio actionis*) against the *promisor.*—See CONDICTIO OB TURPEM CAUSAM.

> Siber, *St Bonfante* 4 (1930) 105.

Turpitudo. The quality of a person to be of bad repute (TURPIS PERSONA) because of his profession, immoral or improper conduct. Such persons were condemned by public opinion and branded factually with infamy although legally they were not infamous (*infamis*). In the literature this kind of infamy is called *infamia facti,* to be distinguished from *infamia iuris,* i.e., infamy inflicted by law.—See INFAMIA, EXISTIMATIO, TURPIS PERSONA, ACTIONES FAMOSAE, NOTA CENSORIA, IGNOMINIA.

Sachers, *RE* 7A.

Tuscianus. A jurist of the second century after Christ, successor of Iavolenus in the leadership of the Sabinian school (see SABINIANI). No excerpt of his works is known.

Berger, *RE* 7A, 1462; Guarino, *AnCat* 1 (1947) 331; Kunkel, *Herkunft und soziale Stellung der röm. Juristen,* 1952, 153.

Tutela. See TUTELA IMPUBERUM, the primary type of guardianship.

Tutela agnatorum. See TUTELA LEGITIMA AGNATORUM.

Tutela dativa. See TUTELA TESTAMENTARIA, TUTOR DATIVUS.

Tutela fiduciaria. Fiduciary guardianship. One instance of *tutela fiduciaria* occurs in connection with the COËMPTIO FIDUCIAE CAUSA. Another instance was connected with EMANCIPATIO, when the person who purchased a son from his father for the third time did not remancipate him to the father but manumitted him himself (*manumissor extraneus*); this gave the manumitter fiduciary guardianship over the emancipated.—Inst. 1.19.

Sachers, *RE* 7A, 1595; W. W. Buckland, *Textbook²* (1932) 147.

Tutela impuberum. Guardianship over persons *sui· iuris* (not under paternal power) who were below the age of puberty (see IMPUBES). The definition of *tutela,* given by the Republican jurist Servius Sulpicius Rufus (and quoted by Justinian in his Inst. 1.13.1), runs: "a right and power over a free person, granted and allowed under *ius civile,* to protect him who, because of his age, is not able to defend himself" (D. 26.1.1. pr.). The guardian (*tutor = tuitor*) had to protect the person and the property of· the ward (*pupillus*) and his functions are qualified as a power (*potestas*) although it was not so extensive as the paternal power (*patria potestas*). "A *tutor* does not only administer the property of the ward (*res pupilli*) but he also has to take care of his moral behavior" (*mores,* D. 26.7.12.3). *Tutela* is not only a right; it created on the part of the *tutor* duties for the fulfillment of which he was responsible. Consequently guardianship was considered a *munus* (a charge); under the later Principate it was designated as a *munus publicum* (= a public service) inasmuch as the protection of young people unable to manage their affairs was also in the public interest. The further development of the institution was dominated by the tendency to extend the liability of the guardians

and to submit them more and more to the control of the public authorities. The original independence of the *tutor* in the administration of the ward's affairs— he was then considered *domini loco* (taking the place of the owner)—was in the course of time restricted in many ways, although, as a matter of principle, he was authorized to manage all matters connected with the ward's property (*negotia pupilli gerere*). Certain acts of the tutor were prohibited, such as donations (except small ones, usual in family events and in social relations), transactions in which the guardian himself was interested (*in re propria*), and what was most important, the alienation and hypothecation of the ward's landed property; see ORATIO SEVERI. For specific purposes, however, when the interests of the ward required it, permission to alienate could be given by a magistrate. The principal function of the *tutor* was his cooperation in legal acts performed by the ward himself who as a person *sui iuris* could, if he was beyond the age of infancy (*infantia maior*) validly conclude but only with the authorization (approval, *auctoritas*) of the guardian (see AUCTORITATEM INTERPONERE, AUCTORITAS TUTORIS). The *auctoritas* was unnecessary when the act concluded by the *pupillus* was exclusively to his advantage. In civil lawsuits the *tutor* was authorized to represent the ward but not without certain restrictions depending either on the form of procedure (under the regime of *legis actiones* he could represent only an *infans,* under the formulary procedure there were no restrictions) or on the age of the *impubes* (e.g., a mature *impubes* could sue his adversary *sine tutore auctore*). The earliest form of the appointment of a *tutor* was the testamentary one (*tutela testamentaria*) which occurred when a father or the person who had paternal power (*patria potestas*) over the *impubes* nominated a *tutor* in his testament (by which the *impubes* normally was instituted as an heir, *heres*). In the absence of a testamentary appointment, the tutor was designated by the law (*tutela legitima*). There was also an appointment by a magistrate; see TUTELA DATIVA. For the requirements concerning the personal ability to be a guardian, see TUTOR. Originally not responsible at all, the guardian was later made liable for damages caused by fraudulent (*dolus, fraus*) or negligent (*culpa*) administration of the ward's property. He could be removed under an accusation to be suspect (see TUTOR SUSPECTUS), sued by the *actio (de) rationibus distrahendis* in the case of fraud committed in the management of the guardianship, and by the *actio tutelae* (*arbitrium tutelae*) for rendering an account of what he had done for the ward, for the restitution of the ward's property and for indemnifying the ward for losses which resulted from fraudulent and (later) negligent administration. The latter action was a *bonae fidei actio* and involved infamy to the guardian if he was condemned. For security given by the guardian, see CAUTIO REM PUPILLI SALVAM FORE. From the time of Constantine the ward had a general hypothec (*hypotheca omnium bonorum*) on the guardian's property. The guardian could seek a reimbursement of his expenses made in the interest of ward through *actio tutelae contraria*.—In Justinian's codification the law of guardianship was thoroughly reformed. Alterations of classical texts obscured many details in the development of the institution and in the field of the guardian's duties and responsibilities. Moreover, the tendency towards equalization of the different types of *tutela* with respect to the forms of appointments contributed considerably to the confusion of the picture.—Inst. 1.13–15, 17–22, 24–26; D. 26.2.1–10, 27.1–9; C. 5.28–68, 71–75; 9.10.—See moreover, EXCUSATIO, POTIORIS NOMINATIO, PRAETOR TUTELARIS, ACTIO SUBSIDIARIA, INVENTARIUM, PERICULUM TUTELAE, ABDICATIO, IN IURE CESSIO TUTELAE, ACTIO RATIONIBUS DISTRAHENDIS, CONTUTORES, USURAE PUPILLARES, and the following items.

Sachers, *RE* 7A; Beauchet and Collinet, *DS* 5; Solazzi, *NDI* 12, 2; Berger, *OCD* 400 (*s.v.* guardianship); Renard, *NRH* (1901) 634; Peters, *ZSS* 32 (1911) 188; R. Taubenschlag, *Studien* (1913); Solazzi, *Tutele e curatele, RISG* 53 (1913) 263, 54 (1914) 17, 273; *idem, RendLomb* 49 (1916) 638, 53 (1920) 121; *idem, Istituti tutelari* (1929); *idem, StPav* 6 (1921) 115; *idem, St sulla tutela, Pubbl. Univ. Modena* 9 (1925), 13 (1926); E. Levy, *Die Konkurrenz der Aktionen* 1 (1918) 143; La Pira, *BIDR* 38 (1929) 53; Vazny, *ACDR Roma* 2 (1935) 529; Lauria, *St Riccobono* 3 (1936) 283; Kübler, *St Besta* 1 (1939) 75; V. Arangio-Ruiz, *Rariora* (1946) 149; Siber, *ZSS* 65 (1947) 162; Lévy-Bruhl, *St Solazzi* (1948) 318; Guarino, *ibid.* 31; Biondi, *Fschr Schulz* 1 (1951) 52; Provera, *Iudicia contraria, MemTor Ser. II,* 75 (1952) 45.

Tutela legitima. Guardianship in which the choice of the guardian was fixed by law (*lex*). Under "law" the Twelve Tables are meant (see LEGITIMUS). If a testator failed to appoint a *tutor* to his son or descendant who was below the age of puberty (*impubes*) and was to become *sui iuris* at the death of the testator, the nearest agnates, the same who succeeded *ab intestato*, had to be the guardians of the persons mentioned. If such relatives were lacking, the Twelve Tables called members of the testator's *gens* (*gentiles*) nearest in relationship. Justinian's reform of the succession on intestacy (Nov. 118) devolved guardianship to the cognates of the deceased.—Inst. 1.15; 17; 18; D. 26.4; C. 5.30.

Tutela legitima parentis. A father who emancipated his son (*parens manumissor*) before the latter became *pubes* was under the law (see LEGITIMUS) the guardian of the son.—Inst. 1.18.—See PARENS MANUMISSOR, EMANCIPATIO.

Tutela legitima patroni. A patron (and after his death his son) became guardian of his freedman whom he manumitted from slavery when the slave was below the age of puberty.—Inst. 1.17.

Tutela mulierum. Guardianship over women *sui iuris*, i.e., who were neither under paternal power (*patria potestas*) nor under that of her husband (*manus*). In the developed stage of the institution the principal function of the *tutor mulieris* was to give his authorization (*auctoritas*) to more important transactions or acts performed by the woman, such as manumission of slaves, acceptance of an inheritance, making a testament, assuming an obligation, alienations, constitution of a dowry, and the like. The women's weakness of sex (see INFIRMITAS SEXUS), light-mindedness, and ignorance of business and court-affairs are given as grounds for their protection through tutelage. The appointment of a woman's guardian was made in the same way as the TUTELA IMPUBERUM: by testament of the person in whose power (paternal or marital) she was, by law (*tutela legitima* of the agnates and of members of the *gens*, *gentiles*, in earlier times) or by a magistrate (*tutela dativa*). The woman could enforce the *auctoritas* of the guardian in the case of an unjustified refusal of approval by applying to a magistrate. The *tutela mulierum* was still in force under Diocletian. In the Theodosian Code there is no mention thereof.—See COËMPTIO FIDUCIAE CAUSA, OPTIO TUTORIS, IUS LIBERORUM, VESTALES, TUTOR AD CERTAM REM, LEX CLAUDIA DE TUTELA MULIERUM, USUCAPIO EX RUTILIANA CONSTITUTIONE.

Sachers, *RE* 7A, 1588; Solazzi, *Aeg* 2 (1921) 155.

Tutela testamentaria. Appointment of a tutor by a testator in his last will for his son or a descendant in his paternal power below the age of puberty who at his death would become *sui iuris* (independent of paternal power). If there was no guardian appointed by testament or if the appointed guardian was excused, legitimate guardianship (*tutela legitima*) entered into account. The appointment had to be made by name (*nominatim*). Guardians appointed by testament were treated by legislation with favorable regard as deserving particular confidence inasmuch as they had been selected by the testator.—Inst. 1.14; D. 26.2; C. 5.28.—See CAUTIO REM PUPILLI SALVAM FORE, CONFIRMARE TUTOREM, TUTOR DATIVUS.

Tutelaris (tutelarius). See PRAETOR TUTELARIUS.

Schneider, *RE* 7A, 1608.

Tutor. A guardian. Only Roman citizens could be guardians (some exceptions were admitted in favor of Latins, see LATINI). Minority was a ground for exemption from assuming a guardianship; Justinian set the age of twenty-five as the minimum age for tutors. Persons with physical defects (dumbness, deafness) were excluded whereas mental defects were only a ground for excuse. Soldiers could not be appointed as guardians. Women were not admitted to guardianship, since it was considered a man's work (*munus masculorum, munus virile*). From A.D. 390 grandmothers and mothers were permitted to assume the tutorship of their grandchildren or children if they were widows and solemnly declared not to marry again, and if there was no testamentary or legitimate tutor (C. 5.35.2).—For the rights and duties of a *tutor*, see TUTELA.—D. 26.5; C. 5.34; 35.—See NOMINATIO POTIORIS.

Solazzi, *RISG* 64 (1920) 2; Frezza, *StCagl* 22 (1934).

Tutor ad augmentum datus. An additional guardian appointed to assist the primary guardian when the ward's property substantially increased (e.g., through an inheritance).

Tutor ad certam rem. A guardian could not be appointed for one specific affair. An exception was the *tutor praetorius,* appointed for a woman under guardianship, for the constitution of dowry if the guardian under law (*tutor legitimus*) was unable to exercise his functions. In the case of larger estates consisting of distant properties the appointment of a tutor for certain locally delimited affairs was admissible; see TUTOR AD AUGMENTUM DATUS, TUTOR ADIUNCTUS.

Tutor adiunctus. An additional *tutor* appointed by a magistrate when the principal *tutor* was temporarily unable to fulfill his duties (e.g., he became a prisoner of war).—C. 5.36.

Sachers, *RE* 7A, 1524.

Tutor Atilianus. See LEX ATILIA.

Tutor cessans. One of two or more guardians (see CONTUTORES) who did not participate in the management of the ward's affairs at all. Originally he was not liable but later he could be compelled by the praetor to fulfill his duties, and from the time of Marcus Aurelius he could be sued by an *actio tutelae utilis* for damages if he did not excuse himself within fifty days.—See TUTOR GERENS.

Sachers, *RE* 7A, 1577; Solazzi, *RISG* 54 (1914) 35.

Tutor cessicius. See IN IURE CESSIO TUTELAE.

Tutor dativus (datus). A guardian appointed by a magistrate: in Rome by the *praetor urbanus* (see LEX ATILIA), in the provinces by the governor under the *Lex Iulia et Titia.* Under the Principate consuls and praetors appointed guardians, and from the time of Marcus Aurelius a special praetor was concerned with tutelary matters; see PRAETOR TUTELARIUS. The term *tutor dativus* refers sometimes to a *tutor* appointed in a testament.—D. 26.5; C. 5.47.

Sachers, *RE* 7A, 1512; Solazzi, *RISG* 54 (1914) 17, 273.

Tutor ex lege Iulia et Titia. See LEX IULIA ET TITIA.—Inst. 1.20.

Tutor falsus. See FALSUS TUTOR, PRO TUTORE GERERE, ACTIO PROTUTELAE.

Tutor fiduciarius. See TUTELA FIDUCIARIA.

Tutor gerens. A guardian who factually administered the ward's property (*gerere*), alone or together with another tutor (see CONTUTORES) and performed acts connected with the guardianship as a whole (*administratio tutelae*). Ant. *tutor cessans.*—D. 26.7.

Sachers, *RE* 7A, 1523; Solazzi, *RISG* 54 (1914) 35.

Tutor honorarius (honoris causa datus). An honorary tutor. He was free from any responsibility since he actually did not participate in the management of the ward's affairs.

Sachers, *RE* 7A, 1522, 1578; Levy, *ZSS* 37 (1916) 71.

Tutor in litem. A tutor especially appointed for the defense of the ward's interest in a trial against his guardian. In Justinian's law a *curator* accomplished such a task.—See TUTOR PRAETORIUS.—C. 5.44.

Tutor legitimus. See TUTELA LEGITIMA.

Tutor mulieris. See TUTELA MULIERUM.

Tutor notitiae causa datus. A guardian appointed in a testament, in addition to the principal guardian, who had to assist and instruct the latter (*ad instruendos contutores*) in the administration of the ward's affairs. Normally he was the testator's freedman who was acquainted with the ward's affairs.

Sachers, *RE* 7A, 1552; Levy, *ZSS* 37 (1916) 49.

Tutor optivus. See OPTIO TUTORIS.

Tutor praetorius. In the case of a controversy between the guardian and the ward during the guardianship the praetor appointed a special *tutor* who protected the ward's interests in the trial. Under Justinian's law a *curator* was appointed for this purpose. —See TUTOR IN LITEM.

Peters, *ZSS* 32 (1911) 221.

Tutor suspectus. A person who for various reasons (primarily of moral or financial nature) was not suitable for a specific guardianship. A guardian could be considered *suspectus* not only before he started the administration of the ward's property, but also when he later performed an act or concluded a transaction from which by his fraud or negligence a considerable loss resulted for the ward, or when through his inexcusable absence he proved that he did not care for the ward's interest. There were also other cases which rendered the tutor suspect, among them his open enmity against the *pupillus* and his family or his moral conduct (*mores*) which clearly indicated that he did not deserve confidence. A *tutor suspectus* could be denounced to the tutelary authority (*postulare, accusare tutorem suspectum*) by any one, but not by the ward himself; when the allegations of the accuser proved true in a special proceeding (*de suspecto tutore cognoscere*), he could be removed (*removere, remotio*) from the guardianship. The removed *tutor* was branded with infamy only when his actions were fraudulent. The *accusatio suspecti tutoris* (called also *crimen suspecti tutoris*) known already in the Twelve Tables, was in postclassical law extended to curators.—Inst. 1.26; D. 26.10; C. 5.43.

Sachers, *RE* 7A, 1556; Solazzi, *La minore età* (1912) 259; R. Taubenschlag, *Vormundschaftliche Studien* (1913) 27; Berger, *ZSS* 35 (1914) 39; Solazzi, *BIDR* 28 (1915) 131; *idem, Istituti tutelari* (1929) 207; R. Laprat, *Crimen suspecti tutoris* (1926); Kaden, *ZSS* 48 (1928) 699; Cardascia, *RHD* 28 (1950) 312.

Tutor temporarius. A guardian temporarily appointed when the *tutor testamentarius* or *legitimus* was absent (e.g., in the interest of the state) or temporarily unable to fulfill his duties (e.g., because of sickness).

Sachers, *RE* 7A, 1521.

Tutore auctore. Refers to acts of the ward which could be performed only with the authorization of his guardian; see AUCTORITAS TUTORIS, TUTELA, TUTELA MULIERUM.

Tutorio nomine agere. To act in court as a guardian in the interest of the ward.

Tutrix. A woman appointed as guardian. In classical law women were excluded from guardianship. Exceptions were introduced in postclassical law.—C. 3.27.—See TUTOR.

U

U.R. Abbreviation for *uti rogas*. See A.

Ugo (Ugolino dei Presbiteri). A glossator of the first half of the twelfth century.

Kuttner, *NDI* 12, 2, 680.

Ulpianus, Domitius. A jurist whose works were excerpted in a large measure by the compilers of the Digest; nearly one-third thereof originates from Ulpian's pen. He was born in Tyre (Phoenicia). He held various high imperial offices, was prefect of the praetorians from A.D. 222, and died in 228, assassinated by his subordinates. Contemporary with Paul (see PAULUS) and like Paul a very productive author, he had a perfect knowledge of the juristic literature; opinions of other jurists are amply quoted by him, but no quotation from Paul occurs in his works. He was an elegant writer, more of a compiler than an original thinker, but far from being a slavish copyist. He wrote many treatises, monographs (some of which are quite extensive) on topics, such as particular statutes, public law, imperial offices (e.g., proconsuls, consuls, *praefectus urbi, praetor tutelarius*), on procedural problems, etc. In addition, elementary works (*Institutiones*) and collections of legal rules (REGULAE), definitions (see DEFINITIONES) and opinions (see OPINIONES) are among his writings. Two collections of *Regulae* appear under the name of Ulpian, one (in 7 books) represented in the Digest by a few texts only, and another, *Liber singularis Regularum,* preserved in a manuscript under the title "Selections from Ulpian's works"; see TITULI EX CORPORE ULPIANI. On Ulpian's Notes to the writings of Papinian, whose younger contemporary he was, see NOTAE. Ulpian's standard works were a commentary on the praetorian Edict (*Libri ad edictum,* in 81 books) and an incomplete treatise on the *ius civile* (*Libri ad Sabinum,* in 51 books).

Jörs, *RE* 5, 1435 (no. 88); Berger, *OCD*; Orestano, *NDI* 12, 2; Pernice, *Ulpian als Schriftsteller, SbBerl* (1885) 443; H. Fitting, *Alter und Folge der Schriften röm. Juristen²* (1908) 99; F. Schulz, *Sabinusfragmente in Ulpians Sabinuskommentar* (1906); H. Krüger, *St Bonfante* 2

(1930) 303; Buckland, *LQR* 38 (1922) 38; 53 (1937) 508; Volterra, *SDHI* 3 (1937) 158; F. De Zulueta, *St Besta* 1 (1939) 137; Schulz, *History of R. legal science* (1946) *passim*; Solazzi, *AG* 133 (1948) 3 (on *Libri Disputationum*); Wolff, *Zur Überlieferungsgesch. Ulp. Libri ad Sab., Fschr Schulz* 2 (1951) 145; W. Kunkel, *Herkunft und soziale Stellung der röm. Juristen,* 1952, 245.

Ultimum supplicium. The death penalty. Syn. *summum supplicium.*

Ultimus. See DISPOSITIO ULTIMA, VOLUNTAS ULTIMA.

Ultro. Voluntarily, spontaneously, i.e., without any obligation, authorization or mandate. The term is applied to acts accomplished for another by a *negotiorum gestor.*

Ultro citroque. Reciprocal, on both sides. The expression is used of reciprocal obligations arising from a bilateral agreement and of the pertinent actions which are available to each party against the other.

Ultro tributa. Public works (constructions and buildings) assigned at a public auction to contractors who offered to build them at the lowest price.—See REDEMPTORES, OPERA PUBLICA.

Kübler, *Gesch. des röm. Rechts* (1925) 92; *idem, RE* 4A, 484; Mommsen, *Staatsrecht* 2, 1³ (1887) 432, 443.

Uncia. One-twelfth of an AS. Hence the twelfth part of a whole, in particular of an inheritance. *Heres unciarius* or *heres ex uncia* = an heir whose share in the inheritance was one-twelfth.

Babelon, *DS* 5, 590.

Unciae usurae. One-twelfth of *usurae centesimae* (= 12 per cent), i.e., one per cent per annum.

Unciarium fenus. See FENUS UNCIARIUM.

Unciarius heres. See UNCIA..

Unde cognati (legitimi, liberti, vir et uxor). The sections of the praetorian Edict which fixed the four groups of successors under praetorian law (see BONORUM POSSESSIO INTESTATI).—D. 38.6–8; C. 6.14; 15; 18.

Unde vi. Three interdicts against dispossession through violence were proposed under this title in the praetorian Edict; see INTERDICTUM DE VI.—D. 43.16; C. 8.4.

Berger, *RE* 9, 1677.

Universaliter venire. To be sold at a lump sum.

Universi cives. See POPULUS ROMANUS.

Universitas. A union of persons or a complex of things, treated as a unit (a whole). As far as a *universitas* of persons is concerned, the term is applied by the jurists in the field of both public (persons associated in a community, *civitas, municipia, collegia* of a public character) and private law (private *collegia, societates*). *Universitas* of persons is distinguished from its members (*singuli*). As a *universitas* of things are treated things which economically (e.g., a herd = *grex*, a building = *universitas aedificii, aedium*) or socially are considered a whole. In the last instance *universitas* comprises the complex of things and rights connected with an individual, such as an inheritance (*hereditas, universitas bonorum*), or in a more restricted sense, a *peculium,* a dowry. In this sense *universitas* is opposed to *singulae res, singula corpora* which refer to the individual things embraced by the term *universitas* as a whole. In later imperial constitutions *universitas* occurs in connections such as *fideicommissum universitatis, donatio universitatis.* The term *universitas* has been suspected as non-classical for various (not always convincing) reasons.—D. 3.4; 38.3; 403.—See ACTOR UNIVERSITATIS, INTERDICTA DE UNIVERSITATE, RES HEREDITARIAE, PIAE CAUSAE.

Cuq, *DS* 5; Bortolucci, *NDI* 12, 2; Guarneri-Citati, *Indice²* (1927) 88, *St Riccobono* 1 (1936) 742, *Fschr Koschaker* 1 (1939) 155 (for interpolations); F. Milone, *Le universitates rerum* (1894); C. Longo, *St Fadda* 1 (1906) 123; Bonfante, *Scr giuridici* 1 (1926) 250, 277; Bortolucci, *BIDR* 42 (1934) 150, 43 (1935) 128; Schnorr v. Carolsfeld, *Zur Gesch. der juristischen Person* 1 (1933) 59; Albertario, *St* 5 (1937) 323, 4 (1946) 65; P. W. Duff, *Personality in R. private law* (1938) 35; Carcaterra, *Rend-Lomb* 73 (1939–40) 701; B. Biondi, *Istituti fondamentali di dir. ereditario* 1 (1946) 42; V. Olivecrona, *Three essays in R. law,* 1949, 5; *Volterra, CambLJ* 10 (1949) 202.

Universitas agrorum. All plots of land within the limits of one city (*civitas*). They are the territory (*territorium*) of the *civitas* (D. 50.16.239.8).

Universitas facti—Universitas iuris. These non-Roman terms were coined in the literature to distinguish a group of things which though physically separated are treated as a whole, their single components not being taken in consideration, *universitas facti* (e.g., a library, a collection of pictures), from a group of persons or things which as a whole has a legal existence, distinct from that of its members or parts (*universitas iuris*).

Universitas hominum. A rather vague term indicating a larger group of persons organized along social lines.

Universitas Iudaeorum. Occurs only in a rescript of the emperor Caracalla (C. 1.9.1) in connection with a legacy bequeathed to it. The emperor declared the legacy not suable. In the case in question the term was used by a *testatrix* with reference to the Jews living in Antioch, and evidently not as a legal technical term, but in the meaning *universi Iudaei.*

Schnorr v. Carolsfeld, *Zur Gesch. der Juristischen Person* 1 (1933) 69.

Universitas iuris. See UNIVERSITAS FACTI.

Bortolucci, *NDI* 12, 2.

Universum ius. See SUCCESSIO IN UNIVERSUM IUS, HEREDITAS, UNIVERSITAS.

Univira (univiria). A woman who after the death of her husband remained unmarried. Women twice married were socially less esteemed. Augustus' legislation (LEX IULIA DE MARITANDIS ORDINIBUS), however, compelled widows and divorced women to marry a second time by inflicting on them considerable material disadvantages.—See LUCTUS, SECUNDAE NUPTIAE.

Frey, *Recherches de science réligieuse* 20 (1930) 48.

Unus casus. A unique case. Contrary to the basic rule concerning the REI VINDICATIO in one case only (*unus casus*)—according to Justinian's Institutes, 4.6.2.—a plaintiff could sue his adversary although he himself had possession of the thing vindicated. The case has remained unknown despite the various attempts on the part of scholars to find it in the Digest where it should be found according to Justinian's assertion.

R. Henle, *U. c.* (1915); Berger, *GrZ* 42 (1916) 725; Scialoja, *St Simoncelli* (1917) 511 (= *St* 2 [1934] 273); Nicolau, *RHD* 13 (1934) 597, 14 (1935) 184.

Unus iudex. See IUDEX UNUS, IUDICIUM LEGITIMUM.

Unus testis. See TESTIMONIUM UNIUS.

Urbana familia. See FAMILIA RUSTICA.

Urbana (urbicaria) praefectura. *Praefectura urbis,* see PRAEFECTUS URBI.

Urbanus. See PRAEDIA URBANA, SEDES, PRAETOR, VILLA.

Urbicarius. Connected with, or pertinent to, the capital (Rome, and later Constantinople). The adjective occurs only in imperial constitutions.

Urbicum edictum. The edict of the *praetor urbanus.* —See EDICTUM PRAETORIS.

Urbicus. Refers only to Rome (see URBS); the term does not occur in Justinian's Code.

Urbs. In the Digest this refers to Rome, in later imperial constitutions to Constantinople. Distinction is made between *urbs* = the city surrounded by walls, and *Roma* as a topographical concept: it is the complex of buildings (*continentia aedificia*) regardless of the walls (*muri,* D. 50.16.2 pr.; 87).—See REGIONES URBIS, MURUS, CONTINENTIA, VICARIUS IN URBE, VICARIUS URBIS.

Urbs Constantinopolitana. See CONSTANTINOPOLITANA URBS.

Urere. To burn.—See CADAVER.

Urgere (urguere). To press, to urge. The term is very rare in the Digest, but frequent in imperial constitutions, particularly in those of Diocletian. It is used in the sense of suing an adversary (debtor) in court in order to obtain satisfaction.

Urseius Ferox. A jurist of the late first century after Christ. He is primarily known through a commentary by Julian (*Ad Urseium Ferocem,* in four books); the title of Urseius' work itself—apparently of a casuistic nature—is unknown.

Ferrini, *Opere* 2 (1929) 505; Baviera, *Scr giur.* 1 (1909) 99; Guarino, *Salvius Julianus* (1946) 48.

Usitatum (usitatius, usitatissimum) est. It is usual, customary, it is generally held. The adjective is used of both legal customs and common juristic opinions.

Ustrina (ustrinum). A place for burning the dead. The establishment of such places was subject to various restrictions (not within the boundaries of a city). With regard to Rome, according to Augustus' order, they had to be located at least two thousand steps beyond the city.

Usuarius. (Adj.) A thing (*res usuaria*) or a slave (*servus usuarius*) of whom a person other than the owner had the right of USUS.

Usuarius. (Noun.) A person who has the right of USUS on another's thing or slave.

Usucapere (usu capere). To acquire ownership over another's thing through USUCAPIO.—See the following items.

Usucapio. Acquisition of ownership of a thing belonging to another through possession of it (*possessio*) for a period fixed by law. Further requirements of *usucapio* under *ius civile* were (*a*) *bona fides* (good faith), i.e., the possessor's honest belief that he acquired the thing from the owner (while, in fact, he acquired it from a non-owner, *a non domino*), and through a transaction which legally was suitable for the transfer of ownership (while, in fact, it was not, if, e.g., the thing which was a *res mancipi* was conveyed by *traditio*). Good faith was required on the part of the possessor only at the beginning of his possession. If he lost later his good faith by getting knowledge of the true situation, the completion of the *usucapio* was not impaired; (*b*) a just cause (*iusta causa*, also called *iustus titulus*); see PRO in connection with possession. Such a just cause was either an act of liberality (*donatio*) of the owner or an agreement with him (a purchase) which would justify the acquisition of ownership if there were not a defect in the transaction itself (e.g., *traditio* of a *res mancipi* instead of *mancipatio*) or in the person of the transferor (a non-owner). An erroneous belief of the usucaptor that there was a just cause (e.g., a valid sale or donation) did not suffice for *usucapio*. Possession of the usucaptor had to be continuous and uninterrupted. If he lost possession during the period required for *usucapio* (according to the Twelve Tables two years for immovables, one year for other things) the previous time during which he possessed under conditions sufficient for *usucapio* did not count any longer. *Usucapio* was accessible only to Roman citizens and on things on which Quiritary ownership was admissible. Things belonging to the fisc and *res publicae* were excluded from usucaption. For provincial land and the later development, see PRAESCRIPTIO LONGI TEMPORIS. In Justinian's law the term *usucapio* refers only to usucaption of movables for which possession for three years was required. Excluded from *usucapio* were stolen things (*res furtivae*, see LEX ATINIA) and things taken by violence (*res vi possessae*, see LEX IULIA ET TITIA) even when possessed by a person who acquired them *bona fide* from the wrongdoers. —D. 41.3; Inst. 2.6; C. 7.30; 31.—See POSSESSIO, MANCIPATIO, ACTIO AUCTORITATIS, INTERPELLATIO, EXPLERE, ACCESSIO POSSESSIONIS, SUCCESSIO IN POSSESSIONEM, BONA FIDES, MALA FIDES, USURPATIO, ACTIO

PUBLICIANA, PRAESCRIPTIO LONGI TEMPORIS, and the subsequent items.

Cuq, *DS* 5; Bortolucci, *NDI* 12, 2; Zanzucchi, *AG* 72 (1904) 177; see Galgano, *I limiti subbiettivi dell'antica usucapio* (1913); Suman, *RISG* 59 (1917) 225; Bonfante, *Scr. giur.* 2 (1926) 469-758; Collinet, *Mél Fournier* (1929) 71; Voci, *St Ratti* (1934) 367; *idem, SDHI* 15 (1949) 159; *idem, St Carnelutti* 4 (1950) 155; J. Faure, *Iusta causa et bonne foi* (Lausanne, 1936); M. Kaser, *Eigentum und Besitz* (1943) 293; Meyers, *Scr Ferrini* 4 (Univ. Sacro Cuore, Milan, 1949) 203.

Usucapio ex Rutiliana constitutione. If a man bought a *res mancipi* from a woman who acted without the *auctoritas* of her guardian (see TUTELA MULIERUM), he did not acquire ownership, but he could usucapt the thing. The woman could, however, interrupt the *usucapio* if she paid back the buyer the price.—See CONSTITUTIO.

Usucapio libertatis. Refers to landed property encumbered by a predial servitude. The owner of a land on which another had a servitude could free his land from the servitude if through a construction or a definite action he prevented the person entitled from exercising his right and the latter tolerated it for a certain time (two years in classical law, ten or twenty under Justinian law), D. 41.3.4.28.—See NON USUS.

Grosso, *Foro Italiano* 62 (1937) part 4, 266; B. Biondi, *Servitù prediali* (1946) 267.

Usucapio pro derelicto. Usucaption of a thing abandoned by a non-owner and possessed by the usucaptor *pro derelicto* (as if abandoned by the owner).—D. 41.7.—See PRO (in connection with possession).

H. Krüger, *Mnem. Pappulia* (1934) 163; A. Cuénod, *U. p. d.* (Thèse Lausanne, 1943).

Usucapio pro donato. Usucaption of a thing received as a gift from a person who was not the owner of it and possessed by the usucaptor *pro donato* (as if donated by the owner).—D. 41.6; C. 7.27.

Bonfante, *Scr giur.* 2 (1926) 563; Levet, *RHD* 11 (1932) 387, 12 (1933) 1.

Usucapio pro dote. Usucaption of a thing which a husband received among the things constituted as a dowry and which was not owned by the person who constituted the dowry. This *usucapio* starts from the time of the conclusion of the marriage.—D. 41.4; C. 7.28.—See DOS, PRO (in connection with possession).

Bonfante, *Scr giuridici* 2 (1926) 569.

Usucapio pro emptore. Usucaption of a thing by the buyer to whom it was sold and delivered and who, however, did not acquire ownership thereof because of a legal defect in the act of transfer or because the seller was not the owner. The possession of the thing by the buyer is *pro emptore* (as if the purchase were valid).—See D. 41.4; C. 7.26.—See EMPTIO, PRO (in connection with possession).

P. Bonfante, *Scr giuridici* 2 (1926) 575.

Usucapio pro herede. If a person possessed a thing which was a part of an inheritance and of which the heir did not yet obtain possession, he acquired ownership thereof by *usucapio,* called *pro herede* (= as if an heir). For this kind of *usucapio* possession for a year sufficed even for immovables. Knowledge on the part of the usucaptor that the thing belonged to an heir, was not a hindrance since neither *bona fides* nor *iusta causa* were required. The reason for this unfair form of acquisition of ownership on another's thing—it was considered by the jurists *"lucrativa"* (= profitable, gratuitous)—was, according to Gaius (Inst. 2.55), that the ancient Romans wanted inheritances to be accepted by the heir as soon as possible in order that the familiar religious rites (see SACRA FAMILIARIA) be continued soon after the death of a head of a family, and that the creditors be satisfied without delay. Under Hadrian a *senatusconsultum* abolished the *usucapio pro herede.*—D. 41.5; C. 7.29.—See HERES, CAUSA LUCRATIVA.

H. Krüger, *ZSS* 54 (1934) 80; Collinet, *St Riccobono* 4 (1931) 131; Kamps, *Arch. d'histoire du droit oriental* 3 (1948) 264; Biondi, *Istituti fondamentali di dir. ereditario* 2 (1948) 114; Albanese, *AnPal* 20 (1949) 276.

Usucapio pro legato. A *usucapio* based on possession of a thing, bequeathed in a valid testament in the form of a *legatum per vindicationem,* of which, however, the legatee could not acquire ownership because the testator had no ownership of it. The possession of the usucaptor is *pro legato* (as if the legacy were valid).—D. 41.8.—See LEGATUM PER VINDICATIONEM, PRO (in connection with possession).

P. Bonfante, *Scr. giuridici* 2 (1926) 611; Bammate, *RIDA* 1 (1948) 27.

Usucapio pro soluto. Usucaption of a thing which one received from his debtor in repayment of a debt and of which the creditor did not acquire ownership because of a legal defect in the transfer of the thing to him.

P. Bonfante, *Scr giuridici* 2 (1926) 555.

Usucapio pro suo. *Usucapio* of a thing which one possessed "as his own" on the ground of any just cause. The term *pro suo* is a general one and was applied whenever there was not a specific title indicated by an appropriate term (see the foregoing items).—D. 41.10.

P. Bonfante, *Scr giur.* 2 (1926) 631; Albertario, *Studi* 2 (1941) 185; H. H. Pflüger, *Erwerb des Eigentums* (1937) 42.

Usucapio servitutis. The acquisition of a servitude (see SERVITUS) through the exercise (*usus*) of the rights connected with it for a certain period of time. *Usucapio servitutis* was admitted in earlier law probably only with regard to rustic servitudes, namely *iter, actus, via,* and *aquaeductus;* it was later forbidden by the LEX SCRIBONIA.

Ascoli, *AG* 38 (1887) 51, 198; B. Biondi, *Le servitù prediali* (1946) 233.

Usucapionem rescindere. See ACTIO RESCISSORIA.

Usufructuarius. See USUSFRUCTUS.

Usurae. Interest generally paid periodically in money (or in fungibles) by the debtor to the creditor as long as the principal (*sors, caput*) was not repaid. *Usurae* are regarded to be proceeds (see FRUCTUS) of the capital. Interest was due when agreed upon by the parties (normally through *stipulatio*), a simple informal pact (*usurae ex pacto*) did not suffice, but could be taken into consideration in trials governed by good faith (see IUDICIA BONAE FIDEI). An agreement was superfluous when the obligation to pay interest was imposed by the law (USURAE LEGITIMAE). Interest paid in an amount higher than permitted by law or though prohibited by law (see LEX GENUCIA) could be claimed back by the debtor who had paid them, through CONDICTIO OB INIUSTAM CAUSAM (see LEX MARCIA).—D. 22.1; C. 4.32.—See FENUS, FENUS NAUTICUM, FENUS UNCIARIUM, MUTUUM, INTERUSURIUM, VERSURA.

Cuq, *DS* 5; De Villa, *NDI* 7, 51; Butera, *NDI* 12, 2, 801; Heichelheim, *OCD* 455; G. Billeter, *Gesch. des Zinsfusses im Altertum* (1898); Garofalo, *AG* 66 (1901) 157; V. A. Cottino, *Usura* (1908); Rotondi, *Scr* 3 (1922 ex 1911) 389; G. Cassimatis, *Les intérêts dans la législation de Justinien* (1931); De Villa, *Usurae ex pacto* (1937).

Usurae centesimae. Monthly interest of one-hundredth of the sum due, i.e., twelve per cent per annum. The Romans counted interest by a fraction of the principal and monthly. *Usurae dimidiae centesimae* = six per cent per annum (syn. *usurae semisses*).

Usurae ex mora (usurae morae). Interest to be paid by the debtor on account of his default. In contracts based on good faith (*contractus bonae fidei*) interest for default could be claimed by the creditor. The judge decided upon it in the judgment about the principal debt. *Usurae ex mora* were due under the law in case of default in fulfillment of a *fideicommissum,* but not when a *legatum* under *ius civile* was concerned. Justinian abolished the distinction.—C. 6.47.—See MORA DEBITORIS.

G. Billeter, *Gesch. des Zinsfusses* (1898) 284; E. Balogh, *Zur Frage der Verzugszinsen,* in *Acta Academiae universalis iurisprud. comparatae* 1 (1928).

Usurae ex pacto. Interest promised by a simple pact. Generally such *usurae* were not enforceable. "If interest was agreed upon by a mere pact (*pactum nudum*), the pact is invalid" (Paul. *Sent.* 2.14.1). If the interest agreement was connected with a contract governed by good faith (*contractus bonae fidei*) the judge could take into consideration the question of interest and condemn the defendant to pay it according to the agreement, especially if such payment was customary. In certain specific cases, as in loans given by cities, in loans of fungibles other than money (in later classical law), or in loans made with bankers (under Justinian), a pact concerning interest was considered valid.

De Villa, *Le u. ex pacto,* 1937.

Usurae fiscales. The fisc could claim interest from his debtors (e.g., from tax farmers) who failed to pay in due time. The fisc, however, did not pay interest at all except when it inherited a debt from which interest was due.—C. 10.8.—See FISCUS.

Usurae legitimae. The rate of interest which was imposed or fixed by law. In the late Republic the highest admissible rate was twelve per cent (USURAE CENTESIMAE). Higher interest was granted in a FENUS NAUTICUM until Justinian limited it to twelve per cent. Under his law the normal rate was six per cent (C. 4.32.26.2); merchants could demand eight per cent, persons of higher social rank (*personae illustres*) only four per cent.—See LEGITIMUS.

G. Billeter, *Gesch. des Zinsfusses* (1898) 267.

Usurae maritimae. See FENUS NAUTICUM.

Usurae morae. See USURAE EX MORA.

Usurae pupillares. Interest which a guardian was liable to pay to his ward if he negligently failed to place the ward's money at interest, if he lent it to insolvent debtors, or used it for his own profit (D. 26.7.7.10).—C. 5.56.—See TUTELA IMPUBERUM.

Usurae quae in obligatione consistunt. Interest which was promised in a separate *stipulatio* and was enforceable independently from the principal obligation. Ant. *usurae, quae officio iudicis praestantur,* actionable only together with the principal obligation and as far as the latter was enforceable, but the decision as to whether they are due or not, and to what extent, lay with the judge (*officium iudicis*). To the latter category belonged USURAE EX MORA; interest to be paid by a manager of another's property (a guardian, a mandatary) when he used money entrusted to him for his own profit or when, through negligence, he failed to place the administered funds at interest; interest due to minors, to the fisc or to charitable institutions.

Usurae quae officio iudicis praestantur. See the foregoing item.

C. Fadda, *St e questioni di diritto,* 1 (1910) 229.

Usurae quincunces. Five-twelfths of USURAE CENTESIMAE, i.e., five per cent per annum.

Usurae rei iudicatae. Justinian ordered that a debtor who did not pay a judgment debt within four months after the judgment was rendered or confirmed on appeal, had to pay twelve per cent interest from the judgment sum.—C. 7.54.

P. De Francisci, *Saggi romanistici,* 1913, 61.

Usurae semisses. See USURAE CENTESIMAE.

Usurae ultra duplum. Interest exceeding the principal. Syn. *usurae ultra alterum tantum.* The accumulation of interest due and not paid could not exceed the amount of the debt; a debtor never had to pay in overdue interest more than the amount of the debt. Justinian extended the rule to interest already paid, to wit, no interest could be demanded by the creditor once the interest paid equaled the sum due.

Usurae usurarum. Compound interest.—See ANATOCISMUS.

Usurarius. (Adj.) A debtor who had to pay interest on the sum he owed. *Usuraria pecunia* = money lent at interest.

Usureceptio. Regaining ownership through USUCAPIO (*usu recipere*) of a thing of which one was previously the owner, as, e.g., if one had transferred the ownership of a thing legally (through *mancipatio* or *in iure cessio*) to another (a relative or a friend) to look after it as a trustee (*fiduciae causa*) and later regained possession of the thing without the ownership being retransferred to him. A *usureceptio* also took place when a thing was given to the creditor as a pledge in the form of FIDUCIA (i.e., ownership thereof was transferred to him) and later, after the debt was paid, possession of the thing (but not ownership) was returned to the debtor, its former owner (Gaius, Inst. 2.59–61). The *usureceptio* disappeared when *fiducia* as a form of pledge and the transfer of ownership as a trust (*fiduciae causa*) went out of use. There is no mention of *usureceptio* in Justinian's legislation.

Manigk, *RE* 6, 2305; Cuq, *DS* 5, 607; Grosso, *RISG* 4 (1929) 260; Bortolucci, *NDI* 12, 2; W. Erbe, *Fiduzia* (1940) 64; Levy, *St Albertario* 2 (1950) 221.

Usureceptio ex praediatura. *Usucapio* of a thing by its former owner who had given it to the fisc as a pledge. If the latter sold it afterwards at auction and the former owner regained possession, no matter how, he could acquire ownership through *usucapio* (Gaius, Inst. 2.61).—See PRAEDIATOR.

Bortolucci, *NDI* 12, 2, 806; Cuq, *DS* 5, 607.

Usurpare. To usurp, to take unlawfully (physical power over a thing). In a quite different meaning (= to interrupt) the term is used with regard to USUS (a form of acquisition of marital power, *manus* over the wife) as a result of the so-called TRINOCTIUM (*abesse a viro usurpandi causa* = to leave the husband in order to interrupt sc. the *usus*, Gellius, *Noct. Att.* 3.2.12–13). Similarly *usurpare* is used of the interruption of USUCAPIO.—See USURPATIO (USUCAPIONIS).

Lévy-Bruhl, *Revue de philologie* 62 (1936).

Usurpatio (usucapionis). An interruption of an *usucapio.* It occurred when the usucaptor lost possession of the thing to be usucapted.—D. 41.3.—See USUCAPIO, INTERPELLATIO.

Cuq, *DS* 5.

Usus. (From *uti.*) In a general sense, the act of using a thing. See FURTUM USUS, RES QUAE USU CONSUMUNTUR. *In usu esse* = to be used by an individual or by all (*in usu publico*). The locution *in usu* is applied to legal institutions that are in general use (e.g., a testament), primarily those connected with civil procedure (*actiones, legis actiones, exceptiones*). In a more specific sense *usus* and the locution *in usu esse* refer to customs and customary rules in legal relations. *Usu receptum est* is said of a rule which has been established by custom.—See CONSUETUDO, IUS SCRIPTUM, LONGAEVUS USUS, USUS LOCI.

Usus. As a personal servitude, the right to use (*ius utendi*) another's property, without a right to the produce (*fructus*) of the thing (contrary to usufruct). *Usus* was strictly personal. When it was granted for dwelling in another's house, the beneficiary (*usuarius*) could reside therein together with his family, household, slaves and guests, but he could not leave the house and let it as a whole to others. Normally *usus* was left as a legacy. If no other use of the thing was possible than by taking the fruits (e.g., a vegetable garden or an orchard), the *usuarius* could use the fruits for himself and his household but not sell them to others.—See OPERAE ANIMALIUM.—Inst. 2.5; D. 7.4; 6; 8; 33.2.

Cuq, *DS* 5, 611; Ricci, *NDI* 1, 36 (*s.v. abitazione e uso*); Riccobono, *St Scialoja* 1 (1905) 579; Pampaloni, *RISG* 49 (1911) Ch. III e V; Meylan, *St Albertoni* 1 (1935) 95; G. Grosso, *Uso, abitazione* (*Corso*, 1939) 139; *idem*, *SDHI* 5 (1939) 139; Solazzi, *SDHI* 7 (1941) 373; Villers, *RHD* 28 (1950) 538; Lauria, *St Arangio-Ruiz* 4 (1953) 225.

Usus. In the law of marriage, a formless acquisition of marital power (*manus*) over the wife through an uninterrupted cohabitation of a man and a woman for one year with the intention of living as husband and wife (*affectio maritalis*). However, a deliberate absence of the woman from the common household for three consecutive nights produced the interruption of the *usus* which was considered as a kind of *usucapio* of the *manus*. The marriage based on living together as husband and wife remained valid but without the husband's power over the wife (*sine manu*) if the latter repeated the practice of three-night absence every year.—See TRINOCTIUM.

Kunkel, *RE* 14, 2261; C. W. Westrup, *Quelques observations sur les origines du mariage par usus*, 1926; E. Volterra, *La conception du mariage* (Padova, 1940) 5; H. Lévy-Bruhl, *Nouvelles Études* (1947) 64; Köstler, *ZSS* 65 (1947) 50; Villers, *RHD* 28 (1950) 538; M. Kaser, *Das altröm. Ius* (1949) 316; *idem*, *Iura* 1 (1950) 70.

Usus auctoritas. According to Cicero (Top. 4.23) the expression was used in the Twelve Tables in reference to the earliest USUCAPIO. The exact meaning of the term is not quite clear. *Usus* seemingly alludes to the uninterrupted possession (use) and physical control over the thing which was to be acquired by *usucapio*.—See ACTIO AUCTORITATIS.

Leifer, *ZSS* 57 (1937) 124; M. Kaser, *Eigentum und Besitz* (1943) 86; F. De Visscher, *Nouvelles Études* (1949) 179; P. Noailles, *Du droit sacré au droit civil* (1950) 256; Kaser, *ZSS* 68 (1951) 155.

Usus iudiciorum. See CONSUETUDO FORI.

Usus iumenti, ovium, pecoris. See OPERAE SERVORUM.

Usus iuris. The exercise of a right, e.g., of a servitude.—See POSSESSIO IURIS, USUCAPIO SERVITUTIS.

Usus loci. A local custom, see USUS.

Usus longaevus. See LONGAEVUS USUS.

Ususfructus. The right to use (*uti, ius utendi*) another's property and to take produce (*fructus*) therefrom (*ius fruendi*), without impairing (i.e., destroying, diminishing, or deteriorating) its substance (*salva*

rerum substantia, D. 7.1.1). The usufruct is reckoned by Justinian among personal servitudes (see SERVITUS). As a strictly personal right the *ususfructus* is neither transferable nor alienable. A transfer of a *ususfructus* through IN IURE CESSIO was possible only from the beneficiary of the *ususfructus* (*usufructuarius, fructuarius*) to the owner of the thing. A usufruct was usually constituted in the last will of the owner through a legacy, but it could arise from a transaction between the owner and the usufructuary through *in iure cessio* and, later, under praetorian law, by formal or formless agreement; see PACTIONES ET STIPULATIONES. A *ususfructus* was extinguished by the death or by *capitis deminutio, maxima* or *media,* of the usufructuary. Perishable things and those used by consumption (see RES QUAE USU CONSUMUNTUR) could not be the object of *ususfructus*; see, however, QUASI USUSFRUCTUS. *Ususfructus* is characterized by the jurists as a part of ownership (*pars dominii*), since practically it comprised all the benefits connected with ownership. The owner retained mere ownership (*nuda proprietas*) and he might dispose of the thing without violating the rights of the *fructuarius*. The limitation *salva rerum substantia* imposed certain duties on the usufructuary: he could not change the economic function or destiny of the property, construct a building thereon, or encumber the property with a servitude or acquire one on behalf of it. But his *ius fruendi* was extended to all kinds of proceeds (see FRUCTUS), hence he could let the property or a part of it to another person.—Inst. 2.4; D. 7.1; 2; 4–6; 9; 33.2; C. 3.33.—See CAUTIO USUFRUCTUARIA, DEDUCTIO USUSFRUCTUS, FRUCTUARIUS, SILVA, INTERDICTUM QUAM HEREDITATEM, MUTATIO REI, VENATIO.

Beauchet and Collinet, *DS* 5; De Dominicis, *NDI* 12, 2; Pampaloni, *BIDR* 22 (1910) 109; *idem*, *RISG* 49 (1911) ch. IV–VI; Albertario, *BIDR* 25 (1912) 5 (= *Studi* 2, 1941, 309); W. W. Buckland, *LQR* 43 (1927) 326; De Francisci, *St Ascoli* (1931) 55; P. E. Cavin, *L'extinction de l'usufruit rei mutatione* (Lausanne, 1933); P. Frezza, *Appunti esegetici in tema di modi pretorii di costituzione dell'usufrutto*, *StCagl* 22 (1935) 92; Masson, *RHD* 13 (1934) 1, 161; Meylan, *St Albertoni* 1 (1933) 122; Bohacek, *BIDR* 44 (1936–37) 19; G. Grosso, *L'usufrutto* (*Corso*, 1938); *idem*, 5 (1939) 483, 9 (1943) 157; Kaser, *Fschr Koschaker* 1 (1939) 458; R. F. Vaucher, *Usufruit et pars dominii* (Thèse Lausanne, 1940); P. Ramelet, *L'acquisition des fruits par l'usufruitier* (Thèse Lausanne, 1945); Kagan, *CambLJ* 9 (1946) 159; *idem*, *TulLR* 22 (1947) 94; Riccobono, *BIDR* 49–50 (1948) 33; Sanfilippo, *ibid.* 58; Kaser, *ZSS* 65 (1947) 363; Solazzi, *SDHI* 6 (1940) 162; *idem*, *La tutela delle servitù prediali* (1949) 93; *idem*, *SDHI* 16 (1950) 277; 18 (1952) 229; Ambrosino, *ibid.* 183; Albanese, *AnPal* 21 (1951) 21; Levy, *West Roman vulgar law*, 1951, *passim*; Reggi, *AG* 142 (1952) 229; Biondi, *St Arangio-Ruiz* 2 (1952) 86.

Ut. (Conj.) When followed by an indicative or an accusative with an infinitive in lieu of a subjunctive, this occurs in interpolated phrases. But as a criterion of an interpolation it is not fully reliable because in corrupt texts the erroneous construction may have originated from a copyist's error or negligence. It can hardly be assumed that the compilers did not know that *ut* had to be followed by a subjunctive.

Guarneri-Citati, *Indice²* (1927) 80 and *Fschr Koschaker* 1 (1939) 155.

Ut puta. See UTPUTA.

Uterini. Brothers (*uterinus frater*) and sisters (*uterina soror*) born of the same mother.—See FRATER.

Uterus. *In utero* = in the womb. Syn. *venter.*—See NASCITURUS.

Usani, *Bollettino di filol. classica* 16 (1910) 85.

Uti. To use.—See USUS, USUSFRUCTUS.

Uti. Technical term for the use of procedural remedies (e.g., *uti actione, interdicto, formula, exceptione, defensione*) or of benefits granted by specific laws (e.g., *uti lega Falcidia* = to claim the *quarta Falcidia* according to LEX FALCIDIA).—See UTIMUR HOC IURE.

Uti frui habere possidere. To use, to take proceeds, to hold, to possess. The four words (sometimes with omissions) are used in leases of public land and in treaties with autonomous cities (*civitates liberae*) to indicate the most important functions of ownership of landed property which are granted to a lessee to be exercised by him without the right of ownership.

Kaser, *ZSS* 62 (1942) 22.

Uti optimus maximus. See OPTIMUS MAXIMUS.

Uti possidetis. See INTERDICTUM UTI POSSIDETIS.

Uti rogas. (Abbreviation U.R.) See A.

Uti iure suo. To make use of (to exercise) one's right. Several legal rules empower a person to make use of his right regardless of whether or not another person suffers a loss thereby. "No one is considered to act fraudulently (*dolo facere*), to commit a wrong (*damnum facere*), or to use violence (*vim facere*) who avails himself of his right (*qui iure suo utitur*)" (D. 50.17.55 and 155.1).—See AEMULATIO, NEMO DAMNUM FACIT, NEMO VIDETUR DOLO, etc.

Riccobono, *BIDR* 46 (1939) 3.

Utilis. Used of legal acts, transactions, and procedural steps which have been, or can be, successfully accomplished in a given situation. In a technical sense the adjective is used in the following connections: ANNUS UTILIS, DIES UTILES, TEMPUS UTILE, IMPENSAE UTILES, ACTIONES UTILES, INTERDICTA UTILIA.—See UTILITER.

Seckel, in Heumann's *Handlexikon⁹* (1907) 608.

Utilis (utile, utilia) publice. In the public interest. Syn. *utilis in commune* (= in the interest of the community), *publice interest.* Ant. *privatim utilis* in the interest of private persons.—See UTILITAS PUBLICA, INTEREST ALICUIUS.

Utilitas. With regard to an individual, his interest, benefit (see INTEREST ALICUIUS). *Utilitas privatorum* = the interest of private persons. Ant. *utilitas publica (communis)*. Some legal rules are qualified as having been established *utilitatis causa* (*propter utilitatem*), i.e., either for public utility (welfare), or on behalf of certain categories of individuals (such as minors, lunatics, absent persons) or for general expediency and suitableness for practical purposes. "When new rules are introduced, their utility must be evident as to whether a law which has been considered just for a long time is to be changed" (D. 1.4.2).

Orestano, *AnMac* 11 (1937) 56; Biondi, *Scr Ferrini* (Univ. Pavia, 1946) 219.

Utilitas communis. See UTILITAS PUBLICA. "It can be proved by innumerable instances that many rules have been introduced by the *ius civile* in the public interest against the principles of reasoning" (D. 9.2.51.2).

Utilitas contrahentium. The benefit of the contracting parties.—See CULPA.

Utilitas publica. The welfare (interest) of the state. "Consideration of the public interest is preferable to the convenience of private individuals (*commodis privatorum*)," Paul, *Sent.* 2.19.2. "Public welfare is to be preferred to private agreements (*privatorum contractibus*)," Diocl., C. 12.62.3.—*Utilitates publicae* (in the later Empire) = public services (contributions in money or labor, so-called liturgies) rendered by the citizens or certain groups of them for the benefit of the state or municipalities.—C. 1.22.—See MUNERA.

F. M. De Robertis, *L'espropriazione per pubblica utilità*, 1936; v. Premerstein, *Vom Wesen und Werden des Prinzipats* (1937) 194; Steinwenter, *Fschr Koschaker* 1 (1939) 84; v. Lübtow, *ZSS* 66 (1948) 486; Berger, *Iura* 1 (1950) 110; Gaudemet, *RHD* 29 (1951) 466; Levy, *West Roman vulgar law*, 1951, 100.

Utiliter. See UTILIS. *Utiliter agere* = either to sue successfully (syn. *utiliter experiri, petere, intendere*) or to sue with an *actio utilis*; see ACTIONES UTILES, INTERDICTA UTILIA. *Utiliter* in connection with other verbs, indicates the validity of an act performed or to be performed (e.g., *utiliter testari, instituere heredem, dare legata, legare, relinquere fideicommissum,* all in the law of succession; *utiliter obligari, gerere negotium, stipulari,* in the law of obligations).

Utimur hoc (eo) iure. This is the law we apply. It is a typical phrase in juristic writings indicating a legal rule which is generally observed. Ant. *alio iure utimur*. The locution is frequent in Gaius' Institutes. At times the compilers of the Digest applied the phrase, which they learned from the classical jurists, especially when they wished to shorten the discussion in a classical text. By no means, however, can the phrase be considered a criterion of an interpolation.

Guarneri-Citati, *Indice²* (1927) 51, *s.v. ius*; Berger, *KrVj* 14 (1912) 440.

Utputa (ut puta). As, for instance; suppose that; as in the case. The adverbial phrase was used by both classical jurists and Justinian's compilers to introduce illustrative material.

Guarneri-Citati. *Indice²* (1927) 72 (*s.v. puta*, Bibl.).

Utraque Roma. See ROMA.

Utrubi. See INTERDICTUM UTRUBI.

Uxor. A wife, a married woman. Strictly speaking *uxor* refers only to a woman married to a Roman citizen. The term is also used, however, with reference to a Latin or to a wife living with a husband in a marriage without CONUBIUM (*uxor iniusta*, as opposed to an *uxor iusta*, i.e., a woman living with a husband in a MATRIMONIUM IUSTUM). Even a female slave living with a slave in a marriage-like union (see CONTUBERNIUM) is occasionally called *uxor*. *Uxorem ducere* = to marry a woman.—C. 4.12.—See MATER FAMILIAS, MATRONA, MARITUS, BONORUM POSSESSIO INTESTATI (for the right of a wife to the intestate succession of her husband, *unde vir et uxor*), INTERDICTUM DE LIBERIS EXHIBENDIS.

V

Vacans possessio. See VACUA POSSESSIO.

Vacantes. With reference to public officials in the later Empire, see HONORARII.

> Kübler, *RE* 7A.

Vacantia (vacua) bona. See BONA VACANTIA.

Vacare. To be accessible to all. See RES COMMUNES OMNIUM. *Vacare a(muneribus)* = to be exempt from (certain charges or duties); see VACATIO.

Vacarius. A professor at the law school of Bologna in the twelfth century, founder of the school of law at Oxford, author of summaries of Justinian's Institutes and Digest.

> F. Liebermann, *Engl. Historical Rev.* 11 (1896) 305; F. De Zulueta, *The liber pauperum of V.* (1927); Ferrari, *RStDIt* 3 (1930) 468; P. Koschaker, *Europa und das röm. Recht* (1947) 74; Ambrosino, *RISG* 57 (1950) 414.

Vacatio. The period of time granted a widow or a divorced woman to remain unmarried after the husband's death or the divorce, according to the *Lex Iulia et Papia Poppaea* (two years or one year and a half, respectively).—See SECUNDAE NUPTIAE, UNIVIRA.

Vacatio. Exemption from public charges, services, or taxes, exemption from the duty to assume a guardianship.—C. 10.45.—See VACATIO MUNERUM, EXCUSATIONES A TUTELA.

> Lammert, *RE* 7A.

Vacatio a forensibus negotiis. See FERIAE.

Vacatio bonorum. See BONA VACANTIA.

Vacatio militiae. See IMMUNIS.

Vacatio munerum (a muneribus). Exemption from compulsory public services and charges (see MUNERA). It expired when the reason therefor (sickness, old age, absence in the interest of the state) disappeared.—D. 50.5; C. 10.46.

> Kübler, *RE* 16, 648.

Vacatio tutelae (a tutela). See EXCUSATIONES A TUTELA.

Vacillare. To hesitate, to be unsteady in bearing testimony. A witness who is unsettled in his testimony does not deserve belief and "should not be heard" (D. 22.5.2).

Vacua pecunia. Money not placed at interest.—See USURAE.

Vacua possessio. Free and unimpeded possession of an immovable, which the buyer might enter without being disturbed by the seller or by a third person. Delivery of such possession (*vacuam possessionem tradere*) by putting the immovable under the purchaser's control was the primary duty of the seller. With reference to the buyer, the sources speak of *in vacuam possessionem ire* (or *intrare* = to enter).—See EMPTIO VENDITIO, TRADITIO.

> V. Scialoja, *Scr giur.* 2 (1934, ex 1907) 247; Seckel and Levy, *ZSS* 47 (1927) 226; M. Bussmann, *L'obligation de délivrance du vendeur* (Lausanne, 1933) 98; J. De Malafosse, *L'interdit momentariae possessionis* (Thèse Toulouse, 1949) 90.

Vacuus. Syn. VACANS.

Vades. See VAS.

Vadimonium. A promise in the form of a *stipulatio* made by a defendant in a trial already under way, or by a debtor summoned by his creditor, concerning due appearance in court. In the case of summons by the plaintiff (see IN IUS VOCATIO) to go with him immediately to court, when the defendant was not able or willing to do so and did not offer a personal surety (see VINDEX), the *vadimonium* took place extrajudicially. The *vadimonium*-promise was made in court if the proceedings before the magistrate were not concluded on the first day and the defendant had to guarantee his reappearance on another day. In certain cases the *vadimonium* was a *vadimonium purum* (i.e., without security), in others it was strengthened by an oath or a real security. The *vadimonium* could not exceed half the value of the object in dispute, and in no case one hundred thousand sesterces. If the defendant failed to appear, the plaintiff could sue him for payment of the *vadimonium* on the ground of his stipulatory promise, unless the defendant could justify his absence. The changes in civil procedure in the later law rendered the *vadimonium* obsolete. It does not appear in Justinian's legislative work, where it was replaced by the *cautio (satisdatio) iudicio sisti*.—See VAS and the following items.

> Steinwenter, *RE* 7A; Fliniaux, *DS* 5; Aru, *NDI* 12, 2; R. Jacquemier, *Le v.* (Thèse Paris, 1900); A. Fliniaux, *Le v.* (Thèse Paris, 1908); Debray, *NRHD* 34 (1910) 521; G. Cicogna, *Vindex e v.*, 1911; Lenel, *Edictum perpetuum*[3] (1927) 80; A. Palermo, *Il procedimento cauzionale* (1942) 17.

Vadimonium desertum. (From *deserere*.) Occurred when the defendant did not appear in court on the date fixed, contrary to his *vadimonium* promise.—See VADIMONIUM.

> Steinwenter, *RE* 7A, 2059; Herzen, *NRHD* 35 (1911) 145.

Vadimonium facere adversario. An extrajudicial declaration ("*vadimonium tibi facio*") made by a creditor to his debtor on the occasion of IN IUS VOCATIO, by which he imposed on the latter, who did not follow him immediately to court, the duty to appear on a certain day and hour *"ante tribunal praetoris urbani"* (= before the tribunal of the urban praetor). The declaration was followed by a *stipulatio* under which the summoned debtor assumed the pertinent obligation.

Arangio-Ruiz, *La parola del passato,* fasc. 8 (1948) 138.

Vadimonium iureiurando. In provincial practice (only in Egypt?) the stipulatory promise of a *vadimonium* was strengthened by an oath.

La Pira, *St Albertoni* 1 (1935) 443.

Vadimonium Romam faciendum. A promise of a *vadimonium* made in a municipal court, before which the plaintiff's claim was brought, to appear on a fixed day before the praetor in Rome in the same matter.

Fliniaux, *DS* 5, 621; Lenel, *Edictum perpetuum*[3] (1927) 55; La Pira, *St Albertoni* 1 (1935) 443.

Vadimonium recuperatoribus suppositis. A promise of a *vadimonium* in which it was stipulated that, in the case of the defendant's non-appearance in court, the matter was to be presented immediately to the tribunal of RECUPERATORES who could condemn him to the sum of the *vadimonium* without delay.

Yvonne Bongert, in *Varia (Publications de l'Institut de droit rom. de l'Univ. de Paris,* 9) 1952, 165.

Vagari. To stroll from place to place. A vagrant slave = ERRO.

Valens. See ABURNIUS.

Valere. With regard to legal transactions and acts, to be legally valid (effective). Syn. *effectum, vires habere (tenere), iure consistere, ratum esse.* Ant. *non valere, nullius esse momenti.* With regard to things *valere* = to have a certain value.

Hellman, *ZSS* 23 (1902) 423.

Valerius Probus. See NOTAE IURIS.

Valerius Severus. (Also mentioned as Severus Valerius.) An unknown jurist of the first century of the Principate. He is cited by Julian and Ulpian.

Kunkel, *Herkunft und soziale Stellung der röm. Juristen,* 1952, 154.

Valetudo. Health. The term is generally used for bad health, physical or mental disease. In specific circumstances sickness was recognized as an excuse for non-appearance in court or for exemption from assuming a guardianship.—See MORBUS.

Validus. Strong, important, legally valid. Ant. *invalidus, nullus, nullius momenti.*—See VALERE.

Vallare. To strengthen the efficiency or validity of a legal transaction or act by a *stipulatio,* or by 'some better means of evidence. The term occurs in the language of the imperial chancery.

Vanus. Legally worthless, useless. For *vanus homo, timor vanus,* see METUS.

Variae causarum figurae. Various types of causes. This general expression includes all sources of obligations (D. 44.7.1 pr.) beyond the typical ones (*consensus, res, verba, litterae*).—See OBLIGATIO.

Variare. See IUS VARIANDI.

Varius Lucullus. An unknown jurist of the first century of the Principate (?), mentioned but once in the Digest.

Kunkel, *Herkunft und soziale Stellung der röm. Juristen,* 1952, 140.

Varro, Marcus Terentius. (Died 27 B.C.) The famous author of *De lingua Latina* (On the Latin Language) and *Res rusticae* (Country-life), cited as the author of a treatise (in fifteen books), *De iure civili,* which is not preserved. Valuable juristic material is to be found in the works just mentioned above.

Dahlmann, *RE* Suppl. 6, 1254; Sanio, *Varroniana in den Schriften röm. Juristen* (1867); Conrat, *ZSS* 30 (1907) 412; Bonfante, *BIDR* 20 (1908) 254; idem, *RendLomb* 42 (1909) 318; Stella-Maranca, *ACSR* 1935, 4 (1938) 45; F. Schulz, *History of R. legal science* (1946) 41, 169; Weiss, *ZSS* 67 (1950) 501.

Varus. See ALFENUS VARUS.

Vas. (Pl. *vades.*) A surety which guaranteed the appearance of the defendant before the magistrate in the earliest law, in the procedure by LEGIS ACTIO. Origin and details are obscure but a connection with VADIMONIUM is beyond any doubt. According to Varro, *de l. Lat.* 6.74, *vas = qui pro altero vadimonium promittebat* (he who promised a *vadimonium* for another). A *vas* could himself offer security through a surety, *subvas. Vades* were also acceptable in criminal matters in the earlier procedure.

Steinwenter, *RE* 7A, 2054 (*s.v. vadimonium*); Fliniaux, *DS* 12, 2, 615; Lenel, *ZSS* 23 (1902) 97; Schlossmann, *ZSS* 26 (1905) 285; E. Levy, *Sponsio, fideiussio* (1906) 26; Mitteis, *Fschr Bekker (Aus röm. und burgerl. Recht,* 1912) 285; De Martino, *SDHI* (1940) 141; L. Maillet, *La théorie de Schuld et Haftung en droit rom.* (1944) 91; M. Kaser, *Das altröm. Ius* (1949) 270.

Vasa. Vessels. In a legacy of wine, the testator's vessels in which the wine was kept were understood to be included.

Vasaria publica. Public archives in which the records concerning the census of the population were preserved (from the fifth century after Christ on).

Vasarium. Allowance of money given to the provincial governor for food, transportation, clothing, domestic establishment, and salary of his staff.—See SALARIUM, CIBARIA.

Vates. See VATICINATOR.

Vaticana fragmenta. See FRAGMENTA VATICANA.

Vaticinatio. Fortune-telling, prophecy; see VATICINATOR, DIVINATIO.

Vaticinator. A fortune-teller, a soothsayer. The profession of a *vaticinator* was reckoned among *artes magicae* which endangered the public order since "through human credulity public morals were corrupted and the minds of the people confused" (Paul, *Sent.* 5.21.1). A *vaticinator* was punished in the later Empire by exile, after castigation, and by death if he prophesied about the health of the emperor or the welfare of the state. The same penalty was inflicted on anyone who asked about such matters.— See MAGIA, MATHEMATICI.

> Bouché-Leclercq, *DS* 2, 317; Pease, *OCD* 292 (*s.v. divination, no. 4*).

Vectigal. The rent paid by the lessee of an *ager publicus.*—See AGER VECTIGALIS, ACTIO VECTIGALIS, IUS VECTIGALE.

Vectigal (vectigalia). A general term denoting all sorts of public revenues, such as rents and periodic payments made by lessees of public land (*ager publicus,* see the foregoing item), pastures, woods, salt mines, lakes, rivers, etc., as well as all kinds of taxes, imposts, and custom duties, collected by tax-farmers (see PUBLICANI), whether they were paid in kind (originally) or in money.—D. 39.4; C. 4.61; 62.— See AURUM VICESIMARIUM, VICESIMA MANUMISSIONUM, VICESIMA HEREDITATIUM, PORTORIUM, CENTESIMA RERUM VENALIUM, FRAUDARE VECTIGAL, CRIMEN FRAUDATI VECTIGALIS, RELIQUATOR VECTIGALIUM, CONDUCTORES VECTIGALIUM.

> Schwahn, *RE* 7A, 25; Cagnat, *DS* 5; Anon., *NDI* 12, 2; Stevenson, *OCD*; Bonelli, *Le imposte indirette in R. antica, StDocSD* 21 (1900) 27, 287; R. Cagnat, *Les impôts indirects chez les Romains,* 1882; Pugliese, *CentCodPav* 1934, 527; Tibiletti, *Ath* 26 (1948) 182.

Vectigal frumentarium. A tax levied in kind (grain) in certain provinces, primarily Egypt in order to supply Rome.

> Rostowzew, *RE* 7, 157.

Vectigal rerum venalium. A sales tax. See CENTESIMA RERUM VENALIUM. Under the later Principate the sales-tax, originally introduced for auctions, became more general (Ulpian, D. 50.16.17.1).—See SILIQUATICUM.

Vectigalis. Connected with, or pertinent to, any kind of VECTIGALIA.—See ACTIO VECTIGALIS.

Vectigalis ager (fundus, vectigale praedium). See AGER VECTIGALIS.

Vector. A ship passenger or an owner of merchandise being shipped.

> Solazzi, *RDNav* 6 (1940) 248.

Vectura. Goods to be transported or the sum paid (or charged) for their transportation. The term is primarily used with regard to transportation by sea. If the ship was lost, restoration of any freight charges paid in advance could be claimed.

Vel. Or, also, even. The conjunction, which frequently occurs in Justinian's constitutions and in doubtless interpolated passages in various combinations and structures (*vel etiam, vel maxime, vel . . . aut . . . , vel . . . sive . . .* , and the like), is nevertheless not a reliable criterion of alterations made by Justinian's compilers on classical texts accepted into the Digest.

> Guarneri-Citati, *Indice²* (1927) 90; De Martino, *ANap* 58 (1937) 292 (on *vel etiam*).

Velamentum. A pretext, an excuse (real or false). *Velamento* under the pretext (syn. *sub praetextu*). The term which occurs only in imperial constitutions, particularly of Diocletian) was used when a person under a true or false excuse tried to rescind the consequences of his former acts (e.g., on the excuse his lawyer's absence or of lack of experience). In all cases the decision was against him.—See EXCUSATIONES.

Velati. See ACCENSI.

Velites. Light armed troops, 1,200 (later 1,500) men in the four earliest legions of the Roman army, recruited from poor citizens. They disappeared about the end of the second century B.C.

> Cagnat, *DS* 5.

Velitis iubeatis. A request addressed to the gathered people by a magistrate, presiding over a popular assembly for approval of a proposed statute ("please, approve and order").—See ROGATIO LEGIS.

Velle (volo). Refers to the wish (will) of a person, to the expression of his will, and more narrowly to the declaration of will by a person who had a right to choose (*eligere, optare,* see ELECTIO, LEGATUM OPTIONIS, OPTIO SERVI) between two or more things. The expression of will was taken into consideration only when it was free from compulsion or fear. "He who obeys his father's or master's command is not held to express his own will" (D. 50.17.4). *"Volo"* (= I wish) was the expression a testator used in his testament when he ordered a manumission, designated a guardian, or bequeathed a legacy (*"dari volo"*).—See VOLUNTAS, NOLLE.

Venaliciarius. A dealer in slaves.

> V. Arangio-Ruiz, *La società* (1950) 141.

Venalicium. See VECTIGAL RERUM VENALIUM.

Venalis (venalicius). Offered for sale at a market or public auction. In another sense = venal, capable of being bought for money (bribed), e.g., *venalis sententia* (a judgment which could be obtained by bribing the judge).

Venatio. Hunting. A hunter acquired ownership of a wild animal (see FERAE), not domesticated by another, even when he killed or caught it on another's property. If the animal was only wounded, it was held to belong to the hunter as long as he had chased it. Justinian decided that only the capture of an animal made it the property of the hunter. Among other controversial questions was whether game was among the proceeds (*fructus*) of the landed property and consequently belonged to the usufructuary or not (see USUSFRUCTUS). The prevailing opinion was in the affirmative, if hunting was the only source of profit of the usufructuary who had no other proceeds from the land. The owner of a land could prohibit hunting on his property, but even then a hunter acquired ownership of an animal he caught or killed. He could, however, be repelled by the owner acting in self-defense. Weapons used for hunting were considered part of the INSTRUMENTUM FUNDI when the chief gain from the land came from hunting.— C. 11.45.—See INGREDI IN FUNDUM ALIENUM, OCCUPATIO.

Kaser, *RE* Suppl. 7, 684 (*s.v. occupatio*); Reinach, *DS* 5; Landucci, *NDI* 2, 588 (*s.v. caccia*); Schirmer, *ZSS* 3 (1882) 23; B. Kayser, *Jagd und Jagdrecht in Rom* (1895); V. Ragusa, *Brevi appunti sulla v.,* 1929; P. Bonfante, *Corso* 2, 2 (1928) 57; Lombardi, *BIDR* 53–54 (1948) 273.

Vendere, venditio. See EMPTIO.—See EXCEPTIO REI VENDITAE ET TRADITAE, LEX VENDITIONIS.

Vendere actionem. To sell a claim against someone to a third person. Syn. *venditio nominis.* Such a transaction was possible either as part of the sale of one's whole property (see BONORUM VENDITIO, VENDITIO HEREDITATIS) or as the cession of a single claim (see CESSIO).—D. 18.4; C. 4.39.

Vendere hereditatem. See EMPTIO HEREDITATIS.— D. 18.4; C. 4.39.

Venditio bonorum. See BONORUM VENDITIO.

Venditio nominis. See VENDERE ACTIONEM.

Venditio sub corona. Sale of a war prisoner into slavery. He was crowned with a chaplet.
Ehrhardt, *RE* Suppl. 7, 96.

Venditio sub hasta. See HASTA, AUCTIO.—Syn. SUBHASTATIO.

Venditio trans Tiberim. See SERVUS, ADDICTUS, TIBERIS.

Venefici. Poisoners. According to the LEX CORNELIA DE SICARIIS ET VENEFICIS (under Sulla's dictatorship) a *veneficus* was "one who killed a man by the hateful means of poison or magic practices, or one who publicly sold poisonous drugs" (Inst. 4.18.5). *Venefici* were also those who prepared or kept poison for killing men.—D. 48.8; C. 9.16.—See VENEFICIUM, VENENUM.

Veneficium. A murder by poison. Capital punishment was inflicted on the poisoner. Persons of lower social status (*humiliores*) were crucified or condemned to fight wild animals.—See VENENUM, VENEFICI.
Lécrivain, *DS* 5.

Venenum. Poison. A poison to be used for criminal purposes, *venenum malum,* was distinguished from *venenum bonum,* a drug which, although poisonous, was used for treatment in certain diseases. *Venenum amatorium* = a love potion. Severe penalties (deportation, forced labor in the mines) were inflicted for giving a woman such a drink to cause an abortion (syn. *poculum, venenum amatorium*), the death penalty if she died.

Venerabilis. Worthy of veneration. In the later Empire the adj. is applied to the emperor and his family, to the senate, and to the Church (also *veneranda Ecclesia*). Similar was the use of *venerari* and *veneratio.*

Venia. In criminal matters, remission of a penalty by way of indulgence and forbearance for particular personal reasons (mental deficiency, error, or juvenile imprudence of the culprit) or because of circumstances which recommended forgiveness. *Venia* was granted by the senate, later by the emperor (see INDULGENTIA PRINCIPIS). *Venia* might also be granted in civil wrongdoings with regard to the liability of the defendant if his act, though of a delictual nature, was excusable for specific reasons.—See RESTITUTIO INDULGENTIA PRINCIPIS.
Gatti, *AG* 115 (1936) 44.

Venia aetatis. A privilege granted by the emperor to a minor whereby he was considered to have attained his majority before the age of twenty-five; the honesty of his life and his sagacity could recommend such a benefit. *Venia aetatis* gave the minor full capacity to conclude legal transactions (except alienation and hypothecation of immovables); in addition, he was freed from curatorship. In the later Empire, *venia aetatis* was granted only to men over twenty and to women over eighteen. *Venia aetatis* is also used as syn. with *beneficium aetatis* = the advantage of being a minor and enjoying protection through *restitutio in integrum.*—C. 2.44.
Berger, *RE* 15, 1888 (*s.v. minores*); R. C. Fischer, *Entwicklung der v. ae.* (1908).

Venire. (From *veneo.*) To be sold, to be offered for sale.—See VENUM DARE.

Venire. For *dies venit,* see CEDERE.

Venire ad aliquem. To come (fall) to a person (by inheritance or legacy). In another sense, the expression means to sue a person in court, to hold one responsible.—*Venire ad aliquid* = to obtain (e.g., possession, inheritance, ownership, freedom).

Venire contra aliquem. To sue a person, to go to court as a plaintiff against another person. *Venire contra (adversus) aliquid* = to act against the law or contrary to an agreement.

Venire ex. To originate from; hence *venientes ex aliquo* = one's descendants.

Venire in aliquid. To be taken into consideration (e.g., in *actionem, iudicium, compromissum, stipulationem, collationem*), to be computed (*in hereditatem* = in an inheritance). The phrase *venit in iudicium* is used of the object of a judicial trial to be considered by the judge.

Venter. The womb. Syn. *uterus. Qui in ventre est* = NASCITURUS.—D. 37.9.—See BONORUM POSSESSIO VENTRIS NOMINE, MISSIO IN POSSESSIONEM VENTRIS NOMINE, INSPICERE VENTREM, SENATUSCONSULTUM PLANCIANUM.

Venuleius Saturninus. A jurist of the second half of the second century after Christ, author of extensive treatises on actions, on interdicts, and on stipulations. Minor works of his deal with the proconsulship and with criminal procedure (*iudicia publica*). No details about his official career are known. He has frequently been identified with two other jurists by the name of Saturninus, Claudius S., and Quintus S.—See SATURNINUS.

> H. Krüger, *GrZ* 41 (1915) 318; W. Kunkel, *Herkunft und soziale Stellung der röm. Juristen*, 1952, 181.

Venum dare (venumdare). *Vendere* (to sell); *venum ire, venire* (from *veneo*) = to be sold privately or at a public auction.

Verba. Words. When referring to an oral declaration of a person, the *verba* are distinguished from either his intention (VOLUNTAS, MENS, ANIMUS, SENSUS) or a written document (see SCRIPTURA). Another distinction is *verba—consensus*, as sources creating a contract: on the one hand contracts concluded through the use of prescribed oral formulae, on the other hand contracts arising from a simple formless consent of the parties.—See CONCEPTA VERBA, CONCEPTIO VERBORUM, ACTIO PRAESCRIPTIS VERBIS, OBLIGATIO VERBORUM, INTERPRETATIO, and the following items.

Verba certa ac (et) sollemnia. Words the use of which is prescribed for the validity of an act concluded (e.g., *stipulatio, acceptilatio, dictio dotis, confarreatio*, appointment of a *cognitor* in a trial, etc.). In the earlier law, the use of words other than the *certa ac sollemnia*, rendered the whole transaction void. Gradually, minor changes became permissible. For the development of the *stipulatio*, the most typical act performed by the use of *certa et sollemnia verba*, see STIPULATIO.—See OBLIGATIO VERBORUM.

Verba facere. In the senate, to make a report, as the presiding magistrate or as the proponent of a law, on the topic submitted to the senate for discussion or vote. The report was followed either by an immediate vote or by an exchange of opinion among the senators upon request of the chairman (*sententias rogare*). Senators who were functioning magistrates could participate in the discussion but could not vote.—See DISCESSIO.

> O'Brien-Moore, *RE* Suppl. 6, 709.

Verba facere ad populum. See CONTIO.

Verba formulae. The text of the procedural FORMULA.—See CONCEPTA VERBA, ACTIO PRAESCRIPTIS VERBIS.

Verba legis (edicti, senatusconsulti). The text of a statute (an edict of a magistrate or a *senatusconsultum*). Sometimes the reference to the *verba legis* is followed by a literal quotation. From the text of a legal enactment is distinguished its spirit, its intention (*ratio, mens, sententia*).

Verberare (verberatio). See CASTIGARE, FUSTIS, FLAGELLUM.

> Lécrivain, *DS* 5.

Verbi gratia. For example. The locution is frequent in Gaius.

Verborum obligatio. See OBLIGATIO VERBORUM.

Verecundia. Respect, reverence for another person (a parent or a patron), conscientiousness, honesty.

> Lécrivain, *NRHD* 14 (1890) 487; Cicogna, *StSen* 54 (1940) 53.

Veredi. See ANGARIA.

Verginia. The tragic story of Verginia, as related by Livy (book 44) and Dionysios of Halicarnassus (11.28–37), is connected with the history of the Twelve Tables (see LEX DUODECIM TABULARUM) and the downfall of the decemvirs (see DECEMVIRI LEGIBUS SCRIBUNDIS). It gives an interesting picture of a *causa liberalis*, a trial over the personal status of a girl Verginia, whom the tyrannical decemvir Appius Claudius (450 B.C.) wanted to have declared a slave in court (*vindicatio in servitutem*). The presentation of the case by the historians touches upon a series of problems connected with the earliest procedure in a CAUSA LIBERALIS, no matter whether the story is true or legendary.

> C. Appleton, *RHD* 24 (1924) 592; M. Nicolau, *Causa liberalis* (Thèse Paris, 1933) 98; P. Noailles, *Ius et Fas* (1949) 187; v. Oven, *TR* 18 (1950) 159.

Veritas. Truth. The search for truth (*veritatem quaerere, exquirere, perquirere, inquirere, requirere, spectare*) is frequently stressed in both criminal and civil trials. For the rule *res iudicata pro veritate accipitur*, see RES IUDICATA. *In veritate esse* = to be real, true. The phrase occurs in discussions about the real value of a thing which is the object of a judicial trial, as opposed to the value (interest) it represents to the plaintiff. Hence, *ex veritate aestimationem facere* = to estimate a thing according to its real value (*vera aestimatio rei*).

Verna. A slave born in the house of his parents' master. Such slaves generally received better treatment.

> Starr, *ClPhilol* 1942, 314.

Versari. To act. The term is used primarily of persons who administer the affairs of others (guardians, curators, *negotiorum gestores*) when their management is incorrect or to the disadvantage of the beneficiaries because of fraud, negligence, or lack of experience on the part of the managers. *Versari* (in passive voice) = to be taken into account, to be examined (e.g., the factual and legal elements of a case by a judge or by a magistrate when he was requested to grant an action or in the course of a *cognitio*). Syn. *verti*.

Versum in rem. (*Sc. patris*, or *domini*.) What turned to the advantage of a father (or master of a slave) from a transaction concluded by a son (*filius familias*) or slave. Under the *actio de in rem verso* (see PECULIUM) the father was liable only to the extent of the enrichment he obtained through the transaction (even when he had given his consent thereto), if the son (or slave) did not fulfill the obligation assumed in the transaction. The term *versio in rem*, used in the literature, is not Roman.—C. 4.26.

> Solazzi, *St Brugi* (1910) 205.

Versura. The conversion of a loan at interest into another loan at a different rate of interest.

G. Billeter, *Gesch. des Zinsfusses* (1898) 138.

Verti. See VERSARI.

Verum est. It is true, it is correct. Through this expression which occurs very frequently in juristic writings, the jurists either underscored indisputable opinions or limited a previous rule by referring it solely to a specific situation: "this holds true only when . . ." (*quod ita demum verum est, si . . .*, or *totiens quotiens* = in any case whenever . . .). The jurists also used a negative formula with *verum est* (*quod non,* or *minime verum est*) to express their disagreement with another opinion. Sometimes an approval expressed in the form of *verum est* may originate from the pen of Justinian's compilers, especially when two divergent opinions are cited. The same is true of the locution *quod verum* (*verius, verissimum*) *est,* when a discussion is closed by such a statement (or *quae sententia vera est*). The decision as to whether such a clause in a specific text is interpolated or not is a very difficult one, since, after all, the jurists must have had and used certain expressions to stress their agreement with another author's opinion.—See VERUS.

Guarneri-Citati, *Indice*[2] (1927) 91 and *St Riccobono* 1 (1936) 719 (*s.v. esse*).

Verus. Real, true, authentic. It is opposed to *falsus* (e.g., *verus tutor, verum testamentum, veri codicilli, verum testimonium*). For *vera rei aestimatio,* see VERITAS. The adjective is also used to indicate the real (not simulated or fictitious) legal quality of a transaction or personal situation (e.g., *verus emptor, debitor, heres, dominus, vera donatio, verum divortium*). *Sententia vera* = a just, correct legal opinion; see VERUM EST.

Vestales virgines. Priestesses (originally five or even fewer, later six) of the goddess Vesta, the symbol of chastity. Their legal situation was similar to that of the *pontifices* and *flamines*. They were not subject to *patria potestas* nor bound by any family ties. Nor were they under TUTELA MULIERUM. They were subject to the jurisdiction of the pontiffs for negligence in the fulfillment of their religious duties; there was no appeal from the judgment of the *pontifices*. For unchastity they were scourged to death. The *Vestales* were selected among girls of six to ten years of age, born of patrician parents whose marriage had been concluded through *confarreatio*. Normally their service lasted thirty years, thereafter they were permitted to leave and to marry.—See LEX PAPIA, LEX VOCONIA.

Hild, *DS* 5; Rose, *OCD*; G. Wissowa, *Religion und Kultus der Römer*[2] (1902) 433; Aron, *NRHD* 28 (1904) 5; Brassloff, *Zeitschr. für vergleichende Rechtswissenschaft* 22 (1909); T. C. Worsfold, *The history of the Vestal Virgins of Rome,* London (1934); Münzer, *Philologus* 92 (1937) 47, 199; Solazzi, *SDHI* 9 (1943) 113.

Vestis collatio (vestis militaris). A tax for military equipment.

Cagnat, *DS* 5, 773.

Vestis forensis. See TOGA.

Vestis militaris. Clothes for soldiers; they were to be furnished by the provincial population (in the Empire) in the same way as food (see ANNONA MILITARIS).—C. 12.39.

Cagnat, *DS* 5; A. W. Persson, *Staat und Manufaktur im röm. Reiche* (Lund, 1923) 97.

Vetare. To forbid, to prohibit. The term is used of legal enactments (statutes, imperial constitutions) which forbade a transaction or act (*lex vetat*), of magistrates who issued a prohibitive order, or of private persons (a principal, a master, a father) who within the framework of their authority forbade persons depending upon them to do something. For the formula *vim fieri veto* (or a simple *veto*), see INTERDICTA PROHIBITORIA, VIM FIERI VETO.—See IUDICARE VETARE.

Veteranum mancipium. See NOVICIUS.

Veteranus. A soldier who completed his years of service and was honorably discharged. According to an enactment of Augustus, a legionnaire was discharged after twenty years of service. The *veterani* were united in an elite detachment which had its own standard, *vexillum*; hence the unit was called *vexillatio veteranorum*. It could be called to service in the event of emergency; see EVOCATI. The veterans enjoyed various privileges among which the most important was exemption from compulsory personal services to the state (*munera*); they were, however, not exempt from charges which were imposed on real property (*munera patrimonii*) and they paid taxes. In penal law certain more humiliating penalties (such as flogging, *castigatio fustibus,* forced labor in mines or public works) were not applicable to veterans. Generally they were not compelled to assume a guardianship or curatorship except when the ward was a child of a soldier or of a veteran. Veterans were permitted to have their own associations, *collegia veteranorum*. Syn. *vetus miles*.—D. 38.12; 49.18; C. 5.65; 12.46.—See PECULIUM CASTRENSE, MISSIO, EMERITUS, EXCUSATIONES A MUNERIBUS.

Mispoulet, *DS* 5; Waltzing, *DE* 2, 350, 368; Schehl, *Das Edict Diocletians über die Immunitäten der Veteranen, Aeg* 13 (1933) 137.

Veterator. See NOVICIUS.

Veteres. The ancestors. With regard to earlier jurists, the term is used of jurists who lived in more or less remote times. In postclassical and Justinian sources the term refers to the classical jurists without distinction as to whether they lived in the Republic or the early or late Principate.—See ANTIQUI.

Vetus consuetudo. See CONSUETUDO. Syn. *veteribus moris fuit* (= the ancients used to).

Vetus ius. Ancient law, the law of past times, an old legal principle. The term may refer to a legal norm which originating in earlier times was still in force or to an earlier legal norm which was amended by later law. *Imitatio veteris iuris* = a new law which followed the pattern of former law.—See IUS ANTIQUUM.

Vetustas. Ancient times in Justinian's constitutions, e.g., *iura vetustatis.* Syn. *antiquitas.* In the language of the jurists *vetustas* is used of situations of very long duration which were considered as legal if there was no evidence to the contrary. The rule that *"vetustas* is considered as a law" (*pro lege habetur,* D. 39.3.2 pr.) was of particular importance in relations between neighbors when the owner of land from time immemorial had certain profits from a neighbor's property (e.g., use of water). In another sense, *vetustas* indicates the bad state of a building (e.g., dilapidation) which required repair because of its "old age." The owner was bound to repair the defects for the benefit of the tenants.

Vetustiores. Ancestors.

Vetustus. Ancient, old. *Vetustum (vetustissimum) ius, vetustae leges* = the ancient law (laws).

Vexare. To molest, to harass (*vexare adversarium litibus* = to harass one's adversary with lawsuits). —See CALUMNIA.

Vexillarius. The soldier who bore the standard or a soldier of a military detachment (see VEXILLATIO).

Vexillatio. (From *vexillum* = a military banner.) A military detachment. The term applies to infantry units, cavalry squadrons, auxiliary troops and marines, even to smaller units to which a special military task was assigned. Sometimes *vexillum* is used in the sense of *vexillatio.* For *vexillatio veteranorum,* see VETERANUS. In the later Empire, military units serving in the imperial palace (*vexillationes palatinae.*

Cagnat, *DS* 5; Liebenam, *RE* 6, 1606; M. Mayer, *Vexillum and vexillarius* (Diss. Strassburg, 1910).

Vi bona rapta. Goods taken away from the owner (or possessor) by force.—See RAPINA.

Via. A rustic servitude (see SERVITUTES PRAEDIORUM RUSTICORUM) which entitled the owner of a land to use a road on his neighbor's land for driving in a carriage or riding on horseback. The *servitus viae* automatically implied the right to walk and pass through (see ITER) as well as to drive draught animals and vehicles (see ACTUS) through the other's property.

Severini, *NDI* 12, 2; Arangio-Ruiz, *St Brugi* (1910) 247; Aru, *StCagl* 24 (1936) 405; Biondi, *St Besta* 1 (1939) 267; Solazzi, *SDHI* 17 (1951) 257.

Viae. Roads. A distinction was made between private and public roads. Private roads (*viae privatae,* called also *agrariae*) were the roads which led through private land. Use could be granted by the owner to private individuals or to groups of neighbors, in an unlimited or limited measure (see VIA, ITER, ACTUS). Public roads (*viae publicae*) were open to the use of the people. They are also called *viae consulares* or

viae praetoriae when their construction was ordered by a consul or praetor. Several Republican statutes dealt with the construction and maintenance of public roads. Construction was in the hands of the higher magistrates and the censors, the administration and supervision was assigned to the *aediles,* later (under the Principate) to special CURATORES VIARUM. In the later Empire, the owners of bordering property were generally bound to maintain the roads running along their property (Cod. Theod. 15.3). Erection of monuments on public roads was prohibited. The use of *viae publicae* by the population was under interdictal protection; see INTERDICTUM DE VIIS PUBLICIS. —D. 43.8; 10; 11.—See QUATTUORVIRI VIIS IN URBE PURGANDIS, DUOVIRI VIIS EXTRA URBEM PURGANDIS.

Chapot, *DS* 5; Voigt, *Röm. System der Wege, BerSächGW* 1872.

Viae consulares, praetoriae. See VIAE.

Viae militares. Roads built for military purposes.

Viae vicinales. Roads which are in, or lead to, villages. They were generally public if they served for traffic to, and from, the village even when maintained by the owners of the adjacent lands.

Viasii vicani. Beneficiaries of public land (AGER PUBLICUS) to whom plots situated alongside a public road were assigned. They were bound to maintain the corresponding sections of the road.

Grenier, *DS* 5, 857.

Viaticum. Travel expenses. A plaintiff who inconsiderately (*temere*) summoned another to court had to reimburse him for the expenses connected with his appearance before the magistrate. Expenses also had to be paid to a partner in a *societas* who made a journey in its interest. A small amount of money which exiled persons were permitted to take with them when going into exile, was also called *viaticum.* Finally, *viaticum* was the travel money given to ambassadors sent on an official mission abroad.

Lécrivain, *DS* 5.

Viatores. Subordinate officials, assigned to the office of a high magistrate or of a plebeian tribune, who carried out orders of their superiors, summoned or arrested persons and brought them to court, transmitted messages to senators or other magistrates, intervened in the convocation of the senate, and the like. They belonged to the lower official personnel (see APPARITORES).—See LEX CORNELIA DE VIGINTI QUAESTORIBUS.

Lengle, *RE* 6A, 2488; Lécrivain, *DS* 5.

Vicanus. An inhabitant of a village (VICUS).—C. 11.57.—See VIASII.

Vicarianus. (Or VICARIUS, adj.) Connected with, or pertinent to, a *vicarius,* the governor of a *dioecesis* (in the later Empire).

Vicarius. One who acts in another's place as his substitute. Syn. *vice agens.*—See VICE.

Vicarius. In public law, the chief of the administration (governor) of a DIOECESIS in the later Empire.

They were purely civil officials also charged with the administration of justice.—C. 1.38.

Lécrivain, *DS* 5; De Villa, *NDI* 12, 2.

Vicarius in urbe (Roma). Following Diocletian's reform of the administration, the *vicarius* residing in Rome was the head of the administration of the southern part of the *dioecesis Italia* (the so-called *suburbicariae regiones* and the islands) except for the district subject to the *praefectus urbi*. Under Constantine he assumed the functions of the former *vicarius praefecturae urbis* and had from that time the title of *vicarius urbis Romae*.

Kornemann, *RE* 5, 731; F. M. De Robertis, *La repressione penale nella circoscrizione dell'urbe* (1937) 43; idem, *Studi di diritto penale rom.* (1943) 43.

Vicarius Italiae. The chief of the administration of the northern part of the *dioecesis Italia* (the districts north of the Apennines) after Diocletian's reform of the administration. His residence was in Milan. —See VICARIUS IN URBE.

Kornemann, *RE* 5, 731.

Vicarius iudex. In the later Empire, a judge (jurisdictional official) acting in the place of the *iudex ordinarius*. Since the latter title was used for provincial governors, the *vicarius* was in fact the substitute of the governor. In the first two centuries of the Principate the title *vicarius* was already being used for officials who substituted for provincial governors in their absence or upon their death.

Vicarius praefecti praetorio. A permanent deputy of the *praefectus praetorio* after Diocletian's reform of administration. One was appointed by the emperor in each *dioecesis* of the Empire.

Lécrivain, *DS* 5, 821; Cuq, *NRHD* 23 (1899) 393.

Vicarius praefecturae urbis. A deputy of the *praefectus urbi*. The office was abolished by Constantine and its functions transferred to the VICARIUS IN URBE.

Ensslin, *Byzantinische Zeitschrift* 36 (1936) 320.

Vicarius servus. See SERVUS VICARIUS.

Vicarius urbis Romae. See VICARIUS IN URBE.

Vice. Added to the title of a high administrative official (e.g., *vice praesidis, legati, proconsulis*) this indicates an official (a *procurator*) in the provinces who temporarily assumed the functions of an absent or dead governor. Syn. *agens vices (partes) praesidis, partibus praesidis fungi. Vice alicuius fungi* = to act in place of another. *Vice alicuius rei* (e.g., *testamenti, legati, pignoris*) = to be considered as being in the place of (a testament, a legacy, a pledge). —See the following items.

Vice (or vices agens) praefecti praetorio. The deputy *praefectus praetorio* appointed (from the time of Diocletian) by the emperor. Appeals from his judicial decisions went directly to the emperor and not to the *praefectus praetorio*.—See VICARIUS PRAEFECTI PRAETORIO.

De Ruggiero, *DE* 1, 354; Cantarelli, *Bull. Comm. Archeol. Comunale di Roma*, 1890, 28; Cuq, *NRHD* 23 (1899) 393; A. Stein, *Hermes* 60 (1925) 97.

Vice sacra. (Acting) in place of the emperor. The *praefecti praetorio* in the *praefecturae* of the Empire and the *praefectus urbi* in Rome (after Diocletian's reform of the administration) were considered as acting *vice sacra*.—See IUDICANS VICE SACRA.

Vicem legis obtinere. See LEGIS VICEM OBTINERE.

Vices (vicem, vice) agens. A deputy official in provincial and military administration.

De Ruggiero, *DE* 1, 353.

Vicesima hereditatium. A five per cent inheritance tax paid by Roman citizens on testamentary and intestate successions worth 200,000(?) sesterces or more. It was introduced by Augustus. Responsibility for collecting the *vicesima hereditatium* was in the hands of special officers, *procuratores hereditatium*.—C. 6.33. —See APERTURA TESTAMENTI, LEX IULIA (?) DE VICESIMA HEREDITATIUM, STATIO VICESIMAE, MISSIO IN POSSESSIONEM EX EDICTIO HADRIANI, EDICTUM HADRIANI.

Cagnat, *DS* 5; Severini, *NDI* 12, 2 (*s.v. vigesima*); De Ruggiero, *DE* 3, 726; Catinell, *StDocSD* 6 (1885) 273, 7 (1886) 33; Bonelli, *ibid.* 21 (1900) 288; E. Guillaud, *Étude sur la v. h.* (Thèse Paris, 1895); Stella-Maranca, *RendLinc* 33 (1924) 263; *Acta Divi Augusti* 1 (Rome, 1945) 219; De Laet, *AntCl* 16 (1947) 29; Gilliam, *AmJPhilol* 73 (1952) 397.

Vicesima libertatis. See VICESIMA MANUMISSIONUM.

Vicesima manumissionum. A manumission tax of five per cent of the slave's value, paid by the master if freedom was granted by him, but paid by the slave if he redeemed himself by his own money; see REDEMPTUS SUIS NUMMIS. Syn. *vicesima libertatis, aurum vicesimarium*.

Lécrivain, *DS* 3, 1220; Humbert, *DS* 1 (*s.v. aurum vicesimarium*); Bonelli, *StDocSD* 21 (1900) 52; Wlassak, *ZSS* 28 (1907) 89; L. Clerici, *Economia e finanza dei Romani* 1 (1943) 505.

Vicinus. A neighbor. In relations between neighbors, owners of land, praedial servitudes were of great importance (see SERVITUTES PRAEDIORUM RUSTICORUM, SERVITUTES PRAEDIORUM URBANORUM) inasmuch as they determined the extent to which one neighbor might use the property of the other. Controversies between neighbors arose for various reasons involving actual or threatened violation of the rights of one by the other.—See CAUTIO DAMNI INFECTI, OPERIS NOVI NUNTIATIO, ACTIO AQUAE PLUVIAE ARCENDAE, PARIES COMMUNIS, TIGNUM IUNCTUM, ACTIO FINIUM REGUNDORUM, CONTROVERSIA DE FINE, IMMISSIO, INTERDICTA.

P. Bonfante, *Scr giuridici* 2 (1926) 783; S. Solazzi, *Requisiti e modi di costituzione delle servitù prediali* (1947) 29.

Vicomagistri. See REGIONES URBIS ROMAE.

Grenier, *DS* 5.

Victor. Used of the successful party in a lawsuit. Syn. *victrix pars*. Similarly, *victoria* may refer to a victory in court.

Victus. Nourishment, all that is necessary for living (*ad victum necessaria, ad vivendum homini necessaria*), hence not only the necessary food, drink, and clothing, but also "anything else which we use for the protection and the care of our body" (D. 50.16.44). This interpretation of the term was important in cases when one was obligated to take care of a person (e.g., a father, a guardian) or to furnish *victus* to another (e.g., as a legacy or under another title).

Vicus. A settlement, a village, a territorial unit, smaller than a *municipium* or an *oppidum,* occupied by a group of families forming a rural community. In larger cities *vicus* indicated a street, a block of buildings.—See PAGUS, REGIONES URBIS ROMAE.

Schulten, *RE* 4, 799; Grenier, *DS* 5; Anon., *NDI* 12, 2; F. De Zulueta, *De patrociniis vicorum* (Oxford, 1909).

Videbimus. We shall examine. The jurists used this word to stress a point to which they wanted to devote particular attention or an important problem that arose from a case under discussion. Similar locutions are *videamus* (= let us see whether), *videndum est* (= it is to be examined).

Videtur (alicui). A favorite term of the jurists to introduce their own ("*mihi videtur*" = it seems to me) or another jurist's (e.g., "*Iuliano videtur*") opinion. In reporting a judge's decision expressions like *videbatur, visum est,* are used.

Vidua. A widow or a woman who has never been married. *Viduitas* = widowhood.—C. 3.14; 6.40; 9.13.—See LUCTUS, SECUNDAE NUPTIAE, TUTELA MULIERUM, RAPTUS.

L. Caes, *Le statut juridique de la sponsalicia largitas échue à la mère veuve, Courtrai,* 1949.

Vigiles. The fire brigade of Rome. Augustus created seven divisions (*cohortes*) of firemen, totaling seven thousand men. Each *cohors* had seven *centuriae* under the command of tribunes. The commander of all the *vigiles* was the PRAEFECTUS VIGILUM. One *cohors* was assigned to two districts of Rome (see REGIONES URBIS ROMAE. The *vigiles* also exercised police functions, chiefly at night time.—D. 1.15; C. 1.45.—See LEX VISELLIA.

Cagnat, *DS* 5; Balsdon, *OCD*; De Magistris, *La militia vigilum nella Roma imperiale* (1898); P. K. Baillie Reynolds, *The v. of imperial Rome* (1926); G. Mancini, *I vigili dell'antica Roma* (1939).

Vigintiviri. See VIGINTISEXVIRI.

Lécrivain, *DS* 5.

Vigintisexviri. A collective term embracing 26 minor magistrates in the Republic with different functions. Among them were: the DECEMVIRI STLITIBUS IUDICANDIS, TRESVIRI CAPITALES, (previously called *tresviri nocturni*), the TRESVIRI MONETALES, the *quattuorviri viis in urbe purgandis*) (four officials who had to keep the streets of Rome clean), the DUOVIRI VIIS EXTRA URBEM PURGANDIS (who had similar duties with regard to the roads around the capital), and the *quattuorviri praefecti Capuam, Cumas* (who acted as representatives of the praetorian jurisdiction in the region of Campania). The latter six magistracies (the *duoviri* and the *quattuorviri praefecti*) were abolished by Augustus, henceforth the remaining twenty magistrates were collectively called *vingintiviri.*

Vilicus (villicus). The administrator of a country estate (*villa*), normally a slave who supervised all the personnel (slaves, see FAMILIA RUSTICA).

Lafaye, *DS* 5.

Villa. A country estate, a country house. *Villa urbana* = the residential part of a country establishment; *villa rustica* = farm buildings, quarters for slaves working in the agricultural part of the estate.—See AGER.

Villicus. See VILICUS.

Vim fieri veto. "I forbid force to be used." The so-called prohibitory interdicts (see INTERDICTA PROHIBITORIA) were provided with this clause by which the praetor forbade the defendant to hinder the plaintiff in the exercise of his right. *Vis* does not mean violence (physical force) here; it indicates any activity of the defendant which might prevent the plaintiff from making use of a right to which he was entitled.

Berger, *RE* 9, 1613.

Vim vi repellere licet. Force may be repelled by force. "All statutes and all laws allow this" (D. 9.2.45.4). The principle admits self-defense by force against an aggressor. A well-known instance was self-defense against a thief (see FUR, FURTUM): the victim could kill a burglar at night, but in the daytime only if the thief defended himself with a weapon (*telum*).—See VINDICATIO.

Aru, *NDI* 12, 2, 1041; idem, *La difesa privata, AnPal* 15 (1936) 128; 381.

Vincire. To fetter.—See VINCTUS, VINCULA.

Vinctus. Fettered. Ant. *solutus* = liberated from fetters.—See VINCULA.

Wenger, *ZSS* 61 (1941) 655.

Vincula. Fetters. Fettering (*vincire*) was applied as a punishment of slaves by their masters. Fettering a free citizen was considered a *crimen plagii* (see PLAGIUM) and punished according to the LEX FABIA. It was permitted, however, as a means of coercion (see COËRCITIO) or as an additional punishment in prison. *Vincula* are mentioned in the Twelve Tables (see LEX DUODECIM TABULARUM) as a coercive measure applied by a creditor against a debtor who did not fulfill a judgment debt. The law permitted shackling the debtor *nervo aut compedibus* (with fetters of iron or wood) but limited their weight to fifteen pounds. —See NEXUM.

Vollgraff, *DS* 5; Wenger, *ZSS* 61 (1941) 655.

Vincula publica. A public prison. Syn. CARCER. Persons suspected of a crime were held in prison until the matter was cleared up. Incarceration was, however, not a punishment for a culprit condemned. Ant. *vincula privata* = fetters applied by private persons, see VINCULA.—See CUSTODIA REORUM.

Vinculum iuris. A legal tie (bond). The expression is used in the definition of OBLIGATIO.

Vinculum pignoris. The tie by which a pledge (*pignus*) is bound on behalf of the creditor. *Vinculum pignoris* is also the right of a ransomer over the prisoner of war whom he redeemed from the enemy; see REDEMPTUS AB HOSTE.

G. Faiveley, *Redemptus ab hoste* (Thèse Paris, 1942) 112.

Vindemia. The vintage season (*tempus vindemiae, vindemiarum*). · It was taken into consideration by the law in the same way as the harvest period (*tempus messis vindemiaeve*). During these seasons jurisdictional activity was exercised only in cases which might be lost to the plaintiff because of lapse of time (*praescriptio*, or *usucapio* on the part of the defendant) or when perishable things were involved. —See ORATIO MARCI on IN IUS VOCATIO.

Vindex. For the *vindex* intervening for a person summoned to court, see IN IUS VOCATIO. The *vindex* guaranteed the appearance of the defendant at a fixed later date. Should the defendant fail to do so, the *vindex* was liable to the plaintiff and could be sued under the formulary procedure by a praetorian *actio in factum*. A *vindex* was acceptable to the magistrate only if he was wealthy enough to guarantee the eventual payment.—A *vindex* (guarantor) was also permissible in the LEGIS ACTIO PER MANUS INIECTIONEM to save the defendant, who had been condemned in a previous trial and did not pay the judgment debt, from being led off to the plaintiff's house and put in fetters. The *vindex* had either to pay the judgment debt of the principal debtor at once or to defend him by denying that the *manus iniectio* was justified. When defeated in the trial, the *vindex* had to pay the plaintiff double. Both kinds of *vindices* disappeared in later law. In Justinian's legislation they were replaced by the *fideiussor iudicio sistendi causa* (*qui aliquem iudicio sisti promiserit* = one who promised to bring another to court).—D. 2.10.—See VADIMONIUM, IUDICATUM, MANUS INIECTIO.

Cuq, *DS* 5; Severini, *NDI* 12, 2; F. Kleineidam, *Die Personalexekution der Zwölf Tafeln* (1904) 146; Lenel, *ZSS* 26 (1905) 232; Schlossmann, *ibid.* 308; G. Cicogna, *V. e vadimonium* (1911); N. Corodeanu, *Sur la fonction du v.* (Bucharest, 1919); Lenel, *Edictum perpetuum*[3] (1927) 65; Düll, *ZSS* 54 (1934) 112; Leifer, *Ztschr. für vergl. Rechtswiss.* 50 (1935) 5; L. Maillet, *La théorie de Schuld et Haftung* (Thèse Aix-en-Provence, 1944) 84; Pugliese, *RIDA* 2 (1949) 251; Kaser, *Das altröm. Ius* (1949) 194; P. Noailles, *Du droit sacré au droit civil* (1950) 143.

Vindex civitatis. ·See DEFENSOR CIVITATIS.

Vindicare (vindicatio). Eventually assumed a general meaning—beyond the domain of REI VINDICATIO —of laying claim to, asserting one's right to.—See the following items.

Juncker, *Gedächtnisschrift für E. Seckel* (1927) 209; Düll, *ZSS* 54 (1934) 98; P. Noailles, *Du droit sacré au droit civil* (1950) 52.

Vindicare necem (mortem). To avenge the assassination of a man by an unknown murderer by prosecuting all the slaves who lived with him in the same household.—See SENATUSCONSULTUM SILANIANUM, QUAESTIO PER TORMENTA, TECTUM.

Vindicatio (vindicare). In earlier times, the act of avenging an offense, self-defense against the violence of an aggressor. Later, the term was applied to the defense of one's property by seeking its recovery in court. Gaius (Inst. 4.5) called all *actiones in rem* (see ACTIONES IN PERSONAM) *vindicationes* and Justinian accepted his terminology (Inst. 4.6.15). See REI VINDICATIO. *Vindicatio* is also. used for the prosecution of certain wrongdoings, such as ADULTERIUM, or *corruptio albi* (see ACTIO DE ALBO CORRUPTO). For other applications of the term, see the following items.—See LEGATUM PER VINDICATIONEM.

Vindicatio coloni (or in colonatum). In the later Empire, the claim of a landowner asserting that a certain person was his COLONUS.

Vindicatio familiae pecuniaeque. The earliest form of HEREDITATIS PETITIO.

Vindicatio filii. The claim of the head of a family for the delivery of his son held by another. Analogous was the *vindicatio* of a wife being under the marital power (*in manu*) of her husband, by the latter since her legal situation was that of a daughter (*filiae loco*).—See INTERDICTUM DE LIBERIS EXHIBENDIS.

Vindicatio gregis. See GREX.

Vindicatio hereditatis. See HEREDITATIS PETITIO, VINDICATIO FAMILIAE PECUNIAEQUE.

Vindicatio in ingenuitatem. See the following item.

Vindicatio in libertatem. An action in favor of a free person held by another as a slave. See ADSERTIO, CAUSA LIBERALIS. A similar case was the *vindicatio in ingenuitatem* whereby one defended the status of another man as free-born; see INGENUITAS. Ant. *vindicatio in servitutem* whereby the claimant asserted that another man was his slave though generally considered free.

Vindicatio in servitutem. See VINDICATIO IN LIBERTATEM, VERGINIA.

Vindicatio pignoris. Often applied to the action of a creditor who claimed the recovery of a pledge from the debtor on the ground that his obligation had been discharged.—See HYPOTHECA, ACTIO QUASI SERVIANA.

Vindicatio servitutis. The action of a person against the owner of land on which the plaintiff claims a servitude. The action is also called *actio confessoria*. On the other hand, the landowner was protected against any one to whom he denied a servitude on his property by an action called *actio negatoria* or *actio negativa*. Similar was the use of an action termed *actio prohibitoria* (its origin is controversial) by which the landowner asserted his right to prevent another from exercising a servitude on his land.

Leonhard, *RE* 4, 871 (*s.v. confessoria actio*); V. Arangio-Ruiz, *Rariora* (1946, ex 1908) 1; G. Segrè, *Mél Girard* 2 (1912) 511; Biondi, *AnMes* 3 (1929) 93; Buckland, *LQR* 46 (1930) 447; Bohácek, *BIDR* 44 (1937) 19, 46 (1939) 142; Solazzi, *Tutela delle servitù prediali* (1949) 1; Albanese, *AnPal* 21 (1950) 24; Grosso, *St Albertario* 1 (1951) 593.

Vindicatio tutelae. The claim for guardianship of a person who was entitled by law to be the guardian (*tutor legitimus*) of a near relative.—See TUTELA LEGITIMA.

Vindicatio ususfructus. Analogous to *vindicatio servitutis* when a usufruct on another's man property is claimed.—See VINDICATIO SERVITUTIS.

G. Grosso, *I problemi dei diritti reali* (1944) 132; Sciascia, *BIDR* 49–50 (1948) 471.

Vindicatio uxoris. See VINDICATIO FILII.

Vindiciae. Possession of a thing which was the object of a judicial trial under the procedure of LEGIS ACTIO SACRAMENTO and which was assigned for possession (*vindicias dicere*) to one of the parties, normally to the actual possessor, by the jurisdictional magistrate. If this party lost the case (VINDICIAE FALSAE), he had to hand over the thing together with double the proceeds he may have received from it in the meantime. In earlier Latin *vindiciae* (or *vindicia*) was the thing itself about which there was a controversy.—See PRAEDES LITIS ET VINDICIARUM, CAUTIO PRO PRAEDE LITIS ET VINDICIARUM.

Cuq, *DS* 5; E. Weiss, *Fschr Peterka* (Prague, 1929) 69.

Vindiciae falsae. Occurred if the party to a trial who received temporary possession of the thing in dispute from the praetor (see VINDICIAE) lost the case under the judgment. According to the Twelve Tables he had to restore to the adversary the thing itself and double the proceeds (*fructus duplio*). The assignment of possession by the praetor to the wrong party was termed *vindicias falsas dicere*.

E. Petot, *Etudes Girard* (1912) 229; Weiss, *Fschr Peterka* (Prague, 1929) 72; Ratti, *St Riccobono* 2 (1936) 421; Levy, *ZSS* 54 (1934) 306; M. Kaser, *Restituere als Prozessgegenstand* (1932) 16; idem, *Eigentum und Besitz* (1943) 72.

Vindicias dicere. See VINDICIAE, VINDICIAE FALSAE.

M. Kaser, *Eigentum und Besitz,* 1943, 76.

Vindicias dicere secundum libertatem. Occurred in a trial over the status of liberty (*status libertatis*) of a person, the praetor ordering that he be considered a free man until the final decision.—See CAUSA LIBERALIS, VINDICATIO IN LIBERTATEM, VINDICATIO IN SERVITUTEM, VERGINIA.

P. Noailles, *Du droit sacré au droit civil* (1950) 192; Van Oven, *TR* 18 (1950) 172.

Vindicta. A rod used for symbolic gestures in the enfranchisement, called MANUMISSIO VINDICTA, and in the LEGIS ACTIO SACRAMENTO *in rem* in which the question of Quiritary ownership of a thing was examined. The controversial object was touched with a rod by the person asserting his ownership. Gaius (Inst. 4.16) identifies *vindicta* with FESTUCA. According to a recent opinion, the term is derived from *vim dicere* (*vis dicta*), indicating the act by which the parties emphasized their power over the thing in dispute.—D. 40.2; C. 7.1.

Cuq, *DS* 5; Beseler, *Hermes* 77 (1942) 79; M. Kaser, *Das altröm. Ius* (1949) 327; P. Noailles, *Ius et Fas* (1948) 46 (= *RHD* 19–20 [1940–41] 1); P. Meylan, *Mél F. Guisan* (Lausanne, 1950) 29.

Vindicta. With regard to criminal offenses, vengeance, retribution, a penalty inflicted in return for an offense, criminal prosecution.

Vindius Verus. A little known jurist of the second century, member of the council of the emperor Antoninus Pius.

Kunkel, *Herkunft und soziale Stellung der röm. Juristen* 1952, 167.

Vinum. For crimes committed by intoxicated person (*per vinum*), see IMPETUS. Drunkenness = *ebrietas temulatio*.

Violatio sepulcri. Violation, desecration, of a grave Different offenses were punished as a *crimen viola sepulcri*, in the first place burglarizing a grave belonging to another or opening one in order to bur a dead body therein. The wrongdoer could be sue for damages by the person who had the IUS SEPULC over the grave under the ACTIO SEPULCRI VIOLA. This was an *actio popularis* so that if the pers interested in the first place did not accuse the culpr any Roman citizen could do so. Penalty for mir infractions was a fine of 100,000 sesterces and infan Major violations, such as taking away a corpse robbery committed with the help of armed acco plices, were punished by death.

Pfaff, *RE* 2A, 1625; Gerner, *RE* 7A, 1742; Lécrivain, 4, 1208; Cuq, *RHD* 11 (1932) 109; E. Wesenberg, *strafrechtliche Schutz der geheiligten Gegenstände* (I Göttingen, 1912) 95; A. Parrot, *Malédiction et viol des tombes* (1939); Arangio-Ruiz, *FIR* 3 (1943) no

Violentia. Violence, use of physical force.—See Niedermeyer, *St Bonfante* 2 (1930) 281.

Vir bonus. An honest, upright man (a Roman zen). In certain contractual relations, particularl those governed by good faith (*bona fides*), the j ment (*arbitrium*) of a third impartial and hc person was decisive whether a party had fulfille obligation or not, e.g., the approval of a work by a contractor or an artisan (*locatio cond operis*). The moral qualifications of a *vir b* were honesty and righteousness.—See BONUS FAMILIAS, ARBITRIUM BONI VIRI.

T. Sinko, *De Romanorum viro bono, Transactions prawy) of the Academy of Sciences in Cracow* 36 251; v. Lübtow, *ZSS* 66 (1948) 520.

Vires. (Pl. of *vis*.) The financial strength (m of a person, an inheritance, or of a separate co of goods (a dowry, a *peculium*).—See FACUL

Virga. A rod, a whip used for flogging.—See CASTI-GARE.

Virgo Vestalis. See VESTALES VIRGINES.

Virilis. Befitting a man (not a woman); see OFFICIUM VIRILE; a share in an intestate inheritance pertaining to one heir and equal to the shares of other heirs = *pars virilis.*—See PORTIO HEREDITARIA.

Viripotens. A marriageable woman.—See IMPUBES.

Viritim. Personally, individually. *Viritim donatus civitate Romana* (in inscriptions) = a foreigner who was personally granted Roman citizenship. *Viritim distribuere* = to divide (e.g., an inheritance) among several persons in equal shares.—See VIRILIS.

Virtus. Bravery, courage. Competition in athletic games was considered a contest in bravery (*certamen in virtute*).—See LEX CORNELIA DE ALEATORIBUS.

Vis. The power one has over a free person (*vis ac potestas*). With reference to legal enactments (*vis legis*), to contractual relations (*vis stipulationis*), or unilateral acts (*vis testamenti*) = validity, effectiveness. Hence *vim* (*vires*) *habere* = to be valid; *vim* (*vires*) *accipere, optinere* = to become legally valid. Ant. *nullas vires habere.*

Vis. Violence, force. The term occurs in both private and penal law, but it is defined differently for the two provinces. Whereas in the first the concept of *vis* is taken in a broader sense and even in different implications, for the penal law it is understood as a major infraction and qualified as *crimen vis* (crime of violence). In the law of obligations, *vis* (the use of physical force or moral compulsion by one person against another) might provoke fear (*metus*) in the latter. Hence the two elements "force and fear" (*vis ac metus*) are mentioned together in discussions of the influence of METUS on legal transactions. The praetorian Edict dealt with *vis* not only in the section concerning duress (*metus*) but also with regard to possession when a person was dispossessed by force. In several provisions the praetor forbade the use of force to disturb existing possessory situations (see VIM FIERI VETO), or he protected public works and institutions against any hindrance ("*ne vis fiat*") which might impair their public use. Such actions were considered as *vis,* no matter whether real force was actually applied or not. See INTERDICTA PRO-HIBITORIA, INTERDICTUM QUOD VI AUT CLAM, INTER-DICTUM DE VI. Thus arose the rule: "All that one has done when he was prohibited (from doing it) is considered to have been done with violence" (D. 50.17.73.2). *Vis* appears among the so-called *vitia possessionis* (legal defects of possession) inasmuch as possession acquired by force was qualified as *pos-sessio vitiosa* (*iniusta*). See EXCEPTIO VITIOSAE POS-SESSIONIS, INTERDICTUM UTI POSSIDETIS, RES VI POS-SESSAE. He who uses force to defend and retain his possession, when illegally attacked by another, is not regarded as possessing by force (*vi*). In the field of penal law, the distinction between *vis pri-vata* and *vis publica* is fundamental: "whatever is done by violence is either a crime of *vis publica* or of *vis privata*" (D. 50.17.152 pr.). The *vis privata,* force used against a private individual in order to commit robbery, was considered a private delict, like theft (*furtum*), and was prosecuted by a penal action (*actio poenalis*) of the person injured, the *actio vi bonorum raptorum*; see RAPINA. The concept of *vis publica,* a crime committed with vio-lence and prosecuted by the state in a criminal trial (*iudicium publicum*), was first established in the LEX PLAUTIA DE VI (78–63 B.C.?) and, later, by the com-prehensive legislation of Augustus, LEX IULIA DE VI PUBLICA and LEX IULIA DE VI PRIVATA. The distinc-tion which was neatly defined in this legislation was later distorted through imperial enactments and in Justinian's compilation. The sources are frequently contradictory in the qualification of certain outrageous acts as *vis publica* or *privata.* The original distinc-tion may have been based on whether the crime vio-lated direct interests of the state (*vis publica*) or those of a private person (*vis privata*). "Many crim-inal offenses are covered by the term of violence" (C. 9.12.6); among the instances of *vis publica* are mentioned acts of violence committed in public with the assistance of armed bands in order to provoke a riot or sedition, disturbing a trial in court, a popular assembly during a vote or election, or the senate, exercising pressure on a judge, appearance in public with arms or armed bands to prepare an attack against temples or city gates, disturbing a funeral, etc. Various kinds of abuses committed by officials and major breaches of official duty were also punished as *vis publica.* Even in certain cases of *vis privata* (more atrocious assaults, the use of arms) public prosecution of the crime was possible in addition to the private penal action of the individual injured. Together with the extension of the instances of *vis publica* more severe punishment was inflicted in the later imperial legislation (deportation combined with confiscation of property became the normal penalty, and from the time of Constantine the death penalty was very frequent).—D. 4.2; 43.16; C. 2.19; 8.4; 5. For *vis publica* Inst. 4.2; D. 47.8; C. 9.33.—See UTI SUO IURE, INTROIRE DOMUM, VIS ARMATA, VI BONA RAPTA, LEX POMPEIA DE VI, TUMULTUM, TURBA, and the following items.

Lécrivain, *DS* 5; Berger, *RE* 9, 1614, 1663, 1677; Nieder-meyer, *St Bonfante* 2 (1930) 400; U. v. Lübtow, *Der Edictstitel quod metus causa* (1932) 101; C. Longo, *BIDR* 42 (1934) 99; Nardi, *SDHI* 2 (1936) 120; Castello, *RISG* 14 (1939) 279; M. David, *Interdit quod vi aut clam* (1947) 25. For *vis publica*: Mommsen, *Röm. Strafrecht,* 1899, 653; J. Coroï, *La violence en droit crim. rom.* (1915); Berger, *Göttingische Gelehrte Anzeigen,* 1917, 344; Costa, *RendBol* 2 (1917/18) 23; Flore, *St Bonfante* 4 (1930) 335; Aru, *AnPal* 15 (1936) 163.

Vis armata. Violence committed with the use of arms (*arma*). By arms are understood not only all kinds of weapons (see TELUM) but also stones and clubs (*fustis*). The term *vis armata* occurs in connection with the dispossession of another from his property. If the aggressor was armed but did not make use of the arms, his assault was nevertheless considered as *vis armata* since his having arms alone produced fear (*terror armorum*) in the person attacked.—D. 43.16. See INTERDICTUM DE VI.

   Berger, *RE* 9, 1680.

Vis atrox. Violence committed in a particularly atrocious manner.—See INIURIA ATROX.

Vis divina. See VIS MAIOR.

Vis ex conventu. Violence under agreement, a simulated violence used by one of the parties to a controversy about possession of an immovable after the pertinent interdict (e.g., *uti possidetis*) was issued. The interdict being only a provisory settlement of the case, it was necessary, in order to bring the controversy to an end, that one of the parties act against the order of the praetor *vim fieri veto* by dispossessing the actual possessor. Instead of using real force, this was accomplished by agreement of the parties through a violenceless, peaceful dispossession which made the post-interdictal procedure possible. See INTERDICTUM SECUNDARIUM. The connection of the *vis ex conventu* (to which only Gaius, Inst. 4.170, alludes, without using the term itself) with an institution mentioned solely by Cicero (*pro Caec.* 7.20; 10.27; 11.32; 32.95; *pro Tullio* 8.20; *vis ex conventu:* Cic. *pro Caec.* 8.22), *deductio quae moribus fit* (putting one out [of possession] according to the customs), is not quite clear.

   Berger, *RE* 9, 1696; Saleilles, *NRHD* 16 (1892) 32; Mitteis, *ZSS* 23 (1902) 298; Chabrun, *NRHD* 32 (1908) 5; Costa, *Cicerone giureconsulto*[2] 1 (1927) 125.

Vis fluminis. A great flow of water in a river, a flood. It is considered equal to an earthquake or storm as a FORTUITUS CASUS which excused a person from appearance in court at a fixed date.—See VIS MAIOR, CASUS.

Vis maior. Superior force, an accident which cannot be foreseen or averted because of "human infirmity" (D. 44.7.1.4), such as an earthquake (see TERRAE MOTUS), a flood (see VIS FLUMINIS), a storm (see TEMPESTAS), incursion of an enemy, violent attack by robbers or pirates (not a simple theft) which cannot be repulsed, and the like.—See RECEPTUM NAUTARUM, CASUS, TUMULTUS.

   De Medio, *BIDR* 20 (1908) 157; D. Behrens, *Die vis m. und das klassische Haftungssystem,* Giessen (1936); G. I. Luzzatto, *Caso fortuito e forza maggiore* 1 (1938); Condanari-Michler, *Fschr Wenger* 1 (1944) 236.

Vis privata, vis publica. See VIS.

Vita. See IUS VITAE NECISQUE.

Vitellius. A little known jurist of the time of Augustus, contemporary with Labeo. The jurist Paul wrote a commentary on the work of Vitellius (*ad Vitellium*); it seems, however, that he did not use Vitellius' writings directly, but Sabinus' commentary *ad Vitellium.*

   Berger, *RE* 10, 713; Kunkel, *Herkunft und soziale Stellung der röm. Juristen,* 1952, 117.

Vites. Vines. Gaius used vines as an example to illustrate the necessity imposed by the Twelve Tables of applying the precise words of that legislation in the *legis actiones.* "If one sued another for having cut down his vines and used the word *vites,* he lost the claim because the Twelve Tables, on which his claim was based, spoke of 'trees' and therefore he had to refer to trees cut down in his claim" (Inst. 4.11).

Vitiari. To be legally defective, to have no legal effectiveness.

   Hellmann, *ZSS* 23 (1902) 413.

Vitiose. Used of acts, transactions, possession, securities, etc., which suffer from a legal defect (see VITIUM) and, consequently, are invalid. Ant. *sine vitio.*

Vitiosus. See VITIOSE. "What is defective (*vitiosum*) from the very beginning cannot become valid by a lapse of time" (D. 50.17.29).—See TRACTUS TEMPORIS, POSSESSIO INIUSTA, VITIUM POSSESSIONIS.

Vitium. When referring to a legal act or transaction, a legal defect resulting from non-observance of the prescribed formalities or the legal inability of the acting person. Hence *sine vitio* = blameless, without any defect. *Vitium* is also used in the sense of a loss, damage (*damnum*), as, e.g., *vitium facere,* or of a fault (*culpa*).—See the following items.

   Cuq, *DS* 5.

Vitium aedium. A defective and dangerous condition of a building or other construction (of a work done *vitium operis*). Syn. *aedes vitiosae.*—See DAMNUM INFECTUM.

   G. Branca, *Danno temuto* (1937) 105 and *passim.*

Vitium animi. A mental (psychical) defect or disease. Ant. *vitium corporis (corporale)* = a chronic physical defect (e.g., blindness, deafness). The distinction is discussed in connection with the sale of slaves and the remedies granted by the aedilician Edict in the case of unvisible defects of slaves sold. —See ACTIONES AEDILICIAE, MORBUS, ERRO, SERVUS FUGITIVUS, REDHIBITIO, ACTIO QUANTI MINORIS.

   H. Vincent, *Le droit des édiles* (1922) 43; R. Monier, *La garantie contre les vices cachés dans la vente romaine* (1930).

Vitium corporis (corporale). See VITIUM ANIMI.

Vitium operis. See VITIUM AEDIUM. *Vitium operis,* when referring to a construction of a building, is distinguished from *vitium soli* = the bad condition of the soil on which the construction was built. If the building (construction, *opus*) collapsed because of a defect in the construction, the contractor was liable; if, however, this happened because of the bad state of the soil, the owner had to bear the loss.

Vitium possessionis. See POSSESSIO INIUSTA, EXCEPTIO VITIOSAE POSSESSIONIS, CLAM.

Vitium rei. A legal "defect" in a thing which renders its acquisition through *usucapio* impossible (e.g., stolen things = *res furtivae*, things taken by violence = *res vi possessae*, things belonging to the fisc).

Vitium soli. See VITIUM OPERIS.

Vitium verborum. A defect in a written or oral declaration, resulting from the use of words other than those prescribed by law.

Vivianus. A little known jurist of the first century after Christ, author of a commentary on the praetorian and aedilician Edicts.

Vocare (vocatio). To summon a person to appear in court. A magistrate could summon a witness to testify, a guardian to render an account of his administration of a ward's property, an accused in a criminal matter (*vocare in crimen*).

Cuq, *DS* 5.

Vocare ad hereditatem. To designate an heir. The term is used both of an intestate inheritance (*lex vocat*) and of the appointment of an heir by a testator in his will.

Vocari ad munus. To be called by an official order to render compulsory personal service or to assume a certain charge (*munus*) in the interest of the state.

Vocatio. See EVOCATIO.

Vocatio in ius. See IN IUS VOCATIO.

Vociferatio. See CONVICIUM.

Voconiana ratio. See LEX VOCONIA, RATIO VOCONIANA.

Volcatius. An unknown jurist of the early first century B.C., a disciple of the renowned jurist Quintus Mucius Scaevola.

Kunkel, *Herkunft und soziale Stellung der röm. Juristen,* 1952, 20.

Volens. One who agrees, who gives his consent. "There is no injury done to a person who consents (*in volentem*)" (D. 47.10.1.5).—See FRAUDARE.

Severino, *NDI* 12, 2, 1135.

Volgo. See VULGO.

Volo. See VELLE.

Voluntaria iurisdictio. See IURISDICTIO CONTENTIOSA.

Voluntarii. Voluntary soldiers organized in special units, *cohortes voluntariorum.*

Voluntarius heres. See HERES VOLUNTARIUS.

Voluntas. A wish, a desire, a will, an intention. *Voluntas* as an element of one's action in the legal field acquires importance in the legal life of a social group and of an individual when it is expressed orally or in writing or is manifested in some other manner in a clear, unambiguous way, either in a unilateral act (a testament) or in a contract. The manifestation of will is taken into consideration as valid only if the person involved is able to express his will. Infants and lunatics (see FURIOSUS) were considered not to have a will at all. The will of a person, appropriately expressed, produced legal effects only if it was free, i.e., not produced by error (see ERROR), fraud (see DOLUS) or by violence (see VIS, METUS). Except for cases for which the law prescribed a specific form (words, witnesses, writing) the formless manifestation of will could be expressed orally (*verbis*), in writing (*in scriptis, scriptura*), by signs (see NUTUS) or by acting in a way which did not admit of any doubt about the person's will (*tacite,* see SILENTIUM). Hence the distinction between a *voluntas* factually expressed in one way or another and the *voluntas* the person really had. "There is a difference between a will which was expressed (*voluntas expressa*) and one which really exists" (D. 45.1.138.1). "If there is no ambiguity in the words used, a query about the will (*voluntas*) should not be admitted" (D. 32.25.1). Doubts arise when one's *voluntas* was expressed in obscure, ambiguous words, written or spoken. "In an ambiguous (equivocal) saying we do not say both one and another thing, but only that one we want to say; but he who says anything other than what he wished, neither says what the words (*vox*) signify because he does not want it, nor what he wants because he did not say it" (D. 34.5.3). In the earlier law a contrast between *voluntas* and its expression through *verba* or *scripta* was not taken into consideration. In a formalistic legal system, only what had been expressly said had legal value. But already at the end of the Republic a contradiction between *voluntas* and *verba* became a problem which did not escape the jurists' interest. The remark in Quintilian (*Inst. orat.* 7.6.1) "the jurists very frequently raise the question of written words and intention (*voluntas*) and a major part of controversial law (*ius controversum*) depends upon it," was not a fantasy of the famous rhetorician, who expressly states (7.5.6) that his saying refers not only to statutes but "also to testaments, agreements, stipulations and any written documents, and to oral declarations as well." The once widely diffused doctrine in the Romanistic literature to the effect that expressions like *animus, affectio, mens, voluntas,* concerned with the individual will of a person, as well as decisions based on taking it into consideration, are suspect in the writings of classical jurists, may now be considered exaggerated and misleading. The rules set by Papinian, "It has been held that in agreements between contracting parties the will should be rather taken into consideration than the words" (D. 50.16. 219), and with regard to testaments, "in conditions settled in a testament the will (*sc.* of the testator) should be considered (*considerari*) rather than the words" (D. 35.1.101 pr.) doubtless reflect the opinion prevailing in his time in favor of the element of volition. In Justinian's law *voluntas* reached its climax in the whole legal system as a decisive element in the evaluation of the validity, and in the interpretation, of manifestations of will.—*Voluntas* sometimes means consent, approval (*voluntatem dare*). For *voluntas* of persons committing crimes or illicit acts (= evil intention), see DOLUS MALUS, ANIMUS, CONATUS, CONSILIUM, INTENTIO.—See, moreover, VERBA, NUDA VOLUNTAS, ANIMUS, MENS, AFFECTIO, SILENTIUM, SIMULATIO, IOCUS, INTERPRETATIO, and the following items.

Guarneri-Citati, *Indice*² (1927) 91; *idem, St Riccobono* 1 (1936) 743; *idem, Fschr Koschaker* 1 (1939) 156 (for interpolations).—Donatuti, *BIDR* 34 (1925) 185; Sokolowski, *Mél Cornil* 2 (1926) 425; Brasiello, *StUrb* 3 (1929) 103; Levy, *ZSS* 48 (1928) 74; Jolowicz, *LQR* 48 (1932) 180; Albertario, *St Bonfante* 1 (1930) 645 (= *Studi* 5, 1937, 112); Himmelschein, *Symb Frib Lenel* (1931) 373; Pringsheim, *LQR* 49 (1933) 43, 379; Grosso, *St Riccobono* 3 (1936) 163; Riccobono, *Mél Cornil* 2 (1926) 357; *idem, ACDR* Roma 1 (1934) 177; *idem, BIDR* 53/4 (1948) 356; *idem, Scr Ferrini* 4 (Univ. Sacro Cuore, Milan, 1949) 55; *idem, Fschr Schulz* 1 (1951) 302; Dulckeit, *ibid.* 158; Flume, *ibid.* 210.

Voluntas contrahentium. See VOLUNTAS.

E. Costa, *Papiniano* 4 (1898).

Voluntas defuncti. The wish of the deceased expressed in his testament.—See VOLUNTAS, VOLUNTAS TESTANTIS, MENS TESTANTIS.

Voluntas legis. The intention of a statute.—See MENS LEGIS, RATIO LEGIS, SENTENTIA LEGIS.

Voluntas postrema. A testament. Syn. *voluntas suprema, ultima.*

Voluntas sceleris. The intention to commit a crime. Syn. *voluntas maleficii.*—See VOLUNTAS, COGITATIO, CONATUS.

Voluntas testantis. The wish of a testator expressed in his last will. Syn. *voluntas defuncti.* See VOLUNTAS. Very frequently the jurists stress that the decision in a specific case concerned with a testamentary disposition depends upon the inquiry into the testator's wish (*quaestio voluntatis*).

E. Costa, *Papiniano* 3 (1896); A. Suman, *Favor testamenti e v. testantium*, 1916; *idem, La ricerca della v. t., Fil* 1917; Donatuti, *BIDR* 34 (1925) 185; G. Dulckeit, *Erblasserwille und Erwerbswille,* 1934; *idem, Fschr Koschaker* 2 (1939) 316; Grosso, *St Riccobono* 3 (1936) 155; C. A. Maschi, *St sull'interpretazione dei legati. Verba e voluntas* (1938); *idem, Scr Ferrini* 1 (Univ. Sacro Cuore, Milan, 1947) 317; Koschaker, *ConfCast* (1940) 106.

Voluptariae impensae. See IMPENSAE VOLUPTARIAE.

Volusius. See MAECIANUS.

Vota. (In the later Empire.) Gifts offered to the emperor on New Year's Day. *Vota pro salute imperatoris* (from the time of Augustus) = vows on the occasion of prayers for the health of the emperor and his family.

Vota matrimonii (nuptiarum). In later imperial constitutions, syn. with NUPTIAE.

Votum. (From *vovere*.) A solemn vow (promise) made in favor of a divinity. A *votum* was not suable under the law, but the promisor (and after his death, his heir) was obligated to the divinity (*numini obligatus*) under sacral law. It is doubtful whether the priests of the divinity had any action against the promisor.

Toutain, *DS* 5; Ferrini, *NDI* 12, 2, 932; Eitrem, *OCD*; Brini, *RendBol* 1908; Wissowa, *Religion und Kultus der Römer*² (1912) 380.

Vox. A spoken word, an oral declaration.—See VOLUNTAS.

Vulgare. To make public officially (e.g., an imperial rescript). The term is found in the language of the imperial chancery.

Vulgaris. Common, commonly used. The term also refers to actions (*vulgaris formula, actio, vulgare iudicium*) but has no technical meaning. It indicates an ordinary action as opposed to those granted exceptionally in specific circumstances (as *actiones utiles, actiones in factum*).

Vulgaris cretio. See CRETIO.

Vulgaris mulier. See MERETRIX.

Vulgaris substitutio. See SUBSTITUTIO.

Vulgata. (*Sc. littera.*) Manuscripts of the Digest of the eleventh and following centuries. They are also called *Littera Bononiensis* because they were used in the University of Bologna.

Kantorowicz, *Die Entstehung der Digesten-Vulgata, ZSS* 30 (1909) 183, 31 (1910) 14; P. Kretschmar, *ZSS* 48 (1928) 88; *idem, Mittelalterliche Zahlensymbolik und die Entstehung der Digesten-Vulgata* (1930); *idem, ZSS* 58 (1938) 202; Mor, *CentCodPav* (1924) 559.

Vulgo. Generally, commonly. It is used of legal rules and sayings generally recognized (*vulgo dicitur, receptum est, respondetur*).

Vulgo conceptus (or quaesitus). A child born out of wedlock, neither in a legitimate marriage nor in a concubinage (see CONCUBINATUS) or CONTUBERNIUM, the offspring of a promiscuous intercourse. Such a child had no father, since the latter was unknown. The mother was bound to maintain the child who was admitted to her intestate inheritance.

X

Xenia. Small gifts (also called *xeniola*) made to a provincial governor; they were originally permitted. Later imperial legislation, however, forbade, donations to governors and higher officials of the provincial administration, except on the occasion of their leaving the post.

Brillant, *DS* 5.

Xenodochium. A hospital. *Xenodochia* were reckoned among PIAE CAUSAE. Legacies and donations to them were favored by the later imperial legislation.—C. 1.3.

Z

Zenonianae constitutiones. Enactments of the emperor Zeno (A.D. 474–491). Some of them are mentioned by Justinian in his Institutes; they are inserted in full in his Code. The most renowned among this emperor's enactments is C. 8.10.12 (the exact date is unknown). It was concerned with the construction of buildings in Constantinople and contained provisions about the height of buildings, the distance between neighboring houses, staircases, etc. There were also procedural rules concerning controversies among neighbors. Penalties for contravention were set not only against the owner of the ground but also the architects and workmen. A contractor who re-fused to finish the construction he was obligated to build was punished by a fine; in the case of insolvency and consequent impossibility of continuing the work, he was castigated and expelled from the city. Jurisdiction in all these matters was vested in the *praefectus urbi.*—See AEDIFICATIO.

H. E. Dirksen, *Hinterlassene Schriften* 2 (1871) 229; Brugi, *RISG* 4 (1887) 395; Voigt, *BerSächGW* 1903, 190; Biondi, *BIDR* 44 (1937) 362.

ENGLISH–LATIN GLOSSARY

Abandon a child. *Exponere filium*

Abandonment. *Derelictio*

Abduction of a woman. *Raptus*

Abettor. See Accomplice

Abolish a statute. *Tollere legem*

Abortion. *Partus abactus*

Absence in a trial. *Contumacia, eremodicium*

Absent without leave. *Emansor*

Abuse of rights. *Aemulatio*

Accept a stipulatory promise. *Stipulari*

Acceptance of an inheritance. *Aditio hereditatis*

Access to a grave. *Iter ad sepulcrum*

Accident. *Casus*

Accomplice. *Socius, conscius, particeps, minister*, see OPE ET CONSILIO

Account-book. *Rationes, codex accepti et expensi*

Accrual. See IUS ADCRESCENDI

Accusation, malicious. *Calumnia*

Accusation, written. *Libellus inscriptionis, subscriptio*

Acknowledge a seal. *Agnoscere (recognoscere) signum*

Acknowledge paternity. *Agnoscere liberum*

Acquittal. *Absolutio*

Act in court. *Postulare*

Actor. *Scaenicus, mimus, qui artem ludicram exercet*

Adjournment of a trial. *Dilatio*

Administrator. *Procurator, curator*; administrator of another's property = *procurator omnium bonorum*

Adoption. *Adoptio, adrogatio*

Advantage. *Commodum, emolumentum*

Adversary in a trial. *Pars diversa*

Advice. *Consilium*

Adviser, legal (of magistrates, judges). *Adsessor*

Adviser of the emperor. *Consiliarius*

Advocate. *Advocatus, patronus causae, orator, causidicus, scholasticus*

Against good customs. *Contra bonos mores*

Against one's will. *Invito (aliquo)*

Age. *Aetas*

Age below puberty. *Aetas pupillaris*

Agent. *Actor, procurator*

Agreement not to sue in court. *Pactum de non petendo*

Agreement. *Pactum, contractus, placitum, conventio*

Agreement, extrajudicial about a controversy. *Transactio*

Agreement with reciprocal obligations. *Synallagma*

Air, airspace. *Aër, coelum*

Alliance. *Foedus*

Ally. *Socius populi Romani*

Ambassador. *Legatus*

Amnesty. *Indulgentia principis*

Ancestors. *Maiores*

Animal, domestic. *Pecus, quadrupes, animal*

Animal, wild. *Fera (bestia)*

Announce (publicly). *Proscribere (palam)*

Annul a statute. *Abrogare, tollere legem*, see DEROGARE

Anonymous. *Sine nomine*, see LIBELLUS FAMOSUS

Answer (decision) of the emperor. *Rescriptum*

Answers (opinions) of the jurists. *Responsa prudentium*

Appeal. *Appellatio, provocatio*

Appeal, written. *Libelli appellatorii*, see APPELLO

Application (written) to court. *Libellus conventionis*

Appointment of an heir. *Institutio heredis*

Appointment of a substitute heir. *Substitutio*

Approval. *Approbatio, probatio, auctoritas*

Approval by a principal. *Ratihabitio*

Appurtenance of a land. *Instrumentum, instructum fundi*

Arbitration, agreement on. *Compromissum*

Arbitrator. *Arbiter, iudex compromissarius*

Archive. *Tabularium, tabulae publicae*

Armistice. *Indutiae*

Army. *Exercitus*

Arrest. *Prensio*

Arson. *Incendium*

Ascendants. *Maiores, superiores*

Assemblies of the people. *Comitia*

Assembly, plebeian. *Concilium plebis*

Assessment of taxes. *Descriptio*

Assistance. *Auxilium*, see IUS AUXILII

Association. *Collegium, sodalicium*

Assume an obligation. *Suscipere obligationem*

Astrologus. *Astrologer, mathematicus*

Asylum. See CONFUGA

Attempt, criminal. *Conatus*

Auction. *Subhastatio*

Authentic. *Verus*

Authority. *Auctoritas*

Authorization. *Iussum, mandatum*

Avenge an offense. *Vindicare*

Bad faith. *Mala fides*

Bad (forged) money. *Adulterina, reproba, falsa pecunia*

Bakers. *Pistores*

Bandit. *Latro*

Banishment. *Deportatio, relegatio, exilium*

Bank of a river. *Ripa*

Banker. *Argentarius, nummularius, mensularius*

Bankrupt. *Decoctor*

Barter. *Permutatio*

Beam. *Tignum*, see TIGNUM IUNCTUM
Beginner in a (lawyer's) profession. *Tiro*
Below puberty. *Impubes*
Betrothal. *Sponsalia*
Beyond the normal order. *Extra ordinem*
Birthplace. *Origo*
Bishop. *Episcopus*
Bishop's court. *Episcopalis audientia*
Blame by the censors. *Nota censoria*
Blind. *Caecus*, see TESTIMONIUM CAECI
Board, advisory, of magistrates. *Consilium magistratuum*
Board, white, for official announcements. *Album*
Body-guard of the emperor. *Protectores*
Bookkeeper. *Ratiocinator*
Booty. *Praeda*
Borrow. *Mutuari*
Bottomry loan. *Fenus nauticum, pecunia traiecticia*
Boundary of a land. *Fines, confinium, modus agri*
Boundary stone. *Terminus, cippus*
Bribe. *Corrumpere*
Bribery at elections. *Ambitus*
Bribery in office. *Repetundae*
Brother. *Frater*
Building. *Aedes, aedificium*
Building materials. *Tignum*, see TIGNUM IUNCTUM
Building regulations. See ZENONIANAE CONSTITUTIONES
Buildings, public. *Opera publica*
Burdens (expenses) of a marriage. *Onera matrimonii*
Burden of the proof. *Onus probandi*
Bureau of the imperial chancery. *Scrinium*
Burglar. *Effractor*
By-laws of an association. *Pactio collegii*

Captain of a ship. *Magister navis*
Case. *Causa, res iudicialis*
Cash-book. *Codex accepti et expensi, rationes*
Cash payment. *Numeratio pecuniae, pecunia numerata*
Cast horoscopes. *Ars mathematica*
Census declaration (return), oral. *Professio censualis*
Chair used by high magistrates. *Sella curulis*, see SUBSELLIUM
Chairman of a criminal jury. *Iudex quaestionis*
Chancery, imperial. See A COGNITIONIBUS and the following entries
Change a testament. *Mutare testamentum*
Change in the family status. *Mutatio familiae*
Charitable institutions. *Piae causae*
Charter of a colony (province). *Lex coloniae (provinciae)*
Chastity, crimes against chastity. *Pudicitia*
Chicanery. *Calumnia*

Chief of the palace offices. *Magister officiorum*
Child. *Infans, liber*
Child, unborn (in the womb). *Nasciturus, in utero*
Child of an unknown father. *Spurius, vulgo conceptus*
Childless. *Orbus*
Children. *Liberi*, see IUS LIBERORUM
Choice. *Optio*
Church. *Ecclesia*
Citizen *Civis*
Citizens of a municipality. *Municipes*
Citizenship. *Civitas*
Civilian. *Paganus*
Claim. *Petitic*
Claim back. *Repetere, reposcere*
Claim for the recovery of a pledge. *Vindicatio pignoris*
Claim of a servitude. *Vindicatio servitutis*
Claim of an inheritance. *Hereditatis petitio*
Class, equestrian (senatorial) *Ordo equester (senatorius)*
Classes, social higher. *Potentiores, honestiores*
Classes, social lower. *Humiliores, tenuiores*
Clerk, in a court. *Scriba, exsecutor*
Coercive measures. *Coercitio*
Co-heirs. *Coheredes*
Coins. *Nummi*
Collapse of a building. *Ruina*
Collusion between accuser and accused. *Praevaricatio*
Command. *Iussum*
Commander. *Praepositus, praefectus*
Commander, military. *Imperator, regens exercitum*
Commander of a fleet unit. *Nauarchus (classis)*
Commander of a ship. *Magister navis*
Commander of the cavalry. *Magister equitum*
Commander of the infantry. *Magister peditum*
Commissioner. *Procurator, curator*
Common ownership. *Communio*
Common thing. *Res communis*
Complain. *Queri*
Complaint. *Querela, querimonia*
Complex of things as a unit. *Universitas (rerum), corpus ex distantibus*
Conceal another's slave. *Celare, suscipere, supprimere servum alienum*
Concealer. *Occultator*
Conceived. *Conceptus, in utero*
Conclude a fictitious transaction. *Simulare*
Concurrent crimes. *Delicta concurrentia*
Confer a higher rank. *Promovere*
Confiscation. *Ademptio, publicatio, proscriptio (bonorum)*
Construction of a house. *Aedificatio.* See SUPERFICIES
Contempt of court. *Contumacia*, see OBTEMPERARE
Contractor. *Redemptor, conductor (operis)*

Control of public morals. *Regimen morum*

Controversy in court. *Lis,* see IURGIUM

Conveyance of a *res mancipi*. *Mancipatio, in iure cessio*

Conveyance of property. *Translatio dominii*

Copper and scales. See PER AES ET LIBRAM

Copy, make a copy. *Describere*

Copy of a document. *Exemplum*

Corporal punishment. *Castigatio, verberatio, fustigatio*

Corporate body. *Universitas, corpus, collegium*

Corpse. *Cadaver*

Correality. See DUO REI PROMITTENDI

Corruption of a slave. See ACTIO SERVI CORRUPTI

Council. *Consilium*

Council, municipal. *Ordo (consilium) decurionum, curia*

Counterfeit money. *Moneta (pecunia) adulterina, falsa*

Court days. *Actus rerum,* see FERIAE, DIES FASTI

Court hall. *Secretarium*

Court practice. *Consuetudo fori*

Creditor by stipulatio. *Reus stipulandi, stipulator*

Crime. *Crimen, delictum, maleficium*

Crime through cheating, fraud, deceit. *Stellionatus*

Crimes prosecuted by the person injured. *Delicta (privata)*

Crimes prosecuted by the state. *Crimina publica*

Criminal courts. *Quaestiones*

Criminal offense. *Admissum, flagitium*

Crown property of the emperor. *Patrimonium Caesaris*

Customary law. *Consuetudo, mos, mores maiorum, ius moribus constitutum*

Custom duties. *Portoria*

Customs (good). *Mores (boni)*

Customs, local. *Usus loci, mores civitatis (regionis)*

Damage done by domestic animals. *Pauperies*

Damage done to property. *Damnum iniuria datum,* see LEX AQUILIA

Damage, threatened. *Damnum infectum*

Danger. *Periculum,* see DAMNUM INFECTUM

Daughter. *Filia*

Deaf. *Surdus*

Death. *Mors*

Death penalty. *Supplicium (ultimum), poena capitis (capitalis)*

Death, upon (because of). *Mortis causa*

Debt. *Debitum*

Debt, non existing. *Indebitum*

Debt-book. *Kalendarium*

Debtor. *Reus (debendi), debitor*

Debtor through stipulation. *Reus promittendi, promissor*

Debtors, joint. *Correi, duo rei.*

Decapitation. *Decollatio, capitis amputatio*

Deceased. *Defunctus*

Deceipt. *Dolus, fraus*

Deceitfully. *Dolo, dolose, subdole*

Deceive creditors. *Fraudare creditores*

Decemviral legislation. *Lex duodecim tabularum*

Decision of a magistrate (emperor). *Decretum*

Decision of an arbitrator. *Arbitrium, sententia arbitri*

Decision of the senate. *Sententia senatus*

Declaration before censors. *Professio censualis*

Declaration before officials. *Professio*

Declaration before witnesses. *Testatio*

Declarations concerning the birth of children. *Professiones liberorum natorum*

Decree. *Decretum*

Defamation. *Iniuria, convicium*

Defamatory letter (poem). *Libellus famosus (carmen famosum)*

Default. *Mora, contumacia, absentia*

Defect, legal. *Vitium*

Defect mental. *Vitium animi*

Defective condition of a building (construction). *Vitium aedium (operis)*

Defective, legally. *Vitiosus*

Defects concealed (latent) in a sale. See ACTIO REDHIBITORIA

Defendant. *Reus, is cum quo agitur*

Defenseless in trial. *Indefensus*

Defraud. *Fraudare*

Defrauding young men. *Circumscriptio adulescentium*

Degree of relationship. *Gradus*

Denial of a claim. *Infitiatio, negatio*

Denouncer. *Delator, nuntiator*

Dependant upon another's paternal power. *Alieni iuris, in potestate*

Deputy official. *Vices (vice) agens, vicarius, proximus*

Descendants. *Descendentes, posteri, progenies*

Desecration of a grave. *Violatio sepulcri*

Deserter. *Perfuga, transfuga,* see DESERERE

Designation of an heir. *Institutio heredis*

Destruction. *Demolitio*

Determination by lot. *Sortitio*

Disapprove. *Reprobare*

Discharge, honorable, from military service. *Missio honesta*

Disease. *Morbus;* chronic disease. *Morbus perpetuus*

Disherison. *Exheredatio*

Dishonest. *Improbus, contra bonam fidem*

Disinherit. *Exheredare*

Dismissal from military service. *Reiectio militia*

Disobedience to a magisterial order. See OBTEMPERARE

Dispossess. *Deicere de possessione*

Dissolve a legal tie. *Solvere*

Distinctive insignia (titles). *Ornamenta*

Distribution of money among people. *Missilia, iactus missilium*

Districts, administrative in Rome (Italy). *Regiones*

Disuse of a law. *Desuetudo*

Divine law. *Ius divinum, ius sacrum, fas*

Division of common inheritance. See ACTIO FAMILIAE ERCISCUNDAE

Division of common property. See ACTIO COMMUNI DIVIDUNDO

Division of process (bipartition). See IN IURE, APUD IUDICEM

Divorce. *Divortium, repudium, separatio*

Document. *Instrumentum, charta, scriptura*

Door. *Ostia*

Dowry. *Dos, res uxoria*

Draft by lot. *Sortitio*

Draft, written of a judgment. *Pariculum*

Drunkenness. *Ebrietas, temulatio,* see VINUM

Dumb. *Mutus*

Duress. See METUS

Duties, public, for the state or city. *Munera*

Earnest (money). *Arra*

Earthquake. *Terrae motus*

Easement. *Servitus*

Ecclesiastical jurisdiction. See EPISCOPALIS AUDIENTIA

Elected magistrate (for the next term). *Designatus*

Election between alternative obligations. *Optio,* see IUS VARIANDI

Elections, dishonest practices in. *Ambitus*

Embezzler. *Decoctor*

Embezzlement in office. *Peculatus*

Emergency. *Necessitas*

Emergency tax. *Tributum temerarium*

Emperor. *Princeps, imperator*

Enactment, imperial, of particular importance. *Sanctio pragmatica*

Enactment of a plebeian assembly. *Plebiscitum*

Enactments of the emperors. *Constitutiones principum, statuta imperialia*

Endow with a dowry. *Dotare*

Enemy. *Hostis*

Enforce payment. *Exigere*

Enfranchisement of a slave. *Manumissio*

Enriched. *Locupletior factus*

Enrichment. *Id quod pervenit, versum in rem alicuius*

Enrichment, unjustified. See CONDICTIO

Enslavement by penalty. See SERVUS POENAE

Entry in a cash-book. *Nomen,* see NOMINA TRANSCRIPTICIA

Equal legal situation. *Par causa*

Equipment of a house (land). *Instrumentum, instructum domus (fundi)*

Equity. *Aequitas*

Error concerning law. *Ignorantia (error) iuris*

Estate (inheritance). *Hereditas, res hereditariae*

Estate tax. *Vicesima hereditatium*

Esteem. *Existimatio*

Estimation. *Taxatio, aestimatio*

Evade law. *Circumvenire, fraudare legem, in fraudem legis agere*

Evade summons in court by hiding. *Latitare*

Evidence. *Probatio*

Evidence, circumstantial. *Indicium*

Examination of a case in court. *Causae cognitio*

Examine (confirm) the correctness of a copy. *Recognoscere*

Excessive claim. *Pluspetitio*

Exchange. *Permutatio*

Exclude from the senate. *Senatu movere*

Excuse. *Excusatio, velamentum*

Execution of a judgment. See ACTIO IUDICATI, MANUS INIECTIO

Execution through taking a pledge. See PIGNUS IN CAUSAM IUDICATI

Execution of a criminal. See POENA CAPITALIS, POENA

Executioner. *Speculator*

Exemption, excuse, from guardianship or public charges. *Excusatio*

Exemption from law. *Solutio legibus*

Exemption from taxes. *Immunitas, vacatio*

Exercise of a right. *Usus iuris, uti suo iure.*

Exile, voluntary. See INTERDICERE AQUA ET IGNI

Ex-master of a slave. *Patronus*

Expenses. *Impensae, impendium, sumptus*

Expenses connected with a lawsuit. *Sumptus litis*

Explanation of laws (or last wills). *Interpretatio*

Expose to public view. *Proponere, publicare, proscribere, promulgare*

Expropriation. *Emptio ab invito*

Expulsion. *Relegatio*

Extinction of obligations. See SOLUTIO, LIBERATIO, ACCEPTILATIO, DATIO IN SOLUTUM, CONFUSIO

Extrajudicial oath. *Iusiurandum voluntarium*

Extort. *Torquere, extorquere*

Extortion. *Concussio, crimen repetundarum*

Factual situation. *Res facti*

Fair and just. *Bonum et aequum*

Faith (good, bad). *Fides (bona, mala)*

False judgment. See Unjust judgment

Family council. *Consilium propinquorum, domesticum*

Farmers of public revenues. *Publicani*

Father. *Pater (familias), parens*

Fear. *Metus, timor*

Fees, judicial. *Sportulae*

Female slave. *Ancilla*

Festivities, public. *Ludi publici*

Fetters. *Vincula*

Fiancé (fiancée). *Sponsus (sponsa)*

Fiduciary agreement. *Pactum fiduciae*

Financial matters. *Rationes*

Financial means of a person. *Facultates, modus facultatum*

Fine. *Multa, poena nummaria (pecuniaria)*

Fire. *Incendium*

Fire brigade. *Vigiles*

First name. *Praenomen*

Fishing. *Piscari*

Fleet. *Classis*

Flock of animals. *Grex*

Flowing water. *Aqua profluens*

Food administration. *Annona*

Forbid. *Prohibere, vetare*

Force (physical). *Vis, violentia*

Foreclosure of pledge. See LEX COMMISSORIA, IMPETRATIO DOMINII

Foreigner. *Peregrinus*

Forgery. *Falsum*

Formalities, legal. *Sollemnitates iuris*

Formless agreement. *Pactum (nudum), placitum*

Formless promise of a dowry. *Pollicitatio dotis*

Formularies for documents. *Formulae*

Formulary procedure. See FORMULA

Fortune-teller. *Vaticinator*

Foster parent. *Nutritor*

Foundations, charitable. *Piae causae*

Four-footed animal. *Quadrupes*

Fracture of a bone. *Os fractum*

Fraud. *Dolus*

Fraudulently. *Subdole, dolose*

Free. *Liber*

Free a slave. *Manumittere*

Free from charges. *Immunis*, see OPTIMO IURE

Free man enslaved through condemnation. *Servus poenae*

Free will. *Libera voluntas*

Freeborn. *Ingenuus*

Freedman. *Libertus, libertinus*

Freedman's services. *Operae liberti*

Fruits. *Fructus*

Funeral. *Funus*

Funeral association. *Collegium funeraticium*

Funeral oration. *Oratio funebris*

Furlough. *Commeatus*

Gain. *Lucrum*

Gain in a transaction. *Lucrari, lucrifacere*

Gambler. *Aleator*, see ALEA

Games (public). *Ludi (publici)*

Gates of a city. *Portae*

General authorization. *Mandatum generale*

Gift. *Donatio, donum, munus*

Gifts between spouses. *Donationes inter virum et uxorem*

Give a dowry. *Dotare*

Give notice. *Denuntiare*

Give security. *Cavere*

Good customs (manners). *Boni mores*

Good faith. *Bona fides*

Goods transported by sea. *Vectura*

Governor of a diocese. *Vicarius*

Governor of a province. *Praeses (rector) provinciae*

Grace of the emperor. *Indulgentia principis*

Gratuitous loan of things for use. *Commodatum*

Grant an action. *Dare actionem*

Grant of majority rights to a minor. *Venia aetatis*

Grave. *Sepulcrum*

Gross negligence. *Magna (lata) culpa, magna neglegentia*

Group of persons as a unit. *Universitas*

Guaranties in process. See VADIMONIUM, CAUTIO IUDICIO SISTI

Guaranty for eviction. See ACTIO AUCTORITATIS, STIPULATIO DUPLAE

Guardian. *Tutor*

Guardianship. *Tutela*

Guild. *Collegium, ordo*

Guilty. *Reus*

Harbor. *Portus*

Harvest. *Messis*

Head of an office. *Praefectus, praepositus, magister, curator*

Head of the fiscal administration. *Rationalis*

Health (bad). *Valetudo*

Heir. *Heres*

Heirless estate. *Bona vacantia*

Help through procedural measures. *Succurrere, subvenire*

Herald. *Praeco*

Herd. *Grex*

Hesitate in testimony. *Vacillare*

High treason. *Crimen maiestatis, perduellio, proditio*

Higher in rank. *Superior*

Highway robber. *Latro, grassator*

Hire another's labor. *Locatio conductio operarum (operis)*

Hold a thing. *Detinere, naturaliter possidere*
Holidays. *Feriae*
Honest man. *Vir bonus*
Honesty. *Bona fides, probitas*
Honorarium for intellectual services. *Salarium*
Hospital. *Xenodochium*
Hostage. *Obses*
House. *Domus, aedes*
Hunting. *Venatio*
Husband. *Maritus*

Ignorance of a fact (law). *Error, ignorantia facti (iuris)*
Illegal. *Illicitus*
Illegitimate child (father). *Filius (pater) naturalis*
Illiterate. *Ignarus litterarum* (see LITTERAE)
Imaginary marriage. *Nuptiae simulatae*
Immovables. *Res immobiles*
Imperial council. *Consilium principis, consistorium*
Imperial enactments. *Constitutiones principum*
Impulse. *Impetus*
In court. *Pro tribunali*
Inaction. *Silentium*
Incapable to be a witness. *Intestabilis*
Income. *Reditus*
Independent of another (legally). *Sui iuris*
Individual thing. *Species*
Ineffective, legally. *Inutilis*
Infamous. *Qui notatur infamia*
Infantrymen. *Pedites*
Informal proceedings, out of court. *De plano*
Informer. *Denuntiator, index, delator*
Inhabitant. *Incola*
Inheritance. *Hereditas*
Inheritance tax. *Vicesima hereditatium*
Innkeeper. *Caupo,* see RECEPTUM NAUTAE
Inquire. *Quaerere*
Insane. *Demens, furiosus, mente captus*
Insubordination. *Contumacia*
Insult. *Contumelia, iniuria, convicium*
Intellectual profession (services). *Artes (operae) liberales*
Intent to commit a crime. *Consilium, voluntas sceleris*
Intention. *Animus, affectio, mens, cogitatio, voluntas, propositum*
Intention of a statute. *Mens, sententia legis*
Intentionally (with evil intention). *Dolo malo, dolose*
Intercourse with an unmarried woman. *Stuprum*
Interest. *Usurae, fenus*
Interest for default. *Usurae morae*
Interest from interest. *Usurae usurarum, anatocismus*
Interest of twelve per cent. *Usurae centesimae*

Interest, public. *Utilitas publica,* see INTERESTE UTILIS
Intermediary. *Interposita persona*
Interruption (of usucaption). *Interpellatio, usurpatio*
Intestate succession. *Hereditas legitima (ab intestato), bonorum possessio intestati*
Intoxication. *Ebrietas, temulatio.* See VINUM
Inundation. *Vis fluminis*
Invade another's property. *Introire, ingredi*
Invalid, legally. *Irritus, invalidus, nullus, nullius momenti*
Invest money. *Collocare pecuniam*
Investigator. *Quaesitor*
Inviolable. *Sacrosanctus*
Island. *Insula*
Issue a decree. *Decernere*
Issue an interdict. *Reddere interdictum*

Jail. *Carcer*
Jettison. *Iactus mercium*
Joinder of issue. *Litis contestatio*
Joinder of possessions. *Accessio possessionis*
Joint debtors. *Correi, duo rei promittendi*
Joint creditors. *Duo rei stipulandi*
Judge. *Iudex*
Judgment. *Sententia*
Judgment debt. *Iudicatum*
Judicial matter. *Causa*
Jurist. *Iurisprudens, prudens, iurisconsultus, iuris peritus*
Just title. *Iusta causa*

Keeper of stables. *Stabularius,* see RECEPTUM NAUTAE
Keys. *Claves*
Kidnapper. *Plagiarius, plagiator*
Kidnapping. *Plagium*
Kind of things. *Genus*
King. *Rex*
Kingship. *Regnum*
Kiss. *Osculum*
Knowledge. *Scientia*
Knowledge of law. *Iuris scientia, iurisprudentia*

Labor (manual and intellectual). *Operae*
Lack of knowledge of the law. *Ignorantia iuris*
Lack of professional skill. *Imperitia*
Lampoon. *Carmen famosum, libellus famosus*
Land (plot of land). *Ager, fundus, praedium*
Land dedicated to the gods. *Locus sacer*
Land for agricultural production. *Praedium rusticum*
Land for urban utilization. *Praedium urbanum*
Land in Italy (provinces). *Fundus Italicus (provincialis), solum, praedium Italicum (provinciale)*

Land-register. *Libri censuales*
Land-tax (in provinces). *Tributum soli, stipendium*
Large estate. *Latifundium*
Last will. *Postrema, ultima voluntas, testamentum*
Law. *Ius, lex*
Law, customary. See Customary law
Law originating in edicts of magistrates (praetors). *Ius honorarium (praetorium)*
Lawsuit. *Actio, petitio, persecutio*
Lawfully. *Iure, recte, rite, licite*
Lawyer. See Advocate
Lawyer pleading in court. *Togatus fori*
Lease. *Locatio conductio*
Lease in perpetuity. See EMPHYTEUSIS
Leave (inheritance, legacy). *Relinquere*
Leave of absence. *Commeatus*
Legacy. *Legatum*, see FIDEICOMMISSUM
Legacy of a fraction of the estate. *Partitio legata*
Legacy, additional, to an heir. *Praelegatum*
Legal rule. *Regula iuris, norma, canon*
Legally. See Lawfully
Legitimate son. *Filius legitimus*
Lend money. *Credere pecuniam*
Lessee. *Conductor*
Lessor. *Locator*
Letter. *Epistula, litterae*
Letter of commendation. *Prosecutoria*
Liable, to be. *Teneri*
Liberation from an obligation. *Solutio*
List of property. *Inventarium*
Litigation. *Lis, controversia*
Litigation tax. *Quadragesima litium*
Loan for consumption. *Mutuum, creditum*
Loan of a thing for use. *Commodatum*
Long-term lease. *Emphyteusis, ius in agrò vectigali*
Loss. *Damnum*
Loss of profit. *Lucrum cessans*
Lower imperial officials. *Proximi*
Lunatic. *Furiosus, demens, mente captus*
Luxury, laws against. *Leges sumptuariae*

Majority in a corporation. *Maior pars*
Make a copy. *Describere*
Make a gift. *Donare*
Make a testament. *Testari, testamentum facere*
Make good losses. *Resarcire, sarcire*
Malicious trial. *Calumnia*
Manage another's affairs. *Negotia (aliena) gerere, administrare*
Management of another's affairs without authorization. *Negotiorum gestio*
Manager of a commercial enterprise. *Institor*

Manager of another's affairs. *Procurator;* without authorization = *negotiorum gestor*
Manslaughter. *Homicidium*
Manumission tax. *Vicesima manumissionum*
Maritime loan. *Fenus nauticum, pecunia traiecticia*
Market. *Nundinae*
Market place. *Forum*
Marriage. *Matrimonium, nuptiae*
Marriage contract, written. *Tabulae nuptiales (dotales)*
Marriage, incestuous. *Nuptiae incestae*, see INCESTUS
Marriage-like union of slaves. *Contubernium*
Master of a slave. *Dominus*
Master of ceremonies. *Magister admissionum*
Matter of fact. *Res (quaestio) facti*
Matter of law. *Res (quaestio) iuris*
Meeting, informal, of the people. *Contio*
Members of a corporation (association). *Socii, sodales, corporati, collegiati*
Merchandise. *Merx*
Merchants. *Negotiatores, mercatores*
Messenger. *Nuntius*
Messengers in office. *Viatores*
Milestone. *Milliarium*
Military court. *Iudices militares*
Military delicts. *Delicta militum*
Military law. *Ius militare (militum)*
Military service. *Militia*
Mines. *Metalla*
Minor magistrates. See VIGINTISEXVIRI
Minority. *Minor aetas*
Mint. *Moneta*
Mistake. *Error*
Money. *Pecunia, nummi*
Money lent. *Pecunia credita*
Monk. *Monachus*
Moral duty. *Officium pietatis*
Motive of a statute. *Ratio legis*
Mourning. *Luctus*
Movables. *Res mobiles*
Move to another place. *Migrare*, see INTERDICTUM DE MIGRANDO
Municipal senate (council). *Consilium (ordo) decurionum*
Municipality. *Municipium*
Murder. *Homicidium*, see PARRICIDIUM
Murder by poison. *Veneficium*
Murderer. *Sicarius*

Name. *Nomen*
Natural law. *Ius naturale (naturae)*
Navy. *Classis*
Negligence. *Culpa*

Neighbor. *Vicinus*
Newborn child. *Partus*
Norm, legal. *Praeceptum (regula) iuris, praescriptum*
Non-appearance in court. *Contumacia*
Non-use of a right. *Non usus*
Notary. *Tabellio, tabularius*
Notification of action to the defendant. *Editio actionis*
Notify. *Denuntiare*
Nourishment. *Victus*
Null. *Nullus, nullius momenti, invalidus*

Oath. *Iuramentum, iusiurandum*
Oath in a civil trial. See IURAMENTUM NECESSARIUM
Oath of a magistrate. See IURARE IN LEGES, EIURATIO
Oath of soldiers. *Sacramentum*
Object of a lawsuit. *Res de qua agitur, lis*
Object of a pending trial. *Res litigiosa*
Objection in trial. *Exceptio*
Obsolescence. *Desuetudo*
Offense against the state. *Maiestas, perduellio*
Offense, personal. *Iniuria*
Offenses, military. *Delicta militum*
Offer. *Oblatio*
Office, public. *Ministerium*
Officers, highest, in the legion. *Tribuni militum*
Offices, regional, of the fisc. *Stationes fisci*
Official duties. *Officium*
Official, highest, in an imperial office. *Primicerus, princeps*
Officials in the fiscal administration. *Rationales*
Officials in the imperial palace. *Palatini*
Omission, negligent. *Neglegentia, culpa in non faciendo*
Omit a person in a will. *Praeterire, omittere*
Opening of a will. *Apertura testamenti*
Opposing an exception. *Excipere*
Oral solemn declaration. *Nuncupatio*
Oral will. *Testamentum per nuncupationem*
Orator. *Rhetor*
Ordain. *Statuere*
Order (authorization). *Iussum*
Order of a magistrate. *Decretum, iussum*
Order of payment from a bank deposit. *Relegare pecuniam, delegare ab argentario*
Order, public. *Disciplina*
Order to lend money. *Mandatum pecuniae credendae*
Order to take possession, issued by a praetor. *Missio in possessionem*
Ordinary civil procedure. *Ordo iudiciorum privatorum*
Ordinary criminal procedure. *Ordo iudiciorum publicorum*
Original of a document. *Exemplar, authenticum*
Outlawed. *Proscriptus, interdictus aqua et igni, sacer*

Outside the court. *Extra iudicium*
Owner. *Dominus, proprietarius*
Ownerless estate (inheritance). *Bona vacantia*
Ownerless things. *Res nullius*
Ownership. *Dominium, proprietas*
Ownership protected by praetorian law. See IN BONIS

Pace. *Passus*
Painting. *Pictura*
Panel of judges. *Album iudicum*
Parcel of public land. *Locus publicus*
Partition. *Divisio*
Partner. *Socius*
Partnership. *Societas*
Party to a trial. *Pars, litigator*
Party wall. *Paries communis*
Pasquil. *Libellus famosus*
Pass a judgment. *Sententiam ferre, iudicare*
Pasture land. *Pascuum*
Pasture servitude. *Ius pascendi*
Paternal power. *Patria potestas*
Patronage. *Patrocinium*
Pay a debt. *Solvere, retro dare*
Payment by installment. *Pensio*
Payment of a debt. *Solutio*
Peace. *Pax*
Pederasty. *Stuprum cum masculo*
Penalty. *Poena*
Period of time. *Tempus, intervallum*
Periods, lucid (in an insane person). *Dilucida (lucida) intervalla*
Perjury. *Periurium*
Person not belonging to a family. *Extraneus*
Personal offense. *Iniuria, contumelia*
Personnel, auxiliary, in an office. *Apparitores*
Petition. *Preces, libellus, supplicatio*
Physical things. *Res corporales*
Physician. *Medicus*
Plaintiff. *Actor, petitor, is qui agit*
Platform for the court. *Tribunal*
Plead in court a case. *Causam dicere, perorare*
Plebeian assembly. *Concilium plebis*
Plot of land. *Ager, fundus, praedium*
Plurality of creditors. *Duo rei stipulandi*
Plurality of debtors. *Duo rei promittendi*
Plurality of guardians. *Contutores*
Plurality of heirs. *Coheredes*
Poison. *Venenum*
Poisoner. *Veneficus*
Police officials. *Curiosi*
Poll-tax. *Tributum capitis*
Popular assembly. *Comitia*

Possession of a right. *Possessio iuris, quasi possessio*
Possessor in good (bad) faith. *Possessor bonae fidei*
Possessory remedies. See INTERDICTA
Postal service. *Cursus publicus*
Poster. *Propositum*
Posthumous child. *Postumus*
Postpone. *Prorogare*
Poverty. *Egestas*
Power. *Potestas*
Power of higher magistrates. *Imperium*
Praetorian Edict, commentaries on. *Libri ad edictum*
Precedent. *Exemplum,* see RES IUDICATA
Predecessor in title. *Auctor*
Preliminary decision in litigation. *Interlocutio*
Prescription, acquisitive. *Usucapio*
Prescription, extinctive. *Longi temporis praescriptio*
Presentation of the case by plaintiff. *Narratio*
Pretext. *Obtentus, velamentum,* see SPECIES
Price. *Pretium*
Priests. *Sacerdotes, flamines, augures, haruspices*
Principal. *Dominus negotii*
Principal (sum). *Sors, caput*
Prison. *Carcer, vincula publica*
Prisoner of war. *Captivus*
Privy purse of the emperor. *Res privata principis*
Procedural stipulations. *Stipulationes praetoriae,* see
    IUDICIALES
Proceeds. *Fructus*
Proclamation. *Programma*
Products. *Fructus*
Professional association. *Collegium, ordo*
Professional services. *Operae*
Profit. *Commodum, lucrum*
Prohibit. *Vetare, prohibere*
Prohibited by law or custom. *Illicitus*
Prolongation of magisterial power. *Prorogatio imperii*
Promise. *Promissio, promissum, pollicitatio*
Promise of a dowry. *Dictio, promissio, pollicitatio dotis*
Promissory note. *Chirographum*
Proof. *Probatio*
Proof, burden of. *Onus probandi*
Property of a person. *Bona, patrimonium*
Proposal of a statute. *Rogatio legis (ferre legem)*
Propose a candidate. *Nominare*
Proposer of a statute. *Rogator, auctor legis*
Prosecutor in a criminal trial. *Denuntiator, accusator*
Prostitute. *Meretrix, mulier quae corpore quaestum
    facit*
Protest against a new construction. *Operis novi nun-
    tiatio*
Prove. *Probare*
Provincial land. *Praedium (solum) provinciale*

Public constructions. *Opera publica*
Public interest (welfare). *Utilitas publica*
Public law. *Ius publicum*
Publicly. *Palam, publice*
Punishment. *Poena*
Punishment, capital. *Poena capitalis, supplicium*
Purchase. *Emptio*
Purpose of a statute. *Ratio legis*
Pursue a claim. *Experiri actione*

Question. *Interrogatio*
Quinquennal period. *Lustrum*

Rain drip. *Stillicidium*
Rate of interest fixed by law. *Usurae legitimae*
Ratification. *Ratihabitio, ratum habere*
Ratification by the senate. *Auctoritas senatus (patrum)*
Read in court. *Recitare*
Real. *Verus*
Real right. *Ius in re (aliena)*
Real security. See FIDUCIA, PIGNUS, HYPOTHECA
Reason, natural. *Naturalis ratio*
Receipt, written. *Apocha, securitates*
Reciprocal claims. *Mutuae petitiones*
Reciprocally. *Invicem*
Recompense. *Remunerare*
Records, official. *Acta, commentarii, tabulae publicae,
    gesta, monumenta*
Recourse. *Regressus*
Recovery of property, action for. *Rei vindicatio*
Recovery of unjustified enrichment, action for. *Con-
    dictio*
Recruit. *Tiro*
Redeem a pledge. *Emere pignus*
Redeemed from the enemy. *Redemptus ab hoste*
Reduction of rent. *Remissio mercedis*
Refusal of action by the praetor. *Denegatio actionis*
Refuse an inheritance. *Abstinere (se) hereditate*
Registered as taxpayer. *Censitus*
Reimburse. *Refundere*
Reinstatement to the former (legal) condition. *Resti-
    tutio in integrum*
Reiteration of evidence. *Ampliatio*
Relationship (kinship). *Necessitudo,* see AGNATIO,
    COGNATIO
Relationship among slaves. *Cognatio servilis*
Release of debt. *Acceptilatio*
Release from an obligation. *Remissio debiti*
Remitting a penalty. *Remissio poenae*
Remnant, unpaid of a debt. *Residuum, reliquatio, re-
    liquum*
Removal of a boundary stone. *Termini motio*

Render judgment. *Iudicare, sententiam ferre.*
Renew. *Renovare redintegrare*
Renewal of an accusation. *Repetere accusationem*
Renewal of a lease. *Reconductio, relocatio*
Rent. *Merces*
Rent in a long-term lease. *Canon, pensio*
Renunciation. *Abdicatio*
Repair. *Reficere*
Replacement of a judge. *Mutatio iudicis,* see TRANS-
LATIO IUDICII
Reply of the defendant. *Contradictio, responsio, libel-*
lus contradictionis
Report to a higher judge. *Referre*
Represent a person. *Sustinere personam alicuius*
Representative of a corporate body. *Syndicus, actor*
Representative of a party in a trial. *Cognitor, pro-*
curator
Request a magistrate. *Postulare*
Request for opinion. *Consultatio*
Rescind. *Rescindere, resolvere, revocare*
Rescission of a sale. *Redhibitio*
Reserve a servitude (usufruct) for the alienator. *De-*
ducere, excipere servitutem (usumfructum)
Residence. *Domicilium, sedes*
Responsibility (risk) of a guardian. *Periculum tutoris*
Responsible for damages. *Obnoxius*
Restore. *Restituere*
Retaliation. *Talio*
Retention of a dowry. *Retentiones dotales*
Return (give back). *Reddere*
Revenues of the state. *Vectigalia*
Revocation of a legacy. *Ademptio legati*
Revolt. *Tumultus, seditio*
Rhetorician. *Rhetor, orator*
Right. *Ius*
Right and just. *Bonum et aequum*
Right of life and death. *Ius vitae necisque*
Right on another's property. *Ius in re aliena*
Right to promulgate edicts. *Ius edicendi*
Right to take produce of another's property. *Ius fru-*
endi, see USUSFRUCTUS
Right to use another's property. *Ius utendi,* see USUS
Right to vote. *Ius suffragii*
Rights of way on another's property. See ITER, VIA,
ACTUS
Riot. *Tumultus, seditio*
Risk. *Periculum*
Risk in a sale. *Periculum rei venditae*
River. *Flumen, rivus*
River bed. *Alveus*
Roads. *Viae*
Robber. *Praedo*
Robbery. *Rapina*

Roman people. *Populus Romanus*
Rome, city of. *Urbs*
Rule, legal. *Regula iuris*
Runaway (slave). *Servus fugitivus*

Salary. *Merces*
Sale. *(Emptio) venditio, distractio*
Sale of a free man. *Plagium*
Sale (purchase) of a future thing. *Emptio spei, emptio*
rei speratae
Sale of a pledge. *Distractio pignoris,* see IUS DISTRA-
HENDI
Sale of a war prisoner. *Venditio sub corona*
Sale of the property of an insolvent debtor. *Bonorum*
venditio
Sale, public, by auction. *Auctio*
Sales tax. *Centesima (vectigal) rerum venalium*
Schedule (inventory) of an estate. *Inventarium, re-*
pertorium
Sea. *Mare*
Seal. *Signum, sigillum*
Seal a document. *Signare, obsignare, consignare*
Search for stolen things. *Perquisitio,* see LANCE ET
LICIO
Seashore. *Litus*
Second marriage. *Secundae nuptiae*
Second marriage between the same persons. *Matri-*
monium redintegratum
Security. *Cautio, satisdatio*
Security for appearance in court. *Cautio iudicio sisti,*
vadimonium
Seizure by the fisc. *Confiscatio, occupatio a fisco*
Selection. *Electio, optio*
Selection by lot. *Sortitio*
Selection of jurors. *Editio iudicum*
Selection of senators. *Lectio senatus*
Self-defense. See VIM VI REPELLERE, VINDICARE
Sell at a public auction. *Publice vendere;* to be sold =
publice venire
Senators. *Patres* ("fathers"), *senatores*
Senility. *Senectus*
Sequence in magisterial career. *Cursus honorum*
Serfdom. See COLONATUS
Servitude of dwelling in another's house. *Habitatio*
Servitudes, rustic. *Servitutes praediorum rusticorum*
Servitudes, urban. *Servitutes praediorum urbanorum*
Set off. See COMPENSATIO
Settle a controversy. *Transigere*
Share of an inheritance. *Portio (pars) hereditatis*
Ship. *Navis*
Shipowner. *Navicularius, nauta,* see RECEPTUM NAU-
TAE
Shipper. *Exercitor navis, nauclerus*

Shipwreck. *Naufragium*

Shorthand writing. *Notae*

Shrewdness. *Dolus bonus*

Sign. *Subscribere, subnotare*

Signature. *Subscriptio*

Silence. *Silentium,* see TACERE

Slander. See DEFAMATIO

Slanderous poem. *Carmen famosum, libellus famosus,* see OCCENTARE

Slave. *Servus, homo, mancipium, puer*

Slave, female. *Ancilla*

Slave manumitted on condition. *Statuliber*

Slave of a slave. *Servus vicarius*

Slave of the state. *Servus publicus*

Slavery. *Servitus*

Social classes, higher. *Potentiores, honestiores, altiores*

Social classes, lower. *Humiliores, tenuiores*

Soil. *Solum*

Soldier. *Miles*

Soldier's pay. *Stipendium*

Soldier's will. *Testamentum militis*

Solidarity in obligations. See Correality

Solvent. *Solvendo esse, facere posse*

Son under paternal power. *Filius familias*

Sorcery. *Magia,* see EXCANTARE

Space between neighboring houses. *Ambitus*

Speech of the emperor. *Oratio principis*

Spendthrift. *Prodigus*

Sphere of competence. *Provincia*

Spy. *Explorator, proditor*

State. See RES PUBLICA

State land. *Ager publicus*

Status of a freeborn. *Ingenuitas*

Statute. *Lex*

Statute of a collegium (association). *Lex collegii*

Statute of limitations. *Praescriptio longi temporis*

Statutes against luxury. *Leges sumptuariae*

Statutes on voting. *Leges tabellariae*

Statutory norm. *Placitum legis*

Steal. *Furari, subripere*

Stepson. *Privignus*

Stipulatory promise. *Stipulatio*

Storehouse. *Horreum, thesaurus*

Storm. *Tempestas*

Straw man. *Interposita (supposita) persona*

Subject to another's power. *Alieni iuris, in potestate*

Submission to arbitration. *Compromissum*

Subordinate personnel in offices. *Apparitores*

Subscribe. *Signare*

Substitute heir. *Heres substitutus, heres secundus*

Substitute of an official. *Vice agens, vicarius*

Substitute of a provincial governor. See IUDEX

Succeed as an heir. *Succedere hereditario iure*

Succession according to praetorian law. *Bonorum possessio*

Sue in court. *Venire contra aliquem, convenire*

Suicide. *Suicidium, consciscere sibi mortem, libera facultas mortis*

Suit, written. *Libellus conventionis*

Sum lent at interest. *Sors, caput*

Summary. *Index*

Summary civil proceeding. *Summatim cognoscere*

Summons to court. *In ius vocatio, denuntiatio, evocatio*

Supposititious child. *Partus subditicius, subiectus, suppositus*

Superior force. *Vis maior*

Supervision. *Cura, curatio*

Surety. *Sponsor, fideiussor, fideipromissor,* see ADPROMISSIO, PRAEDES

Surety in process. *Vindex, vas, praes*

Surname. *Cognomen*

Surrender of a son or slave for damages. *In noxam dedere*

Surrender of an enemy. *Deditio*

Survive. *Supervivere,* see COMMORIENTES

Suspension of judicial activity. *Iustitium*

Sustenance. *Alimenta*

Taking possession of an ownerless thing. *Occupatio*

Taking upon death of a person. *Mortis causa capio*

Tax. *Vectigal*

Tax assessment officials. *Censuales*

Tax collector. *Susceptor*

Tax evasion. *Fraudare vectigal*

Tax farmer. *Publicanus redemptor, conductor*

Tax farmers' association. *Societas publicanorum*

Tax office, regional. *Statio*

Tax officials. *Tabularii*

Tax on inheritance. *Vicesima hereditatium*

Tax on manumissions. *Vicesima manumissionum*

Tax on sales. See Sales tax

Tax payer. *Tributarius*

Taxes in provinces. See TRIBUTUM, CAPITATIO, STIPENDIUM

Teachers. *Magistri, praeceptores, professores, antecessores*

Ten-men group. *Decuria*

Tenant. *Habitator, inquilinus, conductor*

Tenement house. *Insula*

Territory of Rome. See POMERIUM

Testament, capacity to make one or to take under one. *Testamenti factio*

Testify. *Testari*

Testimony. *Testimonium, testatio, attestatio*

Testimony, written. *Testimonium per tabulas, tabulae signatae*

Theatrical art. *Ars ludicra*

Theft. *Furtum*

Theft of sacred things. *Sacrilegium*

Things stolen. *Res furtivae, subreptae*

Things of the husband, stolen by his wife. *Res amotae*

Things without an owner. *Res nullius*

Time, fixed. *Tempus certum, statutum*

Time for the payment of a judgment debt. *Tempus iudicati*

Tomb. *Sepulcrum*

Torture. *Tormentum*

Token (ticket). *Tessera*

Touch the debtor's shoulder. *Manum inicere*

Trade. *Commercium*

Tradesman. *Mercator, negotiator*

Traitor. *Proditor*

Transaction. *Negotium, transactio*

Transfer of a claim. *Cessio*

Transfer of jurisdiction. *Iurisdictio mandata, delegata*

Transfer of ownership. *Translatio dominii*

Transfer of ownership, formless. *Traditio*

Transfer of the right to an inheritance. *Transmissio*

Transferee (transferor) in a *mancipatio*. *Mancipio accipiens (dans)*

Travel expenses. *Viaticum*

Treason. *Perduellio, crimen maiestatis*

Treasure-trove. *Thesaurus*

Treasury. *Aerarium, arca*

Treasury, imperial. *Fiscus, largitiones*

Treaty, international, for protection of citizens. *Reciperatio*

Treaty of alliance. *Foedus*

Treaty of friendship. *Foedus amicitiae*

Trial, civil. *Lis*, see LEGIS ACTIONES, FORMULA, COGNITIO EXTRA ORDINEM

Trial, civil, bipartition of. See IN IURE, APUD IUDICEM

Trial concerning freedom. *Causa liberalis*

Truth. *Veritas*

Try a case in court anew. *Retractare causam*

Turmoil. *Turba, rixa*

Twelve Tables. *Lex duodecim tabularum*

Unborn child. *Nasciturus*

Undutiful will, gift. *Inofficiosus*, see QUERELA INOFFICIOSI TESTAMENTI (INOFFICIOSAE DONATIONIS)

Ungrateful. *Ingratus*

Unjust. *Iniquus, iniustus*

Unjust judgment intentionally rendered by a judge. See IUDEX QUI LITEM SUAM FACIT

Unlawful. *Illegitimus, illicitus*

Unlawfully. *Iniuria, non iure, illicite*

Unlimited in time. *Perpetuus*

Unnamed contracts. *Contractus innominati*

Unseal. *Resignare*

Unworthy heir. *Indignus heres*

Uprising. *Seditio*

Uproar. *Tumultus*

Urge a debtor to pay. *Interpellare*

Usage, use. *Usus*

Usage, legal. *Consuetudo, mos*

Usufructuary. *Fructuarius, usufructuarius*

Vacant inheritance (legacy). *Caducum*

Vagrant slave. *Erro*

Valid, to be legally. *Valere, vim (vires) habere*

Valid marriage. *Iustae nuptiae*

Valuation in money. *Aestimatio*

Vessel. *Navis*

Veteran. *Vetus miles, veteranus*

Veto. *Intercessio*

Vexation with a suit, malicious. *Calumnia*

Village. *Vicus*

Vintage. *Vindemiae*

Violence. *Vis*

Void. *Nullus, irritus, inefficax, nullius momenti, nullas vires habere*

Vote. *Suffragium*

Voting. *Ferre suffragium*

Voting place. *Saeptum, ovile*

Vow. *Votum*

Wages. *Merces*

Walls of a city. *Muri*

War. *Bellum*

War booty. *Praeda*

War, to declare. *Denuntiare, indicere bellum*

Warranty against latent defects in a sale. See EDICTUM AEDILIUM CURULIUM, ACTIO REDHIBITORIA

Warranty against eviction. See ACTIO AUCTORITATIS, STIPULATIO DUPLAE

Water conduits. *Aquaeductus*

Wax-covered tablets. *Cerae, tubulae ceratae, tabellae*

Wealth. *Facultates*

Wealthy. *Locuples, assiduus*

Weapon. *Telum, arma*

Welfare, public. *Utilitas publica*

Whole. See CORPUS

Widow. *Vidua*

Wife. *Uxor*

Wild animals. *Ferae (bestiae)*

Will. *Voluntas, animus, mens*, see VELLE

Will (last). *Testamentum, ultima (postrema) voluntas*

Wink. *Nutus*

Withdraw from a transaction. *Recedere*

Withdrawal of a peculium.   *Ademptio peculii*

Withdrawal of an action.   *Cedere actione, resistere, deserere actionem*

Without (against) one's will.   *Invito*

Witness.   *Testis*

Witness to a will who signed and sealed it.   *Signator testamenti*

Words, solemn and prescribed by law.   *Certa et sollemnia verba*

Words, spoken or written.   *Verba*

Woman.   *Femina, mulier*

Wooden tablet.   *Lignum, tabula, tabella*

Work (construction).   *Opus*

Workman.   *Operarius, mercennarius, opifex*

Writer of a testament.   *Scriptor testamenti*, see QUAESTIO DOMITIANA

Written law.   *Ius scriptum*

Written stipulation.   *Cautio stipulatoria*

Written unilateral divorce.   *Libellus repudii*

Wrongful damage to another's property.   *Damnum iniuria datum*

Wrongful possession.   *Possessio iniusta*

Youth.   *Pueritia, iuvenis*

GENERAL BIBLIOGRAPHY

I. TEXTBOOKS, MANUALS AND GENERAL PRESENTATIONS OF ROMAN LAW. HISTORY OF SOURCES

ALBERTARIO, E. 1935. Introduzione storica allo studio del diritto giustinianeo. Milan, Giuffrè.
——. 1940. Il diritto romano. Milan, Principato.

ALVAREZ, SUAREZ, U. 1944. Horizonte actual del derecho romano. Madrid, Estudios Matritenses de derecho romano.
——. 1948. Curso elemental de derecho romano. 2 v. Madrid, Istituto de estudios politicos.

ALZAMORA, L. 1946. Derecho romano (revised by Alzamora Silva, L.). Lima, Peru, Taller di Linotipia.

ARANGIO-RUIZ, V. 1950. Storia del diritto romano. 6th ed. Naples, Jovene. (Spanish translation by De Pelsmaeker and Ivanez, Madrid, 2nd ed. 1943.)
——. 1951. Istituzioni di diritto romano. 10th ed. Naples, Jovene.

ARIAS, RAMOS, J. 1947. Derecho romano. 3rd ed. Madrid, Editorial Revista de derecho privado.

ARNÒ, C. 1937. Introduzione allo studio delle Pandette. Turin, Giappichelli.

ARU, L., and R. ORESTANO. 1947. Sinossi di diritto romano. Rome, La Navicella.

BAVIERA, G. 1914–1916. Lezioni di storia di diritto romano. 2 v. Palermo, Castiglia.

BETTI, E. 1935. Diritto romano. 1. Parte generale. Padua, Cedam.
——. 1942. Istituzioni di diritto romano. 1. 2nd ed. Padua, Cedam.

BIONDI, B. 1952. Istituzioni di diritto romano. 2nd ed. Milan, Giuffrè.

BISCARDI, A. 1942. Studi sulla legislazione del Basso Impero. *StSen* **54–56**.
——, P. 1925–1933. Corso di diritto romano. Vol. 1, 2, Rome, Sampaolesi; vol. 3, 6. Rome, Foro Italiano.
——. 1934. Storia del diritto romano. 2 v. Rome, Istituto di diritto romano. (French translation by Carrière and Fournier, 1928; Spanish translation by Santa Cruz Teijeiro, Madrid, 1944.)
——. 1946. Istituzioni di diritto romano. 10th ed. Turin, Giappichelli.

BRINZ, A. 1873–1892. Lehrbuch der Pandekten. 4 v. Erlangen, Deichert.

BRUGI, B. 1926. Istituzioni di diritto privato giustinianeo, 3rd ed. Turin, Utet.

BRY, J. 1927–1929. Principles de droit romain, 6th ed. Paris, Sirey.

BUCKLAND, W. W. 1931. The main institutions of Roman private law. Cambridge, Univ. Press.
——. 1932. A text-book of Roman Law from Augustus to Justinian. (Reprinted 1950.) 2nd ed. Cambridge, Univ. Press.
——. 1939. A manual of Roman private law. 2nd ed. Cambridge, Univ. Press.

BURDICK, W. L. 1938. The principles of Roman Law and their relation to modern law. Rochester, N. Y., Lawyers' Coop. Publishing Co.

CAMUS, E. F. 1937. Principios fundamentales del derecho romano, 2nd ed. La Habana, Montero.
——. 1941–1946. Curso de derecho romano. 4th ed., 6 v. La Habana, Universidad.

CARAMES, FERRO, J. M. 1943. Derecho privado romano. 4th ed. 2 v. Buenos Ayres, Perrot.

CASTILLEJO, J. 1935. Historia del derecho romano. Madrid, Suarez.

CHIAZZESE, L. 1947. Introduzione allo studio del diritto romano privato. 3rd ed. Palermo, Palumbo.

CLARK, E. C. 1906–1919. History of Roman private law. 1. Sources. 2. Jurisprudence. 3. Regal period. Cambridge, Univ. Press.

COCK, ARANGO, A. 1943. Curso de derecho romano. 2nd ed. Medellin, Colombia, Ediciones Univ. Catol. Bolivariana.

COGLIOLO, P. 1911. Manuale delle fonti del diritto romano. 2nd ed. Turin, Utet.

COLLINET, P., and A. GIFFARD. 1929–1930. Précis de droit romain. 1 (3rd ed.), 2 (2nd ed.). Paris, Dalloz.

CORNIL, G. 1921. Droit romain. Aperçu historique sommaire. Brussels, Imprimerie méd. et scientifique.

COSTA, E. 1909. Le fonti del diritto romano. Milan, Bocca.
——. 1925. Storia del diritto romano dalle origini alle compilazioni giustinianee. 2nd ed. Turin, Bocca.

CROME, C. 1922. Grundzuege des römischen Privatrechts. Bonn, Marcus.

CUQ, E. 1908. Manuel des institutions juridiques des Romains. 2nd ed. Paris, Plon.

CZYHLARZ, K. v. 1924. Lehrbuch der Institutionen des römischen Rechts. 18th ed. (by M. San Nicolò). Vienna, Hölder.

DECLAREUIL, J. 1924. Rome et l'organisation de droit. Paris, La Renaissance du livre. (Engl. translation under the title Rome, the law-giver, by C. K. Ogden. N. Y., Knopf.)

DIHIGO, E. 1944. Apuntes de derecho romano. La Habana, Editorial Lex.

DULCKEIT, G. 1952. Römische Rechtsgeschichte. Munich, Beck.

DUMONT, F. 1947. Manuel de droit romain. Paris, Librairie Générale de droit.

ENDEMANN, F. 1925. Römisches Privatrecht. Berlin, Gruyter.

FERRINI, C. 1885. Storia delle fonti e della giurisprudenza romana. Milan, Hoepli.

FERRINI, C. 1898. Diritto romano. Milan, Hoepli.
——. 1908. Manuale di Pandette. 3rd ed. Milan, Società Editrice Libraria.

DE FRANCISCI, P. 1929–1939. Storia del diritto romano. **1** (2nd ed., 1939): 2, 1 (2nd ed., 1938); **3**, 1 (revised ed., 1940). Milan, Giuffrè.
——. 1948. Sintesi storica del diritto rom. Rome, Ateneo.

GIFFARD, A. 1950. Précis de droit romain. 4th ed. Paris, Dalloz.

GIRARD, P. F. 1929. Manuel élémentaire de droit romain. 8th ed. (by F. Senn). Paris, Rousseau.

GROSSO, G. 1940. Premesse generali al corso di diritto romano. Bologna, Giappichelli.
——. 1952. Storia del diritto romano (Lezioni). 2nd ed. Turin, Giappichelli.

GUARINO, A. 1945. Profilo storico delle fonti di diritto romano. 2nd ed. Catania, Crisafulli.
——. 1948. Storia del diritto romano. Milan, Giuffrè.
——. 1949. Ordinamento giuridico romano. 1 (Lezioni) Naples, Giovene.

HEILFRON, E. 1920. Römisches Recht. 7th ed. Mannheim, Bensheimer.

HERMESDORF, R. H. D. 1945. Schets der uitwendige geschiedenis van het Romeinsch recht. 2nd ed. Utrecht, Dekker.

HUBRECHT, G. 1943. Manuel de droit romain. 2 v. Paris, Librairie générale de droit.

HUNTER, W. A. 1934. Introduction to Roman law. Revised by F. H. Lawson. 9th ed. London, Sweet & Maxwell.

HUVELIN, P. 1927–1929. Cours élémentaire de droit romain (ed. by R. Monier). 2 v. Paris, Sirey.

IGLESIAS, J. 1950–1951. Instituciones de derecho romano. 2 v. Barcelona.

IHERING, R. v. 1906–1923. Geist des römischen Rechts. 6th ed. 3 v. Leipzig, Breitkopf & Härtel. (Spanish translation by Principe y Latorre, French translation by Meulenaere.)

JOLOWICZ, H. P. 1952. Historical introduction to the study of Roman law. 2nd ed. Cambridge, Univ. Press.

JÖRS, P., and W. KUNKEL. 1949. Römisches Privatrecht (in Enzyklopädie der Rechts- und Staatswissenschaft). 3rd ed. Berlin, Springer.

KARLOWA, O. 1885–1901. Romische Rechtsgeschichte. Leipzig, Veit.

KASER, M. 1950. Römische Rechtsgeschichte. Göttingen, Vanderhoek & Ruprecht.

KIPP, T. 1919. Das romische Recht (in Das gesamte römische Recht, ed. by Stammler), 89–314. Berlin, Stilke.

——. 1919. Geschichte der Quellen des römischen Rechts. 4th ed. Leipzig, Deichert.

KRELLER, H. 1936. Römische Rechtsgeschichte. Tübingen, Mohr.

——. 1950. Romisches Recht und Grundlehren des gemeinen Rechts. Vienna, Springer.

KRÜGER, P. 1912. Geschichte der Quellen und Literatur des römischen Rechts (in Handbuch der deutschen Rechtswissenschaft). 2nd ed. Munich-Leipzig, Duncker & Humblot.

KUHLENBECK, L. 1910–1913. Entwicklungsgeschichte des römischen Rechts. 2 v. Munich, Lehmann.

KUNKEL, W. 1948. Römische Rechtsgeschichte. 2nd ed. Heidelberg, Scherer.

LANDUCCI, L. 1925. Appunti di storia del diritto romano con elementi di Istituzioni. Padua.

LAURIA, M. 1947. Corso di diritto romano. 2. Diritto privato, Età arcaica, Età Augustea. Naples, Morano.

LEAGE, R. W. 1930. Roman private law founded on the Institutes of Gaius and Justinian. 2nd ed. Edited by C. H. Ziegler. London, MacMillan.

LEE, R. W. 1952. The elements of Roman law. With a translation of the Institutes of Justinian. 3rd ed. London, Sweet & Maxwell.

LENEL, O. 1915. Geschichte und Quellen des romischen Rechts (in Enzyklopädie des Rechts, ed. by Holtzendorff and Kohler, 1). Munich-Leipzig, Duncker & Humblot.

——. 1927. Das Edictum perpetuum. 3rd ed. (2nd ed. in French by Peltier). Leipzig, Tauchnitz.

LONGO, C. 1935. Corso di diritto romano. Fatti, negozi giuridici. Milan, Giuffrè.

LONGO C., and G. SCHERILLO. 1944. Storia del diritto romano. Costituzione e fonti. Milan, Giuffrè.

LONGO, G. 1939–1941. Diritto romano. 4 v. Rome, Foro Italiano.

MARTINEZ, J. M. 1945. Los principios orientadores de la compilacion Justinianea. Murcia (Spain).

DI MARZO, S. 1946. Istituzioni di diritto romano. 5th ed. Milan, Giuffrè.

MAY, G. 1935. Éléments de droit romain. 18th ed. Paris, Sirey.

MAYNZ, C. 1891. Cours de droit romain approfondi. 3rd ed. 3 v. Brussels, Bruylant.

MAYR, R. v. 1912–1913. Romische Rechtsgeschichte (in Sammlung Goeschen, nos. 577/8, 645/8, 697). Leipzig, Goeschen.

MELVILLE, R. W. 1921. Manual of principles of Roman law. 3rd ed. Edinburgh, Green.

MITTEIS, L. 1891. Reichsrecht und Volksrecht in den östlichen Provinzen des romischen Kaiserreichs (reprinted with a Preface by L. Wenger, 1935). Leipzig, Teubner.

——. 1908. Romisches Privatrecht bis auf die Zeit Diokletians 1. Leipzig, Hirzel.

MONIER, R. 1947–1948. Manuel élémentaire de droit romain. 1 (6th ed.), 2 (4th ed.). Paris, Domat Montchrestien.

MOREY, W. C. 1914. Outlines of Roman law. 2nd ed. N. Y. & London, Putnam.

MUIRHEAD, J. S. 1947. An outline of Roman law. 2nd ed. London, Hodge.

D'ORS PEREZ-PEIX, A. 1943. Presupuestos criticos para el estudio de derecho romano. Salamanca, Colegio trilingue de la Universidad.

VAN OVEN, J. C. 1946. Leerboek van Romeinsch Privaatrecht. 2nd ed. Leiden, Brill.

——. 1947. Oversicht van Romeinsch Privaatrecht. 4th ed. Zwolle, Tjeenk Willink.

PACCHIONI, G. 1918–1922. Corso di diritto romano. 3 v. Turin, Utet.

——. 1935. Manuale di diritto romano. 3rd ed. Turin, Utet. (Spanish translation by Martinez e Roverte Moreno, Valladolid, 1942.)

PARADISI, B. 1951. Storia del diritto italiano. Le fonti nel Basso Impero e nell' epoca romano-barbarica. Lezioni. Naples, Jovene.

PERNICE, A. 1873–1900. Marcus Antistius Labeo. Romisches Privatrecht im ersten Jahrhundert der Kaiserzeit. 3 v. Halle, Waisenhaus.

PEROZZI, S. 1928. Istituzioni di diritto romano. 2nd ed. Rome, Athenaeum.

PERROT, E. 1927. Précis elementaire de droit romain. Paris, Presse Universitaire.

PETIT, E. 1925. Traité élémentaire de droit romain. 9th ed. Paris, Rousseau.

PETROPOULOS, G. A. 1944. History and institutions (Historia kai exegeseis) of Roman law (in Greek). Athens.

PUCHTA, G. P. 1893. Cursus der Institutionen. 10th ed. (by P. Krüger). Leipzig, Breitkopf & Haertel.

RABEL, E. 1915. Grundzüge des römischen Privatrechts, in Enzyklopädie des Rechts 1 (7th ed.), ed. by Holtzendorff and Kohler, 399–540. Munich-Leipzig, Duncker & Humblot.

RADIN, M. 1924. Fundamental concepts of Roman law. TulLR 12–13.

——. 1927. Handbook of Roman law. St. Paul (Minn.), West Publishing Co.

RICCOBONO, S. 1913. Istituzioni di diritto romano. Ed. by A. Guarneri-Citati. Palermo.

——. 1933–1934. Formazione e sviluppo del diritto romano dalle XII Tavole a Giustiniano. Corso. Milan, Giuffrè.

——. 1949. Lineamenti della storia delle fonti e del diritto romano. 2nd ed. Milan, Giuffrè.

RICCOBONO, S., JR. 1948. Lezioni di storia del diritto romano. Introduzione. Messina, Ferrara.

RIZZI, M. A. 1936. Tratado de derecho privado romano. Buenos Ayres, Menendez.

ROBERTI, M. 1942. Storia del diritto romano. 2nd ed. Milan, Collezione univ. Cetim.

ROBY, H. J. 1902. Roman private law in the time of Cicero and the Antonines. 2 v. Cambridge, Univ. Press.

SALKOWSKI, C. 1907. Institutionen des römischen Privatrechts. 9th ed. by O. Lenel. Leipzig, Tauchnitz.

SAVIGNY, F. K. v. 1840–1851. System des heutigen römischen Rechts. 8 v. Berlin, Veit.

SANFILIPPO, C. 1946. Istituzioni di diritto romano. 2nd ed. Naples, Humus.

SANTA CRUZ TEIJEIRO, J. 1946. Manuel elemental de instituciones de derecho romano. Madrid, Editorial Revista de derecho privado.

SCHERILLO, G. 1948. Lezioni di istituzioni di diritto romano. Milan, Ceum.

SCHERILLO, G., and A. DELL' ORO. 1948. Manuale di storia del diritto romano. Milan, Cisalpina.

SCHILLER, A. A. 1936, 1946. Text and commentary for the study of Roman law. Meccanisms of development (mimeographed). 2 v. N. Y., Columbia Univ.

SCHULZ, F. 1936. Principles of Roman Law. Translated from a text revised and enlarged by the author, by M. Wolf. Oxford, Clarendon Press (Italian translation by V. Arangio-Ruiz, 1946. Firenze, Sansoni).

——. 1946. History of Roman legal science. Oxford, Clarendon Press.

——. 1951. Classical Roman law. Oxford, Clarendon Press.

SCHWIND, F. v. 1950. Römisches Recht 1. Geschichte, Rechtsgang, System des Privatrechts. Vienna, Springer.

SCIALOJA, V. 1934. Corso di istituzioni di diritto romano. Rome, Anonima Romana Editoriale.

SEIDL, E. 1949. Römische Rechtsgeschichte und römisches Zivilprozessrecht. Hannover, Wissenschaftliche Verlagsanstalt.

SERAFINI, F. 1920. Istituzioni di diritto romano. 10th ed. Turin, Utet.

SHERMAN, C. P. 1937. Roman law in the modern world. 2nd ed. N. Y., Baker & Voorhis.

SIBER, H. 1925–1928. Römisches Recht in Grundzügen. 2 v. Berlin, Sack.

SOHM, R. 1928. Institutionen des romischen Rechts. 17th ed. (by L. Wenger and L. Mitteis). Berlin, Duncker & Humblot (English translation by Ledlie, 3rd ed. Oxford, Clarendon Press; New York, Frowde; Spanish translation by W. Roces. Madrid, Suarez).

STEPHENSON, A. 1912. History of Roman law with a commentary on the Institutes of Gaius and Justinian. Boston, Little & Brown.

TAUBENSCHLAG, R. 1920. Das romische Recht zur Zeit Diokletians. Bulletin of the Polish Academy in Cracow.

VOCI, P. 1946. Diritto romano. 3 v. Milan, Giuffrè.

——. 1949. Istituzioni di diritto romano. Milan, Giuffrè.

VOIGT. M. 1892–1902. Römische Rechtsgeschichte. Stuttgart, Cotta.

WALTON, F. P. 1920. Introduction to Roman law. 4th ed. Edinburgh-London, Green.

WEISS, E. 1936. Grundzüge der römischen Rechtsgeschichte. Reichenberg, Stiepel.

——. 1949. Institutionen des rom. Privatrechts. 2nd ed. Basel, Recht und Gesellschaft.

WENGER, L. 1953. Die Quellen des römischen Rechts. Vienna, Akademie der Wissenschaften. (In press.)

VAN WETTER, P. 1909–1911. Pandectes. 5 v. Paris, Librairie Générale de droit.

WINDSCHEID, B. 1906. Lehrbuch des Pandektenrechts. 9th ed. (by T. Kipp). Frankfurt, Rütten and Loening (Italian translation by Fadda, Bensa and Bonfante, richly enlarged. 5 v. 1925–1930, Turin, Utet; Greek translation by Polygenes, 2 v. 1932–1934).

WOLFF, H. J. 1951. Roman law. An historical introduction. Oklahoma Univ. Press.

II. ROMAN PRIVATE LAW

A. LAW OF PERSONS

(Family, marriage, guardianship, slavery, corporations)

ALBERTARIO, E. 1933. Studi di diritto romano 1. Persone e famiglia. Milan, Giuffrè.

——. 1942. Matrimonio e dote. Corso. Milan, Giuffrè.

ALLARD, P. 1914. Les esclaves chrétiens depuis les premiers temps de l'Église. 5th ed. Paris, Lecoffre.

BARROW, R. H. 1928. Slavery in the Roman Empire. London, Methuen.

BERGER, A. 1914, 1922. Streifzüge durch das römische Sklavenrecht. Philol. 73: 61–108; ZSS 43: 398–416.

BONFANTE, P. 1925. Corso di diritto romano 1. Diritto di famiglia. Rome, Sampaolesi.

BRINI, G. 1887. Matrimonio e divorzio nel diritto romano. Bologna, Zanichelli.

BUCKLAND, W. W. 1908. The Roman law of slavery. Cambridge, Univ. Press.

CASTELLO, C. 1940. In tema di matrimonio e concubinato nel mondo romano. Milan, Giuffre.

——. 1942. Studi sul diritto familiare e gentilizio romano. Milan, Giuffrè.

COLI, U. 1913. Collegia e sodalitates. Bologna, Seminario giur. dell' Università. ·

CORBETT, G. 1930. The Roman law of marriage. Cambridge, Univ. Press.

COSTA, E. 1894. Papiniano. 2. Bologna, Zanichelli.

DUFF, A. M. 1928. Freedmen in the early Roman Empire. Oxford, Clarendon Press.

DUFF, P. W. 1938. Personality in Roman private law. Cambridge, Univ. Press.

ELIACHEVITCH, B., 1942. La personnalité juridique en droit privé romain. Paris, Sirey.

FADDA, C. 1910. Diritto delle persone e della famiglia. Naples, Alvano.

KÜBLER, B. 1938. Die vormundschaftliche Gewalt im römischen Recht. St.Besta 1.

LAUM, B. 1914. Stiftungen in der griechischen and romischen Antike. Leipzig, Teubner.

LAURIA, M. 1952. Matrimonio, Dote. Naples. Arte Tipografica.

LEVY, E. 1925. Der Hergang der rom. Ehescheidung. Weimar, Böhlau.

LONGO, G. 1940. Diritto romano. 3. Diritto di famiglia. Rome, Forgo Italiano.

MORIAUD, P. 1910. Le la simple famille paternelle en droit romain. Geneva, Georg.

ORESTANO, R. 1951. La struttura giuridica del matrimonio romano dal diritto classico al diritto giustinianeo. Milan, Giuffrè.

DE ROBERTIS, F. M. 1934. Contributi alla storia delle corporazioni a Roma. AnBari 6–7.

——. 1938. Il diritto associativo romano. Bari, La Terza.

SALEILLES, R. 1910. De la personnalité juridique. Paris, Rousseau.

SCHNORR V. CAROLSFELD, L. 1933. Geschichte der juristischen Person, 1. Munich, Beck.

SCHUPFER, F. 1876. La famiglia secondo il diritto romano. Padua, Sacchetto.

SOLAZZI, S. 1913–1914. Tutele e curatele. RISG 53–54.

——. 1921. Fantasie e riflessioni sulla storia della tutela. StPav 6.

——. 1923, 1926. Studi su tutela. PubMod 9, 13.

——. 1926. Istituti tutelari. Naples, Jovene.

——. 1939, 1942. Sui divieti matrimoniali delle leggi Augustee. ANap 59, 61.

TAUBENSCHLAG, R. 1913. Vormundschaftsrechtliche Studien. Leipzig, Teubner.

VOLTERRA, E. 1946. Diritto di famiglia. Lezioni. Bologna, Edizioni Universitarie.

WALTZING, J. P. 1895–1899. Étude historique sur les corporations professionnelles chez les Romains. Louvain, Peeters.

WESTRUP, C. W. 1934–1944. Introduction to early Roman law. Comparative sociological studies. The patriarchal joint family. 1. The house community (1944); 2. Family property (1934); 3. Patria potestas (1939). Copenhagen.

WOLFF, H. J. 1939. Written and unwritten marriages in Hellenistic and postclassical Roman law. Haverford, Cost.

B. LAW OF THINGS

(Ownership, possession, servitudes, real securities)

ALBERTARIO, E. 1941. Studi di diritto romano. 2. Diritti reali e possesso. Milan, Giuffrè.

——. 1946. Corso di diritto romano. Possesso e quasi-possesso. Milan, Giuffrè.

ARNÒ, C. 1936. Il possesso. Corso. Turin, Giappichelli.

BERGER, A. 1912. Zur Entwicklungsgeschichte der Teilungsklagen im klassischen röm. Recht. Weimar, Böhlau.

BIONDI, B. 1938. La categoria romana delle servitutes. Milan, Vita e Pensiero.
——. 1946. Le servitu prediali. Corso di diritto romano. Revised ed. Milan, Giuffrè.
BISCARDI, A. 1942. Studi sulla legislazione del Basso Impero. Diritti reali e possesso. Rome, Foro Italiano.
BONFANTE, P. 1926-1933. Corso di diritto romano. La proprietà **2** (two parts, 1926, 1928) ; Diritti reali **3** (1933). Roma, Sampaolesi.
BRANCA, G. 1941. Le cose extra patrimonium humani iuris. *AnTriest* **12**. Trieste, Università.
BRASIELLO, U. 1941. La estensione e la limitazione della proprietà. Corso. Milan, Giuffrè.
CARCATERRA, A. 1942. Il possesso dei diritti nel diritto romano. Milan, Giuffrè.
COSTA, E. 1919. Le acque nel diritto romano. Bologna, Zanichelli.
EBRARD, F. 1917. Die Digestenfragmente ad formulam hypothecariam und die Hypothekarrezeption. Leipzig, Veit.
FEHR, M. 1910. Beiträge zur Lehre vom römischen Pfandrecht. Uppsala, Berling.
FERRARI, G. 1932. I diritti reali. Lezioni. Padua, Milani.
DE FRANCISCI, P. 1924. Il trasferimento della proprietà. Padua, La Lito-tipo Editrice Universitaria.
GAUDEMET, J. 1934. Étude sur le regime de l'indivision en droit romain. Paris, Sirey.
GROSSO, G. 1944. I problemi di diritti reali nell' impostazione romana. Turin, Giappichelli.
KASER, M. 1943. Eigentum und Besitz im älteren römischen Recht. Weimar, Böhlau.
LEVY, E. 1951. West Roman vulgar law. The law of property. Philadelphia, *Mem. Amer. Philos. Soc.* **29**.
LONGO, C. 1938. Le cose. La proprietà e suoi modi d'acquisto. Corso. (Reprinted 1946.) Milan, Giuffrè.
LONGO, G. 1935. La distinzione delle cose. Proprietà. Corso. Catania, Muglia.
OLIVECRONA, K. 1938. The acquisition of possession in Roman law. Lund, Gleerup; Leipzig, Harrassowitz.
RODDI, C. 1936. I mutamenti della cosa e le loro conseguenze giuridiche. Turin, Istituto giur. Università.
SANFILIPPO, C. 1944. Servitutes personarum. Corso. Catania, Crisafulli.
SCHERILLO, G. 1945. Lezioni di diritto romano. Le cose. Parte 1. Concetto di cosa, cose extra patrimonium. Milan, Giuffrè.
SEGRÈ, G. 1926-1929. Le cose. La proprietà. Corso. 3 v. Parma.
——. 1935. Le garenzie reali. Corso. Parma.
SIBER, H. 1907. Die Passivlegitimation bei der rei vindicatio. Leipzig, Deichert.
SOKOLOWSKI, P. 1902-1907. Die Philosophie im Privatrecht. Sachbegriff und Körper in der klassischen Jurisprudenz. 2 v. Halle, Niemeyer.
VERMOND, E. 1928. De iure rerum corporalium privatarum. 2 v. Paris, Broccard.
VOCI, P. 1952. Modi di acquisto di proprietà. Corso. Milan, Giuffrè.
DE ZULUETA, F. 1950. Digest 41.1,2. De adquirendo rerum dominio. 2nd ed. Oxford, Clarendon Press.

C. LAW OF OBLIGATIONS

ALBERTARIO, E. 1936. Studi di diritto romano. 3. Milan, Giuffrè.
——. 1944-1947. Le obbligazioni. Corso. Le obbligazioni solidali; Le obbligazioni alternative, generiche, indivisibili. Milan, Giuffrè.
ARANGIO-RUIZ, V. 1933. Responsabilità contrattuale in diritto romano. 2nd ed. Naples, Jovene.

ARCHI, G. G. 1946. Indirizzi e problemi del sistema contrattuale nella legislazione da Constantino a Giustiniano. *Scr. Ferrini Univ. Pavia,* 661-727.
ARNÒ, C. 1931. Obbligazioni. Corso. Pavia, Cucchi.
BERNARD, A. 1935. La remunération des professions libérales en droit romain classique. Paris, Domat-Montchrestien.
BERTOLINI, C. 1905-1909. Appunti didattici di diritto romano. Obbligazioni. 2 v. Turin, Utet.
BISCARDI, A. 1935, 1938. Il dogma della collisione alla luce del diritto romano. Città di Castello; *SDHI* **4**.
BONFANTE, P. 1924-1925. Lezioni di storia del commercio. 2 v. Rome, Sampaolesi.
BOYER, G. 1924. Recherches historiques sur la résolution des contrats. Paris, Presses Universitaires.
BRINI, G. 1905. L'obbligazione nel diritto romano. Bologna, Zanichelli.
——. 1923-1925. Sulle fonti delle obbligazioni nel diritto romano. *RendBol,* ser. 2, **8** : 154.
COLLINET, P. 1932. Evolution of contract as illustrating the general evolution of Roman law. *LQR* **48**.
CORNIL, G. 1912. Debitum et obligatio. Recherches sur la formation de la notion de l'obligation romaine. *Mél Girard* 1. Paris, Rousseau.
COSTA, E. 1898. Papiniano, **4**. Voluntas contrahentium. Bologna, Zanichelli.
CUGIA, S. 1922. La nullità parziale del negozio giuridico. Naples, Alvano.
FADDA, C. 1908. Istituti commerciali del diritto romano. Lezioni. Naples.
FELGENTRÄGER, W. 1933. Antikes Lösungsrecht. Berlin, De Gruyter.
DE FRANCISCI, P. 1923, 1926. Storia e dottrina dei cosidetti contratti innominati. 2 v. Pavia, Mattei.
GEORGESCU, V. A. 1932. Essai d'une théorie générale des leges privatae. Thèse Paris, Rousseau.
GROSSO, G. 1947. Obbligazioni. Contenuto e requisiti. Corso. Turin, Giappichelli.
——. 1950. Il sistema romano dei contratti. 2nd ed. Torino, Giappichelli.
GUARNERI-CITATI, A. 1921. Studi sulle obbligazioni indivisibili nel diritto romano. *AnPal* **9**.
HÄGERSTRÖM, A. 1927, 1941. Der römische Obligationsbegriff im Lichte der römischen Rechtsanschauung. 2 v. Uppsala, Almquist.
HELDRICH, K. 1924. Das Verschulden beim Vertragsabschluss. Leipzig, Weicher.
HIJMANS, I. H. 1927. Romeinsch verbintenissenrecht. Zwolle, Tjeenk Willink.
HUVELIN, P. 1929. Études d'histoire du droit commercial romain. Histoire externe. Droit maritime. Paris, Sirey.
KRETSCHMAR, P. 1906. Die Erfüllung. Leipzig, Veit.
LEIFER, F. 1933. Kritik zur Lehre von Schuld und Haftung. *KrVj* **26**.
LEVY, E. 1915. Privatstrafe und Schadensersatz. Berlin, Vahlen.
LOBINGIER, C. S. 1935. Maritime Law of Rome. *JurR* **47** : 1-32.
LONGO, C. 1936. Classificazione dei rapporti obbligatori. Corso. Milan, Giuffrè.
LONGO, G. 1936. I contratti reali. Corso. Catania, Muglia.
——. 1950. Diritto delle obbligazioni. Turin, Utet.
LUZZATTO, G. I. 1938. Caso fortuito e forza maggiore come limite alla responsabilità contrattuale. Milan, Giuffrè.
——. 1934. Per un' ipotesi sulle origini e la natura delle obbligazioni romane. Milan, Giuffrè.
MAILLET, J. 1944. Le théorie de Schuld et Haftung en droit romain. Aix-en-Provence, Roubaud.
MARCHI, A. 1912. Storia dell'obbligazione romana. Rome, Athenaeum.

——. 1913. Figure e realtà nella terminologia dell'obbligazione romana. *Annuario dell'Università Macerata,* Bianchini.

DE MARTINO, F. 1940. L'origine delle garenzie personali e il concetto dell'obbligazione. *SDHI* **6**.

NOCERA, G. 1942. Insolvenza e responsabilità sussidiaria nel diritto romano. Rome, Edizioni Italiane.

OLIVER, D. T. 1937. Digest XII 1 and 4–7, XIII 1–3, De condictionibus. Cambridge, Univ. Press.

PACCHIONI, G. 1912. Concetto e origine dell'obbligazione romana. La pecuniarietà dell'obbligazione. App. I and III to the Italian translation of C. F. v. Savigny, Das Obligationenrecht. Padua, Milani.

PARTSCH, J. 1931. Das Dogma des Synallagma im römischen und byzantinischen Recht. Aus nachgelassenen Schriften, 3–96. Berlin, Springer.

PASTORI, F. 1951. Profilo dogmatico e storico dell'obbligazione romana. Varese, Istituto editoriale Cisalpino.

PEROZZI, S. 1903. Le obbligazioni romane. Bologna, Zanichelli.

PRINGSHEIM, F. 1916. Kauf mit fremdem Geld. Leipzig, Veit.

RICCOBONO, S. 1929. La formazione della teoria generale del contractus nel periodo della giurisprudenza classica. *St. Bonfante* **1**. Milano, Treves.

——. 1930. Lineamenti della dottrina della rappresentanza diretta in diritto romano. *AnPal* **14** (St. Vivante, 1931)

——. 1935. Stipulatio, contractus, pacta. Corso, Milan, Giuffre.

——. 1939. La teoria dell'abuso nella dottrina romana. *BIDR* **46**.

DE ROBERTIS, F. M. 1946. I rapporti di lavoro nel diritto romano. Milan, Giuffrè.

ROTONDI, G. 1922. Scritti giuridici. 2. Studi sul diritto romano delle obbligazioni. Milan, Hoepli.

SCHLOSSMANN, S. 1904. Altrömisches Schuldrecht und Schuldverfahren. Leipzig, Deichert.

SCIALOJA, V. 1933. Negozi giuridici. Rome, Foro Italiano.

SCIASCIA, G. 1947. Lineamenti del sistema obbligatorio romano. Camerino, Università, Facoltà di giurisprudenza.

SOLAZZI, S. 1935. L'estinzione dell'obbligazione. 2nd ed. Naples, Jovene.

——. 1936. Appunti di diritto romano marittimo. *RDNav* **2**: 113, 168.

——. 1937–1943. Il concorso dei creditori. 4 v. Naples, Jovene.

——. 1944–1945. Revoca degli atti fraudolenti nel diritto romano. 2 v. 3rd ed. Naples, Jovene.

TEDESCHI, G. 1899. Il diritto marittimo dei Romani. Montefiascone.

VERMOND, E. 1937. De iure obligationum. Principes fondamentaux. 2 v. Paris, Boccard.

VIARD, P. E. 1919. Les pactes adjoints aux contrats en droit romain classique. Paris, Sirey.

DE VISSCHER, F. 1931. Les origines des obligations ex delicto, in Études de droit romain. Paris, Sirey.

VOCI, P. 1938. Risarcimento del danno e processo formulare. Milan, Giuffre.

——. 1939. Risarcimento del danno e pena privata nel diritto romano classico. Milan, Giuffrè.

——. 1946. La dottrina romana del contratto. Milan, Giuffrè.

WYLIE, J. K. 1923. Studies in Roman Law 1. Solidarity e correality. Edinburgh, Oliver.

D. LAW OF SUCCESSION

ALBANESE, B. 1949. La successione ereditaria in diritto romano antico. *AnPal* **20**.

ALBERTARIO, E. 1946. Studi di diritto romano **4**. Eredità. Milan, Giuffrè.

ARNÒ, C. 1938. Diritto ereditario. Turin, Giappichelli.

BIONDI, B. 1943. Successione testamentaria. Milan, Giuffrè.

——. 1946, 1948. Istituti fondamentali di diritto ereditario romano. 2 v. Milan, Vita e Pensiero.

CAMUS, E. F. 1942. Derecho succesorio. 2nd ed. La Habana, Universidad.

CARCATERRA, A. 1948. L'azione ereditaria nel diritto romano. 2 v. Rome.

COSTA, E. 1897. Papiniano. **3**. Favor testamentorum e voluntas testantium. Bologna, Zanichelli.

CUGIA, S. 1910. Indagini sulla dottrina della causa del negozio giuridico. L'espressione mortis causa nel diritto romano. Napoli, Sangiovanni.

DAVID, M. 1930. Studien zur heredis institutio ex re certa im klassischen römischen und justinianischen Recht. Leipzig, Weicher.

DROPSIE, M. A. 1892. The Roman law of testaments, codicils, etc. Philadelphia, Johnson.

DULCKEIT, G. 1934. Erblasserwille bei Antretung der Erbschaft. Weimar, Böhlau.

——. 1939. Voluntas and fides im Vermachtnisrecht. *Fschr. Koschaker* **1**. Weimar, Böhlau.

FADDA, C. 1900, 1902. Concetti fondamentali del diritto ereditario romano. Milan, Giuffrè. (Reprinted 1949.)

FERRINI, C. 1889. Teoria generale dei legati e fedecommessi. Milan, Hoepli.

KOROSEC, V. 1927. Die Erbenhaftung nach römischem Recht. Leipzig, Weicher.

LA PIRA, G. 1930. La successione ereditaria intestata e contro il testamento. Firenze, Vallecchi.

LÉVY-BRUHL, H. 1947. Observations generales sur le regime successoral de Douze Tables, in Nouvelles Études de droit romain. Paris, Sirey.

LONGO, C. 1901, 1903. L'origine della successione particolare. *BIDR* **14, 15**.

MASCHI, C. A. 1938. Studi sull'interpretazione dei legati. Verba e voluntas. Milan, Vita e Pensiero.

MICHON, L. 1921. La succession ab intestat dans le plus ancien droit romain. *NRH* **45**.

NARDI, E. 1938. La reciproca posizione dei coniugi privi di conubium. Milan, Giuffrè.

RABEL, E. 1930. Die Erbrechtstheorie Bonfante's. *ZSS* **50**.

SANFILIPPO, C. 1937. Studi sull'hereditas. *AnPal* **17**.

——. 1946. Evoluzione storica dell'hereditas. Corso. Naples, Humus.

SCHULZ, M. 1935. Einfluss Kaiser Justinians auf das Erbrecht. Diss. Erlangen.

SCIALOJA, V. 1933. Diritto ereditario romano. Concetti fondamentali. Rome, Anon. Romana Editoriale.

SEGRÈ, A. 1930. Ricerche di diritto ereditario romano. Rome, Foro Italiano.

SEGRÈ, G. 1905. Note esegetiche sui legati in diritto romano. *St Scialoja* **1**.

SOLAZZI, S. 1932–1933. Diritto ereditario romano. 2 v. Naples, Jovene.

SUMAN, A. 1916. Favor testamenti e voluntas testantium. Rome, Athenaeum.

TIMBAL, P. 1940–1941. Questions de droit successoral romain du Bas-Empire. *RHD* **19–20**.

VACCARU-DELOGU, R. 1941. L'accrescimento nel diritto ereditario romano. Milan, Giuffrè.

DE VILLA, V. 1939. La liberatio legata nel diritto classico e giustinianeo. Milan, Giuffrè.

VOCI, P. 1935. La responsabilità dell'erede nell'adempimento dei legati per damnationem e nei fedecommessi. *SDHI* **48**.

WLASSAK, M. 1933. Studien zum altromischen Erb- und Vermächtnisrecht. *SbWien* **215**.

WOESS, F. v. 1911. Das römische Erbrecht und die Erbanwärter. Berlin, Vahlen.

E. CIVIL PROCEDURE

ALBERTARIO, E. 1946. Studi di diritto romano. 4. Processo. Milan, Giuffrè.

ALVAREZ SUAREZ, U. 1951. Curso del derecho romano. 2. Derecho procesal civil. Madrid.

ANDT, E. 1920. La procédure par rescrit. Paris, Sirey.

APELT, H. 1937. Die Urteilsnichtigkeit im römischen Prozess. Schramberg (Schwarzwald), Salzer & Hahn.

ARANGIO-RUIZ, V. 1935. Cours de droit romain. Les actions. Naples, Jovene.

——. 1920. La privata difesa del proprio diritto. RISG 65.

ARU, L. 1934. Il processo civile contumaciale. Rome, Anon. Rom. Editoriale.

——. 1936. Appunti sulla difesa privata in diritto romano. AnPal 15.

BALOGH, E. 1936. Beiträge zum justinianischen Libellprozess. St Riccobono 2. Palermo, Castiglia.

BEKKER, E. I. 1871, 1873. Die Aktionen des römischen Privatrechts. 2 v. Berlin, Vahlen.

BETHMANN-HOLLWEG, M. A. 1864–1866. Der römische Civilprozess. 3 v. Bonn, Marcus.

BIONDI, B. 1935. Il processo civile giustinianeo. ACDR Roma 2. Pavia, Fusi.

CHECCHINI, A. 1923–1924. Studi sull'ordinamemto processuale. Il processo romano. StCagl 14.

COLLINET, P. 1947. La nature des actions, dès interdits et des exceptions dans l'œuvre de Justinien. Paris, Sirey.

COSTA, E. 1918. Profilo storico del processo civile. Rome, Athenaeum.

DÜLL, R. 1931. Der Gütegedanke im römischen Zivilprozess. Munich, Beck.

EISELE, F. 1889. Abhandlungen zum romischen Zivilprozess. Freiburg i. Br., Mohr.

GIFFARD, A. 1932. Leçons de procédure civile romaine. Paris, Domat Monchrestien.

GIRARD, P. F. 1901. Histoire de l'organisation judiciaire des Romains. Les six premiers siècles de Rome. Paris, Rousseau.

GREENIDGE, A. H. J. 1901. Legal procedure in Cicero's time. Oxford, Clarendon Press.

HAJJE, A., Histoire de la justice seigneuriale. La justice privée dans les domaines des empereurs. Paris, Boccard.

HERDLITCZKA, A. 1934. Skizzen zum römischen Zivilprozess. Vienna, Höfels.

JOBBÉ-DUVAL, E. 1896. Études sur l'histoire de la procédure civile chez les Romains. Paris, Rousseau.

JÖRS, P. 1892. Untersuchungen zur Gerichtsverfassung der römischen Kaiserzeit. Leipzig, Hirschfeld.

JUNCKER, J. 1927. Haftung und Prozessbegründung im altrömischen Rechtsgang. Gedächtnisschrift für E. Seckel. Berlin, Springer.

LEIFER, F. 1947. Vorlesungen über römischen Zivilprozess. Vienna, Österreichische Staatsdruckerei.

LEMOSSE, M. 1944. Cognitio sur le rôle du juge. Paris, Lesot.

LEVY, E. 1918, 1922. Die Konkurrenz der Aktionen und Personen. 2 v. Berlin, Vahlen.

LUZZATTO, G. I. 1946–1950. Procedura civile romana. 3 v. Bologna, Zuffi.

DE MARTINO, F. 1937. La giurisdizione nel diritto romano. Padua, Cedam.

PALERMO, A., 1942. Il procedimento cauzionale. Milan, Giuffrè.

PARTSCH, J. 1905. Die Schriftformel im römischen Provinzialprozess. Breslau, Fock.

PUGLIESE, G. 1939. Actio e diritto subbiettivo. Milan, Giuffrè.

——. 1948. Lezioni sul processo civile romano. Il processo formulare. Milan, Montuoro.

REDENTI, E. 1907. Pluralità di parti nel giudizio civile. Diritto romano. AG 79.

SAMTER, R. 1911. Nichtförmliches Gerichtsverfahren. Weimar, Böhlau.

SANTA-CRUZ TEIJEIRO, J. 1947. Principios de derecho procesal romano, Valencia.

SCHOTT, R. 1903. Gewähren des Rechtsschutzes im römischen Zivilprozess. Jena, Fischer.

STEINWENTER, A. 1914. Studien zum römischen Versäumnisverfahren. Munich, Beck.

——. 1947. Rhetorik und römischer Zivilprozess. ZSS 65.

VOLKMANN, H. 1935. Zur Rechtssprechung im Prinzipat des Augustus. Munich, Beck.

WENGER, L. 1935. Abriss des römischen Zivilprozessrechts. 2nd ed. (Appendix to Joers and Kunkel, Römisches Privatrecht). English translation of the 1st ed. by A. A. Schiller, TulLR 5, 1931.

——. 1940. Institutes of the Roman law of civil procedure (translation by O. H. Fisk). N. Y., Veritas Press. German ed. Institutionen des römischen Zivilprozessrechts. Munich, Hüber, 1925. Italian translation by R. Orestano. Milan, Giuffrè, 1938.

WLASSAK, M. 1888, 1891. Römische Prozessgesetze. 2 v. Leipzig, Duncker & Humblot.

——. 1919. Zum römischen Provinzialprozess. SbWien 190.

——. 1921. Der Judikationsbefehl der römischen Prozesse. SbWien 197.

——. 1924. Die römische Prozessformel. SbWien 202.

III. CRIMINAL LAW AND PROCEDURE

BRASIELLO, U. 1937. La repressione penale in diritto romano. Naples, Jovene.

——. 1938. Linee e fattori dello sviluppo del diritto penale romano. AG 120.

——. 1946. Note introduttive allo studio dei crimina romani. SDHI 12: 148.

BUSEK, V. 1935. Die Gerichtsbarkeit in Strafsachen im römischen Recht. ACII 1.

COSTA, E. 1921. Crimini e pene da Romolo a Giustiniano. Bologna, Zanichelli.

——. 1921. Il conato criminoso. BIDR 31.

FALCHI, G. F. 1932–1937. Diritto penale romano. 3 v. (1st v. in 2nd ed.) Padua, Zannoni.

FERRINI, C. 1899. Diritto penale romano. Teorie generali. Milan, Hoepli.

——. 1909. Esposizione storica e dottrinale del diritto penale romano (Enciclopedia di diritto penale, 1, ed. Pessina).

HITZIG, H. 1909. Die Herkunft des Schwurgerichts im römischen Strafprozess. Zurich, Orell & Füssli.

LAURIA, M. 1934. Accusatio-inquisitio. ANap 56.

LEVY, E. 1931. Die römische Kapitalstrafe. SbHeid.

——. 1938. Gesetz und Richter im kaiserlichen Strafprozess. BIDR 45. (See Statute and judge in Roman criminal law, Washington Law Jour. 13.)

LOTMAR, P. 1918. Litiscontestation im römischen Accusationsprozess. Schweizerische Ztschr. für Strafrecht 31.

DI MARZO, S. 1898. Storia della procedura criminale romana. La giurisdizione dalle origini alle XII Tavole. Palermo, Reber.

MOMMSEN, T. 1899. Römisches Strafrecht. Leipzig, Duncker & Humblot. (French translation by Duquesne, 1909.)

PUGLIESE, G. 1939. Appunti sui limiti dell'imperium nella repressione penale. MemTor. Turin, Istituto giur. dell'Università.

DE ROBERTIS, F. M. 1939. La variazione della pena pro qualitate personarum nel diritto penale romano. RISG 14.

——. 1940. La variazione della pena pro modo admissi nella cognitio extra ordinem e nel processo postclassico. Bari.

——. 1942. Studi di diritto penale romano. Bari, Macri.

——. 1947. La variazione della pena e la sua causa determinante. AnBari 9.

——. 1950. La variazione della pena nel diritto romano. Bari, Cacucci.

SCHISAS, F. M. 1926. Offences against the state in Roman law. London, Univ. Press.

SIBER, H. 1936. Analogie, Amtsrecht und Rückwirkung im Strafrechte des römischen Freistaates. *ASächGW* **43**.

STRACHAN-DAVIDSON, J. L. 1912. Problems of the Roman criminal law. 2 v. Oxford, Univ. Press.

VRIJHEID, H. M. 1918. Schuld en schuldverband in het Romeinsche Strafrecht. Amsterdam, Kruyt.

WLASSAK, M. 1917, 1920. Anklage und Streitbefestigung im Kriminalrecht der Romer. *SbWien* **184**, **194**.

IV. ROMAN PUBLIC LAW

(Constitution, administration, international relations)

ABBOTT, F. F. 1915. History and description of Roman political institutions. Boston-London, Ginn.

ABBOTT, F. F., and A. C. JOHNSON. 1926. Municipal administration in the Roman Empire. Princeton Univ. Press.

ARIAS ROMOS, J. 1948. Compendio de derecho publico romano e historia de las fuentes. 4th ed. Valladolid, Martin.

ARNOLD, W. T. 1914. The Roman system of provincial administration to the accession of Constantine the Great. 3rd ed. Oxford, Blackwell.

BAVIERA, G. 1914. Il diritto pubblico romano. Lezioni. Palermo, Castiglia.

BESTA, E. 1946. Il diritto internazionale nel mondo antico *Communicazioni e studi dell'Istituto di Diritto internazionale dell'Univ. di Milano.* **2**.

BOTT, H. 1928. Grundzüge der diokletianischen Steuervefassung. Darmstadt, Wittich.

BRASSLOFF, S. 1928. Der römische Staat und seine internationalen Beziehungen. Vienna, Perles.

BUECHNER, K. 1947. Die römische Republik im römischen Staatsdenken. Freiburg i. Br., Alber.

BURY, J. 1910. Constitution of the Later Empire. Cambridge, Univ. Press.

BUSSELL, F. W. 1910. The Roman Empire. Essays on the constitutional history from A.D. 81 to A.D. 1081. London, N. Y., Longman & Green.

CAGNAT, R. 1882. Études historiques sur les impots indirects chez les Romains. Paris, Imprimerie Nationale. (Italian translation, Biblioteca della storia economica 5. Milan, Soc. Editr. Libraria).

CANAVESI, M. 1942. La politica estera di Roma. 2 v. Milan, Istituto per gli Studi di politica internazionale.

CARDINALI, G. 1932. Alcuni caratteri fondamentali della costituzione politica ed imperiale di Roma. *Hist* **6**.

CHAVEAU, A. 1891. Le droit des gens dans les rapports de Rome. *NRHD* **15**.

COLI, U. 1938. Sul parallelismo del diritto pubblico a del diritto privato. *SDHI* **4**.

COSTA, E. 1920. Storia del diritto romano pubblico. 2nd ed. Firenze, Barbera.

DAVID, M. 1946. The treaties between Rome and Carthage and their significance for our knowledge of Roman international law. Symb van Oven, Leiden.

EGGER, E. 1866. Études historiques sur les traités publics chez les Romains jusqu'au premiers siècles de l'ère chrétienne. Paris, Durand.

ENSSLIN, W. 1927. Die Demokratie in Rom. *Phil.* **82**.

FRACCARO, P. 1934. Organizzazione politica dell' Italia romana. *ACDR Roma* **1**. Pavia, Fusi.

DE FRANCISCI, P. 1947-1948. Arcana imperii. 3 v. Milan, Giuffrè.

GREENIDGE, A. H. J. 1930. Roman public life. London, Macmillan.

GROAG, E. 1939. Die Reichsbeamten von Achaia bis auf Diokletian. Wien-Leipzig, Hölder, Pichler, Tempsky.

——. 1946. Die Reichsbeamten von Achaia in spätromischer Zeit. Budapest, *Dissertationes Pannonicae*, ser. I, **14**.

GROSSE, R. 1920. Römische Militärgeschichte von Gallienus bis zum Reginn der byzantinischen Themenverfassung. Berlin, Weidmann.

GUARINO, A. 1947. La democrazia romana. *AnCat* **1**.

HAMMOND, M. 1951. City state and world state in Greek and Roman political theory until Augustus. Cambridge (Mass.), Harvard Univ. Press.

HERZOG, E. 1884. Geschichte und System der römischen Staatsverfassung. I. Königszeit und Republik. Leipzig, Teubner.

HEUSS, A. 1933. Die völkerrechtlichen Grundlagen der römischen Aussenpolitik in republikanischer Zeit. *Klio, Beiheft* **33**.

——. 1934. Abschluss und Beurkundung des romischen Staatsvertrages. *Kl* **27** : 14, 218.

HIRSCHFELD, O. 1905. Die kaiserlichen Verwaltungsbeamten bis auf Diokletian. 2nd ed. Berlin, Weidmann.

HOMO, L. 1950. Les institutions politiques romaines. De la cité à l'État. 2nd ed. Paris, Michel. (English translation by Dobie, N. Y., Knopf, 1929.)

HORNICKEL, O. 1930. Ehren- und Rangpraedikate in den Papyrusurkunden. Römisches und byzantinisches Titelwesen. Diss. Giessen.

HOWE, L. L. The praetorian Prefects from Commodus to Diocletian. Chicago, Univ. Press.

KOCH, P. 1903. Byzantinische Beamtentitel von 400 bis 700. Jena, Universitätsbuchdruckerei.

KOLIAS, G. 1939. Ämter-und Würdenkauf im frühbyzantinischen Reich. (*Texte und Forschungen zur byzantinisch-neugriechischen Philologie* **35**.) Athens.

KORNEMANN, E. Doppelprinzipat und Reichsteilung im Imperium Romanum. Leipzig, Teubner.

——. 1940. Prinzipat und Dominat. *Forschungen und Fortschritte* **75**.

LARIVIÈRE, L. 1892. Les traités conclus par Rome avec les rois étrangers. Paris, Rousseau.

LAURIA, M. 1946. Diritto pubblico. Corso I. Naples, Morano.

LEIFER, F. 1914. Die Einheit des Gewaltgedankens im römischen Staatsrecht. Munich, Duncker & Humblot.

——. 1931. Studien zum antiken Ämterwesen. I. Vorgeschichte des Führeramtes. *Klio, Beiheft* **23**.

LEVI, M. A. 1928. La costituzione romana dai Gracchi a Cesare. Firenze, Vallecchi.

LEWALD, H. 1946. Conflits de lois dans le monde grec et romain. *Archeion idiotikou dikaiou* (Athens) **13** : 30–78.

LIEBENAM, W. 1900. Städteverwaltung im römischen Kaiserreich. 2nd ed. Leipzig, Duncker & Humblot.

LOMBARDI, G. 1939. Lo sviluppo costituzionale dalle origini alla fine della Repubblica. Rome, Edizioni Italiane.

——. 1942. Concetti fondamentali del diritto pubblico romano. Rome, Colombo.

LUZZATTO, G. I. 1948. Le organizzazioni preciviche e lo Stato. *Pubbl. Fac. Giur. Università Modena.*

MADVIG, J. N. 1881–1882. Verfassung und Verwaltung des römischen Staates. 2 v. Leipzig, Teubner.

MATTINGLY, H. 1910. The imperial civil service of Rome. Cambridge, Univ. Press.

MARQUARDT, J. 1881–1885. Römische Staatsverwaltung. 3 v. Leipzig, Hirzel.

MEYER, E. 1948. Römischer Staat und Staatsgedanke. Zurich, Artemis.

MOMIGLIANO, A. 1931–1933. Ricerche sulle magistrature romane. *Bull. della Commissione archeologica comunale di Roma*, 88–90.

MOMMSEN, T. 1887–1888. Römisches Staatsrecht. 3rd ed. 3 v. Leipzig, Hirzel. (French translation by P. F. Girard, Paris 1889–1890.)

——. 1907. Abriss des römischen Staatsrechts. 2nd ed. Leipzig, Duncker & Humblot. (Italian translation by Bonfante, 1904, 2nd ed. by V. Arangio-Ruiz, 1944, *Biblioteca storica* **3**. Milan, ISPI.)

MOORE, R. W. 1946. The Roman Commonwealth. London, English Universities Press.

NIEDERER, W. 1952. Ceterum censeo de legum Imperii Romani conflictu. Festschrift H. Fritsche, Fragen des Verfahrens und des Kollisionsrechts. Zurich, Polygraphischer Verlag.

NIESE, B. 1923. Staat und Gesellschaft der Römer. 2nd ed. Kultur der Gegenwart. Teil II, Abt. IV 1: 208–262. Leipzig, Teubner.

NOCERA, G. 1940. Aspetti teoretici della costituzione repubblicana. *RISG* **15**.

NUSSBAUM, A. 1952. The significance of Roman law in the history of international law. *Univ. of Pennsylvania Law Rev.* **100**.

DELL'ORO A. 1950. Formazione dello stato patrizio-plebeo. Milan, Istituto Edit. Cisalpino.

PACCHIONI, G. 1944. Breve storia dell'impero vista da un giurista. Padua, Milani.

PAIS, E. 1915–1921. Ricerche sulla teoria e sul diritto pubblico di Roma. 4 v. Rome, Loescher.

PHILIPPSON, C. 1911. The international law and custom of ancient Greece and Rome. 2 v. London, MacMillan.

PREMERSTEIN, A. v. 1937. Vom Wesen und Werden des Prinzipats. *ABayAW*.

RAUMER, F. 1923. Die romische Staatsverfassung. Munich, Allgemeine Verlagsanstalt.

DE REGIBUS, L. 1949. L'evoluzione politica del governo romano da Augusto a Diocleziano. Corso. Genoa, Di Stefano.

REID, J. S. 1913. The municipalities of the Roman Empire. Cambridge, Univ. Press.

REVON, M. 1891. De l'existence du droit international sous la République romaine. *Revue générale de droit* **15**: 394, 504.

DE ROBERTIS, F. M. 1942. Dal potere personale alla competenza dell' ufficio. *SDHI* **8**.

——. 1946. Il potere di imperio dalla concezione personalistica a quella istituzionale. Bari, Luce.

ROSENBERG, A. 1913. Der Staat der alten Italiker. Berlin, Weidmann.

ROSTOWZEW, M. 1903. Geschichte der Staatspacht in der Kaiserzeit. *Philologus, Suppl.* **9**. Leipzig, Dieterich.

ROTONDI, G. 1920. Problemi di diritto pubblico romano (republished in *Scritti giuridici* 1, 1922, Milan, Hoepli).

RUDOLPH, H. 1933. Stadt und Staat im römischen Italien. Leipzig, Dieterich.

DE RUGGIERO, E. 1921. La patria nel diritto pubblico romano. Rome, Maglione.

SCALA, R. v. 1898. Die Staatsvertrage des Altertums. Leipzig, Teubner.

SCHULZ, O. T. 1916. Das Wesen des romischen Kaisertums in den ersten zwei Jahrhunderten. Paderborn, Schöningh.

——. 1919. Vom Prinzipat zum Dominat. Paderborn, Schöningh.

SEGRÈ, G. 1934. Alcune osservazioni sulla costituzione dell' Impero da Diocleziano a Giustiniano. *ACDR Roma* **1**: 209–233. Pavia, Fusi.

SERAFINI, F. 1896. Il diritto pubblico romano. L'età regia. L'età repubblicana. Pisa, Mariotti.

SHERWIN-WHITE, A. N. 1939. The Roman citizenship. Oxford, Clarendon Press.

SIBER, H. 1933. Zur Entwicklung der römischen Staatsverfassung. *ASächGW* **42**.

SIBER, H. 1936. Die plebeischen Magistraturen bis zur Lex Hortensia. (*Leipziger Rechtswissenschaftliche Studien* **100**.) Leipzig, Weicher.

STARR, C. G. 1941. The Roman imperial navy (31 B.C.–A.D. 324). Ithaca, Cornell Univ. Press.

STELLA-MARANCA, F. 1928. Il diritto pubblico romano nella storia delle istituzioni e delle dottrine politiche. *Hist* **2**.

STEVENSON, G. H. 1949. Roman provincial administration till the age of the Antonines. 2nd ed. Oxford, Blackwell.

STUART JONES, H. 1920. Fresh light on Roman bureaucracy. Oxford, Clarendon Press.

TÄUBLER, E. 1935. Der romische Staat (in Gercke and Norden, Einleitung in die Altertumswissenschaft **3** part 4) 3rd ed. Leipzig, Teubner.

WENGER, L. 1935. Von der Staatskunst der Romer. Munich, Huber.

WILLEMS, P. 1910. Le droit public romain. 7th ed. Louvain, Peeters.

WYLIE, J. K. 1948. Roman constitutional history from the earliest times to the death of Justinian. Capetown, Bookman.

ZWICKY, H. 1944. Zur Verwendung des Militärs in der Verwaltung der Kaiserzeit. (Diss. Zurich.) Winterthur.

V. MISCELLANY

(Economy, public finances, social conditions, labor, industry, numismatics. For commercial institutions see under Law of Obligations, Chapter II C.)

BERNHART, M. 1926. Handbuch zur Münzkunde der römischen Kaiserzeit. 2 v. Halle, Reichman.

BONELLI, G. 1900. Le imposte indirette di Roma antica. *StDocSD* **21**: 27, 287.

CAGNAT, R. 1882. Étude historique sur les impots indirects chez les Romains. Paris, Imprimerie Nationale.

CHARLESWORTH, M. P. 1926. Trade-routes and commerce of the Roman Empire. 2nd ed. Cambridge, Univ. Press. (Italian translation, Milan, 1940.)

CLARK, E. C. 1913. Numismatic illustrations of the history of Roman law, Essays in legal history (ed. Vinogradoff). Oxford, Univ. Press.

CLERICI, L. 1943. Economia e finanza dei Romani, 1. Bologna, Zanichelli.

CULLEN, C. 1921. The Roman revenue system. *Washington Univ. Studies*. St. Louis, Missouri.

FRANK, T. 1935–1940. An economic survey of ancient Rome. 5 v. Baltimore, Johns Hopkins Press.

GRANT, M. 1946. From imperium to auctoritas. A historical study of aes coinage in the Roman Empire (49 B.C.–A.D. 14). Cambridge, Univ. Press.

HEICHELHEIM, F. 1938. Wirtschaftsgeschichte des Altertums. 2 v. Leiden, Sijthoff.

JONKERS, E. J. 1933. Economische en sociale toestanden in het Romeinsche rijk, blijkende uit het Corpus iuris. Thesis Utrecht. Wageningen, Veenman.

LANDUCCI, L. 1932. Il diritto agrario nelle Istituzioni di Giustiniano. *Atti della Soc. ital. per il progresso delle scienze* **1**: 442.

LOANE, H. J. 1938. Industry and commerce of the city of Rome, 50 B.C.–A.D. 200 Baltimore, Johns Hopkins Univ. Press.

LOUIS, P. 1922. Le travail dans le monde romain. Paris, Alcan.

MAUNIER, R., and A. GIFFARD. 1930. Sociologie et droit romain. Paris, Domat-Montchrestien.

MAXEY, M. 1930. Occupation of the lower classes in Roman society. Chicago, Univ. Press.

MICKWITZ, G. 1932. Geld und Wirtschaft im romischen Reich des IV. Jahrhunderts. Helsingfors, Akad. Buchhandlung.

OERTMANN, P. 1891. Volkswirtschaftslehre des Corpus Iuris Civilis. Berlin.

PERNICE, A. 1898. Über wirtschaftliche Voraussetzungen römischer Rechtssätze. *ZSS* **19**: 82–139.

PERSSON, A. W. 1933. Staat und Manufaktur im römischen Reiche. Lund, Bloms.

PÖHLMANN, R. v. 1925. Geschichte der sozialen Frage und des Sozialismus in der antiken Welt. Munich, Beck.

DI RENZO, F. 1950. Il sistema tributario di Roma. Naples, Libreria Intern. Treves.

DE ROBERTIS, F. M. 1945. Lineamenti di storia sociale romana. Bari.

ROSTOWZEW, M. 1910. Studien zur Geschichte des romischen Kolonats. Leipzig, Teubner.

ROSTOFTZEFF, M. 1926. The social and economic history of the Roman Empire. Oxford, Clarendon Press. (Spanish translation by Lopez Ballesteros, Madrid, 1937. Italian translation by Sasena, 1933.)

SALEILLES, R. 1905. Le droit romain et la démocratie. St Scialoja 2: 711. Milan, Hoepli.

SALVIOLI, G. 1929. Il capitalismo antico. Bari, Laterza. (French translation by Bonnet. Paris, Viard.)

SCHEEL, H. v. 1867. De Corporis Iuris Civilis principiis economicis. Halle (Italian translation: I concetti economici fondamentali del Corpus Iuris, *Biblioteca di storia economica*, 1. Milan, Soc. Edit. Libr.).

SCHULZ, O. T. 1925. Die Rechtstitel und Regierungsprogramme der römischen Kaisermunzen von Caesar bis Severus. Paderborn, Schöningh.

SEGRÈ, A. 1922. Circolazione monetaria e prezzi nel mondo antico. Rome, Libreria di Cultura.

——. 1928. Metrologia e circolazione monetaria degli antichi. Bologna, Zanichelli.

THIBAULT, F. 1900. Les impôts directs sous le Bas-Empire romain. Paris, Fontemoing.

VINOGRADOFF, P. 1924. Social and economic conditions of the Roman Empire in the fourth century. *Cambridge Medieval History* 1.

WEBER, M. 1891. Römische Agrargeschichte in ihrer Bedeutung für das Staats- und Privatrecht. Stuttgart, Enke. (Italian translation, *Biblioteca di storia economica* 2, 1891, 1894.)

VI. LEGISLATIVE ACTIVITY AND LEGAL POLICY OF THE EMPERORS.

AUGUSTUS

ACTA DIVI AUGUSTI. 1945. (Ed. S. Riccobono.) Regia Academia Italica. Rome.

ALVAREZ SUAREZ, U. 1942. El principado de Augusto. Revista de Estudios politicos 2.

ARANGIO-RUIZ, V. See under Augustus.

AUGUSTUS. 1938. Studi in onore del Bimillenario Augusteo. Milan, Vita e Pensiero (see V. Arangio-Ruiz, La legislazione; P. De Francisci, La costituzione Augustea).

BIONDI, B. See under Conferenze Augustee.

Conferenze Augustee nel Bimillenario della nascita. 1939. Milan, Pubbl. dell'Univ. Cat. del Sacro Cuore. Vita e Pensiero (see Biondi, La legislazione di Augusto).

CICCOTTI, E. 1938. Profilo di Augusto. Turin, Einaudi.

DE FRANCISCI, P. See above under Augustus.

——. 1941. Genesi e struttura del Principato Augusteo. *Atti Accad. d'Italia*, Ser. VII, v. 2.

——. 1948. Arcana imperii. 3 (1): 169. Milan, Giuffrè.

HAMMOND, M. 1933. The Augustean Principate in theory and practice. Cambridge (Mass.), Harvard Univ. Press.

HOLMES, T. R. E. 1928, 1931. The architect of the Roman Empire. 2 v. Oxford, Clarendon Press.

HOMO, L. 1935. Auguste. Paris, Payot.

HÖNN, K. 1938. Augustus. 2nd ed. Vienna, Seidel.

JONES, A. H. M. 1951. The imperium of Augustus. *JRS* 41: 112.

KORNEMANN, E. 1937. Augustus, der Mann und sein Werk. (*Breslauer Historische Forschungen*) Breslau, Friebatsch.

RICCOBONO, S., JR. 1936. Augusto e il problema della costituzione. *AnPal* 15.

——. 1939. L'opera di Augusto e lo sviluppo del diritto imperiale. *AnPal* 18: 363-507.

SIBER, H. 1933. Das Führeramt des Augustus. *Abhandlungen Sächsische Ges. der Wissenschaften* 42.

——. 1935. Cäsars Diktatur und das Prinzipat des Augustus. *ZSS* 55: 99.

DE VISSCHER, F. 1938. Auguste et la réforme de la justice. *Annales de droit et de sciences politiques* (Louvain).

VOLKMANN, H. 1935. Zur Rechtssprechung im Prinzipat des Augustus. Munich, Beck.

For further bibliography see PRINCEPS, RES GESTAE DIVI AUGUSTI; B. Biondi, Diritto rom. Guida bibl. (1944) 127; Alvarez Suarez, Horizonte actual de derecho rom., 59 (1944); Magdelain, Auctoritas principis, 117 (1947).

TIBERIUS

CIACERI, E. 1934. Tiberio, successore di Augusto. Milan, Albrighi & Segati.

ROGERS, R. S. 1936. Criminal trials and criminal legislation under Tiberius. Middletown, Conn., Amer. Philol. Assoc.

SIBER, H. 1939. Die Wahlreform des Tiberius. *Fschr Koschaker* 1. Weimar, Böhlau.

CLAUDIUS

MAY, G. 1936, 1944. L'activite juridique de l'empereur Claude. *RHD* 15: 56, 213; 23: 101.

MOMIGLIANO, A. 1932. L'opera dell' imperatore Claudio. Firenze, Vallecchi. (English translation by W. D. Hogarth. Oxford, Clarendon Press, 1934.)

SCRAMUZZA, V. M. 1940. The Emperor Claudius. Cambridge (Mass.), Harvard Univ. Press; Oxford, Univ. Press.

VESPASIAN

LEVI, M. A. 1938. I principi dell' impero di Vespasiano. *Rivista di filol. classica* 66.

MENRAD, K. 1911. Gestaltung des römischen Staats- und Privatrechts unter Vespasian (Diss. Erlangen). Munich, Kastner und Callwey.

HADRIAN

CORBETT, P. E. 1926. The legislation of Hadrian. *Univ. of Pennsylvania Law Rev.* 74.

HITZIG, H. F. 1893. Die Stellung des Kaisers Hadrian in der römischen Rechtsgeschichte. Zurich, Schulten.

PRINGSHEIM, F. 1934. The legal policy and reforms of Hadrian. *JRS* 24.

VOGT, H. 1951. Hadrians Justizpolitik im Spiegel der römischen Reichsmünzen. *Fschr Schulz* 2. Weimar, Böhlau.

WIEACKER, F. 1935. Quellen zur Hadrianischen Justizpolitik. *Romanistische Studien* (Freiburger Rechtsgeschichtliche Abhandlungen 5) 33.

ANTONINUS PIUS

HÜTTL, W. 1933-1936. Antoninus Pius. 2 v. Prague, Calve.

MARCUS AURELIUS AND LUCIUS VERUS (DIVI FRATRES)

SCARLATA FAZIO, M. 1939. Principi vecchi e nuovi di diritto privato nell' attività giuridica dei Divi Fratres. Catania, Crisafulli.

MARCUS AURELIUS

DUMERIL, A. 1882. De constitutionibus M. Aurelii Antonini. (Thèse Paris) Toulouse, Impr. Douladoure-Privat.

GORDIAN III

TOWNSEND, P. W. 1934. The administration of Gordian III. *Yale Classical Studies* **4**.

DIOCLETIAN

ALBERTARIO, E. 1937. Le classicisme du Dioclétien. *SDHI* **3**. (Italian translation, in *Studi di diritto romano* **5**: 195, La Romanità di Diocleziano.)

SCHÖNBAUER, E. 1942. Diokletian in einem verzweifelten Abwehrkampfe. *ZSS* **62**.

SESTON, W. 1946. Dioclétien et la tetrarchie. I. Guerres et réformes, 284–300. *Bibliothèque Écoles françaises Athènes et Rome,* **162**.

TAUBENSCHLAG, R. 1923. Das romische Privatrecht zur Zeit Diokletians. *Bull. de l'Académie polonaise de Cracow.*

CONSTANTINE

ALBERTARIO, E. 1935. Alcune osservazioni sulla legislazione di Constantino. *ACII* **1**: 69 (*Studi di diritto romano* **5**: 155, 1937).

CHENON, E. 1914. Les conséquences juridiques de l'Édit de Milan. *NRHD* **38**: 255.

DUPONT, C. 1937. Les constitutions de Constantin et le droit privé au debut du quatrième siecle. Les personnes. Lille, Danel.

GAUDEMET, J. 1947. La législation religieuse de Constantin. *Revue d'histoire de l'Église de France.*

——. 1948. Constantin, restaurateur de l'ordre. *St. Solazzi.* Naples, Jovene.

HÖNN, K. 1945. Konstantin der Grosse. 2nd ed. Leipzig, Hinrichs.

SARGENTI, M. 1938. Il diritto privato nella legislazione di Constantino. Persone e famiglia. Milan, Giuffrè.

SEECK, O. 1889. Zeitfolge der Gesetze Konstantins. *ZSS* **10**.

SEUFFERT, L. 1891. Konstantins Gesetze und das Christentum. Würzburg.

VOGT, J. 1948. Zur Frage des christlichen Einflusses auf die Gesetzgebung Konstantins. *Fschr Wenger* **2**. Munich, Beck.

JULIAN

ANDREOTTI, R. 1930. L'opera legislativa e amministrativa dell' imperatore Giuliano. *Nuova Rivista storica* **14**.

BIDEZ, J., and F. CUMONT. 1922. Imperatoris Flavii Claudii Iuliani epistulae, leges, etc. Paris, Les Belles Lettres.

ENSSLIN, W. 1922. Die Gesetzgebungswerke des Kaisers Julian. *Kl* **18**.

SOLARI, A. 1931. Coerenza ideale nell' attività legislativa dell' imperatore Giuliano. *ACNSR* (III).

JUSTIN I

VASILIEV, A. A. 1950. Justin the First. Cambridge (Mass.), Harvard Univ. Press.

VALENTINIAN I

ANDREOTTI, R. 1931. Incoerenza della legislazione dell' imperatore Valentiniano I. *Nuova Rivista storica* **15**.

VOLTERRA, E. 1952. Una misteriosa legge attribuita a Valentiniano I. *St Arangio-Ruiz* **3**: 139. Naples, Jovene.

JUSTINIAN

ALIVISATOS, H. S. 1913. Die kirchliche Gesetzgebung Justinians. Berlin, Tröwitsch.

——. 1935. Les rapports de la législaton ecclésiastique de Justinien avec les canons de l'Église. *ACDR Roma* **2**: 79–87. Pavia, Fusi.

BERGER, A. 1936. Intorno alle pretese tendenze arcaiche di Giustiniano riguardo alle XII Tavole. *St Riccobono* **1**: 587–639. Palermo, Castiglia.

BIONDI, B. 1935. Religione e diritto canonico nella legislazione di Giustiniano. *ACII* **1**: 99–117. Rome.

——. 1936. Giustiniano I, Principe e legislatore cattolico. Vita e Pensiero.

ERMAN, H. 1939. Zu Justinian. *Fschr. Koschaker* **1**. Weimar, Böhlau.

DE FRANCISCI, P. 1910–1914. La legislazione giustinianea durante la compilazione delle Pandette. *BIDR,* **22, 23, 26**.

FRITZ, K. H. 1937. Studien zur justinianischen Reformgesetzgebung (Diss. Berlin). Quackenbrück, Trute.

KNECHT, A. 1905. System des justinianischen Kirchenvermogensrechts. (*Kirchenrechtliche Abhandlungen,* **22**.) Stuttgart, Enke.

D'ORS PEREZ-PEIX, A. 1947. La actitud del Emp. Justiniano. *Orientalia Christiana,* **119**.

PFANNMÜLLER, G. 1903. Die kirchliche Gesetzgebung Justinians, hauptsächlich auf Grund der Novellen. Berlin, Schwetschke.

PRINGSHEIM, F. 1930. Die archaistische Tendenz Justinians. *Studi Bonfante* **1**: 549. Milan, Treves.

RICCOBONO, S. 1931. La verità sulle pretese tendenze arcaiche di Giustiniano. *ConfMil* 237. Milan, Vita e Pensiero.

SCHÄFER, T. 1935. Justinianus I et vita monachica. *ACII* **1**: 173–188. Rome.

SCHULZ, M. 1935. Einfluss Kaiser Justinians auf das Erbrecht. Diss. Erlangen. Munich, Salesianische Offizin.

SCHWARTZ, E. 1940. Zur Kirchenpolitik Justinians. *AbhBayAW.*

VII. PROBLEMS CONNECTED WITH THE DEVELOPMENT OF ROMAN LAW. FOREIGN INFLUENCES

(For Christianity see Chapter VIII)

ALBERTARIO, E. 1937. Il diritto privato romano nella sua formazione storica e nella sua elaborazione giustinianea. *Studi* **5**. Milan, Giuffrè.

ALVAREZ SUAREZ, U. 1944. Horizonte actual del derecho romano. Madrid, Instituto Francisco di Vitoria.

ARANGIO-RUIZ, V. 1946–1947. L'application du droit romain en Égypte après la Constitution Antoninienne. *Bull. de l'Institut de l'Égypte* **19**.

BARTOŠEK, M. 1952. Concezione naturalistica e materialistica dei giuristi classici. *St. Albertario* **2**.

BRASSLOFF, S. 1933. Sozialpolitische Motive der römischen Rechtsentwicklung. Vienna, Perles.

BUCKLAND, W. W. 1939. Ritual acts and words in Roman Law. *Fschr. Koschaker* **1**. Weimar, Böhlau.

CARUSI, E. 1928. I rapporti tra diritto romano e diritti greco-orientali. *Scr Salandra,* 155–187. Rome, Fac. giuridica dell'Università.

COING, H. 1952. Einfluss der Philosophie des Aristoteles auf die Entwicklung des römischen Rechts. *ZSS* **69**.

COLLINET, P. 1912. Études historiques sur le droit de Justinien. 1. Le caractère oriental de l'œuvre législative de Justinien. Paris, Sirey.

CORNIL, G. 1930. Ancien droit romain. Les problèmes des origines. Paris, Sirey.

CHIAZZESE, L. 1930. Nuovi orientamenti nella storia del diritto romano. *AG* **103**: 87.

COSTA, E. 1891. La filosofia greca nella giurisprudenza romana. Parma, Battei.

DE FRANCISCI, P. 1925. L'azione degli elementi stranieri sullo sviluppo e sulla crisi del diritto romano. *AG* **93**.

——. 1947. Idee vecchie e nuove intorno alla formazione del diritto romano. *Scritti Ferrini* 1. (Univ. Sacro Cuore) Milan, Vita e Pensiero.

GOUDY, H. 1906. L'artificiality of Roman juristic classifications. *St Fadda* 5. Naples, Pierro.

——. 1910. Trichotomy in Roman law. Oxford Univ. Press. (German translation by E. Ehrlich. Leipzig, Duncker & Humblot.)

GROSSO, G. 1948. Problemi generali di diritto attraverso il diritto romano. Turin, Giappichelli.

GUARNERI-CITATI, A. 1927. Fattori del diritto romano giustinianeo ed il problema della sua codificazione. *AnMac.*

GUIBAL, M. P. 1937. De l'influence de la philosophie sur le droit romain et la jurisprudence de l'époque classique. Paris, Sirey.

JOLOWICZ, H. F. 1932. Academic elements in Roman Law. *LQR* 48 : 171.

KAMPHUISEN, P. W. 1922. De codificationsgedachte in het Romeinsche rijk. (Thesis Leiden.) Celeen, Erkens-Franssen.

KÜBLER, B. 1930. Der Einfluss der griechischen Philosophie auf die Entwicklung der Verschuldungsgrade im römischen Recht. Rechtsidee und Staatsgedanke. *Fg Binder*, 63.

——. 1934. Griechische Einflüsse auf die Entwicklung des römischen Privatrechts. *ACDR Roma* 1: 79–98. Pavia, Fusi.

LAURIA, M. 1936. Indirizzi e problemi romanistici. *Il Foro Italiano* 4 : 491.

LEVY, E. 1929. Westen und Osten in der nachklassischen Entwicklung des römischen Rechts. *ZSS* 49.

——. 1943. Vulgarisation of Roman law in the early Middle Ages. *Medievalia et Humanistica* 1: 14 (= *BIDR* 55–56, Post- Bellum, 222, 1951).

——. 1951. West Roman vulgar law. The law of property. Philadelphia, *Mem. Amer. Philos. Soc.* 29.

DE MARTINO, F. 1943. Individualismo e diritto romano privato. *Annuario di diritto comparato e di studi legislativi* 16.

MASCHI, C. A. 1937. La concezione naturalistica del diritto e degli istituti giuridici romani. Milan, Vita e Pensiero.

MEYER, E. 1951. Die Quaestionen der Rhetorik und die Anfänge juristischer Methodenlehre. *ZSS* 68 : 30.

MITTEIS, L. 1891. Reichsrecht und Volksrecht in den östlichen Provinzen des römischen Kaiserreichs. Leipzig, Teubner. (Reprinted 1935.)

MONIER, R. 1938. Méthodes de reconstruction de l'évolution historique du droit romain. Mémoires de la Société des Sciences de Lille.

PITTS, T. J. 1929. The rise and progress of the Roman Law. *Amer. Law Rev.* 63 : 200.

PRINGSHEIM, F. 1940. The character of Justinian's legislation. *LQR* 56.

——. 1944. The unique character of Roman classical law. *JRS* 34.

RICCOBONO, S. 1925. Outlines of the evolution of Roman Law. *Univ. of Pennsylvania Law Rev.* 74.

——. 1926. Fasi e fattori dell'evoluzione del diritto romano. *Mél Cornil* 2. Gand-Paris, Sirey.

——. 1929. Punti di vista critici e ricostruttivi a proposito della dissertazione di Mitteis, Storia del diritto antico. *AnPal* 12.

——. 1934. La prassi nel periodo postclassico. *ACDR Roma* 1 : 317–350.

RICCOBONO, S., JR. 1950. L'esperienza etica della storia politica e giuridica di Roma. Palermo, Palumbo.

SCHILLER, A. A. 1933. Sources and influences of the Roman Law in the third to sixth centuries. *Georgetown Law Jour.* 21.

SENN, F. 1934. L'influence grecque sur le droit romain de la fin de la République. *ACDR Roma* 1: 99–110. Pavia, Fusi.

STROUX, J. 1934. Griechische Einflüsse auf die Entwicklung der römischen Rechtswissenschaft gegen Ende der republikanischen, Zeit. *ACDR Roma* 1 : 111–132 (republished in the following book). Pavia, Fusi.

——. 1949. Römische Rechtswissenschaft und Rhetorik. Potsdam. (See RHETOR.)

TAUBENSCHLAG, R. 1934. Einfluss der Provinzialrechte auf das römische Privatrecht. *ACDR Roma* 1 : 281–316. Pavia, Fusi.

VILLEY, M. 1951. Logique d'Aristote et droit romain. *RHD* 29 : 309.

VOLTERRA, E. 1937. Diritto romano e diritti orientali. Bologna, Zanichelli.

——. 1949. Western postclassical schools. *Cambridge LJ*, 10 : 196.

——. 1949. Introduction à l'histoire du droit romain dans ses rapports avec l'Orient. *Archives d'hist. du droit oriental* 4 : 117.

——. 1951. Storia del diritto romano e storia dei diritti orientali. *RISG* 88 : 134.

WEISS, E. 1934. Der Einfluss der hellenistischen Rechte auf das römische. *ACDR Roma* 1 : 243–254. Pavia, Fusi.

VIII. CHRISTIANITY AND ROMAN LAW

ALLARD, P. 1925. Le Christianisme et l'Empire romain de Nerva à Théodose. 9th ed. Paris, Lecoffre.

ALVAREZ SUAREZ, U. 1941. La influencia del Cristianismo. *Revista del derecho privado* 28.

BAVIERA, G. 1912. Concetto e limiti dell'influenza del Cristianesimo sul diritto romano. *Mél Girard* 1 : 67–121. Paris, Rousseau.

——. 1935. La codificazione giustinianea e il Cristanesimo. *ACDR Roma* 2 : 125–128. Pavia, Fusi.

BECK, A. 1935. Christentum und nachklassische Rechtsentwicklung. *ACDR Roma* 2 : 91–122. Pavia, Fusi.

——. 1939. Zur Frage der religiösen Bestimmtheit des römischen Rechts. *Fschr Koschaker* 1. Weimar, Böhlau.

BOUCAUD, C. 1914. La première ébauche d'un droit chrétien dans le droit Romain. Paris, Trolin.

BRASIELLO, U. 1946. Sull'influenza del Cristianesimo in materia dell'elemento subbiettivo nei contratti. *Scr Ferrini* (Univ. Pavia) 505. Milan, Hoepli.

——. 1947. Premesse relative allo studio dell'influenza del Cristianesimo sul diritto romano. *Scr Ferrini* (Univ. Sacro Cuore) 2. Milan, Vita e Pensiero.

BUSSI, E. 1935. L'influenza cristiana nello svolgimento storico dei patti. Cristianesimo e diritto romano (*Pubbl. dell'Univ. del Sacro Cuore* 43). Milan, Vita e Pensiero.

CHIAZZESE, L. 1948. Cristianesimo e diritto. *BIDR* 51–52 : 222.

FERRERO, M. 1911. Il Cristianesimo nel diritto civile romano. S. Damiano d'Asti, Calosso.

GAUDEMET, J. 1947. La législation réligieuse de Constantin. *Revue d'histoire de l'Église de France*, 25.

GRAY, C. 1922. Il diritto nel Vangelo e l'influenza del Cristianesimo nel diritto romano. Turin, Bocca.

HOHENLOHE, C. 1937. Einfluss des Christentums auf das Corpus Iuris Civilis. Vienna, Pichler.

IMBERT, J. 1949. Refléxions sur le Christianisme et l'esclavage en droit romain. *RIDA* 2 : 444.

JONKERS, E. J. 1934. De l'influence du Christianisme sur la legislation rélative à l'esclavage dans l'antiquité. *Mn* N. S. 1 : 240–280.

——. 1938. Invloed van het Christendom op de Romeinsche wetgewing betreffende het concubinaat en de echtscheiding. Amsterdam, Veeman.

KÜBLER, B. 1909. Die Einwirkung der älteren christlichen Kirche auf die Entwicklung des römischen Rechts. *Theo-*

logische Arbeiten aus dem rheinischen wissenschaftlichen Prediger-Verein, 11.

LE BRAS, G. 1949. Le droit romain au service de la domination pontificale. *RHD* 27 : 377.

LEIFER, F. 1938. Christentum und römisches Recht seit Konstantin. *ZSS* **58** : 185.

MARCHI, A. 1924. Dell'influenza del Cristianesimo sulla codificazione giustinianea. *StSen* **38** : 61–103.

MASCHI, C. A. 1948. Humanitas. *AnTriest* **18** : 31–133.

MEDINA DELLA TORRE, P. 1935. La influencia de las ideas cristianas en la evolucion del derecho romano. *ACII* **2** : 7–21.

MERA MANZANO, R. D. 1948. La influencia de la religion en el derecho romano de familia. Santiago (Chile).

NAZ, R. 1949. Droit romain et droit canonique. *Dictionnaire de droit canonique* 4 : 1502.

RENARD, G. 1938. Droit romain et pensée chrétienne. *Revue des sciences philosophiques et théologiques* 27 : 53.

RICCOBONO, S. 1909. L'influenza del Cristianesimo nella codificazione di Giustiniano. *Scientia* 9.

——. 1911. Cristianesimo e diritto privato. *Rivista di diritto civile,* 3.

——. 1913. Dalla communio del diritto quiritario alla comproprietà moderna. Essays in legal history (ed. by Vinogradoff), 33. London, Humphrey Milford.

——. 1935. L'influsso del Cristianesimo sul diritto romano. *ACDR Roma* 2 : 59. Pavia, Fusi.

ROBERTI, M. 1935. Patria potestas e paterna pietas. Contributo allo studio dell'influenza del Cristianesimo sul diritto romano. *St Albertoni* 1 : 257. Padua, Cedam.

——. 1935. Cristianesimo e collezioni giustinianee. Cristianesimo e diritto romano. (*Pubbl. dell'Univ. del Sacro Cuore* 43.) Milan, Vita e Pensiero.

RUTGERS, V. H. 1940. De invloed van het Christendom on het Romeinsche recht. Amsterdam.

TOSO, A. 1935. Emilio Papiniano e le influenze cristiane nell'evoluzione del diritto romano classico. *ACII* 2 : 21.

TROPLONG, R. 1843. De l'influence du Christianisme sur le droit civil des Romains (first published in 1843, new edition by Abbé Bayle, 1902). Tours, Cattier.

WENGER, L. 1946. Über die ersten Berührungen des Christentums mit dem römischen Recht. *Miscellanea G. Mercati,* 5. Città del Vaticano.

WESSELS BOEHR, J. 1924 Eenige opmerkungen over het Christendom en het Romeinsche recht. Thesis, Leiden.

WESTBURY-JONES, J. 1939. Roman and Christian imperialism. London. MacMillan.

See, moreover, Ch. XIV under Patristic Literature

IX. ROMAN LAW AND MODERN LEGAL SYSTEMS

(Byzantine and Medieval Law included.)

ABELLO, L. 1906. Dottrina giuridica romana e diritto civile odierno. Turin, Vinciguerra.

ALBERTONI, A. 1927. Per un'esposizione del diritto bizantino con riguardo all' Italia. Imola, Cooperative Tipografica.

BERGER, A. 1944. Pourquoi ius Graeco-Romanum? Autour d'une terminologie. *Annuaire de l'Institut de Philologie et d'Histoire orientales et slaves* 7 : 357–368. New York. (= *BIDR* **55–56**, Post-Bellum 1951 : 290–301.)

BESTA, E. 1938. Introduzione al diritto comune. Milan, Giuffrè.

BIONDI, B. 1934. Intorno alla romanità del processo civile moderno. *BIDR* **42** : 355.

BLAESE, H. 1936. Bedeutung und Geltung des römischen Privatrechts in den Baltischen Staaten. (*Leipziger rechtswissenschaftliche Studien* 99.) Leipzig, Weicher.

BRANDILEONE, F. 1921. Il diritto romano nella storia del diritto italiano. *AG* **86** : 6 (= *Scritti* **1** : 19).

BRUCK, E. F. 1930. Römisches Recht und Rechtsprobleme der Gegenwart. Tübingen, Mohr.

BUSSI, E. 1940. La formazione dei dogmi del diritto comune. 2 v. Padua, Cedam.

CALASSO, F. 1937. Il problema storico del diritto comune. *St. Besta* 2 : 459. Milan, Giuffrè.

CALISSE, C. 1935. Influsso di diritto romano nell' evoluzione delle leggi barbariche. *ACII* 2 : 259.

CARUSI, E. 1913. Sui rapporti fra il diritto romano e diritto mussulmano. *Atti Società ital. per il progresso delle Scienze.*

CHIAZZESE, L. 1948. Diritto romano e civiltà moderna. *BIDR* **51–52** : 187.

CHIOVENDA, G. 1935. Sull'influenza delle idee romane nella formazione dei processi civili moderni. *ACDR Bologna* **2** : 411–438. Pavia, Fusi.

CONRAT, M. 1891. Geschichte der Quellen und Literatur des römischen Rechts im früheren Mittelalter. Leipzig, Hinrichs.

CORNIL, G. 1912. Les Codes modernes et le droit romain. *Bull. Acad. Royale de Belgique. Cl. Lettres,* 284–326.

D'EMILIA, A. 1945, 1947. Appunti di diritto bizantino. 1. Le fonti. Rome, Libreria dell'Università, Tumminelli; Lezioni di diritto Bizantino. Parte speciale. 1. Le successioni. 2. Il possesso. Rome, Ferri.

ELGUERA, R. E. 1952. Influencia del derecho romano en el Codigo civil Argentino. *St Arangio-Ruiz* 2 : 405–417.

FEENSTRA, R. 1950. Verkenningen of het gebied der receptie van het Romeinse recht. Zwolle, Tjeenk Willink.

FISHER, M. G. 1947. Scotland and the Roman Law. *TulLR* **22** : 12–23.

FITZGERALD, S. V. 1951. The alleged debt of Islamic to Roman law. *LQR* 67.

FLACH, J. 1890. Études critiques sur l'histoire du droit romain au Moyen Age, avec textes inédits. Paris, Larose.

FLEISCHMANN, M. 1908. Über den Einfluss des römischen Rechts auf das deutsche Staatsrecht. *Mél Fitting* 2 : 635. Montpellier.

DE FRANCISCI, P. 1936. Il diritto romano negli stati moderni. Rome. Istituto Nazionale di Cultura.

GENZMER, E. 1941. Kritische Studien zur Mediaevistik. 1. Renaissance des römischen Rechts. *ZSS* **61** : 276.

GSOVSKI, V. 1939. Roman private law in Russia. *BIDR* **46** : 363–375.

HALBAN, A. v. 1899–1907. Das römische Recht in den germanischen Volksstaaten. 3 v. Breslau, Marcus.

ION, T. P. 1908. Roman law and Mohammedan jurisprudence. *Michigan Law Rev.* **6** : 197, 371.

KOSCHAKER, P. 1947. Europa und das römische Recht. Munich, Biberstein.

LARRAONA, A., and A. TABERA. 1935. El derecho Justinianeo en España. *ACDR Bologna* **3** : 83–182. Pavia, Fusi.

LEE, R. W. 1935. Roman Law in the British Empire, particularly in the Union of South Africa. *ACDR Bologna* **2** : 251–297. Pavia, Fusi.

LEVY, E. 1942. Reflections on the first reception of Roman law in Germanic states. *Amer. Hist. Rev.* **48** : 19.

DI MARZO, S. 1950. Le basi romanistiche del Codice civile. Turin, Unione tipografica-editrice.

MUTO, T. 1934. La recezione e gli studi di diritto romano in Giappone. *AG* **111** : 215.

——. 1935. Il diritto romano e il diritto giapponese. *ACDR Bologna* **2** : 297–320. Pavia, Fusi.

NALLINO, C. 1942. Rapporti fra diritto romano e diritto musulmano. *Raccolta di scritti* 4 : 84. Rome, Istituto per l'Oriente.

NUSSBAUM, A. 1952. The significance of Roman law in the history of international law. *Univ. of Pennsylvania Law Rev.* **100** : 678–688.

VAN OVEN, J. C. 1935. Le droit romain aux Pays-Bas. *ACDR Bologna* **2**: 23–56. Pavia, Fusi.

PATETTA, F. 1891. Per la storia del diritto romano nel Medio Evo. *RISG* **12**.

——. 1891–1892. Contributi alla storia del diritto romano nel Medio Evo. *BIDR* **3**: 4.

PITZORNO, B. 1934. Il diritto romano come diritto consuetudinario. *CentCodPav*. Pavia, Tipografia Cooperativa.

RABEL, E. 1935. Die Rezeption des römischen Rechts in Deutschland. *ACDR Bologna* **2**: 183–190. Pavia, Fusi.

RICCOBONO, S. 1917. Dal diritto romano classico al diritto moderno. *AnPal* **3–4**.

SAVIGNY, F. C. v. 1834–1851. Geschichte des römischen Rechts im Mittelalter. 2nd ed. Heidelberg, Mohr. (Italian translation by Bollati. Turin, Gianini, 1853–1857; French translation by Guenoux, 1839.)

SCIASCIA, G. 1947. Direito romano e direito civil Brasileiro. Textos e apontamentos extravagantes. São Paulo.

SICILIANO-VILLANUEVA, L. 1912. Diritto Bizantino. *Enciclopedia giuridica Italiana* **4** (5): 36–95. Milan, Soc. Editrice Libraria.

SIMONIUS, A. 1934. Was bedeuten für uns die Pandekten. *Ztschr. für Schweizerisches Recht* **53**.

STEINWENTER, A. 1934. Der Einfluss des römischen Rechts auf den antiken kanonischen Prozess. *ACDR Bologna* **1**: 225–242. Pavia, Fusi.

STOICESCO, C. 1935. L'influence du droit romain sur le droit civil roumain. *ACDR Bologna* **2**: 191–202. Pavia, Fusi.

TRIFONE, R. 1934. Il diritto giustinianeo nel mezzogiorno d'Italia. *ACDR Bologna* **1**: 1–16. Pavia, Fusi.

——. 1938. Roma communis patria nel pensiero dei giuristi dell'età intermedia. *RStDIt* **11**.

VACCARI, P. 1936. Dall'unità romana al particolarismo giuridico del Medio Evo. Pavia, Università. Collana di studi storico-politici.

VAZNY, J. 1935. Idee romane nel diritto civile moderno. *ACDR Bologna* **2**: 439–450. Pavia, Fusi.

VINOGRADOFF, P. 1929. Roman law in medieval Europe. 2nd ed. by F. De Zulueta. (Italian translation by S. Riccobono, Milan, Giuffrè, 1950.)

DE VISSCHER, F. 1935. Le droit romain en Belgique. *ACDR Bologna* **2**: 203–214. Pavia, Fusi.

WENGER, L. 1947. Römisches Recht als Weltrecht. *Osterreichische Ztschr. für öffentliches Recht* **1**: 241.

YNTEMA, H. E. 1949. Roman law and its influence on Western civilization. *Cornell Law Quart.* **35**: 77.

ZACHARIAE v. LINGENTHAL, K. E. 1892. Geschichte des griechisch-römischen Rechts. 3rd ed. Berlin, Weidmann.

X. ROMAN LAW AND THE ANGLO-AMERICAN WORLD

ALBERTI, A. 1937. Scuole italiane e giuristi italiani nello sviluppo storico del diritto inglese. Bologna, Zanichelli.

BALDWIN, S. E. 1911. The study of Roman law in American law schools. *Amer. Bar Association Report*.

BRYCE, J. 1901. Methods of law making in Rome and England.—The history of legal development at Rome and in England.—Extension of Roman and English law throughout the world. In Studies in History and Jurisprudence, N. Y., Oxford Univ. Press.

BUCKLAND, W. W., and A. D. McNAIR. 1952. Roman law and common law. 2nd ed. by H. F. Lawson. Cambridge Univ. Press.

CAMPBELL, J. 1942. Romanization of Scottish law. *Boston Univ. Law Rev.* **22**.

COLEMAN-NORTON, P. R. 1950. Why study Roman Law? *Jour. Legal Education* **2**: 473.

COLVIN, H. M. 1938. Roman and civil elements in sources of the law of the United States. *St Albertoni* **3**: 113. Padua, Cedam.

COLVIN, H. M. 1943. Participation of the United States of America with the Republics of Latin America in the common heritage of Roman and civil law. *Proc. Eighth Amer. Scientific Congress, Washington, May 1940*, **10**: 467.

COOPER, T. M. 1950. The Common Law and the Civil Law. A Scot's view. *Harvard Law Rev.* **63**: 468.

DORSEY, R. J. C. 1935. The Roman and common law. *ACDR Bologna* **2**: 361. Pavia, Fusi.

DUFF, P. W. 1947. Roman law today. *TulLR* **22**.

FISHER, M. G. 1947. Scotland and the Roman law. *TulLR* **22**: 12–23.

HALL, A. R. 1927. The common law, its debt to Rome. *Canadian Bar Rev.* **5**: 639, 715.

HANBURY, R. L. 1931. The place of Roman law in teaching of law today. *Jour. Society Public Teachers of Law* **1**: 14–25.

HART, W. G. 1930. Roman law and the custom of London. *LQR* **46**: 49.

HOLDSWORTH, W. S. 1939. Roman law and English common law. *Toronto Law Jour.* **3** (reprinted in *Essays in law and history* 1946, 71). Oxford, Clarendon Press.

HOWE, W. W. 1902–1903. Roman and civil law in America. *Harvard Law Rev.* **16**: 342.

——. 1905. Studies in civil law and its relations to the jurisprudence of England and America. 2nd ed. Boston, Little & Brown.

——. 1907. The study of Roman and civil law. *Amer. Law Rev.* **41**.

IRELAND, G. 1945. Roman and comparative law in the Americas after the war. *TulLR* **19**: 553.

LEE, R. W. 1935. Roman law in the British Empire, particularly in the Union of South Africa. *ACDR Bologna* **2**: 251. Pavia, Fusi.

——. 1944. Interaction of Roman and Anglo-Saxon law. *South African Law Jour.* **61**: 155.

LEONHARD, R. 1908–1909. American remembrances of a German teacher of Roman Law. *Yale Law Jour.* **18**: 584.

——. 1912–1913. The vocation of America for the science of Roman Law. *Harvard Law Review* **26**: 389.

LOBINGIER, C. S. 1916. The value and place of Roman law in the technical curriculum. *Amer. Law Rev.* **49**: 349.

——. 1932. Modern expansion of the Roman law. *Univ. of Cincinnati Law Rev.* **6**: 152.

LYMAN, R. W. 1921. Roman responsa prudentium and English case law. *Dickinson Law Rev.* **25**: 153.

McGINLEY, G. J. 1927. Roman law and its influence in America. *Notre Dame Lawyer* **3**: 70–88.

McILWAIN, C. H. 1941. Our heritage from the law of Rome. *Foreign Affairs* **19**: 597.

MACKINTOSH, J. 1926. Our debt to Roman law. *Juridical Rev.* **38**.

MACKINTOSH, J. 1934. Roman law in modern practice. Edinburgh, Green.

MAINE, H. S. 1880. Roman law, and legal education. Village-communities in the East and West, 330–383. N. Y., Holt.

MUNRO, W. B. 1908–1909. The genesis of Roman law in America. *Harvard Law Rev.* **22**: 579.

NEFF, C. M. 1937. Influence of Roman law upon American jurisprudence. *BIDR* **44**: 433.

NYS, E. 1910. Le droit romain. Le droit des gens. Pages d'histoire du droit en Angleterre. Brussels, Weissenbruch.

OLIVER, D. T. 1926. Roman law in modern cases of English law. *Cambridge legal essays in honor of Bond, Buckland and Kenny*. Cambridge, Heffer.

PLUCKNETT, T. F. T. 1940. Relations between Roman law and English common law down to the sixteenth century. *Univ. of Toronto Law Jour.* **3**: 24.

POWELL, R. 1952. Roman contributions to the reform of English law. *Current Legal Problems* **5**: 229–250. London, Stevens.

PRINGSHEIM, F. 1935. The inner relationship between English and Roman law. *CambLJ* **5**: 347.

RABEL, E. 1950. Private laws of Western civilization. Part 1. The significance of Roman law. *Louisiana Law Rev.* **10**.

RADIN, M. 1935. Roman law in the United States. *ACDR Bologna* **2**: 343–360. Pavia, Fusi.

RICCOBONO, S. 1935–1939. Diritto romano in America. *BIDR* **43**: 314; **44**: 419. **45**: 335; **46**: 328.

ROBINSON, J. E. 1915. American recognition of the Roman and civil law. *Illinois Law Rev.* **9**.

RUSSELL, F. 1937. The practical value of the study of Roman law. *BIDR* **44**: 445.

SARFATI, M. 1938. Influenza reciproca del diritto romano e del diritto anglo-sassone. *St Albertoni* **3**: 563–575.

SCRUTTON, T. E. 1885. The influence of Roman law on the law of England. Cambridge, Univ. Press.

SENIOR, W. 1930. The Roman law in England before Vacarius. *LQR* **46**: 191.

SHERMAN, C. P. 1911. The value of the Roman law to the American lawyer. *Univ. of Pennsylvania Law Rev.* **60**: 174.

——. 1935. Roman law in the United States of America, the present revival of Roman law study. *ACDR Bologna* **2**: 321–341. Pavia, Fusi.

——. 1937. Roman law in the modern world. 3rd ed. N. Y., Baker & Voorhis.

——. 1945. Roman law in the Quebec Civil Code. *Boston Univ. Law Rev.* **25**: 196.

WENGER, L. 1939. Römisches Recht in America. *St. Besta* **1**: 151–169.

WILKE, G. 1927. Römisch-rechtliche Einflüsse auf die Rechtsentwicklung im britischen Weltreich. *Archiv für Rechts- und Wirtschaftsphilosophie* **20**: 293.

WILLIAMS, J. 1904. Roman law in English decisions. Law in English decisions. *Law Magazine and Rev.* **29**: 139.

WILSON, J. D. 1897. On the reception of Roman law in Scotland. *JurR* **9**: 361.

YNTEMA, H. E. 1937. Roman law as the basis of comparative law. *A century of progress, 1835–1935,* **2**: 346. New York University, School of Law.

——. 1950. Roman law and its influence on Western civilization. *Cornell Law Quart.* **357**.

See also Berger, A., and A. A. Schiller. 1945, 1947. Bibliography of Anglo-American studies in Roman law, etc., 1943–1947. *Sem* **3**: 75–94; **5**: 62–85.

XI. ROMAN LAW AND LEGAL EDUCATION.

(Ancient legal history, methods of instruction, the so-called "crisis" of Roman law study.)

APPLETON, C. 1926. Notre enseignement du droit romain, ses ennemis et ses défauts. *Méi Cornil* **1**. Gand-Paris, Sirey.

BERGER, A., 1915. L'indirizzo odierno degli studi di diritto romano. Prolusione. *Rivista critica di scienze sociali* **2**: 1–40. Florence.

BELVAUX, P. A. 1925. Le rôle du droit romain dans la formation du latiniste. *Revue de l'Université Libre de Bruxelles* **30**: 205.

BETTI, E. 1937. Methode und Wert des heutigen Studiums des römischen Rechts. *TR* **15**: 137–174.

——. 1939. La crisi odierna della scienza romanistica in Germania. *RDCom* **37**: 120–128.

BIONDI, B. 1933. Prospettive romanistiche. Milan, Vita e Pensiero.

——. 1950. Crisi e sorti dello studio di diritto romano. *An Triest* **20**: 11.

BISCARDI, A. 1951. Il diritto romano e l'ora presente. *Ius*, N. S., **2**: 287.

DE BLÉCOURT, A. S. 1937. Pro excolendo en de rechtsgeschiedenis. Groningen, Wolters.

BRASIELLO, U. 1951. Lo studio storico del diritto romano in rapporto al diritto moderno. *AG* **141**: 58–78.

CARRELLI, O. 1943. A proposito di una crisi del diritto romano. *SDHI* **9**: 1–20.

CHIAZZESE, L. 1930. Nuovi orientamenti della storia del diritto romano. *AG* **103**: 87–115, 165–228.

DAVID, M. 1937. Der Rechtshistoriker und seine Aufgabe. Leiden, Sijthoff.

FEENSTRA, R. 1952. Interpretatio multiplex. Een beschouwing over de zgn. crisis van het Romeinse recht. Zwolle, Tjeenk Willink.

DE FRANCISCI, P. 1923. Dogmatica e storia nell'educazione giuridica. *Rivista internazionale di filosofia del diritto*.

——. 1949. Punti di orientamento per lo studio del diritto. *RISG* **86**: 69.

GAUDEMET, J. 1947. Méthode historique et droit romain. *RHD* **24–25**: 67–95.

GEORGESCU, V. A. 1939. Remarques sur la crise des etudes de droit romain. *TR* **16**: 403–433.

GROSSO, G. 1946. Premesse generali al corso di diritto romano. Turin, Giappichelli.

——. 1950. Crisi e sorti del diritto romano. *AnTriest* **20**: 13.

HENRION, R. 1947. La recherche scientifique en ancien droit romain. *Latomus* **6**(2) : 97.

JOLOWICZ, H. F. 1949. Utility and elegance in civil law studies. *LQR* **49**: 323.

KOSCHAKER, P. 1938. Die Krise der römischen Rechtswissenschaft. Munich, Beck.

——. 1940. Probleme der heutigen romanistischen Rechtswissenschaft. Deutsche Rechtswissenschaft (Hamburg) **5**.

——. 1947. Europa und das römische Recht. Munich, Biberstein.

LAURIA, M. 1938. Indirizzi e problemi romanistici. Rome, Foro Italiano.

LAUTNER, J. G. 1927. Die Methoden einer antik-rechtsgeschichtlichen Forschung. *ZVR* **47**: 27–76.

LEVY-BRUHL, H. 1925. Pour le droit romain. *Revue internationale d'enseignement* **79**: 88.

MITTEIS, L. 1918. Antike Rechtsgeschichte und romanistisches Rechtsstudium. *Mitteilungen des Vereins der Freunde des humanistischen Gymnasiums (Vienna)* **18**: 56–76. (Italian translation by B. Biondi and G. Funaioli, *AnPal.* **12**: 477–499, 1928, followed by an article by S. Riccobono, Punti di vista critici e ricostruttivi, 500–637).

NOAILLES, P. 1943. La crise du droit romain. *Memorial des Études Latines*, offertes à Marouzeau.

ORESTANO, R. 1950. Diritto romano, tradizione romanistica e studio storico del diritto. *RISG*, 3 ser., **4**: 156.

——. 1951. Il diritto romano nella scienza del diritto. *Ius*, N. S., **2**: 141.

PUGLIESE, G. 1941. Diritto romano e scienza del diritto. *An Mac* **15**: 1.

RICCOBONO, S. 1935. Mos italicus e mos gallicus nella Interpretazione del Corpus iuris. *ACII* **2**: 377–398.

——. 1930. Nichilismo storico e critico nel campo del diritto Discorso. *Annuario Univ. Palermo*.

——. 1942. Vom Schicksal des römischen Rechts. Studia Humanitatis. *Fschr. zur Eröffnung des Instituts Studia Humanitatis* 33. Berlin, Küpper.

DE SARLO, L. 1934. Indirizzi, metodi e tendenze della moderna scienza del diritto romano. *AG* **111**: 98–117.

SCHÖNBAUER, E. 1939. Zur Krise des römischen Rechts. *Fschr. Koschaker* **2**: 385–410.

SCHWARZ, A. B. 1928. Pandektenwissenschaft und heutiges romanistisches Studium. *Festgabe Schweizer Juristenverein.* Zurich.

SECKEL, E. 1921. Das romische Recht und seine Wissenschaft im Wandel der Jahrhunderte. Berlin, Norddeutsche Buchdruckerei.

SIMONIUS, A. 1934. Was bedeuten für uns die Pandekten. Vortrag. Basel, Helbing & Lichtenhahn.

STELLA-MARANCA, F. 1927. Sul metodo di insegnamento delle Pandette. *AnBari*.

WENGER, L. 1907. Die Stellung des öffentlichen romischen Rechts im Universitätsunterricht. Vienna, Manz.

——. 1905. Römische und antike Rechtsgeschichte. Graz, Leuscher.

——. 1927. Heutiger Stand der romischen Rechtswissenschaft. Erreichtes und Erstrebtes. Munich, Beck.

——. 1930. Wesen und Ziele der antiken Rechtsgeschichte. *St Bonfante* 2. Milan, Treves.

——. 1938. Sur le droit romain, le droit comparé et l'histoire du droit. Études du droit comparé E. Lambert 1. Paris, Sirey.

——. 1947. Römisches Recht in historischer und juristischer Anschauung. *Forschungen und Fortschritte* 22.

——. 1951. Um die Zukunft des römischen Rechts. *Fschr Schulz* 2: 364–386.

DE ZULUETA, F. 1920. Study of Roman law today. Lecture. Oxford, Clarendon Press.

——. 1929. L'histoire de droit de l'antiquité. *Mél Fournier*. Paris, Sirey.

XII. SOURCES

(Editions, textual criticism, juristic language. For interpolations, see Ch. XIII)

ACTA DIVI AUGUSTI. 1945. Ed. Riccobono, Festa, Biondi, Arangio-Ruiz. Rome, Regia Academia Italica.

ALBERTARIO, E. 1937. Glossemi e interpolazioni pregiustinianee. *Studi* 5: 377. See also p. 385. Milan, Giuffrè.

——. 1937. Elementi postgaiani nelle Istituzioni di Gaio. *Studi* 5: 439. Milan, Giuffrè.

——. 1937. Glossemi nei Frammenti Vaticani. *Studi* 5: 551–559. Milan, Giuffrè.

APPLETON, C. 1929. Les interpolations dans Gaius. *RHD* 8: 197–241.

ARANGIO-RUIZ, V. See under Fontes iuris Romani anteiustiniani.

——. 1946. La compilazione giustinianea e i suoi commentatori bizantini. *Scr Ferrini* (Univ. Pavia), 81. Milan, Hoepli.

ARANGIO-RUIZ, V., and A. GUARINO. 1943. Breviarium iuris Romani. (Reprint 1951.) Milan, Giuffrè.

ARCHI, G. G. 1937. L'Epitome Gai. Studio del tardo diritto romano in Occidente. Milan, Giuffrè.

BAVIERA, G. (J.) See under Fontes iuris Romani anteiustiniani.

BIONDI, B. 1952. La terminologia romana come prima dommatica giuridica. *St Arangio-Ruiz* 2: 73. Naples, Giovene.

BIZOUKIDES, P. C. 1938–1939. Gaius. 3 v. (Prolegomena, Institutiones, Adnotationes, Fragmenta Gaiana; written in Greek). Salonika; Leipzig, Harrassowitz.

BREMER, F. P. 1896–1901. Iurisprudentiae Romanae quae supersunt. 3 v. Leipzig, Teubner.

BRUNS, C. G., and T. MOMMSEN. 1909–1912. Fontes iuris Romani antiqui. 7th ed. by O. Gradenwitz. 3 v. (Additamenta, Simulacra.) Tübingen, Mohr.

BRUNS, C. G., and E. SACHAU. 1880. Syrisch-romisches Rechtsbuch. Berlin, Reiner.

BUCKLAND, W. W. 1930. Digest 47.2 (De furtis) and the methods of the compilers. *TR* 10: 117–142.

CECI, L. 1892. Le etimologie degli giureconsulti romani. Turin, Loescher.

Codex Gregorianus et Hermogenianus. Ed. P. Krueger. 1890. *Collectio librorum iuris anteiustiniani* 3. Berlin, Weidmann.

Codex Theodosianus cum Constitutionibus Sirmondianis et Leges Novellae ad Theodosianum pertinentes. Ed. T. Mommsen and P. M. Meyer. 1905. 3 v. Berlin, Weidmann.

COGLIOLO, P. 1911. Manuale delle fonti del diritto romano secondo i risultati della più recente critica filologica. Turin, Utet.

Corpus Iuris Civilis. 1. Institutiones. Ed. P. Krueger. Digesta. Ed. T. Mommsen and P. Krueger. 15th stereotype edition, 1928. 2. Codex Iustinianus. Ed. P. Krueger. 10 ster. ed., 1929. 3. Novellae. Ed. R. Schöll and G. Kroll. 5th ster. ed., 1928. Berlin, Weidmann.

Corpus Iuris Civilis. French translation. 1803–1811. Le Digeste (by M. Hulot, **1–7**). Les Institutes (by M. Hulot, **8**). Le Code (by P.-A. Tissot, **9–12**). Les Nouvelles (by M. Bérenger, **13–14**). Metz.

Corpus Iuris Civilis. German translation by C. E. Otto, B. Schilling, C. F. F. Sintenis, 1831–1839. 7 v. Leipzig, Focke.

Corpus Iuris Civilis. Italian translation. 1858–1862. Corpo del diritto corredato dalle note di D. Gotofredo e di C. E. Freiesleben . . . a cura di G. Vignoli. Latin text and translation into Italian. Contains also translations of Gaius' Institutes, Ulpian, Paul, Fragmenta Vaticana etc. Naples, Morelli.

Corpus Iuris Civilis. Spanish translation. 1874. By R. de Fonseca, J. M. de Ortega, A. de Bacardi. 2 v. Barcelona.

Corpus Iuris Civilis. English translation by S. P. Scott. 1931. The Civil Law including the Twelve Tables, the Institutes of Gaius, the Rules of Ulpian, the Opinions of Paulus, the enactments of Justinian and the Constitutions of Leo. 17 v. Cincinnati, Central Trust Company.

DAVID, M. 1948. Gai Institutiones. 1. Leiden, Brill.

Digesta Iustiniani Augusti. 1918, 1931. Ed. P. Bonfante, C. Fadda, C. Ferrini, S. Riccobono, V. Scialoja. 2 v. Milan, Società Editrice Libraria.

EISELE, F. 1896. Zur Latinität Justinians. Beiträge zur romischen Rechtsgeschichte. Freiburg–Leipzig, Mohr.

FELGENTRÄGER, W. 1932. Die Literatur zur Echtheitsfrage der romischen Juristenschriften. *Symbolae Friburgenses Lenel*. Leipzig, Tauchnitz.

——. 1935. Zur Entstehungsgeschichte der Fragmenta Vaticana. Romanistische Abhandlungen. (*Freiburger Rechtsgeschichtliche Abhandlungen* 5: 27.) Freiburg i.B., Waibel.

FERRINI, C. 1884, 1889. Institutionum Graeca Paraphrasis Theophilo vulgo tributa. 2 v. Milan, Hoepli. Berlin, Calvary.

FITTING, H. 1908. Alter und Folge der Schriften der römischen Juristen. 2nd ed. Halle, Niemeyer.

Fontes Iuris Romani Anteiustiniani. 1940–1943. 1. Leges (ed. S. Riccobono). 2nd ed. 1941. 2. Auctores, Leges saeculares (ed. J. Baviera, C. Ferrini, J. Furlani). 2nd ed. 1940. 3. Negotia (ed. V. Arangio-Ruiz). 1st ed. 1943. Florence, Barbèra.

Fontes Iuris Romani antiqui. See above under Bruns and Mommsen.

GIRARD, P. F. 1937. Textes de droit romain. 6th ed. by F. Senn. Paris, Rousseau.

GRUPE, E. 1895–1897. Zur Sprache der Gaianischen Institutionenfragmente in Justinians Digesten. *ZSS* **16–18**.

GUARINO, A. 1952. Guida allo studio delle fonti giuridiche romane. Naples, Pellerano.

HAENEL, G. 1857. Corpus legum ad imperatoribus Romanis ante Iustinianum latarum. Leipzig, Hinrichs.

HARDY, E. G. 1912. Roman laws and charters. Oxford, Clarendon Press.

——. 1912. Three Spanish charters and other documents. Oxford, Clarendon Press.

HEIMBACH, G. E. 1833–1870. Basilicorum libri LX. 5 v.; Prolegomena, Manuale, v. 6; Suppl. 1. ed. K. E. Zachariae

v. Lingenthal, 1846. Leipzig, Barth; Suppl. 2 ed. C. Ferrini and G. Mercati. Milan, Hoepli, 1897.

Huschke, P. E. 1908–1927. Iurisprudentiae anteiustinianae reliquiae. 6th ed. by E. Seckel and B. Kübler. 1 (1908), 2, 1 (1911), 2, 2 (1927) Leipzig, Teubner.

Kalb, W. 1888. Das Juristenlatein. 2nd ed. Nuremberg, Ballhorn.

——. 1890. Roms Juristen nach ihrer Sprache dargestellt. Leipzig, Teubner.

—— 1911. Wegweiser in die römische Rechtssprache. Leipzig, Nemnich.

——. 1923. Spezialgrammatik zur selbständigen Erlernung der römischen Sprache für Rechtsstudierende. Munich, Nemnich.

Kipp, T. 1919. Geschichte der Quellen des römischen Rechts. 4th ed. Leipzig, Deichert.

Kniep, F. 1911–1917. Gai Institutionum commentarii. 5 v. Jena, Fisher.

Kooiman, C. L. 1913. Fragmenta iuris Quiritium. Amsterdam.

Krüger, P. See above under Corpus Iuris Civilis.

——. 1877. Codex Iustinianus (ed. maior). Berlin, Weidmann.

——. 1923, 1926. Codex Theodosianus, libri I-VIII. Berlin, Weidman.

——. See above under Huschke.

Krüger, P., T. Mommsen, and G. Studemund, 1878–1923. Collectio librorum iuris anteiustiniani. 1. Gai Institutiones (6th ed. 1923). 2. Ulpiani Regulae. Pauli Sententiae (1878). 3. Fragmenta Vaticana, Mosaicarum et Romanarum Legum Collatio, Consultatio, Codices Gregorianus et Hermogenianus, etc. (1890). Berlin, Weidmann.

Kübler, B., and E. Seckel. 1939. Gai Institutiones. 8th ed. Leipzig, Teubner.

Lenel, O. 1899. Palingenesia iuris civilis. 2 v. Leipzig, Tauchnitz.

——. 1927. Das Edictum perpetuum. Ein Versuch zu seiner Herstellung. 3rd ed. Leipzig, Tauchnitz.

Lévy-Bruhl, H. 1924. Le Latin et le droit romain. *Revue des Études Latines* 2: 103.

Mommsen, T. See above under Codex Theodosianus and Corpus Iuris Civilis.

——. 1866–1870. Digesta Iustiniani Augusti. 2 v. (Ed. maior). Berlin, Weidmann.

Monro, C. H. 1904, 1909. The Digest of Justinian. 2 v. (Books I-XV.) Cambridge, Univ. Press.

Moyle, J. B. 1913. The Institutes of Justinian. 5th ed. Oxford, Clarendon Press.

Niedermeyer, H. 1934. Vorjustinianische Glossen und Interpolationen und Textüberlieferung. *ACDR Roma* 1: 351–384. Pavia, Fusi.

Novellae Iustiniani. See above under Corpus Iuris Civilis.

Pharr, C., M. B. Pharr, and T. S. Davidson. 1952. The Theodosian Code and Novels and the Sirmondian constitutions. A translation with commentary, glossary and bibliography. Princeton, Univ. Press.

Riccobono, S. See above under Fontes Iuris Romani Anteiustiniani.

——. 1936. La Codificazione di Giustiniano e la critica contemporanea. *AnMac* 10.

Rotondi, G. 1912. Leges publicae populi Romani. Elenco cronologico con una introduzione sull'attività legislativa dei comizi romani (Estr. dall' Enciclopedia giuridica italiana.) Milan, Società Editrice Libraria.

Sachau, E. 1907–1908. Syrische Rechtsbücher. 2 v. Berlin, Reiner. (See above Bruns and Sachau.)

Sandars, T. C. 1934. Institutes of Justinian. 17th impr. London, Longmans & Green.

Scherillo, G. 1939. Contributi alla storia delle Novelle Postteodosiane. *St Besta* 1: 297–321. Milan, Giuffrè.

Schulz, F. 1926. Die Epitome Ulpiani des Cod. Vat. Reginae 1128. Bonn, Marcus & Weber.

Seckel, E. See above under Huschke, Kübler.

Siber, H. 1934. Das Problem vorjustinianischer Textveränderungen. *ACDR Roma* 1: 413–430. Pavia, Fusi.

Solazzi, S. 1934–1953. Glosse a Gaio. *St Riccobono* 1: 71, 1936; Per il XIV Centenario della Codificazione Giustinianea, Pavia (1934) 293–450; *SDHI* 6: 320–356, 1940; *Scr Ferrini*, 139–199, Università Pavia, 1946; *St Arangio-Ruiz* 3: 89–113 (Naples, Jovene, 1953).

Theophili Paraphrasis. See above under Ferrini.

Thiele, G. 1910, 1912. Lateinkursus für Juristen. 2 v. Berlin, Vahlen.

De Visscher, F. 1935. Les sources du droit selon le Code de Justinien. *ACII* 1: 51–68 (= Nouvelles Études, 1949, 353).

Volterra, E. 1935–1936. Indice delle glosse, interpolazioni nelle fonti pregiustinianee occidentali. 1. Pauli Sententiae, 2. Consultatio, 3. Tituli ex corpore Uliani, 4. Collatio. *Rivista di storia di diritto italiano* 8–9.

Warmington, E. H. 1940. Remains of old Latin 4. Loeb Classical Library.

Weiss, E. 1914. Studien zu den römischen Rechtsquellen. Leipzig, Meiner.

Wlassak, M. 1884. Kritische Studien zur Theorie der Rechtsquellen. Graz, Lubensky.

Zachariae v. Lingenthal, C. E. 1856–1884. Ius Graeco-Romanum. 7 v. Leipzig. (Greek edition by J and P. Zepos, 8 v. Athens, 1931.)

De Zulueta, F. 1946, 1953. The Institutes of Gaius. 2 v. 1. Text with critical notes and translation. 2. Commentary. Oxford, Clarendon Press.

XIII. INTERPOLATIONS IN JUSTINIAN'S LEGISLATIVE WORK

(For glosses and so-called pre-Justinian interpolations, see Ch. XII)

Albertario, E. 1935. Introduzione storica allo studio del diritto romano, 39–79. Milan, Giuffrè.

——. 1937. A proposito di "Interpolationenjagd." *Studi di diritto romano* 5: 309. Milan, Giuffrè.

——. 1937. La critica della critica. *Studi cit.* 5: 321.

——. 1937. Giustiniano interpolante se stesso. *Studi cit.* 5: 345.

——. 1937. Ancora sulle interpolazioni giustinianee nelle costituzioni giustinianee. *Studi cit.* 5: 355.

——. 1953. Several articles in *Studi cit.* 6: 1–55, 427.

Ambrosino, R. 1939–1940. In tema di interpolazioni. *Rend Lomb* 73: 69.

Appleton, C. 1916. Les negations intruses ou omises dans les Pandectes Florentini. *RHD* 40: 1–61.

Appleton, H. 1895. Des interpolations dans les Pandectes et des méthodes à les découvrir. Paris, Lerose.

Arangio-Ruiz, V. 1938. Romanisti e Latinisti. *St Mancaleoni, StSas* 16: 15–34.

Berger, A. 1912. Review of G. Beseler, Beitraege zur Kritik der römischen Rechtsquellen 1–2 (see below). *KrVj* 14: 397–445.

Beseler, G. v. 1910–1931. Beiträge zur Kritik der römischen Rechtsquellen. 5 v. Tübingen, Mohr.

——. 1923–1937. Several articles in *ZSS* 43–47, 50–53, 56, 57.

——. 1929. Juristische Miniaturen. Leipzig, Noske.

——. 1929. Subsiciva. Leipzig, Noske.

——. 1930. Opora. Leipzig, Noske.

——. 1928–1936. *TR* 8, 10; *St Riccobono* 1. Palermo, Castiglia.

Bonfante, P. 1934. Storia del diritto romano. 4th ed. 2: 121. Rome, Istituto di diritto romano.

BUCKLAND, W. W. 1924. Interpolations in the Digest. *Yale Law Jour.* **33**: 343.
——. 1941. Interpolations in the Digest. *Harvard Law Rev.* **54**: 1273.
COLLINET, P. 1952. La génèse du Digeste, du Code et des Institutes de Justinien. (Posthumous edition.) Paris, Sirey.
CHIAZZESE, L. 1931. Confronti testuali. Contributo alla dottrina delle interpolazioni giustinianee. Parte generale. *AnPal* **16**.
EBRARD, F. 1918. Die Grundsätze der modernen Interpolationenforschung. *ZVR* **36**: 1.
GRADENWITZ, O. 1887. Interpolationen in den Pandekten. Berlin, Weidmann.
——. 1889. Interpolazioni e interpretazioni. *BIDR* **2**: 3–15.
——. 1886, 1893. Interpolationen in den Pandekten. *ZSS* **7, 14**.
GUARNERI-CITATI, A. 1927–1939. Indice delle parole, frasi e costrutti, ritenuti indizio di interpolazione nei testi giuridici romani. Milan, Hoepli. Suppl. 1, *St Riccobono* **1**: 701, Palermo, Castiglia, 1936; Suppl. 2, *Fschr Koschaker* **1**: 117, Weimar, Böhlau, 1939.
Index Interpolationum quae in Iustiniani Digestis inesse dicuntur. Editionem a L. Mitteis inchoatam et ab aliis viris doctis perfectam curaverunt E. Levy et E. Rabel. 1929–1935. 3 v., Suppl. 1 (1929). Weimar, Böhlau.
KALB, W. 1897. Jagd nach Interpolationen in den Pandekten. Sprachliche Beiträge zur Digestenkritik. *Fschr Autenrieth.* Nuremberg. Programm des Melanchtongymnasiums.
KALINKA, E. 1927. Digestenkritik und Philologie. Philologische Anmerkungen zu Beselers Methode. *ZSS* **47**: 319–354.
KASER, M. 1952. Zum heutigen Stand der Interpolationenforschung. *ZSS* **69**: 60–101.
KRETSCHMAR, P. 1939. Kritik der Interpolationenkritik. *ZSS* **59**: 102–218.
KRÜGER, P. 1910. Interpolationen im Justinianischen Codex. *Fg Güterbock.* Berlin, Vahlen.
LENEL, O. 1925. Interpolationenjagd. *ZSS* **45**: 17–38.
——. 1929. Kritisches und Antikritisches. *ZSS* **49**: 1–23.
——. 1930. Wortforschung. *ZSS* **50**: 1–17.
MARCHI, A. 1906. Le interpolazioni risultanti dal confronto tra il Gregoriano, l'Ermogeniano, il Teodosiano, le Novelle Postteodosiane e il Codice Giustinianeo. *BIDR* **18**.
MITTEIS, L. 1912. Interpolationenforschung. *ZSS* **33**: 180–211.
PETROPOULOS, G. 1940. On traces of Interpolations in Justinian's Code (in Greek). *Mémoires Andréades,* 433. Athens.
RICCOBONO, S. 1952. Fine e conquiste delle indagini interpolazionistiche. *BIDR* **55–56**: 396–408.
SCHULZ, F. 1930. Interpolationen in den Justinianischen Reformgesetzen des Codex Iustinianus vom J. 534. *St. Bonfante* **1**. (See also *ZSS* 30: 212–248.)
——. 1935. Umarbeitungen Justinianischer Gesetze bei ihrer Aufnahme in den Codex Iustinianus von 534. *ACII* **1**: 83.
——. 1951. Die Ulpianfragmente des Papyrus Rylands 474 und die Interpolationenforschung. *ZSS* **68**: 1–29.
SIBER, H. 1925. Beiträge zur Interpolationenforschung. *ZSS* **45**: 146–187.
SOLAZZI, S. 1936. L'interpolazione della rubrica. *SDHI* **2**: 325–332.
STROUX, J. 1950. Die neuen Ulpianfragmente und ihre Bedeutung für die Interpolationenforschung. *Miscellanea Academica Berolinensia* 2 (2): 1.

XIV. ROMAN LAW IN NON-JURISTIC SOURCES

GENERAL

ROTONDI, G. 1922. La codificazione giustinianea attraverso le fonti extragiuridiche. *Scritti giuridici* **1**: 340. Milan, Hoepli.
——. 1922. Indice dei richiami al diritto nei testi extragiuridici. (Posthumous edition.) *Scritti giuridici* **1**: 490. Milan, Hoepli.

ACTA MARTYRUM

LIEBERMAN, S. 1945. Roman legal institutions in early Rabbinics and Acta Martyrum. *Jewish Quart. Rev.* **35**: 1–58.
RAMBAUD, J. 1907. Le droit criminel romain dans les Actes des Martyrs. 2nd ed. Lyons-Paris, Witte.
DE REGIBUS, L. 1926. Storia del diritto negli Acta Martyrum. Turin, Società Editrice Internazionale.

AGRIMENSORES

See Land-surveyors.

APULEIUS

NORDEN, F. 1912. Apuleius von Madaura und das römische. Privatrecht. Leipzig, Teubner.

BOËTHIUS

DIRKSEN, H. E. 1871. Hinterlassene Schriften **1**: 163–184. Leipzig, Teubner.

CASSIUS DIO

VRIND, G. 1923. De Cassii Dionis vocabulis quae ad ius publicum pertinent. Diss. Amsterdam. The Hague, Mensing.

CATO MAIOR (M. PORCIUS)

ARCANGELI, A. 1927. I contratti agrari nel De agricultura di Catone. St. Zanzucchi. Milan, Vita e Pensiero

CICERO

COLEMAN-NORTON, P. R. 1950. Cicero's contribution to the text of the Twelve Tables. *ClJ* **46**: 51.
COSTA, E. 1899. Le orazioni di diritto privato di Cicerone (Pro Quinctio, Pro Roscio, Pro Tullio, Pro Caecina). Bologna, Zanichelli.
——. 1927–1928. Cicerone giureconsulto. 2nd ed. 2 v. Bologna, Zanichelli.
GASQUY, P. 1887. Cicéron jurisconsulte. Thèse Lettres, Aix-en-Provence.
LENGLE, J. 1934. Römisches Strafrecht bei Cicero und den Historikern. Leipzig, Teubner.
PALLASSE, M. 1945. Cicéron et les sources de droit. *Annales Univ. Lyon,* 3 sér.
ROBY, H. J. 1902. Essay on the law in Cicero's private orations. Cambridge, Univ. Press.

COUNCILS OF THE CHURCH

CASTELLO, C. 1937–1939. Raffronti fra Concilii della Chiesa e diritto romano. *RendLomb* **71, 72**.
JONKERS, E. J. 1952. Application of Roman law by councils in the sixth century. *TR* **20**: 340–343.
LARDONE, F. G. 1935. Il diritto romano e i Concilii. *ACII* **2**: 101–122.
STEINWENTER, A. 1934. Die Konzilsakten als Quellen profanen Rechts. *Mnemosyna Pappoulia.* Athens.

ENNIUS

STELLA-MARANCA, F. 1928. Quinto Ennio e lo studio del diritto romano. *Hist.* **1**.

GELLIUS

DIRKSEN, H. E. 1871. Hinterlassene Schriften **1**: 21–63. Leipzig, Teubner.

DE GLOEDEN, J. 1843. Auli Gellii quae ad ius pertinent. Rostock.

HERTZ, M. 1868. Auli Gellii quae ad ius pertinent capita. Breslau, Friedrich.

OLIVER, D. T. 1933. Roman law of Aulus Gellius. *CambLJ* 5.

GRAMMARIANS

DIRKSEN, H. E. 1871. Hinterlassene Schriften 1: 64–108. Leipzig, Teubner.

MORASSO, M. 1894. Studi sui grammatici latini in relazione al diritto romano. *RISG* 17: 101–125.

GRATIANI DECRETUM

VETULANI, A. 1937. Les Nouvelles de Justinien dans le Décret de Gratien. *RHD* 16: 461–479.

——. 1947. Gratien et le droit romain. *RHD* 24–25: 11–48.

HORACE

DIRKSEN, H. E. 1871. Hinterlassene Schriften 1: 335–341 (on the scholia to Horace). Leipzig, Teubner.

STELLA-MARANCA, F. 1933. Il diritto romano nell' opera di Orazio. *AnBari*, Parte II: 71–89.

——. 1935. Introduzione allo studio del diritto romano nelle opere di Orazio. *Hist.* 9: 3, 369, 531.

——. 1935. Orazio e la giurisprudenza romana. *Eloquenza* 25.

——. 1935. Per le studio del diritto romano nell'opera di Orazio. *AGII* 4: 31–88.

——. 1936. Orazio e la legislazione romana. Conferenze Oraziane (Università del Sacro Cuore). Milan, Vita e Pensiero.

JOSEPHUS FLAVIUS

MENDELSSOHN, L. 1874. De senatusconsultis Romanorum a Josepho relatis, Antiqu. VIII 9, 2–XIV 10, 22. Leipzig, Teubner.

JUVENAL

RAZZINI, C. S. 1913. Il diritto romano nelle Satire di Jovenale. Turin, Anfossi.

LAND-SURVEYORS (AGRIMENSORES)

BRUGI, B. 1897. Le dottrine giuridiche degli agrimensori romani comparate a quelle del Digesto. Padua, Drucker.

——. 1903. Nuovi studi sugli agrimensori romani. *RendLinc* 1902/3.

LIBANIUS

BESELER, G. v. 1938. *Byzantinische-neugriechische Jahrbücher* 14: 1–40.

LIVY

BISCARDI, A. 1942. Tito Livio e la storia della costituzione di Roma. *StSen* 56: 346.

EVANS, A. E. 1910. Roman law studies in Livy. Roman history and mythology. *Univ. of Michigan Studies, Hum. Series* 4.

LENGLE, J. See above under Cicero.

SCHERILLO, G. 1943. Il diritto pubblico romano in Livio. Milan, Liviana.

OVIDIUS

VAN IDDEKINGE, J. 1811. De insigni in poeta Ovidio Romani iuris peritia. Amsterdam, Hengst.

STELLA-MARANCA, F. 1927. Ius pontificium nei Fasti di Ovidio. *AnBari*, 1927/I :6.

PATRISTIC LITERATURE. NEW TESTAMENT

BALL, W. E. 1901. Paul and the Roman law. Edinburgh, Clark.

BECK, A. 1930. Römisches Recht bei Tertullian und Cyprian. *Schriften der Königsberger Gelehrten Gesellschaft*, 2. Halle, Niemeyer.

BIONDI, B. 1940. L'influenza di San Ambrogio sulla legislazione religiosa del suo tempo. Sant'Ambrogio nel XVI centenario della nascita. Milan, Vita e Pensiero.

——. 1951. La giuridicità del Vangelo. *Ius* 2: 23.

BRUCK, E. F. 1944. Ethics v. Law. St. Paul, the Fathers of the Church and the cheerful giver. *Trad* 2.

BUSS, S. 1901. Roman law and history in the New Testament. N. Y.-London.

CARUSI, E. 1906. Diritto romano e Patristica. *St Fadda* 2: 69–97. Napoli, Pierro.

CAVIGLIOLI, G. 1935. Impronte di diritto romano nel carteggio di S. Paolo e nella Vulgata del Nuovo Testamento. *ACII* 2: 89–100.

CONRAT, M. 1904. Das Erbrecht in Galaterbrief. *Zeitschr. für neutestamentliche Wissenschaft* 5: 204.

CUMONT, F. 1903. Ambrosiaster et le droit romain. *Revue d'histoire et de littérature réligieuses* 8: 437.

DIRKSEN, H. E. 1871. Hinterlassene Schriften 1: 149–162, 185–203. (On Sidonius Apollinaris and Isidore of Seville.) Leipzig, Teubner.

DUVAL-ARNOULD, L. P. E. 1888. Études sur quelques points d'histoire de droit romain d'après les lettres et les poèmes de Sidoine Apollinaire. These Paris.

EGER, O. 1917. Rechtsworter und Rechtsbilder in den Paulinischen Briefen. *Ztschr. für neutestamentliche Wissenschaft* 8.

——. 1919. Rechtsgeschichtliches zum Neuen Testament. Basel.

ESMEIN, A. 1886. Sur quelques lettres de Sidone. *Mélanges d'histoire de droit*, 359. Paris, Larose.

FERRINI, C. 1929. Su le idee giuridiche nei libri V e VI delle Istituzioni di Lattanzio. *Opere* 2: 481–486. Milan, Hoepli.

——. 1929. Le cognizioni giuridiche di Lattanzio, Arnobio e Minuzio Felice. *Opere* 2: 467–480. Milan, Hoepli.

GASPARINI-FOGLIANI, T. 1928. Cipriano. Contributo alle ricerche di riferimenti legali nei testi extragiuridici del secolo III d.C. Modena, Bossi.

GRUPE, E. 1926. Sidonius Apollinaris. *ZSS* 46: 19–31.

JONKERS, E. J. 1952. Pope Gelasius and civil law. *TR* 20: 335–339.

DE LABRIOLLE, P. 1906. Tertullien jurisconsulte. *NRHD* 30: 5–27. See TERTULLIANUS.

LARDONE, F. 1933. Roman law in the works of St. Augustine. *Georgetown Law Jour.* 21: 435.

MAROI, F. 1943. Il diritto romano agrario nelle fonti cristiane. Rome, Osservatorio ital. di diritto agrario. *Collana di Conferenze* 7.

MASCHI, C. A. 1940. Un problema generale del diritto in S. Ambrogio. Sant'Ambrogio nel XVI centenario della nascita. Milan, Vita e Pensiero.

MEYER, W. 1889. Epistolae imperatorum Romanorum ex collectione canonum Avellana. Göttingen, Dieterich.

NONNOI, D. 1934. San Agostino e il diritto romano. *RISG* 9: 531–622.

ROBERTI, M. 1931. Contributo allo studio delle relazioni fra diritto romano e patristica dall' esame delle fonti agostiniane. *Rivista do filosofia neoscolastica* 24, Suppl.

STANGHELLINI, G. 1910. Il diritto matrimoniale nelle opere dei Padri della Chiesa. *AG* 84: 77–140.

STELLA-MARANCA, F. 1927. Jurisprudentiae Romanae reliquiae quae Isidori Hispalensis Etimologiarum libris continentur. Lanciano.

VIOLARDO, G. 1937. Il pensiero giuridico di San Gerolamo. Milan, Vita e Pensiero.

VITTON, P. 1924. I concetti giuridici nelle opere di Tertulliano. Rome, Tipografia dei Lincei.

WESTBURY-JONES, J. 1939. St. Paul, the Roman jurist, in Roman and Christian imperialism, 104–181. London, Macmillan.

PETRONIUS

DEBRAY, L. 1919. Pétrone et le droit prive romain. *NRHD* **43**: 5–70; 127–186.

SOLIMENA, C. 1905. Il diritto nelle colonie d'Italia nelle satire di Petronio. *St Fadda* **6**: 391. Naples, Pierro.

PLAUTUS

BEKKER, E. I. 1892. Die römischen Komiker als Rechtszeugen. *ZSS* **13**: 53–118.

COSTA, E. 1890. Il diritto romano nelle commedie di Plauto. Turin, Bocca.

DEMELIUS, G. 1861, 1863. Plautinische Studien. *Ztschr. für Rechtsgeschichte* **1**: 351–372; **2**: 177–238.

FREDERSHAUSEN, O. 1906. De iure Plautino et Terentiano. Göttingen, Goldschmidt; *idem, Hermes* **47**: 210, 1912.

GREEN, W. M. 1929. Greek and Roman law in the Trinummus of Plautus. *Cl. Philol*, 24.

VAN KAN, J. 1926. La possession dans les comédies de Plaute. *Mél Cornil* **2**: 1–11. Gand-Paris, Sirey.

PARTSCH, J. 1910. Römisches Recht in Plautus' Persa. *Hermes* **45**.

PERNARD, L. 1900. Le droit romain et le droit grec dans le théâtre de Plaute et Térence.

STELLA-MARANCA, F. 1932. Il diritto ereditario e le commedie di Plauto. *Hist.* **10**.

STEVENS, A. P. 1913. Roman law in the Roman drama. *Jour. Soc. Comparative Legislation* **15**: 542.

PLINY THE OLDER

DIRKSEN, H. E. 1871. Die Quellen der Historia naturalis, insbesondere die römisch-rechtlichen. Hinterlassene Schriften **1**: 133–148. Leipzig, Teubner.

PLINY THE YOUNGER

OLIVER, D. T. 1932. Roman law as illustrated in Pliny's letters. *Camb. Law Jour.*

PULCIANO, C. E. 1913. Il diritto privato nelle epistole di Plinio il Giovane. Excerpta iuridica Pliniana. Turin, Anfossi.

SCHNEITHER, J. A. 1827. Loca e Plinii junioris scriptis quae ad ius civile pertinent. Groningen, Van Boekeren.

SOLIMENA, C. 1905. Plinio il Giovine e il diritto pubblico di Roma. Naples, Pierro.

ZANE, J. M. 1914. A Roman lawyer. *Illinois Law Jour.* **8**: 575.

PLUTARCH

DIRKSEN, H. E. 1871. Hinterlassene Schriften **1**: 281–312. Leipzig, Teubner.

POETS

COSTA, E. 1898. Il diritto nei poeti di Roma. Bologna, Zanichelli.

HENRIOT, E. 1865. Mœurs juridiques et judiciaires de l'ancienne Rome d'après les poètes latins. 3 v. Paris, Firmin-Didot.

MURISON, A. F. 1935. The law in the Latin poets. *ACDR Roma* **2**: 609–639. Pavia, Fusi.

RHETORICIANS

DIRKSEN, H. E. 1871. Hinterlassene Schriften **1**: 243–253 (on Fronto), 254–280 (Über die durch die lateinischen Rhetoren angewendete Methode der Auswahl von Beispielen romisch-rechtlichen Inhalts).

LANFRANCHI, F. 1938. Il diritto nei retori romani. Milan, Giuffrè.

RASI, P. 1943. Il diritto matrimoniale nelle opere dei retori romani. *RStDIt* **16**: 5–24.

SPRENGER, J. 1911. Quaestiones in rhetorum Romanorum declamationes juridicae. Halle, Karras.

STEINWENTER, A. 1947. Rhetorik und römischer Zivilprozess. *ZSS* **65**: 69–120.

SENECA

SANTA CRUZ, J. 1943. Seneca y la esclavidud. *AHDE* **14**: 612–620.

STAMPA-BRAUN, J. M. 1950. Las ideas penales y criminologicas de L. A. Seneca. Valladolid.

STELLA-MARANCA, F. 1924. Seneca Giureconsulto. Prolusione. Rome.

SUETONIUS

DIRKSEN, H. E. 1871. Auslegung einzelner Stellen des Suetonius. Hinterlassene Schriften **1**: 213–242. Leipzig, Teubner.

INVREA, E. 1913. Ricerche di diritto pubblico nelle Vite dei Cesari di Suetonio. *Fil* **481**.

LENGLE. See above under Cicero.

SUIDAS

DIRKSEN, H. E. 1871. Hinterlassene Schriften **1**: 287–296.

SYMMACHUS

DIRKSEN, H. E. 1871. Hinterlassene Schriften **1**: 149–162. Leipzig, Teubner.

TACITUS

DIRKSEN, H. E. 1871. Die romisch-rechtlichen Mitteilungen in Tacitus' Geschichtsbuchern. Hinterlassene Schriften **1**: 204–212. Leipzig, Teubner.

LENGLE. See above under Cicero.

TERENTIUS

See above under Plautus (Bekker, Fredershausen, Pernard, Stevens).

COSTA, E. 1893. Il diritto privato nelle commedie di Terenzio. Bologna, Fava. (See *AG* **50**, 1893.)

VARRO

SANIO, F. D. 1867. Varroniana in den Schriften romischer Juristen. Leipzig.

STELLA-MARANCA, F. 1934. Varrone giureconsulto. *AnBari* **167**.

VIRGIL

See above under Poets.

STELLA-MARANCA, F. 1930. Il diritto romano e l'opera di Virgilio. Bari. See also *Hist* **4**, 1930.

XV. LATIN INSCRIPTIONS

ALIBRANDI, I. 1896. Dell' uso dei monumenti epigrafici per l'interpretazione delle leggi romane, 23–46. Rome, Tipografia Polyglotta.

ARANGIO-RUIZ, V. 1936, 1939. Epigrafia giuridica greca e romana. *SDHI* **2**: 429–520, 1933–1935; **5**: 521–633, 1936–1938.

Dizionario epigrafico di antichità romane. Ed. by De Ruggiero, 5 v. (to be continued by G. Cardinali). Rome.

GATTI, G. 1885. Dell' utilità che lo studio del diritto romano può trarre dall' epigrafia. *StDocSD* **6**: 3–23.

GIRARD, P. F. 1912. L'épigraphie latine et le droit romain. *Mél de droit romain* **1**: 342–414. Paris, Sirey.

LUZZATTO, G. I. 1942. Epigrafia giuridica greca e romana. Rome, Pubblicazioni dell' Istituto di diritto romano.

——. 1951. Epigrafia giuiridica greca e romana, 1939–1949. *SDHI* **17**, Suppl. Rome, Apollinaris.

STELLA-MARANCA, F. 1926. Epigrafia giuridica romana. Prolusione. Rome, Bardi.

XVI. JURISTIC PAPYROLOGY

(General presentations of the law of Greco-Roman Egypt, introductory manuals, comprehensive bibliographical surveys)

ARANGIO-RUIZ, V. 1910–1948. Rivista di papitorogia giuridica. *BIDR* **22**: 208–266, 1910; **24**: 204–276, 1911; *Doxa* **1**: 248, 1948.

BOYÉ, A. J. 1929. Droit romain et papyrus d'Égypte. *L'Égypte contemporaine* **20**: 529.

CALDERINI, A. 1920. Bibliografia metodica degli studi di papirologia. *Aegyptus* **1** ff. (since 1920).

——. 1944. Papyri. Guida allo studio della papirologia greca e latina. 2nd ed. Milan, Vita e Rensiero.

COLLINET, P. 1934. La papyrologie et l'histoire du droit. *Münchener Beiträge zur Papyrusforschung* **19**: 186. Munich, Beck.

DAVID, M., and B. A. VAN GRONINGEN. 1946. Papyrological primer. 2nd ed.

FRESE, B. 1909. Aus dem graeko-aegyptischen Rechtsleben. Halle, Niemeyer.

GRADENWITZ, O. 1900. Einführung in die Papyruskunde. Leipzig, Hirzel.

HENNE, H. 1950. La papyrologie et les études juridiques. Conférences à l'Institut de droit romain en 1947, 77–102. Paris, Sirey.

HOMBERT, M. 1946 ff. Bulletin Papyrologique. *Revue des Études grecques*. Latest survey for 1950 in **65** (1952): 383–463. Previous surveys by P. Collart.

HOMBERT, M., and C. PRÉAUX. 1926. Regular bibliographical surveys in *Chronique d'Égypte. Bulletin périodique de la Fondation Égyptologique Reine Elisabeth, Brussels* (since 1926).

MEYER, P. M. 1921 ff. Juristische Papyrusberichte. *ZVR* **39** (220); **40**: 174, 1922; *ZSS* **44**: 581, 1924; **45**: 305, 1926; **48**: 587, 1928; **50**: 503, 1930; **52**: 356, 1932; **54**: 339, 1934.

——. 1920. Juristische Papyri. Erklärung von Urkunden zur Einführung in die juristische Papyruskunde. Berlin, Weidmann.

MITTEIS, L. 1912. Second Part: Juristischer Teil of Grundzüge und Chrestomathie der Papyruskunde by U. Wilcken and L. Mitteis (two parts in four volumes). Leipzig, Teubner.

MODICA, M. 1914. Introduzione allo studio della papirologia giuridica. Milan, Vallardi.

D'ORS, A. 1948. Introduccion al estudio de los documentos del Egipto romano. Madrid.

PEREMANS, W., and J. VERGOTE. 1942. Papyrologisch Handboek. Leuven. Beheer van Philologische Studiën.

PREISENDANZ, K. 1933. Papyrusfunde und Papyrusforschung. Leipzig, Hiersemann.

——. 1950. Papyruskunde. Handbuch der Bibliothekswissenschaft **1**: 163–248. Stuttgart, Koehler.

SCHUBART, W. 1918. Einführung in die Papyruskunde. Berlin, Weidmann.

SEIDL, E. 1935–1949. Juristische Papyruskunde. *SDHI* **1**: 450, 1935; **2**: 239, 1936; **3**: 213, 487, 1937; **4**: 278, 580, 1938; **5**: 293, 634, 1939; **6**: 206, 433, 1940; **15**: 319, 1949.

STEINWENTER, A. 1952. Was bedeuten die Papyri für die praktische Geltung des justinianischen Rechts. *Aeg* **32**: 131–137.

TAUBENSCHLAG, R. 1929. Geschichte der Rezeption des römischen Privatrechts in Agypten. *St Bonfante* **1**: 369: 440. Milan, Treves.

——. 1944, 1948. The law of Greco-Roman Egypt in the light of the papyri, 322 B.C.-840 A.D. **1**, N. Y., Herald Square Press; **2**, Warsaw, Polish Philological Society.

——. 1945. Survey of juristic papyrological literature and publications of papyri in *Journal of Juristic Papyrology* **1** and ff., since 1945.

——. 1952. Introduction to the law of the papyri. *ADORIDA* **1**: 279–376.

WENGER, L. 1929. Die rechtshistorische Papyrusforschung. Ergebnisse und Aufgaben. *Archiv für Kulturgeschichte* **19**: 10.

——. 1936. Nationales, griechisches und römisches Recht in Aegypten. *Atti del Congresso Internazionale di papirologia, Firenze, 1935*, 159–182. Milan, Vita e Pensiero.

——. 1930–1941. Juristischer Literaturübersicht. *ArPap* **9**: 103, 257, 1930; **10**: 98, 279, 1932; **12**: 103, 247, 1937; **13**: 155, 243, 1939; **14**: 181, 1941.

DE ZULUETA, F. 1928–1935. Survey of juristic papyrology in *Jour. Egyptian Archaeol.* **14**: 131, 1928; **15**: 110, 1929; **16**: 120, 1930; **17**: 117, 1931; **18**: 77, 1932; **19**: 67, 1933; **20**: 94, 1934; **21**: 91, 1935;. Continued by H. F. Jolowicz, **22**: 74, 1936; **23**: 97, 1937; **24**: 105, 1938, and by F. Pringsheim, **26**: 139, 1941.

XVII. COLLECTIONS OF SOURCE MATERIAL FOR TEACHING PURPOSES

ARANGIO-RUIZ, V., and A. GUARINO. 1943. Breviarium iuris Romani. (Reprinted with corrections 1950.) Milan, Giuffre.

ARIAS ROMOS, J. 1947. Seleccion de testos latinos con su version castellana, in Derecho romano, 3rd ed. 623–1064. Madrid, Editorial Revista de derecho privado.

BERGMANN, W. 1910. Das römische Recht aus dem Munde seiner Verfasser. Paderborn, Jungfernmannsche Buchdruckerei.

DÜLL, R. 1939. Corpus Iuris. Eine Auswahl der Rechtsgrundsätze der Antike. Munich, Heimeran.

KÜBLER, B. 1925. Lesebuch des römischen Rechts. 3rd ed. Leipzig, Deichert.

LEVET, A., E. PERROT, and A. FLINIAUX. 1931. Textes et documents pour servir à l'enseignement du droit romain. Paris, Sirey.

MISPOULET, J. B. 1889. Manuel des textes de droit romain. Paris, Plon-Nourrit.

PARTSCH, J. 1909. Formules de procédure civile romaine. Geneva, Kundig.

POUND, R. 1914. Readings in Roman law and the civil law and modern codes as developments thereof. 2nd ed. Cambridge, Harvard Univ. Press.

SCHOTT, R. 1931. Hilfsbüchlein für die Vorlesungen über Institutionen, Geschichte und Zivilprozess des römischen Rechts. Berlin, De Gruyter.

SCHULZ, F. 1916. Einführung in das Studium der Digesten. Tübingen, Mohr.

——. 1925. Texte und Übungen im römischen Privatrecht. Bonn, Marcus & Weber.

SHERMAN, C. P. 1937. Epitome of Roman Law in a single book. A concise collection of almost 700 selected texts. N. Y., Baker & Vorhis.

STAMMLER, R. 1919. Aufgaben aus dem römischen Recht. 4th ed. Leipzig, Veit.

ZEVENBERGEN, C. 1947. Texten ten gebruijke bij de studie van het Romeinsche Recht. Utrecht, De Vroede.

ZITELMANN, E. 1925. Digestenexegese. Zwanzig Fälle aus dem römischen Recht. Berlin-Grunewald, Rothschild.

XVIII. COLLECTIVE WORKS

A. STUDIES IN HONOR OF SCHOLARS

(In alphabetical order of the names of the persons honored)

Studi in memoria di Emilio Albertario. 1952. 3 v. (part still in press). Milan, Giuffrè.

Studi in memoria di Aldo Albertoni. 1935–1938. 3 v. Padua, Cedam.

Études dédiées à la memoire d'André Andréades. 1940. Athens.

Mélanges Charles Appleton. 1903. Lyons, Rey; Paris, Rousseau.

Studi in onore di Vincenzo Arangio-Ruiz. 1952–1953. 4 v. Naples, Jovene.

Scritti vari dedicati al Professore Carlo Arnò. 1928. *PubMod* **30**. Modena, Università.

Studi in onore di Alfredo Ascoli. 1931. Messina, Principato.

Aus römischem und bürgerlichem Recht. Gewidmet Ernst Immanuel Bekker. 1907. Weimar, Böhlau.

Studi di storia e diritto in onore di Enrico Besta. 1937–1938. 4 v. Milan, Giuffrè.

Studi in onore di Pietro Bonfante. 1929–1930. 4 v. Milan, Treves.

Studi in memoria di Guido Bonolis. 1942–1945. 2 v. Milan, Giuffrè.

Studi in onore di Biagio Brugi. 1910. Palermo, Gaipa.

In memory of W. W. Buckland. 1947. *TulLR* **22**.

Studi di storia e diritto in onore di Carlo Calisse. 1940. 3 v. Milan, Giuffrè.

Scritti giuridici in onore di Francesco Carnelutti. 1950. 4 v. Padua, Cedam.

Conferenze romanistiche tenute nella R. Università di Pavia nell' anno 1939 a ricordo di Guglielmo Castelli. 1940. Milan, Giuffrè.

Scritti giuridici dedicati a Giampietro Chironi. 1915. 3 v. Turin, Bocca.

Mélanges de droit romain dédies a Georges Cornil. 1926. 2 v. Gand-Paris, Sirey.

Scritti giuridici in onore di Carlo Fadda. 1906. 6 v. Naples, Pierro.

Studi in memoria di Francesco Ferrara. 1943. 2 v. Milan, Giuffrè.

Scritti di diritto romano in onore di Contardo Ferrini, pubblicati dalla R. Università di Pavia. 1946. Milan, Hoepli.

Scritti in onore di Contardo Ferrini pubblicati in occasione della sua beatificazione. 1947–1949. 4 v. *Pubblicazioni dell' Univ. Cattolica del Sacro Cuore, Milan,* **17, 18, 23, 28**. Milan, Vita e Pensiero.

Mélanges Hermann Fitting 1907–1908. 2 v. Montpellier, Imprimerie du Midi.

Mélanges Paul Fournier. 1929. Paris, Sirey.

Recueil d'Études sur les sources du droit en l'honneur de François Gény. 1934. 3 v. Paris, Sirey.

Mélanges E. Gérardin. 1907. Paris, Sirey.

Études d'histoire juridique offertes à Paul Frédéric Girard par ses élèves. 1913. 2 v. Paris, Geuthner.

Mélanges P. F. Girard. 1912. 2 v. Paris, Rousseau.

Abhandlungen zur antiken Rechtsgeschichte. 1905. Festschrift Gustav Hanausek. Graz, Moser.

Mélanges à la mémoire de Paul Huvelin. 1938. Livre du XXV anniversaire de l'École française de Beyrouth. Paris, Sirey.

Festschrift Paul Koschaker. 1939. 3 v. Weimar, Böhlau.

Studi in memoria di P. Koschaker. L'Europa e il Diritto Romano. 1953. (In press.) Milan, Giuffrè.

Recueil d'études en l'honneur d'Edouard Lambert. 1938. 3 v. Paris, Sirey.

Symbolae Friburgenses in honorem Ottonis Lenel. 1931. Leipzig, Tauchnitz.

Scritti di diritto ed economia in onore di Flaminio Mancaleoni. 1938. *StSas*, ser. 2, **16**. Sassari, Gallizzi.

Miscellanea Giovanni Mercati 5. 1946. Città del Vaticano.

Symbolae ad ius et historiam antiquitatis pertinentes J. C. van Oven dedicatae. 1946. Leiden, Brill.

Mnemosyna Pappoulia. 1934. Athens, Pyrsos.

Studi in onore di Silvio Perozzi. 1925. Palermo, Castiglia.

Studi in memoria di Umberto Ratti. 1934. Milan, Giuffrè.

Studi in onore di Enrico Redenti. 1951. 2 v. Milan, Giuffrè.

Studi in onore di Salvatore Riccobóno. 1936. 4 v. Palermo, Castiglia.

Scritti giuridici in onore di Santi Romano 4. 1940. Padua, Cedam.

Scritti della Facoltà giuridica dell'Univ. di Roma in onore di Antonio Salandra. 1928. Milan, Vallardi.

Festschrift Fritz Schulz. 1951. 2 v. Weimar, Böhlau.

Studi di diritto romano pubblicati in onore di Vittorio Scialoja. 1905. 2 v. Milan, Hoepli.

Studi in memoria di Bernardino Scorza. 1940. Rome, Foro Italiano.

Gedächtnisschrift für Emil Seckel. 1927. Berlin, Springer.

Studi giuridici in onore di Vittorio Simoncelli. 1917. Naples, Jovene.

Studi in onore di Siro Solazzi. 1948. Naples, Jovene.

Studi di storia e diritto in onore di Arrigo Solmi. 1941. 2 v. Milan, Giuffrè.

Mélanges Fernand De Visscher. 1949–1950. 4 v. (*RIDA* **2–5**). Courtrai, Imprimerie Groeninghe.

Festschrift für Leopold Wenger zu seinem 70. Geburtstag. 1944–1945. 2 v. (*Münchener Beitrage zur Papyrusforschung,* **34–36**). Munich, Beck.

Studi dedicati alla memoria di Pier Paolo Zanzucchi. 1927. *Pubblicazioni dell'Univ. Cattolica Sacro Cuore, Milan,* **14**). Milan, Vita e Pensiero.

B. STUDIES PUBLISHED ON PARTICULAR OCCASIONS

(Congresses, anniversaries)

Acta Congressus Iuridici Internationalis (Romae 12–17 Novembris 1934) 1935. 2 v. Rome, Pontificium Institutum utriusque iuris.

Atti del Congresso Internazionale di diritto romano. Bologna e Roma, 17–27 Aprile 1933. 1934–1935. 2 v. Pavia, Fusi.

Atti del Congresso Internazionale di diritto romano e di storia del diritto, Verona, 27–28–29 Settembre 1948. 1951–1953. 4 v. Milan, Giuffrè.

Augustus. Studi in onore del bimillenario Augusteo. 1938. Rome, Accademia del Lincei.

Conférences faites à l'Institut de droit romain en 1947. 1950. Paris, Sirey.

Conferenze Augustee nel bimillenario della nascita, 1939. (*Pubblicazioni dell'Univ. Cat. del Sacro Cuore, Milan.*) Milan, Vita e Pensiero.

Conferenze per il XIV centenario delle Pandette. 1931. (*Pubblicazioni dell'Univ. Cat. del Sacro Cuore, Milan* **33**.) Milan, Vita e Pensiero.

Essays in Legal History read before the International Congress of historical studies in London, in 1913. Ed. P. Vinogradoff. 1914. London, Humphrey Milford.

Per il Centenario della Codificazione giustinianea. Studi di diritto pubblicati dalla Facoltà di giurisprudenza dell' Università di Pavia. 1934. Pavia, Tipografia Cooperativa.

C. COLLECTED WORKS OF INDIVIDUAL SCHOLARS

ALBERTARIO, E. 1933–1953. Studi di diritto romano. 1. Persone e famiglia, 1933. 2. Cose, diritti reali, possesso, 1941. 3. Obbligazioni, 1938. 4. Eredità e processo, 1946. 5. Storia, metodologia, esegesi, 1937. 6. Saggi critici e studi vari, 1953. Milan, Giuffrè.

ALIBRANDI, I. 1896. Opere giuridiche. Rome, Tipografia Polyglotta.

ARANGIO-RUIZ, V. 1947. Rariora. Rome, Edizioni Storia e Letteratura.

BAVIERA, G. 1909. Scritti giuridici. Palermo, Gaipa.

BONFANTE, P. 1916–1926. Scritti giuridici vari. 4 v. Rome, Sampaolesi.

BORTOLUCCI, G. 1906. Studi romanistici. Padua, Gallina.

BRASSLOFF, S. 1925. Studien zur römischen Rechtsgeschichte. Vienna, Fromme.

CASTELLI, G. 1923. Scritti giuridici. Milan, Hoepli.

EISELE, F. 1896. Beiträge zur römischen Rechtsgeschichte. Freiburg i.B.-Leipzig, Mohr.

——. 1912. Studien zur römischen Rechtsgeschichte. Tübingen, Mohr.

ESMEIN, A. 1886. Mélanges d'histoire du droit. Paris, Larose.

FADDA, C. 1910. Studi e questioni di diritto. Pavia, Mattei.

FERRINI, C. 1929–1930. Opere. 5 v. Milan, Hoepli.

GIRARD, P. F. 1912, 1923. Mélanges de droit romain. 2 v. Paris, Sirey.

LÉVY-BRUHL, H. 1934. Quelques problèmes du très ancien droit romain. Paris, Domat-Montchrestien.

——. 1947. Nouvelles études sur le très ancien droit romain. Paris, Sirey.

MOMMSEN, T. 1905–1907. Juristische Schriften. 3 v. Berlin, Weidmann.

PAMPALONI, M. 1941. Scritti giuridici, 1. Pisa-Rome, Vallerini.

PARTSCH, J. 1931. Aus nachgelassenen und kleineren verstreuten Schriften. Berlin, Springer.

NOAILLES, P. 1948. Fas et ius. Études de droit romain. Paris, Les Belles Lettres.

PEROZZI, S. 1938. Scritti giuridici. 3 v. Milan, Giuffre.

ROTONDI, G. 1922. Scritti giuridici. Milan, Hoepli.

SCIALOJA, V. 1932–1936. Studi giuridici. 7 v. Rome, Anonima Romana Editoriale.

SEGRÈ, G. 1930, 1938. Scritti giuridici. Vol. 1, 2, 4. Cortona, Stabilimento Tipografico Commerciale.

VASSALLI, F. 1939. Studi giuridici. 2 v. Rome, Foro Italiano.

DE VISSCHER, F. 1931. Études de droit romain. Paris, Sirey.

——. 1949. Nouvelles études de droit romain public et privé. Milan, Giuffrè.

WIEACKER, F. 1944. Vom romischen Recht. Leipzig, Köhler & Amelung.

XIX. ENCYCLOPEDIAS, DICTIONARIES, VOCABULARIES

AMBROSINO, R. 1942. Vocabularium Institutionum Iustiniani. Milan, Giuffrè.

BORTOLUCCI, G. 1906. Index verborum Graecorum quae in Institutionibus et Digestis occurrunt. AG 76: 353–396.

DAREMBERG, C., and E. SAGLIO, 1879–1918. Dictionnaire des antiquités grecques et romaines. 5 v. Paris, Hachette.

DIRKSEN, H. E. 1837. Manuale Latinitatis fontium iuris civilis Romanorum. Berlin, Duncker.

GRADENWITZ, O. 1925, 1929. Heidelberger Index zum Theodosianus.—Ergänzungsband 1929. Berlin, Weidmann.

——. 1912. Index ad partem primam Brunsii Fontium iuris Romani antiqui. Tübingen, Mohr.

GUARNERI-CITATI, A. Indice delle parole, etc. See Ch. XIII.

LEVY, E. 1930. Erganzungsindex zu Ius und Leges. Weimar, Böhlau.

LONGO, G. 1899. Vocabolario delle costituzioni latine di Giustiniano. BIDR 10.

MAYR, R. v. 1923–1925. Vocabularium Codicis Iustiniani. Pars Latina I. Pars Graeca II, ed. M. San Nicolò.—Corrections noted by P. Krüger, ZSS 47: 387–396. 1927. Prague, Česká Grafická Unie.

MONIER, R. 1949. Petit vocabulaire de droit romain. 4th ed. Paris, Domat-Montchrestien.

Nuovo Digesto Italiano. 1934–1940. Turin, Unione Tipografica Editrice.

Oxford Classical Dictionary. 1949. Ed. by M. Cary and others. Oxford, Clarendon Press.

Pauly's Realenzyklopadie der klassischen Altertumswissenschaft. New edition by G. Wissowa, W. Kroll, K. Mittelhaus. 1894–1953. 1–21 (A- Pont), 1A–7A (R- Val), Suppl. 1–7. To be continued under the direction of K. Ziegler. Stuttgart, Metzler (Druckenmüller).

DE RUGGIERO, E. 1886–1953. Dizionario epigrafico. 1–5 (A-L). Continuation under the direction of G. Cardinali. Rome, Pasqualucci.

SAN NICOLÒ, M. See above under Mayr, R. v.

SECKEL, E. 1907. Heumann's Handlexikon zu den Quellen des römischen Rechts. 9th ed. (Reprints 1914, 1926.) Jena, Fischer.

Vocabularium Iurisprudentiae Romanae. 1903–1939. Ed. by O. Gradenwitz, B. Kübler, and others. Incomplete. 1, A–C, 1903; 2, D–G, 1933; 3, H–ipse, 1910–1933; 4, N–per, 1914–1933; 5, R–Z, 1910–1939. Berlin, De Gruyter.

WENGER, L. 1928. Aus Novellenindex und Papyruswörterbuch. SbMünch 28 (4).

ZANZUCCHI, P. P. 1910. Vocabolario delle Istituzioni di Gaio. Milan, Vallardi.

XX. BIBLIOGRAPHIES

ARANGIO-RUIZ, V. 1948. Diritto romano e papirologia giuridica. Doxa 1: 97, 193.

BERGER, A., and A. A. SCHILLER. 1945, 1947. Bibliography of Anglo-American studies in Roman Law, etc. Sem 3: 75–94, for 1939–1945; 5: 62–85, for 1945–1947.

BERTOLINI, C. 1912. Bibliografia 1895–1899. Diritto romano 1900–1906. Diritto greco e romano. Libri e periodici. Rome, Istituto di diritto romano.—See also BIDR 20: 111–156, 264–303, 1908; 22: 267–334, 1910; 23: Appendix, pp. I–LIV, 1911; 24: 281–329, 1911; 25: 273–318, 1912; 26: 289–358, 1913. F. Vassalli, ibid. 29: 185–216, 1916. For the continuation of this bibliography see below under Romano, S.

Bibliografia giuridica internazionale, ed. by Istituto Italiano di studi legislativi, Rome. Each volume has a section on Roman Law (since 1932).

BIONDI, B. 1944. Diritto romano. Guide bibliografiche (published by Università Cattolica del Sacro Cuore, Milan). Ser. III, Discipline giuridiche. Milan, Vita e Pensiero.

BOHAČEK, M. 1930. Les ouvrages modernes tchèques sur le droit romain. In the Polish periodical Czasopismo historyczno-prawne, 1. Poznań.

Bulletin Bibliographique in NRHD and RHD. Latest issue for 1932–1933 and 1934, published as supplements to 13 and 14 (1934, 1935).

CAES, L., and R. HENRION. 1949 ff. Collectio bibliographica operum ad ius Romanum pertinentium. Ser. I, 1–3: Opera edita in Periodicis, Miscellaneis, Encyclopaediisque. 1949, 1951. Ser. II, 1: Theses Gallicae. Brussels, Office International de Librairie.

COLLINET, P. 1930. Bibliographie des travaux de droit romain en langue française. Paris, Les Belles Lettres. Completed by P. Ciapessoni, Ath 10: 93–96, 1932.

——. 1947. Repertoire des Bibliographies, Vocabulaires, Index, Concordance et Palingénésies du droit romain. *RHD* **24–25**: 109–118.

Cosentini, C. 1949. Guida alla consultazione delle fonti giuridiche romane e dei mezzi ausiliari d'indagine. Catania, Università.

De Francisci, P. 1923. Il diritto romano. Rome, Fondazione Leonardo.

Georgescu, V. A. 1943. Bibliografia de drept roman, 1940–1942. Bucharest.

Iura. Rivista internazionale di diritto romano e antico. 1950 ff. This recently founded periodical contains in each volume an extensive Rassegna bibliografica. **1**: 540–663, 1950; **2**: 348–471, 1951; **3**: 399–490, 1952. Naples, Jovene.

Monier, R. 1944. Bibliographie des travaux récents de droit romain en français, en anglais, en allemand, en italien et en roumain. Paris, Domat-Montchrestien.

Romano, S. 1928–1932. Bibliografia. *BIDR* **36**: 159–314, 1928; **39**: 63–104, 1931; **40**, 253–378, 1932.

Sachers, E. 1932. Generalregister zu den Bänden 1–50 der *ZSS*. Weimar, Böhlau.

Sanfilippo, C. 1949. Bibliografia romanistica italiana, 1939–1949. *Pubblicazioni della Facoltà di Giurisprudenza dell'Univ. di Catania* **12**.

Tardif, J., and F. Senn. 1908. Table des cinquante premiers volumes de la Revue Historique de droit français et étranger, 1855–1905. Paris, Sirey.

Volterra, E. 1937–1951. Saggio bibliografico di diritto agrario romano. New edition: Bibliografia di diritto agrario romano, 1951. Florence, Coppini.

Wenger, L. 1930–1941. Juristische Literaturübersicht in *ArPap* (see Ch. XVI) contains many references to Romanistic literature.

Wisłocki, J. 1945. Prawo rzymskie w Polsce (Roman law in Poland), History of the study of Roman law in Poland. Warsaw, Gebethner & Wolff.

For Bibliography on Roman law in the Middle Ages see Alvarez, U. Horizonte actual del derecho romano. Madrid, 1944, 7–11.

For Bibliography concerning single texts of Justinian's Digest consult Index Interpolationum, see Ch. XIII.

CORRIGENDA